Fodor's 2026

ESSENTIAL ITALY

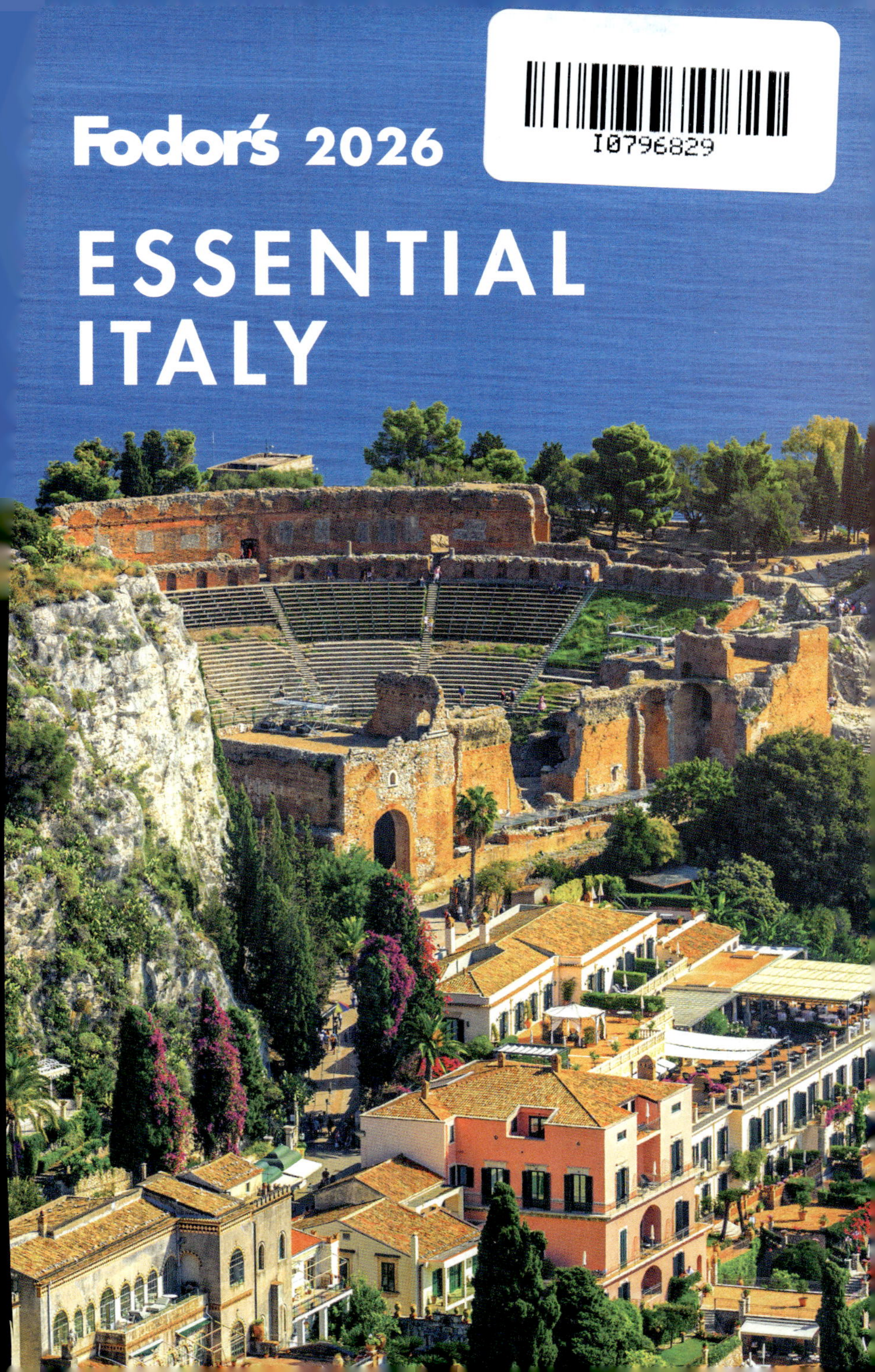

TOP REASONS TO GO

★ **Food:** Italy is a pasta lover's paradise; but don't forget the pizza and the gelato.

★ **Romance:** Whether you're strolling atmospheric Venice or sipping wine, Italy enchants.

★ **History:** The ruins of ancient Pompeii and the Leaning Tower of Pisa breathe antiquity and ingenuity.

★ **Art:** The big hitters—Botticelli, Michelangelo, Raphael, Caravaggio, and more.

★ **Shopping:** Few things say quality or style like "made in Italy."

Welcome to Italy

Italy is patchwork of regions and islands you return to again and again. "Il Bel Paese" (Beautful Country) has awe-inspiring art, culture, and architecture, and stunning historical ruins. From *agnolotti* (stuffed pasta) to zabaglione, it serves among the world's best food and wine. Think sun-kissed olive groves and vineyards, mountains, and beaches lapped by the sparkling Mediterranean Sea. Often animated and engaging, Italians' *campanilismo* (local patriotism) makes them fiercely proud of their traditions ranging from the local cheese to the town's bell tower.

Shaped by Romans, Greeks, Etruscans, and many invaders and native peoples, Italy is awash with ancient treasures and cultural traces. At its heart Rome's Colosseum and Vatican City provide a rich legacy of Catholic and imperial power. As a modern unified country Italy has only been around since 1861, and its 20 regions retain disparate, centuries-old linguistics, influences, and quirks. Geography, climate, and foreign domination shape each: from the Europe-facing alpine north, down its Apennine mountain spine to the Greek-Arabic-African flavored, volcanic south and Sicily.

Interspersed with mountains and lakes—Liguria, Piedmont, Lombardy, and Veneto have outward-looking historic cities: the buzzy, northern economic powerhouses Turin and Milan are flanked by medieval maritime rivals Genoa and Venice. And Florence, pivotal to Italy's 15th-century Renaissance in art and thought sits central amid the urbane and undulating delights of Tuscany.

Open-hearted Naples is an intoxicating mix of beauty, abundance, and danger. Amalfi Coast and Capri provide escape, as do Pompeii's time-capsule ruins dug from Vesuvius' AD 79 eruption. Join holidaying Italians on the gorgeous beaches of Puglia, Calabria, and Basilicata.

Infinitely captivating, complex, compelling, and at times exasperating, this is Italia. Buon Viaggio!

As you plan your travels to Italy, please confirm that places are still open and let us know when we need to make updates by writing to us at corrections@fodors.com.

Contents

Fodor's Features

MAPS

About Our Writers

Portofino

Born of Sicilian stock, **Robert Andrews** has been living and working in various parts of Italy for most of his adult life. He has written articles and guidebooks on this multifaceted peninsula, and provides travel consultancy services as well as leading individual and small-group tours in Sicily and Sardinia. For this edition, Robert updated the Sardinia and Italian Riviera chapters.

Nick Bruno is an Italy specialist and frequent Fodor's contributor. As well as authoring and updating books and features, he makes radio packages for the BBC. A lifelong interest in history and Italian language has led to a project researching his paternal Italian family during the Il Ventennio Fascista period. Nick updated the Experience; Travel Smart; Veneto and Friuli-Venezia Giulia; Puglia, Basilicata, and Calabria; Naples and Campania; and Emilia-Romagna chapters. Follow him on Instagram and Twitter @nickjgbruno and at *barbruno.com.*

Liz Humphreys is a transplant to Europe from New York City, where she edited for media companies including Condé Nast and Time Inc. Since then she's written for publications including *Condé Nast Traveler, Michelin Green Guides,* and *Forbes Travel Guide.* Liz has an advanced certificate in wine studies from WSET (Wine & Spirit Education Trust), which comes in handy when exploring her beloved Italian wine regions. Liz updated the Dolomites; Piedmont and the Valle D'Aosta; Umbria and the Marches; and Venice chapters. Follow her online @winederlust_wanderings

The Colosseum in Rome

Laura Itzkowitz is a freelance writer and editor based in Rome with an MFA in creative writing and a passion for covering travel, arts and culture, lifestyle, design, food, and wine. Her writing has appeared in *Travel + Leisure, Architectural Digest, Vogue, GQ, Departure, AFAR,* and others. Laura updated Rome. Follow her on Instagram and Twitter @lauraitzkowitz.

Originally from California, **Natalie Kennedy** moved to Rome planning to stay for only a year, but has now called the Eternal City home for nearly a decade and runs a popular blog about Roman life (🌐 *www.anamericaninrome.com*). For this edition she updated Rome.

Elizabeth Shemaria is an Italy-based journalist and third-generation Northern Californian who has trekked solo in Himalaya, interviewed artists in military-ruled Burma, and once rode an overnight train across Egypt on her birthday. She has contributed to more than a dozen travel and news publications including Fodor's guidebooks, *AFAR, BBC Travel,* and *Roads & Kingdoms.* Spontaneous dance parties are essential to her creative process. For this edition, Liz updated the Milan, Lombardy, and the Lakes; Tuscany; and Florence chapters. Follow her on Instagram @lizshemaria.

Chapter 1

EXPERIENCE ITALY

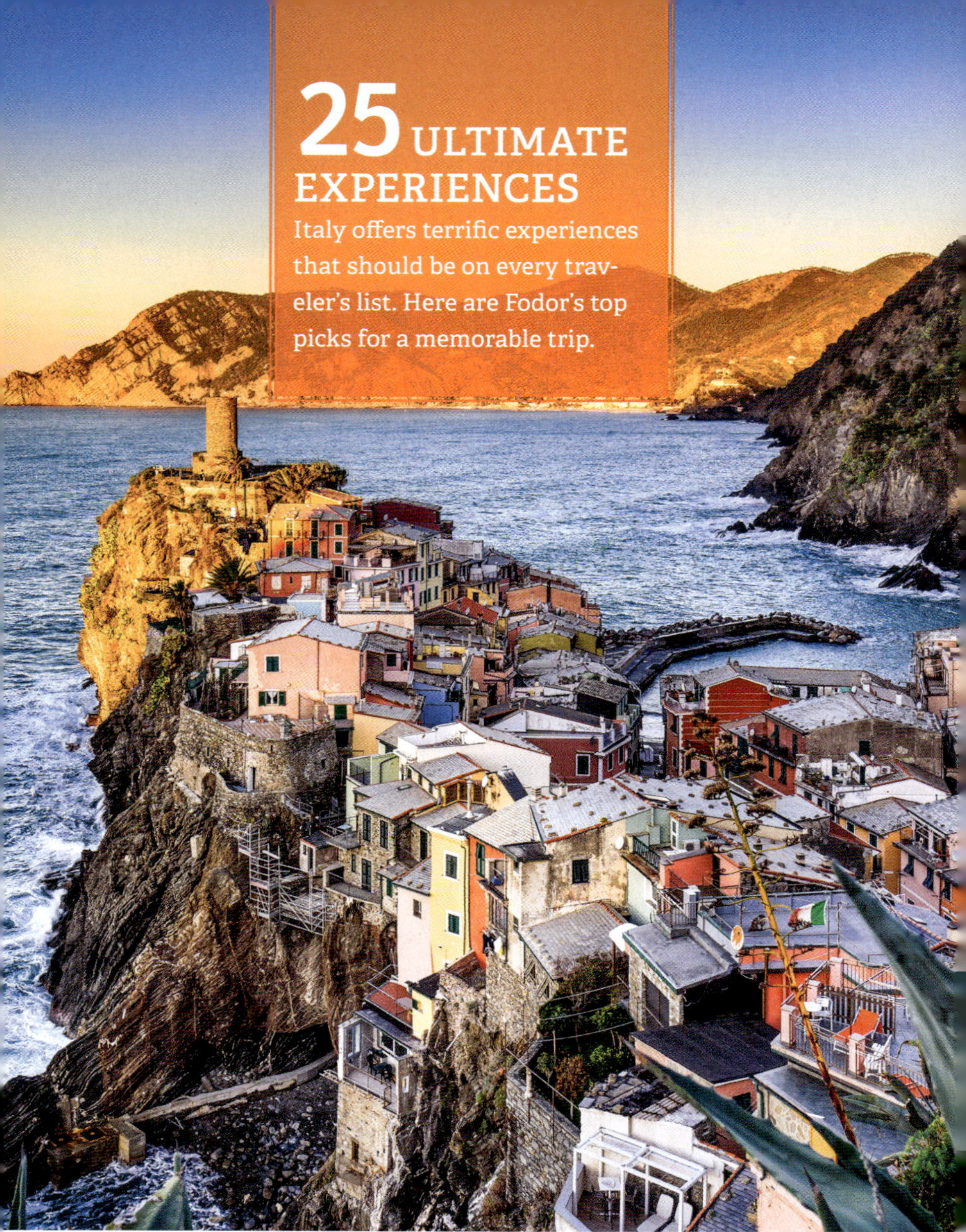

1 Hike the Cinque Terre

Walk the scenic footpaths that connect the five former fishing villages that make up the Cinque Terre; each one appears to hang off the cliffs, allowing for absolutely stunning views of the vineyards above and blue waters below. *(p. 410)*

2 People-Watch in Venice

Venice's Piazza San Marco (St. Mark's Square), flanked by the gorgeous Basilica di San Marco, is certainly one of the world's loveliest squares for people-watching. *(p. 157)*

3 Shop in Milan

In Italy's fashion capital of Milan, you'll find the highest of high-end designers in the Quadrilatero della Moda district, north of the Duomo. *(p. 324)*

4 See Assisi's Frescoes

The medieval town of Assisi is home to enormous Basilica di San Francesco, which includes 28 frescoes showing the life of St. Francis. *(p. 603)*

5 Sail Away to Capri

This fabled island off the coast of Naples has long stood for glitz and glamour. It's a lovely place to escape to. *(p. 671)*

6 Ponder *The Last Supper*

Restoration work has returned *The Last Supper* to its original glory, so the painting is clear and luminous. *(p. 319)*

7 Roam a Medieval City

Perhaps Italy's best-preserved medieval city, Siena's narrow streets are fun to explore. The Piazza del Campo is one of the most beautiful squares in the country. *(p. 577)*

8 Discover Ravello

Wander the Amalfi Coast's refined mountaintop village and discover lush, hidden gardens, medieval fountains, and Mediterranean views. *(p. 689)*

9 Rent a Villa in Tuscany

One of the supreme pleasures of a visit to the countryside of Tuscany is the chance to stay in a villa—preferably one with a swimming pool and vineyard views. *(p. 551)*

10 Admire the Architecture

The city of Lecce is a jewel of Baroque architecture, but that is by no means its only style. Stand in Piazza Sant'Oronzo to best see and appreciate the blend. *(p. 719)*

11 Marvel at Mosaics

Some of the greatest Byzantine mosaics can be found in the unassuming city of Ravenna. You can view the most elaborate ones in the 5th-century Mausoleo di Galla Placidia. *(p. 483)*

12 Go Wine Tasting

The Barolo region produces excellent wine and is filled with hill towns. Make an appointment for a tour and tasting at one of the many wineries. *(p. 384)*

13 Explore Lava Fields

The largest and highest volcano in Europe, Sicily's Mount Etna, has moonlike dunes that you can walk across or view from the comfort of a cable car (the Funivia dell'Etna). *(p. 787)*

14 Enjoy Magical Views

Nowhere inspires as many oohs and aahs as the magnificent town of Positano, with its pastel-color houses seemingly spilling off the mountainside. *(p. 682)*

15 See Great Art

Florence's Galleria degli Uffizi contains the collection of art from the Medicis, including Botticelli's *Birth of Venus*, Michelangelo's *Doni Tondo*, and Caravaggio's *Bacchus*. *(p. 500)*

16 Relax by the Sea

The lovely village of Portofino hugs the coast of the Italian Riviera, with the Santa Margherita cliffs on one side and the Ligurian Sea on the other. *(p. 422)*

17 Feel Romantic

Set on the shores of beautiful Lake Como, Bellagio is often considered one of the loveliest towns in Italy. Its steep streets, lined with cobblestones, are supremely romantic. *(p. 353)*

18 Visit a Volcanic Island

Just a ferry away from Sicily's northeast coast sit the Aeolian Islands, seven volcanic islands offering dramatic scenery and wonderful snorkeling and scuba diving. *(p. 796)*

19 Hit the Slopes

The gorgeous craggy peaks of the Dolomites make the perfect place for an unforgettable ski holiday in the winter or a rejuvenating hike in the spring and summer. *(p. 295)*

20 Toss a Coin in Trevi Fountain

The can't-miss Trevi Fountain in Rome is a Baroque fantasy of sea beasts, seashells, and mermaids in front of a triumphal arch. *(p. 117)*

21 Step Back in Time

The best-preserved excavated site in the world, the commercial center of Pompeii was frozen in time when Vesuvius erupted in AD 79. *(p. 666)*

22 Explore a Hill Town

Wander the narrow winding streets of the walled city of San Gimignano, which is filled with 14 soaring medieval towers (originally there were more than 70). *(p. 570)*

23 Enjoy the Coastline

In the southernmost region of Puglia is a dramatic coastline, with sandstone cliffs crashing into the ocean and beautiful beaches, especially in Gallipoli. *(p. 723)*

24 Lounge on a Beach

Sardinia is justly famed for its white-sand beaches. Spend the day soaking up the sun on these beautiful strands. *(p. 812)*

25 Stand in Awe

Dominating Florence's skyline, the magnificent Duomo is an architectural marvel that took almost 600 years to complete. *(p. 500)*

WHAT'S WHERE

1 Rome. Italy's capital is one of the greatest cities in Europe. It's a busy, modern metropolis where you'll encounter powerful evocations of its storied and spectacular past, from the Colosseum to St. Peter's.

2 Venice. One of the world's most unusual—and beautiful—cities, Venice has canals instead of streets, along with an atmosphere of faded splendor.

3 The Veneto and Friuli–Venezia Giulia. The green plains stretching west of Venice hold three of northern Italy's most artistically significant midsize cities: Padua, Vicenza, and Verona. Farther north and east, Alpine foothills are dotted with welcoming villages and some of Italy's finest vineyards.

4 The Dolomites. Along Italy's northeast border, the Dolomites are the country's finest mountain playground, with gorgeous cliffs, curiously shaped peaks, lush meadows, and crystalline lakes.

5 Milan, Lombardy, and the Lakes. The lakes of Lombardy have been attracting vacationers since the days of ancient Rome. At the center of Lombardy is Milan, Italy's second-largest city and its business capital. It's also the hub of Italian fashion and design.

6 Piedmont and the Valle d'Aosta. Here you'll find great Alpine peaks, one of the most highly esteemed food-and-wine cultures in Italy, and an elegant regional capital in Turin.

7 The Italian Riviera. Northern Italy's most attractive coastline runs along the Italian Riviera in the region of Liguria. The best beaches and temperate winter climate are west of Genoa, but the main appeal lies to the east, where fishing villages dot the seaside cliffs and coves.

8 Emilia-Romagna. Many of Italy's signature foods come from the Emilia-Romagna region. Bologna is a significant cultural center, and the mosaics of Ravenna are glittering Byzantine treasures.

WHAT'S WHERE

9 Florence. The hub of the 15th-century Renaissance, Florence is awash with artistic treasures, exceptional restaurants, and first-rate shopping, as well as a never-ending stream of tourists.

10 Tuscany. Nature outdid herself in Tuscany. The central Italian region has Florence as its principal city and many other interesting midsize towns, but the region's greatest appeal lies in the smaller towns, often perched on hilltops and not significantly altered since the Middle Ages.

11 Umbria and the Marches. A number of the smaller towns, particularly Assisi, Perugia, Spoleto, and Orvieto are fun to explore, and Umbria's Roman past is everywhere—expect to see Roman villas, aqueducts, and temples. Urbino's Ducal Palace reveals more about the Renaissance than a shelf of art history books.

12 Naples and Campania. Campania is the gateway to southern Italy. Dream away two magical weeks on the pint-size islands of Capri and Ischia and at the fabled resorts of the Amalfi Coast. Or explore the past at the archaeological ruins of Pompeii, Herculaneum, and Paestum. Naples is a fun, chaotic metropolis.

13 Puglia, Basilicata, and Calabria. The southernmost regions of the peninsula—Puglia, Basilicata, and Calabria—are known for their laid-back medieval villages, shimmering seas, and varied landscapes. The coastline of Puglia, along the heel of Italy's boot, is popular with beachgoers, but for the most part you're off the beaten path here.

14 Sicily. The breezes are sultry and everyday life is without pretense, as witnessed in the workaday stalls of the fish markets in ports all along the Tyrrhenian and Ionian coasts, bursting with tuna, swordfish, and sardines.

15 Sardinia. The beaches here rank among the Mediterranean's finest, and ancient sites, including the Carthaginian and Roman settlements of Nora and Tharros, add to the island's distinctive character.

Italy Today

ENDURING CUISINE

The old joke goes that three-quarters of the food and wine served in Italy is good—and the rest is amazing. In some sense, that's still true, and the "good" 75% has gotten even better. Those pundits would claim that ingredients that in the past were available only to the wealthy can now be found even in the remotest parts of the country at reasonable prices. Dishes originally conceived to make the most of inferior cuts of meat or the least flavorful part of vegetables are now made with the best.

But many Italians would say that the food in Italy is getting worse. There's a proliferation of fast-food establishments, and increasing tourism has allowed many restaurants to lower their standards while raising their prices. This is true not only in Rome, but in most other tourist centers as well. The good news is Italy is home to one of the world's greatest cuisines, and its traditional favorites still put meat on bones and smiles on faces. Italian restaurateurs seem determined to make the most of the country's reputation for good food. Although quaint, family-run trattorias with checkered tablecloths, traditional dishes, and an informal atmosphere are still common if on the decline, nearly every town has a newer eatery with matching flatware, a proper wine list, and an innovative menu.

This also holds for Italian wine. Today, through investment and experimentation, Italy's winemakers are figuring out how to get the most from their gorgeous vineyards. It's fair to say that Italy now produces more types of high-quality wine from more different grape varieties than any other country in the world.

SOCCER RULES

Soccer (or, as the Italians say, *calcio*—which means "kick") stands without rival as the national sport of Italy, though some complain that big-money influence and loose financial regulations are polluting the beautiful game. That aside, Italy did win its fourth World Cup in 2006, giving the country more world titles than any other this side of Brazil. More recently, Italy won the prestigious UEFA Euro 2020 championship (though due to COVID-19 it was played in 2021). Italy's major clubs have fared better in European competition of late, but the predominance of foreign players means a smaller pool of talent to pick at national level. More games in the schedule and a dwindling fan base mean fewer people are seen at the stadium. Still, fans can't stop watching the game on television. Indeed the allure of its famed teams like Juventus, Inter, and Napoli and their *ultras* (vociferous fans) means the top league, Serie A, has a worldwide following.

AN AGING POPULATION

Italy's population is the oldest in Europe (as percentage of population)—the result of its low birth rate and one of the highest life-expectancy rates in the world. The median age of an Italian in 2024 was 48.7; by 2050, 34.5% of the population is forecast to be over 65.

Italy's famously stable population is now aging and set to contract according to recent estimates, putting a strain on the country's pension system and on families because elderly family members are likely to live with their children or grandchildren as retirement homes are rare. Underfunding of the public health-care system has left older Italians vulnerable.

The trend also has an impact in other areas, including politics (where older politicians are eager to promote policies aimed at older voters), the popular culture (where everything from fashion to television programming takes older consumers into consideration), and a kind of far-reaching nostalgia. Thanks to a long collective memory, it's common to hear even younger Italians celebrate or rue something that happened 50 or 60 years earlier as if it had just taken place.

THE BLACK-MARKET ECONOMY

Nobody knows how big Italy's black-market economy is, though experts all agree it's massive. The presence of the black market isn't obvious to the casual observer, but whenever a customer isn't given a printed receipt in a store or restaurant, tobacco without a tax seal is bought from a street seller, or a product or service is exchanged for another product or service, that means the transaction goes unrecorded, unreported, and untaxed. But that's all penny-ante stuff compared to what many professionals evade by neglecting to declare all they earn.

Austerity measures imposed in recent years have led to much disgruntlement among the population; now most shopkeepers insist that you take a receipt. If you don't, you could be fined, as could the shopkeeper. These measures remain in place, but the country still struggles to meet the 3% limit to its budget deficit as mandated by European Union (EU) agreements, and it is pretty certain that Italy will continue to struggle to meet it in coming years.

A GROWING PARKS SYSTEM

Italy has 25 national parks covering a total of around 1½ million hectares (5,800 square miles), or about 6% of the entire surface area of the country—more than twice as much as 25 years ago. Part of the reason for the expansion has been a growing environmental movement in Italy, which has lobbied the government to annex undeveloped land for parks, thus protecting against development. The trend is a boon for visitors and nature lovers, who can enjoy huge expanses of unspoiled territory.

STAYING HOME IN AUGUST

Italy used to be the best example of Europe's famous August exodus, when city dwellers would spend most of the month at the seaside or in the mountains, leaving the cities nearly deserted. Today the phenomenon is less prevalent, as economic pressures have forced companies to keep operating through August.

The loss of shared vacation time for Italian workers means good things for visitors: in August there's a little more room on beaches and mountains; in addition, cities promote events for nonvacationing natives. Summers in Italy now offer a plethora of outdoor concerts and theatrical events, extended museum hours, and local festivals.

WINTER OLYMPICS AND PARALYMPICS 2026

In February and March 2026 thousands of the world's athletes from 93 countries descend on northern Italy's mountain ski slopes, ice rink venues, and buzzing off-pistes for the Olympic and Paralympic Winter Games Milano Cortina. Milan's Stadio San Siro and Verona's Roman Arena will host the opening and closing ceremonies. Can the games and their legacy match that of the hugely successful Torino 2006, which transformed the Piedmont capital? The country—and the world—shall see.

Best Hilltop Villages in Tuscany and Umbria

SAN GIMIGNANO, TUSCANY
Most medieval towers have given way to war and erosion through the centuries, but San Gimignano retains so many that it has been dubbed the Town of Fine Towers and its historic center, which is packed with examples of medieval architecture, is a UNESCO World Heritage site. (*p. 570*)

VOLTERRA, TUSCANY
Twenty kilometers (12 miles) from the better-known village of San Gimignano is the less visited Volterra. Although there are some serious medieval remnants in this village, especially its narrow streets in the town center, it's much more famous for the historical periods before and after. Some of its ancient Etruscan fortification walls still surround Roman ruins. (*p. 568*)

TODI, UMBRIA
Compact and ancient Todi is a hilltop citadel town with a beautiful patchwork of architecture that includes three sturdy walls, begun by the 3rd-century-BC Etruscans followed by Roman and medieval dynasties. The Piazza del Popolo features a 12th-century Romanesque-Gothic Duomo. (*p. 621*)

ORVIETO, UMBRIA
Although medieval architectural wonders adorn Orvieto, the labyrinth of subterranean tunnels beneath the town is even more fascinating. Orvieto is also recognized for its white and red wines, its olive oils, and its culinary classics—from boar and dove to pastas and pastries. (*p. 622*)

ASSISI, UMBRIA
Assisi claims history as ancient as 1000 BC and is probably best known for its most famous resident, St. Francis, whose 13th-century basilica is now a UNESCO World Heritage site, as is the entire village itself. Plenty of other impressive churches, Roman ruins, and not one but two castles top the extensive list of the town's architectural offerings. (*p. 603*)

Best Beaches in Italy

MARASUSA, CALABRIA

The area around the lovely town of Tropea has some of Calabria's most recognizable seascapes, including those on Marasusa, where the water is a remarkable greenish-blue, the sand light-hued and ultrafine, and buildings seem to grow from the rock atop sheer cliffs. (*p. 734*)

BAIA DEL SILENZIO, LIGURIA

Line a curvy bay with a sandy beach and warm-hued buildings, and you have Baia del Silenzio, one of Liguria's most captivating seaside amphitheaters. This very popular spot in the resort town of Sestri Levante is a fabulous place to people-watch. (*p. 420*)

SPIAGGIA NERA–CALA JANNITA, BASILICATA

Maratea is one of the Tyrrhenian coast's most alluring towns, where the fabulous Spiaggia Nera (Black Beach) has limpid waters and dramatic scenery. Spread your towel out on the dark volcanic gravel, and float amid igneous boulders. (*p. 727*)

TORRE GUACETO, PUGLIA

The color palate at Torre Guaceto is classic and calming: blue waters lapping chalky sands near the so-called Città Bianca (White City) of Ostuni. The beach is part of a marine reserve that extends 20 km (12 miles) along the coast and 6 km (4 miles) inland. (*p. 714*)

SPIAGGIA DI FEGINA, ITALIAN RIVIERA

Hikers tackling the famous Cinque Terre often take a breather on the beautiful, pebbly Spiaggia di Fegina. If you're feeling sprightly, clamber over *faraglioni* (sea stacks) amid the waves or trek down to one end of the beach to see the 46-foot *Statua del Gigante* (Giant Statue) hewn into the rock. (*p. 414*)

Fantastic Cooking Classes in Italy

TASTE BOLOGNA (BOLOGNA, EMILIA-ROMAGNA)
Any cook worth their *sale* (salt) should spend time in Italy's foodie capital, and Taste Bologna provides a fulsome introduction to its riches. Combine their Classic Bologna Tour with the Cooking Class to get a feel for life in the market and in the kitchen.

MONTESE COOKING EXPERIENCE (SAN GIMIGNANO, TUSCANY)
Situated just outside San Gimignano, the well-loved Montese Cooking Experience is blessed with fabulous facilities, chefs, and views. The intensive four-hour Pasta Fatta in Casa session highlights not only long pastas, but also stuffed varieties.

TASTING SARDINIA: THE CENTENARIANS MEAL (CAGLIARI, SARDINIA)
The enlightening Centenarians Meal session, one of many offerings from Tasting Sardinia, takes its premise—that cooking with fresh ingredients is essential to living long and well—straight from the island's centenarians.

BUCA DI BACCO (POSITANO, CAMPANIA)
The venerable Hotel Buca di Bacco opened in the 1950s, but tucked within is the even older eponymous restaurant, established in 1916, which hosts Buca di Bacco cooking classes. You'll learn about pizza and pasta making, as well as the restaurant's signature antipasto: *gamberetti alla Clark*. The dish was created for U.S. General Mark Clark, who was stationed here at the end of World War II. When he requested a prawn cocktail, the chef combined shrimp, lettuce, and a sauce to create a version that reflected the local climate and wartime larder.

COOKING TAORMINA (TAORMINA, SICILY)
In addition to helping you hone your cooking skills, the animated young chef at Cooking Taormina explains the many exotic influences that shaped *la cucina siciliana*. The first part of the lesson stimulates the senses on a visit to Taormina's produce and fish market. Afterward, you'll use your fresh ingredients in classic Sicilian specialties.

MAMA ISA'S COOKING SCHOOL (PADUA, VENETO)
In Padua, a 30-minute drive inland from Venice, Mama Isa and family offer a tempting array of courses—from half-day introductory lessons to six-day extravaganzas—covering many of the Veneto region's culinary traditions. There are weeks' worth of classes, including bread and pasta making, vegan

Bari Walking Tour in Puglia

and vegetarian cooking, and dessert and pastry creation—even how to prepare the perfect risotto.

BARI WALKING TOUR WITH PASTA-MAKING (BARI, PUGLIA)

Deep in Bari's atmospheric *centro storico*, you'll learn about the art of making orecchiette, which is still practiced on the city's streets. The two-hour Bari Walking Tour with Pasta-Making starts with a tour of the city and its food market before heading to the chef's house to get fiddly with the dough. By the end of the session, you will have created hundreds of edible "little ears" to enjoy with a few bottles of Puglia's red Primitivo wine during the all-important tasting lunch.

ITALIANNA COOKING CLASS (ALBA, PIEDMONT)

Renowned for its rich tradition of food and wine, greatly influenced by nearby France, Piedmont is a fine destination for a foodie adventure. ItaliAnna's beginner pasta-making class, for example, is fun, flour filled, and interactive—and just one of their offerings.

COOK WITH US IN ROME (ROMA, LAZIO)

The enthusiasm of the two Roman chefs who conduct the Cook with Us in Rome classes is contagious, making it truly fun to learn about the city's food in a morning or afternoon session.

SLOW COOKING CLASS (PACIANO, UMBRIA)

The family-run Slow Cooking School is based in an organic olive press, Il Fontanaro. Its most popular offering involves a tour of the mill, a rummage around the verdant market garden to select ingredients, and then a chance to get messy: mixing and kneading dough, shaping pasta, and creating the accompanying *sugo* (sauce) from scratch.

Architectural Wonders in Venice

PONTE DI RIALTO
The iconic Ponte di Rialto was completed in 1591. Its generous arch, central portal, and Renaissance arcade make it appear so beautifully balanced that Palladio himself would surely have approved. (p.160)

SAN FRANCESCO DELLA VIGNA
The harmonious combination of architectural designs by two Renaissance maestri and the tranquil neighborhood setting make this church a wonderful place to escape the crowds. (*p. 190*)

HILTON MOLINO STUCKY
This neo-Gothic, warehouselike building, formerly a flour mill and pasta factory (but now a hotel), on the western end of the Giudecca, certainly stands out on the Venetian skyline. (*p. 199*)

SANTA MARIA DELLA SALUTE
One of the city's most beloved and iconic churches, La Salute was built to mark the end of the 1630 plague that took almost 50,000 Venetian lives. (*p. 167*)

PUNTA DELLA DOGANA
There has been a Punta della Dogana (Sea Customs House) situated between the Grand and Giudecca Canals since the 15th century, although the building you see today was designed in the 1860s. Above the entrance tower, two Atlases lift a bronze sphere topped by the figure of Fortune. (*p. 167*)

ARSENALE
For centuries, the colossal Arsenale complex of shipyards, warehouses, and armories was Europe's largest military-industrial compound. Although many areas are still cordoned off as military zones, the southern side is open to the public during the Biennale Arte e Architettura. (*p. 190*)

JEWISH GHETTO
Originally the site of a foundry (*geto* in the local dialect), both the atmosphere and the architecture set the Jewish Ghetto apart: palazzi and *case* are taller here than elsewhere, with story upon story piled high in an effort to make the best use of limited space. (*p. 182*)

Palazzo Ducale

PALAZZO DUCALE
Adorned with a series of soaring Gothic arches topped by an ornately columned arcade, the labyrinthine Doge's Palace has a wedding-cake-like delicacy when viewed from the Piazza San Marco or the waterside Bacino di San Marco. A palace has been here since the 9th century: its present palatial pink Verona marble and Istrian limestone splendor was the vision of architect Filippo Calendario (1315–55). (*p. 157*)

MADONNA DELL'ORTO
An alluring, redbrick Gothic church with ornate marble decoration, it was dedicated to St. Christopher, the patron saint of travelers, until a Madonna statue was found in a nearby *orto* (kitchen vegetable garden). Tintoretto's local church is where he learned his craft as a young man. Seek out the powerful *Martyrdom of St. Paul*, which captures the tension between the violent sword act of a Roman soldier and Paul's saintly calmness below rays of holy light. (*p. 183*)

CA' DA MOSTO
As you drift along the Grand Canal, you'll see palazzi far more eye-catching than the Ca' da Mosto, but none more enduring—the crumbling Byzantine-style palace has been here since the 13th century. The ground and first floors are an example of a *casa-fondaco* (a house-warehouse). A 2019–21 restoration and renovation transformed the palace into an exorbitantly luxe and pricey hotel filled with innovative design and interesting artworks. (*p. 162*)

What to Watch and Read

ITALIAN FOLKTALES BY ITALO CALVINO

In 1956 the celebrated, Cuban-born and Liguria-raised magical realist published this fabulous collection of some 200 traditional folktales from across the archipelago. The prose in the 800-page *Fiabe italiane* tome is simple yet evocative, and the stories appeal to young and old alike. They're largely fantastical morality tales involving love, loss, revenge, and adventure on the part of kings, princesses, saints, and peasants. The book is a fabulous bedtime or beach read.

AMARCORD, DIRECTED BY FEDERICO FELLINI

Amarcord ("I remember," in the Romagnol dialect) is filled with comic archetypes and dreamlike excursions inspired by Fellini's 1930s adolescence in Rimini. The rosy-cheeked protagonist, Titta, and his pals have humorous encounters with authority figures—pompous schoolteachers, frustrated fathers, cruel Fascist officials—as well as with the buxom hairdresser, Gradisca. The 1973 movie, which won the Oscar for Best Foreign Language Film, offers poignant, entertaining, and often bonkers insight into the Italian psyche, family dynamics, and interwar society. Nino Rota's wistful soundtrack adds to the feeling of nostalgia.

THE ITALIANS BY JOHN HOOPER

In this 2015 book, longtime Rome correspondent John Hooper addresses the complexities of contemporary Italy, attempting to reveal "what makes the Italian tick." Here you'll learn the lexicon needed to negotiate and understand Italian culture. Of course, food, sex, and the weather—among other things—are heartily embraced in everyday life, but there is also an *amaro* (bitter) side. Hooper illustrates how the power of the *famiglia* (family) and the *chiesa* (church) has produced a society in which *furbizia* (cunning) is rewarded and meritocracy is replaced with *raccomandazioni* (favors) to get ahead in the world.

THE LEOPARD BY GIUSEPPE TOMASI DI LAMPEDUSA

Il gattopardo, an Italian literary classic, chronicles the tumultuous, revolutionary years of the Risorgimento (1860s–early 20th century). Lampedusa was the last in a line of minor princes, and the novel, born of a lengthy depression, was published in 1958, a year after his death. Set in Sicily, the epic story of decay amid a changing society centers on the ebbing influence and power of Don Fabrizio, Prince of Salina, and his family, and hints at the emergence of the Mafia. One particularly insightful quote in the book—spoken by the prince's young nephew, Tancredi—sheds light on how Italy adapts to shifting political forces and class struggle: "For everything to stay the same, everything must change."

COSA NOSTRA BY JOHN DICKIE

Journalist and academic John Dickie packs a lot of gruesome detail into this fast-paced history of the Mafia. He traces the Cosa Nostra's origins during the Risorgimento years, its infiltration and corruption of the First Republic, and the curious and notorious role of the town of Corleone in its development. Dickie also recounts the organization's birth and rise in America, the Mafia Wars, and the recent crises and tragedies connected to Italy's corrupt political system.

THE CONFORMIST, DIRECTED BY BERNARDO BERTOLUCCI

Il conformista, Bertolucci's stylish psychological thriller set in 1930s Fascist Italy, is considered a postwar cinematic classic. As its name suggests, the 1970 film tackles the issue of conformity through the lens of the cruel, febrile political atmosphere created by Mussolini and his followers. Despite its dark themes, the movie is beautifully lit and shot, filled with vibrant colors, exquisite costuming, and atmospheric locations. It has inspired many directors of the American New Wave and beyond, including Martin Scorsese, Francis Ford Coppola, and the Coen brothers.

DELIZIA! BY JOHN DICKIE

If you think you know all there is to know about Italian food, you'll think again after reading this book. Dickie's gastronomic journey across the regions of Italy through the ages covers everything from *pastasciutta* in 12th-century Palermo to today's Slow Food movement in Turin. Carry this book with you as you travel, so you can compare your menu to, say, that for a 1529 Ferrara banquet, which featured "105 soused sea bream" and "15 large salted eels" for starters, followed by "104 roasted capon livers" and "sweet pastry tarts deep-filled with the spleens of sea bass, trout, pike and other fish." *Che delizia!*

THE GREAT BEAUTY, DIRECTED BY PAOLO SORRENTINO

Although directed by a Neapolitan, this Oscar-winning 2013 film is set in Rome and serves as a kind of contemporary *La Dolce Vita.* The lead character in *La grande bellezza,* Jep Gambardella (Toni Servillo), is an aging hedonistic journalist, who, while pining for his glory days, comes to realize the superficiality of his bourgeois lifestyle. Beset by Roman ennui after his raucous rooftop 65th-birthday bash, Jep goes in search of beauty beyond the vanity of his milieu.

THE NEAPOLITAN NOVELS

Elena Ferrante's novels (2012–15) and the HBO TV series bring multilayered postwar Naples to life, going beyond postcard beauty to portray the grim, savage reality of growing up in a rough *rione* (district). The four books explore the complexities of friendship and Italian society. With vivid depictions—mixing the palatial and the squalid—the pseudonymous author details the lifetime bond and inner lives of Elena and Lila and their interactions with a cast of characters across Italy as well as in Naples.

1992, 1993, AND *1994*

The 10-episode television series *1992* and its follow-ups *1993* and *1994* (originally aired in 2015, 2017, and 2019, respectively) are political dramas that follow the intertwined lives of six people amid the tumult of early-1990s Italy. Massive cracks appear in the postwar political compromise, with the Mani Pulite (Clean Hands) investigation led by prosecutor Antonio Di Pietro initiating the fall of the First Republic. As the country is rocked by the so-called Tangentopoli (Bribesville) scandal, marketing man Stefano Accorsi sees an opportunity for an outside figure to seize power. And so up steps media tycoon Silvio Berlusconi and his populist Forza Italia party. Sound familiar?

STANLEY TUCCI: SEARCHING FOR ITALY (2021–22)

Italian-American actor Stanley Tucci goes on a culinary and cultural adventure around the Italian regions in this CNN TV production. In the first series he visits six regions, their urban centers, and fecund hinterlands. In Naples and the Amalfi Coast he visits a San Marzano tomato farm on the shadows of Vesuvius and discovers the art of mozzarella making. In Rome he samples imaginative *quinto-quarto* offal creations and Roman classics rigatoni *all'amatriciana* and *guanciale*-laden *carbonara.* Trips to Tuscany, Bologna, and Milan yield engaging encounters and mouthfuls of *bistecca alla Fiorentina,* the most sought-after Parmigiana-Reggiano cheese, and a cool hangout for an *aperitivo Milanese.* Tucci rounds off the series meeting young female vintner Arianna Occhipinti in Sicily.

Making the Most of Your Euros

TRANSPORTATION

Italy's state-sponsored train system has been given a run for its money by a private company. Sadly, the competitor (Italo) only operates major, high-speed connections (such as Rome to Naples, Florence to Venice, Milan to Bologna) and not local routes. Because of the competition, Trenitalia and Italo engage in price wars, which only plays to the consumer's advantage; depending on time of day and how far in advance you purchase the tickets, great bargains can be had.

No such good news exists for the *regionali* trains. These are trains connecting cities, highly frequented by commuters and used often by visitors who want to get to less visible towns. These trains are habitually late and almost always crowded. Patience is a virtue, and much needed when taking them, particularly during high season.

FOOD AND DRINK

Always remember, when you enter a bar, that there is almost always a two-tier pricing system: one if you stand and one if you sit. It's always cheaper to stand, but sometimes sitting is not only necessary but fun: you can relax and watch the world go by.

Italians love a good sandwich for lunch. Seek out popular sandwich shops (long lines signify that the place is worth visiting) or go to a *salumeria* (delicatessen) and have them make a sandwich for you. It will be simple—cheese and/or cold cuts with bread, no trimmings—but it will be made while you wait, fresh, delicious, and inexpensive.

SIGHTS

There are plenty of free wonderful things to see. Visit the Musei Vaticani, the Uffizi, and the Accademia in Florence (book ahead whenever possible), but don't forget that many artistic gems are found in churches, most of which can be visited with no charge (some of Caravaggio's best work can be found in various churches in Rome). Also, consider renting audio guides if you want direction to any specific place; if you find the idea of joining an organized tour daunting, most museums sell official guidebooks that can help you target what to see. Walking in *centri storici* (historic centers) is also a joy, and free. Seek out piazzas, climb towers, and look for views.

LODGING

High season in Italy runs from Easter to mid-October. If you want to have Florence practically to yourself, come in November or February (most Italian cities are very crowded during the Christmas holidays, which begin around Christmas and finish on January 6). Many hotels in cities offer bargain rates in July and August because most people are off to the beach or the mountains. Remember to factor in great heat and massive crowds, along with the money you'll save. If you decide to travel then, ensure that you have access to a pool and/or air-conditioning.

A great budget-conscious way to travel is via Airbnb (🌐 *airbnb.com*), although prices have soared in recent years, making pads in popular places pricier than many hotels. You can sleep on someone's couch, rent a private room in an apartment (sometimes with en suite bathroom), or spread out in an entire apartment or house. One of the best things about Airbnb is that many of these accommodations come with refrigerators and kitchens, which means you don't have to spend all your money eating out.

In general, whatever your lodging choice, book sooner rather than later. You'll often find better deals that way.

Chapter 2

TRAVEL SMART

Updated by
Nick Bruno

★ CAPITAL:
Rome

POPULATION:
58,971,220

LANGUAGE:
Italian

$ CURRENCY:
Euro

COUNTRY CODE:
39

⚠ EMERGENCIES:
112

DRIVING:
On the right

ELECTRICITY:
220v/50 cycles; electrical plugs have two round prongs

TIME:
6 hours ahead of New York

WEB RESOURCES:
www.italia.it
www.beniculturali.it

Know Before You Go

A TALE OF TWO COUNTRIES

Italy as we know it is just over 160 years old, united by Giuseppe Garibaldi in 1861, and traditions and customs die hard. Differences and rivalries between the wealthier north and the more relaxed south abound, but you will need to spend time in both for the full Italian experience.

DRINK YOUR FILL

Bottled water is available everywhere but often at an inflated price. Carry a refillable bottle and fill up for free at the strategically placed water fountains in cities. In restaurants you can ask for tap water (*acqua del rubinetto*), although you may have to insist.

GO FOOTBALL CRAZY

Soccer—*calcio*—is taken very seriously in Italy, with rivalries running deep. A little knowledge of a local team's performance makes for great conversation. Just avoid wearing your Juventus shirt in Naples if you want to make new friends. To get a taste for the football fervor, its songs and excitement, visit the *stadio* of the local *squadra* (team) and join the *tifosi* (fans) on the *curve* (in the stands).

BOOK IN ADVANCE

Avoid waiting in line for hours by buying museum tickets online before your visit. Also, the earlier you buy train tickets, the less expensive they're likely to be. Trenitalia and Italo offer substantial first-come-first-served discounts on high-speed services; check their websites, and prepare to be flexible with your travel times. Discounts aren't offered on regional trains, and neither is seat reservation. Unless bought online, tickets for regional trains must be stamped before boarding.

TAKE THE BACK ROADS

So you've rented a car. Why stick to the highways? Much of Italy's beauty is along winding mountain roads or coastal secondary routes, so take your time and wander a little. Not only will you save on tolls but you'll save on fuel, too, as gas prices are generally lower than on the *autostrade*. Also, if you're renting a car between November 15 and April 15, remember to ask for snow chains (obligatory on many roads).

EAT FOR (NEARLY) NOTHING

The *aperitivo* is a staple of many areas of the north, where, for little more than the price of a drink, you can partake of a vast buffet to substitute for your evening meal. Bars vie with each other to provide the best array of pasta dishes, *pizzette*, and panini , so check out a few of them before sitting down. Look out for signs like "Aperitivo Happy Hour" and "Stuzzichini": there are bite-size snacks like *patatine* (potato chips), olives, and *grissini* (breadsticks) either served with your drink at the table, or else in a buffet-style spread replete with pasta, rice, and other dishes.

PLAN YOUR DAY

Although breakfast (*la colazione*) is generally served from 7 to 10:30, other mealtimes vary by region. In the north, lunch (*il pranzo*) is noon to 2, whereas restaurants in the south often serve it until 3. You may have difficulty finding dinner (*la cena*) in the north after 9 pm, when most southerners are just sitting down to eat (restaurants there tend not to open until 7:30). And shoppers take note: many stores close from 1 to 4:30.

LACE UP YOUR WALKING SHOES

The best—and often the only—way to see a city is on foot. Public transport works well (albeit generally better in the north), and in recent years many city and town centers have been pedestrianized. Parking costs and fines can add up (avoid ZTL or limited traffic zones), so when possible don your most comfortable shoes and prepare to pound the pavement. Fall in with a weekend afternoon *passeggiata* in smaller towns, where Italians stroll the main street.

DRINK LOCAL

Italy offers a vast array of fine wines, with each region boasting its own appellation. While you may see Chianti on a wine list in Catania, it will probably be no different to what you find at home; for a more authentic taste of the area, try a local Sicilian wine instead.

YOU GET A COFFEE IN A BAR

Coffee culture is different here. Italians take their single-shot espresso standing at a bar—where snacks and alcoholic drinks are also served, and which usually closes in the evening. Pay the cashier, then set your receipt on the counter and place your order. If you choose to sit, there is usually a surcharge, whether there is table service or not. Also, if you order a latte you'll get a glass of milk.

NEVER PASS A RESTROOM

Public restrooms in train stations usually cost €1, and bars frown on the use of theirs without making a purchase, so before you leave the hotel, restaurant, or museum, use the facilities.

DAY-TRIPPER

Lodging in tourist hot spots is at a premium during high season, but deals can be found a little farther from the action. Consider booking outside town and taking a local train or bus to see the sights—you might miss the evening atmosphere, but you'll have more to spend on lunch.

TAKE YOUR TIME

The Italian experience differs from region to region. Try to plan an itinerary that leaves time to explore each destination at leisure. Sure, quick in-and-out visits to cities will allow you to see the major sights, but rushing things means missing out on each area's unique atmosphere.

BE ITALIAN

Food is one of Italy's defining features, and locals continue to be horrified by the idea of pineapple on pizza or (heaven forbid!) ketchup on pasta. You don't need a knife to eat spaghetti (although using a spoon to help wind the pasta around a fork is allowed), and it's fine to pick your pizza up. Most restaurants set a per-person fee for *pane e coperto* (bread and cover charge), although waiters also appreciate a tip—which is standard (around 10%) in the south.

BEWARE OF SCAMS

Larger train stations are notorious for porters insisting on carrying your bags, then charging a fee, so be firm if you're not interested. Also, be careful where you store your wallet and valuables and avoid purchasing from illegal street vendors.

LOOK INTO SIGHT PASSES

Many cities and towns sell multiday passes for access to different museums and sights. These offer great savings if you plan to visit several attractions; some include deals on public transport.

LEARN THE LINGO

Most Italians have some command of English, although this isn't a fail-safe rule, particularly in the south. You can get by on hand gestures and pointing, but a *grazie* or *buongiorno* here and there can't hurt.

SPECIAL SUNDAYS FOR CULTURE

A fabulous Ministero della Cultura initiative, "Domenica al Museo," allows free entry to state-run museums, galleries, and archaeological sites throughout Italy on the first Sunday of the month. For the latest upcoming "Sunday at the Museum" details consult the list of participating institutions at 🌐 *cultura.gov.it/domenicalmuseo* and look out for the hashtag #DomenicaAlMuseo. Naturally, there are lots of crowds and families on these days.

FOOD-SHOP SAVVY

Save money on restaurant and hotel food, and pricey drinks bills, by seeking out stores to stock up. Head to the *alimentari*, the local food and general store, to buy groceries, cheese, cold cuts, and essential refreshments for hot days out, such as water in bottles. The *supermercato* has a wider selection and may stock interesting housewares and other items that make fab gifts to take home. For picnic supplies the *panificio* or *fornaio* is essential for bakery goods such as *pane* (bread) and *panini* (rolls).

Getting Here and Around

A plethora of airlines provide nonstop flights between North American cities (including Boston, Chicago, Dallas, LA, Miami, New York, Philadelphia, San Francisco, and Washington) and Italy, mostly serving Rome's Aeroporto Internazionale Leonardo da Vinci (FCO), better known as Fiumicino (🌐 *www.adr.it)* and Milan's Aeroporto Malpensa *(MXP; 🌐 www.milanomalpensa-airport.com).*

Other popular destinations such as Venice and Naples also accommodate nonstop flights from the United States. In 2025 Delta, United and American have opened new routes connecting JFK with Bari, Palermo, and Catania; Atlanta-Napoli and Washington-Nice (handy for Liguria). Many of these services are seasonal and may change year to year according to demand. Flying time to Milan or Rome is approximately 8–81⁄2 hours from New York, 10–11 hours from Chicago, and 11 1⁄2 hours from Los Angeles.

ITA Airways (🌐 *www.ita-airways.com*) has direct flights from London to Milan and Rome, while British Airways and smaller budget carriers provide services between Great Britain and other locations in Italy. EasyJet connects London's Gatwick and Stansted airports with a dozen or so Italian destinations. Ryanair flies from Stansted to even more airports. Since tickets are frequently sold at discounted prices, investigate the cost of flights within Italy (even one-way) where you're faced with a long, multichange train journey—a potentially time-saving alternative (although less green) way to travel.

You can take the Ferrovie dello Stato Italiane (FS) airport train or bus to Rome's Termini station or to Cadorna or Centrale in Milan; from the latter you can then catch a train to any other location in Italy. It will take about 40 minutes to get from Fiumicino to Roma Termini, less than an hour from Malpensa to Milano Centrale.

A helpful website for information (location, phone numbers, local transportation, etc.) about all the airports in Italy is 🌐 *www.italianairportguide.com.*

Italy's far-reaching regional bus network, often operated by private companies, isn't as attractive an option as in other European countries, partly due to convenient train travel. Schedules are often drawn up with commuters and students in mind and can be sketchy on weekends. But, car travel aside, regional bus companies often provide the only means of getting to out-of-the-way places. Even when this isn't the case, buses can be faster and more direct than local trains, so it's worth taking time to compare bus and train schedules. Busitalia–Sita Nord (🌐 *www.fsbusitalia.it*) covers Tuscany, Umbria, Campania, and the Veneto. Sita Sud (🌐 *www.sitasudtrasporti.it*) caters to travelers in Puglia, Basilicata, and Campania. FlixBus (🌐 *www.flixbus.com*) offers a low-cost long-distance service.

Italy has an extensive network of *autostradas* (toll highways), complemented by equally well-maintained but free *superstradas* (expressways). You'll need your autostrada ticket from entry to pay the toll when you exit; on some shorter autostradas, you pay the toll when you enter. The condition of provincial roads varies, but maintenance is generally good.

Most gas stations have self-service options. Those on autostradas are open 24 hours; others are generally open

Monday through Saturday 7–7, with a break at lunchtime. Automobile Club Italiano offers 24-hour road service. To call the police in an emergency, dial ☎ *112*. Autogrill provides decent highway catering across the country.

PARKING

Curbside spaces are marked by blue lines; pay at a nearby *parcometro* machine, and leave the printed ticket on your dashboard. Fines for violations are high, and towing is common. It's best to park in designated (preferably attended) lots; even small towns often have them just outside their historic centers.

Most towns and cities have a ZTL (Zone a Traffico Limitato: Limited Traffic Zone) that restricts traffic to registered permit holders, local residents, and businesses, within certain hours. These zones are marked by signs (sometimes positioned high on posts so can be missed) and monitored by video camera and a system that takes note of license plates. Should you enter without authorization, the result can be a fine arriving at your home address weeks and sometimes months later. Hotels will usually register your vehicle with the local police, so giving ZTL access.

TIP If you have baggage in your car, always park your car in an attended car park or garage.

RULES OF THE ROAD

You can rent a car with a U.S. driver's license, but Italy also requires non-Europeans to carry an International Driver's Permit (IDP), available for a nominal fee via the AAA website (🌐 *www.aaa.com*). Speed limits are generally 130 kph (80 mph) on autostradas, 90 kph (55 mph) on state roads, and 50 kph (30 mph) in towns; this can drop to 10 kph (6 mph) in congested areas. Exceed the speed limit by more than 60 kph (37 mph), and your license could be confiscated. Right turns on red lights are forbidden. Headlights must be kept on outside municipalities, and you must wear seat belts. Fines for using mobile phones while driving exceed €1,300. The blood alcohol limit is 0.05% (stricter than in the United States).

 Train

The fastest trains on the Ferrovie dello Stato Italiane (FS), or Italian State Railways, are the Frecciarossa. Their privately owned competitor, Nuovo Trasporto Viaggiatori (NTV), or Italo (🌐 *www.italotreno.it*), also runs high-speed service between all major northern cities and as far as Reggio Calabria in the south. Seat reservations are mandatory for these bullet trains, just as they are for the Eurostar and slower Intercity (IC) trains; tickets for the latter are about half the price of those for the faster trains.

You can buy your tickets at machines in the station or on 🌐 *www.trenitalia.com*—consider downloading the Trenitalia app to have tickets on your phone that are automatically validated on departure. Reservations are not available on Regionale and Espresso trains, which are slower, make more stops, and are less expensive. For these trains, you must validate your ticket before boarding by punching it at a wall- or pillar-mounted yellow or green box—if you forget to do this, find a conductor immediately. Fines for attempting to ride a train without a ticket are €50–€200.

TRAIN PASSES

A rail pass (🌐 *www.italiarail.com*, 🌐 *www.eurail.com*) can save you money on train travel. Generally, the more often you plan to travel long distances on high-speed trains, the more sense a pass makes.

Travel Times by Train and Ferry

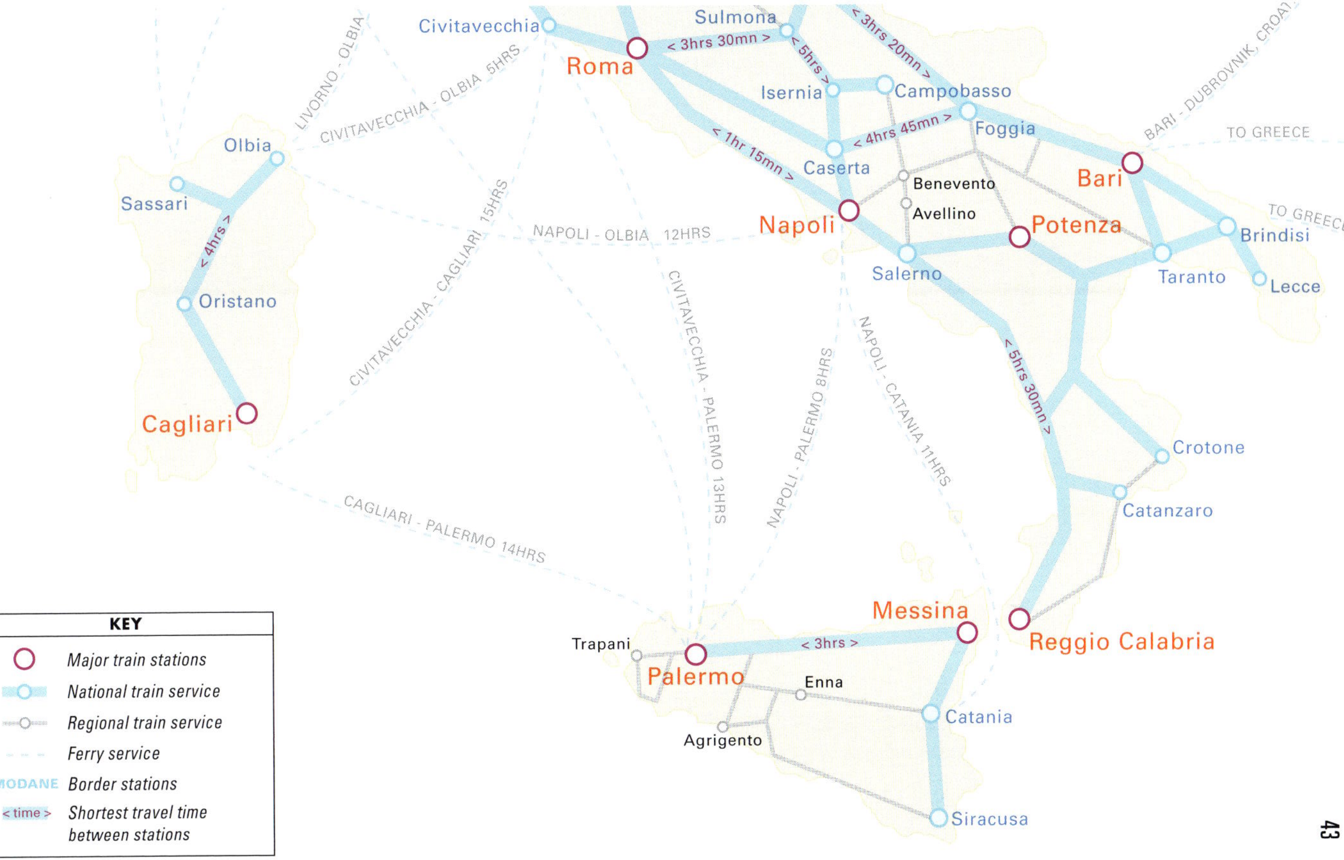

Civitavecchia
Sulmona
Roma
< 3hrs 30mn >
< 5hrs >
< 3hrs 20mn >
Isernia
Campobasso
Foggia
< 4hrs 45mn >
< 1hr 15mn >
Caserta
Benevento
Avellino
Napoli
Potenza
Bari
Salerno
Taranto
Brindisi
Lecce
BARI - DUBROVNIK, CROAT.
TO GREECE
TO GREECE
LIVORNO - OLBIA
CIVITAVECCHIA - OLBIA 5HRS
Olbia
Sassari
< 4hrs >
Oristano
Cagliari
CIVITAVECCHIA - CAGLIARI 15HRS
NAPOLI - OLBIA 12HRS
CIVITAVECCHIA - PALERMO 13HRS
NAPOLI - PALERMO 8HRS
NAPOLI - CATANIA 11HRS
< 5hrs 30mn >
Crotone
Catanzaro
CAGLIARI - PALERMO 14HRS
Messina
Reggio Calabria
Trapani
Palermo
< 3hrs >
Enna
Catania
Agrigento
Siracusa
KEY
Major train stations
National train service
Regional train service
Ferry service
MODANE Border stations
< time > Shortest travel time between stations

Essentials

Dining

Italian cuisine is still largely regional, so try spaghetti *alla carbonara* (with cured pork jowl and egg yolk) in Rome, pizza in Naples, *cinghiale* (wild boar) in Tuscany, or *tartufi* (truffles) in Piedmont. Nowadays, vegetarian and gluten-free options are widely available. Still, if you have dietary restrictions, ask about ingredients; not everything is listed in menu descriptions.

The restaurants we list are the finest in each price category. Unless otherwise noted, they're open for lunch and dinner, closing one or two days a week.

MEALS

Although the distinction has blurred, *ristoranti* tend to be more elegant and expensive than trattorias or *osterie,* which serve traditional, home-style fare. Meals generally consist of an antipasto (starter) followed by a *primo* (first course), a *secondo* (main course) or *contorno* (vegetable side dish), and *dolce* (dessert). You can, of course, eat less (perhaps just a primo or secondo and a dolce). Single dishes are more the norm at an enoteca or pizzeria, and you can grab affordable snacks at bars, cafés, and spots for pizza *al taglio* (by the slice).

PAYING

Most restaurants have a cover charge per person, usually listed at the top of the check as *coperto* or *pane e coperto.* It should be modest (€2–€3 per person) except at the most expensive restaurants. Whenever in doubt, ask before you order to avoid unpleasant discussions later.

The price of fish in restaurants is often given by weight (before cooking), so the price quoted on the menu is for 100 grams of fish, not the whole fish. (an average portion is about 350 grams). So be extra careful when ordering fish as you could be presented with a huge check at the end of your meal.

Major credit cards are widely accepted; more restaurants take Visa and MasterCard than American Express or Diners Club. If you become a regular customer, you may find that the restaurant owner will give you a discount, without you asking for one.

RESERVATIONS AND DRESS

Although reservations are only specifically mentioned when they're essential (there's no other way you'll ever get a table) or when they're not accepted, it's always safest to make one for dinner. Large parties should always call ahead to check the reservations policy. If you change your mind, be sure to cancel, even at the last minute. Some restaurants may require a deposit or charge a fee for no-shows.

When it comes to dress, men being required to wear a jacket or a jacket with tie has been largely phased out in recent years so that even the most old-fashioned smart restaurants tend to have a relaxed dress policy. Only a few places will turn away patrons because they are are wearing shorts.

WINES, BEER, AND SPIRITS

The grape has been cultivated here since the time of the Etruscans, with Tuscany, Piedmont, the Veneto, Puglia, Calabria, Sicily, Le Marche, and Umbria among the renowned areas. Beer is readily available, and Italy has some excellent microbreweries, so ask about local brews. In addition, Italians are imaginative with their cocktails, so consider trying the *aperitivo della casa* (house aperitif). The legal drinking age in Italy is 18.

Italians have a relaxed attitude to alcohol consumption. In many homes, wine is seen as an essential accompaniment to any main meal, like salt or olive oil. All bars and cafés are licensed to serve alcohol, and even takeaway pizzas can be enjoyed with a beer in a city park.

⇨ *Restaurant reviews throughout this guide have been shortened. For full information, visit Fodors.com. Restaurant prices are the average cost of a main course at dinner or, if dinner is not served, at lunch.*

What It Costs in Euros

$	$$	$$$	$$$$
AT DINNER			
under €20	€20–€30	€31–€40	over €40

Health/Safety

EMERGENCIES

No matter where you are in Italy, dial ☎ *112* for all emergencies. Key words to remember for emergency situations are *aiuto* for "help" (pronounced aye-*you*-toh) and *pronto soccorso,* which means "first aid." When confronted with a health emergency, head straight for the Pronto Soccorso department of the nearest hospital or dial ☎ *118.* To call a Red Cross *ambulanza* (ambulance), dial ☎ *800/065510.* If you just need a doctor, ask for *un medico.* Ask the physician for *una fattura* (an invoice) to present to your insurance company for reimbursement.

HEALTH

Smoking is banned inside all public places, so sit indoors (where there's also often air-conditioning) if the smoke in outdoor seating areas bothers you.

It's always best to travel with your own trusted medications. Should you need prescription medication while in Italy, speak with a physician to ensure it's the proper kind. Aspirin (*l'aspirina*) can be purchased at any pharmacy, as can over-the-counter medicines such as ibuprofen or acetaminophen.

Lodging

Many Italian lodgings, some quite luxurious, are in palazzi, villas, monasteries, and smaller historic buildings that have been restored to blend modern comforts with original atmosphere. Another option is renting a vacation property—although, in addition to budget, you should keep in mind location (street noise and neighborhood ambience in cities and towns, degree of isolation in the countryside), the availability of an elevator or the number of stairs, the utility costs, and what's supplied (furnishings, including pots and linens, as well as sundries like dish detergent).

If you're intrigued by the "locavore" movement, ask local tourism offices about *agriturismo* accommodations. Rural farm-stay properties range from luxury villas to farmhouses with basic facilities.

The lodgings we list are the cream of the crop in each price category. Properties are assigned price categories based on the rate for two people sharing a standard double room in high season, including tax and service.

Essentials

⇨ *Hotel reviews throughout this guide have been shortened. For full information, visit Fodors.com. Hotel prices are for a standard double room in high season.*

What It Costs in Euros			
$	$$	$$$	$$$$
LODGING FOR TWO			
under €175	€175–€400	€401–€600	over €600

Money

Of Italy's major cities—where, as in other countries, prices are higher than in the countryside—Milan is by far the most expensive. Resort areas like Capri, Portofino, and Cortina d'Ampezzo cater to wealthy vacationers and also charge top prices. Good value can be found in the scenic Trentino–Alto Adige region of the Dolomites and in Umbria and Le Marche. With a few exceptions, southern Italy and Sicily also offer bargains for those who do their homework before they leave home.

Item	Average Cost
Cup of coffee	€1–€1.60
Soft drink (glass/can/bottle)	€2.50–€3.50
Glass of beer	€3.50–€7
Sandwich	€5–€10
2-km (1-mile) taxi ride in Rome	€11

Passport

A U.S. passport is valid for 10 years. You must apply in person if you're getting a passport for the first time; if your previous passport was lost, stolen, or damaged; or if it has expired and was issued more than 15 years ago or when you were under 16. The cost of a new passport is $165 for adults, $135 for children under 16; renewals are $130.

Tipping

In restaurants a service charge of 10%–15% may appear on your check, but it's not a given that your server will receive this; consider leaving a tip of 5%–10% (in cash) for good service. Taxi drivers also appreciate a euro or two.

In hotels, give the *portiere* (concierge) about 10% of the bill for services or €3–€5 for help with dinner reservations and such. In moderately priced hotels, leave maids about €1 per day, and tip a minimum of €1 for valet or room service. In expensive hotels, double these amounts. Guides should receive €1.50 at least per person for a half-day group tour, more if they're especially knowledgeable.

 U.S. Embassy/Consulate

In addition to the embassy in Rome, the United States has consulates general in Florence, Milan, and Naples. If you're arrested or detained, ask Italian officials to notify the embassy or nearest consulate immediately. Consider participating in the U.S. Department of State's Smart Traveler Enrollment Program (STEP) (*step.state.gov/step*) to receive alerts and make it easier to locate you in an emergency.

 Visa

From 2026, entry for visa-exempt nationals from 60 countries including the United States and Canada requires travel authorization from ETIAS (European Travel Information and Authorization System). It is linked to your current passport and valid for three years, allowing stays up to 90 days in any 180-day period. Most applications should be approved in a few minutes via the website (*etias.com*) for a cost of €7 (free for those under 18 and over 70) but do allow at least 30 days should further evidence and an interview be required (in late 2026 the fee is expected to increase to €20). Just note that the program's implementation has been delayed several times, so confirm in advance that ETIAS registration is required for your trip.

 When to Go

High Season: June through September is expensive and busy. In August, most Italians take their own summer holidays; cities are less crowded, but many shops and restaurants close. July and August can be uncomfortably hot.

Low Season: Unless you're skiing, winter offers the least appealing weather, although it's the best time for airfare and hotel deals and to escape the crowds. Temperatures in the south can be mild.

Value Season: By late September, temperate weather and saner airfares can make for a happier trip. October is also great, but November is often rainy. March and early April weather is changeable. From late April to early May, the masses have not yet arrived.

Helpful Italian Phrases

BASICS

Yes/no	SÍ/No	see/no
Please	Per favore	pear fa-**vo**-ray
Thank you	Grazie	**grah**-tsee-ay
You're welcome	Prego	**pray**-go
I'm sorry (apology)	Mi dispiace	mee dis-pee-**atch**-ay
Excuse me, sorry	Scusi	**skoo**-zee
Good morning/ afternoon	Buongiorno	bwohn-**jor**-no
Good evening	Buona sera	**bwoh**-na **say**-ra
Good-bye	Arrivederci	a-ree-vah-**dare**-chee
Mr. (Sir)	Signore	see-**nyo**-ray
Mrs. (Ma'am)	Signora	see-**nyo**-ra
Miss	Signorina	see-nyo-**ree**-na
Pleased to meet you	Piacere	pee-ah-**chair**-ray
How are you?	Come sta?	**ko**-may-**stah**
Hello (phone)	Pronto?	**proan**-to

NUMBERS

one-half	mezzo	**mets**-zoh
one	uno	**oo**-no
two	due	**doo**-ay
three	tre	Tray
four	quattro	**kwah**-tro
five	cinque	**cheen**-kway
six	sei	Say
seven	sette	**set**-ay
eight	otto	**oh**-to
nine	nove	**no**-vay
ten	dieci	dee-**eh**-chee
eleven	undici	**oon**-dee-chee
twelve	dodici	**doh**-dee-chee
thirteen	tredici	**trey**-dee-chee
fourteen	quattordici	kwah-**tor**-dee-chee
fifteen	quindici	**kwin**-dee-chee
sixteen	sedici	**say**-dee-chee
seventeen	dicissette	dee-chah-**set**-ay
eighteen	diciotto	dee-chee-**oh**-to
nineteen	diciannove	dee-chee-ahn-**no**-vay
twenty	venti	**vain**-tee
twenty-one	ventuno	**vent**-oo-no
thirty	trenta	**train**-ta
forty	quaranta	kwa-**rahn**-ta
fifty	cinquanta	cheen-**kwahn**-ta
sixty	sessanta	seh-**sahn**-ta
seventy	settanta	seh-**tahn**-ta
eighty	ottanta	o-**tahn**-ta
ninety	novanta	no-**vahn**-ta
one hundred	cento	**chen**-to
one thousand	mille	**mee**-lay
one million	un milione	oon **mill**-oo-nay

COLORS

black	Nero	**nair**-ro
blue	Blu	bloo
brown	Marrone	ma-**rohn**-nay
green	Verde	**ver**-day
orange	Arancione	ah-rahn-**cho**-nay
red	Rosso	**rose**-so
white	Bianco	bee-**ahn**-koh
yellow	Giallo	**jaw**-low

DAYS OF THE WEEK

Sunday	Domenica	do-**meh**-nee-ka
Monday	Lunedi	loo-ne-**dee**
Tuesday	Martedi	mar-te-**dee**
Wednesday	Mercoledi	**mer**-ko-le-**dee**
Thursday	Giovedi	jo-ve-**dee**
Friday	VenerdÌ	ve-ner-**dee**
Saturday	Sabato	**sa**-ba-toh

MONTHS

January	Gennaio	jen-**ay**-o
February	Febbraio	feb-**rah**-yo
March	Marzo	**mart**-so
April	Aprile	a-**pril**-ay
May	Maggio	**mahd**-joe
June	Giugno	**joon**-yo
July	Luglio	**lool**-yo
August	Agosto	a-**gus**-to
September	Settembre	se-**tem**-bre
October	Ottobre	o-**toh**-bre
November	Novembre	no-**vem**-bre
December	Dicembre	di-**chem**-bre

USEFUL WORDS AND PHRASES

Do you speak English?	Parla Inglese?	**par**-la een-**glay**-zay
I don't speak Italian	Non parlo italiano	non **par**-lo ee-tal-**yah**-no
I don't understand	Non capisco	non ka-**peess**-ko
I don't know	Non lo so	non lo **so**
I understand	Capisco	ka-**peess**-ko
I'm American	Sono Americano(a)	**so**-no a-may-ree-**kah**-no(a)
I'm British	Sono inglese	so-no een-**glay**-zay
What's your name?	Come si chiama?	**ko**-may see kee-**ah**-ma
My name is ...	Mi chiamo...	mee kee-**ah**-mo
What time is it?	Che ore sono?	kay **o**-ray **so**-no
How?	Come?	**ko**-may
When?	Quando?	**kwan**-doe
Yesterday/today/ tomorrow	Ieri/oggi/domani	**yer**-ee/ **o**-jee/ do-**mah**-nee

This morning	Stamattina/Oggi	sta-ma-**tee**-na/ **o**-jee
Afternoon	Pomeriggio	po-mer-**ee**-jo
Tonight	Stasera	sta-**ser**-a
What?	Che cosa?	kay **ko**-za
What is it?	Che cos'è?	kay ko-**zey**
Why?	Perchè?	pear-**kay**
Who?	Chi?	**Kee**
Where is …	Dov'è…	doe-**veh**
the train station?	la stazione?	la sta-tsee-**oh**-nay
the subway?	la metropolitana?	la may-tro-po-lee-**tah**-na
the bus stop?	la fermata dell'autobus?	la fer-**mah**-ta del-ow-tor-**booss**
the airport	l'aeroporto	la-er-roh-**por**-toh
the post office?	l'ufficio postale	loo-**fee**-cho po-**stah**-lay
the bank?	la banca?	la **bahn**-ka
the hotel?	l'hotel…?	lo-**tel**
the museum?	Il museo	eel moo-**zay**-o
the hospital?	l'ospedale?	lo-spay-**dah**-lay
the elevator?	l'ascensore	la-shen-**so**-ray
the restrooms?	…il bagno	eel **bahn**-yo
Here/there	Qui/là	kwee/la
Left/right	A sinistra/a destra	a see-**neess**-tra/a **des**-tra
Is it near/far?	È vicino/lontano?	ay vee-**chee**-no/ lon-**tah**-no
I'd like …	Vorrei…	vo-**ray**
a room	una camera	**oo**-na **kah**-may-ra
the key	la chiave	la kee-**ah**-vay
a newspaper	un giornale	oon jore-**nah**-vay
a stamp	un francobollo	oon frahn-ko-**bo**-lo
I'd like to buy …	Vorrei comprare…	vo-**ray** kom-**prah**-ray
a city map	una mappa della città	**oo**-na **mah**-pa **day**-la chee-**tah**
a road map	una carta stradale	**oo**-na **car**-tah stra-**dahl**-lay
a magazine	una revista	**oo**-na ray-**vees**-tah
envelopes	buste	**boos**-tay
writing paper	carta de lettera	**car**-tah dah **leyt**-ter-rah
a postcard	una cartolina	**oo**-na car-tog-**leen**-ah
a ticket	un biglietto	oon bee-**yet**-toh
How much is it?	Quanto costa?	**kwahn**-toe **coast**-a
It's expensive/ cheap	È caro/ economico	ay **car**-o/ ay-ko-**no**-mee-ko
A little/a lot	Poco/tanto	**po**-ko/**tahn**-to
More/less	Più/meno	pee-**oo**/**may**-no
Enough/too (much)	Abbastanza/ troppo	a-bas-**tahn**-sa/tro-po
I am sick	Sto male	sto **mah**-lay
Call a doctor	Chiama un dottore	kee-**ah**-mah-oondoe-**toe**-ray
Help!	Aiuto!	a-**yoo**-to
Stop!	Alt!	ahlt

DINING OUT

A bottle of …	Una bottiglia di…	**oo**-na bo-**tee**-lee-ah dee
A cup of …	Una tazza di…	**oo**-na **tah**-tsa dee
A glass of …	Un bicchiere di…	oon bee-key-**air**-ay dee
Beer	La birra	la **beer**-rah
Bill/check	Il conto	eel **cone**-toe
Bread	Il pane	eel **pah**-nay
Breakfast	La prima colazione	la **pree**-ma ko-la-**tsee**-oh-nay
Butter	Il burro	eel **boor**-roh
Cocktail/aperitif	L'aperitivo	la-pay-ree-**tee**-vo
Dinner	La cena	la **chen**-a
Fixed-price menu	Menù a prezzo fisso	may-**noo** a **pret**-so **fee**-so
Fork	La forchetta	la for-**ket**-a
I am vegetarian	Sono vegetariano(a)	**so**-no vay-jay-ta-ree-**ah**-no/a
I cannot eat …	Non posso mangiare	non **pose**-so mahn-gee-**are**-ay
I'd like to order	Vorrei ordinare	vo-**ray** or-dee-**nah**-ray
Is service included?	Il servizio è incluso?	eel ser-**vee**-tzee-o ay een-**kloo**-zo
I'm hungry/ thirsty	Ho fame/sede	oh **fah**-meh/**sehd**-ed
It's good/bad	È buono/cattivo	ay **bwo**-bo/ka-**tee**-vo
It's hot/cold	È caldo/freddo	ay **kahl**-doe/**fred**-o
Knife	Il coltello	eel kol-**tel**-o
Lunch	Il pranzo	eel **prahnt**-so
Menu	Il menu	eel may-**noo**
Napkin	Il tovagliolo	eel toe-va-lee-**oh**-lo
Pepper	Il pepe	eel **pep**-peh
Plate	Il piatto	eel pee-**aht**-toe
Please give me …	Mi dia…	mee **dee**-a
Salt	Il sale	eel **sah**-lay
Spoon	Il cucchiaio	eel koo-kee-ah-yo
Tea	tè	tay
Water	acqua	**awk**-wah
Wine	vino	**vee**-noh

Great Itineraries

Northern Italy

Northern Italy is a region with high fashion, big wines, and beautiful lakes.

DAY 1: MILAN

Start off in **Milan,** Italy's capital of art, fashion, and design. Explore elegant shops around the **Duomo** and **Via Montenapoleone.** Some of Europe's great art treasures are housed in the **Brera Gallery.** The elegant **Basilica di Santa Maria presso San Satiro** is about a 20-minute walk from **Santa Maria delle Grazie,** where Leonardo's stunning *Last Supper* is housed. Spend a night at the opera in **La Scala,** Italy's most illustrious opera house.

Logistics: Central Milan is compact, with excellent public transportation.

DAY 2: BELLAGIO

Lake Como combines some of Italy's most beautiful scenery with elegant historic villas and gardens, making it truly worthy of a full-day excursion. **Bellagio** is a pretty village from which you can ferry to other points along the lake, take walking tours, hike, or just sit on a terrace watching the light play on the sapphire water and the snowcapped mountains.

Logistics: Como's San Giovanni station is just one hour by train from Milan, and Bus C10/C30 leaves hourly from here for the one-hour lakeside journey to Bellagio—you won't need a car, since most touring is on foot, by ferry, or by bus.

DAYS 3 TO 5: VERONA/MANTUA/VICENZA

Take an early train to **Verona** (75 minutes from Milan) and settle into your hotel. Start your exploration of northern Italy's three most important art cities with Verona's ancient Roman arena, theater, and city gates; its brooding medieval palaces and castle; and its graceful bridge spanning the Adige.

The next day, make the 45-minute train trip to **Mantua,** arriving in time for lunch featuring a local specialty: *tortelli di zucca* (pumpkin-filled ravioli) served with sage butter. Check out the Mantegna frescoes in the **Palazzo Ducale,** or visit Giulio Romano's **Palazzo Te,** a 16th-century pleasure palace. Take the train back to Verona in time for dinner and, perhaps, an opera in the Roman amphitheater.

On Day 5, head to **Vicenza** (35 minutes by train) to see the palaces, villas, and public buildings of the lion of late-16th-century architecture, Andrea Palladio. Don't miss **Palladio's Basilica, Teatro Olimpico** and his famous villa, **La Rotonda,** slightly out of town. If time allows, try to see the frescoes by Gianbattista and Giandomenico Tiepolo in the **Villa Valmarana ai Nani,** near La Rotonda. For lunch, try *baccalà alla vicentina,* the local salt-cod dish.

DAY 6: PADUA

Most people visit this important art and university center on a day trip out of Venice, but then they miss one of **Padua's** main attractions: the nightlife that goes on in the city's wine bars and cafés from evening until quite late. See the Giotto frescoes in the **Cappella degli Scrovegni** and the **Basilica di Sant'Antonio** before lunch, then spend a relaxing afternoon at the **Villa Pisani,** enjoying its gardens and important Tiepolo fresco.

Logistics: Trains run frequently to Padua from Verona (one hour) and Vicenza (30 minutes); you don't really have to schedule ahead.

DAY 7: VENICE

The first things you'll probably want to do in **Venice** are to take a vaporetto ride down the **Grand Canal** and see **Piazza San Marco.** After that, move on to the adjacent **Palazzo Ducale** and Sansovino's **Biblioteca Marciana,** across the piazzetta.

For lunch, take Vaporetto No. 1 to Ca' Rezzonico, and have a sandwich and a *spritz* in **Campo Santa Margherita.** From here, make your way to the **Galleria dell'Accademia** to take in its wonderful collection of Venetian paintings. In the evening, walk up the Zattere and have a drink at one of the cafés overlooking the **Canale della Giudecca.**

Logistics: Seeing the Grand Canal and Piazza San Marco in relative tranquillity will be your reward for getting up at the crack of dawn (arrive at the vaporetto before 8:30 to avoid the rush) and doing a little extra planning.

DAY 8: VENICE

If the Galleria dell'Accademia has whetted your appetite for Venetian painting, start the day by visiting churches and institutions where you can see more. If your taste runs to modern art, head to the **Peggy Guggenheim Collection** and, down the street, the Pinault Collection in the refashioned **Punta della Dogana.**

In the afternoon, head for the Fondamenta Nuova station to catch a vaporetto to the outer islands: **Murano,** where you can shop for Venetian glass and visit a glass museum and workshops; **Burano,** known for lace making and colorful houses; and **Torcello,** Venice's first inhabited island and home to a beautiful cathedral.

DAY 9: VENICE

Pay a visit to the **Rialto,** one of Europe's most atmospheric fish markets, where Venetians buy their fruit and vegetables as well as, of course, their fish. Note that the Rialto Market is closed on Sunday and Monday; since there is no fishing on Sunday, there can be no fresh fish available on Monday.

Have lunch in one of the excellent market-area restaurants. Then, on your last afternoon in Venice, leave time to sit with a coffee or spritz in a lively square or in a café along the **Fondamenta della Misericordia** in Cannaregio or **Campo Santa Margherita** in Dorsoduro. Alternatively, visit the Lombardo family's lyrical **Miracoli,** a short walk from the San Marco end of the Rialto Bridge, or Palladio's masterpiece, the **Redentore** church on **Giudecca.**

DAY 10: VENICE/DEPARTURE

Take one last vaporetto trip up the Grand Canal to **Piazzale Roma** and, after saying *arrivederci* to Venice, catch ATVO bus or Alilaguna boat to the airport.

Great Itineraries

Central Italy

Visit central Italy for the great art, sumptuous countryside, and outstanding food and wine.

DAY 1: FLORENCE

If you're coming in on an international flight, you'll probably settle in Florence in time for an afternoon stroll or siesta (depending on your jet-lag strategy) before dinner.

Logistics: Begin anticipating the first dinner of your trip. Look for a place near your hotel, and when you arrive, reserve a table (or have your concierge do it for you). Making a meal the focus of your first day is a great way to ease into Italian life.

DAY 2: FLORENCE

Begin at the **Uffizi Gallery,** whose extensive collection will occupy much of your morning. Next, take in the neighboring **Piazza della Signoria,** then head a few blocks north to the **Duomo** to check out Ghiberti's famous bronze doors on the **Battistero** (actually high-quality copies; the originals are in the **Museo dell'Opera del Duomo**). Climb up Brunelleschi's cathedral dome to the cupola. Spend the afternoon wandering Florence's medieval streets; or head out to **Fiesole** to see the ancient amphitheater.

Logistics: Reserve Uffizi tickets online ahead of your visit; climbs up Brunelleschi's dome must also be reserved in advance.

DAY 3: FLORENCE

Spend your morning seeing Michelangelo's *David* at the **Galleria dell'Accademia,** the **Medici Chapels,** the **Palazzo Pitti** and **Boboli Gardens,** and the churches of **Santa Maria Novella** and **Santa Croce.** If it's a clear day, spend the afternoon making your way up to **Piazzale Michelangelo** for sweeping views of the idyllic Florentine countryside. Recharge with a dinner featuring *bistecca alla fiorentina.*

Logistics: You can reach Piazzale Michelangelo by taxi or by taking Bus No. 12 or 13 from the Lungarno. Otherwise, do your best to get around on foot; Florence is a brilliant city for walking.

DAY 4: SAN GIMIGNANO

After breakfast, pick up your car and make the lazy drive from Florence to **San Gimignano.** Upon arriving in town, you'll no doubt be awed by its towers—medieval skyscrapers that provided security and served as symbols of wealth and power. After finding your way to a hotel in the old town, set out on foot to check out the city's turrets and alleyways, then enjoy a leisurely dinner.

Logistics: San Gimignano is only 57 km (35 miles) to the southwest. Consider taking a detour on the SS222 (Strada Chiantigiana) to a winery in one of the Chianti wine towns.

DAY 5: SIENA

In the morning, set out for nearby **Siena,** which is known worldwide for its Palio, a horse race involving the city's 17 *contrade* (medieval neighborhoods). You will be blown away by the precious medieval streets and memorable fan-shape **Piazza del Campo.** Don't miss the spectacular **Duomo,** the **Battistero,** and the **Spedale di Santa Maria della Scala,** an old hospital and hostel that now contains an underground archaeological museum.

Logistics: Parking can be a challenge. Look for the *stadio* (soccer stadium), where there's a parking lot that often has space.

DAY 6: AREZZO/CORTONA

From Siena you'll first head to **Arezzo,** home to the **Basilica di San Francesco,** which contains important frescoes by Piero della Francesca. Check out the **Piazza Grande** along with its beautiful Romanesque church of **Santa Maria della Pieve.** Try to do all of this before lunch, after which you'll head straight to **Cortona.** Cortona is a town for walking and relaxing, not sightseeing, so enjoy yourself as you wander through the **Piazza della Repubblica** and **Piazza Signorelli,** perhaps doing a bit of shopping.

Logistics: Siena to Arezzo is 70 km (43½ miles) on the SS715 and A1 autostrada. From Arezzo to Cortona, it's just 30 km (18 miles)—take SR71.

DAY 7: ASSISI

Cross over into Umbria and see **Assisi,** the home of St. Francis that today hosts many religious pilgrims. After arrival and check-in, head straight for the **Basilica di San Francesco,** which displays the tomb of St. Francis and some unbelievable frescoes. From here, take Via San Francesco to **Piazza del Comune** and see the **Tempio di Minerva.** Break for lunch and then see **San Rufino,** the cathedral, before returning through the piazza to Corso Mazzini and **Santa Chiara.**

Logistics: From Cortona, take the SR71 to the A1 autostrada toward Perugia. After about 40 km (24 miles), take the Assisi exit (E45), and it's another 14 km (8 miles) to Assisi.

DAY 8: SPOLETO

This morning takes you to the walled city of **Spoleto,** renowned for its summer arts festival; its wonderful **Duomo**; its impressive **La Rocca** fortress; and its marvelous **Ponte delle Torri,** the 14th-century bridge that separates the town from Monteluco. Save your appetite for a serious last dinner in Italy. Try to sample black truffles, a proud product of the region, especially from mid-November to mid-March.

Logistics: The trip from Assisi to Spoleto is a pretty 47-km (29-mile) drive (SS75 to SS3) that should take less than an hour.

DAY 9: SPOLETO/DEPARTURE

It's a fair distance from Spoleto to the Florence airport, your point of departure. One alternative is to fly out of the tiny airport in Perugia. If you prefer to drive, get an early start and allow at least 2½ hours for the trip along the A1 autostrada.

Great Itineraries

Southern Italy

Come for the archaeological wonders, azure sea, and excellent Neapolitan fare.

DAY 1: NAPLES

Fly into Naples's **Aeroporto Capodichino,** a scant 5 km (3 miles) from the city. Naples is classic Italy, and many visitors end up falling in love with its alluring palazzi and spectacular pizza. If you can get over the shock of the initial cacophony and its sketchy reputation, you'll likely get hooked on its lively characters and irresistibly languid, stop-start rhythm.

Recharge with a nap and, after that, a good *caffè*—Naples has some of the world's best. You should be back on your feet in time for an evening stroll down the city's bustling shopping street, Via Toledo, to Piazza Plebiscito, before dinner and bed.

DAY 2: NAPLES

Start the day at the **Museo Archeologico Nazionale,** budgeting at least two hours for its collection, before stopping for coffee at a café in Piazza Bellini. From here, head down Via dei Tribunali, crossing Via Duomo to see Caravaggio's *The Seven Works of Mercy* at **Pio Monte della Misericordia.** Make your way back along Spaccanapoli with a brief stop at the **Cappella Sansevero** for a look at the pinnacle of Masonic sculpture. Continue on to the port and the **Castel Nuovo** and then past the **Teatro San Carlo** to the enormous **Palazzo Reale** in **Piazza Plebiscito.** Just beyond this is the **Santa Lucia** waterfront area, with the **Castel dell'Ovo.** Join the passeggiata along *lungomare* (seafront) as far as Mergellina, soaking up the atmosphere and spectacular views, and perhaps grab an aperitivo or gelato. Return to your hotel for a short rest before dinner and perhaps a night out at one of Naples's lively bars or clubs.

Logistics: This entire day is easily done on foot.

DAY 3: POMPEII/SORRENTO

After breakfast, pack your luggage, and head from Naples to **Pompeii,** one of Europe's true archaeological gems. If it's summer, be prepared for sweltering heat as you make your way through the incredible preserved ruins of a city that was devastated by the whims of **Mt. Vesuvius** nearly 2,000 years ago. You'll see the houses of noblemen and merchants, brothels, political graffiti, and more. **Sorrento,** on the way to the fabled Amalfi Coast, is touristy, but it may well be the Italian city of your imagination: cliff hanging, cobblestone paved, and graced with an infinite variety of fishing ports and coastal views. Stop here for a relaxing dinner of fish and white wine.

Logistics: Rather than rent a car, take the Circumvesuviana, a twice-hourly train to Sorrento that stops near the ruins at Pompeii's Villa dei Misteri.

DAY 4: POSITANO/RAVELLO

Positano, your next stop, is one of Italy's most visited towns for good reason: its blue-green seas, stairs "as steep as ladders," and white Moorish-style houses are all memorable. Walk, gaze, and eat (lunch), before heading on to the less visited, yet even loftier town of **Ravello.** This aerie "closer to the sky than it is to the sea" is an Amalfi Coast dream come true. Don't miss the **Duomo, Villa Rufolo,** and **Villa Cimbrone** before settling in for dinner in the sky.

Logistics: Sorrento to Positano is a slow 15-km (9½-mile) jaunt, and then Ravello is another 26 km (16 miles) to the east, with the winding roads drawing it out for the better part of an hour. The SITA bus is your best option. Motorists should be prepared to use low gears if driving a stick shift.

DAY 5: MATERA

Those with a car will have a bit of a drive from the Amalfi Coast; leaving Campania and entering Basilicata is generally a lonely experience. Little-traveled roads, wild hills, and distant farms are the hallmarks of this province, which has perfected the art of peasant food and the deep, dark *aglianico* wines to go with it. The lengthy journey to **Matera** is worthwhile, however, to see this beautiful ancient city full of Paleolithic **Sassi** (cave-like dwellings hewn out of rock). Spend the afternoon exploring them, then enjoy a relaxing dinner at one of Matera's excellent restaurants.

Logistics: It's a long haul from Ravello to Matera—if using public transportation you may find it easier to return first to Naples—but the effort is worth it, as Basilicata's landscape is so pretty.

DAY 6: LECCE

Get an early start for your journey to the Baroque city of **Lecce,** which will mark your introduction to Puglia, the heel of Italy's boot. It's one of the country's best-kept secrets, as you'll soon find out upon checking out the spectacular church of **Santa Croce,** the ornate **Duomo,** and the harmonious **Piazza Sant'Oronzo.** The shopping, the food, and the evening passeggiata are all great.

Logistics: It's not far from Matera to Lecce as the crow flies, but the 2½-hour trip is more involved than you might think; patience is required. Those without a car should head to Bari, then take the train south. The best driving route is via Taranto, *not* up through Bari.

DAY 7: BARI

It is a two-hour drive from Lecce to **Bari,** and many make a pit stop halfway at the beautiful hilltop town of **Ostuni.** Spend the day wandering through Bari's historic center and finish with a good fish dinner.

Logistics: Take a direct train or the coastal SS16 for 154 km (95 miles) until you hit Bari.

DAY 8: BARI/DEPARTURE

Bari's Aeroporto Karol Wojtyla is small but quite serviceable, with frequent connections through Rome and Milan.

Logistics: Bari hotels offer easy airport transfers; take advantage of them.

Great Itineraries

Venice, Florence, Rome, and Highlights in Between

Think of this itinerary as a rough draft for you to revise according to your interests and time constraints.

DAY 1: VENICE

Arrive in Venice's Marco Polo Airport, and hop on the Alilaguna boat or bus to Venice. Check into your hotel, get out, and get lost along the canals for a couple of hours before dinner.

Logistics: At the main bus station, you can immediately transfer to the most delightful "bus" in the world: the vaporetto. Enjoy your first ride up the Grand Canal, and make sure you're paying attention to the *fermata* (stop) where you need to get off.

DAY 2: VENICE

If you like photography, rise before dawn to catch a vaporetto to Giudecca and walk along the long Fondamenta, observing the golden hour hues bathe Palladio's Redentore and the stunning canal views. Grab a coffee at a real Italian coffee bar before taking in the top sights, including the **Basilica di San Marco, Palazzo Ducale,** and **Galleria dell'Accademia.** Don't forget **Piazza San Marco**: the intense anticipation as you near the giant square climaxes in a stunning view of the piazza. Stop for lunch, sampling the traditional Venetian specialty *sarde in saor* (sardines in a mouthwatering sweet-and-sour preparation with onions and raisins), and check out the fish market at the foot of the **Rialto Bridge**; then see the sunset at the **Zattere** before dinner. Later, stop at a bar on the **Campo San Luca** or **Campo Santa Margherita,** where you can mingle with the students and families enjoying the open space, and toast to being free of automobiles.

Logistics: Venice is best seen on foot, with the occasional vaporetto ride. Always carry a city map: it's very easy to get totally lost here.

DAY 3: FERRARA/BOLOGNA

The ride to **Ferrara,** your first stop in Emilia-Romagna, is about 90 minutes. Visit the **Castello Estense** and **Duomo** before grabbing lunch. Wander Ferrara's cobblestone streets, then hop on the train to **Bologna** (less than an hour away). Check into your hotel, and walk around **Piazza Maggiore** before dinner, soaking up the bustle and architectural gems including the **Fontana del Nettuno.** Later check out some of Italy's best nightlife.

Logistics: The train station lies a bit outside the center of Ferrara, so you may want to take a taxi or a less expensive city bus into town.

DAY 4: BOLOGNA/FLORENCE

After breakfast, visit some of Bologna's churches and piazzas, and walk the porticoed streets admiring the city's medieval towers and tempting delis. After lunch, take the short train ride to **Florence.** You'll arrive in time for an afternoon siesta and an evening passeggiata.

DAY 5: FLORENCE

Start with the **Uffizi Gallery,** where you'll see Botticelli's *Primavera* and *Birth of Venus,* the *Madonna of the Goldfinch* by Raphael, and *Bacchus* by Caravaggio, among other works. Next, walk to **Piazza del Duomo,** site of Brunelleschi's spectacular dome, which you can climb for an equally spectacular view. After a simple trattoria lunch, either devote the afternoon to art or hike up to **Piazzale Michelangelo,** which overlooks the city. Finish the evening in style with a traditional *bistecca alla Fiorentina* (grilled T-bone steak with olive oil).

Logistics: It's best to reserve Uffizi Gallery tickets in advance; you *must* reserve in advance to climb Brunelleschi's dome.

DAY 6: LUCCA/PISA

After breakfast, board a train for a 90-minute ride to the walled medieval city of **Lucca.** Don't miss the Romanesque **Duomo** or a walk along the city's ramparts. Have lunch at a trattoria before continuing on to **Pisa** (30 minutes away) and its **Campo dei Miracoli,** where you'll spend an afternoon seeing the **Leaning Tower,** along with the **Duomo** and **Battistero.** Walk down to the banks of the Arno River and dine at one of the inexpensive local restaurants in the real city center.

Logistics: Lucca's train station is conveniently situated just outside the walled city. Although across town from the Leaning Tower, Pisa's train station isn't far from the city center.

DAY 7: ROME

Take a high-speed train bound for **Rome,** a 90-minute trip from Florence or three hours from Pisa. Although the Eternal City took millennia to build, on this whirlwind trip you'll have just two days to tour it. Make your way to your hotel and relax for a bit before heading to the **Piazza Navona, Campo de' Fiori,** and **Trevi Fountain**—it's best in the evening—and have a stand-up aperitivo (Campari and soda is a classic) at an unpretentious local bar. For dinner, you can't go wrong at any of Rome's popular local pizzerias.

DAY 8: ROME

In the morning, head to the **Vatican Museums** to see Michelangelo's glorious frescoes at the **Sistine Chapel.** Visit **St. Peter's Basilica and Square** before heading for lunch near the Pantheon. Next, visit the magnificent **Pantheon,** and then the **Colosseum,** stopping along Via dei Fori Imperiali to check out the **Roman Forum** from above. From the Colosseum, walk or take a taxi to **Piazza di Spagna,** a good place to shop at stylish boutiques.

Logistics: Avoid lines and waits by buying tickets online.

DAY 9: ROME/DEPARTURE

Head by taxi to Termini station and catch the train to Fiumicino airport.

Logistics: For most people, the train from Termini station is preferable to a taxi ride.

Great Itineraries

Rome in 3 Days

Rome wasn't built in a day—so don't try to see it all in a day. Three days is a doable, if jam-packed, amount of time to visit the ancient city's major attractions.

Logistics: Much of the city shuts down on Sunday (including the Vatican Museums, except for the last Sunday of the month), and many restaurants and state museums are closed on Monday. To skip lines and better enjoy your experiences, reservations are a good idea at the Colosseum and the Vatican Museums; they're required for the Galleria Borghese.

DAY 1: ANCIENT ROME

Spend your first day in Rome exploring the likes of the **Roman Forum, Musei Capitolini,** and the **Colosseum.** This area is pretty compact, but you can easily spend a full morning and afternoon exploring its treasures. It's best to try and beat the crowds at the Colosseum by getting there right when it opens at 8:30 am (advance tickets help, too). A guided tour of the Forum is also a good way to make the most out of your afternoon. After your day of sightseeing, stop for a classic Roman dinner in nearby Monti.

DAY 2: THE VATICAN AND PIAZZA NAVONA

Another full day of sightseeing awaits when you make your way to the city-state known as the **Vatican.** You'll once again want to try and avoid the biggest crowds here, especially for a glimpse of the Sistine Chapel (the best way to do this is to make online reservations ahead of time). Booking a tour of the **Vatican Museums** is a good way to take full advantage of the site; most tours last two hours. Be sure to stop in and marvel at **St. Peter's Basilica,** too. Stop for lunch in nearby Prati, but after you're done with the Vatican, cross the river to **Piazza Navona.** Spend some time exploring this glorious piazza and its sculptures, but make sure to stop by the **Pantheon** before heading to Campo de' Fiori for dinner at an outdoor restaurant. Afterward, there are plenty of nearby bars to keep you occupied.

DAY 3: PIAZZA DI SPAGNA, VILLA BORGHESE, AND TRASTEVERE

Start your morning with breakfast near the **Trevi Fountain** before doing some window-shopping up Via Condotti and along the many surrounding backstreets as you make your way to the **Spanish Steps.** Pose for some postcard-worthy photos there before heading to nearby **Villa Borghese.** If you're sick of museums, feel free to explore Rome's main park and enjoy the great views; if you're up for some more art, the **Galleria Borghese** is one of the city's best art museums. Afterward, head to trendy Trastevere for dinner, and soak up the cobblestone streets and charming medieval houses as you barhop your last night in town.

IF YOU HAVE MORE TIME

If you want to make the most of your time in the city itself, take your time exploring the many churches and cathedrals, like **Sant'Ignazio** or **San Clemente.** You can also stop by to explore gorgeous palaces, like the **Palazzo Doria Pamphilij,** and check out lesser known but just as impressive museums, like the MAXXI or the MACRO. Visiting the ancient Roman road known as the Via Appia Antica and its spooky yet mesmerizing catacombs is a great way to spend an afternoon immersed in Roman history. Make time for some shopping: early evenings are a good time to saunter around the big-label boutiques of Piazza di Spagna and historic independents of Piazza Navona. For flea market bargains check out the Mercato di Porta Portese.

On the Calendar

Winter

Carnevale. Venice earned its international reputation as the "city of Carnevale" in the 18th century, when partying would begin several months before Lent and the city seemed to be one continuous masquerade. The celebration was revived for good in the 1970s, and each year over the 15- to 17-day Carnevale period (ending on the Tuesday before Ash Wednesday), more than a half-million people attend concerts, theater and street performances, masquerade balls, historical processions, fashion shows, and contests.

If you're not planning on joining in the revelry, you'd be wise to choose another time to visit Venice. Crowds throng the streets (which become one-way, with police directing foot traffic), bridges are designated "no-stopping" zones to avoid gridlock, and prices skyrocket. 🌐 *www.carnevale.venezia.it.*

Carnevale di Acireale. With fantastical floats and entertaining parades, Acireale's carnival celebrations are known as being the best in Sicily. The exact dates depend on Easter, but events are held over the course of three weekends before the start of Lent (Ash Wednesday), when thousands of revelers pack the streets of the coastal town. 🌐 *carnevaleacireale.eu.*

Festa di Santa Lucia. The feast of Siracusa's patron, Santa Lucia, is held from December 13 to 20 at the Church of Santa Lucia alla Badia. A splendid silver statue of the saint is carried from the church to the Duomo: a torchlight procession and band music accompany the bearers, while local families watch from their balconies. 🌐 *www.basilicasantalucia.com.*

Sagra del Mandorlo in Fiore. In late February and early March, when most of the almond trees are in blossom, Agrigento hosts the Sagra del Mandorlo in Fiore, with international folk dances, a costumed parade, and the sale of marzipan and other sweet treats made from almonds. 🌐 *www.lavalledeitempli.it/mandorlo-in-fiore.*

Sant'Orso Fair. On the last weekend of January, the streets of Aosta are brightened by an arts-and-crafts market that brings artisans from all over the Valle d'Aosta. All the traditional techniques are featured: wood carving and sculpture, soapstone work, wrought iron, leather, wool, lace, and household items of all kinds. Food and wine are sold at outdoor stands and wandering minstrels enliven the whole event. 🌐 *www.fieradisantorso.it.*

Spring

Biennale di Venezia. Come springtime every two years (the even-numbered) the contemporary art world and the curious descend on Venice's Giardini pavilions, Arsenale dockside warehouses, and scattered palazzi. In odd years it's the turn of the world's leading architects to display their creations. 🌐 *www.labiennale.org.*

Festa della Madonna a Cavallo. In Scicli, Sicily, the last Saturday in May brings the festival of the town's savior, Madonna delle Milizie (Virgin Mary of Militias), celebrating the supposed moment in the 11th century when the Virgin Mary descended on horseback to rescue the Norman-ruled town from a Saracen invasion. The weekend festival includes parading a statue of the Madonna on horseback through the main piazza to intervene in a mock battle before reveling in salvation by indulging in a sweet pastry towering with whipped cream, known as a *testa di turco*. 🌐 *www.visitvigata.com.*

On the Calendar

Festa di Sant'Efisio. On May 1, thousands of costumed villagers parade through town during Sardinia's greatest annual festival, the Festa di Sant'Efisio, named after the martyred saint who saved the city from the plague in the 17th century. The saint's statue is carried aloft through Cagliari's flower-lined streets, part of a four-day procession from Cagliari to Nora and back again (64 km [40 miles] round-trip), and is accompanied by colorful costumed groups from throughout the island in an enthusiastic celebration of traditional culture. Ask at Cagliari's tourist office about viewing the grand spectacle along the main route in Cagliari. From April on, you can find tickets at 🌐 *www.festadisantefisio.it*.

Milan Design Week. For a week in April Italy's northern powerhouse city hosts the biggest gathering of the design world. Pride of place in the calendar is the Salone di Mobile, a furniture fair like no other, staged in the cavernous Fiera Milano exhibition center and in dozens of venues across this design-mad city. 🌐 *www.salonemilano.it*.

Sagra del Pesce. The highlight of the festival of San Fortunato is held on the second Sunday of May each year in Camogli. It's a crowded, colorful, and free-to-the-public feast of freshly caught fish, cooked outside at the port in a 12-foot frying pan. 🌐 *www.camogliturismo.it*.

Scoppio del Carro (Explosion of the Cart). On Easter Sunday, Florentines and foreigners alike flock to the Piazza del Duomo to watch as the Scoppio del Carro, a monstrosity of a carriage pulled by two huge oxen decorated for the occasion, makes its way through the city center and ends up in the piazza. Through an elaborate wiring system, an object representing a dove is sent from inside the cathedral to the baptistery across the way. The dove sets off an explosion of fireworks that come streaming from the carriage. You have to see it to believe it. 🌐 *www.visittuscany.com*.

Vinitaly. This widely attended international wine and spirits event in Verona takes place for a few days in April. Recent gatherings have attracted more than 4,000 exhibitors from two dozen countries. The festivities kick off with Opera Wine, a showcase for the top 100 Italian wines as chosen by *Wine Spectator* magazine, which takes place in the Palazzo della Gran Guardia, in Piazza Bra. 🌐 *www.vinitaly.com*.

Summer

Arena di Verona Opera Festival. During the venue's summer season (June to August), as many as 16,000 attendees sit on the original stone terraces or in modern cushioned stalls. Most of the operas presented are big and splashy, like *Aida* or *Turandot*, demanding huge choruses, and, if possible, camels, horses, or elephants. Order tickets by phone or through the arena website: if you book a spot on the cheaper terraces, be sure to take or rent a *cuscino*. 🌐 *www.arena.it*.

Estate Fiesolana. From June through August, Estate Fiesolana, a festival of theater, music, dance, and film, takes place in Fiesole's churches and in the Roman amphitheater—demonstrating that the ancient Romans knew a thing or two about acoustics (🌐 *www.visittuscany.com*).

Festa del Redentore. On the third Sunday in July, crowds cross the Canale della Giudecca by means of a pontoon bridge, built every year to commemorate the doge's annual visit to Palladio's Chiesa del Santissimo Redentore to offer thanks for the end of a 16th-century plague. The evening before, Venetians—accompanied each year by an increasing number of tourists—set up tables and chairs along the canals. As evening falls, practically the whole city takes to the streets and tables, and thousands more take to the water. Boats decorated with colored lanterns (and well provisioned with traditional Redentore meals) jockey for position to watch the grand event. Half an hour before midnight, Venice kicks off a fireworks display over the Bacino, with brilliant reflections on its waters. You'll find good viewing anywhere along the Riva degli Schiavoni; you could also try Zattere, as close to Punta Dogana as you can get, or on the Zitelle end of the Giudecca. After the fireworks, join the young folks and stay out all night, greeting the sunrise on the Lido beach, or rest up and make the procession to mass on Sunday morning. If you're on a boat, allow a couple of hours to dislodge yourself from the nautical traffic jam when the festivities break up. 🌐 *www.redentorevenezia.it.*

Festa di San Giovanni (Feast of St. John the Baptist). On June 24 Florence mostly grinds to a halt to celebrate the Festa di San Giovanni in honor of its patron saint. Many shops and bars close, and at night a fireworks display lights up the Arno and attracts thousands. 🌐 *www.visittuscany.com.*

Festival dei Due Mondi. Each summer Umbria hosts one of Italy's biggest arts festivals: Spoleto's Festival of the Two Worlds. Starting out as a classical music festival, it has now evolved into one of Italy's brightest gatherings of arts aficionados. Running from late June through mid-July, it features modern and classical music, theater, dance, and opera. Increasingly there are also a number of small cinema producers and their films. 🌐 *www.festivaldispoleto.com.*

Luminaria. Pisa is at its best during the Luminaria feast day, on June 16. The day honors St. Ranieri, the city's patron saint. Palaces along the Arno are lit with white lights, and there are plenty of fireworks. 🌐 *www.turismo.pisa.it/en/events.*

Ravello Festival. This festival was first staged in 1953 and partly inspired by composer Richard Wagner's declaration on setting foot in Villa Rufolo grounds: "The magical garden of Klingsor is found!" Sitting in this lofty terrace in serene Ravello, the striking Oscar Niemeyer Auditorium is the breathtaking venue for wonderful concerts. For the most uplifting musical experience secure a seat at the much-sought-after Sunrise Concert each August, where the dawning sun, divine sounds, and Amalfi Coast vistas intertwine. 🌐 *ravellofestival.info.*

Taormina Film Festival. Sicily's famous festival takes place in late June and early July. 🌐 *www.visitsicily.info.*

Umbria Jazz Festival. Perugia is hopping for 10 days in July, when more than a million people flock to see famous names in contemporary music perform—often in novel collaborations—at the Umbria Jazz Festival. In recent years the stars have included Wynton Marsalis, Sting with Gil Evans, Grace Jones, B52s, Jeff Beck with Johnny Depp, and Nile Rodgers with Chic. There's also a shorter Umbria Jazz Winter Festival from late December to early January. 🌐 *www.umbriajazz.com.*

Fall

Douja d'Or National Wine Festival. For 10 days in mid-September, Asti is host to a popular wine festival—an opportunity to see Asti and celebrate the product that made it famous. 🌐 *visit.asti.it/en/september-in-asti/douja-dor.*

On the Calendar

Eurochocolate Festival. If you've got a sweet tooth and are visiting in fall, book early and head to Perugia for the Eurochocolate Festival. This is one of the biggest chocolate festivals in the world, with a million visitors, and is held over a week in October or November. Fill your cheeks again at Eurochocolate Spring in March. 🌐 *www.eurochocolate.com.*

Fiera Internazionale del Tartufo Bianco (International White Truffle Fair). From early October to early December, Alba hosts an internationally famous truffle fair. Merchants, chefs, and other aficionados of this pungent yet delicious fungus come from all over the world to buy and taste white truffles at the height of their season. The fourth Sunday of September sees the **Palio degli Asini**, a hilarious donkey race, a lampoon of Asti's eminently serious horse race. Tickets to watch this competition between Alba's districts, with riders dressed in medieval garb astride their stubborn beasts, can be hard to get. **TIP→ Hotel and restaurant reservations for October and November should be made well in advance.** 🌐 *www.fieradeltartufo.org.*

Funghi Fest. Spanning two weekends in October, friendly hilltop medieval town Castelbuono in the Madonie mountains of northern Sicily celebrates the area's bountiful mushroom harvest, including its prized porcini and Fungo di Ferla, with tastings, music, and street-food stalls galore. 🌐 *www.funghifest.it.*

Palio di Asti. September is a month of fairs and celebrations in Asti, and this horse race that runs through the streets of town is the highlight. First mentioned in 1275, this annual event has been going strong ever since. After an elaborate procession in period costumes, nine horses and jockeys representing different sections of town vie for the honor of claiming the *palio*, a symbolic flag of victory. The race happens on a Sunday at the beginning of September each year. 🌐 *visit.asti.it.*

Sagra Musicale Umbra. Held mid-September, the Sagra Musicale Umbra celebrates sacred music in Perugia and in several towns throughout the region. 🌐 *www.perugiamusicaclassica.com.*

Chapter 3

ROME

Updated by
Natalie Kennedy and Laura Itzkowitz

WELCOME TO ROME

TOP REASONS TO GO

★ **The Vatican:** Although its population numbers only in the hundreds, the Vatican makes up for it with the millions who visit each year. Marvel at Michelangelo's Sistine Chapel and St. Peter's Basilica.

★ **The Colosseum:** The largest amphitheater of the Roman world was begun by Emperor Vespasian and inaugurated by his son Titus in AD 80.

★ **Piazza Navona:** You couldn't concoct a more Roman street scene: crowded café tables at street level, wrought-iron balconies above, and, at the center, Bernini's Fountain of the Four Rivers and Borromini's Sant'Agnese.

★ **Roman Forum:** This fabled labyrinth of ruins variously served as a political playground, a center of commerce, and a place where justice was dispensed during the Roman Republic and Empire.

★ **Trastevere:** This neighborhood is a maze of jumbled alleyways, traditional Roman trattorias, cobblestone streets, and medieval houses.

1 Ancient Rome with Monti and Celio. The Forum and Palatine Hill were once the hub of Western civilization.

2 The Vatican with Borgo and Prati. St. Peter's Basilica and the Sistine Chapel draw millions.

3 Piazza Navona, Campo de' Fiori, and the Jewish Ghetto. This is the heart of the historic quarter. The Ghetto still preserves the flavor of Old Rome.

4 Piazza di Spagna. Travel back to the days of the Grand Tour in this area.

5 Repubblica and the Quirinale. These areas house government offices, churches, and sights.

6 Villa Borghese and Environs. Rome's most famous park is home to the Galleria Borghese.

7 Trastevere. Rome's left bank has kept its authentic roots.

FLAMINIO
VILLA BORGHESE
PIAZZA DEL POPOLO
PIAZZA DI SPAGNA
PRATI
SAN LORENZO
REPUBBLICA
QUIRINALE
PIAZZA NAVONA
CAMPO DE' FIORI
JEWISH GHETTO
MONTI
ANCIENT ROME
CELIO
TRASTEVERE
SAN GIOVANNI
AVENTINO
VIA APPIA ANTICA
1
2
3
4
5
6
7
Villa Giulia
Villa Strohl Fern
Giardino Zoologico
Giardino D.Lago
Parco D.Daini
Villa Borghese
Villa Medici
Castel Sant'Angelo
Trevi Fountain
Sant'Andrea al Quirinale
Pantheon
Colosseum
Parco Traiano
Isola Tiberina
Circo Massino
Villa Celimontana
Parco di Porta Capena
Fiume Tevere
V. Giuseppe Mazzini
V. G. Nicotera
V. L. Settembrini
V. delle Milize
Lgt. Michelangelo
Lgt. A. da Brescia
Via Flaminia
Viale delle Belle Arti
Via Ulisse Aldrovandi
Via L. di Savoia
Viale del Muro Torto
Via Pinciana
Via Salaria
Via Piave
Corso d'Italia
Via Boncompagni
Via Vitt. Veneto
Via Ludovisi
Via L. Bissolati
Via XX Settembre
Via Gernaia
Via Barberini
Via Sistina
Via d. Quattro Fontane
Via del Tritone
Via del Quirinale
Via del Viminale
Via A. Depretis
Via Cavour
Via Nazionale
V. XXIV Maggio
Via M. Colonna
Via Cicerone
Lgt. Mellini
Lgt. in Augusta
Via del Corso
Pte. Margherita
Pte. Cavour
Via Triboniano
Lgt. Prati
Lgt. Castello
Pte. Umberto
Lgt. Tor di Nona
C. so Vittorio Emanuele II
Lgt. Sangallo
Corso del Rinascimento
Vittorio Emanuele II
V.d. Plebiscito
V. delle Sotteghe Oscure
Via Merulana
Via G. Lanza
Via Cavour
V. del Monte Oppio
Via dei Fori
Lgt dei Tebaldi
Lgt. della Farnesina
Via Arenula
Lgt. dei Vallati
Lgt. dei Cenci
Via del Teatro di Marcello
Pte. Garibaldi
Lgt. Raff. Sanzio
Lgt. d. Anguillara
Lgt. d. Pierleoni
Via Garibaldi
Via L. Manara
Via Labicana
Via C. Vibenna
Via d. Navicella
Via di S.Gregorio
Via del Circo Massimo
Lgt. Ripa
Porto di Risa
Lgt. Testaccio
Viale G. Trastevere
Via Portuense
Pte. Sublicio
Viale Aventino
Villa Sciarra

EAT LIKE A LOCAL IN ROME

A local salumeria or cured meat shop

In Rome, tradition is the dominant feature of the cuisine, with a focus on freshness and simplicity, so when Romans continue ordering the standbys, it's easy to understand why. That said, the influx of residents to the capital from other regions has yielded many variations on the staples.

ARTICHOKES

There are two well-known preparations of *carciofo,* or artichoke, in Rome. Carciofi *alla romana* are stuffed with wild mint, garlic, and pecorino, then braised in olive oil, white wine, and water. Carciofi *alla giudia* (Jewish-style) are whole artichokes, deep-fried twice, so that they open like a flower, the outer leaves crisp and golden brown, while the heart remains tender. When artichokes are in season—late winter through the spring—they're served everywhere.

BUCATINI ALL'AMATRICIANA

It might look like spaghetti with red sauce, but there's much more to *bucatini all'amatriciana*. It's a spicy, rich, and complex dish that owes its flavor to *guanciale*, or cured pork jowl, as well as tomatoes and crushed red pepper flakes. It's often served over bucatini, a hollow, spaghetti-like pasta, and topped with grated pecorino Romano.

CODA ALLA VACCINARA

Rome's largest slaughterhouse in the 1800s was in the Testaccio neighborhood, and that's where you'll find dishes like *coda alla vaccinara*, or "oxtail in the style of the cattle butcher." This dish is made from ox or veal tails stewed with tomatoes, carrots, celery, and wine, and it's usually seasoned with cinnamon. It's simmered for hours and then finished with raisins and pine nuts or bittersweet chocolate.

GELATO

Its consistency is often said to be a cross between regular American ice cream and soft-serve. The best versions of gelato are extremely flavorful, and almost always made fresh daily. When choosing a *gelateria*, watch for signs that say *gelato artigianale* (artisan- or homemade); otherwise, keep an eye out for the real deal by avoiding gelato that looks too bright or fluffy.

PIZZA

There are two kinds of Roman pizza: *al taglio* (by the slice) and *tonda* (round pizza). The former has a thicker, focaccia-like crust and is cut into squares; these are sold by weight and generally available all day. The typical Roman pizza tonda has a very thin crust and is served almost charred. Because they're so hot, the ovens are usually fired up only in the evening, which is why Roman *pizzerie* tend to open for dinner only.

Gelato

Artichokes

CACIO E PEPE

The name means "cheese and pepper," and this is a simple pasta dish from the *cucina povera*, or rustic cooking, tradition. It's a favorite Roman primo, usually made with *tonnarelli* (fresh egg pasta a bit thicker than spaghetti), which is coated with a pecorino-cheese sauce and lots of freshly ground black pepper. Some restaurants serve the dish in an edible bowl of paper-thin baked cheese.

FRITTI

The classic Roman starter in a trattoria and especially at the pizzeria, is *fritti*: an assortment of fried treats, usually crumbed or in batter. Often, before selecting a pizza, locals will order their fritti: *filetti di baccalà* (salt cod in batter), *fiori di zucca* (zucchini flowers, usually stuffed with anchovy and mozzarella), *supplì* (rice balls stuffed with mozzarella and other ingredients), or *olive ascolane* (stuffed olives).

LA GRICIA

This dish is often referred to as a "white amatriciana" because it's precisely that: pasta (usually spaghetti or rigatoni) served with pecorino cheese and guanciale—thus amatriciana without the tomato sauce. It's a lighter alternative to carbonara in that it doesn't contain egg, and its origins date back further than the amatriciana.

The timeless city to which all roads lead, Mamma Roma enthralls visitors today as she has since time immemorial. Here the ancient Romans made us heirs-in-law to what we call Western Civilization; where centuries later Michelangelo painted the Sistine Chapel; and where Gian Lorenzo Bernini's Baroque nymphs and naiads still dance in their marble fountains.

Today the city remains a veritable Grand Canyon of culture. Ancient Rome rubs shoulders with the medieval, the modern runs into the Renaissance, and the result is like nothing so much as an open-air museum.

But always remember: *"Quando a Roma vai, fai come vedrai"* (When in Rome, do as the Romans do). Don't feel intimidated by the press of art and culture. Instead, contemplate the grandeur from a table at a sun-drenched café on Piazza della Rotonda; let Rome's colorful life flow around you without feeling guilty because you haven't seen everything. It can't be done, anyway. There's just so much here that you'll have to come back, so be sure to throw a coin in the Trevi Fountain.

Planning

Addresses

In the *centro storico* (old town/historic center), most street names are posted on ceramic-like plaques on the sides of buildings, which can make them hard to see. Addresses are fairly straightforward: the street name is followed by the street number, but it's worth noting that Roman street numbering, even in the newer outskirts of town, can be erratic. Usually numbers are even on one side of the street and odd on the other, but sometimes numbers are in ascending consecutive order on one side of the street and descending order on the other side.

Etiquette

Although you may find Rome much more informal then many other European cities, Romans will nevertheless appreciate attempts to abide by local etiquette. When entering an establishment, the key words to know are: *buongiorno* (good morning), *buona sera* (good evening), and *buon pomeriggio* (good afternoon). These words can also double as a goodbye upon exit. Italians greet friends with a kiss, usually first on the right cheek, and then on the left. When you meet a new person, shake hands and say *piacere* (*pee*-ah -*chair*-ay).

Getting Around

Although most of Rome's sights are in a relatively circumscribed area, the city is too large to be seen solely on foot. Try to avoid rush hour when taking the Metro (subway) or a bus, as public transport can be extremely crowded. Midmorning or midday through early afternoon tends to be less busy. Otherwise, it's best to take a taxi to the area you plan to visit if it is across town. You should always expect to do a lot of walking in Rome, especially considering how little ground the subway actually covers, so plan on wearing a pair of comfortable, sturdy shoes to cushion the impact of the *sampietrini* (cobblestones). You can get free city and transit maps at municipal information booths.

BUS AND TRAM

Although not as fast as the Metro, bus and tram travel is more scenic. With reserved bus lanes and numerous tram lines, surface transportation is surprisingly efficient, given the volume of Roman traffic. At peak times, however, buses can be very crowded. If the distance you have to travel is not too great, walking can be a more comfortable alternative. ATAC city buses are red or gray; trams are green. Remember to board at the rear and to exit at the middle: some bus drivers may refuse to let you out the front door, leaving you to scramble through the crowd to exit the middle or rear doors. Don't forget that you must buy your ticket before boarding, and be sure to stamp it in a machine as soon as you enter. The ticket is good for a transfer and one Metro trip within the next 100 minutes. Buses and trams run 5:30 am–midnight, after which time there's an extensive network of night buses with service throughout the city.

The bus system is a bit complicated to navigate due to the number of lines, but ATAC has a website (🌐 *www.atac.roma.it*) that will help you calculate the number of stops and bus route needed, and even give you a map directing you to the appropriate stops. To navigate the site, look for the British flag in the upper right-hand corner to change the website into English. Or do as the locals do and use the Moovit app.

METRO

Rome's integrated transportation system includes buses and trams (ATAC), the Metropolitana (the subway, or Metro), suburban trains and buses (COTRAL), and the commuter rail run by the state railway (Trenitalia). A ticket (BIT), valid for 100 minutes on any combination of buses and trams and one entrance to the Metro, costs €1.50. Tickets are sold at tobacco shops, newsstands, some coffee bars, automatic ticket machines in Metro stations, some bus stops, in machines on some buses, and at ATAC ticket booths. You can purchase individual or multiple tickets. It's always a good idea to have a few tickets handy so you don't have to hunt for a vendor when you need one. All tickets must be validated by time-stamping in the yellow meter boxes aboard buses and in Metro stations, immediately prior to boarding. Failure to validate your ticket will result in a fine of €54.90. You can now pay for fines on the ATAC website. Pay immediately, or the fine will increase to €104.90 if you pay after five days. You can also pay fines in post offices, authorized shops, or by wire transfer. Do not pay the ticket inspectors in cash; some may be equipped for payment by mobile POS.

A Roma24H ticket, or *biglietto integrato giornaliero* (integrated daily ticket), is valid for 24 hours (from the moment you stamp it) on all public transit and costs €7. You can also purchase a Roma48H (€12.50), a Roma72H (€18), and a CIS (Carta Integrata Settimanale), which is valid for one week (€24). Each option gives unlimited travel on ATAC buses, COTRAL urban bus services, trains for the Lido and Viterbo, and Metro. There's an ATAC kiosk at the bus terminal in front of Termini station. If you're going farther afield, or planning to spend more than a week in Rome, think about getting a BIRG (daily regional ticket) or a CIRS (weekly regional ticket) from the railway station. These give you unlimited travel on all state transport throughout the region of Lazio. This can take you as far as the Etruscan city of Tarquinia or medieval Viterbo.

Hotels

When it comes to accommodations, Rome offers a wide selection of high-end hotels, bed-and-breakfasts, and designer boutique hotels—options that run the gamut from whimsical to luxurious. Whether you want a simple place to rest your head or a complete cache of exclusive amenities, you have plenty to choose from.

Luxury hotels are justly renowned for sybaritic comfort: postcard views over Roman rooftops, silver flatware on white linen atop a groaning breakfast-buffet table, and the fluffiest towels. But in more modest categories, very often Rome's hotels are not up to the standards of space, comfort, quiet, and service taken for granted in the United States: you'll still find places with tiny rooms, lumpy beds, and anemic air-conditioning. The good news: if you're flexible, there are happy mediums aplenty.

One thing to figure out before you arrive is which neighborhood you want to stay in. There are obvious advantages to staying in a hotel within easy walking distance of the main sights. If a picturesque location is your main concern, stay in one of the small hotels around Piazza Navona or Campo de' Fiori. If luxury is a high priority, head for Piazza di Spagna or beyond the city center, where quality/price ratios are higher and some hotels have swimming pools.

⇨ *Hotel and restaurant reviews have been shortened. For full information, visit Fodors.com. Prices in the lodging reviews are the lowest cost of a standard double room in high season. Prices in the dining reviews are the average cost of a main course at dinner, or, if dinner is not served, at lunch.*

What It Costs in Euros

$	$$	$$$	$$$$
RESTAURANTS			
under €20	€20–€30	€31–€40	over €40
HOTELS			
under €175	€175–€400	€401–€600	over €600

Restaurants

In Rome, simple yet traditional cuisine reigns supreme. Most chefs prefer to follow the mantra of freshness over fuss, and simplicity of flavor and preparation over complex cooking techniques. Rome has been known since antiquity for its grand feasts and banquets, and dining out has always been a favorite Roman pastime. Until recently, the city's *buongustaii* (gourmands) would have been the first to tell you that Rome is distinguished more by its enthusiasm for eating out than for a multitude of world-class restaurants—but this is changing. There is an ever-growing promotion of slow-food practices, a focus on sustainably and locally sourced produce. The economic crisis forced the food industry in Rome to adopt innovative ways to maintain a clientele who were increasingly looking to dine out but wanting to spend less; the result has been the rise of "street food" restaurants, selling everything from inexpensive and novel takes on the classic *supplì* (Roman fried-rice balls) to sandwich shops that use a variety of organic ingredients.

Generally speaking, Romans like Roman food, and that's what you'll find in many of the city's trattorias and wine bars. For the most part, today's chefs cling to the traditional and excel at what has taken hundreds, sometimes thousands, of years to perfect. This is why the basic trattoria menu is more or less the same wherever you go. And it's why even the top Roman chefs feature their versions of simple trattoria classics like carbonara, sometimes in a "deconstructed" or slightly varied way. To a great extent, Rome is still a town where the Italian equivalent of "What are you in the mood for?" still gets the answer, "Pizza or pasta."

Nevertheless, Rome is the capital of Italy, and because people move here from every corner of the Italian peninsula, there are more variations on the Italian theme in Rome than you'd find elsewhere in Italy: Sicilian, Tuscan, Pugliese, Bolognese, Marchegiano, Sardinian, and northern Italian regional cuisines are all represented. And reflecting the increasingly cosmopolitan nature of the city, you'll find a growing number of good-quality international foods here as well—particularly Japanese, Indian, and Ethiopian.

Oddly enough, though, for a nation that prides itself on *la bella figura* ("looking good"), most Romans don't fuss about music, personal space, lighting, or decor. After all, who needs flashy interior design when so much of Roman life takes place outdoors, when dining alfresco in Rome can take place in the middle of a glorious ancient site or a centuries-old piazza?

Roman Hours

In Italy, almost nothing starts on time except for (sometimes) a theater, opera, or movie showing. Italians even joke about a "15-minute window" before actually being late somewhere. In addition, the day starts a little later than normal here, with many shops not opening until 10 am, lunch never happens before 1 pm, and dinner rarely starts before 8 pm. On Sunday, Rome virtually shuts down, and on Monday, most state museums and exhibition halls, plus many restaurants, are closed. Daily food shop hours generally run 10 am–1 pm and 4 pm–7:30 pm or 8 pm; but other stores in the center usually observe continuous opening hours. Pharmacies tend to close for a lunch break and keep night hours (*ora rio notturno*) in rotation. As for churches, most open at 8 or 9 in the morning, close noon–3 or 4, then reopen until 6:30 or 7. St. Peter's, however, has continuous hours 7 am–7 pm (until 6 pm in the fall and winter); and the Vatican Museums are open Monday but closed Sunday (except for the last Sunday of the month).

Roma Pass

In addition to single- and multiday transit passes, a three-day Roma Pass (*€52*) covers unlimited use of buses, trams, and the Metro, plus free admission to two museums or archaeological sites of your choice and discounted entrance to others. A two-day pass is €32 and includes one museum. The pass also allows you to skip the line at the Colosseum and Castel Sant'Angelo. Purchase the pass at either of Rome's airports, at tourist information offices, or at any of the participating attractions.

Tours

Some might consider them kitsch, but guided bus tours can prove a blissfully easy way to enjoy a quick introduction to the city's top sights—if you don't feel like being on your feet all day. Sitting in a bus, with friendly tour-guide commentary (and even friendlier fellow sightseers from every country under the sun), can make for a fun experience—so give one a whirl even if you're an old Rome hand. Of course, you'll want to savor these incredible sights at your own leisure later on.

The least expensive organized sightseeing tour of Rome is the one run by **CitySightseeing Roma** (*www.city-sightseeing.it/rome*). Double-decker buses leave from Via Marsala, beside Termini station, but you can pick them up at any of their nine stopping points. A day ticket costs €30 and allows you to get off and on as often as you like. The price includes an audio guide system in six languages. The total tour takes about two hours and covers the Colosseum, Piazza Navona, St. Peter's, the Trevi Fountain, and Via Veneto. Tickets can be bought on board. Two- and three-day tickets are also available. Tours leave from Termini station every 20 minutes 9–7:30.

All operators can provide a luxury car for up to three people, a limousine for up to seven, or a minibus for up to nine, all with an English-speaking driver, but guide service is extra. Almost all operators offer "Rome by Night" tours, with or without dinner and entertainment. You can book tours through travel agents.

Visitor Information

The Department of Tourism in Rome, called Roma Capitale, staffs green information kiosks (with multilingual personnel) near important sights, as well as at Termini station and Leonardo da Vinci Airport.

When to Go

Spring and fall are the best times to visit, with mild temperatures and many sunny days. Summers are often sweltering, so come in July and August if you like, but we advise doing as the Romans do—get up and out early, seek refuge from the afternoon heat, resume activities in early evening, and stay up late to enjoy the nighttime breeze.

Most attractions are closed on major holidays. Come August, many shops and restaurants shutter as locals head out for vacation. Remember that air-conditioning is still a relatively rare phenomenon in this city, so carrying a small paper fan in your bag can work wonders. Roman winters are relatively mild, with persistent rainy spells.

Ancient Rome with Monti and Celio

Time has reduced ancient Rome to fields of silent ruins, but the powerful impact of what happened here, of the genius and power that made Rome the center of the Western world, echoes across the millennia. In this one compact area of the city, you can step back into the Rome of Cicero, Julius Caesar, and Virgil. You can walk along the streets they knew, cool off in the shade of the Colosseum that loomed over the city, and see the sculptures poised over their piazzas. Today, this part of Rome, more than any other, is a perfect example of the layering of historic eras, the overlapping of ages, of religions, of a past that is very much a part of the present.

Outside the actual ancient sites, you'll find neighborhoods like Monti and Celio, *riones* (districts) that are just as much part of Rome's history as its ruins. These are the city's oldest neighborhoods, and today they are a charming mix of the city's past and present. Once you're done exploring ancient Rome, these are the easiest places to head for a bite to eat or some shopping.

GETTING HERE AND AROUND

The Colosseo Metro station is right across from the Colosseum and a short walk from both the Roman and the Imperial Forums, as well as the Palatine Hill. Walking from the very heart of the historic center will take about 20 minutes, much of it along the wide Via dei Fori Imperiali. The little electric Bus No. 117 from the center or No. 85 from Termini will also deliver you to the Colosseum's doorstep. Any of the following buses will take you to or near the Roman Forum: Nos. 60, 75, 85, and 170.

 Sights

Arco di Costantino (*Arch of Constantine*)
RUINS | This majestic arch was erected in AD 315 to commemorate Constantine's victory over Maxentius at the Milvian Bridge. It was just before this battle, in AD 312, that Constantine—the emperor who converted Rome to Christianity—legendarily had a vision of a cross and heard the words "In this sign thou shalt conquer." Many of the costly marble decorations for the arch were scavenged from earlier monuments, both saving money and placing Constantine in line with the great emperors of the past. It is easy to picture ranks of Roman centurions marching under the great barrel vault. ✉ *Piazza del Colosseo, Colosseo* Ⓜ *Colosseo.*

Basilica di Santa Maria in Aracoeli
CHURCH | Perched atop 124 steps, on the north slope of the Capitoline Hill, Santa Maria in Aracoeli occupies the site of the temple of Juno Moneta (Admonishing Juno), which also housed the Roman mint. According to legend, it was here that the Sibyl, a prophetess, predicted to Augustus the coming of a Redeemer. Augustus responded by erecting an altar, the Ara Coeli (Altar of Heaven). This was eventually replaced by a Benedictine monastery and then by a church, which was passed in 1250 to the Franciscans, who restored and enlarged it in Romanesque-Gothic style.

Today, the Aracoeli is best known for the Santo Bambino, a much-revered olive-wood figure of the Christ Child (a copy of the 15th-century original, which was stolen in 1994). At Christmas, everyone pays homage to the "Bambinello" as children recite poems from a miniature pulpit. In true Roman style, the church interior is a historical hodgepodge, with classical columns and large marble fragments from pagan buildings, as well as a 13th-century cosmatesque pavement. The richly gilded Renaissance ceiling commemorates the naval victory at Lepanto in 1571 over the Turks. The first chapel on the right is noteworthy for Pinturicchio's frescoes of St. Bernardino of Siena (1486). ✉ *Scala dell'Arce Capitolina 14, Campitelli* ☎ *06/69763839* 🌐 *sanmarcoevangelista.it* Ⓜ *Colosseo.*

★ The Campidoglio
PLAZA/SQUARE | Your first taste of ancient Rome should start from a point that embodies some of Rome's earliest and greatest moments: the Campidoglio. Here, on the Capitoline Hill (which towers over the traffic hub of Piazza Venezia), a meditative Edward Gibbon was inspired to write his 1764 tome, *The History of the Decline and Fall of the Roman Empire.* Of Rome's famous seven hills, the Capitoline is the smallest and the most sacred. It has always been the seat of Rome's government, and its Latin name echoes in the designation of the national and state capitol buildings of every country in the world. While there are great views of the Roman Forum from the terrace balconies to either side of the Palazzo Senatorio, the best view is from the 1st-century-BC Tabularium, now part of the Musei Capitolini. The museum café is on the Terrazza Caffarelli, with a magical view toward Trastevere and St. Peter's, and is accessible without a museum ticket. ✉ *Piazza del Campidoglio, including the Palazzo Senatorio and the Musei Capitolini, the Palazzo Nuovo, and the Palazzo dei Conservatori, Piazza Venezia* Ⓜ *Colosseo.*

Circo Massimo (*Circus Maximus*)
RUINS | From the belvedere of the Domus Flavia on the Palatine Hill, you can see the Circus Maximus; there's also a great

free view from Piazzale Ugo La Malfa on the Aventine Hill side. The giant space where 300,000 spectators once watched chariot races while the emperor looked on is ancient Rome's oldest and largest racetrack; it lies in a natural hollow between the two hills. The oval course stretches about 650 yards from end to end; on certain occasions, there were as many as 24 chariot races a day, and competitions could last for 15 days. The charioteers could amass fortunes rather like the sports stars of today. (The Portuguese Diocles is said to have totted up winnings of 35 million sestertii.)

The noise and the excitement of the crowd must have reached astonishing levels as the charioteers competed in teams, each with their own colors—the Reds, the Blues, etc. Betting also provided Rome's majority of unemployed with a potentially lucrative occupation. The central ridge was the site of two Egyptian obelisks (now in Piazza del Popolo and Piazza San Giovanni in Laterano). Picture the great chariot race scene from MGM's *Ben-Hur* and you have an inkling of what this was like. **■TIP→ The "Circo Massimo Experience," a 40-minute augmented and virtual reality experience through the stadium, costs €12.** ✉ *Between Palatine and Aventine Hills, Aventino* ☎ *06/0608* 🎟 *Free* Ⓜ *Circo Massimo.*

★ Colosseum (*Colosseo*)

RUINS | The most spectacular extant edifice of ancient Rome, the Colosseum has a history that is half gore, half glory. Once able to house 50,000 spectators, it was built to impress Romans with its spectacles involving wild animals and fearsome gladiators from the farthest reaches of the empire. Senators had marble seats up front, the vestal virgins took the ringside position, the plebs sat in wooden tiers at the back, and the masses watched from the top tier. Looming over all was the amazing velarium, an ingenious system of sail-like awnings rigged on ropes and maneuvered by sailors from the imperial fleet, who would unfurl them to protect the arena's occupants from sun or rain. **■TIP→ To enter, book a combination ticket (with the Roman Forum and Palatine Hill) in advance online, though if you have a Roma Pass, you can use it.**

Tickets cost €18. Aim for early or late slots to minimize lines, as even the preferential lanes get busy in the middle of the day. Alternatively, you can book a tour online with a company (do your research to make sure it's reputable) that lets you skip the line. Avoid the tours sold on the spot around the Colosseum; although you can skip the lines, the tour guides tend to be dry, the tour groups huge, and the tour itself rushed. To see the arena or the underground, you must purchase a special timed-entry ticket with those features, though the arena is included if you buy the Roman Forum–Palatine complex €24 two-day Full Experience ticket. ✉ *Piazza del Colosseo, Colosseo* 🌐 *www.colosseo.it* 🎟 *Requires either the €18 24-hr ticket or the €24 Full Experience ticket (can include the arena, the underground, and/or the attic for no additional fee, but it must be specified during the purchase)* Ⓜ *Colosseo.*

Domus Aurea (*Golden House of Nero*)

RUINS | Legend has it that Nero fiddled while Rome burned. Fancying himself a great actor and poet, he played, as it turns out, his harp to accompany his recital of "The Destruction of Troy" while gazing at the flames of Rome's catastrophic fire of AD 64. After the fire, Nero built this new palace, the extravagant Domus Aurea (Golden House)—a vast "suburban villa" that was inspired by the emperor's pleasure palace at Baia on the Bay of Naples. His new digs were huge and sumptuous, with a facade of pure gold; seawater piped into the baths; decorations of mother-of-pearl, fretted ivory, and other precious materials; and vast gardens. It was said that after completing this gigantic house, Nero exclaimed,

"Now I can live like a human being!" Note that access to the site is exclusively via guided tours that use virtual-reality headsets for part of the presentation. Booking ahead is essential. ✉ *Viale della Domus Aurea, 1, Monti* ☎ *06/21115843* 🌐 *www.colosseo.it* 🎫 *€18; €26 including guided visit and virtual reality experience* ⏲ *Closed Mon.–Thurs.* ✍ *Reservations essential* Ⓜ *Colosseo.*

Fori Imperiali

RUINS | A compound of five grandly conceived complexes flanked with colonnades, the Fori Imperiali contain monuments of triumph, law courts, and temples. The complexes were tacked on to the Roman Forum, from the time of Julius Caesar in the 1st century BC until Trajan in the very early 2nd century AD, to accommodate the ever-growing need for administrative buildings as well as grand monuments.

From Piazza del Colosseo, head northwest on Via dei Fori Imperiali toward Piazza Venezia. Now that the road has been closed to private traffic, it's more pleasant for pedestrians (it's closed to all traffic on Sunday). On the walls to your left, maps in marble and bronze, put up by Benito Mussolini, show the extent of the Roman Republic and Empire. The dictator's own dreams of empire led him to construct this avenue, cutting brutally through the Fori Imperiali and the medieval and Renaissance buildings that had grown upon the ruins, so that he would have a suitable venue for parades celebrating his expected military triumphs. Among the Fori Imperiali along the avenue, you can see the Foro di Cesare (Forum of Caesar) and the Foro di Augusto (Forum of Augustus). The grandest was the Foro di Traiano (Forum of Trajan), with its huge semicircular Mercati di Traiano and the Colonna Traiana (Trajan's Column). You can walk through part of Trajan's Markets on the Via Alessandrina and visit the Museo dei Fori Imperiali, which presents the Imperial Forums and shows how they would have been used through ancient fragments, artifacts, and modern multimedia. ✉ *Via dei Fori Imperiali, Monti* ☎ *06/0608* 🌐 *www.mercatiditraiano.it* 🎫 *Museum €11.50* Ⓜ *Colosseo.*

Foro di Traiano (*Forum of Trajan*)

RUINS | Of all the Fori Imperiali, Trajan's was the grandest and most imposing, a veritable city unto itself. Designed by architect Apollodorus of Damascus, it comprised a vast basilica, two libraries, and a colonnade laid out around the square—all at one time covered with rich marble ornamentation. Adjoining the forum were the Mercati di Traiano (Trajan's Markets), a huge multilevel brick complex of shops, taverns, walkways, and terraces, as well as administrative offices involved in the mammoth task of feeding the city.

The Museo dei Fori Imperiali (Imperial Forums Museum) takes advantage of the Forum's soaring vaulted spaces to showcase archaeological fragments and sculptures while presenting a video re-creation of the original complex. In addition, the series of terraced rooms offers an impressive overview of the entire forum. A pedestrian walkway, the Via Alessandrina, also allows for an excellent (and free) view of Trajan's Forum.

To build a complex of this magnitude, Apollodorus and his patrons clearly had great confidence, not to mention almost unlimited means and cheap labor at their disposal (readily provided by slaves captured in Trajan's Dacian Wars). The complex also contained two semicircular lecture halls, one at either end, which are thought to have been associated with the libraries in Trajan's Forum. The markets' architectural centerpiece is the enormous curved wall, or *exedra*, that shores up the side of the Quirinal Hill excavated by Apollodorus's gangs of laborers. Covered galleries and streets were constructed at various levels, following the exedra's curves and giving the complex a strikingly modern appearance.

Rome Metro and Suburban Railway

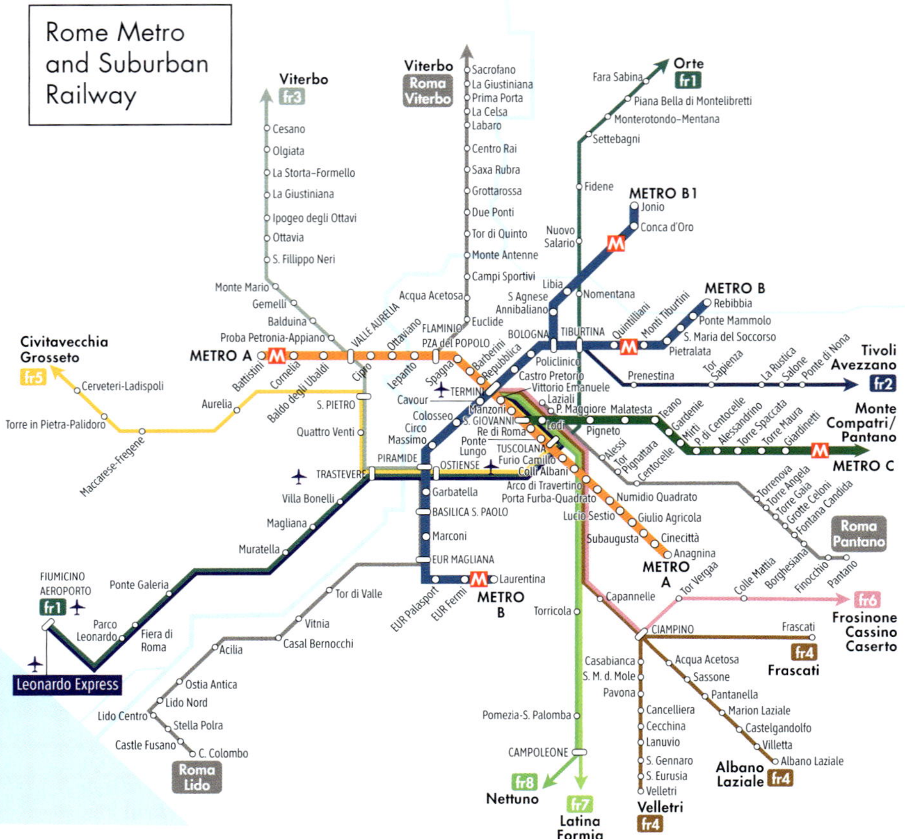

Tickets

A ticket (BIT) valid for 100 minutes on any combination of buses and trams and one entrance to the metro costs €1.50. Tickets are sold at newsstands, some coffee bars, ticket machines in metro stations, and ATAC and COTRAL ticket booths. Time-stamp your ticket when boarding the first vehicle, and stamp it again when boarding for the last time within 75 minutes. You stamp the ticket at Metro sliding electronic doors, and in the little yellow machines on buses and trams.

Fare fees	Price
Single fare	€1.50
Biglietto integrato giornaliero (Integrated Daily Ticket) BIG	€7
Biglietto turistico integrato (Three-Day Pass) BTI	€18
Weekly pass	€24
Monthly unlimited pass	€35

As you enter the markets, a large vaulted hall stands in front of you. Two stories of shops and offices rise up on either side. Head for the flight of steps at the far end that leads down to Via Biberatica. (*Bibere* is Latin for "to drink," and the shops that open onto the street are believed to have been taverns.) Then head back to the three retail and administrative tiers that line the upper levels of the great exedra and look out over the remains of the Forum. Empty and bare today, the cubicles were once ancient Rome's busiest market stalls. Though it seems to be part of the market, the Torre delle Milizie (Tower of the Militia), the tall brick tower that is a prominent feature of Rome's skyline, was actually built in the early 1200s. ✉ *Via IV Novembre, 94, Monti* ☎ *06/0608* 🌐 *www.mercatiditraiano.it* 🎫 *€13* Ⓜ *Cavour.*

★ Musei Capitolini

ART MUSEUM | Surpassed in size and richness only by the Musei Vaticani, the world's first public museum—with the greatest hits of Roman art through the ages, from the ancients to the Baroque—is housed in the Palazzo dei Conservatori and the Palazzo Nuovo, which mirror one another across Michelangelo's famous piazza. The collection was begun by Pope Sixtus IV (the man who built the Sistine Chapel) in 1473, when he donated a room of ancient statuary to the people of the city. This core of the collection includes the She Wolf, which is the symbol of Rome, and the piercing gaze of the Capitoline Brutus. Buy your ticket and enter the Palazzo dei Conservatori, where in the first courtyard, you'll see the giant head, foot, elbow, and imperially raised finger of the fabled seated statue of Constantine, which once dominated the Basilica of Maxentius in the Forum. As you walk between the two halves of the museum, be sure to take the staircase to the Tabularium gallery and its unparalleled view over the Forum. ✉ *Piazza del Campidoglio, 1, Campitelli* ☎ *06/0608* 🌐 *www.museicapitolini.org* 🎫 *€13 (€20.50 with exhibitions); €15.50 with access to Centrale Montemartini; €4 audio guide* Ⓜ *Colosseo.*

★ Palatine Hill

RUINS | Just beyond the Arch of Titus, the Clivus Palatinus gently rises to the heights of the Colle Palatino (Palatine Hill)—the oldest inhabited site in Rome. Despite its location overlooking the Forum's traffic and attendant noise, the Palatine was the most coveted address for ancient Rome's rich and famous. Augustus was born on the hill, and the Houses of Livia and Augustus are today the hill's best-preserved structures, replete with fabulous frescoes. Later emperors built even bigger, and much of what we see today dates from the reign of Domitian, in the late 1st century AD. ✉ *Entrances at Piazza del Colosseo and Via di San Gregorio 30, Monti* ☎ *06/39967700* 🌐 *www.coopculture.it* 🎫 *€18 combined ticket, includes single entry to Palatine Hill–Forum site and single entry to Colosseum (if used within 24 hrs); S.U.P.E.R. ticket €22 (€24 with online reservation) includes access to the Houses of Augustus and Livia, the Palatine Museum, Aula Isiaca, Santa Maria Antiqua, and Temple of Romulus* Ⓜ *Colosseo.*

★ The Roman Forum

RUINS | Whether it's from the main entrance on Via dei Fori Imperali or by the entrance at the Arch of Titus, descend into the extraordinary archaeological complex that is the Foro Romano and the Palatine Hill, once the very heart of the Roman world. Hundreds of years of plunder reduced the Forum to its current desolate state. But this enormous area was once Rome's pulsating hub, filled with stately and extravagant temples, palaces, and shops and crowded with people from all corners of the empire. What you see today are not the ruins from just one period but from a span of almost 900 years, from about 500 BC to AD 400. Nonetheless, the enduring

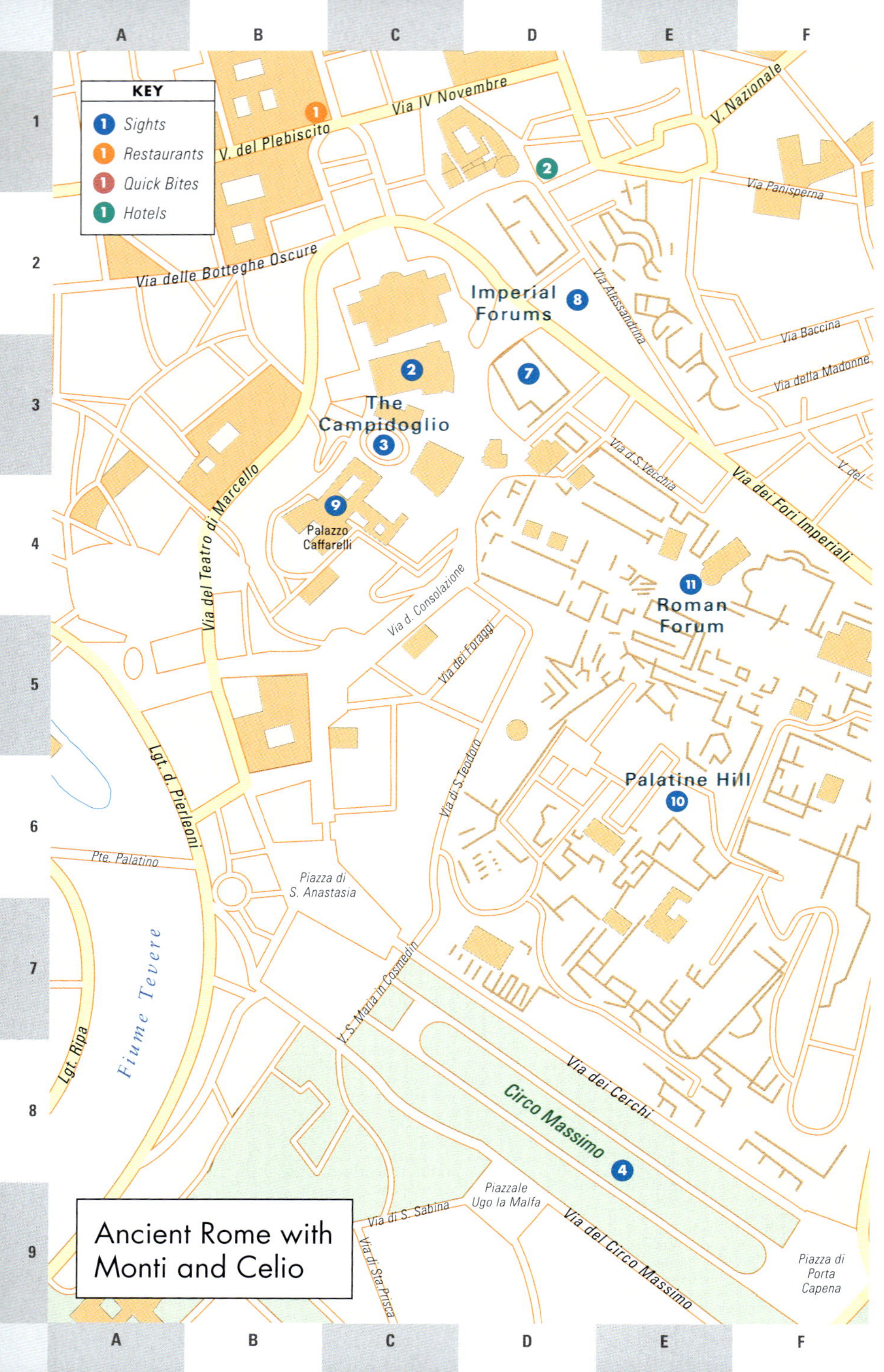

Ancient Rome with Monti and Celio

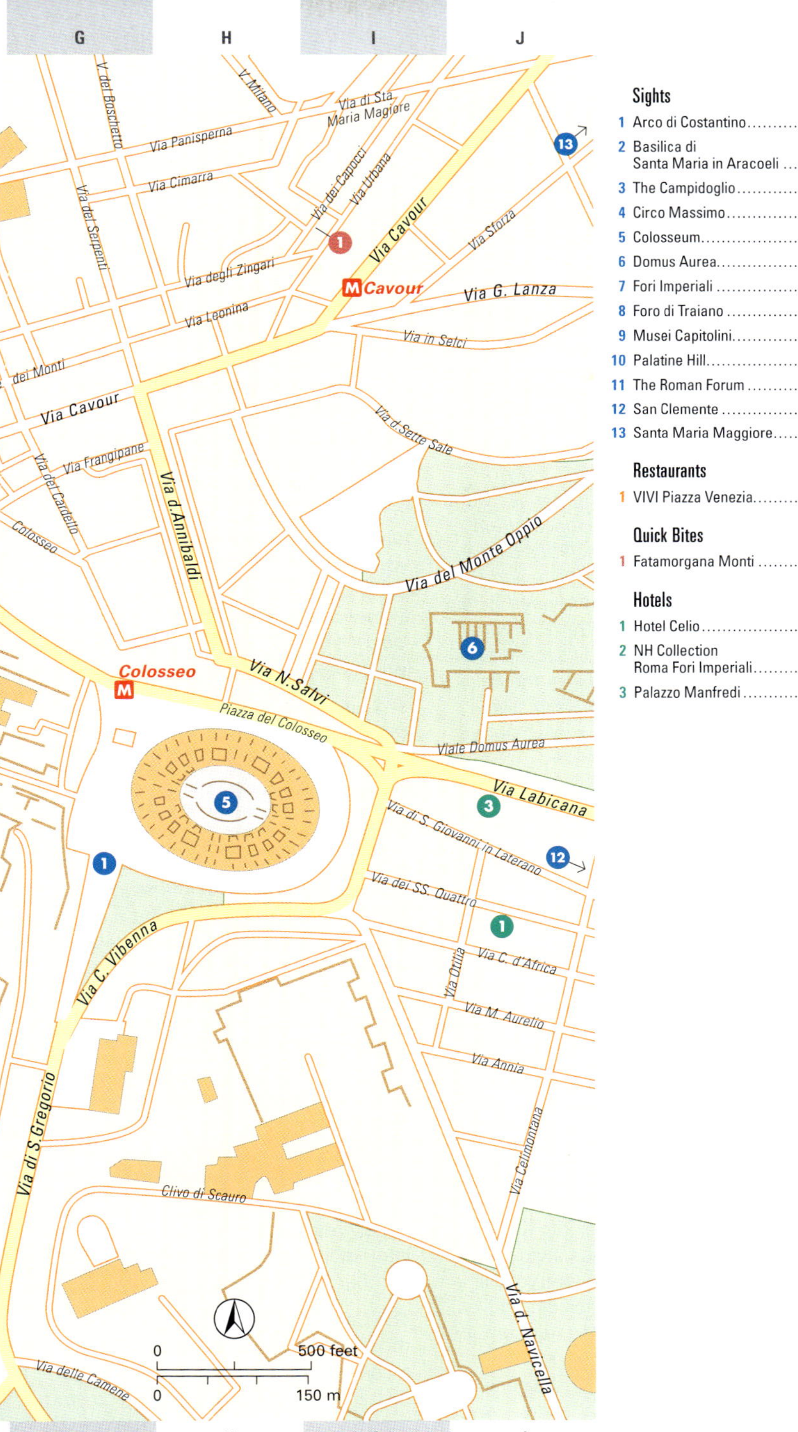

Sights

1 Arco di Costantino G6
2 Basilica di Santa Maria in Aracoeli C3
3 The Campidoglio C3
4 Circo Massimo E8
5 Colosseum H5
6 Domus Aurea J4
7 Fori Imperiali D3
8 Foro di Traiano D2
9 Musei Capitolini C4
10 Palatine Hill E6
11 The Roman Forum E4
12 San Clemente J6
13 Santa Maria Maggiore J1

Restaurants

1 VIVI Piazza Venezia B1

Quick Bites

1 Fatamorgana Monti I2

Hotels

1 Hotel Celio J6
2 NH Collection Roma Fori Imperiali D1
3 Palazzo Manfredi J5

romance of the place, with its lonely columns and great broken fragments of sculpted marble and stone, makes for a quintessential Roman experience. Lines, especially in high season, are not uncommon. Those who don't want to risk waiting in line can book their tickets online in advance, for a €2 surcharge. Choose the print-at-home option (a PDF on a smartphone works, too) and avoid the line to pick up tickets. Your ticket is valid for one entrance to the Roman Forum and the Palatine Hill, which are part of a single continuous complex. Certain sites within the Forum require a S.U.P.E.R. ticket. ✉ *Entrance at Via dei Fori Imperiali, Monti* ☎ *06/39967700* 🌐 *www.coopculture.it* 🎫 *€18 combined ticket, includes single entry to Palatine Hill–Forum site and single entry to Colosseum (if used within 24 hrs); S.U.P.E.R. ticket €22 (€24 with online reservation) includes access to the Houses of Augustus and Livia, the Palatine Museum, Aula Isiaca, Santa Maria Antiqua, and Temple of Romulus; audio guide €5* Ⓜ *Colosseo.*

★ San Clemente

CHURCH | One of the most impressive archaeological sites in Rome, San Clemente is a historical triple-decker. A 12th-century church was built on top of a 4th-century church, which had been built over a 2nd-century pagan temple to the god Mithras and 1st-century Roman apartments. The layers were uncovered in 1857, when a curious prior, Friar Joseph Mullooly, started excavations beneath the present basilica. Today, you can descend to explore all three.

The upper church (at street level) is a gem in its own right. In the apse, a glittering 12th-century mosaic shows Jesus on a cross that turns into a living tree. Green acanthus leaves swirl and teem with small scenes of everyday life. Early Christian symbols, including doves, vines, and fish, decorate the 4th-century marble choir screens. To the right of the sacristy (and bookshop), descend the stairs to the 4th-century church, used until 1084, when it was damaged beyond repair during a siege of the area by the Norman prince Robert Guiscard. Still intact are some vibrant 11th-century frescoes depicting stories from the life of St. Clement.

Descend an additional set of stairs to the Mithraeum, a shrine dedicated to the god Mithras. His cult spread from Persia and gained a foothold in Rome during the 2nd and 3rd centuries AD. Mithras was believed to have been born in a cave and was thus worshipped in cavernous, underground chambers, where initiates into the all-male cult would share a meal while reclining on stone couches, some visible here along with the altar block. ✉ *Via Labicana, 95, Celio* ☎ *06/7740021* 🌐 *basilicasanclemente.com* 🎫 *Archaeological area €10* ✍ *Reservations required* Ⓜ *Colosseo.*

★ Santa Maria Maggiore

CHURCH | Despite its florid 18th-century facade, Santa Maria Maggiore is one of the city's oldest churches, built around 440 by Pope Sixtus III. One Rome's four great pilgrimage churches, it's also the city center's best example of an early Christian basilica—one of the immense, hall-like structures derived from ancient Roman civic buildings and divided into thirds by two great rows of columns marching up the nave. The other three major basilicas in Rome (San Giovanni in Laterano, St. Peter's, and St. Paul Outside the Walls) havelargely been rebuilt. Paradoxically, the major reason why this church is such a striking example of early Christian design is that the same man who built the undulating exteriors circa 1740, Ferdinando Fuga, also conscientiously restored the interior, throwing out later additions and, crucially, replacing a number of the great columns.

The Cappella Sistina (Sistine Chapel), in the right-hand transept, was created by architect Domenico Fontana for Pope Sixtus V in 1585. Elaborately decorated with precious marbles "liberated" from the monuments of ancient Rome, the chapel includes a lower-level museum with some 13th-century sculptures by Arnolfo da Cambio that survived the Sack of Rome in 1527. Borgia popes Paul V and Clement VIII are buried here, as is Gian Lorenzo Bernini, under a simple engraved slab as humble as the tombs of his patrons are grand. The outside mosaic of Christ raising his hand in blessing is one of Rome's most beautiful sights, especially when lighted at night. *Piazza di Santa Maria Maggiore, Monti* *06/69886800* *basilicasantamaria-maggiore.va* *Termini.*

Restaurants

VIVI Piazza Venezia

$ | **BISTRO** | For an alternative to the heavy pastas typically found in Roman restaurants, this cheerful bistro inside Palazzo Bonaparte is a great choice. There are plenty of healthy options like excellent salads and poké bowls, as well as heartier fare such as burgers and, yes, pasta. **Known for:** fresh, healthy food; vegan and gluten-free desserts; shabby-chic design. *Average main: €16* *Piazza Venezia, 5, Piazza Venezia* *06/69228769* *www.vivi.it* *Colosseo.*

Coffee and Quick Bites

★ Fatamorgana Monti

$ | **ICE CREAM** | **FAMILY** | The emphasis is on all-natural ingredients at this woman-owned gelateria, which has several locations in Rome, including one near Campo de' Fiori and another in Trastevere. Flavors change often but might include favorites like stracciatella (with chocolate shavings) and hazelnut as well as more unusual flavors like matcha or carrot cake. **Known for:** all natural ingredients; unusual flavors; gluten-free with many vegan options. *Average main: €3* *Piazza degli Zingari, 5, Monti* *06/48906955* *www.gelateriafatamorgana.com* *Cavour.*

Hotels

Hotel Celio

$$ | **HOTEL** | At this hotel near the Colosseum, each of the small guest rooms is named after a famous Italian painter (Tiziano, Cellini, Michelangelo) and features decor that evokes the work of its namesake. **Pros:** beautiful rooftop garden; good location; comfortable beds. **Cons:** very small bathrooms; no elevator; breakfast not that substantial. *Rooms from: €180* *Via dei Santissimi Quattro, 35/c, Celio* *06/70495333* *www.hotelcelio.com* *20 rooms* *Free Breakfast* *Colosseo.*

NH Collection Roma Fori Imperiali

$$$ | **HOTEL** | It would be hard to find a modern hotel closer to the Roman Forum—the ancient ruins are practically right outside the door. **Pros:** incredible views of ancient Rome; rooftop serves a great aperitivo and refined dinners; restaurant Oro Bistrot by renowned chef Natale Giunta. **Cons:** breakfast foods are prepackaged; not much public space; no spa or gym. *Rooms from: €600* *Via di Santa Eufemia, 19, Monti* *06/697689911* *www.nh-collection.com/en/hotel/nh-collection-roma-fori-imperiali* *42 rooms* *No Meals* *Colosseo.*

Palazzo Manfredi

$$$$ | **HOTEL** | If you dream of waking up to head-on views of the Colosseum, book into this boutique hotel, which is set in a 17th-century palazzo built over the ruins of the Ludus Magnus, the gymnasium used by Roman gladiators, and offers refined luxury. **Pros:** incredible views; unparalleled location; excellent restaurant and cocktail bar. **Cons:** not all rooms have Colosseum views; some guests complain about noise; no spa. *Rooms from: €726* *Via Labicana, 125, Colosseo* *06/77591380* *www.*

palazzomanfredi.com *23 rooms* *No Meals* *Colosseo.*

Nightlife

★ Ai Tre Scalini

WINE BAR | An ivy-covered wine bar in the center of Monti, Rome's trendiest 'hood, Ai Tre Scalini has a warm and cozy menu of delicious antipasti and light entrées to go along with its enticing wine list. After about 8 pm, be prepared to wait—this is one extremely popular spot with locals, and they don't take reservations. *Via Panisperna, 251, Monti* *06/48907495* *www.aitrescalini.org* *Cavour.*

★ The Court

COCKTAIL BARS | For a winning combination of creative cocktails and incredible views of the Colosseum, this bar in Palazzo Manfredi can't be beat. Bar manager Matteo "Zed" Zamberlan cut his teeth in New York's top drinking establishments, and here his creativity is on full display. The cocktails are pricey, but they come with a bounty of snacks from the hotel's acclaimed restaurant. *Via Labicana, 125, Colosseo* *06/69354581* *www.manfredihotels.com/the-court-new* *Colosseo.*

Shopping

Sacripante

CLOTHING | This tiny Monti art gallery/boutique/bar has some of the most sophisticated retro-inspired garments in Rome. Its owner, Carlotta Cerulli, sells clothes by her mother, Wilma Silvestri, who cleverly combines vintage and contemporary fabrics for her label Le Gallinelle, creating stylish fashions with a modern edge made for everyday wear. *Via Panisperna, 59, Monti* *06/48903495* *www.facebook.com/sacripantegallery* *Cavour.*

The Vatican with Borgo and Prati

Climbing the steps to St. Peter's Basilica feels monumental, like a journey that has reached its climactic end. Suddenly, all is cool and dark … and you are dwarfed by the gargantuan nave and its magnificence. Above is a ceiling so high it must lead to heaven itself. Great, shining marble figures of saints frozen mid-whirl loom from niches and corners. And at the end, a throne for an unseen king whose greatness, it is implied, must mirror the greatness of his palace. For this basilica is a palace, the dazzling center of power for a king and a place of supplication for his subjects. Whether his kingdom is earthly or otherwise may lie in the eye of the beholder.

For good Catholics and sinners alike, the Vatican is an exercise in spirituality, requiring patience but delivering joy. Some come here for a transcendent glimpse of a heavenly Michelangelo fresco; others come in search of a direct connection with the divine. But what all visitors share, for a few hours, is an awe-inspiring landscape that offers a famous sight for every taste: rooms decorated by Raphael, antique sculptures like the Apollo Belvedere, famous paintings by Giotto and Bellini, and, perhaps most of all, the Sistine Chapel—for the lover of beauty, few places are as historically important as this epitome of faith and grandeur.

The Borgo and Prati are the neighborhoods immediately surrounding the Vatican, and it's worth noting that, while the Vatican may well be a priority, these neighborhoods are not the best places to choose a hotel, as they're quite far from other top sights in the city.

GETTING HERE AND AROUND

Metro stop Cipro or Ottaviano will get you within about a 10-minute walk of the entrance to the Musei Vaticani. Or, from Termini station, Bus No. 40 Express or the famously crowded No. 64 will take you to Piazza San Pietro. Both routes swing past Largo Argentina, where you can also get Bus No. 46.

A leisurely meander from the centro storico, across the exquisite Ponte Sant'Angelo, will take about a half hour.

Sights

★ Basilica di San Pietro

CHURCH | The world's largest church, built over the tomb of St. Peter, is the most imposing and breathtaking architectural achievement of the Renaissance (although much of the lavish interior dates to the Baroque period). No fewer than five of Italy's greatest artists—Bramante, Raphael, Peruzzi, Antonio da Sangallo the Younger, and Michelangelo—died while striving to erect this new St. Peter's. In 1503, Pope Julius II instructed the architect Bramante to raze all the existing buildings of the original St. Peter's, which had stood for over 1,000 years, and build a new basilica, one that would surpass even Constantine's for grandeur. It wasn't until 1626 that the new basilica was completed and consecrated. Highlights include the Loggia delle Benedizioni (Benediction Loggia), the balcony where newly elected popes are proclaimed; Michelangelo's *Pietà*; and Bernini's great bronze baldacchino, a huge, spiral-columned canopy—at 100,000 pounds, perhaps the largest bronze object in the world—as well as many other Bernini masterpieces. For views of both the dome above and the piazza below, take the elevator or stairs to the roof. Those with more stamina (and without claustrophobia) can then head up more stairs to the apex of the dome.

TIP→ The basilica is free to visit, but a security check at the entrance can create very long lines. Arrive before 8:30 or after 5:30 to minimize the wait and avoid the crowds. ✉ *Piazza San Pietro, Vatican* 🌐 *basilicasanpietro.va* 🎫 *Free* 🕓 *Closed during Papal General Audience (Wed. until 1 pm) and during other ceremonies in piazza* Ⓜ *Ottaviano.*

★ Cappella Sistina (*Sistine Chapel*)

ART MUSEUM | In 1508, the redoubtable Pope Julius II commissioned Michelangelo to fresco the more than 10,000 square feet of the Sistine Chapel's ceiling. The task took four years, and it's said that for many years afterward Michelangelo couldn't read anything without holding it over his head. The result, however, was the greatest artwork of the Renaissance. A pair of binoculars helps greatly, as does a small mirror—hold the mirror facing the ceiling and look down to study the reflection. More than 20 years after his work on the ceiling, Michelangelo was called on again, this time by Pope Paul III, to add to the chapel's decoration by painting the *Last Judgment* on the wall over the altar. By way of signature on this, his late great fresco, Michelangelo painted his own face on the flayed-off human skin in St. Bartholomew's hand.

TIP→ The chapel is entered through the Musei Vaticani, and lines are slightly shorter after 2:30 (reservations are always advisable)—except free Sundays, which are extremely busy and when admissions close at 12:30. ✉ *Musei Vaticani, Vatican* 🌐 *www.museivaticani.va* 🎫 *€20 (part of the Vatican Museums)* 🕓 *Closed Sun.* Ⓜ *Ottaviano.*

Castel Sant'Angelo

CASTLE/PALACE | **FAMILY** | Standing between the Tiber and the Vatican, this circular castle has long been one of Rome's most distinctive landmarks. Opera lovers know it well as the setting for the final scene of Puccini's *Tosca*. Started in AD 135, the structure began as a mausoleum for the emperor Hadrian

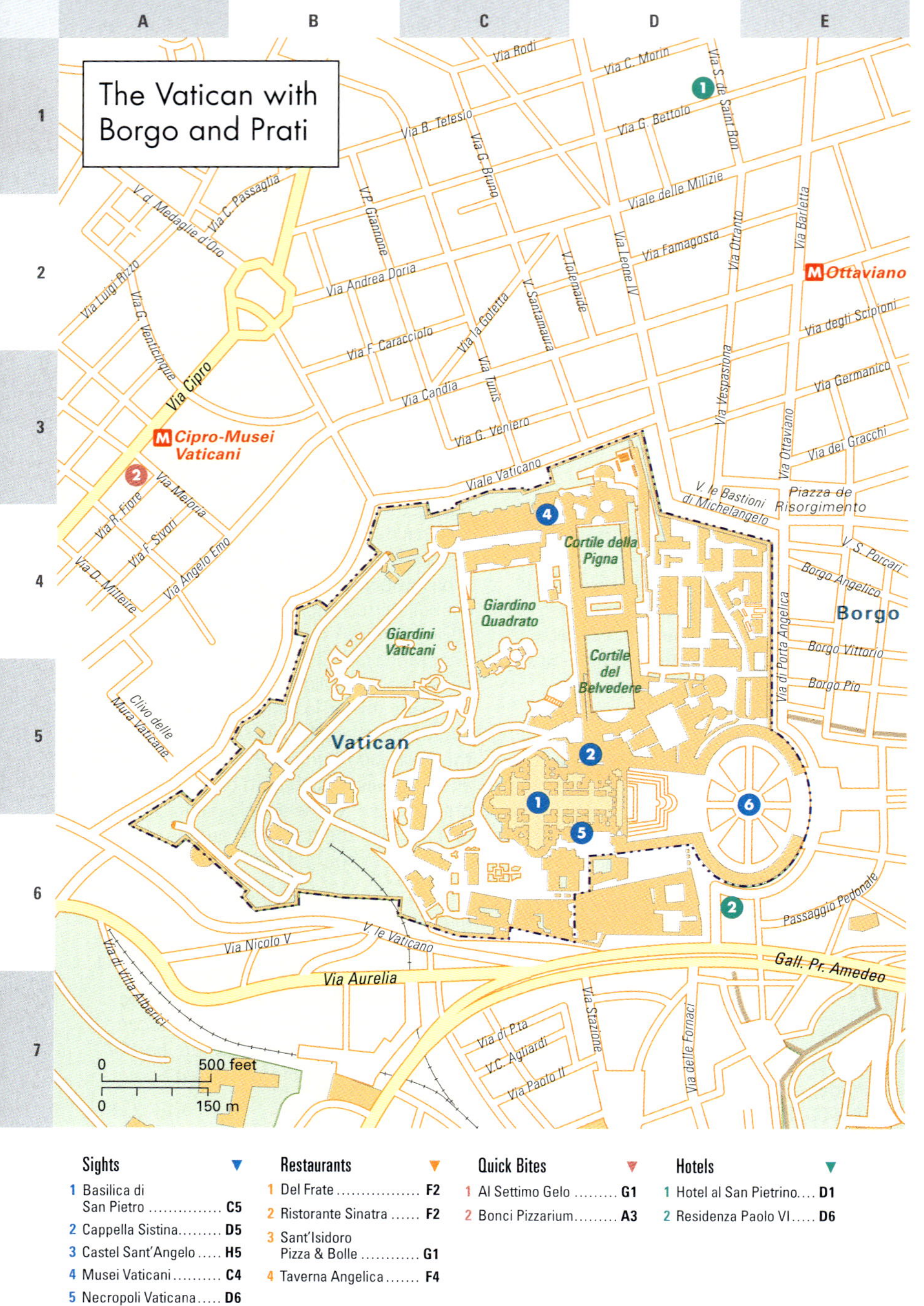

Sights

1 Basilica di San Pietro C5
2 Cappella Sistina......... D5
3 Castel Sant'Angelo H5
4 Musei Vaticani C4
5 Necropoli Vaticana D6
6 Piazza San Pietro E5

Restaurants

1 Del Frate F2
2 Ristorante Sinatra F2
3 Sant'Isidoro Pizza & Bolle G1
4 Taverna Angelica F4

Quick Bites

1 Al Settimo Gelo G1
2 Bonci Pizzarium......... A3

Hotels

1 Hotel al San Pietrino.... D1
2 Residenza Paolo VI D6

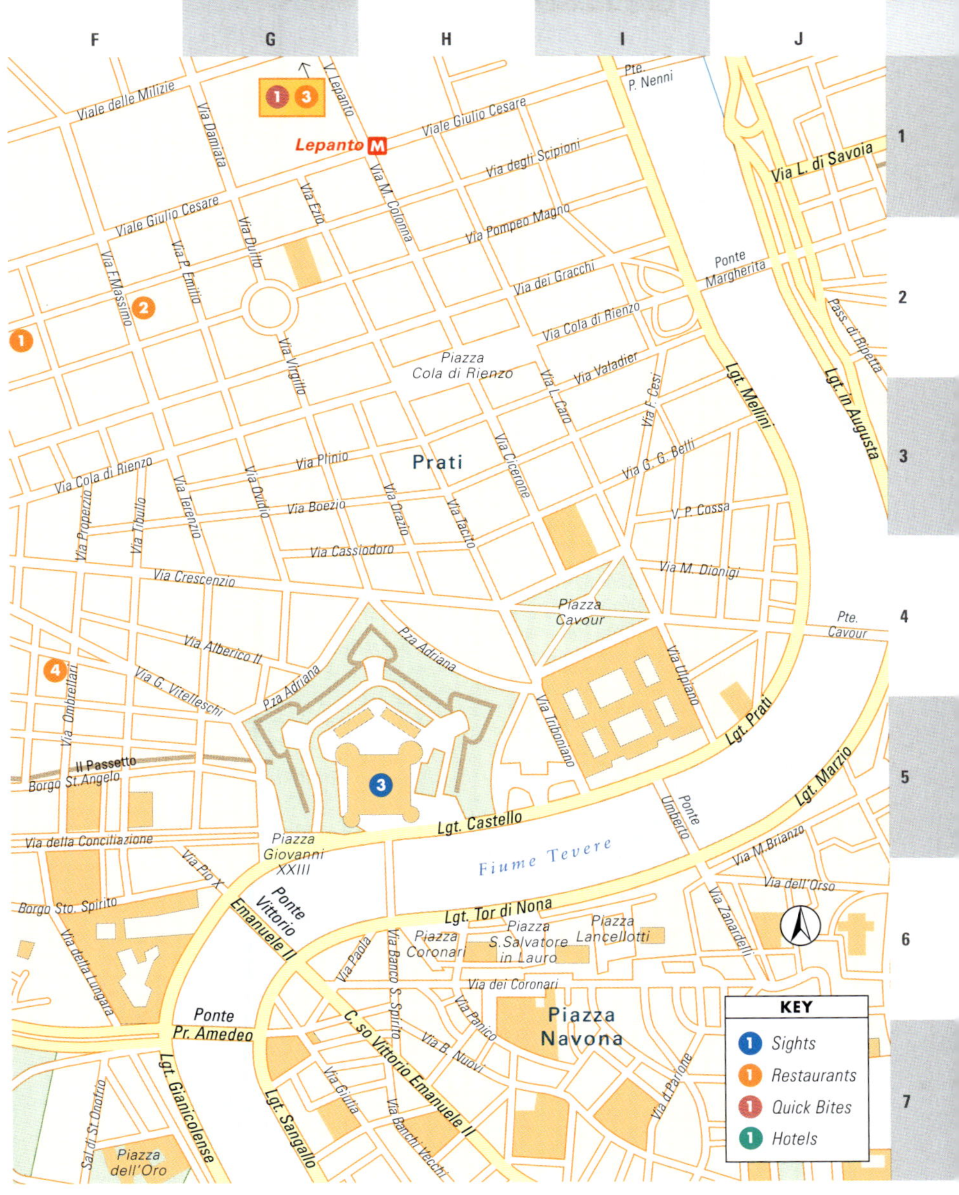
F
G
H
I
J
1
2
3
4
5
6
7
Lepanto
Viale delle Milizie
Via Damiata
V. Lepanto
Viale Giulio Cesare
Via degli Scipioni
Via L. di Savoia
Pte. P. Nenni
Via M. Colonna
Via Ezio
Via Duilio
Via P. Emilio
Via F. Massimo
Via Pompeo Magno
Via dei Gracchi
Ponte Margherita
Via Cola di Rienzo
Via Virgilio
Piazza Cola di Rienzo
Via L. Caro
Via Valadier
Via F. Cesi
Lgt. Mellini
Pass. di Ripetta
Lgt. in Augusta
Prati
Via Plinio
Via Cicerone
Via G. G. Belli
Via Ovidio
Via Terenzio
Via Boezio
Via Orazio
Via Tacito
V. P. Cossa
Via Properzio
Via Tibullo
Via Cassiodoro
Via M. Dionigi
Via Crescenzio
Piazza Cavour
Pte. Cavour
Pza Adriana
Via Alberico II
Via Ulpiano
Via G. Vitelleschi
Via Ombrellari
Via Triboniano
Lgt. Prati
Il Passetto
Borgo St. Angelo
Lgt. Castello
Ponte Umberto
Lgt. Marzio
Via della Conciliazione
Piazza Giovanni XXIII
Fiume Tevere
Via M. Brianzo
Via Pio X
Via dell'Orso
Borgo Sto. Spirito
Ponte Vittorio Emanuele II
Lgt. Tor di Nona
Via Zanardelli
Via della Lungara
Via Paola
Via Banco S. Spirito
Piazza Coronari
Piazza S. Salvatore in Lauro
Piazza Lancellotti
Via dei Coronari
Via Panico
Piazza Navona
Ponte Pr. Amedeo
C. so Vittorio Emanuele II
Via B. Nuovi
Via d. Parione
Lgt. Gianicolense
Sal. di St. Onofrio
Lgt. Sangallo
Via Giulia
Via Banchi Vecchi
Piazza dell'Oro
KEY
Sights
Restaurants
Quick Bites
Hotels

and was completed by his successor, Antoninus Pius. From the mid-6th century the building became a fortress, a place of refuge for popes during wars and sieges. Its name dates to AD 590, when Pope Gregory the Great, during a procession to plead for the end of a plague, saw an angel standing on the summit of the castle, sheathing his sword. Taking this as a sign that the plague was at an end, the pope built a small chapel at the top, placing a statue next to it to celebrate his vision—thus the name, Castel Sant'Angelo. Look for the Cappella di Papa Leone X (Chapel of Pope Leo X), with a facade by Michelangelo. The stairs at the far end of the courtyard lead to the open terrace for a view of the Passetto, the fortified corridor connecting Castel Sant'Angelo with the Vatican. In the *appartamento papale* (papal apartment), the Sala Paolina (Pauline Room) was decorated in the 16th century by Perino del Vaga. ✉ *Lungotevere Castello, 50, Borgo* ☎ *06/6819111 central line* 🌐 *www.castelsantangelo.beniculturali.it* 🎫 *€16* 🕒 *Closed Mon.* Ⓜ *Lepanto, Ottaviano.*

★ **Musei Vaticani** (*Vatican Museums*)
ART MUSEUM | Other than the pope and his papal court, the occupants of the Vatican are some of the most famous artworks in the world. Indeed, most of the Vatican Palace estimated 1,400 rooms, chapels, and galleries are given over to the Vatican Library and Museums. Beyond the glories of the Sistine Chapel, the collection is extraordinarily rich: highlights include the great antique sculptures (including the celebrated *Apollo Belvedere* in the Octagonal Courtyard and the *Belvedere Torso* in the Hall of the Muses); the Stanze di Raffaello (Raphael Rooms), with their famous gorgeous frescoes; and the Old Master paintings, such as Leonardo da Vinci's beautiful (though unfinished) *St. Jerome in the Wilderness,* some of Raphael's greatest creations, and Caravaggio's gigantic *Deposition in the Pinacoteca* ("Picture Gallery"). Guided tours start at €35, including entrance tickets, and can also be booked online. Other offerings include a regular two-hour guided tour of the Vatican gardens. ✉ *Viale Vaticano, near intersection with Via Leone IV, Vatican* ☎ *06/69883145* 🌐 *www.museivaticani.va* 🎫 *€20* 🕒 *Closed Sun. (except the last Sun. of each month) and Roman Catholic holidays* Ⓜ *Cipro, Ottaviano.*

Necropoli Vaticana (*Vatican Necropolis*)
CEMETERY | With advance notice you can take a one-hour guided tour in English of the Vatican Necropolis, under the Basilica di San Pietro, which gives a rare glimpse of early Christian Roman burial customs and a closer look at the tomb of St. Peter. Apply via the contact form online, specifying the number of people in the group (all must be age 10 or older), preferred language, preferred time, available dates, and your contact information in Rome. Each group will have about 12 participants. Visits are not recommended for those with mobility issues or who are claustrophobic. ✉ *Ufficio Scavi, Vatican* ☎ *06/69885318* 🌐 *www.necropolivaticana.org* 🎫 *€20* 🕒 *Closed Sun. and Roman Catholic holidays* ✍ *Reservations required* Ⓜ *Ottaviano.*

★ **Piazza San Pietro**
PLAZA/SQUARE | Mostly enclosed within high walls that recall the papacy's stormy history, the Vatican opens the spectacular arms of Bernini's colonnade to embrace the world only at St. Peter's Square, scene of the pope's public appearances and another of Bernini's masterpieces. The elliptical Piazza di San Pietro was completed in 1667 and holds about 100,000 people. It's surrounded by a pair of quadruple colonnades and is gloriously studded with 140 statues of saints and martyrs. At its center is the 85-foot-high Egyptian obelisk, which was brought to Rome by Caligula in AD 37 and moved here in 1586 by Pope Sixtus V. The Vatican post offices can be found on both sides of the square and inside the Vatican Museums complex.

■ TIP→ The main information office is just left of the basilica as you face it. ✉ *Piazza di San Pietro, Vatican* 🌐 *www.vaticanstate.va* Ⓜ *Ottaviano.*

Restaurants

Del Frate

$$ | **MODERN ITALIAN** | This impressive wine bar pairs modern decor with creative cuisine and three dozen wines available by the glass. There are some fantastic seasonal specialties, but you can also get cheeses, smoked meats, and composed salads. **Known for:** shares space with one of Rome's noted wine shops; daily aperitivo with a nice selection of wines by the glass; wide selection of after-dinner drinks, including mezcal and amari (bitter cordial). Ⓢ *Average main: €25* ✉ *Via degli Scipioni, 118, Prati* ☎ *06/3236437* 🌐 *www.enotecadelfrate.it* ⏲ *Closed 2 wks in Aug.* Ⓜ *Ottaviano.*

Ristorante Sinatra

$ | **MODERN ITALIAN** | Named in homage to the Italian-American crooner, this intimate restaurant has a refined yet casual atmosphere, with wine bottles lining the walls, black-and-white photographs of jazz musicians, and vintage touches like rotary telephones. The menu emphasizes Italian classics, with options like raw meat and fish, fried artichokes, carbonara, meatballs, and steaks. **Known for:** charming vintage setting; classic Italian dishes; live music. Ⓢ *Average main: €16* ✉ *Via Fabio Massimo, 68, Prati* ☎ *06/3219657* 🌐 *www.ristorante-sinatra.it* Ⓜ *Lepanto, Ottaviano.*

Sant'Isidoro Pizza & Bolle

$ | **PIZZA** | **FAMILY** | More upscale than a typical pizzeria but casual enough for a weeknight, this establishment pairs its pies with sparkling wines instead of beer. Opt for a classic pizza, or go with an innovative option, like one topped with squash, speck, pomegranate, and mint. **Known for:** wide selection of sparkling wines; creative pizzas; chic, modern design. Ⓢ *Average main: €14* ✉ *Via Oslavia, 41, Prati* ☎ *06/89822607* 🌐 *www.pizzaebolle.it* ⏲ *No lunch weekends* Ⓜ *Lepanto.*

Taverna Angelica

$$ | **MODERN ITALIAN** | The Borgo area near St. Peter's Basilica hasn't been known for culinary excellence, but Taverna Angelica was one of the first refined restaurants in this part of town. The dining room is small, which allows the chef to create a menu that's inventive without being pretentious. **Known for:** eclectic Italian dishes; high-quality cuisine; ravioli with salt cod in arrabbiata oil spiced with red chili. Ⓢ *Average main: €26* ✉ *Piazza Amerigo Capponi, 6, Borgo* ☎ *06/6874514* 🌐 *www.tavernaangelica.com* ⏲ *Closed Mon.* Ⓜ *Ottaviano.*

Coffee and Quick Bites

Al Settimo Gelo

$ | **ICE CREAM** | **FAMILY** | The unusual flavors of gelato scooped up here include cinnamon and ginger and fig with cardamom and walnut, but the classics also get rave reviews. Ask for a taste of the *passito* flavor, if it's available; it's inspired by the popular sweet Italian dessert wine. **Known for:** organic Sicilian lemon sorbetto; homemade whipped cream; completely gluten-free shop. Ⓢ *Average main: €5* ✉ *Via Vodice, 21/A, Prati* ☎ *06/3725567* 🌐 *www.alsettimogelo.it* ⏲ *Closed Mon. and 1 wk in Aug.* Ⓜ *Lepanto.*

★ Bonci Pizzarium

$ | **PIZZA** | **FAMILY** | This tiny storefront by famed pizzaiolo Gabriele Bonci is the city's most famous place for pizza *al taglio* (by the slice). It serves more than a dozen versions, from the standard margherita to slices piled high with prosciutto and other tasty ingredients. **Known for:** Rome's best pizza al taglio; over a

Continued on page 96

HEAVENS ABOVE:
THE SISTINE CEILING

Forming lines that are probably longer than those waiting to pass through the Pearly Gates, hordes of visitors arrive at the Sistine Chapel daily to view what may be the world's most sublime example of artistry:

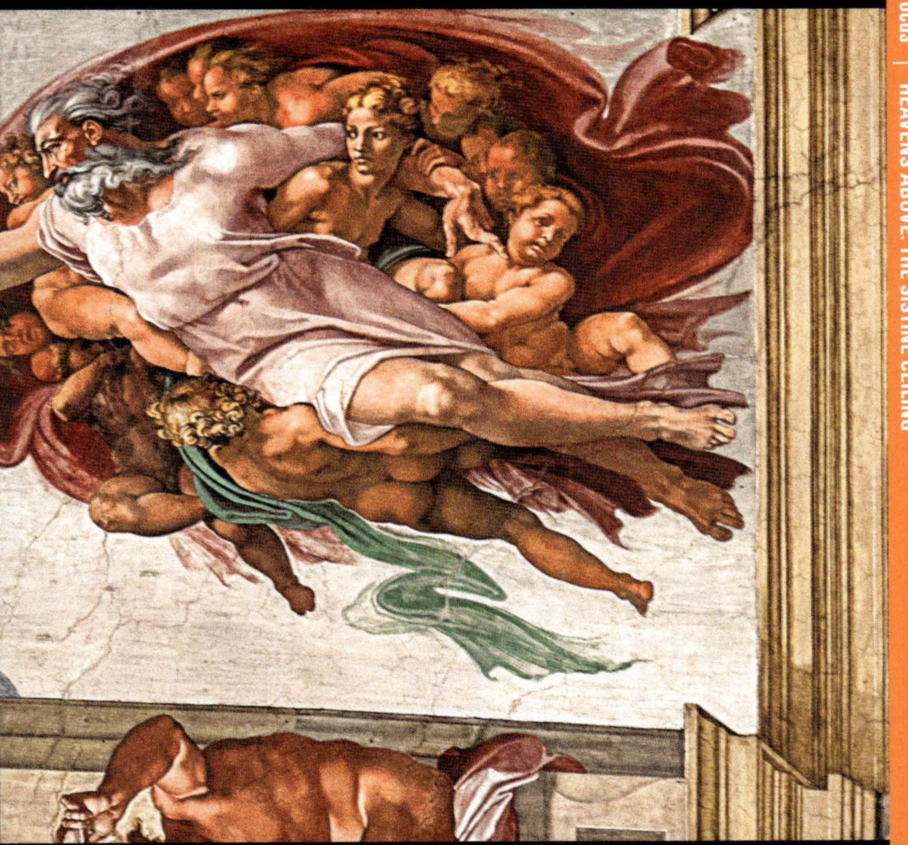

Michelangelo: *The Creation of Adam*, Sistine Chapel, The Vatican, circa 1511.

Michelangelo's Sistine Ceiling. To paint this 12,000-square-foot barrel vault, it took four years, 343 frescoed figures, and a titanic battle of wits between the artist and Pope Julius II. While in its typical fashion, Hollywood focused on the element of agony, not ecstasy, involved in the saga of creation, a restoration of the ceiling, completed in 1994, and the installation of LEDs for better illumination, completed in 2018, have revolutionized our appreciation of the masterpiece of masterpieces.

By Martin Bennett

View of the Cappella Sistina

MICHELANGELO'S MISSION IMPOSSIBLE

Designed to match the proportions of Solomon's Temple described in the Old Testament, the Sistine Chapel is named after Pope Sixtus VI, who commissioned it as a place of worship for himself and as the venue where new popes could be elected. Before Michelangelo, the barrel-vaulted ceiling was an expanse of azure fretted with golden stars. Then, in 1504, an ugly crack appeared. Bramante, the architect, managed do some patchwork using iron rods, but when signs of a fissure remained, the new Pope Julius II summoned Michelangelo to cover it with a fresco 135 feet long and 44 feet wide.

Taking in the entire span of the ceiling, the theme connecting the various scenes in this painted universe is seemingly mankind's need for redemption. The majestic panel depicting the Creation of Adam leads through the stages of the Fall and the expulsion from Eden to the tragedy of Noah found naked and mocked by his own sons. Witnessing all from the side and end walls, a chorus of ancient Prophets and Sibyls peers anxiously forward, awaiting the Redeemer who will come to save both the Jews and the Gentiles.

APOCALYPSE NOW

The sweetness and pathos of his *Pietà*, carved by Michelangelo only ten years earlier, have been left behind. The new work foretells an apocalypse, its congregation of doomed sinners facing the wrath of heaven through hanging, beheading, crucifixion, flood, and plague. Michelangelo, by nature a misanthrope, was already filled with visions of doom thanks to the fiery orations of Savonarola, whose thunderous preachments he had heard before leaving his hometown of Florence. Vasari, the 16th-century art historian, coined the word *terrabilità* to describe Michelangelo's tension-ridden style, a rare case of a single word being worth a thousand pictures.

Michelangelo wound up using a condensed "Reader's Digest" version of the stories from Genesis, with the dramatis personae overseen by a punitive and terrifying God. In real life, poor Michelangelo answered to a flesh-and-blood taskmaster who was almost as vengeful: Pope Julius II. Less vicar of Christ than latter-day Caesar, he was intent on uniting Italy under the power of the Vatican and was eager to do so by any means, including riding into pitched battle. Yet this "warrior pope" considered his most formidable adversary to be Michelangelo. Applying a form of blackmail, Julius threatened to wage war on Michelangelo's Florence, to which the artist had fled after Julius canceled a commission for a grand papal tomb unless Michelangelo agreed to return to Rome and take up the task of painting the Sistine Chapel ceiling.

MICHELANGELO, SCULPTOR

A sculptor first and foremost, however, Michelangelo considered painting an inferior genre—"for rascals and sissies" as he put it. Second, there was the sheer scope of the task, leading Michelangelo to suspect he'd been set up by a rival, Bramante, chief architect of the new St. Peter's Basilica. As Michelangelo was also a master architect, he regarded this fresco commission as a Renaissance mission-impossible. Pope Julius's powerful will prevailed—and six years later the work of the Sistine Ceiling was complete. Irving Stone's famous novel *The Agony and the Ecstasy*—and the granitic 1965 film that followed—chart this epic battle between artist and pope.

THINGS ARE LOOKING UP

To better view the ceiling, bring binoculars or even just a mirror (to prevent your neck from becoming bent like Michelangelo's). Note that photos are not permitted. Admission and entry to the Sistine Chapel is only through the Musei Vaticani (Vatican Museums). To avoid crowds, visit at lunchtime or during the papal blessings and public audiences held in St. Peter's Square. Alternatively, book the Prime Experience Tour, which starts one hour before the museums open, or purchase the Extra Hours–Sistine Chapel ticket, which allows time in the chapel after the museums close.

SCHEMATIC OF THE SISTINE CEILING

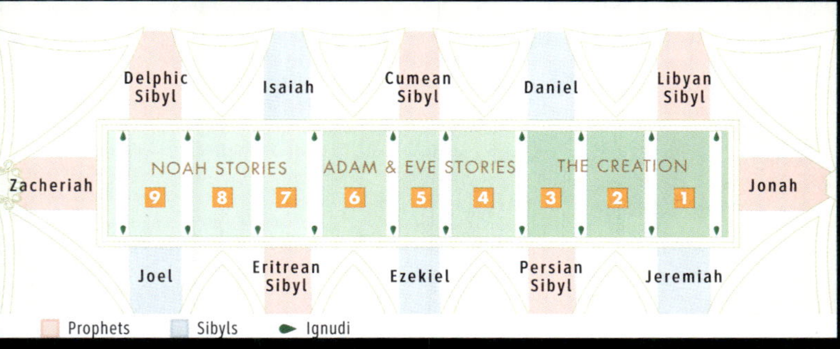

PAINTING THE BIBLE

The ceiling's biblical symbols were ideated by three Vatican theologians, Cardinal Alidosi, Egidio da Viterbo, and Giovanni Rafanelli, along with Michelangelo. As for the ceiling's painted "framework," this quadratura alludes to Roman triumphal arches because Pope Julius II was fond of mounting "triumphal entries" into his conquered cities (in imitation of Christ's procession into Jerusalem on Palm Sunday).

THE CENTER PANELS

Prophet turned art-critic or, perhaps doubling as ourselves, the ideal viewer, Jonah the prophet (painted at the altar end) gazes up at the Creation, or Michelangelo's version of it.

1 The first of three scenes taken from the Book of Genesis: God separates Light from Darkness.

2 God creates the sun and a craterless, pre-Galilean moon, while the panel's other half offers an unprecedented rear view of the Almighty creating the vegetable world.

3 In the panel showing God separating the Waters from the Heavens, the Creator tumbles towards us as in a self-made whirlwind.

4 Pausing for breath, next admire probably Western Art's most famous image—God giving life to Adam.

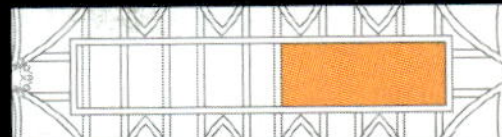

The Creation of Eve from Adam's rib leads to the sixth panel.

6 In a sort of diptych divided by the trunk of the Tree of Knowledge of Good and Evil, Michelangelo retells the Temptation and the Fall.

Illustrating Man's fallen nature, the last three panels narrate, in un-chronological order, the Flood. In the first Noah offers a pre-Flood sacrifice of thanks.

8 Damaged by an explosion in 1794, next comes Michelangelo's version of Flood itself.

Finally, above the monumental Jonah, you can just make out the small, wretched figure of Noah, lying drunk—in pose, the shrunken anti-type of the majestic Adam five panels down the wall.

THE CREATION OF ADAM

Michelangelo's Adam was partly inspired by the Creation scenes Michelangelo had studied in the sculpted doors of Jacopo della Quercia in Bologna and Lorenzo Ghiberti's Doors of Paradise in Florence. Yet in Michelangelo's version Adam's hand hangs limp, waiting God's touch to impart the spark of life. Facing his Creation, the Creator—looking a bit like the pagan god Jupiter—is for the first time ever depicted as horizontal, mirroring the biblical "in his own likeness." Decades after its completion, a crack began to appear, amputating Adam's fingertips. Believe it or not, the most famous fingers in Western art are the handiwork, at least in part, of one Domenico Carnevale.

dozen flavors; long lines. $ *Average main: €8* ✉ *Via della Meloria, 43, Prati* ☎ *06/39745416* 🌐 *www.bonci.it* ⏲ *Closed Mon.* Ⓜ *Cipro.*

Hotels

Hotel al San Pietrino

$ | **HOTEL** | This simple budget hotel on the third floor of a 19th-century palazzo offers rock-bottom rates and is just a five-minute walk from the Vatican. **Pros:** heavenly rates near the Vatican; air-conditioning and Wi-Fi; free parking nearby. **Cons:** a couple of Metro stops from the centro storico; flat pillows and basic bedding; no bar. $ *Rooms from: €98* ✉ *Via Giovanni Bettolo, 43, Prati* ☎ *06/3700132* 🌐 *www.hotelsanpietrino.it* *11 rooms* *No Meals* Ⓜ *Ottaviano.*

Residenza Paolo VI

$$ | **HOTEL** | Set in a former monastery—still an extraterritorial part of the Vatican—abutting Bernini's colonnade of St. Peter's Square, the Paolo VI (pronounced "Sesto," a reference to Pope Paul VI) is unbeatably close to St. Peter's, with basic, quiet guest rooms. **Pros:** direct views of St. Peter's from the rooftop terrace; quiet rooms; lovely staff and service. **Cons:** some rooms are really small; bathrooms are a tight space; far away from Rome's historical attractions. $ *Rooms from: €345* ✉ *Via Paolo VI, 26, Borgo* ☎ *06/684870* 🌐 *www.residenzapaolovi.com* *35 rooms* *Free Breakfast* Ⓜ *Ottaviano.*

Nightlife

Emerald's Bar

COCKTAIL BARS | This classy cocktail bar a few blocks from the Vatican makes you feel transported to a cozy salon in New York or London. In addition to some original creations, the bartenders make reliably good classics, including excellent dirty martinis. The kitchen stays open until midnight, so it's also a good spot for a late bite. ✉ *Via Crescenzio, 91C, Prati* ☎ *06/88654275* 🌐 *www.emeraldsbar.it* Ⓜ *Ottaviano.*

Shopping

★ Castroni

FOOD | Opening its flagship shop near the Vatican in 1932, this gastronomic paradise has long been Rome's port of call for decadent delicacies from around the globe; there are now 13 locations throughout the city. Jonesing expats and study-abroad students pop in for local sweets, 300 types of tea, and even good old-fashioned Betty Crocker red velvet cake mix. If you need a pick-me-up, try the house-roasted espresso, which is some of the best coffee in Rome. ✉ *Via Cola di Rienzo, 196/198, Prati* ☎ *06/6874383* 🌐 *www.castronicoladirienzo.com* Ⓜ *Lepanto.*

Savelli Arte e Tradizione

SOUVENIRS | Here you'll find a fully stocked selection of religious gifts: everything from rosaries and crosses to religious artwork and Pope memorabilia. Founded in 1898, this family business provides a place for pilgrims to pick up a souvenir from the Holy See and also specializes in mosaics. There's another location at the Self-Service Restaurant in Piazza del Sant'Uffizio, 6/7. Both locations are closed on Sunday afternoon. ✉ *Via Paolo VI, 27–29, Borgo* ☎ *06/631164* 🌐 *savellireligious.com* Ⓜ *Ottaviano.*

Piazza Navona, Campo de' Fiori, and the Jewish Ghetto

Set between Via del Corso and the Tiber bend, these time-burnished districts are some of the city's most beautiful. They're filled with airy piazzas, half-hidden courtyards, and narrow streets bearing curious names. Some of Rome's most coveted residential addresses are nestled here. So, too, are the ancient Pantheon and the Renaissance square of Campo de' Fiori, but the spectacular, over-the-top Baroque monuments of the 16th and 17th centuries predominate.

The hub of the district is the queen of squares, Piazza Navona—a cityscape adorned with the most jaw-dropping fountain by Gian Lorenzo Bernini, father of the Baroque. Streets running off the square lead to many historic must-sees, including noble churches by Borromini and Caravaggio's greatest paintings at San Luigi dei Francesi. This district has been an integral part of the city since ancient times, and its position between the Vatican and Lateran palaces, both seats of papal rule, put it in the mainstream of Rome's development from the Middle Ages onward. Craftsmen, shopkeepers, and famed artists toiled in the shadow of the huge palaces built to consolidate the power of leading figures in the papal court. Artisans and artists still live here, but their numbers are diminishing as the district becomes increasingly posh and—so critics say—"Disneyfied." But three of the liveliest piazzas in Rome—Piazza Navona, Piazza della Rotonda (home to the Pantheon), and Campo de' Fiori—are lodestars in a constellation of some of the city's finest cafés, stores, and wine bars.

Although today most of Rome's Jews live outside the Ghetto, the area remains the spiritual and cultural home of Jewish Rome, and that heritage permeates its small commercial area of Judaica shops, kosher bakeries, and restaurants. The Jewish Ghetto was established by papal decree in the 16th century. It was by definition a closed community, where Roman Jews lived under lock and key until Italian unification in 1870. In 1943–44, the already small Jewish population there was decimated by deportations. Today there are a few Judaica shops and kosher groceries, bakeries, and restaurants (especially on Via di Portico d'Ottavia), but the neighborhood mansions are now being renovated and much coveted by rich and stylish expats.

GETTING HERE AND AROUND

The Piazza Navona and Campo de' Fiori are an easy walk from the Vatican or Trastevere, or a half-hour stroll from the Spanish Steps. From Termini or the Vatican, take Bus No. 40 Express or the No. 64 to Largo Torre Argentina; then walk 10 minutes to either piazza. Bus No. 62 winds from Piazza Barberini past the Trevi Fountain to Campo de' Fiori.

From the Vatican or the Spanish Steps, it's a 30-minute walk to the Jewish Ghetto, or take the No. 40 Express or the No. 64 bus from Termini station to Largo Torre Argentina.

 Sights

Chiesa del Gesù

CHURCH | With an overall design by Vignola and a facade and dome by Della Porta, the first Jesuit church in Rome influenced the city's ecclesiastical architecture for more than a century. Consecrated in 1584—after the Council of Trent (1545–63) solidified the determination of the Roman Catholic Church to push back against northern Europe's Reformed Protestants—Il Gesù also became the prototype for Counter-Reformation churches throughout not only Italy but also Europe and the Americas.

Although low lighting underplays the brilliance of everything, the inside of the church drips with gold and lapis lazuli, gold and precious marbles, and gold and more gold. The interior was initially left plain to the point of austerity; when it was finally fully embellished 100 years later, no expense was spared to inspire believers with pomp and majesty. The most striking element is the ceiling, where frescoes swirl down from on high and merge with painted stucco figures at the base. The artist Baciccia achieved extraordinary effects, especially over the nave in the *Triumph of the Holy Name of Jesus*. Here, the figures representing evil who are being cast out of heaven seem to hurtle down onto the observer.

The founder of the Jesuit order himself is buried in the Chapel of St. Ignatius, in the left-hand transept. This is surely one of the most sumptuous altars in Rome, though as is typical of Baroque decoration, which is renowned for its illusions, the enormous globe of lapis lazuli that crowns the altar is really only a shell of lapis over a stucco base. Note, too, architect Carlo Fontana's heavy bronze altar rail, which is in keeping with the surrounding opulence. ✉ *Via degli Astalli, 16, Campo de' Fiori* ☎ *06/697001* 🌐 *www.chiesadelgesu.org* Ⓜ *Barberini; Bus Nos. 30, 40, and 64.*

Crypta Balbi

RUINS | The fourth component of the magnificent collections of the Museo Nazionale Romano, this museum is unusual because it represents several periods of Roman history. The crypt is part of the Balbus Theater complex (13 BC), and other parts of the complex are from the medieval period, up through the 20th century. Though the interior lacks the lingering opulence of some other Roman sites, its evolution via continuous use over centuries offers a unique archaeological glimpse at how the city transformed. Note that recent restoration works have resulted in closures here; check for updates before visiting. ✉ *Via delle Botteghe Oscure, 31, Jewish Ghetto* ☎ *06/684851* 🌐 *museonazionaleromano.beniculturali.it/crypta-balbi* 🎫 *€8 Crypta Balbi only; €12 includes three other Museo Nazionale Romano sites over a 1-wk period (Palazzo Altemps, Palazzo Massimo, Museo Diocleziano)* ⏲ *Closed Mon.* Ⓜ *Colosseo; Bus Nos. 64 and 40; Tram No. 8.*

Fontana delle Tartarughe

FOUNTAIN | **FAMILY** | Designed by Giacomo della Porta in 1581 and sculpted by Taddeo Landini, this fountain, set in pretty Piazza Mattei, is one of Rome's most charming. Its focal point consists of four bronze boys, each grasping a dolphin spouting water into a marble shell. Bronze turtles just out of reach of the boys' hands drink from the upper basin. The turtles were added in the 17th century by Bernini. ✉ *Piazza Mattei, Jewish Ghetto* Ⓜ *Colosseo; Bus Nos. 85, 170, and H; Tram. No. 8.*

Galleria Spada

ART MUSEUM | In this neighborhood of huge, austere palaces, Palazzo Spada strikes an almost frivolous note, with its pretty ornament-encrusted courtyard and its upper stories covered with stuccoes and statues. Although the palazzo houses an impressive collection of Old Master paintings, it's most famous for its trompe-l'oeil garden gallery, a delightful example of the sort of architectural games that rich Romans of the 17th century found irresistible.

Even if you don't go into the gallery, step into the courtyard and look through the glass window of the library to the colonnaded corridor in the adjacent courtyard. You'll see—or seem to see—a statue at the end of a 26-foot-long gallery, seemingly quadrupled in depth in a sort of optical telescope that takes Renaissance's art of perspective to another level. In fact the distance is an illusion: the corridor grows progressively narrower and the columns progressively smaller as they near a statue, which is just 2 feet tall. The Baroque period is known for its special effects, and this is rightly one of the most famous. Borromini was responsible for the ruse, but it was only made possible thanks to the careful mathematical calculations completed by a science-minded Augustinian priest Giovanni Maria da Bitonto.

Upstairs is a seignorial picture gallery with the paintings shown as they would have been: hung one over the next clear to the ceiling. Outstanding works include Brueghel's *Landscape with Windmills,* Titian's *Musician,* and Andrea del Sarto's

Visitation. Look for the fact sheets that have descriptive notes about the objects in each room. ✉ *Piazza Capo di Ferro, 13, Campo de' Fiori* ☎ *06/6874896* 🌐 *galleriaspada.cultura.gov.it* 🎫 *€6; free the first Sun. of the month* ⏲ *Closed Tues.* Ⓜ *Colosseo; Bus Nos. 40, 64, and 70.*

★ Palazzo Altemps

CASTLE/PALACE | Containing some of the world's finest ancient Roman marbles, Palazzo Altemps is part of the Museo Nazionale Romano. The palace's sober exterior belies a magnificence that appears as soon as you walk into the majestic courtyard, studded with statues and covered in part by a retractable awning. The restored interior hints at the Roman lifestyle of the 16th–18th centuries while showcasing the most illustrious pieces from the Museo Nazionale, including the collection of the Ludovisi noble family.

In the frescoed salons you can see the *Galata Suicida,* a poignant sculptural work portraying a barbarian warrior who chooses death for himself and his wife rather than humiliation by the enemy. Another highlight is the large Ludovisi sarcophagus, magnificently carved from marble. In a place of honor is the *Ludovisi Throne,* which shows a goddess emerging from the sea and being helped by her acolytes. For centuries this was heralded as one of the most sublime Greek sculptures, but today at least one authoritative art historian considers it a colossally overrated fake. Look for the framed explanations of the exhibits that detail (in English) how and exactly where Renaissance sculptors, Bernini among them, added missing pieces to the classical works.

In the lavishly frescoed loggia stand busts of the Caesars. In the wing once occupied by early-20th-century poet Gabriele d'Annunzio (who married into the Altemps family), three rooms host the museum's Egyptian collection. ✉ *Piazza di Sant'Apollinare, 46, Piazza Navona* ☎ *06/684851* 🌐 *museonazionaleromano.beniculturali.it* 🎫 *€8; €16 combined ticket includes 3 other Museo Nazionale Romano sites over 1 wk (Crypta Balbi, Palazzo Massimo alle Terme, and Museo delle Terme di Diocleziano)* ⏲ *Closed Mon.* Ⓜ *Spagna; Bus Nos. 40, 64, 70, 85, and 492.*

★ Palazzo Farnese

CASTLE/PALACE | Rome's most beautiful Renaissance palace is fabled for its Galleria Carracci, whose ceiling is to the Baroque age what the Sistine Chapel ceiling is to the Renaissance. The Farnese family rose to great power and wealth during the Renaissance, in part because of the favor Pope Alexander VI showed to the beautiful Giulia Farnese. The massive palace was begun when, with Alexander's aid, Giulia's brother became cardinal; it was further enlarged on his election as Pope Paul III in 1534.

The uppermost frieze decorations and main window overlooking the piazza are the work of Michelangelo, who also designed part of the courtyard, as well as the graceful arch over Via Giulia at the back. The facade on Piazza Farnese has geometrical brick configurations that have long been thought to hold some occult meaning. When looking up at the palace, try to catch a glimpse of the splendid frescoed ceilings, including the Galleria Carracci vault painted by Annibale Carracci between 1597 and 1604.

The Carracci gallery depicts the loves of the gods, a supremely pagan theme that the artist painted in a swirling style that announced the birth of the Baroque. Other opulent salons are among the largest in Rome, including the Salon of Hercules, which has an impressive replica of the ancient *Farnese Hercules.* The French Embassy, which occupies the palace, offers tours (in English) on Monday, Wednesday, and Friday; book at least a few weeks (and up to eight months) in advance through the website and bring a photo ID. ✉ *French Embassy, Servizio*

A
B
C
D
E
F
1
2
3
4
5
6
7
8
9
Piazza Cavour
Via V. Colonna
Pte. Cavour
Pza. Adriana
Ex. Palazzo di Giustizia
V. Triboniano
Via Ulpiano
Lgt. Prati
Fiume Tevere
Lgt. Marzio
Castel S. Angelo
Piazza Giovanni XXIII
Lgt. Castello
Ponte Umberto
Via della Scrofa
Via M. Brianzo
Pte. S. Angelo
Via dell'Orso
Via Zanardelli
Lgt. Tor di Nona
Ponte Vittorio Emanuele II
Piazza Coronari
Piazza S.Salvatore in Lauro
Piazza Lancellotti
Via B.S.Spirito
Piazza Navona
Via dei Coronari
Piazza dell'Oro
San Giovanni dei Fiorentini
Via B.Nuovi
V. d. Cimatori
V. del Fico
V. d. Parione
V. d. Sta. M. d. Anima
Corso del Rinascimento
Vic. d. Palle
Corso Vittorio Emanuele II
V. d. Filippini
Via del G. Vecchio
Via dei Banchi Vecchi
V. d. Bresciani
V. d. Gonfalone
Via Giulia
Via del Pellegrino
V. d. T. Valle
Lgt. Gianicolense
Vic d. Prigioni
V.S. Fil. Neri
Via di Monserrato
Campo de' Fiori
V. d. Cappellari
Sant' Andrea della Valle
Via della Lungara
Pte. G. Mazzini
Via Giulia
V. in Caterina
V. dei Farnesi
Piazza Farnese
Lgt dei Tebaldi
Palazzo Farnese
Via dei Giubbonari
V. del Monte della Farina
V. d. Mascherone
Palazzo Spada
Piazza d. Monte di Pietá
Via degli Specchi
Vic. d. Polverone
Via Pettinari
Lgt. della Farnesina
Via dei Riari
Villa Farnesina
Pte. Sisto
Lgt. dei Vallati
0
500 feet
0
150 m
KEY
Sights
Restaurants
Quick Bites
Hotels

Piazza Navona, Campo de' Fiori, and the Jewish Ghetto

Sights

1 Chiesa del Gesù..................... I7
2 Crypta Balbi........................ H7
3 Fontana delle Tartarughe......... H8
4 Galleria Spada...................... E8
5 Palazzo Altemps.................... E3
6 Palazzo Farnese.................... D8
7 Pantheon............................ G5
8 Piazza Campo de' Fiori............ E7
9 Piazza Navona...................... E5
10 Portico d'Ottavia.................. H9
11 San Luigi dei Francesi............ F4
12 Santa Maria sopra Minerva...... H5
13 Sant'Andrea della Valle........... F6
14 Sant'Ivo alla Sapienza............ F5
15 Sinagoga............................ H9
16 Via Giulia........................... C7

Restaurants

1 Armando al Pantheon............. G5
2 Ba'Ghetto........................... J3
3 BellaCarne.......................... H9
4 Cul de Sac.......................... E6
5 Da Fransceso....................... D5
6 Dar Filettaro a Santa Barbara..... F8
7 Ditirambo........................... E6
8 Emma Pizzeria...................... F7
9 Enoteca Corsi...................... H6
10 Il Convivio Troiani................ E3
11 Il Pagliaccio....................... B5
12 Il Sanlorenzo...................... F7
13 La Ciambella....................... G6
14 L'Angolo Divino.................... E8
15 Osteria dell'Ingegno.............. I4
16 Pierluigi............................ C6
17 Roscioli Salumeria con Cucina... F8

Quick Bites

1 Bar del Fico........................ D5
2 Gelateria Del Teatro.............. D4
3 Giolitti.............................. H3
4 Pasticceria Boccione............. G8
5 Sant'Eustachio il Caffè........... G5

Hotels

1 Albergo Santa Chiara............. G6
2 Casa di Santa Brigida............ D7
3 D.O.M. Hotel Roma................ B6
4 Hotel Chapter Roma............... G9
5 Hotel de' Ricci..................... C7
6 Hotel Genio......................... E4
7 Hotel Ponte Sisto.................. E9
8 The Pantheon Iconic Rome Hotel, Autograph Collection.............. G5

Culturale, Piazza Farnese, 67, Campo de' Fiori ☎ *06/686011* 🌐 *www.visite-palazzo-farnese.it* 🎫 *€15* ⏲ *Closed Tues., Wed., Sat., and Sun.* Ⓜ *Colosseo; Bus Nos. 40, 64, and 70.*

★ Pantheon

RELIGIOUS BUILDING | The city's best-preserved ancient building, this former Roman temple is a marvel of architectural harmony and proportion. It was entirely rebuilt by the emperor Hadrian around AD 120 on the site of a Pantheon (from the Greek: *pan,* all, and *theon,* gods) erected in 27 BC by Augustus's right-hand man and son-in-law, Agrippa. The most striking thing about the Pantheon is not its size, immense though it is, nor even the phenomenal technical difficulties posed by so massive a construction; rather, it's the remarkable unity of the building. The diameter described by the dome is exactly equal to its height. It's the use of such simple mathematical balance that gives classical architecture its characteristic sense of proportion and its nobility. The opening at the apex of the dome, the *oculus,* is nearly 30 feet in diameter and was intended to symbolize the "all-seeing eye of the heavens." On a practical note, this means when it rains, it rains inside: look out for the drainage holes in the floor. One of the reasons the Pantheon is so well preserved is that it was consecrated as a church in AD 608. The Pantheon is also one of the city's important burial places. Its most famous tomb is that of Raphael (between the second and third chapels on the left as you enter). Mass takes place on Sunday and on religious holidays at 10:30; it's open to the public, but you are expected to arrive before the beginning and stay until the end. General access usually resumes at about 11:30. At most times (especially in high season or weekends), you can purchase tickets online in advance. Alternatively, coming prepared with both cash and a credit card will allow you to select the faster-moving line that day. ✉ *Piazza della Rotonda, Piazza Navona* ☎ *06/68300230* 🌐 *www.museiitaliani.it* 🎫 *€5; audio guide €8.50* Ⓜ *Barberini; Bus Nos. 40, 64, and 70.*

Piazza Campo de' Fiori

MARKET | **FAMILY** | A bustling marketplace in the morning (Monday through Saturday from 8 to 2) and a trendy meeting place the rest of the day and night, this piazza has plenty of down-to-earth charm. After lunch, it becomes a circus of bars particularly favored by study-abroad students, tourists, and young expats. Brooding over the piazza is a hooded statue of the philosopher Giordano Bruno, who was burned at the stake here in 1600 for heresy. ✉ *Intersection of Via dei Baullari, Via Giubbonari, Via del Pellegrino, and Piazza della Cancelleria, Campo de' Fiori* Ⓜ *Colosseo; Bus Nos. 30, 40, 64, and 70.*

★ Piazza Navona

PLAZA/SQUARE | Always camera-ready, this beautiful plaza has Bernini sculptures, three gorgeous fountains, and a magnificently Baroque church (Sant'Agnese in Agone), all built atop the remains of a Roman athletics track. Pieces of the arena are still visible near the adjacent Piazza Sant'Apollinare, and the ancient spirit of entertainment lives on in the buskers and artists who populate the piazza today. The piazza took on its current look during the 17th century, after Pope Innocent X of the Pamphilj family decided to make over his family palace (now the Brazilian embassy and an ultraluxe hotel) and its surroundings. Center stage is the Fontana dei Quattro Fiumi, created for Innocent by Bernini in 1651. Bernini's powerful figures of the four rivers represent the longest rivers of the known continents at the time: the Nile (his head covered because the source was unknown); the Ganges; the Danube; and the Plata (the length of the Amazon was then unknown). Popular legend has it that the figure of the Plata—the figure closest to Sant'Agnese in Agone—raises his hand before his eyes because he can't bear to look upon the church's "inferior" facade designed by Francesco Borromini, Bernini's rival. It's a beautiful spot to linger over a coffee, but you can find cheaper, more authentic, and far better meals elsewhere. ✉ *Piazza Navona* Ⓜ *Spagna; Bus Nos. 40, 64, 70, 85, and 492.*

Portico d'Ottavia

RUINS | Looming over the Jewish Ghetto, this huge portico, with a few surviving columns, is one of the area's most picturesque set pieces, with the church of Sant'Angelo in Pescheria built right into its ruins. Named by Augustus in honor of his sister Octavia, it was originally 390 feet wide and 433 feet long; encompassed two temples, a meeting hall decorated with bronze statues, and a library; and served as a kind of grandiose entrance foyer for the adjacent Teatro di Marcello.

In the Middle Ages, the cool marble ruins of the portico became Rome's *pescheria* (fish market). A stone plaque on a pillar (it's a copy as the original is in the Musei Capitolini) states in Latin that the head of any fish surpassing the length of the plaque was to be cut off "up to the first fin" and given to the city fathers or else the vendor was to pay a fine of 10 gold florins. The heads, which were used to make fish soup, were considered a great delicacy. ✉ *Via Portico d'Ottavia, 29, Jewish Ghetto* ☎ *06/0608* Ⓜ *Colosseo; Bus Nos. 85, 170, and H; Tram. No. 8.*

★ San Luigi dei Francesi

CHURCH | San Luigi's Contarelli Chapel (the fifth and last chapel on the left, toward the main altar) is adorned with three stunningly dramatic works by Caravaggio (1571–1610), the Baroque master of the heightened approach to light and dark. They were commissioned for the tomb of Mattheiu Cointerel in one of Rome's French churches (San Luigi is St. Louis, patron saint of France). The inevitable coin machine will light up his *Calling of Saint Matthew, Saint Matthew and the Angel,* and *Martyrdom of Saint Matthew* (seen from left to right), and Caravaggio's mastery of light takes it from there.

When painted, they caused considerable consternation among the clergy of San Luigi, who thought the artist's dramatically realistic approach was scandalously disrespectful. A first version of the altarpiece was rejected; the priests were not particularly happy with the other two, either. Time has fully vindicated Caravaggio's patron, Cardinal Francesco del Monte, who secured the commission for these works and staunchly defended them. ■ **TIP→ This church regularly enforces the rule of covered knees and shoulders, and turns away those who do not abide.** ✉ *Piazza di San Luigi dei Francesi, Piazza Navona* ☎ *06/688271* 🌐 *saintlouis-rome.net* Ⓜ *Barberini; Bus Nos. 40, 64, and 70.*

★ Santa Maria sopra Minerva

CHURCH | The name of the church reveals that it was built *sopra* (over) the ruins of a temple of Minerva, the ancient goddess of wisdom. Erected in 1280 by Dominicans along severe Italian Gothic lines, it has undergone a number of more or less happy interior restorations. Certainly, as the city's major Gothic church, it provides a refreshing contrast to Baroque flamboyance. Have a €1 coin handy to illuminate the Cappella Carafa in the right transept; the small investment is worth it to better see Filippino Lippi's (1457–1504) glowing frescoes featuring a deep azure expanse of sky and musical angels hovering around the Virgin.

Under the main altar is the tomb of St. Catherine of Siena, one of Italy's patron saints and a major destination for faithful locals who drop written prayers on her final resting place. Left of the altar you'll find Michelangelo's *Risen Christ* and the tomb of the gentle artist Fra Angelico. Bernini's unusual and little-known monument to the Blessed Maria Raggi is on the fifth pier of the left-hand aisle.

In front of the church, Bernini's *Elephant and Obelisk* is perhaps the city's most charming sculpture. An inscription on the base references the church's ancient patroness, reading something to the effect that it takes a strong mind to sustain solid wisdom. ✉ *Piazza della Minerva, Piazza Navona* ☎ *333/7468785* 🌐 *www.santamariasopraminerva.it* Ⓜ *Barberini; Bus Nos. 40, 64, and 70.*

Sant'Andrea della Valle

CHURCH | Topped by the highest dome in Rome after St. Peter's (designed by Maderno), this imposing 17th-century church is remarkably balanced in design. Fortunately, its facade, which had turned a sooty gray from pollution, has been cleaned to a near-sparkling white. Use one of the handy mirrors to examine the early-17th-century frescoes by Domenichino in the choir vault and those by Lanfranco in the dome. One of the earliest ceilings done in full Baroque style, its upward vortex was influenced by Correggio's dome in Parma, of which Lanfranco was also a citizen. (Bring a few coins to light the paintings, which can be very dim.) The three massive paintings of St. Andrew's martyrdom are by Mattia Preti (1650–51). Richly marbled and decorated chapels flank the nave, and in such a space, Puccini set the first act of *Tosca*. ✉ *Piazza Vidoni, 6, Corso Vittorio Emanuele II, Campo de' Fiori* ☎ *06/6861339* 🌐 *santandrea.teatinos.org* Ⓜ *Barberini; Bus Nos. 64, 70, and 628.*

Sant'Ivo alla Sapienza

CHURCH | This eccentric Baroque church, probably Borromini's best, has one of Rome's most delightful "domes"—a dizzying spiral said to have been inspired by a bee's stinger. The apian symbol is a reminder that the church was commissioned by the Barberini pope Urban VIII (a swarm of bees figure on the Barberini family crest), although it was completed by Alexander VII. The interior, open only for two hours on Sunday morning, is worth a look, especially if you share Borromini's taste for complex mathematical architectural idiosyncrasies. "I didn't take up architecture solely to be a copyist," he once said. Sant'Ivo is certainly the proof. ✉ *Corso del Rinascimento, 40, Piazza Navona* 🌐 *www.sivoallasapienza.eu* 🕒 *Closed Mon.–Sat., July, and Aug.* Ⓜ *Barberini; Bus Nos. 40, 64, 70, and 85.*

Sinagoga

RELIGIOUS BUILDING | This synagogue has been the city's largest Jewish temple, and a Roman landmark with its distinctive aluminum dome, since its construction in 1904. The building also houses the Jewish Museum on its lower floor, with displays of precious ritual objects and exhibits that document the uninterrupted presence of a Jewish community in the city for nearly 22 centuries. Until the 16th century, Jews were esteemed citizens of Rome. Among them were bankers and physicians to the popes, who had themselves given permission for the construction of synagogues. But, in 1555, during the Counter-Reformation, Pope Paul IV decreed the building of the walls of the Ghetto, confining the Jews to this small flood-prone area and imposing restrictions, some of which continued to be enforced until 1870. For security reasons, entrance is via guided visit only, and tours in English are available twice a day but should be booked online ahead of time. Entrance to the synagogue is through the museum on Via Catalana. ✉ *Lungotevere de' Cenci, 15, Jewish Ghetto* ☎ *06/68400661* 🌐 *www.museoebraico.roma.it* 🎫 *€11* 🕒 *Museum closed Sat. and Jewish holidays* Ⓜ *Colosseo; Bus Nos. 85, 170, and H; Tram. No. 8.*

★ Via Giulia

STREET | Straight as a die and still something of a Renaissance-era diorama, Via Giulia was the first street in Rome since ancient times to be deliberately planned. It was named for Pope Julius II (of Sistine Chapel fame), who commissioned it in the early 1500s as part of a scheme to open up a grandiose approach to St. Peter's Basilica. Although the pope's plans were only partially completed, Via

Giulia became an important thoroughfare in Renaissance Rome. It's still, after more than four centuries, the address of choice for Roman aristocrats, despite a recent, controversial addition: a large parking lot along one side of the street (creating it meant steamrolling through ancient and medieval ruins underneath).

A stroll around and along Via Giulia reveals elegant palaces and churches, including one, **San Eligio**, on the little side street Via di Sant'Eligio, that was designed by Raphael himself. Note also the **Palazzo Sacchetti** (✉ *Via Giulia, 66*), with an imposing stone portal and an interior containing some of Rome's grandest staterooms; it remains, after 300 years, the private quarters of the Marchesi Sacchetti. The forbidding brick building that housed the **Carceri Nuove (New Prison)** (✉ *Via Giulia, 52*), Rome's prison for more than two centuries, now contains the offices of the Direzione Nazionale Antimafia. Near the bridge that arches over Via Giulia's southern end is the church of **Santa Maria dell'Orazione e Morte** (Holy Mary of Prayer and Death), with stone skulls on its door. These are a symbol of a confraternity that was charged with burying the bodies of the unidentified dead found in the city streets.

Designed by Borromini and home, since 1927, to the Hungarian Academy, the **Palazzo Falconieri** (✉ *Via Giulia, 1* ☎ *06/68896700*) has Borromini-designed salons and loggia that are sporadically open as part of guided tours; call for information. The falcon statues atop its belvedere are best viewed from around the block, along the Tiber embankment. Remnant of a master plan by Michelangelo, the arch over the street was meant to link massive **Palazzo Farnese,** on the east side of Via Giulia, with the building across the street and a bridge to the Villa Farnesina, directly across the river. Finally, on the right and rather green with age, dribbles that star of many a postcard, the **Fontana del Mascherone.** ✉ *Via Giulia, between Piazza dell'Oro and Piazza San Vincenzo Palloti, Campo de' Fiori* Ⓜ *Spagna; Bus Nos. 30, 62, and 160.*

Restaurants

★ Armando al Pantheon

$$$ | **ROMAN** | In the shadow of the Pantheon, this small family-run trattoria, open since 1961, delights tourists and locals alike. There's an air of authenticity to the Roman staples here, and the quality of the ingredients and the cooking mean booking ahead through the website is a must. **Known for:** beautifully executed traditional Roman cooking; spaghetti alla gricia (with guanciale, pecorino cheese, and black pepper); reservation list that opens 30 days at a time. $ *Average main: €35* ✉ *Salita dei Crescenzi, 31, Piazza Navona* 🌐 *www.armandoalpantheon.it* ⏲ *Closed Sun. and Aug.* Ⓜ *Barberini; Bus Nos. 30, 40, and 64.*

★ Ba'Ghetto

$$ | **ITALIAN** | **FAMILY** | This well-established hot spot on the Jewish Ghetto's main promenade has pleasant indoor and outdoor seating. The kitchen is kosher (many places featuring Roman Jewish fare are not) and is known for its Judeo-Roman meat dishes mixed with Middle Eastern recipes. **Known for:** carciofi alla giudia (deep-fried artichokes) and other Roman-Jewish specialties; casual family atmosphere; tables on the pedestrianized street. $ *Average main: €22* ✉ *Via del Portico d'Ottavia, 57, Jewish Ghetto* ☎ *06/68892868* 🌐 *www.baghetto.com* ⏲ *Dinner Fri. and lunch Sat. are strictly for those who observe Shabbat with advance payment* Ⓜ *Colosseo; Bus Nos. 85 and 170; Tram. No. 8.*

BellaCarne

$ | **ROMAN** | *Bellacarne* means "beautiful meat," and that's the focus of the menu here (though it's also what a Jewish Italian grandmother might say while pinching her grandchild's cheek). The kosher kitchen makes its own pastrami, but the setting is more fine dining than deli. **Known for:** pastrami; shabbat menu; kosher carbonara with dried beef. *Average main: €19 ✉ Via Portico d'Ottavia, 51, Jewish Ghetto ☎ 06/6833104 🌐 www.bellacarne.it ⏲ No dinner Fri. No lunch Sat. except limited Shabbat seating that must be prepaid Ⓜ Colosseo; Bus Nos. 85, 170, and H; Tram. No. 8.*

★ Cul de Sac

$$ | **WINE BAR** | This popular wine bar a stone's throw from Piazza Navona is among the city's oldest and has a book-length binder listing wines from Italy, France, the Americas, and elsewhere. It offers great value and pleasant service and is a lovely spot for a light late lunch or an early dinner when most restaurants aren't open yet. **Known for:** great wine list (and wine bottle–lined interior); eclectic Italian and Mediterranean fare; relaxed atmosphere and outside tables. *Average main: €21 ✉ Piazza di Pasquino, 73, Piazza Navona ☎ 06/68801094 🌐 www.enotecaculdesacroma.it Ⓜ Barberini; Bus Nos. 40, 64, and 70.*

Da Francesco

$$ | **ROMAN** | **FAMILY** | For good, hearty Roman cuisine in an area filled with mediocre touristy restaurants, head to this trattoria that's been on the scene since the late 1950s. Stick with the classics, perhaps starting off with a mixed salumi plate featuring Parma ham and buffalo mozzarella before moving on to a *primi* (first course)—the amatriciana (with tomato sauce, guanciale, and pecorino cheese) is one of the standouts. **Known for:** authentic and informal atmosphere; outside tables in summer; truffle-topped pasta alla gricia. *Average main: €24 ✉ Piazza del Fico, 29, Piazza Navona ☎ 06/6864009 🌐 www.dafrancesco.it Ⓜ Spagna; Bus Nos. 40, 64, 70, 85, and 492.*

Dar Filettaro a Santa Barbara

$ | **ITALIAN** | The window reads "Filetti di Baccalà," but the official name of this small restaurant that specializes in one thing—deliciously battered and deep-fried fillets of salt cod—is Dar Filettaro a Santa Barbara. If it's in season, be sure to try the *puntarelle* (crisp chicory) tossed with garlic and anchovy dressing. **Known for:** piping hot filetti di baccalà; functional "hole-in-the-wall" interior; tables outside on the pretty square. *Average main: €8 ✉ Largo dei Librari, 88, Campo de' Fiori ☎ 06/6864018 🌐 www.facebook.com/FilettiDiBaccala ⏲ Closed Sun. and Aug. No lunch. Ⓜ Colosseo; Tram No. 8.*

Ditirambo

$$ | **ITALIAN** | Don't let the country-kitchen feel fool you. This little spot off of Campo de' Fiori goes a step beyond the ordinary with constantly changing offbeat takes on Italian classics. **Known for:** cozy and casual; hearty meat and pasta dishes; perfectly grilled octopus and other seafood dishes. *Average main: €25 ✉ Piazza della Cancelleria, 74, Campo de' Fiori ☎ 06/6871626 🌐 www.ditiramboristorante.it ⏲ Closed Aug. No lunch Mon. Ⓜ Barberini; Bus Nos. 30, 40, and 64.*

★ Emma Pizzeria

$$ | **ROMAN** | **FAMILY** | Smack in the middle of the city, with the freshest produce right outside its door, this pizzeria features pies made with dough by Rome's renowned family of bakers, the Roscciolis. The menu also offers a good selection of pastas, mains, and local Lazio wines. **Known for:** light, airy, and casual; thin-crust Roman pizza; tasty fritti (classic fried Roman pizzeria appetizers). *Average main: €25 ✉ Via Monte della Farina, 28–29, Campo de' Fiori ☎ 06/64760475 🌐 www.emmapizzeria.com Ⓜ Colosseo; Tram No. 8.*

Enoteca Corsi

$ | **ITALIAN** | Although this old-school, centro storico trattoria has been renovated, you wouldn't know it, and that's part of its charm. At lunchtime, it's often packed with a mix of civil servants from the nearby government offices, construction workers, and in-the-know tourists enjoying classic pastas, octopus salad, and *secondi* (second courses) such as roast veal with peas. **Known for:** casual atmosphere; Roman specialties; brusque but friendly service. *Average main: €18 ✉ Via del Gesù, 88, Piazza Navona ☎ 06/6790821 ⊕ www.enotecacorsi.com ⏲ Closed Sun. and 3 wks in Aug. No dinner Sat. Ⓜ Barberini; Bus Nos. 40, 64, and 70.*

★ Il Convivio Troiani

$$$$ | **MODERN ITALIAN** | The three Troiani brothers—Angelo in the kitchen and Giuseppe and Massimo presiding over the dining room and wine cellar—have been quietly redefining the experience of Italian *alta cucina* (haute cuisine) since 1990 at this well-regarded establishment in a tiny, nondescript alley north of Piazza Navona. The service is attentive without being overbearing, and the wine list is exceptional. **Known for:** fine dining in elegant surroundings; inventive modern Italian cooking with exotic touches; amazing wine cellar and a great sommelier. *Average main: €80 ✉ Vicolo dei Soldati, 31, Piazza Navona ☎ 06/6869432 ⊕ www.ilconviviotroiani.it ⏲ Closed Sun. and 1 wk in Aug. No lunch Ⓜ Spagna; Bus Nos. 40, 64, 70, 85, and 492.*

Il Pagliaccio

$$$$ | **MODERN ITALIAN** | Some of the most innovative interpretations of fine Roman cookery can be found in this starkly chic restaurant on a backstreet between upscale Via Giulia and the Campo de' Fiori. Chef Anthony Genovese was born in France to Calabrese parents and spent time cooking in Japan and Thailand, so his dishes make use of nontraditional spices, ingredients, and preparations—garnering him a loyal following and multiple accolades. **Known for:** elaborate tasting menus; fine dining in elegant surroundings; discreet location. *Average main: €250 ✉ Via dei Banchi Vecchi, 129a, Piazza Navona ☎ 06/68809595 ⊕ www.ristoranteilpagliaccio.com ⏲ Closed Sun., Mon., and Aug. No lunch Tues.–Fri. Ⓜ Spagna; Bus Nos. 30, 40, and 64.*

Il Sanlorenzo

$$$$ | **SEAFOOD** | A gorgeous space, with chandeliers and soaring original brickwork ceilings, is the setting for one of Rome's best seafood restaurants. Order à la carte, or if you're hungry, the eight-course tasting menu (given the quality of the fish, a relative bargain at €90), which might include cuttlefish-ink tagliatelle with mint, artichokes, and roe or shrimp from the island of Ponza with rosemary, bitter herbs, and porcini mushrooms. **Known for:** top-quality fish and seafood; spaghetti con ricci (sea urchins); elegant surroundings. *Average main: €85 ✉ Via dei Chiavari, 4/5, Campo de' Fiori ☎ 06/6865097 ⊕ www.ilsanlorenzo.it ⏲ Closed 2 wks in Aug. No lunch Mon. Ⓜ Spagna; Bus Nos. 30, 40, and 64.*

La Ciambella

$$$ | **ITALIAN** | A large glass wall to the kitchen and massive skylight in the dining room hint at the contemporary leanings of this restaurant built atop the ruins of the Baths of Agrippa behind the Pantheon. The emphasis here is on high-quality ingredients and classic Italian culinary traditions interpreted for modern diners. **Known for:** elegant setting in a great location near the Pantheon; sophisticated Italian cuisine; expert wine pairings. *Average main: €35 ✉ Via dell'Arco della Ciambella, 20, Piazza Navona ☎ 06/6832930 ⊕ www.la-ciambella.it ⏲ Closed Tues. and Wed. Ⓜ Barberini; Bus Nos. 30, 40, 64, and 70.*

L'Angolo Divino

$ | **WINE BAR** | There's something about this cozy wine bar that makes it feel as if it's in a small traditional village instead of a bustling metropolis. The walls are lined with a tempting array of bottles from around the Italian peninsula, and the counter is stocked with cheese and salumi that can be sliced and piled on plates to order. **Known for:** excellent wine selection and advice; cozy atmosphere;

late-night snacks. [$] *Average main: €19* ✉ *Via dei Balestrari, 12, Campo de' Fiori* ☎ *06/6864413* 🌐 *www.angolodivino.it* 🕒 *Closed 2 wks in Aug.* Ⓜ *Colosseo; Tram No. 8.*

Osteria dell'Ingegno

$$ | MODERN ITALIAN | This casual, trendy place—vibrant with colorful paintings by local artists—is a great spot to enjoy an ancient piazza while savoring a glass of wine or a gourmet meal. The simple but innovative menu includes dishes like Roman artichokes with baccalà, beef *tagliata* (sliced grilled steak) with a red-wine reduction, and a perfectly cooked duck breast with red fruit sauce. **Known for:** a mix of traditional and inventive pastas; a great spot both for aperitifs and/or a meal; outdoor seating with views of ancient ruins. [$] *Average main: €22* ✉ *Piazza di Pietra, 45, Piazza Navona* ☎ *06/6780662* 🌐 *www.osteriadellingegno.com* 🕒 *Closed Mon.* Ⓜ *Barberini; Bus Nos. 40, 64, 85, and 492.*

★ Pierluigi

$$$$ | SEAFOOD | This chic seafood restaurant is a fun spot on balmy summer evenings, where elegant diners sip crisp white wine at tables out on the pretty Piazza de' Ricci. The carpaccio selection is exquisite, but there is also a large selection of pastas extravagantly topped with white truffles. **Known for:** top-quality fish and seafood; tables on the pretty pedestrianized piazza; elegant atmosphere with great service. [$] *Average main: €60* ✉ *Piazza de' Ricci, 144, Campo de' Fiori* ☎ *06/6868717* 🌐 *www.pierluigi.it* Ⓜ *Spagna; Bus Nos. 30, 40, and 64.*

★ Roscioli Salumeria con Cucina

$$ | WINE BAR | The shop in front of this beloved restaurant will beckon you in with top-quality comestibles like hand-sliced cured ham from Italy and Spain, more than 300 cheeses, and a dizzying array of wines—but venture farther inside to try an extensive selection of unusual dishes and interesting takes on the classics. There are tables in the cozy wine cellar downstairs, but try to bag a table at the back on the ground floor (reserve well ahead; Roscioli is very popular). **Known for:** extensive wine list; arguably Rome's best spaghetti alla carbonara; unrivaled prosciutto selection. [$] *Average main: €25* ✉ *Via dei Giubbonari, 21, Campo de' Fiori* ☎ *06/6875287* 🌐 *www.salumeriaroscioli.com* 🕒 *Closed 1 wk in Aug.* Ⓜ *Colosseo; Tram No. 8.*

Coffee and Quick Bites

Bar del Fico

$ | ITALIAN | FAMILY | Everyone in Rome knows Bar del Fico, located right behind Piazza Navona, so if you want to hang out with the locals, come here for a drink or something to eat at any time of day or night. In the mornings, chess players sit at tables outside under the shade of the fig tree that gives the bar its name; after sunset, the bar is packed with people sipping cocktails. **Known for:** outside tables in a pretty square; Italian-style brunch; buzzy atmosphere. [$] *Average main: €15* ✉ *Piazza del Fico, 26, Piazza Navona* ☎ *06/68891373* 🌐 *www.bardelfico.com* Ⓜ *Spagna; Bus Nos. 40, 64, 70, 85, and 492.*

★ Gelateria Del Teatro

$ | ICE CREAM | FAMILY | In a window next to the entrance of this renowned gelateria, you can see the fresh fruit being used to create the day's flavors, which highlight the best of Italy—from Amalfi lemons to Alban hazelnuts. In addition to traditional options, look for interesting combinations like raspberry and sage or white chocolate with basil. **Known for:** sublime gelato; seasonal, all-natural ingredients; charming location on a cobblestone street. [$] *Average main: €4* ✉ *Via dei Coronari, 65/66, Piazza Navona* ☎ *06/45474880* 🌐 *www.gelateriadelteatro.it* Ⓜ *Spagna; Bus Nos. 30, 40, 64, and 70.*

★ Giolitti

$ | **ICE CREAM** | **FAMILY** | Open since 1900, Giolitti near the Pantheon is Rome's old-school gelateria par excellence. Pay in advance at the register by the door; take your receipt to the counter; and choose from dozens of flavors, including chocolate, cinnamon, and pistachio. **Known for:** excellent gelato; old-school setting; wide selection of flavors. *Average main: €5* *Via degli Uffici del Vicario, 40, Piazza Navona* *06/6991243* *www.giolitti.it* *Barberini; Bus Nos. 40, 64, 70, and 492.*

Pasticceria Boccione

$ | **BAKERY** | **FAMILY** | This tiny, old-school bakery famed for its Roman-Jewish sweet specialties doesn't have a sign but is easy to spot because there is always a line snaking out the door. Service is brusque, choices are few, what's available depends on the season, and when it's sold out, it's sold out. **Known for:** ricotta and cherry tarts; pizza ebraica ("Jewish pizza," a dense baked sweet rich in nuts and raisins); no frills and no seats. *Average main: €6* *Via del Portico d'Ottavia, 1, Jewish Ghetto* *06/6878637* *Closed Sat.* *Colosseo; Bus Nos. 60, 170, and H; Tram. No. 8.*

Sant'Eustachio il Caffè

$ | **CAFÉ** | **FAMILY** | Frequented by tourists and government officials from the nearby Senate alike, this caffè is considered by many to make Rome's best coffee. Take it at the counter Roman-style—servers are hidden behind a huge espresso machine, where they vigorously mix the sugar and coffee to protect their secret method for the perfectly prepared cup (if you want yours without sugar here, ask for it *senza zucchero*). **Known for:** gran caffè (large sugared espresso); old-school Roman coffee bar vibe; 1930s interior. *Average main: €4* *Piazza Sant'Eustachio, 82, Piazza Navona* *06/68802048* *www.caffesanteustachio.com* *Barberini; Bus Nos. 40, 64, and 70.*

Hotels

Albergo Santa Chiara

$$ | **HOTEL** | Guests choose this hotel, run by members of the same family for 200 years, not only for its prime location, but also for its welcoming staff, top-notch service, and comfy beds. **Pros:** near the Pantheon and Santa Maria sopra Minerva; free Wi-Fi; lovely sitting area in front, overlooking the piazza. **Cons:** some rooms are on the small side; design is a bit basic given the higher price point; street-side rooms can be noisy. *Rooms from: €330* *Via Santa Chiara, 21, Piazza Navona* *06/6872979* *www.albergosantachiara.com* *96 rooms* *Free Breakfast* *Barberini; Bus Nos. 40, 64, and 70.*

Casa di Santa Brigida

$ | **B&B/INN** | The friendly sisters of Santa Brigida oversee simple, straightforward, and centrally located accommodations in one of Rome's loveliest convents, with a rooftop terrace overlooking Palazzo Farnese. **Pros:** insider papal audience tickets; large library and sunroof; free Wi-Fi. **Cons:** weak air-conditioning; no TVs in the rooms (though there is a common TV room); payment at structure only. *Rooms from: €150* *Piazza Farnese, 96, entrance around the corner at Via Monserrato 54, Campo de' Fiori* *06/68892596* *www.casabrigidaroma.it* *20 rooms* *Free Breakfast* *Spagna; Bus Nos. 30, 40, and 64.*

D.O.M Hotel Roma

$$$ | **HOTEL** | In an old convent on Via Giulia, one of Rome's romantic ivy-covered streets, the D.O.M (Deo Optimo Maximo) is an ultrachic luxury hotel that resembles an aristocratic *casa nobile*. The interior design is cool and eclectic, with wood beam ceilings that date from the1600s, original Andy Warhol silkscreens, exposed brick walls, and scripture-inscribed marble slabs from the 15th century. **Pros:** complimentary Acqua di Parma toiletries; heated towel racks; hip

decor in historic setting. **Cons:** an armed guard at the anti-mafia headquarters opposite the hotel may be off-putting for some; delicious but expensive cocktails; standard rooms are small for a five-star hotel. *Rooms from: €530 Via Giulia, 131, Campo de' Fiori 06/6832144 www.domhotelroma.com 18 rooms Free Breakfast Spagna; Bus Nos. 30, 40, and 64.*

Hotel Chapter Roma

$$ | **HOTEL** | The edgy, of-the-moment design at this boutique hotel juxtaposes plush mid-century Italian furnishings with street art murals and industrial touches. **Pros:** trendy design; in-room mixology station; lively rooftop bar in summer. **Cons:** no gym; no spa; most room arrangements are suited for 2 guests maximum. *Rooms from: €320 Via di Santa Maria de' Calderari, 47, Jewish Ghetto 06/89935351 www.chapter-roma.com 47 rooms No Meals Colosseo; Bus Nos. 85, 170, and H; Tram. No. 8.*

Hotel de' Ricci

$$$$ | **HOTEL** | This intimate boutique hotel from the team behind the Pierluigi restaurant is a top spot for wine lovers. **Pros:** excellent wine cellar and cigar lounge; great location on a quiet street; perks include complimentary aperitivo and priority reservations at Pierluigi. **Cons:** there's a charge of €50 per day to bring pets; moody lighting is dim throughout; no spa or gym. *Rooms from: €605 Via della Barchetta, 14, Campo de' Fiori 06/6874775 www.hotelderricci.com 8 rooms No Meals Spagna; Bus Nos. 30, 40, and 64.*

Hotel Genio

$ | **HOTEL** | Just off the beautiful Piazza Navona, this aging but pleasant hotel has a lovely rooftop terrace that's the perfect place to enjoy a cappuccino or a glass of wine while taking in the view. **Pros:** homey buffet breakfast; moderate prices for the area; nice views from terrace. **Cons:** rather weak AC in summer; spotty Wi-Fi; some furnishings need to be updated. *Rooms from: €170 Via Giuseppe Zanardelli, 28, Piazza Navona 06/6833781 www.hotelgenioroma.it 60 rooms Free Breakfast Spagna; Bus Nos. 40, 64, 70, 85, and 492.*

Hotel Ponte Sisto

$$ | **HOTEL** | Situated in a remodeled Renaissance palazzo with one of the prettiest patio-courtyards in Rome, this hotel is a relaxing retreat close to Campo de' Fiori and Trastevere. **Pros:** rooms with views (and some with balconies and terraces); great location between Trastevere and Campo de' Fiori; beautiful courtyard garden. **Cons:** street-side rooms can be noisy; some upgraded rooms are small and not worth the price difference; a/c is controlled centrally and requires a call to the front desk to adjust. *Rooms from: €290 Via dei Pettinari, 64, Campo de' Fiori 06/6863100 www.hotelponte-sisto.it 106 rooms Free Breakfast Colosseo; Bus Nos. 40, 64, and H.*

The Pantheon Iconic Rome Hotel, Autograph Collection

$$$ | **HOTEL** | A member of Marriott's Autograph Collection, this boutique hotel is a sleek retreat in the center of the action. **Pros:** modern design and amenities; exceptional year-round roof terrace; Marriott Bonvoy members can redeem points. **Cons:** some rooms lack external views; relatively high fees for extras like a rollaway bed; design might be considered a bit cold and corporate. *Rooms from: €600 Via di Santa Chiara, 4A, Piazza Navona 06/87807070 www.thepantheonhotel.com 79 rooms No Meals Barberini; Bus Nos. 40, 64, and 70.*

Nightlife

Enoteca al Parlamento Achilli

WINE BAR | The proximity of this traditional *enoteca* (wine bar) to Montecitorio, the Italian Parliament building, makes it a favorite with journalists and politicos, who often stop in for a glass of wine after work. But it's the tantalizing smell of truffles from the snack counter, where a sommelier waits to organize your tasting, that will probably lure you inside. There's also a celebrated restaurant where you can book a table and enjoy a parade of elegant Italian plates. Don't forget to check out the wineshop, too. ✉ *Via dei Prefetti, 15, Piazza Navona* ☎ *06/6873446* 🌐 *achilli.restaurant* Ⓜ *Spagna; Bus Nos. 64, 70, 85, and 492.*

Il Goccetto

WINE BAR | Specializing in the vintages produced by smaller vineyards from Sicily to Venice, this historical wine bar also has a menu of Italian delicacies (meats and cheeses) that likewise represents the entire Italian peninsula. The burrata with sun-dried tomatoes is a perennial favorite. The tiny bar is well designed but is always busy and never accepts reservations. If all the seats are taken, you might be able to sip wine on the step outside while taking in the snippets of Roman life passing by. ✉ *Via dei Banchi Vecchi, 14, Campo de' Fiori* ☎ *06/99448583* 🌐 *www.facebook.com/Ilgoccetto* Ⓜ *Spagna; Bus Nos. 30, 40, and 64.*

Jerry Thomas Speakeasy

COCKTAIL BARS | One of just a handful of hidden bars in Rome, this intimate bar looks like a Prohibition-era haunt and serves the kind of classic cocktails you find in New York speakeasies. It's seating room only, so reservations must be made online in advance. Upon booking, you'll receive a password via email. Serious cocktail aficionados can also purchase specialty bitters and mixology tools at the Emporium across the alley from the drinks spot. ✉ *Vicolo Cellini, 30, Campo de' Fiori* ☎ *340/7332980 WhatsApp only* 🌐 *www.thejerrythomasproject.it* Ⓜ *Spagna; Bus Nos. 30, 40, and 64.*

The Sofa Bar Restaurant & Roof Terrace

BARS | The romantic rooftop terrace at I Sofà has a 360-degree view of the Eternal City, so it's no surprise that it's a prime spot for a late-afternoon cocktail (weather permitting). The bar takes its name from the historic stone benches carved into the wall at the entrance to the Hotel St. George. Head downstairs in the cooler months for a wide selection of craft beers on tap inside the Hotel Indigo. ✉ *Hotel Indigo Rome—St. George, Via Giulia, 62, Campo de' Fiori* ☎ *06/68661846* 🌐 *www.isofadiviagiulia.com* Ⓜ *Spagna; Bus Nos. 30, 40, and 64.*

Vinoteca Novecento

WINE BAR | Salami-and-cheese tasting menus and a seemingly unlimited selection of wines, Prosecco, vini santi, and grappe are highlights of this lovely (albeit tiny) enoteca with a very old-fashioned vibe. Inside, it's standing-room only; in good weather, you can sit outside at an oak barrique on a quiet cobblestone street leading to one of Rome's prettiest small squares. ✉ *Piazza delle Coppelle, 47, Piazza Navona* ☎ *06/6833078* Ⓜ *Spagna; Bus Nos. 40, 64, 70, 85, and 492.*

Performing Arts

★ Teatro Argentina

THEATER | The 18th-century Teatro Argentina evokes glamour and sophistication with its velvet upholstery, large crystal chandeliers, and beautifully dressed theatergoers, who come to see international productions of stage and dance performances. This is one of the oldest theaters in Italy, but its foundation is ancient: it sits on the site of the Theater of Pompey, which was completed in AD 55. ✉ *Largo di Torre Argentina, 52, Campo de' Fiori* ☎ *06/684000314* 🌐 *www.teatrodiroma.net* Ⓜ *Colosseo; Bus Nos. 30, 40, and 70.*

BEAUTY

Antica Erboristeria Romana

HEALTH & BEAUTY | Complete with hand-labeled wooden drawers holding more than 200 varieties of herbs, flowers, and tinctures, Antica Erboristeria Romana has maintained its old-world apothecary feel (it's the oldest shop of its kind in Rome, dating back to 1752). The shop stocks an impressive array of teas and herbal infusions, more than 700 essential oils, bud derivatives, and powdered extracts. ✉ *Via Torre Argentina, 15, Piazza Navona* ☎ *06/6879493* 🌐 *www.anticaerboristeriaromana.it* Ⓜ *Barberini; Bus Nos. 30, 40, 64, and 492.*

CERAMICS AND DECORATIVE ARTS

★ INOR dal 1952

HOUSEWARES | For more than 50 years, INOR dal 1952 has served as a trusted friend for Romans in need of an exclusive wedding gift, delicate stemware, or oh-so-perfect china place settings for a fancy Sunday lunch. Entrance is via a secluded 15th-century courtyard and up a flight of stairs. The store specializes in work handcrafted by the silversmiths of Pampaloni and Bastianelli in Florence. ✉ *Via della Stelletta, 23, Piazza Navona* ☎ *06/6878579* 🌐 *www.inor.it* ⏲ *Closed Sun.* Ⓜ *Spagna; Bus Nos. 64, 70, 85, and 492.*

CLOTHING

★ L'Archivio di Monserrato

CLOTHING | Tailored jackets with exotic trims, dresses in eclectic prints and bold colors, and smart linen suits are some of the offerings at this airy, spacious boutique curated by Soledad Twombly (daughter-in-law of painter Cy Twombly). In addition to her original designs, look for a sophisticated mix of antique Turkish and Indian textiles, jewelry, shoes, and small housewares picked up on her travels. ✉ *Via di Monserrato, 150, Campo de' Fiori* ☎ *06/45654157* 🌐 *www.soledadtwombly.com* ⏲ *Closed Sun.* Ⓜ *Spagna; Bus Nos. 30, 40, and 64.*

Le Tartarughe

CLOTHING | A familiar face at the city's fashion shows, designer Susanna Liso, a Rome native, mixes raw silks or cashmere and fine merino wool to create captivating, enveloping garments that sometimes feature seductive or playful elements. Both her haute-couture and ready-to-wear lines are much loved by Rome's elite. ✉ *Via Piè di Marmo, 17, Piazza Navona* ☎ *06/6792240* 🌐 *www.letartarughe.eu* Ⓜ *Barberini; Bus Nos. 30, 40, 64, and 492.*

Morgana

CLOTHING | When strolling down Via del Governo Vecchio, a street popular for funky and edgy clothing boutiques, you can't help but stop and stare at this shop's windows, where the family-run business displays some of its best hippie-chick and bridal-chic gowns, as well as Japanese Noh theater–inspired coats. The highly original and highly coveted clothes are carefully crafted and hand-painted with one-of-a-kind designs. ✉ *Via del Governo Vecchio, 27, Piazza Navona* ☎ *334/7960281* 🌐 *www.fabiotruffa.it* Ⓜ *Spagna; Bus Nos. 40, 64, 70, and 85.*

Vestiti Usati Cinzia

CLOTHING | Vintage-clothes hunters, costume designers, and stylists alike love browsing through the racks at this fun, inviting shop, which is stocked wall to wall with funky 1960s and '70s apparel. There's definitely no shortage of goofy sunglasses, flower-power bell-bottoms, embroidered hippie tops, psychedelic boots, and other trippy merchandise from the days of peace and love. ✉ *Via del Governo Vecchio, 45, Piazza Navona* ☎ *06/6832945* 🌐 *cinziavestitiusati.wordpress.com* Ⓜ *Spagna; Bus Nos. 40, 64, 70, and 85.*

FOOD AND WINE

Moriondo e Gariglio

CANDY | FAMILY | Dating from 1850 and adhering strictly to family recipes passed on from generation to generation, this shop makes some of Rome's finest chocolate delicacies and other sweet treats. The selection of more than 80 confections includes everything from dark-chocolate truffles to marrons glacés. The chocolates shaped like every letter of the alphabet are perennial favorites, though. ✉ *Via Piè di Marmo, 21, Piazza Navona* ☎ *06/6990856* 🌐 *moriondoegariglio.com* Ⓜ *Barberini; Bus Nos. 40, 64, and 70.*

JEWELRY

Massimo Maria Melis

JEWELRY & WATCHES | Drawing heavily on ancient Roman and Etruscan designs, the jewelry from former costume designer Massimo Maria Melis will carry you back in time. Working with 21-karat gold, he often incorporates antique coins in many of his exquisite bracelets and necklaces. Some of his pieces are done with an ancient technique, much loved by the Etruscans, in which tiny gold droplets are fused together to create intricately patterned designs. ✉ *Via dell'Orso, 57, Piazza Navona* ☎ *06/6869188* 🌐 *www.massimomariamelis.com* ⏲ *Closed Sun.* Ⓜ *Spagna; Bus Nos. 64, 70, 85, and 492.*

Quattrocolo

JEWELRY & WATCHES | Dating from 1938, this shop showcases exquisite, antique, micro-mosaic jewelry painstakingly crafted in the style perfected by the masters at the Vatican mosaic studio. The small works were beloved by cosmopolitan clientele of the Grand Tour age and offer modern-day shoppers a taste of yesteryear's grandeur. You'll also find 18th- and 19th-century cameos and beautiful engraved stones, one-of-a-kind rings from the 1960s and '70s, as well as contemporary jewelry. ✉ *Via della Scrofa, 48, Piazza Navona* ☎ *06/68801367* 🌐 *www.quattrocolo.com* ⏲ *Closed Sun. and Mon.* Ⓜ *Spagna; Bus Nos. 64, 70, 85, and 492.*

SHOES AND ACCESSORIES

★ Chez Dede

SPECIALTY STORE | Husband-and-wife duo Andrea Ferolla and Daria Reina (he's a fashion illustrator, she's a photographer) curate a selection of clothes, bags, vintage jewelry, books, home decor, and anything else you might need in this cult favorite lifestyle-concept shop. Their signature fabric bags are designed to go from the plane straight to the beach club, and they regularly release collectible items featuring Ferolla's whimsical illustrations. ✉ *Via di Monserrato, 35, Campo de' Fiori* ☎ *06/83772934* 🌐 *www.chezdede.com* ⏲ *Closed Sun.* Ⓜ *Spagna; Bus Nos. 40, 64, and 87.*

Ibiz

LEATHER GOODS | In business since 1972, this family team creates colorful, stylish leather handbags, belts, keychains, and sandals near Piazza Campo de' Fiori. Choose from the premade collection, or order something in the color of your choice; their workshop is visible in the boutique. ✉ *Via dei Chiavari, 39, Campo de' Fiori* ☎ *06/68307297* 🌐 *ibizroma.it* ⏲ *Closed Sun.* Ⓜ *Colosseo; Tram No. 8.*

★ Maison Halaby

HANDBAGS | Lebanese designer and artist Gilbert Halaby was featured in fashion magazines like *Vogue* and created jewelry for Lady Gaga before giving up the rat race and opening his own shop, where the ethos is all about slow fashion. His boldly colored leather handbags incorporate suede, python, fringe, raffia, or jeweled handles, and his silk scarves are printed with his original watercolors, some of which are also on sale. The small, homey boutique—with a velvet sofa and lots of books, plants, and art by Halaby himself—is mainly open by appointment. But try passing by and ringing the bell; if Gilbert is there, he might just invite you in for coffee or Campari. ✉ *Via di Monserrato, 21, Campo de' Fiori* ☎ *06/96521585* 🌐 *www.facebook.com/halaby.official* Ⓜ *Spagna; Bus Nos. 30, 40, and 64.*

STATIONERY

★ Cartoleria Pantheon dal 1910

STATIONERY | Instead of sending a postcard home, why not send a letter written on sumptuous handmade Amalfi paper purchased from this shop? It also sells hand-bound leather journals in an extraordinary array of colors and sizes. There is a second location on Piazza Navona. ✉ *Via della Maddalena, 41, Piazza Navona* ☎ *06/6795633* 🌐 *www.cartoleriapantheon.it* Ⓜ *Barberini; Bus Nos. 30, 40, 64, and 82.*

TOYS

Al Sogno

TOYS | **FAMILY** | This Navona jewel, around since 1945, is crammed top to bottom with artistic, well-crafted puppets, dolls, masks, stuffed animals, and other toys for children of all ages that encourage imaginative (and low-tech) play and learning. ✉ *Piazza Navona, 53, corner of Via Agonale, Piazza Navona* ☎ *06/6864198* 🌐 *www.alsogno.com* Ⓜ *Spagna; Bus Nos. 40, 64, 85, and 492.*

Piazza di Spagna

In spirit (and in fact) this section of the city is its most grandiose. The overblown Vittoriano monument, the labyrinthine treasure-chest palaces of Rome's surviving aristocracy, even the diamond-draped denizens of Via Condotti's shops—all embody the exuberant ego of a city at the center of its own universe. Here's where you'll see ladies in furs gobbling pastries at café tables and walk through a thousand snapshots as you climb the famous Spanish Steps, admired by generations from Byron to Versace. Cultural treasures abound around here: gilded 17th-century churches, glittering palazzi, and the greatest example of portraiture in Rome, Velázquez's incomparable *Innocent X* at the Galleria Doria Pamphilj. Have your camera ready—along with a coin or two—for that most beloved of Rome's landmarks, the Trevi Fountain.

Favorite Places

Laura Itzkowitz: Palazzo Doria Pamphilj has somehow remained under the radar. See paintings by Raphael, Titian, and Caravaggio and soak up the beauty in the spectacular Hall of Mirrors.

GETTING HERE AND AROUND

Piazza di Spagna is a short walk from Piazza del Popolo, the Pantheon, and the Trevi Fountain. One of Rome's handiest subway stations, Spagna, is tucked just left of the steps. Buses No. 117 (from the Colosseum) and No. 119 (from Piazza del Popolo) hum through the area; the latter tootles up Via del Babuino, famed for its shopping.

Sights

★ Ara Pacis Augustae

(*Altar of Augustan Peace*)

MONUMENT | This pristine monument sits inside one of Rome's contemporary architectural landmarks: a gleaming, rectangular, glass-and-travertine structure designed by American architect Richard Meier. It overlooks the Tiber on one side and the ruins of the marble-clad Mausoleo di Augusto (Mausoleum of Augustus) on the other and is a serene, luminous oasis right in the center of Rome.

This altar itself dates from 13 BC and was commissioned to celebrate the Pax Romana, the era of peace ushered in by Augustus's military victories. When viewing it, keep in mind that the spectacular reliefs would have been painted in vibrant colors, now long gone. The reliefs on the short sides portray myths associated with Rome's founding and glory; those on the long sides display a procession of the imperial family. Although half of his body is missing, Augustus is identifiable as the first full figure at the procession's head on the south-side frieze; academics still argue over exact identifications of most of the figures. Be sure to check out the small downstairs museum, which hosts rotating exhibits on Italian culture, with themes ranging from design to film. ✉ *Lungotevere in Augusta, at the corner of Via Tomacelli, Piazza di Spagna* ☎ *06/0608* 🌐 *www.arapacis.it* 🎫 *€12, €13 when there is an exhibition* ✍ *Reservations essential for groups of 11 to 25 persons* Ⓜ *Flaminio, Spagna.*

Galleria d'Arte Moderna

ART MUSEUM | Located in a former monastery, this small museum displays a capsule collection of modern art, with an emphasis on Italian artists. The permanent collection is too large to be displayed at once, so exhibitions rotate, displaying paintings, drawings, prints, and sculptures by artists of the 19th and 20th centuries, including Giorgio de Chirico, Mario Mafai, Scipione, Gino Severini, and Giorgio Morandi. ✉ *Via Francesco Crispi, 24, Piazza di Spagna* ☎ *06/0608* 🌐 *www.galleriaartemodernaroma.it* 🎫 *€9; €11.50 if there's a special exhibit* ⏲ *Closed Mon.* Ⓜ *Spagna.*

Keats-Shelley Memorial House

HISTORIC HOME | Sent to Rome in a last-ditch attempt to treat his consumptive condition, English Romantic poet John Keats—celebrated for such poems as "Ode to a Nightingale" and "Endymion"—lived in this house at the foot of the Spanish Steps. At the time, this was the heart of Rome's colorful bohemian quarter, an area favored by English expats. He took his last breath here on February 23, 1821, and is now buried in the Non-Catholic Cemetery in Testaccio. On a visit to his final home, you can see his death mask, though local authorities had all his furnishings burned after his death as a sanitary measure. You'll also find a quaint collection of memorabilia of other English literary figures of the period—Lord Byron, Percy Bysshe Shelley, Joseph Severn, and Leigh Hun—and an exhaustive library of works on the Romantics. ✉ *Piazza di Spagna 26, Piazza di Spagna* ☎ *06/6784235* 🌐 *ksh.roma.it* 🎫 *€6* ⏲ *Closed Sun.* Ⓜ *Spagna.*

★ Monumento a Vittorio Emanuele II, or Altare della Patria (*Victor Emmanuel II Monument, or Altar of the Nation*)

MONUMENT | The huge white mass known as the "Vittoriano" is an inescapable landmark that has been likened to a giant wedding cake or an immense typewriter. Present-day Romans joke that you can only avoid looking at it if you are standing on it. Built to honor the unification of Italy and the nation's first king, Victor Emmanuel II, it also shelters the eternal flame at the tomb of Italy's Unknown Soldier, killed during World War I. Alas, to create this elaborate marble behemoth and the vast surrounding piazza, its architects blithely destroyed many ancient and medieval buildings and altered the slope of the Campidoglio (Capitoline Hill), which abuts it. The truly enticing feature of the Vittoriano is its rooftop terrace, which offers some of the best panoramic views of Rome. The only way up is by elevator (the entrance is located several flights of stairs up on the right as you face the monument). ✉ *Entrances on Piazza Venezia, Piazza del Campidoglio, and Via di San Pietro in Carcere, Trevi* ☎ *06/0608* 🌐 *vive.cultura.gov.it* 🎫 *Main building free; €17 for the terrace* Ⓜ *Colosseo.*

★ Palazzo Colonna

CASTLE/PALACE | Rome's grandest private palace is a fusion of 17th- and 18th-century buildings that have been occupied by the Colonna family for more than 20 generations. The immense residence faces Piazza dei Santi Apostoli on one side and the Quirinale (Quirinal Hill) on the other—with a little bridge over Via della Pilotta linking to gardens on the hill—and contains an art gallery that's open to the public on Saturday morning or by guided tour on Friday morning. The gallery is itself a setting of aristocratic grandeur; you might recognize the Sala Grande as the site where Audrey Hepburn meets the press in *Roman Holiday.* The most spectacular feature is the ceiling fresco of the Battle of Lepanto painted by Giovanni Coli and Filippo Gherardi. Adding to the opulence are works by Poussin, Tintoretto, and Veronese. ✉ *Via della Pilotta, 17, Trevi* ☎ *06/6784350* 🌐 *www.galleriacolonna.it* 🎫 *€15 for gallery and gardens, €25 to also visit the Princess Isabelle Apartment, €35 for a guided tour on Friday* ⏲ *Closed Sun.–Thurs.* ☞ *Friday for guided tour only* Ⓜ *Barberini.*

★ Palazzo Doria Pamphilj

CASTLE/PALACE | Like the Palazzo Colonna and the Galleria Borghese, this dazzling 15th-century family palace provides a fantastic glimpse of aristocratic Rome. The understated beauty of the graceful facade barely hints at the interior's opulent halls and gilded galleries, which are filled with Old Master works. The 550 paintings here include three by Caravaggio: *St. John the Baptist, Mary Magdalene,* and the breathtaking *Rest on the Flight to Egypt.* Off the eye-popping Galleria degli Specchi (Gallery of Mirrors)—a smaller version of the one at Versailles—are the famous Velázquez *Pope Innocent X,* considered by some historians to be the greatest portrait ever painted, and the Bernini bust of the same Pamphilj pope. ✉ *Via del Corso, 305, Trevi* ☎ *06/6797323* 🌐 *www.doriapamphilj.it* 🎫 *€16* ⏲ *Closed the 3rd Wed. of the month* Ⓜ *Barberini.*

★ Sant'Ignazio

CHURCH | Rome's second Jesuit church, this 17th-century landmark set on a Rococo piazza harbors some of the city's most magnificent trompe l'oeils. To get the full effect of the illusionistic ceiling by priest-artist Andrea Pozzo, stand on the small yellow disk set into the floor of the nave. The heavenly vision that seems to extend upward almost indefinitely represents the *Allegory of the Missionary Work of the Jesuits.* It's part of Pozzo's cycle of works in this church exalting the early history of the Jesuit order, whose founder was the reformer Ignatius of Loyola. The saint soars heavenward, supported by a cast of thousands, creating a jaw-dropping effect that was fully intended to rival that of the glorious ceiling by Baciccia in the nearby mother church of Il Gesù. Be sure to have coins handy for the machine that switches on the lights so you can marvel at the false dome, which is actually a flat canvas—a trompe l'oeil trick Pozzo used when the architectural budget drained dry.

Scattered around the nave are several awe-inspiring altars; their soaring columns, gold-on-gold decoration, and gilded statues are pure splendor. Splendid, too, are the occasional sacred music concerts performed by choirs from all over the world. Look for posters by the main doors, or check the website for more information. ✉ *Piazza S. Ignazio, Trevi* ✥ *Via del Caravita 8A* ☎ *06/6794406* 🌐 *santignazio.gesuiti.it* Ⓜ *Barberini.*

★ The Spanish Steps

OTHER ATTRACTION | **FAMILY** | The iconic Spanish Steps (often called simply *la scalinata,* or "the staircase," by Italians) and the Piazza di Spagna from which they ascend both get their names from the Spanish Embassy to the Vatican on the piazza—even though the staircase was built with French funds in 1723. In honor of a diplomatic visit by the King of Spain, the hillside was transformed by architect Francesco de Sanctis to link the church of Trinità dei Monti at the top with the Via Condotti below. In an allusion to the church, the staircase is divided by three landings (beautifully lined with potted azaleas from mid-April to mid-May). Bookending the bottom of the steps are beloved holdovers from the 18th century, when the area was known as the "English Ghetto": the 18th-century Keats-Shelley House and Babington's

Tea Rooms, both beautifully redolent of the Grand Tour era. ✉ *Plazza di Spagna, Piazza di Spagna* Ⓜ *Spagna.*

★ Trevi Fountain

FOUNTAIN | FAMILY | Alive with rushing waters commanded by an imperious sculpture of Oceanus, the Fontana di Trevi has been all about theatrical effects from the start; it is an aquatic marvel in a city filled with them. The fountain's unique drama is largely due to its location: its vast basin is squeezed into the tight confluence of three little streets (the *tre vie,* which may give the fountain its name), with cascades emerging as if from the wall of Palazzo Poli.

Everyone knows the famous legend that if you throw a coin into the Trevi Fountain you will ensure a return trip to the Eternal City, but not everyone knows how to do it the right way. You must toss a coin with your right hand over your left shoulder, with your back to the fountain. One coin means you'll return to Rome; two, you'll return *and* fall in love; three, you'll return, find love, and marry. The fountain grosses some €1,500,000 a year, with every cent going to the Catholic charity Caritas. ✉ *Piazza di Trevi, Trevi* Ⓜ *Barberini.*

Restaurants

Baccano

$$$ | BRASSERIE | For good food at reasonable prices around the Trevi Fountain, this Paris-inspired brasserie—open for lunch, dinner, and everything in between—is a great bet. Although it emphasizes seafood, the extensive menu has something for everyone, from salads to pasta and entrées. **Known for:** oyster bar; excellent carbonara; classic international cocktails. $ *Average main: €33* ✉ *Via delle Muratte, 23, Trevi* ☎ *06/69941166* 🌐 *www.baccanoroma.com* Ⓜ *Barberini.*

★ Il Marchese

$$ | ITALIAN | This rustic-meets-glamorous bistro attracts locals for its flawless execution of Roman classics (many served photogenically in metal cooking pans) as well as original dishes. Its bar is known among amaro connoisseurs for having the largest selection in Rome, and the bitter liquors are the stars of the expertly crafted cocktail menu. **Known for:** beautiful design; well-executed classics; extensive selection of amari and great cocktails. $ *Average main: €22* ✉ *Via di Ripetta, 162, Piazza di Spagna* ☎ *06/90218872* 🌐 *www.ilmarcheseroma.it* Ⓜ *Spagna.*

Matricianella

$$ | ROMAN | Family-owned neighborhood staple with its quintessentially Roman wooden tables and wood-beamed ceilings, Matricianella charms with hearty Roman dishes and a biblical wine list. Try any of the Roman pasta trifecta—amatriciana, cacio e pepe, and carbonara—or other classics like crispy fried artichokes or saltimbocca alla romana (thin veal slices with prosciutto and sage). **Known for:** rustic charm; classic Roman dishes; extensive wine list. $ *Average main: €25* ✉ *Via del Leone, 4, Piazza di Spagna* ☎ *06/6832100* 🌐 *www.matricianella.it* ⏲ *Closed Sun.* Ⓜ *Spagna.*

★ Moma

$$$ | MODERN ITALIAN | In front of the American embassy and a favorite of the design *trendoisie,* Michelin-starred Moma attracts well-heeled businessmen at lunch but shifts to a more intimate affair for dinner. The kitchen turns out hits as it creates *alta cucina* (haute cuisine) made using Italian ingredients sourced from small producers. **Known for:** pasta with a twist; creative presentation; affordable fine dining. $ *Average main: €39* ✉ *Via San Basilio, 42/43, Piazza di Spagna* ☎ *06/42011798* 🌐 *www.ristorantemoma.it* ⏲ *Closed Sun.* Ⓜ *Barberini.*

Ristorante Nino

$$ | TUSCAN | A favorite among international journalists and the rich and famous since 1934, this elegant Tuscan restaurant with wood-paneled walls and white tablecloths does not seem to

Piazza di Spagna
A
B
C
D
E
F
1
2
3
4
5
6
7
8
9
Villa Borghese
Monte Pincio
Viale Trinità dei Monti
Villa Medici
Via Margutta
Via del Babuino
Via del Corso
Via di Ripetta
Lgt. Mellini
Fiume Tevere
Lgt. in Augusta
Via S. Giacomo
Via dei Greci
Via d. Frezza
Via Vittoria
Via M. Clementi
Piazza di Spagna
Spagna
Via Mario de' Fiori
V. Bocca di Leone
Via d. Croce
Via d. Carrozze
Via M. Dionigi
Via V. Colonna
Pte. Cavour
Via Tomacelli
Via dell'Arancio
Via Condotti
Via Borgognona
Via Gregoriana
Lgt. Prati
Via d. F. Borghese
Via Frattina
Via della Vite
Via C.le Case
V. Due Macelli
Lgt. Marzio
Via delle Mercede
Piazza S. Silvestro
Via del Pozzetto
Via Nazareno
Via M. Brianzo
Via dei Perfetti
Piazza Parlamento
V. del Maroniti
Via dell'Orso
Via del Tritone
Via Zanardelli
Via della Scrofa
Via d. C. Marzio
Piazza Accad. di S. Luca
Via d. Stamperia
Via d. Panetteria
V. d. Lavatore
St. Agostino
Piazza di Montecitorio
Piazza Colonna
V. del Crocoferi
Piazza Navona
Via del Coppelle
Via d. Muratte
V. Minghetti
Vergini
Via delle Vergini
V. d. Umiltà
V. della Dataria
Piazza Pietra
Piazza Navona
Corso del Rinascimento
V. d. Sta. M. d. Anima
Via d. Vecchia
V. Caravita
Via dell'Archetto
Via S. Marcello
Via Lucchesi
Piazza Pilotta
Via Seminario
V. d. St. Ignazio
Via della Pilotta
Piazza St. Eustachio
Piazza di Minerva
Via del Corso
Piazza dei Santi Apostoli
Via d. T. Valle
Via Monterone
Via di Torre Argentina
Via dei Costari
V. della Pigna
Via del Gesù
Piazza Grazioli
Via IV Novembre
Palazzo Massimo
Museo Barracco
Corso Vittorio Emanuele II
Via d. Plebiscito
Piazza Venezia
V. del Sudario
Area Sacra
Via Astalli
Via dei Fori
Campo de' Fiori
Teatro di Pompeo
Via delle Botteghe Oscure
Piazza del Campidoglio
Via dei Giubbonari
Palazzo Mattei
Musei Capitolini
Piazza d. Monte di Pietà
V. d. Delfini
Via dei Funari

Sights

1 Ara Pacis Augustae **B3**
2 Galleria d'Arte Moderna **G4**
3 Keats-Shelley Memorial House... **E3**
4 Monumento a Vittorio Emanuele II, or Altare della Patria **E9**
5 Palazzo Colonna **F7**
6 Palazzo Doria Pamphilj............. **E7**
7 Sant'Ignazio **D7**
8 The Spanish Steps.................. **E3**
9 Trevi Fountain **F6**

Restaurants

1 Baccano **E6**
2 Il Marchese **B4**
3 Matricianella **C4**
4 Moma **I3**
5 Ristorante Nino **E3**
6 Settimo............................. **G2**

Quick Bites

1 Antico Caffè Greco................. **E3**
2 Il Gelato di San Crispino **F5**

Hotels

1 Babuino 181 .... **C1**
2 Baglioni Hotel Regina **H2**
3 Hassler Roma **F3**
4 Hotel de la Ville **F3**
5 Hotel d'Inghilterra **D3**
6 Hotel Eden.......................... **G2**
7 Hotel Vilòn **C4**
8 Il Palazzetto **E2**
9 Maalot Roma **E6**
10 Margutta 19 .... **D1**
11 Scalinata di Spagna................ **F3**

have changed at all over the decades. Its menu is meat-focused with many Tuscan classics: try the meat-filled *cannelloni alla Nino* or *bistecca di costa all'arrabbiata,* a flavorful rib-eye steak cooked with chili and garlic. **Known for:** warm crostini spread with pâté; upscale old-school Italian vibe; ribollita (Tuscan bean soup). *Average main: €26* *Via Borgognona, 11, Piazza di Spagna* *06/6786752* *ristorantenino.it* *Closed Sun. and Aug.* *Spagna.*

Settimo

$$$ | **ITALIAN** | Crowning the Sofitel Rome Villa Borghese hotel, this chic restaurant serves fancy takes on Rome's *cucina povera* (peasant cooking) in a chic space with graphic punches of color. The terrace offers fantastic views that stretch from Villa Borghese to the dome of St. Peter's, but the interior dining room, with its floor-to-ceiling windows and terrazzo-inspired floors, is lovely, too. **Known for:** amped-up versions of classic Roman recipes; colorful, modern design; terrace with great views. *Average main: €38* *Sofitel Rome Villa Borghese, Via Lombardia, 47, Piazza di Spagna* *06/478021* *www.settimoristorante.it* *Spagna, Barberini.*

Coffee and Quick Bites

★ Antico Caffè Greco

$ | **CAFÉ** | The red-velvet chairs and marble tables of one of Rome's oldest caffès have seen the likes of Byron, Shelley, Keats, Goethe, and Casanova. Locals love basking in the more than 260 years of history held within its dark-wood walls lined with antique artwork; tourists appreciate its location amid the shopping madness of upscale Via Condotti. **Known for:** lavish historic design; perfect espresso; crystal goblets and high prices to match. *Average main: €12* *Via dei Condotti, 86, Piazza di Spagna* *06/6791700* *anticocaffegreco.eu* *Spagna.*

Il Gelato di San Crispino

$ | **ICE CREAM** | **FAMILY** | Many people say this place—which is around the corner from the Trevi Fountain and had a cameo in the movie *Eat, Pray, Love*—serves the best gelato in Rome. Creative flavors like black fig, chocolate rum, Armagnac, and ginger-cinnamon all incorporate top-notch ingredients, and the shop is known for keeping its gelato hidden under metal covers to better preserve the quality. **Known for:** seasonal fruit flavors; offering only cups and no cones; wine-based gelato. *Average main: €4* *Via della Panetteria, 42, Trevi* *06/69489518* *www.ilgelatodisancrispino.it* *Barberini.*

Hotels

Babuino 181

$$ | **HOTEL** | On chic Via del Babuino, known for its high-end boutiques, jewelry stores, and antiques shops, this discreet and stylish hotel is an ideal pied-à-terre, with spacious rooms spread over two historic buildings. **Pros:** spacious suites; nice breakfast served on the rooftop; helpful, attentive staff. **Cons:** rooms can be a bit noisy; no spa or fitness center; annex rooms feel removed from service staff. *Rooms from: €373* *Via del Babuino, 181, Piazza del Popolo* *06/32295295* *www.romeluxury-suites.com/it/babuino-181* *25 rooms* *Free Breakfast* *Flaminio, Spagna.*

Baglioni Hotel Regina

$$$$ | **HOTEL** | The former home of Queen Margherita of Savoy, the Baglioni Hotel Regina, which enjoys a prime spot on the Via Veneto, is still a favorite among today's jet-setters. **Pros:** chic decor; luxury on-site spa; excellent restaurant and bar. **Cons:** internal rooms overlook air-conditioning ducts; extra charge for breakfast à la carte; location isn't as prestigious as it once was. *Rooms from: €772* *Via Veneto, 72, Piazza di Spagna* *06/421111* *rome.baglionihotels.com* *117 rooms* *No Meals* *Barberini.*

★ Hassler Roma

$$$$ | **HOTEL** | When it comes to million-dollar views, the best place to stay in the whole city is the Hassler, so it's no surprise many of the rich and famous (Tom Cruise, Jennifer Lopez, and the Beckhams among them) are willing to pay top dollar for a room at this exclusive hotel atop the Spanish Steps. **Pros:** prime location and panoramic views; exceptional service; sauna access included with each reservation. **Cons:** VIP rates (10% VAT not included); some rooms are rather small; rooms are updated on a rolling basis, leaving some feeling dated. *$ Rooms from: €1,500 ✉ Piazza Trinità dei Monti, 6, Piazza di Spagna ☎ 06/699340 ⊕ www.hotelhasslerroma.com 87 rooms and suites No Meals M Spagna.*

★ Hotel de la Ville

$$$$ | **HOTEL** | Occupying a prime position atop the Spanish Steps, this glamorous sister property of the beloved Hotel de Russie near the Piazza del Popolo has a Grand Tour–inspired design featuring antiques, custom wallpaper stamped with Piranesi prints, and plenty of silk. **Pros:** must-visit rooftop bar with panoramic views; prestigious location atop the Spanish Steps; pampering spa uses signature made-in-Italy organic products. **Cons:** some rooms are a bit small for the price; service can be a bit slow at the bar; no pets allowed. *$ Rooms from: €1,500 ✉ Via Sistina, 69, Piazza di Spagna ☎ 06/977931 ⊕ www.roccofortehotels.com 104 rooms and suites Free Breakfast M Spagna.*

★ Hotel d'Inghilterra

$$$$ | **HOTEL** | Situated in a stately 16th-century building and founded in 1845, this storied hotel served as a guesthouse for aristocratic travelers visiting the noble Torlonia family (who still lives across the cobblestone street) and has since been the home away from home for various monarchs, movie stars like Elizabeth Taylor, and several great writers—Lord Byron, John Keats, Mark Twain, and Ernest Hemingway among them. **Pros:** distinct character and opulence; turndown service (with chocolates); excellent in-house restaurant and bar. **Cons:** rooms are on the smaller side; ultraluxury price point; location might be too busy for some. *$ Rooms from: €1,100 ✉ Via Bocca di Leone, 14, Piazza di Spagna ☎ 06/699811 ⊕ www.starhotelscollezione.com 80 rooms and suites No Meals M Spagna.*

★ Hotel Eden

$$$$ | **HOTEL** | At what was once a favorite haunt of Ingrid Bergman, Ginger Rogers, and Fellini, dashing elegance, exquisite decor, and stunning vistas of Rome combine with true Italian hospitality. **Pros:** gorgeous rooftop terrace restaurant; tranquil spa facilities; 24-hour room service. **Cons:** breakfast not included (and very expensive, at €50); gym is standard but small; some rooms overlook an unremarkable courtyard. *$ Rooms from: €1,360 ✉ Via Ludovisi, 49, Piazza di Spagna ☎ 06/478121 ⊕ www.dorchestercollection.com 98 rooms and suites No Meals M Spagna.*

★ Hotel Vilòn

$$$$ | **HOTEL** | Set in a 16th-century mansion annexed to Palazzo Borghese and tucked behind a discreet entrance, this intimate hotel might be Rome's best-kept secret. **Pros:** gorgeous design; attentive staff; fantastic location. **Cons:** not much communal space; no spa or gym; some rooms are a bit small. *$ Rooms from: €780 ✉ Via dell'Arancio, 69, Piazza di Spagna ☎ 06/878187 ⊕ www.hotelvilon.com 17 rooms and suites Free Breakfast M Spagna.*

Il Palazzetto

$$$ | **B&B/INN** | Formerly the retreat of a rich noble family, this 15th-century house is now one of Rome's most intimate and luxurious hotels, with gorgeous terraces and a rooftop bar affording views of the never-ending theater of the Spanish Steps. **Pros:** location and view; free Wi-Fi;

guests have full access to the Hassler's services. **Cons:** often books up far in advance, particularly in high season; bedrooms do not access communal terraces; breakfast is served in the main building at the Hassler. *$ Rooms from: €550 ✉ Vicolo del Bottino, 8, Piazza di Spagna ☎ 06/69934560 🌐 www.ilpalazzettoroma.com 4 rooms 🍴 No Meals Ⓜ Spagna.*

Maalot Roma

$$$$ | **HOTEL** | This boutique property inside the former residence of opera composer Gaetano Donizetto aims to be a restaurant with rooms above rather than a hotel with a restaurant below. **Pros:** chic design with original art; great food at Don Pasquale restaurant; central location just steps from the Trevi Fountain. **Cons:** no spa; service can be a bit slow; some rooms look directly onto the McDonald's across the street. *$ Rooms from: €750 ✉ Via delle Murate, 78, Trevi ☎ 06/878087 🌐 www.hotelmaalot.com 30 rooms and suites 🍴 Free Breakfast Ⓜ Barberini.*

Margutta 19

$$$ | **HOTEL** | At this all-suites property, tucked away on a leafy street known for its art galleries, the amenities are top drawer, the design is contemporary, the restaurant features a verdant terrace, and the accommodations have a hip New York–loft feel. **Pros:** studio-loft feel in the center of Rome; complete privacy; deluxe furnishings. **Cons:** no spa or gym; entry-level rooms lack views; no elevator in the annex to reach rooms on higher floors. *$ Rooms from: €486 ✉ Via Margutta, 19, Piazza del Popolo ☎ 06/97797979 🌐 www.romeluxury-suites.com/margutta-19 22 suites 🍴 Free Breakfast Ⓜ Flaminio, Spagna.*

Scalinata di Spagna

$$ | **HOTEL** | Perched atop the Spanish Steps, this charming boutique hotel is so popular that it's often booked far in advance. **Pros:** friendly and helpful concierge; free bottles of water in the minibars; free Wi-Fi throughout. **Cons:** hike up the hill to the hotel; some rooms are small; no elevator in the main building. *$ Rooms from: €257 ✉ Piazza Trinità dei Monti, 17, Piazza di Spagna ☎ 06/45686150 🌐 www.hotelscalinata.com 40 rooms 🍴 Free Breakfast Ⓜ Spagna.*

Nightlife

Antica Enoteca

WINE BAR | Piazza di Spagna's historic wine bar literally corners the market on prime people-watching. Cozy up to the counter to sip a drink under the charming frescoes, or snag a coveted outdoor table. In addition to a vast selection of wine, Antica Enoteca has delectable antipasti, perfect for a snack or a light lunch, as well as a full menu of pastas and pizzas. *✉ Via della Croce, 76/b, Piazza di Spagna ☎ 06/6790896 🌐 anticaenoteca.superbexperience.com Ⓜ Spagna.*

Il Palazzetto Wine Bar

WINE BAR | This rooftop wine bar and restaurant wins the prize for the perfect aperitivo spot, with excellent drinks and appetizers, as well as a breathtaking view of the comings and goings on the Spanish Steps. Reach it by climbing the monumental staircase that it overlooks, or getting a lift from the elevator by the entrance to the Spagna Metro station. *✉ Il Palazzetto, Vicolo del Bottino, 8, Piazza di Spagna ✣ The main entrance is a small gate at the top of the Spanish Steps ☎ 342/1507215 🌐 ilpalazzettoroma.com Ⓜ Spagna.*

Shopping

ACCESSORIES

Furla

HANDBAGS | Furla might very well be the best deal in Italian leather, selling high-quality purses and wallets at comparatively affordable prices. Be prepared to fight your way through crowds of passionate handbag lovers, all eager to possess one of the delectable bags, wallets, or whimsical key chains in trendy sherbet hues or timeless bold color combos. ✉ *Piazza di Spagna, 22, Piazza di Spagna* ☎ *06/6797159* 🌐 *www.furla.com* Ⓜ *Spagna.*

CLOTHING

★ Brioni

CLOTHING | Founded in 1945, Brioni is hailed for its impeccably crafted menswear. Italy's best tailors create bespoke suits to exacting standards, measured to the millimeter and completely personalized from a selection of more than 5,000 spectacular fabrics. A single made-to-measure wool suit will take a minimum of 32 hours to make. The brand's prêt-à-porter line is also praised for peerless cutting and stitching. Past and present clients include Clark Gable, Barack Obama, and, of course, James Bond. ✉ *Via Condotti, 21A, Piazza di Spagna* ☎ *06/6783428* 🌐 *www.brioni.com* ⏲ *Closed Sun.* Ⓜ *Spagna.*

Elena Mirò

CLOTHING | Elena Mirò is a high-end brand that offers curvy women sophisticated, beautifully feminine clothes in sizes 42 (U.S. size 6, U.K. size 10) and up. There are several locations in Rome, including one on Via Nazionale. ✉ *Via Frattina 11, Piazza di Spagna* ☎ *06/6784367* 🌐 *www.elenamiro.com* Ⓜ *Spagna.*

Fendi

CLOTHING | Fendi has been a fixture of the Roman fashion landscape since "Mamma" Fendi first opened shop with her husband in 1925. With an eye for genius, she hired Karl Lagerfeld, whose furs and runway antics made him one of the most influential designers of the 20th century and brought international acclaim to Fendi. More recently, the atelier has gotten new life in the Italian press for its "Fendi for Fountains" campaign, which included funding the restoration of Rome's Trevi Fountain, and for moving its global headquarters to a striking Mussolini-era building known as the "square Colosseum" in the city's EUR neighborhood. The flagship store in Rome is on the ground floor of Palazzo Fendi. Upper floors contain the brand's seven private suites (the first ever Fendi hotel), and the rooftop is home to Zuma, a modern Japanese restaurant with an oh-so-cool bar that has sweeping views across the city. ✉ *Largo Carlo Goldoni, 420, Piazza di Spagna* ☎ *06/33450896* 🌐 *www.fendi.com* Ⓜ *Spagna.*

Patrizia Pepe

CLOTHING | Patrizia Pepe first emerged on the scene in Florence in 1993 with an aesthetic that's both minimalist and bold. Jackets with oversize lapels, playful pleats, mesmerizing mesh, and the occasional feathered poof set the designs apart. Spending time in the shop of this relative newcomer to the Italian fashion scene gives you the opportunity to pick up an item or two before the brand becomes the next fast-tracked craze. ✉ *Via Frattina, 5, Piazza di Spagna* ☎ *06/6781851* 🌐 *www.patriziapepe.com* Ⓜ *Spagna.*

★ Schostal

CLOTHING | A Piazza di Spagna fixture since 1870, this was once the go-to shop for corsets, petticoats, stockings, and bonnets. Today, it's the place to stop for essential basics that are increasingly difficult to find, like fine-quality pajamas, underwear, and handkerchiefs made of wool and pure cashmere. ✉ *Via della Fontanella di Borghese, 29, Piazza di Spagna* ☎ *06/6791240* 🌐 *www.schostaloriginals.com* Ⓜ *Spagna.*

Valentino

CLOTHING | Valentino fills most of Piazza di Spagna, where the designer lived for decades in a lovely palazzo next to one of the multiple boutiques showcasing his eponymous designs with a romantic edginess—think studded heels or prêt-à-porter evening gowns worthy of the Oscars. Rock stars and other music lovers can also have their Valentino guitar straps personalized when they buy one at this enormous boutique. ✉ *Piazza di Spagna,*

38, Piazza di Spagna ☎ *06/94515710* 🌐 *www.valentino.com* Ⓜ *Spagna.*

Versace

CLOTHING | Versace's Rome flagship is a gem of architecture and design, with Byzantine-inspired mosaic floors, futuristic interiors with transparent walls, and merchandise that has a sexy rocker-Gothic-underground vibe. Here you'll find apparel, accessories, and home furnishings in designs every bit as flamboyant as Donatella and Allegra (Gianni's niece). ✉ *Piazza di Spagna, 12, Piazza di Spagna* ☎ *06/6784600* 🌐 *www.versace.com* Ⓜ *Spagna.*

DEPARTMENT STORES

★ La Rinascente

DEPARTMENT STORE | **FAMILY** | Set in a dazzling, seven-story space, Italy's best-known department store is packed top to bottom with luxury goods, from cosmetics, handbags, and accessories to ready-to-wear designer sportswear to kitchen items and housewares. Even if you're not planning on buying anything, the basement excavations of a Roman aqueduct and the roof terrace bar with its splendid view are well worth a visit. There's also a location at Piazza Fiume. ✉ *Via del Tritone, 61, Trevi* ☎ *02/91387388* 🌐 *www.rinascente.it* Ⓜ *Barberini.*

HEALTH & BEAUTY

Modàfferi Barber Shop

HEALTH & BEAUTY | Run by two friendly brothers, who took over the business from their father, this barbershop is preferred by actors performing at the nearby Teatro Sistina. It was founded in the 1970s and still has charmingly retro decor. They offer haircuts, beard care, manicures, pedicures, facials, and massages and have their own line of products. For extra privacy, you can request the private room. ✉ *Via dei Cappuccini 11, Piazza di Spagna* ☎ *06/4817077* 🌐 *www.modafferibarbershop.it* Ⓜ *Barberini.*

JEWELRY

Bvlgari

JEWELRY & WATCHES | The jewelry giant Bvlgari is to Rome what Tiffany is to New York and Cartier is to Paris. In the middle of the 19th century, company founder Sotirio Bulgari began working as a silversmith in his native Greece and is said to have moved to Rome with less than 1,000 lire in his pocket. This store's temple-inspired interior pays homage to the jeweler's ties to both places. Downstairs, a gallery called DOMVS displays archival creations in themed exhibitions, often including jewels that belonged to jet-setters and movie stars like Elizabeth Taylor. ✉ *Via dei Condotti, 10, Piazza di Spagna* ☎ *06/696261* 🌐 *www.bulgari.com* ⏲ *Closed Wed.* Ⓜ *Spagna.*

SHOES

Braccialini

HANDBAGS | Founded in 1954 by Florentine stylist Carla Braccialini and her husband, Robert, this outfit makes bags that are authentic works of art in bright colors and delightful shapes, such as rotary phones or mountain chalets. Be sure to check out the eccentric Temi (Theme) creature bags; the snail-shaped version made out of python skin makes a true fashion statement. There is another location on Via dei Condotti. ✉ *Via Frattina, 117, Piazza di Spagna* ☎ *342/0338947* 🌐 *www.braccialini.it* Ⓜ *Spagna.*

Fausto Santini

SHOES | Shoe lovers with a passion for minimalist design flock to Fausto Santini to get their hands on his nerdy-chic footwear with its statement-making lines. An outlet at Via Cavour 106, named for Fausto's father, Giacomo, sells last season's shoes at a big discount. ✉ *Via Frattina, 120, Piazza di Spagna* ☎ *06/6784114* 🌐 *www.faustosantini.com* Ⓜ *Spagna.*

Giuseppe Zanotti

SHOES | Giuseppe Zanotti creates sought-after women's and men's shoes ranging from pencil-thin stilettos (often with a bit of sparkle or other bling) to colorful loafers to couture sneakers. The footwear here is placed on a literal pedestal so the craftsmanship can be admired from all angles. ✉ *Piazza di Spagna, 33, Piazza di Spagna* ☎ *06/69924220* 🌐 *www.giuseppezanotti.com* Ⓜ *Spagna.*

Repubblica and the Quirinale

This sector of Rome stretches down from the 19th-century district built up around the Piazza della Repubblica—originally laid out to serve as a monumental foyer between the Termini train station and the rest of the city—and over the rest of the Quirinale. The highest of ancient Rome's famed seven hills, the Quirinale is crowned by the massive Palazzo Quirinale, home to the popes until 1870 and now Italy's presidential palace. Along the way, you can see ancient Roman sculptures, early Christian churches, and highlights from the 16th and 17th centuries, when Rome was conquered by the Baroque—and by Bernini.

Although Bernini's work feels omnipresent in much of the city center, the Renaissance-man range of his creations is particularly notable here. The artist as architect considered the church of Sant'Andrea al Quirinale one of his best; Bernini the urban designer and water worker is responsible for the muscle-bound sea god who blows his conch so provocatively in the fountain at the center of whirling Piazza Barberini. And Bernini the master gives religious passion a joltingly corporeal treatment in what is perhaps his greatest work, the *Ecstasy of St. Teresa,* in the church of Santa Maria della Vittoria.

GETTING HERE AND AROUND

Located between Termini station and the Spanish Steps, this area is about a 15-minute walk from either. Bus No. 40 will get you from Termini to the Quirinale in two stops; from the Vatican take Bus No. 64. The very central Repubblica Metro stop is on the piazza of the same name.

Sights

Capuchin Museum
CEMETERY | Devoted to teaching visitors about the Capuchin order, this museum is mainly notable for its strangely touching and beautiful crypt under the church of Santa Maria della Concezione. The bones of some 4,000 friars are arranged in odd decorative designs around the shriveled and decayed remains of their kinsmen, a macabre reminder of the impermanence of earthly life. As one sign proclaims: "What you are, we once were. What we are, you someday will be."

Upstairs in the church, the first chapel on the right contains Guido Reni's mid-17th-century *Archangel St. Michael Trampling the Devil.* The painting caused great scandal after an astute contemporary observer remarked that the face of the devil bore a surprising resemblance to Pope Innocent X, archenemy of Reni's Barberini patrons. Compare the devil with the bust of the pope that you saw in the Palazzo Doria Pamphilj and judge for yourself. ✉ *Via Veneto, 27, Quirinale* ☎ *06/88803695* 🌐 *www.museoecriptacappuccini.it* 🎟 *€10* Ⓜ *Barberini.*

Fontana delle Api (*Fountain of the Bees*)
FOUNTAIN | The upper shell and inscription of this fountain, which is decorated with the famous heraldic bees of the Barberini family, are from a fountain that Bernini designed for Pope Urban VIII; the rest was lost when the fountain was moved to make way for a new street. The inscription caused considerable uproar when the fountain was first built in 1644. It said that the fountain had been erected in the 22nd year of the pontiff's reign, although, in fact, the 21st anniversary of Urban's election to the papacy was still

some weeks away. The last numeral was hurriedly erased, but to no avail—Urban died eight days before the beginning of his 22nd year as pope. The superstitious Romans, who had regarded the inscription as a foolhardy tempting of fate, were vindicated. ✉ *Piazza Barberini, Quirinale* Ⓜ *Barberini.*

★ MACRO

ART MUSEUM | Formerly known as Rome's Modern and Contemporary Art Gallery, and before that as the Peroni beer factory, this redesigned industrial space has brought new life to the gallery and museum scene of a city hitherto hailed for its "then," not its "now." The collection here covers Italian contemporary artists from the 1960s through today. The goal is to bring current art to the public in innovative spaces and, not incidentally, to support and recognize Rome's contemporary art scene, which labors in the shadow of the city's artistic heritage. After a few days—or millennia—of dusty marble, it's a breath of fresh air. **■ TIP→ Check the website for occasional late-night openings and events.** ✉ *Via Nizza, 138, Repubblica* ☎ *06/696271* 🌐 *www.museomacro.it* 🎫 *€6* 🕒 *Closed Mon.* Ⓜ *Castro Pretorio.*

★ Palazzo Barberini/Galleria Nazionale d'Arte Antica

ART MUSEUM | One of Rome's most splendid 17th-century buildings is a Baroque landmark. The grand facade was designed by Carlo Maderno (aided by his nephew, Francesco Borromini), but when Maderno died, Borromini was passed over in favor of his great rival, Gian Lorenzo Bernini. The palazzo is now home to the Galleria Nazionale d'Arte Antica, with a collection that includes Raphael's *La Fornarina,* a luminous portrait of the artist's lover (a resident of Trastevere, she was reputedly a baker's daughter). Also noteworthy are Guido Reni's portrait of the doomed Beatrice Cenci (beheaded in Rome for patricide in 1599)—Nathaniel Hawthorne called it "the saddest picture ever painted" in his Rome-based novel, *The Marble Faun*—and Caravaggio's dramatic *Judith Beheading Holofernes.*

The showstopper here is the palace's Gran Salone, a vast ballroom with a ceiling painted in 1630 by the third (and too-often-neglected) master of the Roman Baroque Pietro da Cortona. It depicts the *Glorification of Urban VIII's Reign* and has the spectacular conceit of glorifying Urban VIII as the agent of Divine Providence, escorted by a "bomber squadron" (to quote art historian Sir Michael Levey) of huge Barberini bees, the heraldic symbol of the family. ✉ *Via delle Quattro Fontane, 13, Quirinale* ☎ *06/4814591* 🌐 *www.barberinicorsini.org* 🎫 *€15, includes Galleria Corsini* 🕒 *Closed Mon.* Ⓜ *Barberini.*

★ Palazzo Massimo alle Terme

ART MUSEUM | The Museo Nazionale Romano, with items ranging from striking classical Roman paintings to marble bric-a-brac, has four locations: Palazzo Altemps, Crypta Balbi, the Museo delle Terme di Diocleziano, and this, the Palazzo Massimo alle Terme—a vast structure containing the great ancient treasures of the archaeological collection and also the coin collection. Highlights include the *Dying Niobid,* the famous bronze *Boxer at Rest,* and the *Discobolus Lancellotti.*

Among the museum's most intriguing attractions, however, are the ancient frescoes on view on the top floor. They're stunningly set up to "recreate" the look of the homes they once decorated, and their colors are remarkably preserved. You'll see stuccoes and wall paintings found in the area of the Villa Farnesina (in Trastevere), as well as those depicting a garden in bloom and an orchard alive with birds that once covered the walls of cool sunken rooms at Empress Livia's villa in Prima Porta, just outside the city. ✉ *Largo di Villa Peretti, 2, Repubblica* ☎ *06/39967700* 🌐 *www.museonazionaleromano.beniculturali.it* 🎫 *€8, or €12 for a combined ticket including access to Crypta Balbi, Museo delle Terme di*

Diocleziano, and Palazzo Altemps (valid for 1 wk) ⏲ *Closed Mon.* Ⓜ *Repubblica, Termini.*

Piazza del Quirinale

PLAZA/SQUARE | This strategic location atop the Quirinale has long been important. Indeed, it served as home of the Sabines in the 7th century BC—when they were deadly enemies of the Romans, who lived on the Campidoglio and Palatino (all of 1 km [½ mile] away). Today, it's the foreground for the presidential residence, Palazzo del Quirinale, and home to the Palazzo della Consulta, where Italy's Constitutional Court sits.

The open side of the piazza has a vista over the rooftops and domes of central Rome and St. Peter's. The Fontana di Montecavallo, or Fontana dei Dioscuri, has a statuary group of Dioscuri trying to tame two massive marble steeds that was found in the Baths of Constantine, which once occupied part of the Quirinale's summit. Unlike many ancient statues in Rome, this group survived the Dark Ages intact, becoming one of the city's great sights during the Middle Ages. The obelisk next to the figures is from the Mausoleo di Augusto (Tomb of Augustus) and was put here by Pope Pius VI in the late 18th century. ✉ *Piazza del Quirinale, Quirinale* Ⓜ *Barberini.*

Piazza della Repubblica

PLAZA/SQUARE | Often the first view that spells "Rome" to weary travelers walking from Termini station, this round piazza was laid out in the late 1800s and follows the line of the caldarium of the vast ancient public baths, the Terme di Diocleziano. At its center, the exuberant Fontana delle Naiadi (Fountain of the Naiads) teems with voluptuous bronze ladies happily wrestling with marine monsters. The nudes weren't there when the pope unveiled the fountain in 1888—sparing him any embarrassment—but when the figures were added in 1901, they caused a scandal. It's said that the sculptor, Mario Rutelli, modeled them on the ample figures of two musical-comedy stars of the day. The colonnades now house the luxe hotel Anantara Palazzo Naiadi and various shops and caffès. ✉ *Repubblica* Ⓜ *Repubblica.*

San Carlo alle Quattro Fontane

CHURCH | Sometimes known as San Carlino because of its tiny size, this is one of Borromini's masterpieces. In a space no larger than the base of one of the piers of St. Peter's Basilica, he created a church that is an intricate exercise in geometric perfection, with a coffered dome that seems to float above the curves of the walls. Borromini's work is often bizarre, definitely intellectual, and intensely concerned with pure form. In San Carlo, he invented an original treatment of space that creates an effect of rippling movement, especially evident in the double-S curves of the facade. Characteristically, the interior decoration is subdued, in white stucco with no more than a few touches of gilding, so as not to distract from the form. Don't miss the cloister: a tiny, understated Baroque jewel, with a graceful portico and loggia above, echoing the lines of the church. ✉ *Via del Quirinale, 23, Quirinale* ☎ *06/48907729* ⏲ *Closed Sun.* Ⓜ *Barberini.*

★ Santa Maria della Vittoria

CHURCH | Designed by Carlo Maderno, this church is best known for Bernini's sumptuous Baroque decoration of the Cappella Cornaro (Cornaro Chapel, the last on the left as you face the altar), which houses his interpretation of divine love in the *Ecstasy of St. Teresa.* Bernini's masterly fusion of sculpture, light, architecture, painting, and relief is a multimedia extravaganza, with the chapel modeled as a theater, and one of the key examples of the Roman High Baroque. The members of the Cornaro family meditate on the communal vision of the great moment of divine love before them: the swooning saint's robes appear to be on fire, quivering with life, and the white marble group seems

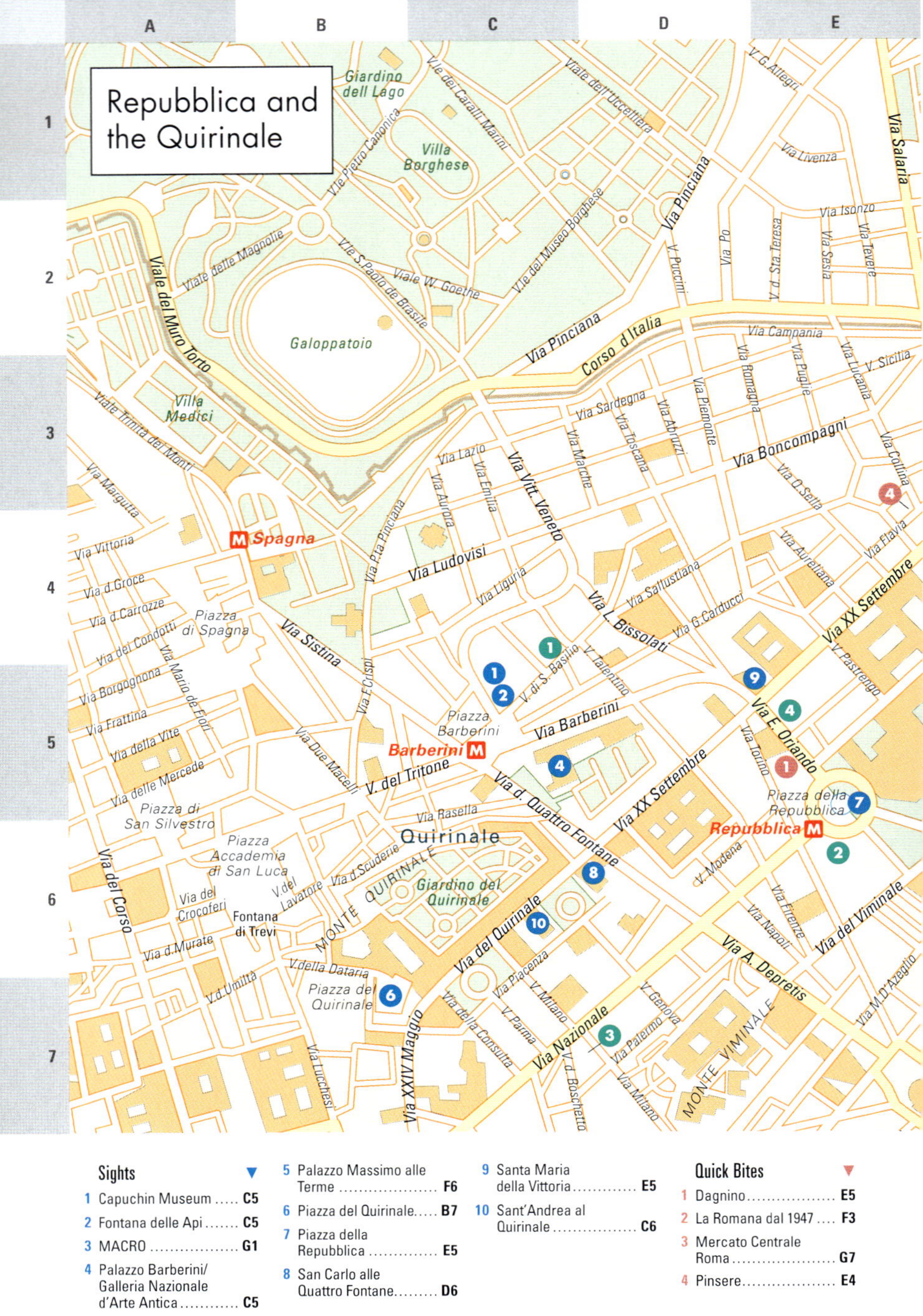

Sights

1 Capuchin Museum **C5**

2 Fontana delle Api **C5**

3 MACRO **G1**

4 Palazzo Barberini/ Galleria Nazionale d'Arte Antica **C5**

5 Palazzo Massimo alle Terme **F6**

6 Piazza del Quirinale..... **B7**

7 Piazza della Repubblica **E5**

8 San Carlo alle Quattro Fontane......... **D6**

9 Santa Maria della Vittoria............. **E5**

10 Sant'Andrea al Quirinale **C6**

Quick Bites

1 Dagnino.................. **E5**

2 La Romana dal 1947 .... **F3**

3 Mercato Centrale Roma...................... **G7**

4 Pinsere.................... **E4**

Hotels

1 Aleph Rome Hotel, Curio Collection by Hilton **C4**

2 Anantara Palazzo Naiadi Rome Hotel...... **E6**

3 Rome Times Hotel **D7**

4 The St. Regis Rome..... **E5**

suspended in the heavens as golden rays illuminate the scene. An angel assists as Teresa abandons herself to the joys of heavenly love. To modern eyes, Bernini's representation of the saint's experience may seem more earthly than mystical. As the visiting French dignitary Charles de Brosses put it in the 18th century, "If this is divine love, I know all about it." ✉ *Via XX Settembre, 17, Largo Santa Susanna, Repubblica* ☎ *06/42740571* Ⓜ *Repubblica.*

Sant'Andrea al Quirinale

CHURCH | Designed by Bernini, this small church is one of the triumphs of the Roman Baroque period. His son wrote that Bernini considered it his best work and that he used to come here occasionally, just to sit and contemplate. Bernini's simple oval plan, a classic form in Baroque architecture, is given drama and movement by the decoration, which depicts St. Andrew's martyrdom and ascension into heaven and starts with the painting over the high altar, up past the figure of the saint above, to the angels at the base of the lantern and the dove of the Holy Spirit that awaits on high. ✉ *Via del Quirinale, 30, Quirinale* ☎ *06/4819399* 🌐 *www.santandrea.gesuiti.it* ⏲ *Closed Mon.* Ⓜ *Barberini.*

Coffee and Quick Bites

Dagnino

$ | **BAKERY** | Hidden inside a covered arcade, this Sicilian pasticceria, which opened in 1955, has pastry cases filled with cannoli, cassata, cakes, and marzipan as well as savory items like sandwiches and arancini. Go for breakfast, and try the cornetto filled with ricotta and chocolate chips—this might be the only place in Rome where you can find it. **Known for:** Sicilian desserts; mid-century-modern design; cornetti filled with ricotta and chocolate chips. $ *Average main: €5* ✉ *Via Vittorio Emanuele Orlando, 75, Repubblica* ☎ *06/4818660* 🌐 *www.dagnino.com* Ⓜ *Repubblica.*

La Romana dal 1947

$ | **ICE CREAM** | **FAMILY** | In summer, the line at this gelateria stretches out the door and around the corner. Though it's a franchise that originated in Rimini, it's loved by Romans for its rich, creamy gelato made with organic milk, fresh fruit, nuts, and chocolate. **Known for:** reasonably priced; big portions; modern decor. $ *Average main: €3* ✉ *Via XX Settembre, 60, Repubblica* ☎ *06/42020828* 🌐 *www.gelateriaromana.com* Ⓜ *Repubblica.*

Mercato Centrale Roma

$ | **INTERNATIONAL** | **FAMILY** | This gourmet food hall is in the last place you'd expect—Termini Station—and it's great for a quick bite even if you're not catching a train. There are stalls from some of Rome's best food purveyors, including Stefano Callegari (of *trapizzino* fame), pizzaiolo Marco Quintili, and fritti by Arcangelo Dandini. **Known for:** gourmet food hall; trapizzino (stuffed triangle-shaped pizza dough) outpost; Sicilian specialties. $ *Average main: €12* ✉ *Termini Station, Via Giovanni Giolitti, 36, Esquilino* ☎ *06/46202900* 🌐 *www.mercatocentrale.it* Ⓜ *Termini.*

Pinsere

$ | **PIZZA** | **FAMILY** | In Rome, you'll usually find either pizza *tonda* (round) or pizza *al taglio* (by the slice), but there's also pizza *pinsa*—an oval-shaped individual pie that's a little thicker than the classic Roman pizza. Pinsere is mostly a take-out shop, with people eating on the street for their lunch break, so it's the perfect quick meal. **Known for:** budget-friendly options; seasonal toppings; mortadella and pistachio pizzas. $ *Average main: €6* ✉ *Via Flavia, 98, Repubblica* ☎ *06/42020924* 🌐 *www.pinsereroma.it* ⏲ *Closed weekends and 2 wks in Aug.* Ⓜ *Castro Pretorio.*

Hotels

Aleph Rome Hotel, Curio Collection by Hilton

$$$ | **HOTEL** | Fashionable couples and families tend to favor the Aleph, a former bank–turned–luxury hotel, where the motto seems to be "more marble, everywhere." The abundant facilities include a rooftop pool and bar, a cigar lounge, a lobby bar, the casual 1930s Restaurant for breakfast and lunch, and the more upscale Sky Restaurant. **Pros:** spa with Finnish sauna, hammam, and Jacuzzi; award-winning design; terrace with small pool. **Cons:** spa access is free only for guests in suites and Gold or Diamond Hilton Honors members; rooftop views don't showcase Rome's most flattering side; buffet breakfast not included. *Rooms from: €549* *Via San Basilio, 15, Quirinale* *06/4229001* *alephrome.com* *80 rooms and suites* *No Meals* *Barberini.*

Anantara Palazzo Naiadi Rome Hotel

$$$$ | **HOTEL** | You'll experience exquisite service and pampering at this neoclassical landmark on the Piazza della Repubblica built on the foundations of the Baths of Diocletian—it's now run by Anantara, a luxury hotel brand with roots in Thailand. **Pros:** top-notch concierge and staff; multiple romantic dining options; spa with both Asian- and European-style treatments. **Cons:** food and beverages are expensive; beyond the immediate vicinity of many sights; rooms are a different style than public spaces. *Rooms from: €750* *Piazza della Repubblica, 47, Repubblica* *06/489381* *www.anantara.com* *232 rooms* *Free Breakfast* *Repubblica, Termini.*

Rome Times Hotel

$$$ | **HOTEL** | This modern hotel has large, soundproofed rooms with contemporary furnishings, hardwood floors, and huge fluffy beds. **Pros:** late checkout if booked through site; free use of Samsung smartphone for calls and internet during your stay; large bright bathrooms. **Cons:** lower floors can be noisy; not much storage space in rooms; lighting in rooms is not optimal. *Rooms from: €425* *Via Milano, 42, Quirinale* *06/99345101* *www.rometimeshotel.com* *81 rooms* *No Meals* *Repubblica.*

★ The St. Regis Rome

$$$$ | **HOTEL** | Originally opened by César Ritz in 1894, this grande dame has a Belle Epoque lobby filled with classic and contemporary art, a ballroom with painstakingly restored ceiling frescoes, and an intimate library where you can sip a cup of tea or something stronger. **Pros:** houses the Roman location of international art gallery Galleria Continua; every room comes with 24/7 butler service; the library lounge serves a lovely afternoon tea. **Cons:** food and drinks are pricey; location is a bit far from most tourist sites; restaurant feels more like a lounge than a proper restaurant. *Rooms from: €800* *Via Vittorio E. Orlando, 3, Repubblica* *06/47091* *www.stregisrome.com* *161 rooms* *No Meals* *Repubblica.*

Performing Arts

★ Teatro dell'Opera

OPERA | The company at this theater, a far younger sibling of La Scala in Milan and La Fenice in Venice, commands an audience during its mid-November–May season. In the hot summer months, it moves to the Terme di Caracalla for an outdoor opera series. As you might expect, the oft-preferred performance is *Aida,* for its spectacle, which once included real elephants. The company has lately taken a new direction, using projections atop the ancient ruins to create cutting-edge sets. *Piazza Beniamino Gigli, 7, Repubblica* *06/481601, 06/4817003 tickets* *www.operaroma.it* *Repubblica.*

Villa Borghese and Environs

Touring Rome's artistic masterpieces while staying clear of its hustle and bustle can be, quite literally, a walk in the park. Some of the city's finest sights are tucked away in or next to green lawns and pedestrian piazzas, offering a breath of fresh air for weary sightseers, especially in the Villa Borghese park. One of Rome's largest, this park can alleviate gallery gout by offering an oasis in which to cool off under the ilex, oak, and umbrella pine trees. If you feel like a picnic, have an *alimentari* (food shop) make you some panini before you go; food carts within the park are overpriced.

GETTING HERE AND AROUND

The Metro stop for Piazza del Popolo is Flaminio on Line A. The Villa Giulia, the Galleria Nazionale d'Arte Moderna e Contemporanea, and the Bioparco in Villa Borghese are accessible from Via Flaminia, 1 km (½ mile) from Piazza del Popolo. Tram No. 19 and Bus No. 3 stop at each. Bus No. 160 and No. 628 connect Piazza del Popolo to Piazza Venezia. Bus No. 116 goes into Villa Borghese.

Sights

★ Galleria Borghese

ART MUSEUM | The luxury-loving Cardinal Scipione Borghese had this museum custom-built in 1612 as a showcase for his fabulous collection of both antiquities and more "modern" works. One of the collection's most famous works is Canova's neoclassical sculpture, *Pauline Borghese as Venus Victorious.* Nearby are three key early Baroque sculptures by Bernini: *David, Apollo and Daphne,* and *The Rape of Persephone.* You'll also find masterpieces by Caravaggio, Raphael (including his moving *Deposition*), Pinturicchio, Perugino, Bellini, and Rubens. Probably the gallery's most famous painting is Titian's allegorical *Sacred and Profane Love.* **TIP→ Admission to the Galleria Borghese is by reservation only. Visitors are admitted in two-hour shifts 9–5. Prime-time slots sell out days in advance, so reserve and directly (and early) through the museum's website.** ✉ *Piazzale Scipione Borghese, 5, off Via Pinciana, Villa Borghese* ☎ *06/32810 reservations, 06/8413979 info* 🌐 *www.galleriaborghese.beniculturali.it* 🎫 *€15, including €2 reservation fee; increased fee during temporary exhibitions* ⏲ *Closed Mon.* ✍ *Reservations essential.*

★ MAXXI—Museo Nazionale delle Arti del XXI Secolo (*National Museum of 21st-Century Arts*)

ART MUSEUM | Designed by the late Iraqi-British architect Zaha Hadid, this modern building plays with lots of natural light and has curving and angular lines, big open spaces, glass ceilings, and steel staircases that twist through the air—all meant to question the division between "within" and "without." The MAXXI hosts temporary exhibitions of art, architecture, film, and more. The permanent collection, displayed on a rotating basis, has more than 350 works from modern and contemporary artists, including Andy Warhol, Francesco Clemente, and Gerhard Richter. ✉ *Via Guido Reni, 4/A, Flaminio* ☎ *06/3201954* 🌐 *www.maxxi.art* 🎫 *€15* ⏲ *Closed Mon.* Ⓜ *Flaminio, then Tram No. 2 to Apollodoro.*

★ Museo Nazionale Etrusco di Villa Giulia (*National Etruscan Museum*)

ART MUSEUM | The world's most outstanding collection of Etruscan art and artifacts is housed in Villa Giulia, built around 1551 for Pope Julius III. Among the team called in to plan and construct the villa were Michelangelo and fellow Florentine Vasari. Most of the actual work, however, was done by Vignola and Ammannati. The villa's *nymphaeum*—or sunken sculpture garden—is a superb example of a refined late-Renaissance setting for princely pleasures. Among the most striking pieces are the terra-cotta statues, such as the *Apollo of Veii* and the serenely beautiful *Sarcophagus of the Spouses*; the cinematic frieze from a later temple (480 BC) in Pyrgi; the displays of Etruscan jewelry; and the beautiful gardens. ✉ *Piazzale di Villa Giulia, 9, Villa Borghese* ☎ *06/3226571* 🌐 *www.museoetru.it* 🎫 *€12* 🕓 *Closed Mon.* Ⓜ *Flaminio.*

★ Piazza del Popolo

PLAZA/SQUARE | **FAMILY** | With its obelisk and twin churches, this immense square marks what was, for centuries, Rome's northern entrance, where all roads from the north converged and where visitors, many of them pilgrims, got their first impression of the Eternal City. The desire to make this entrance to Rome something special was a pet project of popes and their architects for more than three centuries. Although it was once crowded with fashionable carriages, the piazza today is a pedestrian zone. At election time, it's the scene of huge political rallies, and on New Year's Eve, Rome stages a mammoth alfresco party here. ✉ *Piazza del Popolo* Ⓜ *Flaminio.*

★ Santa Maria del Popolo

CHURCH | Standing inconspicuously in a corner of the vast Piazza del Popolo, this church often goes unnoticed, but the treasures inside make it a must for art lovers. Bramante enlarged the apse, which was rebuilt in the 15th century on the site of a much older place of worship. Inside, in the first chapel on the right, you'll see some frescoes by Pinturicchio from the mid-15th century; the adjacent Cybo Chapel is a 17th-century exercise in decorative marble.

Raphael designed the famous Chigi Chapel, the second on the left, with vault mosaics—showing God the Father in Benediction—as well as statues of Jonah and Elijah. More than a century later, Bernini added the oval medallions on the tombs and the statues of Daniel and Habakkuk. Finally, the Cerasi Chapel, to the left of the high altar, holds two Caravaggios: *The Crucifixion of St. Peter* and *The Conversion of St. Paul*. Exuding drama and realism, both are key early Baroque works that show how "modern" 17th-century art can appear. Compare their style with the much more restrained and classically "pure" *Assumption of the Virgin* by Annibale Carracci, which hangs over the altar of the chapel. ✉ *Piazza del Popolo 12, near Porta del Popolo, Piazza del Popolo* ☎ *06/3610836* 🌐 *www.agostiniani.it* Ⓜ *Flaminio.*

★ Villa Borghese

CITY PARK | **FAMILY** | Rome's Central Park, the Villa Borghese was originally laid out as a recreational garden in the early 17th century by Cardinal Scipione Borghese. The word "villa" was used to mean suburban estate, of the type developed by the ancient Romans and adopted by Renaissance nobles. Today's gardens cover a much smaller area—by 1630, the perimeter wall was almost 5 km (3 miles) long. At the end of the 18th century, Scottish painter Jacob More remodeled the gardens into the English style popular at the time. In addition to the gloriously restored Galleria Borghese, the highlights of the park are Piazza di Siena, a graceful amphitheater, and the botanical garden on Via Canonica, where there is a pretty little lake as well as the neoclassical faux–Temple of Aesculapius, the Biopark zoo, Rome's own replica of London's Globe Theatre, and the Villa Giulia museum.

The Carlo Bilotti Museum (🌐 *www.museocarlobilotti.it*) is particularly attractive for Giorgio de Chirico fans, and there is more modern art in the nearby Galleria Nazionale d'Arte Moderna e Contemporanea. The 63-seat children's movie theater, Cinema dei Piccoli, shows films for adults in the evening. There's also Casa del Cinema, where film buffs can screen films or sit at the sleek, cherry-red, indoor-outdoor café (you can find a schedule of events at 🌐 *www.casadelcinema.it*). ✉ *Main entrances at*

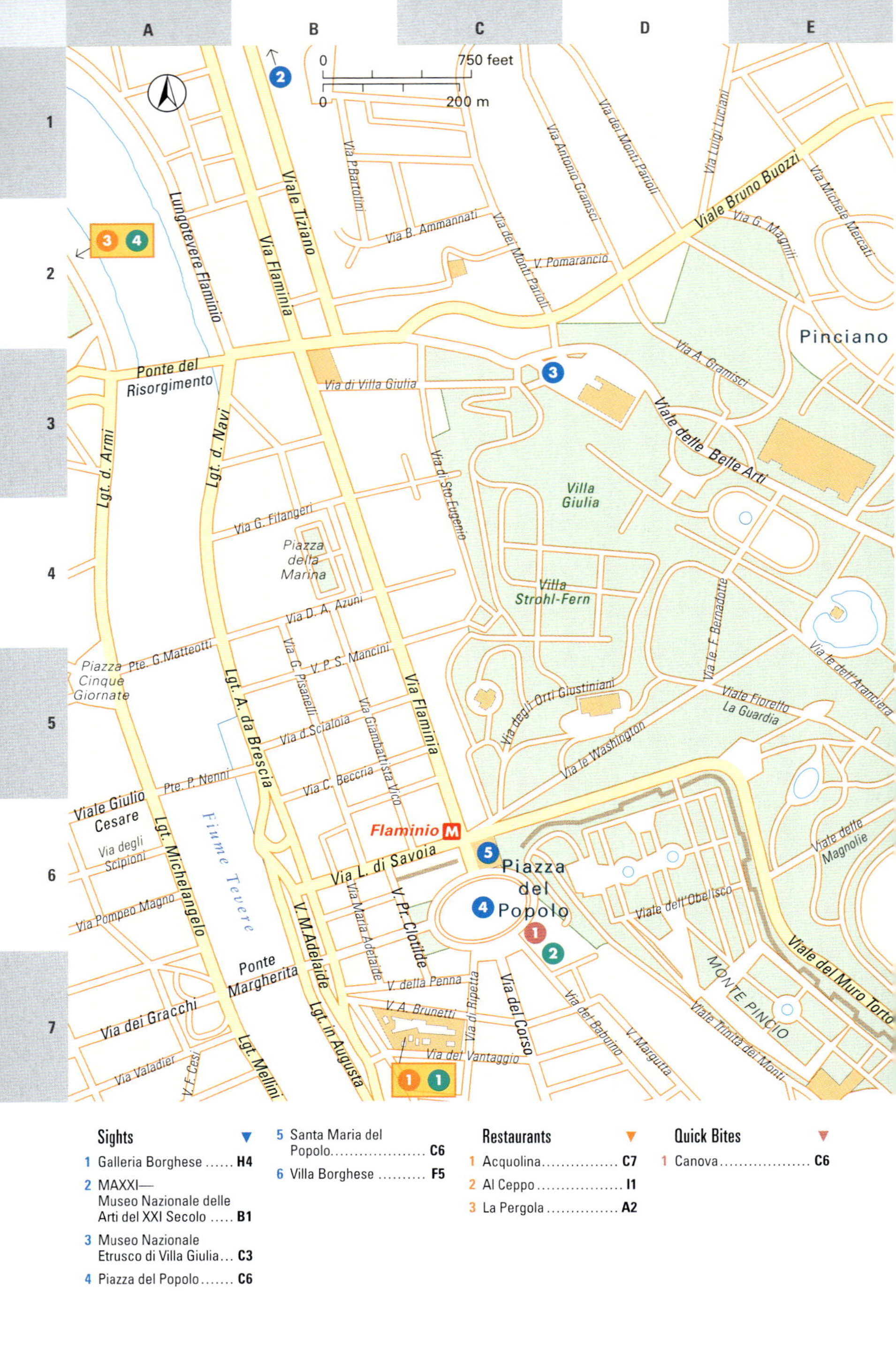

Sights

1 Galleria Borghese **H4**

2 MAXXI—Museo Nazionale delle Arti del XXI Secolo **B1**

3 Museo Nazionale Etrusco di Villa Giulia... **C3**

4 Piazza del Popolo **C6**

5 Santa Maria del Popolo.................... **C6**

6 Villa Borghese **F5**

Restaurants

1 Acquolina................ **C7**

2 Al Ceppo.................. **I1**

3 La Pergola **A2**

Quick Bites

1 Canova.................. **C6**

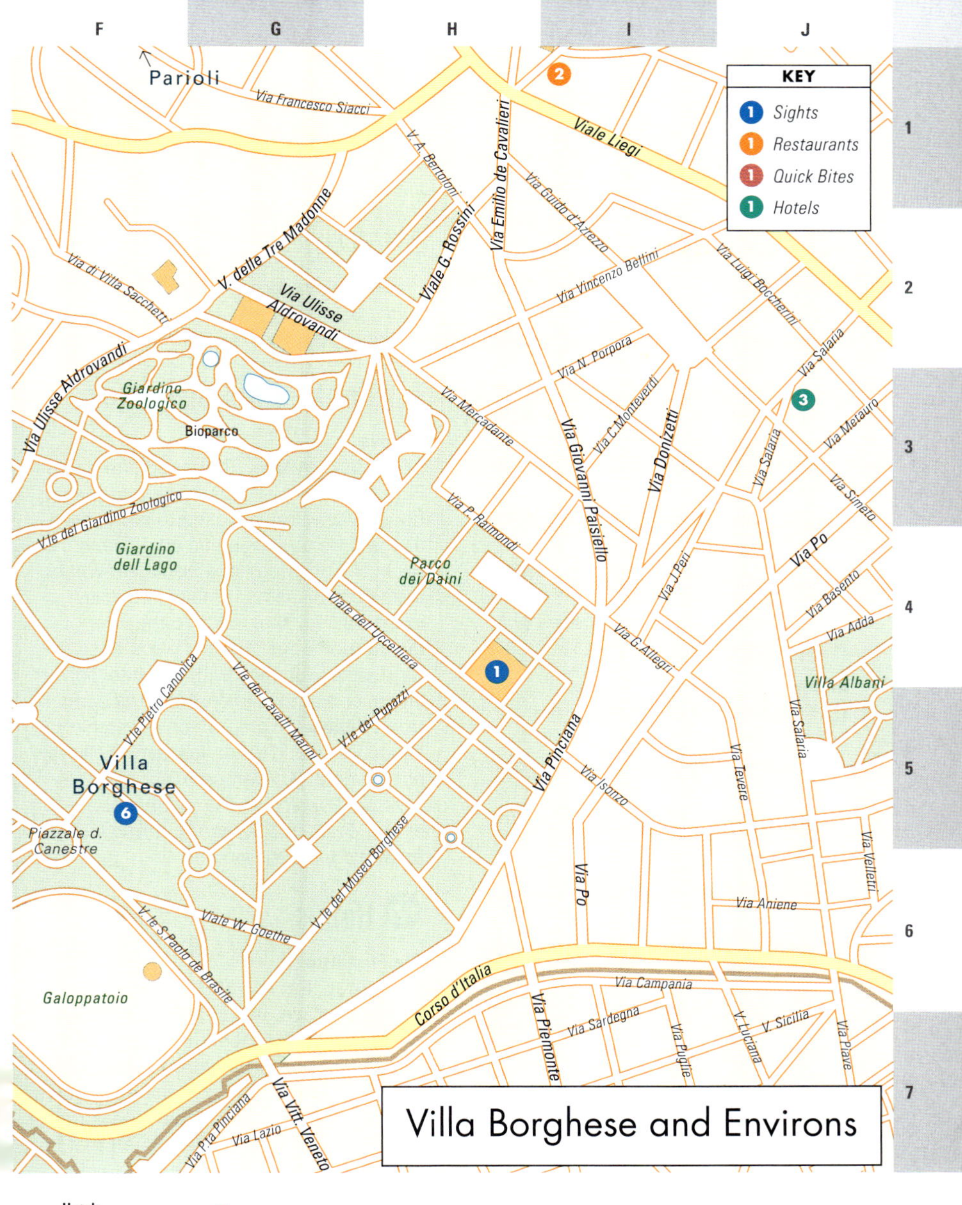

Hotels ▼

1 The First Arte **C7**

2 Hotel de Russie **C7**

3 The Hoxton, Rome **J3**

4 Rome Cavalieri, A Waldorf Astoria Hotel **A2**

Porta Pinciana, the Pincio, Piazzale Flaminio (Piazza del Popolo), Viale delle Belle Arti, and Via Mercadante, Villa Borghese Ⓜ *Flaminio.*

Restaurants

Acquolina

$$$$ | MODERN ITALIAN | This two-Michelin-starred restaurant turns out delicious and high-quality seafood dishes that surprise and evoke a sensory experience. Spaghetti is served with citrus and sea urchin, and all the dishes are artfully presented. **Known for:** elaborate, seasonal tasting menus; spaghetti with sea urchin; sophisticated desserts. *Average main: €220 ✉ The First Arte, Via del Vantaggio, 14, Piazza del Popolo ☎ 06/3201590 🌐 www.acquolinaristorante.it ⏲ Closed Sun. and Mon. ☞ Tasting menus only* Ⓜ *Flaminio.*

Al Ceppo

$$$ | ITALIAN | The well-heeled, the business-minded, and those with refined palates frequent this outpost of tranquility. The owners hail from Le Marche, the region northeast of Rome that encompasses inland mountains and the Adriatic coastline, so dishes from their native region feature alongside seafood and meats ready to be grilled. **Known for:** grilled meat and fish; authentic Le Marche cuisine; excellent wine list. *Average main: €32 ✉ Via Panama, 2, Villa Borghese ☎ 06/8419696 🌐 www.ristorantealceppo.it ⏲ No lunch Mon. Closed 3 wks in Aug.*

★ La Pergola

$$$$ | MODERN ITALIAN | Dinner here is a truly spectacular and romantic event, with incomparable views across the city matched by a stellar dining experience that includes top-notch service as well as sublimely inventive fare. The difficulty comes in choosing from among Michelin-starred chef Heinz Beck's *alta cucina* (high cuisine) specialties. **Known for:** fagotelli La Pergola stuffed with pecorino, eggs, and cream with guanciale and zucchini; award-winning wine list with 3,600 labels; weekend reservations that book up three months in advance. *Average main: €80 ✉ Rome Cavalieri, A Waldorf Astoria Resort, Via Alberto Cadlolo, 101, Monte Mario ☎ 06/35092152 🌐 www.romecavalieri.com ⏲ Closed Sun. and Mon., 3 wks in Jan., and 3 wks in Aug. No lunch Jacket required. No shorts.*

Coffee and Quick Bites

Canova

$ | ITALIAN | FAMILY | Esteemed director Federico Fellini, who lived around the corner on Via Margutta, used to come here all the time and even had an office in the back. His drawings and black-and-white stills from his films remain on display in the hallway that leads to the interior dining room, but the best place to sit for people-watching with a coffee, light lunch, or aperitivo is on the terrace out front. **Known for:** great people-watching; sandwiches and other light fare; Fellini's old hangout. *Average main: €15 ✉ Piazza del Popolo, 16, Piazza del Popolo ☎ 06/3612231 🌐 facebook.com/canovapiazzadelpopolo* Ⓜ *Flaminio.*

Hotels

The First Arte

$$$ | HOTEL | Set in a 19th-century neoclassical palace, this cozy boutique hotel was remodeled to feature high-tech, elegant guest rooms while keeping the core structure, including unique windows and tall ceilings, intact. **Pros:** fitness room with Technogym equipment; staff that is eager to please; more than 200 works of art by Italian artists on display. **Cons:** some rooms are on the small side; rooftop bar can get quite crowded; no spa. *Rooms from: €500 ✉ Via del Vantaggio, 14, Piazza del Popolo ☎ 06/45617070 🌐 www.pavilionshotels.com 26 rooms Free Breakfast* Ⓜ *Flaminio.*

★ Hotel de Russie

$$$$ | **HOTEL** | Occupying a 19th-century building that once hosted royalty, Picasso, and Cocteau, the Hotel de Russie is now the first choice in Rome for government bigwigs and Hollywood high rollers seeking ultimate luxury in a secluded retreat. **Pros:** big potential for celebrity sightings; well-equipped gym and world-class spa; excellent Stravinskij cocktail bar has outdoor tables on the Piazzetta Valadier. **Cons:** some rooms are small, especially for the price; breakfast not included; very expensive. *Rooms from: €1,700* *Via del Babuino, 9, Piazza del Popolo* *06/328881* *www.roccofortehotels.com* *117 rooms* *No Meals* *Flaminio.*

The Hoxton, Rome

$$$ | **HOTEL** | British brand The Hoxton's first foray into Italy is a design lover's dream filled with 1970s-inspired bespoke furniture, art tomes, and plants that transform the large lobby into intimate seating nooks perfect for socializing and coworking. **Pros:** stylish design; friendly staff; great food and drinks. **Cons:** far from main sights, with the closest Metro stop a mile away; rooms have little storage space for clothes; no gym or spa. *Rooms from: €417* *Largo Benedetto Marcello, 220, Parioli* *06/94502700* *www.thehoxton.com/rome* *192 rooms* *No Meals.*

Rome Cavalieri, A Waldorf Astoria Hotel

$$$ | **RESORT** | **FAMILY** | Set in a quiet residential neighborhood amid 15 acres of lush Mediterranean parkland, the Rome Cavalieri is a true hilltop oasis with magnificent views as well as three outdoor pools, one indoor pool, and a palatial spa. **Pros:** famed art collection, including a Tiepolo triptych from 1725; complimentary shuttle to city center; impressive on-site restaurant. **Cons:** you definitely pay for the luxury of staying here—everything is expensive; outside the city center; not all rooms have great views. *Rooms from: €490* *Via Alberto Cadlolo, 101, Monte Mario* *06/3509* *www.romecavalieri.com* *370 rooms* *No Meals.*

Nightlife

★ Stravinskij Bar at the Hotel de Russie

COCKTAIL BARS | This bar may be the best place in the city to sample la dolce vita. Celebrities, blue bloods, and VIPs hang out in the gorgeous Piazzetta Valadier where cocktails are well above par. There's also a selection of coffees, teas, healthy smoothies, and a full food menu if you need to refuel. It's especially popular for aperitivo, when canapés are served alongside the drinks. *Hotel de Russie, Via del Babuino, 9, Piazza del Popolo* *06/3288874* *www.roccofortehotels.com* *Flaminio.*

Performing Arts

★ Auditorium Parco della Musica

CONCERTS | Architect Renzo Piano conceived and constructed the Auditorium Parco della Musica, a futuristic complex made up of three enormous, pod-shaped concert halls, which have hosted some of the world's greatest music acts. The Sala Santa Cecilia is a massive hall for grand orchestra and choral concerts; the Sala Sinopoli is more intimately scaled for smaller troupes; and the Sala Petrassi was designed for alternative events. All three are arrayed around the Cavea (amphitheater), a vast outdoor Greco-Roman-style theater. The Auditorium also hosts seasonal festivals, including the Rome Film Fest. *Viale Pietro de Coubertin, 30, Flaminio* *06/80241281* *www.auditorium.com* *Flaminio, then Tram No. 2 to Apollodoro.*

Teatro Olimpico

THEATER | Part of Rome's theater circuit, the 1930s-era Teatro Olimpico is one of the main venues for cabaret, contemporary dance companies, visiting international ballet companies, and touring Broadway shows. *Piazza Gentile da Fabriano, 17, Flaminio* *349/2378200* *www.teatroolimpico.it* Ⓜ *Flaminio, then Tram 2 to Mancini.*

Shopping

★ Il Marmoraro

SPECIALTY STORE | This tiny shop is a hold-out of Via Margutta's days as a street full of artists and artisans. Sandro Fiorentino's father opened the shop in 1969 (he carved plaques like the one that marks Federico Fellini's house up the street), and Sandro still engraves the marble by hand. The shop is packed full of plaques, many with clever phrases, which make a great souvenir. Sandro will also engrave a message of your choice upon request. ✉ *Via Margutta, 53B, Piazza del Popolo* ☎ *335/6593612* ⏲ *Closed Sun.* Ⓜ *Spagna, Flaminio.*

Trastevere

Across the Tiber from the Jewish Ghetto is Trastevere (literally "across the Tiber"), long cherished as Rome's Greenwich Village and now subject to rampant gentrification. In spite of this, Trastevere remains about the most tightly knit community in the city, the Trasteverini proudly proclaiming their descent from the ancient Romans. Ancient bridges—the Ponte Fabricio and the Ponte Cestio—link Trastevere and the Ghetto to Isola Tiberina (Tiber Island), a diminutive sandbar and one of Rome's most picturesque sights.

GETTING HERE AND AROUND

From the Vatican or Spanish Steps, expect a 30- to 40-minute walk to reach Trastevere. From Termini station, take Bus No. 40 Express or No. 64 to Largo di Torre Argentina, where you can switch to Tram No. 8 to get to Trastevere. If you don't feel like climbing the steep Gianicolo, take Bus No. 115 from Largo dei Fiorentini, then enjoy the walk down to the northern reaches of Trastevere or explore the leafy residential area of Monteverde Vecchio on the other side of the hill.

Sights

Isola Tiberina (*Tiber Island*)

ISLAND | FAMILY | It's easy to overlook this tiny island in the Tiber, but you shouldn't. In terms of history and sheer loveliness, charming Isola Tiberina—shaped like a boat about to set sail—gets high marks. Cross onto the island via Ponte Fabricio, Rome's oldest remaining bridge, constructed in 62 BC. On the north side of the island crumbles the romantic ruin of the Ponte Rotto (Broken Bridge), which dates from 179 BC. Descend the steps to the lovely river embankment to see a Roman relief of the intertwined-snakes symbol of Aesculapius, the great god of healing.

In imperial times, Romans sheathed the entire island with marble to make it look like Aesculapius's ship, replete with a towering obelisk as a mast. Amazingly, a fragment of the ancient sculpted ship's prow still exists. You can marvel at it on the downstream end of the embankment. Today, medicine still reigns here. The island is home to the hospital of Fatebenefratelli (literally, "Do good, brothers"). Nearby is San Bartolomeo, built at the end of the 10th century by the Holy Roman Emperor Otto III and restored in the 18th century.

During summer, the island hosts an outdoor cinema, while its walkway is dotted with white tented bars and pop-up eateries. ✉ *Trastevere* ✣ *Isola Tiberina can be accessed by Ponte Fabricio or Ponte Cestio* Ⓜ *Bus No. 170.*

Palazzo Corsini

ART MUSEUM | A brooding example of Baroque style, the palace (once home to Queen Christina of Sweden) is across the road from the Villa Farnesina and houses part of the 16th- and 17th-century sections of the collection of the Galleria Nazionale d'Arte Antica. Among the star paintings in this manageably sized collection are Rubens's *St. Sebastian Healed by Angels* and Caravaggio's *St. John the Baptist.* Stop in if only to climb the 17th-century stone staircase, itself a drama of architectural shadows and sculptural voids. Behind, but separate from, the palazzo is the University of Rome's Orto Botanico, home to 3,500 species of plants, with various greenhouses around a stairway/fountain with 11 jets. ✉ *Via della Lungara, 10, Trastevere* ☎ *06/68802323 Galleria Corsini, 06/39967500 Galleria Corsini tickets, 06/49917107 Orto Botanico* 🌐 *www.barberinicorsini.org* 🎫 *€15 Galleria Corsini, including entrance to Palazzo Barberini within 20 days; €5 Orto Botanico* ⏲ *Closed Mon.* Ⓜ *Tram 8.*

★ Santa Cecilia in Trastevere

CHURCH | This basilica commemorates the aristocratic St. Cecilia, patron saint of musicians. One of ancient Rome's most celebrated early Christian martyrs, she was most likely put to death by the Emperor Diocletian just before the year AD 300. After an abortive attempt to suffocate her in the baths of her own house (a favorite means of quietly disposing of aristocrats in Roman days), she was brought before the executioner. But not even three blows of the executioner's sword could dispatch the young girl. She lingered for several days, converting others to the Christian cause, before finally dying. In 1595, her body was exhumed—it was said to look as fresh as if she still breathed—and the heart-wrenching sculpture by eyewitness Stefano Maderno that lies below the main altar was, he insisted, exactly how she looked.

The basilica is built atop the ruins of a Republican-age home that purportedly belonged to the martyr herself. It is possible to descend to the ruins, as well as to an underground gilt chapel via the bookstore. Time your visit in the morning to also enter the cloistered convent to see what remains of Pietro Cavallini's *Last Judgment,* dating from 1293. It's the only major fresco in existence known to have been painted by Cavallini, a contemporary of Giotto. To visit the frescoes, ring the bell of the convent to the left of the church entrance between 10 am and 12 pm. ✉ *Piazza di Santa Cecilia, 22, Trastevere* ☎ *06/45492739* 🌐 *www.benedettinesantacecilia.it* 🎫 *Frescoes €3, underground €2.50* ⏲ *Access to frescoes closed in the afternoon* Ⓜ *Tram 8.*

★ Santa Maria in Trastevere

CHURCH | Built during the 4th century and rebuilt in the 12th century, this is one of Rome's oldest and grandest churches. It is also the earliest foundation of any Roman church to be dedicated to the Virgin Mary. The 18th-century portico draws attention to the facade's 800-year-old mosaics, which represent the parable of the Wise and Foolish Virgins. They enhance the whole piazza, especially at night, when the church front and bell tower are illuminated.

With a nave framed by a processional of two rows of gigantic columns (22 in total) taken from the ancient Baths of Caracalla and an apse studded with gilded mosaics, the interior conjures the splendor of ancient Rome. Overhead is Domenichino's gilded ceiling (1617). The church's most important mosaics, Pietro Cavallini's six panels of the *Life of the Virgin,* cover the semicircular apse. Note the building labeled "Taberna Meritoria" just under the figure of the Virgin in the Nativity scene, with a stream of oil flowing from it; it recalls the legend that a fountain of oil appeared on this spot, prophesying the birth of Christ. Off the piazza's northern side is a street called Via delle Fonte dell'Olio in honor of this miracle. ✉ *Piazza Santa Maria in Trastevere, Trastevere* ☎ *06/5814802* 🌐 *www.santamariaintrastevere.it* Ⓜ *Tram 8.*

★ Villa Farnesina

CASTLE/PALACE | Money was no object to the extravagant Agostino Chigi, a banker from Siena who financed many papal

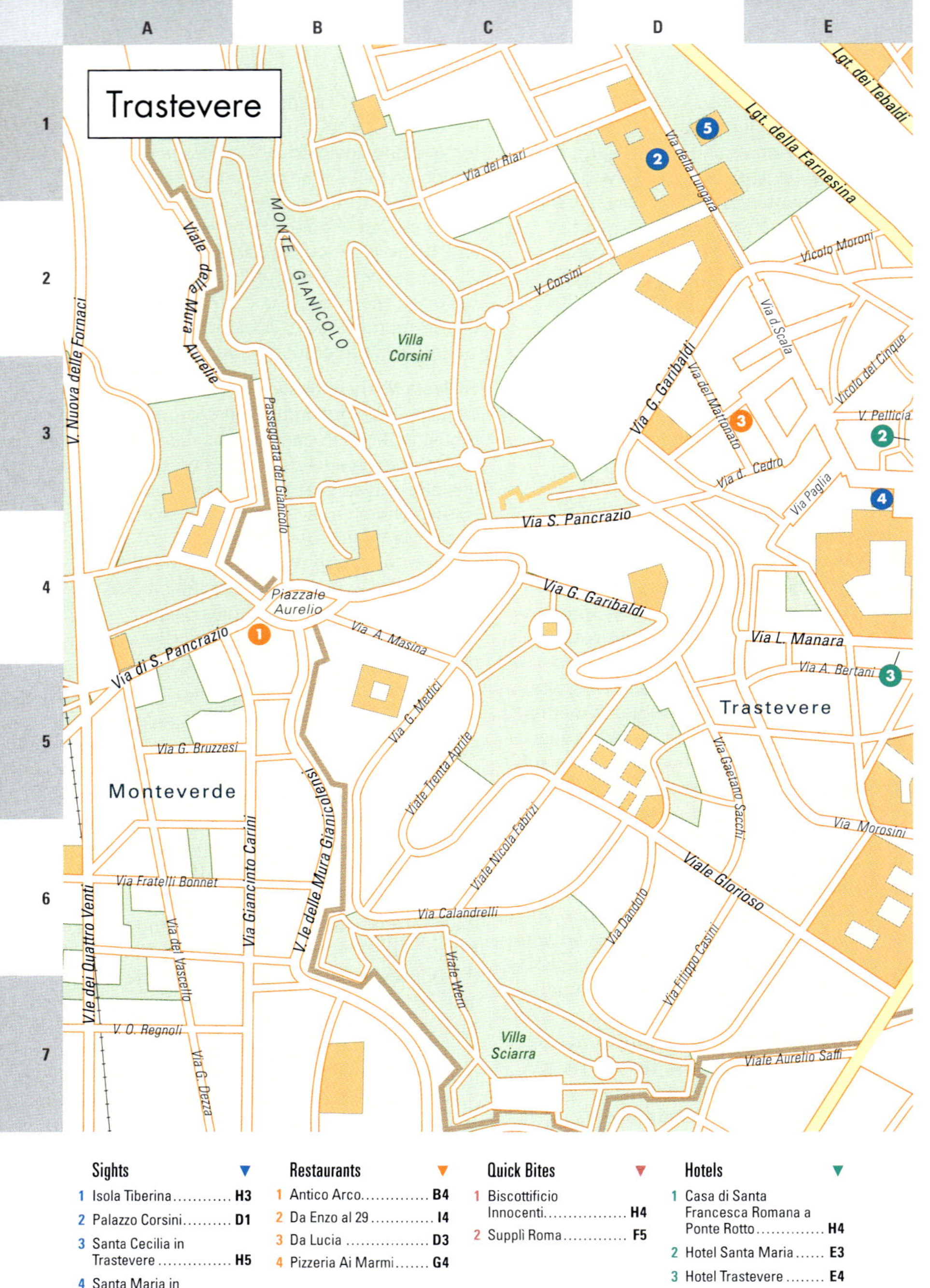

Sights

1 Isola Tiberina **H3**
2 Palazzo Corsini **D1**
3 Santa Cecilia in Trastevere **H5**
4 Santa Maria in Trastevere **E3**
5 Villa Farnesina **D1**

Restaurants

1 Antico Arco **B4**
2 Da Enzo al 29 .... **I4**
3 Da Lucia **D3**
4 Pizzeria Ai Marmi **G4**

Quick Bites

1 Biscottificio Innocenti **H4**
2 Supplì Roma **F5**

Hotels

1 Casa di Santa Francesca Romana a Ponte Rotto **H4**
2 Hotel Santa Maria **E3**
3 Hotel Trastevere **E4**
4 Relais Le Clarisse **F5**

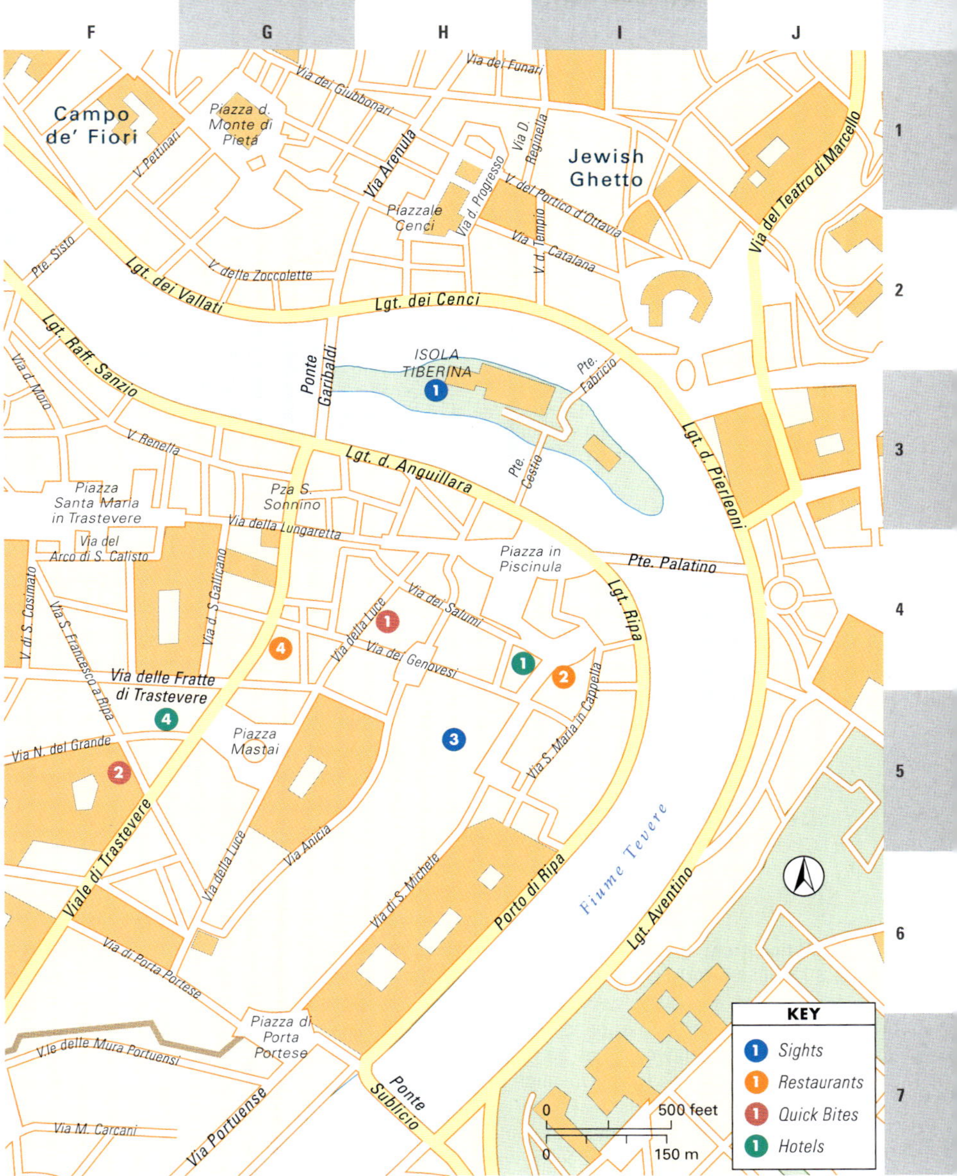
F
G
H
I
J
1
2
3
4
5
6
7
Campo de' Fiori
Piazza d. Monte di Pietà
Via dei Giubbonari
Via dei Funari
V. Pettinari
Via Arenula
Via D. Reginella
Jewish Ghetto
Via d. Progresso
V. del Portico d'Ottavia
Piazzale Cenci
Via Catalana
V. d. Tempio
Via del Teatro di Marcello
Pte. Sisto
V. delle Zoccolette
Lgt. dei Vallati
Lgt. dei Cenci
Lgt. Raff. Sanzio
Via d. Moro
Ponte Garibaldi
ISOLA TIBERINA
Pte. Fabricio
V. Renella
Lgt. d. Anguillara
Pte. Cestio
Lgt. d. Pierleoni
Piazza Santa Maria in Trastevere
Pza S. Sonnino
Via della Lungaretta
Via del Arco di S. Calisto
Piazza in Piscinula
Pte. Palatino
V. di S. Cosimato
Via S. Francesco a Ripa
Via d. S. Gallicano
Via della Luce
Via dei Salumi
Lgt. Ripa
Via dei Genovesi
Via delle Fratte di Trastevere
Via S. Maria in Cappella
Piazza Mastai
Via N. del Grande
Viale di Trastevere
Via della Luce
Via Anicia
Via di S. Michele
Porto di Ripa
Fiume Tevere
Lgt. Aventino
Via di Porta Portese
Piazza di Porta Portese
V.le delle Mura Portuensi
Via M. Carcani
Via Portuense
Ponte Sublicio
0
500 feet
0
150 m
KEY
Sights
Restaurants
Quick Bites
Hotels

projects. His munificence is evident in this elegant villa, built for him in about 1511. Agostino entertained the popes and princes of 16th-century Rome, impressing his guests at riverside suppers by having his servants clear the table by casting the precious silver and gold dinnerware into the Tiber (indeed, nets were unfurled a foot or two beneath the water's surface to retrieve the valuable ware).

In the magnificent Loggia of Psyche on the ground floor, Giulio Romano and others created the frescoes from Raphael's designs. Raphael's lovely *Galatea* is in the adjacent room. On the floor above you can see the trompe-l'oeil effects in the aptly named Hall of Perspectives by Peruzzi. Agostino Chigi's bedroom, next door, was frescoed by Il Sodoma with the *Wedding of Alexander and Roxanne,* which is considered to be the artist's best work. The palace also houses the Gabinetto Nazionale delle Stampe, a treasure trove of old prints and drawings. *Via della Lungara, 230, Trastevere 06/68027268 www.villafarnesina.it €10; €15 with special exhibits Closed Mon. Tram 8.*

Restaurants

★ Antico Arco

$$$ | **MODERN ITALIAN** | Founded by three friends with a passion for wine and fine food, Antico Arco attracts diners from Rome and beyond with its refined culinary inventiveness. The location on top of the Janiculum Hill makes for a charming setting, and inside, the dining rooms are plush, modern spaces, with whitewashed brick walls, dark floors, and black velvet chairs. **Known for:** changing seasonal menu; molten chocolate soufflé cake; extensive wine celler. *Average main: €35 Piazzale Aurelio, 7, Trastevere 06/5815274 anticoarco.it Closed Tues. Bus Nos. 75 and 115.*

★ Da Enzo al 29

$$ | **ROMAN** | In the quieter part of Trastevere, the family-run Da Enzo is everything you would imagine a classic Roman trattoria to be. There are just a few tables, but diners from around the world line up to eat here—a testament to the quality of the food. **Known for:** cacio e pepe (pasta with pecorino-cheese sauce and black pepper), carbonara, and other Roman classics; boisterous, authentic atmosphere; small space with long waits. *Average main: €24 Via dei Vascellari, 29, Trastevere 06/5812260 www.daenzoal29.com Closed Sun. and 2 wks in Aug. Tram 8.*

Da Lucia

$ | **ROMAN** | **FAMILY** | There's no shortage of old-school trattorias in Trastevere, but this one has a strong following. Both locals and expats enjoy the brusque but "authentic" service and the hearty Roman fare; snag a table outside in warm weather for the true Roman experience of cobblestone-terrace dining. **Known for:** bombolotti (a tubular pasta) all'amatriciana; homemade gnocchi; involtini (beef rolls). *Average main: €16 Vicolo del Mattonato, 2, Trastevere 06/5803601 Closed Mon.–Wed. and Aug. Tram 8.*

Pizzeria Ai Marmi

$ | **PIZZA** | **FAMILY** | This place is packed pretty much every night with diners munching on crisp pizzas that come out of the wood-burning ovens at top speed. It's best not to go during peak dining hours, so go early or late if you don't want to wait. **Known for:** excellent wood-oven pizzas; fried starters such as supplì (breaded fried rice balls); open until midnight for a late-night bite. *Average main: €13 Viale Trastevere, 53, Trastevere 06/5800919 www.facebook.com/aimarmi Closed Wed. and 3 wks in Aug. No lunch Tram 8.*

Coffee and Quick Bites

★ Biscottificio Innocenti

$ | **ITALIAN** | **FAMILY** | The scent of cookies wafts out into the street as you approach this family-run bakery, where a small team makes sweet treats the old-school way in a massive oven bought in the 1960s. There are dozens of varieties of baked goods, mostly sweet but some savory. **Known for:** old-school, family-run bakery; dozens of varieties of baked goods; brutti ma buoni ("ugly but good") hazelnut cookies. $ *Average main: €3* ✉ *Via della Luce, 21, Trastevere* ☎ *06/5803926* 🌐 *www.facebook.com/BiscottificioInnocenti* ⏲ *Closed Sun. and 3 wks in Aug.* Ⓜ *Tram 8.*

Supplì Roma

$ | **ROMAN** | **FAMILY** | Trastevere's best supplì (Roman-style rice croquettes) have been served at this hole-in-the-wall take-out spot since 1979. At lunchtime, the line spills out onto the street with locals who've come for the namesake treats, as well as fried baccalà fillets and stuffed zucchini flowers. **Known for:** old-fashioned baked pizza with spicy marinara sauce; gnocchi on Thursday (the traditional day for it in Rome); classic fried risotto ball with ragù or cacio e pepe. $ *Average main: €6* ✉ *Via di San Francesco a Ripa, 137, Trastevere* ☎ *06/5897110* 🌐 *www.suppliroma.it* ⏲ *Closed Sun. and 2 wks in Aug.* Ⓜ *Tram 8.*

Hotels

Casa di Santa Francesca Romana a Ponte Rotto

$ | **HOTEL** | In the heart of Trastevere but tucked away from the hustle and bustle of the medieval quarter, this basic, affordable hotel in a former monastery is centered on a lovely green courtyard and still has a chapel off the corridor. **Pros:** rates can't be beat; triple rooms for small groups; substantial breakfast buffet. **Cons:** a bit far from Metro, but there are tram and bus stops nearby; few amenities besides TV room and reading room; main door locks at midnight, requiring guests to ring the bell. $ *Rooms from: €165* ✉ *Via dei Vascellari, 61, Trastevere* ☎ *06/5812125* 🌐 *www.sfromana.it* *37 rooms* *No Meals* Ⓜ *Tram 8.*

Hotel Santa Maria

$$ | **HOTEL** | A Trastevere treasure with a pedigree going back four centuries, this ivy-covered, mansard-roofed, rosy-brick-red, erstwhile Renaissance-era convent—just steps away from the glorious Santa Maria in Trastevere church and a few blocks from the Tiber—has sweet and simple guest rooms: a mix of brick walls, "cotto" tile floors, oak furniture, and matching bedspreads and curtains. **Pros:** a quaint and pretty oasis in a central location; spacious rooms for groups; lovely rooftop terrace with views across the city. **Cons:** tricky to find; some noise from adjoining bedrooms; church bells may wake light sleepers. $ *Rooms from: €270* ✉ *Vicolo del Piede, 2, Trastevere* ☎ *06/5894626* 🌐 *www.hotelsantamariatrastevere.it* *20 rooms* *Free Breakfast* Ⓜ *Tram 8.*

Hotel Trastevere

$$ | **HOTEL** | This hotel captures the villagelike charm of the Trastevere district and offers basic, clean, comfortable rooms. **Pros:** good rates for location; convenient to tram and bus; friendly staff. **Cons:** rooms are a little worn around the edges; modest amenities; standard rooms are quite small. $ *Rooms from: €190* ✉ *Via Luciano Manara, 24/a, Trastevere* ☎ *06/5814713* 🌐 *www.hoteltrastevere.net* *14 rooms* *Free Breakfast* Ⓜ *Tram 8.*

Relais Le Clarisse

$$ | **B&B/INN** | Set within the former cloister grounds of the Santa Chiara order, with beautiful gardens, Le Clarisse makes you feel like you're staying at a close friend's villa, thanks to the comfortable size of the guest rooms and personalized service. **Pros:** spacious rooms with comfy beds; high-tech

showers/tubs with good water pressure; breakfast in the lush private courtyard. **Cons:** this part of Trastevere can be noisy at night; check when booking as you may be put in neighboring building; no restaurant or bar. *Rooms from: €250* *Via Cardinale Merry del Val, 20, Trastevere* *06/58334437* *www.leclarissetrastevere.com* *17 rooms* *Free Breakfast* *Tram 8.*

Nightlife

★ Freni e Frizioni

COCKTAIL BARS | This hipster hangout is great for a sunset aperitivo (the vegetarian buffet is hugely popular) or for late-night socializing. Though the vibe is artsy and laid-back, the bartenders take their cocktails seriously—and have the awards to prove it. In warmer weather, the crowd overflows into the large terrazza overlooking the Tiber and the side streets of Trastevere. *Via del Politeama, 4, Trastevere* *06/45497499* *www.freniefrizioni.com* *Tram 8.*

Shopping

BOOKSTORES

Almost Corner Bookshop

BOOKS | Bursting at the seams with not an inch of space left on its shelves, this tiny little bookshop is a favorite meeting point for English speakers in Trastevere. Irish owner Dermot O'Connell goes out of his way to find what you're looking for, and if he doesn't have it in stock he'll make a special order for you. The shop carries everything from popular best sellers to translated Italian classics, as well as lots of good books about Rome. *Via del Moro, 45, Trastevere* *06/5836942* *www.facebook.com/AlmostCornerBookshop* *Tram 8.*

MARKETS

Porta Portese

MARKET | **FAMILY** | One of the biggest flea markets in Italy welcomes shoppers in droves every Sunday from 7 am to 2 pm. Treasure seekers and bargain hunters love scrounging around the hundreds of tents for new and vintage clothing and accessories, antique furniture, used books, and other odds 'n' ends. Bring your haggling skills, and cash (preferably small bills—it'll work in your favor when driving a bargain); many stallholders don't accept credit cards, and the nearest ATM is a hike. *Via Portuense and adjacent streets between Porta Portese and Via Ettore Rolli, Trastevere* *Tram 8.*

Chapter 4

VENICE

Updated by
Liz Humphreys

WELCOME TO VENICE

TOP REASONS TO GO

★ **Cruising the Grand Canal:** The beauty of its palaces, enhanced by the play of light on the water, make a trip down Venice's "Main Street" unforgettable.

★ **Basilica di San Marco:** Don't miss the gorgeous mosaics inside—they're worth standing in line for.

★ **Santa Maria Gloriosa dei Frari:** Its austere, cavernous interior houses Titian's *Assumption*—one of the world's most beautiful altarpieces—plus several other spectacular art treasures.

★ **Gallerie dell'Accademia:** Legendary masterpieces of Venetian painting will overwhelm you in this fabled museum.

★ **Sipping wine and snacking at a bacaro:** For a sample of tasty local snacks and excellent Veneto wines in a uniquely Venetian setting, head for one of the city's many wine bars.

1 San Marco. The neighborhood at the center of Venice is filled with fashion boutiques, art galleries, and grand hotels.

2 Dorsoduro. This graceful residential area is home to renowned art galleries; the Campo Santa Margherita is a lively student hangout.

3 San Polo and Santa Croce. These bustling *sestieri* (districts) have all sorts of shops, several major churches, and the Rialto fish and produce markets.

4 Cannaregio. This sestiere has some of the sunniest open-air canal-side walks in town; the Jewish Ghetto has a fascinating history.

5 Castello. With its gardens, park, and narrow, winding walkways, it's the sestiere least influenced by Venice's tourist culture.

6 San Giorgio Maggiore and Giudecca. San Giorgio is graced with its magnificent namesake church, and Giudecca has wonderful views of Venice.

7 Islands of the Lagoon. Each island in Venice's northern lagoon has its own allure.

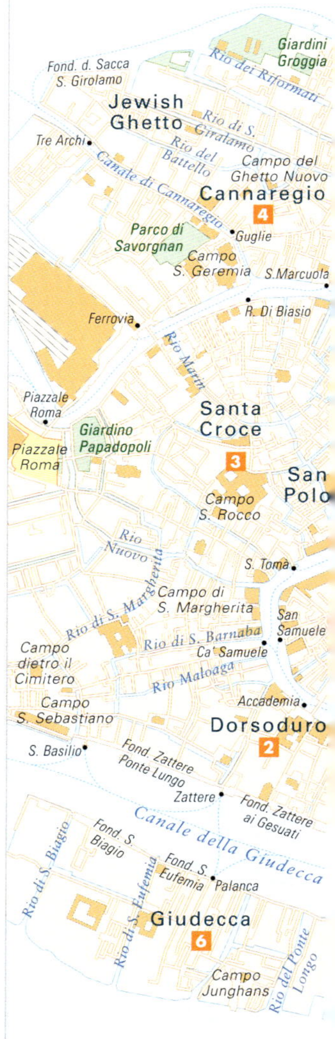

Sant'Alvise
Canale delle Navi
Madonna dell'Orto
Rio d. Zecchini
Rio della Sensa
Sacca della Misericordia
Canale della Misericordia
Fond. Nuove
Fond. Nuove
Rio di Noale
Rio dei Gesuiti
CIMITERO SAN MICHELE
Cimitero
7
Canale delle Fondamento Nuove
San Stae
Ca' d'Oro
Campo dei SS. Apostoli
Rio della Panada
Rio dei Mendicanti
Rio di S. Polo
Rialto Mercato
Riod di S. Giustina
Celestia
Bacini
Campo di S. Polo
Campo di S. Silvestro
Rialto
S.Silvestro
Grand Canal
Campo S. Maria Formosa
San Zaccaria
Darsena Grande
S. Angelo
Campo S. Angelo
Rio Canonica
Rio del Vin
Campo S. Zaccaria
Rio della Pietà
Campo dell' Arsenale
Rio dell' Arsenale
ISOLA DI S. PIETRO
5
Castello
Piazza San Marco
Campo S. Stefano
San Marco
Giardini Ex Reali
Rio di S. Moisè
1
San Zaccaria
Riva di Ca' di Dio
Arsenale
Tana
Rio della Tana
Rio di S. Daniele
Canale di S. Pietro
San Marco
Vallaresso
Riva S. Biagio
Via Giuseppe Garibaldi
Giglio
Salute
Canale di San Marco
Giardini Garibaldi
Riva dei Sette Martiri
Rio della Fornace
Fond. Zattere al Saloni
Campo S. Giorgio
S. Giorgio
S. GIORGIO MAGGIORE
Giardini
Giardini Pubblici
Fond. Zattere allo Spirito Santo
Campo Nanie Barbaro
Canale di S. Giorgio
6
Bacino di S. Giorgio
Riva dei Partigiani
Zitelle
Fond. delle Zitelle
Giardini di Castello
Redentore
Fond. della Croce
Fond. di S. Giacomo
R. d. Croce
LAGUNA VENETA

EATING AND DRINKING WELL IN VENICE

Pescheria (fish market)

The catchword in Venetian restaurants is "fish." How do you learn about the catch of the day? A visit to the Rialto's *pescheria* (fish market) is more instructive than any book, and when you're dining at a well-regarded restaurant, ask for a recommendation.

Traditionally, fish is served with a bit of salt, maybe some chopped parsley, and a drizzle of olive oil—no lemon; lemon masks the flavor. Ask for an entire wild-caught fish; it's much more expensive than its farmed cousin but certainly worth it. Antipasto may be prosciutto *di San Daniele* (from the Veneto region) or *sarde in saor* (fresh pan-fried sardines marinated with onions, raisins, and pine nuts). Risotto, cooked with shellfish or veggies, is a great first course. Pasta? Enjoy it with seafood: this is *not* the place to order spaghetti with tomato sauce. Other pillars of regional cooking include *pasta e fagioli* (thick bean soup with pasta); polenta, often with *fegato alla veneziana* (liver with onion); and that dessert invented in the Veneto, tiramisu.

GOING BACARO

You can sample regional wines and scrumptious *cicheti* (small snacks) in *bacari* (wine bars), a great Venetian tradition. Crostini and *polpette* (meat, fish, or vegetable croquettes) are popular cicheti, as are small sandwiches, seafood salads, *baccalà mantecato* (creamy, whipped salt cod), and toothpick-speared items like roasted peppers, marinated artichokes, and mozzarella balls.

SEAFOOD

Granseola (crab), *moeche* (tiny, locally caught soft-shell crabs), sweet *canoce* (mantis shrimp), *capelunghe* (razor clams), calamari, and *seppie* or *seppioline* (cuttlefish) are all prominently featured, as well as *rombo* (turbot), *branzino* (sea bass), *San Pietro* (John Dory), *sogliola* (sole), *orate* (gilthead bream), and *triglia* (mullet). Trademark dishes include sarde in saor, *frittura mista* (tempura-like fried fish and vegetables), and baccalà mantecato.

RISOTTO, PASTA, POLENTA

As a first course, Venetians favor the creamy rice dish risotto *all'onda* ("undulating," as opposed to firm), prepared with vegetables or shellfish. When pasta is served, it's generally accompanied by seafood sauces, too: *pasticcio di pesce* is lasagna-type pasta baked with fish, and *bigoli* is a strictly local whole-wheat pasta shaped like thick spaghetti, usually served *in salsa* (an anchovy-onion sauce with a dash of cinnamon), or with *nero di seppia* (cuttlefish-ink sauce). Pasta e fagioli is another classic first course, and polenta is a staple—served creamy or fried in wedges, generally as an accompaniment to stews or *seppie in nero* (cuttlefish in black ink).

Tiramisu

Linguine with clam sauce

VEGETABLES

The larger islands of the lagoon are known for their legendary vegetables, such as the Sant'Erasmo *castraure*, sinfully expensive but heavenly tiny white artichokes that appear for a few days in spring. Spring treats include the fat white asparagus from neighboring Bassano or Verona, and artichoke bottoms (*fondi*), usually sautéed with olive oil, parsley, and garlic. From December to March the prized local radicchio *di Treviso* is grilled and frequently served with a bit of melted Taleggio cheese from Lombardy. Fall brings small wild mushrooms called *chiodini* and *zucca di Mantova,* a yellow squash with a gray-green rind used in soups, puddings, and ravioli stuffing.

SWEETS

Tiramisu lovers will have ample opportunity to sample this creamy delight made from ladyfingers soaked in espresso and rum or brandy and covered with mascarpone cream and cinnamon. Gelato, *sgroppino* (prosecco, vodka, and lemon sorbet), and *semifreddo* (soft homemade ice cream) are other sweets frequently seen on Venetian menus, as are almond cakes and dry cookies served with dessert wine. Try *focaccia veneziana,* a sweet raised cake made in the late fall and winter.

Venice is often called La Serenissima, or "the most serene," a reference to the majesty, wisdom, and power of this city that was for centuries a leader in trade between Europe and Asia and a major center of European culture. Built on water by people who saw the sea as defender and ally, and who constantly invested in its splendor with magnificent architectural projects, Venice is a city unlike any other.

No matter how often you've seen it in photos and films, the real thing is more dreamlike than you could ever imagine. Its most notable landmarks, the Basilica di San Marco and the Palazzo Ducale, are exotic mixes of Byzantine, Romanesque, Gothic, and Renaissance styles, reflecting Venice's ties with the rest of Italy and with Constantinople to the east. Shimmering sunlight and silvery mist soften every perspective here; it's easy to understand how the city became renowned in the Renaissance for its artists' use of color. It's full of secrets, inexpressibly romantic, and frequently given over to pure, sensuous enjoyment.

You'll see Venetians going about their daily affairs in vaporetti, in the *campi* (squares), and along the *calli* (narrow streets). Despite their many challenges (including more frequent flooding and overcrowding), they are proud of their city and its history and are still quite helpful to those who show proper respect for Venice and its way of life.

Planning

Getting Here and Around

After arriving at Aeroporto Marco Polo (🌐 *www.veniceairport.it*), it's a mostly covered seven-minute walk to the dock where boats (🌐 *www.alilaguna.it*) depart for Venice's historic center. The ride is in a closed boat so you won't get much of a view; plus, it's more expensive and generally slower than the bus to Piazzale Roma (unless your hotel is near a boat station).

CAR

Venice is at the end of the SR11, just off the east–west A4 autostrada. There are no cars in Venice; if possible, return your rental when you arrive.

A warning: don't be waylaid by illegal touts, often wearing fake uniforms, who try to flag you down and offer to arrange parking and hotels; use one of the established garages, mainly clustered at Piazzale Roma. Consider reserving a space in advance. The **Autorimessa Comunale** (☎ *041/2722111* 🌐 *avm.avmspa.it*) costs €35 for 24 hours with online reservation. **Garage San Marco** (☎ *041/5232213* 🌐 *parclick.it*) €45 for 24 hours with online reservation. For brief stays, opt for **Parcheggio Sant'Andrea** (☎ *041/2727304* 🌐 *avm.avmspa.it*), where up to two hours costs €7. On its own island, **Isola del Tronchetto** (☎ *041/5207555* 🌐 *www.tronchettoparking.it*) charges €29 for 24 hours. Watch for signs coming over the bridge—you turn right just before Piazzale Roma.

Many hotels and the casino have guest discounts with the San Marco or Tronchetto garages. A perfectly convenient alternative is to park in Mestre, on the mainland, and take a train (10 minutes, €1.50) or bus into Venice. The garage across from the station and the Bus 2 stop costs €24 per day.

WATER BOATS AND TAXIS

Water buses are offered through ACTV (🌐 *actv.avmspa.it*). A *motoscafo* or water taxi isn't cheap: you'll spend about €70 for a short trip in town, €90 to the Lido, and €100 or more per hour to visit the outer islands. It is strongly suggested to book through the **Consorzio Motoscafi Venezia** (☎ *041/2406712* 🌐 *www.motoscafivenezia.com*) to avoid an argument with your driver over prices. A water taxi can carry up to 10 passengers, with an additional charge of €10 per person for more than four people, so if you're traveling in a group, it may not be that much more expensive than a vaporetto.

TRAIN

Venice has rail connections with many major cities in Italy and Europe. Note that Venice's train station is **Venezia Santa Lucia,** not to be confused with Venezia Mestre, which is the mainland stop prior to arriving in the historic center. Some trains don't continue beyond the Mestre station; in such cases you can catch the next Venice-bound train. Get a ticket on the Trenitalia app or a paper ticket from the kiosk on the platform and validate it (in the yellow time-stamp machine) to avoid a fine.

Getting Oriented

Venice proper is quite compact, and you should be able to walk across it in a couple of hours, even counting a few minutes for getting lost. Vaporetti will save wear and tear on tired feet but won't always save you much time.

Venice is divided into six sestieri: Cannaregio, Castello, Dorsoduro, San Marco, San Polo, and Santa Croce. More sedate outer islands float around them—San Giorgio Maggiore and Giudecca just to the south; beyond them the Lido, the barrier island; and to the north, Murano, Burano, and Torcello.

Hotels

Venetian magic lingers when you retire for the night, whether you're staying in a grand hotel or budget *locanda* (inn). Hotels usually occupy very old buildings, often without elevators or lounge areas. It's not at all unusual for each room to be different, even on the same floor: windows overlooking charming canals and bleak alleyways are both common. Venice is one of the most popular destinations on Earth—so book your lodging as far in advance as possible.

In terms of location, the area in and around San Marco is the most crowded and expensive. Still convenient but more tranquil areas include Dorsoduro, Santa Croce, and Cannaregio (though the area around the train station can be hectic), or even Castello in the area beyond the Pietà church. Also take into consideration the proximity of a vaporetto stop, especially if you have heavy baggage. Regardless of where you stay, it's essential that you have detailed directions to your hotel: note not only its street address but also its sestiere as well as a nearby landmark or two. Even if you arrive by water taxi, you may still have a bit of a walk.

⇨ *Hotel and restaurant reviews have been shortened. For full information, visit Fodors.com. Prices in the lodging reviews are the lowest cost of a standard double room in high season. Prices in the dining reviews are the average cost of a main course at dinner, or, if dinner is not served, at lunch.*

What It Costs in Euros

$	$$	$$$	$$$$
RESTAURANTS			
under €20	€20–€30	€31–€40	over €40
HOTELS			
under €175	€175–€400	€401–€600	over €600

Making the Most of Your Time

The hordes of tourists here are legendary, especially in spring and fall but during other seasons, too—there's really no "off-season" in Venice. Unfortunately, tales of impassable tourist-packed streets and endless queues to get into the Basilica di San Marco are not exaggerated. A little bit of planning, however, will help you avoid the worst of the crowds.

Most tourists do little more than take the vaporetto down the Grand Canal to Piazza San Marco, see the piazza and the basilica, and walk up to the Rialto and back to the station. You'll want to visit these areas, too, but do so in the early morning, before most tourists have finished their breakfast cappuccinos. Because many tourists are other Italians who come for a weekend outing, you can further decrease your competition for Venice's pleasures by choosing to visit the city on weekdays.

Away from San Marco and the Rialto, the streets and quays of Venice's beautiful medieval and Renaissance residential districts receive only a moderate amount of traffic. Besides the Grand Canal and the Piazza San Marco, and perhaps Torcello, the other historically and artistically important sites are seldom overcrowded. Even on weekends you probably won't have to queue up for the Gallerie dell'Accademia.

Starting in 2024, Venice introduced a tourist tax of €5 per day for daytrippers; visitors who stay overnight are exempt. For certain days (mostly Friday to Sunday) from April and July, you pay online and get a QR code proving payment. The tax increases to €10 per day if you pay less than four days before your visit (🌐 *cda.veneziaunica.it/en/access-fee*).

Nightlife

Nightlife offerings in Venice are, even by rather sedate standards, fairly tame. Most bars must close by midnight, especially those that offer outdoor seating. Piazza San Marco is a popular meeting place in nice weather, when the cafés stay open relatively late and all seem to compete to offer the best live music. The younger crowd, Venetians and visitors alike, tend to gravitate toward the area around the Ponte di Rialto, with Campi San Bartolomeo and San Luca on one side and Campo Rialto Nuovo on the other. Especially popular with university students and young people from the mainland are the bars around Campo Santa Margherita.

Passes and Discounts

Avoid lines and hassle with the online **Venezia Unica City Pass** (🌐 *www.veneziaunica.it*). This all-in-one pass can be used for public transportation and entry to museums, churches, and other attractions; you only pay for the services you wish to add. You'll receive an email with the pass, which you can show for entry at sights, though you'll still need to physically collect your transportation pass at an ACTV automatic ticket machine or ticket point located around the city.

Fifteen of Venice's most significant churches covered by the Venezia Unica City Pass are part of the **Chorus Foundation** umbrella group (☎ *041/2750462* 🌐 *www.chorusvenezia.org*), which coordinates their administration, hours, and admission fees. Churches in this group are open to visitors every day except Sunday. Single church entry costs €3.50; you have a year to visit all 20 with the €14 Chorus Pass, which you can get at any participating church or online.

The Museum Pass (€40) from **Musei Civici** (☎ *041/2405211* 🌐 *www.visitmuve.it/en/tickets*) includes single entry to 11 Venice city museums for six months.

Performing Arts

Visit 🌐 *www.agendavenezia.org* for a preview of musical, artistic, and sporting events. *Venezia News* (*VENews*), available at newsstands, has similar information but also includes in-depth articles about noteworthy events. The tourist office publishes a handy, free quarterly *Calendar* in Italian and English, listing daily events and current museum and venue hours. *Venezia da Vivere* (🌐 *www.veneziadavivere.com*) is a seasonal guide listing cool cultural happenings and places. And don't ignore the posters you see plastered on the walls as you walk—often they contain the most up-to-date information you can find.

⇨ *For more information on festivals in Venice, see On the Calendar in Travel Smart.*

CARNEVALE

Although Carnevale has traditionally been associated with the time leading up to the Roman Catholic period of Lent, it originally started out as a principally secular annual period of partying and feasting to celebrate Venice's victory over Ulrich II, Patriarch of Aquileia, in 1162. To commemorate the annual tribute Ulrich was forced to pay, a bull and 12 pigs were slaughtered in Piazza San Marco each year on the day before Lent. Since then, the city has marked the days preceding *Quaresima* (Lent) with abundant feasting and wild celebrations. The word *carnevale* is derived from the words *carne* (meat) and *levare* (to remove), as eating meat was restricted during Lent. The use of masks for Carnevale was first mentioned in 1268, and its direct association with Lent was not made until the end of the 13th century.

Venice earned its international reputation as the "city of Carnevale" in the 18th century, when partying would begin several months before Lent and the city seemed to be one continuous masquerade. During this time, income from tourists became a major source of funds in La Serenissima's coffers. With the Republic's fall in 1797, Carnevale was prohibited by the French and the Austrians. From Italian reunification in 1866 until the fall of Fascism in the 1940s, the event was alternately allowed or banned, depending on the government's stance.

It was revived for good in the 1970s, when residents began taking to the calli and campi in their own impromptu celebrations. It didn't take long for the tourist industry to embrace Carnevale as a means to stimulate business in low season. And their faith is well placed: each year over the 10- to 12-day Carnevale period (ending on the Tuesday before Ash Wednesday), more than a half-million people attend concerts, theater and street performances, masquerade balls, historical processions, fashion shows, and contests. Stop by any tourist office (☎ *041/2424* 🌐 *www.veneziaunica.it*) for information, but be aware it can be mobbed. If you're not planning on joining in the revelry, you'd be wise to choose another time to visit Venice. Crowds throng the streets (which become one-way, with police directing foot traffic), bridges are designated "no-stopping" zones to avoid gridlock, and prices skyrocket.

Restaurants

Dining options in Venice range from ultrahigh-end establishments, where jackets are required, to very casual eateries. Once staunchly traditional, many restaurants have revamped their dining rooms and their menus, creating dishes that blend classic elements with ingredients and methods less common to the region. Mid- and upper-range restaurants often offer innovative options as well as mainstays.

Unfortunately, Venice also has its share of overpriced, mediocre eateries. Restaurants catering to tourists have little motivation to maintain quality since most diners are one-time patrons. You are better off at a restaurant frequented by locals, who are interested in the food, not the views. Avoid places with cajoling waiters outside, as well as those that don't display their prices or have showy tourist menus translated into a dozen languages. For the same €15–€20 you'd spend at such places, you could do better at a bacaro making a meal of cicheti.

Shopping

Alluring shops abound in Venice. You'll find countless vendors of such trademark wares as glass, lace, and high-end textiles. The authenticity of some goods can be suspect, but they're often pleasing to the eye, regardless of origin. You will also find interesting craft and art studios with high-quality, one-of-a-kind articles. Antiques, especially antique Venetian glass, are almost invariably cheaper outside of Venice, because Venetians are ready to pay high prices for their own heritage.

The San Marco area is full of shops and couture boutiques, such as Armani, Missoni, Valentino, Fendi, and Versace. Leading from Piazza San Marco, you'll find some of Venice's busiest shopping streets—Le Mercerie, the Frezzeria, Calle dei Fabbri, and Calle Larga XXII Marzo. Other good shopping areas surround Calle del Teatro and Campi San Salvador, Manin, San Fantin, and San Bartolomeo. You can find somewhat less expensive, more varied, and more imaginative shops between the Ponte di Rialto and San Polo and in Santa Croce, and art galleries in Dorsoduro from the Salute to the Accademia. Regular store hours are usually 9 to 12:30 and 3:30 or 4 to 7:30; some stores close Saturday afternoon or Monday morning.

Tours

Venice has a variety of tours with expert guides; just be sure to choose a guide that's authorized if you book a private tour. Some excursions also include a boat tour as a portion of a longer walking tour. And, of course, a gondola ride is always an excellent way to take in the sights of the city.

GONDOLA RIDES

The best location to hire a gondola depends on your preference. For a waterside view of Grand Canal palaces, board a boat at one of the main gondola stations, such as Santa Maria del Giglio or San Toma. For a quieter experience, start your tour from a peaceful *fondamenta* (quay) in Cannaregio or Castello, like the Fondamenta S. Severo. The price of a 30-minute ride is €90 for up to six passengers, increasing to €110 between 7 pm and 3 am. Every 20 minutes extra is an additional €40. ■ **TIP➔ Agree with your gondolier on price and duration of the ride beforehand to avoid confusion and unexpected costs.**

PRIVATE TOURS

A Guide in Venice

GUIDED TOURS | This popular company offers a wide variety of innovative, entertaining, and informative themed tours—including master artisan, art, and architecture tours—for private groups of up to eight people. Guided tours generally last two to three hours, with a fee of €90 per hour, which does not include admissions or transportation fees. ☎ *0348/5927974* 🌐 *www.aguideinvenice.com.*

See Venice

GUIDED TOURS | Luisella Romeo is a delightful guide capable of bringing to life even the most convoluted aspects of Venice's art and history. She can customize tours depending on guests' areas of interest, including Murano and glass art, music in Venice, and photography. ☎ *0349/0848303* 🌐 *www.seevenice.it.*

Walks Inside Venice

GUIDED TOURS | For a host of particularly creative group and private tours—from history to art to gastronomy—check out Walks Inside Venice. The maximum group size is six, and tour guides include people with advanced university degrees and published authors. ☎ *0342/1665205,* 🌐 *www.walksinsidevenice.com.*

Visitor Information

The multilingual staff of the Venice tourism office (☎ *041/2424* 🌐 *www.veneziaunica.it*) can provide directions and up-to-the-minute information. Branches can be found at Marco Polo Airport; the Venezia Santa Lucia train station; Garage Comunale, on Piazzale Roma; and at Piazza San Marco near Museo Correr at the southwest corner. The train station branch is open daily 7:10 am–9 pm; other branches have similar hours.

San Marco

Extending from Piazza San Marco (St. Mark's Square) to the Ponte di Rialto, this sestiere is the historical and commercial heart of Venice. Restaurants in its eponymous square—the only one in Venice given full stature as a "piazza" and, hence, often referred to simply as "the Piazza"—heave with tourists, but enjoying an *aperitivo* (pre-dinner drink) here is an unforgettable experience.

This sestiere is also graced with some of Venice's loveliest churches, best-endowed museums, and finest hotels (often with Grand Canal views). In addition, it's the city's main shopping district. Some of the famous Venetian glass producers from Murano have boutiques in San Marco, as do many Italian designers. Its maze of streets is also lined with shops that sell elegantly wrought jewelry among other items.

TIMING

You can easily spend several days seeing the historical and artistic monuments in and around Piazza San Marco alone, but at a bare minimum, plan on at least an hour for the basilica and its wonderful mosaics. Add on another half hour if you want to see its Pala d'Oro, Galleria, and Museo di San Marco. You'll want at least an hour to appreciate the Palazzo Ducale. Leave another hour for the Museo Correr, through which you also enter the archaeological museum and the Libreria Sansoviniana. If you choose to simply take in the piazza itself from a café table at an establishment with an orchestra, keep in mind there will be an additional charge for the music.

★ Basilica di San Marco

(St. Mark's Basilica)

CHURCH | The Basilica di San Marco is not only the religious center of a great city, but also an expression of the political, intellectual, and economic aspiration and accomplishments of a place that, for centuries, was at the forefront of European culture. It is a monument not just to the glory of God, but also to the glory of Venice. The basilica was the doges' personal chapel, linking its religious function to the political life of the city, and was endowed with all the riches the Republic's admirals and merchants could carry off from the Orient (as the Byzantine Empire was then known), earning it the nickname "Chiesa d'Oro" (Golden Church). The glory of the basilica is, of course, its medieval mosaic work; about 30% of the mosaics survive in something close to their original form. The earliest date from the late 12th century, but the great majority date from the 13th century. A 4th- or 5th-century treasure—the Cotton Genesis, the earliest illustrated Bible—was brought from Constantinople and supplied the designs for the exquisite mosaics of the Creation and the stories of Abraham, Joseph, and Moses that adorn the narthex (entrance hall). Remember that this is a sacred place: guards may deny admission to people in shorts, sleeveless dresses, and tank tops. ✉ *Piazza San Marco, San Marco 328, San Marco* ☎ *041/2708311* 🌐 *www.basilicasanmarco.it* 🎟 *Basilica €6; Basilica and Pala d'Oro €12; Basilica and museum €15; museum and Loggia dei Cavalli €10; Basilica, Pala d'Oro, museum, and Loggia dei Cavalli €20; bell tower €10* ⏲ *Basilica and Pala d'Oro closed for tourist visits (church services only) Sun. till 2 pm* Ⓜ *Vaporetto: Zaccaria, Vallaresso.*

Campanile di San Marco

(St. Mark's Bell Tower)

VIEWPOINT | Construction of Venice's famous brick bell tower (325 feet tall, plus the angel) began in the 9th century; it took on its present form in 1514. During the 15th century, the tower was used as a place of punishment: immoral clerics were suspended in wooden cages from the tower, some forced to subsist on bread and water for as long as a year; others were left to starve. In 1902, the tower unexpectedly collapsed, taking with it Jacopo Sansovino's marble loggia (1537–49) at its base. The largest original bell, called the Marangona, survived. The crushed loggia was promptly reconstructed, and the new tower, rebuilt to the old plan, reopened in 1912. On a clear day the stunning view includes the Lido, the lagoon, and the mainland as far as the Alps, but strangely enough, none of the myriad canals that snake through the city. ✉ *Piazza San Marco, San Marco* ☎ *041/2708311* 🌐 *www.basilicasanmarco.it* 🎟 *€12* Ⓜ *Vaporetto: San Zaccaria, Vallaresso.*

★ Museo Correr

HISTORY MUSEUM | This museum of Venetian art and history contains an impressive sculpture collection by Antonio Canova and important paintings by Giovanni Bellini, Vittore Carpaccio (Carpaccio's famous painting of the Venetian courtesans is here), and other major local painters in the Neoclassical Rooms and Picture Gallery. The museum's highlights are the 20 sumptuously decorated and meticulously restored Royal Rooms, home to three ruling dynasties from the 19th century to 1920, and where Sissi, the empress of Austria, once stayed; English visits take place at 10:30 am and 3:30 pm daily and can be booked online. Several rooms also convey the city's proud naval history through highly descriptive paintings and numerous maritime objects, including ships' cannons and some surprisingly large iron mast-top navigation lights. ✉ *Piazza San Marco*

52, Ala Napoleonica, opposite Basilica, San Marco ☎ 041/2405211 🌐 correr.visitmuve.it 🎫 Royal Rooms Itinerary Ticket €14, including Museo Correr, Museo Archeologico, and Biblioteca Nazionale Marciana (book online in advance). Museums of San Marco Pass €30 (€25 when booked online at least 30 days in advance), includes Museo Correr, Museo Archeologico, Biblioteca Nazionale Marciana, and Palazzo Ducale. Museum Pass €40, includes all four museums plus seven civic museums. Royal Rooms tour only, €5 with Museums of San Marco Pass or Museum Pass Ⓜ Vaporetto: San Zaccaria, Vallaresso.

★ **Palazzo Ducale** (*Doge's Palace*)

CASTLE/PALACE | Rising majestically above Piazzetta San Marco, this Gothic fantasia of pink-and-white marble—the doges' residence from the 10th century and the central administrative center of the Venetian Republic—is a majestic expression of Venetian prosperity and power. Upon entering, you'll find yourself in an immense courtyard with some of the first evidence of Venice's Renaissance architecture, including Antonio Rizzo's 15th-century Scala dei Giganti (Stairway of the Giants). The palace's sumptuous chambers have walls and ceilings covered with works by Venice's greatest artists. In the Anticollegio you'll find *The Rape of Europa* by Veronese and Tintoretto's *Bacchus and Ariadne Crowned by Venus*. The ceiling of the Sala del Senato (Senate Chamber), featuring *The Triumph of Venice* by Tintoretto, is magnificent, but it's dwarfed by his masterpiece *Paradise* in the Sala del Maggiore Consiglio (Great Council Hall), the world's largest oil painting. The popular Secret Itineraries tour lets you visit the doge's private apartments and hidden passageways. ✉ *Piazza San Marco 1, San Marco* ☎ *041/2715911* 🌐 *palazzoducale.visitmuve.it* 🎫 *Museums of San Marco Pass €30 (€25 when booked online at least 30 days in advance), includes Museo Correr, Museo Archeologico, Biblioteca Nazionale Marciana, and Palazzo Ducale. Museum Pass €40, includes all four museums plus seven civic museums. Secret Itineraries or Doge's Hidden Treasures tour €32* Ⓜ *Vaporetto: San Zaccaria, Vallaresso.*

★ **Palazzo Grassi**

ART MUSEUM | Built between 1748 and 1772 by Giorgio Massari for a Bolognese family, this palace is one of the last of the great noble residences on the Grand Canal. Once owned by auto magnate Gianni Agnelli, it was bought by French businessman François Pinault in 2005 to showcase his highly esteemed collection of modern and contemporary art (which has now grown so large that Pinault rented the Punta della Dogana, at the entryway to the Grand Canal, for his newest acquisitions). Pinault brought in Japanese architect Tadao Ando to remodel the Grassi's interior. Check online for a schedule of temporary art exhibitions. ✉ *Campo San Samuele 3231, San Marco* ☎ *041/2401308* 🌐 *www.palazzograssi.it* 🎫 *€18, includes Punta della Dogana* Ⓜ *Vaporetto: San Samuele, Sant'Angelo.*

★ **Piazza San Marco** (*St. Mark's Square*)

PLAZA/SQUARE | **FAMILY** | One of the world's most beautiful squares, Piazza San Marco (St. Mark's Square) is the spiritual and artistic heart of Venice, a vast open space bordered by an orderly procession of arcades marching toward the fairy-tale cupolas and marble lacework of the Basilica di San Marco. From midmorning on, it is generally packed with tourists. (If Venetians have business in the piazza, they try to conduct it in the early morning, before the crowds swell.) At night the piazza can be magical, especially in winter, when mists swirl around the lampposts and the campanile.

Facing the basilica, on your left, the long, arcaded building is the Procuratie Vecchie, renovated to its present form in 1514 as offices and residences for the powerful procurators, or magistrates.

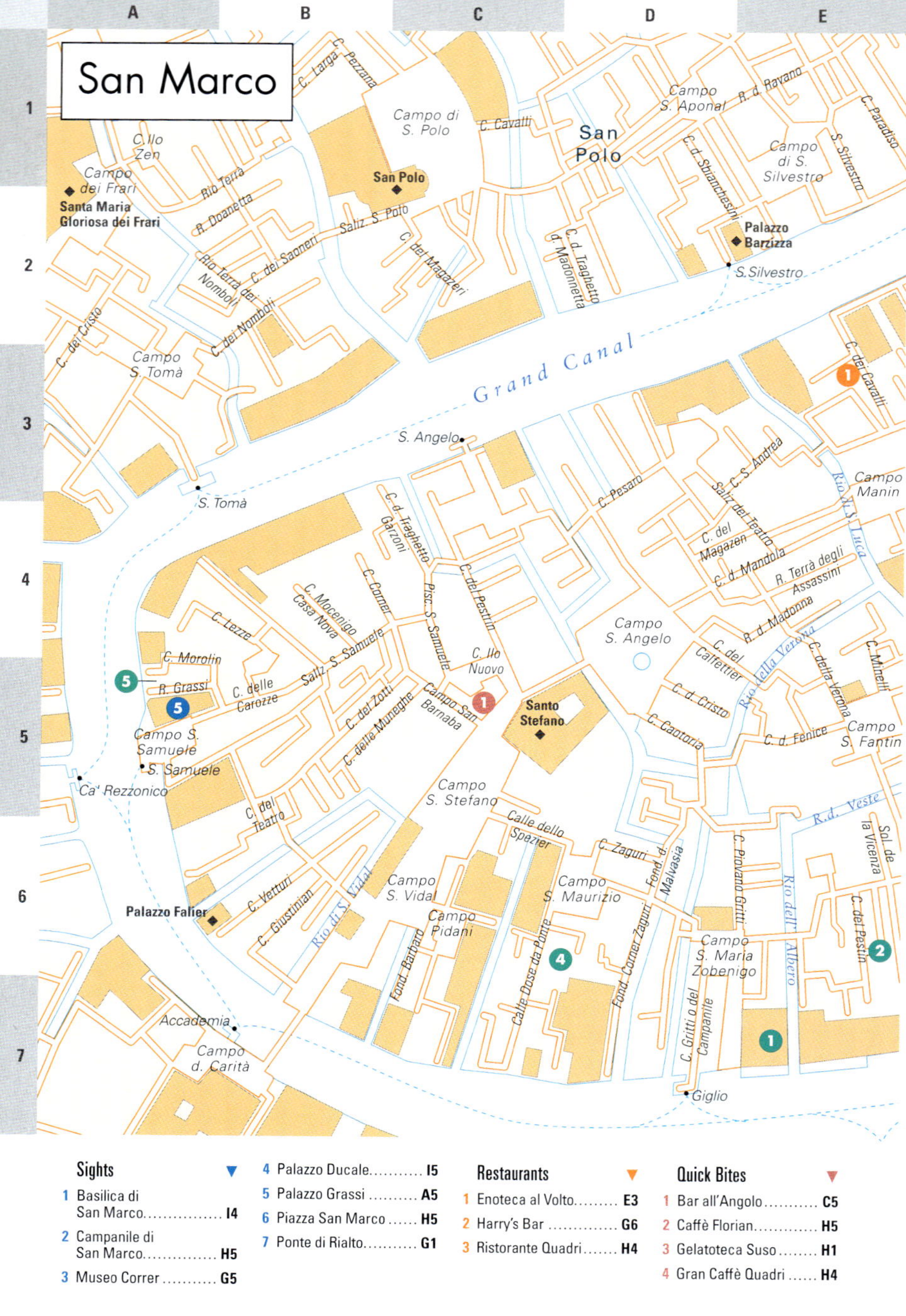

San Marco
A
B
C
D
E
1
2
3
4
5
6
7
Campo dei Frari
Santa Maria Gloriosa dei Frari
C.llo Zen
Rio Terrà
R. Doanetta
Rio Terrà dei Nomboli
C. dei Saoneri
C. dei Nomboli
C. Larga
C. Pezzana
Campo di S. Polo
San Polo
Saliz. S. Polo
C. dei Magazeri
C. Cavalli
San Polo
C. d. Traghetto d. Madonnetta
Campo S. Aponal
R. d. Ravano
C. d. Sbianchesini
Campo di S. Silvestro
S. Silvestro
C. Paradiso
Palazzo Barzizza
S.Silvestro
C. dei Cristo
Campo S. Tomà
S. Tomà
Grand Canal
S. Angelo
C. dei Cavalli
Campo Manin
Rio di S. Luca
C. Pesaro
C. S. Andrea
Saliz. del Teatro
C. del Magazen
C. d. Mandola
R. Terrà degli Assassini
R. d. Madonna
C. d. Traghetto Garzoni
C. Corner
C. Mocenigo Casa Nova
C. Lezze
C. Morolin
R. Grassi
C. delle Carozze
Saliz. S. Samuele
Pisc. S. Samuele
C. del Pestrin
C. llo Nuovo
Campo S. Angelo
C. del Calfettier
Rio della Verona
C. della Verona
C. Minelli
C. d. Cristo
C. Caotorta
C. d. Fenice
Campo S. Fantin
Santo Stefano
Campo San Barnaba
C. del Zotti
C. delle Muneghe
Campo S. Samuele
S. Samuele
Ca' Rezzonico
C. del Teatro
Campo S. Stefano
Calle dello Spezier
C. Zaguri
Fond. d. Malvasia
R.d. Veste
Sol. de la Vicenza
C. Piovano Gritti
Rio dell' Albero
C. del Pestin
Palazzo Falier
C. Vetturi
C. Giustinian
Rio di S. Vidal
Campo S. Vidal
Campo Pidani
Campo S. Maurizio
Calle Dose da Ponte
Fond. Corner Zaguri
Campo S. Maria Zobenigo
Fond. Barbaro
C. Gritti o del Campanile
Accademia
Campo d. Carità
Giglio
Sights
1 Basilica di San Marco I4
2 Campanile di San Marco H5
3 Museo Correr G5
4 Palazzo Ducale I5
5 Palazzo Grassi A5
6 Piazza San Marco H5
7 Ponte di Rialto G1
Restaurants
1 Enoteca al Volto E3
2 Harry's Bar G6
3 Ristorante Quadri H4
Quick Bites
1 Bar all'Angolo C5
2 Caffè Florian H5
3 Gelatoteca Suso H1
4 Gran Caffè Quadri H4

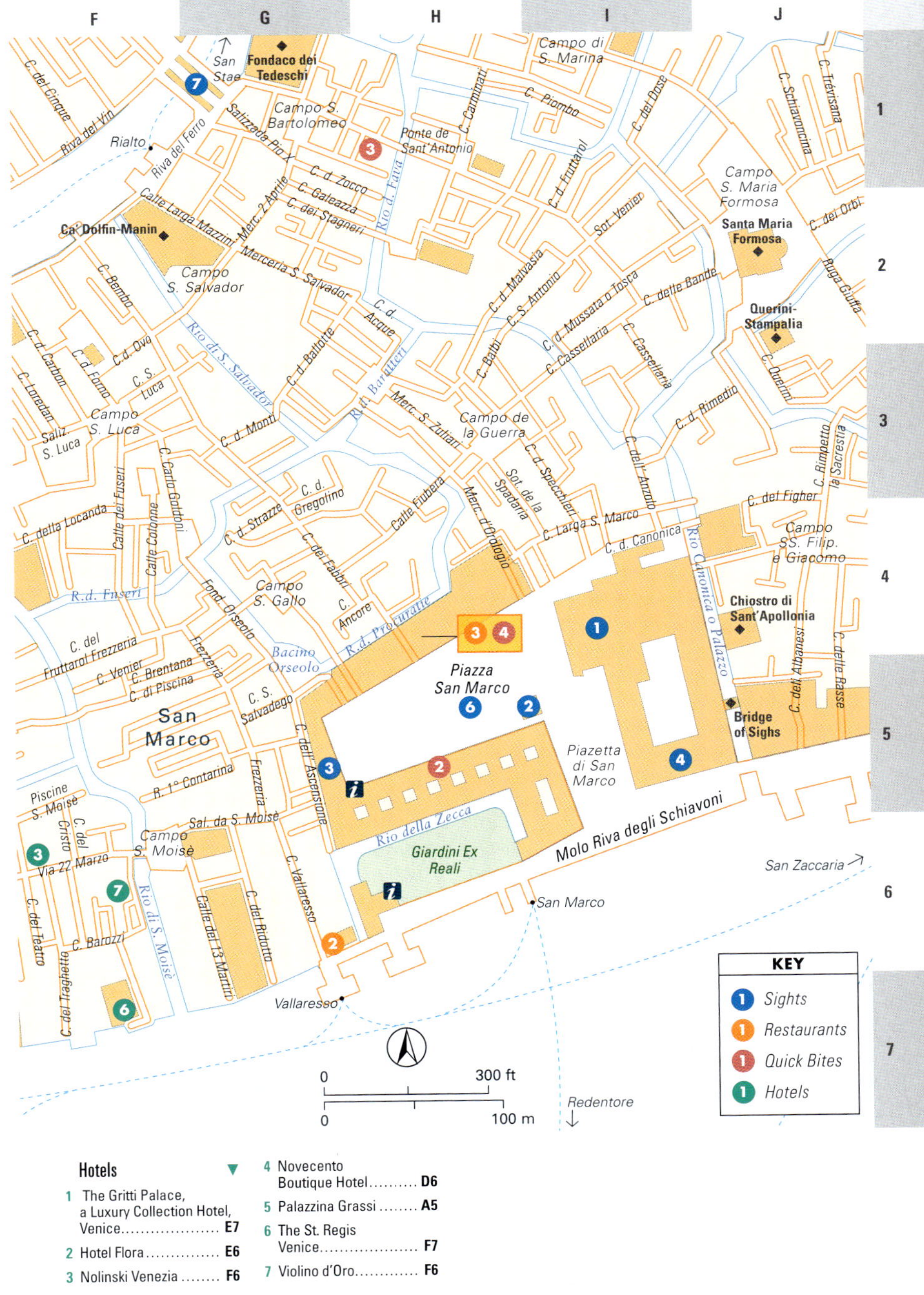

Hotels

1 The Gritti Palace, a Luxury Collection Hotel, Venice **E7**

2 Hotel Flora **E6**

3 Nolinski Venezia **F6**

4 Novecento Boutique Hotel **D6**

5 Palazzina Grassi **A5**

6 The St. Regis Venice **F7**

7 Violino d'Oro............. **F6**

On your right is the Procuratie Nuove, built half a century later in a more imposing, classical style. It was originally planned by Venice's great Renaissance architect Jacopo Sansovino (1486–1570), to carry on the look of his Libreria Sansoviniana (Sansovinian Library), but he died before construction on the Nuove had begun. Vincenzo Scamozzi (circa 1552–1616), a pupil of Andrea Palladio (1508–80), completed the design and construction. Still later, the Procuratie Nuove was modified by architect Baldassare Longhena (1598–1682), one of Venice's Baroque masters.

When Napoléon (1769–1821) entered Venice with his troops in 1797, he expressed his admiration for the piazza and promptly gave orders to alter it. His architects demolished a church with a Sansovino facade in order to build the Ala Napoleonica (Napoleonic Wing), or Fabbrica Nuova (New Building), which linked the two 16th-century procuratie and effectively enclosed the piazza.

Piazzetta San Marco is the "little square" leading from Piazza San Marco to the waters of Bacino San Marco (St. Mark's Basin); its *molo* (landing) once served as the grand entrance to the Republic. Two imposing columns tower above the waterfront. One is topped by the winged lion, a traditional emblem of St. Mark that became the symbol of Venice itself; the other supports St. Theodore, the city's first patron, along with his dragon. (A third column fell off its barge and ended up in the bacino before it could be placed alongside the others.) Although the columns are a glorious vision today, the Republic traditionally executed convicts here—and some superstitious Venetians still avoid walking between them. ✉ *Piazza San Marco, San Marco* Ⓜ *Vaporetto: San Zaccaria, Vallaresso.*

★ **Ponte di Rialto** (*Rialto Bridge*)

BRIDGE | **FAMILY** | The competition to design a stone bridge across the Grand Canal attracted the best architects of the late 16th century, including Michelangelo, Palladio, and Sansovino, but the job went to the less famous (if appropriately named) Antonio da Ponte (1512–95). His pragmatic design, completed in 1591, featured shop space and was high enough for galleys to pass beneath. Putting practicality and economy over aesthetic considerations—unlike the classical plans proposed by his more famous contemporaries—da Ponte's bridge essentially followed the design of its wooden predecessor. But it kept decoration and cost to a minimum at a time when the Republic's coffers were low, due to continual wars against the Turks and competition brought about by the Spanish and Portuguese opening of oceanic trade routes. Along the railing you'll enjoy one of the city's most famous views: the Grand Canal vibrant with boat traffic. ✉ *San Marco* Ⓜ *Vaporetto: Rialto.*

Restaurants

Enoteca al Volto

$$ | **VENETIAN** | A short walk from the Ponte di Rialto, this bar has been around since 1936, and the satisfying cicheti and *primi* have a lot to do with its staying power. Grab a table out front, or take refuge in one of the two small, dark rooms with a ceiling plastered with wine labels that provide a classic backdrop for simple fare, including a delicious risotto that is served daily from noon, plus a solid wine list of both Italian and foreign vintages. **Known for:** great local and international wine selection; tasty and inexpensive cicheti; fantastic main courses, including risotto and pasta with seafood. Ⓢ *Average main: €17* ✉ *Calle Cavalli, San Marco 4081, San Marco* ☎ *041/5228945* 🌐 *enotecaalvolto.com* Ⓜ *Vaporetto: Rialto.*

★ Harry's Bar

$$$$ | **VENETIAN** | For those who can afford it, lunch or dinner at Harry's Bar is as much a part of a visit to Venice as a walk across Piazza San Marco or a vaporetto ride down the Grand Canal. Inside, the

suave, subdued beige-on-white decor is unchanged from the 1930s, and the classic Venetian fare is carefully and excellently prepared. **Known for:** being the birthplace of the Bellini cocktail; see-and-be-seen atmosphere; signature crepes flambées and famous Cipriani chocolate cake. *Average main: €70 ✉ Calle Vallaresso, San Marco 1323, San Marco ☎ 041/5285777 www.cipriani.com Ⓜ Vaporetto: Vallaresso.*

★ Ristorante Quadri

$$$$ | VENETIAN | Although the lavish interior has been updated by designer Philippe Starck, this restaurant above the famed café of the same name is still steeped in Venetian ambience and history (it was where Turkish coffee was introduced to the city in the 1700s). When the Alajmo family (of the celebrated Le Calandre near Padua) took over, they put their accomplished sous-chef from Padua in charge of the kitchen, resulting in the addition of dishes—best sampled with a tasting menu—that are complex and sophisticated, with a wonderful wine list to match. **Known for:** sophisticated and modern Italian cuisine; seasonal tasting menus; revitalized designer decor. *Average main: €185 ✉ Piazza San Marco 121, San Marco ☎ 041/5222105 alajmo.it Closed Mon., Tues., and 3 wks in Jan. No lunch Wed.–Fri. Ⓜ Vaporetto: Giardinetti, Vallaresso.*

Coffee and Quick Bites

Bar all'Angolo

$ | CAFÉ | This corner of Campo Santo Stefano is a pleasant place to sit and watch the Venetian world go by. The café staff are in constant motion, so you'll receive your coffee, spritz, panino (a sandwich warmed on a griddle), or *tramezzino* (sandwich on untoasted white bread, usually with a mayonnaise-based filling) in short order; consume it at your leisure at one of the outdoor tables, at the bar, or at the tables in the back. **Known for:** simple yet satisfying fare, like tramezzini and panini; tasty homemade desserts, including tiramisu and cakes; good people-watching. *Average main: €12 ✉ Campo Santo Stefano, San Marco 3464, just in front of Santo Stefano church, San Marco ☎ 041/5220710 Closed Sun. and Jan. Ⓜ Vaporetto: Sant'Angelo.*

★ Caffè Florian

$ | CAFÉ | Florian is not only Italy's first café (1720), but also one of its most beautiful, with glittering, neo-Baroque decor and 19th-century wall panels depicting Venetian heroes. The coffee, drinks, and snacks are good, but most people come for the atmosphere and history: this was the only café to serve women during the 18th century; it was frequented by artistic notables like Wagner, Goethe, Goldoni, Lord Byron, Marcel Proust, and Charles Dickens; and it was the birthplace of the international art exhibition that became the Venice Biennale. **Known for:** prime location on St. Mark's Square; beautiful, historic interior; hot chocolate, coffee, and quick nibbles. *Average main: €18 ✉ Piazza San Marco 57, San Marco ☎ 041/5205641 caffeflorian.com Closed early Jan. Ⓜ Vaporetto: Giardinetti, Vallaresso.*

★ Gelatoteca Suso

$ | ICE CREAM | FAMILY | Try this fun shop for gelato that's out of the ordinary: think walnut cream with caramelized fig, or vanilla with rum raisins and Malaga wine; sorbets and milk shakes are also on offer. There's a second location on Salizada S Giovanni Grisostomo, in Cannaregio. **Known for:** unusual flavors; vegan ice-cream options; convenient location on way to Rialto Bridge. *Average main: €5 ✉ Sotoportego de la Bissa, San Marco 5453, San Marco ☎ 041/3084136 suso.gelatoteca.it Ⓜ Vaporetto: Rialto.*

★ Gran Caffè Quadri

$$ | CAFÉ | Come for breakfast, a predinner aperitivo, or anything in between at this always lively historic coffeehouse—opened in 1775 and taken over by the

Taking a Gondola Ride

Riding a gondola along the canals is an iconic Venetian experience—and one that's still very much worth doing, despite the expense. It's not hard to find a gondolier, donned in traditional striped garb, beckoning from the helm of a docked boat to take you on a relaxing ride along the city's waterways. Venture away from the busy area around the Grand Canal and look for a boat on one of the smaller, quieter waterways so you can nestle into the plushly upholstered seats and float by Venice's legendary facades including the 13th-century Ca' Da Mosto palazzo without being distracted by the crowds. Go in the morning to watch the city come to life, in the late afternoon when the colors of the buildings are especially vibrant, or at sunset for maximum romance. Boats sit six people, and signs posted on the red-and-white striped poles throughout the city list the standard rates for a 30-minute gondola ride (€80 during the day, €100 after 7 pm; 20-minute increments can be added for an additional fee).

famous culinary Alajmo family in 2011—in the center of the action on Piazza San Marco. Choose from a wide selection of pastries at breakfast (though the cappuccino and brioche combo is always a classic), pizzas at lunch, and tramezzini and cicheti all day long. **Known for:** extensive (though pricey) aperitivo; celebrity owners; prime people-watching. *$ Average main: €22 ✉ Piazza San Marco 121, San Marco ☎ 041/5222105 ⊕ alajmo.it Ⓜ Vaporetto: Giardinetti, Vallaresso.*

Hotels

★ The Gritti Palace, a Luxury Collection Hotel, Venice

$$$$ | **HOTEL** | With handblown chandeliers, sumptuous textiles, and sweeping canal views, this grande dame (whose history dates from 1525, when it was built as the residence of the prominent Gritti family) represents aristocratic Venetian living at its best. **Pros:** truly historical property; Grand Canal location; classic Venetian experience. **Cons:** major splurge; some find service a tad snooty; few spa amenities. *$ Rooms from: €1,058 ✉ Campo Santa Maria del Giglio 2467, San Marco ☎ 041/794611 ⊕ www.thegrittipalace.com 82 rooms No Meals Ⓜ Vaporetto: Giglio.*

★ Hotel Flora

$$ | **HOTEL** | The elegant and refined facade announces a charming, and reasonably priced, place to stay; the hospitable staff, the tastefully decorated rooms, and the lovely garden, where guests can breakfast or drink, do not disappoint. **Pros:** central location; peaceful hidden garden; excellent breakfast. **Cons:** some rooms can be on the small side; no water views; old-fashioned lobby doesn't invite hanging out. *$ Rooms from: €258 ✉ Calle Bergamaschi, San Marco 2283/A, just off Calle Larga XXII Marzo, San Marco ☎ 041/5205844 ⊕ www.hotelflora.it 40 rooms Free Breakfast Ⓜ Vaporetto: Vallaresso.*

★ Nolinski Venezia

$$$$ | **HOTEL** | Right off Venice's main shopping street and a stone's throw from Piazza San Marco, the former 20th-century stock exchange now houses this supremely comfortable hotel with an art deco flair, charming rooms with private terraces, and a glittering enclosed rooftop pool. **Pros:** ultraconvenient location; extremely helpful and friendly service;

elegant, inviting decor. **Cons:** overall hotel lighting a bit dark for some; no saunas or steam room in the spa; expensive cocktails. *Rooms from: €1,050* *Calle Larga XXII Marzo, San Marco* *041/4062459* *nolinskivenezia.com* *43 rooms* *No Meals* *Vaporetto: Vallaresso.*

★ Novecento Boutique Hotel

$$ | **HOTEL** | A stylish yet intimate retreat tucked away on a quiet *calle* (street) midway between Piazza San Marco and the Accademia Bridge offers exquisite rooms tastefully decorated with original furnishings and tapestries from the Mediterranean and Far East. **Pros:** intimate, romantic atmosphere; unique design sensibility; complimentary afternoon tea. **Cons:** most rooms only have showers, not tubs; no elevator; some rooms can be noisy. *Rooms from: €267* *Calle del Dose, San Marco 2683/84, off Campo San Maurizio, San Marco* *041/2413765* *www.novecento.biz* *9 rooms* *Free Breakfast* *Vaporetto: Santa Maria del Giglio.*

Palazzina Grassi

$$$$ | **HOTEL** | The only hotel in Italy outfitted by famed French designer Philippe Starck boasts a clubby atmosphere, over-the-top contemporary rooms lined with Murano glass, and so-close-you-can-touch-them Grand Canal views. **Pros:** fun, modern take on Venetian design; next door to Palazzo Grassi art space and walking distance to St. Mark's; friendly, helpful service. **Cons:** bathrooms smaller than they should be; can be loud when parties are in full swing; food in restaurant not up to par. *Rooms from: €630* *Ramo Grassi, San Marco* *041/5284644* *www.palazzinagrassi.com* *26 rooms* *Free Breakfast* *Vaporetto: San Samuele.*

★ The St. Regis Venice

$$$$ | **HOTEL** | Whimsical design details evoking the Venetian landscape abound in this elegant, contemporary hotel constructed from five historic palazzi with phenomenal views onto the Grand Canal. **Pros:** wonderful central location; terraces with unbeatable views; St. Regis butler service for all guests. **Cons:** sleek modern style not for fans of Venetian opulence; standard rooms on the small side; few spa amenities (no pool or saunas). *Rooms from: €946* *San Marco 2159, San Marco* *041/2400001* *www.marriott.com* *169 rooms* *No Meals* *Vaporetto: Vallaresso.*

★ Violino d'Oro

$$$$ | **HOTEL** | Hoteliers Sara and Elena Maestrelli partnered with solely Italian designers on every aspect of their 17th-century palazzo-turned-hotel, from ceramics to window frames to wall paintings, in what they call an "Italian artisanal product," overlooking Rio San Moise canal. **Pros:** sublime sense of Venetian style; charming, cozy atmosphere; short stroll to Piazza San Marco and Harry's Bar. **Cons:** limited restaurant menu; prices can be on the steep side; lacks amenities of some larger hotels, like a spa and gym. *Rooms from: €937* *San Marco 2091, San Marco* *Off the Rio San Moise Canal* *041/2770841* *violinodoro.com* *32 rooms* *Free Breakfast* *Vaporetto: Vallaresso.*

Nightlife

Bacarando in Corte dell'Orso

WINE BAR | It is easy to see why this place is popular with the locals, offering fairly priced cocktails, a reasonable assortment of cicheti, and a good selection of Italian wine, but the warm ambience, friendly staff, and occasional live jazz are the main draws. The kitchen stays open until late. *Corte Dell'Orso, San Marco 5495, San Marco* *Tucked away in alley across from Church of San Giovanni Grisostomo* *041/5238280* *www.bacarando.com* *Vaporetto: Rialto.*

Bacaro Jazz

BARS | This Venetian-style dive bar has strong cocktails, a jazz soundtrack, and hundreds of bras hanging from the ceiling. The lively daily happy hour is a great time to visit. ✉ *San Marco 5546, San Marco* ☎ *041/5285249* 🌐 *bacarojazz.it* Ⓜ *Vaporetto: Rialto.*

★ Bar Longhi

BARS | The Gritti Palace is home to one of the most exclusive watering holes in town (though thankfully open to the public), lined with 18th-century paintings and Murano chandeliers. You can also enjoy your cocktail on the patio with prime views onto the Grand Canal. ✉ *The Gritti Palace, Campo Santa Maria del Giglio, San Marco 2467, San Marco* ☎ *041/794611* 🌐 *www.thegrittipalace.com* Ⓜ *Vaporetto: Giglio.*

Shopping

★ Al Duca d'Aosta

CLOTHING | The most stylish of Venetians and visitors alike come here for women's and men's designer labels for every taste. Brands include Burberry, Fendi, Givenchy, Lanvin, Loewe, Moncler, and many others; be prepared to be wowed. ✉ *San Marco 284, San Marco* ☎ *041/5220733* 🌐 *www.alducadaosta.com* Ⓜ *Vaporetto: San Marco, Zaccaria.*

★ Atelier Segalin di Daniela Ghezzo

SHOES | This artist turned master shoemaker produces one-of-a-kind creations from exotic leathers. Though the shoes start at €650 and usually take at least six weeks to finish, you'll truly feel like you're wearing a masterpiece. ✉ *Calle dei Fuseri, San Marco 4365, San Marco* ☎ *041/5222115* 🌐 *www.danielaghezzo.it* Ⓜ *Vaporetto: Rialto.*

★ Friulane Dittura

SHOES | Run by a second-generation shoemaker, this shop is one of the only places left in the city still producing Venice's iconic *friulane* slippers, invented in the 19th century and hand-stitched from velvet and rubber. The shoes are still worn by gondoliers today. ✉ *Calle Fiubera, San Marco 943, San Marco* ☎ *0323/3657673* 🌐 *www.instagram.com/friulanedittura* Ⓜ *Vaporetto: San Marco.*

★ Giuliana Longo

HATS & GLOVES | A hat shop that's been around since 1901 offers an assortment of Venetian and gondolier straw hats, Panama hats from Ecuador, caps and berets, and some select scarves of silk and fine wool; there's even a special corner dedicated to accessories for antique cars. ✉ *Calle del Lovo, San Marco 4813, San Marco* ☎ *041/5226454* 🌐 *www.giulianalongo.com* Ⓜ *Vaporetto: San Marco.*

★ Jesurum Venezia 1870

FABRICS | A great deal of so-called Burano Venetian lace is now machine-made in China—and there really is a difference. Unless you have some experience, you're best off going to a trusted place. Jesurum has been the major producer of handmade Venetian lace since 1870, and now specializes in lace incorporated into elegant home linens, such as beautiful bedsheets, bath towels, and placemats. ✉ *Calle Veste, San Marco 2024, San Marco* ☎ *0434/997963* 🌐 *www.jesurum.it* Ⓜ *Vaporetto: Vallaresso.*

★ MuranoVitrum

GLASSWARE | You'll find Murano-made glassworks, including glasses, vases, chandeliers, mirrors, and sculptures, in this friendly family-owned shop. ✉ *San Marco 1229, San Marco* ☎ *041/5206358* 🌐 *www.muranovitrum.com* Ⓜ *Vaporetto: Vallaresso.*

T Fondaco dei Tedeschi

DEPARTMENT STORE | This 15th-century Renaissance commercial center served as Venice's main post office for many years, but was remodeled and returned to its historical roots as a luxury department store. Here you can find a large assortment of high-end jewelry, clothing, and other luxury items. Plus, fabulous views can be had from the rooftop terrace—book a free 15-minute visit online; reservations open 21 days before the visit date. ✉ *Calle Fondaco dei Tedeschi,*

Venetian Art Glass

The glass of Murano is Venice's number one product, and you'll be confronted by mind-boggling displays of traditional and contemporary glassware—much of it kitsch and not made in Venice. Traditional Venetian glass is hot blown glass, not lead crystal; it comes in myriad forms that range from the classic ornate goblets and chandeliers, to beads, vases, sculpture, and more. Beware of paying "Venetian" prices for glass made elsewhere. A piece claiming to be made in Murano may guarantee its origin, but not its value or quality; the prestigious Venetian glassmakers—like Venini, Seguso, Salviati, and others—sign their pieces, but never use a "made in Murano" label. To make a smart purchase, take your time and be selective. You can learn a great deal without sales pressure at the Museo del Vetro (🌐 *museovetro.visitmuve.it*) on Murano; unfortunately, you'll likely find the least attractive glass where public demonstrations are offered. Although prices in Venice and on Murano are comparable, shops in Venice with wares from various glassworks may charge slightly less.

■TIP→ A "free" taxi to Murano always comes with sales pressure. Take the vaporetto included in your transit pass, and, if you prefer, a private guide who specializes in the subject but has no affinity to any specific furnace.

near San Marco end of Ponte di Rialto, San Marco ☎ 041/3142000 🌐 www.dfs.com Ⓜ Vaporetto: Rialto.

Dorsoduro

The sestiere Dorsoduro (named for its "hard back" solid clay foundation) is across the Grand Canal to the south of San Marco. It is a place of meandering canals, the city's finest art museums, monumental churches, and *scuole* (Renaissance civic institutions) filled with works by Titian, Veronese, and Tiepolo, and a promenade called the Zattere, where on sunny days you'll swear half the city is out for *passeggiata* (a stroll). The eastern tip of the peninsula, the Punta della Dogana, is capped by the dome of Santa Maria della Salute and was once the city's customs point; the old customs house is now a museum of contemporary art.

TIMING

You can easily spend a full day in the neighborhood. Devote at least a half hour to admiring the Titians in the imposing and monumental Santa Maria della Salute, and another half hour to the wonderful Veroneses in the peaceful, serene church of San Sebastiano. The Gallerie dell'Accademia demands a few hours, but if time is short an audio guide can help you cover the highlights in about an hour. Ca' Rezzonico deserves at least an hour, as does the Peggy Guggenheim Collection.

Sights

Campo Santa Margherita

PLAZA/SQUARE | Lined with cafés and restaurants generally filled with students from the two nearby universities, Campo Santa Margherita also has produce vendors and benches where you can sit and take in the bustling local life of the campo. Also close to Ca' Rezzonico and the Scuola Grande dei Carmini, and only a 10-minute walk from the Gallerie dell'Accademia, the square is the center of Dorsoduro social life. It takes its name from the church to one side, closed since the early 19th century and now used as an auditorium. On weekend evenings, especially in the summer, it attracts hordes of students, even from the mainland. ✉ *Campo Santa Margherita, Dorsoduro* Ⓜ *Vaporetto: Zattere, Ca' Rezzonico.*

★ Ca' Rezzonico

HISTORY MUSEUM | Designed by Baldassare Longhena in the 17th century, this gigantic palace was completed nearly 100 years later by Giorgio Massari and became the last home of English poet Robert Browning (1812–89). Stand on the bridge by the Grand Canal entrance to spot the plaque with Browning's poetic excerpt ("Open my heart and you will see graved inside of it, Italy …") on the left side of the palace. The spectacular centerpiece is the eye-popping Grand Ballroom, which has hosted some of the grandest parties in the city's history, from its 18th-century heyday to the 1969 Bal Fantastica (a Save Venice charity event that attracted every notable of the day, from Elizabeth Taylor to Aristotle Onassis). Today the upper floors of the Ca' Rezzonico are home to the especially delightful Museo del Settecento (Museum of Venice in the 1700s). Its main floor successfully retains the appearance of a magnificent Venetian palazzo. ✉ *Fondamenta Rezzonico, Dorsoduro 3136, Dorsoduro* ☎ *041/2410100* 🌐 *carezzonico.visitmuve.it* 🎟 *€10 (free with Museum Pass)* ⏲ *Closed Tues.* Ⓜ *Vaporetto: Ca' Rezzonico.*

★ Gallerie dell'Accademia

ART MUSEUM | The greatest collection of Venetian paintings in the world hangs in these galleries founded by Napoléon in 1807 on the site of a religious complex he had suppressed. The galleries were carefully and subtly restructured between 1945 and 1959 by the renowned Venetian architect Carlo Scarpa. Highlights include works by Jacopo Bellini, the father of the Venetian Renaissance, as well as the richly colored paintings of his more accomplished son Giovanni; *The Tempest* by Giorgione, a revolutionary work that has intrigued viewers and critics for centuries; *Feast in the House of Levi,* which got Veronese summoned to the Inquisition; and several of Tintoretto's finest works. Don't miss the views of 15th- and 16th-century Venice by Carpaccio and Gentile Bellini, Giovanni's brother—you'll recognize many places you've seen on your walks. Booking tickets in advance isn't essential but does free you from having to stand in line, as you choose the time you want to come when you book. ✉ *Campo de la Carità, Dorsoduro 1050, Campo della Carità just off Accademia Bridge, Dorsoduro* ☎ *041/5222247, 041/5243354 reservations when calling from outside Italy* 🌐 *www.gallerieaccademia.it/en* 🎟 *€15; subject to increases for special exhibitions* ⏲ *Closed Mon. afternoon* Ⓜ *Vaporetto: Accademia, Zattere.*

Gesuati (*Church of Santa Maria del Rosario*)

CHURCH | After the Dominicans took over the church of Santa Maria della Visitazione from the suppressed order of Gesuati laymen in 1668, Giorgio Massari, the last of the great Venetian Baroque architects, was commissioned to build this structure between 1726 and 1735. It has an important Gianbattista Tiepolo (1696–1770) illusionistic ceiling and several other of his works, plus those of his contemporaries Giambattista Piazzetta (1683–1754) and Sebastiano Ricci (1659–1734). Outside on the right-hand wall above a small staircase is a bronze door decorated with a series of panels showing scenes from the life of Jesus by noted Venetian sculptor Francesco Scarpabolla. ✉ *Fondamenta Zattere ai Gesuati, Dorsoduro* ☎ *041/5205921 church office, 041/2750462* 🌐 *www.chorusvenezia.org* 🎟 *€3.50 (free with Chorus Pass)* ⏲ *Closed Sun.* Ⓜ *Vaporetto: Zattere.*

Peggy Guggenheim Collection

ART MUSEUM | FAMILY | Housed in the incomplete but nevertheless charming Palazzo Venier dei Leoni, this choice selection of 20th-century painting and sculpture represents the taste and extraordinary style of the late heiress Peggy Guggenheim. Through wealth, social connections, and a sharp eye for artistic trends, Guggenheim (1898–1979) became an important art dealer and collector from the 1930s through the 1950s, and her personal collection here includes works by Picasso, Kandinsky, Pollock, Motherwell, and Ernst (her onetime husband). The museum serves beverages, snacks, and light meals in its refreshingly shady and artistically sophisticated garden. ✉ *Fondamenta Venier dei Leoni, Dorsoduro 701–704, Dorsoduro* ☎ *041/2405411* 🌐 *www.guggenheim-venice.it* 🎟 *€16* 🕓 *Closed Tues.* Ⓜ *Vaporetto: Accademia, Salute.*

★ Punta della Dogana

ART MUSEUM | Funded by the billionaire who owns a major share in Christie's Auction House, the François Pinault Foundation commissioned Japanese architect Tadao Ando to redesign this fabled customs house—sitting at the *punta,* or point of land, at the San Marco end of the Grand Canal—now home to a changing roster of works from Pinault's renowned collection of contemporary art. The streaming light, polished surfaces, and clean lines of Ando's design contrast beautifully with the massive columns, sturdy beams, and brick of the original Dogana. Even if you aren't into contemporary art, a visit is worthwhile just to see Ando's amazing architectural transformation. Be sure to walk down to the punta for a magnificent view of the Venetian basin. Check online for a schedule of temporary exhibitions. ✉ *Punta della Dogana, Dorsoduro* ☎ *041/2401308* 🌐 *www.pinaultcollection.com/palazzograssi/en* 🎟 *€18 with Palazzo Grassi* 🕓 *Closed Tues.* Ⓜ *Vaporetto: Salute.*

★ San Sebastiano

CHURCH | Paolo Veronese (1528–88), though still in his twenties, was already the official painter of the Republic when he began the ceiling oil panels and wall frescoes at San Sebastiano in 1555. For decades he continued to embellish the church with very beautiful illusionistic scenes. The cycles of scenes in San Sebastiano are considered to be his supreme accomplishment. His three oil paintings in the center of the ceiling depict scenes from the life of Esther, a rare theme in Venice. Veronese is buried beneath his bust near the organ. ✉ *Campazzo San Sebastiano, Dorsoduro* ☎ *041/2750462* 🌐 *www.chorusvenezia.org* 🎟 *€3.50 (free with Chorus Pass)* 🕓 *Closed Sun.* Ⓜ *Vaporetto: San Basilio.*

★ Santa Maria della Salute

CHURCH | The most iconic landmark of the Grand Canal, La Salute (as this church is commonly called) is best viewed from the Riva degli Schiavoni at sunset or from the Accademia Bridge by moonlight. Baldassare Longhena (later Venice's most important baroque architect) won a competition in 1631 to design a shrine honoring the Virgin Mary for saving Venice from a plague that over two years (1629–30) killed 47,000 residents, or one-third of the city's population. Outside, this ornate white Istrian stone octagon is topped by a colossal cupola with snail-like ornamental buttresses. Check the website for information on guided tours. ✉ *Punta della Dogana, Dorsoduro* ☎ *041/2743928* 🌐 *basilicasalutevenezia.it* 🎟 *Church free, sacristy €6, sacristy and art gallery €10, balustrade of the prophets €5, dome €8* Ⓜ *Vaporetto: Salute.*

Scuola Grande dei Carmini

HISTORIC SIGHT | When the order of Santa Maria del Carmelo commissioned Baldassare Longhena to finish the work on the Scuola Grande dei Carmini in the 1670s, their confraternity was one of the largest and wealthiest in Venice. Little expense was spared in the stuccoed ceilings and

Dorsoduro
A
B
C
D
E
F
1
2
3
4
5
6
7
8
9
Giardino Papadopoli
Rio Nuovo
C. dei Amai
Campo dei Tolentini
San Nicola da Tolentino
Fond. Condulmer
Fond. d. Gaffaro
Fond. Minotto
Fond. del Gaffaro
R. Cimesin
C. C. Falier
C. Vinanti
C. Molin
C. d. Laca
Santa Grande di San Giovanni Evangelista
Campo S. Stin
Campo di S. Agostin
Rio di S. Polo
San Polo
Campo di San Polo
San Polo
Rio Terrà
Campo dei Frari
Campo S. Rocco
Santa Maria Gloriosa dei Frari
Scuola Grande di San Rocco
Campo S. Tomà
C. d. Preti Crosera
C. de Basego
Rio Nuovo
Fond. del Rio Nuovo
Campo S. Pantalon
Grand Canal
S. Angelo
S. Tomà
Cor. Contarini
Fond. Rossa
C. Ragusei
Rio Briati
Campo S. Margherita
Rio di S. Margherita
C. Lezze
C. del Pestrin
Palazzo Grassi
C. Bernardo
Campo S. Samuele
S. Samuele
Ca' Samuele
Campo Santo Stefano
Campo S. Stefano
Fond. del Soccorso
Carmini
Fond. dello Squero
Fond. Gerardini
Campo S. Barnaba
C. Lunga S. Barnaba
Rio Maloaga
R. Cerchieri
Palazzo Falier
Rio di S. Vidal
Campo S. Vidal
Campo Pidani
C. Avogaria
C. Balastro
Campo S. Sebastiano
Dorsoduro
Accademia
Campo d. Carità
Ognissanti
Campo di S. Basegio
C. del Pistor
S. Basilio
Fond. Zattere Ponte Lungo
Rio degli Ognissanti
Fond. Bontini
Campo S. Trovaso
Fond. Venier
Fond. Bragadin
Campo di S. Agnese
Zattere
Fond. Zattere ai Gesuati
Canale della Giudecca
Fond. Zattere allo
Fond. S. Biagio
Rio di S. Biagio
Fond. S. Eufemia
Palanca
Rio delle Convertite
Fond. delle Convertite
Campazzo S. Cosmo
Campo di S. Cosmo
S. Cosmo
C. dei Nicoli
C. del Forno
C. dell' Olio
C. del Ferro
Fond. di S. Giacomo

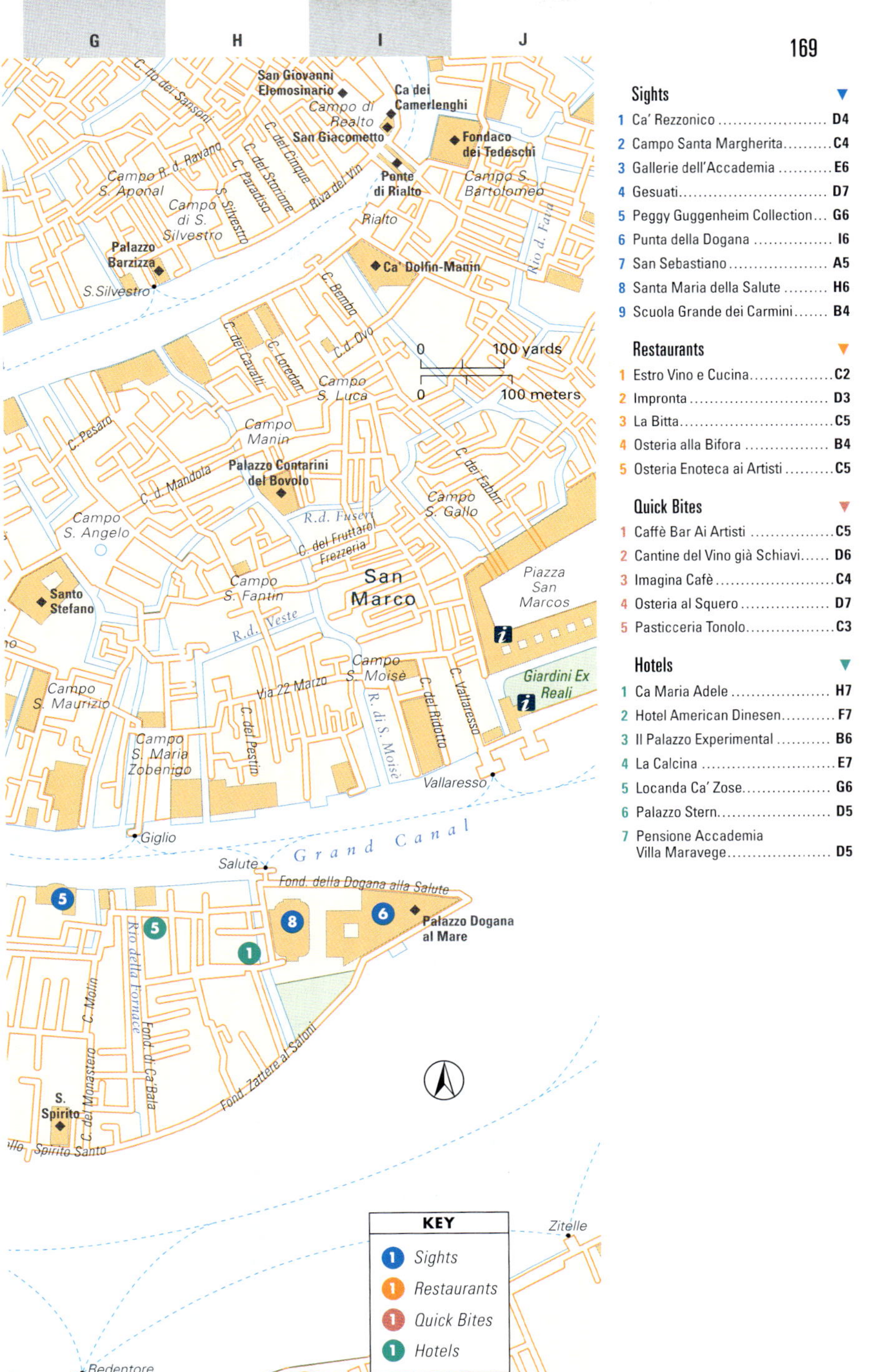

Sights

1 Ca' Rezzonico D4
2 Campo Santa Margherita C4
3 Gallerie dell'Accademia E6
4 Gesuati D7
5 Peggy Guggenheim Collection ... G6
6 Punta della Dogana I6
7 San Sebastiano A5
8 Santa Maria della Salute H6
9 Scuola Grande dei Carmini B4

Restaurants

1 Estro Vino e Cucina C2
2 Impronta D3
3 La Bitta C5
4 Osteria alla Bifora B4
5 Osteria Enoteca ai Artisti C5

Quick Bites

1 Caffè Bar Ai Artisti C5
2 Cantine del Vino già Schiavi D6
3 Imagina Cafè C4
4 Osteria al Squero D7
5 Pasticceria Tonolo C3

Hotels

1 Ca Maria Adele H7
2 Hotel American Dinesen F7
3 Il Palazzo Experimental B6
4 La Calcina E7
5 Locanda Ca' Zose G6
6 Palazzo Stern D5
7 Pensione Accademia Villa Maravege D5

carved wooden paneling, and the artwork is remarkable. The paintings by Gianbattista Tiepolo that adorn the Baroque ceiling of the **Sala Capitolare** (Chapter House) are particularly alluring. In what many consider his best work, the artist's nine canvases vividly transform some rather conventional religious themes into dynamic displays of color and movement. ✉ *Campo dei Carmini, Dorsoduro 2617, Dorsoduro* ☎ *041/5289420* 🌐 *www.scuolagrandecarmini.it* 🎫 *€10* Ⓜ *Vaporetto: Ca' Rezzonico.*

Restaurants

★ Estro Vino e Cucina

$$ | **MODERN ITALIAN** | Wine lovers shouldn't miss this cozy and compact gastro-bistro run by the Spezzamonte brothers, which offers wine from more than 700 vineyards along with modern takes on classic Venetian dishes, such as *scampi in saor* (marinated langoustines) and grilled local amberjack. If you can't choose, let the helpful servers suggest the perfect vino to pair with your à la carte dishes or tasting menu. **Known for:** extensive natural wine list; ambitious local cuisine; vibrant atmosphere. $ *Average main: €28* ✉ *Crosera San Pantalon, Dorsoduro 3778, Dorsoduro* ☎ *041/4764914* 🌐 *www.estrovenezia.com* ⏲ *Closed Tues.* Ⓜ *Vaporetto: San Tomà, Piazzale Roma.*

Impronta

$$ | **VENETIAN** | This sleek café is a favorite lunchtime haunt for professors from the nearby university and local businesspeople, when you can easily have a beautifully prepared *primo* (first course) or *secondo* (second course), plus a glass of wine, for a reasonable price; there's also a good selection of sandwiches and salads. Unlike most local eateries, this spot is open from breakfast through late dinner, and you can dine well in the evening on imaginative pasta, seafood, and meat dishes. **Known for:** imaginative dishes; contemporary decor; all-day dining. $ *Average main: €27* ✉ *Dorsoduro 3815, Calle Crosera by Calle San Pantalon, Dorsoduro* ☎ *041/2750386* 🌐 *improntarestaurantvenice.com/en/* ⏲ *Closed Sun. and 2 wks in Aug.* Ⓜ *Vaporetto: San Tomà, Piazzale Roma.*

★ La Bitta

$$ | **NORTHERN ITALIAN** | For a break from all the fish and seafood options in Venice, this is your place; the meat- and veggie-focused menu (inspired by the cuisine of the Venetian mainland) presents a new temptation at every course, and market availability keeps the dishes changing almost every day. The homemade desserts are all luscious (it's been said that La Bitta serves the best panna cotta in town), and you can trust the owner's selections from her excellent wine and grappa lists, which tend to favor small local producers. **Known for:** meat dishes (no seafood); seasonally inspired menus; friendly and efficient service. $ *Average main: €25* ✉ *Calle Lunga San Barnaba, Dorsoduro 2753/A, Dorsoduro* ☎ *041/5230531* 🌐 *www.instagram.com/labittavenezia* 💳 *No credit cards* ⏲ *Closed weekends. No lunch* Ⓜ *Vaporetto: Ca' Rezzonico, Zattere.*

★ Osteria alla Bifora

$ | **VENETIAN** | A beautiful and atmospheric bacaro, Alla Bifora has such ample, satisfying fare that most Venetians consider it a full-fledged restaurant. Offerings include overflowing trays of cold, sliced meats and cheeses; various preparations of *baccalà* (cod); and Venetian classics, such as *polpette* (croquettes), and marinated anchovies. **Known for:** good selection of regional wines by the glass; seppie in nero con polenta (cuttlefish in ink with polenta); warm and friendly owners. $ *Average main: €18* ✉ *Campo Santa Margherita, Dorsoduro 2930, Dorsoduro* ☎ *041/5236119* ⏲ *Closed Jan. and Aug.* Ⓜ *Vaporetto: Ca' Rezzonico.*

★ Osteria Enoteca ai Artisti

$$ | **VENETIAN** | Pop into this canal-side restaurant at lunch for a satisfying

primo or come for dinner to sample fine and fresh offerings; the candlelit tables that line the *fondamenta* (quay) suggest romance, and the service is friendly and welcoming. The posted menu—with choices like tagliatelle with porcini mushrooms and tiger prawns, or a filleted John Dory with tomatoes and pine nuts—changes daily (spot the date at the top) and seasonally. **Known for:** delicious pasta and seafood offerings; superlative tiramisu; truly helpful service. *$ Average main: €26 ✉ Fondamenta della Toletta, Dorsoduro 1169a, Dorsoduro ☎ 041/5238944 🌐 www.enotecaartisti.com ⏲ Closed Sun. and Mon. Ⓜ Vaporetto: Ca' Rezzonico, Zattere.*

Coffee and Quick Bites

Caffè Bar Ai Artisti

$ | **CAFÉ** | Caffè Ai Artisti gives locals, students, and travelers alike good reason to pause and refuel. The location is central, pleasant, and sunny—perfect for people-watching and taking a break before the next destination—and the hours are long. **Known for:** relaxing with a coffee; evening Aperol spritz or wine; chilling with the locals. *$ Average main: €8 ✉ Campo San Barnaba, Dorsoduro 2771, Dorsoduro ☎ 0376/2265420 Ⓜ Vaporetto: Ca' Rezzonico.*

★ Cantine del Vino già Schiavi

$ | **WINE BAR** | A mainstay for anyone living or working in the area, this beautiful, family-run, 19th-century bacaro across from the *squero* (gondola boatyard) of San Trovaso has original furnishings and one of the city's best wine cellars, and the walls are covered floor to ceiling with bottles for purchase. The cicheti (small snacks) here are some of the most inventive—and freshest—in Venice (feel free to compliment the signora, who makes them up to twice a day); everything's eaten standing up, as there's no seating. **Known for:** excellent quality cicheti; plenty of wine choices; boisterous local atmosphere. *$ Average main: €8 ✉ Fondamenta Nani, Dorsoduro 992, Dorsoduro ☎ 041/5230034 🌐 www.cantinaschiavi.com ⏲ Closed Sun. and 3 wks in Aug. Ⓜ Vaporetto: Accademia, Zattere.*

Imagina Cafè

$ | **ITALIAN** | This friendly café and art gallery, located between Campo Santa Margherita and Campo San Barnaba, is a great place to stop for a spritz, or even for a light lunch or dinner. The highlights are the freshly made salads, but their panini and *tramezzini* (triangle-shape Italian sandwich) are also among the best in the area. **Known for:** tasty sandwiches and salads; good wines and cocktails; pleasant outdoor seating. *$ Average main: €10 ✉ Rio Terà Canal, Dorsoduro 3126, Dorsoduro ☎ 041/2410625 🌐 www.imaginacafe.it Ⓜ Vaporetto: Ca' Rezzonico.*

Osteria al Squero

$ | **ITALIAN** | It wasn't long after this lovely little wine bar (not a restaurant) appeared across from Squero San Trovaso that it became a neighborhood—and city-wide—favorite. The Venetian owner has created a personal vision of what a good bar should offer: a variety of sumptuous cicheti, panini, and cheeses to be accompanied by just the right regional wines (ask for his recommendation). **Known for:** tasty cicheti; good veggie options; pretty canal views. *$ Average main: €10 ✉ Fondamenta Nani, Dorsoduro 943/944, Dorsoduro ☎ 041/2960479 🌐 osteriaalsquero.wordpress.com ⏲ Closed Sat. evening and Sun. Ⓜ Vaporetto: Zattere, Accademia.*

Pasticceria Tonolo

$ | **BAKERY** | One of Venice's premier confectioneries has been in operation since 1886. During Carnevale it's still one of the best places in town for *frittelle,* or fried doughnuts (traditional raisin or cream-filled), and at Christmas and Easter, this is where Venetians order their focaccia veneziana, the traditional raised cake—well in advance. **Known for:** arguably the best pastries in Venice; excellent coffee; can't-miss doughnuts. *$ Average main: €5 ✉ Calle San Pantalon, Dorsoduro 3764, Dorsoduro ☎ 041/5237209 🌐 pasticceria-tonolo.foodjoyy.com ⏲ Closed Mon. Ⓜ Vaporetto: San Tomà, Ca' Rezzonico.*

Hotels

★ Ca Maria Adele

$$ | **HOTEL** | One of the city's most intimate and elegant getaways blends terrazzo floors, dramatic Murano chandeliers, and antique-style furnishings with contemporary touches, particularly in the African-wood reception area and breakfast room. **Pros:** quiet and romantic; imaginative decor; tranquil yet convenient spot near Santa Maria della Salute. **Cons:** no elevator and lots of stairs; bathrooms on the small side; no restaurant (just breakfast room). *$ Rooms from: €379 ✉ Campo Santa Maria della Salute, Dorsoduro 111, Dorsoduro ☎ 041/5203078 🌐 www.camariaadele.it ⏲ Closed 3 wks in Jan. 🛏 12 rooms 🍽 Free Breakfast Ⓜ Vaporetto: Salute.*

Hotel American Dinesen

$$ | **HOTEL** | If you're in Venice to see art, you can't beat the location of this hotel, where all the spacious rooms have brocade fabrics and Venetian-style lacquered furniture. **Pros:** near Gallerie dell'Accademia and Peggy Guggenheim Collection; on a bright, quiet, exceptionally picturesque canal; some rooms have canal-view terraces. **Cons:** canal-view rooms are more expensive; style could be too understated for those expecting Venetian opulence; bathrooms can feel cramped. *$ Rooms from: €221 ✉ Fondamenta Bragadin, Dorsoduro 628, Dorsoduro ☎ 041/5204733 🌐 www.hotelamerican.it 🛏 34 rooms 🍽 No Meals Ⓜ Vaporetto: Accademia, Salute, Zattere.*

Il Palazzo Experimental

$$ | **HOTEL** | Of-the-moment Parisian designer Dorothée Meilichzon composed the striped pastel color palette at this hip boutique hotel—the first Experimental Group property in Italy—hidden inside a Renaissance palazzo facing Giudecca Canal. **Pros:** fun, whimsical decor; quiet location away from the Venice crowds; trendy cocktail bar on-site. **Cons:** not all rooms have water views; little storage space in bathrooms; no gym. *$ Rooms from: €288 ✉ Fondamenta Zattere Al Ponte Lungo, Dorsoduro 1411, Dorsoduro ☎ 041/0980200 🌐 www.palazzoexperimental.com 🛏 32 rooms 🍽 No Meals Ⓜ Vaporetto: Zattere, San Basilio.*

La Calcina

$$ | **HOTEL** | Many notables (including Victorian-era art critic John Ruskin) have stayed at this hotel, though they might not recognize it after its series of upscale renovations; it has an enviable location along the sunny Zattere, as well as comfy rooms and apartments with parquet floors, original 19th-century furniture, and firm beds. **Pros:** panoramic views from some rooms; quiet, peaceful atmosphere; well-regarded restaurant with terrace over Giudecca Canal. **Cons:** not for travelers who prefer ultramodern surroundings; no elevator; most rooms on the small side. *$ Rooms from: €185 ✉ Zattere ai Gesuati, Dorsoduro 780, Dorsoduro ☎ 041/5206466 🌐 www.lacalcina.com 🛏 25 rooms 🍽 Free Breakfast Ⓜ Vaporetto: Zattere, Accademia.*

Locanda Ca' Zose

$ | **HOTEL** | The idea that the Campanati sisters named the 15 rooms in their renovated 17th-century locanda after the stars and constellations of the highest magnitude in the Northern Hemisphere says something about how personally this place is run. **Pros:** quiet but convenient location; canal views; efficient, personal service. **Cons:** no outdoor garden or terrace; no Wi-Fi in rooms (but free in lounge, as is computer use); unimpressive breakfast. *$ Rooms from: €144 ✉ Calle Barbaro, Dorsoduro 193/B, Dorsoduro ☎ 041/5226635 🌐 www.*

hotelcazose.com *15 rooms* *No Meals* *Vaporetto: Salute.*

★ Palazzo Stern

$$ | **HOTEL** | This opulently refurbished neo-Gothic palazzo features marble-column arches, terrazzo floors, frescoed ceilings, mosaics, and a charming carved staircase, and some rooms have tufted walls and parquet flooring. **Pros:** excellent hotel service; lovely views from many rooms; modern renovation retains historic ambience. **Cons:** standard rooms don't have views; Grand Canal–facing rooms can be a bit noisy; no restaurant, gym, or spa. *Rooms from: €294* *Calle del Traghetto, Dorsoduro 2792/A, Dorsoduro* *041/2770869* *www.palazzostern.it* *24 rooms* *No Meals* *Vaporetto: Ca' Rezzonico.*

Pensione Accademia Villa Maravege

$ | **HOTEL** | Behind iron gates in one of the busiest parts of the city is this renowned Gothic-style villa with gardens and charmingly decorated accommodations with Venetian-style antique reproductions and fine tapestry. **Pros:** a unique villa in the heart of Venice; two gardens where guests can breakfast, drink, and relax; complimentary drinks and snacks at the bar. **Cons:** no guest rooms have Grand Canal views; bathrooms can be on the small side; no restaurant. *Rooms from: €146* *Fondamenta Bollani, Dorsoduro 1058, Dorsoduro* *041/5210188* *www.pensioneaccademia.it* *27 rooms* *Free Breakfast* *Vaporetto: Accademia.*

Nightlife

Al Chioschetto

BARS | Although this popular place consists only of a kiosk set up to serve some outdoor tables, it is located on the Zattere and thus provides a wonderful view of Giudecca Canal. It's a handy meet-up spot for locals, especially students from the nearby university, and a useful stop-off for tourists in nice weather for a spritz or a panino. Keep in mind, though, that "the kiosk" exists for quick refreshments and not for lingering. The view and the sunshine (and especially the sunset) are the main draw; the food and drink, while acceptable, are not exceptional. *Fondamenta delle Zattere al Ponte Lungo, Dorsoduro 1406/A, Dorsoduro* *348/3968466* *Vaporetto: San Basilio, Zattere.*

★ Il Caffè Rosso (*Bar Rosso*)

BARS | The sign above the door simply says "CAFFÈ," but it has long since been called "Bar Rosso" for its bright-red exterior. The ideal people-watching spot on one of the busiest campos, it has far more tables outside than inside. A favorite with students and faculty from the nearby university, it's a good place to start the day with coffee and croissant, or later to enjoy a drink. *Campo Santa Margherita, Dorsoduro 2963, Dorsoduro* *041/5287998* *www.facebook.com/cafferosso.venezia* *Vaporetto: Ca' Rezzonico, Piazzale Roma, San Tomà.*

Shopping

Il Grifone

HANDBAGS | Of Venice's few remaining artisan leather shops, Il Grifone is the standout with respect to quality, tradition, and the guarantee of an exquisite product. For more than 30 years, Antonio Peressin has been making bags, purses, belts, and smaller leather items that have a wide following because of his precision and attention to detail. His goods remain reasonably and accessibly priced. *Fondamenta del Gafaro, Dorsoduro 3516, Dorsoduro* *041/5229452* *www.ilgrifonevenezia.it* *Closed Sun. and Mon.* *Vaporetto: Piazzale Roma.*

Marina e Susanna Sent

JEWELRY & WATCHES | The beautiful and elegant glass jewelry of Marina and Susanna Sent has been featured in *Vogue*. Look also for vases and other exceptional design pieces. Other locations are on the Fondamenta Serenella on Murano and in San Polo under the Sotoportego dei Oresi at Rialto. ✉ *Campo San Vio, Dorsoduro 669, Dorsoduro* ☎ *041/5208136* 🌐 *www.marinaesusannasent.com* Ⓜ *Vaporetto: Salute, Accademia, Zattere.*

San Polo and Santa Croce

The two smallest of Venice's six sestieri, San Polo and Santa Croce, were named after their main churches, although the Chiesa di Santa Croce was demolished in 1810. The city's most famous bridge, the Ponte di Rialto, unites San Marco (east) with San Polo (west). The Rialto takes its name from Rivoaltus, the high ground on which it was built. You'll find some of Venice's most lauded restaurants here, and shops abound in the area surrounding the Ponte di Rialto. On the San Marco side you'll find fashion, on the San Polo side, food.

TIMING

To do the area justice requires at least half a day. If you want to take part in the food shopping, come early to beat the crowds. Campo San Giacomo dell'Orio, west of the main thoroughfare that takes you from the Ponte di Rialto to Santa Maria Gloriosa dei Frari, is a peaceful place for a drink and a rest. The museums of Ca' Pesaro are a time commitment—you'll want at least two hours to see them both.

Sights

Campo San Polo

PLAZA/SQUARE | Only Piazza San Marco is larger than this square, and the echo of children's voices bouncing off the surrounding palaces makes the space seem even bigger. Campo San Polo once hosted bullfights, fairs, military parades, and packed markets, and now comes especially alive on winter days when a temporary ice-skating rink is installed. In the summer, an outdoor cinema is set up with 1,300 seats.

The Chiesa di San Polo has been restored so many times that little remains of the original 9th-century church, and the 19th-century alterations were so costly that, sadly, the friars sold off many great paintings to pay bills. Although Gianbattista Tiepolo is represented here, his work is outdone by 16 paintings by his son Giandomenico (1727–1804), including the *Stations of the Cross* in the oratory to the left of the entrance. The younger Tiepolo also created a series of expressive and theatrical renderings of the saints. Look for altarpieces by Tintoretto and Veronese that managed to escape auction.

San Polo's bell tower (begun 1362), across the street from the entrance to the church, remained unchanged over the centuries—don't miss the two lions, playing with a disembodied human head and a serpent, on the wall just above the tower's doorway. Tradition has it that the head refers to that of Marino Faliero, the doge executed for treason in 1355. ✉ *Campo San Polo* ☎ *041/2750462* 🌐 *www.chorusvenezia.org* 🎫 *Chiesa di San Polo €3.50 (free with Chorus Pass)* 🕑 *Closed Sun.* Ⓜ *Vaporetto: San Silvestro, San Tomà.*

Ca' Pesaro

ART MUSEUM | Baldassare Longhena's grand Baroque palace, begun in 1676, is the beautifully restored home of two impressive collections. The Galleria Internazionale d'Arte Moderna has works by 19th- and 20th-century artists, such as Klimt, Kandinsky, Matisse, and Miró. It also has a collection of representative works from the Venice Biennale that amounts to a panorama of 20th-century art. The pride of the Museo Orientale is its collection of Japanese art—and especially armor and weapons—of the Edo period (1603–1868). It also has a small but striking collection of Chinese and Indonesian porcelains and musical instruments. ✉ *Fondamenta Pesaro, Santa Croce 2076* ☎ *041/721127* 🌐 *capesaro.visitmuve.it* 🎫 *€10, includes both museums (free with Museum Pass)* 🕒 *Closed Mon.* Ⓜ *Vaporetto: San Stae.*

San Giacomo de l'Orio

PLAZA/SQUARE | Theories abound on this lovely square's unusual name; one hypothesis is that there was once a laurel tree here and the Venetian dialect has thoroughly transformed the word (*lauro* in Italian). In any case, today's trees lend it shade and character. Add benches and a fountain (with a drinking bowl for dogs), and the pleasant, oddly shaped campo becomes a welcoming place for friendly conversation and neighborhood kids at play. The church of San Giacomo dall'Orio (another common spelling) was founded in the 9th century on an island still populated (the legend goes) by wolves. The current church dates from 1225. ✉ *Campo San Giacomo dall'Orio* ☎ *041/2750462* 🌐 *www.chorusvenezia.org* 🎫 *Church €3.50 (free with Chorus Pass)* 🕒 *Church closed Sun.* Ⓜ *Vaporetto: San Stae, Riva de Biasio.*

San Giovanni Elemosinario

CHURCH | Storefronts make up the facade, and market guilds—poulterers, messengers, and fodder merchants—built the altars at this church intimately bound to the Rialto markets. The original church was completely destroyed by a fire in 1514 and rebuilt in 1531 by Scarpagnino, who had also worked on the Scuola di San Rocco. During a more recent restoration, workers stumbled upon a frescoed cupola by Pordenone (1484–1539) that had been painted over centuries earlier. Don't miss Titian's *St. John the Almsgiver* and Pordenone's *Sts. Catherine, Sebastian, and Roch.* ✉ *Rialto Ruga Vecchia San Giovanni, San Polo 479* ☎ *041/2750462* 🌐 *www.chorusvenezia.org* 🎫 *€3.50 (free with Chorus Pass)* 🕒 *Closed Fri.–Tues.* Ⓜ *Vaporetto: San Silvestro, Rialto Mercato.*

San Stae

CHURCH | The church of San Stae—the Venetian name for Sant' Eustachio (St. Eustace)—was reconstructed in 1687 by Giovanni Grassi and given a new facade in 1707 by Domenico Rossi. Renowned Venetian painters and sculptors of the early 18th century decorated this church around 1717 with the legacy left by Doge Alvise II Mocenigo, who's buried in the center aisle. San Stae affords a good opportunity to see the early works of Gianbattista Tiepolo, Sebastiano Ricci, and Giovanni Battista Piazzetta, as well as those of the previous generation of Venetian painters, with whom they had studied. ✉ *Campo San Stae* ☎ *041/2750462* 🌐 *www.chorusvenezia.org* 🎫 *€3.50 (free with Chorus Pass)* 🕒 *Closed Fri.–Tues.* Ⓜ *Vaporetto: San Stae.*

★ Santa Maria Gloriosa dei Frari

CHURCH | Completed in 1442, this immense Gothic church of russet-color brick, known locally as "I Frari," is famous for its array of spectacular Venetian paintings and historic tombs. In the sacristy, see Giovanni Bellini's 1488 triptych *Madonna and Child with Saints.* The Corner Chapel is graced by Bartolomeo Vivarini's altarpiece *St. Mark Enthroned* and *Saints John the Baptist, Jerome, Peter, and Nicholas.* In the first south chapel of the chorus, there is a fine sculpture of St. John the Baptist by Donatello, dated 1438, with a psychological intensity rare for early Renaissance sculpture. Titian's renowned *Assumption,* unveiled in 1518, is at the far end of the nave, above the altar. ✉ *Campo dei Frari* ☎ *041/2728618* 🌐 *www.basilicadeifrari.it* 🎫 *€5* 🕒 *Closed Sun. morning* Ⓜ *Vaporetto: San Tomà.*

★ Scuola Grande di San Rocco

ART MUSEUM | This elegant example of Venetian Renaissance architecture was built between 1516 and 1549 for the essentially secular charitable confraternity bearing the saint's name. The

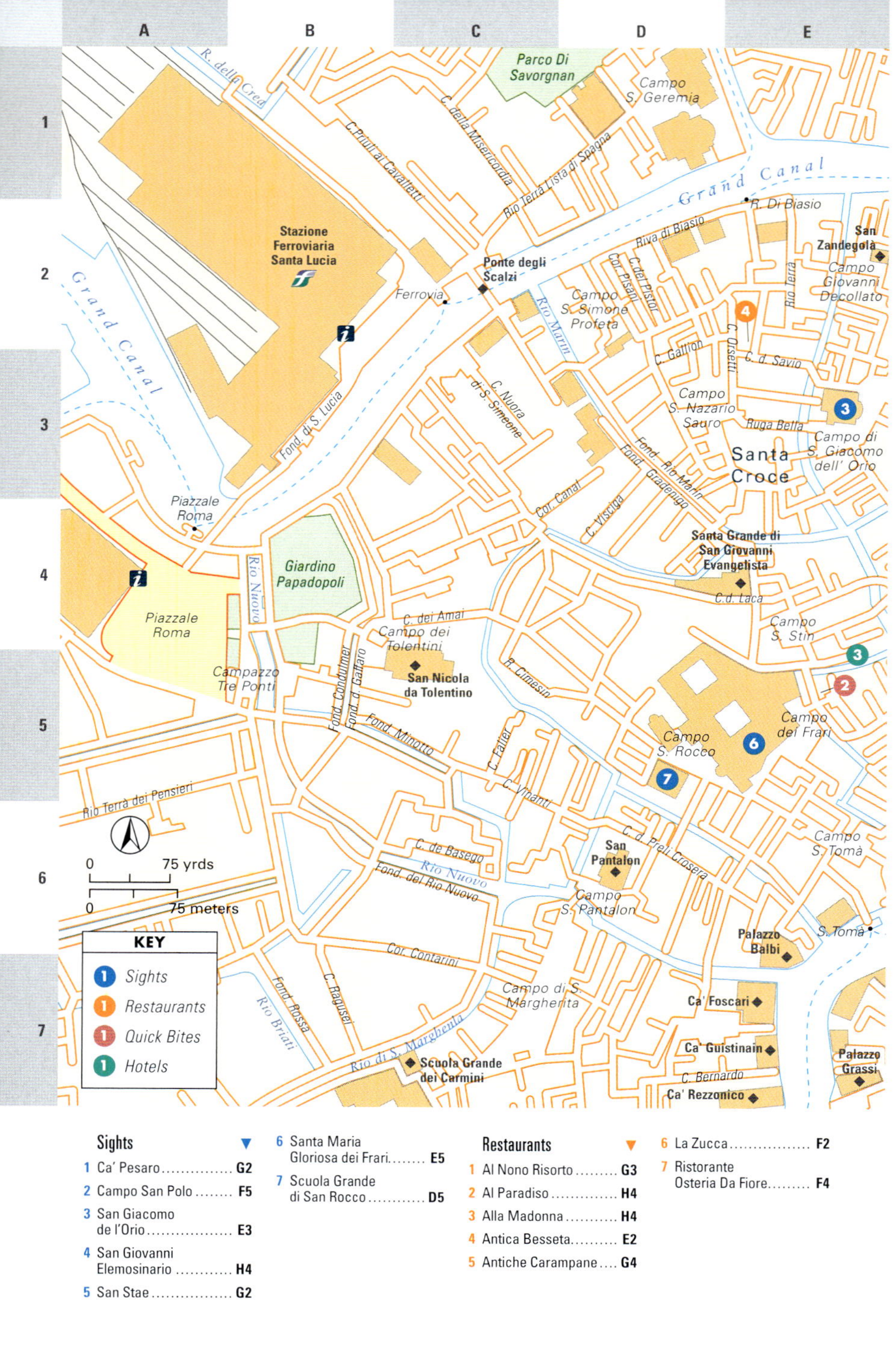

Sights

1 Ca' Pesaro G2

2 Campo San Polo F5

3 San Giacomo de l'Orio E3

4 San Giovanni Elemosinario H4

5 San Stae G2

6 Santa Maria Gloriosa dei Frari........ E5

7 Scuola Grande di San Rocco D5

Restaurants

1 Al Nono Risorto G3

2 Al Paradiso H4

3 Alla Madonna H4

4 Antica Besseta.......... E2

5 Antiche Carampane G4

6 La Zucca F2

7 Ristorante Osteria Da Fiore......... F4

Quick Bites ▼

1 All'Arco **H4**

2 Caffè dei Frari........... **E5**

3 Cantina Do Mori **H4**

Hotels ▼

1 Hotel al Ponte Mocenigo................ **F2**

2 La Villeggiatura **H4**

3 Oltre il Giardino **E5**

Venetian *scuole* were organizations that sometimes had loose religious affiliations, through which the artisan class could exercise some influence upon civic life. San Rocco was a protector against the plague, and his scuola was one of the city's most magnificent. While the building is bold and dramatic outside, its contents are even more stunning—a series of more than 60 paintings by Tintoretto. *Moses Striking Water from the Rock, The Brazen Serpent,* and *The Fall of Manna* represent three afflictions—thirst, disease, and hunger—that San Rocco sought to relieve. *Campo San Rocco, San Polo 3054 041/5234864 www.scuolagrandesanrocco.it €10 Vaporetto: San Tomà, Piazzale Roma.*

Restaurants

Alla Madonna

$ | VENETIAN | "The Madonna" used to be world-famous as *the* classic Venetian trattoria, but in recent decades has settled into middle age. Owned and operated by the Rado family since 1954, this Venetian institution looks like one, with wood beams, stained-glass windows, and a panoply of paintings on white walls. **Known for:** freshly prepared seafood; traditional Venetian cuisine; old-time atmosphere. *Average main: €18 Calle della Madonna, San Polo 594 041/5223824 www.ristoranteallamadonna.com Closed Wed. and Jan. Vaporetto: San Silvestro, Rialto Mercato.*

Al Nono Risorto

$ | VENETIAN | FAMILY | This friendly trattoria popular with the locals is only a short walk from the Rialto markets. The pizza—not a Venetian specialty, generally speaking—is pretty good here, but the star attractions are the generous appetizers and excellent shellfish pastas. (The "reborn *nono*" refers to a small lagoon sea snail, a Venetian favorite.) In good weather, you can enjoy your meal in the pergola-covered courtyard (do reserve if you want to snag a table there). **Known for:** traditional starters and pastas; quite tasty pizzas; pretty outdoor garden seating. *Average main: €16 Sotoportego de Siora Bettina, Santa Croce 2338 041/5241169 alnonorisortovenezia.com Closed Jan. Vaporetto: Rialto Mercato, San Stae.*

★ Al Paradiso

$$ | MODERN ITALIAN | In a small dining room made warm and cozy by its pleasing and unpretentious decor, proprietor Giordano makes all diners feel like honored guests. Unlike many elegant restaurants, Al Paradiso serves generous portions, and many of the delicious antipasti and primi are quite satisfying; you may want to follow the traditional Italian way of ordering and wait until you've finished your antipasto or your primo before you order your secondo. **Known for:** large appetizer and pasta portions; tasty meat and fish mains; central location near the Ponte di Rialto. *Average main: €26 Calle del Paradiso, San Polo 767 041/5234910 www.ristoranteal-paradiso.com Closed 3 wks Jan. and Feb. Vaporetto: San Silvestro.*

Antica Besseta

$$ | VENETIAN | Tucked away in a quiet corner of Santa Croce, with a few tables under an ivy shelter, the Antica Besseta dates from the 19th century, and it retains some of its old feel. The menu focuses on vegetables and fish, according to what's at the market, with some pasta and meat dishes, too. **Known for:** classic Italian pastas, like spaghetti con vongole (with clams); simple menu of fish and meat choices; charming old-fashioned feel. *Average main: €30 Salizzada de Ca' Zusto, Santa Croce 1395 041/721687 www.anticabesseta.it Closed Tues. No lunch Mon. and Wed. Vaporetto: Riva de Biasio.*

★ Antiche Carampane

$$$ | SEAFOOD | Judging by its rather modest and unremarkable appearance, you wouldn't guess that Piera Bortoluzzi Librai's trattoria is among the finest fish

restaurants in the city both because of the quality of the ingredients and because of the chef's creative magic. You can choose from a selection of classic dishes with a modern and creative touch. **Known for:** superlative fish and seafood; modernized Venetian dishes; popular with visitors and locals (so book ahead). *Average main: €31 Rio Terà delle Carampane, San Polo 1911 041/5240165 www.antichecarampane.com Closed Sun. and Mon., 10 days in Jan., and 3 wks July and Aug. Vaporetto: San Silvestro.*

La Zucca

$$$ | NORTHERN ITALIAN | Simple place settings, wood lattice walls, and a mélange of languages make La Zucca (The Pumpkin) feel much like a typical, somewhat sophisticated vegetarian restaurant that you could find in any European city. What makes La Zucca special is simply great cooking and the use of fresh, local ingredients—many of which, like the particularly sweet zucca itself, aren't normally found outside northern Italy. **Known for:** seasonal vegetarian-focused dishes; homestyle Italian cooking; flan di zucca (pumpkin pudding). *Average main: €31 Calle del Tentor, at Ponte del Megio, Santa Croce 1762 041/5241570 www.lazucca.it Closed Sun. Vaporetto: San Stae.*

★ Ristorante Osteria Da Fiore

$$$$ | VENETIAN | The understated atmosphere, simple decor, and quiet elegance featured alongside Da Fiore's modern take on traditional Venetian cuisine certainly merit its international reputation. With such beautifully prepared cuisine, you would expect the kitchen to be run by a chef with a household name; however, the kitchen is headed by owner Maurizio Martin's wife, Mara, who learned to cook from her grandmother. **Known for:** sophisticated traditional Venetian dishes; delicious tasting menus; reservations required. *Average main: €52 Calle del Scaleter, San Polo 2202 041/721308 www.ristorantedafiore.com Closed Sun. and 3 wks in Jan. No lunch Mon.–Thurs. Vaporetto: San Tomà, San Silvestro.*

Coffee and Quick Bites

All'Arco

$ | WINE BAR | Just because it's noon and you only have enough time between sights for a sandwich doesn't mean that it can't be a satisfying, even an exceptional, one. There's no menu at All'Arco, but a scan of what's behind the glass counter is all you need; order what entices you, or have Roberto or Matteo (father and son) suggest a cicheto or panino. **Known for:** top-notch cicheti; platters of meats and cheeses; friendly and helpful service. *Average main: €10 Calle Arco, San Polo 436 041/5205666 Closed Wed. Vaporetto: Rialto Mercato, San Silvestro.*

Caffè dei Frari

$ | CAFÉ | Just over the bridge in front of the Frari church is this old-fashioned place where you'll find an assortment of sandwiches and snacks, but it is the atmosphere, and not the food, that is the main attraction. Established in 1870, it's one of the last Venetian tearooms with its original decor, and while prices are a bit higher than in cafés in nearby Campo Santa Margherita, the vibe and the friendly "retro" atmosphere make the added cost worthwhile. **Known for:** lovely historic setting; well-made cocktails; quality cicheti. *Average main: €10 Fondamenta dei Frari, San Polo 2564 041/4767305 Closed Sun. and Mon. No dinner Vaporetto: San Tomà.*

Cantina Do Mori

$ | WINE BAR | This is the original bacaro, in business continually since 1462; cramped but warm and cozy under hanging antique copper pots, it has served generations of workers from the Rialto markets. In addition to young local whites and reds, the well-stocked cellar offers reserve labels, many available by the glass; between sips you can choose to munch the wide range of cicheti on offer, or a few tiny well-stuffed tramezzini, appropriately called *francobolli* (postage stamps). **Known for:** good choice of wines by the glass; fine selection of cicheti and sandwiches; delicious baccalà mantecato, with or without garlic and parsley. *Average main: €12 Calle dei Do Mori, San Polo 429 041/5225401 Closed Sun. Vaporetto: Rialto Mercato.*

Hotels

★ Hotel al Ponte Mocenigo

$ | **HOTEL** | At this hotel—once home to the Santa Croce branch of the Mocenigo family, which counts a few doges in its lineage—a columned courtyard welcomes you, and guest room decor nods to the building's history, with canopied beds, striped damask fabrics, lustrous terrazzo flooring, and gilt-accented furnishings. **Pros:** fantastic value; friendly and helpful staff; enchanting courtyard (the perfect spot for an aperitivo). **Cons:** beds are on the hard side; standard rooms are small; rooms in the annex can be noisy. *Rooms from: €150 Salizzada San Stae, Santa Croce 1985 041/5244797 www.alpontemocenigo.com 11 rooms Free Breakfast Vaporetto: San Stae.*

La Villeggiatura

$$ | **HOTEL** | If eclectic Venetian charm is what you seek, this luminous residence near the Rialto has it: each of the individually decorated guest rooms has its own theater-theme wall painting by a local artist. **Pros:** relaxed atmosphere and friendly, personalized service; meticulously maintained; well located near markets, artistic monuments, and restaurants. **Cons:** no elevator and lots of stairs; no view to speak of, despite the climb; no restaurant (though breakfast is served). *Rooms from: €185 Calle dei Botteri, San Polo 1569 041/5244673 www.lavilleggiatura.it 6 rooms Free Breakfast Vaporetto: Rialto Mercato.*

★ Oltre il Giardino

$$ | **HOTEL** | Behind a brick wall, just over the bridge from the Frari church, this palazzo named "Beyond the Garden" is hard to find but well worth the effort: a sheltered location, large canal-side garden, and individually decorated guest rooms make it feel like a country house. **Pros:** peaceful, gracious, and convenient setting; glorious walled garden; friendly owners happy to share their Venice tips. **Cons:** a beautiful, though not particularly Venetian, ambience; rooms book up quickly; no in-house restaurant (though breakfast served). *Rooms from: €340 Fondamenta Contarini, San Polo 2542 041/2750015, 331/5460266 WhatsApp www.oltreilgiardino-venezia.com Closed Jan. 6 rooms Free Breakfast Vaporetto: San Tomà.*

Nightlife

★ Il Mercante

COCKTAIL BARS | When the clock strikes 6 pm, historic Caffè dei Frari transforms into this lively craft cocktail bar that will dazzle your inner adventurer. Relax on a velvet sofa while savoring remarkably inventive drinks paired with flavorful small bites. Each pairing has a distinctive name; "Amatriciana" is composed of vodka, dry vermouth, and black tea, served with Parmesan foam, pineapple gel, and balsamic vinegar (billed as "strong, smoky, tasty"). *Fondamenta dei Frari, San Polo 2564 347/8293158 mobile www.ilmercantevenezia.com Vaporetto: San Tomà.*

Naranzaria

BARS | At the friendliest of the several bar-restaurants that line the Erbaria, near the Rialto markets, enjoy a cocktail outside, along the Canal Grande, or at a cozy table inside the renovated 16th-century warehouse. Although the food is acceptable, the ambience is really the main attraction. The kitchen closes at 11, and occasionally there is live music (usually jazz, Latin, or rock) on Sunday evening. On summer evenings, especially the weekend, the market area draws crowds of young people from Venice, the lagoon islands, and the mainland. ✉ *Sotoportego del Bancogiro, L'Erbaria, San Polo 130* ☎ *041/7241035* 🌐 *www.naranzaria.it* Ⓜ *Vaporetto: Rialto Mercato.*

Shopping

Gilberto Penzo

CRAFTS | FAMILY | The gondola and lagoon boat expert in Venice creates scale models of a wide variety of Venetian boats in his nearby *laboratorio* (workshop). (If the retail shop is closed, a sign posted on the door will explain how to find Signor Penzo.) When he's not busy sawing and sanding, Mr. Penzo writes historical and technical books about traditional Venetian boats, including the gondola. Here you'll also find gondola model kits, as well as some forcole (Venetian rowing oarlocks). ✉ *Calle Seconda dei Saoneri, San Polo 2681* ☎ *041/5246139* 🌐 *www.veniceboats.com* Ⓜ *Vaporetto: San Tomà.*

★ Il Tabarro San Marco di Monica Daniele

SPECIALTY STORE | This petite shop is the best place in town to find traditional Venetian wool capes, known as *tabarro*, and classic hats, such as the Ezra Pound (soft fedora), the *tricorno* (three-cornered hat), and the *cilindro* (top hat). ✉ *Calle del Scaleter, San Polo 2235* ☎ *041/5246242, 0349/1395987 WhatsApp* 🌐 *www.monicadaniele.com* Ⓜ *Vaporetto: San Stae, San Silvestro.*

Laberintho

JEWELRY & WATCHES | A tiny bottega near Campo San Polo is run by a team of young goldsmiths and jewelry designers specializing in inlaid stones. The work on display in their shop is exceptional, and they also create customized pieces. ✉ *Calle del Scaleter, San Polo 2236* ☎ *041/710017* 🌐 *www.laberintho.com* Ⓜ *Vaporetto: San Stae, San Silvestro.*

Cannaregio

Seen from above, this part of town seems like a wide field plowed by several long, straight canals linked by perpendicular streets—not typical of Venice, where the shape of the islands usually defines the shape of the canals. Cannaregio's main thoroughfare, the Strada Nova (New Street, converted from a canal in 1871), is the longest street in Venice; it runs parallel to the Grand Canal.

TIMING

Although it's more residential and less sight-rich than other Venice neighborhoods, you'll still need several hours here to explore the Ca' d'Oro palace and Madonna dell'Orto and Santa Maria dei Miracoli churches, and to wander the Jewish Ghetto. Cannaregio is a great place to spend a morning before taking the vaporetto to Murano and Burano, which departs from the Fondamente Nove stop.

Sights

Ca' d'Oro

HISTORY MUSEUM | One of the classic postcard sights of Venice, this exquisite Venetian Gothic palace was once literally a "Golden House," when its marble tracery and ornaments were embellished with gold. It was created by Giovanni and Bartolomeo Bon between 1428 and 1430 for the patrician Marino Contarini, who had read about the Roman emperor Nero's golden house in Rome, the Domus Aurea, and wished to imitate it as a present to his wife. Her family owned the land and the Byzantine *fondaco* (palace–trading house) previously standing on it; you can still see the round Byzantine arches incorporated into the Gothic building's entry porch. ✉ *Calle Ca' d'Oro, Cannaregio 3933, Cannaregio*

041/5222349 www.cadoro.org €8 Closed Mon. Vaporetto: Ca' d'Oro.

Casino di Venezia—Palazzo Vendramin-Calergi

CASINO | Hallowed as the site of Richard Wagner's death and today Venice's most glamorous casino, this magnificent edifice found its fame centuries earlier: Venetian star architect Mauro Codussi (1440–1504) essentially invented Venetian Renaissance architecture with this design. Built for the Loredan family around 1500, Codussi's palace married the fortresslike design of the Florentine Alberti's Palazzo Rucellai with the lightness and delicacy of the Venetian Gothic. Note how Codussi beautifully exploits the flickering light of Venetian waterways to play across the building's facade and to pour in through the generous windows. Consult the website to book a guided tour of the small Museo Wagner upstairs, where an archive, events, and concerts may interest Wagnerians.

Venice has always prized the beauty of this palace. In 1652 its owners were convicted of a rather gruesome murder, and the punishment would have involved, as was customary, the demolition of their palace. The murderers were banned from the Republic, but the palace, in view of its beauty and historical importance, was spared. Only a newly added wing was torn down. *Cannaregio 2040, Cannaregio 041/5297111 www.casinovenezia.it Casino ticket €50: includes €20 playing credit, vaporetto ticket, parking, and a drink; free for visitors staying at a Venice hotel (with prior written confirmation from the hotel, by 6 pm that day) Vaporetto: San Marcuola.*

★ **Gesuiti** (*Chiesa di Santa Maria Assunta*)

CHURCH | The interior walls of this early-18th-century church (1715–30) resemble brocade drapery, and only touching them will convince skeptics that rather than embroidered cloth, the green-and-white walls are inlaid marble. This trompe-l'oeil decor is typical of the late Baroque's fascination with optical illusion. Toward the end of his life, Titian tended to paint scenes of suffering and sorrow in a nocturnal ambience. A dramatic example of this is on display above the first altar to the left: Titian's daring *Martyrdom of St. Lawrence* (1578), taken from an earlier church that stood on this site. Tintoretto's *Assumption* (1555), originally commissioned for the destroyed Crociferi church, demands reverence. The Crociferi's surviving oratory, or prayer hall (Oratorio dei Crociferi), located across from the church, features some of Palma Giovane's best work, painted between 1583 and 1591. The oratory can be visited only with reservations at least three days in advance requested on the website or by email. *Campo dei Gesuiti, Cannaregio 041/3096605 oratory, 041/5286579 Gesuiti www.gioiellinascostidivenezia.it Gesuiti €1; Oratorio dei Crociferi €3 plus €60 per group with guided tour and €40 per group without guided tour Reservations needed to visit oratory Vaporetto: Fondamente Nove.*

★ **Jewish Ghetto**

HISTORIC DISTRICT | The very first Jewish Ghetto in Europe also contains the continent's highest density of Renaissance-era synagogues, and visiting them on a guided tour is interesting not only culturally but also aesthetically. In 1516, the Venetian Senate voted to confine Jews to an island in Cannaregio, whose gates were locked at night and whose canals were patrolled. In the 16th century, the community grew with refugees from the Inquisition. Although the gates were pulled down after Napoléon's 1797 arrival, the Ghetto was reinstated during the Austrian occupation. Full freedom wasn't realized until 1866 with the founding of the Italian state. Many Jews fled Italy after Mussolini's 1938 racial laws, but of the remainder, all but eight were killed by the Nazis. You can visit some of the historic buildings of the Ghetto on guided tours, which run in English every hour from 10 am to 5 pm (9 am to 3 pm on Friday), every day except Saturday. ✉ *Campo del Ghetto Nuovo, Cannaregio* ☎ *041/5246083* 🌐 *www.ghettovenezia.com* 🎫 *€15 for guided tour* 🕑 *No guided tours on Sat. or Jewish holidays.*

★ Madonna dell'Orto

CHURCH | Though built toward the middle of the 14th century, this church takes its character from its beautiful late-Gothic facade, added between 1460 and 1464; it's one of the most beautiful Gothic churches in Venice. Tintoretto lived nearby, and this, his parish church, contains some of his most powerful work. Lining the chancel are two huge (45 feet by 20 feet) canvases, *Adoration of the Golden Calf* and *Last Judgment.* In glowing contrast to this awesome spectacle is Tintoretto's *Presentation of the Virgin at the Temple* and the simple chapel where he and his children, Marietta and Domenico, are buried. Paintings by Domenico, Cima da Conegliano, Palma Giovane, Palma Vecchio, and Titian also hang in the church. A chapel displays a photographic reproduction of a precious *Madonna and Child* by Giovanni Bellini. The original was stolen one night in 1993. Don't miss the beautifully austere, late-Gothic cloister (1460), which you enter through the small door to the right of the church; it is frequently used for exhibitions but may be open at other times as well. ✉ *Campo della Madonna dell'Orto, Cannaregio* ☎ *041/719933 church office, 041/2750462* 🌐 *www.chorusvenezia.org* 🎫 *€3.50 (free with Chorus Pass)* 🕑 *Closed Sun.* Ⓜ *Vaporetto: Orto.*

Museo Ebraico (*Jewish Museum*)

SYNAGOGUE | The "dispersed museum" comprises three of the Ghetto's five synagogues (the 16th-century Tedesca, Canton, and Italiana) plus a compact, well-arranged museum that highlights centuries of Venetian Jewish culture. Among the artifacts on display are splendid silver Hanukkah lamps and Torahs, beautifully decorated wedding contracts handwritten in Hebrew, and an important library. The recently created and wonderful Giardino Segreto della Scuola Spagnola, a secret garden with rich plant life and a sukkah, is also open to the public occasionally. Tours of the Ghetto and its synagogues in Italian and English leave from the museum hourly. ✉ *Campo del Ghetto Nuovo, Cannaregio 2902/B, Cannaregio* ☎ *055/2989815* 🌐 *www.ghettovenezia.com* 🎫 *€15 with guided tour* 🕑 *Closed Sat.* Ⓜ *Vaporetto: San Marcuola, Guglie.*

★ Santa Maria dei Miracoli

CHURCH | Tiny yet harmoniously proportioned, this Renaissance gem, built between 1481 and 1489, is sheathed in marble and decorated inside with exquisite marble reliefs. Architect Pietro Lombardo (circa 1435–1515) miraculously compressed the building to fit its lot, then created the illusion of greater size by varying the color of the exterior, adding extra pilasters on the building's canal side, and offsetting the arcade windows to make the arches appear deeper. The church was built to house *I Miracoli,* an image of the Virgin Mary by Niccolò di Pietro (1394–1440) that is said to have performed miracles—look for it on the high altar. ✉ *Campo Santa Maria Nova, Cannaregio* ☎ *041/2750462* 🌐 *www.chorusvenezia.org* 🎫 *€3.50 (free with Chorus Pass)* 🕑 *Closed Sun.* Ⓜ *Vaporetto: Rialto.*

Restaurants

★ Algiubagiò

$$$ | **ITALIAN** | Established in 1950, this restaurant along the quiet, northern outlier of Fondamente Nove has grandstand views of the San Michele island and various menus showcasing seasonal fish, meat, and pasta dishes. The friendly staff also serve ice cream, drinks, and sandwiches, making its modern bar, chic dining rooms, and lagoon-side platform restful environs to pause any time of day. **Known for:** airy respite for lunch or a snack; romantic spot for dinner;

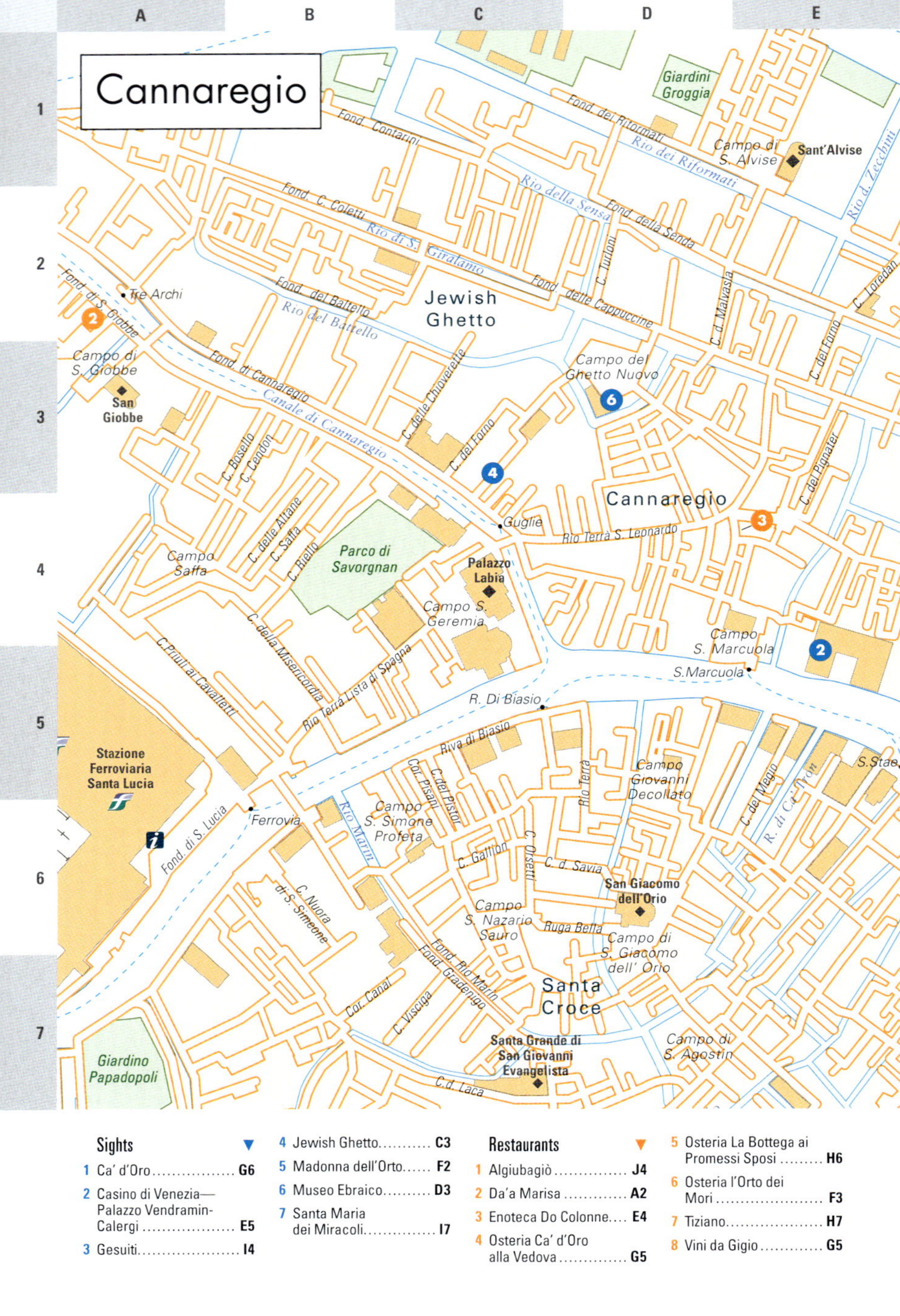

Sights ▼

1 Ca' d'Oro **G6**
2 Casino di Venezia—Palazzo Vendramin-Calergi **E5**
3 Gesuiti **I4**
4 Jewish Ghetto........... **C3**
5 Madonna dell'Orto...... **F2**
6 Museo Ebraico.......... **D3**
7 Santa Maria dei Miracoli............... **I7**

Restaurants ▼

1 Algiubagiò **J4**
2 Da'a Marisa **A2**
3 Enoteca Do Colonne.... **E4**
4 Osteria Ca' d'Oro alla Vedova **G5**
5 Osteria La Bottega ai Promessi Sposi **H6**
6 Osteria l'Orto dei Mori **F3**
7 Tiziano..................... **H7**
8 Vini da Gigio **G5**

Quick Bites

1 Vino Vero **G4**

Hotels

1 Al Palazzetto **G5**
2 Al Ponte Antico **H7**
3 Ca' Amadi................ **H7**
4 Ca' Sagredo Hotel **G6**
5 Hotel Antico Doge **H6**
6 Palazzo Abadessa **G5**
7 3749 Ponte Chiodo...... **G5**

innovative dishes like spaghetti alla spirulina. [$] *Average main: €32* ✉ *Fondamente Nove, Cannaregio 5039, Cannaregio* ☎ *041/5236084* 🌐 *www.algiubagio.net* 🕙 *Closed Tues.* [M] *Vaporetto: Fondamente Nove.*

Da'a Marisa

$$ | **ITALIAN** | This is the most famous restaurant in Venice for the city's working class; if you can get a table for lunch, you'll eat, without any choice, what Marisa prepares for her local clientele—generally, big portions of excellent pasta followed by a hearty roast meat course (frequently game, more infrequently fish), for an inexpensive fixed price. Dinner is more expensive, and you may have some choice, but not much; for the authentic "Marisa experience," go for lunch. **Known for:** Venetian classics like baccalà mantecato; limited menu choices and cramped inside; genuine local atmosphere and gruff service. [$] *Average main: €20* ✉ *Fondamenta di San Giobbe 652B, Cannaregio* ☎ *041/720211* 🕙 *No dinner Sun., Mon., and Wed.*

Enoteca Do Colonne

$ | **WINE BAR** | Venetians from the neighborhood frequent this friendly bacaro, not just for a glass of very drinkable wine, but also because of its bountiful selection of traditional Venetian cicheti for lunch. There's a large assortment of sandwiches and panini, as well as luscious tidbits like grilled vegetables, breaded and fried sardines and shrimp, and a decent version of baccalà mantecato, along with Venetian working-class specialties, such as *musetto* (a sausage made from pigs' snouts served warm with polenta) and *nervetti* (veal tendons with lemon and parsley). **Known for:** a cozy place for locals to hang out; classic cicheti and sandwiches; traditional offal dishes. [$] *Average main: €13* ✉ *Rio Terà Cristo, Cannaregio 1814, Cannaregio* ☎ *041/5240453* 🌐 *www.docolonne.it* [M] *Vaporetto: San Marcuola.*

Osteria Ca' d'Oro alla Vedova

$$ | **VENETIAN** | "The best *polpette* in town," you'll hear fans of the venerable Vedova say, and that explains why it's an obligatory stop on any *giro d'ombra* (bacaro tour); the polpette are always hot and crunchy—and also gluten-free, as they're made with polenta. Ca' d'Oro is a full-fledged trattoria as well, but make sure to reserve ahead: it's no secret to those seeking traditional Venetian fare at reasonable prices, locals and travelers alike. **Known for:** famous polpette; classic Venetian meat, fish, and cicheti; traditional bacaro decor and wine glasses. [$] *Average main: €20* ✉ *Calle del Pistor, Cannaregio 3912, off Strada Nova, Cannaregio* ☎ *041/5285324* 🌐 *www.facebook.com/allavedova* 🕙 *Closed Thurs. No lunch Sun.* [M] *Vaporetto: Ca' d'Oro.*

Osteria La Bottega ai Promessi Sposi

$$ | **VENETIAN** | Join locals at the *banco* (counter) premeal for an *ombra* (small glass of wine) and cicheti like polpette or violet eggplant rounds, or reserve a table for a full meal in the dining room or the intimate courtyard. A varied, seasonal menu includes local standards like calf's liver, along with creative variations on classic Venetian fare, such as homemade ravioli stuffed with radicchio di Treviso or orecchiette with a scrumptious minced-duck sauce. **Known for:** creative cicheti and wine; regularly changing menu with both traditional and modern choices; friendly, helpful service. [$] *Average main: €22* ✉ *Calle de l'Oca, just off Campo Santi Apostoli, Cannaregio 4367, Cannaregio* ☎ *041/2412747* 🌐 *www.facebook.com/aipromessisposi* 🕙 *No lunch Mon.* [M] *Vaporetto: Ca' d'Oro.*

★ Osteria l'Orto dei Mori

$$ | **ITALIAN** | This small, popular neighborhood osteria—located canal-side, just under the nose of the campo's famous corner statue—specializes in creative versions of classic Italian (but not necessarily Venetian) dishes; keep it Venetian with baccala mantecato then

fegato alla veneziana (liver with onions) or push the experimental boat out with their Sicilian king prawns swimming in curry and fennel followed by duck breast with grapefruit and rosemary sauce. Don't skip dessert, as their boozy tiramisu with Moscato di Pantelleria wins raves. **Known for:** traditional Italian dishes with modern accents; choice local wine selection; buzzing atmosphere with locals and tourists alike. *Average main: €27 Campo dei Mori, Fondamenta dei Mori, Cannaregio 3386, Cannaregio 041/5243677 www.osteriaortodeimori.com Closed Tues. and Wed. Vaporetto: Orto, Ca' d'Oro, San Marcuola.*

Tiziano

$ | ITALIAN | A fine variety of excellent *tramezzini* (sandwiches made of untoasted white bread triangles) lines the display cases at this busy *tavola calda* (roughly the Italian equivalent of a cafeteria) on the main thoroughfare from the Rialto to Santi Apostoli; inexpensive salad plates and daily pasta specials are also served. This is a great place for a light meal or snack before a performance at the nearby Teatro Malibran. **Known for:** quick meals or snacks, especially tramezzini; noisy spot; efficient (if occasionally grumpy) service. *Average main: €10 Salizada San Giovanni Crisostomo, Cannaregio 5747, Cannaregio 041/5235544 Vaporetto: Rialto.*

★ Vini da Gigio

$$ | VENETIAN | A brother-sister team run this refined trattoria, where you're made to feel as if you've been personally invited to lunch or dinner. Indulge, perhaps, in spaghetti with clams and cod roe or arugula-stuffed ravioli, seafood risotto made to order for two, or sesame-encrusted tuna. Just note, though, that it's the meat dishes that steal the show: the steak with red-pepper sauce and *fegato alla veneziana* (liver and onions) are among the best in town. **Known for:** superb meat dishes like fegato alla veneziana; one of the city's best wine cellars; helpful and professional service. *Average main: €26 Fondamenta San Felice, Cannaregio 3628/A, Cannaregio 041/5285140 www.vinidagigio.com Closed Mon., Tues., and 2 wks in Aug. Vaporetto: Ca' d'Oro.*

Coffee and Quick Bites

★ Vino Vero

$ | WINE BAR | Swing by this pint-sized wine bar for cicheti and crostini that are just a bit different and fresher than what you'll find elsewhere, along with a fine selection of natural wines. Though there's not much space inside, try to snag one of the coveted seats by the canal, which becomes a buzzy evening spot at *aperitivo* time. **Known for:** large selection of both Italian and international natural wines; delectable small bites; pretty canal-side seating. *Average main: €14 Fondamenta de la Misericordia, Cannaregio 2497, Cannaregio 041/2750044 vinovero.wine No lunch Mon. Vaporetto: Madonna dell'Orto, Ca' d'Oro.*

Hotels

Al Palazzetto

$ | B&B/INN | FAMILY | Understated Venetian decor, original exposed-beam ceilings and terrazzo flooring, and large rooms suitable for families or small groups are hallmarks of this intimate, family-owned guesthouse. **Pros:** authentic 18th-century palace; clean and quiet; good value for Venice. **Cons:** old-fashioned decor; not many amenities; a bit rough around the edges. *Rooms from: €159 Calle delle Vele, Cannaregio 4057, Cannaregio 041/2750897 www.guesthouse.it 5 rooms Free Breakfast Vaporetto: Ca' d'Oro.*

★ Al Ponte Antico

$$ | HOTEL | The intimate upstairs terrace of this hospitable 16th-century palace inn is a perfect spot to survey the nearby Rialto scene while enjoying evening *aperitivi* and their fabulous homemade

breakfasts. **Pros:** unique upper-level terrace overlooks Grand Canal; Peruch family-run warmth and attentive service; Matteo and Barbara's made-to-order omelets and Venetian pastries. **Cons:** in one of the busiest areas of the city (although not particularly noisy); beds a little hard for some; books up quickly. *Rooms from: €390 Calle dell'Aseo, Cannaregio 5768, Cannaregio 041/2411944 www.alponteantico.com 9 rooms Free Breakfast Vaporetto: Rialto.*

Ca' Amadi

$$ | **HOTEL** | A historic 13th-century palazzo near the Rialto markets is a welcome retreat on a tranquil *corte* (court), and individually decorated rooms have tufted walls and views of a lively canal or a quiet courtyard. **Pros:** classic Venetian style; some canal-view rooms; handy for sightseeing. **Cons:** rooms vary a lot in size and quality; no restaurant (simple continental breakfast served, though); reception staff not always helpful or available. *Rooms from: €180 Corte Amadi, Cannaregio 5815, Cannaregio 041/5285210 www.caamadi.it 6 rooms Free Breakfast Vaporetto: Rialto.*

Ca' Sagredo Hotel

$$ | **HOTEL** | This expansive palace has been the Sagredo family residence since the mid-1600s and has the decor to prove it: a massive staircase has Longhi wall panels soaring above it; large common areas are adorned with original art by Tiepolo, Longhi, and Ricci; and a traditional Venetian style dominates guest rooms, many of which have canal views and some of which have original art and architectural elements. **Pros:** canal views from some rooms; some of the city's best-preserved interiors; rooftop terrace and indoor bar. **Cons:** impersonal, formal atmosphere; heat in rooms controlled by front desk; no coffee- or tea-making facilities in rooms. *Rooms from: €374 Campo Santa Sofia, Cannaregio 4198/99, Cannaregio 041/2413111 www.casagredohotel.com 42 rooms No Meals Vaporetto: Ca' d'Oro.*

Hotel Antico Doge

$$ | **HOTEL** | Once the home of Marino Faliero, a 14th-century doge who was executed for treason, this palazzo has been attentively "modernized" in elegant 18th-century Venetian style: all rooms are adorned with brocades, damask-tufted walls, gilt mirrors, and parquet floors—even the breakfast room has a stuccoed ceiling and Murano chandelier. **Pros:** romantic, atmospheric decor; convenient to the Rialto and beyond; some rooms have whirlpool tubs. **Cons:** no outdoor garden or terrace; no elevator; area outside hotel is very busy and noisy. *Rooms from: €253 Campo Santi Apostoli, Cannaregio 5643, Cannaregio 041/7799990 www.anticodoge.com 20 rooms No Meals Vaporetto: Ca' d'Oro, Rialto.*

Palazzo Abadessa

$$ | **HOTEL** | At this atmospheric late-16th-century palazzo, you can experience warm hospitality, a lush private garden, and unusually spacious guest rooms well appointed with antique-style furniture, frescoed or stuccoed ceilings, and silk fabrics. **Pros:** enormous walled garden, a rare and delightful treat in crowded Venice; unique and richly decorated guest rooms; superb guest service. **Cons:** many of the bathrooms need a refurb; no restaurant (buffet breakfast served); poor soundproofing. *Rooms from: €292 Calle Priuli, Cannaregio 4011, off Strada Nova, Cannaregio 041/2413784 www.abadessa.com Closed last 2 wks in Jan. 15 rooms Free Breakfast Vaporetto: Ca' d'Oro.*

3749 Ponte Chiodo

$ | **B&B/INN** | Spending time at this charming guesthouse secreted away down narrow Calle Racheta near the Ca' d'Oro vaporetto stop is like staying with a friend: service is warm and helpful, with lots of suggestions for dining and sightseeing. **Pros:** highly attentive service; relaxed atmosphere; pretty private garden. **Cons:** bathroom decor dated; no restaurant, though breakfast is served in the garden; not for those looking for large-hotel amenities (no spa or gym). *Rooms from: €130* *Calle Racheta, Cannaregio 3749, Cannaregio* *041/2413935, 348/2473520 mobile* *www.pontechiodo.it* *6 rooms* *Free Breakfast* *Vaporetto: Ca' d'Oro.*

Nightlife

El Sbarlefo

WINE BAR | The odd name is Venetian for "smirk," although you'll be hard-pressed to find one at this cheery, familiar bacaro with a wine selection as ample as the cicheti on offer. The spread of delectables ranges from classic polpette of meat and tuna to tomino cheese rounds to speck and robiola rolls, and the selection of wines is equally intriguing. There's often live jazz and blues on Friday and Saturday nights. El Sbarlefo has a second location in Dorsoduro, in the calle just behind the church of San Pantalon. *Salizada del Pistor, off Campo Santi Apostoli, Cannaregio 4556/C, Cannaregio* *041/5246650* *www.elsbarlefo.it* *Vaporetto: Ca' d'Oro.*

Time Social Bar

COCKTAIL BARS | The seasonal cocktails at this charming mixology bar, many of which use fruit and homemade bitters, win rave reviews from visitors and locals alike. There are also small nibbles on offer if hunger strikes. *Rio Terà Farsetti, Cannaregio 1414, Cannaregio* *338/3636951 mobile* *www.timesocialbar.it* *Vaporetto: San Marcuola Casino.*

Un Mondo di Vino

WINE BAR | Recharge with some wine or a cicheto or two—meat, fish, and vegetarian choices are on offer—at this cozy, friendly spot near the Miracoli church. Numerous wines are available by the glass, and the helpful servers are often happy to crack open a bottle for sampling if there's something you fancy. *Salizzada San Cancian, Cannaregio* *041/5211093* *www.bacarounmondodivino.it* *Vaporetto: Rialto, Ca' d'Oro.*

Shopping

★ Gianni Basso Stampatore

STATIONERY | Beloved of artists and celebrities, this traditional printer run by amiable Gianni and his son creates handmade business cards, stationery, and invitations using vintage letterpress machinery. You can choose from the selection on offer or have your own custom designed and shipped to you at home. Ask Gianni about the history of the place and his loyal global clientele, and he'll likely regale you with tales and a tour of his lovingly curated museum-workshop. Don't touch the antique equipment, though. *Calle del Fumo, Cannaregio 5306, Cannaregio* *041/5234681* *Vaporetto: Fondamente Nove.*

★ Vittorio Constantini

ANTIQUES & COLLECTIBLES | **FAMILY** | This glass artist's workshop features unusual, intricate pieces inspired by nature—birds, butterflies, beetles, and other insects—appreciated by adults and children alike. *Calle del Fumo, Cannaregio 5311, Cannaregio* *041/5222265* *www.vittoriocostantini.com* *Vaporetto: Fondamente Nove.*

Castello

Castello, Venice's largest sestiere, includes all of the land from east of Piazza San Marco to the city's easternmost tip. Its name probably comes from a fortress that once stood on one of the eastern islands. Not every well-off Venetian family could find a spot or afford to build a palazzo on the Grand Canal. Many who couldn't instead settled in western Castello, taking advantage of its proximity to the Rialto and San Marco, and built the noble palazzi that today distinguish this area from the fisher's enclave in the more easterly streets of the sestiere. During the days of the Republic, eastern Castello was the primary neighborhood for workers in the shipbuilding Arsenale located in its midst and now home to the Venice Biennale. Foodies flock here for some of the city's most creative modern Italian cuisine.

TIMING

Unless you're here during the Biennale—in which case, you'll be spending at least a full day or two at the Arsenale—you can check out the neighborhood's three gorgeous churches (San Francesco della Vigna, Santi Giovanni e Paolo, and San Zaccaria), as well as the lovely rooms in the Scuola di San Giorgio degli Schiavoni (if it's open, which it isn't always), in half a day.

Sights

Arsenale

MILITARY SIGHT | Visible from the street, the Porta Magna (1460), an impressive Renaissance gateway designed by Antonio Gambello, was the first classical structure to be built in Venice. It is guarded by four lions—war booty of Francesco Morosini, who took the Peloponnese from the Turks in 1687. The Arsenale is said to have been founded in 1104 on twin islands. The immense facility that evolved—it was the largest industrial complex in Europe built prior to the Industrial Revolution—was given the old Venetian dialect name *arzanà,* borrowed from the Arabic *darsina'a,* meaning "workshop." At the height of its activity, in the early 16th century, it employed as many as 16,000 *arsenalotti,* workers who were among the most respected shipbuilders in the world. The Arsenale developed a type of pre–Industrial Revolution assembly line, which allowed it to build ships with astounding speed and efficiency. The Arsenale's efficiency was confirmed time and again—whether building 100 ships in 60 days to battle the Turks in Cyprus (1597) or completing one perfectly armed warship, start to finish, while King Henry III of France attended a banquet. ✉ *Campo de la Tana 2169, Castello* Ⓜ *Vaporetto: Arsenale.*

★ San Francesco della Vigna

CHURCH | Although this church contains some interesting and beautiful paintings and sculptures, it's the architecture that makes it worth the hike through a lively, middle-class residential neighborhood. The Franciscan church was enlarged and rebuilt by Jacopo Sansovino in 1534, giving it the first Renaissance interior in Venice; its proportions are said to reflect the mystic significance of the numbers three and seven dictated by Renaissance neo-Platonic numerology. The soaring but harmonious facade was added in 1562 by Palladio. The church represents a unique combination of the work of the two great stars of 16th-century Veneto architecture. The complex contains three cloisters that house vegetable plots and the city's oldest vineyard. ✉ *Campo di San Francesco della Vigna, Castello* ☎ *041/5222476* 🌐 *www.facebook.com/sanfrancescodellavignavenezia* Ⓜ *Vaporetto: Celestia.*

★ Santi Giovanni e Paolo

CHURCH | This gorgeous Italian Gothic church of the Dominican order, consecrated in 1430, looms over one of the most picturesque squares in Venice: the Campo Giovanni e Paolo, centered around the magnificent 15th-century equestrian statue of Bartolomeo Colleoni by the Florentine Andrea Verrocchio. Bartolomeo Bon's portal, combining Gothic and classical elements, was added between 1458 and 1462, using columns salvaged from Torcello. The 15th-century Murano stained-glass window near the side entrance is breathtaking for its beautiful colors and figures. ✉ *Campo dei Santi Giovanni e Paolo, Castello* ☎ *041/5235913* 🌐 *www.santigiovanniepaolo.it* 🎫 *€3.50* 🕒 *Closed weekends* Ⓜ *Vaporetto: Fondamente Nove, Rialto.*

★ San Zaccaria

CHURCH | More a museum than a church, San Zaccaria has a striking Renaissance facade, with central and upper portions representing some of Mauro Codussi's best work. The lower portion of the facade and the interior were designed by Antonio Gambello. The original structure of the church was 14th-century Gothic, with its facade completed in 1515, some years after Codussi's death in 1504, and it retains the proportions of the rest of the essentially Gothic structure. Inside is one of the great treasures of Venice, Giovanni Bellini's celebrated altarpiece, *La Sacra Conversazione*, easily recognizable in the left nave. Completed in 1505, when the artist was 75, it shows Bellini's ability to incorporate the aesthetics of the High Renaissance into his work. ✉ *Campo San Zaccaria, 4693 Castello, Castello* ☎ *041/2750462, 041/5221257 church office* 🌐 *chorusvenezia.org* 🎫 *Church free, chapels and crypt €3.50 (free with Chorus Pass)* ⏲ *Closed Sun. morning* Ⓜ *Vaporetto: San Zaccaria.*

★ Scuola di San Giorgio degli Schiavoni (Scuola Dalmata)

HISTORIC SIGHT | Founded in 1451 by the Dalmatian community, this small scuola, or confraternity, was, and still is, a social and cultural center for migrants from what is now Croatia. It contains one of Italy's most beautiful rooms, harmoniously decorated between 1502 and 1507 by Vittore Carpaccio. Although Carpaccio generally painted legendary and religious figures against backgrounds of contemporary Venetian architecture, here is perhaps one of the first instances of "Orientalism" in Western painting. ■ **TIP→ Opening hours are quite flexible. Since this is a must-see site, book in advance so you won't be disappointed.** ✉ *Calle dei Furlani, Castello 3259/A, Castello* ☎ *041/5228828* 🌐 *www.scuoladalmatavenezia.com* 🎫 *€6* ⏲ *Closed Tues.* Ⓜ *Vaporetto: Arsenale, San Zaccaria.*

Restaurants

Al Covo

$$$ | **VENETIAN** | For years, Diane and Cesare Benelli's Al Covo has set the standard of excellence for traditional, refined Venetian cuisine; the Benellis are dedicated to providing their guests with the freshest, highest-quality fish from the Adriatic, and vegetables, when at all possible, from the islands of the Venetian Lagoon and the fields of the adjacent Veneto region. Although their cuisine could be correctly termed "classic Venetian," it always offers surprises, like the juicy crispness of their legendary fritto misto (fried mixed seafood and vegetables)—reliant upon an unconventional secret ingredient in the batter—or the heady aroma of their fresh anchovies marinated in wild fennel, an herb somewhat foreign to Veneto. **Known for:** sophisticated Venetian flavors; top-notch local ingredients; Diane's chocolate cake for dessert. 💲 *Average main: €33* ✉ *Campiello Pescaria, Castello 3968, Castello* ☎ *041/5223812* 🌐 *www.ristorantealcovo.com* ⏲ *Closed Tues. and Wed., 3 wks in Jan., and 10 days in Aug.* Ⓜ *Vaporetto: Arsenale.*

★ Alle Testiere

$$ | **VENETIAN** | The name is a reference to the old headboards that adorn the walls of this tiny, informal restaurant, but the food (not the decor) is undoubtedly the focus. Local foodies consider this one of the most refined eateries in the city thanks to chef Bruno Gavagnin's gently creative take on classic Venetian fish dishes; the chef's artistry seldom draws attention to itself but simply reveals new dimensions of familiar fare, creating dishes that stand out for their lightness and balance. **Known for:** daily changing fish offerings, based on what's fresh at the market; excellent pasta with seafood; wonderful wine selection. 💲 *Average main: €29* ✉ *Calle del Mondo Novo, Castello 5801, Castello* ☎ *041/5227220* 🌐 *www.osterialletestiere.it* ⏲ *Closed*

Castello, San Giorgio Maggiore, and Giudecca
A
B
C
D
E
F
1
2
3
4
5
6
7
8
9
Fond. Nuove
Ospedale
Canale
C. Bandi
S. Canciano
Campo S. Maria Nova
Rio della Panada
C. della Testa
Rio dei Mendicanti
Fondamenta dei Mendicanti
C. Larga Giacinto Gallina
Santa Maria dei Miracoli
Ospedaletto
Barbaria delle Tole
C. Nicolò Mazza
C. delle Cappuccine
C. Cavalli
Rio di S. Giustina
Fond. S. Giustina
Celestia
C. S. Francesco
Campo di S. Marina
C. delle Fava
C. del Dose
C. Trevisana
C. Pinelli
C. Lunga S. Maria Formosa
Rio d. Fava
Salizzada di S. Lio
C. d. Paradiso
Campo S. Maria Formosa
San Zaccaria
Borgoloco S. Lorenzo
Campo S. Lorenzo
Salizzada S. Giustina
Cor. Nuova
C. dell' Olio
Ruga Giuffa
Fond. di S. Severo
Fond. di S. Giorgio d. Schiavoni
C. Cassellaria
Campo S. Severo
C. del Lion
C. dei Preti
C. Mandolin
C. d. Scudi
Campo de la Guerra
San Marco
C. Fiubera
C. Rimpetto la Sacrestia
Fond. dell' Osmarin
San Giorgio dei Greci
San Antonio
Campo S. Provolo
Rio della Pietà
Sal. S. Antonin
Torre dell'Orologio
Basilica di San Marco
Rio Canonica o Palazzo
Rio dei Greci
C. dei Greci
Procuratie Vecchie
C. dell' Albanesi
C. delle Rasse
Rio del Vin
Campo S. Zaccaria
Campo Bandiera
San Giovanni in Bragora
Piazza San Marco
Campanile
Palazzo Ducale
C. della Pietà
C. del Dose
C. Morosina
Museo Archeologico
Piazzetta di San Marco
Schiavoni
San Zaccaria
Riva di Ca' di Dio
Biblioteca Marciana
Molo Riva degli
C. dei Forni
Giardini Ex Reali
San Marco
Arsenale
Salute
Canale di San Marco
Campo S. Giorgio
S. Giorgio
San Giorgio Maggiore
S. GIORGIO MAGGIORE
Redentore
Zitelle

Sights

1 Arsenale I7
2 Fondazione Giorgio Cini C9
3 San Francesco della Vigna F3
4 San Giorgio Maggiore D9
5 San Zaccaria D6
6 Santi Giovanni e Paolo C3
7 Santissimo Redentore A9
8 Scuola di San Giorgio degli Schiavoni (Scuola Dalmata) E5

Restaurants

1 Al Covo F6
2 Alle Testiere B4
3 Cip's Club & Oro B9
4 Corte Sconta F6
5 Il Ridotto C5
6 La Palanca A9
7 Local E5
8 L'Osteria di Santa Marina A3

Quick Bites

1 El Rèfolo H8
2 Wine Bar 5000 .... D5

Hotels

1 Belmond Hotel Cipriani B9
2 Ca' dei Dogi B6
3 Ca' di Dio F7
4 Hilton Molino Stucky Venice A9
5 Hotel Danieli C6
6 Hotel La Residenza E6
7 Metropole E6
8 Ruzzini Palace Hotel B4

Sun. and Mon., 3 wks in Jan. and Feb., and 4 wks in July and Aug.

★ Corte Sconta

$$ | **SEAFOOD** | The heaping seafood antipasti alone is reason enough to visit this classic seafood-focused eatery close to the Biennale—think tuna and swordfish carpaccio, spider crab, clams, crab pâté, and a variety of fish. But you'll also want to stay for the excellent mains, particularly soft-shell crab, mixed grilled fish, and spaghetti vongole, plus the lovely courtyard setting. **Known for:** some of the best seafood in town; charming atmosphere with outdoor seating; service with a sense of humor. *$ Average main: €28 ✉ Calle del Pestrin, Castello 3886, Castello ☎ 041/5227024 🌐 www.cortescontave.com ⏲ Closed Sun. and Mon. M Vaporetto: Arsenale.*

Il Ridotto

$$$ | **MODERN ITALIAN** | Longtime restaurateur Gianni Bonaccorsi has established an eatery where he can pamper a limited number of lucky patrons with his imaginative cuisine and impeccable taste in wine. *Ridotto* means "small, private place," which this very much is, evoking an atmosphere of secrecy and intimacy; the innovative menus tend toward lighter but wonderfully tasty versions of classic dishes. **Known for:** some of the most creative cuisine in Venice; excellent five- or seven-course tasting menus; extensive wine recommendations. *$ Average main: €40 ✉ Campo SS. Filippo e Giacomo, Castello 4509, Castello ☎ 041/5208280 🌐 www.ilridotto.com ⏲ Closed Wed. No lunch Tues. and Thurs. M Vaporetto: San Zaccaria.*

Local

$$$$ | **VENETIAN** | In a simple yet charming setting with beamed ceilings and terrazzo floors, a sister and brother team oversee their "new Venetian cuisine," where local ingredients are used to prepare reinvented traditional dishes, often with Japanese influences. It's tasting-menu only, with seven or nine courses (or a less expensive four-course option at weekday lunch), and wine pairings from their extensive list are a recommended treat. **Known for:** tiramisù dessert: coffee, marsala, and mascarpone; ingredients from Italian producers and daily catch; highly attentive staff. *$ Average main: €160 ✉ Salizzada dei Greci, Castello 3303, Castello ☎ 041/2411128 🌐 www.ristorantelocal.com ⏲ Closed Tues. and Wed. No lunch Sun. and Thurs. M Vaporetto: San Zaccaria.*

L'Osteria di Santa Marina

$$$ | **VENETIAN** | The candlelit tables on this romantic campo are inviting enough, but it's the intimate restaurant's imaginative kitchen that's likely to win you over; you can order consistently excellent pasta, fish, or meat dishes à la carte or opt for one of the rewarding tasting menus. The wine list is ample and well thought out, and the service is gracious, warm, and professional. **Known for:** innovative and artfully presented modern Venetian food; charming setting; wonderful wine pairings. *$ Average main: €33 ✉ Campo Santa Marina, Castello 5911, Castello ☎ 041/5285239 🌐 www.osteriadisantamarina.com ⏲ Closed Sun. and 2 wks in Aug. No lunch Mon. M Vaporetto: Rialto.*

Coffee and Quick Bites

★ El Rèfolo

$ | **WINE BAR** | At this contemporary cantina and hip hangout in a very Venetian neighborhood, the owner pairs enthusiastically chosen wines and artisanal beers with select meat, savory cheese, pasta dishes, and seasonal vegetable combos. With outside-only seating (not particularly comfortable), it's more appropriate for an aperitivo and a light meal. **Known for:** good selection of wine and beer; filling panini, meat and cheese plates; boisterous atmosphere outside in nice weather. *$ Average main: €16 ✉ Via Garibaldi, Castello 1580, Castello ☎ 320/3267536 mobile 🌐 www.facebook.com/elrefolo ⏲ Closed Mon. M Vaporetto: Arsenale.*

Wine Bar 5000

$ | **WINE BAR** | Nibble on a selection of cicheti or a cheese or meat plate at this cozy wine bar on Campo San Severo, near the Basilica dei Frari. You can either dine inside the brick-walled, Murano glass–chandeliered space, or watch the gondolas sail by at a table outdoors next to the quiet adjacent Severno canal. **Known for:** large wine list, including biodynamic options; lovely outdoor seating area; small but well-prepared choice of cicheti and salads. *Average main: €16* *Campo San Severo, Castello 5000, Castello* *041/3097891* *winebar5000.it* *Vaporetto: San Zaccaria.*

Hotels

Ca' dei Dogi

$$ | **HOTEL** | A quiet courtyard secluded from the San Marco melee offers an island of calm in six guest rooms and two apartments (some with private terraces overlooking the Doge's Palace), which are individually decorated with contemporary furnishings and accessories. **Pros:** amazing location close to Doge's Palace and Piazza San Marco; balconies with wonderful views; traditional Italian restaurant on-site. **Cons:** rooms are on the small side; no elevator and lots of stairs; bathrooms can feel cramped. *Rooms from: €180* *Corte Santa Scolastica, Castello 4242, Castello* *041/2413751* *www.cadeidogi.it* *Closed 3 wks in Dec.* *6 rooms* *No Meals* *Vaporetto: San Zaccaria.*

Ca' di Dio

$$$ | **HOTEL** | Housed in a palace dating from 1272, with interiors updated by of-the-moment architect Patricia Urquiola, this deluxe hotel offers rooms with views of San Giorgio Maggiore island, two restaurants, and two internal courtyards, all within striking distance of the Venice Biennale grounds. **Pros:** most guest rooms are suites; convenient to the Biennale; on-site gym and spa. **Cons:** staff can be a tad aloof; not for fans of traditional design; a walk from traditional Venetian sights. *Rooms from: €578* *Riva Ca' di Dio, Castello 5866, Castello* *041/0980238* *vretreats.com/en/ca-di-dio* *66 rooms* *No Meals* *Vaporetto: Arsenale.*

★ Hotel Danieli

$$$$ | **HOTEL** | One of the city's most famous lodgings—built in the 14th century and run as a hotel since 1822—lives up to its reputation: the chance to explore the wonderful, highly detailed lobby is itself a reason to book an overnight stay, plus the views along the lagoon are fantastic, the rooms gorgeous, and the food fabulous. **Pros:** historical and inviting lobby; amazing rooftop views; tasty cocktails at Bar Dandolo. **Cons:** lots of American tourists; some rooms feel dated; service can be indifferent. *Rooms from: €810* *Riva degli Schiavoni, Castello 4196, Castello* *041/5226480* *hoteldanieli.com* *210 rooms* *No Meals* *Vaporetto: San Zaccaria.*

Hotel La Residenza

$ | **HOTEL** | Set in a quiet campo, this renovated 15th-century Gothic-Byzantine palazzo has simple but spacious rooms and lovely public spaces filled with chandeliers, 18th-century paintings, and period reproduction furnishings. **Pros:** lavish salon and breakfast room; quiet residential area, steps from Riva degli Schiavoni and 10 minutes from Piazza San Marco; affordable rates. **Cons:** no elevator; basic, dated guest room decor; average breakfast. *Rooms from: €170* *Campo Bandiera e Moro, Castello 3608, Castello* *041/5285315* *www.venicelaresidenza.com* *15 rooms* *No Meals* *Vaporetto: Arsenale.*

Metropole

$$ | **HOTEL** | Atmosphere prevails in this labyrinth of opulent, intimate spaces featuring classic Venetian decor combined with Eastern influences: common areas and guest rooms are filled with an assortment of antiques and curiosities. **Pros:** hotel harkens back to the gracious Venice

of a bygone era; suites have private roof terraces with water views; gorgeous Oriental Bar & Bistrot. **Cons:** one of the most densely touristed locations in the city; some standard rooms and bathrooms are small; quirky, eccentric collections on display not for everyone. *Rooms from: €300 Riva degli Schiavoni, Castello 4149, Castello 041/5205044 www.hotelmetropole.com 67 rooms Free Breakfast Vaporetto: San Zaccaria.*

Ruzzini Palace Hotel

$$ | HOTEL | Renaissance- and Baroque-style common areas are soaring spaces with Venetian terrazzo flooring, frescoed and exposed-beam ceilings, and Murano chandeliers; guest rooms tastefully mix historical style with contemporary furnishings and appointments. **Pros:** a luminous, aristocratic ambience; located on a lively Venetian campo not frequented by tourists; cheaper rates for standard rooms often available. **Cons:** plain bathrooms; relatively far from a vaporetto stop; no restaurant on-site. *Rooms from: €260 Campo Santa Maria Formosa, Castello 5866, Castello 041/2410447 www.ruzzinipalace.com 28 rooms No Meals Vaporetto: San Zaccaria, Rialto.*

Nightlife

Bar Dandolo

COCKTAIL BARS | Even if you're not staying at Hotel Danieli, it's worth a stop to marvel at its bar's over-the-top decor—replete with ornate ceilings, stained glass, marble columns, and chandeliers—inside a 14th-century palace. Though pricey, it's a highly atmospheric place to sample their signature Vesper martini or another cocktail of your choice, usually accompanied by live piano music. *Hotel Danieli, Riva degli Schiavoni, Castello 4196, Castello 041/5226480 www.hoteldanieli.com Vaporetto: San Zaccaria.*

Zanzibar

BARS | This kiosk bar is very popular on warm summer evenings with Venetians and tourists drinking spritz and nibbling popcorn. It's all about the location under the soaring church of Santa Maria Formosa, which makes it an atmospheric place for people-watching; plus, if you like a boogie, they stage occasional music (mainly reggae and dub) nights, and carnival events. Although there's food, it's mostly limited to conventional Venetian sandwiches and commercial ice cream. *Campo Santa Maria Formosa, Castello 5840, Castello 345/2885654 www.facebook.com/zanzibar5840 Vaporetto: San Zaccaria.*

Shopping

Kalimala

LEATHER GOODS | This shop should not be missed if you are looking for soft leather bags that are a perfect match for almost any outfit, handmade leather shoes, or quality belts. *Salizzada San Lio, Castello 5387, Castello 041/5283596 Vaporetto: Rialto.*

★ Papier Mache—Laboratorio di Artigianato Artistico

SPECIALTY STORE | FAMILY | If you're looking for an authentic Venetian mask, this is the place to go. Owner Stefano and his talented team of artists create exquisite handmade masks that can be custom ordered if you don't see what you want, as well as shipped worldwide. *Calle Lunga Santa Maria Formosa, Castello 5174/B, Venice 041/5229995 www.papiermache.it Vaporetto: Ospedale.*

San Giorgio Maggiore and Giudecca

Beckoning travelers across St. Mark's Basin is the island of San Giorgio Maggiore, separated by a small channel from Giudecca. A tall brick campanile on that distant bank nicely complements the Campanile of San Marco. Beneath it looms the stately dome of one of Venice's greatest churches, San Giorgio Maggiore, the creation of Andrea Palladio. To the west, on Giudecca, is Palladio's other masterpiece, the church of the Santissimo Redentore.

You can reach San Giorgio Maggiore via Vaporetto Line 2 from San Zaccaria. The next three stops on the line take you to Giudecca. The island's past may be shrouded in mystery, but despite recent gentrification by artists and well-to-do bohemians, it's still down-to-earth and one of the city's few remaining primarily working-class neighborhoods. Interestingly, you find that most Venetians don't even consider the Giudecchini Venetians at all.

TIMING

A half day should be plenty of time to visit the area. Allow about a half hour to see each of the churches and an hour or two to look around Giudecca.

Sights

★ Fondazione Giorgio Cini (*Cini Foundation*)

SPECIALTY MUSEUM | Adjacent to San Giorgio Maggiore is a complex that now houses the Cini Foundation, established in 1951 as a cultural center dedicated to humanist research. It contains a beautiful cloister designed by Palladio in 1560, his refectory, a library designed by Longhena, and various archives. In a woodland area you can wander amid 10 "Vatican Chapels" created for the 2018 Architecture Biennale by renowned architects, including Norman Foster. Another stunning feature is the Borges Labyrinth, a 1-km (½-mile) path through a boxwood hedge that allows visitors to take a 45-minute contemplative walk. It was designed by Randoll Coate and inspired by the Jorge Luis Borges short story "The Garden of Forking Paths." An evocative audio guide, composed by Antonio Fresa and performed by Teatro La Fenice's orchestra, may accompany your pensive stroll. Guided tours are given daily (except Wednesday), and reservations are required. ✉ *Isola di San Giorgio Maggiore, San Giorgio Maggiore* ☎ *366/4202181* 🌐 *www.visitcini.com* 🎫 *Each tour is €15 (Foundation buildings, Borges Labyrinth, and the Vatican Chapels with Teatro Verde); combine two tours for €22; and three tours for €28* ⏲ *Closed Wed.* ✍ *Reservations required* Ⓜ *Vaporetto: San Giorgio.*

★ San Giorgio Maggiore

CHURCH | There's been a church on this island since the 8th century. Today's refreshingly airy and simply decorated church of brick and white marble was begun in 1566 by Palladio and displays his architectural hallmarks of mathematical harmony and classical influence. *The Last Supper* and the *Gathering of Manna*, two of Tintoretto's later works, line the chancel. To the right of the entrance hangs *The Adoration of the Shepherds* by Jacopo Bassano. Book ahead for a tour of the private rooms to view Carpaccio's *St. George and the Dragon* (1516) and what is considered to be Tintoretto's final work, *The Entombment of Christ* (1594). The campanile (bell tower) dates from 1791. **■ TIP→ Take an elevator to the top of the campanile for unparalleled 360-degree views of the lagoon, islands, and Venice itself.** ✉ *Isola di San Giorgio Maggiore, San Giorgio Maggiore* ☎ *0375/6323595* 🌐 *www.abbaziasangiorgio.it* 🎫 *Church free, campanile €6* Ⓜ *Vaporetto: San Giorgio.*

Santissimo Redentore

CHURCH | After a plague in 1576 claimed some 50,000 people—nearly one-third of the city's population (including Titian)—Andrea Palladio was asked to design a commemorative church. Giudecca's Capuchin friars offered land and their services, provided the building's design was in keeping with the simplicity of their

Did You Know?

The nobility in Venice used to be extremely competitive about their gondolas, decorating them in flamboyant colors and over-the-top ornaments. A law in the 16th century put an end to that. Today, all gondolas in Venice must be painted boring black, though they are allowed three flourishes: a curly tail, a pair of seahorses, and a multi-pronged prow.

hermitage. Consecrated in 1592, after Palladio's death, the Redentore (considered Palladio's supreme achievement in ecclesiastical design) is dominated by a dome and a pair of slim, almost minaretlike bell towers. Its deceptively simple, stately facade leads to a bright, airy interior. There aren't any paintings or sculptures of note, but the harmony and elegance of the interior makes a visit worthwhile. ✉ *Fondamenta San Giacomo, Giudecca* ☎ *041/5231415 church office, 041/2750462* 🌐 *www.chorusvenezia.org* 🎫 *€3.50 (free with Chorus Pass)* ⏲ *Closed Sun.* Ⓜ *Vaporetto: Redentore.*

Restaurants

Cip's Club & Oro

$$$$ | VENETIAN | Located on the water's edge, looking out at the Venice skyline, the Belmond Cipriani's exclusive outdoor-indoor Cip's Club bar and Oro restaurant is best known for its breathtaking views, but the exquisite and very pricey tasting menu (from €250) of Venetian classics and extensive wine list certainly don't play second fiddle. Taking the complimentary 10-minute boat ride to and from San Marco also adds to the thoroughly James Bond sense of drama and romance. **Known for:** sublime Venice vistas with a Bellini; sophisticated service; relaxing lunch destination. $ *Average main: €60* ✉ *Belmond Hotel Cipriani, Giudecca 10, Giudecca* ☎ *041/240801* 🌐 *www.belmond.com* Ⓜ *Vaporetto: Zitelle.*

★ **La Palanca**

$ | ITALIAN | It's all about the views at this classic, informal wine bar–restaurant, where tables perched on the water's edge are often filled with chatty patrons, particularly at lunchtime. The homemade pasta and fish dishes are highly recommended, and although they don't really serve dinner, a filling selection of *cicheti* is offered in the evening. **Known for:** sea bass ravioli, grilled seafood, and baccalà; good, affordable wine list; superlative views. $ *Average main: €19* ✉ *Isola della Giudecca 448, Giudecca* ☎ *041/5287719* 🌐 *www.facebook.com/lapalancagiudecca* ⏲ *Closed Sun.* Ⓜ *Vaporetto: Palanca.*

Hotels

★ **Belmond Hotel Cipriani**

$$$$ | HOTEL | With amazing service, wonderful rooms, fab restaurants, and a large pool and spa—all just a five-minute boat ride from Piazza San Marco (the hotel water shuttle leaves every 15 minutes, 24 hours a day)—the Cipriani is Venetian luxe at its best. **Pros:** old-world charm meets modern luxury; Olympic-size heated saltwater pool; Michelin-starred restaurant. **Cons:** very expensive; may be too quiet for some; gym not open 24 hours. $ *Rooms from: €1,385* ✉ *Giudecca 10, Giudecca* ☎ *041/240801* 🌐 *www.belmond.com* ⏲ *Closed mid-Nov.–early Apr.* 🛏 *96 rooms* 🍽 *Free Breakfast* Ⓜ *Vaporetto: Zitelle.*

Hilton Molino Stucky Venice

$$ | HOTEL | FAMILY | Wooden beams and iron columns are some of the original details still visible in this redbrick former flour mill–turned-hotel, which also features sublime views across the lagoon to Venice, particularly from the lively rooftop bar. **Pros:** extremely helpful staff; shuttle boat to San Marco; ample breakfast buffet. **Cons:** can hear noise from other rooms; hotel itself a bit confusing to navigate; food offerings on the pricey side. $ *Rooms from: €355* ✉ *Giudecca 810, Giudecca* ☎ *041/2723311* 🌐 *www.hilton.com* 🛏 *379 rooms* 🍽 *No Meals* Ⓜ *Vaporetto: Palanca.*

Nightlife

Skyline Rooftop Bar

COCKTAIL BARS | For arguably the best views of Venice anywhere, visit this buzzy eighth-floor hotel cocktail bar. There are regular DJ and live music events during the summer months. Their cocktails, such as their signature gin martini The Gentlemen (€22), are not cheap. ✉ *Hilton Molino Stucky Venice, Giudecca 810, Giudecca* ☎ *041/2723316* 🌐 *www.skylinebarvenice.it* Ⓜ *Vaporetto: Palanca.*

Fortuny Tessuti Artistici

FABRICS | The original Fortuny textile factory, built on former convent grounds, has been converted into a showroom. Prices are over-the-top, but it's worth a trip to see the extraordinary colors and textures of their hand-printed silks and velvets. Call in advance to arrange a tour of the buildings and gorgeous gardens. ✉ *Fondamenta San Biagio, Giudecca 805, Giudecca* ☎ *041/5287697* 🌐 *fortuny.com* Ⓜ *Vaporetto: Palanca.*

Islands of the Lagoon

The perfect vacation from your Venetian vacation is an escape to Murano, Burano, and sleepy Torcello, the islands of the northern lagoon, or to the Lido, Venice's barrier island that forms the southern border of the Venetian Lagoon. Torcello is legendary for its beauty and breathing room, and makes a wonderful destination for a picnic (be sure to pack a lunch). Burano, which has a long history of lace production, is an island of fishing traditions and houses painted in a riot of colors—blue, yellow, pink, ocher, and dark red. Murano is renowned for its glass, and you can tour a glass factory here, but be warned that you will be pressured to buy. San Michele, a vaporetto stop on the way to Murano, is the cemetery island of Venice, the resting place of many international artists who have chosen to spend eternity in this beautiful city. Finally, the Lido, which protects Venice from the waters of the Adriatic, forms the beach of Venice, and is home to a series of elegant bathing establishments.

TIMING

Hitting all the sights on all the islands takes a busy, full day. If you limit yourself to Murano and San Michele, you can easily explore for an ample half day; the same goes for Burano and Torcello. In summer the express Vaporetto Line 7 will take you to Murano from San Zaccaria (the Jolanda landing) in 25 minutes; Line 3 will take you from Piazzale Roma to Murano via the Canale di Cannaregio in 21 minutes; otherwise, local Line 4.1 makes a 45-minute trip from San Zaccaria every 20 minutes, circling the east end of Venice, stopping at Fondamente Nove and San Michele on the way. To see glassblowing, get off at Colonna; the Museo stop will put you near the Museo del Vetro.

Line 12 goes from Fondamente Nove direct to Murano and Burano every 30 minutes (from there, Torcello is a five-minute ferry ride on Line 9); the full trip takes 45 minutes each way. To get to Burano and Torcello from Murano, pick up Line 12 at the Faro stop (Murano's lighthouse). Line 1 runs from San Marco to the Lido in about 20 minutes.

★ Cimitero di San Michele (San Michele Cemetery)

CEMETERY | It's no surprise that serenity prevails on San Michele in Venice's northern lagoon. The city's island cemetery is surrounded by ocher brick walls and laced with cypress-lined pathways amid plots filled with thousands of graves; there's also a modern extension completed by British architect David Chipperfield in 2017. Among those who have made this distinctive island their final resting place are such international arts and science luminaries as Igor Stravinsky, Sergei Diaghilev, Ezra Pound, and the Austrian mathematician Christian Doppler (of the Doppler effect). You're welcome to explore the grounds if you dress respectfully and adhere to a solemn code

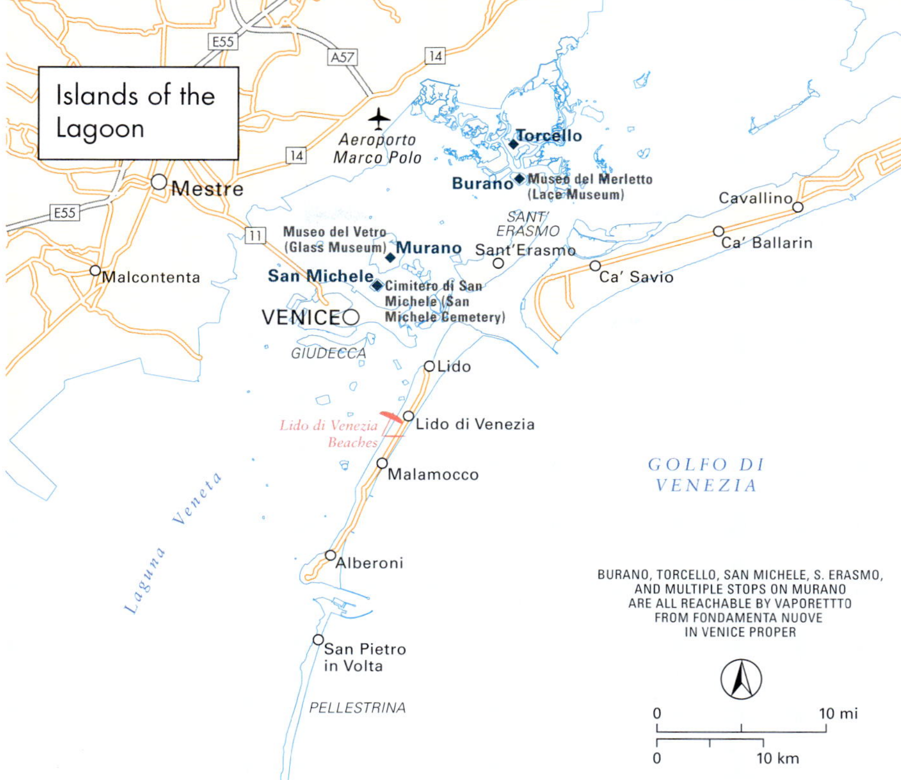

of conduct. Photography and picnicking are not permitted. ✉ *Isola di San Michele* ☎ *041/7292841* 🌐 *www.comune.venezia.it/it/content/cimitero-smichele* 🎫 *Free* Ⓜ *Vaporetto: San Michele.*

Museo del Merletto (Lace Museum)
HISTORY MUSEUM | FAMILY | Home to the Burano Lace School from 1872 to 1970, the palace of Podestà of Torcello now houses a museum dedicated to the craft for which this island is known. Detailed explanations of the manufacturing process and Burano's distinctive history as a lace-making capital provide insight into displays that showcase everything from black Venetian Carnival capes to fingerless, elbow-length "mitten gloves" fashionable in 17th-century France. Portraits of Venice's aristocracy as well as embroidered silk and brocade gowns with lace embellishments provide greater societal context on the historical use of lace in European fashion. You can also watch interesting lace-making demonstrations. ✉ *Piazza Galuppi 187* ☎ *041/730034* 🌐 *museomerletto.visitmuve.it* 🎫 *€5, Island Museums Ticket €12 (also includes Murano Glass Museum), free with Museum Pass* ⏲ *Closed Mon.* Ⓜ *Vaporetto: Burano.*

★ **Museo del Vetro (Glass Museum)**
ART MUSEUM | FAMILY | This compact yet informative museum displays glass items dating from the 3rd century to today. You'll learn all about techniques introduced through the ages (many of which are still in use), including 15th-century gold-leaf decoration, 16th-century filigree work that incorporated thin bands of white or colored glass into the crystal, and the 18th-century origins of Murano's iconic chandeliers. A visit here will help

you to understand the provenance of the glass you'll see for sale—and may be tempted to buy—in shops around the island. ✉ *Fondamenta Marco Giustinian 8* ☎ *041/739586 office, 041/2434914 tickets* 🌐 *museovetro.visitmuve.it* 🎫 *€10; Island Museums Ticket €12 (also includes Burano Lace Museum); free with Museum Pass* Ⓜ *Vaporetto: Murano Museo.*

 Beaches

Lido di Venezia Beaches

BEACH | **FAMILY** | Most hotels on the Lido have access to charming beach clubs with cabanas, striped umbrellas, and chaise longues—all of which are often available for nonguests to use for a fee. On either end of the long barrier island, the public beaches offer a more rustic but still delightful setting for nature lovers to dig their toes in the sand. **Amenities:** food and drink; lifeguards; showers; toilets. **Best for:** swimming; walking. ✉ *Lido di Venezia* ☎ *041/8627117* 🌐 *www.visitlido.it* Ⓜ *Vaporetto: Lido.*

 Restaurants

Acquastanca

$$ | **VENETIAN** | Grab a seat among locals at this charming, intimate eatery—the perfect place to pop in for a lunchtime *primo* or to embark on a romantic evening. The name, referring to the tranquillity of the lagoon at the turn of the tide, reflects this restaurant's approach to food and service, and you'll find such tempting seafood-based dishes as gnocchi with scallops and zucchini and curried scampi with black rice; tasteful decor sets the mood with exposed brick, iron and glass accents, and charming fish sculptures. **Known for:** light and fresh traditional food; focus on seafood dishes; relaxing atmosphere. $ *Average main: €28* ✉ *Fondamenta Manin 48* ☎ *041/3195125* 🌐 *www.acquastanca.it* 🕒 *Closed Sun. No dinner Tues.–Thurs. and Sat.* Ⓜ *Vaporetto: Murano Colonna, Murano Faro.*

Favorite Places

Liz Humphreys: Gorgeous winery-restaurant-hotel Venissa rescued the native dorona grape from near-extinction. Catching the vaporetto from Venice to drink, dine, and sleep here is always the highlight of my trip.

Busa alla Torre da Lele

$ | **VENETIAN** | If you're shopping for glass on Murano and want to sample some first-rate home cooking for lunch, you can't do better than stopping in this unpretentious trattoria in the island's central square. Friendly waiters will bring you ample portions of pasta, with freshly made seafood-based sauces, and a substantial variety of carefully grilled or baked fish. **Known for:** tasty local fish and seafood; reliable lunch stop in Murano; outdoor dining on a square. $ *Average main: €18* ✉ *Campo Santo Stefano 3* ☎ *041/739662* 🕒 *No dinner* Ⓜ *Vaporetto: Murano Colonna.*

Trattoria Al Gatto Nero

$$$ | **SEAFOOD** | Since 1965, Al Gatto Nero has offered the best fish on Burano; no matter what you order, though, you'll savor the pride the owner and his family have in their lagoon, their island, and the quality of their *cucina* (maybe even more so when enjoying it on the picturesque fondamenta). The fish is top quality and couldn't get any fresher; all pastas and desserts are made in-house; the fritto misto is outstanding for its lightness and variety of fish; risotto alla Buranella features gò (short for ghiozzo fish), a Burano *cucina povera* ("kitchen of the poor") standard that had almost disappeared from local menus until Anthony Bourdain introduced it to travelers. **Known for:** the freshest fish and seafood around; risotto Burano style, using local ghiozzi fish; tagliolini (thin spaghetti) with spider crab. *Average main: €36 Fondamenta della Giudecca 88 041/730120 www.gattonero.com Closed Mon., 1 wk in July, and 3 wks in Nov. No dinner Sun., Wed., and Thurs. Vaporetto: Burano.*

★ Venissa

$$$$ | **MODERN ITALIAN** | Stroll across the bridge from Burano to the islet of Mazzorbo to see some of the Venetian islands' only working vineyards, amid which sits this charming restaurant where seasonal dishes incorporate vegetables, herbs, and flowers fresh from the garden and fish fresh from the lagoon, served in seven- or 10-course tasting menus (there's also a more casual osteria). To accompany your meal, pick out a local wine like the Dorona di Venezia, made with the island's native grape. **Known for:** creative, sometimes avant-garde dishes; relaxed setting with tables overlooking the vines; perfect wine pairings. *Average main: €150 Fondamenta Santa Caterina 3 041/5272281 www.venissa.it Closed Wed. in Sept.; Tues. and Wed. the rest of the year; 10 days in late July–early Aug.; 10 days in late Nov.; and early Jan.–early Mar. Vaporetto: Mazzorbo.*

Hotels

Hotel Excelsior Venice Lido Resort

$$$ | **HOTEL** | **FAMILY** | Built in 1908, this grand hotel with Moorish decor has old-fashioned charm and loads of amenities—from a private beach with white cabanas and a seasonal bar and restaurant to a swimming pool, gym, and tennis courts (though, oddly, no spa). **Pros:** lovely beachfront location; convenient water shuttle every 30 minutes to and from Venice proper; friendly, welcoming staff. **Cons:** could do with a refresh; restaurants on the expensive side; can get very busy in summer and around the Venice Film Festival. *Rooms from: €595 Lungomare Marconi 41 041/5260201 www.hotelexcelsiorvenezia.com 196 rooms Free Breakfast Vaporetto: Lido.*

★ Hyatt Centric Murano Venice

$ | **HOTEL** | Befitting its location on Murano, this well-situated hotel is in a former glassmaking factory and has vitreous works of art throughout; it also has spacious, contemporary guest rooms with dark-wood floors and brown-and-cream color schemes. **Pros:** excellent breakfast buffet; vaporetto stop right outside the hotel, free airport transfers; easy walk to restaurants and shops. **Cons:** most rooms have no views; gym is basic; extra charge for using sauna and steam room. *Rooms from: €136 Riva Longa 49 041/2731234 www.hyatt.com/hyatt-centric/vcect-hyatt-centric-murano-venice 119 rooms No Meals Vaporetto: Murano Museo.*

★ JW Marriott Venice Resort & Spa

$$$ | **RESORT** | Once you get a taste of the resort's lush gardens, fabulous spa, and fantastic pools—all set on an exclusive island called Isole Delle Rose, a 20-minute boat ride from Venice—you may find yourself quickly settling in to la dolce vita. **Pros:** relaxed vibe; spacious rooms; loads of amenities. **Cons:** getting to and from Venice can feel like a hassle; not much Venetian style in rooms; extra charge for spa. *Rooms from: €553 Isola delle Rose, Laguna di San Marco, Venezia Succursale 12 041/8521300 www.jwvenice.com Closed mid-Nov.–Feb. 266 rooms Free Breakfast.*

Shopping

★ Davide Penso

JEWELRY & WATCHES | This Venice-born, Murano-based artist makes gorgeous glass necklaces, earrings, and bracelets using the lampwork technique, where he shapes colored glass rods over a flame. ✉ *Fondamenta Riva Longa 48* ☎ *041/739819* 🌐 *www.davidepenso.info* Ⓜ *Vaporetto: Museo Murano.*

★ Emilia Burano

FABRICS | This is not your grandmother's lace—these fourth-generation lace makers have updated their designs to produce exquisite bed linens, lampshades, and other items. ✉ *Piazza Galuppi 205* ☎ *0351/6810761* 🌐 *emiliaburano.it* Ⓜ *Vaporetto: Burano.*

★ MaMa Salvadore Murano

GLASSWARE | To see more of glassmaking's artistic side, visit this gallery-shop that highlights works from international contemporary glass artists. ✉ *Fondamenta da Mula 148* ☎ *331/6224359 mobile* 🌐 *www.mamamurano.com* Ⓜ *Vaporetto: Murano.*

★ Salviati

GLASSWARE | One of the oldest and most prestigious Italian glassmakers (founded in 1859), Salviati partners with renowned international designers, including Tom Dixon, to create beautiful contemporary pieces. ✉ *Fondamenta Radi 16* ☎ *041/5274085* 🌐 *www.salviati.com* Ⓜ *Vaporetto: Murano Museo, Murano Navagero.*

★ Simone Cenedese

GLASSWARE | This talented second-generation glass master produces intricately designed and often whimsical glass chandeliers and sculptures. ✉ *Calle Bertolini 6* ☎ *041/5274455* 🌐 *simonecenedese.it* Ⓜ *Vaporetto: Murano Faro, Murano Colonna.*

Chapter 5

THE VENETO AND FRIULI–VENEZIA GIULIA

Updated by
Nick Bruno

WELCOME TO THE VENETO AND FRIULI–VENEZIA GIULIA

TOP REASONS TO GO

★ **Giotto's frescoes in the Cappella degli Scrovegni:** In this Padua chapel, Giotto's expressive and innovative frescoes foreshadowed the Renaissance.

★ **Villa Barbaro in Maser:** Master architect Palladio's graceful creation meets Veronese's splendid frescoes in a one-time-only collaboration.

★ **Opera in Verona's ancient arena:** The performances may not be top-notch, but even serious opera fans can't resist the spectacle of these shows.

★ **Roman and early Christian ruins at Aquileia:** Aquileia's beautiful ruins offer a glimpse of the transition from pagan to Christian Rome and are almost entirely free of tourists.

★ **The wine roads north of Treviso:** A series of routes takes you through beautiful hillsides to some of Italy's finest wines.

1 **Padua.** An old university city brimming with art and history, Padua is most noted for Giotto's Cappella degli Scrovegni frescoes.

2 **Verona.** One of the best preserved and most beautiful cities in Italy.

3 **Vicenza.** This elegant art city bears the signature of the great 16th-century architect Andrea Palladio.

4 **Marostica.** A small hilltop-citadel town renowned for a biennial human-scale chess game.

5 **Asolo.** The "City of a Hundred Horizons" is in the wine-producing hills.

6 **Treviso.** This town with beguiling canals has more than a touch of Venetian style.

7 **Udine.** This city has medieval and Renaissance splendors, including works by Tiepolo.

8 **Cividale del Friuli.** The Natisone River and ravine and the Julian Alps provide a ravishing backdrop to this town.

9 **Aquileia.** This was a pivotal port town in Augustus's Rome.

10 **Trieste.** This port city has Belle Époque cafés and palaces.

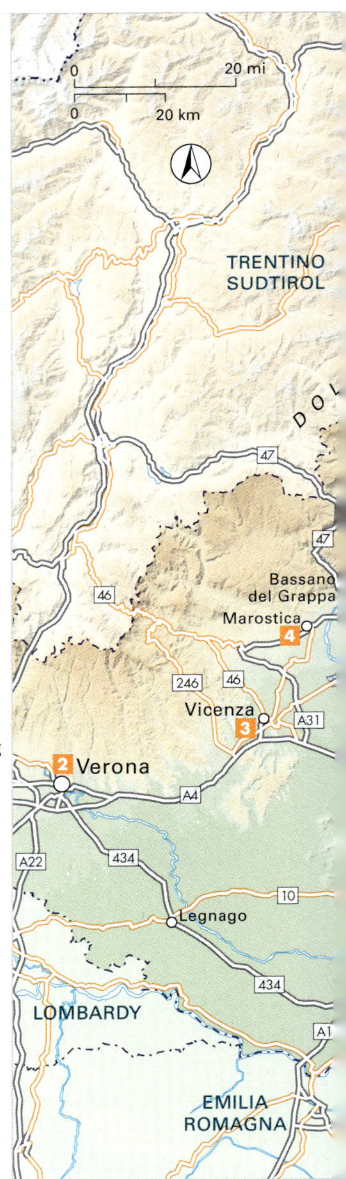

AUSTRIA
SLOVENIA
CROATIA
ADRIATIC SEA
CARNIA
FRIULI-VENEZIA GIULIA
VENETO
DOLOMITES
Tarvisio
Tolmezzo
Gemona del Friuli
Cividale del Friuli
Udine
Cormóns
Gorizia
Monfalcone
Aquileia
Grado
Trieste
Lignano Sabbiadoro
Caorle
Lido di Jesolo
Pordenone
Vittorio Veneto
Conegliano
Belluno
Feltre
Mt. Grappa
Villa Barbaro
Asolo
Treviso
Cittadella
Mestre
Mira
Venice
Padua
Laguna Veneto
Chioggia
Adria
Rovigo
Contarina
Tagliamento
Piave River
Adige River
Po River
River
A23
A27
A28
A4
A13
52
50
13
14
53
348
354
47
309
1
5
6
7
8
9
10

EATING AND DRINKING WELL IN THE VENETO AND FRIULI–VENEZIA GIULIA

Baked sea bream

With the decisive seasonal changes of the Venetian Arc, it's little wonder that many restaurants shun printed menus. Elements from field and forest define much of the region's cuisine, including white asparagus, herbs, chestnuts, radicchio, and wild mushrooms.

Restaurants of the Venetian Arc tend to cling to tradition, not only in the food they serve, but also when they serve it. From 2:30 in the afternoon until about 7:30 in the evening most places are closed (though you can pick up a snack at a bar during these hours), and on Sunday afternoon restaurants are packed with Italian families and friends indulging in the weekly ritual of lunching out.

Meals are still sacred for most Italians, so don't be surprised if you get disapproving looks as you gobble down a sandwich or a slice of pizza while seated on the church steps or a park bench. (In many places it's actually illegal to do so.)

THE BEST IN BEANS

Pasta e fagioli (a thick bean soup with pasta, served slightly warm or at room temperature) is made all over Italy. Folks in the Veneto, though, take special pride in their version, made from particularly fine beans grown around the village of Lamon, near Belluno. *Il fagiolo di Lamon* derives from the *Borlotto di Vigevano* bean and was first introduced by a monk in the 1500s via the Spanish court's colonial links to Mexico and Guatemela.

FISH

The catch of the day is always a good bet, whether it's sweet and succulent Adriatic shellfish, sea bream, bass, or John Dory, or freshwater fish from Lake Garda, near Verona. A staple in the Veneto is *baccalà*: this is dried salt cod, which, alongside *stoccafisso,* air-dried cod, was introduced to Italy during the Renaissance by northern European traders. Dried cod is soaked in water or milk and then prepared in a different way in each city. In Vicenza, baccalà *alla vicentina* confusingly uses stoccafisso, which is cooked with onions, milk, and cheese, and is generally served with polenta.

MEAT

In the Veneto, traditional dishes feature offal as much as the prime cuts. Beef (including veal), pork, rabbit, horse, and donkey meat are standard, while goose, duck, and guinea fowl are common poultry options. In Friuli–Venezia Giulia, menus show the influence of Austria-Hungary: you may find deer and hare on the menu, as well as Eastern European–style goulash. One unusual treat served throughout the Veneto is *nervetti*—cubes of gelatin from a calf's knee prepared with onions, parsley, olive oil, and lemon.

Radicchio

Creamed salted cod

PASTA, RISOTTO, POLENTA

For *primi* (first courses), the Veneto dines on *bigoli* (thick whole-wheat pasta), generally served with an anchovy-onion sauce delicately flavored with cinnamon, or creamy risotto flavored with vegetables or shellfish. Polenta is everywhere, whether it's a stiff porridge topped with Gorgonzola, or a stew, or a patty grilled and served alongside meat or fish.

RADICCHIO DI TREVISO

In fall and winter be sure to try the radicchio di Treviso, a red endive grown near that town but popular all over the region. Cultivation is very labor-intensive, so it can be expensive. It's best in a veal or chicken stew, in a risotto, or just grilled or baked with a drizzle of olive oil and perhaps a little Taleggio cheese from neighboring Lombardy.

WINE

The Veneto produces more D.O.C. (Denominazione di Origine Controllata) wines than any other region in Italy. Amarone, the region's crowning achievement, is a robust, full-bodied red. The best of the whites are Soave, prosecco, and *pinot bianco* (pinot blanc). In Friuli–Venezia Giulia, local wines include *friulano,* a dry, lively white made from the sauvignon vert grape, and *picolit,* a dessert wine.

The arc around Venice—stretching from Verona to Trieste, encompassing the Veneto and Friuli–Venezia Giulia regions—is indisputably one of the most culturally rich areas in Italy, an intellectual and spiritual feast of architecture, painting, and sculpture. Since the 16th century, the art, architecture, and way of life here have all reflected Venetian splendor. It wasn't always this way. Back in the Middle Ages, Padua and Verona were independent cities that developed substantial cultural traditions of their own.

They left behind many artistic treasures. And even while it was under Venice's political domination, 16th-century Vicenza contributed more to the cultural heritage of La Serenissima than it took from her—in large part because of its master architect, Andrea Palladio.

This region is primarily flat, green farmland. As you move inland, though, you encounter low hills, which swell and rise in a succession of plateaus and high meadows, culminating in the snowcapped Dolomite Alps. Much of the pleasure of exploring here comes from discovering the variations on the Venetian theme that give a unique character to each of the towns. Some, such as Verona, Treviso, and Udine, have a solid medieval look at their heart. Padua, with its narrow arcaded streets, tree-lined canals, and large student population, is romantic and youthful. Vicenza, ennobled by the architecture of Palladio, is elegant and wealthy. Udine, in Friuli–Venezia Giulia, is genteel yet rustic, an intricately sculpted city that's home to the first important frescoes by Gianbattista Tiepolo. In Trieste, once the main port of the Austro-Hungarian Empire, you can find survivors of those days in its Viennese-inspired coffeehouses and *buffets*—hole-in-the-wall eateries serving sausages and other pork dishes.

Unlike the western regions of northern Italy, the Veneto and Friuli–Venezia Giulia were slow to move from an agricultural to an industrial economy, and even now the region depends upon small- and medium-size businesses, many of which are still family-run. The area, therefore, has attracted far fewer migrants from elsewhere in Italy and thus maintained its cultural identity; local dialects, for example, may have all but died out in places like Milan and Turin, but they still thrive in the Veneto and Friuli–Venezia Giulia. Even when residents speak standard Italian, it is frequently laced with local words and pronounced with a distinctive nasal-sounding musicality.

MAJOR REGIONS

The Veneto. Influenced by the city of Venice on the marshy Adriatic coast, the Veneto is a prosperous region dotted by fortified cities with captivating history and undulating vineyards. Padua's alluring architecture, art, and canal network may reflect the Venetian influence as the closest terra firma dominion, but its ancient, pioneering university—famed for its humanist alumni—creates a beguiling buzz of cycling students, food markets, and commerce. With the cooling Dolomite Alpine waters of the Adige River snaking through its medieval, Roman, and Venetian heart, Verona combines splendor with intimacy. Perfectly formed and wealthy Vicenza is where the peerless Palladio put his harmonious architectural plans into bricks, mortar, and gleaming marble. Heading north toward the snowcapped Dolomites, Marostica draws visitors moved by commanding views and an biannual human-scale game of chess on a colossal board. Set amid verdant hills, Asolo dines out on its 19th-century heyday as an idyllic village muse for artists and poets. Moated and medieval Treviso retains a thriving and tranquil air in arcaded streets and leafy canals.

Friuli–Venezia Giulia. Heading northeast of the Veneto, the atmosphere of the Friuli–Venezia Giulia region derives from its fascinating mix of Italian, Slavic, and Central European influences. Sitting atop foothills below the Carnic Alps, the university city of Udine mixes semirural provincial charms with the grandeur of Venetian architecture and the rococo riches of 18th-century artist Gianbattista Tiepolo. A short hop east and set amid scenic wooded valleys, Cividale del Friuli brims with Roman, Celtic, and Lombard archaeological artifacts. Following the Natisone River down to tranquil Aquileia, you'll hear echoes of ancient Rome in this erstwhile port and spot signs of early Christianity in its mosaics. Bordering Slovenia, the strategic Adriatic port city of Trieste mixes Eastern, Central, and Western European cultures, giving it a liminal atmosphere of nostalgia and intrigue, beloved by writers and artists.

Planning

Getting Here and Around

BUS

There are interurban and interregional connections throughout the Veneto and Friuli–Venezia Giulia, handled by nearly a dozen private bus lines. To figure out which line will get you where, the best strategy is to seek assistance from local tourist offices.

CAR

Padua, Vicenza, and Verona are on the highway (and train line) between Venice and Milan. Seeing them without a car isn't a problem; in fact, having a car can even complicate matters. The cities and some towns have Traffic Limited Zones (ZTL) that limit vehicular access to those with a permit within certain hours. The best strategy is to check with your hotel before arrival for an update and check the relevant ZTL websites for each city. You will need a car to get the most out of the hill country that makes up much of the Venetian Arc, and it will be particularly useful for visiting Aquileia, a rather interesting archaeological site with limited public transportation.

The two main access roads to the Venetian Arc from southern Italy are both linked to the A1 (Autostrada del Sole), which connects Bologna, Florence, and Rome. They are the A13, which ends in Padua, and the A22, which passes through Verona running north–south. Linking the region from east to west is the A4, the primary route from Milan to Trieste, skirting Verona, Padua, and Venice along the way. The distance from Verona to Trieste via the A4 is 263 km (163 miles; 2½ hours), with one break in the autostrada near Venice/Mestre. Branches link the A4 with Treviso (A27) and Udine (A23).

TRAIN

Trains (🌐 *www.trenitalia.com*) on the main routes from the south stop twice hourly in Verona, Padua, and Venice. From northern Italy and the rest of Europe, trains usually enter via Milan or through Porta Nuova in Verona. Treviso and Udine both lie on the main line from Venice to Tarvisio. Unfortunately, there are no daytime express trains between Venice and Tarvisio, only the slower interregional and regional service with at least two changes. There is now a regional three-hour through-train service between Trieste and the neighboring Slovenian capital Ljubljana (Lubiana in Italian). To the west of Venice, the main line running across the north of Italy stops at Padua (30 minutes from Venice), Vicenza (45–75 minutes), and Verona (75 minutes); to the east is Trieste (two hours). Local trains link Vicenza to Treviso (one hour) and Udine to Trieste (one hour).

Be sure to take Regionale Veloce (fast regional) trains whenever possible; a local "milk run" or Regionale that stops in every village along the way can take considerably longer. The fastest trains are the Frecce, but reservations are mandatory and fares are much higher than on regional services. Private operator Italo (🌐 *www.italotreno.com*) provides an alternative high-speed network across the region.

Hotels

Rates tend to be higher in Padua and Verona; in Verona especially, seasonal rates vary widely and soar during trade fairs and the opera season. There are fewer good lodging choices in Vicenza, perhaps because overnighters are drawn to the better restaurant scenes in Verona and Padua. *Agriturismo* (farm stay) information is available at tourist offices and sometimes on their websites. Ask about weekend discounts, often available at hotels catering to business clients. Substantial savings can sometimes be had by booking through reservation services on the Internet.

⇨ *Hotel and restaurant reviews have been shortened. For full information, visit Fodors.com. Prices in the hotel reviews are the lowest cost of a standard double room in high season. Prices in the dining reviews are the average cost of a main course at dinner, or, if dinner is not served, at lunch.*

What It Costs in Euros

	$	$$	$$$	$$$$
RESTAURANTS				
	under €20	€20–€30	€31–€40	over €40
HOTELS				
	under €175	€175–€400	€401–€600	over €600

Planning Your Time

Lined up in a row west of Venice are Padua, Vicenza, and Verona—three prosperous small cities that are worth at least one day each on a northern Italy itinerary. Verona has the most grandeur and most varied attractions, as well as the widest selection of hotels and restaurants. It's probably the best choice for a base in the area, even though it also draws the most tourists. The hills north of Venice make for good driving, with appealing villages set in a visitor-friendly wine country.

East of the Veneto, the region of Friuli–Venezia Giulia is off the main tourist circuit. You probably won't go here on a first trip to Italy, but by your second or third visit you may be drawn by its caves and castles, its battle-worn hills, and its mix of Italian and Central European culture. The port city of Trieste, famous for its elegant cafés, has a quiet character that some people find dull but others find alluring.

Note that several of the most interesting and important sights in the Venetian Arc require reservations or are open only at limited times, so plan ahead. For instance, reservations are required in advance to see the Giotto frescoes in Padua's Cappella degli Scrovegni. On the outskirts of Vicenza, the Villa della Rotonda, one of Palladio's masterpieces, is not open in winter and has very limited hours when it is open. Another important Palladian conception, Villa di Maser or Villa Barbaro, also has limited hours.

Restaurants

Although the Veneto is not considered one of Italy's major culinary destinations, the region offers many opportunities for exciting gastronomic adventures. The fish offerings are among the most varied and freshest in Italy (and possibly Europe), and the vegetables from the islands in the Venetian lagoon are considered a national treasure. Carnivores are spoiled for choice here with donkey and horse on many menus, from donkey ragù with bigoli pasta to lean equine preparations like *sfilacci di cavallo* (dry shredded horsemeat), carpaccio, and more hearty *pastissada de caval* (stew). Take a break from pasta and try the area's wonderful, creamy risottos and hearty polenta.

When to Go

The towns and services of the Veneto and Friuli–Venezia Giulia are generally busy all year, with all but a few attractions accessible to visitors. Summer months are generally very humid but dry and hot. The most precipitation and fog fall between November and March, although these months can be rewarding for city sightseeing and immersion in local culture and seasonal food. Toward the foothills of the Dolomites, there are cooler summers and snowfall in winter, while the northeast Adriatic corner around the Gulf of Trieste can have year-round breezy days from eastern winds.

Padua

42 km (25 miles) west of Venice.

A romantic warren of arcaded streets, Padua has long been one of the major cultural centers of northern Italy. It has first-rate artistic monuments and, along with Bologna, is one of the few cities in the country where you can catch a glimpse of student life.

Its university, founded in 1222 and Italy's second oldest, attracted such cultural icons as Dante (1265–1321), Petrarch (1304–74), and Galileo Galilei (1564–1642), thus earning the city the sobriquet *La Dotta* (The Learned). Padua's Basilica di Sant'Antonio, begun around 1238, attracts droves of pilgrims, especially on his feast day, June 13. Three great artists—Giotto (1266–1337), Donatello (circa 1386–1466), and Mantegna (1431–1506)—left significant works in Padua, with Giotto's Scrovegni Chapel being one of the best-known, and most meticulously preserved, works of art in the country. Today, a cycle-happy student body—some 60,000 strong—flavors every aspect of local culture. Don't be surprised if you spot a *laurea* (graduation) ceremony marked by laurel leaves, mocking lullabies, and X-rated caricatures.

GETTING HERE AND AROUND

The train trip between Venice and Padua is short, and regular bus service originates from Venice's Piazzale Roma. By car from Venice, Padua is on the Autostrada Torino–Trieste A4/E70. Take the San Carlo exit and follow Via Guido Reni to Via Tiziano Aspetti into town. Regular bus service connects Venice's Marco Polo airport with downtown Padua.

Padua is a walker's and cyclist's city, with an excellent tram and bus network. If you arrive by car, leave your vehicle in one of the parking lots on the outskirts or at your hotel. Unlimited bus and tram service is included with the Urbs Picta Card (€28 or €35, valid for 48 or 72 hours), which allows entry to all the city's eight principal sights. It's available at tourist information offices and at some museums and hotels. Join the cycling throngs by hiring a bike or e-bike with Forever Bike (*www.foreverbike.com* *049/8717574*).

VISITOR INFORMATION

CONTACT **Padua Tourism Office.** *Padova Railway Station, Piazzale Stazione, Padua* *049/5207415* *www.turismopadova.it.*

Sights

Abano Terme

HOT SPRING | A very popular hot-springs spa town about 12 km (7 miles) southwest of Padua, Abano Terme lies at the foot of the Euganean Hills among hand-tilled vineyards. If a bit of pampering sounds better than traipsing through yet another church or castle, indulge yourself with a soak, a massage, or mud treatments, which are especially recommended for joint aches. A good-value weekday pass (€45) is available at Hotel Antiche Terme Ariston Molino Buja for access to their thermal pools (*aristonmolino.it*). *Abano Terme* *Take Padua West exit off A4, or Terme Euganee exit off A13* *049/8669061* *www.abano.it; aristonmolino.it.*

★ Basilica di Sant'Antonio

(*Basilica del Santo*)

CHURCH | Thousands of faithful make the pilgrimage here each year to pray at the tomb of St. Anthony, while others come to admire works by the 15th-century Florentine master Donatello. His equestrian statue (1453) of the condottiere Erasmo da Narni, known as Gattamelata, in front of the church is one of the great masterpieces of Italian Renaissance sculpture. The huge church, which combines elements of Byzantine, Romanesque, and Gothic styles, was probably begun around 1238, seven years after the death of the Portuguese-born saint. The Cappella del Santo (housing the tomb of the saint) dates from the 16th century. *Piazza del Santo, Padua* *049/8225652* *www.basilicadelsanto.it* *Basilica free, museum complex €10* *Museum complex closed Mon.*

Burchiello Excursion, Brenta Canal

BODY OF WATER | During the 16th century the Brenta was transformed into a mainland version of Venice's Grand Canal with the building of nearly 50 waterside villas. Back then, boating parties viewed them from *burchielli*—beautiful river barges. Today the Burchiello excursion boat makes full- and half-day tours along the Brenta in season, departing from Padua and Venice; tickets can also be bought at travel agencies. You visit three houses, including the Villas Pisani and Foscari, with a lunchtime break in Oriago (€26 or €30 extra). There is also the option to rent or bring your own bike to explore partly on wheels as part of a trip. Note that most houses are on the left side coming from Venice, or the right from Padua. *Via Porciglia 34, Padua* *049/8760233* *www.ilburchiello.it* *€79 half day, €139 full day; lunch extra* *Closed Mon. and Nov.–Feb.*

★ Cappella degli Scrovegni
(The Arena Chapel)

CHURCH | The emotional intensity and naturalism of the frescoes illustrating the lives of Mary and Jesus in this world-famous chapel broke new ground in Western art. Enrico Scrovegni commissioned these frescoes to atone for the sins of his deceased father, Reginaldo, the usurer condemned to the Seventh Circle of the Inferno in Dante's *Divine Comedy.* Giotto and his assistants worked on the frescoes from 1303 to 1305, arranging them in tiers to be read from left to right. To preserve the artwork, doors are opened only every 15 minutes. ✉ *Piazza Eremitani 8, Padua* ☎ *049/2010020 reservations* 🌐 *www.cappelladegliscrovegni.it* 🎟 *€16, includes Musei Civici and Palazzo Zuckermann.*

Chiesa degli Eremitani

CHURCH | This 13th-century church houses substantial fragments of Andrea Mantegna's frescoes (1448–50), which were damaged by Allied bombing in World War II. Despite their fragmentary condition, Mantegna's still beautiful and historically important depictions of the martyrdom of St. James and St. Christopher show the young artist's mastery of extremely complex problems of perspective. ✉ *Piazza Eremitani, Padua* ☎ *049/8756410.*

Montegrotto Terme

HOT SPRING | At this spa town about 13 km (8 miles) southwest of Padua, you can luxuriate in thermal mineral pools. Montegrotto Terme has several hotels whose treatments vary from simple massage and thermal and mud baths to hydrokinetic therapy. Scuba enthusiasts head here for the world's deepest indoor pool, Y-40 Deep Joy. The verdant hills of the nearby Parco dei Colli Euganei provide opportunities for walking, cycling, and other outdoor pursuits. The nearest railway stop, on the Bologna–Padua line, is Terme Euganee–Montegrotto. Taxis are available outside the station. ✉ *Montegrotto Terme* ✥ *Terme Euganee exit off A13* ☎ *049/8928311* 🌐 *www.visitabanomontegrotto.com.*

★ Musei Civici degli Eremitani
(Civic Museum)

SPECIALTY MUSEUM | Usually visited along with the neighboring Cappella degli Scrovegni, this former monastery houses a rich array of exhibits and has wonderful cloister gardens with a mix of ancient architectural fragments and modern sculpture. The Pinacoteca displays works of medieval and modern masters, including some by Tintoretto, Veronese, and Tiepolo. Standouts are the *Giotto Crucifix*, which once hung in the Cappella degli Scrovegni, and the *Portrait of a Young Senator*, by Giovanni Bellini (1430–1516). ✉ *Piazza Eremitani 8, Padua* ☎ *049/8204551* 🌐 *www.padovanet.it* 🎟 *€11, €16 with Scrovegni Chapel and Palazzo Zuckermann.*

★ Orto Botanico *(Botanical Garden)*

GARDEN | **FAMILY** | The Venetian Republic ordered the creation of Padua's botanical garden in 1545 to supply the university with medicinal plants, and it retains its original layout. You can stroll the arboretum—still part of the university—and wander through hothouses and beds of plants that were introduced to Italy in this late-Renaissance garden. A St. Peter's palm, planted in 1585, inspired Goethe to write his 1790 essay, "The Metamorphosis of Plants." The wonderful museum opened here in 2023, contains fascinating botanical collections and multimedia displays that explore the garden's history and evolution of plant use in medicine. ✉ *Via Orto Botanico 15, Padua* ☎ *049/8273939* 🌐 *www.ortobotanicopd.it* 🎟 *€10* ⏲ *Closed Mon.*

★ Palazzo del Bo

CASTLE/PALACE | The University of Padua, founded in 1222, centers on this predominantly 16th-century palazzo with an 18th-century facade. It's named after the Osteria del Bo (*bo* means "ox"), an inn that once stood on the site. It's worth a visit to see the perfectly proportioned anatomy theater (1594), the beautiful Old Courtyard, and a hall with a lectern

Sights

1 Abano Terme A5
2 Basilica di Sant'Antonio D4
3 Burchiello Excursion, Brenta Canal E1
4 Cappella degli Scrovegni D1
5 Chiesa degli Eremitani D2
6 Montegrotto Terme A5
7 Musei Civici degli Eremitani D2
8 Orto Botanico D5
9 Palazzo del Bo D3
10 Palazzo della Ragione C2
11 Piazza dei Signori C2
12 Villa Pisani E4

Restaurants

1 Enoteca dei Tadi B3
2 L'Anfora C3
3 Le Calandre A1
4 Osteria dal Capo C3

Quick Bites

1 Bar Romeo C2

Hotels

1 Al Fagiano D5
2 Albergo Verdi B2
3 Palazzo Mantua Benavides E2

The Venetian Arc, Past and Present

Long before Venetians made their presence felt on the mainland in the 15th century, Ezzelino III da Romano (1194–1259) laid claim to Verona, Padua, and the surrounding lands and towns. He was the first of a series of brutal and aggressive rulers who dominated the cities of the region until the rise of Venetian rule. Because of Ezzelino's cruel and violent nature, Dante consigned his soul to Hell.

After Ezzelino was ousted, powerful families such as Padua's Carrara and Verona's della Scala (Scaligeri) vied throughout the 14th century to dominate these territories. Venetian rule ushered in a time of relative peace, when noble families from the lagoon and the mainland commissioned Palladio and other accomplished architects to design their palazzi and villas. This rich classical legacy, superimposed upon medieval castles and fortifications, is central to the identities of present-day Padua, Vicenza, and Verona.

The region remained under Venetian control until the Napoleonic invasion and the fall of the Venetian Republic in 1797. The Council of Vienna ceded it, along with Lombardy, to Austria in 1815. The region revolted against Austrian rule and joined the Italian Republic in 1866.

Friuli–Venezia Giulia has been marched through, fought over, hymned by patriots, and romanticized by writers that include James Joyce, Rainer Maria Rilke, Pier Paolo Pasolini, and Jan Morris. The region has seen Fascists and Communists, Romans, Hapsburgs, and Huns. It survived by forging sheltering alliances—Udine beneath the wings of San Marco (1420), Trieste choosing Duke Leopold of Austria (1382) over Venetian domination.

Some of World War I's fiercest fighting took place in Friuli–Venezia Giulia, where memorials and cemeteries commemorate hundreds of thousands who died before Italian troops arrived in 1918 and liberated Trieste from Austrian rule. Trieste, along with the whole of Venezia Giulia, was annexed to Italy in 1920. During World War II the Germans occupied the area and placed Trieste in an administrative zone along with parts of Slovenia. The only Nazi extermination camp on Italian soil, the Risiera di San Sabba, was in a suburb of Trieste. After the war, during a period of Cold War dispute, Trieste was governed by an allied military administration; it was officially reannexed to Italy in 1954, when Italy ceded the Istrian peninsula to the south to Yugoslavia. These arrangements were not finally ratified by Italy and Yugoslavia until 1975.

used by Galileo. You can enter only as part of a guided tour; weekend/public holiday tours allow access to other parts of the university including the gorgeous 1930–40s interiors by Milanese architect-designer Gio Ponti; most guides speak English, but it is worth checking ahead by phone. ✉ *Via 8 Febbraio, Padua* ☎ *049/8275111 university switchboard, 049/8273939* 🌐 *heritage.unipd.it/bo-teatroanatomico* 🎫 *Historical tour €8.70; €16.50 extended "Gio Ponti" tour with expert guide weekends and public holidays.*

Palazzo della Ragione

CASTLE/PALACE | Also known as Il Salone, the spectacular arcaded reception hall in Padua's original law courts is as notable for its grandeur—it's 85 feet high—as for its colorful setting, surrounded by shops, cafés, and open-air fruit and vegetable markets. Nicolò Miretto and Stefano da Ferrara, working from 1425 to 1440, painted the frescoes after Giotto's plan, which was destroyed by a fire in 1420. The stunning space hosts art shows, and an enormous wooden horse, crafted for a public tournament in 1466, commands pride of place. It is patterned after the famous equestrian statue by Donatello in front of the Basilica di Sant'Antonio, and may, in fact, have been designed by Donatello himself in the last year of his life. ✉ *Piazza della Ragione, Padua* ☎ *049/8205006* 🌐 *padovacultura.padovanet.it* 🎫 *€8 (free with Urbs Picta Card)* 🕒 *Closed Mon.*

Piazza dei Signori

PLAZA/SQUARE | Some fine examples of 15th- and 16th-century buildings line this square. On the west side, the **Palazzo del Capitanio** (facade constructed 1598–1605) has an impressive **Torre dell'Orologio,** with an astronomical clock dating from 1344 and a portal made by Falconetto in 1532 in the form of a Roman triumphal arch. The 12th-century **Battistero del Duomo** (Cathedral Baptistry), with frescoes by Giusto de' Menabuoi (1374–78), is a few steps away. ✉ *Piazza dei Signori, Padua* ☎ *049/656914* 🌐 *kalata.it/esperienza/battistero-padova* 🎫 *Battistero €12 (free with Urbs Picta Card).*

Villa Pisani

CASTLE/PALACE | FAMILY | Extensive grounds with rare trees, ornamental fountains, and garden follies surround this extraordinary palace in Stra, 13 km (8 miles) southeast of Padua. Built in 1721 for the Venetian doge Alvise Pisani, it recalls Versailles more than a Veneto villa. This was one of the last and grandest of many stately residences constructed along the Brenta River from the 16th to 18th centuries by wealthy Venetians. Gianbattista Tiepolo's (1696–1770) spectacular fresco on the ballroom ceiling, *The Apotheosis of the Pisani Family* (1761), alone is worth the visit. For a relaxing afternoon, explore the gorgeous park and maze. ✉ *Via Doge Pisani 7, Stra* ☎ *049/502074* 🌐 *villapisani.beniculturali.it* 🎫 *€12, €6 park only* 🕒 *Closed Mon.*

Restaurants

★ Enoteca dei Tadi

$$ | ITALIAN | In this cozy and atmospheric cross between a wine bar and a restaurant, you can put together a fabulous, inexpensive dinner from various classic dishes from all over Italy. Portions are small, but prices are reasonable—just follow the local custom and order a selection, perhaps starting with fresh *burrata* (mozzarella's creamier cousin) with tomatoes, or a selection of prosciutti or salami. **Known for:** several kinds of lasagna; intimate and rustic setting; bountiful wine and grappa list. 💲 *Average main: €22* ✉ *Via dei Tadi 16, Padua* ☎ *338/4083434 mobile* 🌐 *www.enotecadeitadi.it* 🕒 *Closed Mon. No dinner Sun; no lunch Tues.–Sat.*

L'Anfora

$ | WINE BAR | This mix between a traditional *bacaro* (wine bar) and an osteria is a local institution, opened in 1922. Stand at the bar with a cross section of Padovano society, from construction workers to professors, and peruse the reasonably priced menu of simple *casalinga* (home-cooked dishes), plus salads and a selection of cheeses. **Known for:** atmospheric art-filled osteria with wood interior; no-nonsense traditional Veneto food; hearty pasta dishes like pasta con fagioli. 💲 *Average main: €17* ✉ *Via Soncin 13, Padua* ☎ *049/656629* 🌐 *osteria-lanfora.eatbu.com* 🕒 *Closed Sun. (except in Dec.).*

Le Calandre

$$$$ | **MODERN ITALIAN** | Traditional Veneto recipes are given a highly sophisticated and creative treatment here, and the whole theatrical tasting-menu experience and gorgeous table settings can seem by turns revelatory or overblown at this high-profile place. Owner-chef Massimiliano Alajmo's creative, miniscule-portion dishes, passion for design (bespoke lighting, carved wooden tables, and quirky plates), and first-class wine list make this an option for a pricey celebratory meal. **Known for:** theatrical, sensory dining experience; playful (or to some, pretentious) touches; reservations essential. *Average main: €280 Via Liguria 1, Sarmeola 7 km (4 miles) west of Padua 049/630303 alajmo.it Closed Sun. and Mon. No lunch Tues.*

Osteria dal Capo

$ | **VENETIAN** | Located in the heart of what used to be Padua's Jewish ghetto, this friendly trattoria serves almost exclusively traditional Veneto dishes, and it does so with refinement and care. Everything from the well-crafted dishes to the unfussy ship's dining cabin–like decor and elegant plates reflect decades of Padovano hospitality. **Known for:** intimate and understated dining at decent prices; meaty-sauced pasta dishes; limited tables mean reservations essential. *Average main: €19 Via degli Obizzi 2, Padua 049/663105 www.osteriadalcapo.it Closed Sun. No dinner Sat.; no lunch Mon.*

Coffee and Quick Bites

Bar Romeo

$ | **NORTHERN ITALIAN** | Deep in the atmospheric Sotto Salone market, this busy bar does a fab selection of filled *tramezzini* (triangular sandwiches), panini, and other snacks. It's a great place to hear the local dialect and mingle with the market workers and shoppers any time of day; grab a breakfast coffee and brioche, a glass of Falanghina, or a bit later—after 11 am perhaps—an apertivo with snacks. **Known for:** good-value sandwiches; friendly staff and Padovano vibe; superb selection of wine by the glass. *Average main: €7 26 Sotto Salone, Padua 340/5560611 mobile.*

Hotels

Al Fagiano

$ | **HOTEL** | The refreshingly funky surroundings in this self-styled art hotel include sponge-painted walls, brush-painted chandeliers, and views of the spires and cupolas of the Basilica di Sant'Antonio. **Pros:** great for art lovers or those after a unique ambience; relaxed, quirky, homey atmosphere; convenient location. **Cons:** not all rooms have views; some find the way-out-there (some risqué) art a bit much; lots of stairs. *Rooms from: €100 Via Locatelli 45, Padua 049/8750073 www.alfagiano.com 40 rooms No Meals.*

Albergo Verdi

$ | **HOTEL** | One of the best-situated hotels in the city provides understated modern rooms and public areas that tend toward the minimalist without being severe, while the intimate breakfast room with mid-century Eames Eiffel chairs and adjoining terrace is a tranquil place to start the day. **Pros:** excellent location close to Piazza dei Signori; bountiful breakfast selection; 24-hour bar service. **Cons:** student noise in piazza-facing rooms; few views; steep stairs and small elevator. *Rooms from: €120 Via Dondi dell'Orologio 7, Padua 049/8364163 www.albergoverdipadova.it 14 rooms Free Breakfast.*

Palazzo Mantua Benavides

$$ | **HOTEL** | Housed within a 16th-century palace, where renowned Florentine architect Bartolomeo Ammannati carved colossal statuary, the four spacious suites and three apartments with kitchenettes here offer a wonderful atmospheric alternative to regular hotel

accommodation. **Pros:** palatial surroundings; verdant grounds; near the Scrovegni and Musei Eremitani. **Cons:** no in-room safes; pricey €25 parking; lack of hotel services and amenities. *Rooms from: €250 ✉ Piazza Eremitani 18, Padua ☎ 380/8932289 mobile 🌐 palazzomantuabenavides.com 7 suites No Meals.*

Nightlife

CAFÉS AND WINE BARS

★ Caffè Pedrocchi

WINE BAR | No visit to Padua is complete without taking time to sit in this historic café and iconic Padovano venue, patronized by luminaries like the French novelist Stendhal in 1831. Nearly 200 years later, it remains central to the city's social life. The café was built in the Egyptian Revival style, and it's now famed for its innovative aperitivi and signature mint coffee. The accomplished, innovative restaurant serves breakfast, lunch, and dinner. The grand salons and terrace provide a backdrop for the occasional jazz, swing, and cover bands. *✉ Piazzetta Pedrocchi, Padua ☎ 049/8781231 🌐 www.caffepedrocchi.it.*

Shopping

★ Mercato Sotto il Salone

FOOD | Under the Salone there's an impressive food market where shops sell choice salami and cured meats, local cheeses, wines, coffee, and tea. With the adjacent Piazza delle Erbe fruit and vegetable market, you can pick up all the makings of a fine picnic. On weekends and public holidays, the buzzy piazza is often filled with a cornucopia of street food options, as well as wine and beer stalls, many run by the makers themselves. *✉ Piazza della Ragione, Padua 🌐 mercatosottoilsalone.it.*

Cocktail Hour on Padua's Piazzas

One of Padua's greatest traditions is the outdoor en masse consumption of aperitifs: a spritz mixing Aperol or Campari with soda water and wine, prosecco (sparkling wine), or wine. It all happens in Piazza delle Erbe and Piazza della Frutta. Several bars there provide drinks in plastic cups, so you can take them outside and mingle among the crowds. The ritual, practiced primarily by students, begins at 6 or so, at which hour you can also pick up a snack from one of the outdoor vendors.

Zotti Antiquariato

ANTIQUES & COLLECTIBLES | Owned by antiques dealer Pietro Maria Zotti—who has worked for more than 40 years in the trade—this always-changing shop has fascinating finds from Venetian artworks to stylish mid-century furniture, plus lots of smaller, more affordable items, including books, prints, jewelry, militaria, and coins. *✉ Selciato San Nicolò 5, Padua ☎ 338/2930830 mobile 🌐 www.antichitazotti.com.*

Activities

LoVivo Tours

CULTURAL TOURS | A local tour operator offers a wealth of interesting tours and experiences that won't break the bank, covering Padua's cultural and UNESCO sites, a tour of the Riviera di Brenta villas, the area's intriguing garden labyrinths (including a lavender maze), and various excursions (including hiking and bike adventures) in the Euganean Hills. *✉ Via A. Vespucci 17, Abano Terme, Padua ☎ 049/2969340 🌐 www.lovivo.it From €45.*

Verona

114 km (71 miles) west of Venice, 60 km (37 miles) west of Vicenza.

On the banks of the fast-flowing River Adige, enchanting Verona has timeless monuments, a picturesque town center, and a romantic reputation as the setting of Shakespeare's *Romeo and Juliet*. With its lively Venetian air and proximity to Lake Garda, it attracts hordes of tourists, especially Germans and Austrians. Tourism peaks during summer's renowned season of open-air opera in the arena and during spring's Vinitaly, one of the world's most important wine expos. For five days you can sample the wines of more than 4,000 wineries from dozens of countries.

Verona grew to power and prosperity within the Roman Empire as a result of its key commercial and military position in northern Italy. With its Roman arena, theater, and city gates, it has the most significant monuments of Roman antiquity north of Rome. After the fall of the empire, the city continued to flourish under the guidance of barbarian kings, such as Theodoric, Alboin, Pepin, and Berenger I, reaching its cultural and artistic peak in the 13th and 14th centuries under the della Scala (Scaligero) dynasty. (Look for the *scala*, or ladder, emblem all over town.) In 1404 Verona traded its independence for security and placed itself under the control of Venice. (The other recurring architectural motif is the lion of St. Mark, a symbol of Venetian rule.)

If you're going to visit more than one or two sights, it's worth purchasing a Verona Card, available at museums, churches, and tobacconists for €27 (for 24 hours) or €32 (48 hours). It buys a single admission to most of the city's significant museums and churches, plus you can ride free on city buses. If you're mostly interested in churches, a €8 Chiese Vive cumulative ticket is sold at Verona's major houses of worship and gains you entry to the Duomo, San Fermo Maggiore, San Zeno Maggiore, and Sant'Anastasia. Note that Verona's churches strictly enforce their dress code: no sleeveless shirts, shorts, or short skirts.

GETTING HERE AND AROUND

Verona is midway between Venice and Milan. Several trains per hour depart from any point on the Milan–Venice line. By car, from Venice, take the Autostrada Trieste–Torino A4/E70 to the SS12 and follow it north into town.

VISITOR INFORMATION

CONTACT Verona Tourism Office (IAT Verona). ✉ *Palazzo Barbieri, Via Leoncino 61, Piazza Bra, Verona* ☎ *045/8068680* 🌐 *www.veronatouristoffice.it/en.*

Sights

In addition to ancient Verona's famous Roman theater and arena, two of its city gates (Porta dei Leoni and Porta dei Borsari) and a beautiful triumphal arch (Arco dei Gavi) have survived. These graceful and elegant portals provide an idea of the high aesthetic standards of their time. Look, too, beyond the main sights of the Città Antica (historic center): take time to wander the streets, and be sure not to miss out on the many leafy stretches of the riverside Lungadige. Away from the crowds there's a wealth of varied architecture from ancient Rome to the Fascist era to the contemporary, as well as tranquil spots for feeding the ducks.

Arche Scaligere

TOMB | On a little square off Piazza dei Signori are the fantastically sculpted Gothic tombs of the della Scala family, who ruled Verona during the late Middle Ages. The 19th-century English traveler and critic John Ruskin described the tombs as graceful places where people who have fallen asleep live. The tomb of Cangrande I (1291–1329) hangs over the portal of the adjacent church and is the work of the Maestro di Sant'Anastasia.

Sights

1 Arche Scaligere F2
2 Arco dei Gavi D3
3 Arena di Verona E3
4 Castelvecchio D3
5 Duomo F1
6 Funicular of Castel San Pietro G1
7 Loggia del Consiglio F2
8 Museo Archeologico and Teatro Romano G1
9 Palazzo degli Scaligeri ... F2
10 Palazzo della Ragione and Torre dei Lamberti ... F2
11 Piazza delle Erbe F2
12 Porta dei Borsari E2
13 Porta dei Leoni G3
14 San Zeno Maggiore B2
15 Sant'Anastasia G1

Restaurants

1 Antica Osteria al Duomo F1
2 Il Desco G2

Quick Bites

1 Caffè Borsari F2

Hotels

1 Escalus Luxury Suites E3
2 Gabbio d'Oro F2
3 Hotel Accademia F3
4 Hotel Indigo Verona – Grand Hotel Des Arts E3

The tomb of Mastino II, begun in 1345, has an elaborate baldachin, originally painted and gilded, and is surrounded by an iron grillwork fence and topped by an equestrian statue. The latest and most elaborate tomb is that of Cansignorio (1375), the work principally of Bonino da Campione. Visitors with a Verona civic sight ticket can enter the compact gated grounds for a closer view, although all the major tombs are visible from the street. ✉ *Via Arche Scaligere, Verona* 🎫 *Free entrance only to those with a current day ticket for any civic museum/ monument or Verona Card.*

Arco dei Gavi

RUINS | This stunning structure is simpler and less imposing, but also more graceful, than the triumphal arches in Rome. Built in the 1st century by the architect Lucius Vitruvius Cerdo to celebrate the accomplishments of the patrician Gavia family, it was highly esteemed by several Renaissance architects, including Palladio. ✉ *Corso Cavour, Verona.*

Arena di Verona

RUINS | **FAMILY** | Only Rome's Colosseum and Capua's arena would dwarf this amphitheater, built for gymnastic competitions, choreographed sacrificial rites, and games involving hunts, fights, battles, and wild animals. Although four arches are all that remain of the arena's outer arcade, the main structure is complete and dates from AD 30. In summer, you can join up to 16,000 for spectacular opera productions and pop or rock concerts (extra costs for these events). **TIP→ The opera's the main thing here: when there is no opera performance, you can still enter the interior, but the arena is less impressive inside than the Colosseum or other Roman amphitheaters.** ✉ *Piazza Bra 5, Verona* ☎ *045/8005151 performance tickets, 045/8003204 visit* 🌐 *www.arena.it* 🎫 *€12 (free with VeronaCard).*

★ Castelvecchio

CASTLE/PALACE | This crenellated, russet brick building with massive walls, towers, turrets, and a vast courtyard was built for Cangrande II della Scala in 1354 and presides over a street lined with attractive old buildings and palaces of the nobility. Only by going inside the Museo di Castelvecchio can you really appreciate this massive castle complex with its vaulted halls. You also get a look at a significant collection of Venetian and Veneto art, medieval weapons, and jewelry. The interior of the castle was restored and redesigned as a museum between 1958 and 1975 by Carlo Scarpa, one of Italy's most accomplished architects. **TIP→ Behind the castle is the fortified Ponte Scaligero (1355), which spans the River Adige and is a fab spot for taking photos.** ✉ *Corso Castelvecchio 2, Verona* ☎ *045/7110129* 🌐 *museodicastelvecchio.comune.verona.it* 🎫 *€9 (free with VeronaCard)* 🕒 *Closed Mon.*

Duomo

CHURCH | The present church dedicated to Santa Maria Assunta was begun in the 12th century in the Romanesque style; there are paleo-Christian remains under the Sant' Elena and Canons' cloister, while later additions are mostly Gothic. On pilasters guarding the main entrance are 12th-century carvings thought to represent Oliver and Roland, two of Charlemagne's knights and heroes of several medieval epic poems. Inside, Titian's *Assumption* (1530) graces the first chapel on the left. ✉ *Via Duomo, Verona* ☎ *045/592813* 🌐 *www.chieseverona.it* 🎫 *€4 (€8 Chiese Vive Cumulative Ticket or free with VeronaCard).*

★ Funicular of Castel San Pietro

VIEWPOINT | Opened in 2017, this funicular ride ascends 500 feet from near the Teatro Romano up to a panoramic terrace in just 90 seconds, affording fabulous Veronese views. For the adventurous, there's scope for long walks around the parkland paths and quiet lanes crisscrossing the elevated city walls. ✉ *Via Fontanelle S. Stefano, Verona* ☎ *342/8966695 mobile* 🌐 *www.funicolarediverona.it* 🎫 *€3 round-trip, €2 one-way.*

Loggia del Consiglio

GOVERNMENT BUILDING | This graceful structure on the north flank of Piazza dei Signori was finished in 1492 and built to house city council meetings. Although the city was already under Venetian rule, Verona still had a certain degree of autonomy, which was expressed by the splendor of the loggia. Very strangely for a Renaissance building of this quality, its architect remains unknown, but it's the finest surviving example of late-15th-century architecture in Verona. The building is not open to the public, but the exterior is worth a visit. ✉ *Piazza dei Signori, Verona.*

Museo Archeologico and Teatro Romano

HISTORY MUSEUM | The archaeological holdings of this museum in a 15th-century former monastery consist largely of the donated collections of Veronese citizens proud of their city's classical past. You'll find few blockbusters here, but there are some noteworthy pieces (especially among the bronzes), and it is interesting to see what cultured Veronese collected between the 17th and 19th centuries. The museum complex includes the Teatro Romano, Verona's 1st-century theater, which is open to visitors and an atmospheric music venue. ✉ *Rigaste del Redentore 2, Verona* ☎ *045/7110129* 🌐 *museoarcheologico.comune.verona.it* 🎫 *€9 (free with VeronaCard)* 🕑 *Closed Mon.*

Palazzo degli Scaligeri (*Palazzo di Cangrande*)

CASTLE/PALACE | The della Scala family ruled Verona from this stronghold built (over Roman ruins) at the end of the 13th century and then inhabited by Cangrande I. At that time Verona controlled the mainland Veneto from Treviso and Lombardy to Mantua and Brescia, hence the building's alternative name as a seat of Domini di Terraferma (Venetian administration): Palazzo del Podestà. The portal facing Piazza dei Signori was added in 1533 by the accomplished Renaissance architect Michele Sanmicheli. You have to admire the palazzo from the outside, as it's not open to the public. ✉ *Piazza dei Signori, Verona.*

★ Palazzo della Ragione and Torre dei Lamberti

VIEWPOINT | An elegant 15th-century pink-marble staircase leads up from the *mercato vecchio* (old market) courtyard to the magistrates' chambers in this 12th-century palace, built at the intersection of the main streets of the ancient Roman city. The interior now houses exhibitions and the 1,600-strong artwork collection of the **Galleria d'Arte Moderna Achille Forti,** including the alluring Meditazione (1851) by Francesco Hayez. You can get the highest view in town from atop the attached 270-foot-high Romanesque Torre dei Lamberti. About 50 years after a lightning strike in 1403 knocked its top off, it was rebuilt and extended to its current height. ✉ *Piazza dei Signori, Verona* ☎ *045/9273027* 🌐 *www.torredeilamberti.it; gam.comune.verona.it* 🎫 *€6 gallery only; €6 tower only (both free with VeronaCard)* 🕑 *Gallery closed Mon.* ✍ *Book the tower visit in advance by phone.*

Favorite Places

Nick Bruno: For Veronese vistas I love ascending the San Pietro funicular. From the panoramic hilltop terrace you can enjoy wonderful views over terracotta rooftops, bell towers, and the River Adige.

Piazza delle Erbe

PLAZA/SQUARE | Frescoed buildings surround this medieval square, where a busy Roman forum once stood; during the week it's still bustling, as vendors sell produce and trinkets, much as they have been doing for generations. Eyes are drawn to the often sun-sparkling Madonna Verona fountain (1368) and its Roman statue (the body is from AD 380, with medieval additions). ✉ *Piazza delle Erbe, Verona.*

★ Porta dei Borsari

RUINS | As its elegant decoration suggests, this is the main entrance to ancient Verona—dating, in its present state, from the 1st century. It's at the beginning of the narrow, pedestrianized Corso Porta Borsari, now a smart shopping street leading to Piazza delle Erbe. ✉ *Corso Porta Borsari, Verona.*

Porta dei Leoni

RUINS | The oldest of Verona's elegant and graceful Roman portals, the Porta dei Leoni (on Via Leoni, just a short walk from Piazza delle Erbe) dates from the 1st century BC, but its original earth-and-brick structure was sheathed in local marble during the early imperial era. It has become the focus of a campaign against violence—there are often flowers and messages by the monument—in memory of the murder of a young Veronese here in 2009. ✉ *Via Leoni, Verona.*

★ San Zeno Maggiore

CHURCH | One of Italy's finest Romanesque churches is filled with treasures, including a rose window by the 13th-century sculptor Brioloto that represents a wheel of fortune, with six of the spokes formed by statues depicting the rising and falling fortunes of mankind. The 12th-century porch is the work of Maestro Niccolò; it's flanked by marble reliefs by Niccolò and Maestro Guglielmo depicting scenes from the Old and New Testaments and from the legend of Theodoric. The bronze doors date from the 11th and 12th centuries; some were probably imported from Saxony, and some are from Veronese workshops. They combine allegorical representations with scenes from the lives of saints.

Inside, look for the 12th-century statue of San Zeno to the left of the main altar. In modern times it has been dubbed the "Laughing San Zeno" because of a misinterpretation of its conventional Romanesque grin. A famous *Madonna and Saints* triptych by Andrea Mantegna (1431–1506) hangs over the main altar, and a peaceful cloister (1120–38) lies to the left of the nave. The detached bell tower was finished in 1173. ✉ *Piazza San Zeno, Verona* ☎ *045/592813* 🌐 *www.chieseverona.it* 🎫 *€4 (€8 Chiese Vive Cumulative Ticket or free with VeronaCard).*

Sant'Anastasia

CHURCH | Verona's largest church, begun in 1290 but only consecrated in 1471, is a fine example of Gothic brickwork and has a grand doorway with elaborately carved biblical scenes. The main reason for visiting this church, however, is *St. George and the Princess* (dated 1434, but perhaps earlier) by Pisanello (1377–1455). It's above the Pellegrini Chapel off the main altar. As you come in, look also for the *gobbi* (hunchbacks) supporting the holy-water basins. ✉ *Piazza Sant'Anastasia, Verona* ☎ *045/592813* 🌐 *www.chieseverona.it* 🎫 *€4 (€8 Chiese Vive Cumulative Ticket or free with VeronaCard).*

Restaurants

★ Antica Osteria al Duomo

$$ | NORTHERN ITALIAN | This side-street eatery, lined with old wood paneling and decked out with musical instruments, serves traditional Veronese classics, like bigoli (thick whole wheat spaghetti) with donkey ragù and *pastissada con polenta* (horsemeat stew with polenta). Don't be deterred by the unconventional meats—they're tender and delicious, and this is

probably the best place in town to sample them. **Known for:** blackboard menu, bar, and wooden interiors; occasional live music; rustic courtyard. *Average main: €20 Via Duomo 7/A, Verona 045/8004505 Closed Sun. except in Dec. and during wine fair.*

★ Il Desco

$$$$ | **MODERN ITALIAN** | Opened in 1981 by Elia Rizzo, the nationally renowned fine-dining Desco cuisine is now crafted by talented son Matteo. True to Italian and Rizzo culinary traditions, he preserves natural flavors through careful ingredient selection, adding daring combinations inspired by stints in kitchens around the world. **Known for:** inventive, colorful plates of food; elegant, arty surroundings fit for a modern opera; pricey three-, four-, or five-course tasting menus. *Average main: €120 Via Dietro San Sebastiano 7, Verona 045/595358 www.ristoranteildesco.it Closed Sun. and Mon.*

Coffee and Quick Bites

★ Caffè Borsari

$ | **NORTHERN ITALIAN** | This bustling café-bar is famed for its excellent creamy coffee and freshly made brioche—it's cheek by jowl *al banco* (at the counter/bar), with Veronese patrons spilling outside. The narrow space with star-vaulted ceiling on the charming Corso Borsari cobbles is packed with coffee- and tea-making pots and cups, as are its walls with colorful gifts and oddities according to the time of year. **Known for:** indulgent hot chocolate; selection of coffee, tea, candies, and chocolates for gift giving; famed for their schiuma (froth) creations. *Average main: €5 Corso Portoni Borsari 15, Verona 045/8031313 facebook.com/caffeborsari.*

Hotels

Book hotels months in advance for spring's Vinitaly, usually in early April, and for opera season. Verona hotels are also very busy during the January and September gold fairs in neighboring Vicenza. Hotels jack up prices considerably at all these times.

Escalus Luxury Suites

$$ | **HOTEL** | **FAMILY** | Near the Arena and Verona's marble-paved main shopping street, Via Mazzini, these suites and mini-apartments offer contemporary minimalist style in muted colors; the larger ones have handy kitchenettes, and all have swank bathrooms. **Pros:** chic location near sights and shopping; family-friendly Glamour Deluxe Suite with balcony; large showers. **Cons:** checkout is before 11 am; constant passeggiata hum from Via Mazzini; minimalist decor not to everyone's taste. *Rooms from: €360 Vicolo Tre Marchetti 12, Verona 045/8036754 www.escalusverona.com 6 suites Free Breakfast.*

Gabbia d'Oro

$$$ | **HOTEL** | Occupying a historic building off Piazza delle Erbe in the ancient heart of Verona, this hotel is a romantic fantasia of ornamentation, rich fabrics, and period-style furniture. **Pros:** central location; great breakfast; romantic atmosphere. **Cons:** some very small rooms, especially considering the price; small bathrooms; some guests may find the decor overly ornate, even stuffy. *Rooms from: €425 Corso Porta Borsari 4/a, Verona 045/8003060 www.hotelgabbiadoro.it 27 rooms Free Breakfast.*

Hotel Accademia

$$ | **HOTEL** | The Palladian facade of columns and arches here hint at the well-proportioned interior layout: expect an elegant contemporary take on Art Deco in public spaces and immaculate if impersonal traditional-style decor in

guest rooms. **Pros:** central location; good fitness room; rooftop solarium. **Cons:** expensive parking; some may find the decor lacking; lack of views in some rooms and breakfast under-par. $ *Rooms from: €285* ✉ *Via Scala 12, Verona* ☎ *045/596222* 🌐 *www.hotelaccademia-verona.it* *96 rooms* *Free Breakfast.*

Hotel Indigo Verona – Grand Hotel Des Arts

$$ | HOTEL | Handily placed near both the Arena and train station, the art-inspired Indigo is a handsome 1920s Stile Liberty palazzo with stylish design touches and a sophisticated loungy feel throughout. **Pros:** good parking and transport links; cool bar and courtyard; warm customer service. **Cons:** limited breakfast choice; smallish rooms; on busy Corso Porta Nuova. $ *Rooms from: €240* ✉ *Corso Porta Nuova 105, Verona* ☎ *0800/9880220* 🌐 *www.ihg.com/hotelindigo* *62 rooms* *Free Breakfast.*

Performing Arts

★ Arena di Verona Opera Festival

OPERA | Milan's La Scala and Naples's San Carlo offer performances more likely to attract serious opera fans, but neither offers a greater spectacle than the Arena di Verona. During the venue's summer season (June to August), as many as 16,000 attendees sit on the original stone terraces or in modern cushioned stalls. Most of the operas presented are big and splashy, like *Aida* or *Turandot,* demanding huge choruses, lots of color and movement, and, if possible, camels, horses, or elephants. Order tickets by phone or through the arena website. ✉ *Box office, Via Dietro Anfiteatro 6/b, Verona* ☎ *045/8005151* 🌐 *www.arena.it* *From €38 (for general admission).*

Vinitaly

FESTIVALS | This widely attended international wine and spirits event takes place in Verona over four days in April. ✉ *Fiera di Verona, Viale del Lavoro 8, Verona* ☎ *045/8298111* 🌐 *www.vinitaly.com.*

Shopping

De Rossi

FOOD | Opened in 1947, De Rossi is a Veronese institution producing oven-hot bread, cakes, pastries, biscotti, and other specialties like fresh pasta. ✉ *Corso Porta Borsari 3, Verona* ☎ *045/8002489* 🌐 *www.derossi.it.*

Libreria del Novecento

BOOKS | All bibliophiles should make a beeline to this small bookshop with its fascinating selection of secondhand volumes spanning many subjects. Have a rummage to unearth paperbacks with alluringly designed covers, collectibles, first editions, and intriguing art books. They also have a selection of overpriced vinyl records and CDs. ✉ *Via Santa Maria in Chiavica 3/A, Verona* ☎ *045/8008108* 🌐 *www.libreriadelnovecento.it.*

Activities

★ Adige Rafting

RAFTING | FAMILY | Briefed by expert guides and issued with paddles and life jackets, the adventurous can set off on a *gommone* (dinghy) from the Chievo (eastern) area of town and navigate the cool waters of the Adige, finishing up at the picnic area of Boschetto. Along the 8-km (5-mile) stretch of river there are wonderful water-level views of Verona's architectural and natural riches. The trip takes around three hours, with two hours spent on the water, including a fun race along the way. ✉ *Centro Sportivo Bottagisio, Via del Perloso 14/A, Verona* ☎ *347/8892498 mobile* 🌐 *adigerafting.it* *€30.*

Vicenza

74 km (46 miles) west of Venice, 43 km (27 miles) west of Padua.

A visit to Vicenza is a must for any student or fan of architecture. This elegant, prosperous city bears the distinctive signature of the 16th-century architect Andrea Palladio, whose name has been given to the "Palladian" style of architecture. He emphasized the principles of order and harmony using the classical style of architecture established by Renaissance architects, such as Brunelleschi, Alberti, and Sansovino. He used these principles and classical motifs not only for public buildings but also for private dwellings. His elegant villas and palaces were influential in propagating classical architecture in Europe, especially Britain, and later in America—most notably at Thomas Jefferson's Monticello.

In the mid-16th century Palladio was commissioned to rebuild much of Vicenza, which had been greatly damaged during wars waged against Venice by the League of Cambrai (1505), an alliance of the papacy, France, the Holy Roman Empire, and several neighboring city-states. He made his name with the renovation of the basilica, begun in 1549 in the heart of Vicenza, and then embarked on a series of lordly buildings, all of which adhere to the same classicism and principles of harmony.

GETTING HERE AND AROUND

Vicenza is midway between Padua and Verona; several trains leave from Venice every hour. By car, take the Autostrada Brescia–Padova/Torino–Trieste A4/E70 to SP247 North directly into Vicenza.

VISITOR INFORMATION

CONTACT Vicenza Tourism Office. ✉ *Piazza Giacomo Matteotti 12, Vicenza* ☎ *0444/320854* 🌐 *www.vicenzae.org.*

Sights

★ Basilica Palladiana

NOTABLE BUILDING | At the heart of Vicenza, Piazza dei Signori contains the Palazzo della Ragione (1549), the project with which Palladio made his name by successfully modernizing a medieval building, grafting a graceful two-story exterior loggia onto the existing Gothic structure. Commonly known as Basilica Palladiana, the palazzo served as a courthouse and public meeting hall (the original Roman meaning of the term "basilica"). Walk around the loggia for grandstand views of the piazza, and the cavernous salon which hosts wonderful art exhibitions. Take a look also at the Loggia del Capitaniato, opposite, which Palladio designed but never completed. ✉ *Piazza dei Signori, Vicenza* 🎫 *€6* ⏲ *Closed Mon.*

Museo Civico di Palazzo Chiericati

CASTLE/PALACE | This imposing Palladian palazzo (1550) would be worthy of a visit even if it didn't house Vicenza's Museo Civico. Because of the ample space surrounding the building, Palladio combined elements of an urban palazzo with those he used in his country villas. The museum's important Venetian holdings include significant paintings by Cima, Tiepolo, Piazetta, and Tintoretto, but its main attraction is an extensive collection of rarely found works by painters from the Vicenza area, among them Jacopo Bassano (1515–92) and the eccentric and innovative Francesco Maffei (1605–60), whose work foreshadowed important currents of Venetian painting of subsequent generations. An audio guide QR code (€5) via your smartphone or tablet is available at the entrance. ✉ *Piazza Matteotti, Vicenza* ☎ *0444/222811* 🌐 *www.museicivicivicenza.it* 🎫 *€8; €16 Vicenza Silver Card/£22 Vicenza Gold Card: the former includes 4 sights, the latter all 11 city network sights including Palladio Museum and Teatro Olimpico* ⏲ *Closed Mon.*

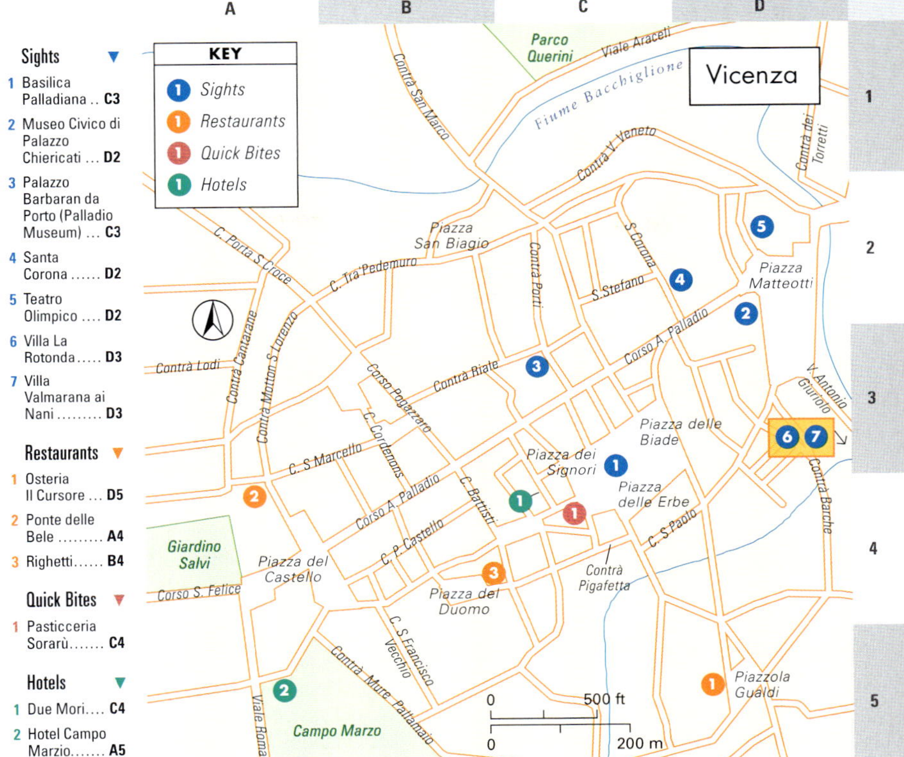

Palazzo Barbaran da Porto (Palladio Museum)

CASTLE/PALACE | Palladio executed this beautiful city palace for the Vicentine noble Montano Barbarano between 1570 and 1575. The noble patron, however, did not make things easy for Palladio; the architect had to incorporate at least two preexisting medieval houses, with irregularly shaped rooms, into his classical, harmonious plan. It also had to support the great hall of the *piano nobile* (moving floor) above the fragile walls of the original medieval structure. The wondrous palazzo is one of Palladio's most harmonious constructions; the viewer has little indication that this is actually a transformation of a medieval structure. The palazzo also contains a museum dedicated to Palladio and is the seat of a center for Palladian studies. ✉ *Contrà Porti 11, Vicenza* ☎ *0444/323014* 🌐 *www.palladiomuseum.org* 🎫 *€8; €16 Vicenza Silver Card/£22 Vicenza Gold Card: the former includes 4 sights, the latter all 11 city network sights* ⏲ *Closed Mon. and Tues.*

Santa Corona

CHURCH | An exceptionally fine *Baptism of Christ* (1502), a work of Giovanni Bellini's maturity, hangs over the altar on the left, just in front of the transept of this 13th Century Gothic-style church. Santa Corona also houses the elegantly simple Valmarana chapel, designed by Palladio, and an *Adoration of the Magi* (1573) by Veronese. Ask about the free audio guide via QR code for smartphone/tablet at the entrance. ✉ *Contrà S. Corona, Vicenza* ☎ *0444/320854* 🌐 *www.museicivicivicenza.it* 🎫 *€4 (free with Vicenza Card)* ⏲ *Closed Mon.*

★ Teatro Olimpico

PERFORMANCE VENUE | Palladio's last, perhaps most spectacular work was begun in 1580 and completed in 1585, after his death, by Vincenzo Scamozzi (1552–1616). Based closely on the model of ancient Roman theaters, it represents an important development in theater and stage design and is noteworthy for its acoustics and the cunning use of perspective in Scamozzi's permanent backdrop. The anterooms are frescoed with images of important figures in Venetian history. One of the few Renaissance theaters still standing, it can be visited (with guided tours) during the day and is used for concerts, operas, and other performances. ✉ *Ticket office, Piazza Matteotti 12, Vicenza* ☎ *0444/964380* 🌐 *www.teatrolimpicovicenza.it* 🎫 *€12; €16 Vicenza Silver Card/£22 Vicenza Gold Card: the former includes 4 sights, the latter all 11 city network sights* 🕒 *Closed Mon.*

★ Villa La Rotonda (*Villa Almerico Capra*)

HISTORIC HOME | Commissioned in 1556 as a suburban residence for Paolo Almerico, this beautiful Palladian is the purest expression of Palladio's architectural theory and aesthetic. More a villa-temple than a residence, it contradicts the rational utilitarianism of Renaissance architecture and demonstrates the priority Palladio gave to the architectural symbolism of celestial harmony over practical considerations. A visit to view the interior can be difficult to schedule—the villa remains privately owned, and visiting hours are limited to the weekend—but this is a worthwhile stop, if only to see how Palladio's harmonious arrangement of smallish interconnected rooms around a central domed space paid little attention to the practicalities of living. The interior decoration, mainly later baroque stuccowork, contains some allegorical frescoes in the cupola by Palladio's contemporary, Alessandro Maganza. Even without a peek inside, experiencing the exterior and the grounds, including the newly restored 19th century woodland *Boschetto Romantico,*is a must for any visit to Vicenza. The villa is a 20-minute walk from town or a cab (€15) or bus ride (No. 8) from Vicenza's Piazza Roma. Private tours are by appointment; see the website for the latest visiting details. ✉ *Via della Rotonda, Vicenza* ☎ *0444/321793* 🌐 *www.villalarotonda.it* 🎫 *€12; €25 with guided tour, in Italian only; €3 Boschetto Romantico* 🕒 *Closed Mon.–Thurs. April–Oct., weekdays Apr. and Nov.* ✍ *Message to WhatsApp no: 351 7922118.*

★ Villa Valmarana ai Nani

HISTORIC HOME | Inside this 17th- to 18th-century country house, named for the statues of dwarfs adorning the garden, is a series of frescoes executed in 1757 by Gianbattista Tiepolo depicting scenes from classical mythology, the *Iliad*, Tasso's *Jerusalem Delivered*, and Ariosto's *Orlando furioso* (The Frenzy of Orlando). They include his *Sacrifice of Iphigenia,* a major masterpiece of 18th-century painting. The neighboring *foresteria* (guesthouse) is also part of the museum; it contains frescoes showing 18th-century life at its most charming and scenes of chinoiserie popular in the 18th century, by Tiepolo's son Giandomenico (1727–1804). The garden dwarfs are probably taken from designs by Giandomenico. You can reach the villa on foot by following the same path that leads to Palladio's Villa La Rotonda. ✉ *Via dei Nani 2/8, Vicenza* ☎ *0444/321803* 🌐 *www.villavalmarana.com* 🎫 *€15.*

Restaurants

Osteria Il Cursore

$ | **NORTHERN ITALIAN** | This cozy 19th-century *locale storico* (historic hostelry) is steeped in Vicentina atmosphere, from the bar serving local wines and *sopressa* (premium salami) to the intimate dark-wood restaurant serving hearty classics.

Grab a table out back for a sit-down meal of robust dishes like bigoli (thick, egg-enriched spaghetti) with duck, spaghetti with baccalà (cod), and, in spring, *risi e bisi* (rice with peas). **Known for:** quality wine and cold cuts; buzzy atmosphere, especially on Vicenza soccer-match days; great-value pasta. *Average main: €16 Stradella Pozzetto 10, Vicenza 0444/323504 www.osteriacursore.it Closed Tues., no dinner Mon.–Thurs., no lunch Fri.*

Ponte delle Bele

$ | **NORTHERN ITALIAN** | Many of Vicenza's wealthier residents spend at least part of the summer in the Alps to escape the heat, and the dishes of this popular and friendly trattoria reflect the hearty influences of neighboring Alpine areas of the Trentino and Tyrol on local cuisine. The house specialty, *stinco di maiale al forno* (roast pork shank), is wonderfully fragrant, with herbs and aromatic vegetables and roast potatoes. **Known for:** hearty Vicentina classics, including baccalà served with polenta; unfussy, relaxed atmosphere and kitschy Alpine decor; mountain cheeses and cold cuts. *Average main: €15 Contrà Ponte delle Bele 5, Vicenza 0444/320647 www.pontedellebele.it Closed Sun. and Mon., and 2 wks in Aug.*

Righetti

$ | **ITALIAN** | Vicentini of all generations gravitate to this popular self-service cafeteria for classic dishes that don't put a dent in your wallet. Expect hearty helpings of fare such as *orzo e fagioli* (barley and bean soup) and baccalà alla vicentina (stockfish Vicenza style) **Known for:** rustic dining area and tables on the piazza; very popular, especially for lunch; entertaining local atmosphere. *Average main: €12 Piazza Duomo 3, Vicenza 0444/543135 www.selfrighetti.it Closed weekends and 1 wk in Jan. and Aug.*

Coffee and Quick Bites

★ Pasticceria Soraru

$ | **NORTHERN ITALIAN** | Nestled under the porticoes of Piazzetta Palladio, the historic Pasticceria Sorarù occupies the former Cafeteria Palladio (1870) and is an ever-reliable spot for the freshest breakfast brioche with cappuccino, and a cornucopia of pastry delights. Inside, you can lean on the handsome old wooden counter and sample a pastry or three while admiring the glass jars filled with colorful candies. **Known for:** traditional Vicentino pastries and gelato; zaèti (polenta and raisin) biscuits and famous plum cake; seating under the porticoes. *Average main: €6 Piazzetta Andrea Palladio 17, Vicenza 0444/320915 www.facebook.com/pasticceriasoraru.*

Hotels

During annual gold fairs in January and September, it may be quite difficult to find lodging. If you're coming then, be sure to reserve well in advance and expect to pay higher rates.

Due Mori

$ | **HOTEL** | The public areas and guest rooms at one of the oldest (1883) hotels in the city, just off Piazza dei Signori, are filled with turn-of-the-20th-century antiques, and regulars favor the place because the high ceilings in the main building make it feel light and airy. **Pros:** traditionally furnished rooms in central location; rate same year-round; free Wi-Fi. **Cons:** no a/c, whirring ceiling fans instead; basic breakfast; no TVs in rooms. *Rooms from: €110 Contrà Do Rode 24, Vicenza 0444/321886 www.albergoduemori.it Closed 2 wks in early Aug. and 2 wks in late Dec. 30 rooms No Meals.*

★ Hotel Campo Marzio

$ | **HOTEL** | Rooms at this comfortable full-service hotel—a five-minute walk from the train station and right in front of the city walls—are ample in size, with a mix of contemporary and traditional accents. **Pros:** great location; free bike hire; set back from the street, so it's quiet and bright. **Cons:** breakfast room a tad uninspiring; businesslike exterior; no in-room tea- or coffeemaking facilities. *$ Rooms from: €130 ✉ Viale Roma 21, Vicenza ☎ 0444/5457000 🌐 www.hotelcampomarzio.com 🛏 36 rooms 🍴 Free Breakfast.*

Activities

Palladian Routes

CULTURAL TOURS | FAMILY | Based in the handsome Palazzo Valmarana Braga, this company offers a wealth of tours around the province of Vicenza. Their one-day Vicenza Landscapes and Soul of Palladio tour is among their most popular e-bike jaunts. Visit their office to pick up your bike and accessories with GPS, and be guided by a narration app via smartphone around gorgeous landscapes, three villas, and the verdant shores of Lago di Fimon. *✉ Palazzo Valmarana Braga, Corso Fogazzaro 16, Vicenza ☎ 0444/1270212 🌐 www.palladianroutes.com 🎫 From €42 for e-bike hire; from €59 for an e-bike tour.*

Marostica

26 km (16 miles) northeast of Vicenza, 93 km (58 miles) northwest of Venice.

From the 14th-century Castello Inferiore, where the town council still meets, an ancient stone wall snakes up the hill to enclose the Castello Superiore, which has commanding views. Marostica's most celebrated feature is the checkerboard-like square made with colored stone, Piazza Castello. The big annual event here, held in September in even-number years, is the Partita a Scacchi, a human-scale chess game.

GETTING HERE AND AROUND

There's no train station in Marostica. The closest rail connection is Bassano del Grappa, about 8 km (5 miles) away. There are regular bus connections from Vicenza's main station on STV Bus No. E05; the trip takes about 45 minutes. By car, take the SS248 northeast from Vicenza, or southwest from Bassano.

VISITOR INFORMATION

CONTACT Associazione Pro Marostica. *✉ Piazza Castello 1, Marostica ☎ 0424/72127 🌐 www.marosticascacchi.it.*

Sights

Castello di Marostica

CASTLE/PALACE | FAMILY | Sitting on the summit of Monte Pauso, the origins of fortifications here stretch back to the turn of the first millennium, and a guided tour of the castle delves into its bloody history, and the lives and tastes of its former residents. The fairytale-like castle form makes it a fine backdrop to the giant chess game staged outside the impressive drawbridge and crenellated, pitted walls. Legend has it that the moat was the watery, muddy realm of an Egyptian crocodile brought here by the town's most famous son, the physician and botanist Prospero Alpini (1553–1617). The atmospheric interiors house collections of court clothing including those of the Venetian Podestà, arms and armature, and a fresco attributed to Mantegna (1454–57). The Sale Espostive stages exhibitions and cultural events, and has a curious sculpture of doge Foscari kneeling before the lion of San Marco. *✉ Via Cansignorio della Scala 4, Marostica ☎ 0424/72127 🌐 www.marosticascacchi.it 🎫 €8 ☞ Book a small group guided tour by phone or online.*

Restaurants

★ Osteria Madonnetta

$ | VENETIAN | Opened in 1904, this ever-reliable osteria serves hearty traditional *cucina veneta* in wonderfully homey, rustic surroundings. Take a seat under the dark wooden beams or in the leafy courtyard, and let the friendly staff guide you through a menu, dominated by meat dishes and seasonal soups, that has barely changed in decades. **Known for:** baccalà alla vicentina; sweet, grappa-infused zaeti biscuits; quirky, history-filled decor including a chess-theme fireplace. *Average main: €16 Via Vajenti 21, Marostica 0424/75859 www.osteriamadonnetta.it Closed Thurs.*

Hotels

Due Mori

$ | B&B/INN | Although this inn dates from the 18th century, the interior is minimalist and clean-lined—Rooms 7, 8, 11, and 12 redress the balance with picture-perfect views of the town's upper castle, while other windows look out onto the city walls or olive-tree-filled terraces. **Pros:** only hotel within the city walls; travel transfers and bikes available; great views of castle from some rooms. **Cons:** limited breakfast choice; noise from Corso Mazzini–facing rooms; bland decoration. *Rooms from: €160 Corso Mazzini 73, Marostica 0424/471777 www.duemori.com 12 rooms Free Breakfast.*

Performing Arts

Partita a Scacchi

THEATER | FAMILY | A human-scale chess game known as the Partita a Scacchi is acted out by players in medieval costume on the second weekend in September in even-number years. The game dates from 1454 and originated as a peaceful way of settling a love dispute for the hand of the daughter of the lord of Marostica Castle. The orders are still given in the local Veneto dialect. A game is presented on Friday and weekend evenings as well as Sunday afternoon. If you book an evening show and do not have a hotel reservation in Marostica, be sure you have a way of getting back afterward. Buses do not run late in the evening, and taxis, if you can find one, may hike up their rates. Tickets go on sale in February; the tourist office can help with bookings. *Piazza Castello 1, Marostica 0424/72127 www.marosticascacchi.it From €50 for an atmospheric 9 pm game.*

Asolo

27 km (17 miles) east of Marostica.

Once considered the most romantic and charming of Veneto towns, the hamlet of Asolo has unfortunately lost much of its appeal, now that it's given over completely to tourism and vacation houses, with almost no local population. It does still make a nice stop for lunch after a visit to the Palladian villa at Maser, but try to avoid it on weekends and holidays, when the crowds pour in.

Through the centuries, Veneto aristocrats built elegant villas on the hillside, and in the 19th century Asolo became the idyllic haunt of musicians, poets, and painters. Back then it was one of Italy's most perfectly situated villages, with views across miles of hilly countryside; now it bears some of the scars of modern development.

Asolo hosts a modest antiques market on the second Sunday of every month.

GETTING HERE AND AROUND

There's no train station in Asolo; the closest one is in Montebelluna, 12 km (7½ miles) away. Bus connections are infrequent, and buses are not coordinated with trains, making it about a 2½-hour trip from Venice via public transportation. The best option is to drive.

By car from Treviso, take Via Feltrina and continue onto Via Padre Agostino Gemelli (SR348). Follow SR348 about 16 km (10 miles), then turn left on SP667, which you follow for almost 4 km (2½ miles). At the roundabout, take the first exit, Via Monte Grappa (SP248), and follow it for 6½ km (4 miles) to Via Loredan, where you turn right and then left onto Via Biordo Vecchio. Asolo is less than 7 km (4½ miles) away from the Palladian Villa Barbaro at Maser.

VISITOR INFORMATION

CONTACT Asolo IAT Tourism Office. ✉ *Piazza Maggiore 73 (aka Piazza Garibaldi), Asolo* ☎ *0423/529046* 🌐 *www.asolo.it.*

Sights

★ Museo Canova (*Gypsoteca*)

ART MUSEUM | The most significant cultural monument in the Asolo area is this museum dedicated to the work of the Italian neoclassical sculptor Antonio Canova (1757–1822), whose sculptures are featured in many major European and North American cultural institutions. Set up shortly after the sculptor's death in his hometown, the village of Possagno, the museum houses most of the original plaster casts, models, and drawings made by the artist in preparation for his marble sculptures. In 1957 the Museo Canova was extended by the Italian architect Carlo Scarpa. ✉ *Via Canova 74, 13½ km (8¼ miles) northwest of Asolo, Possagno* ☎ *0423/544323* 🌐 *www.museocanova.it* 🎫 *€13* ⏲ *Closed Mon.*

Museo Civico, Torre Civica, and La Rocca

HISTORY MUSEUM | In the Piazza Maggiore, the frescoed 15th-century Loggia del Capitano contains the Museo Civico, which displays a collection of eccentric memorabilia—the Italian actress Eleonora Duse's correspondence, the poet Robert Browning's spinet, and portraits of the noble Caterina Cornaro (1454–1510). There is also access to the nearby medieval tower, Torre Civica, partially rebuilt after an earthquake in 1685. It affords great views just above its handsome 18th-century clock, designed by Bartolomeo Ferracina, the genius engineer behind clocks in Venice's Piazza San Marco and Sant'Antonio da Padova. Temporary exhibitions are also staged in the tower, along with guided tours. Those after a woodland stroll should head up to the 1,000-foot Monte Ricco medieval hilltop fortress La Rocca—the views are fabulous but the structure itself is sometimes off-limits. ✉ *Piazza Maggiore, Asolo* ☎ *0423/952313* 🌐 *www.museoasolo.it* 🎫 *€5 Museo Civico; €3 Torre Civica; €3 La Rocca; €9 combined ticket* ⏲ *Closed weekdays.*

Piazza Maggiore

PLAZA/SQUARE | Also known as Piazza Giuseppe Garibaldi, this graceful square is surrounded by Renaissance palaces, historical cafés, and the mosaic-adorned cathedral. The Fontana Maggiore is fed by the remains of a Roman aqueduct; the fountain's latest form combines 16th-century marble with a lion added in 1918, attesting to centuries of Venetian rule here. ✉ *Piazza Maggiore, Asolo* 🌐 *www.asolo.it.*

★ Tempio Canoviano

MONUMENT | One of the most impressive and historically significant neoclassical buildings in Italy, the Tempio Canoviano, a church, was designed by Canova in 1819 and finished in 1830, incorporating motifs from the rotunda of the Roman Pantheon and the pronaos of the Parthenon. The church contains several works by Canova, including his tomb, along with paintings by Luca Giordano, Palma il Giovane, and Il Pordenone. A series of staircases gives access to the cupola roof and wonderful countryside views. ✉ *Piazza Canova, Possagno* ✣ *16 km (10 miles) north of Asolo* ☎ *0423/544323* 🌐 *www.tempiocanoviano.it* 🎫 *Free; cupola €3* ⏲ *Closed Mon.*

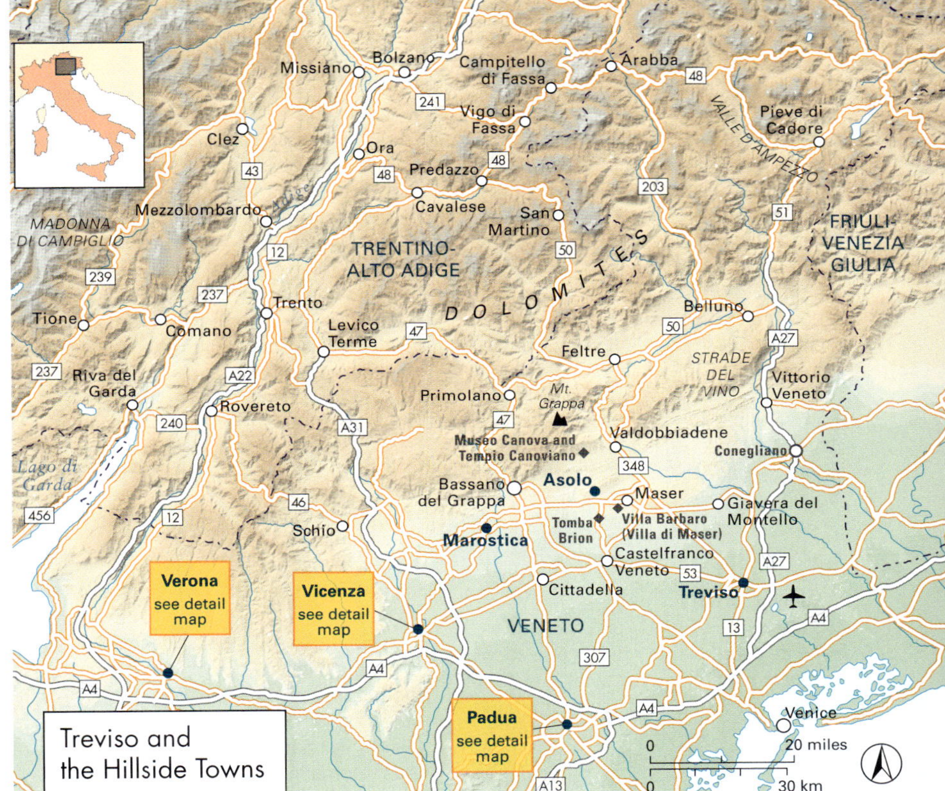

Tomba Brion

MONUMENT | One of the major monuments of contemporary Italian architecture, the Brion family tomb was designed and built by the architect Carlo Scarpa (1906–78) between 1970 and 1972. Combining Western rationalism with Eastern spirituality, Scarpa avoids the gloom and bombast of conventional commemorative monuments, creating, in his words, a secluded Eden. ✉ *SP6 (Via Castellana), about 7 km (4½ miles) south of Asolo, near village of San Vito di Altivole, Asolo* 🌐 *fondoambiente.it/luoghi/memoriale-brion* 🎫 *Guided tours €12* 🕓 *Closed Nov.–Feb.*

Restaurants

Al Bacaro

$ | **ITALIAN** | At this rustic, wood-rich family-style osteria, it's worth giving the robust local specialties, such as tripe, snails, or stewed game, a go—many of them served with polenta. Less adventurous diners can go for other homey options, such as goulash, polenta with cheese and mushrooms, or one of Bacaro's open-face sandwiches, generously topped with fresh salami, speck, or other cold cuts. **Known for:** good, meaty country fare; crammed with local artifacts and patrons' hand-scribbled witticisms; seasonal vegetables and meat. [$] *Average main: €18* ✉ *Via Browning 165, Asolo* ☎ *0423/55150* 🌐 *www.albacaroanticaosteria.it* 🕓 *Closed Wed. No dinner Tues.*

★ Locanda Baggio

$$ | ITALIAN | A fabulous garden setting and warm yet unfussy country-style dining rooms elevate this family-run restaurant, renowned for Nino Baggio's elegant creative take on traditional cuisine. This is the finest restaurant in Asolo, and the prix-fixe menu (you can also order à la carte) delivers one of the best-value top-quality dining options in the Veneto. **Known for:** inventive, tasty food; white truffles and other seasonal specialties; warm hospitality. *Average main: €27 Via Bassane 1, Asolo 0423/529648 www.locandabaggio.it Closed Mon. No dinner Sun.*

Hotels

★ Albergo Al Sole

$$ | HOTEL | This elegant pink-washed hotel in a 16th-century building overlooks the main square and has wide views over picturesque Asolo or its leafy hinterland. **Pros:** central location with beautiful views; free bike hire; shuttle service to the surrounding area. **Cons:** huge rate increase in the high season; standard rooms have less interesting views than more expensive ones; expensive drinks and hidden extras. *Rooms from: €288 Via Collegio 33, Asolo 0423/951332 www.albergoalsole.com Closed early Jan.–late Feb. 23 rooms Free Breakfast.*

Hotel Asolo

$ | HOTEL | FAMILY | This tastefully modernized 18th-century farmhouse just outside Asolo retains exposed stone, brick, and wooden joists creating a calming rural ambience in its spacious public areas, simply furnished rooms, and handsome guesthouse. **Pros:** excellent service; free parking; verdant grounds. **Cons:** simple room furnishings might not be for everyone; some road traffic noise; a longish stroll to Asolo itself. *Rooms from: €105 Via Castellana 9, Asolo 0423/952963 www.hotel-asolo.com 32 rooms Free Breakfast.*

Hotel Duse

$ | HOTEL | A spiral staircase winds its way up this narrow, centrally located building—filled with traditional furnishings like gilded chairs—to rooms with grandstandlike views of the main square. **Pros:** simple, clean, good-value rooms; homey feel and central location; bike rental and tours available. **Cons:** some street noise; not as much of a bargain when you add the cost of breakfast and parking; dated, garish decor in some rooms. *Rooms from: €170 Via Browning 190, Asolo 0423/55241 www.hotelduse.com Closed 3 wks in Jan. and Feb. 14 rooms No Meals.*

Villa Cipriani

$$ | HOTEL | From its 19th-century furnishings to a 21st-century spa and a romantic garden, this luxurious 16th-century villa turned hotel strives for opulence. **Pros:** incomparable views, including from the terrace; truly elegant grounds; spa services and outdoor panoramic pool. **Cons:** small bathrooms; exorbitant parking fees; rooms in the annex are very small. *Rooms from: €302 Via Canova 298, Asolo 0423/523411 www.villacipriani.it Closed Jan.–early Mar. 29 rooms Free Breakfast.*

Treviso

37 km (23 miles) southeast of Asolo, 30 km (19 miles) north of Venice.

Treviso has been dubbed "Little Venice" because of its meandering, moss-bank canals. They can't really compare with Venice's spectacular waterways, but Treviso's historic center, with its medieval arcaded streets, does have a great deal of charm. Treviso is a fine place to stop for a few hours on the way from Venice to the wine country in the north or to the Palladian villas in the hinterland.

Allied bombing on Good Friday in 1944 destroyed half the city—it was bombed by mistake after a report that Hitler would be in Tarvisio, on the Austrian border, was misread. Despite this, Treviso managed to preserve what remained of its old town's narrow streets while introducing modernity far more gently than in many other parts of Italy. These days it's one of the wealthiest small cities in the country, with fashionable shops and boutiques at every turn in the busy city center.

GETTING HERE AND AROUND

Treviso is 30 minutes by train from Venice; there are frequent daily departures. By car from Venice, pick up the SS13 (Via Terraglio) in Mestre and follow it all the way to Treviso; the trip takes about 45 minutes.

VISITOR INFORMATION

CONTACT Treviso IAT Tourism Office. ✉ *Piazza Borsa 4, Treviso* ☎ *0422/595780* 🌐 *www.visittreviso.it.*

Sights

Conegliano

TOWN | This attractive town, with Venetian-style villas and arcaded streets, lies 23 km (14 miles) north of Treviso in wine-producing country and is known for its sparkling white wine, prosecco. Its other claim to fame is its connection with Gianbattista Cima—called Cima di Conegliano. Along with Giovanni Bellini, Cima is one of the greatest painters of the early Venetian Renaissance, and the town's elegant 14th-century Duomo houses an altarpiece he painted in 1492. The front of the Duomo is formed by the frescoed late-medieval facade and Gothic arcade of the Scuola dei Battuti. If you stop in town, be sure to taste the prosecco, sold in local wine bars and shops. There is regular train service from Treviso. ✉ *Conegliano* ☎ *0438/4131* 🌐 *www.visitconegliano.it.*

Duomo

CHURCH | The Cattedrale San Pietro Apostolo, or Duomo, was given a 19th-century neoclassical makeover but retains the Renaissance splendor of the Malchiostro Chapel, with an *Annunciation* by Titian (1520) and Pordenone's (1484–1539) *Adoration of the Magi* frescoes. The crypt has 12th-century columns. Bring a handful of coins for the coin-operated lights that illuminate the artwork. To the left of the Duomo is the Romanesque Battistero di San Giovanni (11th–12th centuries), which is probably quite similar in style to the medieval Duomo; it's open only for special exhibitions. ✉ *Piazza del Duomo, Treviso* ☎ *0422/545720* 🌐 *www.diocesitv.it.*

La Pescheria

HISTORIC DISTRICT | A short walk east of Piazza dei Signori is the *pescheria* (fish market; opened in 1856), set on an island on Cagnan Grande, one of the small canals that flow through town. The picturesque, leafy setting here is completed by the surrounding handsome medieval buildings, including Ca' dei Carraresi, Ca' Brittoni, and the former convent of the Monache Camaldolesi. Seek out two beguiling female statues close to Trevisani hearts around these parts: *La Sirenetta* or Little Mermaid emerges from the Cagnan Grande; and on Vicolo Podestà, Fontana Delle Tette's serene-looking signorina spouts water—and on special occasions, *vino rosso* and *vino bianco*—from her breasts. ✉ *Vicolo Podestà, Treviso.*

Piazza dei Signori

PLAZA/SQUARE | The center of medieval Treviso, this Piazza dei Signori remains the town's social hub, with outdoor cafés and some impressive public buildings. The most important of these, the Palazzo dei Trecento (1185–1268), was the seat of the city government, composed of the Council of 300, during the Middle Ages. It was rebuilt after bombing in 1944. Step inside to view its beautiful loggia, the Salone, replete with impressive wooden roof trusses and elaborate frescoed walls. ✉ *Piazza dei Signori, Treviso.*

Traveling the Wine Roads

You'd be hard-pressed to find a more stimulating and varied wine region than northeastern Italy. From the Valpolicella, Bardolino, and Soave produced near Verona to the superlative whites of the Collio Goriziano region, wines from the Veneto and Friuli–Venezia Giulia earn more Denominazione di Origine Controllata (DOC) seals for uniqueness and quality than those of any other area of Italy.

You can travel on foot, by car, or by bicycle over hillsides covered with *cantine* (vineyards), each field nurturing subtly different grape varieties. Be advised that Italy has become more stringent about its driving regulations; designated drivers can help avoid the risk of fines, embarrassment, or worse.

In the stretch of country north of Treviso, you can follow designated wine roads—tours that blend a beautiful rural setting with the delights of the grape. Authorized wineshops, where you can stop and sample, are marked with a sign showing a triangular arrangement of red and yellow grapes. There are three routes to choose from, and you can do them all comfortably over the course of a day or two.

Montello and Asolo Hills

This route provides a good balance of vineyards and nonwine sights. It winds from Nervesa della Battaglia, 18 km (10 miles) north of Treviso, past two prime destinations in the area, the village of Asolo and the Villa Barbaro at Maser. Asolo produces good prosecco, while Montello, a hill near Nervesa, favors merlot and cabernet. Both areas also yield pinot noir and chardonnay.

Piave River

The circular route follows the Piave River and runs through orchards, woods, and hills. Among the area's gems are the dessert wines Torchiato di Fregona and Refrontolo Passito, both made according to traditional methods.

Raboso del Piave, renowned since Roman times, ages well and complements local dishes such as beans and pasta or goose stuffed with chestnuts. Other reds include merlot and cabernet sauvignon.

Prosecco

La Strada del Prosecco (Prosecco Road) runs for 47 km (29 miles) between Valdobbiadene and Conegliano, home of Italy's first wine institute, winding between knobby hills covered in grapevines. These hang in festoons on row after row of pergolas to create a thick mantle of green.

Turn off the main route to explore the narrower country lanes. They meander past numerous family wineries where you can taste and buy the wines. It's well worth setting aside time to explore the most scenic southern stretches: between Renfrontolo and Col San Martino there's the ancient San Vigilio church and the celebrated Follador winery, while the Cartizze hills afford breathtaking views. Spring is an excellent time to visit, with no fewer than 15 local wine festivals held between March and early June.

Quartiere Latino

HISTORIC DISTRICT | While strolling the city, take in this handsomely restored district between Riviera Garibaldi and Piazza Santa Maria Battuti. It's the site of university buildings, upscale apartments, and restaurants and shops. ✉ *Quartiere Latino, Treviso.*

San Nicolò

CHURCH | The most important church in Treviso, this huge Venetian Gothic structure from the early 14th century has an ornate vaulted ceiling and frescoes (circa 1350) of saints by Tommaso da Modena (circa 1325–79) on the columns. The depiction of St. Agnes on the north side is particularly interesting, combining the naturalism initiated a few decades earlier by Giotto with the grace and elegance of Gothic abstraction. Also worth examining are Tommaso's realistic portraits of 40 Dominican friars, found in the Sala del Capitolo of the seminary next door. They include the earliest known painting of a subject wearing eyeglasses, an Italian invention (circa 1280–1300). ✉ *Seminario Vescovile, Via San Nicolò, Treviso* ☎ *0422/548626* 🌐 *www.sannicolotreviso.it* ⏲ *Closed Sun. morning except to worshippers.*

★ Villa Barbaro (Villa di Maser)

NOTABLE BUILDING | At the Villa Barbaro (1554) near the town of Maser, you can see the exquisite results of a onetime collaboration between two of the greatest artists of their age: Palladio was the architect, and Paolo Veronese did the interiors. You can easily spend a couple of hours here, so set aside time for lingering in the gorgeous grounds, admiring the honey-hue exterior and ornate statuary, including the dreamlike nymphaeum and pool. A visit is particularly immersive because the superb condition of the grounds and interior creates an uncanny atmosphere: nowhere else in the Veneto do you get such a vivid feeling for the combination of grandeur and leisure with a tangible whiff of a working farm. Villa Barbaro, a short drive from Asolo, is most accessible by private car; the closest train station is Montebelluna. Buses leave for Maser from the bus station at Treviso, Montebelluna, or Bassano di Grappa. The bus will leave you at a stop about 1½ km (1 mile) from Maser. Hours can vary, so check the website. ✉ *Via Cornuda 7, Maser, Treviso* ☎ *0432/923004* 🌐 *www.villadimaser.it* 🎫 *€9* ⏲ *Closed Mon., Apr.–Oct., and weekdays Nov.–Mar.*

Restaurants

All'Antico Portico

$$ | ITALIAN | FAMILY | This little old brick trattoria on a beguiling piazza with views of the Santa Maria Maggiore church is a favorite among locals and tourists, who flock to its cozy wood-trimmed interior. The menu changes daily but always features well-executed versions of simple local dishes, from risottos and pastas to a variety of seafood and meat dishes. **Known for:** set under the 15th-century porticoes; homemade pasta and white truffle; mamma's baccalà alla veneziana recipe. $ *Average main: €22* ✉ *Piazza Santa Maria Maggiore 18, Treviso* ☎ *0422/545259* 🌐 *www.anticoportico.it* ⏲ *Closed Tues. No dinner Mon.*

Beccherie

$$$ | ITALIAN | Adventurous foodies with deep pockets should book a table in this stylish blue-and-wood-accented dining room, located behind Treviso's Palazzo dei Trecento old meat market, for an experience that marries Trevigiano culinary traditions with contemporary elegance. It was here back in the late '60s that the famous dessert tiramisu was invented and the Beccherie, opened in 1939, still makes it to the original, featherlight recipe. **Known for:** inventive, beautifully presented food; contemporary design and tasting menus; special tiramisu. $ *Average main: €39* ✉ *Piazza Ancilotto 10, Treviso* ☎ *0422/540871* 🌐 *www.lebeccherie.it* ⏲ *Closed Tues.*

Il Basilisco

$$ | **ITALIAN** | Gastronomically adventurous diners who visit this quirky restaurant filled with stylish mid-century furnishings will find *cucina povera* (peasant food) given an inventive twist. The chef is a passionate slow-food champion, so expect local and seasonal meat and vegetables, as well as excellent seafood and an extensive wine list from Italy and farther afield. **Known for:** inventive use of quinto quarto (offal); vibrant contemporary decor and design; homemade pasta, cured meats, and antipasti. *Average main: €23 Via Bison 34, Treviso 0422/541822 www.ristorantebasilisco.com Closed Sun. and Mon.*

Odeon alla Colonna

$$ | **NORTHERN ITALIAN** | Dine in the atmospheric arcaded canal-side *vicolo* on Odeon's superb-value pasta, meat, and seafood dishes, or amid the columns in the high-ceiling *salone*. As befits the intriguing historic setting and interiors, the menu showcases traditional Trevisano ingredients with the occasional flavorsome twist. **Known for:** take-away dried pasta, risotto, and so on from their deli counter; light lunches, heaped salads, and novel ravioli dishes; special tasting menus and cultural gatherings. *Average main: €21 Vicolo Rinaldi 3, Treviso 0422/541012 www.odeonlacolonna.it.*

Toni del Spin

$ | **ITALIAN** | Wood paneled and with a 1930s-style interior, this bustling trattoria has a wholesome menu based on local Veneto cooking. The "spin" in the restaurant's name refers to the spine of the baccalà, one of several justly famous specialties (served without the titular spine); also try the *sopa coada,* a pigeon-and-bread soup. **Known for:** Veneto specialties and great wine choices; idiosyncratic, sometimes brusque service; terrazza dining in warmer months. *Average main: €17 Via Inferiore 7, Treviso 393/9863597 mobile www.ristorantetonidelspin.com Closed 3 wks in July and Aug. No lunch Mon.*

Coffee and Quick Bites

Vecia Hostaria dai Naneti

$ | **NORTHERN ITALIAN** | Drop into this busy locals favorite for panini bulging with the prized *porchetta Trevigiana* (roast pork) or mortadella with gorgonzola amid a rustic room crammed with fragrant hanging salami, cheese wheels, wine bottles and assorted ephemera. It's a fab spot from morning to mid evening, fulfilling all quick bite and cheeky drink needs from on the hoof-snacks and picnic provisions to laid-back lunches and aperitivo sessions. **Known for:** sharing charcuterie platters; excellent local vino and beer selection; buzzy atmosphere and piazza seating. *Average main: €8 Vicolo Broli 2, Treviso 340/378 3158 mobile www.facebook.com/veciahostariadainaneti Closed Sun.*

Hotels

Hotel San Nicolò

$$ | **HOTEL** | Comfort combines with warm hospitality and distinctive decor—public areas are elegant with choice antiques, while each guest room is themed after a global city—at this well-run central hotel in a handsome palazzo near Chiesa di San Nicolò. **Pros:** individual character in each guest room; warm, family-run customer service; low-season deals. **Cons:** road noise in some rooms; some rooms on the small size; no elevator. *Rooms from: €180 Via Risorgimento 54, Treviso 0422/590114 www.relais-sannicolo.com 10 rooms Free Breakfast.*

Udine

127 km (79 miles) northeast of Venice.

The main reason for devoting some time to Udine is to see works by Gianbattista Tiepolo (1696–1770), one of the greatest European painters of the 18th century. Distributed in several palaces and churches around town, this is the largest assembly of his art outside Venice. In fact, Udine calls itself "la città di Tiepolo."

The largest city on the Friuli side of the region, Udine has a provincial, genteel-meets-rustic atmosphere with oodles of charm. The city sometimes seems completely unaffected by tourism, and things are still done the way they were decades ago. In the medieval and Renaissance historical center of town, you'll find unevenly spaced streets with appealing wine bars and open-air cafés.

Friulani are proud of their culture, with many restaurants featuring local cuisine, and street signs and announcements written in both Italian and Friulano (Furlan), which, although it is classified as a dialect, is really a separate language from Italian.

Commanding a view from the Alpine foothills to the Adriatic Sea, Udine stands on a mound that, according to legend, was erected so Attila the Hun could watch the burning of Aquileia, an important Roman center to the south. Although the legend is unlikely (Attila burned Aquileia about 500 years before the first historical mention of Udine), the view from Udine's castle across the alluvial plane down to the sea is impressive. In the Middle Ages Udine flourished, thanks to its favorable trade location and the right granted by the local patriarch to hold regular markets.

GETTING HERE AND AROUND

There's frequent train service from both Venice and Trieste; the trip takes about two hours from Venice, and a little over an hour from Trieste. By car from Venice, take the SR11 to the E55 and head east. Take the E55 (it eventually becomes the Autostrada Alpe Adria) to SS13 (Viale Venezia) east into Udine. Driving from Trieste, take the SS202 to the E70, which becomes the A4. Turn onto the E55 north, which is the same road you would take coming from Venice. Driving times are 1½ to 2 hours from Venice and 1 hour from Trieste.

The tourist office and website sells the FVG (Friuli Venezia Giulia) Card, which includes admission to most museums in Udine and other important sites in the region. Its price ranges from €30 (for 48 hours) up to €40 (for one week).

VISITOR INFORMATION

CONTACT Udine IAT Tourism Office. ✉ *Piazza I Maggio 7, Udine* ☎ *0432/295972* 🌐 *www.turismofvg.it.*

Sights

★ Castello and Musei Civici

CASTLE/PALACE | The hilltop castle (construction began in 1517) has panoramic views extending to Monte Nero (7,360 feet) in neighboring Slovenia, but head inside to see Udine's civic museums of art and archaeology, with myriad collections that can detain you for hours. On the ground floor are the Museo del Risorgimento (tracing the history of Italian unification) and Museo Archeologico; the third floor is the Museo della Fotografia, with fascinating 19th- and 20th-century images of the Friuli. Particularly worthwhile is the national and regional art collection in the Galleria d'Arte Antica, which has canvases by Venetians Vittore Carpaccio (circa 1460–1525) and Gianbattista Tiepolo, the recently restored (2020) *Il San Francesco Riceve le Stimmate* (St. Francis Receiving the Stigmata) by Caravaggio, and carefully selected works by lesser-known but still interesting Veneto and Friuli artists. **TIP→ The museum's small collection of drawings includes**

several by Tiepolo; some find his drawings even more moving than his paintings. ✉ *Via Lionello 1, Udine* ☎ *0432/1272591* 🌐 *www.civicimuseiudine.it* 🎫 *€10; €12 Unico ticket also includes Casa Cavazzini and Museo Etnografico del Friuli; €15 Unico Musei tickets also includes Museo Diocesano (free with FVG Card)* ⏲ *Closed Mon.*

Duomo

CHURCH | A few steps from the Piazza della Libertà is Udine's 1335 Duomo, with some significant works by Tiepolo (1696–1770). Its Cappella del Santissimo has important early frescoes by Tiepolo, and the Cappella della Trinità has a Tiepolo altarpiece. There is also a beautiful late Tiepolo *Resurrection* (1751) in an altar by the sculptor Giuseppe Toretti. Ask the Duomo's attendant to let you into the adjacent Oratorio della Purità to see Tiepolo's later works: the altarpiece *Immaculate Conception* and ceiling frescoes *Assumption and Glory of the Angels,* alongside eight monochrome, chiaroscuro scenes by son Giandomenico Tiepolo (1726–1804). The Museo del Duomo, housed in two 14th-century chapels and baptistery, contains sculptures (including a fine funereal marble sarcophagus), paintings, textiles, and devotional jewels. ✉ *Piazza del Duomo 1, Udine* ☎ *0432/505302* 🌐 *www.cattedraleudine.it* 🎫 *Free* ⏲ *Museum closed Tues., Oratorio closed Tues. and Sat.*

★ Museo d'Arte Moderna e Contemporanea–Casa Cavazzini

ART GALLERY | Udine's fine civic collection of modern and contemporary art is housed in the handsome and part-modernized 16th-century Casa Cavazzini, which retains some ornate apartment interiors. The first and second floors display the permanent collection: first-floor highlights include bold sculptural works by the three Udinese brothers Dino, Mirko, and Afro Basaldella, with a backdrop of 14th-century frescoes discovered during the 2012 refurbishing. There are also fine works by Giorgio Morandi, Renato Guttuso, and Carlo Carrà. Up a floor is the Collezione Astaldi, spanning the 1920s through the 1960s, and Collezione FRIAM, with '60s and '70s works. Worth seeking out are Giorgio de Chirico's *I Gladiatori* (1931) and pieces by 20th-century American icons Willem de Kooning, Roy Lichtenstein, and Sol LeWitt. ✉ *Via Cavour 14, Udine* ☎ *0432/1273772* 🌐 *www.civicimuseiudine.it* 🎫 *€7; €12 Unico ticket also includes Castello and Museo Etnografico del Friuli; €15 Unico Musei tickets also includes Museo Diocesano (free with FVG Card)* ⏲ *Closed Mon.*

★ Museo Diocesano e Gallerie del Tiepolo

CASTLE/PALACE | The handsome Palazzo Patriarcale o Arcivescovile contains several rooms of frescoes by the young Gianbattista Tiepolo, painted from 1726 to 1732, which comprise the most important collection of early works by Italy's most brilliant 18th-century painter. The Galleria del Tiepolo (1727) contains superlative Tiepolo frescoes depicting the stories of Abraham, Isaac, and Jacob. The *Judgment of Solomon* (1729) graces the Pink Room. There are also beautiful and important Tiepolo frescoes in the staircase, throne room, and palatine chapel of this palazzo. Even in these early works we can see the Venetian master's skill in creating an illusion of depth, not only through linear perspective, but also through subtle gradations in the intensity of the colors, with the stronger colors coming forward and the paler ones receding into space. Tiepolo was one of the first artists to use this method of representing space and depth, which reflected the scientific discoveries of perception and optics in the 17th century.

The Museo Diocesano here features sculptures from Friuli churches from the 13th through 18th centuries; and don't miss the magnificent library, the Biblioteca Arcivescovile Delfiniana. ✉ *Piazza Patriarcato 1, Udine* ☎ *0432/25003 www.musdioc-tiepolo.it €8, includes Museo Diocesano; €15 Unico Musei ticket bundles Museo Diocesano with Musei Civici (free with FVG Card) Closed Tues.*

Piazza della Libertà

PLAZA/SQUARE | Udine was conquered by the Venetians in 1420, so there is a distinctly Venetian stamp on the architecture of the historic center, most noticeably here, in the large main square. The Loggia del Leonello, begun in 1428, dominates the square and houses the municipal government. Its similarity to the facade of Venice's Palazzo Ducale (finished in 1424) is clear, but there is no evidence that it is an imitation of that palace. It's more likely a product of the same architectural fashion. Opposite stands the Renaissance Porticato di San Giovanni (1533–35) and the Torre dell'Orologio, a 1527 clock tower with naked *mori* (Moors), who strike the hours on the top. *Piazza della Libertà, Udine.*

Restaurants

★ Hostaria alla Tavernetta

$$ | FRIULIAN | The trusty Hostaria (open since 1954) has rustic fireside dining downstairs and more elegantly decorated rooms upstairs, where there's also an intimate terrace under the Duomo. It's a great place for sampling regional specialties such as *orzotto* (barley prepared like risotto), delicious *cjalzòns* or *cjarsons* (ravioli from the Carnia), and seasonal meat dishes, accompanied by a fabulous wine list. **Known for:** rustic yet sophisticated atmosphere; Friulian ingredients and traditions; superb local Collio wine, grappa, and regional selections. *Average main: €24 Via di Prampero 2, Udine 0432/501066 www.allatavernetta.com Closed Sun. and Mon.*

★ Vitello d'Oro

$$$ | ITALIAN | Udine's very chic landmark restaurant is the one reserved most by locals for special occasions, and the menu features the freshest meat and fish in sophisticated dishes served with moodily lit culinary stagecraft. You might start with an antipasto of assorted raw shellfish, including the impossibly sweet Adriatic scampi, followed by the fresh fish of the day. **Known for:** seafood served raw and cooked; large terrace popular in summer; multicourse tasting menu. *Average main: €31 Via Valvason 4, Udine 0432/508982 www.vitellodoro.com Closed Tues. No lunch Wed. and Thurs.*

Coffee and Quick Bites

★ Grosmi Caffè

$ | NORTHERN ITALIAN | Under the porticoes of gorgeous Piazza Matteoti, with its vibrant student and dialect-speaking locals, Grosmi is a reliable choice for excellent coffee, pastries, and people-watching. Although the brioche filled with chocolate, custard, or fruit jam are staples, some opt for a small cake or macaroon to accompany their caffeine fix. **Known for:** selection of imported blends; tables on the piazza; brioche, pastries, and cakes. *Average main: €5 Piazza Giacomo Matteotti 9, Udine 0432/506411 biquadrocaffe.it.*

Hotels

Hotel Clocchiatti Next

$ | HOTEL | You have two smart and contrasting choices here: the 19th-century villa, with canopy beds and Alpine-style wood ceilings and paneling; and the more tranquil "Next Wing," with rich colors and spare furnishings in starkly angular rooms. **Pros:** stylish, individually decorated rooms; excellent breakfast for €10 extra; a tranquil Zen-garden haven. **Cons:** 10-minute drive from town center; small bathrooms; some rooms need a refresh. *Rooms from: €120 Via Cividale 29, Udine 0432/505047 www.hotelclocchiatti.it 27 rooms No Meals.*

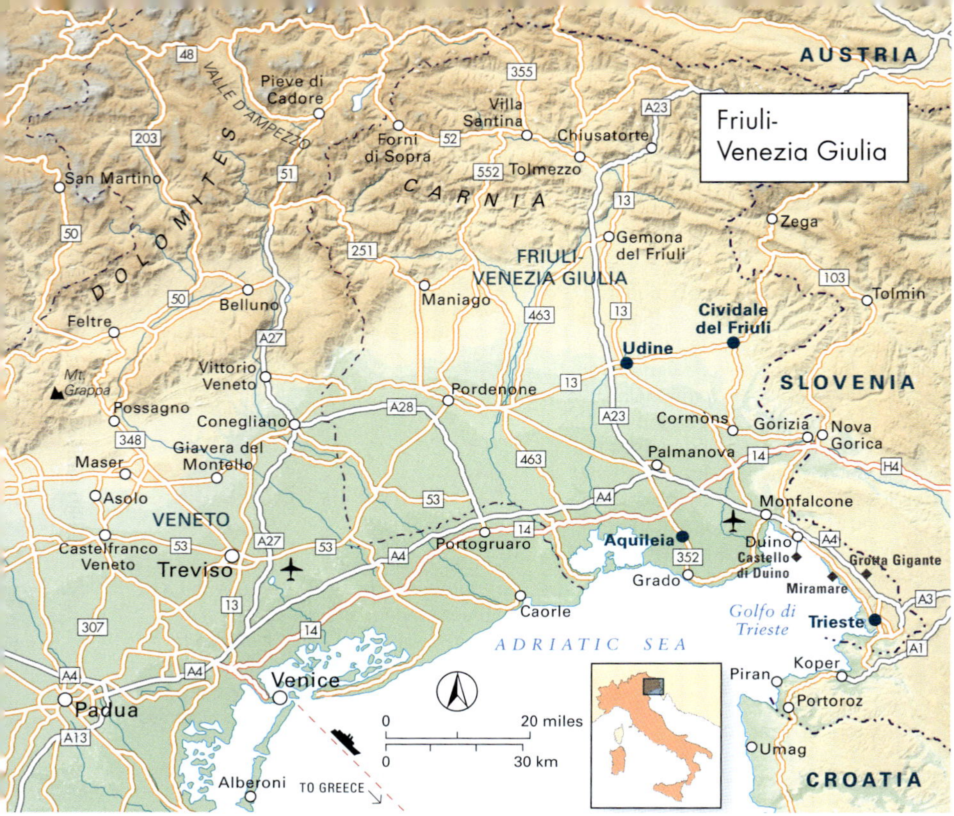

Hotel Ristorante Allegria

$ | **HOTEL** | Renovation of this 15th-century building took a decidedly minimalist approach: the breakfast room, lounges, and guest rooms feature plenty of light wood, mood lighting, and sleek, angular design. **Pros:** well-appointed, neutral-hue rooms; easy access, secure garage; easy walking distance to the center. **Cons:** rooms may be too minimalist for some; fee for parking; a/c can be unreliable. *Rooms from: €132* *Via Grazzano 18, Udine* *0432/201116* *www.hotelallegria.it* *21 rooms* *Free Breakfast.*

Activities

L'Ippovia del Cormor

BIKING | L'Ippovia del Cormor is a 26-km (16-mile) path that allows walkers, runners, cyclists, and horseback riders to immerse themselves in the rural hamlets north of Udine, including Tricesimo, Colloredo di Monte Albano, Cassacco, and Treppo Grande. The path rises and ends at Buja, where the source of the River Cormor bubbles with numerous streams, including the Rio Gelato, and is surrounded by the mountain peaks. Contact Cussigh Bike or X-Zone for suitably robust wheels to hire. *Via del Lavoro, Feletto Umberto-Tavagnacco, Udine* *0432/688268 Cussigh Bike, 0432/1698220 X-Zone Bike* *www.cussighbike.it; www.xzonebike.it.*

Cividale del Friuli

17 km (11 miles) east of Udine, 144 km (89 miles) northeast of Venice.

Cividale is the most important place for taking in the impressive and beautiful art of the Lombards, a Germanic people who entered Italy in 568 and who ruled parts of Italy until the late 8th century. The city was founded in AD 53 by Julius Caesar, then commander of Roman legions in the area. Here you can also find Celtic, Roman, and medieval Jewish ruins alongside Venetian Gothic buildings, including the Palazzo Comunale. Strolling through the part of the city that now occupies the former Gastaldia, the Lombard ducal palace, gives you spectacular views of the medieval city and the river.

GETTING HERE AND AROUND

There's hourly train service from Udine. Since the Udine–Cividale train line isn't part of the Italian national rail system, you have to buy the tickets from the electronic machines, the MPL tobacconist, or the newsstand Edicola 103 within the Udine station. You can't buy a ticket through to Cividale from another city.

By car from Udine, take Via Cividale, which turns into SS54; follow SS54 into Cividale.

VISITOR INFORMATION

CONTACT Informacittà office. ✉ *Palazzo de Nordis, Piazza Duomo 5, Cividale del Friuli* ☎ *0432/710460* 🌐 *www.facebook.com/ufficioturisticocividale.*

Sights

Duomo

CHURCH | Cividale's Renaissance Duomo is largely the work of Pietro Lombardo, principal architect of Venice's famous Santa Maria dei Miracoli. The interior was restructured in the 18th century by another prominent Venetian architect, Giorgio Massari. The church contains a magnificent 12th-century silver gilt altarpiece. ✉ *Piazza Duomo, Cividale del Friuli* ☎ *0432/731144* 🌐 *www.duomocividale.it.*

Museo Archeologico

HISTORY MUSEUM | Trace the area's history here and learn about the importance of Cividale and Udine in the period following the collapse of the Roman Empire. The collection includes Roman mosaics and epigraphs as well as weapons and exquisite jewelry from 6th-century Lombard warriors, who swept through much of what is now Italy. ✉ *Piazza Duomo 13, Cividale del Friuli* ☎ *0432/700700* 🌐 *www.museoarcheologicocividale.beniculturali.it* 🎫 *€6; €15 combined ticket, includes Museo Archeologico, Monastero/Tempietto and Museo Cristiano e Tesoro del Duomo (free with FVG Card).*

Museo Cristiano e Tesoro del Duomo

SPECIALTY MUSEUM | Entered via a courtyard to the right of the Duomo, this museum contains two interesting, important, and surprisingly beautiful monuments of Lombard art: the Altar of Duke Ratchis (737–744) and the Baptistry of Patriarch Callisto (731–776). Both were found under the floor of the present Duomo in the early 20th century. The museum also has two fine paintings by Veronese, one by Il Pordenone, and a small collection of medieval and Renaissance vestments. ✉ *Via Candotti 1, Cividale del Friuli* ☎ *0432/730403* 🌐 *www.mucris.com* 🎫 *€6; €15 combined ticket, includes Museo Archeologico, Monastero/Tempietto and Museo Cristiano e Tesoro del Duomo (free with FVG Card)* 🕓 *Closed Mon. and Tues.*

Palazzo de Nordis: Galleria d'Arte De Martiis

ART GALLERY | Opened in 2020 and housed in a magnificent historic palazzo, originally dating from the 15th century, the Gallery showcases the De Martiis family's exquisite collection of 20th-century art. Among the figurative works is a saucy Toulouse-Lautrec, and there are eye-popping impressionist masterpieces by Karel Appel and Victor Vasarely. **TIP→ For tourist info visit the ground-floor Sportello Informacittà.** *Piazza Duomo 5, Cividale del Friuli 0432/710357 www.instagram.com/palazzodenordis €8; free with FVG Card.*

★ **Tempietto Longobardo** (*Lombard Church*)

CHURCH | Seeing the beautiful and historically important Tempietto Longobardo from the 8th century is more than enough reason to visit Cividale. Now inside the 16th-century Monastery of Santa Maria in Valle, the Tempietto was originally the chapel of the ducal palace, known as the Gastaldia. The west wall is the best-preserved example of the art and architecture of the Lombards, a Germanic people who entered Italy in 568. It has an archway with an exquisitely rendered vine motif, guarded by an 8th-century procession of female figures, showing the Lombard interpretation of classical forms that resembles the style of the much earlier Byzantine mosaics in Ravenna, a town that had passed briefly to Lombard rule in 737. The post-Lombard frescoes decorating the vaults and the east wall date from the 13th and 14th centuries, and the fine carved wooden stalls also date from the 14th century. *Via Monastero Maggiore, Cividale del Friuli 0432/700867 www.tempietto-longobardo.it €6; €15 combined ticket, includes Museo Archeologico, Monastero/Tempietto and Museo Cristiano e Tesoro del Duomo (free with FVG Card).*

Restaurants

Alla Speranza

$$ | NORTHERN ITALIAN | This well-thought-of osteria-trattoria lands the freshest seafood and creates exquisite, beautifully presented plates; the chefs constantly delight with new things to try such as homemade spirulina grissini, unusual flavor combos, and vibrant garnishes. Dine in the rustic yet refined dining room with its exposed stone, wooden beams, and coved ceilings, or outside on the gorgeous terrace with piazza views. **Known for:** fresh seafood with colorful flowers, herbs, and crunchy garnishes; innovative desserts and aperitivi; superb wine list. *Average main: €22 Piazza Foro Giulio Cesare 15, Cividale del Friuli 0432/731131 www.allasperanza.net Closed Mon. No lunch Tues.–Thurs.*

Hotels

B&B dai Toscans

$ | B&B/INN | In a central location, this 15th-century palazzo, once home to the dukes of Tuscany, is now a charming and romantic bed-and-breakfast with parquet flooring throughout, a pleasant if unremarkable breakfast room, and large guest rooms furnished in antique style. **Pros:** large, well-appointed rooms; triples for families; no- or low-fee nearby parking. **Cons:** some noise from the street and the cathedral bells; quirky decor not to everyone's taste; can be a struggle hauling luggage in this pedestrianized area. *Rooms from: €100 Corso Mazzini 15/1, Cividale del Friuli 3490/765288 mobile daitoscans.it 5 rooms Free Breakfast.*

Aquileia

123 km (77 miles) east of Venice, 42 km (25 miles) south of Udine.

This sleepy little town is refreshingly free of the tourists that you might expect at such a culturally historic place. In the time of Emperor Augustus, it was Italy's fourth-most-important city (after Rome, Milan, and Capua), as well as the principal northern Adriatic port of Italy and the beginning of Roman routes north. Aquileia's Roman and early Christian remains offer an image of the transition from pagan to Christian Rome.

GETTING HERE AND AROUND

Getting to Aquileia by public transportation is difficult but not impossible. There's frequent train service from Venice and Trieste to Cervignano di Friuli, which is 8 km (5 miles) away from Aquileia by taxi (about €25) or infrequent bus service. (Ask the newsstand attendant or the railroad ticket teller for assistance.) By car from Venice or Trieste, take Autostrada A4 (Venezia–Trieste) to the Palmanova exit and continue 17 km (11 miles) to Aquileia. From Udine, take Autostrada A23 to the Palmanova exit.

VISITOR INFORMATION

CONTACT **Aquileia Infopoint.** ✉ *Via Giulia Augusta 11, Aquileia* ☎ *0431/919491* 🌐 *www.turismofvg.it.*

Sights

Aquileia Archaeological Site

RUINS | Roman remains of the forum, houses, cemetery, and port are surrounded by cypresses here, and the little stream was once an important waterway extending to Grado. Unfortunately, many of the excavations of Roman Aquileia could not be left exposed, because of the extremely high water table under the site, and had to be reburied after archaeological studies had been conducted; nevertheless, what remains aboveground, along with the monuments in the archaeological museum, gives an idea of the grandeur of this ancient city. The area is well signposted. ✉ *Near basilica, Aquileia* ☎ *0431/917619* 🌐 *www.fondazioneaquileia.it* 🎫 *Free.*

★ La Basilica di Aquileia

CHURCH | The highlight of the Basilica complex is the spectacular 3rd- to 4th-century mosaic covering the entire floor of the basilica and the adjacent crypt, which make up one of the most important early Christian monuments. Theodore, the basilica's first bishop, built two parallel basilicas (now the north and the south halls) on the site of a Gnostic chapel in the 4th century. These were joined by a third hall, forming a "U." The complex later accumulated the Romanesque portico and Gothic bell tower. The mosaic floor of the basilica is the remains of the floor of Theodore's south hall.

In his north hall, Theodore retained much of the floor of the earlier Gnostic chapel, whose mosaics represent the ascent of the soul, through the realm of the planets and constellations, to God, who is represented as a ram. (The ram, at the head of the zodiac, is the Gnostic generative force.) This integration of Gnosticism into a Christian church is interesting, since Gnosticism had been branded a heresy by early church fathers.

The 4th-century mosaics of the Südalle (the south hall is the present-day nave) represent the story of Jonah as prefiguring the salvation offered by the Church. Down a flight of steps, the Cripta degli Affreschi contains 12th-century frescoes.

In Piazza Capitolo, the Domus and Palazzo Episcopale's newest discoveries reveal fascinating layers of the city's history, with beautiful geometric mosaics and frescoes, and original walls. ✉ *Piazza Capitolo 1, Aquileia* ☎ *0431/919719* 🌐 *www.fondazioneaquileia.it* 🎫 *€5 Cripta degli Affreschi with Cripta Scavi; €2 campanile; €10 whole complex; all sites free with FGV card* ⏲ *Campanile closed Oct.–Mar.*

Museo Archeologico Nazionale

SPECIALTY MUSEUM | The museum's wealth of material from Roman times includes portrait busts from the Republican era, semiprecious gems, amber—including preserved flies—and goldwork, and a fine glass collection. Beautiful pre-Christian mosaics are from the floors of Roman houses and palaces. ✉ *Via Roma 1, Aquileia* ☎ *0431/91016* 🌐 *www.museoarcheologicoaquileia.beniculturali.it* 🎫 *€9 (free with FGV card)* ⏲ *Closed Mon.*

Museo Paleocristiano

HISTORY MUSEUM | What started out as an early-Christian 4th-century suburban basilica was transformed in the 9th century into a monastery and then a farmhouse. Now it's a museum: some of the fragments of 4th-century mosaics preserved here are even more delicate than those in the main basilica. It's open Saturday and by appointment on weekdays. ✉ *Località Monastero, Aquileia* ☎ *0431/91035* 🌐 *museoarcheologicoaquileia.beniculturali.it* 🎫 *Free* ⏲ *Closed Sun. By appointment only.*

Trieste

163 km (101 miles) east of Venice, 48 km (77 miles) east of Aquileia.

Trieste is Italy's only truly cosmopolitan city. In a country—perhaps even in a continent—where the amalgamation of cultures has frequently proved difficult, Trieste stands out as one of the few authentic melting pots. Not only do Italian, Slavic, and Central European cultures meet here, they actually merge to create a unique Triestino culture. To discover this culture, visiting Trieste's coffeehouses, local eateries, and piazzas is probably more important than visiting its churches and museums, interesting though they are.

Trieste is built along a fringe of coastline where the rugged Karst Plateau tumbles abruptly into the beautiful Adriatic. The city's history, the sea, and its inhabitants are shaped by the power of the fierce northerly to northeasterly wind, the bora. It was the only port of the Austro-Hungarian Empire and, therefore, a major industrial and financial center. In the early years of the 20th century, Trieste and its surroundings also became famous by their association with some of the most important names of Italian literature, such as Italo Svevo, and Irish and German writers. James Joyce drew inspiration from the city's multiethnic population, and Rainer Maria Rilke was inspired by the coast to the west.

The city has lost its importance as a port and a center of finance, but perhaps because of its multicultural nature, at the juncture of Latin, Slavic, and Germanic Europe, it's never fully lost its role as an intellectual center. In recent years the city has become a center for science and technology. The streets hold a mix of monumental neoclassical and art nouveau architecture, built by the Austrians during Trieste's days of glory, granting an air of melancholy stateliness to a city that lives as much in the past as the present.

Italian revolutionaries of the 1800s rallied their battle cry around Trieste, because of what they believed was foreign occupation of their motherland. After World War II the sliver of land including Trieste and a small part of Istria became an independent, neutral state that was officially recognized in a 1947 peace treaty. Although it was actually occupied by British and American troops for its nine years of existence, the Free Territory of Trieste issued its own currency and stamps. In 1954 a Memorandum of Understanding was signed in London, giving civil administration of Trieste to Italy.

GETTING HERE AND AROUND

Trains to Trieste depart regularly from Venice, Udine, and other major Italian cities. By car, it's the eastern terminus of the Autostrada Torino–Trieste (E70). The city is served by Trieste–Friuli Venezia Giulia Airport, which receives flights from major Italian airports and some European cities. The airport is 33 km (20½ miles) from the city; transfers into Trieste are by train (quickest: 30 minutes), taxi or APT coach G51.

VISITOR INFORMATION

CONTACT Trieste Infopoint. ✉ *Piazza Unità d'Italia 4, Trieste* ☎ *335/7429440 mobile, 040/3478312* 🌐 *www.discover-trieste.it.*

Sights

Castello di Duino

CASTLE/PALACE | This 14th-century castle, the property of the Princes of Thurn and Taxis, contains a collection of antique furnishings and an amazing Palladian circular staircase, but the main attractions are the surrounding gardens and the spectacular views. In 1912 Rainer Maria Rilke wrote much of his masterpiece, the *Duino Elegies,* here. The easy path along the seacoast from the castle toward Trieste has gorgeous views that rival those of the Amalfi Coast and the Cinque Terre. For more spectacular cliff-top views, visit the ruins of the nearby 11th-century Castelvecchio. ✉ *Frazione Duino 32, 12 km (7½ miles) from Trieste, Duino* ✣ *Take Bus No. 44 or 51 from Trieste train station to Duino* ☎ *040/208120* 🌐 *www.castellodiduino.it* 🎫 *€11; €13.50 Castello di Duino and Castello Vecchio* ⏲ *Closed weekdays Nov.–mid-Mar., except a few special days (contact for latest).*

Castello di San Giusto

CASTLE/PALACE | This hilltop castle, built between 1470 and 1630, was constructed on the ruins of the Roman town of Tergeste. Given the excellent view, it's no surprise that 15th-century Venetians turned the castle into a shipping observation point; the structure was further enlarged by Trieste's subsequent rulers, the Hapsburgs. The castle also contains the Civic Museum, which has a collection of furnishings, tapestries, and weaponry, as well as Roman artifacts in the atmospheric Lapidario Tergestino. ✉ *Piazza della Cattedrale 3, Trieste* ☎ *040/309362* 🌐 *www.castellodisangiustotrieste.it* 🎫 *€7 includes all complex museums* ⏲ *Closed Mon. Oct.–Mar.*

Cattedrale di San Giusto

CHURCH | Dating from the 14th century and occupying the site of an ancient Roman forum, the cathedral contains remnants of at least three previous buildings, the earliest a hall dating from the 5th century. A section of the original floor mosaic still remains, incorporated into the floor of the present church. In the 9th and 11th centuries two adjacent churches were built—the Church of the Assumption and the Church of San Giusto. The beautiful apse mosaics of these churches, done in the 12th and 13th centuries by a Venetian artist, still remain in the apses of the side aisles of the present church. The mosaics in the main apse date from 1932. In the 14th century the two churches were joined and a Romanesque-Gothic facade was attached, ornamented with fragments of Roman monuments taken from the forum. The jambs of the main doorway derive from Roman funereal stelae. ✉ *Piazza della Cattedrale 2, Trieste* ☎ *040/2600892* 🌐 *www.sangiustomartire.it.*

Grotta Gigante

CAVE | More than 300 feet high, 900 feet long, and 200 feet wide, this gigantic cave is filled with spectacular stalactites and stalagmites. The required tour takes 50 minutes. Bring a sweater to ward off the year-round chill and be willing (and able) to descend 500 steps and then climb back up. To get here you can take Bus No. 42, which leaves every 30 minutes from the Piazza Oberdan; a more scenic route is to take the tram uphill from Piazza Oberdan to Opicina, where you connect with Bus No. 42. ✉ *Borgo Grotta Gigante 42/A, Trieste* ✣ *10 km (6 miles) north of Trieste* ☎ *040/327312* 🌐 *www.grottagigante.it* 🎫 *€15* ⏲ *Closed Mon. Sept.–Feb.*

★ LETS Museum Literature Trieste

ART MUSEUM | Opened in 2024, Trieste's newest museum brings together various collections exploring multifarious facets of the written word and the lives of literary figures who have become synonymous with the city. Sections include the introductory "History Kiosk," a wonderful space dedicated to cinematic adaptations, and immersive exhibitions dedicated to James Joyce, Italo Svevo, and poet

Umberto Saba. If you fancy a leaf through 1,000 books, there's the "Writers' Bookstore," and listening stations allow visitors to enjoy audiobooks while gazing through picture windows with city views. ✉ *Palazzo Biserini, Piazza Hortis 4, Trieste* ☏ *040/6757240* 🌐 *lets.trieste.it* 🎫 *Free.*

★ Miramare

CASTLE/PALACE | FAMILY | A 19th-century castle on the Gulf of Trieste, this is nothing less than a major expression of the culture of the decaying Austrian Hapsburg monarchy: nowhere else—not even in Vienna—can you savor the decadent opulence of the last years of the empire. Maximilian of Hapsburg, brother of Emperor Franz Josef and the retired commander of the Austrian Navy, built the seafront extravaganza between 1856 and 1860, complete with a throne room under a wooden ceiling shaped like a ship's keel. The rooms are generally furnished with copies of medieval, Renaissance, and French period furniture, and the walls are covered in red damask. In 1864 Maximilian became emperor of Mexico at the initiative of Napoléon III. He was executed three years later by a Mexican firing squad.

During the last years of the Hapsburg reign, Miramare became one of the favorite residences of Franz Josef's wife, the Empress Elizabeth (Sissi). The castle was later owned by Duke Amedeo of Aosta. Changing exhibitions in the revamped Sala Progetti showcase the impressive museum archive. Tours in English are available by reservation via 🌐 *coopculture.it.* Surrounding the castle is a gorgeous 54-acre park. To get here from central Trieste, take Bus No. 36 from Piazza Oberdan; it runs every half hour. ✉ *Viale Miramare, off SS14, Trieste* ✣ *7 km (4½ miles) northwest of Trieste* ☏ *040/224143* 🌐 *miramare.cultura.gov.it* 🎫 *€15.*

Museo d'Antichità J. J. Winckelmann

HISTORY MUSEUM | On the hill near the Castello, this eclectic collection showcases statues from the Roman theater, mosaics, and a wealth of artifacts from Egypt, Greece, and Rome. There's also an assortment of glass and manuscripts. The Orto Lapidario (Lapidary Garden) has classical statuary, pottery, and a small Corinthian temple. The collection was renamed in 2018 after the pioneering art historian and Hellenist J. J. Winckelmann, who was murdered in Trieste in 1768. ✉ *Via Cattedrale 1, Trieste* ☏ *040/310500* 🌐 *museoantichitawinckelmann.it* 🎫 *Free* 🕒 *Closed Mon.*

★ Museo Revoltella–Galleria d'Arte Moderna

ART MUSEUM | Housed in three magnificent buildings and partly remodeled by influential Italian architect Carlo Scarpa, the Revoltella provides a stimulating survey of 19th- and 20th-century art and decoration. Building on the bequeathment of the grand palazzo and art of Triestino collector-industrialist Pasquale Revoltella (1795–1869), the institution has continued to add important artworks from the Venice Biennale by the likes of Carrà, Mascherini, Morandi, de Chirico, Manzù, Fontana, and Burri. In contrast, a gorgeous cochlear staircase connects the three floors of the museum: its history and 1850–60 cityscapes are on the ground floor; 19th-century classical statuary, portraits, and historic scenes take up the first; while the third preserves opulent *saloni.* ✉ *Via Diaz 27, Trieste* ☏ *040/6754350* 🌐 *museorevoltella.it* 🎫 *€8* 🕒 *Closed Tues.*

Piazza della Borsa

PLAZA/SQUARE | A statue of Hapsburg emperor Leopold I looks out over this square, which contains Trieste's original stock exchange, the Borsa Vecchia (1805), an attractive neoclassical building now serving as the chamber of commerce. It sits at the end of the Canal

Grande, dug in the 18th century by the Austrian empress Maria Theresa as a first step in the expansion of what was then a small fishing village of 7,000 into the port of her empire. ✉ *Piazza della Borsa, Trieste.*

Piazza Unità d'Italia

PLAZA/SQUARE | The imposing square, ringed by grandiose facades, was set out as a plaza open to the sea, like Venice's Piazza San Marco, in the late Middle Ages. It underwent countless changes through the centuries, and its present size and architecture are essentially products of late-19th- and early-20th-century Austria. It was given its current name in 1955, when Trieste was finally given to Italy. On the inland side of the piazza, note the facade of the **Palazzo Comunale** (Town Hall), designed by the Triestino architect Giuseppe Bruni in 1875. It was from this building's balcony in 1938 that Mussolini proclaimed the infamous racial laws, depriving Italian Jews of most of their rights. The sidewalk cafés on this vast seaside piazza are popular meeting places in the summer months. ✉ *Piazza Unità d'Italia, Trieste.*

Risiera di San Sabba

HISTORIC SIGHT | In September 1943 the Nazi occupation established Italy's only concentration camp in this rice-processing factory outside Trieste. In April 1944 a crematorium was put into operation. The Nazis destroyed much of the evidence of their atrocities before their retreat, but a good deal of the horror of the place is still perceivable in the reconstructed museum (1975). The site, an Italian national monument since 1965, receives more than 100,000 visitors per year. ✉ *Via Giovanni Palatucci 5, Trieste* ✣ *Take municipal Bus No. 8 or 10; off the Autostrada A4, take exit Valmaura/Stadio/Cimitero* ☎ *040/826202* 🌐 *www.risierasansabba.it* 🎟 *Free.*

San Silvestro

CHURCH | This small Romanesque gem, dating from the 9th to the 12th centuries, is the oldest church in Trieste that's still in use and in approximately its original form. Its interior walls have some fragmentary remains of Romanesque frescoes. The church was deconsecrated under the secularizing reforms of the Austrian emperor Josef II in 1785 and was later sold to the Swiss Evangelical community; it then became, and is still, the Reformed Evangelical and Waldensian Church of Trieste. ✉ *Piazza San Silvestro 1, Trieste* ☎ *040/632770* 🌐 *triestevangelica.org* 🎟 *Free.*

Teatro Romano

RUINS | The ruins of this 1st-century amphitheater, opposite the city's *questura* (police station), were discovered during 1938 demolition work. Its crumbling and partly grassy steps can be viewed from the street, while its statues are now displayed at the Museo Civico. The space is used for summer plays and concerts. ✉ *Via del Teatro Romano, Trieste.*

Restaurants

Al Bagatto

$$ | **SEAFOOD** | At this warm and sophisticated seafood place, going strong since 1966 near Piazza Unità d'Italia, you'll find exquisite dishes that honor the traditions of the Mancussi family. Although now run by the Leonardi family, Roberto Mancussi's culinary ethos remains: integrating nouvelle ingredients without overshadowing the freshness of whatever local fish he bought in the market that morning. **Known for:** freshest seafood beautifully prepared; more than 300 wine labels and spirits; novel culinary experience. $ *Average main: €27* ✉ *Via Luigi Cadorna 7, Trieste* ☎ *040/301771* 🌐 *www.albagatto.it* ⏲ *Closed Sun. No lunch Mon.*

Buffet da Siora Rosa

$ | **NORTHERN ITALIAN** | **FAMILY** | Serving delicious and generous portions of traditional Triestino buffet fare, such as boiled pork and sausages with savory sauerkraut, Siora Rosa is a bit more comfortable than many buffets. In addition to ample seating in the simple dining room, there are tables outside for when the weather is good. **Known for:** well-loved Trieste institution (opened 1921); chatty locals speaking in dialect; meat dishes galore. *Average main: €19 Piazza Hortis 3, Trieste 040/301460 www.facebook.com/buffetdasiorarosa Closed Sun. and Mon.*

★ Suban

$$ | **NORTHERN ITALIAN** | An easy trip just outside town, this landmark trattoria—serving Triestino food with Slovene, Hungarian, and Austrian accents—has been in business since 1865. Sit by the dining room fire or relax on a huge terrace with a pergola, watching the sun set as you tuck into rich soups and roasts spiced with rosemary, thyme, and sweet paprika. **Known for:** meat dishes with Mitteleuropean influences; jota carsolina (a rich soup of cabbage, potatoes, and beans); warm hospitality. *Average main: €24 Via Comici 2, Trieste Take Bus No. 35 from Piazza Oberdan 040/54368 www.suban.it Closed Tues. and 2 wks in early Jan. No lunch weekdays.*

★ Trattoria Nerodiseppia

$$ | **NORTHERN ITALIAN** | For over a decade the Cusma family have been serving Triestini regulars beautifully crafted seafood, alongside a few seasonal meat and vegetarian dishes. Dining in warm, modern interiors under the arches of a refurbished storehouse, choose from Giulio's exquisite but small seafood plates like fish carpaccio, spaghetti *con bottarga e tonno* (cured fish roe and tuna), and fritto misto (fried seafood medley). **Known for:** compact, seasonal menu; Friuli, Carso DOC, and Croatian wines; especially fab seafood starters, mains, and desserts. *Average main: €22 Via Luigi Cadorna 23, Trieste 040/301377 trattorianerodiseppia.com Closed Sun. and Mon.*

Coffee and Quick Bites

Da Pepi

$ | **NORTHERN ITALIAN** | A Triestino institution, this is the oldest and most esteemed of the many "buffet" restaurants serving pork and sausages around town, with a wood-paneled interior and seating outside. It specializes in *bollito di maiale,* a dish of boiled pork and pork sausages accompanied by delicately flavored sauerkraut, mustard, and grated horseradish. **Known for:** porky platter La Caldaia Da Pepi; panino porzina (pork shoulder with mustard and kren [horseradish]); good for a snack on the hoof. *Average main: €15 Via Cassa di Risparmio 3, Trieste 040/366858 www.buffetdapepi.it No dinner Sun.*

Hotels

★ Duchi d'Aosta

$$ | **HOTEL** | Bang smack in regal Piazza Unità d'Italia, this grande dame of a hotel is beautifully furnished in Venetian Renaissance style, with dark-wood antiques, rich carpets, and plush fabrics. **Pros:** lots of charm paired with modern convenience; outstanding indoor pool and spa on grand scale; excellent breakfast. **Cons:** soundproofing not the best; restaurant overpriced; expensive and inconvenient parking. *Rooms from: €304 Piazza Unità d'Italia 2/1, Trieste 040/7600011 duchidaosta.com 55 rooms Free Breakfast.*

★ Hotel Riviera & Maximilian's

$$ | **HOTEL** | Set on gorgeous, verdant grounds with stunning sea views, this cliff-top hotel—a villa with a modern annex—offers a mix of traditional and minimalist rooms, many with private balconies. **Pros:** superb views of the Golfo di Trieste; area for swimming in

sea; Exentia spa facilities. **Cons:** far from town; rooms on the small side; set on a busy road. *$ Rooms from: €230 ✉ Strada Costiera 22, Trieste ✣ 7 km (4½ miles) north of Trieste ☎ 040/224551 🌐 hotelrivieraemaximilian.com ⇨ 67 rooms 🍴 Free Breakfast.*

★ L'Albero Nascosto Hotel Residence
$$ | B&B/INN | There's plenty of architectural character mixed with contemporary, artsy warmth in the guest rooms of this central, 18th-century building, while the nearby annex offers four spacious apartments. **Pros:** very central; spacious and simple but tasteful rooms; friendly, knowledgeable hosts. **Cons:** no elevator; street noise can be a problem (if noise sensitive, ask for a room in the back); tricky parking nearby. *$ Rooms from: €210 ✉ Via Felice Venezian 18, Trieste ☎ 040/300188 🌐 www.alberonascosto.it ⇨ 10 rooms 🍴 Free Breakfast.*

Victoria Hotel Letterario
$ | HOTEL | The former home of James Joyce is a real gem of a hotel—with stylish, unfussy traditional decor and a just-out-of-town location that's convenient for both local sightseeing and trips into the Karst mountains. **Pros:** large, pleasant, light-filled rooms; excellent two-bedroom apartments for longer stays; wellness center and spa. **Cons:** parking fee; a bit removed and a stroll into town; some rooms suffer from traffic noise. *$ Rooms from: €160 ✉ Alfredo Oriani 2, Trieste ☎ 040/362415 🌐 www.hotelvictoriatrieste.com ⇨ 44 rooms 🍴 Free Breakfast.*

Nightlife

Trieste is justly famous for its coffee and some beautiful coffeehouses. The elegant civility of Trieste plays out beautifully in a café culture combining the refinement of Vienna with the passion of Italy. In Trieste, as elsewhere in Italy, ask for a caffè and you'll get a thimbleful of high-octane espresso. Your cappuccino here will come in the Viennese fashion, with a dollop of whipped cream. Many cafés are part of a *torrefazione* (roasting shop), so you can sample a cup and then buy beans to take with you.

★ Antico Caffè San Marco
GATHERING PLACE | Few cafés in Italy can rival Antico Caffè San Marco for its historic and cultured atmosphere. Founded in 1914, it was largely destroyed in World War I and rebuilt in the 1920s, then restored several more times, but some of the original art nouveau interior remains. It became a meeting place for local intellectuals and was the haunt of the Triestino writers Italo Svevo and Umberto Saba: the wonderful bookshop hosts literary events. It remains open until 11:45 pm on Friday and Saturday, and light meals are available. *✉ Via Battisti 18, Trieste ☎ 040/2035357 🌐 www.caffesanmarco.com.*

Caffè degli Specchi
GATHERING PLACE | For a great view of the grand piazza, you can't do better than this café, whose many mirrors make for engaging people-watching. Originally opened in 1839, it was taken over by the British navy after World War II, and Triestini were not allowed in unless accompanied by someone British. Because of its location, the café—which stays open late—is heavily frequented by tourists. It's now owned by the Segafredo Zanetti coffee company, and some feel it has lost its local character. *✉ Piazza Unità d'Italia 7, Trieste ☎ 040/661973.*

Caffè Tommaseo
GATHERING PLACE | Founded in 1830, this classic café is a comfortable place to linger, especially on some evenings and Sunday lunchtimes, when there's live music. Although you can still have just a coffee, Tommaseo has evolved into a restaurant, with an extensive menu. It's open nightly until 10:30. *✉ Piazza Tommaseo 4/C, Trieste ☎ 040/362666 🌐 www.caffetommaseo.it.*

Performing Arts

Teatro Verdi

OPERA | Trieste's main opera house, built under Austrian rule in 1801, is of interest to aficionados of fine architecture as well as music lovers. Gian Antonio Selva, the architect of Venice's Teatro La Fenice, designed the interior, and Matteo Pertsch, responsible for Milan's Teatro alla Scala, designed the facade. You'll have to attend a performance to view Teatro Verdi's interior; guided tours aren't conducted for individuals. **TIP→ Opera season runs from October through May, with a brief operetta festival in June or thereafter.** ✉ *Piazza Verdi 1, Trieste* ☎ *040/6722298* 🌐 *www.teatroverdi-trieste.com.*

Shopping

★ Katastrofa - The Second Life Store

ANTIQUES & COLLECTIBLES | Head to this bonkers emporium for an entertaining and eye-popping perusal of 20th-century antiques and ephemera, from vintage stereo equipment and funky furniture to quirky artworks and designer handbags. ✉ *Via Armando Diaz 19, Trieste* ☎ *338/2272351 mobile* 🌐 *katastrofa.it.*

Rigatteria

ANTIQUES & COLLECTIBLES | Opened in 1981, the fascinating Rigatteria is crammed with antiques, paintings, and a cornucopia of printed matter, including books, newspapers, and magazines, many documenting Triestina life over the decades. ✉ *Via Malcanton 12, Trieste* ☎ *040/630866* 🌐 *www.rigatteria.com.*

Chapter 6

THE DOLOMITES

Updated by
Liz Humphreys

WELCOME TO THE DOLOMITES

TOP REASONS TO GO

★ **Driving in the Dolomites:** Your Fiat rental will think it's a Ferrari on a gorgeous drive through the heart of the Dolomites.

★ **Hiking:** No matter your fitness level, there's an unforgettable walk in store for you here.

★ **Skiing:** The Dolomites are renowned as one of Europe's top locations for winter sports, and will cohost the 2026 Winter Olympics along with Milan.

★ **Museo Archeologico dell'Alto Adige, Bolzano:** The impossibly well-preserved body of the iceman Ötzi, the star attraction at this museum, provokes countless questions about what life was like 5,000 years ago.

★ **Trento:** A graceful fusion of Austrian and Italian styles, this breezy frescoed town is famed for its imposing castle.

1 **Trento.** Piazza del Duomo is a highlight.

2 **Rovereto.** Enjoy the medieval center.

3 **Madonna di Campiglio.** A favorite for skiers and hikers.

4 **Bolzano (Bozen).** High-gabled houses are hallmarks.

5 **Bormio.** History, ski trails, and spa treatments.

6 **Merano (Meran).** Come here for the thermal waters.

7 **Naturno (Naturns).** Known for its hiking trails and castle museum.

8 **Caldaro (Kaltern).** The Strada del Vino runs through this wine town.

9 **Bressanone (Brixen).** The castle is a big draw.

10 **Brunico (Bruneck).** Don't miss the medieval quarter.

11 **Misurina.** The Three Peaks views are lovely.

12 **Canazei.** Come for the hiking and skiing.

13 **Ortisei (St. Ulrich).** Woodcarving workshops dot this town.

14 **Corvara.** Known for skiing and fine hotels.

15 **Cortina d'Ampezzo.** This ski resort has lots of summer activities.

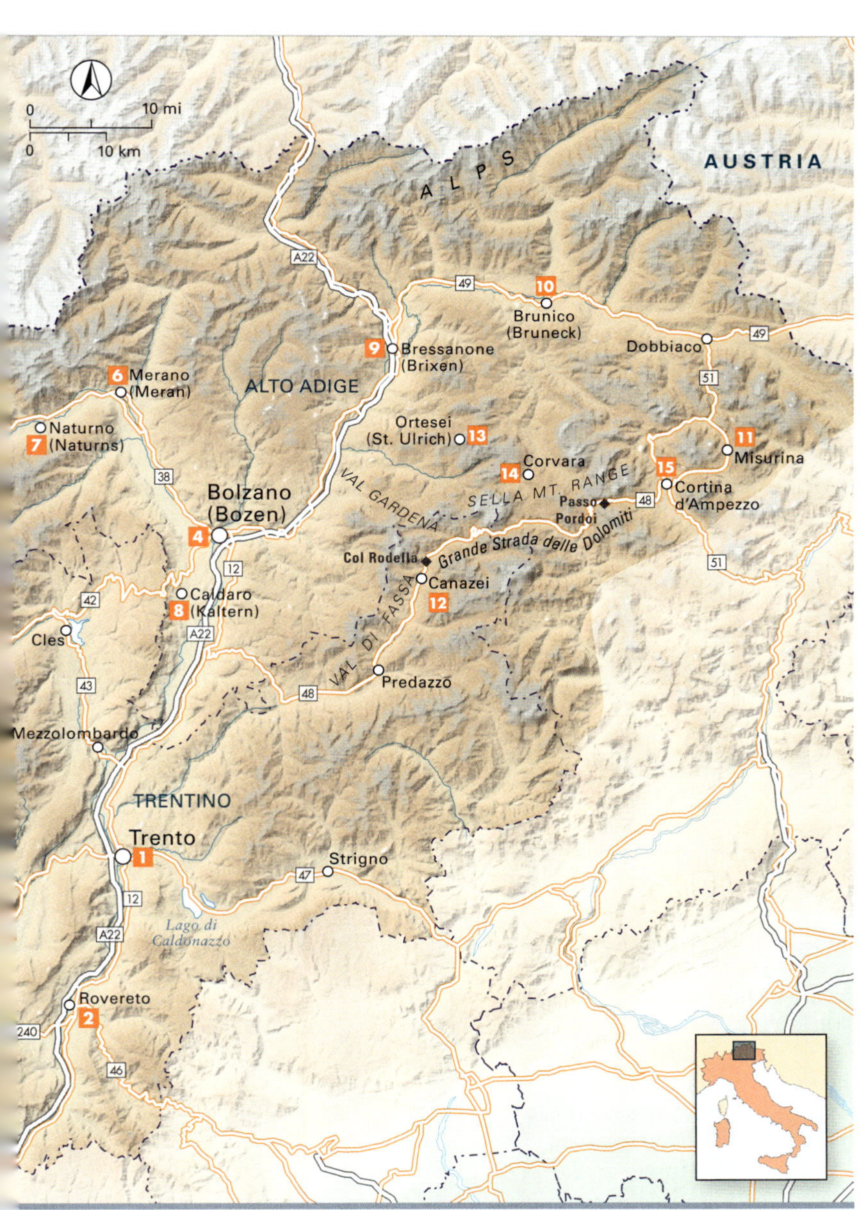
0
10 mi
0
10 km
ALPS
AUSTRIA
A22
49
10
Brunico
(Bruneck)
Dobbiaco
49
9
Bressanone
(Brixen)
6
Merano
(Meran)
ALTO ADIGE
51
Naturno
7
(Naturns)
Ortesei
(St. Ulrich)
13
11
Misurina
14
Corvara
15
Cortina
d'Ampezzo
38
VAL GARDENA
SELLA MT. RANGE
Passo
Pordoi
48
Bolzano
(Bozen)
4
Grande Strada delle Dolomiti
Col Rodella
12
Canazei
12
51
42
Caldaro
8
(Kaltern)
VAL DI FASSA
A22
Cles
43
Predazzo
48
Mezzolombardo
TRENTINO
Trento
1
Strigno
47
12
Lago di
Caldonazzo
A22
Rovereto
2
240
46

EATING AND DRINKING WELL IN THE DOLOMITES

Asiago cheese with pistachios

Everything in Alto Adige (and, to a lesser extent, Trentino) has more than a tinge of the Teutonic—and food is no exception. The rich and creamy cuisine here, including fondue, polenta, and barley soup, reflects the Alpine climate and Austrian and Swiss influences.

The quintessential restaurant is the wood-paneled Tyrolean *stube* (pub) serving hearty meat-and-dumpling fare, and there's also a profusion of pastry shops and lively beer halls.

Although the early dining schedule you'll find in Germany or Austria is somewhat tempered here, your options for late-night meals are more limited than they are in places farther south, where la dolce vita has a firmer grip.

Thankfully, the coffee is every bit as good as in parts south—just expect to hear *"danke, grazie"* when paying for your cappuccino.

BEST OF THE WURST

Not to be missed are the outdoor wurst carts. After placing your order you'll get a sheet of wax paper, followed by a dollop of mustard, a kaiser roll, and your chosen sausage. You can sometimes make your selection by pointing to whatever picture is most appealing; if not, pass on the familiar-sounding Frankfurter and try the local Merane. Carts can reliably be found in Bolzano (try Piazza delle Erbe, or in front of the archaeological museum) and Merano (Piazza del Grano, or along the river).

POLENTA AND DUMPLINGS

Polenta is a staple in the region, in both creamy and firm renditions, often topped with cheese or mushrooms (or both). Dumplings also appear on many menus; the most distinctive to the region are *canederli* (also known as Knödel) made from seasoned bread in many variations, and served either in broth or with a sauce. Other dumplings to look for are the dense *strangolapreti* (literally, "priest-chokers") and *gnocchi di ricotta alla zucca* (ricotta and pumpkin dumplings).

Polenta with porcini mushrooms

CHEESE

Every isolated mountain valley in Trentino–Alto Adige seems to make its own variety of cheese, and the local specialty is often simply called *nostrano* (ours). The best known of them are the mild Asiago and *fontal,* as well as the more pungent *puzzone di Moena* (literally, "stinkpot"). Also try the *schiz*: fresh cheese that's sliced and fried in butter.

PASTRIES AND BAKED GOODS

Bakeries turn out a wide selection of crusty dark rolls and caraway-studded rye breads—maybe not typical Italian bread, but full of flavor. Pastries here are reminiscent of what you'd find in Vienna. Apple strudel is everywhere, and for good reason: the best apples in Italy are grown here. There are other exceptional fruits as well, including pears, plums, and grapes, which make their way into baked goods.

Apple strudel

ALIMENTARI

If you're planning a picnic or getting provisions for a hike, you'll be well served by the fine *alimentari* (food shops) of Trentino and Alto Adige. They stock a bounty of regional specialties, including cheeses, pickles, salami, and smoked meats. These are good places to pick up a sample of *speck tirolese*, the salt-cured, cold-smoked deboned ham hock usually cut in paper-thin slices like prosciutto (though proud speck producers often bristle at the comparison).

WINE

Although Trentino and Alto Adige aren't as esteemed for their wines as many other Italian regions, they produce a wide variety of crisp, dry, and aromatic whites—Kerner, Müller-Thurgau, and Traminer, to name a few—not surprisingly, more like what you'd expect from German vineyards than Italian. Among the reds, look for *lagrein* and the native *teroldego*, a fruity, spicy variety produced only in the tiny valley north of Trento. The Trento D.O.C. appellation yields a marvelous sparkling wine in a class with Champagne.

The Dolomites, those inimitable craggy peaks Le Corbusier called "the most beautiful work of architecture ever seen," are never so arresting as at dusk, when the last rays of sun create a pink hue that languishes into purple—a magnificent transformation locals call the *enrosadira*. You can certainly enjoy this glow from a distance, but the Dolomites are such an appealing year-round destination precisely because of the many ways to get into the mountains themselves. And once there, in short order your perspective—like the peaks around you—will take on a rosy hue.

The Dolomites are strange, rocky pinnacles that jut straight up like chimneys; they are, in fact, the otherworldly pinnacles that Leonardo depicted in the background of his *Mona Lisa*. In spite of this incredible beauty, the vast mountainous domain of northeastern Italy has remained relatively undeveloped. Below the peaks, rivers meander through valleys dotted with peaceful villages, while pristine lakes are protected by picture-book castles. In the most secluded Dolomite vales, unique cultures have flourished: the Ladin language, an offshoot of Latin still spoken in the Val Gardena and Val di Fassa, owes its unlikely survival to centuries of topographic isolation.

The more accessible parts of Trentino–Alto Adige, on the other hand, have a history of near-constant intermingling of cultures. The region's Adige and Isarco Valleys make up the main access route between Italy and Central Europe, and as a result, the language, cuisine, and architecture are a blend of north and south. The province of Trentino is largely Italian-speaking, but Alto Adige is predominantly Germanic: until World War I the area was Austria's Südtirol. As you move north toward the famed Brenner Pass—through the prosperous valley towns of Rovereto, Trento, and Bolzano—the Teutonic influence is increasingly dominant; by the time you reach Bressanone, it's hard to believe you're in Italy at all.

Along with Milan, the region will play host to the 2026 Winter Olympics from February 6 to 22, and the Paralympic Winter Games from March 6 to 15. Events will take place in several locations throughout the Dolomites and Trentino–Alto Adige. Tickets start at €30 and are only available online at 🌐 *tickets.milanocortina2026.org*. If you visit during these times, expect large crowds and limited accommodation availabilities.

MAJOR REGIONS

Trentino. Until the end of World War I, the Trentino–Alto Adige/Südtirol region was part of Austria-Hungary. Although today the province of Trentino remains unmistakably Italian, Germanic influences are palpable in its architecture, cuisine, culture, and language. Visitors are drawn by the historical sites and cosmopolitan nature of Trento, while numerous year-round mountain resorts, like the fashionable Madonna di Campiglio, can be found in the wings of this butterfly-shape region. Culture-hounds will want to visit Rovereto, a town just south of Trento known for its fine contemporary art museum.

Bolzano. With castles and steeples topping the landscape, this quiet city at the confluence of the Isarco (Eisack) and Talvera Rivers has retained its provincial appeal. Proximity to fabulous skiing and mountain climbing—not to mention the world's oldest preserved human body—make it a very worthwhile destination. And its streets are immaculate: after Milan, residents here have the highest per capita earnings of any city in Italy.

The Western Dolomites. The Parco Nazionale dello Stelvio extends through western Trentino and the Altoatesino area of Alto Adige and beyond into eastern Lombardy. It's named for the famed Stelvio, Europe's highest road pass and site of the highest battle fought during World War I (also to ski slopes where the 2026 Winter Olympics downhill skiing competitions will take place). Even if you don't want to ski its trails or indulge in one of its renowned spa treatments, the well-preserved town of Bormio still merits a visit for its history and character.

Alto Adige. In the province of Alto Adige (Südtirol/South Tyrol), Germanic and Italian culture balance harmoniously, as do medieval and modern influences, with ancient castles regularly hosting contemporary art exhibitions. Prosperous valley towns, such as the famed spa center of Merano, the medieval town of Bressanone, and the wine village of Caldaro, entice those seeking both relaxation and the finer pleasures.

The Heart of the Dolomites. This area between Bolzano and the mountain resort Cortina d'Ampezzo—home to many 2026 Winter Olympics events—is dominated by two major valleys, Val di Fassa and Val Gardena. Both share the spectacular panorama of the Sella mountain range. Along the scenic Grande Strada delle Dolomiti (Great Dolomites Road), you'll find Canazei, Ortisei, and Corvara, resort towns with skiing and hiking galore. The Tre Cime (Three Peaks), the best-known symbol of the Dolomites, are visible from the lakeside town of Misurina and worth a gander if not a hike.

Planning

Getting Here and Around

BUS

Regular bus service connects larger cities to the south (Verona, Venice, and Milan) with valley towns in Trentino–Alto Adige (Rovereto, Trento, Bolzano, and Merano). You'll need to change to less frequent local buses to reach resorts and smaller villages in the mountains beyond.

If you're equipped with current schedules and don't mind adapting your schedules to theirs, it's possible to visit even the remotest villages by bus. ATVO (🌐 *www.*

atvo.it), CortinaExpress (🌐 *www.cortinaexpress.it*), and FlixBlus (🌐 *www.flixbus.com*) provide year-round service to Cortina from Venice airport and Mestre train station daily. FlixBus also connects Venice directly with Bolzano and Trento. DolomitiBus (🌐 *dolomitibus.it*) covers the eastern Dolomites, including a number of small towns. SAD (🌐 *www.sad.it*) provides service from Bolzano and Bressanone. Trentino Trasporti (🌐 *www.trentinotrasporti.it*) offers buses within Trento and Rovereto. Südtirolmobil (🌐 *www.suedtirolmobil.info*) provides further information on local services.

CAR

Driving is easily the most convenient way to travel in the Dolomites; it can be difficult to reach the ski areas (or any town outside of Rovereto, Trento, Bolzano, or Merano) without a car. Driving is also the most exhilarating way to get around, as you rise from broad valleys into mountains with narrow, winding roads straight out of a sports-car ad. The most important route in the region is the A22 autostrada, the main north–south highway linking Italy with Central Europe by way of the Brenner Pass. It connects Innsbruck with Bressanone, Bolzano, Trento, and Rovereto, and near Verona joins the A4, which runs east–west across northern Italy, from Trieste to Turin. By car, Trento is 3 hours from Milan and 2½ hours from Venice. Bolzano is another 45-minute drive to the north, with Munich 4 hours farther on.

Caution is essential (tap your horn in advance of hairpin turns), as are chains in winter, when roads are often covered in snow. Sudden closures are common, especially on high mountain passes, and can occur as early as September and as late as May. Even under the best conditions, expect to negotiate mountain roads at speeds no greater than 50 kph (30 mph).

TRAIN

The rail line following the course of the Isarco and Adige Valleys—from Munich and Innsbruck, through the Brenner Pass, and southward past Bressanone, Bolzano, Trento, and Rovereto en route to Verona—is well trafficked, making trains a viable option for travel between these towns. Eurocity trains on the Dortmund–Venice and Munich–Innsbruck–Rome routes stop at these stations, and you can connect with other Italian lines at Verona. Although branch lines from Trento and Bolzano do extend into some of the smaller valleys (including hourly service between Bolzano and Merano), most mountain attractions are beyond the reach of trains. 🌐 *www.italotreno.com, www.trenitalia.com*

Hotels

Classic Dolomite lodging includes restored castles, chalets, and stately 19th-century hotels. The small villages that pepper the Dolomites often have scores of flower-bedecked inns, many of them inexpensive. Hotel information offices at train stations and tourist offices can help if you've arrived without reservations. The Bolzano train station has a 24-hour hotel service, and tourist offices will give you a list of all the hotels in the area, arranged by location, stars, and price. Hotels at ski resorts cater to longer stays at full or half board. Many Italians come to the Dolomites every winter for their Settimana Bianca (White Week), and if you care to join them you should book ski vacations as packages well in advance. Most rural accommodations close from early November to mid- or late December, as well as for two months or so after Easter. The majority of *rifugi* (mountain huts) on hiking trails are operated by the Club Alpino Italiano (🌐 *www.cai.it*). Contact information for both CAI-run and private rifugi is available from local tourist offices; most useful are those in Madonna di Campiglio (🌐 *www.*

campigliodolomiti.it), Cortina d'Ampezzo (🌐 *www.dolomiti.org*), Val di Fassa (🌐 *www.fassa.com*), and Val Gardena (🌐 *www.val-gardena.com*).

⇨ *Hotel and restaurant reviews have been shortened. For full information, visit Fodors.com. Prices in the hotel reviews are the lowest cost of a standard double room in high season. Prices in the dining reviews are the average cost of a main course at dinner, or, if dinner is not served, at lunch.*

What It Costs in Euros

$	$$	$$$	$$$$
RESTAURANTS			
under €20	€20–€30	€31–€40	over €40
HOTELS			
under €175	€175–€400	€401–€600	over €600

Making the Most of Your Time

For a brief stay, your best choice for a base is vibrant Bolzano, where you can get a sense of the region's contrasts—Italian and German, medieval and modern. After a day or two in town, venture an hour south to history-laden Trento, north to the lovely spa town of Merano, or southwest to Caldaro and its Strada di Vino; all are viable day trips from Bolzano, and Trento and Merano make good places to spend the night as well.

If you have more time, you'll want to get up into the mountains, which are the region's main attraction. The trip on the Grande Strada delle Dolomiti through the Heart of the Dolomites from Bolzano to Cortina d'Ampezzo is one of Italy's most spectacular drives. Summer or winter, this is a great destination for mountain sports, with scores of trails for world-class hiking and skiing.

The Brixen Card (free with paid lodging in Bressanone) offers free transportation throughout Trentino and Alto Adige (Südtirol/South Tyrol) and entrance to three Brixen museums, plus one return ride on the Plose lifts (depending on dates) and discounts at partner venues. See 🌐 *www.brixen.org* for a list of participating hotels and bed-and-breakfasts.

Detailed information about *vie ferrate* (mountain paths with steel cables and fixed anchors and ladders) in the eastern Dolomites can be found at 🌐 *www.dolomiti.org*. Capable tour organizers include the Scuola di Alpinismo (Mountaineering School) in Madonna di Campiglio (☎ *0465/442634* 🌐 *www.guidealpine-campiglio.it*) and in Cortina d'Ampezzo (☎ *0436/868505* 🌐 *www.guidecortina.com*).

Restaurants

When dining out in the Dolomites, it's evident you are in a region of Italy that was once part of Austria-Hungary. Although you can still find traditional Italian pasta and pizza, there's a considerable amount of Austro-Germanic flair. Sausages, spaetzle, meats, cheeses, and polenta—foods that will sustain the body through a long day of skiing or hiking—can be found on nearly every menu, although you'll also find more contemporary restaurants using seasonal ingredients in a lighter style. Many restaurants either raise their own crops and livestock or have a direct relationship with their farmers and providers.

Trento

58 km (36 miles) south of Bolzano.

Trento is a prosperous, cosmopolitan university town that retains an architectural charm befitting its historical importance. It was here, from 1545 to 1563, that the structure of the Catholic Church was redefined at the Council of Trent, the starting point of the Counter-Reformation, which brought half of Europe back to Catholicism. Today, the word *consiglio* (council) appears everywhere in Trento—in hotel, restaurant, and street names, and even on wine labels. The Piazza del Duomo remains splendid, and its enormous medieval palazzo dominates the city landscape in virtually its original form.

The 24-hour Trentino Card (🌐 *www.trento.info/en/trentino-guest-card*) is given free (via email or text) to hotel guests, and grants free or discounted admission to museums, castles, parks, and other attractions, as well as all public transportation. Non–hotel guests can make use of the 48-hour Museum Pass (€22), which allows unlimited access to all museums and castles in Trento and Rovereto as well as free public transportation in Trentino. It can be bought online (🌐 *www.trento.info/en/museum-pass*), at tourist offices, or at participating museums, and can even be converted into a three-month card for no extra charge.

GETTING HERE AND AROUND

The A22 autostrada is the main highway to Trento. From the north, take the Trento Nord exit; from the south, take the Trento Sud exit. There are signs directing you to the city center. Trento is easily accessible from Venice (2½ hours) and Verona (just over an hour), and is only 4½ hours from Munich. The city center is pedestrian-friendly, or you can use the transit options in conjunction with the Trentino Card for discounts on the city buses.

TOURS

Guided Tours of Trento

GUIDED TOURS | FAMILY | Two-hour guided tours of Trento's city center depart from the tourist office on Saturday at 10 am, mainly in Italian but with some English. Reserve your place on the tour beforehand online. ✉ *Piazza Dante 24, Trento* ☎ *0461/216000* 🌐 *www.trento.info/en* 🎫 *€10; €8 with Trento Card.*

VISITOR INFORMATION

CONTACT Trento Tourism Office. ✉ *Piazza Dante 24, Trento* ☎ *0461/216000* 🌐 *www.trento.info/en.*

Sights

Belvedere di Sardagna

VIEWPOINT | FAMILY | Take the Funivia Trento–Sardagna cable car up to the Belvedere di Sardagna, a lookout point 1,200 feet above medieval Trento. **TIP→ This is open year-round but can close due to inclement weather.** ✉ *Via Monte Grappa 1, Trento* ☎ *0461/031000* 🌐 *www.trentinotrasporti.it* 🎫 *€5 round-trip.*

★ Castello del Buonconsiglio (*Castle of Good Counsel*)

CASTLE/PALACE | FAMILY | The position and size of this stronghold of the prince-bishops made it easier to defend than the Palazzo Pretorio. Look for the evolution of architectural styles: the medieval fortifications of the Castelvecchio section (on the far left) were built in the 13th century; the fancier Renaissance Magno Palazzo section (on the far right) wasn't completed until 300 years later. The 13th-century **Torre dell'Aquila** (Eagle's Tower) is home to the castle's artistic highlight, a 15th-century *ciclo dei mesi* (cycle of the months). The four-wall fresco is full of charming and detailed scenes of medieval life in both court and countryside. ✉ *Via Bernardo Clesio 5, Trento* ☎ *0461/233770* 🌐 *www.buonconsiglio.it* 🎫 *€10; Torre Aquila €2.50* ⏲ *Closed Mon.* ✍ *Timed visits must be booked online in advance.*

Duomo (*Cattedrale di San Vigilio*)

CHURCH | This massive Romanesque church, also known as the Cathedral of San Vigilio (St. Vigilius), forms the southern edge of the Piazza del Duomo. Locals refer to this square as the city's *salotto* (sitting room), as in fine weather it's always filled with students and residents drinking coffee, sipping an aperitif, or reading the newspaper. The Baroque

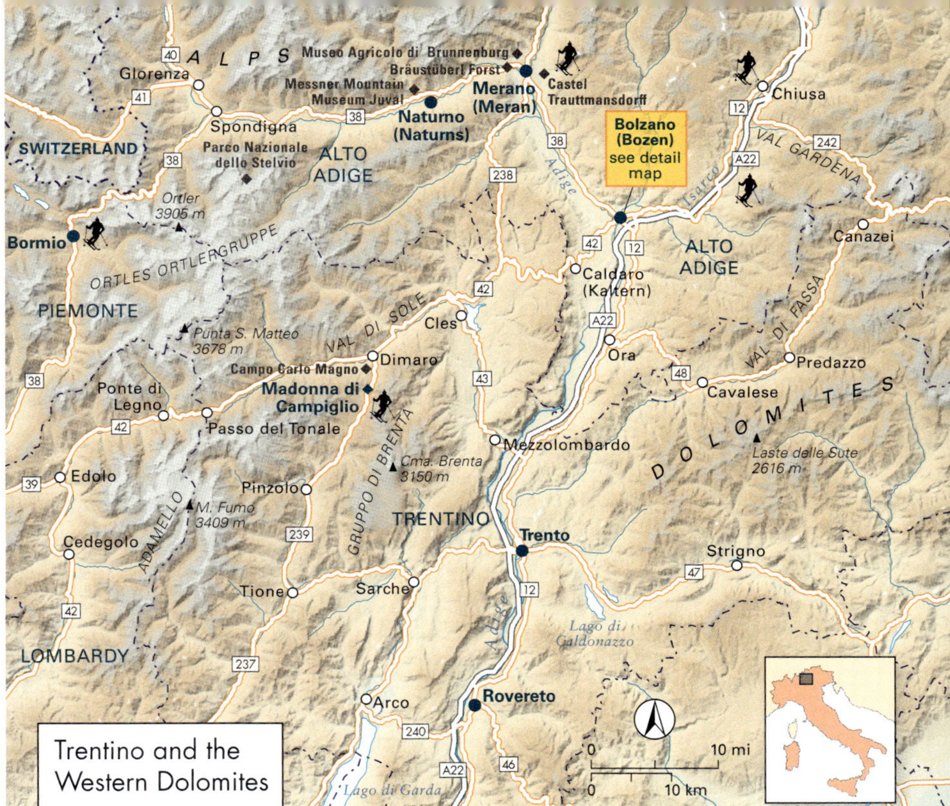

Fontana del Nettuno presides over it all. When skies are clear, pause here to savor the view of the mountaintops enveloping the city.

Within the Duomo unusual arcaded stone stairways border the austere nave. Ahead is the *baldacchino* (altar canopy), a copy of Bernini's masterpiece in St. Peter's in Rome. To the left of the altar is a mournful 16th-century crucifixion, flanked by the Virgin Mary and John the Apostle. This crucifix, by German artist Sisto Frey, was a focal point of the Council of Trent: each decree agreed on during the two decades of deliberations was solemnly read out in front of it. Stairs on the left side of the altar lead down to the 4th-century Paleo-Christian burial vault (Early Christian Basilica). Outside, check out the bronze scale model of the city on the south side of the cathedral, then walk around to the back to see an exquisite display of 14th-century stonemason artistry, from the small porch to the intriguing knotted columns on the graceful apse. ✉ *Piazza del Duomo, Trento* ☎ *0461/231293* 🌐 *www.cattedralesanvigilio.it* 🎫 *Free. Early Christian Basilica €3* ⏲ *Early Christian Basilica closed Sun. morning and Tues.*

★ MUSE – Museo delle Scienze di Trento
(*Science Museum of Trento*)
SCIENCE MUSEUM | FAMILY | Extending over six floors, in a 41,000-foot space, this interactive science museum, designed by Renzo Piano, encourages families of all ages to explore science and nature. As befits the region, mountain imagery plays a big part in the displays and is used to investigate the Dolomites' history and even life on Earth. There's also a sensory experience room for younger kids up

to five years old. ✉ *Corso del Lavoro e della Scienza 3, Trento* ☎ *0461/270311* 🌐 *www.muse.it* 🎫 *€12* ⏲ *Closed Mon.*

Museo Diocesano Tridentino

HISTORY MUSEUM | Located inside the Palazzo Pretorio, the Museo Diocesano Tridentino is where you can see paintings and other objects that come from the treasury of the adjoining Cathedral of San Vigilio. This includes many carved wood altars and statues; an 11th-century sacramentary, or book of services; the seating plan of the prelates during the Council of Trent; and early-16th-century tapestries by Pieter van Aelst (1502–56), the Belgian artist who carried out Raphael's 15th-century designs for the Vatican tapestries. The palazzo itself was built in the 13th century and designed to seem like a wing of the Duomo; it became the fortified residence of the prince-bishops, who enjoyed considerable power and autonomy within the medieval hierarchy. The remarkable palazzo has lost none of its original splendor. Accessible through the museum, a subterranean archaeological area beneath the adjacent cathedral reveals remnants of the Early Christian Basilica of San Vigilio. You can also get good city views by climbing the 156 steps up the attached Torre di Piazza (Civic Tower), accessible only by guided tour. ✉ *Piazza del Duomo 18, Trento* ☎ *0461/234419* 🌐 *www.museodiocesanotridentino.it* 🎫 *Museo and Basilica €7; Museo, Basilica, and Torre di Piazza €12* ⏲ *Closed Tues.* ✍ *Must purchase tickets in advance online or at the ticket office for Torre di Piazza.*

Tridentum — Spazio Archeologico Sotterraneo del Sas (*S.A.S.S.*)

RUINS | **FAMILY** | The ancient Roman city of Tridentum lies beneath much of Trento's city center. Centuries of Adige River flooding buried ruins that only recently have been unearthed on public and private land. Beneath this piazza lies the largest of the archaeological sites, which reveals some marvels of Roman technology, such as underfloor heating and subterranean sewers complete with manhole covers. The Romans also used lead pipes for four centuries before recognizing it was hazardous to health. ✉ *Piazza Cesare Battisti, Trento* ☎ *0461/230171* 🌐 *www.cultura.trentino.it* 🎫 *Tridentum and Villa di Orfeo €5* ⏲ *Closed Mon.*

Via Belenzani

STREET | Locals refer to this street as Trento's outdoor gallery because of the frescoed facades of the hallmark Renaissance palazzi. It's an easy 50-yard walk up the lane behind the church of Santa Maria Maggiore. ✉ *Via Belenzani, Trento.*

★ **Villa di Orfeo** (*Roman Villa of Orpheus*)

HISTORIC SIGHT | **FAMILY** | Just outside the walls of the ancient Roman city of Tridentum, this fascinating residence was built during the 1st century AD. The villa's highlight is a large ceremonial room with a 603-square-foot mosaic of Orpheus playing music to serenade animals. The visit also includes an immersive video that gives you a feel for the villa's look and location at the time it was built, along with a virtual reconstruction of Tridentum. ✉ *Via Antonio Rosmini 2, Trento* ☎ *0461/492161* 🌐 *www.cultura.trentino.it* 🎫 *Villa di Orfeo and Tridentum €5* ⏲ *Closed Mon.*

Restaurants

★ **Locanda Margon**

$$$$ | **MODERN ITALIAN** | Inside an elegant country house perched atop a steep hill and set among the vineyards, about a 10-minute drive south of Trento's center, talented chef Edoardo Fumagalli creates thoroughly modern cuisine that pairs perfectly with the Lunelli family's sparkling Ferrari wines. Choose from three tasting menus, which feature local ingredients such as Garda lemons, ricotta from the surrounding farm, and Dolomite trout roe; for lighter appetites, the more casual bistro next door offers à la carte dishes. **Known for:** panoramic vineyard vistas; liberal use of ingredients from the surrounding area; beautifully plated dishes. *Average main: €185 Via Margone di Ravina 15, Trento 5½ km (3½ miles) south of Trento city center 0461/349401 locandamargon.it Closed Tues. and Wed.*

Osteria a Le Due Spade

$$ | **NORTHERN ITALIAN** | What started out as a Tyrolean tavern around the time of the Council of Trent is today an intimate restaurant that adeptly serves superb innovative dishes, using both local and international ingredients. The menu changes throughout the year and offers a choice of a four-course meat, fish, or vegetarian menu (dishes are also available à la carte); decadent additions of fois gras and cheese are also possible. **Known for:** creative fine dining; knowledgeable, welcoming staff; cozy wood-paneled interior. *Average main: €24 Via Rizzi 11, Trento 0461/234343 www.leduespade.com Closed Sun. No lunch Mon.*

Ristorante Al Vò

$ | **NORTHERN ITALIAN** | Trento's oldest trattoria (it's the descendant of a 14th-century tavern) remains one of its most popular lunch spots. Locals crowd into a simple, modern dining room to enjoy regional specialties like gnocchi with vegetables and *baccalà* (salt cod); an impressive (and inexpensive) selection of local wines is available. **Known for:** Trento's oldest eatery; knowledgeable, welcoming staff; fine selection of wines. *Average main: €13 Vicolo del Vò 11, Trento 0461/985374 www.ristorantealvo.it Closed Sun. No dinner.*

Scrigno del Duomo

$$ | **NORTHERN ITALIAN** | More than 30 wines by the glass, accompanied by an excellent selection of local cheeses, are served in this chic eatery, which has outside seating in the piazza. Salads and regional specialties are prepared in the open kitchen by gourmet chefs; the downstairs room features *graffito* (graffiti) murals from local artist Luigi Senesi, while the Roman wall running under the Duomo is also in clear view. **Known for:** traditional food and local wine; fine views of the cathedral; local art and history. *Average main: €22 Piazza del Duomo 29, Trento 0461/220030 www.scrignodelduomo.com.*

Coffee and Quick Bites

Antica Birreria Pedavena

$ | **NORTHERN ITALIAN** | **FAMILY** | Come for the beer—several varieties are brewed in-house and served in this charismatic beer hall—and stay for the meals that include wursts, meat and cheese platters, pizzas, and huge salads. Smaller wood-paneled dining rooms and a summer terrace allow for more peaceful dining. **Known for:** fine selection of brewed-in-house beers; typical Bavarian meats; enormous beer hall. *Average main: €14 Piazza di Fiera 13, Trento 0461/986255 www.birreriapedavena.com Closed Tues.*

Hotels

Castel Pergine

$$ | **B&B/INN** | **FAMILY** | The stone and brick chambers, prison cells, and chapels in this labyrinthine 13th-century castle (occupied by Trento's prince-bishops in the 16th century) today contain spare, rustic guest rooms with carved-wood trim, lace curtains, and heavy wooden beds—some of them canopied. **Pros:** romantic setting; great restaurant; authentic castle experience. **Cons:** simple accommodations; need a car to get around; bathrooms are very small. *Rooms from: €214 Via al Castello 10, Pergine Valsugana 11 km (7 miles) east of Trento 0461/531158 castelpergine.it Closed Nov.–Mar. Restaurant closed Wed., bistro closed Mon. and Tues. 20 rooms No Meals.*

Grand Hotel Trento

$ | **HOTEL** | This contemporary, rounded facade stands out among the ancient palazzi nearby, but inside you'll find a handsome marble-paved lobby, rich drapery in the restaurant, and ample rooms with clubby wood-trimmed furniture. **Pros:** near train station; professional service; wellness center. **Cons:** busy neighborhood; dated decor; basic bathroom amenities. *Rooms from: €148* ✉ *Piazza Dante 20, Trento* ☎ *0461/271000* 🌐 *www.grandhoteltrento.com* *136 rooms* *Free Breakfast.*

Performing Arts

★ **I Suoni delle Dolomiti** (*The Sounds of the Dolomites*)

FESTIVALS | **FAMILY** | Held from mid-August to mid-September high in the hills of Trentino, this series of free concerts offers the chance to enjoy chamber music performances amid grassy meadows and mountain views. ✉ *Trento* ☎ *0461/219300* 🌐 *www.isuonidelledolomiti.it* *Free, except for certain concerts.*

Shopping

Enoteca del Corso

FOOD | A bit outside the town center, this atmospheric shop is laden with wines, sweets, and other local products. ✉ *Corso 3 Novembre 64, Trento* ☎ *0461/916424.*

Lunelli Specialità Trento

FOOD | This specialty food shop boasts an impressive array of sauces, as well as wines, grappas, and liqueurs. A picnic can be handily assembled from a huge assortment of local salamis and cheeses. ✉ *Via Mazzini 46, Trento* ☎ *0461/238053* 🌐 *www.lunellitrento.it.*

Rovereto

24 km (15 miles) south of Trento, 75 km (47 miles) south of Bolzano.

A 15th-century Venetian castle dominates Rovereto's compact medieval *centro storico* (historic center), with one of Italy's finest contemporary art museums just steps away. **TIP→ The Trento Museum Pass also includes entry to sites here in Rovereto.**

GETTING HERE AND AROUND

By car from Trento, take the A22/E45 for 28 km (17 miles) to Rovereto. Frequent trains run from Trento to Rovereto; the journey takes about 13 minutes.

VISITOR INFORMATION

CONTACT Rovereto Tourism Office. ✉ *Corso Rosmini 21, Rovereto* ☎ *0464/430363* 🌐 *www.visitrovereto.it.*

Sights

Mart Rovereto (*Museo di Arte Moderna e Contemporanea di Trento e Rovereto*)

ART MUSEUM | Most of the 20,000 works of contemporary and modern art in this collection are from the 20th century. Rotating exhibitions and special events throughout the year highlight still more contemporary art. ✉ *Corso Bettini 43, Rovereto* ☎ *0464/438887* 🌐 *www.mart.tn.it* *€15* *Closed Mon.*

Museo Storico Italiano della Guerra (*Italian Historical War Museum*)

HISTORY MUSEUM | This museum was founded after World War I to commemorate the conflict—and to warn against repeating its atrocities. An authoritative exhibition of military artifacts is displayed in the medieval castle perched above Rovereto; the views alone warrant a visit. From June through October you can also see a collection of artillery from the Great War housed in a former air-raid shelter. ✉ *Via Castelbarco 7, Rovereto* ☎ *0464/438100* 🌐 *museodellaguerra.it* *€11* *Closed Mon.*

Hotels

Hotel Rovereto

$ | **HOTEL** | The Zani family runs this modern, centrally located hotel, which has welcoming public spaces, warm-color guest rooms, and one of the city's most appealing restaurants. **Pros:** excellent restaurant; unbeatable location; distinctive decor. **Cons:** some rooms are on the small side; small parking area; design choices, like sinks in some rooms, not to everyone's taste. *Rooms from: €89* *Corso Rosmini 82/D, Rovereto* *0464/435222* *www.hotelrovereto.it* *Restaurant closed Sun. No lunch* *49 rooms* *No Meals.*

Madonna di Campiglio

80 km (50 miles) northwest of Trento, 100 km (62 miles) southwest of Bolzano.

The winter resort of Madonna di Campiglio vies with Cortina d'Ampezzo as the most fashionable place for Italians to ski and be seen in the Dolomites. Madonna's popularity is well deserved, with 62 lifts connecting 156 km (97 miles) of well-groomed ski runs and equally good lodging and trekking facilities. The resort itself is a modest 5,000 feet above sea level, but the downhill runs, summer hiking paths, and mountain-biking trails venture high up into the surrounding peaks (including Pietra Grande at 9,700 feet).

GETTING HERE AND AROUND

By car from Trento, take the SS45 toward Vezzano. After Vezzano, continue to the SS237 until Ragoli, and turn onto the SP34. Follow the SP34 for 6 km (4 miles), and turn onto the SS239 for another 23 km (15 miles) until you arrive at Madonna di Campiglio. The more convenient railway station is at Trento; then you can ride the Trentino Trasporti bus for 2½ hours from Trento (four times daily) or take the FlySki Shuttle during ski season (€29 one-way, €58 round-trip).

VISITOR INFORMATION

CONTACT Madonna di Campiglio Tourism Office. *Via Pradalago 4, Madonna di Campiglio* *0465/447501* *www.campigliodolomiti.it.*

Sights

Campo Carlo Magno

VIEWPOINT | The stunning pass at Campo Carlo Magno (5,500 feet) is 3 km (2 miles) north of Madonna di Campiglio. This is where Charlemagne is said to have stopped in AD 800 on his way to Rome to be crowned emperor. You, too, can stop here to gaze upon the whole of northern Italy. If you continue north, take the descent with caution—in the space of a mile or so, hairpin turns and switchbacks deliver you down more than 2,000 feet. *3 km (2 miles) north of Madonna di Campiglio, Madonna di Campiglio.*

Restaurants

Cascina Zeledria

$$ | **NORTHERN ITALIAN** | Although most of Madonna's visitors dine at resort hotels, Italians consider an on-mountain meal in a remote, rustic refuge like this one to be an indispensable part of a proper ski week. You can drive or hike up in summer months, but in winter, you ski, snowshoe, or are collected by a Sno-Cat and ferried 10 minutes up the slopes; once there, you'll sit down to grill your own meats and vegetables over stone griddles. **Known for:** authentic experience in a rural mountain setting; house specialty mushrooms and polenta; local wine. *Average main: €25* *Località Zeledria, Madonna di Campiglio* *0465/440303* *www.zeledria.it* *Closed May–mid-June and mid-Sept.–Nov.*

Ferrari Spazio Bollicine Nabucco

$$ | **WINE BAR** | Although it has a stylish black-and-white color scheme, this restaurant/wine bar nevertheless has the feel of a rustic, intimate chalet. Settle into pleasant surroundings for an

après-ski aperitif or a light meal made with local ingredients and paired with the sparkling wines of Ferrari, a well-known Trentino vintner. **Known for:** predinner cocktails; intimate atmosphere; central location. *Average main: €30 Piazza Righi B3, Madonna di Campiglio 0465/440756 www.ferraritrento.com Closed May–Nov.*

Hotels

★ Lefay Resort & SPA Dolomiti

$$$ | RESORT | FAMILY | Blending beautifully into the mountain landscape, this deluxe lodging just south of Madonna di Campiglio features one of the largest and most impressive spas in the Alps. **Pros:** exceptional breakfast offerings; wonderful spa facilities; gorgeous architectural design. **Cons:** electric fireplaces in the rooms aren't as charming as real ones (though more sustainable); pools could be more heated in colder seasons; high prices on food and drinks. *Rooms from: €485 Via Alpe di Grual 16, Pinzolo 13 km (8 miles) south of Madonna di Campiglio 0465/768800 dolomiti.lefayresorts.com 88 rooms Free Breakfast.*

TH Madonna di Campiglio Golf Hotel

$$ | HOTEL | FAMILY | You need to make your way north to the Campo Carlo Magno Pass to reach this grand if dated hotel, the former summer residence of Habsburg emperor Franz Josef, replete with verandas, Persian rugs, and bay windows. **Pros:** attractive indoor pool; elegant rooms; kids' club for children ages 3–11 and infant club for ages 3 months–3 years. **Cons:** long walk into town; food not up to par; all rooms are carpeted. *Rooms from: €215 Via Cima Tosa 3, Madonna di Campiglio 0465/441003, 049/2956411 reservations www.thcampiglio.it Closed late Mar.–early July and Sept.–early Dec. 109 rooms Free Breakfast.*

Activities

GOLF

Madonna di Campiglio Golf Club

GOLF | The 9-hole Madonna di Campiglio course is one of the highest in Europe, at 5,400 feet. It's only open mid-June through mid-September. *Via Cima Tosa 16, near Golf Hotel, Madonna di Campiglio 0465/440622 www.golfcampiglio.it €50; €75 mid-July–late Aug. 9 holes, 6,090 yards, par 70.*

HIKING AND CLIMBING

The Madonna di Campiglio tourism office (www.campigliodolomiti.it) has maps of a dozen trails leading to waterfalls, lakes, and stupefying views.

Monte Spinale (*Spinale Peak*)

HIKING & WALKING | FAMILY | The cable car to 6,900-foot-high Monte Spinale offers magnificent views of the Brenta Dolomites in winter; it also runs during peak summer season and leads to many hikes at the vista. Alternatively, you can opt for an intermediate-level hike from town to the top, which takes around two hours to complete. *Off Via Monte Spinale, Madonna di Campiglio 0465/447744 www.ski.it Cable car €20 round-trip.*

SKIING

★ Campiglio Dolomiti di Brenta Val di Sole Val Rendena Skiarea

SKIING & SNOWBOARDING | FAMILY | Miles of interconnecting ski runs—some of the best in the Dolomites—are linked by the cable cars and lifts of Campiglio Dolomiti di Brenta Val di Sole Val Rendena Skiarea. Advanced skiers will like the extremely difficult terrain found on certain mountain faces, and intermediate and beginner skiers will find many runs at their levels, all accessible from town. There are also plenty of off-piste opportunities. Passes can be purchased online or at the main *funivia* (cable car) in town, and multiday passes are available. *Via Presanella 12, Madonna di Campiglio 0465/447744 www.ski.it Passes from €50.40 per day.*

Bolzano (Bozen)

32 km (19 miles) south of Merano, 50 km (31 miles) north of Trento.

Bolzano (Bozen), capital of the autonomous province of Alto Adige, is tucked among craggy peaks in a Dolomite valley 77 km (48 miles) from the Brenner Pass and Austria. Tyrolean culture dominates Bolzano's language, food, architecture, and people. It's hard to remember that you're in Italy when walking the city's colorful cobblestone streets and visiting its lantern-lighted cafés, where you may enjoy sauerkraut and a beer among a lively crowd of German speakers. That said, the fine Italian espresso and the boutiques will help to remind you where you are. The long, narrow arcades of Via dei Portici house shops that specialize in Tyrolean crafts and clothing, as well as many Italian designers.

The Bolzano Bozen Guestcard, free of charge at participating accommodations, grants free transport throughout the region as well as discounts on select activities.

GETTING HERE AND AROUND

By car from Trento, take the A22 for 60 km (37 miles) to Bolzano Sud. The train station is just steps away from Piazza Walther and has regular service from Italy and Munich (four hours). The SASA bus can help you connect between Bolzano and other parts of the region. There is an airport in Bolzano, but its connections are not as convenient as the larger airports serving Venice, Verona, and Munich.

VISITOR INFORMATION

CONTACT Bolzano Tourism Office. ✉ *Via Alto Adige 60, Bolzano* ☎ *0471/307000* 🌐 *www.bolzano-bozen.it.*

Sights

Assumption of Our Lady Cathedral (*Duomo*)
CHURCH | A lacy spire looks down on the mosaic-like roof tiles of the city's Gothic cathedral, built between the 12th and 14th centuries. Inside are 14th- and 15th-century frescoes and an intricately carved stone pulpit dating from 1514. Outside, don't miss the Porta del Vino (Wine Gate) on the northeast side facing the square; decorative carvings of grapes and harvest workers attest to the long-standing importance of wine to this region. ✉ *Piazza della Parrocchia 27, Bolzano* ☎ *0471/978676* 🌐 *dompfarre.bz.it* 🎫 *Free* ⏲ *Closed Sat.*

Castel Roncolo (*Schloss Runkelstein*)
CASTLE/PALACE | **FAMILY** | Green hills and farmhouses north of town surround this meticulously kept castle (also called Runkelstein Castle, or Schloss Runkelstein in German) with a tiled roof. It was built in 1237, destroyed half a century later, and then rebuilt soon thereafter. The world's largest cycle of secular medieval frescoes, beautifully preserved, is inside. A tavern in the courtyard serves excellent local food and wines. To get here from Piazza Walther, take Bus No. 12 (weekdays) or 14 (Sunday and public holidays). Alternatively, it's a 45-minute walk from Piazza delle Erbe: head north along Via Francescani, continue through Piazza Madonna, connecting to Via Castel Roncolo. If you drive or take the bus, be advised that you'll still have a 5- to 10-minute walk up to the castle. ✉ *Via San Antonio 15, Bolzano* ☎ *0471/329808 castle* 🌐 *www.runkelstein.info* 🎫 *€10* ⏲ *Closed Mon. and 3 wks in Jan.*

★ **Messner Mountain Museum Firmian**
ART MUSEUM | **FAMILY** | Perched on a peak overlooking Bolzano, the 10th-century Castle Sigmundskron is home to one of six mountain museums established by Reinhold Messner—the first climber to conquer Everest solo and the first to reach its summit without oxygen. The Tibetan tradition of *kora,* a circular pilgrimage around a sacred site, is an inspiration for the museum, where visitors contemplate the relationship between human and mountain, guided

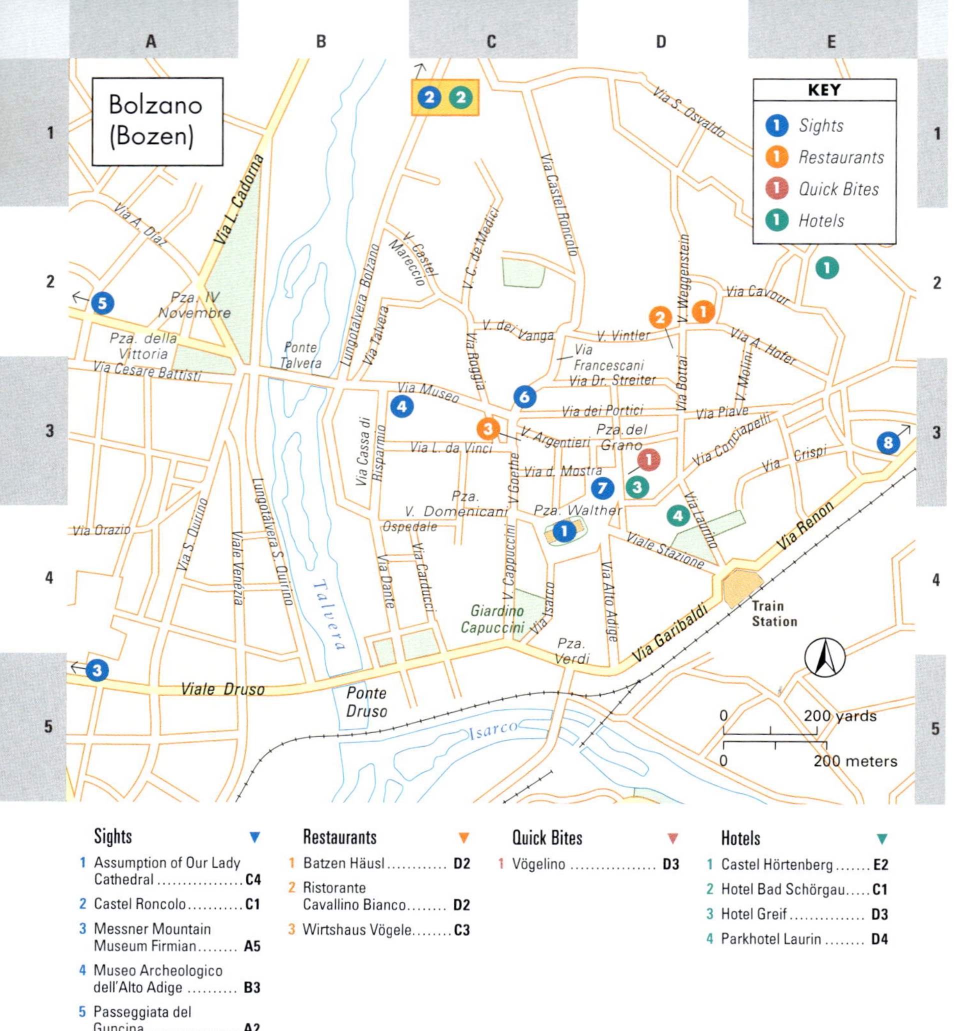

Sights

1 Assumption of Our Lady Cathedral C4
2 Castel Roncolo C1
3 Messner Mountain Museum Firmian A5
4 Museo Archeologico dell'Alto Adige B3
5 Passeggiata del Guncina A2
6 Piazza delle Erbe C3
7 Piazza Walther D3
8 Renon (Ritten) Plateau E3

Restaurants

1 Batzen Häusl D2
2 Ristorante Cavallino Bianco D2
3 Wirtshaus Vögele C3

Quick Bites

1 Vögelino D3

Hotels

1 Castel Hörtenberg E2
2 Hotel Bad Schörgau C1
3 Hotel Greif D3
4 Parkhotel Laurin D4

by images and objects Messner collected during his adventures. The museum is 3 km (2 miles) southwest of Bolzano, just off the Appiano exit on the highway to Merano. ✉ *Sigmundskron Castle 53, Sigmundskronerstrasse, Bolzano* ☎ *0471/631264* 🌐 *www.messner-mountain-museum.it* 🎫 *€15* 🕑 *Closed Thurs. and mid-Nov.–mid-Mar.*

★ Museo Archeologico dell'Alto Adige
HISTORY MUSEUM | FAMILY | This museum has gained international fame for Ötzi, its 5,300-year-old iceman, discovered in 1991 and the world's oldest naturally preserved body. In 1998 Italy acquired it from Austria after it was determined that the body lay 100 yards inside Italian territory. The iceman's leathery remains are displayed in a freezer vault, preserved along with his longbow, ax, and clothing. The rest of the museum relies on models and artifacts from nearby archaeological sites, and exhibitions change regularly. An English audio guide leads you not only through Ötzi's Copper Age, but also into the preceding Mesolithic and Neolithic eras, and the Bronze and Iron Ages that followed. ✉ *Via Museo 43, Bolzano* ☎ *0471/320100* 🌐 *www.iceman.it* 🎫 *€13* 🕑 *Closed Mon. Jan.–June and Sept.–Nov.* ✍ *Online reservations recommended up to 3 days in advance.*

Passeggiata del Guncina
PROMENADE | FAMILY | An 8-km (5-mile) botanical promenade dating from 1892 ends with a panoramic view of Bolzano. Recent updates include signposting for various species of plants and trees, as well as benches and picnic tables. You can choose to return to town along the same path, or you can walk along the River Fago and end up back in the center of Bolzano. ✉ *Entrance near Vecchia Parrocchiale di Gries, across river and up Corsa Libertà, Bolzano* 🎫 *Free.*

Piazza delle Erbe
PLAZA/SQUARE | A bronze statue of Neptune, which dates from 1745, presides over this square's bountiful fruit and vegetable market. Stalls spill over with colorful displays of local produce; bakeries and grocery stores showcase hot breads, pastries, cheeses, and delicatessen meats—a complete picnic. Try the speck tirolese (cured and lightly smoked ham from Tyrol, Austria) and the apple strudel. ✉ *Piazza delle Erbe, Bolzano* 🎫 *Free.*

Favorite Places

Liz Humphreys: The six Messner Mountain Museums, started by Italian mountaineer Reinhold Messner to display his personal collections, are awesome. My fave is Firmian, inside Sigmundskron Castle, dating from 945 AD.

Piazza Walther
PLAZA/SQUARE | This pedestrians-only square is Bolzano's heart; in warmer weather it serves as an open-air living room where locals and tourists can be found at all hours sipping a drink (such as a glass of chilled Riesling). The piazza's namesake was the 12th-century German wandering minstrel Walther von der Vogelweide, whose songs lampooned the papacy and praised the Holy Roman Emperor. In the center of the piazza stands Heinrich Natter's white-marble, neo-Romanesque *Monument to Walther*, built in 1889. ✉ *Piazza Walther, Bolzano* 🎫 *Free.*

★ Renon (Ritten) Plateau
NATURE SIGHT | FAMILY | The earth pyramids of Renon Plateau are a bizarre geological formation where erosion has left a forest of tall, thin, needlelike spires of rock, each topped with a boulder. To get here, take the Soprabolzano cable car from Via Renon, about 300 yards left of the Bolzano train station. At the top, switch to the electric train that takes you to the

plateau, which is in Collalbo, just above Bolzano. The cable car takes about 12 minutes and the train takes around 18 minutes. The final 30-minute hike along gentle Trail No. 24 is free. *Via Renon, Collalbo 0471/356100 www.ritten.com Cable car €10 round-trip, electric train €6 round-trip.*

Restaurants

Batzen Häusl

$ | **ECLECTIC** | Locals hold animated conversations over pints of beer in this modern take on a traditional stube. Tasty South Tyrolean specialties include *bierspeckknodeln* (homemade beer bacon dumplings) and *bauerngröstl* (beef, onion, and potato fry-up), and there's also a wide menu of salads, pastas, and burgers. **Known for:** convivial atmosphere; home-brewed beer on tap; late-night dining. *$ Average main: €16 Via Andreas Hofer 30, Bolzano 0471/050950 www.batzen.it.*

Ristorante Cavallino Bianco

$ | **NORTHERN ITALIAN** | **FAMILY** | A spacious, comfortable dining room near Via dei Portici is a dependable favorite with locals and visitors alike. A wide selection of Italian and German dishes are served to large tables of families enjoying their meals together. **Known for:** generations of cooking; crowded, friendly atmosphere; local dishes, such as canederli in brodo (bread dumplings in broth). *$ Average main: €16 Via Bottai 6, Bolzano 0471/973267 www.weissesroessl.org Closed Sun. No dinner Sat.*

★ Wirtshaus Vögele

$$ | **NORTHERN ITALIAN** | Ask locals where they like to dine out, and odds are they'll tell you Vögele, one of the area's oldest inns, where the menu features Tyrolean standards such as *canederli* (bread dumplings) with speck and venison. The classic wood-paneled dining room on the ground level is often packed, but don't despair—the restaurant has two additional floors. **Known for:** friendly vibe; late dining; local dishes. *$ Average main: €23 Goethestr 3, Bolzano 0471/973938 www.voegele.it Closed Sun. No dinner Sat.*

Coffee and Quick Bites

★ Vögelino

$ | **ITALIAN** | The more casual little sister to long-standing favorite Vögele serves coffee and croissants for breakfast, plus all manner of focaccia, ice cream and cake, and aperitivo (think *stuzzichini*, or savory Italian snacks, and Aperol spritz) all day long. The prime spot on bustling Piazza Walther is perfect for people-watching while catching some rays. **Known for:** focaccia of the day; fine selection of wine and cocktails; pleasant central location. *$ Average main: €13 Piazza Walther 2, Bolzano 0338/8485646 www.voegelino.com Closed Sun.*

Hotels

Castel Hörtenberg

$$$ | **HOTEL** | The modern and the ancient contrast beautifully in the contemporary interiors of this renovated palace, only about a 10-minute walk from lively Piazza Walther, but in a quiet neighborhood that seems a world away. **Pros:** relaxing spa area with outdoor pool; lovely stone-walled restaurant in the old dungeon; large-size guest rooms. **Cons:** service can be standoffish at times; modern interior design a bit generic; no coffee- or teamaking facilities in the guest rooms. *$ Rooms from: €436 Via Monte Tondo 4, Bolzano 0471/1800355 www.castel-hoertenberg.com Closed 1 wk in Mar. 24 rooms Free Breakfast.*

★ Hotel Bad Schörgau

$$ | **HOTEL** | You'll get a warm welcome at this charming family-run hotel in the Sarentino Valley, which has incorporated natural materials into the design and an innovative philosophy into the menus, including a substantial cellar of natural wines. **Pros:** peaceful, relaxing

surroundings; delicious cuisine and wines; large, out-of-the-ordinary spa area. **Cons:** not much else around the immediate area; beds on the hard side; some rooms are carpeted. *Rooms from: €286* ✉ *Via Ronco 24, Sarentino* *17 km (11 miles) north of Bolzano* ☎ *0471/623048* *www.bad-schoergau.com* *Closed Mar.–mid-Apr. and June* *22 rooms* *Free Breakfast.*

★ Hotel Greif

$$ | **HOTEL** | Individually designed guest rooms in a centuries-old Bolzano landmark feature modern furnishings with clean lines, as well as contemporary art paired with 19th-century paintings and sketches. **Pros:** elegant decor; helpful staff; central location. **Cons:** rooms vary in size; some rooms have small windows; no on-site spa. *Rooms from: €243* ✉ *Piazza Walther 1, Bolzano* ☎ *0471/318000* *www.greif.it* *33 rooms* *Free Breakfast.*

Parkhotel Laurin

$$ | **HOTEL** | An exercise in Art Nouveau opulence, presiding over a large park in the middle of town, this elegant hotel features art-filled guest rooms, handsome public spaces, and an exceptional restaurant. **Pros:** convenient location; excellent restaurants; high standard of service. **Cons:** rooms facing park can be noisy; can be packed with business groups; decor a bit old-fashioned. *Rooms from: €241* ✉ *Via Laurin 4, Bolzano* ☎ *0471/311000* *www.laurin.it* *100 rooms* *Free Breakfast.*

Nightlife

Grifoncino

COCKTAIL BARS | The Hotel Greif's sleek, modern cocktail bar (where the actual bar is made out of empty bottles) serves the best libations in town. The drinks menu betrays a particular fondness for gin, but the staff also excel at making cocktails tailored to your preferences. In the summer months, the bar transfers to the hotel's rooftop. ✉ *Via della Rena 28, Bolzano* ☎ *0471/318000* *www.greif.it.*

Parkhotel Laurin Bar

BARS | The Laurin Bar hosts jazz combos on Friday between October and May and a jazz pianist every Saturday evening. In summer, the bar moves outside to the pretty garden, where a DJ spins tunes on Thursday night. ✉ *Via Laurin 4, Bolzano* ☎ *0471/311000* *www.laurin.it.*

Shopping

CRAFTS

Artigiani Atesini

CRAFTS | This is the largest store for locally made handcrafted goods. ✉ *Via Portici 39, Bolzano* ☎ *0471/978590* *www.facebook.com/suedtiroler.werkstaetten.*

MARKETS

Christkindlmarkt (*Christmas market*)

MARKET | **FAMILY** | From the end of November to the first week after New Year's there's a traditional Christkindlmarkt in Piazza Walther, with stalls selling all kinds of Christmas decorations and local handcrafted goods. ✉ *Piazza Walther, Bolzano* ☎ *0471/307000* *www.mercatinodinatalebz.it.*

Piazza della Vittoria

MARKET | A weekly flea market takes place Saturday morning in Piazza della Vittoria. ✉ *Piazza della Vittoria, Bolzano.*

Activities

BIKING

Südtirol Rad Bici Alto Adige

BIKING | **FAMILY** | If you're in decent shape, one great way to see some of the surrounding castles, lakes, and forested valleys of the Dolomites is by bike. Südtirol Rad can help with bike rentals from April till early November. ✉ *Via Renon 45, Bolzano* ☎ *0473/201500* *www.suedtirol-rad.com* *Bike rental from €25 per day.*

Bormio

97 km (60 miles) northwest of Madonna di Campiglio, 100 km (62 miles) southwest of Merano.

At the foot of Stelvio Pass, Bormio is the most famous ski resort on the western side of the Dolomites, with 50 km (31 miles) of long pistes and a nearly 6,000-foot vertical drop; the 2026 Winter Olympics men's downhill skiing and men's and women's ski mountaineering competitions will take place here. In summer its cool temperatures and clean air entice Italians away from cities on the humid Lombard plain. This dual-season popularity supports the plentiful shops, restaurants, and hotels in town. Bormio has been known for the therapeutic qualities of its waters since the Roman era, and there are numerous spas.

GETTING HERE AND AROUND

Take the SS239 North toward Dimaro. Turn onto the SS42 and follow it for 41 km (25 miles). Turn right onto Via Roma, and, after 2 km (1 mile), turn right onto Via Valtellina for 24 km (15 miles), and then turn right at SP78. Merge onto the SS38, and follow it to Bormio. In the summertime, you can choose to turn off the SS42 at Ponte di Legno, onto the SS300, and follow it to the end in Bormio. This takes you through Stelvio National Park. The nearest railway is in Tirano, which is half an hour away by bus. Tirano is serviced by Trenitalia and Italo, as well as the UNESCO World Heritage–designated Rhaetian Railway (Bernina Express).

VISITOR INFORMATION

CONTACT Bormio Tourism Office. ✉ *Via Roma 131/B, Bormio* ☎ *0342/903300* 🌐 *www.bormio.eu.*

Sights

Parco Nazionale dello Stelvio

NATIONAL PARK | FAMILY | The Alps' (and Italy's) biggest national park is spread over 1,350 square km (520 square miles) and four provinces. Opened in 1935 to preserve flora and protect fauna, today it has more than 1,200 types of plants, 600 different mushrooms, and more than 160 species of animals, including the chamois, ibex, and roe deer. There are many entrances to the park and five visitor centers. **TIP→ Bormio makes a good base for exploring—the closest entrance to town is the year-round gateway at Torre Alberti.** ✉ *Via Roma 131, Bormio* ☎ *0473/830430* 🌐 *www.parconazionale-stelvio.it* 🎫 *Free.*

Restaurants

Ristorante Kuerc

$$ | **NORTHERN ITALIAN | FAMILY** | This building was for centuries where justice was publicly served to accused witches, among others. Today, it's a great place to enjoy bewitching specialties like bresaola with rocket salad and Parmesan or *pizzoccheri* (buckwheat pasta) with garlic and winter vegetables. **Known for:** innovative gourmet dishes; pleasant location; interesting history. $ *Average main: €24* ✉ *Piazza Cavour 8, Bormio* ☎ *0342/910787* 🌐 *www.ristorantekuerc.it* ⏲ *Closed Tues.*

Hotels

La Genzianella

$$ | **HOTEL | FAMILY** | Unpretentious Alpine chic meets contemporary decor, with warm pine, ceramics, rich textiles, and wood-beamed ceilings—and all but one of the guest rooms have balconies. **Pros:** great for bikers; handy to slopes and town; excellent on-site restaurant. **Cons:** no pool; some beds are two twins pushed together; rooms can be compact. $ *Rooms from: €192* ✉ *Via Zandilla 6,*

Bormio ☎ 0342/904485 🌐 www.genzianella.com ⏲ Closed mid-Apr.–mid-May and late Sept.–mid-Dec. 39 rooms 🍽 Free Breakfast.

Activities

SKIING

★ Bormio Ski

SKIING & SNOWBOARDING | FAMILY | You can buy a ski pass and pick up a trail map at the base of the funivia (cable car), in the center of town (or buy the pass in advance online), before connecting to the Bormio 2000 station (6,600 feet) on Vallecetta, the main resort mountain. From there, you can ski down intermediate trails (the majority of Bormio's runs), use the extensive lift network to explore secondary ski areas, or get another funivia up to the Bormio 3000 station at Cima Bianca (9,800 feet) for more challenging terrain (the Stelvio slope will be the site of the men's downhill races in the 2026 Winter Olympics). The cable car also runs July to mid-September, when it is used by mountain bikers to reach long trails through breathtaking Alpine terrain; less ambitious visitors can wander around and then ride the cable car back down. ✉ *Via Battaglion Morbegno 25, Bormio* ☎ *0342/901451* 🌐 *www.bormioski.eu* *Ski pass from €54 for 1 day. Cable car Bormio–Bormio 2000 €17 round-trip; cable car Bormio 2000–Bormio 3000 €17 round-trip; cable car Bormio–Cima Bianca €26 round-trip.*

SPAS

Bormio Terme

SPA | FAMILY | From outdoor swimming pools to private baths, there are plenty of ways for the entire family to enjoy the healing qualities of the thermal waters. General admission gets you a full day in the pools, saunas, and Turkish baths. Spa and beauty treatments are also available; book ahead to avoid disappointment. You do not need to pay for the pools if you are only enjoying spa treatments. ✉ *Via Stelvio 14, Bormio* ☎ *0342/901325* 🌐 *www.bormioterme.it* *Entrance fee from €28; massages from €45; facials from €54.*

★ QC Terme Bagni Vecchi (*Old Baths*)

SPA | Ancient Roman baths predate the thermal springs, caves, and waterfalls that are now known as the Bagni Vecchi. Leonardo da Vinci soaked here in 1493, and today you can also take the waters, as well as book massages and treatments. The spa complex includes thermal baths, saunas, aromatherapy, and a salt grotto. Bagni Vecchi only accepts those aged 14 or older. ✉ *Via Bagni Nuovi 7, Molina* ☎ *0289/747201* 🌐 *www.qcterme.com* *Admission fee from €44; massages and facials from €54.*

Merano (Meran)

29 km (18 miles) north of Bolzano, 16 km (10 miles) east of Naturno.

The second-largest town in Alto Adige, Merano (Meran) was once the capital of the Austrian region of Tyrol. When the town and surrounding area were ceded to Italy as part of the 1919 Treaty of Versailles, Innsbruck became Tyrol's capital. Merano continued to be known as a spa town, attracting European nobility for its therapeutic waters and its "grape cure," which consists simply of eating the grapes grown on the surrounding hillsides. Sheltered by mountains, Merano has an unusually mild climate, with summer temperatures rarely exceeding 80°F (27°C) and winters that usually stay above freezing, despite the skiing within easy reach. Along the narrow streets of Merano's old town, houses have little towers and huge wooden doors, and the pointed arches of the Gothic cathedral sit next to neoclassical and Art Nouveau buildings. Merano serves as a good respite from mountain adventures, or from the bustle of nearby Trento and Bolzano.

GETTING HERE AND AROUND

By car from Bolzano, take the SP165 to the SP117 toward Merano (29 km [18 miles]). There is regular service by Trenitalia to the train station in Merano from many points in Italy.

VISITOR INFORMATION

CONTACT Merano Tourism Office. ✉ *Corso Libertà 45, Merano* ☎ *0473/272000* 🌐 *www.merano-suedtirol.it.*

Sights

★ Castel Trauttmansdorff

GARDEN | FAMILY | This Gothic castle was restored in the 19th century and now serves as a museum that celebrates more than 250 years of tourism in South Tyrol. But the real draw is the expansive garden, where exotic flora is organized by country of origin. The castle is about 2 km (1 mile) southeast of town on the Sentiero di Sissi; you can walk in about 45 minutes from the center of Merano on Sissi's Path, or take Bus No. 4 or 1B from the Merano train station. ✉ *Via Valentino 51/a, Merano* ☎ *0473/255600* 🌐 *www.trauttmansdorff.it* 🎫 *€17* 🕒 *Closed mid-Nov.–Mar.*

Chiesa di San Nicolò *(Duomo)*

CHURCH | The 14th-century Gothic cathedral, with a crenellated facade and an ornate campanile, sits in the heart of the old town. The Capella di Santa Barbara, just behind the Duomo, is an octagonal church containing a 15th-century pietà. **■ TIP→ Mass is held in German only.** ✉ *Piazza del Duomo, Merano* ☎ *0473/230174* 🌐 *www.stadtpfarre-meran.it* 🎫 *Free.*

Museo Agricolo di Brunnenburg

HISTORY MUSEUM | FAMILY | Overlooking the town, atop Mt. Tappeinerweg, is Castel Fontana, which was the home of poet Ezra Pound from 1958 to 1964. Still in the Pound family, the castle now houses the Museo Agricolo di Brunnenburg, devoted to Tyrolean country life. Among its exhibits are a smithy and a room with Pound memorabilia. ✉ *Ezra Pound Strada 3, Tirolo* ✣ *Take Bus No. 3, which departs every hr on the hr from Merano to Dorf Tirol (20 minutes)* ☎ *339/1803086 mobile* 🌐 *www.brunnenburg.net* 🎫 *€8* 🕒 *Closed Fri. and Sat., and early Nov.–mid-Apr.*

★ Promenades

PROMENADE | FAMILY | A stroll along one of Merano's well-marked, impossibly pleasant promenades may yield even better relaxation than time in its famous spa. Passeggiata Tappeiner (Tappeiner's Promenade) is a 3-km (2-mile) path with panoramic views from the hills north of the Duomo and diverse botanical pleasures along the way. Passeggiata d'Estate (Summer Promenade) runs along the shaded south bank of the Passirio River, and the Passeggiata d'Inverno (Winter Promenade), on the exposed north bank, provides more warmth and the Wandelhalle—a sunny area decorated with idyllic paintings of surrounding villages. The popular Austrian empress Sissi (Elisabeth of Wittelsbach, 1837–98) put Merano on the map as a spa destination; a trail named in her honor, the Sentiero di Sissi (Sissi's Walk), follows a path from Castel Trauttmansdorff to the heart of Merano. ✉ *Merano.*

Restaurants

★ Prezioso

$$$$ | MODERN ITALIAN | South Tyrol native Egon Heiss uses ingredients from Castel Fragsburg's gardens as well as produce from nearby organic farms, and meat and fish from area producers, to create his beautiful versions of hyperlocal dishes. Delicious items on Prezioso's five-course tasting menus may include potato dumplings with Alpine cheese, Alpine salmon, and lamb from the Funes Valley—traditional cuisine elevated by modern preparations and artful presentations. **Known for:** refined local cuisine; organic ingredients; mountainside setting. $ *Average main: €185* ✉ *Castel Fragsburg, Via Fragsburg 3, Merano* ✣ *8½ km (5 miles) southeast of Merano* ☎ *0473/244071* www.fragsburg.com Closed Sun., Mon., and mid-Nov.–mid-Apr. No lunch.

Saxifraga

$$ | **ITALIAN** | To reach this charming eatery, which occupies an enviable position overlooking Merano and the peaks enveloping the town, climb the stairs behind the Duomo or hike up along the Passeggiata Tappeiner. The kitchen serves well-prepared dumplings, pasta, and other local specialties—just don't leave without trying the homemade breads. **Known for:** charcuterie and cheeses; delicious desserts; beautiful views. *Average main: €20 Via Monte San Zeno 33, Passeggiata Tappeiner (Tappeiner's Promenade), Merano 0473/239249 www.saxifraga.it Closed Tues. and Nov.–Mar. No dinner Oct. and Apr.–mid-May.*

★ Sissi

$$$ | **NORTHERN ITALIAN** | The sterile surroundings of this restaurant, a short walk from Via dei Portici, belie its culinary delights—namely, rustic regional dishes reenergized and prepared with precision. Three-, five-, and seven-course tasting menus change according to the chef's whim and the season, but they usually include a modernized *vitello tonnato* (veal with tuna sauce), delightful homemade pasta and dumplings, and decadent meat dishes such as veal stewed in Lagrein, the area's renowned red wine; vegetarian options are also available. **Known for:** varied tasting menu; fantastic wine list; highly polished service. *Average main: €39 Via Galilei 44, Merano 0473/231062 sissi.andreafenoglio.com Closed Mon. and late Jan.–mid-Mar. No lunch Tues.*

Coffee and Quick Bites

Vinothek Relax

$ | **NORTHERN ITALIAN** | If you have difficulty choosing from the long list of tasty pizzas here, ask the friendly English-speaking staff for help with the menu. You're unlikely to find a better selection of wine, or a more pleasant environment for sampling; you can also buy bottles of the locally produced vintages to take home. **Known for:** large choice of wines; top-notch pizzas and local cuisine; helpful service. *Average main: €15 Via Cavour 31, opposite Palace Hotel, Merano 0473/236735 www.weine-relax.it Closed Thurs., Sun., and 2 wks in Feb. and Mar.*

Hotels

★ Castel Fragsburg

$$$ | **HOTEL** | For a taste of old-school Italian glamour just outside of Merano, you can't do better than this elegant Relais & Chateaux property high up in the mountains, set amid 4 acres of gardens and featuring a Michelin-starred restaurant and spa that both use products sourced from the land. **Pros:** beautiful landscape; wonderful spa concept; discreet, courteous service. **Cons:** not a lot of indoor common space for relaxing; classic decor not to everyone's taste; drive up to hotel not for faint of heart. *Rooms from: €580 Via Fragsburg 3, Merano 8½ km (5 miles) southeast of Merano 0473/244071 www.fragsburg.com Closed mid-Nov.–mid-Apr. 20 rooms Free Breakfast.*

★ Hotel Terme Merano

$$ | **HOTEL** | If you're in Merano to pamper yourself, you can't do much better than the Hotel Terme: as its name suggests, it's connected to the expansive Terme Merano (a stay here includes free, unlimited access via a "bathrobe tunnel"), and it also has the rooftop Sky Spa with indoor and outdoor pools and saunas. **Pros:** delicious breakfast offerings; well-equipped gym; very central location. **Cons:** rooms on the plain side; accommodations above bar can be noisy; staff can be unfriendly at times. *Rooms from: €386 Piazza Terme 1, Merano 0473/259000 www.hoteltermemerano.it 139 rooms Free Breakfast.*

★ **Miramonti Boutique Hotel**
$$$ | HOTEL | FAMILY | Perched up in the hills 4,035 feet above Merano, this striking Alpine hotel takes full advantage of its superlative views with floor-to-ceiling windows in the guest rooms, a panoramic restaurant, and an infinity pool. **Pros:** second-to-none mountain views; tasty and well-presented food at breakfast and dinner; kids' play area and dedicated splash time in the pool. **Cons:** three-night minimum stay; spa not open till noon and forest sauna till 2 pm; no air-conditioning in rooms. *Rooms from: €536 ✉ Via San Caterina 14 ✣ 12 km (7½ miles) southeast of Merano ☎ 0473/279335 ⊕ www.hotel-miramonti.com ⏲ Closed mid-Mar.–mid-Apr. 47 rooms Free Breakfast.*

Shopping

Via dei Portici (*Laubengasse*)
NEIGHBORHOOD | Merano's narrow, arcaded main shopping street runs west from the cathedral. Here you can find regional products—wood carvings, Tyrolean-style clothing, embroidery, cheeses, salami, and fruit schnapps—alongside standard clothing-boutique stock. ✉ *Via dei Portici, Merano.*

Activities

BIKING

Sissi Tours
BIKING | Merano makes for a scenic place to explore by bike, and Sissi Tours offers guided day trips that include e-bike rental and helmet. Tours are usually held in German, so ask in advance if English is preferred. ✉ *Viale Europa, Merano ☎ 0473/424344 ⊕ www.sissitours.it Full-day guided bike tour €104.*

SPAS

★ **Terme Merano**
SPA | FAMILY | This sprawling spa complex has 25 pools (15 indoor pools open year-round and 10 outdoor pools open from mid-May to mid-September) and six saunas (with an indoor "snow room" available for cooling down). Along with the family-friendly options for bathing, personalized services for grown-ups include traditional cures using local products, such as grape-based applications and hay baths. ✉ *Piazza Terme 9, Merano ☎ 0473/252000 ⊕ www.termemerano.it From €17 for 2 hrs in thermal baths; from €26 for 2 hrs in thermal baths and saunas; from €37 for full day's use of baths and saunas. Massages and facials from €72.*

Naturno (Naturns)

44 km (27 miles) northwest of Bolzano, 61 km (38 miles) east of Passo dello Stelvio.

As the name suggests, Naturno is a great location for a nature-based vacation; you can access a number of hiking trails to explore the area by foot. City planners have redesigned the town, reducing traffic and making the town more pedestrian-friendly. The locals take great pride in their produce; the fresh fruit, wine, and cheeses of this area are alone worth the drive.

GETTING HERE AND AROUND

By car from Bolzano, take the SS42 to the SS38 toward Merano. Naturno is 15 km (9 miles) past Merano. The town is very pedestrian-friendly, so talk to your hotel about where to leave your car, or head straight to a parking garage. Naturno is easily accessible by train from Bolzano or Merano.

VISITOR INFORMATION

CONTACT Naturno Tourism Office. ✉ *Via Municipio 1, Naturno ☎ 0473/666077 ⊕ www.merano-suedtirol.it.*

Stumbling on Ötzi

It was at the Similaun rifugio in September 1991 that a German couple arrived talking of a dead body they'd discovered near a "curious pickax." The couple, underestimating the age of the corpse by about 5,300 years, thought it was a matter for the police. This was to be the world's introduction to Ötzi, the oldest mummy ever found. World-famous mountaineers Reinhold Messner and Hans Kammerlander happened to be passing through the same rifugio during a climbing tour, and a few days later they were on the scene, freeing the iceman from the ice, and Ötzi's remarkable story was underway.

Today, you can see Ötzi on display, along with his longbow, ax, and clothes, at Bolzano's Museo Archeologico dell'Alto Adige, where he continues to be preserved at freezing temperatures.

Sights

Bräustüberl Forst (*FORST Brewery*)

BREWERY | The source of the full-flavored beer served throughout the region is the striking FORST Brewery, on the road connecting Naturno and Merano. Tours can be arranged if you call ahead, but you can also just turn up between late April and late September to sample the product line. In high season, cross a flower-lined covered wooden bridge to reach the delightful beer garden (Braugarten Forst), which then becomes a festive Christmas forest from mid-November to early January. ✉ *Via Venosta 10, Lagundo* ☎ *0473/221887* 🌐 *www.forst.it* 🎫 *Free* 🕐 *Beer garden closed late Sept.–late Apr.*

★ **Messner Mountain Museum Juval** (*Castel Juval*)

ART MUSEUM | **FAMILY** | Since 1983 this 13th-century castle in the hills above the hamlet of Stava has been the summer home of the South Tyrolese climber and polar adventurer Reinhold Messner—the first climber to conquer Everest solo. Part of the castle has been turned into one of six in Messner's chain of mountain museums, where visitors can view his collection of Tibetan art and masks from around the world. You can download an app to use as a self-guided tour. It's a 10-minute shuttle ride from the parking lot below, plus a 15-minute walk up to the castle, or a 60- to 90-minute hike on local trails; wear sturdy shoes, even if you take the shuttle, as the paths are uneven. ✉ *Juval 3, Castelbello* ☎ *0471/631264* 🌐 *www.messner-mountain-museum.it* 🎫 *€14, shuttle bus €12 round-trip* 🕐 *Closed Wed. and early Nov.–late Mar.*

St. Prokulus Kirchlein (*St. Proculus Church*)

CHURCH | Frescoes here are some of the oldest in the German-speaking world, dating from the 8th century. A small, modern museum offers multimedia installations (in Italian or German only) presenting four epochs in the region's history: ancient, medieval, Gothic, and the era of the Great Plague of 1636 (which claimed a quarter of Naturno's population, some of whom are buried in the church's cemetery). There are leaflets and other information in English on request. ✉ *Via San Procolo 1/a, Naturno* ☎ *348/673139 mobile* 🌐 *www.prokulus.org* 🎫 *€6* 🕐 *Closed Mon., Wed., weekends, and early Nov.–Mar.*

Did You Know?

There are three different hiking areas in Naturno: in the valley, wide easy paths traverse apple orchards and meadows; on the slopes of the Sonnenberg, trails run along ancient irrigation channels; the most popular hiking trail around Naturno is the Merano High Mountain Trail, a long-distance tour between mountain huts.

Caldaro (Kaltern)

15 km (9 miles) south of Bolzano.

This vineyard village, with clear views of castles high up in the surrounding mountains, represents the centuries of division that forged the unique character of the area. Caldaro architecture is famous for the way it blends Italian Renaissance elements of balance and harmony with the soaring windows and peaked arches of the Germanic Gothic tradition—the church of Santa Caterina, on the main square, is a good example. The warmest bathing lake in the Alps is just 4 km (2½ miles) away.

GETTING HERE AND AROUND

By car from Bolzano, follow the SS42 south toward Caldaro. This road is famously known as the Strada del Vino (Wine Road), and you will pass several vineyards along the way. If you head straight to the Wine Museum in Caldaro, you can pick up maps and plan a route through the vineyards based on specific tastes.

VISITOR INFORMATION

CONTACT Caldaro Tourism Office. ✉ *Marktplatz 8, Caldaro* ☎ *0471/963169* 🌐 *www.kaltern.com.*

Sights

★ Elena Walch

WINERY | This sustainably farmed 148-acre property produces some of the region's most renowned wines, in particular Gewürztraminer and Pinot Nero. It's overseen by Elena herself along with her daughters Julia and Karoline. Stop by their gorgeous Castel Ringberg site for a short vineyard hike (May through mid-October, by reservation), or have lunch at their Ostaria al Castello, which has panoramic views over the vines and down to Lake Caldaro. You can also do tastings in their historical cellar at a second vineyard site closer to Tramin (from May through August); the wine shop and bistro there are open daily year-round. ✉ *Castel Ringberg, San Giuseppe al Lago 1, Caldaro* ☎ *0471/860172* 🌐 *www.elenawalch.com* 🎫 *€25 for 1½-hr vineyard tour with wine tasting* 🕓 *Castel Ringberg wine shop and osteria closed mid-Oct.–Mar.*

★ South Tyrolean Wine Museum

SPECIALTY MUSEUM | Head here to learn how local wine has historically been made, stored, served, and worshipped, through a series of entertaining exhibits. ✉ *Via dell'Oro 1, near main square, Caldaro* ☎ *0471/963168* 🌐 *www.museo-del-vino.it* 🎫 *€6* 🕓 *Closed Sun., Mon., and mid-Nov.–Mar.*

Restaurants

★ Alois Lageder Paradeis

$$ | **NORTHERN ITALIAN** | Just off of the Strada del Vino (Wine Road), this charming eatery and wine bar lets you indulge in seasonal dishes while sampling some of the biodynamic wines produced by one of the Trentino area's most well-known vintners. When the weather's nice, dining in the pretty courtyard among lemon trees, with mountaintops visible just behind, really lives up to the "paradise" name. **Known for:** gorgeous gardenlike setting; organic ingredients, including produce from their veggie garden; chance to sample older vintages for a great price. 💲 *Average main: €22* ✉ *Via Casòn Hirschprunn 1, Margrè* ☎ *0471/809580* 🌐 *en.paradeis-aloislageder.eu* 🕓 *Closed Sun. No dinner.*

Hotels

★ SEELEITEN – Lake Spa Hotel

$$$ | **HOTEL** | **FAMILY** | If you need somewhere to lay your head after a day of visiting the nearby wineries, this ultramodern property near Lake Caldero, owned by the Moser family, has beautiful views, an expansive spa, a private beach area on the lake, and its own vineyards. **Pros:** spectacular views; beautiful

grounds; relaxing spa and beach areas. **Cons:** rooms can be pricey; may hear some traffic noise; only buffet offered for lunch (included in rate). *Rooms from: €568 Strada del Vino 30, Caldaro 0471/960200 www.seeleiten.it 71 rooms All-Inclusive.*

Bressanone (Brixen)

42 km (25 miles) northeast of Bolzano.

Bressanone is an important artistic center and was the seat of prince-bishops for centuries. Like their counterparts in Trento, these medieval administrators had the delicate task of serving two masters—the pope (the ultimate spiritual authority) and the Holy Roman Emperor (the civil and military power), who were virtually at war throughout the Middle Ages. Bressanone's prince-bishops became experts at tact and diplomacy.

The Guestpass BrixenCard offers free transportation throughout Alto Adige (Südtirol/South Tyrol) and includes a free ride on the Plose lift (from late May to mid-October), entry to three local museums, and discounts at partner venues; it's free to guests of local hotels.

GETTING HERE AND AROUND

Driving from Bolzano, follow the SS12 northeast 42 km (26 miles) to Bressanone. Trains run from Bolzano (28 minutes), as does Sudtirol bus No. 350 (75 minutes).

VISITOR INFORMATION

CONTACT Bressanone Tourism Office. *Regensburger Allee 9, Bressanone 0472/275252 www.brixen.org.*

Sights

Abbazia di Novacella

CHURCH | This Augustinian abbey founded in 1142 has been producing wine for at least nine centuries and is most famous for the delicate stone-fruit character of its dry white Sylvaner. As you wander the delightful grounds, note the progression of Romanesque, Gothic, and Baroque building styles. Guided tours of the abbey, in various languages, depart daily except Sunday. Guided tours of the vineyard are also available, in English, by reservation. *Via Abbazia 1, Varna* *3 km (2 miles) north of Bressanone* *0472/836189* *www.kloster-neustift.it* *Abbey visit €12 with audioguide, €17 with guided tour; wine tastings with vineyard tour €25* *Closed Sun.*

Duomo di Bressanone

CHURCH | The imposing town cathedral was built in the 13th century but acquired a baroque facade 500 years later; its 14th-century cloister is decorated with medieval frescoes. *Piazza Duomo 1, Bressanone* *0471/306200* *www.bz-bx.net* *Free.*

Restaurants

★ Fink Restaurant

$$ | **NORTHERN ITALIAN** | This warm, wood-paneled upstairs dining room, under the arcades of the pedestrians-only town center, serves creative Tyrolean dishes made with ingredients grown in the city's monastery gardens. Owner/chef Florian Fink creates seasonally rotating three- to five-course tasting menus along with satisfying plates using local vegetables, meat, and fish, such as black bread ricotta dumplings with venison ragout. **Known for:** using regional and seasonal products; elegant historical atmosphere; central location. *Average main: €29* *Kleine Lauben 4, Bressanone* *0472/834883* *www.fink1896.it* *Closed Sun. and Mon.*

★ Restaurant Apostelstube

$$$$ | **ECLECTIC** | In a pretty art deco setting inside Hotel Elephant, wunderkind chef Mathias Bachmann whips up beautifully presented and creative Italian cuisine with an Asian flair in his nightly six-course tasting menus. Dishes change with the seasons, but if they're on the menu, don't miss the nori tartlet with asparagus or Hokkaido Wagyu with miso and black applesauce. **Known for:** using seasonal products; thoughtful wine pairings; elegant atmosphere. *Average main: €165* *Hotel Elephant, Via Rio Bianco 4, Bressanone* *0472/832750* *www.hotelelephant.com* *Closed Mon.–Thurs. No lunch.*

Hotels

★ Fink Restaurant & Suites

$$ | **B&B/INN** | This friendly, intimate hotel in the center of town combines history with modernity in its spacious, minimalist suites—some with original ceiling frescoes—inside a house dating from 1450. **Pros:** cozy, charming atmosphere; fabulous on-site restaurant; guests (ages 10 and over) can use spa 24 hours a day. **Cons:** hotel lacks accessibility due to the historical structure; no hotel bar; no fitness center. *Rooms from: €284* *Kleine Lauben 4, Bressanone* *0472/834883* *www.fink1896.it* *9 rooms* *Free Breakfast.*

★ Forestis

$$$$ | **HOTEL** | It's all about the views at this minimalistic yet quietly luxurious retreat (for guests age 14 and over) high up in the mountains at 1,800 meters (5,900 feet), reached by winding roads through the pretty forest—rooms in the main building exude cozy mountain chalet vibes, while those in the Tower have a more polished feel along with astounding Alpine views in the suites and penthouses, two of which boast their own fireplace, sauna, and outdoor pool. **Pros:** unbeatable vistas from all guest rooms; delicious food at breakfast and dinner;

Hiking the Dolomites

In 2009 UNESCO (the United Nations Educational, Scientific, and Cultural Organization) added the Dolomites to its list of natural heritage sites. The dramatic terrain, inspiring vistas, and impossibly pleasant climate are complemented by excellent facilities for enjoying the mountains.

Picking a Trail

The Dolomites have a well-maintained network of trails for hiking and rock climbing. As long as you're in reasonably good shape, the number of appealing hiking options can be overwhelming. Trails are well marked and designated by grades of difficulty: T for tourist path, H for hiking path, EE for expert hikers, and EEA for equipped expert hikers. On any of these paths you're likely to see carpets of mountain flowers between clutches of dense evergreens, with chamois and roe deer milling about.

If you're just out for a day in the mountains, you can leave the details of your walk open until you're actually on the spot; local tourist offices (especially those in Cortina and Madonna) can help you choose the right route based on trail conditions, weather, and desired exertion level.

Traveling the Vie Ferrate

If you're looking for an adventure somewhere between hiking and climbing, consider a guided trip along the vie ferrate, or "iron paths" (🌐 *www.ferrate365.it*). These routes offer fixed climbing aids (steps, ladders, bridges, safety cables) left by Alpine divisions of the Italian and Austro-Hungarian armies and later converted for recreational use. Previous experience is generally not required, but vertigo-inducing heights do demand a strong stomach.

Bedding Down

One of the pleasures of an overnight adventure in the Dolomites is staying at a rifugio, one of the refuges that dot the mountainsides, often in remote locations. There are hundreds of them, and they range in comfort from spartan to posh. Most fall somewhere in between—they're cozy mountain lodges with dormitory-style accommodations. Pillows and blankets are provided (there's no need to carry a sleeping bag), but you have to supply your own sheet. Bathrooms are usually shared, with cold showers. Reservations are a must, especially in August, although Italian law requires rifugi to accept travelers for the night if there's insufficient time to reach other accommodations before dark.

Eating Well

Food is as much a draw at rifugi as location. The rustic dishes, such as salami, dumplings, and hearty stews, are all excellent—an impressive feat, made all the more remarkable when you consider that supplies often have to arrive by helicopter. Your bed for the night, with breakfast and dinner included, may cost from €70 to €90 per person. Snacks and packed lunches are available for purchase, but many opt to sit down for the midday meal. Multilingual stories are swapped, food and wine shared, and new adventures launched.

all-inclusive minibar drinks and snacks. **Cons:** sometimes overrun by influencers; Alpine roads to the hotel challenging for some; quite expensive. *Rooms from: €890 ✉ Palmschoss 22, Bressanone ✣ 20 km (12 miles) southeast of Brixen ☏ 0472/521008 ⊕ www.forestis.it ⏲ Closed Apr.–late May 62 rooms Free Breakfast.*

★ Hotel Elephant

$$ | HOTEL | At this recently renovated cozy inn—more than 500 years old and still one of the region's best—each room is unique, and many are filled with antiques and paintings. **Pros:** lovely ambience; good restaurants; lavish breakfast. **Cons:** rooms vary in size; soundproofing in rooms could be better; some bathrooms are small. *Rooms from: €232 ✉ Via Rio Bianco 4, Bressanone ☏ 0472/832750 ⊕ www.hotelelephant.com 44 rooms Free Breakfast.*

Brunico (Bruneck)

33 km (20 miles) east of Bressanone, 65 km (40 miles) northwest of Cortina d'Ampezzo.

Located in the heart of the Val Pusteria, this quiet and quaint town is divided by the Rienza River. The modern part of Brunico is on one side of the river, and on the other is the medieval quarter, nestled below a 13th-century bishop's castle.

GETTING HERE AND AROUND

From Bressanone follow the E66 east for 30 km (19 miles) to Brunico. If driving from Cortina d'Ampezzo, take the SR51 to Toblach and continue to the SS49 toward Brunico. There are bus (SAD) and train (Trenitalia) connections available at Bolzano.

VISITOR INFORMATION

CONTACT Brunico Tourism Office. *✉ Piazza Municipio 7, Brunico ☏ 0474/555722 ⊕ www.bruneck.com.*

Sights

★ Lumen Museum

ART MUSEUM | Take a cable car to the top of Kronplatz to reach this 19,375-square-foot museum dedicated to mountain photography (actually, you have your choice of eight different cable cars, two from the town of Brunico). Once inside, you'll find pictures from Alpine photography's early days all the way to the present, taken by photographers from mountainous regions throughout the world and displayed across four floors. Lumen also houses AlpiNN, a casual restaurant from critically acclaimed chef Norbert Niederkofler of St. Hubertus fame. Note that the museum can be difficult to access in winter if you're not a skier; it's down a slight, rather terrifying incline from the top of the mountain. Be aware that the museum closes at 4 pm (last admission at 3:30), so that you won't miss the last cable car back down. *✉ Kronplatz–Plan de Corones Mountain Station, Brunico ✣ Take a cable car up to Kronplatz ☏ 0474/431090 ⊕ www.lumenmuseum.it €17 ⏲ Closed mid-Apr.–May and mid- to late Nov.*

★ Messner Mountain Museum Corones

SPECIALTY MUSEUM | FAMILY | High atop the Mountain Station Kronplatz–Plan de Corones, almost 7,500 feet above Brunico, the newest museum from mountaineer Reinhold Messner displays climbing equipment and other Alpine paraphernalia from the 1800s until now. It also examines all facets of mountaineering through painting, sculpture, and other media. Equally interesting is the museum's Zaha Hadid–designed concrete building: its sloped roof makes it seem like a miniature mountain, and its outdoor lookout point affords magnificent vistas. Note that the museum closes at 4 pm (last admission at 3:30), so that you won't miss the last cable car back down. *✉ Kronplatz–Plan de Corones Mountain Station, Brunico ✣ Take a cable car up to Kronplatz ☏ 0474/501350 ⊕ www.*

The Three Peaks in Misurina are one of the most famous landmarks in the Dolomites.

messner-mountain-museum.it 🎫 *€14* ⏲ *Closed mid-Apr.–May and early–late Nov.*

★ Messner Mountain Museum Ripa

SPECIALTY MUSEUM | **FAMILY** | This fascinating, comprehensive museum within the 13th-century Bruneck Castle looks at the lives of mountain-dwelling people from Europe, Asia, Africa, and South America through artifacts, tools, statues, paintings, living spaces, and more. Part of the experience is reaching the castle itself: it's a 15-minute hike up to it on a path accessed just off Brunico's pedestrian area. ✉ *Schlossweg 2, Brunico* ☎ *0474/410220* 🌐 *www.messner-mountain-museum.it* 🎫 *€14* ⏲ *Closed Tues., late Apr.–mid-May, and early Nov.–early Dec.*

Restaurants

★ Albergo Oberraut Ristorante

$$ | **ITALIAN** | Drive up into the hills about 12 minutes northeast of Brunico to reach this charming chalet-style family-run eatery, which has an expansive terrace with great views overlooking the mountains. Hearty dishes use local ingredients—including meat from their farm, vegetables from their gardens and greenhouses, and grain from their own mill—and the delightful servers are happy to recommend seasonal specialties. **Known for:** zero-kilometer philosophy; deer and beef dishes; Alpine vistas. $ *Average main: €22* ✉ *Via Ameto 1, Brunico* ☎ *0474/559977* 🌐 *oberraut.it* ⏲ *Closed Thurs.*

★ Atelier Moessmer Norbert Niederkofler

$$$$ | **MODERN ITALIAN** | Renowned Italian chef Norbert Niederkofler, formerly of three-Michelin-star St. Hubertus in San Cassiano, creates zero-kilometer cuisine out of alpine ingredients in an historical villa owned by the Moessmers, a prosperous textile family. The "Cook the Mountain" menu includes 14 dishes that change with the seasons; pair them with fantastic local wines or unique house-made nonalcoholic beverages. **Known for:** superlative tasting menus using hyperlocal ingredients; villa tour, including the kitchen, as part of the experience; signature menu additions, including white fish tartare and beet root gnocchi. *Average main: €320 Via Walther von der Vogelweide 17, Brunico 0474/646629 ateliernorbertniederkofler.com Closed Mon. and Tues. No dinner Sun. No lunch Wed.–Fri.*

Hotels

Falkensteiner Hotel Kronplatz

$$$ | HOTEL | FAMILY | This family-friendly ultramodern hotel near the Plan de Corones chairlift, made up of four sleek connected houses designed by Italian architect Matteo Thun, offers spacious rooms and an expansive spa. **Pros:** eager-to-help staff; extravagant breakfast buffet; wonderful spa area. **Cons:** service can be distracted at times; not all rooms have mountain views; can hear traffic noise in some rooms. *Rooms from: €465 Via Funivia 1/c, Brunico 0474/862400 www.falkensteiner.com Closed late Apr.–late May 97 rooms All-Inclusive.*

Majestic Hotel & Spa

$$ | HOTEL | FAMILY | Right in front of the Plan de Corones chairlift, this is a great base for a skiing or hiking vacation, with bus service to the ski slopes and a spa and pools on-site to unwind after a big day out. **Pros:** convenient for skiers and hikers; nice indoor and outdoor pools; spacious rooms. **Cons:** meal portions are a little small; no covered parking; far from town center. *Rooms from: €312 Via Im Gelände 20, Brunico 0474/410993 www.hotel-majestic.it 60 rooms Free Breakfast.*

Misurina

115 km (71 miles) east of Bolzano.

Nestled on the shores of Lake Misurina, among the Dolomites, Misurina's high altitude, low air humidity, and total absence of dust mites and air pollution has some saying that the "Pearl of the Dolomites" has some of the purest air in the world. The town itself is rather small, but it's a perfect base to explore Lake Misurina and the Tre Cime of Lavaredo. The surrounding mountains are rich in history and artifacts from the First World War and earlier conflicts. Along some of the hikes and vie ferrate (mountain paths with steel cables and fixed anchors and ladders), you can explore caves and trenches complete with informational placards giving details about troop positions and fighting.

GETTING HERE AND AROUND

From Brunico, drive southeast on the SS49/E66 to Dobbiaco. Turn right onto SS51 and drive for 13 km (8 miles). Turn left onto SP49 in the direction of Auronzo. Arrive at Lago di Misurina in 6 km (4 miles).

VISITOR INFORMATION

CONTACT Misurina Tourism Office. *Via Monte Piana 2, Misurina 0435/39016 auronzomisurina.it.*

Sights

★ Tre Cime di Lavaredo

MOUNTAIN | FAMILY | Without a doubt, the Three Peaks—Cima Piccola (9,373 feet), Cima Grande (9,839 feet), and Cima Ovest (9,753 feet)—are the symbols of the Dolomite UNESCO World Heritage site. From the town of Misurina, only two of the Tre Cime are visible. In order to get up close and personal, drive or take a bus along the dedicated toll road (usually open June through October; toll of €30). Once at the top, follow Footpath 101 from Rifugio Auronzo to Forcella Laveredo (easy) for about an hour. There are many other footpaths and vie ferrate which allow you to climb the cime and access the base. Rifugi offer hot meals without a reservation, as well as dorm-style lodging, which is best reserved in advance. ✉ *Parco Naturale Tre Cime, Auronzo di Cadore* ☎ *0435/99603* 🌐 *www.drei-zinnen.info.*

Restaurants

Malga Rin Bianco

$$ | NORTHERN ITALIAN | FAMILY | For fresh, properly cooked regional food, this *malga* (Alpine hut) with great mountain views can't be beat—just make a reservation, especially in winter, when you must be transported over on a snowmobile by day and a shuttle at night (in summer, you can drive all the way). Salamis and cheeses are made on-site, and the bar serves both commercial and homemade grappas, many of which are brewed with local herbs; also try some *capriolo* (mountain goat stew), polenta, *skitz* (grilled cheese that doesn't melt), or fresh local mushrooms. **Known for:** scenic mountain location; local food; great views. $ *Average main: €28* ✉ *Via Monte Piana 35, Strada Tre Cime, Misurina* ☎ *0320/5699375* 🌐 *www.rinbianco.com* ⏲ *Closed 1 month after Easter, and Nov.*

Hotels

Chalet Lago Antorno

$$ | B&B/INN | FAMILY | Located in a quiet, panoramic spot, this chalet is ideal for exploring the mountains or simply relaxing amid the beauty of the Alps. **Pros:** family-run; typical decor and regional flavor; idyllic mountain setting. **Cons:** away from town center; food gets mixed reviews; some rooms are small. $ *Rooms from: €217* ✉ *Località Lago Misurina, Misurina* ☎ *0320/9625700* 🌐 *www.lagoantorno.it* ⏲ *Closed late Oct.–late Dec.* *10 rooms* *Free Breakfast.*

Grand Hotel Misurina

$$ | HOTEL | FAMILY | On the shores of beautiful Lake Misurina and just a few kilometers from renowned winter resort Cortina d'Ampezzo, this grand hotel has simply furnished rooms that range from standard fare to full apartments. **Pros:** amazing scenery; perfect for large groups; shuttle to ski areas. **Cons:** rooms have simple furnishings; dated decor; extra charge and limited time slots for the spa. $ *Rooms from: €185* ✉ *Via Monte Piana 21, Misurina* ☎ *0435/39191* 🌐 *www.grandhotelmisurina.com* ⏲ *Closed mid-Mar.–mid-May and mid-Oct.–mid-Dec.* *125 rooms* *Free Breakfast.*

Activities

BIKING

Cycling enthusiasts flock to the Dolomites for the challenging mountain terrain, and much of the region is used by Olympic athletes to train. Some of the descents along gravelly roads set off a rush of adrenaline, while others follow paved roads and bike paths. The Auronzo-Misurina Cycle Track provides about 32 km (20 miles) of bicycle path between the two towns.

SKIING

Two major ski lifts service the area: the Col de Varda lift in Misurina, and the Monte Agudo lift in Auronzo di Cadore (about a 30-minute drive from Misurina), which takes you from Taiarezze (2,952 feet) to Rifugio Monte Agudo (5,160 feet). The views from Auronzo differ from Misurina in that all Tre Cime are visible. Restaurants and maps are available at the top.

Col de Varda

SKIING & SNOWBOARDING | FAMILY | The major ski lift servicing the area from Misurina climbs to Col de Varda, with a summit of 6,909 feet. Rifugio Col de

Varda, at the top, has a bar and restaurant, as well as rooms to rent. In the summer, the area is an excellent starting point for great hiking and biking excursions. At any time of the year, the views of Lake Misurina, Mt. Cristallo, the Sesto Dolomites, and the Cadini, Sorapiss, and Tofane massifs are breathtaking. ✉ *Misurina* ☎ *0435/39013* 🌐 *auronzomisurina.it* 🎟 *€15 round-trip.*

Monte Cristallo
SKIING & SNOWBOARDING | Some of the most impressive views (and steepest slopes) are on Monte Cristallo. ✉ *Misurina* ☎ *0436/861035* 🌐 *faloriacristallo.it* 🎟 *From €70 for 1-day pass.*

Canazei

45 km (28 miles) southwest of Misurina.

Of the year-round resort towns in the Val di Fassa, Canazei is the most popular. The mountains around this small town are threaded with hiking trails and ski slopes set amid large clutches of conifers.

GETTING HERE AND AROUND

Bus service from Bolzano and Bressanone (the nearest train stations) is infrequent, and schedules are often interrupted or canceled. By car from the A22 autostrada, take the Bolzano Nord exit onto the SS241. Cross the Passo Costalunga into the Val di Fassa. From the town of Vigo, follow signs for Canazei.

VISITOR INFORMATION

CONTACT Canazei Tourism Office. ✉ *Piazza G. Marconi 5, Canazei* ☎ *0462/609500* 🌐 *www.fassa.com.*

Sights

★ Col Rodella
VIEWPOINT | **FAMILY** | An excursion from Campitello di Fassa, about 4 km (2½ miles) west of Canazei, to the vantage point at Col Rodella has unmissable views. A cable car rises some 3,000 feet to a full-circle vista of the Heart of the Dolomites, including the Sasso Lungo and the rest of the Sella range. ✉ *Localita' Ischia 1, Canazei* ☎ *0462/608811* 🌐 *www.valdifassalift.it* 🎟 *Col Rodella cable car €26 round-trip.*

Passo Pordoi
MOUNTAIN | **FAMILY** | At 7,346 feet, Passo Pordoi is the highest surface-road pass in the Dolomites. It connects Arabba, in Val Cordevole (Province of Belluno), with Canazei, in Val di Fossa (Province of Trento). Views from the top include the Sassolungo and Sella group of mountains, and even the Marmolada Glacier. There are several hotels and a ski school located at the pass, as well as some souvenir shops, restaurants, and snack carts. While the hotels are not glamorous, some do offer half-board packages at reasonable rates. The road up to the pass from Canazei has a few scenic and picnic pull-offs, plus 28 hairpin turns.

Skiing is available year-round. The most popular winter skiing areas are Belvedere and Sella Ronda, and much of the area is part of the Dolomiti Superski package. Even if the road for the pass is closed, many of the cable cars in neighboring valley towns will be running to various summits.

From Passo Pordoi you can get a cable car (May through October) to the Sass Pordoi, often called the Terrazza delle Dolomiti (Terrace of the Dolomites). At more than 9,100 feet, it offers myriad hiking trails and vie ferrate with varying degrees of difficulty (none of which are easy), leading to rifugi and the region's other peaks and passes. ✉ *Strada del Pordoi, Canazei* ☎ *0462/608811* 🌐 *www.valdifassalift.it* 🎟 *Sass Pordoi cable car €28 round-trip.*

Hotels

Albergo Alla Rosa
$ | **HOTEL** | Ask for a room with a balcony: the view of the imposing Dolomites is the real attraction in accommodations

that pleasantly blend rustic and contemporary furnishings. **Pros:** in the center of town; great views; plentiful breakfast buffet. **Cons:** five-night minimum stays in summer; extra charge for parking and only by reservation; no restaurant for lunch or dinner. *Rooms from: €161* *Strada del Faure 18, Canazei* *0462/601107* *www.hotelallarosa.com* *Closed late Mar.–mid-June and mid-Sept.–early Dec.* *49 rooms* *Free Breakfast.*

Ortisei (St. Ulrich)

28 km (17 miles) northwest of Canazei.

Ortisei (St. Ulrich), the jewel in the crown of Val Gardena's resorts, is a hub of activity in both summer and winter; there are hundreds of miles of hiking trails and accessible ski slopes. Ortisei has been a family-friendly mountain vacation destination since the 1930s. The most famous cable car in the area, the Alpe di Siusi, operates in summer and winter. As the largest village in the Val Gardena, Ortisei makes a picturesque and practical base for exploring much of the heart of the Dolomites.

For centuries Ortisei has also been famous for the expertise of its wood carvers, and there are still numerous workshops. Apart from making religious sculptures—particularly the wayside calvaries you come upon everywhere in the Dolomites—Ortisei's carvers were long known for producing wooden dolls, horses, and other toys. As itinerant peddlers, they traveled every spring on foot with their loaded packs as far as Paris, London, and St. Petersburg. Shops in town still sell woodcrafts.

GETTING HERE AND AROUND

By car from Bolzano, take the SS12 to the SS242 in the direction of Ortisei. From Canazei, follow the SS242 north to Ortisei. Free bus service is available from participating accommodations on the Val Gardena network from Bolzano and Bressanone and other points around the region. The Gardena Card gives unlimited use of all the lifts (18) of the region for one price (www.gardena-card.com).

VISITOR INFORMATION

CONTACT Ortisei Tourist Office. *Via Rezia 1, Ortisei* *0471/777600* *www.valgardena.it.*

Sights

Alpe di Siusi Cable Car

TRANSPORTATION | FAMILY | First opened in 1935, the cable car from Ortisei to Alpe di Siusi climbs more than 6,100 feet to the widest plateau in Europe. There are more than 57 square km (22 square miles) of Alpine pastures lined with summertime hiking trails. In the winter, 20 ski lifts and cross-country ski paths keep active visitors happy. There is a restaurant at the top of the Mt. Seuc ski lift, or you can pick up a map at the tourist office in Ortisei listing the mountain huts and restaurants that can be reached on foot. Opening days and times depend on the season and daily weather conditions; check the website or call ahead to avoid disappointment. *Setil Strada 9, Ortisei* *0471/797897* *www.funiviaortisei.eu* *€35 round-trip* *Closed early Nov.–early Dec. and early Apr.–mid-May.*

Museo della Val Gardena

ART MUSEUM | FAMILY | Fine historic and contemporary examples of local woodworking are on display here, as well as a retrospective on the life of local film director Luis Trenker. *Via Rezia 83, Ortisei* *0471/797554* *www.museumgherdeina.it* *€8* *Closed early Apr.–mid-May and Sept.–early Dec.; closed Sat.–Mon. early Dec.–early Apr. (except Dec. 26–Jan. 6), Sat. afternoon and Sun. July and Aug., and weekends mid-May–June.*

Hotels

Adler Spa Resort Dolomiti

$$$$ | HOTEL | FAMILY | Set dramatically in the foothills, the Adler Spa Resort Dolomiti is a luxe chalet home base for skiing the magnificent UNESCO World Heritage peaks—with two lifts within walking distance—or exploring the spectacular surroundings with cable car rides, hiking, and mountain- or e-biking. **Pros:** many activities on offer year-round; attentive staff; one of the best spas in the area. **Cons:** rooms can be pricey; standard rooms can be small; kids' club only starts from age four. *Rooms from: €626* *Strada Rezia 7, Ortisei* *0471/775000* *www.adler-resorts.com* *Closed early Apr.–mid-May* *108 rooms* *Free Breakfast.*

★ **Cavallino Bianco Family Spa Grand Hotel**

$$$$ | RESORT | FAMILY | With delicate wooden balconies and an eye-catching wooden gable, the pink Cavallino Bianco (Little White Horse) looks like a gigantic dollhouse, and it is, in fact, marketed toward families. **Pros:** excellent family facilities; cheerful rooms; laundry facilities. **Cons:** in the busy town center; public areas a bit dated; very expensive. *Rooms from: €732* *Via Rezia 22, Ortisei* *0471/783333* *www.cavallino-bianco.com* *Closed mid-Apr.–mid-May* *104 rooms* *All-Inclusive.*

★ **COMO Alpina Dolomites**

$$$$ | HOTEL | FAMILY | This architecturally stunning property in the Alpe di Siusi, with a facade of wood and quartzite, has three restaurants, a serious spa area, and its own ski rental service. **Pros:** ski-in, ski-out, plus hiking right out the door; complimentary minibars; excellent breakfast selection. **Cons:** interior design choices not to everyone's taste; rooms can be too warm at times; a trek to reach Ortisei. *Rooms from: €822* *Localita Compatsch 62/3, Ortisei* *0471/796004* *www.comohotels.com* *Closed Apr.–early June and late Oct.–early Dec.* *60 rooms* *Free Breakfast.*

Activities

SKIING

With almost 600 km (370 miles) of accessible downhill slopes and more than 90 km (56 miles) of cross-country skiing trails, Ortisei is one of the most popular ski resorts in the Dolomites. Prices are good, and facilities are among the most modern in the region. In warmer weather, the slopes surrounding Ortisei are a popular hiking destination, as well as a playground for vehicular mountain adventures like biking, rafting, and paragliding.

Sella Ronda

SKIING & SNOWBOARDING | FAMILY | An immensely popular ski route, the Sella Ronda relies on well-placed chairlifts to connect 26 km (16 miles) of downhill skiing around the colossal Sella massif, passing through several towns along the way. You can ski the loop, which requires intermediate ability and a full day's effort, either clockwise or counterclockwise. Going with a guide is recommended. *Ortisei, Ortisei* *0471/777777* *www.val-gardena.com* *From €75 for 1-day Dolomiti Superski ski pass.*

Corvara

29 km (18 miles) east of Ortesei (St. Ulrich).

Corvara is the main town of the Alta Badia, known for its prime skiing and hiking location in the middle of the Sella Ronda. The first chairlift in Italy opened here in 1946, and today there are two cable cars—the Col Alto and the Boè—along with 11 chairlifts, making Corvara a convenient base for an active holiday in winter or summer. Corvara is also the start of the First World War Ski Tour, a 79-km (49-mile) route around Col di

Lana that takes you past wartime relics like trenches and forts. The town itself is pleasant and walkable, with a smattering of restaurants, bars, and ski rental and sporting goods stores.

GETTING HERE AND AROUND

To get to Corvara from Bolzano, take the A22 north to Bressanone/Pusteral. Turn right on the SS244, and take it all the way to Corvara. From Ortisei, take the SS242 to the SS243 into Corvara. Buses arrive many times daily from Bolzano and Bressanone.

VISITOR INFORMATION

CONTACTS Corvara Tourist Office. ✉ *Strada Col Alt 36, Corvara* ☎ *0471/836176* 🌐 *www.altabadia.org.*

Sights

Boè Cable Car

TRANSPORTATION | FAMILY | This cable car takes hikers and skiers from Corvara up Piz Boè, the highest mountain of the Sella group, at 10,341 feet. Once at the first station, you can hike the Sella Ronda, ski back down, or ride a chairlift farther up to the Vallon Peak for more challenging skiing or hiking in the warmer months. Paragliding is also popular from the Vallon area. ✉ *Strada Burjé 10, Corvara* ☎ *0471/836073* 🌐 *www.moviment.it/en/boe-ski-lift-corvara.php* 🎫 *€21.80 round-trip.*

Col Alto Cable Car

TRANSPORTATION | FAMILY | The site of Italy's first chairlift in 1946 now has modern yellow eight-seater cable cars that ascend to a height of 6,562 feet. From there you have access to ski lifts that take you all over the Alta Badia region and, in summer, to trails that include a 10-km (6-mile) route to the Rifugio Pralongià. You can rent skis and snowboards at the Ski Service Colalto, located at the bottom of the lift. ✉ *Strada Col Alt 36, Corvara* ☎ *0471/836073* 🌐 *www.moviment.it/en/col-alt-ski-lift-corvara.php* 🎫 *€15.70 round-trip.*

Restaurants

La Stüa de Michil

$$$$ | ITALIAN | You'll feel like you're dining in a traditional Alto Adige hut at the Perla hotel's critically acclaimed restaurant, which features wood-beamed ceilings. Items in the seasonally changing six-course tasting menu are complex, modern takes on regional cuisine: even a simple veal dish might be served with reserve Alpine cheese and black truffle. **Known for:** romantic atmosphere; interesting wine pairings (not all Italian); daring ingredient combinations. [$] *Average main: €190* ✉ *Strada Col Alt 105, Corvara* ☎ *0471/831000* 🌐 *www.lastuademichil.it* ⏲ *Closed Apr.–mid-June, and late Sept.–early Dec. No lunch.*

★ Ristorante Rifugio Col Alt

$$ | ECLECTIC | From town, take the Col Alt cable car—or a snowcat (by reservation only) for dinner on Wednesday and Friday—to this surprisingly modern restaurant with amazing panoramas from 6,562 feet. The wide-ranging menu features everything from salads to hearty fried potatoes, eggs, and bacon (perfect after a morning of skiing), and the interesting wine list is heavy on natural producers, since the affable owner is a fan and often has local winemakers in for tastings. **Known for:** unbeatable vistas; an enormous terrace; memorable wines at affordable prices. [$] *Average main: €22* ✉ *Monte Cabinovia, Strada Col Alt 1, Corvara* ✥ *Take Col Alt cable car* ☎ *0471/836324* 🌐 *rifugiocolalt.it* ⏲ *Closed mid-Apr.–mid-June and mid-Sept.–early Dec.*

Hotels

★ Aman Rosa Alpina

$$$$ | HOTEL | From its 1939 beginnings as a modest family inn to its newest incarnation as a luxe Aman property, the Rosa Alpina offers an intimate home-away-from-home feel combined with top culinary and wellness experiences. **Pros:**

highly personalized service; second-to-none attention to details; restorative spa experiences. **Cons:** sky-high prices; vibe too member's clubby for some; more than an hour's drive to Cortina. *Rooms from: €1,600 ✉ Strada Micurà de Rue 20, San Cassiano ☎ 0471/849500 🌐 www.aman.com 51 rooms Free Breakfast.*

Ciasa Salares

$$ | HOTEL | FAMILY | This refined, amenities-filled hotel has a distinctly Germanic vibe and lots of mountain atmosphere—from its outdoor hot tub and sauna to its simple guest rooms, with light-wood paneling, white accents, and balconies, to its underground fondue room–wine cellar (24,000 bottles with a focus on biodynamic producers). **Pros:** a number of top-notch dining choices; lovely spa; more affordable than comparable hotels. **Cons:** some rooms feel a bit cramped; service can be standoffish; not ski-in, ski-out. *Rooms from: €261 ✉ Strada Prè de Vì 31, Località Armentarola, 10 km (6 miles) east of Corvara, San Cassiano ☎ 0471/849445 🌐 www.ciasasalares.it Closed late-Mar.–mid-June 47 rooms Free Breakfast.*

★ Hotel La Perla

$$$$ | HOTEL | Best described as "Alpine country chic," this luxe yet rustic family-run hotel has spacious wood-latticed rooms with mountain-view balconies, a spa, lots of cozy sitting areas, and a much-lauded restaurant. **Pros:** ski-in, ski-out; convenient location next to both the mountains and town; extremely friendly service. **Cons:** rooms can be hot; expensive drinks; ski room could use a refresh. *Rooms from: €648 ✉ Strada Col Alt 105, Corvara ☎ 0471/831000 🌐 www.laperlacorvara.it Closed Apr.–early June and late Sept.–early Dec. 50 rooms Free Breakfast.*

Activities

HIKING

Corvara offers hikes for all levels, including the popular Col Alt Pralongià hike—an easy, level hike that passes through pasture lands—as well as a number of walks in the Puez-Odle nature reserve. Hikers looking for more challenging, steeper routes should start at the top of the Boè cable car.

SKIING

Alta Badia

SKIING & SNOWBOARDING | The Alta Badia ski area, which includes 53 ski lifts and 130 km (80 miles) of slopes, is cheaper and more Austrian in character than the more famous ski destinations in this region. Groomed trails for cross-country skiing (usually loops marked off by the kilometer) accommodate differing degrees of ability. Inquire at the local tourist office. *✉ Alta Badia, Corvara ☎ 0471/836176 Corvara tourism office 🌐 www.altabadia.org Day pass from €70.*

Cortina d'Ampezzo

38 km (24 miles) east of Corvara.

The archetypal Dolomite resort, Cortina d'Ampezzo entices those seeking both relaxation and adventure, and is one of the main sites for the 2026 Winter Olympics along with Milan. Events held here include women's Alpine (downhill) skiing, bobsleigh, skeleton, luge, and curling. In preparation, Cortina has been undergoing a construction wave, which has included many brand-new and refreshed hotels along with the new Cortina Sliding Centre containing the bobsleigh, luge, and skeleton track. The Cortina Olympic Center, which hosted the 1956 Winter Olympics Opening Ceremonies, is being used for curling this time around.

The town is the western gateway to the Strade Grande delle Dolomiti and actually crowns the northern Veneto region and an area known as Cadore in the northernmost part of the province of Belluno. Like Alto Adige to the west, Cadore (birthplace of the Venetian Renaissance painter Titian) was on the Alpine front during World War I, and was the scene of many battles that have been commemorated in refuges and museums. Cortina remains, for many, Italy's most idyllic incarnation of an Alpine ski town.

GETTING HERE AND AROUND

To drive to Cortina d'Ampezzo from Trento or Bolzano, take the A22 autostrada north to Bressanone/Pustertal. Turn right on the SS49/E66, then right on to the SS51 and follow it into Cortina. The Südtirolmobil site (*www.suedtirolmobil.info*) provides itineraries for train and bus arrivals from around the region. The town itself is pedestrian-friendly and has local bus service to area ski slopes. Beware of taxis, as the rates are very high—and the fare may begin from the taxi's point of origin, not necessarily where you get in the vehicle.

VISITOR INFORMATION

CONTACT Cortina d'Ampezzo Tourism Office. *Corso Italia 81, Cortina d'Ampezzo* *0436/869086* *cortina.dolomiti.org.*

Sights

Surrounded by mountains and dense forests, the "Queen of the Dolomites" is in a lush meadow 4,000 feet above sea level. The town hugs the slopes beside a fast-moving stream, and a public park extends along one bank. Higher in the valley, luxury hotels and the villas of the rich are identifiable by their attempts to hide behind stands of firs and spruces. The bustling center of Cortina d'Ampezzo has little nostalgia, despite its alpine appearance, with its tone set by shops and cafés as chic as their well-dressed patrons. Unlike neighboring resorts that have a strong Germanic flavor, Cortina d'Ampezzo is unapologetically Italian and distinctly fashionable.

Restaurants

La Tavernetta di Cortina

$$ | **NORTHERN ITALIAN** | These Tirolean-style wood-paneled dining rooms near the Olympic ice-skating rink are a Cortina institution. Join the local clientele in sampling terrific pizza along with house specialties such as pork cheek in Barolo sauce. **Known for:** typical dishes; nice wine selection; house-made desserts. *Average main: €26* *Via Castello 53, Cortina d'Ampezzo* *0436/060268* *latavernettadicortina.it* *Closed Mon.*

Ristorante Lago Pianozes di Alberti Massimo

$$ | **NORTHERN ITALIAN** | The owner of this small, endearing establishment—just outside Cortina and beside picturesque Lago Pianozes—is friendly and knowledgeable, not only about the food and wine but also about the region. The menu varies according to the seasons, always incorporating local recipes—seating is limited, though, so reservations are recommended. **Known for:** delightful location; meat dishes, including beef tartare, stewed beef cheek, and Tomahawk steak; friendly staff. *Average main: €30* *Campo di Sotto Pianozes 1, Cortina d'Ampezzo* *366/3591737* *lagopianozesrestaurant.it* *Closed Tues., and early May–late June.*

★ SanBrite

$$$$ | **MODERN ITALIAN** | Most of the ingredients, including fabulous handmade cheeses and butter, used at this charming Michelin-starred organic dairy-turned-eatery (whose name means "healthy pasture") come from the family farm, Agriturismo El Brite de Larieto, perched 1,800 meters (5,900 feet) above the sea. Out of this local bounty, chef Riccardo Gaspari and his wife Ludovica craft impressive and highly personal dishes you'll find nowhere else in the Dolomites,

such as the signature spaghetti with mountain pine oil and scent of the forest ice cream. **Known for:** farm-to-table cuisine; six-course tasting menu (plus à la carte dishes); stunning mountain views. *Average main: €50 Via Alverà, Cortina d'Ampezzo 0436/863882 www.sanbrite.it Closed Wed., May–early June, and Nov. No lunch Thurs.*

Hotels

Grand Hotel Savoia Cortina d'Ampezzo, A Radisson Collection Hotel

$$$ | **HOTEL** | Stunning mountain views are the hallmark of this elegant property, dating from 1912, which also has a delightful spa and friendly service. **Pros:** updated rooms with wonderful views; walkable to restaurants and shopping; extensive breakfast buffet. **Cons:** rooms can be too hot; extra charge for breakfast; not ski-in, ski-out. *Rooms from: €522 Via Roma 62, Cortina d'Ampezzo 0436/3201 www.grandhotelsavoiacortina.it 132 rooms No Meals.*

Hotel De la Poste

$$ | **HOTEL** | Loyal skiers return year after year to this old-school mountain retreat, where each unique room has antiques in characteristic Dolomite style (almost all have wooden balconies) and the main terrace bar is one of Cortina's social centers. **Pros:** professional service; charging stations for electric cars; lively atmosphere. **Cons:** no pool or spa; dated furnishings; street noise can be an issue. *Rooms from: €324 Piazza Roma 14, Cortina d'Ampezzo 0436/4271 www.delaposte.it Closed Apr.–late May and early Oct.–early Dec. 72 rooms Free Breakfast.*

Hotel de Len

$$$$ | **HOTEL** | At this mountain-chic inn in the center of Cortina, from the same owners as Puglia's famed Borgo Egnazia resort, sustainable materials and chill vibes add up to the most modern boutique hotel in town. **Pros:** convenient, central location; very friendly staff; lovely spa area with great views. **Cons:** restaurant food could be better; only first hour free at spa, then must pay to use; parking costs extra. *Rooms from: €610 Via Cesare Battisti 66, Cortina d'Ampezzo 0436/4246 hoteldelen.it 22 rooms Free Breakfast.*

Activities

HIKING AND CLIMBING

Cortina has more than 400 km (249 miles) of hiking routes, ranging from forests to Alpine lakes, including the popular Lake Sorapis, famous for its amazing blue colors. Hiking information is available from the excellent local tourism office.

★ Cima Tofana

HIKING & WALKING | **FAMILY** | Cima Tofana is home to the Dolomites' third highest peak, Tofana di Mezzo, at 3,244 meters (10,643 feet). In the summer months, you can access a 360-degree panoramic terrace with phenomenal views, along with hiking trails and vie ferrate. Adventurous types can opt for the moderately difficult 15-minute hike up to the top of Tofana di Mezzo. Reach Cima Tofana by taking three cable cars: from Cortina to Col Durscié up to Ra Valles and then on to Cima Tofana. *Cortina d'Ampezzo 0436/5052 www.freccianelcielo.com From €73 round-trip for cable cars from Cortina to Cima Tofana Closed early Apr.–mid-June and late Sept.–early Dec.*

Gruppo Guide Alpine Cortina Scuola di Alpinismo (*Mountaineering School*)

HIKING & WALKING | This group organizes climbing trips and trekking adventures. *Corso Italia 69/a, Cortina d'Ampezzo 0436/868505 guidecortina.com Guided climbing trips from €330 per person.*

SKIING

Cortina offers ski options—with many long and picturesque runs—for all levels of skier in its three main ski areas:

Cinque Torre (Lagazuoi and Faloria), Cristallo, and Tofana. Along with gondolas directly from the center of town, efficient ski-bus service connects Cortina with the high-speed chairlifts and gondolas that ascend in all directions from the valley.

If you buy a ski pass online, pick up a free refillable My Dolomiti Card at ticket offices and continue to top it up online when you purchase future ski passes.

★ Cinque Torri – Lagazuoi

SKIING & SNOWBOARDING | **FAMILY** | The Cinque (5) Torri – Lagazuoi ski area includes 16 slopes of low and medium difficulty, including the 8.5-km (5.3-mile) Armenterola run, with panoramic views of the Fannes-Sennes-Prags Nature Park. From the Tofana ski area, take the Cortina Skyline gondola to reach the Cinque Torri slopes. ✉ *Between Giau Pass and Falzarego Pass, Cortina d'Ampezzo* ☎ *0436/871178* 🌐 *5torri.it* 🎫 *Cortina Skyline cable car: €18.50 one-way (€19 in Aug.), €25 round-trip (€26 in Aug.)* 🕓 *Closed early Apr.–late June and mid-Sept.–mid-Dec.*

Cortina d'Ampezzo Ski Pass

SKIING & SNOWBOARDING | **FAMILY** | If you only want to ski in and around Cortina, this ski pass that includes 120 km (74 miles) of slopes in the Cortina d'Ampezzo, San Vito di Cadore, Auronzo, and Misurina resorts could be your best bet. You can buy the pass online and pick it up at ticket offices next to ski lifts throughout the area. ✉ *Via Marconi 15, Cortina d'Ampezzo* ☎ *0436/862171* 🌐 *skipasscortina.com* 🎫 *From €70 for 1 day.*

Dolomiti Superski Pass

SKIING & SNOWBOARDING | **FAMILY** | The Dolomiti Superski Pass provides access to the surrounding Dolomites, with 450 lifts and gondolas serving 1,200 km (750 miles) of trails. There's also a Dolomiti Supersummer Card, good for 140 lifts from mid-May to mid-November. Buy the passes online and get them at a pickup box (locations listed on the website). You can also purchase at other outlets in the Dolomites; see the Dolomiti Superski site for details. ✉ *Via Marconi 15, Cortina d'Ampezzo* ☎ *0471/795397* 🌐 *www.dolomitisuperski.com* 🎫 *Superski: from €75 for 1 day, lower rates for longer durations. Supersummer: €65 for 1 day.*

Faloria – Cristallo

SKIING & SNOWBOARDING | **FAMILY** | The Faloria – Cristallo ski area includes seven ski lifts and 15 slopes, ranging from beginner blue trails to advanced black trails. The Faloria gondola runs from the center of town up to Monte Faloria. ✉ *Via Ria de Zeta 10, Cortina d'Ampezzo* ☎ *0436/5889* 🌐 *faloriacristallo.it* 🎫 *Cable car: €27 round-trip.*

★ Passo Falzarego

SKIING & SNOWBOARDING | The topography of the Passo Falzarego ski area, 16 km (10 miles) east of town, is dramatic. From here, a cable car takes you to one of the highest points in the Dolomites (Rifugio Lagazuoi)—where, on a clear day, you'll experience some of the best views. It's also easy to see why this was such a deadly area for soldiers in the Great War. Hiking is uneven in places, and there are vie ferrate that require the use of helmets and flashlights; other paths lead to tunnels that don't require helmets. You can reach Passo Falzarego from Cortina by transferring from the Freccia nel Cielo cable car to the Cortina Skyline cable car, or by taking a car or bus. ✉ *Between Lagazuoi and Col Gallina opposite Sass de Stria, Cortina d'Ampezzo* ☎ *0436/867301 cable car ticket office* 🌐 *lagazuoi.it* 🎫 *Lagazuoi cable car: €25.50 round-trip mid-Dec.–early Apr.; €26.50 round-trip June, July, and Sept.–mid-Oct.; €30 round-trip Aug.* 🕓 *Lagazuoi cable car closed early Apr.–May and mid-Oct.–mid-Dec.*

Chapter 7

MILAN, LOMBARDY, AND THE LAKES

Updated by
Liz Shemaria

WELCOME TO MILAN, LOMBARDY, AND THE LAKES

TOP REASONS TO GO

★ **Lake Como:** Ferries crisscross the waters, taking you from picture-book villages to stately villas to Edenic gardens—all against the backdrop of the snow-capped Alps.

★ **Leonardo's *The Last Supper*:** Behold one of the world's most famous works of art for yourself.

★ **The sky's no limit:** A funicular ride in Bergamo whisks you up to the magnificent medieval city.

★ **Milan alla moda:** As you window-shop the afternoon away in Milan's Quadrilatero della Moda district, catch a glimpse of fashion's latest trends.

★ **A night at La Scala:** What the Louvre is to art, Milan's La Scala is to the world of opera.

★ **Lake Garda and Lake Maggiore:** The former is great for outdoors enthusiasts; the latter has plentiful islands to explore.

★ **Cremona's violins:** If you are in the market for a violin, you'll find the world's best here in more than 150 shops.

1 **Milan.** The international fashion capital.

2 **Bergamo.** A charming medieval quarter.

3 **Cremona.** The birthplace of the violin.

4 **Mantua.** The Palazzo Ducale is a must.

5 **Lake Iseo and Franciacorta.** Lovely views and quaint restaurants.

6 **Sirmione.** A bustling spa town.

7 **Riva del Garda.** Stroll, sunbathe, or windsurf.

8 **Gargnano.** Don't miss the pleasant beach.

9 **Gardone Riviera.** A lovely town set against the Alps.

10 **Bellagio.** The belle of Lake Como.

11 **Tremezzo.** Explore two 18th-century villas.

12 **Cernobbio.** Villa d'Este hotel commands pride of place.

13 **Como.** A former silk town, with an urban vibe.

14 **Stresa and the Isole Borromee.** Grand hotels abound here.

15 **Verbania.** Gorgeous gardens and villas.

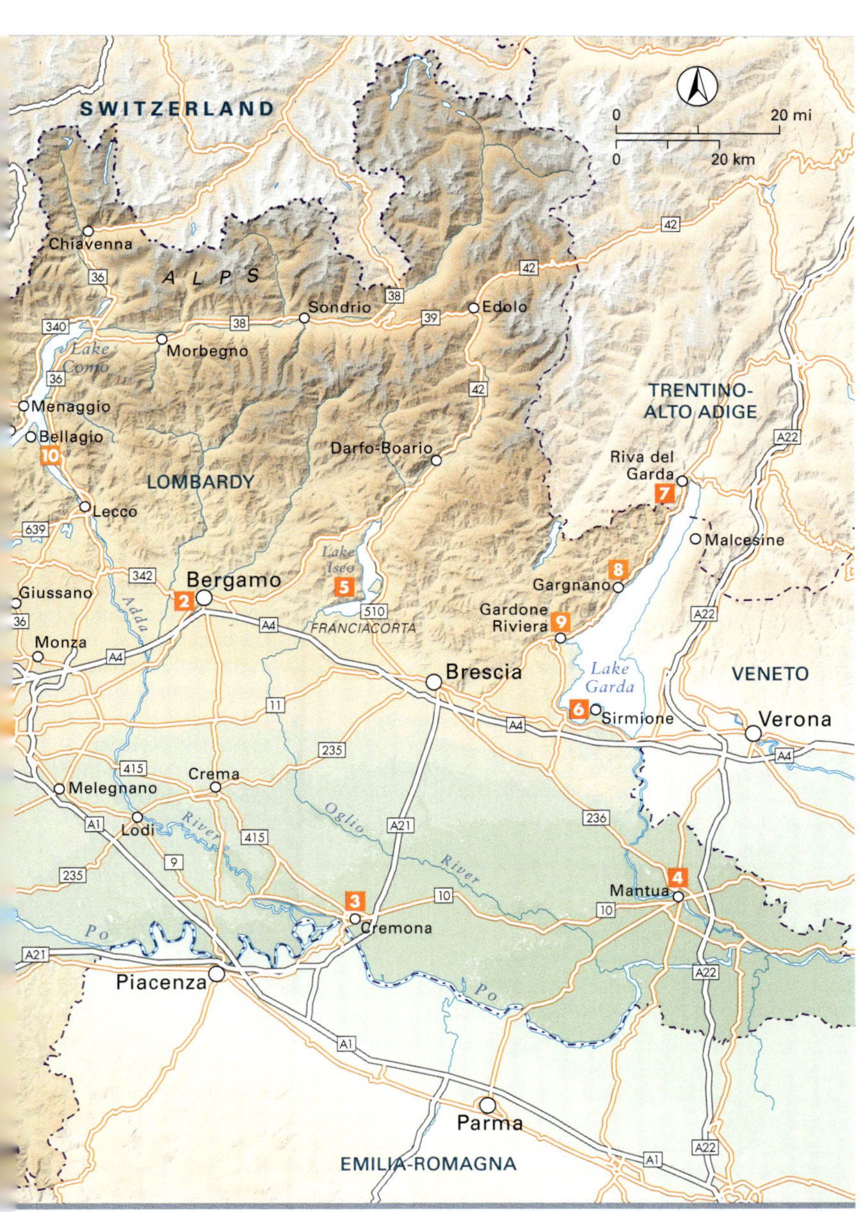
SWITZERLAND
0
20 mi
0
20 km
Chiavenna
ALPS
Sondrio
Edolo
Morbegno
Lake Como
Menaggio
Bellagio
10
Darfo-Boario
TRENTINO-ALTO ADIGE
Riva del Garda
7
LOMBARDY
Lecco
Malcesine
Lake Iseo
5
8
Gargnano
Bergamo
2
Giussano
Adda
Gardone Riviera
9
FRANCIACORTA
Monza
Lake Garda
Brescia
VENETO
6
Sirmione
Verona
Crema
Melegnano
Lodi
River
Oglio River
4
Mantua
3
Cremona
Po
Piacenza
Po
Parma
EMILIA-ROMAGNA
36
340
38
39
42
38
36
639
342
510
A4
A4
A4
A4
11
235
415
A1
415
9
235
10
10
236
A21
A21
A22
A22
A22
A22
A1
A1
36

EATING WELL IN MILAN, LOMBARDY, AND THE LAKES

Rice from the Lombardy region

Lombardy may well offer Italy's most varied, rich, and refined cuisine. Local cooking is influenced by the neighboring regions of the north; foreign conquerors have left their mark; and today, business visitors, industrious immigrants, and well-traveled Milanese are likely to find more authentic ethnic cuisine in Milan than in any other Italian city.

Milan runs counter to many established Italian dining customs. A "real" traditional Milanese meal is a rarity; instead, Milan offers a variety of tastes, prices, and opportunities, from expense-account elegance in fancy restaurants to abundant *aperitivo*-hour nibbles. The city's cosmopolitan nature means trends arrive here first, and things move fast. Meals are not the drawn-out pastime they tend to be elsewhere in Italy. But the food is still consistently good: competition among restaurants is fierce and the local clientele is demanding, which means you can be reasonably certain that if a place looks promising, it won't disappoint.

THE COTOLETTA QUESTION

Everyone has an opinion on *cotoletta*, the breaded veal cutlet known across Italy as *una Milanese*. It's clearly related to Austria's Wiener schnitzel, but did the Austrians introduce it when they seized Milan, or did they take it home when they left? Some think it's best with fresh tomato and arugula on top; others find this sacrilege. Two things unite all camps: the meat must be well beaten until it's thin, and it must never leave a grease spot after it's fried.

REGIONAL SPECIALTIES

Ask an Italian what Lombards eat, and you're likely to hear *cotoletta, càsoeûla,* and *risotto giallo*—all dishes that reinforce Lombardy's status as the crossroads of Italy. *Cotoletta alla Milanese* may very well have Austrian roots. *Càsoeûla* is a cabbage-and-pork stew that resembles French cassoulet, though some say it has Spanish origins. *Risotto giallo* (also known as *risotto Milanese*) is colorful and perfumed with exotic saffron.

BUTTER AND CHEESE

Geography and a strong agricultural tradition mean that animal products are more common here than in southern Italy; butter and cream, for example, take the place of olive oil. One rare point of agreement about cotoletta is that it's cooked in butter, and the first and last steps of risotto making—toasting the rice, then letting it "repose" before serving—use ample amounts of butter. And the second-most-famous name in Italian cheese (after Parmesan) is likely Gorgonzola, named for a town near Milan; the best now comes from Novara.

RISOTTO

Rice is Lombardy's answer to pasta, and the region is the center of Italian (and European) rice production. From Milan's risotto giallo with its saffron tint, to Mantua's risotto with pumpkin or sausage, there's no end to the variety. Canonical risotto should be *all'onda,* flowing off the spoon like a wave. In keeping with the Italian tradition of wasting nothing, yesterday's risotto is flattened in a pan and fried in butter to produce *riso al salto,* which at its best has a crispy crust and a tender middle.

Veal Milanese

Panettone

PANETTONE

Panettone, a tall, fluffy yeast bread, is flavored with candied fruit. Invented in Milan, it graces nearly every table during the Christmas holiday. Consumption begins on December 7, Milan's patron saint's day, and goes until supplies run out at January's end.

WINE

The Franciacorta region around Brescia makes highly regarded sparkling wines, often called the "Champagne of Italy" since they're produced using the same labor-intensive method. The Valtellina area to the northeast of Milan produces two notable reds from the *nebbiolo* grape: Valtellina Superiore and the intense dessert wine Sforzato di Valtellina. Lake breezes yield crisp, smooth whites from the shores of Lake Garda.

Lombardy is one of Italy's most dynamic regions, offering everything from world-class ski slopes to summer lake resorts, and Milan is the pulse of the nation—commercial, fashionable, and forward-looking. The Renaissance cities of the Po Plain—Cremona and Mantua—offer the romantic Italy visitors dream about, embracing their past by preserving national treasures while keeping an eye on the present.

Topping any list of the region's attractions are the glacial lakes at the very feet of the Alps, praised as the closest thing to paradise by writers throughout the ages, from Virgil to Hemingway.

Millions of travelers have concurred: for sheer beauty, the lakes of northern Italy—Como, Maggiore, Garda, Iseo, and Orta—have few equals. Along their shores are 18th- and 19th-century villas, exotic formal gardens, sleepy villages, and dozens of Belle Époque–era resorts that were once Europe's most fashionable and that still retain a powerful allure.

Milan can be disappointingly modern and congested—a little too much like the place you've come to Italy to escape—but its historic buildings and art collections in many ways rival those of Florence and Rome. And if you love to shop, Milan is one of the world's great fashion centers, offering experiences and goods for every taste.

Sports fans are descending on the Italian fashion capital for the Winter Olympic Games, known as Milano Cortina 2026 (🌐 *milanocortina2026.olympics.com*). Though many of the events are happening to the north in Cortina, Bormio, and other mountain resorts, the opening ceremonies, figure skating, and other major events are bringing an extra buzz to the city. Key event venues are in Assago, Fiera, San Siro, and Santa Giulia, and ticket/hospitality packages include hotels in Repubblica, Navigli, Porta Garibaldi, and Cairoli.

MAJOR REGIONS

Milan. Long the country's capital of commerce, finance, fashion, and media, Milan is also Italy's transport hub, with the biggest international airport.

The Po Plain, Lake Garda, and Lake Iseo. Italy's wealthiest, most populous region is home not only to Milan but also to nearby medieval towns that once rivaled Milan in power. Bergamo, set against the Bergamese Alps, is a modern town connected by funicular to its lovely ancient counterpart, and Cremona is renowned for its incomparable violin-making tradition.

An hour's drive from Milan, sleepy Lake Iseo merits a stop for waterfront eateries amid picture-postcard settings. Lake Garda is the region's biggest and, by most accounts, cleanest lake. Places of note include the port town Gargnano (known for its association with Mussolini) and quaint 19th-century Gardone Riviera.

Lakes Como and Maggiore. Palatial villas, rose-laden belvederes, and majestic Alpine vistas are among the treasures of Lake Como—Europe's deepest lake. Many travelers head directly to boats for Bellagio and the *centro di lago,* the beautiful center region of the lake's three branches. Lake Maggiore has a unique geographical position: its mountainous western shore is in Piedmont, its lower eastern shore is in Lombardy, and its northern tip is in Switzerland.

Planning

Getting Here and Around

AIR

The region's main international gateway airport is Aeroporto Malpensa (🌐 *www.milanomalpensa-airport.com*), 48 km (30 miles) northwest of Milan. Some international and domestic flights also fly into more central Aeroporto Linate (🌐 *www.milanolinate-airport.com*), 7 km (4 miles) east of Milan, while European low-cost carriers like Ryanair use Aeroporto Milano Bergamo Orio al Serio (🌐 *www.milanbergamoairport.it*), 55 km (34 miles) northeast of Milan and 5 km (3 miles) south of Bergamo.

BOAT

Frequent daily ferry and hydrofoil services (🌐 *www.navigazionelaghi.it*) link the lakeside towns and villages. Residents take them to get to work and school, while visitors use them for exploring the area. There are also special round-trip excursions.

BUS

Bus service isn't the best way to travel between cities here because trains are faster, cheaper, and more convenient. There's regular bus service (🌐 *www.arriva.it*, 🌐 *www.autostradale.it*) for reaching and traveling between the small towns on the lakes. It's less convenient than going by boat or by car, and it's used primarily by locals (particularly schoolchildren), but sightseers can use it as well. The bus service around Lake Garda serves mostly towns on the western shore.

CAR

Getting almost anywhere by car is a snap, as several major highways intersect at Milan, all connected by the *tangenziale,* the city's ring road. The A4 autostrada runs west to Turin and east to Venice; the A1 leads south to Bologna, Florence, and Rome; the A7 angles southwest down to Genoa. The A8 goes northwest toward Lake Maggiore, and the A9 runs north past Lake Como and into Switzerland's southernmost tip.

To get around the lakes themselves by car, you have to follow secondary roads. The SP572 follows the southern and western shores of Lake Garda, the SS45bis edges the northernmost section of the western shore, and the SR249 runs along the eastern shore. Around Lake Como, follow the SS340 along the western shore, the SS36 on the eastern shore, and the SP583 on the lower arms. The SS33 and SS34 trace the western shore of Lake Maggiore. The SP469 runs on the western side of Lake Iseo, while the SP510 borders the east. Although the roads around the lakes can be beautiful, they're full of harrowing twists and turns, making for a slow, challenging drive—often with an Italian speed racer on your tail.

TRAIN

Milan's majestic Central Station (Milano Centrale), 3 km (2 miles) northwest of the Duomo, has frequent service within the region to Como, Bergamo, Brescia,

Sirmione, Cremona, and Mantua. There are plenty of signs to help you get around, but its sheer size requires considerable amounts of walking and patience, so allow for some extra time here.

Tickets bought without a reservation need to be validated by stamping them in yellow machines on the train platforms, or, for tickets purchased online, by following directions in your email confirmation. Tickets with reservations don't require validation. When in doubt, validate—it can't hurt. For general information on trains and schedules, as well as online ticket purchases, visit the website of the Italian national railway, Trenitalia (🌐 *www.trenitalia.com*), also known as Ferrovie dello Stato (FS).

Hotels

Given that this is the wealthiest part of Italy, most hotels here cater to a clientele willing to pay for extra comfort. Outside Milan, many are converted villas with well-landscaped grounds. Most of the famous lake resorts are expensive; many smaller lakeside hotels are more reasonably priced. Local tourism offices throughout the region are an excellent source of information about affordable lodging.

Please note that the time for "high season" can vary here—in the lakes it's the height of summer, not surprisingly, but in Milan it depends on what fairs and exhibitions are being staged. Prices in almost all hotels can go up dramatically during Salone, the furniture and design fair in early April. Fashion, travel, tech fairs, and in 2026, the Winter Olympics in February will also draw big crowds, raising prices. In contrast to other cities in Italy, however, you can often find discounts on weekends. The lakes, including Como, Maggiore, Iseo, and Garda, have little to offer except quiet from November to March, when most gardens, hotels, and restaurants are closed.

⇨ *Hotel and restaurant reviews have been shortened. For full information, visit Fodors.com. Prices in the hotel reviews are the lowest cost of a standard double room in high season. Prices in the dining reviews are the average cost of a main course at dinner, or, if dinner is not served, at lunch.*

What It Costs in Euros

$	$$	$$$	$$$$
RESTAURANTS			
under €20	€20–€30	€31–€40	over €40
HOTELS			
under €175	€175–€400	€401–€600	over €600

Making the Most of Your Time

Italy's commercial hub isn't usually at the top of the list for visiting tourists, but Milan is the nation's most modern city, with its own sophisticated appeal: its fashionable shops rival those of New York and Paris, its soccer teams are Italy's answer to the Yankees and the Mets, its opera performances set the standard for the world, and its art treasures are well worth the visit.

The biggest draw in the region, though, is the Lake District. Throughout history, the magnificently beautiful lakes of Como, Garda, Maggiore, Iseo, and Orta have attracted their fair share of well-known faces—from Winston Churchill and Russian royalty to George Clooney and Madonna. Each lake town has its own history and distinct character. If you have limited time, visit the lake you think best suits your style, but if you have time to spare, make the rounds to two or three to get a sense of their contrasts.

Restaurants

You'll find lots of traditional northern Italian restaurants in this region, and can pretty much count on menus divided into pasta, fish, and meat options. As in the rest of Italy, it's common for dishes to feature seasonal and local ingredients. Meal prices in Milan tend to be higher than in the rest of the region (and quite high for European cities in general), though this is also where you'll see examples of the latest food trends and more adventurous choices on the menus.

Milan

Rome may be bigger and wield political power, but Milan and the affluent north are what really make the country go. Leonardo da Vinci's *The Last Supper* and other great works of art are here, as well as a spectacular Gothic Duomo, the finest of its kind.

And yet, Milan hasn't won the battle for hearts and minds when it comes to tourism. Most visitors prefer Tuscany's hills and Venice's canals to Milan's hectic efficiency and wealthy indifference. But its secrets reveal themselves slowly to those who look. A side street conceals a garden complete with flamingos (Giardini Invernizzi, on Via dei Cappuccini, just off Corso Venezia; closed to the public, but you can still catch a glimpse), and a renowned 20th-century-art collection hides modestly behind an unspectacular facade a block from Corso Buenos Aires (the Casa-Museo Boschi di Stefano).

Virtually every invader in European history—Gaul, Roman, Goth, Lombard, and Frank—as well as a long series of rulers from France, Spain, and Austria, took a turn at ruling the city. After being completely sacked by the Goths in AD 539 and by the Holy Roman Empire under Frederick Barbarossa in 1157, Milan became one of the first independent city-states of the Renaissance. Its heyday of self-rule proved comparatively brief. From 1277 until 1500 it was ruled first by the Visconti and then the Sforza dynasties. These families were known, justly or not, for a peculiarly aristocratic mixture of refinement, classical learning, and cruelty; much of the surviving grandeur of Gothic and Renaissance art and architecture is their doing. Be on the lookout in your wanderings for the Visconti family emblem—a viper, its jaws straining wide, devouring a child.

GETTING HERE AND AROUND

The city center is compact and walkable; trolleys and trams make it even more accessible, and the efficient Metropolitana (subway) and buses provide access to locations farther afield. Driving in Milan is difficult and parking a real pain, so a car is a liability. In addition, drivers within the second ring of streets (the *bastioni*) must pay a daily congestion charge on weekdays between 7:30 am and 7:30 pm. You can pay the charge at news vendors, tobacconists, Banca Intesa Sanpaolo ATMs, or with the EasyPark app (🌐 *www.easyparkitalia.it*); parking meters and parking garages in the area also include it in the cost. There is also a public bike sharing system called BikeMi (🌐 *www.bikemi.com*).

A standard public transit ticket within the central zones of Milan costs €2.20 and is valid for a 90-minute trip on a subway, bus, or tram. An all-inclusive subway, bus, and tram pass costs €7.60 for 24 hours or €15.50 for three consecutive days. Another option is a Carnet (€19.50), good for 10 tram, bus, or subway rides. Individual tickets and passes can be purchased from news vendors, tobacconists, at ticket machines at all subway stops, at ticket offices at the Duomo and other subway stops, and on your phone via the ATM Milano app. You can also pay for a subway ride using a contactless credit card at the turnstile to avoid ticket purchasing lines.

Once you have your ticket, either stamp it or insert it into the slots in station turnstiles or on poles inside trolleys and buses. (Electronic tickets won't function if they become bent or demagnetized. If you have a problem, contact a station manager, who can usually issue a new ticket.) Trains run from 6 am to 12:30 am.

Taxi fares in Milan are higher than in American cities; a short ride can run about €15 during rush hour or fashion week. You can get a taxi at a stand with an orange "Taxi" sign, or by calling one of the taxi companies (🌐 *www.milanoradiotaxi.it*, 🌐 *www.taxiblu.it*, 🌐 *www.026969.it*). Most also have apps you can download to order taxis from your phone; some let you text or use WhatsApp to hail a cab. Dispatchers may speak some English; they'll ask for the phone number you're calling from, and they'll tell you the number of your taxi and how long it'll take to arrive. If you're in a restaurant or bar, ask the staff to call a cab for you.

TOURS

CONTACT City Sightseeing Milano. ☎ *02/961237* 🌐 *www.city-sightseeing.it/en/milan.*

VISITOR INFORMATION

CONTACT Milan Tourism Office. ✉ *Piazza del Duomo 14, next to Palazzo Reale, Duomo* ☎ *02/88455555* 🌐 *www.yesmilano.it.*

Duomo

Milan's main streets radiate out from the massive Duomo, a late-Gothic cathedral begun in 1386. Heading north is the handsome Galleria Vittorio Emanuele II, an enclosed shopping arcade that opens at one end to the world-famous opera house known as La Scala. Via Manzoni leads northeast from La Scala to the Quadrilatero della Moda, or fashion district. Heading northeast from the Duomo is the pedestrian-only street Corso Vittorio Emanuele II. Northwest of the Duomo is Via Dante, at the top of which is the imposing outline of the Castello Sforzesco.

Sights

Battistero Paleocristiano/Baptistry of San Giovanni alle Fonti

ARCHAEOLOGICAL SITE | More specifically known as the Baptistry of San Giovanni alle Fonti, this 4th-century baptistry is one of two that lie beneath the Duomo. Although opinion remains divided, it is widely believed to be where Ambrose, Milan's first bishop and patron saint, baptized Augustine. Tickets also include a visit to the Duomo and its museum. ✉ *Piazza del Duomo, Duomo* ✥ *Enter through Duomo* ☎ *02/72023375* 🌐 *www.duomomilano.it* 🎟 *€14, including admission to Duomo and museum; €26, including Duomo, museum, and roof with elevator, valid for 72 hrs* Ⓜ *Duomo.*

★ Duomo

CHURCH | There is no denying that for sheer size and complexity, the Duomo is unrivaled in Italy. It is the second-largest church in the country—the largest being St. Peter's in Rome. This intricate Gothic structure has been fascinating and exasperating visitors and conquerors alike since it was begun by Gian Galeazzo Visconti III (1351–1402), first duke of Milan, in 1386. Consecrated in the 15th or 16th century, it was not completed until just before the coronation of Napoléon as king of Italy in 1809.

The building is adorned with 135 marble spires and 2,245 marble statues. The Duomo's most famous sculpture is the gruesome but anatomically instructive figure of *San Bartolomeo* (St. Bartholomew), who was flayed alive. As you enter the apse to admire those splendid windows, glance at the sacristy doors to the right and left of the altar. The lunette on the right dates from 1393 and was decorated by Hans von Fernach. ✉ *Piazza del Duomo, Duomo* ☎ *02/72023375 www.duomomilano.it* *Cathedral, museum, and archaeological area €14; stairs to roof €14; elevator €16; fast-track skip the line with elevator €26* *Duomo.*

★ Galleria Vittorio Emanuele II

STORE/MALL | This spectacular late-19th-century Belle Époque tunnel is essentially one of the planet's earliest and most select shopping malls, with upscale tenants that include Gucci and Prada. This is the city's heart, midway between the Duomo and La Scala. It teems with life, which makes for great people-watching from the tables that spill out from bars and restaurants, where you can enjoy an overpriced coffee. Books, clothing, food, hats, and jewelry are all for sale. Known as Milan's "parlor," the Galleria is often viewed as a barometer of the city's well-being. *Piazza del Duomo, Duomo* *Duomo.*

Milano Osservatorio—Fondazione Prada

SPECIALTY MUSEUM | This contemporary photography and visual languages exhibition space, developed in partnership with Fondazione Prada, is spread over two floors in the Galleria Vittorio Emanuele II. Exhibitions, which rotate several times a year, explore the cultural and social implications of expression. The space itself, bombed after World War II and then fully restored, is worth visiting just for the unique view of the Galleria dome through the large windows. You can reach the gallery via the elevator next to the Prada store. *Galleria Vittorio Emanuele II, Piazza del Duomo, Duomo* *02/56662611* *www.fondazioneprada.org/visit/milano-osservatorio* *€10; €15, including Fondazione Prada* *Closed Tues.* *Duomo.*

Museo del Novecento

ART MUSEUM | Ascend a Guggenheim-esque spiral walkway to reach the modern works at this petite yet dense collection of Italian contemporary art, adjacent to the Duomo. The museum highlights 20th-century Italian artists, including a strong showing of Futurists, like Boccioni and Severini, and sculptures from Marini, along with a smattering of works by other European artists, including Picasso, Braque, and Matisse. *Via Marconi 1, Duomo* *02/88444061* *www.museodelnovecento.org* *€5 (free every 1st and 3rd Tues. of month after 2)* *Closed Mon.* *Duomo.*

★ Palazzo Reale

ART MUSEUM | Elaborately decorated with painted ceilings and grand staircases, this former royal palace close to the Duomo is almost worth a visit in itself; however, it also functions as one of Milan's major art galleries, with a focus on modern artists. Exhibitions have highlighted works by Picasso, Chagall, Warhol, Pollock, and Kandinsky. Check the website before you visit to see what's on; purchase tickets online in advance to save time in the queues, which are often long and chaotic. *Piazza del Duomo 12, Duomo* *02/88445181* *www.palazzorealemilano.it* *Varies by exhibition* *Closed Mon.* *Duomo.*

Pinacoteca Ambrosiana

ART MUSEUM | Cardinal Federico Borromeo, one of Milan's native saints, founded this picture gallery in 1618 with the addition of his personal art collection to a bequest of books to Italy's first public library. The core works of the collection include such treasures as Caravaggio's *Basket of Fruit,* Raphael's monumental preparatory drawing (known as a "cartoon") for *The School of Athens,* which hangs in the Vatican, and Leonardo da Vinci's *Portrait of a Musician.* The highlight for many is Leonardo's *Codex Atlanticus,* which features thousands of his sketches and drawings. *Piazza Pio XI 2, Duomo* *02/806921* *www.ambrosiana.it/en* *€17* *Closed Wed.* *Duomo.*

Santa Maria Presso San Satiro

CHURCH | Just a few steps from the Duomo, this architectural gem was first built in 876 and later perfected by Bramante (1444–1514), demonstrating

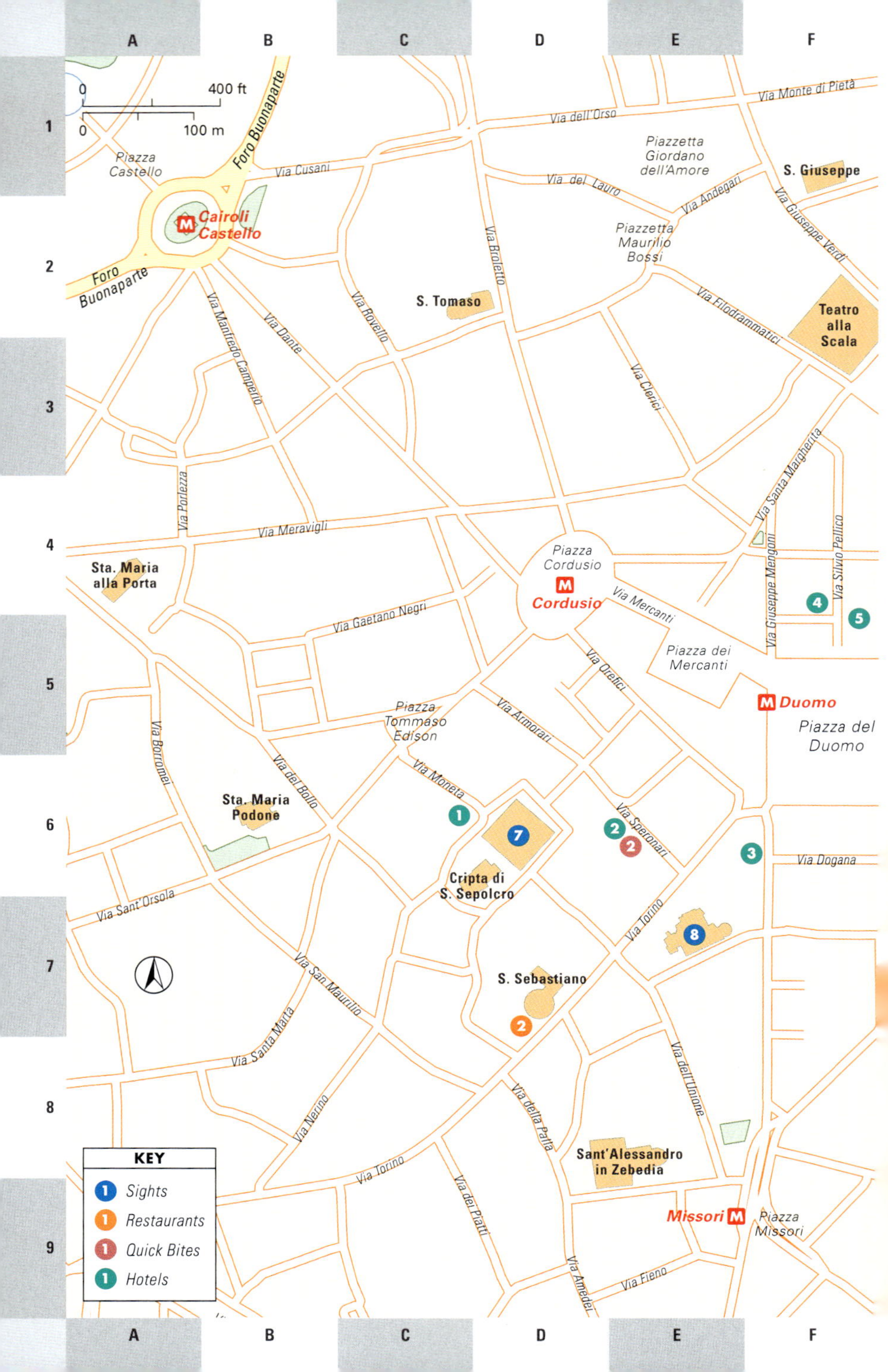

A
B
C
D
E
F
1
2
3
4
5
6
7
8
9
0
400 ft
100 m
Piazza Castello
Foro Buonaparte
Cairoli Castello
Via Cusani
Via dell'Orso
Via Monte di Pietà
Piazzetta Giordano dell'Amore
S. Giuseppe
Via del Lauro
Via Andegari
Via Giuseppe Verdi
Piazzetta Maurilio Bossi
Via Broletto
S. Tomaso
Via Rovello
Via Manfredo Camperio
Via Dante
Via Filodrammatici
Teatro alla Scala
Via Clerici
Via Santa Margherita
Via Porlezza
Via Meravigli
Piazza Cordusio
Cordusio
Sta. Maria alla Porta
Via Giuseppe Mengoni
Via Silvio Pellico
Via Mercanti
Via Gaetano Negri
Piazza dei Mercanti
Via Orefici
Duomo
Piazza del Duomo
Piazza Tommaso Edison
Via Armorari
Via Borromei
Via del Bollo
Via Moneta
Sta. Maria Podone
Via Speronari
Via Dogana
Cripta di S. Sepolcro
Via Sant'Orsola
Via Torino
Via San Maurilio
S. Sebastiano
Via Santa Marta
Via dell'Unione
Via della Palla
Via Nerino
KEY
Sights
Restaurants
Quick Bites
Hotels
Sant'Alessandro in Zebedia
Via dei Piatti
Missori
Piazza Missori
Via Amedei
Via Fieno

G H I J

Sights

1 Battistero Paleocristiano/ Baptistry of San Giovanni alle Fonti **H5**
2 Duomo **H5**
3 Galleria Vittorio Emanuele II........ **G4**
4 Milano Osservatorio— Fondazione Prada **G4**
5 Museo del Novecento **G6**
6 Palazzo Reale **H7**
7 Pinacoteca Ambrosiana **D6**
8 Santa Maria Presso San Satiro **E7**

Restaurants

1 Da Giacomo Arengario........ **G6**
2 Piz **D7**

Quick Bites

1 Camparino in Galleria **G5**
2 Peck........ **E6**

Hotels

1 Hotel Gran Duca di York........ **C6**
2 Hotel Spadari al Duomo........ **E6**
3 Maison Milano | UNA Esperienze **F6**
4 Park Hyatt Milan........ **F4**
5 Room Mate Giulia........ **F5**

G H I J

his command of proportion and perspective—hallmarks of Renaissance architecture. Bramante tricks the eye with a famous optical illusion that makes a small interior seem extraordinarily spacious and airy, while accommodating a beloved 13th-century fresco. ✉ *Via Torino 17–19, Duomo* ☎ *02/874683* Ⓜ *Duomo; Tram No. 2, 3, 4, 12, 14, 19, 20, 24, or 27.*

Restaurants

Da Giacomo Arengario

$$$ | **ITALIAN** | Join businesspeople, ladies who lunch, and in-the-know travelers at this elegant restaurant atop the Museo del Novecento and with a glorious Duomo view (be sure to request a window table, though, or risk being relegated to a viewless back room). To complement the vistas, choose from a selection of well-prepared seafood, pasta, and meat courses for lunch and dinner; the servers are happy to recommend pairings from the extensive wine list. **Known for:** amazing Duomo views from tables by the windows; contemporary Milanese dishes; wine pairings. [$] *Average main: €38* ✉ *Via Marconi 1, Duomo* ☎ *02/72093814* 🌐 *www.giacomomilano.com/en* Ⓜ *Duomo.*

Piz

$ | **PIZZA** | Fun, lively, and usually with a line out the door, this no-frills pizzeria on a side street near the Duomo has just four kinds of thin crust on offer. Choose from *margherita, bianca* (white, with no tomato, and a seasonal vegetarian topping), marinara (with no mozzarella), and a surprise pizza of the day; all are served hot from a wood-burning oven to satisfy locals and tourists alike. **Known for:** pizzas with seasonal toppings; popular with tourists and local lunch crowd; bustling vibe. [$] *Average main: €13* ✉ *Via Torino 34, Duomo* ☎ *02/72096413* 🌐 *www.pizmilano.it* Ⓜ *Duomo; Tram No. 2, 3, or 14.*

Coffee and Quick Bites

Camparino in Galleria

$$$ | **EUROPEAN** | One thing has remained constant in the Galleria: the Camparino, whose inlaid counter, mosaics, and wrought-iron fixtures have been welcoming tired shoppers since 1867. Small plates to be enjoyed with a Campari aperitif are served in pretty Bar di Passo downstairs, while a more extensive range of Campari cocktails paired with food for aperitivo or dinner is available in elegant Sala Spiritello upstairs. **Known for:** contemporary versions of Campari cocktails; high-end aperitivo; prime people-watching. [$] *Average main: €31* ✉ *Galleria Vittorio Emanuele, Piazza del Duomo 21, Duomo* ☎ *02/86464435* 🌐 *www.camparino.com* Ⓜ *Duomo.*

★ Peck

$$ | **SANDWICHES** | The café at this foodie paradise at its original 1883 outpost near the Duomo features Italian specialty foods such as excellent cheeses, charcuterie, vegetables in olive oil, seafood, and sandwiches. It also reinterprets classic dishes like Russian salad and pâté, which can be washed down with a fine selection of wines by the glass or a bottle from its cellar of global labels. **Known for:** wide bakery selection, including classic brioche; delicious Italian treats from the famed Peck deli; casual atmosphere. [$] *Average main: €20* ✉ *Via Spadari 9, Duomo* ☎ *02/8023161* 🌐 *www.peck.it* Ⓜ *Tram No. 2, 12, 14, 16, or 19.*

Hotels

Hotel Gran Duca di York

$$ | **HOTEL** | The classically elegant and efficient rooms at this hotel are arranged around a courtyard—four have private terraces—and offer good value for pricey Milan. **Pros:** central location; friendly staff; good breakfast. **Cons:** limited amenities (no restaurant or gym); many rooms on the small side; showers can be tiny. [$] *Rooms from: €247* ✉ *Via Moneta 1,*

Duomo ☎ *02/874863* 🌐 *www.ducadiyork.com* 🛏 *33 rooms* 🍽 *Free Breakfast* Ⓜ *Cordusio or Duomo; Tram No. 2, 12, 14, 16, or 27.*

Hotel Spadari al Duomo

$$ | **HOTEL** | That this chic city-center inn is owned by an architect's family comes through in details like the custom-designed furniture and paintings by young Milanese artists in the stylish guest rooms. **Pros:** good breakfast; central location; attentive staff. **Cons:** some rooms on the small side; street noise can be a problem; no restaurant. 💲 *Rooms from: €360* ✉ *Via Spadari 11, Duomo* ☎ *02/72002371* 🌐 *www.spadarihotel.com* 🛏 *40 rooms* 🍽 *Free Breakfast* Ⓜ *Duomo; Tram No. 2, 3, 12, 14, 16, 24, or 27.*

Maison Milano | UNA Esperienze

$$ | **HOTEL** | Inside this faithfully restored palazzo dating from the early 1900s, spaciousness is accentuated with soft white interiors, muted fabrics and marble, and contemporary lines. **Pros:** the warmth of a residence and the luxury of a design hotel; lovely bathrooms; friendly staff. **Cons:** breakfast not included; not much of a lobby; no restaurant or bar. 💲 *Rooms from: €227* ✉ *Via Mazzini 4, Duomo* ☎ *02/69826949* 🌐 *www.gruppouna.it/esperienze/maison-milano* 🛏 *27 rooms* 🍽 *No Meals* Ⓜ *Duomo; Tram No. 2, 3, 12, 14, 16, 24, or 27.*

★ Park Hyatt Milan

$$$$ | **HOTEL** | Extensive use of warm travertine stone and modern art creates a sophisticated yet inviting backdrop at the Park Hyatt, where spacious, opulent guest rooms have walk-in closets and bathrooms with double sinks, glass-enclosed rain showers, and separate soaking tubs. **Pros:** central location; contemporary decor and amenities; excellent restaurant. **Cons:** not particularly intimate; very expensive; some rooms showing a little wear. 💲 *Rooms from: €1,000* ✉ *Via Tommaso Grossi 1, Duomo* ☎ *02/88211234* 🌐 *www.hyatt.com/en-US/hotel/italy/park-hyatt-milan/milph* 🛏 *106 rooms* 🍽 *No Meals* Ⓜ *Duomo; Tram No. 1.*

★ Room Mate Giulia

$$ | **HOTEL** | For hip, design-focused lodging with a friendly feel and prime location right next to the Galleria and around the corner from the Duomo, you can't do much better than the city's outpost from Spanish hotel chain Room Mate. **Pros:** amazing location; fresh, appealing design; spa. **Cons:** expensive breakfast and room a bit cramped; gym on the small side; busy location means some noise in rooms. 💲 *Rooms from: €349* ✉ *Via Silvio Pellico 4, Duomo* ☎ *02/80888900* 🌐 *www.room-matehotels.com/gb/hotel-giulia-milan* 🛏 *85 rooms* 🍽 *No Meals* Ⓜ *Duomo; Tram No. 1.*

Nightlife

Bar STRAF

BARS | This architecturally stimulating but dimly lit place has such artistic features as recycled fiberglass panels and vintage 1970s furnishings. The music is an eclectic mix of chill-out tunes during the daytime, with more upbeat and vibrant tracks pepping it up at night. Located on a quiet side street near the Duomo, STRAF, inside the hotel of the same name, draws a young and lively, if tourist-heavy, crowd. ✉ *Via San Raffaele 3, Duomo* ☎ *02/805081* 🌐 *www.straf.it/bar* Ⓜ *Duomo.*

Performing Arts

★ Teatro alla Scala

OPERA | You need know nothing of opera to sense that La Scala is closer to a cathedral than a concert hall. Hearing opera sung in this magical setting is an unparalleled experience: it is, after all, where Verdi established his reputation and where Maria Callas sang her way into opera lore. It stands as a symbol—both for the performer who dreams of singing here and for the opera buff—and its notoriously demanding audiences are apt to jeer performers who do not measure up. At the Museo Teatrale alla Scala you can admire an extensive collection of librettos, paintings of the famous names of Italian opera, posters, costumes, antique instruments, and design sketches for the theater. *Piazza della Scala, Largo Ghiringhelli 1, Duomo 02/72003744 theater, 02/88797473 museum www.teatroallascala.org Museum €12 Ⓜ Duomo or Cordusio; Tram No. 1.*

Shopping

Borsalino

HATS & GLOVES | The kingpin of milliners, Borsalino has managed to stay trendy since it opened in 1857. *Galleria Vittorio Emanuele II 92, Duomo 02/89015436 www.borsalino.com Ⓜ Duomo; Tram No. 1.*

Gucci

CLOTHING | This Florence-born brand attracts lots of fashion-forward tourists in hot pursuit of its monogrammed bags, shoes, and accessories. *Galleria Vittorio Emanuele II, Duomo 02/8597991 www.gucci.com Ⓜ Duomo; Tram No. 1.*

La Rinascente

DEPARTMENT STORE | The flagship location of this always bustling and very central department store—adjacent to both the Duomo and the Galleria Vittorio Emanuele II—carries a wide range of Italian and international brands (both high-end and casual) for men, women, and children. There's also a fine selection of beauty and home products. *Piazza Duomo, Duomo 02/91387388 www.rinascente.it Ⓜ Duomo; Tram No. 1, 2, 12, 14, 16, or 27.*

Castello

This 15th-century castle is home to crypts, battlements, tunnels, and an interesting array of museums.

Sights

Castello Sforzesco

HISTORIC SIGHT | Wandering the grounds of this tranquil castle and park near the center of Milan is a great respite from the often-hectic city, and the interesting museums inside are an added bonus. Highlights include the Sala delle Asse, a frescoed room attributed to Leonardo da Vinci (1452–1519), and Michelangelo's unfinished *Rondanini Pietà*, believed to be his last work. The *pinacoteca* (picture gallery) features 230 paintings from medieval times to the 18th century, and the Museo dei Mobili e delle Sculture Lignee (Furniture Museum) includes a delightful collection of Renaissance treasure chests. *Piazza Castello, Castello 02/88463700 www.milanocastello.it Castle free, museums €5 (free every 1st and 3rd Tues. of month after 2, and 1st Sun. of month) Museums closed Mon. Ⓜ Cadorna, Lanza, or Cairoli; Tram No. 1, 2, 4, 12, 14, or 19; Bus No. 18, 37, 50, 58, 61, or 94.*

Performing Arts

Teatro Dal Verme

CONCERTS | Frequent classical, rock, and jazz concerts by international artists are staged here from October to May. *Via San Giovanni sul Muro 2, Castello 02/87905 www.ipomeriggi.it Ⓜ Cairoli; Tram No. 1 or 4.*

Sempione

Just beyond the Sforzesco Castle grounds is a large park that holds an aquarium, the Triennale museum, and the Torre Branca.

Sights

Parco Sempione

CITY PARK | **FAMILY** | Originally the gardens and parade grounds of the Castello Sforzesco, this open space was reorganized during the Napoleonic era, when the arena on its northeast side was constructed, and then turned into a park during the building boom at the end of the 19th century. It is still the lungs of the city's fashionable western neighborhoods, and the **Aquarium** still attracts Milan's schoolchildren. The park became a bit of a design showcase in 1933 with the construction of the Triennale. ✉ *Piazza Sempione, Sempione* 🌐 *www.yesmilano.it/en/see-and-do/itineraries/explore-parco-sempione* 🎫 *Free* Ⓜ *Cairoli, Lanza, or Cadorna; Tram No. 1, 2, 4, 12, 14, 19, or 27; Bus No. 43, 57, 61, 70, or 94.*

Torre Branca
VIEWPOINT | It is worth visiting Parco Sempione just to see the Torre Branca. Designed by architect Gio Ponti (1891–1979), who was behind so many of the projects that made Milan the design capital that it is, this steel tower rises 330 feet over the Triennale. Take the elevator to get a nice view of the city, then have a drink at the glitzy Justme Milano restaurant and club at its base. ✉ *Parco Sempione, Sempione* ☎ *02/6847122* 🌐 *www.museobranca.it/torre-branca* 🎫 *€6* 🕒 *Closed Mon., Tues., and Thurs., and mid-May–mid-Nov.* Ⓜ *Cadorna; Tram No. 1; Bus No. 61.*

Triennale Design Museum
ART MUSEUM | In addition to honoring Italy's design talent, the Triennale also offers a regular series of exhibitions on design from around the world. A spectacular bridge entrance leads to a permanent collection, an exhibition space, and a stylish café and rooftop restaurant with expansive views. The Triennale also manages the fascinating museum-studio of designer Achille Castiglioni, in nearby Piazza Castello (open only with hour-long prebooked guided tours, available Tuesday through Friday at 10, 11, and noon, and one Saturday a month 🎫 *€15*. Call or email in advance to book: ☎ *02/8053606* ✉ *info@achillecastiglioni.it*). ✉ *Via Alemagna 6, Sempione* ☎ *02/72434244* 🌐 *www.fondazioneachillecastiglioni.it* 🎫 *From €15* 🕒 *Closed Mon.* Ⓜ *Cadorna; Bus No. 61.*

Brera

To the north of the Duomo lie the winding streets of this elegant neighborhood, once the city's bohemian quarter.

Sights

Palazzo Citterio (*Grande Brera*)
ART MUSEUM | Emilio and Maria Jesi were among the great Italian art collectors of the 20th century. Some of their treasured works from Pablo Picasso and Amedeo Modigliani are part of the permanent collection in this four-level museum, which opened at the end of 2024, and merges a modern building by Mario Cucinella (who also designed the Fondazione Luigi Rovati museum in Porta Venezia), with an 18th-century palazzo that was once the Jesi family home. Highlights from the permanent galleries on the first floor also include works by Umberto Boccioni and Georges Braque and paintings from the Pinacoteca di Brera (Brera Art Gallery). Temporary exhibitions on the second and ground floors have focused on contemporary art and the history of the Brera neighborhood. ✉ *Via Brera 12, Brera* ☎ *02/72105141* 🌐 *www.palazzocitterio.org* 🎫 *€12 (€20 includes Pinacoteca di Brera)* 🕒 *Closed Mon.–Wed.* Ⓜ *Cairoli, Lanza, Montenapoleone; Tram No. 1, 4, 12, 14, or 27; Bus No. 61.*

★ **Pinacoteca di Brera** (*Brera Art Gallery*)
ART MUSEUM | The collection here is star-studded even by Italian standards. Highlights include the somber *Cristo Morto* (Dead Christ) by Mantegna, which dominates Room VI with its sparse palette of umber and its foreshortened perspective, Raphael's (1483–1520) *Sposalizio della Vergine* (*Marriage of the Virgin*), and *La Vergine con il Bambino e Santi* (*Madonna with Child and Saints*),

by Piero della Francesca (1420–92), an altarpiece commissioned by Federico da Montefeltro (shown kneeling, in full armor, before the Virgin). *Via Brera 28, Brera* *02/72105141* *www.pinacotecabrera.org* *€15 (€20 includes Plazzo Citterio)* *Closed Mon.* *Montenapoleone or Lanza; Tram No. 1, 4, 12, 14, or 27; Bus No. 61.*

Restaurants

★ Cittamani

$$ | **MODERN INDIAN** | Celebrity chef Ritu Dalmia runs well-regarded Italian restaurants in India, so it's no surprise that her restaurant in Milan offers a mash-up of modern Indian food with Italian and international ingredients; even the decor, with shelves of pottery and terrazzo floors, is a cultural combo. Look for unexpected flavors and a mix of small plates, more substantial mains, and utterly delicious fusion desserts. **Known for:** Indian food quite different from the norm; nontraditional naans; sleek contemporary setting. *Average main: €25* *Piazza Mirabello 5, Brera* *02/38240935* *www.cittamani.com* *Closed Sun. No lunch Sat.* *Moscova or Turati; Bus No. 43 or 94.*

Fioraio Bianchi Caffè

$$ | **MODERN ITALIAN** | A French-style bistro in the heart of Milan, Fioraio Bianchi Caffè was opened more than 40 years ago by Raimondo Bianchi, a great lover of flowers; in fact, eating at this restaurant is a bit like dining in a Parisian boutique with floral decor. Despite the French atmosphere, the dishes have Italian flair and ensure a classy, inventive meal. **Known for:** charming, flower-filled, shabby-chic setting; creative Italian-style bistro food; great spot for morning coffee and pastries. *Average main: €30* *Via Montebello 7, Brera* *02/29014390* *www.fioraiobianchicaffe.it* *Closed Sun. and 3 wks in Aug.* *Turati.*

Coffee and Quick Bites

N'Ombra de Vin

$$ | **WINE BAR** | This enoteca serves wine by the glass and, in addition to the plates of *salumi* (Italian cold cuts) and cheese nibbles, has light food and not-so-light desserts. It's a great place for people-watching on Via San Marco, while indoors offers a more dimly lit, romantic setting; check out the impressive vaulted basement, where bottled wines and spirits are sold. **Known for:** atmospheric setting in an Augustinian refectory; Italian and French wines; solid tapas dishes. *Average main: €25* *Via S. Marco 2, Brera* *02/6599650* *www.nombradevin.it* *Lanza, Turati, or Montenapoleone; Tram No. 1, 2, 4, 12, or 14.*

Hotels

Bulgari Hotel Milano

$$$$ | **HOTEL** | Housed in an 18th-century palazzo on a quiet street a short stroll from Brera and Montenapoleone shopping, the Bulgari offers up chic yet restrained rooms, an enormous garden, and a celebrity-chef-helmed restaurant. **Pros:** excellent spa, with heated pool, sauna, and Jacuzzi; trendy and fashionable guests; convenient location for sightseeing. **Cons:** rooms are a bit bland; service not quite up to par; extremely expensive. *Rooms from: €1,400* *Via Privata Fratelli Gabba 7/b, Brera* *02/8058051* *www.bulgarihotels.com/en_US/milan* *61 rooms* *No Meals* *Montenapoleone.*

Nightlife

Il Bar at Bulgari Hotel Milano

BARS | Having drinks or a light lunch at the Bulgari Hotel bar (Il Bar or The Bar) lets you step off the asphalt and into one of the city's most impressive private urban gardens—even indoors you seem to be outside, separated from the elements by a spectacular wall of glass. The Bar is a great place to run into international hotel guests and jet-setting Milanese, and the staff mix up a wide range of traditional and novel drinks—including the Bulgari Cocktail with gin, Aperol, and orange, pineapple, and lime juices. ✉ *Via Privata Fratelli Gabba 7/b, Brera* ☎ *02/8058051* 🌐 *www.bulgarihotels.com/milan/dining/il-bar* Ⓜ *Montenapoleone; Tram No. 1.*

Shopping

With its narrow streets and outdoor cafés, Brera is one of Milan's most charming neighborhoods. Wander through it to find smaller shops with some appealing offerings from lesser-known names that cater to the well-heeled taste of this upscale area. The densest concentration is along Via Brera, Via Solferino, and Corso Garibaldi.

Mercato di Via S. Marco

MARKET | The Monday- and Thursday-morning markets here cater to the wealthy residents of the central Brera neighborhood. In addition to food stands where you can get cheese, roast chicken, and dried beans and fruits, there are several clothing and shoe stalls that are important stops for some of Milan's most elegant women. ✉ *Via San Marco, near Via Castelfidardo, Brera* Ⓜ *Lanza; Tram No. 2, 4, 12, or 14.*

Sant'Ambrogio

If the part of the city to the north of the Duomo is dominated by shopping, Sant'Ambrogio and other parts to the south are known for art. The most famous piece is *Il Cenacolo*—known in English as *The Last Supper.* If you have time for nothing else, make sure you see this masterpiece, which is housed in the refectory of Santa Maria delle Grazie. Reservations are required to see it, and you should make yours at least three weeks before you depart for Italy, so you can plan the rest of your time in Milan.

Sights

Basilica di Sant'Ambrogio
(*Basilica of St. Ambrose*)

CHURCH | Milan's bishop, St. Ambrose (one of the original Doctors of the Catholic Church), consecrated this church in AD 387. St. Ambroeus, as he is known in Milanese dialect, is the city's patron saint, and his remains—dressed in elegant religious robes, a miter, and gloves—can be viewed inside a glass case in the crypt below the altar. Until the construction of the more imposing Duomo, this was Milan's most important church. Much restored and reworked over the centuries (the gold-and-gem-encrusted altar dates from the 9th century), Sant'Ambrogio still preserves its Romanesque characteristics, including 5th-century mosaics. The church is often closed for weddings on Saturday. ✉ *Piazza Sant'Ambrogio 15, Sant'Ambrogio* ☎ *02/86450895* 🌐 *www.basilicasantambrogio.it* Ⓜ *Sant'Ambrogio; Bus No. 50, 58, or 94.*

Chiesa di San Maurizio al Monastero Maggiore

CHURCH | Next to the Museo Civico Archeologico, you'll find this little gem of a church, constructed starting in 1503 and decorated almost completely with magnificent 16th-century frescoes. The modest exterior belies the treasures inside, including a concealed back room once used by nuns that includes a fascinating fresco of Noah loading the ark with animals, including two unicorns. ✉ *Corso Magenta 15, Sant'Ambrogio* ☎ *02/88445208* 🌐 *www.museoarcheologicomilano.it/oltre-il-museo/la-chiesa-s.-maurizio-al-monastero-maggiore* 🕐 *Closed Mon.* Ⓜ *Cadorna or Cairoli; Tram No. 16 or 27; Bus No. 50, 58, or 94.*

Sights

1. Basilica di Sant'Ambrogio **C5**
2. Castello Sforzesco....... **C3**
3. Chiesa di San Maurizio al Monastero Maggiore ... **C4**
4. The Last Supper/ Il Cenacolo/Santa Maria delle Grazie.............. **B4**
5. Museo Civico Archeologico **C4**
6. Museo Nazionale della Scienza e Tecnologia Leonardo da Vinci **B4**
7. Palazzo Citterio **D3**
8. Parco Sempione **C2**
9. Pinacoteca di Brera.... **D2**
10. Torre Branca **B2**
11. Triennale Design Museum **B2**

Restaurants

1. Altriménti **A2**
2. Cittamani.................. **E1**
3. Fioraio Bianchi Caffè.... **E1**
4. Zibo........................ **C5**

Quick Bites

1. N'Ombra de Vin.......... **E2**

Hotels

1. Antica Locanda Leonardo **B4**
2. Bulgari Hotel Milano **E3**

★ *The Last Supper*/Il Cenacolo/Santa Maria delle Grazie

HISTORIC SIGHT | Leonardo da Vinci's *The Last Supper,* housed in this church and former Dominican monastery, has had an almost unbelievable history of bad luck and neglect. Its near destruction in an American bombing raid in August 1943 was only the latest chapter in a series of misadventures, including—if one 19th-century source is to be believed—being whitewashed over by monks. After years of restorers patiently shifting from one square centimeter to another, Leonardo's masterpiece is free of centuries of retouching, grime, and dust. Astonishing clarity and luminosity have been regained, helped by lighting, and a timed entry system where small groups are ushered into climate-controlled rooms with automatic glass doors, to prevent humidity.

Despite Leonardo's carefully preserved preparatory sketches, in which the apostles are clearly labeled by name, there still remains some small debate about a few identities in the final arrangement. There can be no mistaking Judas, however—small and dark, isolated from the terrible confusion that has taken the hearts of the others. Reservations are required to view the work. Viewings are in 15-minute timed-entry slots, and visitors must arrive 30 minutes before. Reservations can be made online. Reserve at least three weeks ahead if you want a Saturday slot, two weeks for a weekday slot. Some city bus tours include a visit in their regular circuit, which may be a good option. ✉ *Piazza Santa Maria delle Grazie 2, off Corso Magenta, Sant'Ambrogio* ☎ *02/92800360 reservations, 02/4676111 church* 🌐 *www.cenacolovinciano.net* 🎫 *Last Supper €15* ⏲ *Closed Mon.* Ⓜ *Cadorna or Conciliazione; Tram No. 18.*

Museo Civico Archeologico (*Municipal Archaeological Museum*)

HISTORY MUSEUM | Appropriately situated in the heart of Roman Milan, this museum housed in a former monastery displays everyday utensils, jewelry, silver plate, and several fine examples of mosaic pavement from Mediolanum, the ancient Roman name for Milan. The museum opens into a garden that is flanked by the square tower of the Roman circus and the polygonal Ansperto tower, adorned with frescoes dating to the end of the 13th and 14th centuries that portray St. Francis and other saints receiving the stigmata. ✉ *Corso Magenta 15, Sant'Ambrogio* ☎ *02/88445208* 🌐 *www.museoarcheologicomilano.it* 🎫 *€5 (free every 1st and 3rd Tues. of month after 2, and 1st Sun. of month)* ⏲ *Closed Mon.* Ⓜ *Cadorna or Cairoli; Tram No. 16 or 27; Bus No. 50, 58, or 94.*

Museo Nazionale della Scienza e Tecnologia Leonardo da Vinci (*National Museum of Science and Technology*)

SCIENCE MUSEUM | FAMILY | This converted cloister is best known for the collection of models based on Leonardo da Vinci's sketches. One of the most visited rooms features interactive, moving models of the famous *vita aerea* (aerial screw) and *ala battente* (beating wing), thought to be forerunners of the modern helicopter and airplane, respectively. The museum also houses a varied collection of industrial artifacts, including trains, and several reconstructed workshops, including a watchmaker's, a lute maker's, and an antique pharmacy. ✉ *Via San Vittore 21, Sant'Ambrogio* ☎ *02/02485551* 🌐 *www.museoscienza.org* 🎫 *€10* Ⓜ *Sant'Ambrogio; Bus No. 50, 58, or 94.*

Restaurants

Zibo

$ | MODERN ITALIAN | Zibo used to wander Milan, serving up unconventional Italian street food but the demand for Giulio Potestà and Alessandro Cattaneo's *carbonara* ravioli (ravioli filled with black pepper and pecorino Romano fondue and topped with crispy guanciale [beef cheek]), *primo sale* (fresh Sicilian cheese) croquettes with onion jam, and pastrami sandwiches led Zibo to put down roots. On a side street off Via Caminadella, its "Base Camp" has a takeaway window (convenient for grabbing a bite between sightseeing) as a remnant of this van life. **Known for:** traditional Italian recipes reimagined as dumplings; seasonal vegetarian mains; casual neighborhood spot with takeaway window. *Average main: €19* *Via Caminadella 21, Sant'Ambrogio* *02/35999463* *www.zibocuochi.com* *Closed Sun. and Mon.* *Sant'Ambrogio, De Amicis; Tram No. 2 or 14.*

Hotels

Antica Locanda Leonardo

$ | HOTEL | A feeling of relaxation prevails in this 19th-century building, and the neighborhood—the church that houses *The Last Supper* is a block away—is one of Milan's most desired and historic. **Pros:** very quiet and homey; breakfast is ample; friendly, helpful staff. **Cons:** more like a bed-and-breakfast than a hotel; books up in advance; breakfast is an extra fee. *Rooms from: €140* *Corso Magenta 78, Sant'Ambrogio* *02/48014197* *www.anticalocandaleonardo.com* *Closed 1st wk in Jan. and 3 wks in Aug.* *24 rooms* *No Meals* *Conciliazione, Sant'Ambrogio, or Cadorna; Tram No. 1, 16, 19, or 27.*

Fiera and San Siro

Fiera is a quiet suburb northwest of the city center, but it's also home to the convention center, Fiera Milano, and the Milano Ice Park hosting speed skating and hockey events for Milano Cortina 2026. Neighboring San Siro's Stadio Meazza (commonly known as San Siro Stadium) is home to AC and Inter Milan home matches and Winter Olympic opening ceremonies.

Restaurants

Altriménti

$$ | MODERN ITALIAN | Alternative describes more than the decor and name at Altriménti. But there are the scarlet velvet Three Wise Monkeys (See no evil, hear no evil, speak no evil) to greet you, evocative bright prints from contemporary Italian artists, that same scarlet for walls, stairs, and cushions, and fluted cardboard stools for resting handbags table-side in the bright main dining room that can seat 30. **Known for:** unusual combinations of signature ingredients from across Italy; traditional Northern Italian dishes with flair; bistro vibe with friendly service. *Average main: €29* *Via Monte Bianco 2/a, Fiera* *02/82778751* *www.altrimenti.eu* *Closed Sun. and Mon.* *Amendola, Lotto, Tre Torri.*

Activities

San Siro Stadium (Stadio Meazza)

SOCCER | FAMILY | AC Milan and Inter Milan, two of the oldest teams in Europe, vie for the heart of soccer-mad Lombardy. They share the use of San Siro Stadium (Stadio Meazza) during their August–May season. With more than 60,000 of the 80,000 seats appropriated by season-ticket holders and another couple of thousand allocated to visiting fans, tickets to Sunday games can be difficult to come by. Buy advance AC Milan tickets at *www.acmilan.com*, at the Casa Milan ticket office at Via Aldo Rossi 8, or at VivaTicket sales points. They're also sold at the stadium booth on match days. Inter tickets are available at *www.inter.it*. Tours are also available (*www.sansirostadium.com/en/museum-tour/*). *Piazzale Angelo Moratti, San Siro* *02/48798201* *www.sansirostadium.com* *San Siro Stadio; Tram No. 16; Bus No. 49.*

Quadrilatero

Via Manzoni, which lies northeast of La Scala, leads to Milan's Quadrilatero della Moda, or fashion district.

Sights

Museo Bagatti Valsecchi

HISTORIC HOME | Glimpse the lives of 19th-century Milanese aristocrats in a visit to this lovely historic house museum, once the home of two brothers, Barons Fausto and Giuseppe Bagatti. Family members inhabited the house until 1974; it opened to the public as a museum in 1984. The house is decorated with the brothers' fascinating collection of 15th- and 16th-century Renaissance art, furnishings, and objects, including armor, musical instruments, and textiles. The detailed audio guide included with admission provides a thorough insight into the history of the artworks and intriguing stories of the family itself. ✉ *Via Gesu 5, Quadrilatero* ☎ *02/76006132* 🌐 *www.museobagattivalsecchi.org* 🎟 *€12* ⏲ *Closed Mon. and Tues.* Ⓜ *Montenapoleone; Tram No. 1.*

Museo Poldi-Pezzoli

ART MUSEUM | This exceptional museum, opened in 1881, was once a private residence and collection, and contains not only pedigreed paintings but also porcelain, textiles, and a cabinet with scenes from Dante's life. The gem is undoubtedly *Portrait of a Lady* by Piero del Pollaiolo (1431–98), one of the city's most prized treasures and the source of the museum's logo. The collection also includes masterpieces by Botticelli (1445–1510), Andrea Mantegna (1431–1506), Giovanni Bellini (1430–1516), and Fra Filippo Lippi (1406–69). ✉ *Via Manzoni 12, Quadrilatero* ☎ *02/794889* 🌐 *www.museopoldipezzoli.it* 🎟 *€15* ⏲ *Closed Tues.* Ⓜ *Montenapoleone or Duomo; Tram No. 1.*

Restaurants

Don Carlos

$$$ | **ITALIAN** | One of the few restaurants open after La Scala lets out, Don Carlos, in the Grand Hotel et de Milan, is nothing like its indecisive operatic namesake (whose betrothed was stolen by his father). Flavors are bold, presentation is precise and full of flair, service is attentive, and the walls are blanketed with sketches of the theater. **Known for:** veal Milanese; homemade pasta; late-night hours. $ *Average main: €39* ✉ *Grand Hotel et de Milan, Via Manzoni 29, Quadrilatero* ☎ *02/72314640* 🌐 *www.ristorantedoncarlos.it/en* ⏲ *No lunch* Ⓜ *Montenapoleone; Tram No. 1 or 2.*

★ **Seta**

$$$$ | **MODERN ITALIAN** | Modern Italian cuisine made using interesting ingredients is the draw at this restaurant with sophisticated brown-and-turquoise decor in Milan's Mandarin Oriental Hotel. The best way to experience the intricate dishes is through the seven-course tasting menu; for a less expensive option, opt for the three-course "carte blanche" lunch menu. **Known for:** ultracreative dishes; wonderful Italo-centric wine list; top-notch service. $ *Average main: €160* ✉ *Via Andegari 9, Quadrilatero* ☎ *02/87318897* 🌐 *www.mandarinoriental.com/milan/la-scala/fine-dining/restaurants/italian-cuisine/seta* ⏲ *Closed Sun. and Mon., 1st wk of Jan., and 3 wks in Aug.* Ⓜ *Montenapoleone; Tram No. 1.*

Hotels

★ **Armani Hotel Milano**

$$$$ | **HOTEL** | This minimalist boutique hotel looks like it has been plucked from the pages of a sleek magazine, and it should: it was designed by fashion icon Giorgio Armani to evoke the same sculptural, streamlined aesthetic—and tailored comfort—as his signature clothing. **Pros:** complimentary (except for alcohol) minibar; lovely spa area and 24-hour

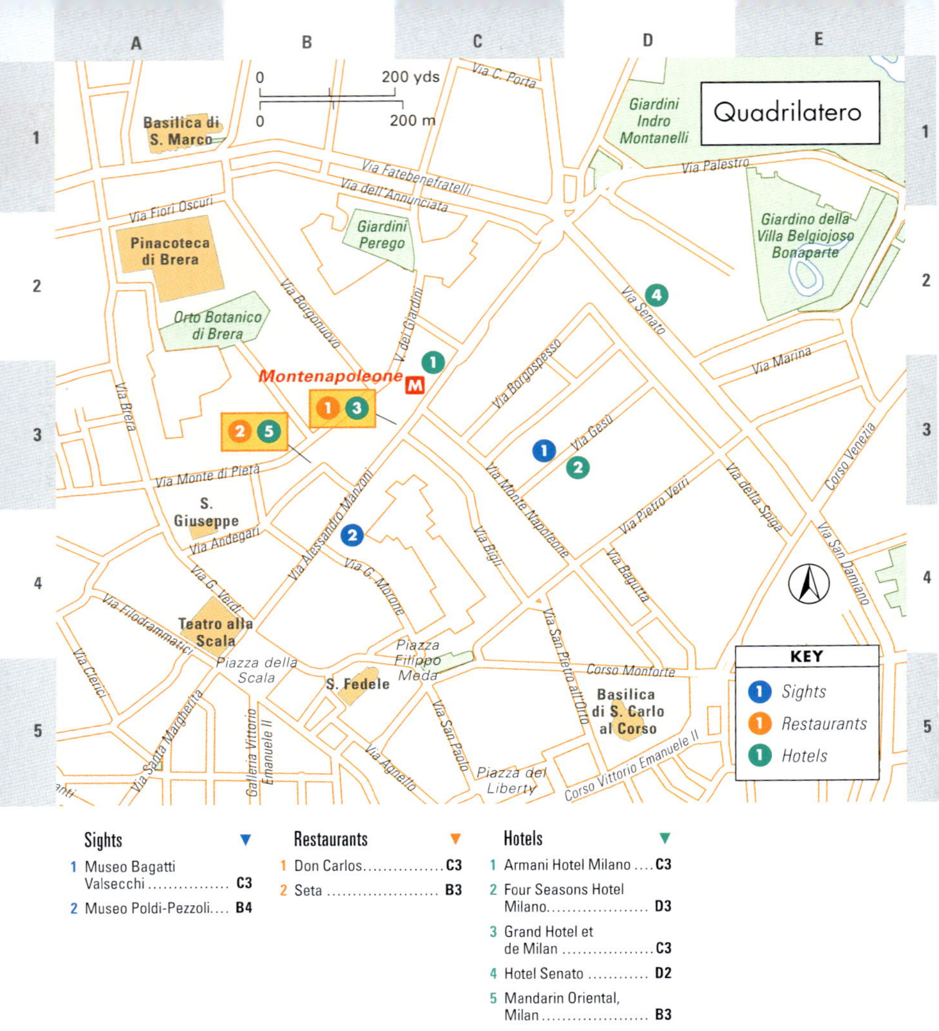

Sights

1 Museo Bagatti Valsecchi **C3**

2 Museo Poldi-Pezzoli.... **B4**

Restaurants

1 Don Carlos................ **C3**

2 Seta **B3**

Hotels

1 Armani Hotel Milano **C3**

2 Four Seasons Hotel Milano.................... **D3**

3 Grand Hotel et de Milan **C3**

4 Hotel Senato **D2**

5 Mandarin Oriental, Milan **B3**

gym; great location near major shopping streets. **Cons:** breakfast (only included in some rates) not up to par; some noise issues from neighboring rooms; a few signs of wear and tear. *$ Rooms from: €1,180 ✉ Via Manzoni 31, Quadrilatero ☎ 02/88838888 🌐 www.armanihotelmilano.com 95 rooms No Meals M Montenapoleone.*

Four Seasons Hotel Milano

$$$$ | **HOTEL** | Built in the 15th century as a convent, with a colonnaded cloister, this sophisticated retreat certainly exudes a feeling that is anything but urban. **Pros:** quiet, elegant setting that feels removed from noisy central Milan; friendly and helpful staff; large rooms. **Cons:** decor is a bit old-fashioned; breakfast isn't included in the rate; expensive. *$ Rooms from: €1,540 ✉ Via Gesù 6–8, Quadrilatero ☎ 02/77088 🌐 www.fourseasons.com/milan 118 rooms No Meals M Montenapoleone; Tram No. 1.*

Grand Hotel et de Milan

$$$$ | **HOTEL** | Only blocks from La Scala, you'll find everything you would expect from a traditionally elegant European hotel, where tapestries and persimmon velvet enliven a 19th-century look without sacrificing dignity and luxury. **Pros:** traditional and elegant; great location off Milan's main shopping streets; staff go above and beyond to meet guest needs. **Cons:** gilt decor may not suit those who like more modern design; no spa; some small rooms. *$ Rooms from: €814 ✉ Via Manzoni 29, Quadrilatero ☎ 02/723141 🌐 www.grandhoteletdemilan.it 72 rooms, 23 suites No Meals M Montenapoleone.*

Hotel Senato

$$$ | **HOTEL** | The central courtyard of this boutique hotel near Milan's fashion district is covered in a layer of water, a cheeky nod to the Naviglio Grande canal that once ran in front of the 19th-century palace, which now has a sleek, minimalist design and artsy touches like brass ginkgo biloba–leaf lamps, serpentine mosaic floor patterns, and flowers and music selected by curators. **Pros:** cool designer touches; lovely breakfast buffet with local products; convenient location. **Cons:** some rooms on the small side; noise can be an issue; basic gym facilities. *$ Rooms from: €480 ✉ Via Senato 22, Quadrilatero ☎ 02/781236 🌐 www.senatohotelmilano.it 43 rooms Free Breakfast M Turati or Palestro; Tram No. 1; Bus No. 61 or 94.*

★ Mandarin Oriental, Milan

$$$$ | **HOTEL** | **FAMILY** | A sense of refined luxury pervades the guest rooms and public spaces of this sophisticated hotel, located just off the main Via Montenapoleone shopping street; from the elegant bedrooms with supercomfortable beds and oversize bathrooms with underfloor heating to the highly rated restaurant and one of the largest spas in Milan (9,700 square feet), you'll be taken care of here. **Pros:** wonderful and attentive service; tranquil spa and 24-hour fitness center; top restaurant on-site. **Cons:** very expensive; only some rooms have views; can be difficult to find. *$ Rooms from: €1,400 ✉ Via Andegari 9, Quadrilatero ☎ 02/87318888 🌐 www.mandarinoriental.com/it/milan 70 rooms, 34 suites No Meals M Montenapoleone; Tram No. 1.*

Armani/Bamboo Bar

BARS | With high ceilings, louvered windows, and expansive views of the city's rooftops, this modern architectural marvel is a great spot to enjoy a relaxing cup of tea or a predinner aperitivo. *✉ Via Manzoni 31, Quadrilatero ☎ 02/88838703 🌐 www.armanihotels.com/it/hotels/armani-hotel-milano/dining M Montenapoleone; Tram No. 1.*

Armani
SPECIALTY STORE | Armani Junior, Emporio Armani, Armani Fiori (flowers), Armani Dolci (chocolate), and Armani Libri (books) are all under this monumental store's roof. ✉ *Via Manzoni 31, Quadrilatero* ☎ *02/62312600* 🌐 *www.armani.com* Ⓜ *Montenapoleone; Tram No. 1.*

★ DMAG Outlet
CLOTHING | This store has some of the best prices in the area for luxury items, such as Prada, Gucci, Lanvin, and Cavalli. DMAG has two other locations, at Via Forcella 13 and Via Bigli 4. ✉ *Via Manzoni 44, Quadrilatero* ☎ *02/36514365* 🌐 *www.dmag.eu* Ⓜ *Montenapoleone; Tram No. 1.*

★ Dolce & Gabbana
CLOTHING | This fabulous duo has created an empire based on sultry designs for men and women. The gorgeous three-story flagship store features clothing for both, plus accessories. ✉ *Via della Spiga 3, Quadrilatero* ☎ *02/77884555* 🌐 *www.dolcegabbana.it* Ⓜ *San Babila; Tram No. 61 or 94.*

Missoni
CLOTHING | Famous for their kaleidoscope-pattern knits, this family-run brand sells whimsical designs for men and women. ✉ *Via Pietro Verri 5, Quadrilatero* ☎ *02/87046300* 🌐 *www.missoni.com* Ⓜ *Montenapoleone or San Babila; Tram No. 1.*

Miu Miu
CLOTHING | Prada's more upbeat, youthful brand has a wide offering of boldly printed women's fashions and accessories. ✉ *Via Sant'Andrea 21, Quadrilatero* ☎ *02/76001799* 🌐 *www.miumiu.com* Ⓜ *Montenapoleone, San Babila, or Palestro; Tram No. 1.*

Prada
CLOTHING | Founded in Milan in 1913 selling steamer trunks and handbags, Prada has several locations throughout the city. Its store on Via Montenapoleone showcase its women's collection. ✉ *Via Montenapoleone 8, Quadrilatero* ☎ *02/7771771* 🌐 *www.prada.com* Ⓜ *Montenapoleone, San Babila, or Palestro; Tram No. 1.*

Roberto Cavalli
CLOTHING | Famous for his wild-animal prints, Roberto Cavalli creates sexy designs for men and women. ✉ *Via Montenapoleone 6, Quadrilatero* ☎ *02/7630771* 🌐 *www.robertocavalli.com* Ⓜ *San Babila.*

Salvatore Ferragamo
LEATHER GOODS | This Florence-based brand is a leader in leather goods and accessories, and carries designs for men and women in this store. ✉ *Via Montenapoleone 3, Quadrilatero* ☎ *02/76000054* 🌐 *www.ferragamo.com* Ⓜ *San Babila.*

Tod's
LEATHER GOODS | This leather-goods leader sells luxury handbags as well as a variety of shoes for men and women. It also offers men's and women's clothing. ✉ *Via Montenapoleone 13, Quadrilatero* ☎ *02/76002423* 🌐 *www.tods.com* Ⓜ *Montenapoleone, San Babila, or Palestro; Tram No. 1.*

Valentino
CLOTHING | Even after the departure of its founding father, Valentino Garavani, this fashion brand still flourishes. ✉ *Via Montenapoleone 20, Quadrilatero* ☎ *02/76006182* 🌐 *www.valentino.com* Ⓜ *Montenapoleone; Tram No. 1.*

Versace
CLOTHING | Run by flamboyant Donatella Versace and known for its rock-and-roll styling, the first store of this fashion house opened on Via della Spiga in 1978, not far from its current location in the Quadrilatero della Moda shopping district. ✉ *Via Monte Napoleone 11, Quadrilatero* ☎ *02/76008528* 🌐 *www.versace.com* Ⓜ *San Babila or Montenapoleone.*

Porta Garibaldi

This stylish, upscale, and buzzing district is home to the colorful and lively Piazza Gae Aulenti, which is a study in Milan's modern architecture, including the 757-foot UniCredit Tower. New construction, stylish restaurants, and urban parks provide a modern break from historical sightseeing.

Sights

ADI Design Museum Compasso d'Oro

SPECIALTY MUSEUM | More than 350 of the most renowned Italian industrial design objects are showcased in this former Enel electricity plant. The items in the permanent collection were selected during biennial judging for Compasso d'Oro (Golden Compass) awards from 1954 until today. Some of the exhibits are grouped by category, like cars (1960 Abarth-Fiat Monza Zagato, 1959 Fiat 500, and 2014 Ferrari F12berlinetta) and coffeemakers (Alessi's 9090 from 1979 and Napoletana from 1981). *✉ Piazza Compasso d'Oro, 1, Garibaldi ☎ 02/36693790 🌐 www.adidesignmuseum.org 🎫 €15 ⏲ Closed Fri. ☞ Tickets may be purchased online, or at the museum with a credit card or mobile wallet (no cash accepted) Ⓜ Garibaldi.*

Piazza Gae Aulenti

PEDESTRIAN MALL | Welcome to the modern era. The piazza named for the famed Italian female architect is a stroll into the future of architectural design. Here you'll find Italy's tallest skyscraper (the 757-foot mirrored and spired UniCredit Tower), IBM Studios (a curved and wood-slatted innovation lab), a Tesla dealership, and an LED tree surrounded by reflective pools. Linger through a botanical garden, *Biblioteca degli Alberi* (library of trees), and join locals picnicking when the weather cooperates. *✉ Piazza Gae Aulenti, Garibaldi Ⓜ Garibaldi.*

Restaurants

★ Ceresio 7 Pools & Restaurant

$$$ | CONTEMPORARY | Book well in advance for one of Milan's most fashionable eateries, where the tables are lacquered red and modern artwork crowds the walls—exactly what you'd expect from the twin brothers, Dean and Dan Caten, behind the fashion label Dsquared2. The food cred matches the scene—with fresh, creative, sophisticated pastas and other dishes. **Known for:** luxe ingredients like lobster, king crab, and truffles; place for seeing and being seen; swimming pools and terrace views. *$ Average main: €39 ✉ Via Ceresio 7, Garibaldi ☎ 02/31039221 🌐 www.ceresio7.com Ⓜ Garibaldi; Tram No. 2, 4, 12, or 14; Bus No. 37 or 190.*

Ratanà

$$ | MODERN ITALIAN | Chef Cesare Battisti infuses the Milanese dishes of his childhood with a contemporary twist at this lively restaurant. Its two patios face a park with skyline views, and its dining room is decorated with vintage items (like an Olivetti typewriter and Scandalli accordion). **Known for:** meat- and fish-focused menu with contemporary and traditional dishes; setting in a former historical house; more than 500 wines. *$ Average main: €28 ✉ Via Gaetano de Castillia 28, Garibaldi ☎ 02/87128855 🌐 www.ratana.it ⏲ Closed 2 wks in Aug. and 2 wks in Dec. Ⓜ Gioia.*

Coffee and Quick Bites

Zàini

$ | DESSERTS | The Zàini family opened its chocolate factory here in 1913, on a side street off Corso Como. Today, its black-and-white marble-tile-floored and chandelier-lit café is a stop for coffee paired with a Zàini classic like Emilia (dark chocolate named after the family's nanny) or Boero (cherry cordial); or dozens of cakes and other sweets. **Known for:** decadent hot chocolate; artfully wrapped chocolate

Sights

1 ADI Design Museum Compasso d'Oro **B3**

2 Piazza Gae Aulenti....... **C2**

Restaurants

1 Ceresio 7 Pools & Restaurant **B3**

2 Mercato Centrale........ **E2**

3 Ratanà **D2**

Quick Bites

1 Pavè........................ **E4**

2 Zàini........................ **C3**

Hotels

1 Hotel Principe di Savoia Milano **D3**

2 Hotel VIU Milan **A3**

3 ME Milan Il Duca **D4**

4 Westin Palace **E4**

gifts; elegant breakfast spot. $ *Average main: €10* ✉ *Via Carlo de Cristoforis 5, Garibaldi* ☎ *02/694914449* 🌐 *www.zainimilano.com* Ⓜ *Garibaldi.*

Hotels

Hotel VIU Milan

$$ | **HOTEL** | A short walk from trendy Corso Como and the historic Cimitero Monumentale, this sleek business-focused hotel features vertical gardens outside and contemporary Italian-designed furnishings within—but its true pièce de résistance is an inviting rooftop pool with panoramic views. **Pros:** stylish modern decor; spacious bathrooms; high-quality food. **Cons:** out-of-the-way location for central Milan; hotel has a signature scent, which may bother perfume-averse guests; rooftop terrace sometimes not useable due to events. $ *Rooms from: €288* ✉ *Via Aristotile Fioravanti 6, Garibaldi* ☎ *02/80010910* 🌐 *www.hotelviumilan.com* *124 rooms* *No Meals* Ⓜ *Monumentale; Tram No. 10, 12, or 14.*

Nightlife

★ Blue Note

LIVE MUSIC | The famous New York nightclub's Milan outpost features regular performances by some of the most well-known names in jazz, as well as blues and rock concerts. Dinner is also available. ✉ *Via Borsieri 37, Garibaldi* ☎ *02/69016888* 🌐 *www.bluenotemilano.com* Ⓜ *Isola; Tram No. 7, 31, or 33.*

Shopping

10 Corso Como

SPECIALTY STORE | A museum-like shrine (taking photos is discouraged) to Milan's creative fashion sense, the concept store 10 Corso Como was founded by the former fashion editor and publisher Carla Sozzani. The clothing and design establishment also includes a restaurant-café, gallery, bookstore, and small hotel. ✉ *Corso Como 10, Corso Como* ☎ *02/29002674* 🌐 *www.10corsocomo.com* Ⓜ *Porta Garibaldi.*

Repubblica

Repubblica, with its stalwart hotels and rooftop bars, is a convenient base if you want a place to unwind near the Central Station.

Restaurants

Mercato Centrale

$ | **FOOD HALL** | Without traveling across the city, you can try the creations of some of the most well-known food purveyors in Milan. Follow neon signs with sketches of the type of food on offer to pick from standbys such as *risotto* from Sergio Barzetti and fish from Pescheria Pedol at Milan's version of the concept food hall that's also in Florence, Rome, and Turin. **Known for:** late-night dining; wide variety of Italian street food; high quality for affordable prices. $ *Average main: €15* ✉ *Via Giovanni Battista Sammartini 2, Repubblica* ☎ *02/37928400* 🌐 *www.mercatocentrale.it/milano* Ⓜ *Central Station; Tram No. 5, 9, or 10.*

Coffee and Quick Bites

★ Pavè

$ | **BAKERY** | Your main problem at Pavè will be deciding what to order among rows of cakes, tarts, classic Italian brioches (with sweet fillings like cream and jam), and other pastries. When everything is this drool-worthy, your best strategy is to come with friends and share your favorites. **Known for:** chocolate and fruit-filled tarts; vegan pastries; sandwiches and crostini on homemade bread. $ *Average main: €10* ✉ *Via Felice Casati 27, Repubblica* ☎ *02/37905491* 🌐 *www.pavemilano.com* Ⓜ *Repubblica.*

Hotels

Hotel Principe di Savoia Milano

$$$ | **HOTEL** | Here, you'll find all the exquisite trappings of a traditional luxury hotel: lavish mirrors, drapes, and carpets; and some of the city's largest guest rooms, outfitted with eclectic fin de siècle furnishings. **Pros:** substantial health club–spa; close to Central Station; shuttle to Duomo and shopping district. **Cons:** located in a not-very-attractive neighborhood; not near major sites; breakfast and other meals overly expensive; showing a bit of wear and tear. *Rooms from: €495* *Piazza della Repubblica 17, Repubblica* *02/91387010* *www.dorchestercollection.com/en/milan/hotel-principe-di-savoia* *301 rooms* *No Meals* *Repubblica; Tram No. 1, 9, or 33.*

ME Milan Il Duca

$$$ | **HOTEL** | This outpost of the Spanish hotel brand ME by Meliá has a lively party atmosphere, with rousing music playing in the lobby, a design-conscious vibe, and a happening rooftop bar with panoramic city views. **Pros:** great rooftop bar; spacious rooms; young, vibrant atmosphere. **Cons:** no spa; may feel overdesigned to some; can be noisy. *Rooms from: €467* *Piazza della Repubblica 13, Repubblica* *02/84220108* *www.melia.com/it/hotels/italia/milano/me-milan-il-duca* *132 rooms* *No Meals* *Repubblica; Tram No. 1, 5, 9, 10, or 33.*

Westin Palace

$$ | **HOTEL** | Don't be fooled by the functional exterior of one of Milan's key business addresses: inside, rooms have a contemporary look with soothing gray walls and marble bathrooms. **Pros:** full-service business hotel with extensive amenities; renovated rooms in both modern and more traditional styles; good-size gym open 24/7. **Cons:** lacking in local character; not in the most central or attractive location; Wi-Fi can be spotty in some rooms. *Rooms from: €329* *Piazza della Repubblica 20, Repubblica* *02/63361* *www.marriott.com/hotels/travel/milwi-the-westin-palace-milan* *231 rooms* *No Meals* *Repubblica; Tram No. 1, 5, 9, or 33.*

Nightlife

Radio Rooftop Bar

COCKTAIL BARS | Some of Milan's most beautiful people congregate for an Aperol spritz and a selection of international tapas on this terrace with panoramic views of the city. Located at the top of the ME Milan Il Duca, the bar has heat lamps to keep visitors here even in cooler weather. *Piazza della Repubblica 13, Repubblica* *02/84220108* *www.melia.com/en/hotels/italy/milan/me-milan-il-duca/restaurants/radio-rooftop-bar* *Repubblica; Tram No. 1, 5, 9, 10, or 33.*

Cinque Giornate

Located just east of the city center, Cinque Giornate marks the location of the Five Days revolt against Austrian rule in Milan.

Restaurants

Da Giacomo

$$$ | **ITALIAN** | The fashion and publishing crowds, as well as international bankers and businesspeople, favor this Milanese-Ligurian restaurant. The emphasis is on fish, and with its tile floor and bank of fresh seafood, the place has a refined neighborhood-bistro style. **Known for:** sophisticated dining; specialty gnocchetti alla Giacomo (with seafood and tomato); extensive wines, cocktails, and after-dinner drinks. *Average main: €40* *Via P. Sottocorno 6, Cinque Giornate* *Entrance in Via Cellini* *02/76023313* *www.giacomomilano.com* *Tram No. 9, 12, 23, or 27; Bus No. 60 or 73.*

Coffee and Quick Bites

De Santis

$ | SANDWICHES | Whether you want to grab a quick sandwich or linger with a glass of wine, since 1964, De Santis is the spot if you're hungry any time of day. There's a selection of traditional sandwiches like Gianmarco with prosciutto, basil, tomato, and soft cow's milk cheese, and the Doralice with mortadella, fontina, and tomato. **Known for:** inventive sandwich fillings; late-night quick meals and drinks; sandwiches made-to-order. *Average main: €12 Via Cesare Battisti 19, Cinque Giornate 02/92862257 www.paninidesantis.it Closed Sun.*

Palestro

Nestled just below the Giardini Pubblici Indro Montanelli park, Palestro is filled with galleries, museums, and historical landmarks.

Sights

GAM: Galleria d'Arte Moderna/Villa Reale

ART MUSEUM | One of the city's most beautiful buildings is an outstanding example of neoclassical architecture, built between 1790 and 1796. After it was donated to Napoléon, who lived here briefly with Empress Josephine, it became known as the Villa Reale. The collection consists of works donated by prominent Milanese art collectors. It emphasizes 18th- and 19th-century Italian works, but also has a smattering of 20th-century Italian pieces. *Via Palestro 16, Palestro 02/88445947 www.gam-milano.com €5 (free every 1st and 3rd Tues. of month after 2 pm) Closed Mon. M Palestro or Turati; Tram No. 1 or 2; Bus No. 94 or 61.*

★ Villa Necchi Campiglio

HISTORIC HOME | In 1932, architect Piero Portaluppi designed this sprawling estate in an Art Deco style, with inspiration coming from the decadent cruise ships of the 1920s. Once owned by the Necchi Campiglio industrial family, the tasteful and elegant three-level home and garden—which sits on Via Mozart, one of Milan's most exclusive streets—is a reminder of the refined, modern culture of the nouveaux riches who accrued financial power in Milan during that era. Don't miss the *Collezione Guido Sforni* on the second floor behind a closed door of one of the bedrooms, where you'll find 21 original drawings by Henri Matisse, Pablo Picasso, and Amedeo Modigliani among other 20th-century artists. There is also a café on the grounds that is open 10 am–6 pm. **TIP→ An audio tour is included with the entrance fee, and can be listened to on a mobile device. Tours in English are available on Saturday at 11:30 am and 2:30 pm with advanced booking.** *Via Mozart 14, Palestro 02/76340121 www.fondoambiente.it/villa-necchi-campiglio-eng €15 (€22 for guided visit) Closed Mon. and Tues. M Palestro, San Babila, or Montenapoleone; Bus No. 54, 61, or 94.*

Porta Venezia

This district is home to parks and gardens, museums, galleries, and one end of the famed Corso Buenos Aires shopping street.

Sights

Fondazione Luigi Rovati

ART MUSEUM | This isn't your typical Etruscan history museum. A seven-year project led by the Luigi Rovati foundation transformed two levels of a palazzo commissioned by the Prince of Piombino in 1871 into a stone-carved contemporary museum where ancient artifacts stand alongside those from the 20th century and beyond. Digital installations translate Etruscan into English and Italian on some of the objects, while an immersive moving floor map shows the civilization's

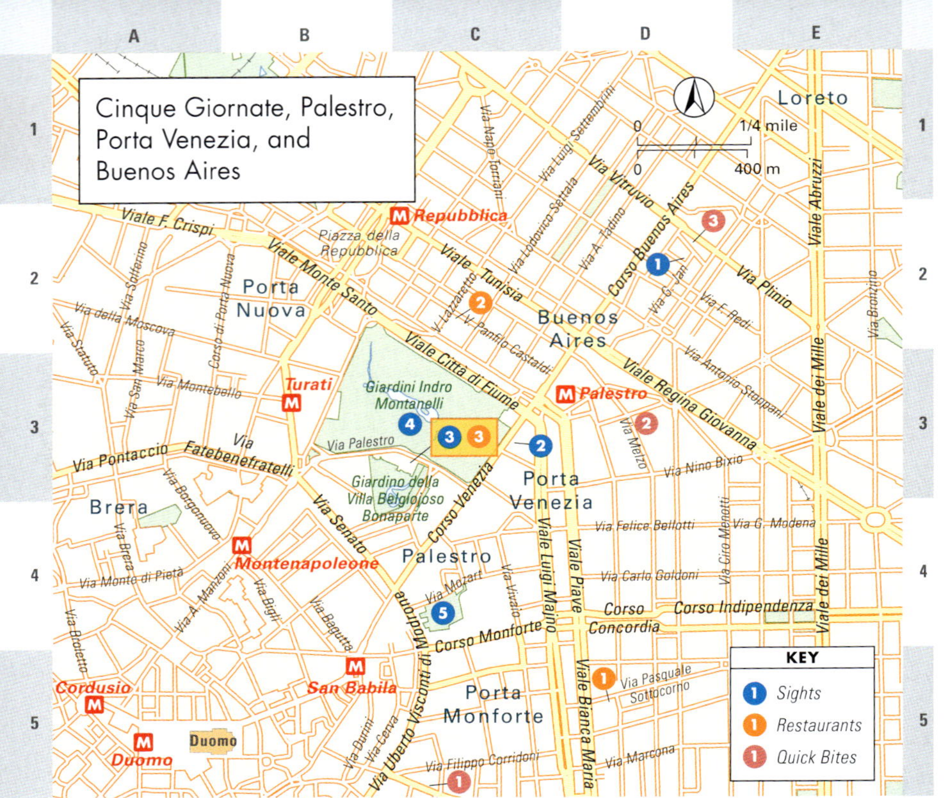

Sights

1 Casa-Museo Boschi di Stefano....... **D2**

2 Fondazione Luigi Rovati............... **C3**

3 GAM: Galleria d'Arte Moderna/Villa Reale **C3**

4 Giardini Pubblici Indro Montanelli......... **C3**

5 Villa Necchi Campiglio................. **C4**

Restaurants

1 Da Giacomo............ **D5**

2 Joia........................ **C2**

3 LùBar...................... **C3**

Quick Bites

1 De Santis................. **C5**

2 Égalité.................. **D3**

3 Marghe.................. **D2**

major cities before its Roman conquest. A rotating display of contemporary exhibits along with permanent works on the main floor continues the play of ancient and modern, such as one where Andy Warhol's interpretation of an Etruscan scene was in the same room as archaeological finds. Giardino Padiglione, and its adjoining Andrea Aprea Bistrot, is an ideal spot for an afternoon aperitif or coffee. ✉ *Corso Venezia 52, Porta Venezia* ☎ *02/38273001* 🌐 *www.fondazioneluigirovati.org* 🎫 *€16* 🕒 *Closed Mon. and Tues.* Ⓜ *Porta Venezia; Tram No. 9.*

Giardini Pubblici Indro Montanelli (*Public Gardens Indro Montanelli*)
GARDEN | **FAMILY** | Giuseppe Piermarini, architect of La Scala, laid out these gardens across Via Palestro from the Villa Reale in 1770. Designed as public pleasure gardens, today they are still popular with families who live in the city center. Generations of Milanese have taken a ride on the miniature train and merry-go-round. The park also contains a small planetarium and the Museo Civico di Storia Naturale (Municipal Natural History Museum). ✉ *Corso Venezia 55, Porta Venezia* ☎ *02/88463337* 🌐 *www.comune.milano.it/aree-tematiche/verde/verde-pubblico/parchi-cittadini/giardini-indro-montanelli* 🎫 *Gardens free, museum €5 (free every 1st and 3rd Tues. of month after 2 pm and 1st Sun. of month)* 🕒 *Museum closed Mon.* Ⓜ *Palestro; Tram No. 9, 29, or 30.*

Restaurants

Joia
$$$$ | **VEGETARIAN** | At this hushed, haute-cuisine vegetarian haven, delicious dishes—all without eggs and many without flour—are served in a minimalist beige room that puts the focus solely on the artistry of the food. Vegetarians, who often get short shrift in Italy, will marvel at the variety of culinary offerings made from many organic and biodynamic ingredients. **Known for:** imaginative presentations; ever-changing menu; well-thought-out wine selection. Ⓢ *Average main: €140* ✉ *Via Panfilo Castaldi 18, Porta Venezia* ☎ *02/29522124* 🌐 *www.joia.it/en* 🕒 *Closed Sun. and Mon., 2 wks in Aug., and Dec. 24–Jan. 6* Ⓜ *Repubblica or Porta Venezia; Tram No. 1, 5, 9, or 33.*

LùBar
$$ | **SICILIAN** | Dining at LùBar, which was started by three children of Milan fashion designer Luisa Beccaria and which is tucked into the side of the Galleria d'Arte Moderna, feels like eating inside a greenhouse—only with fashionable people among the trees and plants. The cozy, chic environs lend themselves perfectly to nibbling on small plates of modern Sicilian food—for lunch, an afternoon snack, or a light dinner. **Known for:** Sicilian street food like arancini and polpette (meatballs); LùBar Spritz made with Amara, a Sicilian blood orange amaro; charming, relaxed atmosphere. Ⓢ *Average main: €21* ✉ *Via Palestro 16, Porta Venezia* ☎ *02/83527769* 🌐 *www.lubar.it* Ⓜ *Palestro or Turati; Tram No. 1 or 2; Bus No. 94 or 61.*

Coffee and Quick Bites

Égalité
$ | **FRENCH** | The 15 different types of daily breads along with tarts, croissants, and a decadent selection of other desserts have a French influence at this bakery with sidewalk tables and chairs and a viewing window into the bakers behind the scenes of it all. Grab an easy breakfast, lunch, or aperitif as you soak up the aroma of fresh-baked baguettes. **Known for:** bread made with Moulin Céard flour; aperitif dishes with cheeses, meats, pickles, and jams; hearty sandwiches. Ⓢ *Average main: €12* ✉ *Via Melzo 22, Porta Venezia* ☎ *02/91763465* 🌐 *www.egalitemilano.it.*

Buenos Aires

This street in northeastern Milan is one of the busiest in the city and has more than 350 stores and outlets to choose from.

Sights

Casa-Museo Boschi di Stefano (*Boschi di Stefano House and Museum*)
HISTORIC HOME | To most people, Italian art means Renaissance art, but the 20th century in Italy was also a time of artistic achievement. An apartment on the second floor of a stunning Art Deco building designed by Milan architect Portaluppi houses this collection, which was donated to the city of Milan in 2003 and is a tribute to the enlightened private collectors who replaced popes and nobles as Italian patrons. The walls are lined with the works of postwar greats, such as Fontana, de Chirico, and Morandi. Along with the art, the museum holds distinctive postwar furniture, sculptures, and stunning Murano glass chandeliers. ✉ *Via Jan 15, Buenos Aires* ☎ *02/88464748* 🌐 *www.casamuseoboschidistefano.it* *Free* ⏲ *Closed Mon.* Ⓜ *Lima; Tram No. 33; Bus No. 60.*

Coffee and Quick Bites

★ **Marghe**
$ | **NEAPOLITAN** | At Marghe, crafting Neapolitan-style pizza is art. Book in advance to grab a table in the rustic and lively dining room with exposed concrete walls, floral-tiled floors, and pendant lights, where pizzas are delivered quickly and piping hot. **Known for:** ingredients from Naples and the Amalfi Coast; local atmosphere; delicious pizza. $ *Average main: €12* ✉ *Via Plinio 6, Buenos Aires* ☎ *02/2047117* 🌐 *www.marghepizza.com* Ⓜ *Lima.*

Formula 1 Racing

Italian Grand Prix. Italy's Formula 1 fans are passionate and huge numbers converge in September for the Italian Grand Prix, held 15 km (9 miles) northeast of Milan in Monza. The racetrack was built in 1922 within the Parco di Monza. Check the website for dates, as well as for special category races, like classic cars and motorcycles. Visitors are allowed to zoom around the track on certain days—guided by a professional driver, of course. ✉ *Monza Eni Circuit, Via Vedano 5, Parco di Monza, Monza* ☎ *24821 in Italy* 🌐 *www.monzanet.it.*

Porta Romana

Porta Romana is a hip and vibrant neighborhood.

Sights

★ **Fondazione Prada**
ART MUSEUM | New structures of metal and glass and revamped buildings once part of a distillery from the 1910s now contain this museum's roughly 205,000 square feet. The modern art showcased here is not for the faint of heart. Permanent pieces, such as *Haunted House,* featuring works by Louise Bourgeois and Robert Gober, are avant-garde and challenging, and temporary exhibitions highlight cutting-edge Italian and international artists. Don't hesitate to ask one of the helpful, knowledgeable staffers for guidance navigating the expansive grounds, which can be confusing. And don't miss the Wes Anderson–designed café, Bar Luce, for a drink or snack, or the restaurant Torre for an aperitivo or a full meal with panoramic views from on high.

The Fondazione is a hike from the city center; expect a 10-minute walk from the metro station to the galleries. ✉ *Largo Isarco 2, Porta Romana* ☎ *02/56662611* 🌐 *www.fondazioneprada.org* 🎟 *€15* ⏲ *Closed Tues.* Ⓜ *Lodi TIBB; Tram No. 24; Bus No. 65.*

Restaurants

Pastamadre

$$ | **MODERN ITALIAN** | Mobiles and natural-wood lanterns decorate this cozy restaurant where house-made pasta is the main event. Start with crusty sourdough bread and small dishes of seasonal salads, vegetables, and fish served on plates crafted in a Milan ceramics studio. **Known for:** vegetarian options; intimate setting; pasta made in-house. $ *Average main: €21* ✉ *Via Bernardino Corio 8, Porta Romana* ☎ *02/55190020* 🌐 *www.pastamadremilano.it* ⏲ *Closed Sun.* Ⓜ *Porta Romana.*

U Barba

$$ | **LIGURIAN** | Simple, fresh, authentic Ligurian specialties will take you back to lazy summer days on the Italian Riviera—even during Milan's gray winters. Such coastal classics as *trofie al pesto* (an egg-free pasta served with pesto) and *bagnun di acciughe* (anchovy soup), coupled with a basket of warm focaccia or a side of *farinata* (a chickpea pancake) reign supreme in this Milan favorite. **Known for:** fresh pasta, also available to take home; charming setting with vintage furniture; seasonal changing menu. $ *Average main: €21* ✉ *Via Pier Candido Decembrio 33, Porta Romana* ☎ *02/45487032* 🌐 *www.ubarba.it* ⏲ *Closed Mon. No lunch weekdays* Ⓜ *Lodi TIBB; Tram No. 16; Bus No. 90.*

Coffee and Quick Bites

Marlà

$ | **BAKERY** | Whether you stop for a cappuccino and one of their gigantic brioche (similar to a croissant) filled with jam, cream, or an unconventional salted-caramel for breakfast, an afternoon break with a selection of minicakes, or to eat a quick sandwich, any craving can be satisfied at Marlà—the acronym for the first names of the two owners, Marco Battaglia and Lavinia Franco. Keep in mind that you may not have room for dinner if you stop by this sea green–and-white modern café in the afternoon. **Known for:** wide selection of breakfast pastries; specialty desserts from Tuscany, Lombardy, and Sicily; mini cheesecakes and tiramisu. $ *Average main: €10* ✉ *Corso Lodi 15, Porta Romana* ☎ *02/36536410* 🌐 *www.marlapasticceria.it* ⏲ *Closed Mon.* Ⓜ *Porta Romana.*

Ticinese

This boho district is also home to the Basilica di San Lorenzo Maggiore and the Basilica di Sant'Eustorgio.

Sights

San Lorenzo Maggiore alle Colonne

CHURCH | Sixteen ancient Roman columns line the front of this sanctuary; remnants of 4th-century Paleo-Christian mosaics survive in the Cappella di Sant'Aquilino (Chapel of St. Aquilinus). ✉ *Corso di Porta Ticinese 35, Ticinese* ☎ *02/89404129* 🌐 *www.sanlorenzomaggiore.com* 🎟 *€2 Chapel of St. Aquilinus* Ⓜ *Missori.*

Restaurants

★ [bu:r] di Eugenio Boer

$$$$ | **MODERN ITALIAN** | Named after the phonetic spelling of the Dutch-Italian chef's last name, this innovative, high-concept restaurant, whose quiet dining rooms are done up in gray and gold, offers a choice of interesting tasting menus and à la carte options. Boer's contemporary Italian food is beautifully presented and full of complex flavors, and the well-matched wines lean toward the

Sights

1 Armani/Silos............ B3
2 Fondazione Prada E4
3 MUDEC (Museo delle Culture) A3
4 Navigli District B4
5 San Lorenzo Maggiore alle Colonne D2

Restaurants

1 Al Fresco................. A3
2 [bu:r] di Eugenio Boer... E3
3 142........................ B3
4 Pastamadre E4
5 U Barba E4

Quick Bites

1 Marià...................... E4

Hotels

1 Aethos Milan............ C3
2 Hotel Magna Pars Suites Milano B3

natural. **Known for:** personalized cuisine; traditional dishes with an ultramodern spin; helpful and well-informed service. *$ Average main: €115 ✉ Via Mercalli 22, Ticinese ☎ 02/62065383 🌐 www.restaurantboer.com ⏱ Closed Mon. and Tues. No lunch weekdays Ⓜ Crocetta; Tram No. 15; Bus No. 94.*

Hotels

★ Aethos Milan

$$ | **HOTEL** | The decor in this eclectic, extremely hip hotel at the foot of the lively Corso di Porta Ticinese and by the Navigli canals features sports memorabilia from golf, horseback riding, boxing, and others. **Pros:** contemporary flair; interesting location near many restaurants and bars; very friendly staff. **Cons:** lacking some of the amenities of large hotels; about a half-hour hike from the Duomo and central attractions; bar noise can be heard in some rooms. *$ Rooms from: €285 ✉ Piazza XXIV Maggio 8, Porta Ticinese ☎ 02/89415901 🌐 www.aethos.com 32 rooms No Meals Ⓜ Tram No. 3 or 9.*

Navigli

One of the oldest neighborhoods in the city, Navigli is a quiet, artistic hub during the weekdays and a lively hot spot on nights and weekends.

Sights

★ Navigli District

HISTORIC DISTRICT | In medieval times, a network of *navigli*, or canals, crisscrossed the city. Almost all have been covered over, but two—Naviglio Grande and Naviglio Pavese—are still navigable. The area's chock-full of boutiques, art galleries, cafés, bars, and restaurants, and at night the Navigli serves up a scene about as close as you will get to southern Italian–style street life in Milan. On weekend nights, it is difficult to walk among the youthful crowds thronging the narrow streets along the canals. Check out the antiques fair on the last Sunday of the month from 9 to 6. **TIP→ During the summer months, be sure to put on some mosquito repellent.** *✉ South of Corso Porta Ticinese, Navigli ☎ 02/89409971 🌐 www.navigliogrande.mi.it/eventi Ⓜ Porta Genova; Tram No. 2, 3, 9, 14, 15, 29, or 30.*

Restaurants

142

$$ | **MODERN ITALIAN** | From day to night, step into the chic living room of 142 for whatever you are craving. Drink coffee and eat a homemade brioche at a bar decorated in crown caps or eat lunch or dinner at tables with a hand-painted Pollock flourish, while browsing a selection of art books. **Known for:** playful plating and setting; all day and late-night dining; seafood dishes with flair. *$ Average main: €26 ✉ Corso Cristoforo Colombo 6, Navigli ☎ 02/47758490 🌐 www.142.restaurant ⏱ Closed Mon. No dinner Sun. Ⓜ Porto Genova: Tram No. 2, 9, 10, or 14.*

Nightlife

Rita

BARS | Though it's a bit difficult to find, on a side street in the popular aperitivo haunt of Navigli, the expertly mixed cocktails, well-prepared snacks, and excellent playlist make this classic worth the hunt. It also serves burgers, sandwiches, and more substantial plates for dinner. *✉ Via Angelo Fumagalli 1, Navigli ☎ 02/8372865 🌐 www.ritacocktails.com Ⓜ Porta Genova; Tram No. 2.*

★ Ugo Bar

BARS | Flanked by a long bar and tables lit by candles, and featuring floral wallpaper and eclectic framed paintings of animals, this bar has a moody living-room vibe. It's a charming place for a drink, if you can squeeze past the crowds. There is also a

Did You Know?

The oldest canal in Milan, the Naviglio Grande was built between 1177 and 1257. It's more than 50 km (31 miles) long and was primarily used for transporting goods. Today, the area around the canal is hopping with charming boutiques, galleries, cafés, and restaurants. Take a boat tour down the waterway and take in the neighborhood.

handful of outdoor tables for prime people-watching. ✉ *Via Corsico 12, Navigli* ☎ *02/39811337* 🌐 *www.ugobar.it* Ⓜ *Porta Genova; Tram No. 9 or 10.*

Performing Arts

Auditorium di Milano Fondazione Cariplo

CONCERTS | This modern hall, known for its excellent acoustics, is home to the Orchestra Sinfonica di Milano (Symphonic Orchestra) and Coro Sinfonico di Milano Giuseppe Verdi (Symphonic Choir). The season, which runs from September to June, includes many top international performers and rotating guest conductors. ✉ *Largo Gustav Mahler, at Corso San Gottardo, Navigli* ☎ *02/83389401* 🌐 *www.sinfonicadimilano.org* Ⓜ *Tram No. 3 or 15; Bus No. 59 or 91.*

Shopping

Antonioli

CLOTHING | Antonioli raises the bar for Milan's top trendsetters. Uniting the most cutting-edge looks of each season, it is among the fashion-forward concept stores in the city. Aside from Italian brands like Valentino, it also stocks a competitive international array of designers, like Ann Demeulemeester, Rick Owens, Givenchy, and Maison Margiela. ✉ *Via Pasquale Paoli 1, Navigli* ☎ *02/36564834* 🌐 *www.antonioli.eu* Ⓜ *Porta Genova; Tram No. 2.*

Tortona

Tortona's former factories, warehouses, and workshops are now a creative hub packed with shops, studios, and the MUDEC, a museum with modern and contemporary art and special exhibitions.

Sights

Armani/Silos

SPECIALTY MUSEUM | About 600 pieces, from about 1980 to the present, by famed Milanese fashion designer Giorgio Armani are displayed on four floors of this airy 48,000-square-foot museum, housed in a 1950s building that was formerly a Nestlé cereal storage facility. The collection includes many of Armani's famous suits and clothes worn to the Oscars and other celebrity-studded events. A digital archive lets you explore Armani's full body of work, and a café lets you stop for a restorative espresso. Temporary exhibitions explore photography, architecture, and other themes related to design. ✉ *Via Bergognone 40, Tortona* ☎ *02/91630010* 🌐 *www.armanisilos.com* 🎫 *€12* 🕒 *Closed Mon. and Tues.* Ⓜ *Sant'Agostino or Porta Genova; Tram No. 2 or 14; Bus No. 68 or 90/91.*

MUDEC (Museo delle Culture)

ART MUSEUM | Home to a permanent collection of ethnographic displays as well as temporary exhibitions of big-name artists such as Basquiat and Miró, MUDEC is in the vibrant Zona Tortona area of the city. British architect David Chipperfield designed the soaring space in a former factory. The permanent collection includes art, objects, and documents from Africa, Asia, and the Americas. Book in advance for the most popular temporary exhibits. There's also a highly rated restaurant, Enrico Bartolini Mudec, as well as a more casual bistro. ✉ *Via Tortona 56, Tortona* ☎ *02/54917* 🌐 *www.mudec.it* 🎫 *Permanent collection free, special exhibitions from €16* 🕒 *Closed Mon. until 2:30 pm* Ⓜ *Sant'Agostino or Porta Genova; Tram No. 2 or 14; Bus No. 68 or 90/91.*

Restaurants

Al Fresco

$$ | **MODERN ITALIAN** | In Italian, *al fresco* means open-air, and when the weather cooperates you can dine in the candlelit garden of this restaurant converted from a former factory. The string lights and wooden tables create a romantic setting, while indoors, a greenhouse with terra-cotta floors is decorated with seasonal floral arrangements, chandeliers, and pendant lights to add to the 19th-century charm. **Known for:** garden setting; fish and tempura courses; extensive menu and many vegetarian options. *Average main: €30* ✉ *Via Savona 50, Tortona* ☎ *02/49533630* 🌐 *www.alfrescomilano.it* Ⓜ *Porto Genova.*

Hotels

Hotel Magna Pars Suites Milano

$$$$ | **HOTEL** | This ultrastylish all-suites boutique hotel in a former perfume factory has Italian-designed furnishings; paintings by local Brera Academy artists; and sleek, white accommodations—each with its own signature scent (such as fruity, woodsy, or floral) and all overlooking one of two tranquil courtyards. **Pros:** modern, design-y feel; attentive service; wonderful food at the attached restaurant. **Cons:** spa on the small side; a bit of a trek to central attractions; perfumed rooms not for everyone. *Rooms from: €650* ✉ *Via Forcella 6, Tortona* ☎ *02/8338371* 🌐 *www.magnapars.it* *60 suites* *Free Breakfast* Ⓜ *Porta Genova; Tram No. 2, 9, or 19.*

Bergamo

52 km (32 miles) northeast of Milan.

If you're driving from Milan to Lake Garda, the perfect deviation from your autostrada journey is the lovely medieval town of Bergamo, which is also a wonderful side trip by train from Milan. With direct service from Milan, you'll be whisked from the restless pace of city life to the medieval grandeur of Bergamo Alta in about an hour.

GETTING HERE AND AROUND

Bergamo is along the A4 autostrada. By car from Milan, take the A51 out of the city to pick up the A4; the drive is 52 km (32 miles) and takes about 45 minutes. By train, Bergamo is about one hour from Milan and 1½ hours from Desenzano del Garda-Sirmione station.

VISITOR INFORMATION

CONTACT Bergamo Tourism Office. ✉ *Torre del Gombito, Via Gombito 13, Bergamo Alta, Bergamo* ☎ *035/242226* 🌐 *www.visitbergamo.net.*

Sights

Accademia Carrara

ART MUSEUM | Bergamo is home to an art collection that's surprisingly rewarding given its size and remote location. Many of the Venetian masters are represented—Mantegna, Bellini, Carpaccio (circa 1460–1525/26), Tiepolo (1727–1804), Francesco Guardi (1712–93), and Canaletto (1697–1768), as well as Botticelli (1445–1510). ✉ *Piazza Carrara 82, Bergamo Bassa, Bergamo* ☎ *035/234396 weekdays, 035/4122097 weekends* 🌐 *www.lacarrara.it* *€10.*

Campanone

CLOCK | The massive 13th-century Torre Civica (Civic Tower), known as the Campanone, offers a great view of the two cities. Climb the stairs or take an elevator to the top of the tower, where the bells ring every half hour and then 100 times each night at 10 to commemorate the closure of the city gates during Venetian rule. ✉ *Piazza Vecchia, Bergamo Alta, Bergamo* ☎ *035/247116* 🌐 *www.museodellestorie.bergamo.it/luogo/campanone* *€7* *Closed Mon.*

The medieval town of Bergamo at sunrise is a stunning sight.

Cappella Colleoni

CHURCH | Bergamo's **Duomo** and **Battistero** are the most substantial buildings in Piazza Duomo. But the most impressive structure is the Cappella Colleoni, which boasts a kaleidoscope of marble decoration and golden accents. ✉ *Piazza Duomo, Bergamo Alta, Bergamo* ☎ *035/210061* ⏲ *Closed Mon.*

Restaurants

★ Al Donizetti

$$ | **NORTHERN ITALIAN** | Find a table in the back of this central, cheerful restaurant before choosing local cured meats and cheeses to accompany your wine. A few versions of polenta, daily pastas, and other heartier dishes are also available; just save room for the desserts, which go well with the sweet wines. **Known for:** beef tartare; 900-bottle wine selection with many by the glass; chocolate desserts. [$] *Average main: €20* ✉ *Via Gombito 17/a, Bergamo Alta, Bergamo* ☎ *035/242661* ⏲ *Closed Tues.*

Villa Elena

$$$$ | **MODERN EUROPEAN** | Walking through the iron gates of Villa Elena, past a Medieval tower and manicured mosaic-pathed garden with sweeping Bergamo views, is like entering a fairy tale. The Liberty villa, with original frescoes, parquet and terrazzo floors and stained glass windows punctuated by Mid-Century Modern lamps, chairs, and credenzas, complements the white-gloved presentation across three dining rooms under the direction of celebrated chef Enrico Bartolini. **Known for:** palatial setting with sweeping views above the Città Alta; refined Italian cuisine with no-waste philosophy; roots and tubers with 20 different types on one plate. [$] *Average main: €155* ✉ *Via San Vigilio 56, Bergamo* ☎ *035/260944* 🌐 *www.enricobartolini.net/i-ristoranti/villa-elena* ⏲ *Closed Mon. and Tues.*

Vineria Cozzi

$$ | **WINE BAR** | The wine list at this romantic but informal *vineria* (wine bar) is exceptional—both by the glass

and by the bottle—and there's also an array of flavorful foods, from snacks to sumptuous full-course meals typical of the region. The atmosphere is warm and charming, harking back more than 150 years to when the spot was first established in Bergamo as a lively meeting place. **Known for:** quirky historical decorations; cellar with more than 300 wines; polenta dishes as starters and mains. *Average main: €27 Via B. Colleoni 22, Bergamo Alta, Bergamo 035/238836 www.vineriacozzi.it Closed Wed.*

 Coffee and Quick Bites

La Marianna

$ | ICE CREAM | FAMILY | *Stracciatella* gelato—a creamy combination of milk, egg yolks, vanilla, sugar, and dark chocolate shavings—is Italy's answer to chocolate-chip ice cream. While you'll see the flavor in gelaterie across Italy, one pastry shop, and city, Bergamo, claims it as its own. **Known for:** upscale gelateria atmosphere; decorated seasonal cookies and cakes; outdoor courtyard away from the crowds of Città Alta. *Average main: €10 Largo Colle Aperto 4, Bergamo 035/237027 www.lamarianna.it.*

 Hotels

Mercure Bergamo Centro Palazzo Dolci

$ | HOTEL | Set in a restored 19th-century palazzo, this Bergamo Basso hotel has modern comforts and a friendly, efficient staff, making it a good choice for both business and leisure travelers. **Pros:** convenient to train station, airport, and some shopping; good value; bountiful breakfast buffet. **Cons:** basic rooms; no parking on-site; no restaurant. *Rooms from: €124 Viale Papa Giovanni XXIII 100, Bergamo Bassa, Bergamo 035/227411 www.mercurebergamocentropalazzodolci.com-hotel.com 92 rooms No Meals.*

Relais San Vigilio

$$ | HOTEL | Brothers Gigi and Paolo Zani transformed a castle and soldiers' barracks dating from the Middle Ages into a retreat just above the Città Alta. **Pros:** lovely views and spacious garden with many sitting areas; quiet location away from the crowds; hotel layout in two buildings offers extra privacy among rooms. **Cons:** 10-minute walk or quick funicular ride to Città Alta; expensive on-site parking in small garage with narrow driveway; some bathrooms are small. *Rooms from: €261 Via al Castello 7/9, Bergamo 035/2650987 www.relaissanvigilio.it 9 rooms Free Breakfast.*

Cremona

100 km (62 miles) southeast of Milan.

Cremona is a classical-music lover's dream. With violin shops on nearly every block along its crooked old streets, it is where the world's best violins are crafted. Andrea Amati (1510–80) invented the modern instrument here in the 16th century. Though cognoscenti continue to revere the Amati name, it was an apprentice of Amati's nephew for whom the fates had reserved wide and lasting fame. In a career that spanned an incredible 68 years, Antonio Stradivari (1644–1737) made more than 1,200 instruments—including violas, cellos, harps, guitars, and mandolins, in addition to his fabled violins. They remain among the most coveted, most expensive stringed instruments in the world.

Cremona's other claim to fame is *torrone* (nougat), which is said to have been created here in honor of the marriage of Bianca Maria Visconti and Francesco Sforza, which took place in October 1441. The new confection, originally prepared by heating almonds, egg whites, and honey over low heat, and shaped and named after the city's tower, was created in symbolic celebration. The annual Festa del Torrone is held in the main piazza over the third or fourth week of November.

GETTING HERE AND AROUND

By car from Milan, start out on the A1 autostrada and switch to the A21 at Piacenza; the drive is about 100 km (62 miles) and takes about 1½ hours. By train, Cremona is about an hour from Milan and 1½ hours from Desenzano, near Sirmione on Lake Garda.

VISITOR INFORMATION

CONTACT Cremona Tourism Office. ✉ *Piazza del Comune 5, Cremona* ☎ *0372/407081* 🌐 *www.turismocremona.it.*

Sights

Duomo

CHURCH | Cremona's Romanesque Duomo was consecrated in 1190. It's an impressive structure in a breathtaking piazza, and certainly one of the most beautiful churches in Italy. Here you can find the *Story of the Virgin Mary and the Passion of Christ,* the central fresco of an extraordinary cycle commissioned in 1514 and featuring the work of local artists, including Boccaccio Boccaccino, Giovanni Francesco Bembo, and Altobello Melone. ✉ *Piazza del Comune, Cremona* ☎ *0373/495082* 🌐 *www.cattedraledicremona.it.*

★ **Museo del Violino**

SPECIALTY MUSEUM | At this lovely and informative museum dedicated to all things violin, even those not already enamored by the instrument will find something to appreciate. Historic violins made in Cremona by masters, including Stradivari, are presented as works of art; be sure to get the audio guide included with admission to listen to recordings as you stroll. An audio chamber lets you hear a musical performance in "3D audio"—and if you're lucky, there will be a live concert going on at the innovative on-site auditorium, where the seats wrap around the stage and musicians for an immersive experience. ✉ *Palazzo dell'Arte, Piazza Marconi 5, Cremona* ☎ *0372/801801, 0372/080809 tickets* 🌐 *www.museodelviolino.org* 🎟 *€12* ⏲ *Closed Mon.*

Piazza del Comune

PLAZA/SQUARE | The Duomo, tower, baptistery, and Palazzo Communale (city hall) surround this distinctive and harmonious square: the combination of old brick, rose- and cream-color marble, terra-cotta, and old copper roofs brings Romanesque, Gothic, and Renaissance together with unusual success. ✉ *Piazza del Comune, Cremona.*

Piazza Roma 1

PLAZA/SQUARE | Legendary violin maker Antonio Stradivari lived, worked, and died near the verdant square at Piazza Roma 1 (not open to the public). According to local lore, Stradivari kept each instrument in his bedroom for a month before varnishing it, imparting part of his soul before sealing and sending it out into the world. In the center of the park is a copy of Stradivari's tombstone, while the original is in the Violin Museum. ✉ *Piazza Roma 1, Cremona.*

Torrazzo (*Big Tower*)

CLOCK | Dominating Piazza del Comune is perhaps the tallest campanile in Italy, visible for a considerable distance across the Po Plain. The tower's astronomical clock is the 1583 original. Climb the 500-plus steps to the top for amazing views; along the way, you can stop at the Museo Verticale for informative displays on astronomy and ancient methods of measuring time. ✉ *Piazza del Comune, Cremona* ☎ *0372/495082* 🌐 *www.museoverticale.it* 🎟 *€10 with baptistery* ⏲ *Closed Mon. during Jan. and Feb.*

The Po Plain, Lake Garda, and Lake Iseo
Lake Lugano
Tremezzo
Lake Como
Lecco
Como
Giussano
Monza
Aeroporto di Milano Malpensa
Legnano
Lainate
Rho
Milan see detail maps
Aeroporto di Milano Linate
Buccinasco
Rozzano
Melegnano
Adda
Ticino
Mortara
Certosa di Pavia
Pavia
Po
Bergamo
Treviglio
LOMBARDY
Crema
Lodi
Casalpusterlengo
TO PARMA
Cremona
Oglio
Darfo-Boario
Monte Isola
Sale Marasino
Sarnico
Lake Iseo
Borgonato
Iseo
Cortefranco
Sarezzo
Franciacorta
Erbusco
Ca' del Bosco
Brescia
TRENTINO-ALTO ADIGE
Riva del Garda
Limone
Malcesine
Tignale
Gargnano
Monte Baldo
Gardone Riviera
Salò
Lake Garda
Punta di San Vigilio
Bardolino
Sirmione
Desenzano
TO VERONA
TO VENICE
VENETO
Mantua
0 10 mi
0 10 km

Restaurants

La Sosta

$$ | **NORTHERN ITALIAN** | This osteria looks to the 16th century for culinary inspiration, with excellent homemade salami and a popular primo—*marubini Cremonesi ai tre brodi* (stuffed meat ravioli in broth)—made according to time-tested recipes. Order the tiramisu and an accompanying dessert wine for a perfect finish. **Known for:** cheese tasting menu; Cremonese sausage and veal osso buco; extensive wine cellar with dessert wines. *Average main: €24 Via Sicardo 9, Cremona 0372/456656 www.osterialasosta.it Closed Mon. and 3 wks in Aug. No dinner Sun.*

Coffee and Quick Bites

★ Pasticceria Duomo

$ | **CAFÉ** | This portal to the past opened in 1883 and still serves up such handmade local delights as *pan torrone* (a loaf cake made with chunks of nougat) and *torta cremona* (a cake made with almond flour and filled with Amarena cherries). A relaxing stop between visiting museums, it's the perfect place to have a cappuccino. **Known for:** torrone (nougat) in many shapes and sizes; old-world charm; seasonal decorated cakes and pastries. *Average main: €10 Via Boccaccino 6, Cremona 0372/22273.*

Hotels

Delle Arti Design Hotel

$ | **HOTEL** | With modern interiors and eclectic but comfortable designer furniture, this aptly named hotel makes a nice counterpoint to the historical surroundings of Cremona. **Pros:** convenient central location; friendly staff; good breakfast options. **Cons:** small bathrooms; hallways can be a little dark; starting to show its age. *Rooms from: €157 Via Bonomelli 8, Cremona 0372/23131 www.dellearti.com 33 rooms Free Breakfast.*

Hotel Impero

$ | **HOTEL** | Just a few minutes' walk from the Duomo and the Museo del Violino, this comfortable hotel with functional yet pleasant rooms (the best of which overlook the piazza) is well equipped to satisfy both leisure and business travelers. **Pros:** central location; highly professional staff; spacious rooms. **Cons:** rooms are a little bland and outdated; outside noise can be a problem, especially on weekends; breakfast is basic. *Rooms from: €127 Piazza della Pace 21, Cremona 0372/413013 www.hotelimpero.cr.it 51 rooms Free Breakfast.*

Shopping

Sperlari

FOOD | Sperlari and parent company Fieschi have grown into a confectionery empire, but it all started at this handsome shop, which has been selling Cremona's famous nougat and its best *mostarda* (a spicy-sweet condiment made of candied fruit in a syrup with mustard mixed in) since 1836. While shopping for these items—as well as teas, marmalades, and other Italian delights—be sure to check out the historical product display at the back of the store. *Via Solferino 25, Cremona 0372/22346 www.sperlari1836.com.*

Mantua

192 km (119 miles) southeast of Milan.

Mantua (Mantova in Italian) stands tallest among the ancient walled cities of the Po Plain; it may not be flashy or dramatic, but its beauty is subtle and deep, hiding a rich trove of artistic, architectural, and cultural gems beneath its slightly somber facade. Its fortifications are circled on three sides by the passing Mincio River, which long provided Mantua with protection, fish, and a steady stream of river tolls on its meandering way from Lake Garda to the Po.

GETTING HERE AND AROUND

Mantua is 5 km (3 miles) west of the A22 autostrada. The drive from Milan, following the A4 to the A22, takes a little more than two hours. The drive from Cremona, along the SP10, is 1¼ hours. Most trains arrive in just under two hours from Milan, depending on the type of service, and in about 1½ hours from Desenzano, near Sirmione on Lake Garda, via Verona.

VISITOR INFORMATION

CONTACT Mantua Tourism Office. ✉ *Piazza Sordello 23, Mantua* ☎ *0376/288208* 🌐 *www.turismo.mantova.it.*

Sights

Be sure to pick up a Mantova Sabbioneta Card (☎ *0376/230339* 🌐 *www.mantova-card.it*) at the tourism office, Palazzo Ducale, or Palazzo Te. It costs €25 and entitles you to visit 17 museums and monuments (with a €5.50 supplement to visit Camera degli Sposi) and also includes access to city buses, including Sabbioneta.

★ Palazzo Ducale

CASTLE/PALACE | The 500-room palace that dominates the Mantua skyline was built for the Gonzaga family, though much of the art within the castle was sold or stolen as the dynasty waned in power and prestige. A glimpse of past grandeur can still be spotted as you enter the palace, turn immediately left, and walk up a steep hallway, arriving in Camera degli Sposi (literally, the "Wedded Couple's Room") where Duke Ludovico and his wife held court. Reservations are recommended, either by phone or online (🌐 *www.ducalemantova.org*). ✉ *Piazza Sordello 40, Mantua* ☎ *041/2411897* 🌐 *www.mantovaducale.beniculturali.it* 🎫 *€9, €15 including Camera degli Sposi (€5.50 with Mantova Sabbioneta Card)* 🕒 *Closed Mon.*

★ Palazzo Te

CASTLE/PALACE | One of the greatest of all Renaissance palaces, built between 1525 and 1535 by Federico II Gonzaga, is the Mannerist masterpiece of artist-architect Giulio Romano. Two highlights are the Camera di Amore e Psiche (Room of Cupid and Psyche), which depicts a wedding set among lounging nymphs, and the gasp-inducing Camera dei Giganti (Room of the Giants) that shows Jupiter expelling the Titans from Mount Olympus. The scale of the latter is overwhelming; the floor-to-ceiling work completely envelops the viewer. Note the etched graffiti from as far back as the 17th century to the left as you enter the room. ✉ *Viale Te 13, Mantua* ☎ *0376/323266* 🌐 *www.centropalazzote.it* 🎫 *€15.*

Sant'Andrea

CHURCH | Mantegna's tomb is in the first chapel to the left in this basilica, most of which was built in 1472. The current structure, a masterwork by the architect Alberti, is the third built on this spot to house the relic of the Precious Blood: the crypt holds two reliquaries containing earth believed to be soaked in the blood of Christ, brought to Mantua by Longinus, the soldier who pierced his side. They are displayed only on Good Friday. ✉ *Piazza di Mantegna 1, Mantua* ☎ *0376/320220* 🌐 *www.parrocchiasantanselmomantova.it.*

Restaurants

Ambasciata

$$$$ | **NORTHERN ITALIAN** | Heralded as one of Italy's classic gourmet restaurants, Ambasciata (Italian for "embassy") emphasizes elegance in tiny Quistello, 20 km (12 miles) southeast of Mantua. Those who are willing to make the trek (and pay the bill) can order à la carte or opt for the tasting menu (from €80) with an ever-changing array of traditionally inspired creations, such as the famed *tortelli di zucca* (pumpkin tortelli with pumpkin cream, almond cookies, and Parmigiano-Reggiano), or mains like guinea fowl with mostarda, and roast pigeon with 25-year reserve balsamic vinegar. **Known for:** intricate cuisine coupled with classics; whimsical setting; attentive service. *Average main: €80* *Piazzetta Ambasciatori del Gusto 1, Quistello* *0376/619169* *www.ristorantelambasciata.eu* *Closed Mon. and Tues.*

Sücar Brüsc

$$ | **MODERN ITALIAN** | In Mantua, *sücar brüsc* (brusque sugar), is another way of saying salt—since sugar and salt are deceptive look-alikes. Savory-sweet also describes the city's culinary stars t *ortelli di zucca* (pumpkin ravioli) and *mostarda mantovana* (relish with apples, pears, and mustard oil). **Known for:** extensive caviar and sparkling wine list; creative spins on Mantua's traditional ingredients; tasting menus for carnivores and vegetarians. *Average main: €24* *Via Camillo Benso Conte di Cavour 49, Mantua* *0333/1848730* *www.sucarbrusc.it.*

Coffee and Quick Bites

Bar Caravatti

$ | **NORTHERN ITALIAN** | A steady crowd has kept Caravatti's baristas pulling espresso shots and mixing up its signature aperitif since 1865. The secret Caravatti concoction of wine and herbs—among them, white wormwood and hibiscus—is paired with snacks during the predinner aperitif hour; for breakfast, there's a wide selection of pastries and sandwiches. **Known for:** Caravatti aperitif; rose-shape cake; lively atmopshere. *Average main: €10* *Via Broletto 16, Mantua* *0376/327826* *www.barcaravatti.it* *Closed Mon.*

Freddi

$ | **BAKERY** | The Freddi family's history in Piazza Cavallotti began more than 100 years ago. On the edge of the historical center of town, it's still where locals queue to buy Mantua's traditional pastas and pastries—don't miss *sbrisolona* (meaning "crumbs" in Italian), a hybrid cookie and pie that you'll see sold everywhere with varying levels of quality. **Known for:** Mantuan almond sweets; friendly local spot; location between the train station and major sites. *Average main: €10* *Piazza Cavallotti 7, Mantua* *0376/321418* *www.panificiofreddi.it* *Closed Sun.*

Hotels

Casa Poli

$ | **HOTEL** | **FAMILY** | A refreshing minimalist influence, attention to detail, and creative touches (like the room number projected onto the hall floor) create a welcoming ambience with contemporary flair. **Pros:** attentive staff; tasteful and modern; families welcome. **Cons:** although convenient, not in the absolute center of the city; some traffic noise in front-facing rooms; no on-site restaurant. *Rooms from: €165* *Corso Garibaldi 32, Mantua* *0376/288170* *www.hotelcasapoli.it* *27 rooms* *Free Breakfast.*

Lake Iseo and Franciacorta

108 km (67 miles) northeast of Milan.

The lesser known of Lombardy's lakes, Iseo is a haven for cyclists and sailors around Monte Isola. With more than 100 cellars and more than 7,000 acres of vineyards across 124 miles, for wine lovers, Franciacorta is a region not to be missed.

GETTING HERE AND AROUND

Frequent trains make the hour-long trip from Milano Centrale to Brescia. From there, hourly trains run to the town of Iseo (about half an hour) and then up Lake Iseo's eastern shore. You'll need a car to reach the western side or the Franciacorta wine region just south of the lake.

To drive from Milan or Bergamo, take the A4/E64; exit at Rovato on SP51 in the direction of Iseo. The trip takes about one hour and 20 minutes from Milan and 30 minutes from Bergamo. Ferries run from Sulzano, Sale Marasino, Iseo, and Tavernola Bergamasca to Monte Isola.

VISITOR INFORMATION

CONTACT Lake Iseo and Franciacorta Tourism Office. ✉ *Lungolago Marconi 2/c, Iseo* ☎ *030/980209* 🌐 *www.visitlakeiseo.info.*

Sights

Ca' del Bosco

WINERY | Modern sculptures adorn the grounds of this respected Franciacorta winery (one of the largest in the region). Enjoyable two-hour-long tours conclude with a tasting; information about tour availability can be requested online. ✉ *Via Albano Zanella 13, Erbusco* ☎ *030/7766111* 🌐 *www.cadelbosco.com* *Tours and tastings from €70.*

★ Monte Isola

ISLAND | The largest island within any European lake, Monte Isola allows no cars (except authorized vehicles), making it the perfect place for leisurely walks and bike rides. The main towns are Siviano, with medieval mansions; Peschiera Maraglio, an old fishing village with 16th-century homes and the Church of St. Michele; and Carzano, with the 18th-century San Giovanni Battista church. Walk around the water and stop at the many restaurants and gelaterie, or, for more exercise, trek uphill to admire the views back to the shore. Frequent ferries from Sulzano stop at Peschiera Maraglio, and ferries from Sale Marasino arrive at Carzano; there are less frequent ferries from Iseo and Tavernola Bergamasca. ✉ *Monte Isola* ☎ *030/9825088* 🌐 *www.visitmonteisola.it.*

Restaurants

★ Due Colombe Ristorante Al Borgo Antico

$$$ | NORTHERN ITALIAN | Visitors to Lake Iseo would do well to follow the locals' lead by sampling the delightful cooking at this cozy restaurant just south of the lake. The elegant dining area, with wood-beam ceilings and stone walls, is juxtaposed with the thoroughly modern menu, which offers a selection of "classic" and "creative" dishes. **Known for:** Franciacorta sauces; countryside setting; more than 900 wines to select from. $ *Average main: €40* ✉ *Via Foresti 13, Borgonato* ☎ *030/9828227* 🌐 *www.duecolombe.com* ⏲ *Closed Mon.–Wed. No dinner Sun. No lunch Thurs.*

Coffee and Quick Bites

Fabio Nazzari

$ | BAKERY | Watch Fabio Nazzari at work in this pastry lab and chocolate shop off Iseo's Piazza Garibaldi. When you do, you'll see why locals fill sleek black tables, both inside and outside in the piazza, to pair coffee with French-inspired sweets along with Italian dessert classics. **Known for:** breakfast spot with a dozen filled croissant flavors; delicately decorated minicakes; exotic fruit ingredients. $ *Average main: €10* ✉ *Piazza Garibaldi 15, Iseo* ☎ *030/9821756.*

Hotels

★ L'Albereta

$$$ | RESORT | Set in an early-20th-century villa amid Franciacorta's hilly vineyards, this Relais & Chateaux property is a true sanctuary, with an enormous spa, a botanical garden, and vast, sculpture-filled grounds to explore. **Pros:** cozy, calm, and luxurious atmosphere; excellent on-site restaurants; beautiful surroundings. **Cons:** rooms quite varied in terms of size and level of renovation; not all rooms have Lake Iseo views; breakfast not included. $ *Rooms from:*

€473 ✉ *Via Vittorio Emanuele 23, Erbusco* ☎ *030/7760550* 🌐 *www.albereta.it* 🛏 *57 rooms* 🍽 *No Meals.*

Sensole Locanda Contemporanea

$ | HOTEL | The tranquillity and flavors of Lake Iseo permeate through this relaxed retreat in the tiny village Sensole on car-free Monte Isola—nine simple rooms in a 19th-century palazzo have black and white contemporary decor and the best have sweeping lake views; or soak up the panorama from the top-floor terrace. **Pros:** affordable prices for the area; serene location; superb on-site restaurant and bistro. **Cons:** only reachable by ferry, with less frequent service to Sensole in the off-season; bathroom design is a bit outdated; not all rooms have lake views. [$] *Rooms from: €100* ✉ *Sensole 10, Monte Isola* ☎ *030/6091762* 🌐 *www.sensole.it* 🕓 *Closed Jan. 8–early Feb.* 🛏 *9 rooms* 🍽 *No Meals.*

Sirmione

138 km (86 miles) east of Milan.

Dramatically rising out of Lake Garda is the enchanting town of Sirmione. *"Paene insularum, Sirmio, insularumque ocelle,"* wrote Catullus in a homecoming poem: "It is the jewel of both peninsulas and islands." The forbidding Castello Scaligero stands guard behind the small bridge connecting Sirmione to the mainland; beyond, cobbled streets wind their way through medieval arches past lush gardens, stunning lake views, and gawking crowds. Originally a Roman resort town, Sirmione served under the dukes of Verona and later Venice as Garda's main point of defense. It has now reclaimed its original function, and is often overcrowded with visitors. Cars aren't allowed into town, and there's extremely limited parking just outside the center. If arriving by car, the best option on weekends and during high season is a 30-minute walk or short bus ride to the historical center from the large parking lot on Via Ederle at the traffic circle at the start of the road into Sirmione.

GETTING HERE AND AROUND

The town of Sirmione, at the south end of the lake, is 10 km (6 miles) from Desenzano, which has regular train service; it's about one hour and 20 minutes by train from Milan and 25 minutes from Verona. The A4 autostrada passes to the south of the lake, and the A22 runs north–south about 10 km (6 miles) from the eastern shore.

VISITOR INFORMATION

CONTACT Sirmione Tourism Office. ✉ *Viale Marconi 8, Sirmione* ☎ *349/7285327 mobile* 🌐 *www.visitsirmione.com.*

Sights

Bardolino

TOWN | This small town—one of the most popular summer resorts on the lake—is 32 km (20 miles) north of Sirmione along Lake Garda's eastern shore, at the wider end. It's most famous for its red wine, which is light, dry, and often slightly sparkling; the Festa dell'Uva e del Vino (Grape and Wine Festival), held here in early October, is a great excuse to indulge in the local product. Bardolino has two handsome Romanesque churches, both near the center: San Severo, from the 11th century, and San Zeno, from the 9th. ✉ *Bardolino* ☎ *045/7210087 tourist office* 🌐 *www.visitbardolino.it.*

Castello Scaligero di Sirmione

CASTLE/PALACE | As hereditary rulers of Verona for more than a century before they lost control of the city in 1402, the Della Scala counted Garda among their possessions. It was they who built this lakeside redoubt, along with almost all the other castles on the lake. You can go inside to take in a lake view from the tower, or you can swim at the nearby beach. ✉ *Piazza Castello 34, Sirmione* ☎ *030/916468* 🌐 *www.beniculturali.it/*

luogo/castello-scaligero-di-sirmione 🎫 *€8* ⏲ *Closed Mon.*

Grotte di Catullo (*Grottoes of Catullus*)
RUINS | Locals will almost certainly tell you that these romantic lakeside ruins were once the site of the villa of Catullus (87–54 BC), one of the greatest pleasure-seeking poets of all time. Modern-day archaeology, however, does not concur, and there is some consensus that this was the site of two villas of slightly different periods, dating from about the 1st century AD. But never mind—the view through the cypresses and olive trees is lovely, and even if Catullus didn't have a villa here, he is closely associated with the area and undoubtedly did have a villa nearby. The ruins are at the top of the isthmus and are poorly signposted: walk through the historic center and past the various villas to the top of the spit; the entrance is on the right. A small museum offers a brief overview of the ruins (on the far wall). ✉ *Piazzale Orti Manara, Sirmione* ☎ *030/916157* 🌐 *museilombardia.cultura.gov.it/musei/grotte-di-catullo-e-museo-archeologico-di-sirmione* 🎫 *€10.*

Restaurants

La Rucola 2.0

$$$$ | **MODERN ITALIAN** | Next to the castle and tucked into three charming rooms, this elegant, intimate restaurant is considered by many to be Sirmione's finest. Its creative tasting menus feature an appealing mix of fish (from the lake or the sea), meat, and vegetarian dishes, all accompanied by a good choice of wines. **Known for:** tasting menus; open kitchen; fantastic wine list. 💲 *Average main: €95* ✉ *Vicolo Strentelle 3, Sirmione* ☎ *030/916326* 🌐 *www.ristorantelarucola.it* ⏲ *June–Oct. closed Sun. and no lunch Mon.; Oct. 7–31, May closed Thurs., no lunch Fri. and no dinner Sun.*

Ristorante Al Pescatore

$$ | **SEAFOOD** | Freshwater fish is the specialty at this simple, popular restaurant in Sirmione's historic center. Try the grilled trout with a bottle of local white, and then settle your meal with a walk in the nearby park. **Known for:** grilled fresh fish from the lake; extensive variety of pasta and seafood; reasonable prices for the area. 💲 *Average main: €22* ✉ *Via Giovanni Piana 20/22, Sirmione* ☎ *030/916216* 🌐 *www.ristorantealpescatore.com* ⏲ *Closed Thurs.*

Hotels

Hotel Sirmione Terme

$$ | **HOTEL** | A homey feel with comfortable beds and upholstered furnishings with matching drapery, along with access to a luxurious thermal spa included in the rates, keeps many guests returning year after year. **Pros:** next to the lake and near Castello; beautiful grounds; nice spa area. **Cons:** not all rooms have lake views; hotel could use a refresh; service can be indifferent. 💲 *Rooms from: €219* ✉ *Piazza Castello 19, Sirmione* ☎ *030/916331, 030/9904922 booking* 🌐 *www.termedisirmione.com* *102 rooms* 🍽 *Free Breakfast.*

★ Palace Hotel Villa Cortine

$$$ | **HOTEL** | This former private villa in a secluded park is known for its bucolic lakeside setting, charming decor of the older rooms, and accommodating staff. **Pros:** an opulent experience; lovely pool area; beautiful grounds. **Cons:** noise heard in some rooms; no spa at hotel but thermal baths a short walk away; no gym. 💲 *Rooms from: €466* ✉ *Viale C. Gennari 2, Sirmione* ☎ *030/9905890* 🌐 *www.hotelvillacortine.com* ⏲ *Closed mid-Oct.–Apr.* *54 rooms* 🍽 *Free Breakfast.*

Riva del Garda

180 km (112 miles) northeast of Milan.

Riva del Garda is set on the northern tip of Lake Garda, against a dramatic backdrop of jagged cliffs and miles of beaches. The old city, surrounding a pretty harbor, was built up during the 15th century, when it was a strategic outpost of the Venetian Republic.

GETTING HERE AND AROUND

Riva del Garda is along Lake Garda's scenic SS45bis. By car from Milan, head to the A35 from SP14. The drive is 167 km (103 miles) and takes approximately three hours.

VISITOR INFORMATION

CONTACT Riva del Garda Tourism Office. ✉ *Largo Medaglie d'Oro al Valor Militare 5, Riva del Garda* ☎ *0464/554444* 🌐 *www.gardatrentino.it.*

Sights

Piazza III Novembre

PLAZA/SQUARE | This lakeside piazza, the heart of Riva del Garda, is surrounded by medieval palazzi. Standing there and looking out over the lake, you can understand why Riva del Garda has become a windsurfing destination: air currents ensure good breezes on even the most sultry midsummer days. ✉ *Piazza III Novembre, Riva del Garda* ☎ *0464/554444* 🌐 *www.gardatrentino.it.*

Torre Apponale

VIEWPOINT | Predating the Venetian period by three centuries, this sturdy tower looms above the medieval residences of the main square; its crenellations recall its defensive purpose. You can climb the 165 steps to see the view from the top. ✉ *Piazza III Novembre, Riva del Garda* ☎ *0464/573869* 🌐 *www.gardatrentino.it* 🎫 *€2.*

Restaurants

Peter Brunel

$$$$ | MODERN EUROPEAN | Walk through a Japanese garden off a country road east of Riva del Garda to enter multiple-Michelin-star-awarded chef Peter Brunel's light-filled, turquoise velvet-chaired restaurant. Each of the dozen sleek white tables are decorated with a unique sculpture, and jazz music sets the tone. **Known for:** dishes inspired by the chef's travels and Northern Italian roots; chic lounge areas to enjoy before and after meal drinks; impeccable service and presentation. 💲 *Average main: €140* ✉ *Vina Linfano 47, Arco* ☎ *0464/076705* 🌐 *www.peterbrunel.com* ⏲ *Closed Sun., Mon., Feb., and 2 wks in Nov.*

Ristorante Castel Toblino

$$ | NORTHERN ITALIAN | A lovely stop for a drink or a romantic dinner, this 16th-century castle is right on a lake in Sarche, about 20 km (12 miles) north of Riva toward Trento. Dishes highlight seasonal local ingredients, including mountain cheeses, salmon, trout, duck, and deer. **Known for:** castle setting; fish tasting menu; wine list featuring Trentino varieties. 💲 *Average main: €30* ✉ *Localita' Castel Toblino 1, Sarche* ☎ *0461/864036* 🌐 *www.casteltoblino.com* ⏲ *Closed mid-Oct.–late Mar.*

Coffee and Quick Bites

★ Eta Beta

$ | ICE CREAM | FAMILY | Matteo Mutti's gelato flavors have personality—like cheesecake with red pepper, rosemary, and pineapple, which might sound strange, but leaves a delightful impression on your taste buds. Other standouts are "Anni '90," inspired by Mutti's favorite tastes of the '90s—sour cherry and chocolate chip—and "Disaronno," swirled with a Lombardy liquor that is infused from apricot pits. **Known for:** gelato flavors that you won't find elsewhere; fun atmosphere; wide selection of cones, sundaes, and sizes. *Average main: €5* *Via Disciplini 14, Riva del Garda* *0464/554614* *www.facebook.com/gelateriaetabeta* *Closed Nov.–Mar.*

Hotels

Du Lac et du Parc Grand Resort

$$ | RESORT | FAMILY | Highly personalized service and well-appointed guest rooms (including bungalows perfect for families) are among the hallmarks of Riva's largest resort; another is the beautifully manicured 17-acre garden with more than 200 species of plants. **Pros:** lush, expansive grounds with two swimming pools, plus kids' pool; pampering and indulgent staff; lovely spa area. **Cons:** not that cozy; no beach of its own; can hear noise in some rooms. *Rooms from: €261* *Viale Rovereto 44, Riva del Garda* *0464/566600* *www.dulacetduparc.com* *Closed mid-Nov.–late Mar.* *163 rooms* *Free Breakfast.*

Hotel Sole Relax & Panorama

$ | HOTEL | A 15th-century palazzo in the center of town is the setting for this classic, comfortable, and relatively affordable hotel, where front rooms have terraces with breathtaking lake views and the rooftop terrace is a perfect retreat from summer's crowded beaches. **Pros:** prime location on the lake; modern hotel conveniences; comfortable beds. **Cons:** sometimes taken over by tour groups; not for those looking for ultracontemporary design; food gets mixed reviews. *Rooms from: €164* *Piazza III Novembre 35, Riva del Garda* *0464/552686, 0464/557809 reservations* *www.hotelsoleriva.it* *Closed Nov.–Dec. 21 and early Jan.–Mar.* *80 rooms* *Free Breakfast.*

Lido Palace

$$$ | HOTEL | In a 19th-century lakeside palace, Riva's most chic hotel has a high-end spa; sleek public spaces with turquoise mod couches and classic floor-to-ceiling windows; and contemporary guest rooms, where slate floors and brown-and-gray color schemes are offset by crisp white linens. **Pros:** friendly service; gorgeous spa and pools; top-notch food. **Cons:** not all rooms have lake views or balconies; on the pricey side; rooms can be hot in the summer. *Rooms from: €450* *Viale Carducci 10, Riva del Garda* *0464/021899* *www.lido-palace.it* *Closed mid-Jan.–late Mar.* *44 rooms* *Free Breakfast.*

★ Luise

$$ | HOTEL | FAMILY | Outdoor perks here include a big garden, a large swimming pool, and an included half-day bike rental to explore paths around the lake; interior draws include unique design touches—such as the lobby's collection of vintage luggage labels—and spacious rooms, all with comfy beds and a playful vibe and some with a whirlpool tub and a balcony. **Pros:** pleasant service; reasonably priced for the area; great for kids. **Cons:** some rooms can be noisy; 10-minute walk to center of Riva; no gym. *Rooms from: €184* *Viale Rovereto 9, Riva del Garda* *0464/550858* *www.hotelluise.com* *Closed mid-Nov.–late Mar.* *68 rooms* *Free Breakfast.*

Gargnano

30 km (19 miles) southwest of Riva del Garda, 144 km (89 miles) northeast of Milan.

This small port town was an important Franciscan center in the 13th century. Today, it comes alive in the summer, when German tourists, many of whom have villas here, crowd the small pebble beach. An Austrian flotilla bombarded the town in 1866, and some of the houses still bear marks of cannon fire. Mussolini owned two houses in Gargnano: one is the luxury hotel Villa Feltrinelli.

GETTING HERE AND AROUND

Gargnano is about a 30-minute drive south of Riva del Garda along the SS45bis.

VISITOR INFORMATION

CONTACT Gargnano Tourism Office. ✉ *Via Roma 45, Gargnano* ☎ *0365/042100* 🌐 *www.thisisgargnano.it.*

Restaurants

La Tortuga

$$$$ | **NORTHERN ITALIAN** | This trattoria is more sophisticated than it first appears: not only does it serve local dishes with novel twists, but it also has an extensive wine cellar. *Capesante scottate con salse ai diversi sapori* (seared scallops with different sauces) and *tavolozza di piccoli campioni di lago e di mare* (mixed lake and sea fish palette) are worthy introductions to regional delights. **Known for:** fish and meat tasting menu; extensive cheese selection; delightful service. $ *Average main: €46* ✉ *Via XXIV Maggio 5, Gargnano* ☎ *0365/71251* 🌐 *www.ristorantelatortuga.it* ⏲ *Closed Tues. and Dec.–Mar. No lunch.*

Hotels

Garni Bartabel

$ | **B&B/INN** | The small rooms at this cozy main-street inn—where breakfast is served on an elegant lake-view terrace—have attractive Venetian-style furnishings and pastel color schemes. **Pros:** attractive lake views; a bargain for this area; delicious breakfast. **Cons:** few luxuries; not all rooms have lake views or terraces; can hear road noise. $ *Rooms from: €95* ✉ *Via Roma 39, Gargnano* ☎ *0365/71300* 🌐 *www.hotelbartabel.it* ⏲ *Closed Nov.–Mar.* *11 rooms* *Free Breakfast.*

Lefay Resort & Spa Lago di Garda

$$$$ | **RESORT** | The first thing you'll notice about this elegant resort in the hills above Gargnano are the stupendous lake and mountain views; the second thing will be its enormous spa, which is so filled with amenities (heated indoor-outdoor pool, saunas, well-equipped lake-view gym, extensive treatment menu) that you might just want to stay all day—and some guests do. **Pros:** fabulously relaxing spa; lovely location; delicious breakfast buffet. **Cons:** village of Gargnano is down a steep and twisty road; restaurant not up to standards of rest of hotel; prices for food and drink excessively high. $ *Rooms from: €605* ✉ *Via Angelo Feltrinelli 136, Gargnano* ☎ *0365/241800* 🌐 *lagodigarda.lefayresorts.com/it* ⏲ *Closed early Jan.–early Feb.* *93 rooms* *Free Breakfast.*

Villa Feltrinelli

$$$$ | **HOTEL** | This 1892 Art Nouveau villa hotel, named for the Italian publishing family who once vacationed here, has attracted the likes of Winston Churchill, D.H. Lawrence, and Benito Mussolini to its private lake-view gardens; extensive library; sumptuous and palatial rooms (as befits the final bill); and overall opulent interior of fresco ceilings, wood paneling, and antique ceramics. **Pros:** first-class luxury hotel; like stepping into a bygone era; amazing service including laundry and valet services, and in-room bar. **Cons:** three-night stay required in summer; children under 12 not permitted; some find the attitude a bit arrogant. $ *Rooms from: €1,800* ✉ *Via Rimembranza 38/40, Gargnano* ☎ *0365/798000* 🌐 *www.villafeltrinelli.com* ⏲ *Closed mid-Oct.–mid-Apr.* *20 suites* *Free Breakfast.*

Gardone Riviera

12 km (7 miles) southwest of Gargnano, 124 km (77 miles) northeast of Milan.

Now pleasantly faded, this once-fashionable 19th-century resort is best known these days for the hilltop estate of the poet Gabriele D'Annunzio, made as an elaborate memorial to himself. The middle-European appearance of its towers and palaces helps set this lakeside town apart from the rest of Italy. With the Italian Alps in the background and crystalline lake views in the summer, it's a gorgeous, albeit underappreciated, destination.

GETTING HERE AND AROUND

Gardone Riviera is about 22 km (13 miles) east of Brescia and 126 km (77 miles) east of Milan. By car from Milan, head for the A35 autostrada from SP14.

VISITOR INFORMATION

CONTACT Gardone Riviera Tourism. ✉ *Corso Repubblica 1, Gardone Riviera* ☎ *348/8954214 mobile* 🌐 *www.rivieradelgarda.com.*

Sights

★ Heller Garden

GARDEN | This 2½-acre garden is a place to get lost while navigating stepping stones over lily ponds, climbing rock formations, and walking across wooden bridges. The treasures to be found are nearly 100 different Alpine, subtropical, and Mediterranean plant species and 30 modern art installations by the likes of Roy Lichtenstein, Joan Mirò, and Auguste Rodin. A former vineyard, Heller Garden was first cultivated in 1903 by Austrian dentist and botanist Arthur Hruska, and bought in 1988 by artist Andrè Heller (although he is no longer the owner). ✉ *Via Roma 2, Gardone Riviera* ☎ *0366/410877* 🌐 *www.hellergarden.com* 🎫 *€12* ⏲ *Closed Nov.–Feb.*

Il Vittoriale

HISTORIC HOME | The estate of the larger-than-life Gabriele D'Annunzio (1863–1938)—one of Italy's major modern poets, and later war hero and supporter of Mussolini—is filled with the trappings of his conquests in art, love, and war. His eccentric house crammed with quirky memorabilia can only be seen during a 35-minute guided tour (available in English), and the extensive gardens are definitely worth a stroll, particularly to see the curious full-size warship's prow. There's also an imposing mausoleum, made of white marble, along with three museums showcasing personal items from D'Annunzio's exploits, including one devoted to his cars. ✉ *Via Vittoriale 12, Gardone Riviera* ☎ *0365/296511* 🌐 *www.vittoriale.it* 🎫 *€18 park, 3 museums, and guided tour of house; €15 park and 3 museums; €12 park and 2 museums* ⏲ *House closed Mon. and Tues. Nov.–Jan. and Mon. in Feb.*

Restaurants

★ Ristorante Lido 84

$$$$ | MODERN ITALIAN | Dining in this bright, airy space feels like enjoying a meal in a fabulous friend's modern lake cottage—if the friend had floor-to-ceiling windows overlooking Lake Garda and a top-notch chef on hand. For an adventure in flavors from across the country, choose from one of the tasting menus and complement your meal with Italian or international wines in four- or five-glass pairings. **Known for:** unusual ingredients from all across Italy; rose cake with zabaglione; exquisite lake setting. 💲 *Average main: €140* ✉ *Corso Zanardelli 196, Gardone Riviera* ☎ *0365/20019* 🌐 *www.ristorantelido84.com* ⏲ *Closed Tues., Wed., and early Jan.–mid-Feb.*

Favorite Places

Liz Shemaria: Getting lost on the stone paths and bridges in the hidden oasis of Heller Garden—where plants mingle with contemporary art—is like entering a world of whimsy.

Hotels

★ Grand Hotel Fasano

$$$ | **RESORT** | Used as a hunting lodge in the 19th century, the Fasano has matured into a seasonal hotel with high standards, opulent rooms, and many amenities—including an Aveda Destination Spa and a well-regarded restaurant, Il Fagiano, in addition to three more casual eateries (one a short walk away). **Pros:** exquisitely stylish rooms; relaxing surroundings; gorgeous spa. **Cons:** not all rooms have lake views; staff can seem indifferent; must book many months in advance. *Rooms from: €434 Corso Zanardelli 190, Gardone Riviera 0365/290220 www.ghf.it Closed Nov.–Mar. 79 rooms Free Breakfast.*

Villa del Sogno

$$$ | **HOTEL** | A narrow winding road takes you from town to this imposing villa, now a luxurious hotel retreat thanks to its valley and lake views and its peaceful grounds, which have an outdoor pool and a tennis court. **Pros:** endless amenities; individually decorated rooms; expansive terrace overlooking the lake. **Cons:** food gets mixed reviews; remote location; staff can be indifferent. *Rooms from: €413 Via Zanardelli 107, Gardone Riviera 0365/290181 www.villadelsogno.it Closed Nov.–mid-Apr. 38 rooms Free Breakfast.*

Villa Fiordaliso

$$ | **HOTEL** | A fine restaurant and five tastefully furnished guest rooms are housed in the pink-and-white lakeside villa given to Benito Mussolini's mistress, Claretta Petacci, by Il Duce himself. **Pros:** combines cinematic charm with the intimacy of a B&B; amazing setting on the lake; elaborate breakfast spread. **Cons:** short on amenities (no spa or pool); can sometimes be noisy; may be too small for some people. *Rooms from: €350 Corso Zanardelli 150, Gardone Riviera 0365/20158 www.relaischateaux.com/it/hotel/villa-fiordaliso Closed mid.-Oct.–mid-Mar. 5 rooms Free Breakfast.*

Bellagio

30 km (19 miles) northeast of Como, 56 km (35 miles) northwest of Bergamo.

Sometimes called the prettiest town in Europe, Bellagio always seems perfectly adorned, with geraniums ablaze in every window and bougainvilleas veiling its staircases, or *montées*. At dusk Bellagio's nightspots—including the wharf, where an orchestra may be serenading dancers under the stars—beckon you to come and make merry. It's an impossibly enchanting location, one that inspired the French composer Gabriel Fauré to call Bellagio "a diamond contrasting brilliantly with the sapphires of the three lakes in which it is set."

GETTING HERE AND AROUND

Boats can take you from here to Tremezzo, where Napoléon's worst Italian enemy, Count Sommariva, resided at Villa Carlotta; and a bit farther south of Tremezzo, to Villa del Balbianello via Lenno. Check timetables at *www.navigazionelaghi.it*.

VISITOR INFORMATION

CONTACT Bellagio Tourism Office. *Piazza della Chiesa 14, Bellagio 031/951555 www.bellagiolakecomo.com.*

Sights

Villa Melzi

GARDEN | The famous gardens of the Villa Melzi were once a favorite picnic spot for Franz Liszt, who advised author Louis de Ronchaud in 1837, "When you write the story of two happy lovers, place them on the shores of Lake Como. I do not know of any land so conspicuously blessed by heaven." The gardens are open to the public, and though you can't get into the 19th-century villa, don't miss the lavish Empire-style family chapel. *Lungo Lario Manzoni, Bellagio 031/950318 www.giardinidivillamelzi.it €10 Closed Nov.–late Mar.*

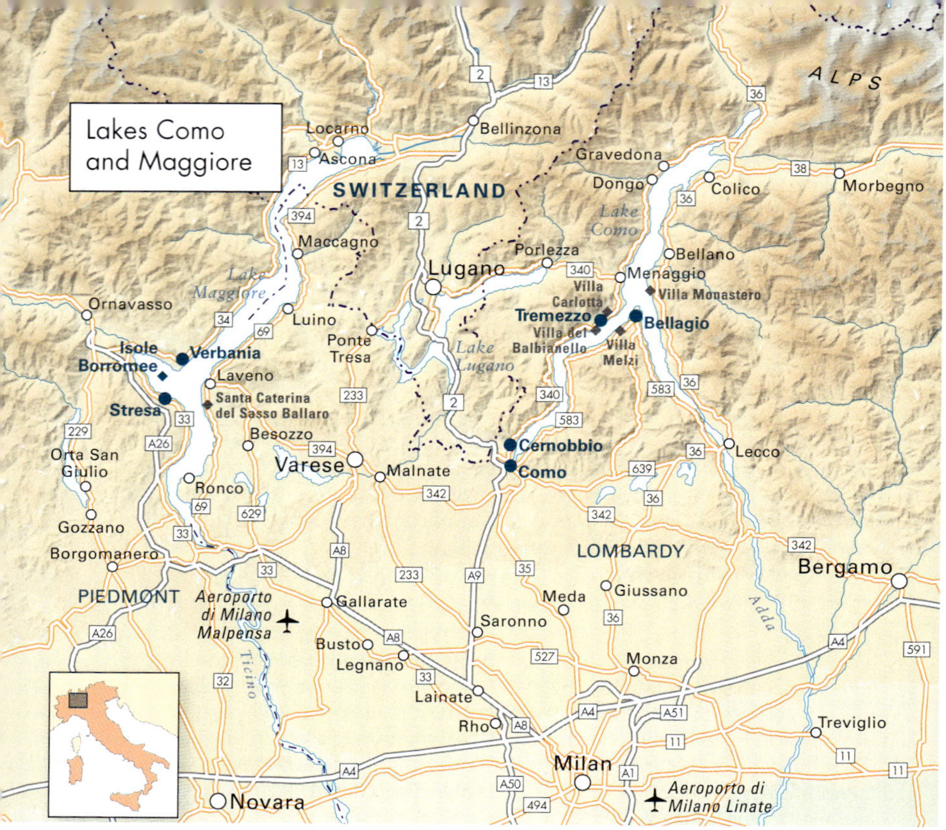

Villa Monastero

GARDEN | By ferry from Bellagio it's a quick trip across the lake to Varenna. The principal sight here is the spellbinding garden of the Villa Monastero, which, as its name suggests, was originally a monastery. There's also a house museum where you can admire 18th-century furnishings, as well as an international science and convention center. ✉ *Viale Giovanni Polvani 4, Varenna* ☎ *0341/295450* 🌐 *www.villamonastero.eu* 🎫 *Garden €10, garden and house €13* 🕒 *Check website for updated seasonal hrs.*

Restaurants

Ristorante La Punta

$$$ | **ITALIAN** | When tourist-heavy Bellagio starts to wear you down, seek respite at this charming restaurant located on the town's very northernmost point, a scenic 10-minute walk from the center, with lake views of Varenna to the north and Tremezzo to the west. As you might expect, the menu is heavy on lake fish; although the dishes aren't innovative, the view makes the experience even better. **Known for:** fresh fish; Lake Como views; friendly service. [$] *Average main: €38* ✉ *Via Eugenio Vitali 19, Bellagio* ☎ *031/951888* 🌐 *www.ristorantelapunta.it* 🕒 *Closed Nov.–Mar.*

Hotels

Du Lac

$$ | **HOTEL** | Most of the modern, inviting guest rooms at this comfortable hotel—owned by an Anglo-Italian family and right in the center of Bellagio's action—have lake and mountain views, and the rooftop terrace garden is a perfect spot for drinks or dozing. **Pros:** pleasant terrace garden; fabulous buffet breakfast; friendly service. **Cons:** beds too hard for some; some of the decor could use a refresh; the boat dock right in front of the hotel can be noisy. *$ Rooms from: €306 ✉ Piazza Mazzini 32, Bellagio ☎ 031/950320 🌐 www.bellagiohoteldu-lac.com ⏲ Closed Nov.–Mar. 42 rooms 🍽 Free Breakfast.*

★ Grand Hotel Villa Serbelloni

$$$$ | **HOTEL** | The 19th-century luxury at this grand lake hotel—originally designed to cradle nobility and still a refined haven for the discreetly wealthy—has not so much faded as mellowed: guest rooms remain immaculate and plush; public areas are still awash with gilt ornamentation and marble; and breakfast is served in a ballroom. **Pros:** old-world grandeur; lovely gardens; great pools. **Cons:** could use some sprucing up; staff helpfulness varies widely; expensive food and drink. *$ Rooms from: €900 ✉ Via T. Olivielli 1, Bellagio ☎ 031/950216 🌐 www.villaser-belloni.com ⏲ Closed Nov.–early Apr. 94 rooms 🍽 Free Breakfast.*

Hotel Belvedere

$$$$ | **HOTEL** | **FAMILY** | In Italian, *belvedere* means "beautiful view," and it's an apt name for this enchanting spot, where the modern rooms have classic touches such as antique furniture, decorative tiles, and marble bathrooms. **Pros:** attention to detail; great views; has a spa and a lovely pool. **Cons:** a climb from the waterfront; must request a lake-view balcony room in advance; fewer on-site amenities than other similarly priced hotels. *$ Rooms from: €750 ✉ Via Valassina 31, Bellagio ☎ 031/950410 🌐 www.belvederebellagio.com ⏲ Closed Nov.–Mar. 63 rooms 🍽 Free Breakfast.*

Hotel Florence

$$ | **HOTEL** | Most of the large and comfortable rooms in this 1880s villa across from the ferry stop are furnished with interesting antiques and have splendid views of the lake. **Pros:** central location; appealing public spaces; lovely bar with outdoor lake-facing seating. **Cons:** location may feel too central if you're looking to get away from it all; some baths only have handheld showers; hotel could use an update. *$ Rooms from: €180 ✉ Piazza Mazzini 46, Bellagio ☎ 031/950342 🌐 www.hotelflorencebellagio.it ⏲ Closed mid-Oct.–Apr. 30 rooms 🍽 Free Breakfast.*

Tremezzo

34 km (21 miles) north of Cernobbio, 79 km (49 miles) north of Milan.

The dreamy lakeside town of Tremezzo is close to two outstanding and magical villas, as well as sprawling gardens and one of the lake's grandest hotels.

GETTING HERE AND AROUND

Tremezzo is along the SS340. By car from Milan, the drive is 79 km (48 miles) following the A8 autostrada and takes about 90 minutes.

VISITOR INFORMATION

CONTACT Tremezzo Tourist Office. *✉ Via Statale Regina 3, Tremezzo ☎ 0344/40493 🌐 www.tremezzinatour-ism.com.*

Sights

Villa Carlotta

GARDEN | If you're lucky enough to visit Tremezzo in late spring or early summer, you will find the magnificent Villa Carlotta a riot of color, with more than 14 acres of azaleas and dozens of varieties of rhododendrons in full bloom. The height of the blossoms is late April to early May. The villa was built between 1690 and 1743 for the luxury-loving marquis Giorgio Clerici. The garden's collection is remarkable, particularly considering the difficulties of transporting delicate plants before the age of aircraft. Palms, banana trees, cacti, eucalyptus, a sequoia, orchids, and camellias are among the more than 500 species.

The villa's interior is worth a visit, particularly if you have a taste for the romantic sculptures of Antonio Canova (1757–1822). The best known is his *Cupid and Psyche,* which depicts the lovers locked in an odd but graceful embrace, with the young god above and behind, his wings extended, while Psyche awaits a kiss that will never come. The villa can be reached by boat from Bellagio and Como. ✉ *Via Regina 2, Tremezzo* ☎ *0344/40405* 🌐 *www.villacarlotta.it* 🎟 *€15* ⏲ *Closed early Nov.–Mar.*

★ Villa del Balbianello

HISTORIC HOME | The relentlessly picturesque Balbianello may be the most magical house in all of Italy; you probably know it from cameos in the movies *Casino Royale* and *Star Wars Episode II: Attack of the Clones*. It sits on its own little promontory, Il Dosso d'Avedo, around the bend from the tiny fishing village of Ossuccio. The villa is composed of loggias, terraces, and *palazzini* (tiny palaces), all spilling down verdant slopes to the shore, where you'll find an old Franciscan church, a magnificent stone staircase, and a statue of San Carlo Borromeo blessing the waters.

The villa is usually reached from Como and Bellagio by boat, which leaves you at the village of Lenno. From there, marked signs lead you to the villa—it's either accessible by foot via a 25-minute walk or a more challenging 45-minute hike. ✉ *Via Guido Monzino 1, Lenno* ✣ *5 km (3 miles) southwest of Tremezzo* ☎ *0344/56110* 🌐 *www.fondoambiente.it/luoghi/villa-del-balbianello* 🎟 *€24 villa and gardens, includes 1-hr guided tour; €14 gardens only* ⏲ *Check the website for seasonal and special event closures.*

Coffee and Quick Bites

Cantina Follie

$ | WINE BAR | This cantina's leafy patio is reached by hiking up the stairs into the neighborhood above Tremezzo. There's a collection of more than 300 wines to sample along with *tagliere* (cutting boards) of local cheeses, preserved meats, and vegetarian and vegan options. **Known for:** shady and quiet setting away from the main street; cheese and wine pairings; local products. 💲 *Average main: €15* ✉ *Via Alessandro Volta 14, Tremezzo* ☎ *0344/42311* 🌐 *www.cantinafollie.it* ⏲ *Closed Tues. and Dec.–Feb.*

Hotels

★ Grand Hotel Tremezzo

$$$$ | RESORT | Creature comforts in this turn-of-the-20th-century building—one of the top grand hotels on the lake—include a lush park, three heated swimming pools (one of them floats on pontoons on the lake), a small private beach, and sumptuous guest rooms where old-world style meets modern amenities. **Pros:** lakeside location with beautiful views; attractive spa; gracious service. **Cons:** not well situated if you're looking for shopping or nightlife; very expensive; somewhat busy road between hotel and lake. 💲 *Rooms from: €1,300* ✉ *Via Regina 8, Tremezzo* ☎ *0344/42491* 🌐 *www.grandhoteltremezzo.com* ⏲ *Closed mid-Nov.–early Apr.* 🛏 *90 rooms* 🍽 *Free Breakfast.*

Hotel Rusall

$ | B&B/INN | Amid a large garden on the hillside above Tremezzo, this hotel offers small, private, comfortably simple rooms; a pool with a nice view; and a popular restaurant that serves tasty Italian classics. **Pros:** lovely walks into town and in the countryside; more intimate than grander lake hotels; good on-site restaurant and half-board rates. **Cons:** takes some effort to reach and walk to town; rooms are fairly basic; air-conditioning can be an issue in rooms and common areas. *Rooms from: €145 Via San Martino 2, Tremezzo 0344/40408 www.rusall-hotel.com Closed Jan.–mid-Mar. 23 rooms Free Breakfast.*

Cernobbio

5 km (3 miles) north of Como, 53 km (33 miles) north of Milan.

The legendary resort of Villa d'Este is reason enough to visit this jewel on the lake, but the town itself is worth a stroll. The place still has a neighborhood feel to it, especially on summer evenings and weekends, when the piazza is full of families and couples strolling.

GETTING HERE AND AROUND

Cernobbio is on the SS340, 6 km (4 miles) north of the city of Como; from Milan take the A9 and follow signs for Como. The drive is 53 km (33 miles) and takes about one hour.

VISITOR INFORMATION

CONTACT Cernobbio Tourism Office. *Largo Alfredo Campanini 2, Cernobbio 347/8818532 www.mylakecomo.co/en/cernobbio.*

Sights

Villa Bernasconi

HISTORIC HOME | Art Nouveau details, such as intricately-carved floral balconies and tile work, are enough to make you get out of the car for a closer look at this villa on the main road from Como to Cernobbio. The turreted two-story former home of textile tycoon Davide Bernasconi was built on the grounds of his company's silk mills in the 1900s and is now an interactive museum. Among the rooms with original wood-inlay ceilings, decorative stained glass, and marble mosaic floors, are audio installations that recount the history of Bernasconi's empire and the Lake Como area's silk industry. Temporary exhibits highlight contemporary Italian artists and fashion design. *Largo Campanini 2, Cernobbio 031/3347209 www.villabernasconi.eu €8 Closed Tues.–Thurs. Reservations recommended.*

Restaurants

Il Gatto Nero

$$$$ | **NORTHERN ITALIAN** | Reservations are a must for this longtime favorite in the hills above Cernobbio. The lake view is splendid, and specialties include homemade pastas and fish dishes with a dash of international flair. **Known for:** classic cotoletta alla Milanese; high-end wine selection; lovely terrace. *Average main: €51 Via Monte Santo 69, Cernobbio 031/512042 www.ristorantegattonero.it Closed Mon. Credit card required for reservations; €30/person no-show fee for missed reservations and €20/person for late cancellations.*

Lido di Cernobbio

$$$ | **ITALIAN** | **FAMILY** | Right next to the Cernobbio ferry stop, this pretty restaurant offers a nice selection of local wines and, whenever possible, uses local ingredients in its pizza, pasta, fish, and meat dishes. Though the modern gray interior is pleasant, try for a table on the terrace, and note that, in season, you can rent a sun bed and use the pools (one for adults and one for kids) before or after your meal. **Known for:** lovely lake scenery; solid Italian dishes; family-friendly atmosphere. *Average main: €31 Piazza Risorgimento 5, Cernobbio 031/4446437 www.lidodicernobbio.com Closed Wed. and Nov.–Mar.*

★ Materia

$$$$ | **MODERN ITALIAN** | This aesthetically simple bistro-style restaurant, spruced up with modern art, draws a mainly local crowd for some of the most inventive food creations and presentation in the Como region. The imaginative vegetable-focused cuisine makes good use of local ingredients, and the frequently changing surprise five- or seven-course tasting menus are a particular delight, especially when paired with the mostly natural wines on offer. **Known for:** use of organic herbs and vegetables from their greenhouse; vegetarian tasting menu; Italian and international wines from small producers. *Average main: €43* *Via Trieste 1/b, Cernobbio* *031/2075548* *www.ristorantemateria.it* *Closed Mon. and Tues.*

Coffee and Quick Bites

Anagramma

$ | ITALIAN | Communal garden tables and atrium seating make for a pleasant stop for a coffee and pastry, light lunch, or aperitif. Baked goods, such as apple and *frangipane* (almond cream) cake and sourdough bread for sandwiches and tagliere plates (with local cheese, salumi, and lake fish), are made daily in-house. **Known for:** relaxed garden setting; house-made breakfast pastries and bread; convenient stop on the way to other lake towns. *Average main: €14* *Largo Alfredo Campanini 1, Cernobbio* *031/4446483* *Closed Mon.*

Hotels

Passalacqua

$$$$ | RESORT | Count Andrea Lucini Passalacqua hosted artists and politicians at this 5-acre lakefront villa in Moltrasio, just north of Cernobbio, until the count's death in 1890; today the Bellini Suite (a 2,700-square-foot suite with an opulent music room reserved for Vincenzo Bellini while he composed operas) and 23 others, have restored frescoes, Murano glass chandeliers, and luxurious soaking tubs. **Pros:** luxurious and quiet retreat; in-room extras such as Dyson hair tools and Aqua Como products; highly attentive staff. **Cons:** books up far in advance; not all rooms have lake views; a bit difficult to find off a side road. *Rooms from: €2,200* *Via Besana 59, Moltrasio* *031/44311* *www.passalacqua.it/en* *Closed Feb.–late Mar.* *24 suites* *Free Breakfast.*

★ Villa d'Este

$$$$ | RESORT | Europe's rich and famous have long favored this hotel, one of Italy's grandest, where rooms are done in Empire style; a broad veranda sweeps out to the lakefront; a swimming pool extends above the water; a restaurant offers top-notch views and cuisine; there are four private villas; and pavilions, miniature forts, and other follies ensure whimsical garden walks. **Pros:** fine service; amazing grounds; excellent restaurant. **Cons:** may feel too formal for some; not all rooms have lake views; all this grandness comes with a hefty price tag. *Rooms from: €1,380* *Via Regina 40, Cernobbio* *031/3481* *www.villadeste.com* *Closed mid-Nov.–mid-Mar.* *152 rooms, 4 private villas* *Free Breakfast.*

Como

5 km (3 miles) south of Cernobbio, 30 km (19 miles) southwest of Bellagio, 50 km (31 miles) north of Milan.

Como commands the south shore of the lake. In its center, elegant cobblestone pedestrian streets wind their way past parks and bustling cafés. However, it's only partly a resort: the city also has an industrial heritage, deeply rooted in the production of textiles, particularly silk and the silk trade. If traveling by car, leave it at the edge of the town center in the well-lit underground parking facility right on the lake.

GETTING HERE AND AROUND

Como is easily reachable by regional trains from Milan from Porta Garibaldi, Cadorna, and Milano Centrale stations, and the ride is about one hour. If driving from Milan, take the A9 and follow signs for Como; the journey is 50 km (31 miles) and takes about one hour.

VISITOR INFORMATION

CONTACT Como Tourism Office. ✉ *Via Pretorio 1, Como* ☎ *031/304137* 🌐 *www.visitcomo.eu/en.*

Sights

Duomo

CHURCH | The splendid 15th-century Renaissance-Gothic Duomo was begun in 1396. The facade was added in 1455, and the transepts were completed in the mid-18th century. The dome was designed by Filippo Juvarra (1678–1736), chief architect of many of the sumptuous palaces of the royal house of Savoy. The facade has statues of two of Como's most famous sons, Pliny the Elder and Pliny the Younger, whose writings are among the most important documents from antiquity. Inside, the works of art include Luini's *Holy Conversation,* a fresco cycle by Morazzone, and the *Marriage of the Virgin Mary* by Ferrari. ✉ *Piazza del Duomo, Como* ☎ *031/3312275* 🌐 *www.cattedraledicomo.it.*

Museo della Seta (*Silk Museum*)

SPECIALTY MUSEUM | From silkworm litters to textile finishing machinery to temporary exhibitions, this small but complete collection preserves the history of a manufacturing region that continues to supply a large proportion of Europe's silk. The friendly staffers will give you an overview of the museum; they are also happy to provide brochures and information about local retail shops. Follow the textile school's driveway around to the low-rise concrete building on the left, and take the shallow ramp down to the entrance. ✉ *Via Castelnuovo 9, Como* ☎ *031/303180* 🌐 *www.museosetacomo.com* 🎫 *€10* ⏲ *Closed Mon.*

San Fedele

CHURCH | At the heart of Como's medieval quarter, the city's first cathedral is well worth a peek. The apse walls and ceiling are completely frescoed, as are the ceilings above the altar. ✉ *Piazza San Fedele, Como* ☎ *031/3868316* 🌐 *www.parrocchiasanfedelecomo.it.*

Restaurants

★ Feel Como

$$$$ | MODERN ITALIAN | Your palate will travel from the lakes to the countryside to the mountains, all from the comfort of your table at this cozy (six-table) stone-arched eatery tucked into Como's commercial district. Expect creative takes on risotto, ravioli, and linguine using both locally harvested and more exotic ingredients, best sampled with a tasting menu. **Known for:** witty variations on local cuisine; gorgeous platings; extensive wine list. 💲 *Average main: €65* ✉ *Via Generale Armando Diaz 54, Como* ☎ *0334/7264545* 🌐 *www.feelcomo.com* ⏲ *Closed Mon. and Tues. No lunch weekdays.*

Rive Enoteca

$$$ | NORTHERN ITALIAN | A former 17th-century convent is now a lively enoteca run by Alberto and Catia Rivetti, offering more than 600 wines, as well as spirits and beers—all from northern Italy. Old and new merge in this warm and friendly spot with sage and rose walls, an original decorative ceiling, and a hallway with an automatic dispenser with more than 30 wines available on demand—get up from your seat to taste as many wines as you'd like using a prepaid card. **Known for:** local wines and spirits, including from the owners' winery; dispenser for wines "on demand" in three sizes, or by the bottle; entirely Lombard-focused cuisine.

$ *Average main: €33* ✉ *Via A. Diaz 56, Como* ☎ *351/7518058 mobile* 🌐 *www.rivenoteca.it* ⏲ *Closed Sun. and Wed. No lunch Mon. and Tues.*

Hotels

Albergo Terminus

$$$ | **HOTEL** | In addition to Lake Como panoramas, this early-20th-century Art Nouveau landmark has marbled public spaces and guest rooms with floral fabrics, walnut wardrobes, and silk-covered sofas. **Pros:** old-world charm; right on the lake; bountiful breakfast. **Cons:** limited number of lake-view rooms; decor in some rooms seems dated; noise from the restaurant and outside can be an issue. $ *Rooms from: €457* ✉ *Lungo Lario Trieste 14, Como* ☎ *031/329111* 🌐 *www.albergoterminus.it* *50 rooms* 🍴 *Free Breakfast.*

★ Il Sereno Lago di Como

$$$$ | **RESORT** | Throughout this, the first European outpost of the luxe Il Sereno Hotel in St. Barths, you'll find floor-to-ceiling lake-view windows and an understated retro-mod aesthetic, with a muted palette of browns and grays complementing a panoply of wood, stone, leather, and copper accents. **Pros:** cool modern design; hushed elegance throughout; fabulous views. **Cons:** extremely expensive; not for lovers of historical villas; can be difficult to find. $ *Rooms from: €3,000* ✉ *Via Torrazza 10, Torno* ☎ *031/5477800* 🌐 *www.ilsereno.com* ⏲ *Closed Nov.–mid-Mar.* *40 suites* 🍴 *Free Breakfast.*

Mandarin Oriental, Lago di Como

$$$$ | **HOTEL** | The nine 19th-century villas that comprise this Lake Como outpost of the extravagant Mandarin chain have been thoroughly updated for the 21st century, offering a quiet setting (just north of the busy town of Como) and luxurious amenities that include a 14,000-square-foot spa and a swimming pool that "floats" above the lake. **Pros:** amazingly peaceful setting; fabulous wellness facilities; complimentary minibar. **Cons:** location a bit isolated from other towns; food not up to par; service can be haphazard. $ *Rooms from: €2,000* ✉ *Via E. Caronti 69, Blevio* ☎ *031/32511* 🌐 *www.mandarinoriental.com/lake-como/blevio* ⏲ *Closed mid-Nov.–mid-Mar.* *75 rooms* 🍴 *Free Breakfast.*

Posta Design Hotel

$$ | **HOTEL** | Just a block from the lake, on downtown Como's pedestrian-only Piazza Volta, this boutique hotel has a minimalist modern interior that's in perfect keeping with its exterior—the 1931 building that houses it was designed by Rationalist architect Giuseppe Terragni. **Pros:** central location; comfortable rooms; friendly service. **Cons:** rooms on lower floors can be noisy; sparse amenities (no minibars in rooms, no breakfast, no gym); Internet must be logged into each time. $ *Rooms from: €285* ✉ *Via Garibaldi 2, Como* ☎ *031/2769011* 🌐 *www.postadesignhotel.com* *14 rooms* 🍴 *No Meals.*

Vista Lago di Como

$$$$ | **HOTEL** | A 19th-century lakefront palazzo steps from pedestrian-only Piazza Cavour has been transformed into an elegant in-town hotel, where a sweeping staircase leads to spacious, sophisticated white-and-gray guest rooms that have pops of color, parquet floors, walk-in closets, and sumptuous marble bathrooms with deep soaking tubs. **Pros:** great central location; lovely views from most rooms; friendly and helpful service. **Cons:** lakefront rooms can be noisy; breakfast can be a bit sparse; Como town can be crowded. $ *Rooms from: €1,212* ✉ *Piazza Cavour 24, Como* ☎ *031/5375241* 🌐 *www.vistapalazzo.com* *18 rooms* 🍴 *Free Breakfast.*

Activities

Lake Como has lots of ways to stay active and outdoors, from windsurfing at the lake's northern end, to boating, sailing, and Jet Skiing at Como and Cernobbio. The lake is also quite swimmable in summer. For hikers there are lovely paths all around the lake. For an easy trek, take the funicular up to Brunate, and walk along the mountain to the lighthouse for a stunning view of the lake.

Stresa and the Isole Borromee

80 km (50 miles) northwest of Milan.

One of the better known resorts on the western shore, Stresa is a tourist town, which provided Hemingway with one of the settings in *A Farewell to Arms*. It has capitalized on its central lakeside position, though the luxurious elegance that distinguished its heyday has faded; grand hotels are still grand, but traffic now encroaches on their parks and gardens.

The best way to escape to yesteryear is to head for the Isole Borromee (Borromean Islands) in Lake Maggiore. Boats to the three islands depart from the dock at Stresa's Piazza Marconi, as well as from Piazzale Lido at the northern end of the promenade. There's also a boat from Verbania; check locally for the seasonal schedule. Although you can hire a private boat, it's cheaper and just as convenient to use the regular service. Make sure you buy a ticket allowing you to visit all the islands—Bella, dei Pescatori (Superiore), and Madre. The islands take their name from the Borromeo family, which has owned them since the 15th century.

GETTING HERE AND AROUND

Trains run regularly from Milan to the town of Stresa on Lake Maggiore; the trip takes 1–1½ hours, depending on the type of train. By car from Milan to Stresa, take the A8 autostrada to the A8dir, and from the A8dir take the A26; the drive is about 1¼ hours.

VISITOR INFORMATION

CONTACT Stresa & Isole Borromee Tourism Office. ✉ *Piazza Marconi 16, Stresa* ☎ *0323/933478* 🌐 *www.terreborromeo.it/en.*

Sights

Isola Bella (*Beautiful Island*)
ISLAND | The most famous of the three Isole Borromee (Borromean Islands), is named after Isabella, whose husband, Carlo III Borromeo (1538–84), built the palace and terraced gardens here for her as a wedding present. Before Count Carlo began his project, the island was rocky and almost devoid of vegetation; the soil for the garden had to be transported from the mainland. For a splendid view of the lake, wander up the 10 terraces of Teatro Massimo. In the gardens, white peacocks roam among the scented shrubs. Visit Palazzo Borromeo to see the rooms where famous guests—including Napoléon and Mussolini—stayed in 18th-century splendor. ✉ *Isola Bella* ☎ *0323/933478* 🌐 *www.terreborromeo.it* 🎫 *Garden and palace €23* 🕒 *Closed early Nov.–mid-Mar.*

Isola dei Pescatori
(*Island of the Fishermen*)
ISLAND | Stop for lunch at the smallest Borromean island, also known as Isola Superiore. It's less than 100 yards wide and only about ½ km (¼ mile) long. It's an ideal place to visit before, after, or in between touring the other two islands. Of the 10 or so restaurants on

this island the two worth visiting are Il Verbano (☎ *0323/31226*) and Belvedere (☎ *0323/32292*). The island with little lanes strung with fishing nets and dotted with shrines to the Madonna is a crowded place filled with souvenir stands and shops in high season. ✉ *Isola dei Pescatori.*

★ **Isola Madre** (*Mother Island*)
GARDEN | All of this Borromean island is a botanical garden, with a season that stretches from late March to late October due to the climatic protection of the mighty Alps and the tepid waters of Lake Maggiore. The cacti and palm trees here, so far north and so near the border with Switzerland, are a beautiful surprise. Two special times to visit are April, for the camellias, and May, for azaleas and rhododendrons. Also on the island is a 16th-century palazzo, where the Borromeo family still lives for part of the year. ✉ *Isola Madre* ☎ *0323/933479* 🌐 *www.terreborromeo.it* 🎟 *€20 palace and garden* ⏲ *Closed early Nov.–mid Mar.*

Parco Pallavicino
GARDEN | **FAMILY** | As you wander around the palms and semitropical shrubs, don't be surprised if you're followed by a peacock or even an ostrich: they're part of the zoological garden and are allowed to roam almost at will. From the top of the hill on which the villa stands you can see the gentle hills of the Lombardy shore of Lake Maggiore and, nearer and to the left, the jewel-like Isole Borromee. In addition to a bar and restaurant, the grounds also have picnic spots and there is a farm that's popular with children. ✉ *Via Sempione 8, Stresa* ☎ *0323/933478* 🌐 *www.terreborromeo.it/en/parco-pallavicino* 🎟 *€16* ⏲ *Closed early Nov.–mid-Mar.*

Restaurants

★ **Ristorante Lastresa**
$$ | **NORTHERN ITALIAN** | The nondescript exterior of this buzzy eatery off one of Stresa's main streets belies its modern interior. Dishes made with seasonal ingredients dominate the menu, but, no matter the season, you'll find local lake fish, both marinated and pan-fried, as well as a solid list of wines from throughout the region and across Italy. **Known for:** locals' favorite; friendly, knowledgeable waitstaff; Piedmont dessert sampler. [$] *Average main: €25* ✉ *Via Principessa Margherita 22, Stresa* ☎ *0323/33240* 🌐 *www.ristorantelastresa.it* ⏲ *Closed Sept.–Mar. No lunch Mon.–Wed.*

Trattoria due Piccioni
$$ | **MODERN ITALIAN** | In a town with an overabundance of touristy pizza and pasta places, this unassumingly modern family-run bistro raises the bar. Although the shabby-chic decor and friendly service entice, the real draw is the short but smart menu of creative Italian dishes and vegetarian options. **Known for:** inventive local cuisine; intriguing desserts; attentive service. [$] *Average main: €22* ✉ *Via P. Tommaso 61, Stresa* ☎ *0323/934556* 🌐 *www.facebook.com/duepiccioni* ⏲ *Closed Wed.*

Coffee and Quick Bites

Cicinin Panini al Metro
$ | **SANDWICHES** | Pick a sandwich size (from a few inches to 40—or a meter—as the name *al metro* implies) to match your appetite, at this *paninoteca* (sandwich shop) off Piazza Luigi Cadorna. There are just four inventive sandwich types on offer each day, with ingredients changing seasonally like lentil cream, fennel, ricotta salata, and orange; or mortadella, pistachio cream, and Toma cheese. **Known for:** portions for any appetite; friendly service; curated menu

of local ingredients. *Average main: €10* *Via Principe Tomaso 24, Stresa* *334/1627769 mobile* *No credit cards* *Closed Mon. and Thurs.*

Pasticceria Marcolini

$ | **BAKERY** | Margheritine cookies were first baked in Stresa for Margherita of Savoy in 1857 while she was still a princess. Named for the first queen of Italy as well as for their decoration like a daisy (*margherita* in Italian), the biscuits' recipe includes cooked egg yolk and an abundant supply of powdered sugar, making them crumble effortlessly in your mouth. **Known for:** sweets made following traditional Stresa recipes; gift boxes to take cookies home; locals' spot for breakfast and special occasions. *Average main: €10* *Via Vincenzo de Vit 14, Stresa* *0323/30364* *www.facebook.com/pasticceriamarcolini* *Closed Tues.*

Hotels

★ Grand Hotel des Iles Borromees

$$ | **HOTEL** | This palatial, Liberty-style hotel has catered to a demanding European clientele since 1863, and although its spacious salons and guest rooms still have lavish turn-of-the-last-century furnishings, there are signs of modernity, including a redesigned bar (Hemingway Bar), low-calorie and gluten-free options at the restaurant, and extensive wellness treatments. **Pros:** bygone-era grace and style plus modern amenities; sumptuous rooms, particularly the fabulous Hemingway Suite; nice pool and spa selection. **Cons:** bathrooms could use a refresh; decor may be over the top for some; Internet can be on the slow side. *Rooms from: €250* *Corso Umberto I 67, Stresa* *0323/938938* *www.borromees.com* *Closed Dec. and Jan.* *179 rooms* *Free Breakfast.*

Verbania

16 km (10 miles) north of Stresa, 102 km (63 miles) northwest of Milan.

The quaint town of Verbania is across the Gulf of Pallanza from its more touristy neighbor, Stresa. It is known for the Villa Taranto, which has magnificent botanical gardens. With its majestic gardens and greenery, Verbania is often called the Garden of Lake Maggiore.

GETTING HERE AND AROUND

By car from Milan take the A8 to Lago Maggiore, traveling 102 km (63 miles); Verbania is on SS34 and the drive takes about one hour and 45 minutes.

VISITOR INFORMATION

CONTACT Verbania Tourism. *Corso Zanitello 6/8, Lungolago di Pallanza, Verbania* *0323/503249* *www.viviverbania.it/en.*

Sights

Santa Caterina del Sasso Ballaro

CHURCH | Near the town of Laveno, this beautiful lakeside hermitage was constructed in the 12th century by a local merchant to express his gratitude for having been saved from the wrath of a storm. Seemingly carved out of its supporting cliff, it's particularly striking as you approach it by boat, although, after docking, you'll need to climb 80 steps. Alternatively, park in the lot above and walk down a 268-step staircase; there's an elevator, though it's not as scenic. *Via Santa Caterina 13, Leggiuno* *0332/647014* *www.eremosantacaterina.it* *€5 (with elevator €6).*

Villa Taranto

GARDEN | **FAMILY** | The Villa Taranto was acquired in 1931 by Scottish captain Neil McEachern, who helped make the magnificent gardens here what they are today, adding terraces, waterfalls, more than 3,000 plant species from all over the world—including 300 varieties of dahlias—and broad meadows sloping gently to the lake. While the gardens can be visited, the villa itself is not open to the public. ✉ *Via Vittorio Veneto 111, Verbania* ☎ *0323/556667* 🌐 *www.villataranto.it* 🎟 *€13* 🕒 *Closed early Nov.–early Mar.*

Hotels

Il Chiostro

$ | **HOTEL** | Using space formed from a 17th-century monastery merged with an adjoining 19th-century textile factory, this hotel offers plain, functional rooms, some overlooking a lovely garden. **Pros:** friendly, efficient staff; lovely breakfast; affordable for the area. **Cons:** rooms are fairly plain; limited amenities; small bathrooms. [$] *Rooms from: €90* ✉ *Via Fratelli Cervi 14, Verbania* ☎ *0323/404077* 🌐 *www.chiostrovb.it* 🛏 *100 rooms* 🍴 *Free Breakfast.*

Il Sole di Ranco

$$ | **HOTEL** | For more than 170 years the same family has run this elegant inn—about an hour's drive from Verbania on the banks of the lake opposite Stresa—where guest rooms are in two late-19th-century villas surrounded by a garden and the chef does the family proud in the exceptional restaurant. **Pros:** classic lake setting; tranquil grounds; lovely pool area. **Cons:** far from the tourist center (hotel offers tours with private drivers); decor on the old-fashioned side; restaurant a bit pricey. [$] *Rooms from: €190* ✉ *Piazza Venezia 5, Ranco* ☎ *0331/976507* 🌐 *www.ilsolediranco.it* 🕒 *Closed Jan.–early Feb.* 🛏 *14 rooms* 🍴 *Free Breakfast.*

Chapter 8

PIEDMONT AND THE VALLE D'AOSTA

Updated by
Liz Humphreys

WELCOME TO PIEDMONT AND THE VALLE D'AOSTA

TOP REASONS TO GO

★ **Sacra di San Michele:** Explore one of the country's most spectacularly situated religious monuments.

★ **Castello di Fénis:** This castle transports you back in time to the Middle Ages.

★ **Monte Bianco:** A cable-car ride over a snowcapped mountain will take your breath away.

★ **Turin's Museo Egizio:** A surprising treasure—one of the world's richest collections of Ancient Egyptian art outside Cairo, Egypt.

★ **Regal wines:** Some of Italy's most revered reds—led by Barolo, the "king of wines"—come from the hills of southern Piedmont.

★ **Turin's Galleria Sabauda:** Witness to the regal splendor of the reigning House of Savoy, this museum is famed for its spectacular collection of Old Masters.

1 **Turin.** Neoclassical piazzas and Baroque palazzi have been restored in grand style.

2 **Asti.** Home of its namesake *spumante*, a sweet sparkling wine.

3 **Alba.** A city that's renowned for its truffles and mushrooms.

4 **The Barolo Region.** Birthplace of the celebrated nebbiolo grape.

5 **Gavi.** This town boasts charming streets and famed white wine.

6 **Bard.** A strategic medieval town with an impressive fortress.

7 **Breuil-Cervinia/The Matterhorn.** This skier's paradise straddles the Swiss border.

8 **Castello di Fénis.** Castello di Fénis is embellished with many towers.

9 **Aosta.** This is one of Italy's most livable cities.

10 **Courmayeur/Monte Bianco.** A cozy mountain town, popular with skiers.

11 **Venaria Reale.** An expansive 16th-century Savoy palace.

12 **Rivoli.** This charming town is a highlight.

13 **Sacra di San Michele.** This 11th-century abbey once controlled 176 European churches.

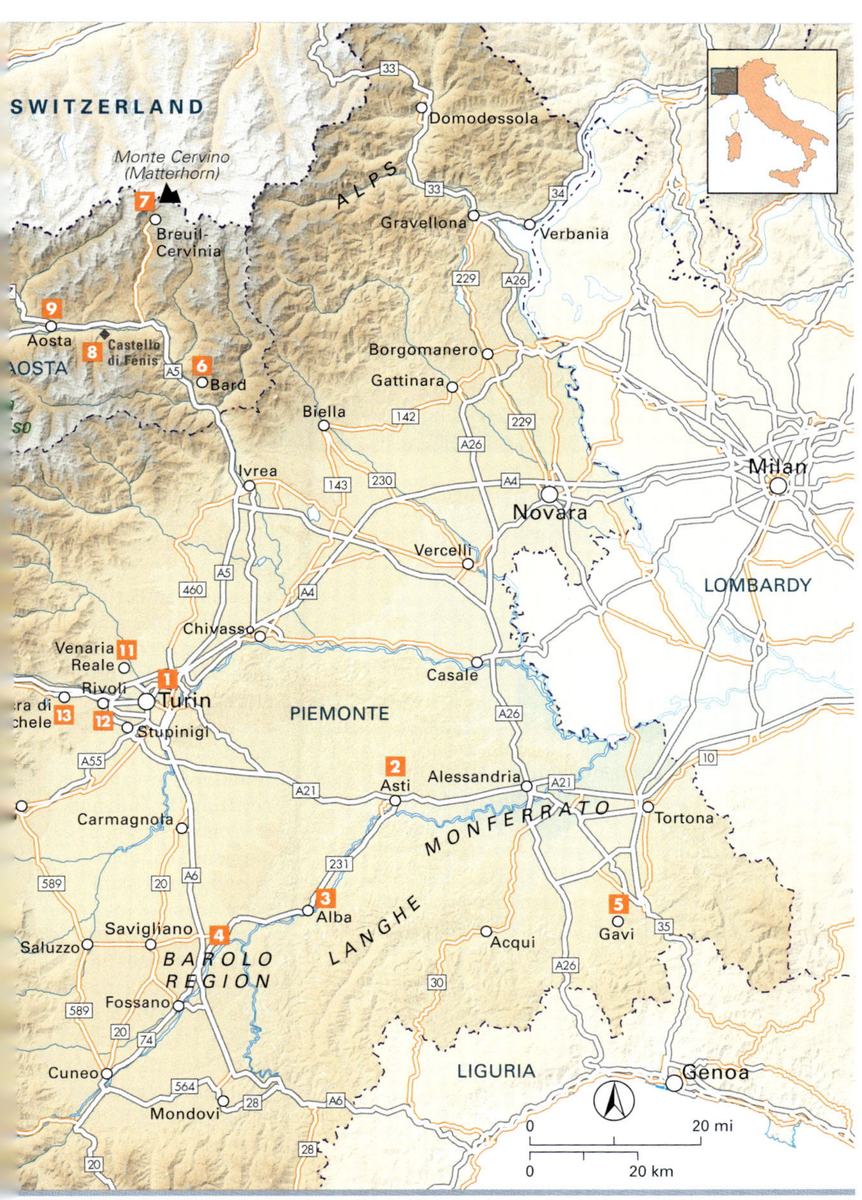
SWITZERLAND
Monte Cervino (Matterhorn)
Domodossola
ALPS
Gravellona
Verbania
Breuil-Cervinia
Aosta
Castello di Fenis
Bard
Borgomanero
Gattinara
Biella
Ivrea
Milan
Novara
Vercelli
LOMBARDY
Chivasso
Venaria Reale
Rivoli
Turin
Casale
Stupinigi
PIEMONTE
Asti
Alessandria
Tortona
MONFERRATO
Carmagnola
Alba
LANGHE
Savigliano
Saluzzo
BAROLO REGION
Gavi
Acqui
Fossano
Cuneo
Mondovi
LIGURIA
Genoa
0
20 mi
0
20 km

EATING AND DRINKING WELL IN PIEDMONT AND THE VALLE D'AOSTA

Selection of grissini (bread sticks)

In Piedmont and the Valle d'Aosta you can find rustic specialties from farmhouse hearths, fine cuisine with a French accent, and everything in between. The Piedmontese take their food and wine very seriously.

There's a significant concentration of upscale restaurants in Piedmont, with refined cuisine designed to showcase the region's fine wines. Wine-oriented menus are prevalent both in cities and in the country, where even simply named trattorias may offer a *menu di degustazione* (a multicourse tasting menu that highlights the chef's specialties) accompanied by wine pairings.

In Turin the ritual of the *aperitivo* (aperitif) has been finely tuned, and most cafés from the early evening onward provide lavish buffets that are included in the price of a cocktail—a respectable substitute for dinner if you're traveling on a limited budget. As a result, restaurants in Turin tend to fill only after 9 pm.

GREAT GRISSINI

Throughout the region—and especially in Turin—you'll find that most meals are accompanied by *grissini* (bread sticks). When they are freshly made and hand-rolled, these renditions are a far cry from the thin and dry, plastic-wrapped versions available elsewhere. Grissini were invented in Turin in the 17th century to ease the digestive problems of little Prince Vittorio Amedeo II (1675–1730). Napoléon called them *petits batons* and was supposedly addicted to them.

TRUFFLES

The *tartufo* (truffle) is a peculiar delicacy—a gnarly clump of fungus that grows wild in forests a few inches underground. It's hunted down using truffle-sniffing dogs. The payoff is a powerful, perfume flavor that makes gourmets swoon and for which they are willing to pay a small fortune. Although truffles are more abundant farther south in Umbria, the most coveted ones are the *tartufi bianchi* (white truffles) from Alba in Piedmont. A thin shaving of truffle often tops pasta dishes; they're also used to flavor soups and other dishes.

POLENTA AND PASTA

The area's best-known dish is probably polenta, creamy cornmeal served with *carbonada* (a meat stew), melted cheese, or wild mushrooms. *Agnolotti*—crescent-shape pasta stuffed with meat filling—is another specialty, often served with the pan juices of roast veal.

CHEESE

In keeping with their northern character, Piedmont and the Valle d'Aosta are both known for *fonduta,* a version of fondue made with melted cheese, eggs, and sometimes grated truffles. Fontina and ham also often deck out the ubiquitous French-style crepes *alla valdostana,* served casserole-style.

Agnolotti (meat-filled pasta)

White truffles

MEAT

The locally raised beef of Piedmont is some of Italy's most highly prized; it's often braised or stewed with the region's hearty red wine. In winter, *bollito misto* (various meats, boiled and served with a rich sauce) shows up on many menus, and fritto misto, a combination of fried meats and vegetables, is another specialty.

DESSERTS AND SWEETS

Although desserts here are less sweet than in some other Italian regions, treats like *panna cotta* (a puddinglike cooked cream), *torta di nocciole* (hazelnut torte), and *bonet* (a pudding made with hazelnuts, cocoa, milk, and macaroons) are delights. Turin is renowned for its delicate pastries and fine chocolates—especially for *gianduiotti,* made with hazelnuts.

WINE

Piedmont is one of Italy's most important wine regions, producing full-bodied reds, such as Barolo, Barbaresco, freisa, barbera, and the lighter dolcetto. Asti Spumante, a sweet sparkling wine, comes from the region, as does the white wine Gavi, from the southeast. The Valle d'Aosta is an up-and-coming wine region and is also famous for brandies made from fruits or herbs.

Northwest Italy's Piedmont and Valle d'Aosta regions come with a large dose of mountain splendor, culinary achievement, and scenic beauty. Two of Europe's most famous peaks, Monte Bianco (Mont Blanc) and Monte Cervino (the Matterhorn), straddle the Valle d'Aosta's borders with France and Switzerland, and the region draws skiers and hikers from all over.

To the south, the mist-shrouded lowlands are home to Turin, a city that may not have the artistic treasures of Rome or the cutting-edge style of Milan but has developed a sense of urban sophistication that makes it a pleasure to visit. The fourth-largest city in the country, it was once overlooked on tourist itineraries as a mere industrial center (Fiat is based here), but the 2006 Winter Olympic Games put Turin on many tourists' map.

Farther south, vineyards carpet the rolling hills of the Langhe, Monferrato, and Gavi regions, where Barolo, Barbaresco, Asti Spumante, and Gavi wines—some of Italy's finest—are produced. It's here, as well, that the prized white truffle of Alba is found and celebrated during an autumn fair.

Piedmont has the longest border with France of any region, and the fact of its having been ruled by the French Savoy for centuries is revealed in a Gallic influence in all walks of life—especially in food and architecture. Turin's mansard roofs and porticoed avenues can make a walk through its streets feel like a stroll down a Parisian boulevard.

MAJOR REGIONS

Southeast of Turin. In the hilly, wooded Monferrato area, and farther south in the Langhe near Alba and in the Gavi region, the landscape is a patchwork of vineyards and dark woods, dotted with hill towns. This area produces some of Italy's most famous red wines, as well as sparkling whites like Asti Spumante and the dry white Gavi.

The Valle d'Aosta. In this region near the French–Swiss border, the unspoiled beauty of the Alps' highest peaks, the Matterhorn and Mont Blanc, competes with the magnificent scenery of Italy's oldest national park, Gran Paradiso. Luckily, the region is so small that you don't have to choose. The main Aosta Valley, largely on an east–west axis, is hemmed in by high mountains. Pont St. Martin, north of Ivrea, is the beginning of bilingual (Italian and French) territory.

West of Turin and beyond. As you head west from Turin into the *colline* ("little hills"), castles and medieval fortifications begin to appear and the Alps come into better view. In this region lie the storybook medieval town of Rivoli; 12th-century abbeys like Sacra di San Michele; and a 16th-century Savoy hunting lodge, Venaria Reale.

Planning

Getting Here and Around

BUS

Turin's main bus station is in Corso Bolzano, near the Porta Susa train station. There's also a major bus station at Aosta, across the street from the train station. The major bus companies include FlixBus (🌐 *www.flixbus.com*), GTT (🌐 *www.gtt.to.it/cms*), and Arriva Italia (🌐 *torino.arriva.it*)

CAR

Like any mountainous region, the Italian Alps can be tricky to navigate by car. Roads that look like highways on the map can be narrow and twisting, with steep slopes and cliff-side drops. Generally, roads are well maintained, but the distance covered by all of those curves tends to take longer than you might expect, so it's best to figure in extra time for getting around. This is especially true in winter, when weather conditions can slow traffic and close roads. Check with local tourist offices or, in a pinch, with the police to make sure roads are passable and safe.

For travel across the French, Swiss, and Italian borders in Piedmont and the Valle d'Aosta, only a few routes are usable year-round: the 12-km (7-mile) Mont Blanc tunnel connecting Chamonix with Courmayeur; the Colle del Gran San Bernardo/Col du Grand-Saint-Bernard (connecting Martigny to Aosta on Swiss highway E27 and Italian highway SS27, with 6 km [4 miles] of tunnel); and the Traforo del Fréjus (between Modane and Susa, with 13 km [8 miles] of tunnel). Other passes become increasingly unreliable between November and April.

TRAIN

Turin is on the main Paris–Rome TGV express line and is also connected with Milan, 60 minutes away on the fast train. The fastest (Frecciarossa) trains cover the 667-km (414-mile) trip to Rome in just over four hours; other trains take between five and seven hours.

Services to the larger cities east of Turin are part of the extensive and reliable train network of the Lombard Plain. In the mountains to the west of the region's capital, however, train service begins to peter out in favor of bus connections; information about train-bus mountain services can be obtained from train stations and tourist information offices, or by contacting Trenitalia (🌐 *www.trenitalia.com*), the Italian national train service, or Italo (🌐 *www.italotreno.it*), the privately owned high-speed train company.

Hotels

High standards and good service are characteristic of Turin's better hotels, and the same is true at top mountain resorts. Hotels in Turin and other major towns are generally geared to business travelers; make sure to ask whether lower weekend rates or special deals for two- or three-night stays are available.

Summer vacationers and winter skiers keep occupancy rates and prices high at resorts during peak seasons. Many mountain hotels require guests to pay for either half or full board and insist on a stay of several nights; some have off-season rates that can reduce the cost by a full price category. If you're planning to ski, ask about packages that give you a discount on lift tickets.

⇨ *Hotel and restaurant reviews have been shortened. For full information, visit Fodors.com. Prices in the hotel reviews are the lowest cost of a standard double room in high season. Prices in the dining reviews are the average cost of a main course at dinner, or, if dinner is not served, at lunch.*

What It Costs in Euros

	$	$$	$$$	$$$$
RESTAURANTS	under €20	€20–€30	€31–€40	over €40
HOTELS	under €175	€175–€400	€401–€600	over €600

Making the Most of Your Time

Turin needs at least two or three days to visit properly. If you have extra time, visit one of the magnificent palaces built by the Savoy family. They surround Turin in the so-called *corona di delizie* (crown of delights) and make for an easy day trip.

Plan on several days to visit the Langhe and Monferrato areas. The towns of Alba and Asti should not be missed, but neither should the smaller wine towns that dot the rolling hills of both regions. You may also want to add a day or two to relax and visit wineries in the Gavi region. You'll need your own car in all these areas, but the rewards are great views, great food, and great wine. If coming in September and October, when there are festivals in both Alba and Asti, make sure to book your trip well in advance.

Unless you are planning on a skiing or hiking holiday, the Valle d'Aosta requires less time to visit. The emphasis here is on the natural beauty of the mountains, but if you are driving between France and Italy, the region certainly merits a one- or two-night stopover, in either Courmayeur or Aosta; be sure not to miss Castello di Fénis and the Forte di Bard on your way.

Restaurants

In this region's restaurants you'll taste a difference between the mountain and the city, but the hearty peasant fare served in tiny stone villages and the French-accented delicacies of the plain are both eminently satisfying.

Turin

128 km (80 miles) west of Milan.

Turin (Torino, in Italian) is roughly in the center of Piedmont–Valle d'Aosta; it's on the Po River, on the edge of the Po Plain, which stretches east all the way to the Adriatic. Turin's flatness and wide, angular, tree-lined boulevards are a far cry from Italian *metropoli* to the south; the region's decidedly northern European bent is quite evident in its nerve center. Aside from its role as northwest Italy's major industrial, cultural, intellectual, and administrative hub, Turin also has a reputation as Italy's capital of black magic and the supernatural. This distinction is enhanced by the presence of Turin's most famous and controversial relic, the Sacra Sindone (Shroud of Turin), still believed by many Catholics to be Christ's burial shroud. (For its part, the Vatican has not taken an official position on its authenticity.)

GETTING HERE AND AROUND

Turin is well served by the Italian autostrada system and can be reached easily by car from all directions: from Milan on the A4 (two hours); from Bologna (four hours) and Florence (five hours) on the A1 and A21; from Genoa on the A6 (two hours). Bus service to and from other major Italian cities is also plentiful, and Turin can be reached by fast train service from Paris in less than six hours. Fast train service also connects the city with Milan, Genoa, Bologna, Venice, Florence, and Rome.

VISITOR INFORMATION

The city's tourist office organizes group and personal guided tours. It also provides maps and details about a wide range of thematic self-guided walks through town. The Torino+Piemonte Card, which provides discounts on transportation and museum entrances for one-, two-, three-, or five-day visits, can be purchased here.

CONTACT Turin Tourist Information Center. ✉ *Piazza Castello, at Via Garibaldi, Turin* ☎ *011/535181* 🌐 *www.turismotorino.org.*

Sights

ALONG THE PO

The Po River is narrow and unprepossessing here in Turin, only a hint of the broad waterway that it becomes as it flows eastward toward the Adriatic. It's flanked, however, by formidable edifices, a park, and a lovely pedestrian path.

★ Museo dell'Automobile

SPECIALTY MUSEUM | FAMILY | No visit to this motor city would be complete without a pilgrimage to see the perfectly preserved Bugattis, Ferraris, and Isotta Fraschinis at this museum. Here you can get an idea of the importance of Fiat—and cars in general—to Turin's economy. There's a collection of antique cars from as early as 1896, and displays show how the city has changed over the years as a result of the auto industry. ✉ *Corso Unità d'Italia 40, Millefonti* ☎ *011/677666* 🌐 *www.museoauto.com* 🎫 *€15* 🕒 *Closed Mon. after 2 pm.*

Parco del Valentino

CITY PARK | FAMILY | This pleasant riverside park is a great place to stroll, bike, or jog. Originally the grounds of a relatively simple hunting lodge, the park owes its present arrangement to Madama Maria Cristina of France, who received the land and lodge as a wedding present after her marriage to Vittorio Amedeo I of Savoy. The building, now home to the University of Turin's Faculty of Architecture, is not open to the public. However, you can visit the Orto Botanico di Torino (Botanical Garden of Turin) just north of the castle. ✉ *Viale Mattioli 25, San Salvario* ☎ *011/6705980 botanical gardens* 🌐 *www.ortobotanico.unito.it* 🎫 *Botanical gardens €5* 🕒 *Botanical gardens closed weekdays except for holidays, and mid-Nov.–late Mar.*

★ Pinacoteca Agnelli

ART MUSEUM | This gallery was opened by Gianni Agnelli (1921–2003), the head of Fiat and patriarch of one of Italy's most powerful families, just four months before his death. There are four magnificent scenes of Venice by Canaletto (1697–1768); two splendid views of Dresden by Canaletto's nephew, Bernardo Bellotto (1720–80); and several works by Manet, Renoir, Matisse, and Picasso. You can also visit La Pista 500, the former Fiat test track on the roof of the Lingotto building, to view rotating exhibits from contemporary artists. ✉ *Via Nizza 230, Lingotto* ☎ *011/0925011* 🌐 *www.pinacoteca-agnelli.it* 🎫 *Pinacoteca and Pista 500 €12, Pinacoteca €10, Pista 500 €4* 🕒 *Closed Mon.*

Sassi-Superga Cog Train

TRAIN/TRAIN STATION | FAMILY | The 18-minute ride from Sassi up the Superga hill is a real treat on a clear day. The view of the Alps is magnificent at the hilltop **Parco Naturale Collina Torinese,** a tranquil retreat from the bustle of the city. If you feel like a little exercise, you can walk back down to Sassi (about two hours) on one of the well-marked wooded trails that start from the upper station. Other circular trails lead through the park and back to Superga. Note that a bus replaces the train on Wednesday, although the ride up the hill is still just as lovely. ✉ *Piazza G. Modena, Sassi* ☎ *800/019152* 🌐 *www.gtt.to.it* 🎫 *€4 one-way and €6 round-trip on weekdays, €6 one-way and €9 round-trip on weekends.*

Sights

1 Duomo di San Giovanni **B2**
2 Galleria Civica d'Arte Moderna e Comtemporanea (GAM).. **A5**
3 Galleria Sabauda **B2**
4 Mole Antonelliana **C3**
5 Museo d'Arte Orientale **A2**
6 Museo dell' Automobile... **A9**
7 Museo di Antichità **B2**
8 Museo Egizio **B3**
9 Palazzo Carignano... **B3**
10 Palazzo Madama **B3**
11 Palazzo Reale **B2**
12 Parco del Valentino.... **B7**
13 Piazza San Carlo......... **B4**
14 Pinacoteca Agnelli....... **A9**
15 Sassi-Superga Cog Train.... **D3**

Restaurants

1 Al Garamond... **B4**
2 Casa Vicina........ **A9**
3 Consorzio ... **A3**
4 Del Cambio...... **B3**
5 Vintage 1997.......... **A3**

Quick Bites

1 Al Bicerin ... **A1**
2 Il Mercato Centrale Torino........ **B1**

Hotels

1 Grand Hotel Sitea......... **B4**
2 Hotel Victoria Torino........ **B4**

DOWNTOWN TURIN

Many of Turin's major sights are clustered around Piazza Castello, and others are on or just off the portico-lined Via Roma, one of the city's main thoroughfares, which leads 1 km (½ mile) from Piazza Castello south to Piazza Carlo Felice, a landscaped park in front of the train station. First opened in 1615, Via Roma was largely rebuilt in the 1930s, during the Mussolini era.

Duomo di San Giovanni

CHURCH | The most impressive part of Turin's 15th-century cathedral is the Cappella della Sacra Sindone (Chapel of the Holy Shroud), where the famous relic is housed in a sealed casket. The Sacra Sindone is a 12-foot-long sheet of linen, thought by millions to be the burial shroud of Christ, bearing the light imprint of his crucified body. The shroud first made an appearance around the middle of the 15th century, when it was presented to Ludovico of Savoy in Chambéry. In 1578 it was brought to Turin by another member of the Savoy royal family, Duke Emanuele Filiberto.

It was only in the 1990s that the Catholic Church began allowing rigorous scientific study of the shroud. Not surprisingly, the results have been hazy. On one hand, three separate university teams—in Switzerland, Britain, and the United States—have concluded, as a result of carbon-14 analysis, that the cloth dates from between 1260 and 1390. On the other hand, they are unable to explain how medieval forgers could have created the shroud's image. Either way, the shroud continues to be revered as a holy relic, exhibited to the public on very rare occasions. ✉ *Piazza San Giovanni, Centro* ☎ *011/4361540* 🌐 *www.facebook.com/parrocchiaduomotorino* 🎫 *Free.*

Galleria Civica d'Arte Moderna e Contemporanea (GAM)

ART MUSEUM | In 1863 Turin was the first Italian city to begin a public collection devoted to contemporary art. Housed in a modern building on the edge of downtown, a permanent display of more than 600 paintings, sculptures, and installation pieces (from a collection of more than 45,000 works of art) provides an exceptional glimpse of how Italian contemporary art has evolved since the late 1800s. The Futurist, Pop, neo-Dada, and Arte Povera movements are particularly well represented, and the gallery has a fine video and art film collection. ✉ *Via Magenta 31, Centro* ☎ *011/4429518* 🌐 *www.gamtorino.it* 🎫 *€11* ⏲ *Closed Mon.*

★ Galleria Sabauda (*Savoy Gallery*)

ART MUSEUM | Housed in the restored Manica Nuova (new wing) of the Palazzo Reale, the gallery displays some of the most important paintings from the vast collections of the house of Savoy. The collection is particularly rich in Dutch and Flemish paintings: note the *Stigmate di San Francesco* (*St. Francis Receiving the Stigmata*) by Jan van Eyck (1395–1441), in which the saint receives the marks of Christ's wounds while a companion cringes beside him. ✉ *Piazetta Reale 1, Centro* ☎ *011/19560449* 🌐 *museireali.beniculturali.it* 🎫 *€15, includes the Royal Museums (Palazzo Reale, Armeria Reale, Cappella della Sindone, Museo di Antichità, Giardini Reali, and Biblioteca Reale)* ⏲ *Closed Wed.*

★ Mole Antonelliana

NOTABLE BUILDING | **FAMILY** | You can't miss the unusual square dome and thin, elaborate spire of this Turin landmark above the city's rooftops. This odd structure, built between 1863 and 1889, was intended to be a synagogue, but costs escalated and eventually it was bought by the city; it now houses the Museo Nazionale del Cinema (National Cinema Museum), a worthy sight for film buffs. At scheduled times on weekends, you can walk all the way up to the top of the dome, a journey not for the faint of heart (and not permitted for children under age six). ✉ *Via Montebello 20, Centro* ☎ *011/8138563* *www.museocinema.it* *Museum €16, elevator to panoramic terrace €9, combination ticket €20, walking by foot to dome €10* *Closed Tues.*

Museo d'Arte Orientale (*Asian Art Museum*)

ART MUSEUM | Housed in the magnificently renovated 17th-century Palazzo Mazzonis, this is a beautifully displayed collection of Southeast Asian, Chinese, Japanese, Himalayan, and Islamic art, including sculptures, paintings, and ceramics. Highlights include a towering 13th-century wooden statue of the Japanese temple guardian Kongo Rikishi and a sumptuous assortment of Islamic manuscripts. *Via San Domenico 11, Centro* *011/443693* *www.maotorino.it* *€10* *Closed Mon.*

Museo di Antichità

HISTORY MUSEUM | A small but fascinating collection of artifacts found at archaeological sites in and around Turin is displayed here. A spiral ramp winds down through the subterranean museum, and as in a real archaeological site, the deeper you go, the older the objects on display. A life-size silver bust of the Roman emperor Lucius Verus (AD 161–169) is one of the masterpieces of the collection. *Via XX Settembre 88, Centro* *011/19560449* *museireali.beniculturali.it* *€15, includes the Royal Museums (Galleria Sabauda, Palazzo Reale, Armeria Reale, Cappella della Sindone, Giardini Reali, and Biblioteca Reale)* *Closed Wed.*

★ **Museo Egizio**

HISTORY MUSEUM | **FAMILY** | The Egyptian Museum's superb collection includes statues of pharaohs and mummies and entire frescoes taken from royal tombs. The striking sculpture gallery, designed by the Oscar-winning production designer Dante Ferretti, is a veritable who's who of ancient Egypt. Look for the magnificent 13th-century-BC statue of Ramses II and the fascinating Tomb of Kha. The latter was found intact with furniture, supplies of food and clothing, and writing instruments. *Via Accademia delle Scienze 6, Centro* *011/4406903* *www.museoegizio.it* *€18* *Closed Mon. afternoon.*

Palazzo Carignano

HISTORY MUSEUM | Half of this building is the Baroque triumph of Guarino Guarini, the priest and architect who designed many of Turin's most noteworthy buildings. Built between 1679 and 1685, his redbrick palace later played an important role in the creation of the modern-day nation. Vittorio Emanuele II of Savoy (1820–78), the first king of a united Italy, was born here, and, after a 19th-century neoclassical extension, Italy's first parliament met here between 1860 and 1865. The palace now houses the Museo del Risorgimento, a museum honoring the 19th-century movement for Italian unity. *Via Accademia delle Scienze 5, Centro* *Entrance at Piazza Carlo Alberto 8* *011/5621147* *www.museorisorgimentotorino.it* *€10* *Closed Mon.*

Palazzo Madama

HISTORY MUSEUM | In the center of Piazza Castello, this castle was named for the Savoy queen Maria Cristina, who made it her home in the 17th century. The building incorporates the remains of a Roman gate with late-medieval and Renaissance additions, and the monumental Baroque facade and grand entrance staircase were added by Filippo Juvarra (1678–1736). The palace now houses the Museo Civico d'Arte Antica, whose collections comprise more than 30,000 items dating from the Middle Ages to the Baroque era. *Piazza Castello 10, Centro* *011/5211788* *www.palazzomadamatorino.it* *Staircase and courtyard free, museum €10* *Closed Tues.*

★ **Palazzo Reale**

CASTLE/PALACE | **FAMILY** | This 17th-century palace, a former Savoy royal residence, is an imposing work of brick, stone, and marble that stands on the site of one of Turin's ancient Roman city gates. In contrast to its sober exterior, the two main floors of the palace's interior are swathed in luxurious rococo trappings, including tapestries and gilt ceilings. The gardens were laid out in the late 17th century by André Le Nôtre, landscape designer at Versailles, and the Armeria Reale (Royal Armory) wing holds a collection of arms and armor. ✉ *Piazzetta Reale 1, Centro* ☎ *011/4361455* 🌐 *museireali.beniculturali.it* 🎟 *€15, includes the Royal Museums (Galleria Sabauda, Armeria Reale, Cappella della Sindone, Museo di Antichità, Giardini Reali, and Biblioteca Reale)* ⏲ *Closed Wed.*

Piazza San Carlo

PLAZA/SQUARE | Surrounded by shops, arcades, fashionable cafés, and elegant Baroque palaces, this is one of the most beautiful squares in Turin. In the center stands a statue of Duke Emanuele Filiberto of Savoy, the victor at the battle of San Quintino, in 1557. The melee heralded the peaceful resurgence of Turin under the Savoy after years of bloody dynastic fighting. The fine bronze statue erected in the 19th century is one of Turin's symbols. At the southern end of the square, framing the continuation of Via Roma, are the twin Baroque churches of San Carlo and Santa Cristina. ✉ *Piazza San Carlo, Centro.*

Restaurants

★ Al Garamond

$$ | PIEDMONTESE | The well-spaced tables and the ancient brick vaulting in this small, bright space set the stage for game, meat, fish, and seafood dishes served with creative flair. The level of service is very high, even by demanding Turin standards. **Known for:** chef's table experience; mix of traditional and inventive dishes; merging Sicilian and Piedmontese cuisine. $ *Average main: €28* ✉ *Via G. Pomba 14, Centro* ☎ *011/8122781* 🌐 *algaramond.it* ⏲ *Closed Sun., Aug., and Jan. 19–26. No lunch Sat., Mon., and Tues.*

★ Casa Vicina

$$$$ | PIEDMONTESE | Tucked away on the third floor of the Green Pea sustainable retail venture (next to Eataly Lingotto), one of Turin's top destinations for fine dining is run by the fourth generation of the Vicina family, with Claudio and wife Anna leading the kitchen and Stefano managing the front of house. Excellent-quality traditional Piedmontese dishes are served with creative style, and the wine list is an encyclopedia, featuring not only the top Barolo producers but also many other small but notable wineries. **Known for:** fresh agnolotti pasta; fixed-price tasting and gastronomic menus; layered bagna càuda served in a martini glass. $ *Average main: €50* ✉ *Via Ermanno Fenoglietti 20/b, 3rd fl. of Green Pea, Lingotto* ☎ *011/6640140* 🌐 *www.casavicina.com* ⏲ *Closed Sun. and Mon.*

Consorzio

$ | PIEDMONTESE | Extremely popular for lunch during the week, this lively and informal osteria is in Turin's business district. The service is relaxed, the decor is low-key, the menu highlights organic meats and vegetables from Piedmont, and there's a good selection of natural wines. **Known for:** wide selection of cheeses from across Europe; Piedmont dishes like agnolotti gobbi (stuffed pasta); creative presentation. $ *Average main: €18* ✉ *Via Monte di Pietà 23, Centro* ☎ *011/2767661* 🌐 *ristoranteconsorzio.it* ⏲ *Closed Sun. and Mon.*

★ Del Cambio

$$$$ | PIEDMONTESE | Set in a palace dating from 1757, this is one of Europe's most beautiful and historic restaurants, with decorative moldings, mirrors, and hanging lamps contrasted with ultramodern takes on Piedmontese cuisine from young Michelin-starred chef Matteo Baronetto. Order an inventive signature dish such as the Piedmontese salad, with around 24 artfully composed ingredients, and an expertly prepared meat or fish dish, or opt for the eight-course

tasting menu to sample more of the chef's innovative cooking. **Known for:** beautifully presented plates; elegant atmosphere; well-selected wine pairings. $ *Average main: €62* ✉ *Piazza Carignano 2, Centro* ☎ *011/546690* 🌐 *delcambio.it* 🕒 *Closed Mon. No dinner Sun. No lunch Tues.–Thurs.*

★ Vintage 1997

$$$ | NORTHERN ITALIAN | The first floor of an elegant town house in the center of Turin makes a fitting location for this sophisticated restaurant. There's an excellent wine list with regional, national, and international vintages well-represented, and tasting menus, including a feast that covers the full range of the restaurant's cuisine and desserts. **Known for:** Piedmontese roasted veal; selection of rare cheeses; tasting menus from three to 10 courses. $ *Average main: €33* ✉ *Piazza Solferino 16/h, Centro* ☎ *011/535948* 🌐 *www.vintage1997.com* 🕒 *Closed Sun. No lunch Sat.*

Coffee and Quick Bites

★ Al Bicerin

$ | CAFÉ | FAMILY | A chocolate lover's pilgrimage to Turin inevitably leads to this café where Nietzsche, Puccini, Dumas, and the political reformer Cavour have all sipped. If you order the house specialty, *bicerin* (a hot drink with layers of chocolate, coffee, and cream), or a flavored *zabaioni* (warm eggnog), and browse the collection of chocolate goodies including chocolate-flavored pasta, you'll understand why. **Known for:** elegant presentation; traditional Gianduiotto chocolates; wide assortment of creative sweet drinks. $ *Average main: €6* ✉ *Piazza della Consolata 5, Centro* ☎ *011/4369325* 🌐 *bicerin.it* 🕒 *Closed Wed. and Aug.*

★ Il Mercato Centrale Torino

$ | INTERNATIONAL | FAMILY | When you're not in the mood for an Italian-style lunch or dinner (read: leisurely), head to the Mercato Centrale for a selection of foods—from more than 20 food stands—like fresh pasta, fish, roast meats, pizza, and fried dishes; more international options including ramen and Peruvian plates; and a good choice of cocktails, wines, and beer. But don't fill up on the mains, as you'll also find a delightful selection of baked goods and, of course, gelato, for a sweet finish. **Known for:** lively crowds; late-night hours (open Sunday–Thursday till 11 pm, and Friday and Saturday till midnight); wide selection of dishes. $ *Average main: €12* ✉ *Piazza della Repubblica 25, Centro* ☎ *011/0898040* 🌐 *www.mercatocentrale.com/turin.*

Hotels

★ Grand Hotel Sitea

$$ | HOTEL | One of the city's finest hotels, the Sitea is in the historic center and decorated in a warm classical style; the common areas and guest rooms are elegant, spacious, and comfortable. **Pros:** central location; well-appointed rooms; large bathrooms. **Cons:** air-conditioning and street noise can be loud in some rooms; carpets are a little worn; bathrooms could use a refresh. $ *Rooms from: €267* ✉ *Via Carlo Alberto 35, Centro* ☎ *011/5170171* 🌐 *www.grandhotelsitea.it* 🛏 *120 rooms* 🍽 *No Meals.*

Hotel Victoria Torino

$$ | HOTEL | Style, attention to detail, and comfort are hallmarks of this retreat that's furnished like a refined English home. **Pros:** tranquil location in the center of town; good spa facilities; wonderful breakfast. **Cons:** standard rooms are small; no on-site restaurant; no gym. $ *Rooms from: €257* ✉ *Via Nino Costa 4, Centro* ☎ *011/5611909* 🌐 *www.hotelvictoria-torino.com* 🛏 *106 rooms* 🍽 *Free Breakfast.*

Piedmont

Nightlife

Caffè Elena

BARS | This café/bar is a trendy place for an aperitif or for a drink before going out to a show or dancing. It's in the large piazza at the end of Via Po. ✉ *Piazza Vittorio Veneto 5, Centro* ☎ *329/5767414 mobile* 🌐 *www.caffeelena.it.*

Pastis

GATHERING PLACE | The Quadrilatero Romano, which roughly corresponds to the grid pattern of Roman Turin near Piazza della Repubblica, is a hopping area filled with nightclubs and international restaurants. Places open and close with startling frequency here, but Pastis has shown considerable staying power. ✉ *Piazza Emanuele Filiberto 9/b, Centro* ☎ *011/5211085* 🌐 *pastistorino.com.*

Performing Arts

MUSIC

★ Lingotto Musica

MUSIC | Classical music concerts are held at this theater designed by Renzo Piano in the renovated Lingotto building; internationally famous conductors and orchestras are frequent guests. ✉ *Via Nizza 280, Lingotto* ☎ *333/9382545 ticket office* 🌐 *www.lingottomusica.it.*

OPERA

★ Teatro Regio

OPERA | Premieres at the Teatro Regio, one of Italy's leading opera houses, sell out well in advance. You can buy tickets for most performances at the box office or on the website, where discounts are often offered on the day of the performance. The season runs from October through July. ✉ *Piazza Castello 215, Centro* ☎ *011/8815241* 🌐 *www.teatroregio.torino.it.*

Shopping

CHOCOLATE

★ Peyrano

CHOCOLATE | FAMILY | The most famous of all Turin chocolates is the wedge-shape gianduiotto, flavored with hazelnuts and first concocted in 1867. The tradition has been continued at this family-run shop, where more than 80 types of chocolates and other sweets are made. ✉ *Corso Moncalieri 47, Centro* ☎ *011/6602202* 🌐 *www.peyrano.com.*

★ Stratta

CHOCOLATE | FAMILY | In business since 1836, this famed shop sells confectionery of all kinds—not just the chocolates in the lavish window displays but also fancy cookies, rum-laced fudges, and magnificent cakes. ✉ *Piazza San Carlo 191, Centro* ☎ *011/547920* 🌐 *stratta1836.it.*

MARKETS

Balon Flea Market

MARKET | Go to this famous market for bargains on secondhand books, antiques, and clothing. There is good browsing to be had among the stands, which spill out of Borgo Dora onto the surrounding side streets. During the second weekend of every month, the market extends its hours into Sunday, becoming the so-called Gran Balon. (Be aware, however, that the market is also famous for its pickpockets.) ✉ *Via Borgo Dora, Centro* ☎ *0373/8030002* 🌐 *www.balon.it.*

★ Mercato di Porta Palazzo

MARKET | For food lovers, people-watchers, or anyone interested in the lively local scene, the immensely popular market in this huge square to the north of town is not to be missed. Outdoors, the keepers of hundreds of vegetable stands vie with one another to create the most appetizing displays. Indoors, the meat vendors provide an equally tantalizing array of local products, while the fishmongers proudly display the fresh catch of the day. ✉ *Piazza della Repubblica, Centro* ☎ *011/5216242.*

SPECIALTY FOOD AND DELIS

★ Borgiattino

FOOD | Specialty food stores and delicatessens abound in central Turin, but for a truly spectacular array of cheeses and other delicacies, this should be your first stop. ✉ *Corso Vinzaglio 29, Centro* ☎ *011/5629075* 🌐 *www.borgiattino.com.*

★ Eataly Turin Lingotto

FOOD | FAMILY | Now with branches in Milan, Florence, Bologna, New York, and Tokyo, the original home of Eataly is probably Turin's most famous food emporium. In addition to the market, there are kitchenware and cookbook stores, plus several different counters and restaurants serving pizza, pasta, gelato, and more Italian goodies. ✉ *Via Ermanno Fenoglietti 14, Lingotto* ☎ *020/9997900* 🌐 *www.eataly.net.*

Asti

60 km (37 miles) southeast of Turin.

Asti is best known outside Italy for its wines—excellent reds as well as the famous sparkling white spumante. In the 12th century Asti began to develop as a republic, at a time when other Italian cities were also flexing their economic and military muscles. It flourished in the following century, when the inhabitants began erecting lofty towers for its defense. In the center of Asti some of these remain, among them the 13th-century Torre Comentina and the well-preserved Torre Troyana. The 18th-century church of Santa Caterina has incorporated one of Asti's medieval towers, the Torre Romana (itself built on an ancient Roman base), as its bell tower.

Hit the Slopes

Skiing is the major sport in both Piedmont and the Valle d'Aosta. Excellent facilities abound at resort towns such as Courmayeur and Breuil-Cervinia. The so-called Via Lattea (Milky Way)—six skiing areas near Sestriere with 400 km (almost 250 miles) of linked runs and 90 ski lifts—provides practically unlimited skiing. Lift tickets, running around €65 for a day's pass, are a good deal compared to those at major U.S. resorts.

To Italian skiers, a weeklong holiday on the slopes is known as a *settimana bianca* (white week). Ski resort hotels in Piedmont and the Valle d'Aosta encourage these getaways by offering six- and seven-day packages, and though they're designed with the domestic market in mind, you can get a bargain by taking advantage of them. The packages usually (though not always) include half or full board.

You should have your passport with you if you plan a day trip into Switzerland—although the odds are that you won't be asked to show it.

GETTING HERE AND AROUND

Asti is less than an hour away from Turin by car on the A21 autostrada. Train service from Turin to Asti is frequent and fast, and Itabus service directly connects the two towns.

VISITOR INFORMATION

CONTACT Asti Tourism Office. ✉ *Piazza Alfieri 34, Asti* ☎ *0141/530357* 🌐 *visit.asti.it.*

Sights

Collegiata di San Secondo

CHURCH | This Gothic church is dedicated to Asti's patron saint, believed by some to have been decapitated by the Emperor Hadrian on this very spot. San Secondo is also the patron of the city's favorite folklore and sporting event, the annual Palio di Asti, a colorful medieval-style horse race that's similar to Siena's. It's held each year on a Sunday in early September in the vast Campo del Palio to the south of the church. ✉ *Piazza San Secondo, south of Corso Vittorio Alfieri, Asti* ☎ *0141/530066* 🌐 *www.cittaecattedrali.it* 🎫 *Free.*

Duomo (*Cattedrale di Santa Maria Assunta*)

CHURCH | Dedicated to the Assumption of the Virgin, the Duomo is an object lesson in Italian Gothic architecture. Completed in the early 14th century, it is decorated so as to emphasize geometry and verticality: pointed arches and narrow vaults are completely covered with frescoes that direct your gaze upward. The porch on the south side of the cathedral facing the square was built in 1470; it represents the Gothic style at its most florid and excessive. ✉ *Piazza Cattedrale, Via San Giovanni 8, Asti* ☎ *0141/592924* 🌐 *www.diocesiasti.it* 🎫 *Free.*

Restaurants

★ Cannavacciuolo Le Cattedrali

$$$$ | MODERN ITALIAN | Renowned Italian chef Antonio Cannavacciuolo, who cooks at three-Michelin-star Villa Crespi on Lake Orta, oversees the menu at this refined ode to contemporary Italian cooking just outside the town of Asti. Chef Gianluca Renzi creates playful riffs on Piedmontese classics, such as pigeon with black garlic, salted peanuts, and Nebbiolo crystals or hen-filled stuffed Piedmontese

pasta (*plin*) with mushrooms, gorgonzola, and saffron, in his three tasting menus, ranging from five to eight dishes; the Menù Freehand includes five creative tastes of the chef's choosing. **Known for:** beautifully presented dishes; encyclopedic wine list (more than 2,000 labels in their cellar); cheese trolley with tempting local choices. *Average main: €50 Le Cattedrali Relais by LAQUA Collection, Frazione Valleandona 1/b, Asti 0141/1858888 www.lecattedrali.com Closed Mon. and Tues. and early Jan.–mid-Feb.*

★ Il Cavallo Scosso

$$ | **MODERN ITALIAN** | In a contemporary villa built entirely of wood on the outskirts of Asti, chef Enrico Pivieri uses a mix of local and international ingredients to create new takes on traditional dishes with a global flair. The Shaken Horse is especially strong in seafood—rare for meat-heavy Piedmont—with such creative plates as gnocchi with cuttlefish ink in miso broth with smoked sardines and fried Sicilian anchovies with *giardiniera* (pickled vegetables in vinegar). **Known for:** modern interpretations of meat and seafood dishes; beef tartare marinated with citrus fruits, seared scampi, and beetroot; choice of three tasting menus. *Average main: €26 Via Al Duca 23/d, Asti 0141/211435 ilcavalloscosso.it Closed Tues.*

Hotels

★ Le Cattedrali Relais by LAQUA Collection

$$ | **HOTEL** | Just outside Asti in the Monferrato hills, this striking contemporary property in a gorgeous natural setting features a Michelin-starred restaurant, designer furnishings, and art-lined walls. **Pros:** magnificent building and grounds; design-forward sensibility; restaurant is a destination in itself. **Cons:** some may consider room design a bit cold and sterile; light control panels in rooms technologically sophisticated but confusing; fragrance smell throughout the hotel may be too strong for some. *Rooms from: €378 Frazione Valleandona 1/b, Asti 0141/1858888 www.lecattedrali.com Closed early Jan.–mid-Feb. 13 rooms Free Breakfast.*

★ Relais Sant'Uffizio

$$ | **HOTEL** | **FAMILY** | You may be surprised to learn that this now delightfully peaceful and elegant retreat—with a luxurious spa and swimming pool, surrounded by vineyards and rolling hills—was once home to the Inquisition in the 16th century. **Pros:** tranquil and beautiful location; excellent spa and exercise facilities; good value for the amenities. **Cons:** a bit isolated; a number of rooms are a walk from the main building; soundproofing could be better in some rooms. *Rooms from: €198 Strada Sant Uffizio 1, Cioccaro di Penango, Asti 20 km (12 miles) north of Asti 0141/916292 www.relaissantuffizio.com 41 rooms Free Breakfast.*

Alba

30 km (18 miles) southwest of Asti.

This small town has a gracious atmosphere and a compact core, studded with medieval towers and Gothic buildings. In addition to being a wine center for the region, Alba is known as the "City of the White Truffle" for delicious little tubers that cost as much as €4,000 a pound. For picking out your truffle and having a few wisps shaved on top of your food, expect to shell out an extra €18 or so—definitely worth doing for a second-to-none foodie experience.

For the true truffle experience, visit during the annual Fiera Internazionale Tartufo Bianco D'Alba (International Alba White Truffle Fair *www.fieradeltartufo.org*) mid-October to mid-December for a truffle market, cooking shows, food with truffles, wine tasting, and even educational games for kids.

GETTING HERE AND AROUND

By car from Turin follow the A6 autostrada south to Marene and then head east on the A33, which connects Asti and Alba. GTT offers frequent bus service between Alba and Turin—the journey takes approximately 1½ hours. Direct trains run to Alba from Turin's Lingotto station; the trip takes about an hour.

VISITOR INFORMATION

CONTACT Alba Tourism Office. ✉ *Piazza Risorgimento 2, Alba* ☎ *0173/35833* 🌐 *www.visitlmr.it.*

Sights

★ Castello di Neive

WINERY | This family-run, 160-acre wine estate produces wine from seven vineyards in the Langhe region. Barbaresco is their star wine, and they also make fine barbera and dolcetto. Visitor tours, by appointment only, include a look inside their 18th-century castle, including the wine cellars, as well as a tasting of three wines. ✉ *Piazzetta Demaria 1, Neive* ☎ *329/2125171 mobile* 🌐 *www.castellodineive.it* 🎫 *Tour and tasting from €10* ⏲ *Closed Tues.* ✍ *Reservations required.*

Restaurants

★ Guido da Costigliole

$$$$ | NORTHERN ITALIAN | Inside atmospheric stone-walled ancient cellars, the latest incarnation of Guido—which began in 1961 in Costigliole d'Asti—is now managed by the son of the original owners. It serves excellent preparations of traditional dishes best sampled with one of the three tasting menus (including one vegan option), along with superlative pairings of wine from the surrounding regions. **Known for:** agnolotti pasta filled with meat; wonderful wine list; gelato of the moment. $ *Average main: €55* ✉ *Relais San Maurizio, Località San Maurizio 59, Santa Stefano Belbo* ✥ *22 km (14 miles) east of Alba* ☎ *0141/844455* 🌐 *www.guidodacostigliole.it* ⏲ *Closed Mon. No lunch Tues.–Sat.*

Lalibera

$ | PIEDMONTESE | Modern and subdued, this small spot on a quiet backstreet is conducive to a leisurely meal while trying a huge selection of Barolo wines. On the menu you'll find Piedmontese starters, pastas, and a variety of tasty meat dishes, and there's also a superb selection of local cheeses. **Known for:** tajarin pasta al ragù; Piedmontese wines and cheeses; locally sourced meat and produce. $ *Average main: €19* ✉ *Via Elvio Pertinace 24/a, Alba* ☎ *0173/293155* 🌐 *lalibera.com* ⏲ *Closed Sun. and Mon., 3 wks in Aug., and late Dec.–mid-Jan.*

★ L'Inedito Vigin Mudest

$ | PIEDMONTESE | Delicious regional specialties with tartufo-focused and fixed-price tasting menus are served at this bustling family-run restaurant in the center of Alba. Seasonal recipes emphasize local vegetables, nuts (particularly hazelnuts), and meats like rabbit and venison. **Known for:** agnolotti del plin (stuffed ravioli) with truffles; fresh tajarin (tagliolini with egg dough); braised beef marinated in Barolo. $ *Average main: €19* ✉ *Via Vernazza 11, Alba* ☎ *0173/441701* 🌐 *www.lineditoviginmudest.it* ⏲ *Closed Wed.*

Vincafè

$ | WINE BAR | This excellent *enoteca,* with a contemporary casual atmosphere, has a whole range of Piedmont specialties to pair with local wines. You'll find more than 60 labels, as well as grappas and liqueurs, on the menu. **Known for:** Langhe wine pairings; Piedmontese crudos; late-night dining. $ *Average main: €16* ✉ *Via Emanuele 12, Alba* ☎ *0173/364603* 🌐 *vincafe.com.*

Hotels

★ Locanda del Pilone

$$ | B&B/INN | It would be hard to imagine a more commanding position for these simply but tastefully decorated accommodations and the Michelin-starred restaurant above Alba. **Pros:** spectacular location with a 360-degree view; excellent restaurant; abundant breakfast. **Cons:** while not far from Alba, you do need a car to get around; parking can be challenging; rooms near common areas can be noisy. *$ Rooms from: €235 ✉ Località Madonna di Como 34, Alba ☎ 0173/366616 🌐 www.locandadelpilone.com ⏲ Closed Jan.–Mar. 🛏 6 rooms 🍽 Free Breakfast.*

★ Relais San Maurizio

$$$$ | HOTEL | FAMILY | The first luxury hotel in Piedmont, opened in 2002 inside a 17th-century monastery, is still one of the most extravagant places to stay in the region, with a 10,764-square-foot spa, an outdoor swimming pool, tennis courts, and a Michelin-star restaurant. **Pros:** ultrarelaxing spa area with unique treatments; wonderful dining options; elegant, old-fashioned charm. **Cons:** bathrooms could use an update; some rooms on the small side; breakfast choices could be more extensive. *$ Rooms from: €600 ✉ Località San Maurizio 39 ✥ 22 km (14 miles) east of Alba ☎ 0141/841900 🌐 www.relaissanmaurizio.it 🛏 36 rooms 🍽 Free Breakfast.*

★ Villa La Madonna

$$ | HOTEL | This art-filled boutique hotel (one of the two sister-owners is a photographer) surrounded by vineyards exudes a sense of casual luxury and a modern design aesthetic, from the sitting room with an open fireplace to the lively outdoor pool with retro snack bar. **Pros:** cozy, comfortable feel; all rooms have outdoor spaces; delicious food at the in-house eatery. **Cons:** no TVs or phones in rooms; minimum-night stays in some seasons; some rooms rather small. *$ Rooms from: €375 ✉ Regione Madonna 21, Monastero Bormida ✥ 45 km (28 miles) southeast of Alba ☎ 348/8366141 mobile 🌐 villalamadonna.com ⏲ Closed mid-Nov.–late Mar. 🛏 18 rooms 🍽 Free Breakfast.*

The Barolo Region

17 km (11 miles) southwest of Alba, 72 km (45 miles) southeast of Turin.

The Langhe district produces some of the top wines in Italy (Barolo and Barbaresco), along with the less-famous but well-regarded dolcetto (from Dogliani) and arneis and nebbiolo (from Roero). Try to schedule a day trip to one or several of the wine estates here.

GETTING HERE AND AROUND

The easiest way to reach Barolo and its wineries is to drive from Alba.

Sights

Famiglia Anselma

WINERY | This winery is known for its steadfast commitment to producing only Barolo—nothing else. The winemaker here, Maurizio Anselma, is something of a prodigy in the Barolo world, and he's quite open to visitors. Contact them by email or phone in advance for an appointment. *✉ Località Castello della Volta, Barolo ☎ 0173/560511 🌐 www.anselma.it ✍ Reservations essential.*

Marchesi di Barolo

WINERY | Right in the town of Barolo, this wine estate makes an easy, if touristy, option for getting to know the local wines. In the estate's user-friendly enoteca you can taste wine, buy some of the thousands of bottles from vintages going way back, and look at display bottles, including an 1859 Barolo. Marchesi di Barolo's *cantine* (wine cellars), at *✉ Via Roma 1*, are open daily; book tours and tastings in advance online. *✉ Via Roma 1, Barolo ☎ 0173/564419 🌐 marchesibarolo.com 🎟 From €45 for tour and tasting ✍ Reservations essential.*

Rocche dei Manzoni

WINERY | A good, accessible example of the new school of Barolo wine making (concrete tanks, blended wines) is this estate, about 6 km (4 miles) south of Barolo. Rocche dei Manzoni's reds include Barolo, dolcetto, Langhe Rosso, and barbera. Visits take about two hours and include a guided tour of the wine cellar plus a tasting of three wines; reserve in advance online. *Località Manzoni Soprani 3, Monforte d'Alba 0173/78421 www.rocchedeimanzoni.it From €40 for tour and tasting Closed Dec. 22–Jan. 8; week of Aug. 9; and weekends in Jan.–Mar. and June–Aug. Reservations required.*

WiMu—Il Museo del Vino a Barolo

SPECIALTY MUSEUM | **FAMILY** | Spread over three floors of the Barolo Castle, this quirky wine museum looks at the emotions behind the region's top tipple. The entertaining interactive exhibits explore such themes as the moon in harmony, the geometry of life, and the history of wine, through films, displays, and art—just don't expect a glass of Barolo at the end. *Castello Comunale Falletti, Piazza Falletti, Barolo 0173/386697 www.wimubarolo.it €9 Closed Feb., and weekdays mid-Jan.–late Jan.*

Restaurants

★ Massimo Camia

$$ | **PIEDMONTESE** | Chef Massimo Camia's restaurant is in an elegant and modern space, with views of the Barolo vineyards that surround the Damilano winery; the service is impeccable and the food is divine. The restaurant is outside the town of La Morra, a 20-minute drive to the southwest of Alba. **Known for:** inventive meat, seafood, and game dishes; extensive cheese menu; amuse-bouches and wine pairings. *Average main: €30 SP122 (Alba–Barolo), La Morra 0173/56355 www.massimocamia.it Closed Tues. and Wed.*

Hotels

Casa di Langa

$$$ | **HOTEL** | Billed as the first sustainable luxury hotel in Barolo, Casa di Langa uses local materials in its architecture, organic ingredients in its restaurant, and recycled water to irrigate the 104 acres of vineyards and land on its property. **Pros:** fabulous outdoor heated pool; convenient location for Barolo area wine tasting; tasty restaurant food. **Cons:** decor rather on the plain side; not all rooms have views; service not up to par. *Rooms from: €557 Località Talloria 1 0173/520520 www.casadilanga.com Closed late Jan.–late Mar. 39 rooms Free Breakfast.*

Gavi

117 km (73 miles) east of Barolo, 100 km (62 miles) southeast of Turin.

This pretty medieval town nestled in the hills of southeastern Piedmont—and very close to the Ligurian border, only about 50 km (30 miles) north of Genoa—is all about the wine: specifically, the cortese grape used to make Gavi, one of Italy's best-known white wines. Since the town of Gavi is less touristed than Piedmont's other wine areas, you can spend a relaxing day or two wandering its charming streets and taking a countryside drive to admire the lovely vineyard scenery.

GETTING HERE AND AROUND

From Barolo, take the A33 autostrada north past Asti and then head east on the E70. Near Tortona, take the A7 south and exit onto the SP161. It's about 1½ hours from Barolo to Gavi by car, and around the same distance from Turin. It's possible to take a combination of buses and trains between Barolo and Gavi (switching in Alba and Turin), but not recommended unless you have lots of time and patience.

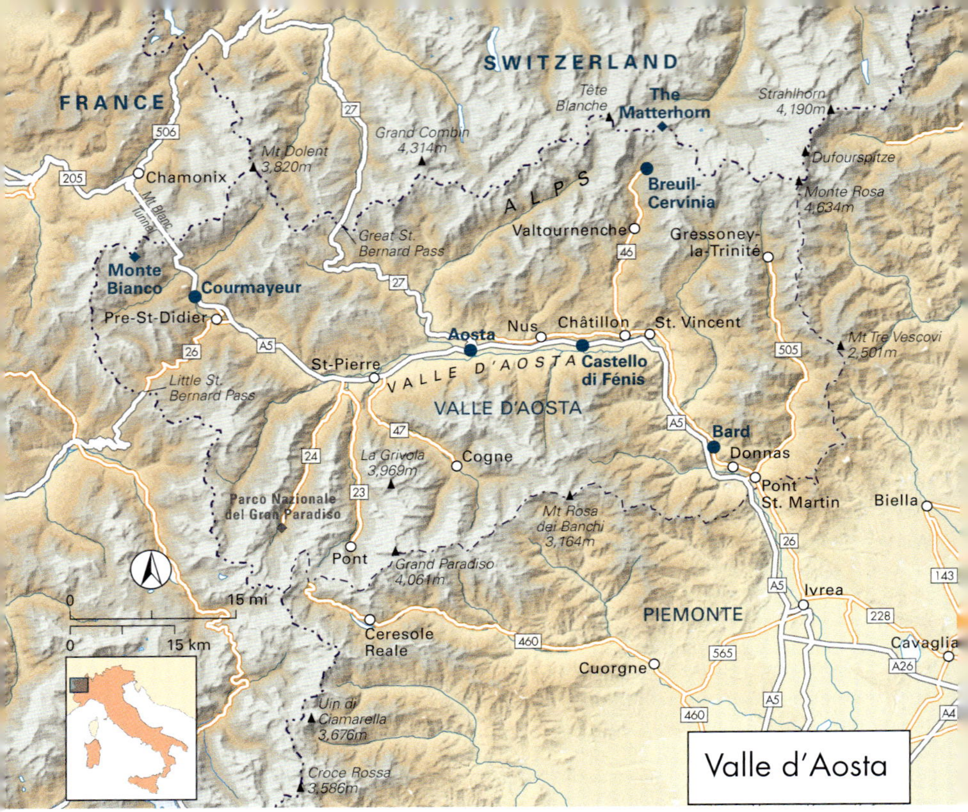

Valle d'Aosta

Sights

★ Forte di Gavi

MILITARY SIGHT | FAMILY | The origins of this imposing military fortress perched on a rocky hilltop above Gavi are rather murky, but it's thought to have first been built atop the ruins of a 10th-century castle before being enlarged between the 16th and 18th centuries. The fortress was used as a military prison during both World Wars, and today you can take a 45-minute tour to learn about its history, as well as tour the courtyards, guards' towers, and other rooms. Tours leave every hour from 8:30 to 4:30 Wednesday to Saturday and from 9:30 to 5:30 on the first Sunday of the month and public holidays. Even if you don't see the inside of the fort, the area around it offers stunning views of the town of Gavi and the Alto Monferrato hills below. ✉ *Via al Forte 14, Gavi* ☎ *0143/643554* 🌐 *www.museiitaliani.it* 🎫 *€5; free 1st Sun. of month* 🕒 *Closed Sun.–Tues., except 1st Sun. of month.*

Restaurants

★ Cantine del Gavi

$$$$ | PIEDMONTESE | FAMILY | Inside an enchanting 18th-century palace with arched ceilings, this zero-kilometer restaurant uses products only from the surrounding area, including vegetables, herbs, and edible flowers from its own gardens, in its weekly changing seven-course tasting menus. In the warmer months, don't miss dining amongst the roses in the romantic courtyard, where a smaller three-course menu with cocktail of the day is also offered. **Known for:** risotto al Gavi, which changes by season; wonderful wine selection, with a focus on Piedmont and France; lovely garden setting. *$ Average main: €65 ✉ Via Goffredo Mameli 69, Gavi ☎ 0143/642458 🌐 www.instagram.com/cantinedelgavi ⏲ Closed Mon.–Wed. No lunch Thurs. and Fri.*

Hotels

Albergo l'Ostelliere

$$ | **HOTEL** | **FAMILY** | An 18th-century farmhouse nestled in the hills of Monterotondo di Gavi is home to this charming hotel—part of the Villa Sparina Resort—surrounded by a park and vineyards with a wonderfully secluded outdoor pool and a gourmet restaurant. **Pros:** quiet, peaceful location; fantastic restaurant with modern dishes; breathtaking vineyard scenery. **Cons:** beds on the hard side; have to drive if you want to eat elsewhere; no coffee or tea in the rooms. *$ Rooms from: €250 ✉ Frazione Monterotondo 56, Gavi ☎ 0143/607801 🌐 www.villasparinaresort.it ⏲ Closed Dec.–late Mar. 33 rooms Free Breakfast.*

★ **Locanda La Raia**

$$$ | **HOTEL** | Atop a hill surrounded by vineyards, this modernized country house–turned–cozy inn offers all the comforts needed for a relaxing stay—large-size guest rooms with comfy beds, a tasty restaurant focused on farm-fresh ingredients, and an inviting indoor/outdoor pool. **Pros:** wonderfully relaxing environment; spectacular views; delicious food and wines. **Cons:** air-conditioning can be loud; can hear some noise from street and other rooms; must book in advance to use spa. *$ Rooms from: €477 ✉ Località Lomellina 26, Gavi ☎ 0143/642860 🌐 www.la-raia.it ⏲ Closed mid-Nov.–late Mar. 12 rooms Free Breakfast.*

★ **Nordelaia**

$$ | **HOTEL** | A stay at this charming, rural-chic hotel surrounded by vineyards is like visiting a stylish friend's country home—one with impeccably good taste in design and cuisine. **Pros:** luxe yet homey atmosphere; gorgeous environs; friendly service. **Cons:** a little out of the way from Piedmont's main wine region; prices on the high side; terrace pool is unheated. *$ Rooms from: €384 ✉ Via Piazze 14–16, Cremolino ⊕ 28 km (17 miles) west of Gavi ☎ 0143/038045 🌐 nordelaia.com ⏲ Closed mid-Dec.–early Apr. 12 rooms Free Breakfast.*

Bard

65 km (40 miles) north of Turin.

This small medieval town clings to a rocky crag that almost completely blocks the entrance to the Valle d'Aosta from Piedmont. Recognized for its strategic importance since prehistoric times, the location was first fully fortified by the Romans, and then by the Ostrogoths in the 6th century. As befits its military heritage, the village is rather gray and somber, but the magnificent fortress that sits atop it makes a visit well worthwhile.

GETTING HERE AND AROUND

Bard is just off the A5 autostrada, which runs north from Turin into the Valle d'Aosta—by car the trip takes about an hour. There are trains about every two hours from Turin and more regular service to and from Aosta. Traveling to Bard by bus is not a viable option.

Sights

★ **Forte di Bard**

SPECIALTY MUSEUM | **FAMILY** | A few minutes beyond the French-speaking village of Pont St. Martin, you pass through the narrow Gorge de Bard to reach the fortress that has stood guarding the valley entrance for more than eight centuries. Take a series of funiculars up the mountain to see the fort's five fascinating museums: Museo delle Alpi, dedicated to the history and culture of the Valle d'Aosta region; Le Prigioni, an interactive walk through the former prisons;

Museo delli Fortificazioni, which looks at defense techniques (fortifications) over the centuries; Museo delle Frontiere, which examines the political, economic, and cultural meaning of borders; and a children's museum, Le Alpi dei Ragazzi. The fort also hosts regularly changing exhibitions featuring contemporary Italian artists. There's also a restaurant with well-prepared local foods, and a hotel if you want to extend your stay. ✉ *Via Vittorio Emanuele II, Bard* ☎ *0125/833811* 🌐 *www.fortedibard.it* 🎫 *€12 for 2 museums, €24 for all museums and exhibitions* ⏲ *Closed Mon. Sept.–July.*

Favorite Places

Liz Humphreys: Driving from Piedmont to Valle d'Aosta, the Forte di Bard never fails to inspire me. I'm in awe of the history, the 360-degree views, and the fascinating museums within.

Breuil-Cervinia/ The Matterhorn

50 km (30 miles) north of Bard, 116 km (72 miles) north of Turin.

Sitting in a huge natural basin at the foot of the Matterhorn, this town, once a high Alpine pasture, grew to become one of Europe's most famous ski areas when a road connecting it to the Valle d'Aosta was completed in 1934. It bustles in the winter and has become a popular spot for hikers in the summer, but it's sleepy for much of the rest of the year.

GETTING HERE AND AROUND

From Aosta take the A5 autostrada and then the SR46 (one hour); from Turin take the A5 and then the SR46 (90 minutes). Arriva Italia has regular bus service from Turin and Milan. Breuil-Cervinia isn't on a train line.

Sights

★ **Matterhorn** (*Monte Cervino in Italian; Mont Cervin in French*)

MOUNTAIN | FAMILY | The famous peak straddles the border between Italy and Switzerland, and all sightseeing and skiing facilities are operated jointly. Splendid views of the peak can be seen from Plateau Rosa, which can be reached by cable car from the center of Breuil-Cervinia. The cable car gives access to climbing and off-trail skiing on ridges that were once inaccessible. The Matterhorn Glacier Ride II cable car from Cervinia directly to Zermatt opened in summer 2023. This 90-minute ride is the highest border crossing in the Alps; ticket prices vary by season. ✉ *Breuil-Cervinia* ☎ *0166/944311* 🌐 *www.cervinia.it* 🎫 *From Breuil-Cervinia to Plateau Rosa: €35 one-way, €55 round-trip. From Breuil-Cervinia to Zermatt: from €130 one-way, from €199 round-trip.*

Restaurants

★ **Ristorante Alpage**

$$ | NORTHERN ITALIAN | Diners can ski or hike (or drive, if they wish) to this charming alpine cabin at the foot of Mount Cervino decorated with a whimsical mix of cowbells and modern art. Alpage specializes in typical Valle d'Aosta cuisine, such as pappardelle with deer ragù and wild boar stew with polenta, using ingredients from small producers, along with a wonderful selection of wines from both local and other Italian producers. **Known for:** traditional meat and cheese plates; polenta with corn ground in a local mill; extensive wine list. 💲 *Average main: €28* ✉ *Loc. Lago Blu 4, Breuil-Cervinia* ☎ *0166/949398* 🌐 *www.alpage-cervinia.com* ⏲ *Closed Tues. No lunch Wed.*

The mighty Matterhorn straddles Switzerland and Italy and has one of the highest summits in Europe.

Hotels

★ Aethos Monterosa

$$ | **HOTEL** | **FAMILY** | Aethos breaks the traditional Alpine lodging mold with ultramodern furnishings, a rock-climbing wall inside and an ice-climbing wall outside (winter only), an indoor-outdoor spa, and even a Japanese steak house and cocktail bar, near the sleepy Alpine village of Champoluc. **Pros:** well-designed exteriors and interiors; hip, young vibe compared to other alpine hotels; unusual activities on offer, such as an indoor climbing, ice climbing, and boxing lessons. **Cons:** in a rather remote area; service can seem harried; split-level rooms not to everyone's taste. *Rooms from: €280* *Strada Regionale 45, 16, Champoluc, Breuil-Cervinia* *63 km (39 miles) southeast of Breuil-Cervinia* *0125/938300* *www.aethos.com/monterosa* *Closed Apr., May, and November* *50 rooms* *Free Breakfast.*

★ Hermitage

$$$ | **RESORT** | The entryway's marble relief of St. Theodolus reminds you that this was once a hermitage, but asceticism has given way to comfort and elegance—a fire is always glowing in the enormous hearth, the dining room is candlelit, the bright bedrooms have balconies, and the suites have antique fireplaces and 18th-century furnishings. **Pros:** superlative staff; refined atmosphere; frequent shuttle service into town and to ski lifts. **Cons:** located 2 km (1 mile) from the town center; books up quickly; expensive for the area. *Rooms from: €591* *Via Piolet 1, Località Chapellette, Breuil-Cervinia* *0166/948998* *hotelhermitage.com* *Closed mid-Apr.–late June and Sept.–late Nov.* *47 rooms* *Free Breakfast.*

Les Neiges d'Antan

$$ | **B&B/INN** | In an evergreen forest at Perrères, just outside Cervinia, this family-run inn is quiet and cozy, with three big fireplaces and a nice view of the Matterhorn. **Pros:** secluded and beautiful

setting; wonderful restaurant; well-designed spa facilities. **Cons:** 5 km (3 miles) outside Breuil-Cervinia (a car is essential); entrance and lobby areas are showing some wear; no elevator. *Rooms from: €366* *Frazione Cret de Perrères 10, Breuil-Cervinia* *0166/948775* *lesneigesdantan.it* *24 rooms* *Free Breakfast.*

VRetreats Cervino

$$ | **HOTEL** | This modern ski chalet-style hotel just south of Cervinia hits all the marks for an active yet relaxing holiday, with on-site equipment rentals, a large spa complete with swimming pool, and even personal saunas in some guest rooms. **Pros:** quiet location just outside town; high-quality food at the restaurants; Matterhorn views from the main restaurant and bar. **Cons:** overall decor a bit generic; beds on the hard side; service can be lacking at times. *Rooms from: €382* *Frazione Avouil, Breuil-Cervinia* *0166/871973* *vretreats.com/cervino* *Closed early May–late June and late Aug.–early Dec.* *66 rooms* *Free Breakfast.*

Activities

CLIMBING

Serious climbers can make the ascent of the Matterhorn from Breuil-Cervinia after registering with the local mountaineering officials at the tourist office. This ascent is for experienced climbers only. Less demanding hikes follow the lower slopes of the Marmore river valley, south of town.

Società Guide Alpine del Cervino

SNOW SPORTS | **FAMILY** | The Society's guides are available to accompany you on treks and also lead skiing, snowshoeing, ice-climbing, and rock-climbing excursions. *Via Circonvallazione 2, Breuil-Cervinia* *0166/948169* *www.guidedelcervino.com* *Ski touring, ice climbing, and rock climbing from €440 per person per day; group snowshoeing from €35 per person for 2 hrs; private snowshoeing from €140 for 1 to 4 people for 2 hrs.*

Road to Gaul

Between Bard and the town of Donnas, 5 km (3 miles) south along the SS26, you can walk a short but fascinating stretch of a 1st-century Roman consular road that passed this way en route to France. Still showing the deeply worn tracks left by the passage of cart and chariot wheels, this section includes an archway carved through solid rock (used during the Middle Ages as the Donnas city gate) and a milestone ("XXXVI," counting 36 Roman miles from Aosta).

SKIING

More than 70 lifts and a few hundred miles of ski runs, ranging from beginner to expert, make Breuil-Cervinia Valtournenche one of the best and most popular resort areas in Italy. Because the slopes border a glacier, there's skiing year-round.

Castello di Fénis

34 km (21 miles) northwest of Bard, 104 km (65 miles) north of Turin.

The tiny town of Fénis owes its origins to the presence of the medieval castle that once provided shelter for the local peasants who lived nearby. Today, the population of the town is less than 1,800, most either farmers or part of the tourist industry.

GETTING HERE AND AROUND

To reach the castle by car, take the Nus exit from the A5 autostrada. Arriva Italia buses provide infrequent service between Aosta and Fénis. It's about a 10-minute train ride from Aosta to the train station in Nus, a 2-km (1-mile) walk from the castle.

Sights

★ Castello di Fénis

CASTLE/PALACE | FAMILY | The best-preserved medieval fortress in Valle d'Aosta, this many-turreted castle was built in the mid-14th century. The 15th-century courtyard surrounded by wooden balconies is elegantly decorated with well-preserved frescoes. Inside you can see the kitchen, with an enormous fireplace that provided central heat in winter; the armory; and the spacious, well-lighted rooms used by the lord and lady of the manor. ✉ *Località Chez-Sapin 1, Fénis* ☎ *0165/764263* 🌐 *valledaostaheritage.com* 🎫 *€10* 🕐 *Closed Mon. Sept.–June (except holidays).*

Aosta

12 km (7 miles) west of Castello di Fénis, 113 km (70 miles) north of Turin.

Aosta stands at the junction of two of the important trade routes that connect France and Italy, the valleys of the Rhône and the Isère. Its significance as a trading post was recognized by the Romans, who built a garrison here in the 1st century BC, and the present-day layout of the streets is the clearest example you'll find of Roman urban planning in Italy. Well-preserved Roman walls form a perfect rectangle around the center, and the regular pattern of streets reflects its role as a military stronghold. Although its gray-stone buildings and slate roofing give the town a rather cold feeling, Aosta has appeared on several lists as one of the most livable towns in Italy.

GETTING HERE AND AROUND

Aosta is off the A5 autostrada and can easily be reached by car or bus from Milan and Turin. Arriva Italia buses regularly travel to and from Milan, Turin, and Chamonix in France. Train service is also available from Turin (two hours) and from Milan (three hours), but you'll have to transfer.

VISITOR INFORMATION

CONTACT Aosta Tourism Office. ✉ *Piazza Porta Praetoria 3, Aosta* ☎ *0165/236627* 🌐 *www.lovevda.it.*

Sights

Arco di Augusto

HISTORIC SIGHT | At the eastern entrance to town, and commanding a fine view over Aosta and the mountains, stands the Arco di Augusto (Arch of Augustus), built in 25 BC to mark Rome's victory over the Celtic Salassi tribe. (The sloping roof was added in 1716 in an attempt to keep rain from seeping between the stones.) ✉ *Piazza Arco d'Augusto, Aosta* 🎫 *Free.*

Cattedrale di Santa Maria Assunta (*Aosta Cathedral*)

CHURCH | Aosta's cathedral dates from the 10th century, but all that remains from that period are the bell towers. The decoration inside is primarily Gothic, but the main attraction of the cathedral predates that era by 1,000 years: among the many ornate objects housed in the treasury museum is a carved ivory diptych from AD 406 portraying the Roman emperor Honorius. You can also see frescoes dating from the 11th century above the Gothic vaults. The treasury and frescoes can only be visited on weekends between 3 and 5:30 pm, or with advance reservation on weekdays. ✉ *Piazza Papa Giovanni XXIII, Aosta* ☎ *0165/40251* 🌐 *cattedraleaosta.it* 🎫 *Duomo free, treasury museum €4, frescoes and treasury museum €5.*

★ Parco Nazionale del Gran Paradiso

NATIONAL PARK | FAMILY | Cogne, 27 km (17 miles) south of Aosta, is the gateway to this huge park, which was once the domain of King Vittorio Emanuele II (1820–78). Bequeathed to the nation after World War I, it is one of Europe's most rugged and unspoiled wilderness areas, with wildlife and many plant species protected by law. The park is one of the few places in Europe where you can see the ibex (a mountain goat with horns up to 3 feet long) and the chamois (a small antelope). The park, which is 703 square km (271 square miles), is open free of charge throughout the year; there's an information office in Cogne. **TIP→ Try to visit in May, when spring flowers are in bloom and most of the meadows are clear of snow.** ✉ *Villaggio Cogne 81, Cogne* ☎ *011/8606211* 🌐 *www.pngp.it* 🎫 *Free.*

Restaurants

Trattoria Praetoria

$$ | NORTHERN ITALIAN | Just outside the Porta Pretoria, this simple and unpretentious restaurant serves hearty local dishes, including homemade pastas and desserts. They're also well-known for their tasty gluten-free recipes. **Known for:** polenta with a variety of sauces and accompaniments; three-layer cake with white chocolate, hazelnut, and pistachio; savory crepes. $ *Average main: €24* ✉ *Via Sant'Anselmo 9, Aosta* ☎ *0165/35473* 🌐 *www.trattoriapraetoria.it* 🕒 *Closed Thurs. No dinner Wed.*

★ Vecchio Ristoro

$$$$ | NORTHERN ITALIAN | Chef Filippo Oggioni took over this traditional restaurant in 2019, adding freshness and creative versions of regional recipes and decadent desserts, available à la carte or as five- or seven-course tasting menus, including a five-course vegetarian option. The elegant, intimate spaces of this converted mill are furnished with antiques, and a traditional ceramic stove provides additional warmth in cool weather. **Known for:** regional tasting menus; wonderful wine pairings; local game dishes. $ *Average main: €50* ✉ *Via Tourneuve 4, Aosta* ☎ *0165/33238* 🌐 *vecchioristoro.com* 🕒 *Closed Sun. and Mon.*

Hotels

★ Bellevue Hotel & Spa

$$ | HOTEL | Opened in 1925 and still run by the same family, the Bellevue provides timeless charm, gracious hospitality, delectable cuisine, and a second-to-none spa, along with astounding views of the Gran Paradiso, the highest mountain entirely within Italy. **Pros:** wonderful attention to details; lovely surroundings near Parco Nazionale del Gran Paradiso; convenient location next to beginner and cross-country ski areas and the village of Cogne. **Cons:** breakfast offerings could be more extensive; some rooms on the small side; not extremely child-friendly. $ *Rooms from: €318* ✉ *Rue Grand Paradis 22, Cogne* ✣ *27 km (17 miles) south of Aosta* ☎ *0165/74825* 🌐 *www.hotelbellevue.it* 🕒 *Closed late Mar.–mid-Apr.* 🛏 *39 rooms* 🍴 *Free Breakfast.*

★ Hotel Milleluci

$$ | B&B/INN | At this small and inviting family-run hotel overlooking Aosta, guest rooms are bright and charmingly decorated; some have balconies and all have splendid views of the city and mountains. **Pros:** panoramic views; great spa amenities; cozy and traditionally decorated rooms. **Cons:** 1 km (½ mile) north of town, so a car is needed to get around; no a/c; small bathrooms. $ *Rooms from: €249* ✉ *Località Porossan Roppoz 15, Aosta* ☎ *0165/235278* 🌐 *www.hotelmilleluci.com* 🛏 *28 rooms* 🍴 *Free Breakfast.*

Courmayeur/ Monte Bianco

35 km (22 miles) northwest of Aosta, 150 km (93 miles) northwest of Turin.

The main attraction of Courmayeur is a knock-'em-dead view of Europe's highest peak, Monte Bianco. The celebrities and the wealthy who come here these days are following a tradition that dates back to the late 17th century, when Courmayeur's natural springs first began to attract visitors. The spectacle of the Alps gradually surpassed the springs as the biggest draw: the Alpine letters of the English poet Percy Bysshe Shelley were almost advertisements for the region. Since 1965, when the Mont Blanc Tunnel opened, ever-increasing numbers of travelers have passed through the area, and it's now hugely popular with both skiers in winter and hikers during the summer. Planners have managed to keep some restrictions on wholesale development within the town, and its angled rooftops and immaculate cobblestone streets maintain a cozy feeling.

GETTING HERE AND AROUND

Courmayeur is on the A5 autostrada and can easily be reached by car from both Turin and Milan by way of Aosta. There is FlixBus service from Milan and Arriva Italia buses run regularly from both Turin and Milan. Train service isn't available.

VISITOR INFORMATION

CONTACT Courmayeur Tourism Office. *Piazzale Monte Bianco 15, Courmayeur 0165/842060 www.lovevda.it.*

Sights

★ **Monte Bianco** (*Mont Blanc*)

MOUNTAIN | FAMILY | Monte Bianco's attraction is not so much its shape, which is much less distinctive than that of the Matterhorn, as its expanse and the awesome vistas from the top. The Skyway Monte Bianco cable car, which ascends from Entrèves, just below the Mont Blanc Tunnel, whisks you up first to the Pavillon in about 10 minutes—a starting point for many beautiful hikes, and also home to the Alpine restaurant and the Mountain Bar. In another 10 minutes, you reach the spectacular viewing platform at Punta Helbronner (more than 11,000 feet), which is also the border post with France and home to the Kartell Panoramic Bistro and the world's highest bookshop.

From Punta Helbronner, in winter, you can ski parts of the route off-piste. In summer, if so inclined, you can switch to the Panoramic Mont Blanc cable car to France, stopping first at Aigulle du Midi (30 minutes). The trip is particularly impressive; you dangle over a huge glacial snowfield (more than 2,000 feet below) and make your way slowly to the viewing station above Chamonix. It's one of the most dramatic rides in Europe. From this point you're looking down into France, and if you change cable cars at the Aiguille du Midi station, you can make your way down into Chamonix itself in about 20 minutes. *SS26, Courmayeur 0165/89196 in Courmayeur, 0450/532275 in Chamonix www.montebianco.com €26 (€24 online) round-trip from Courmayeur to Pavillon, €63 (€58 online) round-trip from Courmayeur to Punta Helbronner, €117.50 round-trip from Punta Helbronner to Chamonix Closed Nov., May, and depending on weather conditions and demand.*

Restaurants

★ **Cadran Solaire**

$$ | NORTHERN ITALIAN | Dominated by stone arches, this welcoming eatery off Courmayeur's pedestrian strip, run by the Garin family of nearby Auberge de la Maison fame, serves up tons of atmosphere along with elevated takes on traditional Valdostan dishes. The large menu offers a choice of hearty tried-and-true plates such as grandma's salad, with ham, eggs, Mont d'Or cheese, and boiled potatoes, along with lighter fare like salmon trout with savoy cabbage. **Known for:** romantic setting; polenta with local fontina cheese; montenapoleone al Monte Bianco (meringue with yogurt froth, mixed berries sauce, and lime). *Average main: €29 Via Roma 122, Courmayeur 0165/844609 www.cadransolaire.it Closed Tues.*

★ Pierre Alexis 1877

$$$$ | **MODERN ITALIAN** | Just off Courmayeur's pedestrian center, this charming restaurant with beamed ceilings and wildlife pictures on the wall is truly a family affair: Stefano Alessandro Marchetto cooks, his wife Monica hosts, and their twin sons are the sommelier and server. The cuisine leans toward modern versions of Valle d'Aosta cuisine with unexpected twists, like the risotto with mountain pine and sturgeon; while you can order à la carte, trying one of the tasting menus lets you sample the full range of their inspired offerings. **Known for:** creative preparations using mainly local ingredients; five- and seven-course tasting menus, plus a four-course vegetarian menu; fine selection of wines, emphasizing Valle d'Aosta and Alsace producers. *Average main: €45* *Via Marconi 50/a, Courmayeur* *0165/846700* *pierrealexis.it* *Closed Mon. No lunch Tues.–Fri.*

Hotels

★ Auberge de la Maison

$$$ | **HOTEL** | Most guest rooms here have balconies with spectacular views of Monte Bianco, and the plush fabrics, wood-burning stoves, and Alpine prints on the walls give the feeling of a cozy country inn. **Pros:** quiet and secluded location, yet very close to the Skyway Monte Bianco; lovely hotel spa with indoor/outdoor pool; charming country decor. **Cons:** shuttle into town can get crowded; not all standard rooms have views of Monte Bianco; unheated outdoor pool can be too cold. *Rooms from: €401* *Via Passerin d'Entrèves 16, Courmayeur* *0165/869811* *www.aubergemaison.it* *Closed Apr.–mid-June and Nov.* *33 rooms* *Free Breakfast.*

Villa Novecento Romantic Hotel - Estella Hotel Collection & Experience

$$ | **HOTEL** | Run with friendly charm and efficiency, the Novecento is a peaceful haven with the style of a comfortable mountain lodge, complete with a log fire in winter, traditional fabrics, wooden furnishings, and early-19th-century prints. **Pros:** frequent shuttle to the slopes and town; good restaurant and excellent breakfast; convenient to the town's pedestrian center. **Cons:** wellness area on the small side; limited parking spaces; no air-conditioning. *Rooms from: €205* *Viale Monte Bianco 64, Courmayeur* *0165/843000* *villanovecento.it* *Closed mid-Apr.–May and mid-Oct.–late Nov.* *22 rooms* *Free Breakfast.*

Activities

SKIING

★ Courmayeur Mont Blanc

SNOW SPORTS | **FAMILY** | Courmayeur pales in comparison to its French neighbor, Chamonix, in both the quality and the number of its ski runs. But with good natural snow cover, the trails and vistas are spectacular. A huge gondola leads from the center of Courmayeur to Plan Chécrouit, where other gondolas and lifts lead to the slopes. The skiing around Monte Bianco is particularly good, and the off-piste options are among the best in Europe. The routes from Cresta d'Arp (the local peak) to Dolonne, and from La Palud into France, should be done with a guide. Contact the Courmayeur tourist office for complete information about lift tickets, ski runs, and weather conditions. *Strada Dolonne La Villette 1, Courmayeur* *0165/841612* *www.courmayeur-montblanc.it* *1-day ski pass €61.*

Società delle Guide Alpine (*Alpine Guide Society*)
SNOW SPORTS | The society provides Alpine guide services year-round, for activities such as skiing, snowshoeing, and ice climbing in the winter and mountaineering, rock climbing, and trekking in the summer. ✉ *Strada Villair 2, Courmayeur* ☎ *0165/842064* 🌐 *www.guidecourmayeur.com* 🎫 *Guides from €55 for 1 day.*

Venaria Reale

10 km (6 miles) northwest of Turin.

This immense palace was built in the 16th century as a hunting lodge.

GETTING HERE AND AROUND

Starting in Turin, take the Venaria Express bus from Piazza Vittorio Veneto or Piazza Castello to reach Venaria; the 40-minute trip runs Tuesday to Sunday, about six times a day. You can also take Bus No. 11 from the north side of Piazza della Repubblica; the trip takes approximately 60 minutes. By car, follow Corso Regina Margherita to the A55 autostrada. Head north and leave the highway at the Venaria exit, following signs for the Venaria Reale.

Sights

★ Reggia di Venaria Reale
CASTLE/PALACE | **FAMILY** | Extensive Italianate gardens surround this magnificent 16th-century UNESCO-protected hunting lodge built for Carlo Emanuele II of Savoy. Inside, its Great Gallery is worthy of Versailles, and the attached chapel (Capella di Sant'Uberto) and stables were designed in the 1720s by Sicilian architect Filippo Juvarra. The Theatre of History and Magnificence houses a fascinating historical exhibition that tells the story of the House of Savoy. The upper floors are reserved for changing exhibitions. ✉ *Piazza della Repubblica 4, Venaria Reale* ☎ *011/4992333* 🌐 *lavenaria.it* 🎫 *€20* ⏲ *Closed Mon. early June–mid-Apr.*

Rivoli

16 km (10 miles) southwest of Venaria, 13 km (8 miles) west of Turin.

The Savoy court was based in Rivoli in the Middle Ages, and the town retains several remnants from that richly dramatic period.

GETTING HERE AND AROUND

GTT buses and trams regularly link central Turin with Rivoli; the journey takes just over one hour. On Saturday, you can take a train from Turin's Porta Nuova station to the Alpignano train station and then a shuttle to Rivoli every hour from 11 to 6 pm (35 minutes). By car, follow Corso Francia from central Turin all the way to Rivoli; unless there's a lot of traffic, the trip should take a half hour.

Sights

Casa del Conte Verde (*House of the Green Count*)
HISTORIC HOME | The richly decorated House of the Green Count, in the oldest part of Rivoli, attests to the wealth and importance of its onetime owner, Amedeo VI of Savoy (1334–83). Legend has it that the count attended tournaments dressed all in green, hence the name. Inside, a small gallery occasionally hosts temporary exhibitions, which may increase the entrance fee. ✉ *Via Fratelli Piol 8, Rivoli* ☎ *011/9563020* 🌐 *www.comune.rivoli.to.it* 🎫 *€5 (varies with exhibitions)* ⏲ *Closed Mon. and Tues., and Wed.–Fri. until 4 pm.*

★ Castello di Rivoli Museo d'Arte Contemporanea and Villa Cerutti (*Castle of Rivoli Museum of Contemporary Art*)
ART MUSEUM | The Baroque castle of Rivoli now houses a fascinating museum of contemporary art. The building was begun in the 17th century and

then redesigned, but never finished, by architect Filippo Juvarra in the 18th century; it was finally converted into a museum in the late 20th century by the minimalist Turin architect Andrea Bruno. Its sister museum, Villa Cerutti, houses 300 paintings (including works by Renoir and Kandinsky) and sculptures, plus rare books and furnishings, in a 20th-century villa not far from the castle; visits are only by prior reservation and guided tour on weekends for adults and children ages 10 and up, with individual nonguided visits offered one Saturday each month. ✉ *Piazzale Mafalda di Savoia, Rivoli* ☎ *011/9565222* 🌐 *www.castellodirivoli.org* 🎫 *Castello €10, Villa Cerutti and Castello €26.50* ⏲ *Castello closed Mon. and Tues., Villa Cerutti closed weekdays.*

Sacra di San Michele

26 km (17 miles) west of Rivoli, 43 km (27 miles) west of Turin.

Perhaps best known as inspiration for the setting of Umberto Eco's novel *The Name of the Rose,* this abbey was built on Monte Pirchiriano in the 11th century so it would stand out: it occupies the most prominent location for miles around, hanging over a 3,280-foot bluff.

GETTING HERE AND AROUND

From Turin, take the train to Avigliana and then a 14-km (9-mile) taxi ride or uphill hike from the station. By car take the Avigliana Est exit from the A32 autostrada (Torino–Bardonecchia).

Sights

★ Sacra di San Michele

CHURCH | To reach the church—built between 983 and 987 AD, and which inspired Umberto Eco to write *The Name of the Rose*—you must climb 150 steps from the Porta dello Zodiaco, a splendid Romanesque doorway decorated with the signs of the zodiac. On the left side of the interior are 16th-century frescoes representing New Testament themes; on the right are depictions of the founding of the church. ✉ *Via Sacra di San Michele 14, Sant'Ambrogio di Torino* ☎ *011/939130* 🌐 *sacradisanmichele.com* 🎫 *€8, €10 with guided tour (in Italian only).*

Chapter 9

THE ITALIAN RIVIERA

Updated by
Robert Andrews

WELCOME TO THE ITALIAN RIVIERA

TOP REASONS TO GO

★ **The Cinque Terre:** Hike the famous Cinque Terre trails past gravity-defying vineyards, colorful rock-perched villages, and the deep blue Mediterranean Sea.

★ **Portofino:** See the world through rose-tinted sunglasses at this glamorous little harbor village.

★ **Genoa's historical center and port:** From the palaces of Via Garibaldi to the labyrinthine backstreets of the old city to the world-class aquarium, the city is full of surprising delights.

★ **Giardini Botanici Hanbury:** A spectacular natural setting harbors one of Italy's largest, most exotic botanical gardens, near Bordighera.

★ **Pesto:** The basil-rich sauce was invented in Liguria, and it's never been equaled elsewhere.

1 Riomaggiore. The first of the Cinque Terre villages has a small harbor and coastal views.

2 Manarola. Terraced vineyards, olive trees, and pastel houses fill the town.

3 Corniglia. Climb (365 steps) to the most remote Cinque Terre town.

4 Vernazza. Enjoy its lively piazza and a postcard-worthy port view.

5 Monterosso al Mare. Come here for festivals, beaches, clear water, and plentiful accommodations.

6 Lerici. White-sand beaches, hiking trails, and seaside cafés are memorable.

7 La Spezia. This busy port city has outdoor markets and palm-lined streets.

8 Portovenere. Quaint passageways and a castle distinguish the port town.

9 Levanto. This makes an ideal base for diving, surfing, hiking, and day trips around Liguria.

10 Sestri Levante. The small seaside village is framed by two bays.

11 Santa Margherita Ligure. Palm trees, attractive hotels, and a yacht-filled marina add appeal.

12 Portofino. This vacation spot for the rich and famous has a castle, cliff-side gardens, and fancy boutiques.

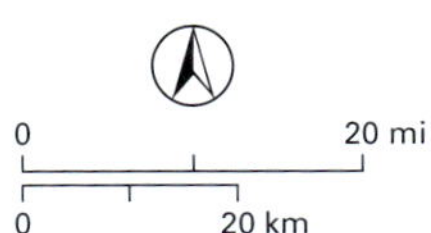

13 Camogli. Multicolor houses and a picturesque historical fishing port are draws here.

14 Genoa. Palaces, superb pesto, and a rich maritime history mark the birthplace of Christopher Columbus.

15 Nervi. A promenade and parks enhance this resort near busy Genoa.

16 Finale Ligure. Explore the Riviera di Ponente in the villages of Finalmarina, Finalpia, and Finalborgo.

17 San Remo. The largest resort in the Riviera di Ponente is known for its casino, glamorous hotels, and seaside promenades.

18 Bordighera. Its many English residents give this town a distinct personality, and it's near a famous botanical garden.

EATING AND DRINKING WELL IN THE ITALIAN RIVIERA

Vegetable-topped focaccia bread

Ligurian cuisine might surprise you. As you'd expect, given the long coastline, it employs all sorts of seafood, but its real claim to fame is the exemplary use of vegetables and herbs.

Basil is practically revered in Genoa—the word is derived from the Greek *basileus,* meaning "king"—and the city is considered the birthplace of pesto, the basil-rich pasta sauce. This and other herbs (laurel, fennel, and marjoram) are cultivated, but also grow wild on the sun-kissed hillsides. Naturally, seafood plays a prominent role on the menu, appearing in soups, salads, and pasta dishes. Vegetables—particularly artichokes, eggplant, and zucchini—are abundant, and usually prepared with liberal amounts of olive oil and garlic.

Like much of Italy, Liguria has a wide range of eating establishments from cafeteria-like *tavole calde* to family-run trattorias to sophisticated *ristoranti*. Lunch is served between 12:30 and 2:30 and dinner between 7:30 and 11. Also popular, especially in Genoa, are *enoteche* (wine bars), which serve simply prepared light meals late into the night.

FABULOUS FOCACCIA

When you're hankering for a snack, turn to bakeries and small eateries serving focaccia. The flatbread is more dense and flavorful here than what's sold as focaccia in American restaurants—it's the region's answer to pizza, usually eaten on the go. It comes simply salted and drizzled with olive oil; flavored with rosemary and olives; covered with cheese or anchovies; and even *ripiena* (stuffed), usually with cheese or vegetables and herbs.

ANTIPASTI

Seafood antipasti are served in abundance at most Ligurian restaurants. Typical dishes include marinated anchovies from Monterosso, *cozze ripiene* (mussel shells stuffed with minced mussel meat, prosciutto, Parmesan, herbs, and bread crumbs), and *soppressata di polpo* (flattened octopus in olive oil and lemon sauce).

PASTA

Liguria's classic sauce is pesto, made from basil, garlic, olive oil, pine nuts, and hard cheese. It's usually served with *trenette* (similar to spaghetti) or the slightly sweet *testaroli* (a flat pasta made from chestnut flour). You can also find *pansotti* (triangular pockets filled with a cheese mixture), and *trofie* (short twists) with *salsa di noci,* a rich sauce of garlic, walnuts, and cream that, as with pesto, is ideally pounded with mortar and pestle. Spaghetti *allo scoglio* has an olive oil, tomato, and white-wine-based sauce containing an assortment of local *frutti di mare* (seafood) like shrimp, clams, mussels, and cuttlefish.

FISH AND MEAT

Fish is the best bet for a second course: the classic preparation is a whole grilled or baked whitefish—branzino and *orata* (dorado) are good

Cheese-filled pansotti pasta

Trofie pasta with tomato sauce

choices—served *alla Ligure,* with olives, potatoes, tomatoes, Ligurian spices, and a drizzle of olive oil. A popular meat dish is *cima alla Genovese,* a veal roll stuffed with a mixture of eggs and vegetables, served as a cold cut.

PANIGACCI

One of the real treats of the region is *panigacci.* Small, terra-cotta dishes known as *testine* are placed in a wood-burning oven or fire to heat at the highest of temperatures. Then balls of dough are laid in the dishes, which are stacked one on top of the other in order to flatten and cook the dough. Panigacci are usually served with *stracchino* cheese, pesto or nut sauce, and cold cuts.

WINE

Local vineyards produce mostly light and refreshing whites, such as *pigato* from the Ponente and *vermentino* from the Levante, although both light reds and appealing *rosato* (Italian rosé) are on the rise. Rossese di Dolceacqua, from near the French border, is considered the best red wine the region has to offer, but for a more robust accompaniment to meats, opt for the full-bodied reds of the neighboring Piedmont region. For a post-dinner or dessert wine, try the *sciacchetrà,* made exclusively in the Cinque Terre.

Nestled between the south of France and the Tuscan border lies the region of Liguria, with verdant mountains to the north and east, and the sapphire-blue Mediterranean to the south and west. In between is a land of lush vegetation, medieval hilltop hamlets, panoramic vistas, colorful seaside villages, pristine beaches, and one of Italy's most underrated cities, Genoa.

There is plenty to do—from hiking and biking, to water sports and fishing, to eating (very) well—and plenty to see, including some of Italy's most aesthetically pleasing architecture. It's also easy to just enjoy la dolce vita along this coast, better known as the Italian Riviera.

The Italian Riviera oozes charm and irresistible allure, with many seaside resort towns and colorful villages that stake intermittent claim to the rocky shores of the Ligurian Sea and seem like the long-lost cousins of newer seaside paradises found elsewhere. It has been a haven for artists, writers, celebrities, and royalty since the 1800s, and continues to fascinate visitors throughout the year due to its mild climate. Here the grandest palazzi share space with frescoed, angular *terratetti* (tall, skinny houses). The rustic and elegant, the provincial and chic, the small-town and cosmopolitan all collide here in a sun-drenched blend that defines the Italian side of the Riviera. There are chic resort towns such as San Remo and Portofino, the unique beauty and outdoor adventures of the Cinque Terre, numerous quaint seaside and hilltop villages to explore, plus the history and architectural charm of Genoa. Mellowed by balmy breezes blowing in from the sea, travelers bask in the sun, explore the picturesque fishing villages, and pamper themselves at the resorts that dot this ruggedly beautiful landscape.

MAJOR REGIONS

Cinque Terre. The beautiful Cinque Terre is the heart of the Italian Riviera. In their rugged simplicity, the five old fishing towns of Monterosso al Mare, Vernazza, Corniglia, Manarola, and Riomaggiore seem to mock the glitzy neighboring resorts. With a blue sea in the foreground, multicolor buildings emerge almost seamlessly from cliffs, and rocky mountains rise precipitously to vineyards and olive groves. The terrain is so steep that for centuries, footpaths were the only way to get around. Since its 1997 UNESCO World Heritage designation, the Cinque Terre has become one of Italy's most popular destinations. Eastward from Genoa to Lerici (encompassing the Cinque Terre and a naval port, La Spezia) stretches the Riviera di Levante (Riviera of the Rising Sun). It has a raw, unpolished feel, and its rugged coastline is dotted with colorful fishing villages like Camogli, Portovenere, and Sestri Levante. It also has one of Europe's well-known playgrounds for the rich and famous, the inlet of Portofino, and nearby Santa Margherita Ligure is popular with well-to-do Italians. From this area's twisting roads, the hills plummet sharply to the sea. Beaches tend to be rocky, yet there are some lovely sandy stretches in Lerici, Monterosso al Mare, Levanto, and Paraggi (near Portofino).

Genoa. The seaside city of Genoa (Genova in Italian), birthplace of Christopher Columbus, has a long history as a major trading station, and in the Middle Ages and the Renaissance, Genoa became a wealthy, prestigious commercial center. Its bankers, merchants, and princes adorned their city with palaces, churches, and impressive art collections. Today Genoa is a cultural center worth a look. Nearby Nervi is a stately resort town.

The Riviera di Ponente. West of Genoa, the Riviera di Ponente (Riviera of the Setting Sun) covers the narrow strip of northwest Liguria from Genoa to the French border. The sapphire Mediterranean Sea to one side and the verdant foothills of the Alps on the other allow for temperate weather, which is why it's also called the Riviera dei Fiori (Riviera of the Flowers). Once filled with seaside villages and elegant homes, this area struggles to balance natural beauty with resort development, as in glitzy San Remo. Highly populated resorts and some overly industrialized areas are jammed into the thin stretch of white-sand and pebble beaches. There are still several worthwhile villages, like Finale Ligure, Albegna, and Bordighera, along the sea and hinterland. Bordighera is near Giardini Botanici Hanbury, one of Italy's most beautiful groupings of gardens. The Riviera di Levante may retain more of its natural beauty, but the Ponente remains popular with visitors looking for sunshine, nightlife, and relaxation.

Planning

Getting Here and Around

BUS

Generally speaking, buses are a difficult way to come and go in Liguria. Although there are local buses that run between some villages along the Riviera Ponente and Riviera Levante, it's not an extensive network and can be a challenge to navigate.

CAR

With the freedom of a car, you could drive from one end of the Riviera to the other on the autostrada in about three hours. Two good roads run parallel to each other along the coast of Liguria. Closer to shore and passing through all the towns and villages is the SS1, or Via Aurelia, which was laid out by the ancient Romans and has excellent views at almost every turn. It's slow, though, particularly in July and August when it gets very crowded. More direct and higher up than SS1 are autostradas A10, west of Genoa, and A12, to the south—engineering wonders with literally hundreds of long tunnels and towering viaducts. These toll routes save time on weekends, in summer, and on days when festivals slow traffic in some resorts to a standstill.

TRAIN

Train travel on the national railway, Ferrovie dello Stato, is by far the most convenient mode of transportation throughout the region. It takes 3½–4½ hours for an express train to cover the entire Ligurian coast. Local trains take upward of five hours or more to get from one end of the coast to the other, stopping in or near all the towns along the way. For schedules, check 🌐 *www.trenitalia.com/en.html.*

Hotels

Liguria has a good selection of Belle Epoque-style luxury palazzi, but in other categories its lodging may be a step behind more developed areas like Positano and Taormina. You'll need to reserve the region's better accommodations well in advance, particularly the relatively limited options in the Cinque Terre. Hotels tend to be pricey in high season, while—outside Genoa—many places close in winter.

⇨ *Hotel and restaurant reviews have been shortened. For full information, visit Fodors.com. Prices in the lodging reviews are the lowest cost of a standard double room in high season. Prices in the dining reviews are the average cost of a main course at dinner, or, if dinner is not served, at lunch.*

What It Costs in Euros

	$	$$	$$$	$$$$
RESTAURANTS	under €20	€20–€30	€31–€40	over €40
HOTELS	under €175	€175–€400	€401–€600	over €600

Hiking

Walking Liguria's extensive network of trails while taking in the gorgeous views is a major outdoor activity and regional attraction. The mild climate and laid-back state of mind can lull you into underestimating just how strenuous such walks can be. Wear good shoes, use sunscreen, and carry plenty of water—you'll be glad you did. Trail maps are available from tourist information offices, or upon entry to the Cinque Terre National Park.

On the Portofino promontory, the relatively easy walk to the Abbazia di San Fruttuoso is popular, and there's a more challenging hike from Ruta to the top of Monte Portofino and back down to Camogli. From Genoa, you can take the Zecca–Righi funicular up to Righi and walk along the ring of fortresses that used to defend the city.

Walking tours can introduce you to lesser-known aspects of the region. For the Cinque Terre and the rest of the Province of La Spezia, Cinqueterre Experience (✉ *Viale Amendola 172, La Spezia* ☎ *0187/739410, landline, or 338/4244882, mobile* 🌐 *www.cinqueterrexperience.com*) is a good source for English-speaking and other foreign-language guides. A day tour (lasting from 1½ hours to a full day) is €350 (not including tips); this price is for a group of up to 20 people. Tours with no hiking are also offered (maximum 35 people) at the same price.

Planning Your Time

Your first decision, particularly given limited time, is between the two Rivieras. The Riviera di Levante (east of Genoa) is more rustic and has a more distinct personality, with the unique Cinque Terre, ritzy Portofino, and the panoramic Gulf of Poets. The Riviera di Ponente (west of Genoa) is a classic European resort experience with some white-sand beaches and more nightlife and accommodation choices—similar to, but not as glamorous as, the French Riviera across the border.

In either case, your second decision is whether to visit Genoa. Despite its rough exterior and (diminishing) reputation as a seamy port town, Genoa's artistic and cultural treasures are significant—you won't find anything remotely comparable elsewhere in the region. Unless your goal is to avoid urban life entirely, consider a night or two in the city, or at least within easy reach of it.

Restaurants

While fine dining can be found in Liguria, you are more likely to enjoy a casual atmosphere, often with an amazing sea view. Expect the dishes to be simple but flavorful; fish and seafood are highlights here, while pesto is ubiquitous.

When to Go

The Italian Riviera is extremely seasonal, apart from Genoa, a city with year-round cultural attractions. The region has a typical Mediterranean climate with warm summers and rainy winters, making high season (Easter and June–August in particular) the best time to visit, though it can be really crowded as well as lively. From April to October, the area bustles with shops, cafés, clubs, and restaurants that stay open late. The rest of the year, the majority of resorts close down, and you'll be hard-pressed to find accommodations or restaurants open.

Riomaggiore

17 km (11 miles) southwest of La Spezia, 101 km (60 miles) southeast of Genoa.

At the eastern end of the Cinque Terre, Riomaggiore is built into a river gorge (hence the name, which means "major river") and is easily accessible from La Spezia by train or car. The landscape is terraced and steep—be prepared for many stairs!—and leads to a small harbor, protected by large slabs of alabaster and marble that serve as tanning beds for sunbathers. The harbor is also the site of several outdoor cafés with fine views. According to legend, the settlement of Riomaggiore dates as far back as the 8th century, when Greek religious refugees came here to escape persecution by the Byzantine emperor.

The village is divided into two parts. If you arrive by train, you will have to pass through a tunnel that flanks the train tracks to reach the historic side of town. To avoid the crowds and get a great view of the Cinque Terre coast, walk straight uphill as soon as you exit the station. This winding road takes you over the hill to the 14th-century **church of St. John the Baptist,** toward the medieval town center and the Genovese-style tower houses that dot the village. Follow Via Roma (the Old Town's main street) downhill, pass under the train tracks, and you'll arrive in the charming fishermen's port. Lined with traditional fishing boats and small trattorias, this is a lovely spot for a romantic lunch or dinner. Unfortunately, Riomaggiore doesn't have as much old-world charm as its sister villages; its easy accessibility has brought traffic and more construction here than elsewhere in the Cinque Terre.

GETTING HERE AND AROUND

The enormous parking problems presented by these cliff-dwelling villages have been mitigated somewhat by a large, covered parking structure at La Spezia Centrale station, which in the summer months costs around €1.50 per hour for the first two hours, then €2 per hour. It's clean and secure (you cannot enter without a ticket code to open the door), and it's open 24/7. This is a good backup solution for those with cars, although others may choose to take a day trip from Pisa or Lucca and rely on bus and train services. Arrive early, as it can fill up by midmorning, especially in high season.

VISITOR INFORMATION

CONTACT Riomaggiore Welcome Center. ✉ *Riomaggiore train station, Piazza Rio Finale, Riomaggiore* ☎ *0187/1857573* 🌐 *www.parconazionale5terre.it.*

Accessing Cinque Terre Trails

When to Go

The ideal times to visit the Cinque Terre are September and May, when the weather is mild and the summer tourist season isn't in full swing (June through August can be unbearably hot and crowded).

Getting Here and Around

There is a local train between La Spezia and Levanto that stops at each of the Cinque Terre villages and runs every 30 minutes between March and October, hourly in winter. Tickets for each leg of the journey (from around €2.50) are available at any of the train stations. In Corniglia, the only one of the Cinque Terre that isn't at sea level, a shuttle service (€1.50) is provided for those who don't wish to climb (or descend) the 300-plus steps that link the train station with the cliff-top town.

The Explora 5 Terre shuttle-bus operates a daily service between La Spezia and the villages; a day ticket costs €18.50.

Along the Cinque Terre coast two ferry lines operate. From June to September, Golfo Paradiso runs from Genoa and Camogli to Monterosso al Mare (a round-trip ticket costs €43 or €48). Other tours are also available. From late March to October, the smaller but more frequent Golfo dei Poeti stops at each village from Lerici (east of Riomaggiore) and La Spezia to Monterosso, with the exception of Corniglia, hourly (a round-trip ticket costs €28–€41); you can also purchase one-way tickets.

Admission

Entrance tickets for using the trails are available at ticket booths located at the start of each section of Trail No. 2, and at information offices in the Levanto, Monterosso, Vernazza, Corniglia, Manarola, Riomaggiore, and La Spezia train stations. A one-day Cinque Terre Card costs €7.50, which includes a trail map and an information leaflet; a two-day pass is €14.50.

The Cinque Terre Carta Treno, which allows access to the park plus unlimited daily use of the regional train between La Spezia, the five villages, and Levanto just north of Monterosso, varies in cost, with higher prices during holidays and summer. Rates are €19.50–€32.50 for a one-day pass, €34–€59 for a two-day pass, and €46.50–€78.50 for a three-day pass. There are also passes for under-13s, over-70s, and families.

For More Information

🌐 *www.lecinqueterre.org; www.parconazionale5terre.it; www.golfoparadiso.it; www.navigazionegolfodeipoeti.it.*

Sights

Riomaggiore

TOWN | This village at the eastern end of the Cinque Terre is built into a river gorge (hence the name, which means "major river"). It has a tiny harbor protected by large slabs of alabaster and marble, which serve as tanning beds for sunbathers as well as being the site of several outdoor cafés with fine views. According to legend, the settlement of Riomaggiore dates as far back as the 8th century, when Greek religious refugees came here to escape persecution by the Byzantine emperor. ✉ *Riomaggiore* 🌐 *www.parconazionale5terre.it.*

Continued on page 410

HIKING THE CINQUE TERRE

FIVE REMOTE VILLAGES MAKE ONE MUST-SEE DESTINATION

"Charming" and "breathtaking" are adjectives that get a workout when you're traveling in Italy, but it's rare that both apply to a single location. The Cinque Terre is such a place, and this combination of characteristics goes a long way toward explaining its tremendous appeal.

The area is made up of five tiny villages (Cinque Terre literally means "Five Lands") clinging to the cliffs along a gorgeous stretch of the Ligurian coast. The terrain is so steep that for centuries footpaths were the only way to get from place to place. It just so happens that these paths provide beautiful views of the rocky coast tumbling into the sea, as well as access to secluded beaches and grottoes.

Backpackers "discovered" the Cinque Terre in the 1970s, and its popularity has been growing ever since. Despite summer crowds, much of the original appeal is intact. Each town has maintained its own distinct charm, and views from the trails in between are as breathtaking as ever.

Monterosso

Corniglia

Terracing around Corniglia

HIKING THE CINQUE TERRE

Monterosso—Vernazza Trail
The most demanding portion of the trail. Often narrow, with significant climbs and descents, particularly near Vernazza. Your labors are rewarded with the Trail No. 2's best views.

Vernazza—Corniglia Trail
Ups and downs interspersed with olive groves and terraced vineyards.

Monterosso
The most resortlike of the villages, with the largest beach.

Vernazza
Pretty and visitor-friendly. The best spot for lingering in a café and watching waves crash against the shore.

THE CLASSIC HIKE

Hiking is the most popular way to experience the Cinque Terre, and Trail No. 2, the Sentiero Azzurro (Blue Trail), is the most traveled path. To cover the entire trail is a full day: it's approximately 13 km (8 miles) in length, takes you to all five villages, and requires about five hours, not including stops, to complete. The best approach is to start at the easternmost town of Riomaggiore and warm up your legs on the easiest segment of the trail. As you work your way west, the hike gets progressively more demanding. Between Corniglia and Manarola take the ferry (which provides its own beautiful views) or the inland train running between the towns instead.

Manarola

Along Lovers' Lane

Via dell'Amore

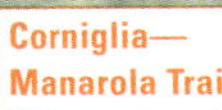

Corniglia—Manarola Trail
This section of the trail is currently closed.

Manarola—Riomaggiore Trail
Known as the Via dell'Amore (Lovers' Lane). A wide, paved, flat path with fine views.

KEY
Major footpaths
Sanctuary footpaths
Connecting footpaths
45min Hiking times
Sanctuaries

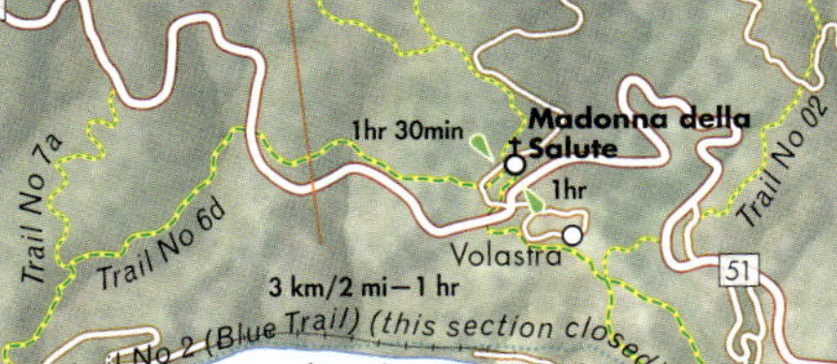

Corniglia
Perched on a cliff 500 feet above the sea, reached by a switchback path (or by shuttle bus).

Manarola
The most photogenic of the villages, best seen from the cemetery a few minutes up the path toward Corniglia.

Riomaggiore
Cliff-clinging buildings are almost as striking as those in Manarola. Stairs to the left of the train station entrance cross over the tracks and lead to the trailhead.

BEYOND TRAIL NO.2

Trail No. 2 is just one of a network of trails crisscrossing the hills. If you're a dedicated hiker, spend a few nights and try some of the other routes. Trail No. 1, the Sentiero Rosso (Red Trail), climbs from Portovenere (east of Riomaggiore) and returns to the sea at Levanto (west of Monterosso al Mare). To hike its length takes from 9 to 12 hours; the ridge-top trail provides spectacular views from high above the villages, each of which can be reached via a steep path. Other shorter trails go from the villages up into the hills, some leading to religious sanctuaries. Trail No. 9, for example, starts from the old section of Monterosso and ends at the Madonna di Soviore Sanctuary.

Hiking the Cinque Terre

Though often described as relaxing and easy, the Cinque Terre also have several hiking options if you wish to exert yourself a little. Many people do not realize just how demanding parts of these trails can be—it's best to come prepared. We recommend bringing a Cinque Terre Card and cash (smaller shops, eateries, and some park entrances may not accept credit cards).

When all trails are completely open, a hike through the villages takes about four to five hours; add time for exploring each village and taking a lunch break—it's an all-day, if not two-day, trek. We recommend an early start, especially in summer when midday temperatures can rise to 90°F. Note that only Sentiero Azzurro (Trail No. 2) requires the Cinque Terre Card. The other 20-plus trails in the area are free. All trails are well marked with a red-and-white sign. Trails from village to village get progressively steeper from south (Riomaggiore) to north (Monterosso). If you're a day-tripper with a car, use the underground lot at La Spezia Centrale train station (from €1.50 per hour) and take the train to Riomaggiore (6–8 minutes).

Our Favorites

Other trails to consider include **Monterosso to Santuario Madonna di Soviore,** a fairly strenuous but rewarding 1½ hours up to a lovely 8th-century sanctuary. There is also a restaurant and a priceless view. **Riomaggiore to Montenero and Portovenere** is one hour up to the sanctuary and another three hours to Portovenere, passing through some gorgeous, less-traveled terrain. **Manarola to Volastra to Corniglia** runs high above the main trail and through vineyards and lesser-known villages. **Monterosso to Levanto** is a good 2½-hour hike, passing over Punta Mesco with glorious views of the Cinque Terre to the south, Corsica to the west, and the Alps to the north.

Each town has something that passes for a beach (usually with lots of pebbles or slabs of terraced rock), but there is only one option for both sand and decent swimming—in Monterosso, just across from the train station. It's equipped with chairs, umbrellas, and snack bars.

Precautions

If you're hitting the trails, carry water with you, wear sturdy shoes (hiking boots are best), and have a hat and sunscreen handy. Note that the lesser-used trails aren't as well maintained as Trail No. 2. If you're undertaking the full Trail No. 1 hike, bring something to snack on as well as your water bottle. Note that currently the Via dell'Amore and the portion of Trail No. 2 between Manarola and Corniglia are closed indefinitely due to landslides.

■ TIP→ **Check weather reports, especially in late fall and winter; thunderstorms can make shelterless trails slippery and dangerous. Rain in October and November can cause landslides and close trails altogether.**

Manarola

16 km (10 miles) southwest of La Spezia, 117 km (73 miles) southeast of Genoa.

The enchanting pastel houses of Manarola spill down a steep hill overlooking a spectacular turquoise swimming cove and a bustling harbor. The whole town is built on black rock. Above the town, ancient terraces still protect abundant vineyards and olive trees. This village is the center of wine and olive oil production in the region, and its streets are lined with shops selling local products.

Surrounded by steep terraced vineyards, Manarola's one road tumbles from the Chiesa di San Lorenzo (14th century) high above the village, down to the rocky port. Since the Cinque Terre wine cooperative is located in Groppo, a hamlet overlooking the village (reachable by foot or by the green park bus; ask at park offices for schedules), the vineyards are accessible. If you'd like to snap a shot of the most famous view of the town, you can walk from the port area to the cemetery above. Along the way you'll pass the town's playground, bathrooms, and a tap with clean drinking water.

GETTING HERE AND AROUND

Though it's possible to drive and park (in a lot above town, which means walking down), it's much easier to arrive by an often overly crowded train. Trains run from La Spezia or Levanto; both are very short journeys and cost around €3.

VISITOR INFORMATION

CONTACT Manarola Welcome Center. ✉ *Manarola train station, Via dell'Amore, Manarola* ☎ *0187/1857573* 🌐 *www.parconazionale5terre.it.*

Sights

Manarola
TOWN | Enchanting pastel houses spill down a steep hill overlooking a spectacular turquoise swimming cove and a bustling harbor. The whole town is built on black rock. Above the town, ancient terraces still protect abundant vineyards and olive trees. This village is the center of the wine and olive oil production of the region, and its streets are lined with shops selling local products. ✉ *Manarola* 🌐 *www.parconazionale5terre.it.*

Hotels

★ La Torretta
$$ | HOTEL | One of the Cinque Terre's few "boutique" hotels is in a 17th-century tower that sits high on the hill above the rainbow-hue village of Manarola, with truly lovely views of the terraced vineyards, colorful village homes, and the Mediterranean sea; inside, decor is chic, sleek, and antiques-bedecked. **Pros:** spectacular views; free luggage transfer; stellar staff. **Cons:** steep walk up to the hotel; some rooms are small; books up quickly. $ *Rooms from: €308* ✉ *Vico Volto 20, Cinque Terre, Manarola* ☎ *0187/920327* 🌐 *www.torrettas.com* ⏲ *Closed Nov.–Mar.* *15 rooms* *Free Breakfast.*

Corniglia

27 km (17 miles) northwest of La Spezia, 100 km (60 miles) southeast of Genoa.

The buildings, narrow lanes, and stairways of Corniglia are strung together amid vineyards high on the cliffs. On a clear day, views of the entire coastal strip are excellent, from Elba in the south to the Italian Alps in the north. The high perch and lack of harbor make this farming community the most remote and therefore least crowded of the Cinque Terre. In fact, the 365 steps that lead up from the train station to the town center dissuade many tourists from making the hike to the village. You can also take the green park bus, but they run infrequently and are usually packed with tired hikers.

Corniglia is built along one road edged with small shops, bars, gelaterias, and restaurants. Midway along Via Fieschi is the Largo Taragio, the main square and heart of the village. Shaded by leafy trees and umbrellas, this is a lovely spot for a mid-hike gelato break.

GETTING HERE AND AROUND

This town has very limited parking and it's much simpler to take the train from either La Spezia or Levanto.

VISITOR INFORMATION

CONTACT Corniglia Welcome Center. ✉ *Corniglia train station, Via alla Stazione, Corniglia* ☎ *0187/1857573* 🌐 *www.parconazionale5terre.it.*

Sights

Corniglia

TOWN | Stone buildings, narrow lanes, and stairways are strung together amid vineyards high on the cliffs; on a clear day views of the entire coastal strip are excellent. The high perch and lack of harbor make this farming community the most remote of the Cinque Terre. ✉ *Corniglia* ☎ *0187/812523* 🌐 *www.parconazionale5terre.it.*

San Pietro

CHURCH | On a pretty pastel square sits the 14th-century church of San Pietro. The rose window of marble imported from Carrara is impressive, particularly considering the work required to get it here. ✉ *Via Fieschi 19, Corniglia* 🎫 *Free.*

Vernazza

27 km (17 miles) west of La Spezia, 96 km (59 miles) southeast of Genoa.

With its narrow streets and small squares, Vernazza is arguably the most charming of the Cinque Terre towns, and usually the most crowded. Historically, it was the most important of them and—since Vernazza was the only one fortunate enough to have a natural port—the wealthiest, as evidenced by the elaborate arcades, loggias, and marble work lining Via Roma and Piazza Marconi.

The village's pink slate-roof houses and colorful squares contrast with the remains of the medieval fort and castle, including two towers, in the old town. The Romans first inhabited this rocky spit of land in the 1st century. Today, Vernazza has a fairly lively social scene. Piazza Marconi looks out across Vernazza's small sandy beach to the sea, toward Monterosso. The numerous restaurants and bars crowd their tables and umbrellas on the outskirts of the piazza, creating a patchwork of sights and sounds that form one of the most unique and beautiful places in the world.

GETTING HERE AND AROUND

Driving to Vernazza is complicated, and it's much easier to take a short train ride from either La Spezia or Levanto. Trains run frequently.

VISITOR INFORMATION

CONTACT Vernazza Welcome Center. ✉ *Vernazza train station, Via Roma 51, Vernazza* ☎ *0187/1857573* 🌐 *www.parconazionale5terre.it.*

Sights

If Mass is not going on (a cord blocks the entrance if it is), take a peek into the church of St. Margaret of Antioch, where little has changed since its enlargement in the 1600s. This 14th-century edifice has simple interiors but truly breathtaking views toward the sea—a stark contrast to the other more elaborate churches of the Cinque Terre.

On the other side of the piazza, stairs lead to a lookout fortress and cylindrical watchtower, built in the 11th century as protection against pirate attacks. For a small fee you can climb to the top of the tower for a spectacular view of the coastline.

Vernazza

TOWN | With narrow streets and small squares, the village that many consider to be the most charming of the five towns has the best access to the sea—a geographic reality that made the village wealthier than its neighbors, as evidenced by the elaborate arcades, loggias, and marble work. The village's pink, slate-roof houses and colorful squares contrast with the remains of the medieval fort and castle, including two towers, in the old town. The Romans first inhabited this rocky spit of land in the 1st century. Today, Vernazza has a fairly lively social scene. It's a great place to refuel with a hearty seafood lunch or linger in a café between links of the seaside hike. ✉ *Vernazza* 🌐 *www.parconazionale5terre.it.*

Restaurants

Gambero Rosso

$$$ | LIGURIAN | Relax on Vernazza's main square at this fine trattoria looking out onto the church of Santa Maria d'Antiochi. Enjoy such delectable dishes as shrimp salad, vegetable torte, and *risotto alla ciccio* (with squid, prawns, and mussels). **Known for:** piazza view; fresh seafood; excellent pesto. *$ Average main: €33 ✉ Piazza Marconi 7, Vernazza ☎ 0187/812265 🌐 www.ristorantegamberorosso.net ⏲ Closed Thurs. and mid-Nov.–mid-Mar.*

★ Ristorante Belforte

$$ | LIGURIAN | High above the sea in one of Vernazza's remaining medieval stone towers is this unique spot serving delicious Cinque Terre cuisine such as branzino *sotto sale* (cooked under salt), *tagliolini al nero di seppia con gamberi* (fresh pasta with squid ink sauce and prawns), and *polpo di scoglio alla griglia* (grilled octopus). There's a good selection of vegetarian dishes, too. **Known for:** incredible views; choice of vegetarian dishes; lively atmosphere. *$ Average main: €20 ✉ Via Guidoni 42, Vernazza ☎ 0187/812222 🌐 www.ristorantebelforte.it ⏲ Closed Tues. and Nov.–late Mar.*

Hotels

La Malà

$$ | B&B/INN | A cut above other lodging options in the Cinque Terre, these small, white-walled guest rooms are equipped with flat-screen TVs, air-conditioning, marble showers, and comfortable bedding and have views of the sea or the port, which can also be enjoyed at their most bewitching from a shared terrace literally suspended over the Mediterranean. **Pros:** clean, fresh-feeling rooms; dreamy views; helpful, attentive staff. **Cons:** many stairs are involved; books up quickly; child-friendly (either a pro or a con). *$ Rooms from: €200 ✉ Via San Giovanni Battista 29, Vernazza ☎ 334/2875718 mobile 🌐 www.lamala.it ⏲ Closed early Jan. and Feb. 🛏 4 rooms 🍽 No Meals.*

Monterosso al Mare

32 km (20 miles) northwest of La Spezia, 89 km (55 miles) southeast of Genoa.

It's the combined draw of beautiful beaches, rugged cliffs, crystal clear turquoise waters, and plentiful small hotels and restaurants that has made Monterosso al Mare the largest of the Cinque Terre villages (population 1,300) and also the busiest in midsummer.

And Monterosso has festivals enough to match its size. They start with the Lemon Festival on the third weekend in May. Then, on the second Sunday after Pentecost, comes the Flower Festival of Corpus Christi: during the afternoon, the streets and alleyways of the historic center are decorated with thousands of colorful flower petals, set in beautiful designs, over which an evening procession passes. Finally, the Salted Anchovy and Olive Oil Festival takes place each year during the third weekend of September.

GETTING HERE AND AROUND

The largest of the "Five Lands," it's possible to drive and park nearby, but it's best to take the train either from La Spezia or Levanto.

VISITOR INFORMATION

CONTACT Monterosso al Mare Welcome Center. ✉ *Monterosso al Mare train station, Via Fegina 40, Monterosso al Mare* ☎ *0187/1857573* 🌐 *www.parconazionale5terre.it.*

 Sights

Heading west from the train station, you pass through a tunnel and exit into the *centro storico* (historic center) of the village.

Monterosso al Mare

TOWN | Nestled into the wide valley that leads to the sea, Monterosso is built above numerous streams, which have been covered to make up the village's main streets. Via Buranco, the oldest street in Monterosso, leads to the most characteristic piazza of the village, Piazza Matteotti. Locals pass through here daily to shop at the supermarket and butcher. This piazza also contains the oldest and most typical wineshop in the village, Enoteca da Eliseo—stop here between 6 pm and midnight to share tables with fellow tourists and locals over a bottle of wine. There's also the Chiesa di San Francesco, built in the 12th century and an excellent example of the Ligurian Gothic style. Its distinctive black stripes and marble rose window make it one of the most photographed sites in the Cinque Terre.

Fegina, the newer side of the village (and site of the train station), has relatively modern homes ranging from the Liberty style (Art Nouveau) to the early 1970s. At the far eastern end of town, you'll run into a private sailing club sheltered by a vast rock carved with an impressive statue of Neptune. From here, you can reach the challenging trail to Levanto (a great 2½-hour hike). This trail has the added bonus of a five-minute detour to the ruins of a 14th-century monastery. The expansive view from this vantage point allowed the monks who were housed here to easily scan the waters for enemy ships that might invade the villages and alert residents to coming danger. Have your camera ready for this Cinerama-like vista. After a day of sightseeing, unwind on Spiaggia di Fegina, a large sandy beach.

The local outdoor market is held on Thursday and attracts crowds of tourists and villagers from along the coast to shop for everything from pots, pans, and underwear to fruits, vegetables, and fish. Often a few stands sell local art and crafts, as well as olive oil and wine. ✉ *Monterosso al Mare* 🌐 *www.parconazionale5terre.it.*

Restaurants

★ Enoteca Internazionale

$ | **WINE BAR** | Located on the main street, this bar offers a large selection of wines, both local and from farther afield, plus delicious light fare; its umbrella-covered patio is a welcoming spot to recuperate after a day of hiking. The bar's certified sommeliers are forthcoming with helpful suggestions on pairing local wines with their tasty bruschette. **Known for:** extensive local wine list; patio dining; helpful staff. *Average main: €13* ✉ *Via Roma 62, Monterosso al Mare* ☎ *0187/817278* 🌐 *www.enotecainternazionale.com* ⏲ *Closed Jan. and Feb.*

★ Miky

$$ | **SEAFOOD** | This is arguably the best restaurant in Monterosso, specializing in tasty, fresh seafood dishes like grilled calamari and monkfish ravioli. If their *catalana* (poached lobster and shrimp with sliced raw fennel and carrot) happens to be on the menu, know that it's a winner. **Known for:** sunny seaside setting; fresh seafood; fine dining. *Average main: €30* ✉ *Via Fegina 104, Monterosso al Mare* ☎ *0187/817608* 🌐 *www.ristorantemiky.it* ⏲ *Closed Tues. and Nov.–Mar.*

Hotels

★ Il Giardino Incantato

$$ | **B&B/INN** | With wood-beam ceilings and stone walls, the stylishly restored and updated rooms in this 16th-century house in the historic center of Monterosso ooze comfort and old-world charm. **Pros:** spacious rooms; gorgeous garden; excellent hosts. **Cons:** no views; no under-14s or pets; there are only four rooms so books up quickly. *Rooms from: €200* *Via Mazzini 18, Monterosso al Mare* *0187/818315* *www.ilgiardinoincantato.net* *Closed Nov.–early Apr.* *4 rooms* *Free Breakfast.*

Porto Roca

$$ | **HOTEL** | Far from the madding crowds, Porto Roca is perched on the famous terraced cliffs right over the main beach, with large balconies to savor panoramic views of the magnificent sea. **Pros:** unobstructed sea views; tranquil location; shuttle bus into town (though walking there is eminently possible). **Cons:** two- or three-night minimum stay in high season; back-facing rooms can be a bit dark; somewhat removed from town. *Rooms from: €264* *Via Corone 1, Monterosso al Mare* *0187/817502* *www.portoroca.it* *Closed early Nov.–early Apr.* *43 rooms* *Free Breakfast.*

Lerici

106 km (66 miles) southeast of Genoa, 65 km (40 miles) west of Lucca.

Lerici, part of the Riviera di Levante, is on the spectacular Bay of La Spezia, otherwise known as the Gulf of Poets, and is famous for its natural beauty. Near Liguria's border with Tuscany, this picturesque village dates back to medieval times when, under the rule of Pisa, it fought cross-bay battles with the Genovese town of Portovenere, as well as with local pirates. The town is set on a magnificent coastline of gray cliffs jutting down into a crystal clear sea and surrounded by a national park that is like an unframed painting of pine forests, olive trees, and tiny colorful hamlets. The waterfront piazza is filled with trompe-l'oeil frescoed buildings, and seaside cafés line a charming little harbor that holds sailboats and *gozzi,* the typical small fishing boats of the area.

Several white-sand beaches and bathing establishments dot the 2-km (1-mile) walk along the bay from the village center to nearby San Terenzo. From the village, you can also reach some beautiful hiking trails that head southeast to both seaside and hilltop villages like Fiascherino, Tellaro, and Montemarcello.

GETTING HERE AND AROUND

By car, Lerici is less than a 10-minute drive west from the A12, with plenty of signage indicating the way. There's a large parking lot (fee) about a 10-minute walk along the seaside promenade from the center. By train, the closest station is either Sarzana (10-minute drive) or La Spezia Centrale (20-minute drive) on the main north–south line between Genoa and Pisa. There are good bus services between Sarzana, La Spezia, and Lerici.

VISITOR INFORMATION

CONTACT Lerici Tourism Office. *Infopoint, Via S. Biaggini 552 (next to Hotel Florida), Lerici* *0187/960700* *www.stlerici.it.*

Sights

Castello di Lerici

CASTLE/PALACE | The promontory is dominated by this 13th-century Pisan castle, which now houses temporary art exhibitions and, with its views overlooking the Gulf of Poets, is a superb location for weddings (for which it is occasionally closed for visits). *Piazza S. Giorgio 1, Lerici* *0187/967840* *www.stlerici.it/castello-di-lerici* *€6* *Closed Mon. Oct.–May.*

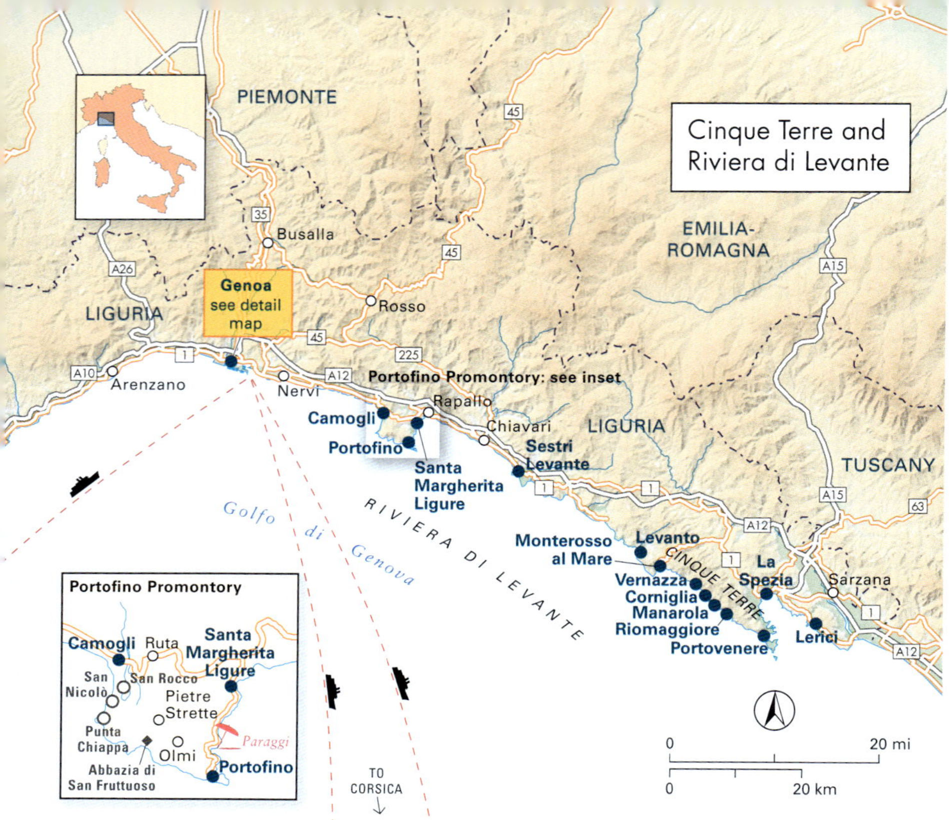

Cinque Terre and Riviera di Levante

Restaurants

Bontà Nascoste

$$ | **ITALIAN** | In the local dialect, *bontà nascoste* means "hidden goodness," a reference to its back-alleyway location and consistently delicious dishes, which feature risotto, fresh pasta, and an abundance of local seafood, including seafood soup and lobster. There is little for non-fish eaters, however, and only six tables (and a couple more outside in summer), so reserve ahead. **Known for:** inventive seafood dishes; cozy atmosphere; discreet and stylish service. *Average main: €26* *Via Cavour 52, Lerici* *0187/965500* *www.bontanascoste.it* *No lunch Mon. and Wed.*

Franceschini Ristorante

$$ | **LIGURIAN** | Across the bay from Lerici, this relaxed and intimate restaurant in the San Terenzo neighborhood has won an enthusiastic following, both for its creative, seafood-leaning menu and its congenial ambience. You can observe the chefs at work in the open kitchen, but the results are always somewhat surprising, whether it's such straightforward dishes as squid-ink risotto or fresh tagliolini with pesto, or more unusual combinations, for example salt cod in a chutney sauce, and there are gluten-free options, too. **Known for:** innovative menu; characterful interior; genial and attentive service. *Average main: €22* *Via XX Settembre 7, Lerici* *371/1999115 mobile* *www.facebook.com/franceschiniristorante* *Closed Mon.*

Hotels

★ Doria Park Hotel

$ | HOTEL | FAMILY | Its location—set amid hills of olive trees yet steps from the village center—makes this hotel with bright rooms and contemporary furnishings one of the best places to stay in Lerici. **Pros:** stunning sea views; varied and excellent breakfasts; free parking and convenient location near town and the beach. **Cons:** stairs, narrow paths, and elevator are not equipped for people with mobility issues; less alluring rooms outside the main building; three-night minimum stay in summer. *Rooms from: €156* *Via Carpanini 9, Lerici* *0187/967124* *www.doriaparkhotel.it* *44 rooms* *Free Breakfast.*

Hotel Florida Lerici

$$ | HOTEL | FAMILY | Prepare to relax at this family-run seaside establishment, where one pleasure is lounging on one of the deck chairs on the hotel's rooftop solarium and enjoying its sea views. **Pros:** beachfront location; bay views from most rooms; abundant breakfast. **Cons:** a bit generic in character; neighborhood can be busy; 15-minute walk to town center. *Rooms from: €210* *Lungomare Biaggini 35, Lerici* *0187/967332* *www.hotelflorida.it* *Closed late Dec.–early Jan.* *40 rooms* *Free Breakfast.*

La Spezia

11 km (7 miles) northwest of Lerici, 103 km (64 miles) southeast of Genoa.

La Spezia is sometimes thought of as nothing but a large, industrialized naval port en route to the Cinque Terre and Portovenere; it does possess some charm, however, and it also gives you a look at a less tourist-focused part of the Riviera. Its palm-lined promenade, fertile citrus parks, renovated Liberty-style palazzi, and colorful balcony-lined streets make parts of La Spezia surprisingly beautiful. Monday through Saturday morning, you can stroll through the fresh fish, produce, and local cheese stalls at the outdoor market on Piazza Cavour, which is also the venue for an antiques market on the first Sunday of the month, while on Friday you can take part in the busy flea market on Via Garibaldi. At the harbor, the modern Porto Mirabello has a pool club, shops, and several restaurants that overlook the fleet of superyachts in the marina.

GETTING HERE AND AROUND

By car, take the exit for La Spezia off the A12. La Spezia Centrale train station is on the main north–south railway line between Genoa and Pisa.

VISITOR INFORMATION

CONTACT La Spezia Tourism Office. *Corso Cavour 20, La Spezia* *0187/026152* *www.visitspezia.it.*

Sights

Castello di San Giorgio

CASTLE/PALACE | FAMILY | The remains of this massive 13th-century castle, atop a small hill above the modern town, now house a small museum dedicated to local archaeology. *Via XXVII Marzo, La Spezia* *0187/751142* *museodelcastello.museilaspezia.it* *€6* *Closed Mon.*

Restaurants

La Pia Centenaria

$ | PIZZA | Considered an institution, this arched, vaulted, and simply decorated pizzeria dates back to 1887. It gets quite busy at lunchtime, with locals inside or, in summer, on the patio munching happily on *farinata* (a chickpea pancake and a Ligurian delicacy) and thick-crust pizza served hot out of the wood-burning oven. **Known for:** affordable lunch menu; traditional Ligurian recipes; variety of pizza toppings. *Average main: €6* *Via Magenta 12, La Spezia* *0187/739999* *www.lapia.it* *Closed Sun.*

Portovenere

12 km (7 miles) south of La Spezia, 114 km (70 miles) southeast of Genoa.

The colorful facades and pedestrian-only *calata* (promenade) make Portovenere the quintessential Ligurian seaside village; it's often called the "sixth town" of the Cinque Terre—but with half the crowds. As a UNESCO World Heritage site, Portovenere is lined with tall, thin *terratetto* houses (town houses), which date from as far back as the 11th century and which were connected in a wall-like formation to protect against attacks by Pisans and local pirates. Its tiny *carruggi* (alleylike passageways) lead to an array of charming shops, homes, and gardens, and eventually to the village's impressive Castle Doria, high on the olive-tree-covered hill. To the west, standing guard over the Mediterranean, is the picturesque medieval Chiesa di San Pietro, once the site of a temple to Venus (Venere in Italian), from which Portovenere gets its name. Nearby, in a rocky area leading to the sea, is Byron's Cave, one of the poet's favorite spots for swimming out into the sea.

GETTING HERE AND AROUND

By car from the port city of La Spezia, follow the signs for Portovenere. It's about a 20-minute winding drive along the sea through small fishing villages. From La Spezia train station you can hire a taxi for about €30. By bus from Via Garibaldi in La Spezia (a 10-minute walk from the train station) it takes about 30 minutes.

VISITOR INFORMATION

CONTACT **Portovenere Tourist Office.** ✉ *Piazza Bastreri 7, Portovenere* 🌐 *www.portovenere.com.*

Sights

Grotto Arpaia

CAVE | Near the entrance to the huge, strange Grotto Arpaia, at the base of the sea-swept cliff, is a plaque recounting the strength and courage of Lord Byron (1788–1824) as he swam across the gulf to the village of San Terenzo, near Lerici, to visit his friend Shelley (1792–1822). The poet is said to have written his lengthy narrative poem *Childe Harold's Pilgrimage* in Portovenere. ✉ *SP530 92, Portovenere.*

★ San Pietro

CHURCH | With its black-and-white-striped exterior, this 13th-century Gothic church is a spectacular landmark recognizable from far out at sea and upon entering the village. It is built on the site of an ancient pagan shrine, on a formidable solid mass of rock above the Grotto Arpaia. There's a fantastic view of the Cinque Terre coastline from the church's front porch. ✉ *Piazza Lazzaro Spallanzani, Portovenere* ☎ *0187/790684* 🌐 *www.parrocchiaportovenere.org.*

Restaurants

Bacicio

$ | WINE BAR | Named after a locally born 19th-century pirate, this maritime-theme enoteca and antipasto bar is popular with locals and tourists looking for typical regional dishes, soups, and fresh seafood. They also offer terrific sandwiches to go, and there's a lengthy wine list. **Known for:** anchovies cooked many ways; fresh fish crostini; generous portions at reasonable prices. $ *Average main: €14* ✉ *Via Cappellini 17, Portovenere* ☎ *0187/793031* ⏲ *Closed evenings.*

★ Il Timone

$ | LIGURIAN | FAMILY | Find some of the best food in Portovenere at this airy, affordable, and casual portside restaurant. The menu is typical "Ligure," ranging from meat to pasta with seafood, and also offers *farinata* (fried pancake), focaccia, and pizza. **Known for:** comfortable patio in summer; portside location; Ligurian farinata and pizza. $ *Average main: €17* ✉ *Via Olivo 29, Portovenere* ☎ *0187/914595* 🌐 *pizzeriailtimone.it* ⏲ *Closed Tues. and mid-Jan. and Feb. No lunch weekdays.*

Hotels

Grand Hotel Portovenere

$$$ | **HOTEL** | This 13th-century Franciscan monastery turned elegant hotel incorporates modern enhancements while retaining the structure's impressive rose facade, arches, and frescoes. **Pros:** excellent location and views; comfortable beds and mostly spacious rooms; wellness center and gym. **Cons:** some rooms are small; some room amenities are limited, no in-room tea or coffeemaker; expensive restaurant and bar. *Rooms from: €465 Via Giuseppe Garibaldi 5, Portovenere 0187/777751 www.portovenereGrand.com Closed early Nov.–late Apr. 46 rooms Free Breakfast.*

Hotel Belvedere

$ | **HOTEL** | True to its name (which means "beautiful view"), the best rooms in this sunny Liberty-style building face the bay of Portovenere, with lovely vistas of Palmaria Island and the Gulf of Poets. **Pros:** sea views from the terrace and some rooms; family rooms available; good value for the location. **Cons:** modernization required; limited parking; rooms facing the street are noisy. *Rooms from: €132 Via Giuseppe Garibaldi 26, Portovenere 0187/790608 www.belvedereportovenere.it 17 rooms Free Breakfast.*

Levanto

47 km (29 miles) northwest of Portovenere, 60 km (36 miles) southeast of Genoa.

Nestled at the end of a valley of pine forests, olive groves, vineyards, and medieval villages lies this sunny seaside town, an alternative and usually less expensive base for exploring the Cinque Terre and the Riviera di Levante.

GETTING HERE AND AROUND

By car, take the Carodanno/Levanto exit off the A12 for 25 minutes to the town center. By train, Levanto is on the main north–south railway, one stop north of Monterosso.

VISITOR INFORMATION

CONTACT Levanto Tourism Office. *Piazza Cavour 1, Levanto 0187/808125 www.visitlevanto.it.*

Levanto

TOWN | With its long sandy beach, colorful old quarter, and breathtakingly beautiful hiking paths, Levanto has become a haven not only for sun worshippers but also for divers, surfers, and hikers. The path between Levanto and Monterosso al Mare, about a 2½-mile hike, is freely accessible. This is also an ideal starting point for day trips by train or boat to many interesting places along the Riviera, such as Portovenere, Lerici, Tellaro, and Fiascherino, in the direction of La Spezia; and Portofino, Santa Margherita, Camogli, and Sestri Levante, in the direction of Genoa. *Levanto 0187/808125 www.visitlevanto.it.*

Sestri Levante

37 km (22 miles) northwest of Levanto, 28 km (17 miles) southeast of Santa Margherita Ligure.

Halfway between the Cinque Terre and Portofino lies this lovely seaside resort. The old village is on a peninsula with the beautiful Baia del Silenzio on one side and the Baia delle Favole and promenade on the other. The Baia delle Favole (*favole* means "fairy tales") was named in honor of the Danish author Hans Christian Andersen, who visited Sestri for a short time.

GETTING HERE AND AROUND

By car, it is a five-minute drive off the A12. The Sestri Levante train station is on the main north–south train line between Genoa and Pisa; it's just a five-minute walk to the beach and old village.

VISITOR INFORMATION

CONTACT **Sestri Levante Tourist Office.** ✉ *Corso Colombo 50, Sestri Levante* ☎ *0185/478530* 🌐 *www.sestri-levante.net.*

Beaches

Baia del Silenzio

BEACH | The Bay of Silence is a sandy cove east of the pedestrian-only street in the old town, with pastel-color bars and restaurants edging the sand and bobbing boats dotting the horizon. It's a picture-postcard public beach and an idyllic setting for a dip in the Mediterranean, frequented mostly by locals and some visiting crowds in summer. You can also take a short walk up to the Convento dei Cappuccini, a church dedicated to the Virgin Mary. The monastery was built at the end of the 17th century and offers a spectacular panoramic view. **Amenities**: food and drink; parking (free). **Best for**: views; walking. ✉ *Baia del Silenzio, Sestri Levante* ☎ *0185/478530* 🌐 *www.sestri-levante.net.*

Restaurants

La Cantina del Polpo

$$ | LIGURIAN | This cozy former cantina with wood paneling, a fireplace, and local maritime memorabilia serves some of the best dishes in town. Using the bounty of the two bays that frame the village, its chefs create inventive menus with standout mains, which include expertly seasoned fish, as well as such starters as spaghetti with anchovies and *gnocchetti alla Sorrentina* (with tomatoes, mozzarella, and basil) and some great desserts. **Known for:** friendly staff; creative seafood-focused dishes at affordable prices; hard-to-find regional wines. [$] *Average main: €24* ✉ *Via Camillo Benso Cavour 2, Sestri Levante* ☎ *0185/485296* 🌐 *www.cantinadelpolpo.com* ⏲ *Closed Wed. and mid-Feb.–mid-Mar.*

Hotels

★ Grand Hotel dei Castelli

$$ | HOTEL | You can see the Baia delle Favole from this castle-turned-hotel on a promontory, and you just might feel you've been transported to a fairy tale here. **Pros:** grand setting with spectacular views of the two bays; beautiful grounds; private inlet. **Cons:** some rooms and public areas have a dated feel; steep walk (or slow elevator) down to the beach; guests are charged for private beach and pool access. [$] *Rooms from: €350* ✉ *Via Penisola di Levante 26, Sestri Levante* ☎ *0185/487020* 🌐 *www.hoteldeicastelli.it/en* ⏲ *Closed Nov.–mid-Mar.* *50 rooms* *Free Breakfast.*

Santa Margherita Ligure

31 km (19 miles) southeast of Genoa.

A lively resort town favored by well-to-do Italians, Santa Margherita Ligure has everything a Riviera playground should have—plenty of palm trees and attractive hotels, cafés, and a marina packed with yachts. Some of the older buildings have trompe-l'oeil frescoed exteriors that are typical of this part of the Riviera. For many people, this pleasant, convenient base represents the perfect balance on the Italian Riviera: more spacious than the Cinque Terre; less glitzy than San Remo; more relaxing than Genoa and environs; and ideally situated for day trips, such as an excursion to Portofino.

GETTING HERE AND AROUND

By car, take the Rapallo exit off the A12 and follow the signs, about a 10-minute drive. The Santa Margherita Ligure train station is on the main north–south line between Genoa and Pisa.

VISITOR INFORMATION

CONTACT Santa Margherita Ligure Tourism Office. *Piazza Vittorio Veneto, Santa Margherita Ligure* *0185/287485* *live-santa.it.*

Restaurants

Oca Bianca

$$ | **EUROPEAN** | In a departure from the local norm, meat dishes, not seafood, are the specialty on the menu at Oca Bianca. Choices include tasty pastas as well as mouthwatering preparations of beef, lamb, pork, and octopus. **Known for:** lively outdoor seating in summer; multiple steak preparations; classic sauces for meat dishes. *Average main: €28* *Via XXV Aprile 21, Santa Margherita Ligure* *0185/288411* *www.ristoranteocabianca.it* *Closed Mon. No lunch.*

U Giancu

$ | **LIGURIAN** | Although the walls of Fausto Oneto's restaurant are covered in original cartoons, and a playground is the main feature of the outdoor seating area, this chef-owner is completely serious about his cooking, which follows the seasons. His own garden provides the freshest possible vegetables, the wine list (ask to visit the cantina) is excellent, and there are lively morning Ligurian cooking lessons. **Known for:** lamb dishes; creative and playful setting; vegetables fresh from the restaurant's garden. *Average main: €18* *Via San Massimo 78, Località San Massimo* *0185/261212* *www.ugiancu.it* *Closed Wed. and Jan. and Feb. No lunch Mon.–Sat.*

Hotels

Grand Hotel Miramare

$$$$ | **RESORT** | Classic Riviera elegance prevails at this palatial hotel overlooking the bay, where antique furniture and crystal chandeliers fill the high-ceiling rooms. **Pros:** top-notch service close to the beach; wellness and fitness centers; well-maintained rooms and marble bathrooms. **Cons:** traffic in summer from the road in front of the hotel; sea access is down the grand entrance staircase and across a busy street; elevated prices. *Rooms from: €1,000* *Via Milite Ignoto 30, Santa Margherita Ligure* *0185/287013* *www.grandhotelmiramare.it* *Closed Nov.–mid-Apr.* *72 rooms* *Free Breakfast.*

Hotel Continental

$$$ | **HOTEL** | A stately seaside mansion surrounded by a lush garden shaded by tall palms and pine trees offers stylish accommodations done in a blend of classic furnishings, mostly inspired by the 19th century. **Pros:** lovely location with extensive garden; convenient private beach; panoramic views from some rooms and the dining area. **Cons:** old-fashioned and outdated in parts; extra charges for lounge chairs and cabanas at the beach; located off a road that gets busy in high season. *Rooms from: €466* *Via Pagana 8, Santa Margherita Ligure* *0185/286512* *www.hotel-continental.it* *Closed Jan.–late Mar.* *68 rooms* *Free Breakfast.*

Hotel Jolanda

$$ | **HOTEL** | They may not have sea views, but the stylish, comfortable rooms here are decorated in a classic style, and some have large balconies. **Pros:** central location near train station and restaurants; outdoor areas for dining and relaxing; spa and massage options. **Cons:** no sea view; street noise can be intrusive; some rooms and indoor common areas feel cramped. *Rooms from: €225* *Via Luisito Costa 6, Santa Margherita Ligure* *0185/287512* *www.hoteljolanda.it* *Closed mid-Oct.–Dec.* *45 rooms* *Free Breakfast.*

Santa Margherita Palace & Spa

$$ | **HOTEL** | Just a short walk from the old town, this well-kept and well-equipped hotel offers modern rooms with contemporary furnishings and spa and gym facilities. **Pros:** handy central location near train station; helpful staff; modern

bathrooms (some rooms have Jacuzzis). **Cons:** neighborhood lacks charm; no views or beach access; expensive breakfast, spa use, and parking. *Rooms from: €256 Via Roma 9, Santa Margherita Ligure 0185/287139 www.santamargheritapalace.com Closed Nov.–Mar. 53 rooms No Meals.*

Portofino

5 km (3 miles) southeast of Santa Margherita Ligure, 36 km (22 miles) east of Genoa.

One of the most photographed villages along the coast, with a decidedly romantic and highly affluent aura, Portofino has long been a popular destination for the rich and famous. Once an ancient Roman colony and taken by the Republic of Genoa in 1229, it has also been ruled by the French, English, Spanish, and Austrians, as well as by marauding bands of 16th-century pirates. Elite British tourists first flocked to the lush harbor in the mid-1800s. Some of Europe's wealthiest drop anchor in Portofino in summer, but they stay out of sight by day, appearing in the evening after buses and boats have carried off the day-trippers.

There's not actually much to *do* in Portofino other than stroll around the wee harbor, see the castle, walk to Punta del Capo, browse at the pricey boutiques, and sip a coffee while people-watching. However, weaving through picture-perfect cliff-side gardens and gazing at yachts framed by the sapphire Ligurian Sea and the cliffs of Santa Margherita can make for quite a relaxing afternoon. There are also several tame, photo-friendly hikes into the hills to nearby villages.

Unless you're traveling on a deluxe budget, you may want to stay in Camogli or Santa Margherita Ligure rather than at one of Portofino's few very expensive hotels. Restaurants and cafés are also pricey: don't expect to have a beer here for much under €10.

GETTING HERE AND AROUND

By car, exit at Rapallo off the A12 and follow the blue signs (about a 20-minute drive mostly along the coast). Trying to reach Portofino by bus or car on the single narrow road can be a nightmare in summer and on holiday weekends. There is only one car park in the village, which is often full.

The nearest train station is Santa Margherita Ligure. No trains go directly to Portofino: you must stop at Santa Margherita, then take public Bus No. 782 from there (€5 each way). Note that the ticket machine for the bus is card-only and doesn't actually issue tickets (instead, a record of your card payment is transmitted to the bus driver). Alternatively, you can take a boat from Santa Margherita.

Portofino can be reached from Santa Margherita on foot: it's about a 60-minute walk along the sea, but be aware that many parts of the narrow road have no sidewalk.

VISITOR INFORMATION

CONTACT Portofino Tourism Office. *Via Roma 35, Portofino 0185/215037 portofinotourism.com.*

Sights

Abbazia di San Fruttuoso (*Abbey of San Fruttuoso*)

CHURCH | A medieval stronghold built by the Benedictines of Monte Cassino protects a minuscule fishing village that can be reached only on foot or by water—a 20-minute boat ride from Portofino and also reachable from Camogli, Santa Margherita Ligure, and Rapallo. The restored abbey is now the property of a national conservation fund (FAI) and occasionally hosts temporary exhibitions; it also contains the tombs of some illustrious members of the Doria family. Plan on spending a few hours enjoying the abbey and grounds, and perhaps lunching at one of the modest beachfront trattorias nearby (open only in summer). Boatloads of visitors can make this place very crowded very fast; you might appreciate it most off-season. ✉ *Via S. Fruttuoso 13, Portofino* ✣ *15-minute boat ride or 2-hr walk northwest of Portofino* ☎ *0185/772703* 🌐 *www.fondoambiente.it/luoghi/abbazia-di-san-fruttuoso* 🎫 *€9* 🕑 *Closed Mon. Nov.–Feb.* ✍ *Reservations essential.*

San Giorgio

CHURCH | This small church, sitting on a ridge above Portofino, is said to contain the relics of its namesake, brought back from the Holy Land by the Crusaders. Portofino enthusiastically celebrates St. George's Day every April 23. ✉ *Above harbor, Salita San Giorgio, Portofino* 🎫 *Free.*

Beaches

Paraggi

BEACH | The only sand beach near Portofino is at Paraggi, a cove on the road between Santa Margherita Ligure and Portofino. The bus will stop here on request. **Amenities:** food and drink; parking (free). **Best for:** swimming; walking. ✉ *Via Strada Provinciale, Portofino.*

Punta Portofino

VIEWPOINT | Pristine views can be had from the deteriorating *faro* (lighthouse) at Punta Portofino, a 15-minute walk along the point that begins at the southern end of the port. Along the seaside path you can see numerous impressive, sprawling private residences behind high iron gates. **Amenities:** none; parking (free). **Best for:** walking. ✉ *Viale Rainusso 1, Portofino.*

Restaurants

Ristorante Puny

$$$ | LIGURIAN | If you want to be in the middle of everything and don't mind spending a small fortune, then you'll want (and need) a reservation at this waterfront restaurant in Portofino. Quite simply, it's *the* place to be seen while dining on baked fish and local pasta dishes. **Known for:** pappardelle al portofino (with tomato and pesto sauce); baked mini-octopus; dining right on the port. $ *Average main: €32* ✉ *Piazza Martiri dell'Olivetta 4–5, on harbor, Portofino* ☎ *0185/269037* 🌐 *www.ristorantepunyportofino.com* 🕑 *Closed Thurs. and Dec.–Feb.*

Coffee and Quick Bites

Canale

$ | BAKERY | If the staggering prices at virtually all of Portofino's cafés and restaurants are enough to ruin your appetite, join the long line outside this family-run bakery where you will find more affordable eats. At this takeaway spot, the focaccia is baked on-site, along with all kinds of sandwiches and other refreshments. **Known for:** takeout only; one of few budget options in Portofino; delicious pastries. $ *Average main: €10* ✉ *Via Roma 30, Portofino* ☎ *0185/269248* 🕑 *Closed Wed. and Nov.*

Hotels

Belmond Hotel Splendido

$$$$ | HOTEL | FAMILY | This 1920s luxury hotel oozes charm, taste, and lovely scenery, with a particular attention to color—from the coordinated floral linens in corals and gold in the guest rooms to the fresh flowers in the reception rooms, the two restaurants, and on the large terrace. **Pros:** rooms have garden or sea views; lovely manicured grounds; attentive staff. **Cons:** be prepared to

spend upward of €100 for a simple lunch for two; pool and other common areas can be noisy because of the kid-friendly atmosphere; selfie-taking influencers may mar the experience. *Rooms from: €2,980 Salita Baratta 16, Portofino 0185/267801 www.belmond.com/hotel-splendido-portofino Closed Nov.–early June 67 rooms Free Breakfast.*

Eight Hotel Portofino

$$$$ | HOTEL | At this intimate hotel, comfortable and soothingly designed guest rooms—some with canopy beds, pastel walls, and ultramodern bathrooms—are spread across two small 19th-century town houses on a quiet backstreet. **Pros:** walking distance to the harbor and village; private garden; comfortable beds and a choice of pillows. **Cons:** some lower-level rooms don't receive much light; no sea views; cheapest rooms are small and basic for the price. *Rooms from: €1,045 Via Del Fondaco 11, Portofino 0185/26991 portofino.eighthotels.it Closed Oct.–Easter 18 rooms Free Breakfast.*

Activities

HIKING

If you have the stamina, you can hike to the Abbazia di San Fruttuoso from Portofino. It's a steep climb at first, and the walk takes about 2½ hours one-way. If you're extremely ambitious and want to make a day of it, you can hike another 2½ hours all the way to Camogli. Much more modest hikes from Portofino include a one-hour uphill walk to Cappelletta delle Gave, a bit inland in the hills, from where you can continue downhill to Santa Margherita Ligure (another 1½ hours); there is also a gently undulating paved trail leading to the beach at Paraggi (½ hour). Finally, there's a 2½-hour hike from Portofino that heads farther inland to Ruta, through Olmi and Pietre Strette. The trails are well marked, and maps are available at the tourist information offices in Rapallo, Santa Margherita Ligure, Portofino, and Camogli.

Camogli

15 km (9 miles) northwest of Portofino, 20 km (12 miles) southeast of Genoa.

Camogli, at the edge of the large promontory and nature reserve known as the Portofino Peninsula, has always been a town of sailors. By the 19th century it was leasing its ships throughout the continent. Today, multicolor houses, staircases with incredible sea views, and a massive 17th-century seawall mark this appealing harbor community, which is perhaps as beautiful as Portofino but without the glamour. When exploring on foot, don't miss the antiquated harbor, reached through a narrow archway at the northern end of the pebble beach and promenade.

GETTING HERE AND AROUND

By car, exit the A12 at Recco and follow the signs. There are several parking lots (fee) near the village center. Camogli is on the main north–south railway line between Genoa and La Spezia.

VISITOR INFORMATION

CONTACT Camogli Tourism Office. *Via XX Settembre 33, Camogli 0185/771066 www.welcomecamogli.it.*

Sights

Ruta

TRAIL | The footpaths that leave from Ruta, 4 km (2½ miles) east of Camogli, thread through rugged terrain and contain a multitude of plant species. Weary hikers are sustained by stunning views of the Riviera di Levante from various vantage points along the way. *Camogli.*

San Rocco, San Nicolò, and Punta Chiappa

TOWN | From Camogli, you can reach these hamlets along the western coast of the peninsula either on foot or by boat. They're more natural and less fashionable than those facing south on the eastern coast. In the small Romanesque church at San Nicolò, sailors who survived dangerous voyages came to offer thanks. *Camogli.*

Restaurants

Vento Ariel

$$ | SEAFOOD | This popular restaurant serves some of the best seafood in town on the harborfront terrace or the indoor patio with wicker chairs, where you can watch the bustling activity in the old port. Only the freshest catches are presented; try the "Bagnun" anchovy soup or any of the pastas. **Known for:** outdoor seating with views; fresh seafood; relaxed atmosphere. *$ Average main: €21 ✉ Calata Porticciolo 1, Camogli ☎ 0185/771080 🌐 www.ventoariel.it ⏲ Closed Wed. and 10 days in Dec.*

Coffee and Quick Bites

Revello

$ | LIGURIAN | You'll know this focacceria and pasticceria by the line out the door, as you walk along the beach before entering the archway to the old port. This tiny spot—where you can see focaccia being baked through a window into its kitchen—specializes in Liguria's favorite bread, *farinata* or chickpea flatbread (baked late afternoons from October to March) and several flavors of *camogliesi* (rum-filled is the original), a sweet that the shop's owner, Giacomo, invented in 1970. **Known for:** camogliesi sweets; wide variety of focaccia flavors; no seating, so take your treats away. *$ Average main: €7 ✉ Via Giuseppe Garibaldi 183, Camogli ☎ 0185/770777 🌐 www.revellocamogli.com ⏲ Closed 3 wks in Jan. and 2 wks in mid-Sept.*

Hotels

★ Cenobio dei Dogi

$$ | HOTEL | Perched majestically above Camogli's beaches, the former summer palace of Genoa's doges features many guest rooms with expansive balconies and commanding vistas of the city's port. **Pros:** location and setting are wonderful; pool and gardens; direct access to private beach. **Cons:** books quickly in high season; plain decor in some rooms; one week minimum stay in peak season. *$ Rooms from: €350 ✉ Via Nicolò Cuneo 34, Camogli ☎ 0185/7241 🌐 www.cenobio.it 105 rooms Free Breakfast.*

★ Locanda I Tre Merli

$ | B&B/INN | In a typical Ligurian terratetto on the old port, this charming *locanda*, or inn, is reminiscent of old-world voyages but with the amenities to make it a comfortable and relaxing stop for today's traveler. **Pros:** friendly management and staff; quaint port location and views; small spa with whirlpool tub and Turkish bath. **Cons:** can be a bit noisy in the summer months; located right on the port, so you have to park a distance away; narrow corridors. *$ Rooms from: €159 ✉ Via Scalo 5, Camogli ☎ 0185/776752 🌐 www.locandaitremerli.com 5 rooms Free Breakfast.*

Villa Rosmarino

$$ | B&B/INN | A beautiful Ligurian villa in the Camogli hills offers chic, contemporary, and comfortable accommodations along with well-manicured gardens and outdoor sitting areas, arbors, and a welcoming pool. **Pros:** stylish modern decor; lovely garden with pool; excellent breakfast. **Cons:** some rooms are small and have minimal storage; the hike uphill is not ideal in summer months; parking can be challenging. *$ Rooms from: €295 ✉ Via Figari 38, Camogli ☎ 0185/771580 🌐 www.villarosmarino.com ⏲ Closed Nov.–Feb. 6 rooms Free Breakfast.*

Genoa

20 km (12 miles) northwest of Camogli, 144 km (89 miles) south of Milan.

Genoa (Genova in Italian) was the birthplace of Christopher Columbus, but the city's proud history predates the famous explorer by hundreds of years. Genoa was already an important trading station by the 3rd century BC, when the Romans conquered Liguria. The Middle Ages and the Renaissance saw it rise to become a jumping-off place for the Crusaders, a commercial center of tremendous wealth and prestige, and a strategic bone of international contention. A network of fortresses defending the city connected by a wall second only in length to the Great Wall of China was constructed in the hills above, and Genoa's bankers, merchants, and princes adorned the city with palaces, churches, and impressive art collections.

Crammed into a thin crescent of land between sea and mountains, Genoa expanded up rather than out, taking on the form of a multilayer wedding cake, with churches, streets, and entire residential neighborhoods built on others' rooftops. Public elevators and funiculars are almost as common as buses and trains.

With its impressive palaces and museums, one of the largest medieval city centers in Europe, and an elaborate network of ancient hilltop fortresses, Genoa may be just the dose of culture you're looking for. Europe's biggest boat show, the annual Salone Nautico Internazionale, is held here. Fine restaurants are abundant, and classical dance and music are richly represented. The Teatro Carlo Felice is the local opera venue, and it's where the internationally renowned annual Niccolò Paganini Violin Contest takes place.

If you're planning to do much sightseeing, consider investing either in a Genova Museum Card (€15), which allows entry to all 28 of the city-administered museums as well as all AMT transport services within a 24-hour period (or buy a 48-hour pass for €25), or the more personalized Genova City Pass (€20 for 24 hours, €35 for 48 hours), which allows free or discounted entry to specific museums and use of AMT transport services, plus a selection of other attractions and activities. Buy these at most of the museums included in the package, at the tourist office, or online at 🌐 *www.museidigenova.it/en/museum-card* or 🌐 *www.genovacitypass.it*. More information on these are available from the tourist office in Via Garibaldi.

GETTING HERE AND AROUND

By car, take the Genoa Ovest exit off the A12 and take the upper bridge (*sopraelevata*) to the second exit, Genova Centro–Piazza Corvetto. Be forewarned: driving in Genoa is harrowing and best avoided whenever possible. If you want to see the city on a day trip, go by train (🌐 *www.trenitalia.com*); regular service operates to and from Genoa's two main stations, Principe and Brignole. If you're staying in the city, park in a garage or by valet and travel by foot and taxi throughout your stay.

The best way by far to get around Genoa is on foot, with the occasional assistance of public transportation. Many of the more interesting districts are either entirely closed to traffic, have roads so narrow that no car could fit, or are, even at the best of times, blocked by gridlock. Although it might seem a daunting task, exploring the city is made simple by its geography. The historical center of Genoa occupies a relatively narrow strip of land running between the mountains and the sea. You can easily visit the most important monuments in one or two days. The main bus station in Genoa is at Piazza Principe. Local buses operated by the municipal transport company, AMT (🌐 *www.amt.genova.it*), serve the steep valleys that run to some of the towns along the western coast. Tickets may be bought at local bus stations or at newsstands. (You must have a ticket before you board.) This company also operates the funicular railways and the elevators that service the steeper sections of the city.

VISITOR INFORMATION

CONTACT Genoa Tourism Office. ✉ *Via Garibaldi 12/r, Maddalena* ☎ *010/5572903* 🌐 *www.visitgenoa.it.*

Sights

THE MEDIEVAL CORE AND POINTS ABOVE

The medieval center of Genoa, threaded with tiny streets flanked by 11th-century portals, is roughly the area between the port and Piazza de Ferrari. This mazelike pedestrian zone is officially called the Caruggi District, but the Genovese, in their matter-of-fact way, simply refer to the area as the place of the *vicoli* (alleys). In this warren of narrow cobbled streets extending north from Piazza Caricamento, the city's oldest churches sit among tiny shops selling antique furniture, coffee, cheese, rifles, wine, gilt picture frames, camping gear, and even live fish. The 500-year-old apartment buildings lean so precariously that penthouse balconies nearly touch those across the street, blocking what little sunlight would have shone through to the cobblestones. Wealthy Genovese built their homes in this quarter in the 16th century, and prosperous guilds—such as the goldsmiths for whom Vico degli Indoratori and Via degli Orefici were named—set up shop here.

Castelletto

VIEWPOINT | To reach this charming neighborhood high above the city center, you take one of Genoa's historical municipal elevators that whisk you skyward from Piazza del Portello, at the end of Galleria Garibaldi, for a spectacular view of the old city. ✉ *Piazza del Portello, Castelletto* 🎫 *Free.*

Cimitero Monumentale di Staglieno

CEMETERY | One of the most famous of Genovese landmarks is this bizarrely beautiful cemetery; its fanciful marble and bronze sculptures sprawl haphazardly across a hillside on the outskirts of town. A pantheon holds indoor tombs and some remarkable works like an 1878 *Eve* by Villa. Don't miss Rovelli's 1896 **Tomba Raggio,** which shoots Gothic spires out of the hillside forest. The cemetery began operation in 1851 and has been lauded by such visitors as Mark Twain and Evelyn Waugh. It covers a good deal of ground (allow at least half a day to explore). Take Bus Nos. 13 or 14 from the Stazione Genova Brignole, Bus No. 34 from Stazione Principe, or a taxi. ✉ *Piazzale Resasco 2, Genoa* ☎ *010/5576470* 🌐 *www.staglieno.comune.genova.it* 🎫 *Free (€5 guided tours).*

Ferrovia Genova–Casella

TRAIN/TRAIN STATION | FAMILY | The Genova–Casella Railroad is a good way to get a sense of the rugged landscape around Genoa; the train departs about every 90 minutes, and a bus supplements some routes. In operation since 1929, it runs from Piazza Manin in Genoa (follow Via Montaldo from the center of town, or take Bus No. 34 or 36 to the piazza) through the beautiful countryside above the city, arriving in the rural hill town Casella. The tiny train traverses precarious switchbacks that afford sweeping views of the Ligurian hills. In Casella Paese (the last stop) you can hike, eat lunch, or check out the view and ride back. Canova (two stops from the end of the line) is the start of two possible hikes: a two-hour (one-way) trek to a small sanctuary, Santuario della Vittoria, and a grueling four-hour hike to the hill town of Creto. Another worthwhile stop is Sant'Olcese Tullo, where you can take a half-hour (one-way) walk through the Sentiero Botanico di Ciaé, a botanical garden and forest refuge with a tiny medieval castle. ✉ *Genoa* ☎ *010/5582414* 🌐 *www.ferroviagenovacasella.it* 🎫 *From €3 one-way.*

Galleria Nazionale di Palazzo Spinola

ART MUSEUM | Housed in the richly adorned Palazzo Spinola north of Piazza Soziglia, this beautiful museum contains masterpieces by Luca Giordano and Guido Reni. The *Ecce Homo,* by Antonello da Messina (1430–79), is a hauntingly beautiful painting, of historical interest because it was the Sicilian Antonello

A
B
C
D
E
F
1
2
3
4
5
6
7
8
9
Stazione Principe
Piazza Acquaverde
Piazza del Principe
Via A. Doria
Principe
Via Adua
Strada Aldo Moro
Via Balbi
Corso Dogali
Piazza E. Brignole
Sal. Pietraminuta
V. Brig. de Ferrari
Via Prè
Via Antonio Gramsci
Piazzale Staz. Marittima
Stazione Marittima
Piazza d. Nunziata
V. delle Fontane
Via P. Bensa
V. Cairoli
Darsena
V. Lomellini
Via del Campo
V. S. Siro
Ponte dei Mille
Ponte Parodi
Marina Porto Antico
Ponte Calvi
Via S. Luca
Ponte Spinola
Bacino Porto Vecchio
Piazza Caricamento
Ponte Embriaco
San Giorgio
Via S.
Molo Vecchio
Via F. Turati
Via di Canneto il Curto
Via del Molo
Via dei
Via S.
KEY
Sights
Restaurants
Quick Bites
Hotels
Piazza Embriaci
Via Santa Croce
Corso M. Quadrio
Strada Aldo Moro
Molo Nuovo
0
200 meters
0
200 yards

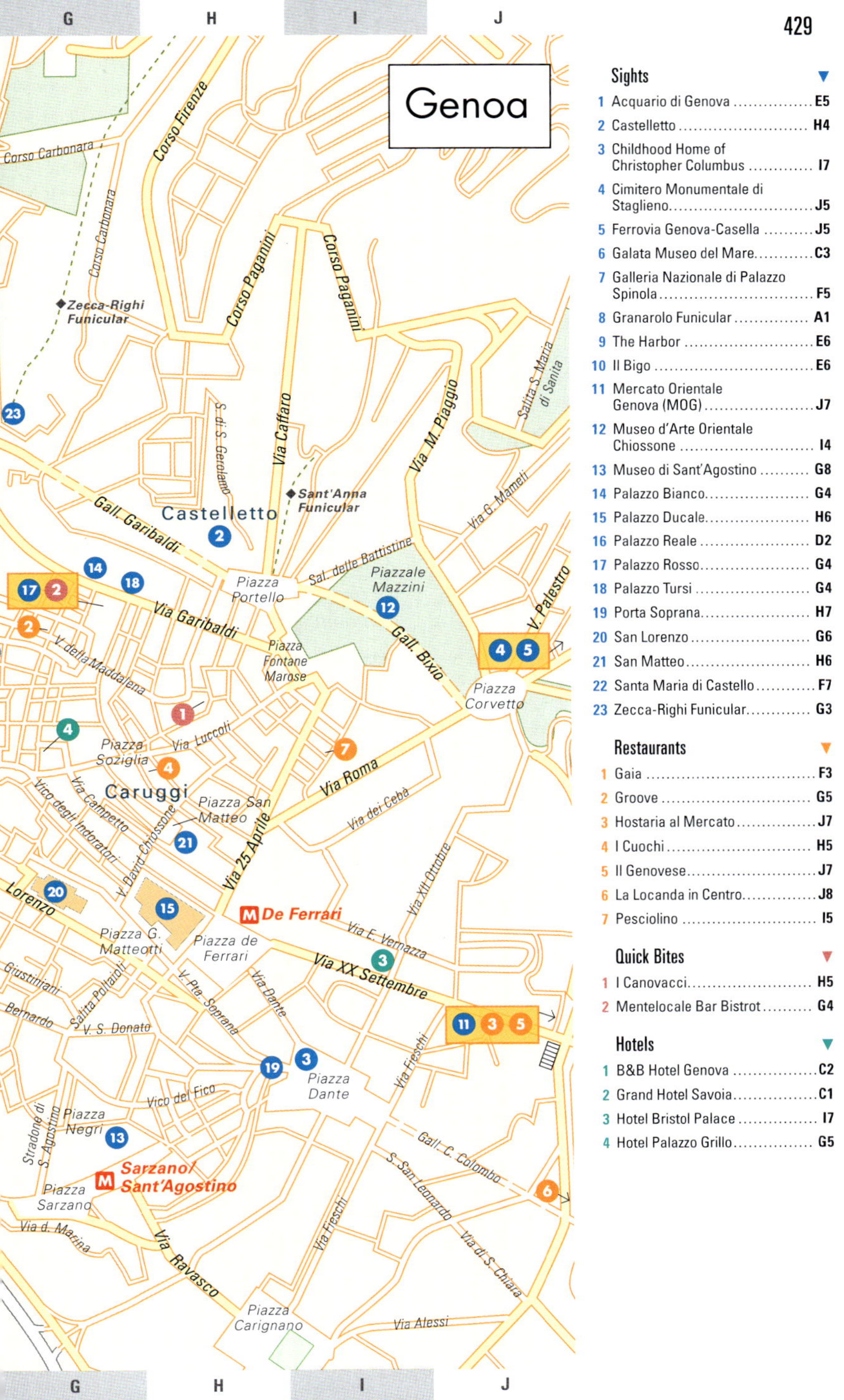

Sights

1 Acquario di Genova E5
2 Castelletto H4
3 Childhood Home of Christopher Columbus I7
4 Cimitero Monumentale di Staglieno............................ J5
5 Ferrovia Genova-Casella J5
6 Galata Museo del Mare............ C3
7 Galleria Nazionale di Palazzo Spinola............................. F5
8 Granarolo Funicular A1
9 The Harbor E6
10 Il Bigo E6
11 Mercato Orientale Genova (MOG)...................... J7
12 Museo d'Arte Orientale Chiossone I4
13 Museo di Sant'Agostino G8
14 Palazzo Bianco..................... G4
15 Palazzo Ducale..................... H6
16 Palazzo Reale D2
17 Palazzo Rosso...................... G4
18 Palazzo Tursi G4
19 Porta Soprana...................... H7
20 San Lorenzo G6
21 San Matteo.......................... H6
22 Santa Maria di Castello............ F7
23 Zecca-Righi Funicular............. G3

Restaurants

1 Gaia F3
2 Groove G5
3 Hostaria al Mercato................ J7
4 I Cuochi H5
5 Il Genovese.......................... J7
6 La Locanda in Centro............... J8
7 Pesciolino I5

Quick Bites

1 I Canovacci......................... H5
2 Mentelocale Bar Bistrot G4

Hotels

1 B&B Hotel Genova C2
2 Grand Hotel Savoia................. C1
3 Hotel Bristol Palace I7
4 Hotel Palazzo Grillo................ G5

who first brought Flemish oil paints and techniques to Italy from his sojourns in the Low Countries. Or so some contend. ✉ *Piazza Pellicceria 1, Genoa* ☎ *010/2477061* 🌐 *palazzospinola.cultura.gov.it* 🎫 *€12 with Palazzo Reale (except 1st Sun. of month when it's free entry)* 🕒 *Closed 2nd and 4th Sun. of month, Mon., and Tues. morning.*

Granarolo Funicular

TRANSPORTATION | FAMILY | Take a cog railway up the steeply rising terrain to another part of the city's fortified walls. It takes 15 minutes to hoist you from Stazione Principe to Porta Granarolo, 1,000 feet above, where the sweeping view gives you a sense of Genoa's size. The funicular departs every 30–40 minutes. ✉ *Piazza del Principe, San Teodoro* ☎ *010/5582414, 848/000030 Call Center* 🌐 *www.amt.genova.it* 🎫 *€2 (ticket valid 110 minutes).*

Museo d'Arte Orientale Chiossone

ART MUSEUM | One of Europe's most noteworthy collections of Japanese, Chinese, and Thai objects is housed in galleries in the Villetta di Negro park on the hillside above Piazza Portello. There's also a fine view of the city from the museum's terrace. ✉ *Piazzale Mazzini 4, Maddalena* ☎ *010/5577950* 🌐 *www.museidigenova.it/en/oriental-museum-e-chiossone* 🎫 *€5* 🕒 *Closed Mon.*

Palazzo Bianco

ART MUSEUM | It's difficult to miss the splendid white facade of this town palace and museum as you walk down Via Garibaldi (also known as Strada Nuova), one of Genoa's most important streets. The building houses a fine collection of 16th- and 17th-century art, with the Spanish and Flemish schools well represented. There's also a textiles collection. ✉ *Via Garibaldi 11, Genoa* ☎ *010/5572193* 🌐 *www.museidigenova.it/en/strada-nuova-museums* 🎫 *€9, includes Palazzo Rosso and Palazzo Tursi* 🕒 *Closed Mon.*

★ Palazzo Reale

CASTLE/PALACE | Lavish rococo rooms provide sumptuous display space for paintings, sculptures, tapestries, and Asian ceramics. The 17th-century palace—also known as Palazzo Balbi Durazzo—was built by the Balbi family, enormously wealthy Genovese merchants. Its regal pretensions were not lost on the Savoy, who bought the palace and turned it into a royal residence in the early 19th century. The gallery of mirrors and the ballroom on the upper floor are particularly decadent. **TIP→ The formal gardens provide a welcome respite from the bustle of the city, as well as great views of the harbor.** ✉ *Via Balbi 10, Pré* ☎ *010/2710236* 🌐 *palazzorealegenova.cultura.gov.it* 🎫 *€12 with Galleria Nazionale di Palazzo Spinola (except 1st Sun. of month when it's free entry)* 🕒 *Closed 2nd and 4th Sun. of month, Mon., and Tues. morning.*

Palazzo Rosso

CASTLE/PALACE | This 17th-century Baroque palace, named for the red stone used in its construction, now contains, apart from a number of lavishly frescoed suites, works by Veronese, Guido Reni, and Sir Anthony van Dyck. ✉ *Via Garibaldi 18, Genoa* ☎ *010/5572193* 🌐 *www.museidigenova.it/en/strada-nuova-museums* 🎫 *€9, includes Palazzo Bianco and Palazzo Tursi* 🕒 *Closed Mon.*

Palazzo Tursi

GOVERNMENT BUILDING | In the 16th century, wealthy resident Nicolò Grimaldi had a palace built of pink stone quarried in the region, and today it has been reincarnated as Genoa's Palazzo Municipale (Municipal Building). Most of the goings-on inside are the stuff of local politics and weddings, but you can visit the richly decorated Sale Paganiniane (Paganini rooms), where the famous Guarnerius violin belonging to Niccolò Paganini (1782–1840) is typically displayed, and the gardens that connect the palace with the neighboring Palazzo Bianco. There is also a collection of five centuries worth of coins, as well as ceramics that were used in homes and pharmacies. ✉ *Via Garibaldi 9, Maddalena* ☎ *010/5572193* 🌐 *www.museidigenova.it/en/strada-nuova-museums* 🎫 *€9, includes Palazzo Bianco and Palazzo Rosso* ⏲ *Closed Mon.*

Zecca-Righi Funicular

OTHER ATTRACTION | A seven-stop commuter funicular begins just off of Piazza della Nunziata and ends at a high lookout on the fortified gates in the 17th-century city walls. Ringed around the circumference of the city are a number of huge fortresses; this gate was part of the city's system of defenses. From Righi you can undertake scenic all-day hikes from one fortress to the next. ✉ *Piazza della Nunziata, Genoa* ☎ *010/5582414, 848/000030 call center* 🌐 *www.amt.genova.it* 🎫 *€2 (ticket valid 110 minutes).*

SOUTHERN DISTRICTS AND THE AQUARIUM

Inhabited since the 6th century BC, the oldest section of Genoa lies on a hill to the southwest of the Caruggi district. Today, apart from a section of 9th-century wall near Porta Soprana, there's little to show that an imposing castle once stood here. Though the neighborhood is quite run-down, some of Genoa's oldest churches make it a worthwhile excursion. Heading down the hill, you can stroll along the harbor. Once squalid and unsafe, the port was given a complete overhaul during Genoa's preparations for the Columbus quincentennial celebrations of 1992, and additional restorations in 2003 and 2004 revitalized the waterfront. You can easily reach the port on foot by following Via San Lorenzo downhill from Genoa's cathedral, Via delle Fontane from Piazza della Nunziata, or any of the narrow vicoli that lead down from Via Balbi and Via Pré.

Acquario di Genova

AQUARIUM | **FAMILY** | Europe's biggest aquarium is a must for children. Fifty tanks of marine species, including sea turtles, dolphins, seals, eels, penguins, jellyfish, and sharks, share space with educational displays, touch pools, and re-creations of marine ecosystems, among them a tank of coral from the Indian Ocean and a wall that replicates a forest in Madagascar. The Aquarium Village complex (additional cost) includes a biosphere with tropical plants and birds, as well as a virtual reality "experience museum," and the Bigo panoramic elevator. **TIP→ Buy tickets online in advance for the lowest prices.** If arriving by car, take the Genova Ovest exit from the autostrada. ✉ *Ponte Spinola, Genoa* ☎ *010/23451* 🌐 *www.acquariodigenova.it* 🎫 *From €26.*

Childhood Home of Christopher Columbus

HISTORIC HOME | The ivy-covered remains of this fabled medieval house—just a very small portion of it—stand in the gardens below the Porta Soprana. A small collection of objects and reproductions relating to the life and travels of Columbus are on display inside. Just outside the house, take a minute to admire the charming remains of the *chiostro di* Sant'Andrea, a medieval cloister dating from the 13th century. ✉ *Piazza Dante, Molo* ☎ *331/2605009 mobile* 🌐 *www.museidigenova.it* 🎫 *€5* ⏲ *Closed Mon.*

Galata Museo del Mare

SPECIALTY MUSEUM | **FAMILY** | Devoted to the city's seafaring history, this museum is probably the best way, at least on dry land, to get an idea of the changing shape of Genoa's busy port. Highlighting the displays is a full-size replica of a 17th-century Genoan galley. ✉ *Calata de Mari 1, Genoa* ☎ *010/2533555* 🌐 *www.galatamuseodelmare.it* 🎫 *€17* ⏲ *Closed Mon. Nov.–Feb.*

The Harbor

OTHER ATTRACTION | A boat tour (with Consorzio Liguria Via Mare, for example) gives you a good perspective on the layout of the harbor, which dates to Roman times. The Genoa inlet, the largest along the Italian Riviera, was also used by the

Phoenicians and Greeks as a harbor and a staging area from which they could penetrate inland to form settlements and to trade. The port is guarded by the Diga Foranea, a striking 5-km-long (3-mile-long) wall built into the ocean. The Lanterna, a lighthouse more than 360 feet tall, was built in 1544; it's one of Italy's oldest lighthouses and a traditional emblem of Genoa. ✉ *Porto Vecchio.*

Il Bigo

VIEWPOINT | FAMILY | Designed by world-renowned architect Renzo Piano, this spiderlike white structure was erected in 1992 to celebrate the Columbus quincentenary. You can take its **Ascensore Panoramico Bigo** (Bigo Panoramic Elevator) up 650 feet for a 360-degree view of the harbor, city, and sea. In winter there's an ice-skating rink next to the elevator, in an area covered by sail-like awnings. Check the website for seasonal opening hours. ✉ *Ponte Spinola, Genoa* ☎ *010/23451* 🌐 *www.acquariodigenova.it/en/bigo* 🎫 *Elevator €6* 🕒 *Closed Mon. morning and weekdays Nov.–Feb.*

Mercato Orientale Genova (MOG)

MARKET | A bustling place, this produce, fish, and meat market in a former church cloister has added a second-floor bar, restaurant, and cooking school. Experience the sensory overload of colorful everyday Genovese life while watching the merchants and buyers banter over prices on the ground floor, and then head upstairs for a craft beer, a cooking lesson, or to try authentic Ligurian cuisine. ✉ *Via XX Settembre 75, Portoria* ☎ *010/8973000* 🌐 *www.moggenova.it* 🕒 *Closed Sun. evening.*

Museo di Sant'Agostino

ART MUSEUM | Damaged during World War II, the 13th-century Gothic church of Sant'Agostino now houses a museum displaying pieces of medieval architecture, sculptures, and frescoes. Highlights of the collection are the enigmatic fragments of a tomb sculpture by Giovanni Pisano (circa 1250–1315). Surviving from the original construction are the fine campanile with a Moorish inlaid marble design and two well-preserved cloisters (one of which is the only triangular cloister in Europe). If you have a ticket for the Childhood Home of Christopher Columbus, present it here for a discounted entry. ✉ *Piazza Sarzano 35, Genoa* ☎ *010/5576757* 🌐 *www.museidigenova.it/en/museum-st-augustine* 🎫 *€5, €3 with ticket to Childhood Home of Christopher Columbus* 🕒 *Closed Thurs.*

Palazzo Ducale

ART GALLERY | This palace was built in the 16th century over a medieval hall, and its facade was rebuilt in the late 18th century and later restored. It now houses temporary exhibitions upstairs and a couple of cocktail bars and restaurants on the ground floor. The amazingly large courtyard (which is free) is worth strolling through. ✉ *Piazza Matteotti 9, Portoria* ☎ *010/8171600* 🌐 *www.palazzoducale.genova.it* 🎫 *Exhibitions from €12* 🕒 *Closed Mon. morning.*

Porta Soprana

NOTABLE BUILDING | A striking 12th-century twin-tower structure, this medieval gateway stands on the spot where a road from ancient Rome entered the city. It is just steps uphill from Christopher Columbus's boyhood home. ✉ *Piazza Dante, Molo.*

Favorite Places

Robert Andrews: It's always a thrill to stand in the Childhood Home of Christopher Columbus in Genoa, absorbing the well-preserved (but not over-restored) surroundings that evoke the great explorer's life.

San Lorenzo

CHURCH | Contrasting black and white marble, so common in Liguria, embellishes the cathedral at the heart of medieval Genoa, inside and out. Consecrated in 1118, the church honors St. Lawrence, who passed through the city on his way to Rome in the 3rd century. For hundreds of years the building was used for state purposes, such as civic elections, as well as religious. Note the 13th-century Gothic portal, the fascinating twisted barbershop columns, and the 15th- to 17th-century frescoes inside. The last campanile dates from the early 16th century. The Museo del Tesoro di San Lorenzo (San Lorenzo Treasury Museum) inside has some stunning pieces from medieval goldsmiths and silversmiths, work for which medieval Genoa was renowned. ✉ *Piazza San Lorenzo, Genoa* ☎ *010/27001 cathedral office, 010/2700295 museum* 🌐 *www.chiesadigenova.it/cattedrale, www.museidigenova.it* 🎫 *Cathedral free, museum €5* ⏲ *Museum closed Sun.*

San Matteo

CHURCH | This typically Genovese black-and-white-striped church dates from the 12th century; its crypt contains the tomb of Andrea Doria (1466–1560), the Genovese admiral who maintained the independence of his native city. The well-preserved Piazza San Matteo was, for 500 years, the seat of the Doria family, which ruled Genoa and much of Liguria from the 16th to the 18th century. The square is bounded by 13th- to 15th-century houses decorated with portals and loggias. ✉ *Piazza San Matteo, Maddalena* ☎ *010/2474361* 🌐 *www.parrocchiasanmatteo.org* 🎫 *Free* ⏲ *Closed Mon.*

Santa Maria di Castello

CHURCH | One of Genoa's most significant churches, this early Christian structure was rebuilt in the 12th century and finally completed in 1513. You can view some fine artwork in the attached museum and in the cloisters, where a wall displays a superb *Annunciation* by the German Justus da Ravensburg. Volunteers may be on hand to guide you around (not during religious services). ✉ *Salita di Santa Maria di Castello 15, Genoa* ☎ *376/1865764 mobile* 🌐 *www.santamariadicastello.it* 🎫 *Free.*

Restaurants

Gaia

$ | LIGURIAN | For a truly Genovese experience, this unassuming restaurant, located in the vaulted basement of an old palazzo in the heart of the centro storico between Strada Nuova and the port, is just the place. You'll find some of the best, most authentic food in the city, with a focus on fish, meat dishes, and, of course, pesto. **Known for:** cozy, old-world atmosphere; stuffed anchovies; Genovese dishes. [$] *Average main: €16* ✉ *Vico dell'Argento 13/r, Maddalena* ☎ *010/2461629* ⏲ *Closed Sun.*

Groove

$ | BURGER | An extensive and highly rated selection of burgers and pizzas is the stock-in-trade of this trendy spot buried in Genoa's *caruggi* (alleys). Bare brick walls hung with LP sleeves, a retro-rock soundtrack, and cheerful staff help to create a good-time feel, while the menu includes plant-based and vegan options as well as hot dogs, steaks, and salads. **Known for:** delicious burgers; rock 'n' roll vibe; late-night opening. [$] *Average main: €12* ✉ *Via ai Quattro Canti di S. Francesco 32/r, Maddalena* ☎ *320/4293658 mobile* 🌐 *www.grooveburger.it.*

★ Hostaria al Mercato

$ | LIGURIAN | An offshoot of the highly regarded (but evenings-only) Hostaria Ducale restaurant off Piazza De Ferrari, this more casual and modern place located on the upper floor of Genoa's Mercato Orientale makes the most of the fresh produce arrayed on the stalls below. The small but select menu of meat and seafood dishes changes all the time; recent

The Art of the Pesto Pestle

You may have known Genoa primarily for its salami or its brash explorer, but the city's most direct effect on your life away from Italy may be through its cultivation of one of the world's best pasta sauces. The sublime blend of basil, extra-virgin olive oil, garlic, pine nuts, and grated pecorino and Parmigiano-Reggiano cheeses that forms *pesto alla Genovese* is one of Italy's crowning culinary achievements, a concoction that the late Italian food writer Marcella Hazan called "the most seductive of all sauces for pasta." Ligurian pesto is served usually over spaghetti, gnocchi, lasagna, or—most authentically—trenette (a flat, spaghetti-like pasta) or trofie (short, doughy pasta twists), typically mixed with boiled potatoes and green beans. Pesto is also occasionally used to flavor minestrone. Sometimes it appears in other tasty guises (like focaccia).

The small-leaf basil grown in the region's sunny seaside hills is considered by many to be the best in the world, and pesto sauce was invented primarily as a showcase for that singular flavor. The simplicity and rawness of pesto is one of its virtues, as cooking (or even heating) basil ruins its delicate flavor. In fact, pesto aficionados refuse even to subject the basil leaves to an electric blender; Genovese (and other) foodies insist that true pesto can be made only with mortar and pestle.

highlights include fried anchovies, ossobuco ravioli, and, for dessert, zabaglione with brioche and salted caramel. **Known for:** fresh local produce; competent and welcoming staff; bird's-eye view of the food market. *Average main: €19* *Mercato Orientale Genova, Via Venti Settembre 75, Brignole* *010/8973000* *www.moggenova.it/hostariaalmercato* *Closed Sun.–Wed. evening.*

I Cuochi

$$ | **LIGURIAN** | This cozy bistro-style restaurant located a few steps from Piazza de Ferrari is popular with locals and visitors alike for its refined, almost elegant menu of primarily seafood dishes, with a few pastas and meats. The decor is art nouveau with exposed brick walls and small, square tables. **Known for:** artistically presented seafood and desserts; romantic setting; contemporary Ligurian dishes. *Average main: €20* *Vico del Fieno 18/r, Maddalena* *010/2476170* *Closed Sun. No lunch weekdays.*

Il Genovese

$ | **LIGURIAN** | At this bright and friendly trattoria with a maritime theme, you can dine on some of the city's best pesto and Ligurian dishes in a casual, comfortable setting. The staff are knowledgeable about the region's specialties and the wines on the always interesting menu, and even if you don't order a pesto dish, taste some with bread before your meal. **Known for:** award-winning pesto; courteous and efficient service; good value for the price. *Average main: €14* *Via Galata 35/r, Brignole* *010/8692937* *www.ilgenovese.com* *Closed Sun.*

La Locanda in Centro

$ | **LIGURIAN** | The cordial welcome and meaty menu at this osteria a short walk from Brignole station have ensured its continuing popularity among locals. The traditional character is enhanced by its setting of chandeliers, bare brick walls, and shelves of wine bottles, but while the menu offers a range of steaks and Genovese favorites, there are seafood and a few novelty options, too, including prawns with cognac and orange and zebra goulash. **Known for:** warm atmosphere; quality meat dishes; traditional setting. *Average main: €19* *Via Domenico Fiasella 70/r, Brignole* *010/8693922* *www.lalocandaincentro.com* *Closed Sun. No lunch Sat.*

Pesciolino

$ | **SEAFOOD** | With its slightly quirky but quality cuisine, attentive staff, moderate prices, and central position near Via Roma, this place ticks all the boxes for a satisfying lunchtime or evening meal-stop. The accent is firmly on seafood, often with an unusual twist, evident in such dishes as roast squid with creamed broccoli, olives, and polenta, fish soup, and grilled octopus. **Known for:** quirky seafood dishes; attentive service; good and affordable wine list. *Average main: €19* *Best Western City Hotel, Piazzetta S. Sebastiano, Genoa* *010/5532131* *www.locandapesciolino.it* *No lunch Sun.*

Coffee and Quick Bites

★ I Canovacci

$ | **LIGURIAN** | There's a steady stream of locals of all ages at this traditional but fashionable spot on a typical vicolo of the old town. The small and reasonably priced daily menu follows the seasons, with generous portions of fish and pasta, sandwiches, vegetables, and homemade desserts. **Known for:** traditional and wholesome dishes; seasonal ingredients, some of which are also sold at the counter; warm and relaxed service. *Average main: €13* *Via dei Macelli di Soziglia 60, Genoa* *010/0985417* *Closed Sun. No dinner.*

Mentelocale Bar Bistrot

$ | **LIGURIAN** | This modern place on Via Garibaldi (Strada Nuova) is located right inside the Palazzo Rosso complex in the heart of the tourist circuit, but it benefits from a large courtyard that makes a wonderfully calm oasis away from the sightseeing throngs. The short menu includes panini, salads, burgers, and pastries, all of which can also be purchased for take-out. **Known for:** relaxing sightseeing stop; coffees, pastries, and snacks; huge courtyard. *Average main: €11* *Via Garibaldi 18, Palazzo Rosso, Genoa* *010/8697047* *mentelocale-bistrot.it/i-bistrot/palazzo-rosso.*

Hotels

★ B&B Hotel Genova

$ | **B&B/INN** | **FAMILY** | This simple and utterly charming inn is a stone's throw away from the main train station (Piazza Principe), and is handily located near most sights. **Pros:** location; charming staff; great value. **Cons:** might be too close to the train station for some; books up quickly; no on-site garage. *Rooms from: €86* *Piazza Acquaverde 1, Genoa* *010/4030343* *www.hotelbb.com* *108 rooms* *No Meals.*

★ Grand Hotel Savoia

$$ | **HOTEL** | As you enter this 1890s-vintage hotel above Piazza Acquaverde, you'll be transported from the modern city to a more glamorous era, thanks to details such as the original marble floors and lush gilt and richly colored velvet furniture in common areas. **Pros:** convenient location near Stazione Principe; rooftop restaurant and bar; comfortable rooms with luxury amenities. **Cons:** Principe station area not the best in the city; rooms on lower floors face next-door buildings; spa on the small side. *Rooms from: €219* *Via Arsenale di Terra 5, Genoa* *010/27721* *www.grandhotelsavoiagenova.it* *117 rooms* *No Meals.*

Hotel Bristol Palace

$$ | **HOTEL** | One of Europe's gracious 19th-century grand hotels, the Bristol Palace guards its reputation for courtesy, service, and elegance, offering mostly spacious, handsomely furnished, high-ceilinged guest rooms and lovely

public spaces. **Pros:** outdoor terrace is lovely in summer months; in the heart of the shopping district; beautiful period details in some rooms. **Cons:** on a busy street that can be noisy; parking is a bit expensive; some standard rooms are small. *Rooms from: €200 Via XX Settembre 35, Portoria 010/592541 www.hotelbristolpalace.it 133 rooms Free Breakfast.*

Hotel Palazzo Grillo

$$ | **HOTEL** | Formerly the Grillo family palace, this sumptuously comfortable boutique hotel integrates architectural details from the 1500s to the 1700s—like an original marble entryway and staircase, frescoed ceilings, and frieze details in some rooms—with clean-lined modern luxury. **Pros:** comfortable rooms with large bathrooms and high-end mattresses; great character and charm; terrace with cathedral views. **Cons:** can be hard to find; understated modern decor not to everyone's taste; parking is a little distant. *Rooms from: €220 Piazza delle Vigne 4, Maddalena 010/2477356 www.hotelpalazzogrillo.it Closed Jan.–mid-Feb. 25 rooms No Meals.*

Nightlife

Biblo's Pub

PUB | Just a few steps from Porta Soprana and the Childhood Home of Christopher Columbus, this cavernous basement space offers cocktails, a selection of draught beers, and live entertainment in the evenings, including cabaret, karaoke, and (on Friday and Saturday evening) local bands. There are succulent hamburgers, Ligurian pasta dishes, and other hot snacks on the menu, and the place makes a handy stop for a sightseeing pause during the day, too. *Piazza Dante 31, Molo 393/1124217 mobile Closed Mon. evening.*

Performing Arts

Teatro Carlo Felice

OPERA | The World War II–ravaged opera house in Genoa's modern center, Piazza de Ferrari, was rebuilt and reopened in 1991 to host the fine Genovese opera company; its massive tower has been the subject of much criticism. Lavish productions of old favorites and occasional world premieres are staged throughout the year. *Piazza de Ferrari, Passo Eugenio Montale 4, Portoria 010/5381433 www.operacarlofelicegenova.it.*

Shopping

Liguria is famous for fine lace, silver-and-gold filigree work, and ceramics. Also look for bargains in velvet, macramé, olive wood, and marble. Genoa is the best spot to find all these specialties. In the heart of the medieval quarter, Via Soziglia is lined with shops selling handicrafts and tempting foods. Via XX Settembre and Via Roma are famous for their exclusive shops. High-end shops line Via Luccoli. The best shopping area for trendy-but-inexpensive Italian clothing is near San Siro, on Via San Luca.

CLOTHING AND LEATHER GOODS

Pescetto

CLOTHING | Look for designer clothes, shoes, belts, and handbags, and fancy gifts like wallets and silk scarves at Pescetto. *Via Scurreria 8, Molo 010/2473433 www.pescetto.it.*

JEWELRY

Luigi Codevilla

JEWELRY & WATCHES | Established in 1830, Codevilla is known as one of the best jewelers in the city. They sell top-of-the-line watches and custom jewelry. *Via Roma 83/r, Maddalena 010/8938278 www.luigicodevilla.it.*

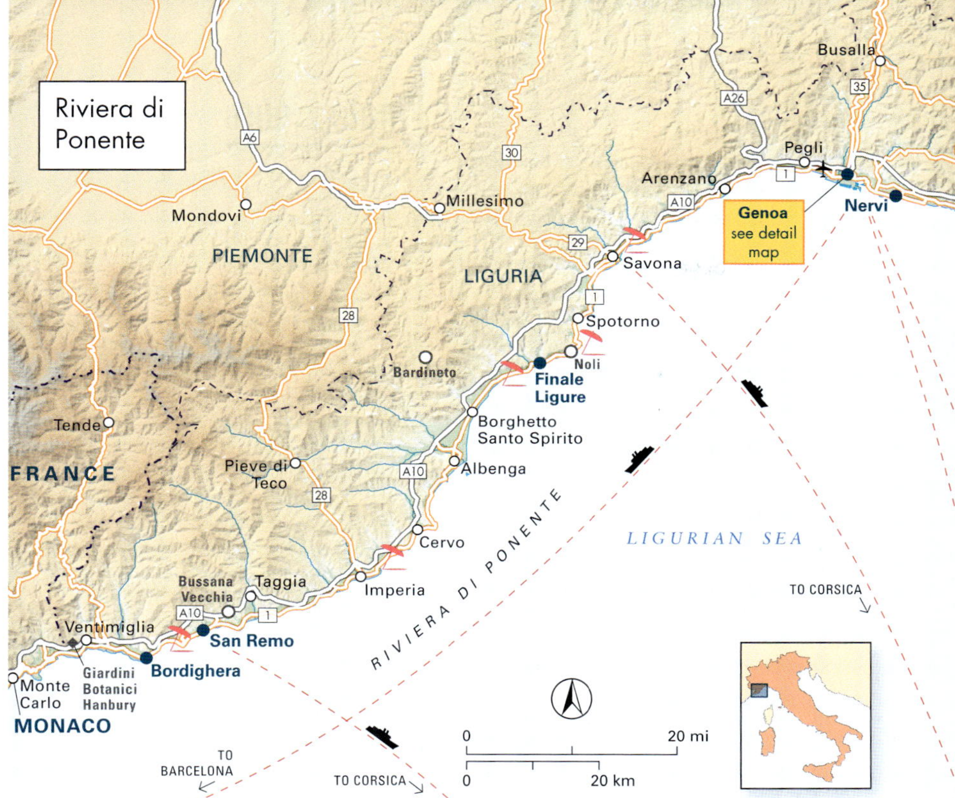

WINES

Vinoteca Sola

WINE/SPIRITS | The owner of this shop specializes in discovering the best wines from across Italy. During the fall you can taste the latest wines, and all year you can purchase your favorites and have them shipped home. You can even buy futures for vintages to come. ✉ *Piazza Colombo 13–15/r, near Stazione Brignole, Brignole* ☎ *010/561329* 🌐 *www.vinotecasola.it.*

Nervi

11 km (7 miles) east of Genoa.

The identity of this stately late-19th-century resort, famous for its 1½-km-long (1-mile-long) seaside Passeggiata Anita Garibaldi, its palm-lined roads, and its 300 acres of orderly parks and gardens, is given away only by the sign on the sleepy train station. Although Nervi is technically part of Genoa, its peace and quiet are as different from the city's hustle and bustle as its clear blue water is from the crowded port. From the centrally located train station, walk east along the seaside promenade to reach the beaches, a cliff-side restaurant, and the 2,000 varieties of rose in the public Parco Villa Grimaldi, all the while enjoying one of the most breath-taking views on the Riviera. Nervi and the road between it and Genoa are known for their nightlife in summer.

GETTING HERE

By car, exit the A12 at Genova Nervi and follow the "Centro" signs. The Nervi train station is on the main Genoa–La Spezia–Pisa line, and you can also take the commuter trains from Genova Principe and Brignole.

Sights

GAM (Galleria d'Arte Moderna di Genova)

ART MUSEUM | Beautifully situated in a 16th-century villa (with a garden and great views), this collection houses a vast amount of paintings, sculptures, and drawings from the very recent past. The artists are largely not household names, but a visit here is well worth it (as are their contemporary exhibitions). *Villa Saluzzo Serra, Via Capolungo 3, Nervi 010/5576976 www.museidigenova.it €6, €8 with Wolfsoniana Closed Mon.*

Wolfsoniana

ART MUSEUM | The private collection of Florida businessman Mitchell Wolfson Jr. has turned into an eclectic museum of art and crafts from the period 1880–1945, not only reflecting its founder's personal tastes but also the additions of later purchases and bequests. Expect to see a diversity of items that take in design, sculpture, and furniture, and there are regular exhibitions. *Via Serra Gropallo 4, Nervi 010/5575595 www.palazzoducale.genova.it/la-wolfsoniana €5, €8 with GAM Closed Mon.*

Hotels

Hotel Esperia

$ | **HOTEL** | Relaxed and friendly, this hotel set in its own grounds just steps from the sea makes a great alternative to staying in Genoa, which is easily accessible by train in just 15 minutes from the station opposite. **Pros:** stress-free alternative to staying in Genoa; close to the train station and sea; free parking. **Cons:** uninspiring restaurant; rather old-fashioned style; minimum stay in summer of 2–3 nights. *Rooms from: €129 Via Val Cismon 1, Nervi 010/321777 www.hotelesperia.it Closed Nov. 27 rooms Free Breakfast.*

Finale Ligure

72 km (44 miles) southwest of Genoa.

Lovely Finale Ligure is actually made up of three small villages—Finalmarina, Finalpia, and Finalborgo—and makes a wonderful base for exploring the Riviera di Ponente. The former two have fine sandy beaches and a mix of traditional and modern resort amenities. Finalborgo, less than 1 km (½ mile) inland, is a medieval walled village, beautifully preserved and now containing characterful shops and restaurants. The surrounding countryside is pierced by deep, narrow valleys and caves; the limestone outcroppings provide the warm pinkish stone found in many buildings in Genoa. Rare reptiles lurk among the exotic flora.

GETTING HERE AND AROUND

By car, take the Finale Ligure exit off the A10 and follow the "Centro" signs. Finale Ligure Marina is a stop on the main train line between Genoa and France.

VISITOR INFORMATION

CONTACT Finale Ligure Tourism Office. *Via San Pietro 14, Finalmarina, Finale Ligure 019/681019 www.visitfinaleligure.it.*

Sights

Noli

TOWN | Just 9 km (5½ miles) northeast of Finale Ligure, the ruins of a castle loom benevolently over Noli, a tiny medieval gem. It's hard to imagine that this charming seaside village was—like Genoa, Venice, Pisa, and Amalfi—a prosperous maritime republic in the Middle Ages. Let yourself get lost among its labyrinth of cobblestone streets filled with shops and cafés or enjoy a day in the sun on its lovely stretch of beach. If you don't have a car, get a bus for Noli at Spotorno, where local trains stop. *Noli 019/7499591.*

Restaurants

Ai Torchi

$$$ | LIGURIAN | This restored 5th-century olive oil mill is now a chic restaurant in the historical center of Finalborgo. The relatively high prices are justified by excellent seafood and meat dishes as well as the pampering setting of clean white, arched and vaulted rooms that foster an air of space and tranquility. **Known for:** traditional Ligurian cuisine with a contemporary twist; delicious fresh fish and vegetables; airy and modern dining area. *Average main: €32 Via dell'Annunziata 12, Finale Ligure 019/690531 www.aitorchi.it Closed Tues., Wed. in Oct.–May, and mid-Jan.–mid-Feb. No lunch.*

Hotels

★ Ca de' Tobia

$$ | B&B/INN | This lovely little guesthouse on the seafront promenade of Noli is stylishly done with wood floors, uncluttered white walls with splashes of bright colors, and modern decor. **Pros:** modern furniture and bathrooms; easy beach access; great breakfast and aperitivo. **Cons:** street noise; parking can be a challenge in high season; not for families. *Rooms from: €205 Via Aurelia 35, Noli 019/7485845 www.cadetobia.it 6 rooms Free Breakfast.*

Hotel Punta Est

$$ | HOTEL | FAMILY | The grand former home of a musician and composer, this 18th-century villa perched on a fragrant hillside above white-sand beaches has since had a wing added, creating a wonderful retreat from the crowds at the water's edge. **Pros:** dining on the terrace with views; close to the beach; relaxing pool and gardens. **Cons:** some rooms are a bit outdated; a busy road must be crossed to walk to or from the sea; some noisy rooms because of their proximity to the terrace. *Rooms from: €260 Via Aurelia 1, Finale Ligure 019/600611 www.puntaest.com Closed mid-Oct.–mid-May 36 rooms Free Breakfast.*

San Remo

146 km (90 miles) southwest of Genoa.

Once the crown jewel of the Riviera di Ponente, San Remo may have lost some of its luster, but is still the area's largest resort, and preserves an impressive number of polished hotels, exotic gardens, and seaside promenades. Even without these remnants of its glamorous past from the late 19th century to World War II, a VIP crowd continues to be drawn to the resort's famous casino, annual music festival, and romantic setting.

While San Remo suffers from the same epidemic of overbuilding that has changed so much of the Ponente for the worse, it remains a lively town, even in the off-season, and is the center of northern Italy's flower-growing industry. The surrounding hills, now blanketed with plastic to form immense greenhouses, produce more than 20,000 tons of carnations, roses, mimosa flowers, and innumerable other kinds of cut flowers each year, and Italy's most important wholesale flower market, the Mercato dei Fiori, is held in a market hall between Piazza Colombo and Corso Garibaldi (though it's open to dealers only).

GETTING HERE AND AROUND

By car, take the San Remo exit off the A10 and follow the "Centro" signs. San Remo is on the main train line between Genoa and France.

VISITOR INFORMATION

CONTACT San Remo Tourism Office. *Corso Garibaldi 1, San Remo 0184/580500 www.lamialiguria.it/localita/sanremo.*

Sights

Bussana Vecchia

TOWN | In the hills where flowers are cultivated for export, this self-consciously picturesque former ghost town is a flourishing artists' colony. The town was largely destroyed by an earthquake in 1877, when the inhabitants packed up and left en masse. For almost a century the houses, church, and crumbling bell tower were empty shells, overgrown by weeds and wildflowers. Since the 1960s, painters, sculptors, artisans, and bric-a-brac dealers have restored the dwellings as houses and studios. You need a car to visit the town. ✉ *8 km (5 miles) east of San Remo, San Remo* 🌐 *www.bussanavecchia.it.*

La Pigna (*The Pinecone*)

NEIGHBORHOOD | San Remo's steep and labyrinthine old town climbs upward to Piazza Castello, which offers a splendid view of the town and sea below. Some lovely old palazzi and squares have been restored, and the neighborhood gives you a sense of what it was like to live in San Remo centuries ago. ✉ *Old Town, San Remo.*

San Remo Casinò

CASINO | In addition to gaming, this lovely 1905 Art Nouveau landmark offers two restaurants, bars, and a theater that hosts concerts. Admission is free, but if you want to try your luck at the gaming tables, bets begin at around €10, depending on the time of day or night. Under-18s are not admitted to any of the gaming rooms. **TIP→ In the upstairs rooms, where the traditional gaming tables are located, dress is elegant ("smart casual")—shorts and sandals are not permitted but there is no jacket-and-tie requirement for men.** ✉ *Corso degli Inglesi 18, San Remo* ☎ *0184/5951* 🌐 *www.casinosanremo.it* 🎫 *Free.*

Restaurants

Antica Trattoria Piccolo Mondo

$ | LIGURIAN | Vintage wooden furniture and peach-color walls evoke the homey charm of this small family-run trattoria in a pedestrians-only alley. A faithful clientele keeps the kitchen busy, so get here early to grab a table and order Ligurian specialties—fresh pasta, pesto, and vegetable and seafood dishes. **Known for:** warm and friendly service; reasonable prices; polpo e patate (stewed octopus with potatoes). $ *Average main: €17* ✉ *Via Piave 7, San Remo* ☎ *0184/509012* ⏲ *No dinner Mon. Closed Sun. and 2 wks in June and July.*

Hotels

Hotel Paradiso

$$ | HOTEL | There's an air of seclusion and a respite from hectic San Remo in these bright, well-equipped rooms—some with balconies and sea views—that face a quiet, palm-fringed garden and pool. **Pros:** nice pool; close to the beach; secluded yet near town. **Cons:** steep walk up some stairs and a hill from seafront; paid parking with restricted space; some rooms are small and dated. $ *Rooms from: €190* ✉ *Via Roccasterone 12, San Remo* ☎ *0184/571211* 🌐 *www.paradisohotel.it* ⏲ *Closed mid-Oct.–late Dec.* 🛏 *41 rooms* 🍴 *Free Breakfast.*

Royal Hotel Sanremo

$$$ | HOTEL | With its heated seawater swimming pool in a tropical garden and guest rooms (some with sea views) with an attention to traditional design and modern amenities, this is considered one of Liguria's most luxurious resorts. **Pros:** the glamour of yesteryear with high-end amenities; choice of restaurants; relaxing pool open April through October. **Cons:** expensive on-site meals and beverages; spa facilities often booked up; pool area can be crowded in high season. $ *Rooms from: €420* ✉ *Corso Imperatrice 80, San Remo* ☎ *0184/5391* 🌐 *www.*

Did You Know?

The gorgeous Hanbury Botanical Gardens were completely devastated in World War II. In 1960, Lady Hanbury sold the property to the State of Italy and in 1987, the University of Genoa began restoration. Today it's considered one of the most beautiful gardens in Italy.

royalhotelsanremo.com ⏲ *Closed early Nov.–early Feb.* *126 rooms* *Free Breakfast.*

Bordighera

12 km (7 miles) southwest of San Remo, 155 km (96 miles) southwest of Genoa.

Bordighera is an attractive seaside resort with panoramas (on a clear day) from Genoa to Monte Carlo. A large English colony settled here in the second half of the 19th century and is still very much in evidence today; you regularly find people drinking afternoon tea in the cafés, and streets are named after Queen Victoria and Shakespeare. Claude Monet, visiting in 1884, declared himself to be "bewitched" by the place.

GETTING HERE AND AROUND

By car, take the Bordighera exit off the A10 and follow the signs for "Centro," about a 10-minute drive. Bordighera is on the main railway line between Genoa and France.

VISITOR INFORMATION

CONTACT Bordighera Tourism Office. ✉ *Via Vittorio Emanuele 172, Bordighera* ☎ *0184/262882* 🌐 *www.visitbordighera.it.*

Sights

★ Giardini Botanici Hanbury

GARDEN | Mortola Inferiore is the site of the world-famous Hanbury Botanical Gardens, one of the largest and most beautiful in Italy. Planned and planted in 1867 by a wealthy English merchant, Sir Thomas Hanbury, and his botanist brother, Daniel, the terraced gardens contain species from five continents, including many palms and succulents. ✉ *Corso Montecarlo 43, Località Mortola Inferiore, Ventimiglia* ☎ *0184/229507* 🌐 *www.giardinihanbury.com* *€10* ⏲ *Closed Mon. Nov.–Feb.*

Restaurants

★ Magiargè

$$ | LIGURIAN | A mix of great charm and great food make this small, bustling osteria in the historic center an absolute dining delight. Dishes are Ligurian with a focus on local fish, but there are some surprises, for example Catalan lobster with mayonnaise and ginger. **Known for:** cozy dining room with curved archways; refined but relaxed ambience; multi-course set menus of Ligurian specialties. $ *Average main: €21* ✉ *Via Dritta 2, Bordighera* ☎ *0184/262946* 🌐 *www.facebook.com/magiargebordighera* ⏲ *Closed Mon. and Tues.*

Hotels

★ Hotel Villa Elisa

$$ | HOTEL | On a street filled with beautiful old villas, this Victorian-era former private residence has a relaxed and friendly atmosphere, beautiful gardens, a spa, and well-appointed rooms (some with balconies). **Pros:** gregarious staff; old-world charm; an amazing breakfast buffet. **Cons:** somewhat removed from the center of things; the spa costs extra for more than 1 hour; books up quickly. $ *Rooms from: €182* ✉ *Via Romana 70, Bordighera* ☎ *0184/261313* 🌐 *www.villaelisa.com* ⏲ *Closed Nov.–mid-Mar.* *30 rooms* *Free Breakfast.*

Chapter 10

EMILIA-ROMAGNA

Updated by Nick Bruno

WELCOME TO EMILIA-ROMAGNA

TOP REASONS TO GO

★ **The signature food of Emilia:** This region's food—prosciutto crudo, Parmesan cheese, balsamic vinegar, and above all, pasta—makes the trip to Italy worthwhile.

★ **Mosaics that take your breath away:** The intricate tiles in Ravenna's Mausoleo di Galla Placidia, in brilliantly well-preserved colors, depict vivid portraits and pastoral scenes.

★ **Arguably Europe's oldest wine bar:** Nicolaus Copernicus tippled here while studying at Ferrara's university in the early 1500s—Enoteca al Brindisi, in the historic center, has been pouring wine since 1435.

★ **The nightlife of Bologna:** This red-roof city has had a lively student culture since the university—Europe's oldest—was founded in the late 11th century.

★ **The medieval castles of San Marino:** Its three castles dramatically perch on a rock more than 3,000 feet above the flat landscape of Romagna.

1 Piacenza. With its majestic piazzas, fine cathedral, and palatial museum, this town at Emilia's northwestern end makes a fitting introduction to the region.

2 Busseto. Opera aficionados visit to pay homage to one of Italy's greatest composers, Giuseppe Verdi.

3 Parma. Internationally known for its foodstuffs, Parma also boasts a battery of sights.

4 Modena. Endowed with a compact, beautifully preserved city center and a magnificent cathedral, this town repays a leisurely wander.

5 Bologna. Emilia's principal cultural and intellectual center is famed for its arcaded sidewalks, medieval towers, and sublime restaurants.

6 Ferrara. This prosperous, tidy town north of Bologna has a rich medieval past and distinctive cuisine.

7 Imola. There is plenty more to this place than its famous Formula One racetrack, including an attractive city center.

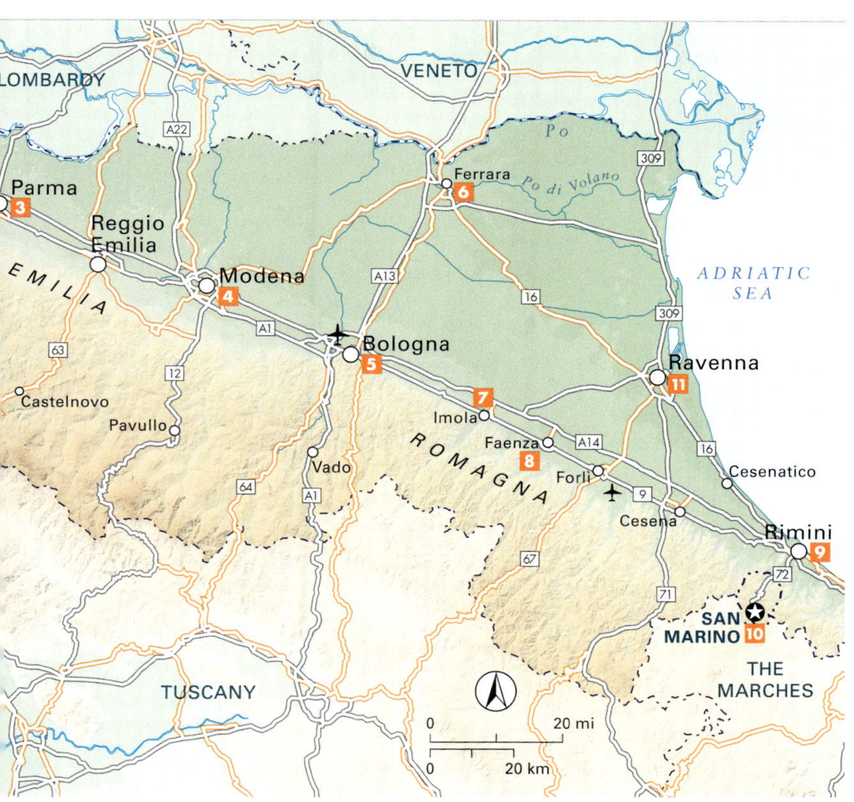

8 Faenza. This handsome settlement has bequeathed its name to the majolica ceramics, or *faience*, for which it is best known.

9 Rimini. A beach resort on the Adriatic coast, Rimini has noteworthy Roman and Renaissance monuments.

10 San Marino. Officially an independent republic, this quirky enclave is a tourist hot spot.

11 Ravenna. The main attractions of this well-preserved Romagna city are its mosaics—glittering treasures left from Byzantine rule.

EATING AND DRINKING WELL IN EMILIA-ROMAGNA

Homemade tortellini

Italians rarely agree about anything, but many concede that some of the country's finest foods originated in Emilia-Romagna. Tortellini, fettuccine, Parmesan cheese, prosciutto crudo, and balsamic vinegar are just a few of the Italian delicacies born here.

One of the beauties of Emilia-Romagna is that its exceptional food can be had without breaking the bank. Many trattorias serve up classic dishes, mastered over the centuries, at reasonable prices. Cutting-edge restaurants and wine bars are often more expensive; their inventive menus are full of *fantasia*—reinterpretations of the classics. For the budget-conscious, Bologna, a university town, has great places for cheap eats.

Between meals, you can sustain yourself with the region's famous sandwich, the *piadina*. It's made with pitalike thin bread, usually filled with prosciutto or mortadella, cheese, and vegetables, then put under the grill and served hot, with the cheese oozing at the sides. These addictive sandwiches can be savored at sit-down places or ordered to go.

THE REAL RAGÙ

Emilia-Romagna's signature dish is *tagliatelle al ragù* (flat noodles with meat sauce), which inspired the "spaghetti Bolognese" eaten outside Italy. This *primo* (first course) is on every menu, and no two versions are the same. The sauce starts in a sauté pan with finely diced carrots, onions, and celery. Purists add nothing but minced beef, but some use *guanciale* (pork cheek), sausage, veal, or chicken. Broth is added, and sometimes wine, milk, or cream.

PORK PRODUCTS

It's not just mortadella and cured pork products like prosciutto crudo and *culatello* that Emilia-Romagnans go crazy for—they're wild about the whole hog. You'll frequently find *cotechino* and *zampone*, both *secondi* (second courses), on menus. Cotechino is a savory, thick, fresh sausage served with lentils on New Year's Eve (the combination is said to augur well for the new year) and with mashed potatoes year-round. Zampone, a stuffed pig's foot, is redolent of garlic and deliciously fatty.

BOLLITO MISTO

The name means "mixed boil," and they do it exceptionally well in this part of Italy. According to Emilia-Romagnans, *bollito misto* was invented here, although other Italians—especially those from Milan, Verona, and Piedmont—might dispute this claim. Chicken, beef, tongue, and zampone are tossed into a stockpot and boiled; they're then removed from the broth and served with a fragrant *salsa verde* (green sauce), made with parsley and spiced with anchovies, garlic, and capers. This simple yet rich dish is usually served with mashed potatoes on the side, and savvy diners will mix some of the piquant salsa verde into the potatoes as well.

Cotechino sausage

Pumpkin-stuffed tortelli

STUFFED PASTA

Among the many Emilian variations on stuffed pasta, tortellini are the smallest. *Tortelli* and *cappellacci* are larger pasta "pillows," about the size of a brussels sprout, but with the same basic form as tortellini. They're often filled with pumpkin or spinach and cheese. *Tortelloni* are, in theory, even bigger, although their size varies. Stuffed pastas are generally served simply, with melted butter, sage, and Parmigiano-Reggiano cheese or, in the case of tortellini, *in brodo* (in beef, chicken, or capon broth or some combination thereof), which brings out the subtle richness of the filling.

WINES

Emilia-Romagna's wines accompany the region's fine food rather than vying with it for accolades. The best-known is *Lambrusco,* a sparkling red produced on the Po Plain that has some admirers and many detractors. It's praised for its tartness and condemned for the same; it does, however, pair brilliantly with the local fare. The region's best wines include Sangiovese di Romagna (somewhat similar to Chianti), from the Romagnan hills, and Barbera from the Colli Piacentini and Apennine foothills. Castelluccio, Bonzara, Zerbina, Leone Conti, and Tre Monti are among the region's top producers.

Gourmets the world over claim that Emilia-Romagna's greatest contribution to humankind has been gastronomic. Birthplace of fettuccine, tortellini, lasagna, prosciutto, balsamic vinegar, and Parmigiano-Reggiano cheese, the region has a spectacular culinary tradition.

But there are many reasons to come here aside from the desire to be well fed: Parma's Correggio paintings, Giuseppe Verdi's villa at Sant'Agata, the medieval splendor of Bologna's palaces, Ferrara's medieval alleys, and, perhaps foremost, the Byzantine beauty of mosaic-rich Ravenna—glittering as brightly today as it did 1,500 years ago.

As you travel through Emilia, the western half of the region, you'll encounter the sprawling plants of Italy's industrial food giants, like Barilla and Fini, standing side by side with the fading villas and farmhouses. Bologna, the principal city of Emilia, is a busy cultural and, increasingly, business center, less visited but in many ways just as engaging as the country's more famous tourist destinations.

The historic border between Emilia to the west and Romagna to the east lies near the fortified town of Dozza. Emilia is flat, but just east of the Romagnan border the landscape gets hillier and more sparsely settled. Finally, it flattens again into the low-lying marshland of the Po Delta, which meets the Adriatic Sea. Each fall, in both Romagna and Emilia, the trademark fog rolls in off the Adriatic to hang over the flatlands in winter, coloring the region with a spooky, gray glow.

MAJOR REGIONS

Emilia. The westernmost part of the region, Emilia, is richly redolent of the history and culture of northern Italy. The Via Emilia, an ancient Roman road, runs through Emilia's heart in a straight shot from medieval Piacenza, southeast of Milan, through Bologna and ultimately to Romagna and the Adriatic Coast. On the way you encounter many of Italy's cultural riches—notably the culinary and artistic treasures of Parma and Modena. Northeast of Bologna, explore the mist-shrouded tangle of streets in Ferrara's charismatic old town.

Romagna. The mostly rural Romagna has rolling hills dotted with handsome farmhouses, giving way at its eastern end to the lively resorts and sandy beaches of the Adriatic coast. Imola, most famed for its Formula One racetrack, is traditionally regarded as the western gateway to Romagna. From here it's a short hop to Faenza, home to dozens of shops selling its well-known ceramics. Most visitors to Romagna make a beeline for Ravenna, the site of shimmering Byzantine mosaics, and the ministate of San Marino, to the south, is a curiosity worth a brief detour for its castles.

Planning

Getting Here and Around

CAR

Driving is the best way to get around Emilia-Romagna. Roads are wide, flat, and well marked; distances are short; and beautiful farmhouses and small villages offer undemanding detours.

A car is particularly useful for visiting the spa towns of Romagna, which aren't well connected by train. Historic centers are off-limits to cars, but they're also quite walkable, so you may just want to park your car and get around on foot once you arrive.

Entering Emilia-Romagna by car is as easy as it gets. Coming in from the northwest on the Autostrada del Sole (A1), you'll first hit Piacenza, a mere 45-minute drive southeast of Milan. On the other side of the region, Venice is about an hour from Ferrara by car on the A13.

Bologna is on the autostrada, so driving between cities is a breeze, though take special care if you're coming from Florence, as the road is winding and the drivers speed. The Via Emilia (SS9), one of the oldest roads in the world, runs through the heart of the region. Although less scenic, the A1 autostrada, which runs parallel to the Via Emilia from Bologna, can get you where you're going about twice as fast. From Bologna, the A13 runs north to Ferrara, and the A14 takes you east to Ravenna. Much of the historic center of Bologna is closed off to cars daily from 7 am to 8 pm—look out for ZTL (Zona Traffico Limitato) road signs.

TRAIN

When it comes to public transportation in the region, trains are better than buses—they're fairly efficient and quite frequent, and most stations aren't too far from the center of town. The railroad track follows the Via Emilia (SS9). In Emilia it generally takes 30–60 minutes to get from one major city to the next. To reach Ferrara or Ravenna, you typically have to change to a local train at Bologna. Ferrara is a half hour north of Bologna on the train, and Ravenna is just over an hour east.

Bologna is an important rail hub for northern Italy and has frequent, fast service to Milan, Florence, Rome, and Venice. The routes from Bologna to the south usually go through Florence, about 40 minutes away on a high-speed train. The high-speed Frecciarossa train service cuts the time from Milan to Bologna to only one hour. On the northeastern edge of the region, Venice is 1½ hours east of Ferrara by train. Check the website of the state railway, the **Trenitalia** (aka Ferrovie dello Stato or FS 🌐 *www.trenitalia.com*), for information, or stop in a travel agency, as many sell train tickets (without a markup) and agents often speak English. **Italo** (🌐 *www.italotreno.it/en*), a privately owned high-speed train line, competes with the state-sponsored service. Italo's Milan–Rome line makes stops in Reggio Emilia, Bologna, and Florence; the Venice–Naples line stops in Padua, Bologna, Florence, and Rome. Some of these also stop at secondary stations.

Hotels

Emilia-Romagna has a reputation for demonstrating a level of efficiency uncommon in most of Italy. Even the smallest hotels are usually well run, with high standards of quality and service. Bologna is very much a businessperson's city, and many hotels here cater to the business traveler, but there are smaller, more intimate hotels as well. It's smart to book in advance—the region hosts many fairs and conventions that can fill up hotels even during low season.

⇨ Hotel and restaurant reviews have been shortened. For full information, visit Fodors.com. Prices in the hotel reviews are the lowest cost of a standard double room in high season. Prices in the dining reviews are the average cost of a main course at dinner, or, if dinner is not served, at lunch.

What It Costs in Euros

	$	$$	$$$	$$$$
RESTAURANTS	under €20	€20–€30	€31–€40	over €40
HOTELS	under €175	€175–€400	€401–€600	over €600

Planning Your Time

Plan on spending at least two days in Bologna, the region's cultural and historical capital. You shouldn't miss Parma, with its stunning food and graceful public spaces. Also plan on visiting Ferrara, a misty, mysterious medieval city. If you have time, go to Ravenna for its memorable Byzantine mosaics and Modena for its harmonious architecture and famous balsamic vinegar.

If you have only a few days in the region, it's virtually impossible to do all five of those cities justice. If you're a dedicated gourmand (or *buona forchetta,* as Italians say), move from Bologna west along the Via Emilia (SS9) to Modena and Parma. If you're more interested in architecture, art, and history, choose the eastern route, heading north on the A13 to Ferrara and then southeast on the SS16 to Ravenna.

If you have more time, you won't have to make such tough choices. You can start in neighboring Lombardy and Milan, go east, and finish on the Adriatic—or vice versa.

Restaurants

Dining options range from mom-and-pop-style informal trattorias to three-star Michelin restaurants. Food in Emilia-Romagna is not for the faint of heart (or those on diets): it is rich, creamy, and cheesy. Local wines pair remarkably well with this sumptuous fare. You may want to rethink Lambrusco, as it marries well with just about everything on the menu.

When to Go

Extending along the valley of the River Po, Emilia-Romagna's predominantly flat and featureless landscape is subject to hot summers and cold, foggy winters. It's humid year-round, so rain is always a possibility and fairly common during the winter months. Tourism is mainly cultural in the region and thus isn't particularly subject to seasonal variations, though you can expect to see some resorts along the Romagna coast close in winter, particularly around Rimini.

Piacenza

67 km (42 miles) southeast of Milan, 150 km (93 miles) northwest of Bologna.

Piacenza has always been associated with industry and commerce. Its position on the Po River has made it an important inland port since the Etruscans, and then the Romans, had thriving settlements here. As you approach the city today, you could be forgiven for thinking that it holds little of interest. Piacenza is surrounded by ugly industrial suburbs (with particularly unlovely concrete factories and a power station), but if you forge ahead you'll discover a well-preserved medieval center and an unusually clean city. Its prosperity is evident in the great shopping along Corso Vittorio Emanuele II. Among its cultural highlights is the annual jazz festival each spring.

Emilia-Romagna Through the Ages

Ancient History. Emilia-Romagna owes its beginnings to a road. In 187 BC the Romans built the Via Aemilia—a long road running northwest from the Adriatic port of Rimini to the central garrison town of Piacenza—and it was along this central spine that the primary towns of the region developed.

Despite the unifying factor of what came to be known as the Via Emilia, this section of Italy has had a fragmented history. Its eastern part, roughly the area from Faenza to the coast (known as Romagna), looked first to the Byzantine east and then to Rome for art, political power, and, some say, national character. The western part, from Bologna to Piacenza (Emilia), looked more to the north with its practice of self-government and dissent.

Bologna was founded by the Etruscans and eventually came under the influence of the Roman Empire. The Romans established a garrison here, renaming the old Etruscan settlement Bononia. It was after the fall of Rome that the region began its fragmentation. Romagna, centered in Ravenna, was ruled from Constantinople. Ravenna eventually became the capital of the empire in the west in the 5th century, passing to papal control in the 8th century. Even today, the city is filled with reminders of two centuries of Byzantine rule.

Family Ties. The other cities of the region, from the Middle Ages on, became the fiefdoms of important noble families—the Este in Ferrara and Modena, the Pallavicini in Piacenza, and the Bentivoglio in Bologna. Today all these cities bear the marks of their noble patrons. When in the 16th century the papacy managed to exert its power over the entire area, some of these cities were divided among the papal families—hence the stamp of the Farnese family on Parma and Piacenza.

A Leftward Tilt. Emilia-Romagna (and Bologna, in particular) has an established and hearty tradition of rebellion and dissent. The Italian socialist movement was born in this region, as was Benito Mussolini. In keeping with the political climate of his home region, he was a firebrand socialist during the early part of his career. Despite having Mussolini as a native son, Emilia-Romagna didn't take to Fascism: it was here that the anti-Fascist resistance was born, and during World War II the region suffered terribly at the hands of the Fascists and the Nazis.

GETTING HERE AND AROUND

Regional trains run often from Milan to Piacenza and take a little less than an hour, and Frecciarossa trains make it from Milan to Bologna in an hour. Services from Bologna to Piacenza take about 1½ hours and closer to 2 hours on some regional trains. Both have frequent service. Piacenza is easily accessible by car via the A1, either from Milan or from Bologna. If you're coming from Milan, take the Piacenza Nord exit; from Bologna, the Piacenza Est exit.

VISITOR INFORMATION

CONTACT Piacenza Tourism Office. ✉ *Piazza Cavalli 7, Piacenza* ☎ *0523/492001* 🌐 *visitpiacenza.it.*

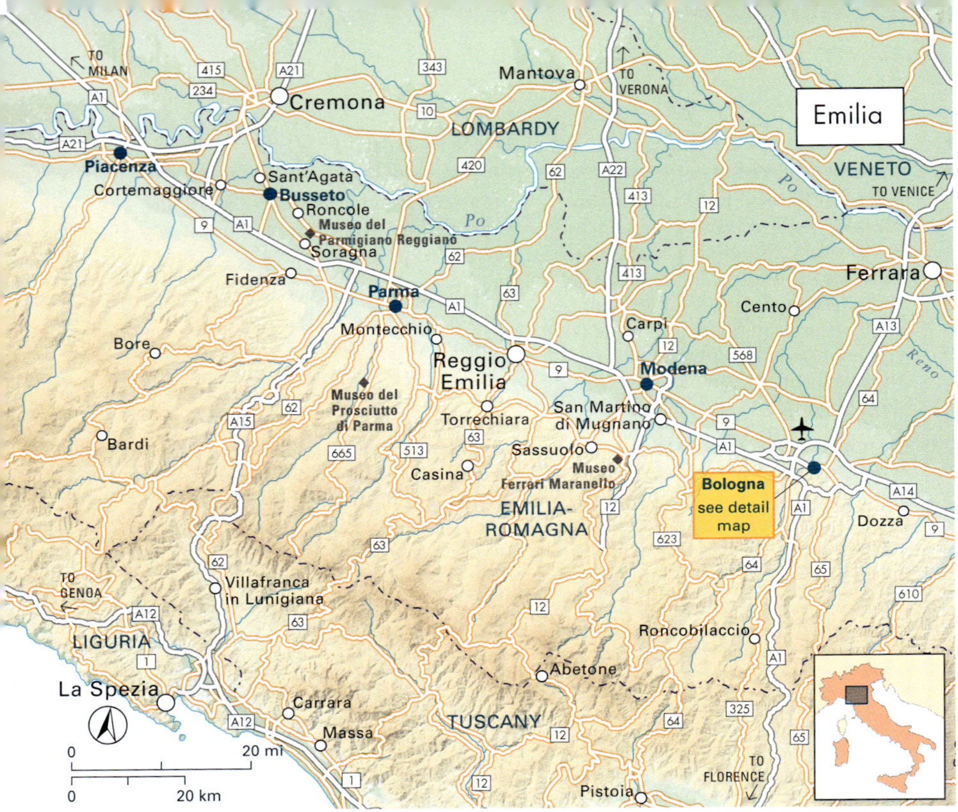

Sights

Cattedrale di Santa Maria Assunta e Santa Giustina

CHURCH | Attached like a sinister balcony to the bell tower of Piacenza's 12th-century Duomo is a *gabbia* (iron cage), where miscreants were incarcerated naked and subjected to the scorn of the crowd in the marketplace below. Inside the cathedral, less evocative but equally impressive medieval stonework decorates the pillars and the crypt, and there are extravagant frescoes in the dome of the cupola begun by Morazzone (1573–1626). Guercino (1591–1666) completed them upon Morazzone's death. If you're feeling strong, you can climb the spiral staircase to the cupola for a closer view. Nearby at Via Prevostura 7, Kronos Museum displays the cathedral's collection of religious artworks, reliquaries, textiles and medieval manuscripts. **TIP→ Take Bus No. 4/17 or walk 20 minutes to the Basilica di Santa Maria di Campagna for more captivating cupola frescos by Pordenone (combined cupola ticket €15), plus panoramic city views.** ✉ *Piazza Duomo 33, Piacenza* ☎ *0523/044542* 🌐 *www.mirabiliprospettive.it* 🎫 *Free; 1 cupola €10; 2 cupole, including Pordenone's €15; Kronos Museum €6; combined ticket €12* ⏲ *Cupola and Kronos closed Mon.*

Galleria d'Arte Moderna Ricci Oddi

ART GALLERY | Housed in a 1930s palazzo and displaying over 400 mainly Italian modern works amassed largely by collector Giuseppe Ricci Oddi (1868–1936), this gallery hit worldwide headlines for the mysterious and labyrinthine saga surrounding centerpiece painting *Portrait of a Lady* by Gustav Klimt (1862–1918). After viewing the vivacious expressionistic canvas and learning about the theft, forgery and reappearance of the Austrian lady 23 years after her theft in 1997, you can join those who like to speculate over the curious, clandestine turn of events. Not be overshadowed, the luminous paintings and sculptures largely spans Romanticism through Expressionism, with works by De Nittis, Grosso, Pellizza da Volpedo, Larsson and Boccioni. ✉ *Via San Siro 13, Piacenza* ☎ *0523/320742* 🌐 *riccioddi.it* 🎫 *€9* 🕑 *Closed Mon.*

Musei di Palazzo Farnese
ART MUSEUM | The eclectic city-owned museum of Piacenzan art and antiquities is housed in the vast Palazzo Farnese, a monumental palace began in 1558, but never completed as planned. The highlight of the museum's collection is the tiny 2nd-century-BC Etruscan Fegato di Piacenza, a bronze tablet shaped like a *fegato* (liver), marked with the symbols of the gods of good and ill fortune. The collection also contains Botticelli's beautiful *Madonna and Child with St. John the Baptist*. The museum's eclectic collections include not only artworks and sculpture but also archaeological, armory, carriages, glass and ceramics, and Risorgimento artifacts. ✉ *Piazza Cittadella 29, Piacenza* ☎ *0523/492658* 🌐 *www.palazzofarnese.piacenza.it* 🎫 *€10; €3 for one section* 🕑 *Closed Mon.*

Piazza dei Cavalli (*Square of the Horses*)
PLAZA/SQUARE | The hub of the city is the Piazza dei Cavalli, with the flamboyant equestrian statues from which the piazza takes its name. These are depictions of Ranuccio Farnese (1569–1622) and, on the left, his father, Alessandro (1545–92). The latter was a beloved ruler, enlightened and fair; Ranuccio, his successor, less so. Both statues are the work of Francesco Mochi, a master Baroque sculptor. Dominating the square is the massive 13th-century Palazzo Pubblico, also known as Il Gotico. This two-tone, marble-and-brick, turreted and crenellated building was the seat of town government before Piacenza fell under the iron fists of the ruling Pallavicini and Farnese families. ✉ *Piazza dei Cavalli, Piacenza.*

Busseto

30 km (19 miles) southeast of Piacenza, 25 km (16 miles) south of Cremona in Lombardy.

Sleepy Busseto's greatest claim to fame is local son Giuseppe Verdi (1813–1901), who was born in nearby Le Roncole, and his "Casa Natale" (birthplace) is now a museum and shrine to the maestro. Bussetto sits in the middle of cultivated countryside, and was known since Carolingian times as Buxetum. In 1533 it attracted the attention of Hapsburg emperor Charles V, who became lord of the city. Now it attracts opera lovers who wish to walk in the grand maestro's footsteps—by hearing one of his works at the local theater or exploring the places he frequented. At the time of this writing, Verdi's former residences, villas Verdi and Pallavicino, remained closed to the public due to legal issues.

GETTING HERE AND AROUND

If you're coming by car from Parma, drive along the A1/E35 and follow signs for the A15 in the direction of Milan/La Spezia. Choose the exit in the direction of Fidenza/Salsomaggiore Terme, following signs to the SP12, which connects to the SS9W. At Fidenza, take the SS588 heading north, which will take you into Busseto. If you're without a car, you'll have to take a bus from Piacenza or Parma, as there's no train service.

VISITOR INFORMATION

CONTACT Busseto Tourism Office. ✉ *Piazza G. Verdi 10, Busseto* ☎ *0524/92487* 🌐 *www.bussetolive.com.*

Sights

Casa Natale di Giuseppe Verdi

HISTORY MUSEUM | An engaging audio-guide itinerary for each of the eight modestly furnished rooms of Verdi's birthplace evokes the atmosphere of his family life here, shared with his seamstress mother and *osteria* (tavern)-running father. Despite Verdi's worldwide success and fame he never forgot his origins. In 1863 he wrote: "Sono stato, sono e sarò sempre un paesano delle Roncole: "I was, am, and always will be a Roncole peasant." ✉ *Via della Processione 1, Roncole Verdi, Busseto* ☎ *0524/801331* 🌐 *www.bussetolive.com/it/poi/casa-natale-giuseppe-verdi* 🎫 *€5* 🕐 *Closed Mon.*

Teatro Giuseppe Verdi

HISTORIC SIGHT | In the center of Busseto is the lovely Teatro Verdi, dedicated, as you might expect, to the works of the hamlet's famous son. Guided tours (in both English and Italian) of the well-preserved, ornate, 19th-century-style theater are offered every half hour. Check with the Busseto tourist office for the performance schedule. ✉ *Piazza G. Verdi 10, Busseto* ☎ *0524/92487* 🌐 *www.bussetolive.com* 🎫 *Tours €5* 🕐 *Closed Mon.*

Parma

40 km (25 miles) southeast of Busseto, 97 km (60 miles) northwest of Bologna.

Parma stands on the banks of a tributary of the Po River. Despite damage during World War II, much of the stately historic center seems untouched by modern times. This is a prosperous city, and it shows in its well-dressed residents, clean streets, and immaculate piazzas.

Bursting with gustatory delights, Parma draws crowds for its sublime cured pork product, *prosciutto crudo di Parma* (known locally simply as "prosciutto crudo"). The pale-yellow Parmigiano-Reggiano cheese produced here and in nearby Reggio Emilia is the original—and best—of a class known around the world as Parmesan.

GETTING HERE AND AROUND

Train service, via Frecciarossa, Intercity, and Regionale trains, runs frequently from Milan and Bologna. It takes slightly less than an hour on fast but pricier Frecciarossa trains from both cities. By car, Parma is just off the A1 autostrada, halfway between Bologna and Piacenza.

VISITOR INFORMATION

CONTACT Parma Welcome Tourism Office. ✉ *Strada Garibaldi, 18, Parma* ☎ *0521/218889* 🌐 *www.parmawelcome.it.*

Sights

Battistero di San Giovanni Battista
(Baptistery)

CHURCH | Baptisms still happen in this octagonal baptistery designed by Benedetto Antelami between 1196 and 1216. It has a simple Pink Verona–marble Romanesque exterior and an uplifting Gothic interior. The doors are richly decorated with figures, animals, and flowers, and inside, the building has stucco figures (probably carved by Antelami) showing the months and seasons, and a vibrantly decorated cupola. Early-14th-century frescoes depicting scenes from the life of Christ grace the walls. ✉ *Piazza del Duomo, Parma* ☎ *0521/208699* 🌐 *www.piazzaduomoparma.com* 🎫 *€12 combined with Museo Diocesano.*

★ Camera di San Paolo e Cella di Santa Caterina

HISTORIC SIGHT | In the former Benedictine covent of San Polo lies a reception room for the erudite abbess Giovanna da Piacenza, who hired Correggio in 1519 to provide its bucolic, cherub-dancing decoration: mythological scenes are depicted in glorious frescoes of the *Triumphs of the Goddess Diana*, the *Three Graces*, and the *Three Fates*. A small room contains a copy of *The Last Supper,* while La Cella di Santa Caterina mixes frescoes of saintly scenes with fantastical figures, all by Araldi (1460–1528). ✉ *Via Melloni 3, off Strada Garibaldi, near Piazza Pilotta, Parma* ☎ *0521/287195* 🌐 *parmawelcome.it/scheda/camera-di-san-paolo-e-cella-di-santa-caterina* 🎫 *€8* 🕒 *Closed Tues. and Wed.*

Cattedrale di Santa Maria Assunta

CHURCH | The magnificent 12th-century duomo has two vigilant stone lions standing guard beside the main door; inside is some notable art in styles from medieval to Mannerist. The arch of the entrance is decorated with a delicate frieze of figures representing the months of the year, a motif repeated inside the baptistery. Some of the church's original artwork still survives, notably the simple yet evocative *Descent from the Cross,* a carving in the right transept by Benedetto Antelami (active 1178–1230), whose masterwork is this cathedral's baptistery. It's an odd juxtaposition to turn from his austere work to the exuberant fresco in the dome, the *Assumption of the Virgin* by Antonio Allegri, better known to us as Correggio (1494–1534). The fresco was not well received when it was unveiled in 1530. "A mess of frogs' legs," the bishop of Parma is said to have called it. Today Correggio is acclaimed as one of the leading masters of Mannerist painting. **■ TIP→ The fresco is best viewed when the sun is strong, as this building is not particularly well lit.** ✉ *Piazza del Duomo, Parma* ☎ *0521/208699* 🌐 *www.piazzaduomoparma.com.*

Museo del Parmigiano Reggiano

SPECIALTY MUSEUM | **FAMILY** | The trademark crumbly cheese is the focus of this museum, which is part of the collective known as Musei del Cibo whose goal is to showcase the region's most famous foods. There's a video that demonstrates the process of making Parmigiano-Reggiano and exhibits that explore the history of the cheese. Tastings are also offered, and cheese is available to purchase. ✉ *Corte Castellazzi, Via Volta 5* ✣ *28 km (17 miles) northwest of Parma* ☎ *0524/507205* 🌐 *www.museidelcibo.it* 🎫 *€5; €12 Musei del Cibo card for all the food museums* 🕒 *Closed weekdays (open by appointment), and Dec.–Feb.*

Museo del Prosciutto di Parma

SPECIALTY MUSEUM | **FAMILY** | Part of the collective known as Musei del Cibo, which works to showcase the region's most famous foods, this museum offers an in-depth look at Italy's most famous cured pork product. It offers tastings, a bit of history on prosciutto, and a tour through the process of making it. A gift shop ensures that you can take some of this marvelous product home. ✉ *Via Bocchialini 7, Parma* ✣ *Langhirano, 22 km (13 miles) from Parma* ☎ *0524/507205* 🌐 *www.museidelcibo.it* 🎫 *€5; €12 Musei del Cibo card for all the food museums* 🕒 *Closed weekdays (open by appointment only) and Dec. 9–Feb. 28.*

Piazza del Duomo

PLAZA/SQUARE | **FAMILY** | The impressive cobblestone piazza scene contains the cathedral and the Battistero, plus the Palazzo del Vescovado (Bishop's Palace). Behind the Duomo is the Baroque church of San Giovanni Evangelista. ✉ *Piazza del Duomo, Parma.*

Piazza Garibaldi

PLAZA/SQUARE | **FAMILY** | This piazza is the heart of Parma, where people gather to pass the time of day, start their *passeggiata* (constitutional), or simply hang out; the square and nearby Piazza del Duomo make up one of the loveliest historic centers in Italy. Strada Cavour, leading off the piazza, is Parma's prime shopping street. It's also crammed with wine bars teeming with locals, so it's a perfect place to stop for a snack or light lunch or a drink. ✉ *Piazza Garibaldi, Parma.*

★ Pilotta Museums

ART GALLERY | With one ticket, you can visit the Pilotta museums. The Galleria Nazionale contains masterpieces by Correggio, Leonardo da Vinci, and Bronzino. The Baroque Teatro Farnese, built in 1617–18, is made entirely of wood—though largely destroyed in a 1944 Allied bombing raid, it's been flawlessly restored. In the Archeological Museum see Etruscan, Roman, and Egyptian artifacts; the Palatina Library houses more than 500 religious manuscripts; and the Bodoniano museum covers printmaking. ✉ *Piazza della Pilotta 15* ☎ *0521/233617* 🌐 *www.complessopilotta.it* 🎫 *€18* 🕑 *Closed Mon.*

San Giovanni Evangelista

CHURCH | Beyond the elaborate Baroque facade of San Giovanni Evangelista, the Renaissance interior reveals several works by Correggio: *St. John the Evangelist* (in the lunette above the door in the left transept) is considered among his finest. Two chapels have works displaying delicate perspective by a twenty-something Parmigianino (1503–40), a contemporary of Correggio's. ✉ *Piazzale San Giovanni 1, Piazza del Duomo, Parma* ☎ *0521/1651508* 🌐 *www.monasterosangiovanni.com.*

Santa Maria della Steccata

CHURCH | Dating from the 16th century, this delightful church has one of Parma's most recognizable domes. In the dome's large arch there's a wonderful decorative fresco by Francesco Mazzola, better known as Parmigianino. He took so long to complete it that his patrons briefly imprisoned him for breach of contract. ✉ *Piazza Steccata 9, off Via Dante near Piazza Garibaldi, Parma* ☎ *0521/380500* 🌐 *www.diocesi.parma.it.*

Restaurants

La Filoma

$$ | EMILIAN | The dining room here evokes the turn of the 19th century with its high ceilings, chandeliers, and damask drapes. The food shines, from the classic *anolini in brodo di manzo e gallina* (a local variation on tortellini in brodo) to the exquisite roast veal stuffed with prosciutto and Parmigiano-Reggiano. **Known for:** regional specialties that don't break the bank; Parmigiana di melanzane (eggplant Parm) and other vegetarian options; excellent wine list. Ⓢ *Average main: €24* ✉ *Borgo XX Marzo 15, Parma* ☎ *0521/206181* 🌐 *www.ristorantelafiloma.it* 🕑 *Closed Wed.*

★ La Forchetta

$$ | ITALIAN | Sicily-born Parma transplant Angelo Cammarata makes magic in his small eatery on the ground floor of a 16th-century palazzo, where the menu teems with Parma classics as well as modern takes on Sicilian dishes. Creatures from the sea play a starring role—from a selection of raw seafood starters to *Mezze maniche ai frutti di mare* (mixed seafood pasta) and catch of the day *al forno* (baked). **Known for:** cozy interior; great choice of quality fish dishes; lip-smacking cannoli. Ⓢ *Average main: €25* ✉ *Borgo San Biagio 6d, Parma* ☎ *0521/208812* 🌐 *laforchettaparma.it* 🕑 *Closed Tues. No dinner Sun.*

La Greppia

$ | EMILIAN | Little-known by tourists but popular with locals in the know, this small and select restaurant just down the street from Palazzo della Pilotta in the historic center offers up traditional Parmesan cooking with stylistic flourishes. The chef has a nice touch with classics like *anolini ripieni di stracotto in brodo di cappone* (dumplings stuffed with stewed meat in a capon stock) but also prepares innovative dishes. **Known for:** impeccable service; good gluten-free choices;

superb antipasti and desserts. *Average main: €19* *Strada Garibaldi 39, Parma* *0521/233686* *www.ristorantelagreppia.axeleroweb.it.*

Ristorante Parizzi

$$ | EMILIAN | Chef-owner Marco Parizzi is the third-generation cook in this elegant restaurant, originally his grandfather's *salumeria* (delicatessen), where he now serves a mix of Parmense classics and contemporary creations. The *anolini alla parmigiana in brodo di manzo e gallina* (pasta with Parmigiano-Reggiano in broth) is a more typical dish, while the *faraona in crosta di frutta secca* (guinea fowl cooked with dried fruits and mushroom sauce) is a flight of fancy. **Known for:** special menu with white truffles from Alba in autumn; inventive tasting menus; affordable, well-curated wine list. *Average main: €24* *Strada della Repubblica 71, Parma* *0521/285952* *www.ristoranteparizzi.it* *Closed Mon., Aug., and Jan. 8–15.*

Coffee and Quick Bites

★ Tabarro

$ | EMILIAN | Convivial, lively, and full of locals, this favorite little wine bar on one of Parma's main drags has a couple of keg tables outside, a few stools on the ground floor, and several more small tables upstairs. The menu is based largely on cheese and pork products (equine as well: people in this part of the world like to eat horse) and is designed to pair with, and accentuate, the fine wines on offer. **Known for:** international wine list; delicious crostini; the ebullient hosts. *Average main: €14* *Strada Farini 5/b* *0521/200223* *www.tabarro.net* *No lunch weekdays.*

Hotels

★ Palazzo dalla Rosa Prati

$ | HOTEL | Marchese Vittorio dalla Rosa Prati has converted part of his family's 15th-century palace on Piazza del Duomo into luxurious, self-catering accommodations, and those with connecting rooms are ideal for families. **Pros:** spacious, well-appointed rooms with small kitchenettes; historical setting; apartments perfect for families or friends traveling together. **Cons:** meager breakfast; parking can sometimes be a problem; books up quickly. *Rooms from: €150* *Strada al Duomo 7, Parma* *0521/386429* *www.palazzodallarosaprati.it* *19 rooms* *Free Breakfast.*

Parizzi Suites and Studio

$ | B&B/INN | A 17th-century palace has been refurbished with 21st-century amenities to provide a lovely place to rest one's head: the suites are under the same management as the Parizzi restaurant (it's a shared entrance), so you can just glide downstairs for a marvelous meal. **Pros:** central location; great staff; breakfast served in rooms. **Cons:** no parking; some parts need a refurb; restaurant can be noisy. *Rooms from: €120* *Strada della Repubblica 71, Parma* *0521/207032* *www.parizzisuite.com* *13 suites* *Free Breakfast.*

Modena

56 km (35 miles) southeast of Parma, 38 km (24 miles) northwest of Bologna.

Modena is famous for local products: Maserati, Ferrari, and opera star Luciano Pavarotti, born near here and buried in his family plot in Montale Rangone in 2007. However, it's Modena's heavenly scented balsamic vinegar, aged up to 40 years, that's probably its greatest achievement. The town has become another Emilian food mecca, with terrific restaurants and *salumerie* (delicatessens) at every turn.

GETTING HERE AND AROUND

Modena, on the Bologna–Milan line, is easily accessible by train, and it's an easy walk from the station to the *centro storico*. The Intercity connection from

Florence takes about 90 minutes. By car, Modena is just off the A1 autostrada.

TOURS

Consorzio Produttori Aceto Balsamico Tradizionale di Modena

FOOD AND DRINK TOURS | Connoisseurs of balsamic vinegar can arrange visits to local producers through the Consorzio. It's best to contact the organization via its website to obtain a list of producers offering tours. One superb option just east of the city is historic Acetaia Gambigliani Zoccoli, which offers a guided tasting tour among its 1,000 barrels for €10 or a tour with lunch for €30. *Strada Vaciglio Sud 1085/1, Modena 059/395633, 338/8233867 mobile/WhatsApp www.balsamico.it; www.acetaiagambiglianizoccoli.com Free.*

VISITOR INFORMATION

CONTACT Modena Tourism Office. *Piazza Grande 14, Modena 059/2032660 www.visitmodena.it.*

Sights

★ Duomo

CHURCH | Begun by the architect Lanfranco in 1099 and consecrated in 1184, the 12th-century Romanesque cathedral has sculptured facade reliefs by Wiligelmo depicting scenes from Genesis. Look over the main portal to enter a medieval world of intricately carved plant shoots teeming with human, heavenly and demonic life, flanked by two column-bearing Roman lions. Walk around to the Piazza Grande side to see graceful arcading and loggias, a rare example of a cathedral having various aspects and four grand entrances. The interior, completely clad in brick, creates a sober ambience and is filled with intricate stonework by generations of the Maestri Campionesi. The tomb of San Geminiano, Modena's patron saint is in the crypt. The white-marble bell tower is known as La Torre Ghirlandina (the Little Garland Tower) because of its distinctive weather vane. *Piazza Grande, Modena 059/216078 www.duomodimodena.it.*

★ Galleria Estense

ART MUSEUM | Modena's principal museum, housed in the Palazzo dei Musei and located just a short walk from the Duomo, has an impressive collection assembled in the mid-17th century by Francesco d'Este (1610–58), Duke of Modena. The Galleria Estense is named in his honor and contains masterpieces by Bernini, Correggio, El Greco, Tintoretto, Velázquez, Veronese, and Salvator Rosa among others. The Biblioteca Estense here is a huge collection of illuminated manuscripts, of which the best known is the beautifully illustrated *Bible of Borso d'Este* (1455–61). *Largo Porta Sant'Agostino 337, Modena 059/4395711 www.gallerie-estensi.beniculturali.it €8 Closed Mon.*

★ Mercato Storico Albinelli

MARKET | FAMILY | Locals and visitors flock to this fruit, vegetable, meat, and fish market with good reason. Ingredients are of the finest and of the freshest, and visually the place is a glorious sight to behold. It's been around in this current incarnation since 1931, and it's pretty easy to see why. *Via Luigi Albinelli 13, Modena mercatoalbinelli.it Closed Sun.*

Museo Enzo Ferrari

SPECIALTY MUSEUM | The home of the much revered founder of the Ferrari automobile marque, Enzo Ferrari, has been imaginatively enlarged and converted into a museum dedicated to his life and work. Besides the various trophies and engines on display, visitors can view an a video that tells the Ferrari story and see the restored workshop belonging to Enzo's father, Alfredo, and, in a futuristic pavilion built alongside, a grand array of contemporary and vintage cars. **TIP→ A joint ticket is available with the Museo Ferrari in Maranello.** *Via Paolo Ferrari 85, Modena 059/4397979 www.ferrari.com*

Continued on page 464

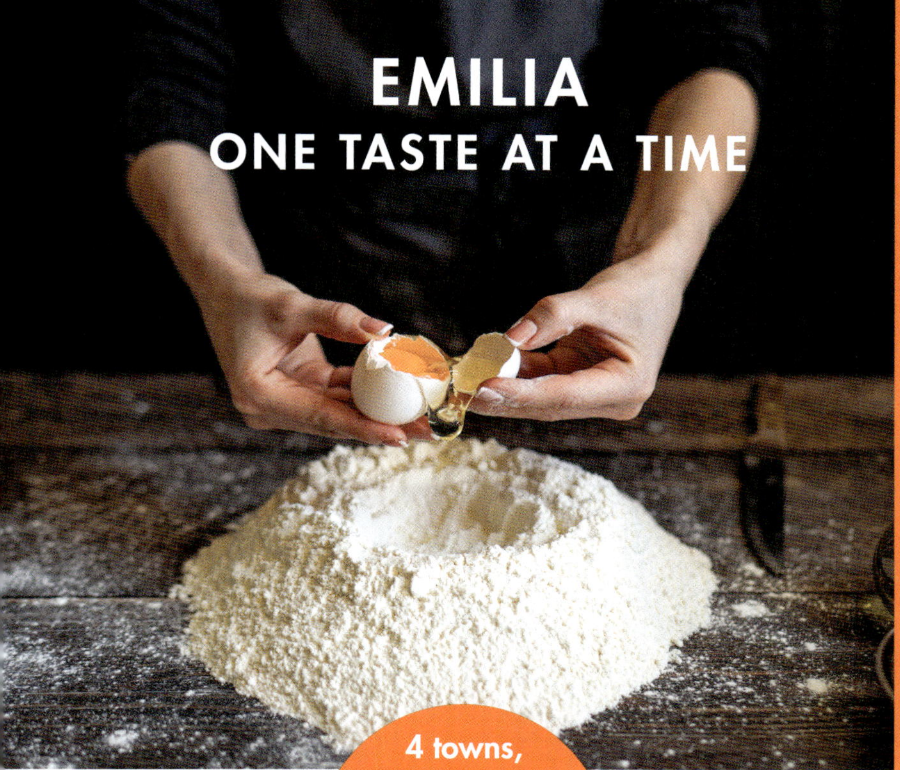

EMILIA
ONE TASTE AT A TIME

4 towns, dozens of foods, and a mouthful of flavors you'll never forget

Imagine biting into the silkiest prosciutto in the world or the most delectable homemade tortellini you've ever tasted. In Emilia, Italy's most famous food region, you'll discover simple tastes that exceed all expectations. Beginning in Parma and moving eastward to Bologna, you'll find the epicenters of such world-renowned culinary treats as *prosciutto crudo*, Parmigiano-Reggiano, *aceto balsamico*, and tortellini. The secret to this region is not the discovery of new and exotic delicacies, but rather the rediscovery of foods you thought you already knew—in much better versions than you've ever tasted before.

TASTE 1 PROSCIUTTO CRUDO

From Piacenza to the Adriatic, ham is the king of meats in Emilia-Romagna, but nowhere is this truer than in **Parma.**

Parma is the world's capital of *prosciutto crudo*, raw cured ham (*crudo* for short). Ask for *crudo di Parma* to signal its local provenance; many other regions also make their own crudo.

CRUDO LANGUAGE

It's easy to get confused with the terminology. Crudo is the product that Americans simply call "prosciutto" or the Brits might call "Parma ham." *Prosciutto* in Italian, however, is a more general term that means any kind of ham, including *prosciutto cotto*, or simply *cotto*, which means "cooked ham." Cotto is an excellent product and frequent pizza topping that's closer to (but much better than) what Americans would put in a deli sandwich.

Crudo is traditionally eaten in one of three ways: in a dry sandwich (*panino*); by itself as an appetizer, often with shaved butter on top; or as part of an appetizer or snack platter of assorted *salumi* (cured meats).

WHAT TO LOOK FOR

For the best crudo di Parma, look for slices, always cut to order, that are razor thin and have a light, rosy red color (not dark red). Don't be shy about going into a simple *salumeria* (a purveyor of cured meats) and ordering crudo by the pound. You can enjoy it straight out of the package on a park bench—and why not?

BEST SPOT FOR A SAMPLE

You can't go wrong with any of Parma's famed salumerie, but **Salumeria Garibaldi** is one of the town's oldest and most reliable. You'll find not only spectacular prosciutto crudo, but also delectable cheeses, wines, porcini mushrooms, and more.

LEARN MORE

For more information on crudo di Parma, contact the **Consorzio del Prosciutto di Parma** through the tourist office, or stop by the famous store, **La Prosciutteria**.

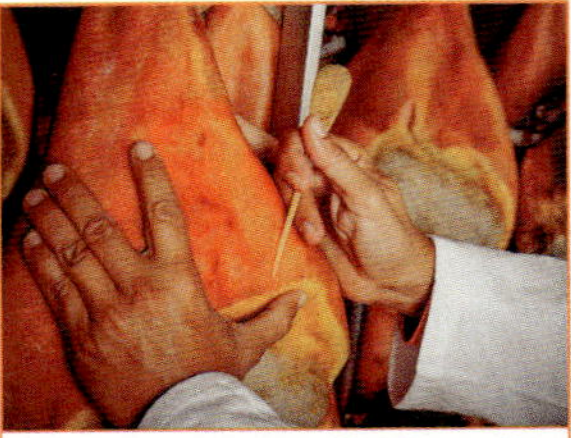
Quality testing

Greasing the ham

Fire branding

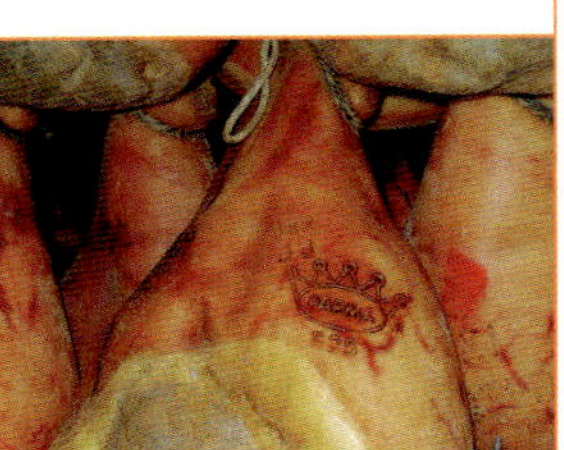
Quality trademark

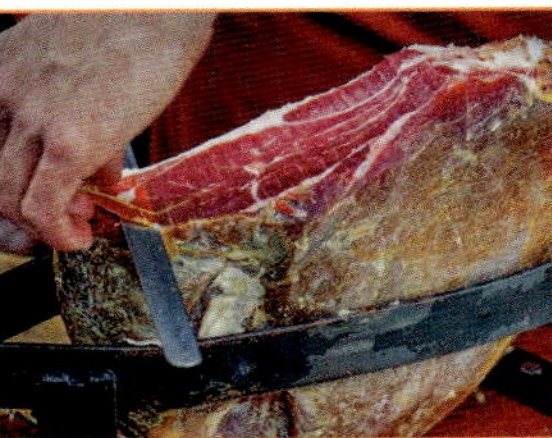
A cut above

TASTE 2 PARMIGIANO-REGGIANO

From Parma, it's only a half-hour trip east to **Reggio Emilia**, the birthplace of the crumbly and renowned Parmigiano-Reggiano cheese. Reggio (not to be confused with Reggio di Calabria in the south) is a charming little Emilian town that has been the center of production for this legendary cheese for more than 70 years.

SAY CHEESE

Grana is the generic Italian term for hard, aged, full-flavored cheese that can be grated. Certain varieties of Pecorino Romano, for example, or Grana Padano, also fall under this term, but Parmigiano-Reggiano, aged for as long as four years, is the foremost example.

NOT JUST FOR GRATING

In Italy, Parmigiano-Reggiano is not only grated onto pasta, but also often served by itself in chunks, either as an appetizer—perhaps accompanied by local salumi—or even for dessert, when it might be drizzled with honey or Modena's balsamic vinegar.

MEET THE MAKERS

If you're a cheese enthusiast, you shouldn't miss the chance to take a free two-hour guided tour of a Parmigiano-Reggiano–producing farm. You'll witness the entire process and get to meet the cheesemakers. Tours can be booked online (🌐 *www.parmigianoreggiano.com*) via the **Consorzio del Formaggio Parmigiano-Reggiano** in Reggio Emilio.

BEST SPOT FOR A SAMPLE

The production of Parmigiano-Reggiano is heavily controlled by the Consorzio del Formaggio, so you can buy the cheese at any store or supermarket in the region and be virtually guaranteed equal quality and price. For a more distinctive shopping experience, however, try buying Parmigiano-Reggiano at the street market on Reggio's central square. The market takes place on Tuesday and Friday from 8 am to 1 pm year-round. You can pick up a small piece to eat while you're in Italy, or have larger pieces shrink-wrapped to take home.

Warming milk in copper cauldrons

Breaking up the curds

Placing cheese in molds

Aging cheese wheels

Parmigiano-Reggiano

TASTE 3 ACETO BALSAMICO DI MODENA

Modena is home to *Aceto Balsamico Tradizionale di Modena*, a kind of balsamic vinegar unparalleled anywhere else on Earth. The balsamic vinegar you've probably tried—even the pricier versions sold at specialty stores—may be good on salads, but it bears only a fleeting resemblance to the real thing.

HOW IS IT MADE?

The *tradizionale* vinegar that passes strict government standards is made with Trebbiano grape must, which is cooked over an open fire, reduced, and fermented from 12 to 25 or more years in a series of specially made wooden casks. As the vinegar becomes more concentrated, so much liquid evaporates that it takes more than 6 gallons of must to produce one quart of vinegar 12 years later. The result is an intense and syrupy concoction best enjoyed sparingly on grilled meats, strawberries, or Parmigiano-Reggiano cheese. The vinegar has such a complexity of flavor that some even drink it as an after-dinner liqueur.

BEST SPOT FOR A SAMPLE

The **Consorzio Produttori Antiche Acetaie** offers tours and tastings by reservation only. The main objective of the consortium is to monitor the quality of the authentic balsamic vinegar, made by only a few licensed restaurants and small producers.

The consortium also limits production, keeping prices sky high. Expect to pay €60 for a 100-ml (3.4 oz) bottle of tradizionale, which is generally aged 12 to 15 years, or €90 and up for the older tradizionale extra vecchio variety, which is aged 25 years.

But perhaps the best place to sample this vinegar, in its various stages and permutations, is in situ—that is, in any one of Modena's remarkable restaurants. You can have a simple trattoria meal at **Ermes**, whose recipes rely heavily on that liquid gold. Or you can splurge at **Osteria Francescana**, where three-starred Michelin chef Massimo Bottura works miracles with local ingredients.

Tasting tradizionale vinegar

Wooden casks for fermenting

OTHER TASTES OF EMILIA

- **Cotechino:** a sausage made from pork and lard, a specialty of Modena
- **Culatello de Zibello:** raw cured ham produced along the banks of the Po River, and cured and aged for more than 11 months
- **Mortadella:** soft, smoked sausage made with beef, pork, cubes of pork fat, and seasonings, a specialty of Bologna
- **Ragù:** a sauce made from minced pork and beef, simmered in milk, onions, carrots, and tomatoes
- **Salama da sugo:** salty, oily sausage aged and then cooked, a specialty of Ferrara
- **Tortelli and cappellacci:** pasta pillows with the same basic form as tortellini, but stuffed with cheese and vegetables

TASTE 4 TORTELLINI

The venerable city of **Bologna** is called "the Fat" for a reason: this is the birthplace of tortellini, not to mention other specialties such as mortadella and ragù. Despite the city's new reputation for chic nightclubs and flashy boutiques, much of the food remains as it ever was.

You'll find the many Emilian variations on stuffed pasta all over the region, but they're perhaps at their best in Bologna, especially the native tortellini.

INSPIRED BY THE GODS

According to one legend, tortellini was inspired by the navel of Venus, goddess of love. As the story goes, Venus and some other gods stopped at a local inn for the night. A nosy chef went to their room to catch a glimpse of Venus. Peering through the keyhole, he saw her lying only partially covered on the bed. He was so inspired after seeing her perfect navel that he created a stuffed pasta, tortellini, in its image.

ON THE MENU

Tortellini is usually filled with beef (sometimes cheese), and is served two ways: *asciutta* is "dry," meaning it is served with a sauce such as ragù, or perhaps just with butter and Parmigiano. *Tortellini in brodo* is immersed in a lovely, savory beef broth.

Tortellini alla panna contains a meat filling and is sauced with cream. Aficionados, however, argue frequently about what to stuff into these little bundles, and no two cooks do it the same. Some purists insist that only beef will do; others mix it up with sausages, mortadella, spices, and cheese (usually Parmigiano).

BEST SPOT TO BUY

Don't miss **Tamburini**, Bologna's best specialty food shop, where aromas of Emilia-Romagna's famous specialties waft out through the room and into the streets.

Simple beginnings

Stretching the dough

Adding the filling

Shaping each piece

Tortellini di Bologna

€27 (Sept.–May), €32 (June and Aug.), combination ticket with Museo Ferrari in Maranello €38/€42.

Museo Ferrari Maranello

SPECIALTY MUSEUM | This museum has become a pilgrimage site for auto enthusiasts. It takes you through the illustrious history of Ferrari, from early 1951 models to the present—the legendary F50 and cars driven by Michael Schumacher in Formula One victories being highlights. You can also take a look at the glamorous life of founder Enzo Ferrari (a re-creation of his office is on-site) and get a glance at the production process. *Via Dino Ferrari 43, Maranello In Maranello, 17 km (11 miles) south of Modena 0536/949713 www.ferrari.com €27 (Sept.–May), €32 (June and Aug.), combination ticket with Museo Enzo Ferrari in Modena €38/€42.*

 Restaurants

Aldina

$ | **EMILIAN** | On the second floor of a building across from the covered market, steps from the Piazza Grande, this simple, typical trattoria is in the very nerve center of the city. Here you'll find exemplary preparations of the region's crown jewels: tortellini in brodo, tagliatelle al ragù, and roasted meats. **Known for:** inexpensive regional food loved by locals; authentically old-fashioned character; tortellini in brodo. *Average main: €18 Via Albinelli 40, Modena 059/236106 www.trattoriaaldina.it No credit cards Closed Sun. in Aug. No dinner.*

★ Danilo

$ | **EMILIAN** | Honest cooking doesn't get much better than this: host Danilo has been at the helm for decades and oversees his restaurant with a keen eye and great spirit. The food here is local, terrific, and unpretentious. **Known for:** il filetto all'aceto balsamico (beef fillet with a sumptous balsamic sauce); well-priced wine list; attentive and courteous staff. *Average main: €19 Via Coltellini 31, Modena 059/216691 www.ristorantedadanilomodena.it Closed Sun.*

Favorite Places

Nick Bruno: Modena's 12th-century Duomo is rich in art and religious symbolism. I like to walk around its four portals greeting the pride of gormless-looking stone lions, while admiring the carving.

Hosteria Giusti

$$$ | **EMILIAN** | In the back room of the Salumeria Giusti, established in 1605 and reportedly the world's oldest deli, you'll find just four tables in a room tastefully done with antique furnishings. You'll also find some of the best food in Emilia-Romagna—perfectly executed takes on traditional dishes such as *gnocco fritto* (fried dough) stuffed with pancetta or prosciutto, and *tortellini in brodo di Cappone* (pasta in possibly the most fragrant broth in the world). **Known for:** gnocco fritto with prosciutto; cozy setting; popular and pricey. *Average main: €31 Via Farini 75 and Vicolo Squallore 46, Modena 059/222533 www.hosteriagiusti.it Closed Sun., Mon., Aug., Dec., and early Jan. No dinner.*

Osteria Francescana

$$$$ | **EMILIAN** | Chef-proprietor Massimo Bottura has done stints with Adrià and Ducasse, takes inspiration from music and literature, and pours all these influences into creating some of the fanciest plates in all of Italy while remaining true to his Modenese roots. The restaurant contains only 12 tables and it's possible to order à la carte; for the full haute cuisine experience opt for the seasonal tasting menu with the accompanying wine pairing (€590). **Known for:** a reverential atmosphere; eye-wateringly

pricey tasting menu; reservations required months in advance. *$ Average main: €110 ✉ Via Stella 22, Modena ☎ 059/223912 🌐 www.osteriafrancescana.it ⏲ Closed 2 wks in Aug.*

Coffee and Quick Bites

★ Mon Café

$$ | ECLECTIC | Locals love this lively café because it does just about everything and does it well, beginning at 7 in the morning with excellent coffee and tasty breakfast pastries and ending long after dark with *aperitivi* (aperitifs), cocktails, and dinner. The fairly limited menu includes Italian tapas and starters and mains with vegetarian and fish options. **Known for:** excellent breakfasts and service; fab selection of mocktails; atmospheric interior. *$ Average main: €20 ✉ Corso Canalchiaro 128, Modena ☎ 059/223257 🌐 mon-cafe.it ⏲ Closed Mon; until 1 pm Sun.*

Hotels

Hotel Rua Frati 48 in San Francesco

$$$ | HOTEL | Set in a Renaissance palazzo in central Modena, this luxurious bolthole combines modern and antique furnishings, and has a selection of spacious room and suites (the Royal has a beautiful frescoed ceiling) with smart marble bathrooms. **Pros:** excellent restaurant and bountiful breakfast; minispa, gym, and fitness center; exceptional service. **Cons:** pricey; may lack character for some; the standard Deluxe decor uninspiring. *$ Rooms from: €492 ✉ Rua dei Frati Minori 48, Modena ☎ 059/7474411 🌐 ruafrati48.com 30 rooms Free Breakfast.*

Phi Hotel Canalgrande

$ | HOTEL | In a calm location within easy walking distance of Modena's main tourist attractions, this hotel housed in an old palazzo has plenty of old-world character in the form of antique paintings, fancy plasterwork, and trompe l'oeil in the public rooms. **Pros:** great central position; spacious gardens; secure garage parking. **Cons:** dated in parts; service is sometimes poor; inadequate soundproofing in some rooms. *$ Rooms from: €157 ✉ Corso Canalgrande 6, Modena ☎ 059/217160 🌐 www.hotelcanalgrandemodena.com 67 rooms Free Breakfast.*

★ Quartopiano

$ | B&B/INN | Proprietor Antonio di Resta shows his impeccable sense of style and love of all things French in a lovely little bed-and-breakfast just a few steps from the Duomo. **Pros:** intimate setup in the heart of town; lovely bath products and fluffy towels; owner provides helpful local advice. **Cons:** with only two rooms, it books up quickly; space a bit cramped; breakfast in a separate establishment. *$ Rooms from: €170 ✉ Via Bonacorsa 27, Modena ☎ 348/0189112 mobile 🌐 www.bbquartopiano.it 2 rooms Free Breakfast.*

Bologna

117 km (72 miles) north of Florence in Tuscany, 57 km (35 miles) southeast of Modena.

Bologna, a city rich with cultural jewels, has long been one of the best-kept secrets in northern Italy. Tourists in the know bask in the shadow of its leaning medieval towers and devour the city's wonderful food.

The charm of the centro storico, with its red-arcaded passageways and sidewalks, can be attributed to wise city counselors who, at the beginning of the 13th century, decreed that roads couldn't be built without *portici* (porticoes). Were these counselors to return to town eight centuries later, they'd marvel at how little has changed.

Bologna, with a population of about 392,000, has a university-town vibe—and it feels young and lively in a way that many other Italian cities don't.

GETTING HERE AND AROUND

Frequent train service from Florence to Bologna makes getting here easy. The Italo and Frecciarossa (high-speed trains) run several times an hour and take just under 40 minutes. Otherwise, you're left with the *regionale* (regional) trains, which putter along and get you to Bologna in around two hours. The historic center is an interesting and relatively effortless walk from the station—though it takes about 20 minutes.

If you're driving from Florence, take the A1, exiting onto the A14, and then get on the RA1 to Exit 7–Bologna Centrale. The trip takes about an hour. From Milan, take the A1, exiting to the A14 as you near the city. The trip takes just under three hours.

VISITOR INFORMATION

Bologna Welcome Easy card (from €35) offers free and discounted entry to many sights, including the Musei Civici for up to 15 days, plus a Discover Bologna walking tour and four-hour bike rental. The Welcome Card Plus (€55) includes extras such as the City Red Bus, and San Luca Express minitourist train to the Sanctuary of San Luca (🌐 *www.bolognawelcome.com/en/information/bologna-welcome-card-eng*).

CONTACT Bologna Tourism Offices. ✉ *Piazza Maggiore 1/e, Bologna* ☎ *051/6583111* 🌐 *www.bolognawelcome.com.*

Sights

Basilica di San Petronio

CHURCH | Construction on this vast cathedral began in 1390, and the work still isn't finished more than 600 years later. Above the center of the door is a Madonna and Child flanked by Saints Ambrose and Petronius, the city's patrons. Michelangelo, Giulio Romano, and Andrea Palladio (among others), submitted designs for the facade, which were all eventually rejected. The Bolognesi had planned an even bigger church but had to tone down construction when the university seat was established next door in 1561. The most important art in the church is in the fourth chapel on the left: these frescoes by Giovanni di Modena date to 1410–15. ✉ *Piazza Galvani 5, Piazza Maggiore* ☎ *051/231415* 🌐 *www.basilicadisanpetronio.org* 🎫 *Free.*

Fontana del Nettuno

FOUNTAIN | Sculptor Giambologna's elaborate 1563–66 Baroque fountain and monument to Neptune occupying Piazza Nettuno has been aptly nicknamed "Il Gigante" (The Giant). Its exuberantly sensual mermaids and undraped god of the sea drew fire when it was constructed—but not enough, apparently, to dissuade the populace from using the fountain as a public washing stall for centuries. ✉ *Piazza del Nettuno, next to Palazzo Re Enzo, Piazza Maggiore.*

Le Due Torri

NOTABLE BUILDING | **FAMILY** | Two landmark medieval towers, mentioned by Dante in *The Inferno,* stand side by side in the compact Piazza di Porta Ravegnana. Once, every family of importance had a tower as a symbol of prestige and power (and as a potential fortress). Now only 24 remain out of nearly 100 that once presided over the city. Torre Garisenda (late 11th century), which tilts 4 degrees (Pisa's leans 3.9), was shortened to 157 feet in the 1300s. Torre degli Asinelli (1119) is 318 feet tall and leans 7½ feet; both towers and the piazza are currently closed to visitors while the tottering Torre Garisenda is being carefully monitored. ✉ *Piazza di Porta Ravegnana, East of Piazza Maggiore* ☎ *051/6583111* 🌐 *www.duetorribologna.com.*

★ MAMbo and Museo Morandi

ART MUSEUM | The museum—the name stands for Museo d'Arte Moderna di Bologna, or Bologna's Museum of

Modern Art—houses a permanent collection of modern art. All of this is set within the sleek minimalist structure built in 1915 as the Forno del Pane, a large bakery. Seek out the powerful Arte e Ideologia section for Guttuso's *Funerali di Togliatti* (1972), a charged symbol of pride and pain for many Bolognesi and Italiani. The work of Bologna's celebrated abstract painter Giorgio Morandi (1890–64), known for his muted still life paintings of domestic objects and landscapes, can be viewed at the Museo Morandi here. The fab bookshop and MAMbo Cafè complete the complex. ✉ *Via Don Minzoni 14, Bologna* ☎ *051/6496611* 🌐 *www.mambo-bologna.org* 🎫 *€6* ⏲ *Closed Mon.*

Museo Internazionale e Biblioteca della Musica di Bologna

SPECIALTY MUSEUM | The music museum in the spectacular Palazzo Aldini-Sanguinetti, with its 17th- and 18th-century frescoes, offers among its exhibits a 1606 harpsichord and a collection of beautiful music manuscripts dating from the 1500s. ✉ *Strada Maggiore 34, University area* ☎ *051/2757711* 🌐 *www.museibologna.it/musica* 🎫 *€5* ⏲ *Closed Mon.*

Palazzo Comunale (*Palazzo d'Accursio*)

GOVERNMENT BUILDING | When Bologna was an independent city-state, this huge palace dating from the 13th to 15th century was the seat of government—a function it still serves today in a building that is a mélange of styles. Over the door is a statue of Bologna-born Pope Gregory XIII (reigned 1572–85), most famous for reorganizing the calendar. The Collezioni Comunali d'Arte museum exhibits medieval paintings as well as some Renaissance works by Luca Signorelli (circa 1445–1523) and Tintoretto (1518–94). You can also explore two panoramic terraces of the Torre dell'Orologio, its clock mechanism and the grand Sala Farnese. The cavernous, light-filled iron-roofed Sala Borsa (1884) now houses the wonderful civic library Salaborsa Biblioteca Multimediale. ✉ *Piazza Maggiore 6, Piazza Maggiore* ☎ *051/2193998 Collezioni Comunali d'Arte, 051/2194400 Sala Borsa* 🌐 *www.museibologna.it; www.bibliotecasalaborsa.it* 🎫 *Collezioni Comunali d'Arte and Torre dell'Orologio €10; Sala Borsa free* ⏲ *Collezioni Comunali d'Arte closed Mon.; Sala Borsa closed Sun. and Mon. morning.*

Palazzo del Podestà

NOTABLE BUILDING | This classic Renaissance palace facing the Basilica di San Petronio was erected from 1484–94, and attached to it is the soaring Torre dell'Arengo. The bells in the tower have rung whenever the city has celebrated, mourned, or called its citizens to arms. It may not be open to the public, but head under the palazzo's atmospheric vaulted arches to experience the resonant magic of the Voltone del Podestà: whisper into the right-angled brick walls below a saintly statue to communicate with a pal opposite. ✉ *Piazza Maggiore 1, Piazza Maggiore.*

Palazzo Re Enzo

CASTLE/PALACE | Built in 1244, this palace became home to King Enzo of Sardinia, who was imprisoned here in 1249 after he was captured during the fierce battle of Fossalta. He died here 23 years later. The palace has other macabre associations as well: common criminals received last rites in the tiny courtyard chapel before being executed in Piazza Maggiore. The colonnaded courtyard is worth a peek, and its two grand *saloni* (salons) are used for events including concerts. ✉ *Piazza del Nettuno 1/c, Piazza Maggiore* ☎ *051/6583192* 🌐 *www.palazzoreenzo.com.*

Pinacoteca Nazionale

ART GALLERY | Bologna's principal art gallery contains many works by the immortals of Italian painting; its prize possession is the *Ecstasy of St. Cecilia* by Raphael (1483–1520). There's also a beautiful polyptych by Giotto (1267–1337), as well as *Madonna with Child and*

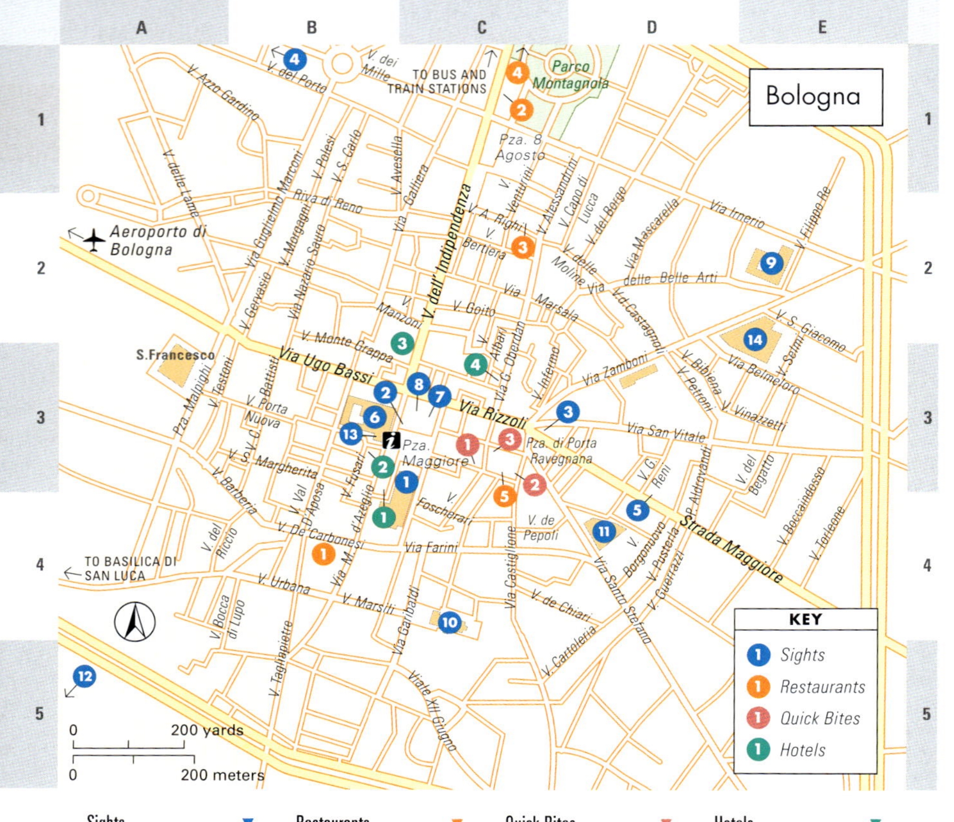

Sights

1 Basilica di San Petronio C3
2 Fontana del Nettuno..... C3
3 Le Due Torri............... C3
4 MAMbo and Museo Morandi......... B1
5 Museo Internazionale e Biblioteca della Musica di Bologna D4
6 Palazzo Comunale...... B3
7 Palazzo del Podestà..... C3
8 Palazzo Re Enzo.......... C3
9 Pinacoteca Nazionale... E2
10 San Domenico C4
11 Santo Stefano........... D4
12 Santuario Madonna di San Luca.............. A5
13 Torre dell'Orologio...... B3
14 Università di Bologna ... E2

Restaurants

1 Da Cesari B4
2 Ristorante I Portici....... C1
3 Trattoria Caffè del Rosso C2
4 Trattoria di Via Serra C1
5 Trattoria Gianni a la Vecia Bulagna....... C3

Quick Bites

1 Mercato di Mezzo C3
2 Sfoglia Rina............... C3
3 Tamburini C3

Hotels

1 Art Hotel Commercianti B3
2 Art Hotel Orologio B3
3 Grand Hotel Majestic già Baglioni.... C3
4 Hotel Corona D'Oro...... C3

Saints Margaret, Jerome, and Petronius (altarpiece of St. Margaret) by Parmigianino (1503–40); note the rapt eye contact between St. Margaret and the Christ child. ✉ *Via delle Belle Arti 56, University area* ☎ *051/4209411* 🌐 *pinacotecabologna.beniculturali.it* 🎫 *€12* ⏲ *Closed Mon.*

San Domenico

CHURCH | The tomb of St. Dominic, who died here in 1221, is called the Arca di San Domenico and is found in this church in the sixth chapel on the right. Many artists participated in its decoration, notably Niccolò di Bari, who was so proud of his 15th-century contribution that he changed his name to Niccolò dell'Arca to recall this famous work. The young Michelangelo (1475–1564) carved the angel on the right and the image of San Petronio. In the right transept of the church is a tablet marking the last resting place of hapless King Enzo, the Sardinian ruler imprisoned in the Palazzo Re Enzo. The attached museum contains religious relics. ✉ *Piazza San Domenico 13, off Via Garibaldi, South of Piazza Maggiore* ☎ *051/6400411* 🌐 *www.sandomenicobologna.it.*

★ Santo Stefano

CHURCH | This splendid and unusual basilica contains between four and seven connected churches (authorities differ). A 4th-century temple dedicated to Isis originally occupied this site, but much of what you see was erected between the 10th and 12th centuries. Just outside the church, which probably dates from the 5th century (with later alterations), is the Cortile di Pilato (Pilate's Courtyard), named for the basin in the center. Despite the fact that the basin was probably crafted around the 8th century, legend has it that Pontius Pilate washed his hands in it after condemning Christ. ✉ *Piazza Santo Stefano, Via Santo Stefano 24, University area* ☎ *051/4983423* 🌐 *www.santostefanobologna.it* ⏲ *Closed during services.*

★ Santuario Madonna di San Luca

CHURCH | With panoramic views and grandiose Baroque architecture atop the forested Colle della Guardia hill some 5 km (3 miles) southwest of Piazza Maggiore, the 1765-consecrated Sanctuary of San Luca church is a symbol of Bologna. For a bona fide Bolognese pilgrimage climb the 950-foot hill on foot from Porta Saragozza protected by the 666 arches (alluding to the Madonna-crushed devil) and 15 chapels of the world's longest portico (3.9 km/2.4 miles). The final ceremonial section (completed in 1721) begins at the monumental Arco del Meloncello, which echoes the orange-hued architecture of the basilica itself. Visitors can ascend a further 110 steps into the cupola for 180-degree views as part of the new San Luca Sky Experience. For a less strenuous route to the sanctuary hop on the No. 20 bus then the 58 minibus (from Villa Spada), or the San Luca Express *trenino* (mini tourist train; €13 return) from the city center. To avoid the crowds set out early morning. ✉ *Via di San Luca 36, Beyond the City Center* ☎ *051/6142339* 🌐 *www.santuariodisanluca.it; www.succedesoloabologna.it/san-luca-sky-experience-en* 🎫 *San Luca Sky Experience €5; free plus San Luca Express with Bologna Welcome Card.*

Torre dell'Orologio (*Clock Tower*)

CLOCK | For a spectacular view of Piazza Maggiore and the Bolognesi hills from two terraces, as well as a look at how Bologna's oldest clock keeps the city punctual, climb the Torre dell'Orologio, or d'Arccursio tower. Opened to the public in 2021, it was built in 1249 as University of Bologna law professor Accursio da Bagnolo's monumental timepiece for his home in the piazza. The clock mechanism you'll see dates from 1773, as found on the horologist's inscription "Rinaldo Gandofli Accademic Clementi Fece 1773," among the clock's movement, gears, and swinging pendulum. ✉ *Piazza Maggiore 6, Bologna* ☎ *051/6583111* 🌐 *www.bolognawelcome.com* 🎫 *€10* *includes Collezioni Comunali d'Arte* ✍ *Reservations required.*

★ Università di Bologna

COLLEGE | Take a stroll through the streets of the university area: a jumble of buildings, some dating as far back as the 15th century and most to the 17th and 18th. The neighborhood, as befits a college town, is full of bookshops, coffee bars, and inexpensive restaurants. Political slogans and sentiments are scrawled on walls all around the university and tend to be ferociously leftist, sometimes juvenile, and often entertaining. Among the 15 university museums, the most interesting is the Museo di Palazzo Poggi, which displays scientific instruments plus paleontological and botanical artifacts. ✉ *Via Zamboni 33, University area* ☎ *051/2099610 museum* 🌐 *sma.unibo.it/it/il-sistema-museale/museo-di-palazzo-poggi* 🎫 *€7 museum* 🕙 *Closed Mon.*

Restaurants

★ Da Cesari

$$ | EMILIAN | Host Paolino Cesari has been presiding over his eatery since 1962, and he and his staff go out of their way to make you feel at home. The food's terrific, and if you love pork products, try anything on the menu with *mora romagnola*: Paolino has direct contact with the people who raise this breed that nearly became extinct (he calls it "my pig"). **Known for:** pork dishes like flavorful salame; wine list with lots of local bottles; traditional setting. 💲 *Average main: €23* ✉ *Via de' Carbonesi 8, South of Piazza Maggiore* ☎ *051/237710* 🌐 *www.da-cesari.it* 🕙 *Closed Sun., Aug., and 1 wk in Jan.*

Ristorante I Portici

$$$$ | EMILIAN | The frescoed ceiling, parquet flooring, and live classical music are clues that this sophisticated restaurant (part of the hotel of the same name) occupies a former theater and *café-chantant,* or musical venue, from the late 19th century. It's the perfect setting for an evening of fine dining featuring mainly Emilian-inspired dishes with modern touches and the vision of chef Nicola Annunziata. **Known for:** sumptuous surroundings in a former theater; sophisticated culinary offerings; refined and attentive service. 💲 *Average main: €110* ✉ *Via dell'Indipendenza 69, North of Piazza Maggiore* ☎ *051/42185* 🌐 *www.iporticihotel.com* 🕙 *Closed Sun. and Mon. No lunch Tues.–Thurs.*

Trattoria Caffè del Rosso

$ | EMILIAN | Here, in the mirrored interior, a mostly young crowd chows down on classic regional fare at affordable prices. Nimble staff bearing multiple plates sashay neatly between the closely spaced tables delivering such standards as *tortellini in brodo* and *cotoletta alla Bolognese* (veal with Parmigiano-Reggiano and prosciutto). **Known for:** student haunt with great-value regional food; affordable wine list; fun atmosphere. 💲 *Average main: €15* ✉ *Via Augusto Righi 30, University area* ☎ *051/236730* 🕙 *No dinner Sun.*

Trattoria di Via Serra

$ | EMILIAN | At this simple trattoria off the main tourist circuit, much care has been taken with the decor: the rooms, overseen by host Flavio, are small and intimate, and the wooden walls painted a creamy whitish gray. Chef Tommaso gives equal care to the menu and deftly turns out Bolognese classics, as well as dishes with a modern twist—among the antipasti, his *tosone avvolto nella pancetta* incorporates roasted Parmigiano-Reggiano trimmings and unsmoked bacon. **Known for:** all locally sourced ingredients; modern riffs on classic dishes; convivial atmosphere. 💲 *Average main: €19* ✉ *Via Serra 9/b, Beyond the City Center* ☎ *051/6312330* 🌐 *www.trattoriadiviaserra.it* 🕙 *Closed Sun. and Mon. No dinner Tues. and Aug.*

★ Trattoria Gianni a la Vecia Bulagna

$$ | EMILIAN | At the bottom of an alley off Piazza Maggiore, this unassuming

place—known to locals as simply "Da Gianni"—is all about hearty traditional food. The usual starters are on hand—including a tasty tortellini in brodo—in addition to daily specials; bollito misto (mixed boiled meat) is a fine option here, and the *cotechino con puré di patate* (pork sausage with mashed potatoes) is elevated to sublimity by the accompanying salsa verde. **Known for:** tortellini in brodo; efficient and friendly service; busy local spot. *Average main: €21 Via Clavature 18, Piazza Maggiore 051/229434 www.trattoria-gianni.it Closed Mon. and 1 wk in early Jan. No dinner Sun.*

Coffee and Quick Bites

Mercato di Mezzo

$ | ITALIAN | FAMILY | This former fruit and vegetable market, established in medieval times and transformed into a covered market after unification, has now morphed into a fancy gourmet food hall. Various outlets offer quality Bologna classics plus some innovations, including tortellini, gnocchi and tortelloni at DeGusto Coop; focaccia from Bologna Food Company; panini, pasta, and cold cuts at L'Antica Bottega; and fried fish and quirky fish hamburgers at Pescheria del Pavaglione. **Known for:** great wines by the glass; buzzy Bolognesi atmosphere; its pork and cheese products. *Average main: €14 Via Clavature 12, Piazza Maggiore 379/1855172 mobile www.facebook.com/mercatodimezzobologna Closed Mon.*

Sfoglia Rina

$ | ITALIAN | FAMILY | The *pastaio* (pasta-maker) tradition in this bright honeycomb tiled pasta shop and casual restaurant—which often has a line around the block—started in 1963 in a town about 9½ km (6 miles) southwest of Bologna. There, Rina De Franceschi rolled *sfoglia* (dough) following family recipes. **Known for:** fresh pasta in many varieties; weekly vegetarian-friendly specials; affordable and wide-ranging menu. *Average main: €13 Via Castiglione 5/b, Bologna 051/9911710 www.sfogliarina.it.*

Tamburini

$ | WINE BAR | Two small rooms inside plus kegs and bar stools outside make up this lively, packed little spot. The overwhelming plate of *affettati misti* is crammed with top-quality local cured meats and succulent cheeses, and the adjacent salumeria offers many wonderful items to take away. **Known for:** cheese and cured meat plates; abundant portions; lively atmosphere with a vast wine selection. *Average main: €13 Via Caprarie 1, Piazza Maggiore 051/234726 www.tamburini.com.*

Hotels

Art Hotel Commercianti

$$ | HOTEL | Set within an historic palazzo dating back to the 12th century, with stained glass and beamed ceilings, this hotel is fitted with stylish interiors and rooms filled with interesting art and antiques. **Pros:** central location next to the San Petronio basilica; beautifully renovated and appointed with quirky arts and antiques; bountiful breakfasts. **Cons:** you may be disturbed by the morning basilica bells next door; classic rooms on the small side; central locations means some street noise. *Rooms from: €227 Via de' Pignattari 11, Bologna 051/7457511 en.art-hotel-commercianti.com 35 rooms Free Breakfast.*

★ Art Hotel Orologio

$$ | HOTEL | FAMILY | The location of this stylish and welcoming family-run hotel can't be beat: it's right around the corner from Piazza Maggiore on a quiet piazza. **Pros:** central location; family-friendly rooms; fresh and bountiful breakfast. **Cons:** some street noise; pet-friendly environment may not appeal to allergy sufferers; limited facilities. *Rooms from: €241 Via IV Novembre 10, Piazza Maggiore 051/7457411 www.*

art-hotel-orologio.com 34 rooms *Free Breakfast.*

Grand Hotel Majestic già Baglioni

$$$ | **HOTEL** | From the marble lobby to the luxury rooftop-terrace suites, Bologna's oldest and grandest hotel, set in an 18th-century palazzo impresses with its classical aristocratic French decor and top-notch food. **Pros:** central location; spa and gym; sophisticated Carracci restaurant dining. **Cons:** poor soundproofing and street noise in some rooms; breakfast could be better; service may feel aloof to some. *Rooms from: €510* *Via dell'Indipendenza 8, Piazza Maggiore* *051/225445* *grandhotelmajestic.duetorrihotels.com* *106 rooms* *Free Breakfast.*

Hotel Corona D'Oro

$$ | **HOTEL** | Elegance and historic charm are the keynotes of this converted medieval palazzo once belonging to the powerful Azzoguidi family, just a short stroll from Piazza Maggiore and all the main attractions. **Pros:** helpful, friendly staff; spacious and silent rooms; historic character. **Cons:** steps on some floors are not ideal for anyone with mobility issues; housekeeping efficiency is patchy; some rooms are small. *Rooms from: €308* *Via Oberdan 12, Bologna* *051/7457611* *www.hco.it* *40 rooms* *Free Breakfast.*

Nightlife

BARS

Caffè Rubik

BARS | Get a taster for Bologna's student life at this quirky joint run by Alessio, Edoardo, and a friendly troupe in an historic *tabaccheria*-bar premises. Take at pew inside by day or night amid an eclectic decor of old cassettes, artworks, and an ever-diverse soundtrack, or outside under the porticoes; choose from a menu of classic cocktails, beers, wine, and their beloved *amari* (Italian digestifs with a twist) plus juices, caffè, pastries, and toasted sandwiches. *Via Marsala 31/d, North of Piazza Maggiore* *051/0140660* *www.cafferubik.com.*

Le Stanze

BARS | At Le Stanze you can sip an aperitivo or a late-night drink amid a young and noisy clientele. The incredibly grand decor includes 17th-century frescoes in what was once the private chapel of the Palazzo Bentivoglio. The adjoining restaurant offers a small selection of Bologna favorites. *Via del Borgo di San Pietro 1, University area* *051/228767* *www.lestanzecafe.it.*

★ Osteria del Sole

WINE BAR | Although "osteria" in an establishment's name suggests that food will be served, such is not the case here. This place is all about drinking wine; the entrance door has warnings such as "He who doesn't drink will please stay outside." It's been around since 1465, and locals pack in, bearing food from outside to accompany the wine. *Vicolo Ranocchi 1/d, Piazza Maggiore* *347/9680171 mobile* *www.osteriadelsole.it.*

MUSIC VENUES

★ Bravo Caffè

LIVE MUSIC | Rub shoulders with artsy celebs, locals, and visitors who dine while listening to intimate jazz, funk, rock, and pop artists from Italy and beyond. It can be a special, intimate place to see legends like Luca Carboni, Tullio de Piscopo, Nicola Conte, Suzanne Vega, Lisa Stansfield, Billy Cobham, and Roy Ayers. *Via Mascarella 1 Bologna, North of Piazza Maggiore* *051/266112* *www.bravocaffe.it.*

Cantina Bentivoglio

LIVE MUSIC | Since 1987, this historic venue has hosted jazz and other musical *maestri*, such as Chet Baker, Max, Roach, Herbie Hancock, and Caetano Veloso. You can enjoy light and more substantial meals here as well. *Via Mascarella 4/b, University area* *051/265416* *www.cantinabentivoglio.it.*

Performing Arts

MUSIC AND OPERA

Teatro Comunale

MUSIC | This 18th-century theater presents concerts by Italian and international orchestras throughout the year, but the highly acclaimed opera performances from January to July and October to December are the main attraction. Reserve seats for those performances well in advance. ✉ *Largo Respighi 1, University area* ☎ *051/529019* 🌐 *www.tcbo.it* 🎫 *From €10 for balcony tickets.*

Shopping

ANTIQUE JEWELRY AND OBJECTS

★ **Nostalgia 1968 - Galleria Antiquaria**

ANTIQUES & COLLECTIBLES | Fascinating emporium run by the amiable antique dealer Giorgio and family, specializing in procuring and selling exquisite jewelry and precious objects for the home since 1968. Even if you don't purchase one of their choice pieces it's worth exploring the ever-changing collection of rings, bracelets, artworks, vases, and clocks. ✉ *Strada Maggiore 13d, Bologna* ☎ *051/223802* 🌐 *nostalgia1968.it.*

CLOTHING

Galleria Cavour

MALL | Opened in 1959, the upscale Galleria houses many of the fashion giants, including Armani, Gucci, Saint Laurent, and Tod's. ✉ *Via Luigi Carlo Farini 14, South of Piazza Maggiore* ☎ *051/226889* 🌐 *www.galleriacavourbologna.com.*

WINE AND FOOD

Bologna is a good place to buy wine. Several shops have a bewilderingly large selection—to go straight to the top, ask the managers which wines have won the prestigious Tre Bicchieri (Three Glasses) award from Gambero Rosso's wine bible, *Vini d'Italia*.

Enoteca Italiana

WINE/SPIRITS | Consistently recognized as one of the best wine stores in the country, Enoteca Italiana (established 1972) lives up to its reputation—as it says, "every good bottle has a good story"—with shelves lined with excellent selections from all over Italy at reasonable prices. In addition, the delicious plates of cured meats served with wines by the glass, make a great light lunch. ✉ *Via Marsala 2/b, North of Piazza Maggiore* ☎ *051/235989* 🌐 *www.enotecaitaliana.it.*

La Baita Vecchia Malga

FOOD | Fresh tagliolini, tortellini, and other Bolognese pasta delicacies are sold here, along with sublime food to eat at small tables here or take away. The cheese counter is laden with superlative local specimens. ✉ *Via Pescherie Vecchie 3/a, Piazza Maggiore* ☎ *051/223940* 🌐 *www.vecchiamalganegozi.com.*

Majani

CANDY | Classy Majani has been producing chocolate since 1796. Its staying power may be attributed to high-quality confections that are as pretty to look at as they are to eat. ✉ *Via de' Carbonesi 5, Piazza Maggiore* ☎ *051/234302* 🌐 *www.majani.it.*

Mercato delle Erbe

FOOD | This food market and food hall that opened in 1910 bustles year-round. ✉ *Via Ugo Bassi 23, Piazza Maggiore* ☎ *335/4112427* 🌐 *www.mercatodelleerbe.it.*

Paolo Atti & Figli

FOOD | This place has been producing some of Bologna's finest pastas, cakes, and other delicacies since 1868. There's a second branch at Via Drapperie 6. ✉ *Via Caprarie 7, Piazza Maggiore* ☎ *051/220425* 🌐 *www.paoloatti.com.*

★ **Roccati**

CANDY | Sculptural works of chocolate, as well as basic bonbons and simpler sweets, have been crafted here since 1909. ✉ *Via Clavature 17/a, Piazza Maggiore* ☎ *051/261964* 🌐 *www.roccaticioccolato.com.*

Ferrara

47 km (29 miles) northeast of Bologna, 74 km (46 miles) northwest of Ravenna.

When the legendary Ferrarese filmmaker Michelangelo Antonioni called his beloved hometown "a city that you can see only partly, while the rest disappears to be imagined," perhaps he was referring to the low-lying mist that rolls in off the Adriatic each winter and shrouds Ferrara's winding knot of medieval alleyways, turreted palaces, and ancient wine bars—once frequented by the likes of Copernicus—in a ghostly fog. But perhaps Antonioni was also suggesting that Ferrara's striking beauty often conceals a dark and tortured past.

Today you're likely to be charmed by Ferrara's prosperous air and meticulous cleanliness, its excellent restaurants and chic bars (for coffee and any other liquid refreshment), and its lively wine-bar scene. You'll find aficionados gathering outside any of the wine bars near the Duomo even on the foggiest of weeknights. Although Ferrara is a UNESCO World Heritage site, the city draws amazingly few tourists—which only adds to its appeal.

GETTING HERE AND AROUND

Train service is frequent from Bologna (usually three trains per hour) and takes either a half hour or 50 minutes, depending on which train type you take. It's around 35 minutes from Florence to Bologna, and then about a half hour from Bologna to Ferrara. The walk from the station is easy (about 20 minutes) and not particularly interesting. You can also take Bus No. 1, No. 6, or No. 9 from the station to the center; buy your ticket onboard with money or contactless card via machines onboard, or at the station newsagent: remember to stamp your ticket upon boarding the bus.

If you're driving from Bologna, take the RA1 out of town, then the A13 in the direction of Padua, exiting at Ferrara Nord. Follow the SP19 directly into the center of town. The trip should take about 45 minutes.

VISITOR INFORMATION

CONTACT Ferrara IAT Tourism Office. ✉ *Castello Estense, Piazza Castello, Ferrara* ☎ *0532/419190* 🌐 *www.ferrarainfo.com.*

Sights

Casa Romei

CASTLE/PALACE | Built by the wealthy banker Giovanni Romei (1402–83), this vast structure with a graceful courtyard ranks among Ferrara's loveliest Renaissance palaces. Mid-15th-century frescoes adorn rooms on the ground floor; the piano nobile contains detached frescoes from local churches as well as lesser-known Renaissance sculptures. The Sala delle Sibille has a very large 15th-century fireplace and beautiful coffered wood ceilings. ✉ *Via Savonarola 30, Ferrara* ☎ *0532/234130* 🌐 *www.ferraraterraeacqua.it* 🎫 *€6.*

★ Castello Estense

CASTLE/PALACE | The former seat of Este power, this massive castle dominates the center of town, a suitable symbol for the ruling family: cold and menacing on the outside, lavishly decorated within. The public rooms are grand, but deep in the bowels of the castle are dungeons where enemies of the state were held in wretched conditions. The prisons of Don Giulio, Ugo, and Parisina have some fascinating features, like 15th-century graffiti. Lovers Ugo and Parisina (stepmother and stepson) were beheaded in 1425 because Ugo's father, Niccolò III, didn't like the fact that his son was cavorting with his stepmother.

The castle was established as a fortress in 1385, but work on its luxurious ducal quarters continued into the 16th century. Representative of Este grandeur are the Sala dei Giochi, painted with athletic scenes, and the Sala dell'Aurora, decorated to show the times of the day. The terraces of the castle and the hanging garden have fine views of the town and countryside. You can traverse the castle's drawbridge and wander through many of its arcaded passages whenever the castle gates are open. ✉ *Piazza Castello, Ferrara* ☎ *0532/419180* 🌐 *www.castelloestense.it* 🎫 *€12* 🕑 *Closed Tues.*

Cattedrale di San Giorgio

CHURCH | The magnificent Gothic cathedral, a few steps from the Castello Estense, has a three-tier facade of slender arches and beautiful sculptures over the central door. Work began in 1135 and took more than 100 years to complete. The interior was completely remodeled in the 17th century. On Palm Sunday 2024, the Duomo reopened having undergone major restoration after the 2012 earthquake; the extensive works uncovered ornately sculpted capitals hidden behind plaster for more than three centuries. ✉ *Piazza della Cattedrale, Ferrara* ☎ *0532/207449* 🌐 *www.cattedralediferrara.it.*

Museo della Cattedrale

ART MUSEUM | Some of the original decorations of the town's main church, the former church, and the cloister of San Romano reside in the Museo della Cattedrale, across the piazza from the Duomo. Inside you'll find 22 codices commissioned between 1477 and 1535; early-13th-century sculptures by the Maestro dei Mesi; a mammoth oil on canvas by Cosmè Tura from 1469; and an exquisite Jacopo della Quercia, the *Madonna della Melagrana.* Although this last work dates from 1403 to 1408, the playful expression on the Christ child seems very 21st century. ✉ *Via San Romano 1, Ferrara* ☎ *0532/244949* 🌐 *www.ferrarainfo.com* 🎫 *€6* 🕑 *Closed Mon.*

Museo Nazionale dell'Ebraismo Italiano e della Shoah (*Museum of Italian Judaism and the Shoah*)

SPECIALTY MUSEUM | The collection of ornate religious objects and multimedia installations at this museum (commonly known as MEIS) bears witness to the long history of the city's Jewish community. This history had its high points—1492, for example, when Ercole I invited the Jews to come over from Spain—and its lows, notably 1627, when Jews were enclosed within the ghetto, where they were forced to live until the advent of a united Italy in 1860. The triangular warren of narrow cobbled streets that made up the ghetto originally extended as far as Corso Giovecca (originally Corso Giudecca, or Ghetto Street). When it was enclosed, the neighborhood was restricted to the area between Via Scienze, Via Contrari, and Via di San Romano. The museum is located about a 15-minute walk from the former Jewish ghetto. Guided tours may be booked in advance by emailing or calling the museum. ✉ *Via Piangipane 81, Ferrara* ☎ *0532/1912039* 🌐 *meis.museum* 🎫 *€10* 🕑 *Closed Mon.*

Palazzo dei Diamanti

(*Palace of Diamonds*)

ART MUSEUM | Named for the 8,500 small pink-and-white marble pyramids (or "diamonds") that stud its facade, this building was designed to be viewed in perspective—both faces at once—from diagonally across the street. Work began in the 1490s and finished around 1504. Inside the palazzo is the Pinacoteca Nazionale which houses 13th- to 17th-century Ferrarese painting, plus temporary shows. ✉ *Corso Ercole I d'Este 21, Ferrara* ☎ *0532/244949* 🌐 *www.palazzodiamanti.it* 🎫 *€15.*

★ **Palazzo Schifanoia**

HISTORIC SIGHT | The oldest, most characteristic area of Ferrara is south of the Duomo, stretching between the Corso Giovecca and the city's ramparts. Here various members of the Este family built pleasure palaces, the best known of which is the Palazzo Schifanoia (*schifanoia* means "carefree" or, literally, "fleeing boredom"). Begun in the late 14th century, the palace was remodeled between 1464 and 1469. Inside is Museo Schifanoia, with its lavish interior—particularly the Salone dei Mesi, which contains an extravagant series of frescoes showing the months of the year and their mythological attributes. ✉ *Via Scandiana 23, Ferrara* ☎ *0532/244949* 🌐 *www.ferrarainfo.com* 🎫 *€12* ⏲ *Closed Mon.*

Via delle Volte

STREET | One of the best-preserved medieval streets in Europe, the Via delle Volte clearly evokes Ferrara's past. The series of ancient *volte* (arches) along the narrow cobblestone alley once joined the merchants' houses on the south side of the street to their warehouses on the north side. The street ran parallel to the banks of the Po River, which was home to Ferrara's busy port. ✉ *Via delle Volte, Ferrara.*

Restaurants

★ Enoteca al Brindisi

$ | WINE BAR | Ferrara is a city of wine bars, beginning with this one (allegedly Europe's oldest), which opened in 1435—Copernicus drank here while a student in the late 1400s, and the place still has an undergraduate aura. The twentysomething staff pours well-chosen wines by the glass, and they serve *cappellacci di zucca* (pasta stuffed with squash) with two different sauces (ragù or butter and sage). **Known for:** set menus at great prices; characterful interior; full of locals, students, and visitors. [$] *Average main: €13* ✉ *Via Adelardi 11, Ferrara* ☎ *0532/473744* 🌐 *www.albrindisi.net* ⏲ *No dinner Mon. and Tues.*

★ L'Oca Giuliva

$$ | EMILIAN | Food, service, and ambience harmonize blissfully at this casual but elegant restaurant inside a 12th-century building. The chef shows a deft hand with area specialties and shines with the fish dishes. **Known for:** creative antipasti and seafood dishes; cappellacci di zucca (pumpkin-stuffed pasta); Ferrarese, meat and seafood tasting menus. [$] *Average main: €21* ✉ *Via Boccacanale di Santo Stefano 38/40, Ferrara* ☎ *0532/207628* 🌐 *www.ristorantelocagiuliva.it* ⏲ *Closed Tues. No lunch Thurs.*

Molto Più Che Centrale

$ | EMILIAN | A winning combination of traditional and innovative dishes is the big draw at this colorful, contemporary restaurant with splashy modern art spread over two floors. Young chef Giacomo Garutti delivers Ferrarese classics like *salamina da sugo con purè* (salami atop creamy mashed potatoes) alongside fried and grilled seafood, and innovations like cappellacci pasta filled with pumpkin, orange, and ginger. There's a good wine list, too. **Known for:** local dishes with modern flourishes; upbeat, contemporary setting; attentive waitstaff. [$] *Average main: €19* ✉ *Via Boccaleone 8, Ferrara* ☎ *0532/1880070* 🌐 *www.moltopiuchecentrale.it* ⏲ *Closed Thurs.*

★ Quel Fantastico Giovedì

$$ | EMILIAN | Locals and other cognoscenti frequent this sleek eatery just minutes away from Piazza del Duomo, where chef Gabriele Romagnoli uses prime local ingredients to create gustatory sensations on a menu that changes daily. Fish and seafood figure prominently among his dishes, such as with a *gratinato* (similar to a French au gratin) with seafood. **Known for:** seasonal menu; notable fish and seafood dishes; excellent service. [$] *Average main: €20* ✉ *Via Castelnuovo 9, Ferrara* ☎ *0532/760570* 🌐 *quelfantasticogiovedi.com* ⏲ *Closed Wed.*

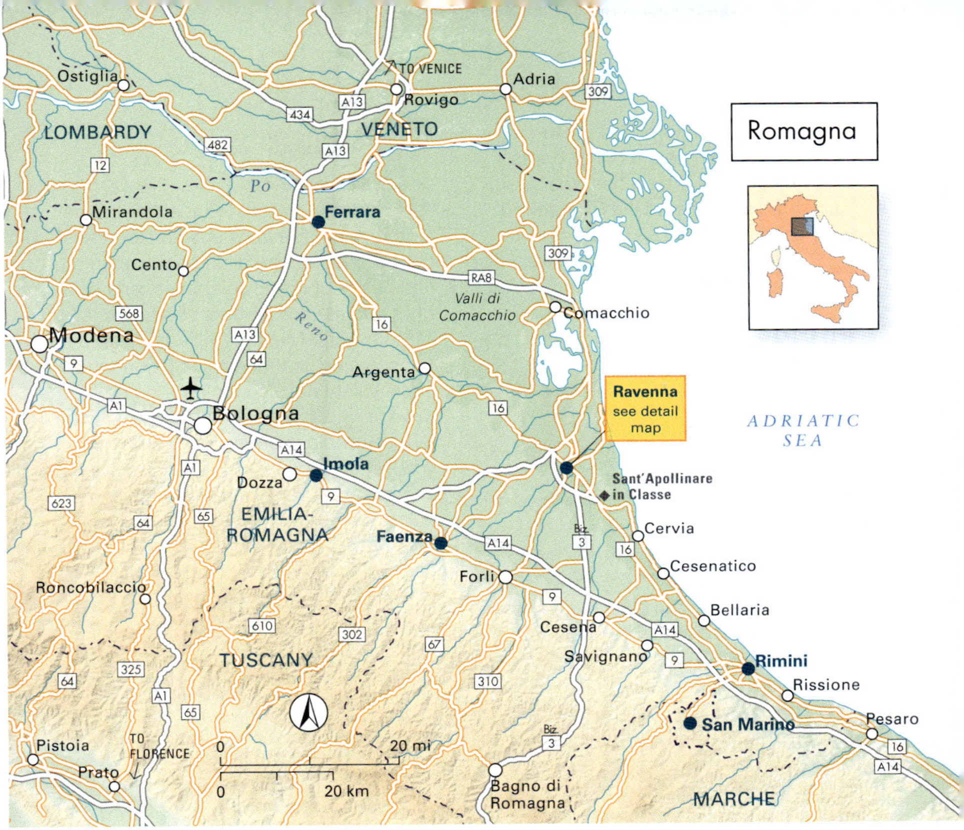

Hotels

Hotel Annunziata

$ | **HOTEL** | Brightly colored fittings enliven the white-walled, hardwood-floor guest rooms—think minimalism with a splash—at this hotel on a quiet little piazza near the forbiddingly majestic Castello Estense. **Pros:** perfect location (you can't get much more central); stellar staff; terrific buffet breakfast. **Cons:** few facilities and limited public spaces; some rooms have uninspiring views; annex 500 feet from main building. *$ Rooms from: €120 ✉ Piazza Repubblica 5, Ferrara ☎ 0532/201111 🌐 www.annunziata.it 🛏 27 rooms 🍽 Free Breakfast.*

★ **Locanda Borgonuovo**

$ | **B&B/INN** | In the early 18th century this lodging began life as a convent (later suppressed by Napoléon), but now it's a delightful city-center bed-and-breakfast, popular with performers at the city's Teatro Comunale. **Pros:** phenomenal breakfast featuring local foods and terrific cakes made in-house; bicycles can be borrowed for free; knowledgeable local advice. **Cons:** steep stairs to reception area and rooms; must reserve far in advance as this place books quickly; decor may be a bit over-fussy for some. *$ Rooms from: €100 ✉ Via Cairoli 29, Ferrara ☎ 0532/211100 🌐 www.borgonuovo.com 🛏 5 rooms 🍽 Free Breakfast.*

Maxxim Hotel

$ | **HOTEL** | **FAMILY** | Though given a stylish modern makeover, the courtyards, vaulted brick lobby, and breakfast room of this 15th-century palazzo retain much of their lordly Renaissance flair. **Pros:** helpful staff; good choice for families; tasteful modern makeover. **Cons:** split-level loft rooms impractical for some; occasional noise from neighboring rooms; some bathrooms are on the small side. *Rooms from: €79* *Via Ripagrande 21, Ferrara* *0532/1770700* *www.maxxim.it* *40 rooms* *Free Breakfast.*

Imola

82 km (51 miles) south of Ferrara, 42 km (26 miles) southeast of Bologna.

Affluent Imola, with its wide and stately avenues, lies on the border between Emilia and Romagna. It was populated as early as the Bronze Age, came under Roman rule, and was eventually annexed to the Papal States in 1504. Imola is best known for its Formula One auto-racing tradition: the San Marino Grand Prix was held here (1981–2006) and it has staged the Emilia Romagna Grand Prix 2020–25. Auto racing as a serious sport in Imola dates to 1953, when, with the support of Enzo Ferrari, the racetrack just outside the city center was inaugurated. As well as hosting the Formula One races, Imola is renowned for its ceramics and the town's world-famous restaurant, San Domenico.

GETTING HERE AND AROUND

Local trains from Bologna run often and take 20–30 minutes. If you're driving from Bologna, take the RA1 to the A14 (following signs for Ancona). Take the exit for Imola. If you're coming from Milan, you can catch the Frecciarossa to Bologna (a little over an hour), and then transfer to the local train.

VISITOR INFORMATION

CONTACT IAT Imola Tourism Office. *Galleria del Centro Cittadino, Via Emilia 135, Imola* *0542/602207* *www.visitareimola.it.*

Restaurants

★ San Domenico

$$$$ | **MODERN ITALIAN** | Year after year this restaurant defends its position as one of Italy's most refined dining destinations, and heads of state, celebrities, and lovers of fine food venture here to savor chef Massimiliano Mascia's wondrous creations. Typical of these is his pioneering uncle Valentino Marcattilii's memorable *uovo in raviolo San Domenico,* in which a large raviolo is stuffed with a raw egg yolk—it cooks only a little, then spills out and mixes with Parmigiano-Reggiano, butter, and black truffles (depending on the season). **Known for:** creative destination dining worth the price; raviolo filled with egg yolk; impeccable service. *Average main: €70* *Via G. Sacchi 1, Imola* *0542/29000* *www.sandomenico.it* *Closed Sun. and Mon.*

Faenza

16 km (10 miles) southeast of Imola, 49 km (30 miles) southeast of Bologna.

In the Middle Ages, Faenza was the crossroads between Emilia-Romagna and Tuscany, and the 15th century saw many Florentine artists working in town. In 1509, when the Papal States took control, Faenza became something of a backwater. It did, however, continue its 12th-century tradition of making top-quality glazed earthenware. In the 16th century local artists created a color called *bianchi di Faenza* (Faenza white), which was widely imitated and wildly desired all over Europe. The Frenchified *faience,* referring to the color and technique, soon entered the lexicon, where it remains to this day. In the central Piazza del Popolo, dozens of shops sell local ceramics.

GETTING HERE AND AROUND

Trains run frequently from Bologna to Faenza, making the trip in 25–50 minutes. There's also sporadic service from

Florence, a beautiful ride of under two hours. The walk to the centro storico, though easy, isn't especially interesting.

By car it takes about an hour from Bologna. Follow the SP253 to the RA1, at which point pick up on the A14/E45 heading in the direction of Ancona. Exit and take the SP8 into Faenza.

VISITOR INFORMATION

CONTACT Pro Loco IAT Faenza Tourism Office. ✉ *Voltone della Molinella 2, Faenza* ☎ *0546/25231* 🌐 *www.prolocofaenza.it.*

Sights

Museo Internazionale delle Ceramiche

ART MUSEUM | One of the largest ceramics museums in the world has a well-labeled, well-lit collection, with objects from the Renaissance among its highlights. Although the emphasis is clearly on local work, the rest of Italy and the globe are also represented. Don't miss the 20th- and 21st-century galleries, which prove that decorative arts often surpass their practical limitations and become genuinely sculptural. ✉ *Viale Baccarini 19, Faenza* ☎ *0546/697311* 🌐 *www.micfaenza.org* 🎟 *€12* ⏲ *Closed Mon.*

Restaurants

Marianaza

$$ | **ITALIAN** | A large open-hearth fireplace dominates this rustic trattoria, and wonderful aromas of grilled meats and garlic greet you as you walk in. Marianaza successfully showcases the best of *la cucina romagnola* (the cuisine of Romagna): the extraordinary primi are mostly made with fresh pasta—tagliatelle or *garganelli* (egg-based and tubular)—while secondi rely heavily on the grill. **Known for:** good-value grilled meats; fresh pasta; Romagna specialties. $ *Average main: €20* ✉ *Via Torricelli 21, Faenza* ☎ *0546/681461* 🌐 *www.marianaza.com* ⏲ *Closed Sun. and Wed. (June–Sept.), and Tues. and Wed. (Oct.–May).*

Rimini

70 km (43½ miles) southeast of Faenza, 52 km (32 miles) southeast of Ravenna, 121 km (75 miles) southeast of Bologna.

Rimini is one of the most popular summer resorts on the Adriatic Coast and one of the most popular in Italy. July and August are the most crowded, packed with people who don't mind crammed beaches and not-terribly-blue water. In the off-season (October through March), Rimini is a cold, windy fishing port with few places open. Any time of year, one of Rimini's least touristy areas is the port; rambling down the Via Sinistra del Porto or Via Destra del Porto past all the fishing boats, you're far from the crush of sunbathers.

The town stands at the junction of two great Roman consular roads, the Via Emilia and the Via Flaminia. In Roman times it was an important port, making it a strategic and commercial center. From the 13th century onward, Rimini was controlled by the Malatesta family, an unpredictable clan equally capable of grand gestures and savage deeds.

GETTING HERE AND AROUND

Trains run hourly from Ravenna to Rimini and take about an hour. By car from Ravenna, take the SS16/E55, then follow the SS3bis/E45/E55 in the direction of Roma/Ancona. Follow directions for Ancona Nord, then follow signs for Ancona. Take the A14/E55 to the Rimini Nord exit, then the SP136 to the SS16, and follow signs for the center of town. Alternatively, take the coastal road, SS16, which hugs the shoreline much of the way, passing through Cervia. Though only 52 km (32 miles), this scenic route is naturally slower (beware of fog in winter). The coast north of Rimini is lined with dozens of small resort towns, but only one really has any charm—the seaport of Cesenatico—the others are mini-Riminis, and in summer the narrow road is hopelessly clogged with traffic.

There's frequent train service (usually three or four trains per hour) from Bologna to Rimini. It takes one to two hours, depending on which train you choose. By car from Bologna, take the SP253 out of town, pick up the RA1, and then enter the A14 heading toward Ancona. Get off at the Rimini Nord exit and follow the SP136 to the SS16 to the center of town.

VISITOR INFORMATION

CONTACT Rimini Tourism Office. ✉ *Piazzale Federico Fellini 3, Rimini* ☎ *0541/53399* 🌐 *www.riminiturismo.it.*

Sights

Arco d'Augusto

HISTORIC SIGHT | Rimini's oldest monument is the Arco d'Augusto, now stranded in the middle of a square just inside the city ramparts. It was erected in 27 BC, making it among the oldest surviving ancient Roman arches. ✉ *Largo Giulio Cesare at Corso d'Augusto, Rimini.*

★ Museo Fellini

ART MUSEUM | The life and magical cinematic oeuvre of Rimini's favorite 20th-century son, the celebrated film director Federico Fellini, is explored in depth at this wonderfully atmospheric and suitably dreamlike museum, opened in 2021. Spread over three sites—Castel Sismondo, Palazzo del Fulgor, and Piazza Malatesta—and through multimedia, sculpture, iconic film props, costumes, playful installations, and archive material, the exhibits chart the maestro's formative and Italian cinema's golden years. Fellini's artistic friends and collaborators are center-stage, too: screens project clips of Giulietta Masina in *La Strada* (1956) and Marcello Mastroianni in *La Dolce Vita* (1960), the evocative music of Nino Rota scores enliven every corner, and there's a Fellini-esque sculpture of a reposing Anita Ekberg. Palazzo del Fulgor, and the cinema immortalized in Fellini's semi-autobiographical love letter to Rimini, *Amarcord* (1973), has a changing program of Fellini's filmography. ✉ *Castel Sismondo, Piazza Malatesta, Rimini* ☎ *0541/793781* 🌐 *www.fellinimuseum.it* 🎟 *€10* ⏲ *Closed Mon.*

Tempio Malatestiano

CHURCH | The Malatesta family constructed the Tempio Malatestiano, also called the Basilica Cattedrale, with a masterful facade by Leon Battista Alberti (1404–72). Inside, the chapel to the right of the high altar contains a wonderful (if faded) fresco by Piero della Francesca (1420–92) depicting Sigismondo Malatesta kneeling before a saint. The two greyhounds in the right corner are significantly less faded than the rest. ✉ *Via IV Novembre 35, Rimini* ☎ *0541/51130* 🌐 *www.diocesi.rimini.it* 🎟 *Free.*

Restaurants

La Marianna

$ | ITALIAN | It's all about fish at this welcoming spot, and aside from vegetable side dishes and dessert there's little on the menu that wasn't recently swimming (or lurking) in the sea. Depending on what's in season you might find a starter like *seppia in umido con fagioli* (steamed octopus with beans), which provides a tasty introduction to more complicated delights. **Known for:** locally caught seafood across all courses; lively outdoor dining; reasonable prices. 💲 *Average main: €18* ✉ *Viale Tiberio 19, Rimini* ☎ *0541/22530* 🌐 *www.trattorialamarianna.it.*

Hotels

Grand Hotel Rimini

$$ | HOTEL | This 1908 extravaganza, made famous by Federico Fellini in his film *Amarcord*, is grander than ever with ongoing restorations that keep the place completely current while maintaining its Belle Époque charm. **Pros:** sumptuous buffet breakfast that starts early (7 am) and ends late (11 am); Fellini's beloved Terrazza; amenities including everything from a spa and a private beach to programs for children in summer. **Cons:** 1 km (½ mile) from Rimini's historic center; sea view rooms cost more; under par services and room decor. $ *Rooms from: €249* ✉ *Parco Federico Fellini, Rimini* ☎ *0541/56000* 🌐 *www.grandhotelrimini.com* *172 rooms* *Free Breakfast.*

San Marino

20 km (12½ miles) southwest of Rimini, 139 km (86 miles) southeast of Bologna.

The world's smallest and oldest republic, as San Marino dubs itself, is surrounded entirely by Italy. It consists of three ancient castles perched on sheer cliffs rising implausibly out of the flatlands of Romagna, and a tangled knot of cobblestone streets below that are lined with tourist boutiques, cheesy hotels and restaurants, and gun shops. A visit here is justified, however, by the sweeping views from the castle of the countryside. The 3,300-foot-plus precipices will make jaws drop and acrophobes quiver.

Visiting San Marino in winter (off-season) increases the appeal of the experience, as tourist establishments shut down and you more or less have the castles to yourself. In August every inch of walkway on the rock is mobbed with sightseers. Don't worry about changing money, showing passports, and the like (although the tourist office in Piazza Garibaldi will stamp your passport for €5). San Marino is, for all practical purposes, Italy—except, that is, for its majestic perch, its lax gun laws, and its high national voter turnout rate.

GETTING HERE AND AROUND

To get to San Marino by car, take highway SS72 west from Rimini. From Borgo Maggiore, at the base of the rock, a cable car will whisk you up to the town. Alternatively, you can drive up the winding road; public parking is available. There is a regular bus service to and from Rimini train station, with service sometime every hour throughout the year (less frequent service on Sunday); a one-way ticket from Rimini to San Marino costs €7. The trip takes about 50 minutes.

VISITOR INFORMATION

CONTACT San Marino Tourism Office. ✉ *Via dei Cappuccini 1, San Marino* ☎ *0549/882914* 🌐 *www.visitsanmarino.com.*

Sights

Piazza della Libertà

PLAZA/SQUARE | One must-see is the Piazza della Libertà, where the Palazzo Pubblico is guarded by soldiers in green uniforms. As you'll notice by peering into the shops along the old town's winding streets, the republic is famous for crossbows and other items (think fireworks or firearms) that are illegal almost everywhere else. ✉ *Piazza della Libertà, San Marino.*

Tre Castelli

CASTLE/PALACE | San Marino's headline attractions are its Tre Castelli—medieval architectural wonders that appear on every coat of arms in the city—and some spectacular views. Starting in the center of town, walk a few hundred yards past the trinket shops, along a paved cliff-top ridge, from the 10th-century Rocca della Guaita to the 13th-century Rocca della Cesta (containing a museum of ancient weapons; worthwhile mostly for the views from its terraces and turrets) and finally to the 14th-century Rocca Montale (closed to the public), the most remote of the castles. Every step of the way affords spectacular views of Romagna and the Adriatic—it's said that on a clear day you can see Croatia. The walk makes for a good day's exercise but is by no means arduous. Even if you arrive after visiting hours, it's supremely rewarding. ✉ *San Marino* ☎ *0549/991369* 🌐 *www.cultura.sm* *La Torre Guaita, La Torre Cesta, and 2 museums €9.*

Ravenna

80 km (50 miles) northwest of San Marino, 93 km (58 miles) southeast of Ferrara.

A small, quiet, and well-heeled city, Ravenna has brick palaces, cobblestone streets, magnificent monuments, and spectacular Byzantine mosaics. The high point in its civic history occurred in the 5th century, when Pope Honorious moved his court here from Rome. Gothic kings Odoacer and Theodoric ruled the city until it was conquered by the Byzantines in AD 540. Ravenna later fell under the sway of Venice, and then, inevitably, the Papal States.

Because Ravenna spent much of its past looking east, its greatest art treasures show that Byzantine influence. Churches and tombs with the most unassuming exteriors contain within them walls covered with sumptuous mosaics. These beautifully preserved Byzantine mosaics put great emphasis on nature, which you can see in the delicate rendering of sky, earth, and animals. Outside Ravenna, the town of Classe hides even more mosaic gems.

GETTING HERE AND AROUND

By car from Bologna, take the SP253 to the RA1, and then follow signs for the A14/E45 in the direction of Ancona. From here, follow signs for Ravenna, taking the A14dir Ancona–Milano–Ravenna exit. Follow signs on the SS309 to the center of Ravenna. From Ferrara the drive is more convoluted, but also more interesting. Take the SS16 to the RA8 in the direction of Porto Garibaldi, taking the Roma/Ravenna exit. Follow the SS309/E55 to the SS309dir/E55, taking the SS253 Bologna/Ancona exit. Follow the SS16/E55 into the center of Ravenna.

By train, there are one or two direct services hourly from Bologna, taking 70 minutes.

VISITOR INFORMATION

CONTACT Ravenna Tourism Office. ✉ *Piazza San Francesco 7, Ravenna* ☎ *0544/35755* 🌐 *www.turismo.ra.it.*

Sights

★ Basilica di San Vitale

CHURCH | The octagonal church of San Vitale was built in AD 547, after the Byzantines conquered the city, and its interior shows a strong Byzantine influence. The area behind the altar contains the most famous works, depicting Emperor Justinian and his retinue on one wall, and his wife, Empress Theodora, with her retinue, on the opposite one. Notice how the mosaics seamlessly wrap around the columns and curved arches on the upper sides of the altar area. **TIP→ School groups can sometimes swamp the site from March through mid-June.** ✉ *Via San Vitale, off Via Salara, Ravenna* ☎ *0544/541688* 🌐 *www.ravennamosaici.it* 🎟 *€11 combination ticket, includes other diocesan monuments.*

Battistero Neoniano

CHURCH | Next door to Ravenna's 18th-century cathedral, this baptistery has one of the town's most important mosaics. It dates from the beginning of the 5th century AD, with work continuing through the century. In keeping with the building's role, the great mosaic in the dome shows the baptism of Christ, and beneath are the Apostles. The lowest register of mosaics contains Christian symbols, the Throne of God, and the Cross. Note the naked figure kneeling next to Christ—he is the personification of the River Jordan. ✉ *Piazza Duomo, Ravenna* ☎ *0544/541688* 🌐 *www.ravennamosaici.it* 🎟 *€11 combination ticket, includes other diocesan monuments (€2 supplement for Baptistery and Mausoleum)* ✍ *Reservations essential.*

Classis Ravenna – Museo della Città e del Territorio

SPECIALTY MUSEUM | FAMILY | In Classe, a short distance outside Ravenna, this museum dazzlingly illustrates the history of Ravenna and its environs from the pre-Roman era to the Lombard conquest in AD 751. The museum occupies a refurbished sugar refinery, and with the help of multimedia presentations and panels in Italian and English, it chronicles the Roman, Ostrogoth, and Byzantine periods. Displays include bronze statuettes, stone sculptures, glassware, and mosaic fragments. A separate room summarizes the building's more recent history. It's an easy walk from Sant'Apollinare in Classe. **■ TIP→ To get here from Ravenna, take Bus No. 4 from the station or the local train to Classe, or use the cycle path from the city center.** ✉ *Via Classense 29, off SS71, Classe* ☎ *0544/473717* 🌐 *www.classisravenna.it* 🎫 *€6* ⏲ *Closed Mon.*

Domus dei Tappeti di Pietra

(House of the Stone Carpets)

RUINS | This archaeological site with lovely mosaics was uncovered in 1993 during digging for an underground parking garage near the 18th-century church of Santa Eufemia. Ten feet below ground level lie the remains of a Byzantine palace dating from the 5th and 6th centuries AD. Its beautiful and well-preserved network of floor mosaics displays elaborately designed patterns, creating the effect of luxurious carpets. ✉ *Via Barbiani 16, Ravenna* ✥ *Enter through Sant'Eufemia church* ☎ *0544/473678* 🌐 *www.domusdeitappetidipietra.it* 🎫 *€6* ⏲ *Closed Mon.*

★ Mausoleo di Galla Placidia

CHURCH | The little tomb and the great church stand side by side, but the tomb predates the Basilica di San Vitale by at least 100 years: these two adjacent sights are decorated with the best-known, most elaborate mosaics in Ravenna. Galla Placidia was the sister of the Roman emperor Honorius, who moved the imperial capital to Ravenna in AD 402. This mid-5th-century mausoleum is her memorial.

The simple redbrick exterior only serves to enhance by contrast the richness of the interior mosaics, in deep midnight blue and glittering gold. The tiny central dome is decorated with symbols of Christ, the evangelists, and striking gold stars. Eight of the Apostles are represented in groups of two on the four inner walls of the dome; the other four appear singly on the walls of the two transepts. There are three sarcophagi in the tomb, none of which are believed to actually contain the remains of Galla Placidia. **■ TIP→ Visit early or late in the day to avoid the school groups that can sometimes swamp the Mausoleo from March through mid-June.** ✉ *Via San Vitale 17, off Via Salara, Ravenna* ☎ *0544/541688* 🌐 *www.ravennamosaici.it* 🎫 *€11 combination ticket, includes other diocesan monuments (€2 supplement for mausoleum and baptistery).*

Museo d'Arte della città di Ravenna (MAR)

ART MUSEUM | Housed in the magnificent former monastery and abbey of Santa Maria in Porto, this municipal art collection with origins in the Napoleonic era has a core of 300 paintings and sculptures, with sections dedicated to late Middle Ages-early Renaissance pious works and the 16th and 17th century, to the Novecento and contemporary works. Seek out the archaic-looking, myth-inspired equine terra-cotta sculpture *L'Assediato* (1999) by Paladino that seems to span the ages. The collection is well displayed and artfully lighted, especially the vibrant contemporary mosaic section, plus there's the *RavennaMosaico* biennial among the changing shows. ✉ *Via di Roma 13,*

Sights

1 Basilica di San Vitale... **B1**

2 Battistero Neoniano.... **B4**

3 Classis Ravenna – Museo della Città e del Territorio.................. **E5**

4 Domus dei Tappeti di Pietra.................. **A2**

5 Mausoleo di Galla Placidia.................. **B1**

6 Museo d'Arte della città di Ravenna (MAR)....... **E5**

7 Museo Nazionale di Ravenna............... **B2**

8 Sant'Apollinare in Classe..................... **E5**

9 Sant'Apollinare Nuovo..................... **E4**

10 Tomba di Dante and Circuito Dante........... **D4**

Restaurants

1 Ca' de Vèn................ **C4**

2 Osteria del Tempo Perso............ **B2**

Hotels

1 Albergo Cappello........ **C2**

2 Hotel Sant'Andrea...... **A3**

3 Palazzo Bezzi............. **E4**

Bologna ☎ 0544/482477 🌐 mar.ra.it 🎟 €6 🕑 Closed Mon.

Museo Nazionale di Ravenna

(*National Museum of Ravenna*)
SPECIALTY MUSEUM | Next to the Church of San Vitale and housed in a former Benedictine monastery, the museum contains artifacts from ancient Rome, Byzantine fabrics and carvings, and pieces of early Christian art. Curiosities include remains of the city's gate Porta Aurea (AD 44) and 14th-century "Giotto School" frescoes by Pietro da Rimini. ✉ *Via San Vitale 17, Ravenna* ☎ *0544/213902* 🎟 *€6* 🕑 *Closed Mon.*

Sant'Apollinare in Classe

CHURCH | This church about 5 km (3 miles) southeast of Ravenna is landlocked now, but when it was built, it stood in the center of the busy shipping port known to the ancient Romans as Classis. The arch above and the area around the high altar are rich with mosaics. Those on the arch, older than the ones behind it, are considered superior. They show Christ in Judgment and the 12 lambs of Christianity leaving the cities of Jerusalem and Bethlehem. In the apse is the figure of Sant'Apollinare himself, a bishop of Ravenna, and above him is a magnificent Transfiguration against blazing green grass, animals in odd perspective, and flowers. ✉ *Via Romea Sud 224, off SS71, Classe* ☎ *0544/527308* 🌐 *info.ravennantica.it* 🎟 *€5 or €9, including Classis Ravenna museum* 🕑 *Closed Mon.*

Sant'Apollinare Nuovo

CHURCH | The mosaics displayed in this church date from the early 6th century, making them slightly older than those in San Vitale. Since the left side of the church was reserved for women, it's only fitting that the mosaics on that wall depict 22 virgins offering crowns to the Virgin Mary. On the right wall, 26 men carry the crowns of martyrdom; they approach Christ, surrounded by angels. ✉ *Via Roma 53, at Via Guaccimanni, Ravenna* ☎ *0544/541688* 🌐 *www.ravennamosaici.it* 🎟 *€11 combination ticket, includes other diocesan monuments.*

Tomba di Dante and Circuito Dante

TOMB | Exiled from his native Florence, the author of *The Divine Comedy* died here in 1321, and Dante's tomb and bones (which over the centuries were secretly stashed in various spots nearby) lies in a small neoclassical building by the church of St. Francis. Nearby a Dante Circuit consists of the immersive, multimedia Museo Dante and more meditative Casa Dante with Dantean artifacts from the Biblioteca Classense and the Uffizi. The Florentines have long been trying to reclaim their famous son, but the Ravennans argue that since Florence did not welcome Dante in life, it does not deserve him in death. Perhaps as penance, every September the Florentine government sends olive oil that's used to fuel the light hanging in the chapel's center. ✉ *Via Dante Alighieri 9, Ravenna* ☎ *0544/215676* 🌐 *vivadante.it* 🎟 *Tomba €5, Circuito Dante €5.*

Restaurants

Ca' de Vèn

$ | ITALIAN | These buildings, joined by a glass-ceilinged courtyard, date from the 15th century, so the setting itself is reason enough to come; that the food is so good makes a visit here all the more satisfying. At lunchtime Ca' de Vèn teems with locals tucking in to *piadine* (a typical Romagnolo flatbread) stuffed or topped with various ingredients, and the grilled dishes—including *tagliata di pollo* (sliced chicken breast tossed with arugula and set atop exquisitely roasted potatoes)—are among the highlights. **Known for:** grilled meats; weekly menu of Romagnolo specialties; majestic, high-ceilinged lively setting. 💲 *Average main: €19* ✉ *Via Corrado Ricci 24, Ravenna* ☎ *0544/30163* 🌐 *www.cadeven.it* 🕑 *Closed Mon.*

★ Osteria del Tempo Perso

$$ | ITALIAN | A couple of jazz-, rock-, and food-loving friends joined forces to open this smart little restaurant in the center. The interior's warm terra-cotta-sponged walls give off an orange glow, and wine bottles line the walls, interspersed with photographs of musical greats—but the food is what counts. **Known for:** terrific seafood dishes; fine wine list; homemade pastas. *Average main: €22 Via Gamba 12, Ravenna 0544/215393 www.osteriadeltempoperso.it Closed Thurs. No lunch.*

Hotels

Albergo Cappello

$ | HOTEL | Originally opened in the late 19th century and restored a century later, this small, charming place exhibits a Venetian influence, with Murano chandeliers hanging from the high coffered wood ceilings in common rooms. **Pros:** good location in historic area and near sights; accommodating staff; wine bar and good restaurant. **Cons:** patchy air-conditioning; parking sometimes hard to find; occasional street noise in some rooms. *Rooms from: €149 Via IV Novembre 41, Ravenna 0544/219813 www.albergocappello.it 7 rooms Free Breakfast.*

Hotel Sant'Andrea

$ | B&B/INN | FAMILY | For a quiet and welcoming lodging on a residential street a stone's throw from the Basilica di San Vitale, look no further—it even has a delightful garden. **Pros:** quiet neighborhood; good-size guest rooms and family suites, some with terraces; cheery and helpful staff. **Cons:** can get a little noisy; limited breakfast choice; few facilities. *Rooms from: €130 Via Carlo Cattaneo 33, Ravenna 0544/215564 www.santandreahotel.com 12 rooms Free Breakfast.*

Palazzo Bezzi

$$ | HOTEL | Set in a historic, central palazzo, Bezzi is the best bet in town for reliable, friendly customer service, and a comfortable stay amid modern surroundings, a quiet garden, and panoramic rooftop solarium. **Pros:** central yet quiet location; small spa and gym; reliable service, cleanliness, and maintenance. **Cons:** no bar or restaurant; some may find the decor soulless; pricey garage parking. *Rooms from: €189 Via di Roma 45, Ravenna 0544/36926 palazzobezzi.it 32 rooms Free Breakfast.*

Chapter 11

FLORENCE

Updated by
Liz Shemaria

WELCOME TO FLORENCE

TOP REASONS TO GO

★ **Galleria degli Uffizi:** Italian Renaissance art doesn't get much better than the contents of this vast collection bequeathed in 1737 by the last Medici, Anna Maria Luisa.

★ **Brunelleschi's Dome:** His work of engineering genius is the city's undisputed centerpiece.

★ **Michelangelo's *David*:** One look, up close, and you'll know why this is one of the world's most famous sculptures.

★ **The view from Piazzale Michelangelo:** From this perch the city is laid out before you. The colors at sunset heighten the experience.

★ **Piazza Santa Croce:** After you've had your fill of Renaissance masterpieces, idle here and watch the world go by.

1 Around the Duomo. You're in the heart of Florence here. Among the numerous highlights are the city's greatest museum (the Uffizi) and arguably its most impressive square (Piazza della Signoria).

2 San Lorenzo. The complex of the basilica of San Lorenzo, the Palazzo Medici-Riccardi, and the Galleria dell'Accademia bears the imprints of the Medici and of Michelangelo, culminating in the latter's masterful statue *David*. Just to the north, the former convent of San Marco is an oasis of artistic treasures decorated with ethereal frescoes.

3 Santa Maria Novella. This part of town includes the train station, 16th-century palaces, and the city's swankest shopping street, Via Tornabuoni.

4 Santa Croce. The district centers on its namesake basilica, which is filled with the tombs of Renaissance (and other) luminaries. The area is also known for its leather shops.

5 The Oltrarno. Across the Arno you encounter the massive Palazzo Pitti and the narrow streets and alleys of the hip Santo Spirito neighborhood.

San Marco
Galleria dell'Accademia/ Michelangelo's David
SAN LORENZO
2
SAN GIOVANNI
Piazza San Lorenzo
San Lorenzo
Battistero
Duomo
Piazza del Duomo
1
Piazza della Repubblica
Piazza Strozzi
Piazza della Signoria
Piazza San Firenze
Galleria degli Uffizi
Piazza degli Uffizi
Ponte Vecchio
Arno River
SANTA CROCE
4
Piazza Santa Croce
Santa Croce
Ponte alle Grazie
OLTRARNO
5
TO PIAZZALE MICHELANGELO
0
150 yards
0
150 meters
Via Panicale
Via Taddea
Via Chiara
Via G.B. Zannoni
Via dell'Ariento
Via Sant'Orsola
Via Rosina
Via San Gallo
Via Guelfa
Via degli Arrazieri
Via degli Alfani
Via della Colonna
Borgo la Noce
Via della Stufa
Via de Ginori
Via Cavour
Via Ricasoli
Via dei Servi
V. del Castellaccio
Via Sant'Antonino
V. Faenza
Via dell' Amorino
V. del Giglio
V. dell' Alloro
V. F. Zannetti
Borgo San Lorenzo
Via Martelli
Via d. Bitti
Via del Pucci
Via dei Pilastri
Borgo Pinti
Via dei Cerretani
Via del Pecori
Via F. Portinari
Via M. Bufalini
Via dell' Orinolo
V. del Tosinghi
Via del Pescioni
Via del Vecchietti
Via Brunelleschi
Via Roma
Via Calzaiuoli
Via S. Elisabetta
Via d. Studio
V. del Proconsolo
Via Giuseppe Verdi
Via dei Pepi
Via d. Speziali
Via del Strozzi
Via del Corso
Borgo degli Albizi
Via Pietrapiana
V. d. Anselmi
Via Calimala
V. del Cerchi
Via d. Giraldi
Via del Pandolfini
Via d. Senglote
Via delTavolini
Via Dante Alighieri
Via dell' Agnolo
Via Monalda
Via del Sassetti
Via Pellicceria
Via del Lamberti
Via Magazzini
Via Ghibellina
Via della Condotta
Via d. Vigna Vecchia
Via d. Burelli
Via Calimaruzza
Ricasoli
Via delle Terme
Borgo Santi Apostoli
V. Por Santa
V. Vacchereccia
Via d. Gondi
V. G. d. Verrazzano
Via d. Pinzochere
Via san Cristofano
Borgo Allegri
Lungarno Acciaioli
V. Lambertesca
Via d. Ninna
Via del Leoni
Via d. Corno
Via Vinegia
Via d. Magalotti
Via de' Rustici
Borgo del Greci
Via dei Benci
Via Antonio Magliabechi
Via San Giuseppe
Lungarno Archibusieri
Via d. Castellani
Via del Neri
Via d. Mosca
V. d. Bracne
Borgo Santa Croce
Via d. Saponai
V. d. Vagellai
V. V. Malenchini
Lungarno Generale Armando Diaz
Corso del Tintori
Via de' Bardi
Lungarno della Grazie
Via Tripoli
Costa di San Giorgio
Costa de' Magnoli
Lungarno Torrigiani
Lungarno Serristori
Via dei Renai

EATING AND DRINKING WELL IN FLORENCE

A well-stocked local wine shop

In Florence, simply prepared meats, grilled or roasted, are the culinary stars, usually paired with seasonal vegetables like artichokes or porcini. *Bistecca* (steak) is popular here, but there's plenty more that tastes great on the grill.

Traditionalists go for their gustatory pleasures in *trattorie* (casual restaurants) and *osterie* (down-home restaurants), places where decor is unimportant and place mats are mere paper. Culinary innovation comes slowly in this town, though some cutting-edge restaurants have been appearing.

By American standards, Florentines eat late: 1:30 or 2 pm is typical for lunch and 9 pm for dinner is considered early. Consuming a *primo* (first course), *secondo* (second course), and *dolce* (dessert) is largely a thing of the past. For lunch, many Florentines simply grab a panino and a glass of wine at a bar. Those opting for a simple trattoria lunch often order a plate of pasta and dessert.

STALE AND STELLAR

Stale bread is the basis for three classic Florentine primi: *pappa al pomodoro*, *ribollita*, and *panzanella*. Pappa is made with either fresh or canned tomatoes and that stale bread. Ribollita is a vegetable soup with *cavolo nero* (Tuscan kale) and cannellini beans, thickened with bread. Panzanella is reconstituted Tuscan bread combined with tomatoes, cucumber, and basil. These dishes are all enhanced with a generous application of fragrant Tuscan olive oil.

A CLASSIC ANTIPASTO: CROSTINI DI FEGATINI

This beloved dish consists of a chicken-liver spread, presented warm or at room temperature, on toasted, garlic-rubbed bread. It can be served smooth, like a pâté, or in a chunkier, more rustic version. It's made by sautéing chicken livers with finely diced carrot and onion, enlivened with the addition of wine, broth, or Marsala reductions, and mashed anchovies and capers.

A CLASSIC SECONDO: BISTECCA ALLA FIORENTINA

The town's culinary pride and joy is a thick slab of beef, resembling a T-bone steak, from large white oxen called Chianina. The meat's slapped on the grill, seared on both sides, and served rare, sometimes with a pinch of salt.

A CLASSIC CONTORNO: CANNELLINI BEANS

Simply boiled, beans provide the perfect accompaniment to bistecca. The small white ones are best when they go straight from the garden into the pot. They should be anointed with a generous dose of Tuscan olive oil; the combination is oddly felicitous, and it goes a long way toward explaining why Tuscans are referred to as *mangiafagioli* (bean eaters) by other Italians.

Biscotti

Bistecca alla Fiorentina

A CLASSIC DOLCE: BISCOTTI DI PRATO

These are sometimes the only dessert on offer. *Biscotti* means twice-cooked (or, in this case, twice-baked). They are hard almond cookies that soften considerably when dipped languidly into *vin santo* ("holy wine"), a sweet dessert wine, or into a simple *caffè*.

A CLASSIC WINE: CHIANTI CLASSICO

This blend from the region just south of Florence relies mainly on the local, hardy Sangiovese grape; it's aged for at least one year before hitting the market. (*Riserve*—reserve—is aged at least an additional six months.)

Chianti is usually the libation of choice for Florentines. Traditionalists opt for the younger, fruitier (and usually less expensive) versions often served in straw flasks. You can sample Chianti Classico all over town and buy it in local supermarkets.

Its magical combination of beauty and history has drawn people to Florence for centuries, and then it draws them back again. It offers myriad moments of personal illumination before its palazzi, its churches, and its art museums, as well as in interaction with the people you meet there.

Florence has captivated visitors for ages now, probably ever since the powerful Medici family first staged jousts and later lavish pageants to celebrate their weddings. Its mostly sober beauty continued to attract people from all over Europe intent on taking in the achievements of the past on their Grand Tour of Europe. Sometimes, this heady combination of art and beauty has proven overwhelming, as it did for French author and diplomat Stendhal in 1817, whose visit to the church of Santa Croce occasioned palpitations and a fainting spell.

Today, however, visitors are more often overwhelmed by the press of their own numbers intent on taking it all in before moving on to the next stop on their tightly scheduled tours. Florence has always been visitor-friendly—the historical center of the city can be crossed on foot in less than half an hour, and the picturesque surrounding hills are a short bus ride away. But the flood of tourists has made the natives more reticent. A visitor is more likely to bump into or to exchange views with other visitors than with native Florentines, all busy catering to tourists' needs. Few Florentines, these days, can afford to live in the center. Even the university has pulled some buildings out to a suburb.

By day, the city is overrun with busloads of day-trippers; come evening by droves of U.S. study-abroad students intent on immersion in the native *aperitivo* (predinner drink) culture. Where have all the Italians gone, you wonder? Fear not, they still come out on Sunday to walk in family groups along the major shopping streets, school groups still pack museums, and they still hold parades in Renaissance costume to mark various historical or religious occasions. Caffè culture still thrives. All this will be revealed to the attentive visitor who sees past the crowds and takes the time to look around the corner onto a quieter street, piazza, or neighborhood.

When the sun sets over the Arno and, as Mark Twain described it, "overwhelms Florence with tides of color that make all the sharp lines dim and faint and turn the solid city to a city of dreams," it's hard not to fall under the city's spell.

Planning

Getting Here and Around

AIR

To get into the city center from Aeroporto A. Vespucci (🌐 *www.aeroporto.firenze.it*) by car, take the autostrada A11. The T2 tram will take you directly to and from the airport and the center of town. Buy tickets at machines outside the tram stops.

BIKE AND MOPED

Brave souls (cycling in Florence is difficult at best) may rent bicycles at easy-to-spot locations at Fortezza da Basso, the Stazione Centrale di Santa Maria Novella, and Piazza Pitti. Otherwise, try **Alinari** (✉ *Via San Zanobi 40/r, San Marco* ☎ *055/280500* 🌐 *www.alinarirental.com*). You'll be up against hordes of tourists and those pesky *motorini* (mopeds). (For a safer ride, try Le Cascine, a former Medici hunting ground turned into a large public park with paved pathways.) The historic center can be circumnavigated via bike paths lining the *viali,* the ring road surrounding the area. If you want to go native, rent a noisy Vespa (Italian for "wasp") or other make of motorcycle or *motorino.* Try **Vespa Hangar** (✉ *Via degli Avelli 2* ☎ *351/5494122 mobile*).

BUS

Florence's flat, compact city center is made for walking, but when your feet get weary you can use the bus system, which includes the small electric buses making the rounds in the center. Buses also climb to Piazzale Michelangelo and San Miniato south of the Arno. Note that buses are often delayed and you may need to flag a bus down if you're the only person waiting for it.

Autolinee Toscana (🌐 *www.at-bus.it*) has updated schedules on its website. Tickets should be bought in advance from tobacco shops, newsstands, automatic ticket machines near main stops, online, or using a mobile app. Paper tickets must be validated in the machine immediately upon boarding. You may also buy tickets on the bus, but the cost is approximately double.

You have several ticket options, all valid for one or more rides on all lines. A €1.70 ticket purchased in advance is good for one hour from the time it is first validated. A Carnet of multiple tickets—each valid for 70 minutes—costs €15.50. A weekly pass costs €14.70.

Autolinee Toscana also provides service to Siena and San Gimignano. Long-distance **FlixBus** (🌐 *www.global.flixbus.com*) provides inexpensive service between Florence and other cities in Italy and Europe.

CAR

Florence is connected to the north and south of Italy by the Autostrada del Sole (A1). It takes about 1½ hours of driving on scenic roads to get to Bologna (although heavy truck traffic over the Apennines often makes for slower going), about 3 hours to Rome, and 3–3½ hours to Milan. The Tyrrhenian Coast is an hour west on the A11.

An automobile in Florence is a major liability. If your itinerary includes parts of Italy where you'll want a car (such as Tuscany), pick the vehicle up on your way out of town.

TAXI

Taxis usually wait at stands throughout the city (in front of the train station and in Piazza della Repubblica, for example). You can also call radio dispatch (☎ *055/4390, 055/4242*) for one to pick you up wherever you are.

The meter start rate depends on what time of day you travel, and extra charges apply at night, on Sundays and holidays, and for luggage. Women out on the town after midnight are entitled to a 10% discount on the fare; you must, however, request it or call radio dispatch (☎ *055/4378557*).

TRAIN

Florence is on the principal Italian train route between most European capitals and Rome, and within Italy it is served frequently from Milan, Venice, and Rome by Intercity (IC) and nonstop Eurostar trains. Avoid trains (🌐 *www.trenitalia.com*) that stop only at the Campo di Marte or Rifredi station, which are not convenient to the city center. The main train station is Stazione Centrale di Santa Maria Novella.

Hotels

Florence is equipped with hotels for all budgets; for instance, you can find both budget and luxury hotels in the *centro storico* (historic center) and along the Arno. Florence has so many famous landmarks that it's not hard to find lodging with a panoramic view. The equivalent of the genteel *pensioni* of yesteryear can still be found, though they are now officially classified as "hotels." Generally small and intimate, they often have a quaint appeal that usually doesn't preclude modern plumbing. Florence's importance not only as a tourist city but also as a convention center and the site of the Pitti fashion collections guarantees a variety of accommodations.

The high demand also means that, except in winter, reservations are a must.

⇨ *Hotel and restaurant reviews have been shortened. For full information, visit Fodors.com. Prices in the hotel reviews are the lowest cost of a standard double room in high season. Prices in the dining reviews are the average cost of a main course at dinner, or, if dinner is not served, at lunch.*

What It Costs in Euros

	$	$$	$$$	$$$$
RESTAURANTS				
	under €20	€20–€30	€31–€40	over €40
HOTELS				
	under €175	€175–€400	€401–€600	over €600

Making the Most of Your Time

With some planning, you can see Florence's most famous sights in a couple of days. Start off at the city's most awe-inspiring architectural wonder, the **Duomo,** climbing to the top of the dome if you have the stamina (and are not claustrophobic: it gets a little tight going up and coming back down). On the same piazza, check out Ghiberti's bronze doors at the **Battistero.** (They're actually high-quality copies; the Museo dell'Opera del Duomo has the originals.) Set aside the afternoon for the **Galleria degli Uffizi** and the **Vasari Corridor ,** making sure to reserve tickets in advance.

On Day 2, visit Michelangelo's *David* in the **Galleria dell'Accademia**—reserve tickets here, too. Linger in **Piazza della Signoria,** Florence's central square, where a copy of *David* stands in the spot the original occupied for centuries, then head east a couple of blocks to **Santa Croce,** the city's most artistically rich church. Double back and walk across Florence's landmark bridge, the **Ponte Vecchio.**

Do all that, and you'll have seen some great art, but you've just scratched the surface. If you have more time, put the **Bargello,** the **Museo di San Marco,** and the **Cappelle Medicee** at the top of your list. When you're ready for an art break, stroll through the **Boboli Gardens** or explore Florence's lively shopping scene, from the food stalls of the **Mercato Centrale** to the chic boutiques of the **Via Tornabuoni.**

HOURS

Florence's sights keep tricky hours. Some are closed Wednesday, some Monday, some every other Monday. Quite a few shut their doors each day (or on most days) by 2 in the afternoon. Things get even more confusing on weekends. Make it a general rule to check the hours closely for any place you're planning to visit; if it's someplace you have your heart set on seeing, it's worthwhile to call to confirm.

Here's a selection of major sights that might not be open when you'd expect (⇨ *consult the Sights listings within this chapter for full details).* And be aware that, as always, hours can and do change. Also note that on the first Sunday of the month, all state museums are free. That means that the Accademia and the Uffizi, among others, do not accept reservations. Unless you are a glutton for punishment (i.e., large crowds), these museums are best avoided on that day.

The **Accademia** and the **Uffizi** (including the **Vasari Corridor**) are both closed Monday. Note, too, that on the first Sunday of the month, all state museums, including these two, are free and do not accept reservations.

The **Bargello** is closed on Tuesday and the second and fourth Sunday of the month. Otherwise, it's open from 8:15 am until 1:50 pm (until 6:50 pm on Saturday).

The **Battistero** is open daily 8:30 am to 7:30 pm.

The **Cappelle Medicee** are closed Tuesday. Otherwise, they're open from 8:15 am to 6:50 pm.

The **Duomo** is closed on Sunday and open from 10:15 am until sunset the rest of the week.

Museo di San Marco closes at 1:50 pm—except for alternating Sundays and Mondays, when it's closed entirely.

Palazzo Medici-Riccardi is closed Wednesday.

RESERVATIONS

At most times of day a line of people snakes around the Uffizi. They're waiting to buy tickets, and you don't want to be one of them. Instead, book online (🌐 *www.uffizi.it*) or call ahead (☎ *055/294883*) for a reservation.

Go to the museum's reservation door (door 3) 10 minutes before the appointed hour (at least 30 minutes before in high season), give the clerk your reservation number, or show your digital ticket, pick up your paper ticket, and go inside. You'll pay €4 for this privilege, but it's money well spent. Money-saving combo tickets are available as well.

You'll also want to book in advance for Galleria dell'Accademia (🌐 *www.galleriaaccademiafirenze.it*), where lines rival those of the Uffizi. Reservations can also be made for the Palazzo Pitti, the Bargello, and several other sights, but they usually aren't needed—although, lately, in summer, lines can be long at Palazzo Pitti. An alternative strategy is to check with your hotel—many will handle reservations.

Restaurants

Florence's popularity with tourists means that, unfortunately, there's a higher percentage of mediocre restaurants here than you'll find in most Italian towns (Venice, perhaps, might win that prize). Some restaurant owners cut corners and let standards slip, knowing that a customer today is unlikely to return tomorrow, regardless of the quality of the meal. So, if you're looking to eat well, it pays to do some research, starting with the recommendations here. Dining hours start at around 1 for lunch and 8 for dinner. Many of Florence's restaurants are small, so reservations are a must. You can sample such specialties as creamy fegatini (a chicken-liver spread) and ribollita (minestrone thickened with bread and beans and swirled with extra-virgin olive oil) in a bustling, convivial trattoria, where you share long wooden tables set with paper place mats, or in an upscale *ristorante* with linen tablecloths and napkins.

Shopping

Window-shopping in Florence is like visiting an enormous contemporary-art gallery. Many of today's greatest Italian artists are fashion designers, and most keep shops in Florence. Discerning shoppers may find bargains in the street markets. **■TIP→ Do not buy any knockoff goods from any of the hawkers plying their fake Prada (or any other high-end designer) on the streets. It's illegal, and fines are astronomical if the police happen to catch you. (You pay the fine, not the vendor.)**

Shops are generally open 9–1 and 3:30–7:30, and are closed Sunday and Monday morning most of the year. Summer (June to September) hours are usually 9–1 and 4–8, and some shops close Saturday afternoon instead of Monday morning. When looking for addresses, you'll see two color-coded numbering systems on each street. The red numbers are commercial addresses and are indicated, for example, as "31/r." The blue or black numbers are residential addresses. Most shops take major credit cards and ship purchases, but because of possible delays it's wise to take your purchases with you.

SHOPPING DISTRICTS

Florence's most fashionable shops are concentrated in the center of town. The fanciest designer shops are mainly on **Via Tornabuoni** and **Via della Vigna Nuova.** The city's largest concentrations of antiques shops are on **Borgo Ognissanti** and the Oltrarno's **Via Maggio.** The **Ponte Vecchio** houses reputable but very expensive jewelry shops, as it has since the 16th century. The area near **Santa Croce** is the heart of the leather merchants' district.

Tours

Alone-in-the-Duomo VIP Tour

SPECIAL-INTEREST TOURS | **FAMILY** | Partnering with international companies such as Walks and Devour Tours, City Experiences (🌐 *www.cityexperiences.com*) is able to offer unique, once-in-a-lifetime tours. On the two-hour Alone-in-the-Duomo experience, for instance, you not only get after-hours access to the cathedral, but you also climb up to the dome, visit private terraces, and watch as the official Key Master locks up for the night—all while accompanied by knowledgeable guides. ☎ *800/4598105 City Experiences Main U.S. contact center, 888/6838670 City Experiences Walks (toll-free in U.S.), 068/5960143 City Experiences Walks (in Italy)* 🌐 *www.takewalks.com/florence-tours* 🎫 *From €195.*

Visitor Information

The Florence tourist office (☎ *039/055000* 🌐 *www.feelflorence.it*), has branches at the airport, across the street from Stazione di Santa Maria Novella (the main train station), and at Via Cavour 1R. The offices are generally open from 9 am until 7 pm (5:30 pm on Sunday and holidays). The multilingual staff will answer questions, give you directions, and provide information on the latest performing-arts happenings and other events. The website also provides information in English.

Around the Duomo

The heart of Florence, stretching from the Piazza del Duomo south to the Arno, is as dense with artistic treasures as any place in the world. Its churches, medieval towers, Renaissance palaces, and world-class museums and galleries contain some of the most outstanding achievements of Western art.

Much of the centro storico is closed to automobile traffic, but you still must dodge mopeds, cyclists, and masses of fellow tourists as you walk the narrow streets, especially in the area bounded by the Duomo, Piazza della Signoria, Galleria degli Uffizi, and the Ponte Vecchio. Via dei Calzaiuoli, between Piazza del Duomo and Piazza della Signoria, is the city's favorite passeggiata.

★ Bargello

ART MUSEUM | This building started out in the Middle Ages as the headquarters for the *capitano del popolo* (captain of the people) during the Middle Ages and was later a prison. It now contains the Museo Nazionale, which has one of Italy's finest collections of Renaissance sculpture. The remarkable masterpieces by Michelangelo (1475–1564), Donatello (circa 1386–1466), and Benvenuto Cellini (1500–71) are distributed amid an eclectic collection of arms, ceramics, and miniature bronzes, among other things. ✉ *Via del Proconsolo 4, Bargello* ☎ *055/0649440* 🌐 *bargellomusei.it* 🎫 *€10* ⏲ *Closed Tues. and 2nd and 4th Sun. of the month.*

★ Battistero (*Baptistery*)

RELIGIOUS BUILDING | The octagonal Baptistery is one of the supreme monuments of the Italian Romanesque style and one of Florence's oldest structures. The round Romanesque arches on the exterior date from the 11th century, and the interior dome mosaics from the beginning of the mid-13th century are justly renowned, but they could never outshine the building's famed bronze Renaissance doors decorated with panels crafted by Lorenzo Ghiberti. Michelangelo declared them so beautiful that they could serve as the Gates of Paradise. ✉ *Piazza del Duomo, Duomo* ☎ *055/2645789* 🌐 *www.duomo.firenze.it* 🎫 *Admission is via one of 3 combo tickets, each valid for 3 days: €30 Brunelleschi Pass (with Campanile, Cupola of the Duomo, Museo dell'Opera del Duomo, and Santa Reparata Basilica Cripta); €20 Giotto Pass (with Campanile, Museo dell'Opera, and Cripta); €15 Ghiberti Pass (with Museo dell'Opera and Cripta).*

Campanile

NOTABLE BUILDING | **FAMILY** | The Gothic bell tower designed by Giotto (circa 1266–1337) is a soaring structure of multicolor marble originally decorated with sculptures by Donatello and reliefs by Giotto, Andrea Pisano, and others (which are now in the Museo dell'Opera del Duomo). A climb of 414 steps rewards you with a close-up of Brunelleschi's cupola on the Duomo next door and a sweeping view of the city. ✉ *Piazza del Duomo, Duomo* ☎ *055/2645789* 🌐 *www.duomo.firenze.it* 🎫 *Admission is via one of 2 combo tickets, each valid for 3 days: €30 Brunelleschi Pass (with Battistero, Cupola of the Duomo, Museo dell'Opera del Duomo, and Santa Reparata Basilica Cripta); €20 for Giotto Pass (with Battistero, Museo dell'Opera, and Cripta).*

Corridoio Vasariano [Vasari Corridor]

BRIDGE | The Corridoio Vasariano (Vasari Corridor), a private Medici elevated passageway, was built by Vasari in 1565. Though the ostensible reason for its construction was one of security, it was more likely designed so that the Medici family wouldn't have to walk amid the commoners—as you can now see following the about half-mile route that glides over one of the most foot-trafficked parts of Florence, across Piazza del Pesce (named for the area's past life as a fish

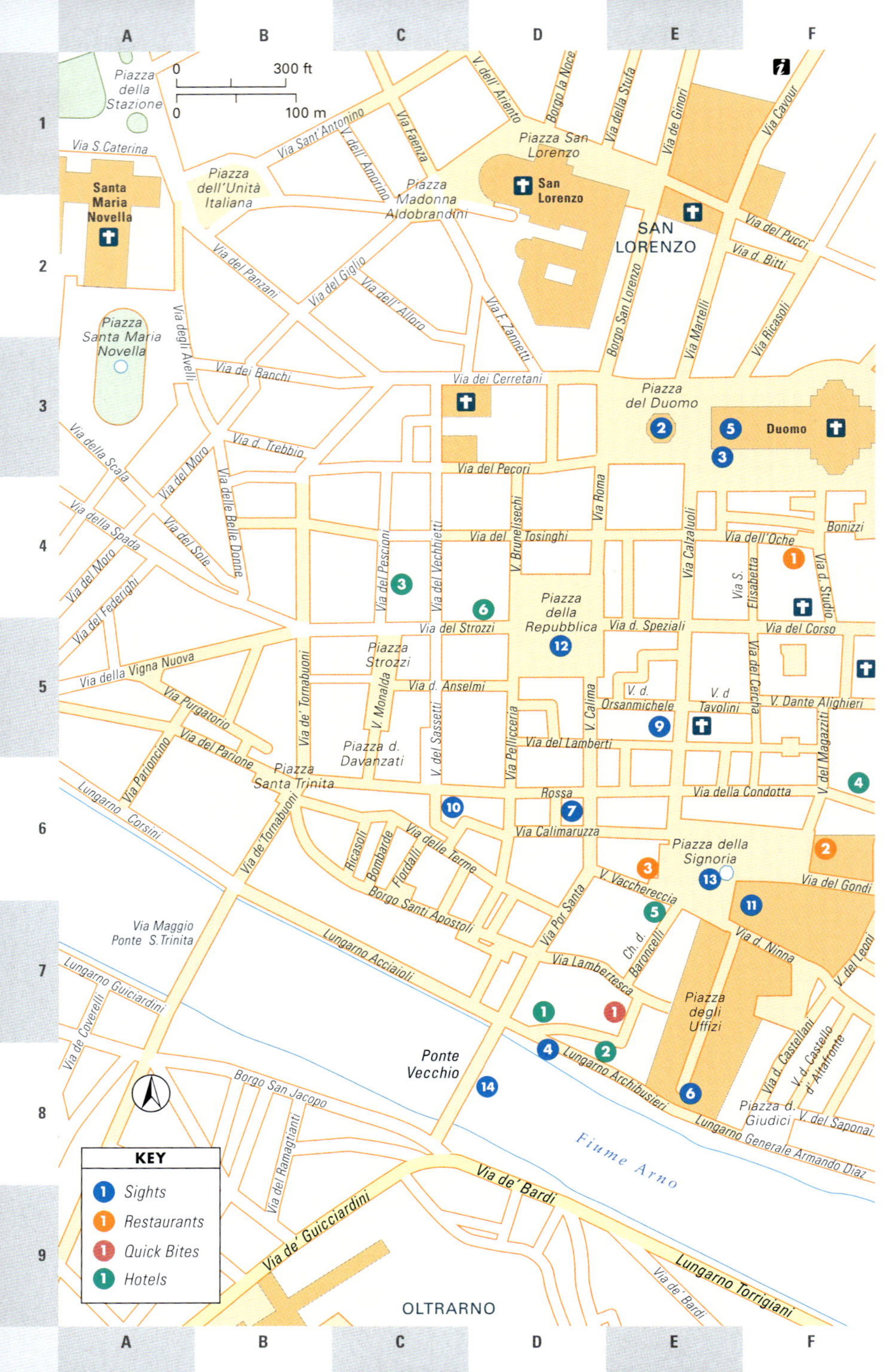

A
B
C
D
E
F
1
2
3
4
5
6
7
8
9
0
300 ft
100 m
Piazza della Stazione
Via S.Caterina
Santa Maria Novella
Piazza dell'Unità Italiana
Via Sant'Antonino
V. dell' Ariento
Via Faenza
V. dell' Amorino
Borgo la Noce
Via della Stufa
Via de Ginori
Via Cavour
Piazza San Lorenzo
San Lorenzo
Piazza Madonna Aldobrandini
SAN LORENZO
Via del Pucci
Via d. Bitti
Via del Panzani
Via del Giglio
Via dell' Alloro
Via F. Zannetti
Borgo San Lorenzo
Via Martelli
Via Ricasoli
Via degli Avelli
Piazza Santa Maria Novella
Via dei Banchi
Via dei Cerretani
Piazza del Duomo
Duomo
Via della Scala
Via d. Trebbio
Via del Moro
Via delle Belle Donne
Via del Pecori
Via della Spada
Via del Sole
Via Roma
Via del Tosinghi
Via Calzaiuoli
Via dell'Oche
Bonizzi
V. Brunelleschi
Via del Pescioni
Via del Vecchietti
Via S. Elisabetta
Via d. Studio
Via del Moro
Via del Federighi
Piazza della Repubblica
Via del Strozzi
Via d. Speziali
Via del Corso
Piazza Strozzi
Via della Vigna Nuova
Via de' Tornabuoni
V. Monalda
Via d. Anselmi
V. d. Orsanmichele
V. d Tavolini
Via del Cerchia
V. Dante Alighieri
Via Purgatorio
Via del Parione
V. Calimala
Piazza d. Davanzati
V. del Sassetti
Via Pellicceria
Via del Lamberti
V. del Magazzini
Via Parioncino
Piazza Santa Trinita
Rossa
Via della Condotta
Lungarno Corsini
Via de' Tornabuoni
Via Calimaruzza
Ricasoli
Bombarde
Fiordalli
Via delle Terme
Piazza della Signoria
V. Vacchereccia
Via del Gondi
Borgo Santi Apostoli
Via Por Santa
Via d. Ninna
Via Maggio
Ponte S. Trinita
Lungarno Acciaioli
Ch. d. Baroncelli
V. del Leoni
Lungarno Guicciardini
Via Lambertesca
Piazza degli Uffizi
Via de Coverelli
Ponte Vecchio
Lungarno Archibusieri
Via d. Castellani
V. d. Castello d'Altafronte
Borgo San Jacopo
Piazza d. Giudici
V. del Saponai
Via del Ramagtianti
Lungarno Generale Armando Diaz
Fiume Arno
Via de' Bardi
Via de' Guicciardini
Lungarno Torrigiani
Via de' Bardi
OLTRARNO
KEY
Sights
Restaurants
Quick Bites
Hotels

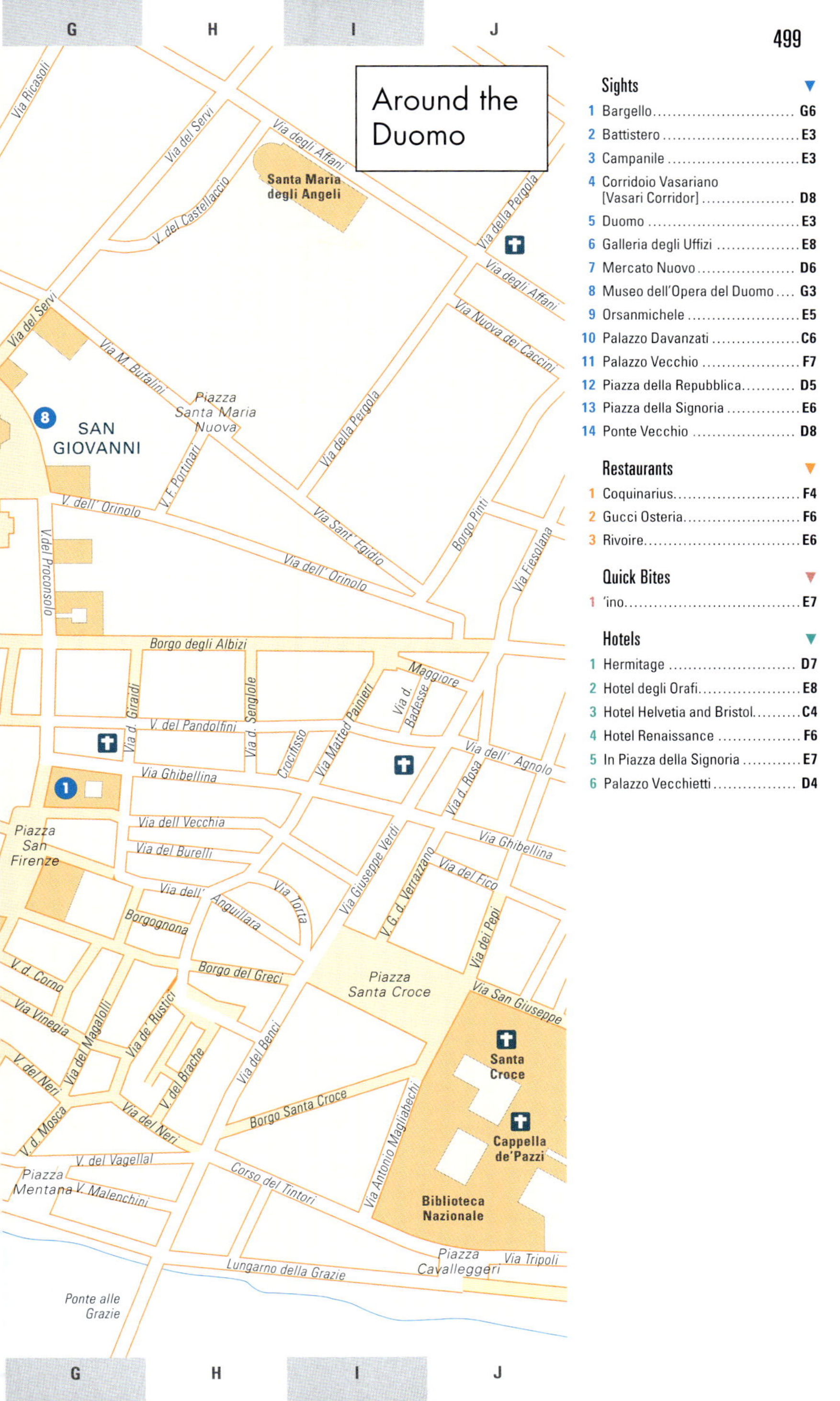
Around the Duomo
G
H
I
J
Via Ricasoli
Via del Servi
V. del Castellaccio
Via degli Alfani
Santa Maria degli Angeli
Via della Pergola
Via degli Alfani
Via Nuova dei Caccini
Via del Servi
Via M. Bufalini
Piazza Santa Maria Nuova
8
SAN GIOVANNI
Via della Pergola
V. F. Portinari
V. dell' Orinolo
Via Sant' Egidio
Borgo Pinti
Via Fiesolana
V.del Proconsolo
Via dell' Orinolo
Borgo degli Albizi
Maggiore
Via d. Badesse
Via Matteo Palmieri
Via d. Giraldi
V. del Pandolfini
Via d. Senglole
Crocifisso
Via dell' Agnolo
Via d. Rosa
Via Ghibellina
1
Via dell Vecchia
Via del Burelli
Piazza San Firenze
Via dell' Anguillara
Via Torta
Via Giuseppe Verdi
V. G. d. Verrazzano
Via Ghibellina
Via del Fico
Via dei Pepi
Borgognona
V. d. Corno
Borgo del Greci
Piazza Santa Croce
Via San Giuseppe
Via Vinegia
Via del Magalolli
Via de' Rustici
V. del Brache
Via del Benci
Santa Croce
V. del Neri
Via del Neri
V. d. Mosca
Borgo Santa Croce
Via Antonio Magliabechi
Cappella de'Pazzi
V. del Vagellal
Piazza Mentana
V. Malenchini
Corso del Tintori
Biblioteca Nazionale
Piazza Cavalleggeri
Via Tripoli
Lungarno della Grazie
Ponte alle Grazie
G
H
I
J

Sights
1 Bargello G6
2 Battistero E3
3 Campanile E3
4 Corridoio Vasariano [Vasari Corridor] D8
5 Duomo E3
6 Galleria degli Uffizi E8
7 Mercato Nuovo D6
8 Museo dell'Opera del Duomo G3
9 Orsanmichele E5
10 Palazzo Davanzati C6
11 Palazzo Vecchio F7
12 Piazza della Repubblica D5
13 Piazza della Signoria E6
14 Ponte Vecchio D8
Restaurants
1 Coquinarius F4
2 Gucci Osteria F6
3 Rivoire E6
Quick Bites
1 'ino E7
Hotels
1 Hermitage D7
2 Hotel degli Orafi E8
3 Hotel Helvetia and Bristol C4
4 Hotel Renaissance F6
5 In Piazza della Signoria E7
6 Palazzo Vecchietti D4

market) and the Ponte Vecchio and on to Palazzo Pitti. The corridor was once filled with art, and today's blank walls are a bit disappointing, though windows along the route provide Arno views on the Ponte Vecchio, and at the Torre de Mannelli, a pass through one of four towers that once defended the "old bridge" from attack. The most interesting part of the walk is when the corridor passes over Santa Felicita, and a window facing the church's altar; this was the Medici's private church entrance. Access to the corridor is through the Galleria degli Uffizi, and ticket-holders need to meet at room D-19 to start the guided visit; Uffizi entry is permitted two hours before the corridor's ticket time to visit the museum since Uffizi reentry isn't permitted after ending the corridor tour in Giardino di Boboli. ✉ *Piazzale degli Uffizi 6, Florence* ☎ *055/294883* 🌐 *www.uffizi.it* 🎫 *€43 (includes access to Uffizi for 2 hrs before entering the corridor)* ⏲ *Closed Mon.*

★ **Duomo** (*Cattedrale di Santa Maria del Fiore*)

CHURCH | In 1296, Arnolfo di Cambio was commissioned to build "the loftiest, most sumptuous edifice human invention could devise" in the Romanesque style. The immense Duomo was not completed until 1436, the year it was consecrated. The imposing facade dates only from the 19th century; its neo-Gothic style somewhat complements Giotto's genuine Gothic 14th-century campanile. The real glory of the Duomo, however, is Filippo Brunelleschi's dome, presiding over the cathedral with a dignity and grace that few domes to this day can match.

Brunelleschi's cupola was one of the great engineering breakthroughs of all time: most of Europe's later domes, including that of St. Peter's in Rome, were built employing Brunelleschi's methods, and today the Duomo has come to symbolize Florence in the same way that the Eiffel Tower symbolizes Paris. The interior is a fine example of Florentine Gothic, though much of the cathedral's best-known art has been moved to the nearby Museo dell'Opera del Duomo. ✉ *Piazza del Duomo, Duomo* ☎ *055/2645789* 🌐 *www.duomo.firenze.it* 🎫 *Church is free. Admission to the cupola is via the €30 Brunelleschi Pass, a 3-day combo ticket that also includes the Battistero, Campanile, Museo dell'Opera del Duomo, and Santa Reparata Basilica Cripta* ⏲ *Closed Sun.* ✍ *Timed-entry reservations required for the cupola.*

★ **Galleria degli Uffizi**

ART MUSEUM | The Medici installed their art collections at Europe's first modern museum, open to the public (at first only by request) since 1591. Among the highlights are Paolo Uccello's *Battle of San Romano*; the *Madonna and Child with Two Angels* by Fra Filippo Lippi; *Birth of Venus* and *Primavera* by Sandro Botticelli; the portraits of the Renaissance duke Federico da Montefeltro and his wife Battista Sforza by Piero della Francesca; the *Madonna of the Goldfinch* by Raphael; Michelangelo's *Doni Tondo*; the *Venus of Urbino* by Titian; and the splendid *Bacchus* by Caravaggio. Late in the afternoon is the least crowded time to visit. For a €4 fee, advance tickets (recommended) can be reserved by phone, online, or, once in Florence, at the Uffizi's reservation booths (✉ *Uffizi presale booth, Piazza Pitti* ☎ *055/294883*), at least one day in advance of your visit. ✉ *Piazzale degli Uffizi 6, Piazza della Signoria* ☎ *055/294883* 🌐 *www.uffizi.it* 🎫 *From €23* ⏲ *Closed Mon.*

Mercato Nuovo (*New Market*)

MARKET | **FAMILY** | The open-air loggia, built in 1551, teems with souvenir stands, but the real attraction is a copy of Pietro Tacca's bronze *Porcellino* (which translates as "little pig" despite the fact the animal is, in fact, a wild boar). The sculpture is Florence's equivalent of the Trevi Fountain: put a coin in his mouth, and if it falls through the grate below (according to one interpretation), it means you'll return to Florence someday. What you're seeing is a copy of a copy: Tacca's original version, in the Museo Bardini, is actually a copy of an ancient Greek work. ✉ *Via Por Santa Maria at Via Porta Rossa, Piazza della Repubblica* ☎ *339/3271143 mobile* 🌐 *www.mercatodelporcellino.it.*

★ Museo dell'Opera del Duomo (*Cathedral Museum*)

ART MUSEUM | A seven-year restoration, completed in 2015, gave Florence one of its most modern, up-to-date museums. The exhibition space was doubled, and the old facade of the cathedral, torn down in the 1580s, was re-created with a 1:1 relationship to the real thing. Both sets of Ghiberti's doors adorn the same room. Michelangelo's *Pietà* finally has the space it deserves, as does Donatello's *Mary Magdalene.* ✉ *Piazza del Duomo 9, Duomo* ☎ *055/2302885* 🌐 *www.duomo.firenze.it* 🎫 *Admission is via one of 3 combo tickets, each valid for 3 days: €30 Brunelleschi Pass (with Battistero, Campanile, Cupola of the Duomo, and Santa Reparata Basilica Cripta); €20 Giotto Pass (with Battistero, Campanile, and Cripta); €15 Ghiberti Pass (with Battistero and Cripta)* 🕓 *Closed 1st Tues. of month.*

Orsanmichele

CHURCH | This structure has served multiple purposes. Built in the 8th century as an oratory, in 1290, it was turned into an open-air loggia for selling grain. Destroyed by fire in 1304, it was rebuilt as a loggia-market. Between 1367 and 1380, its arcades were closed and two stories were added above. Finally, at century's end, it was turned into a church.

Although the interior contains a beautifully detailed 14th-century Gothic tabernacle by Andrea Orcagna (1308–68), it's the exterior that is most interesting. Niches contain sculptures (all copies) dating from the early 1400s to the early 1600s by Donatello and Verrocchio (1435–88), among others, which were paid for by the guilds. ✉ *Via dell'Arte della Lana, Duomo* ☎ *055/0649450* 🌐 *www.bargellomusei.beniculturali.it* 🎫 *€8* 🕓 *Closed Tues.* ✍ *Reservations recommended.*

Palazzo Davanzati

CASTLE/PALACE | The prestigious Davizzi family owned this 14th-century palace in one of Florence's swankiest medieval neighborhoods (it was sold to the Davanzati in the 15th century). The place is a delight, as you can wander through the surprisingly light-filled courtyard and climb the steep stairs to the piano nobile (there's also an elevator), where the family did most of its living. The beautiful Sala dei Pappagalli (Parrot Room) is adorned with trompe-l'oeil tapestries and gaily painted birds. ✉ *Piazza Davanzati 13, Piazza della Repubblica* ☎ *055/0649460* 🌐 *www.bargellomusei.beniculturali.it* 🎫 *€6* 🕓 *Closed Mon. and 1st, 3rd, and 5th Sun. of month.*

Palazzo Vecchio (*Old Palace*)

CASTLE/PALACE | **FAMILY** | Presumably designed by Arnolfo di Cambio and begun in 1299, Florence's forbidding, fortress-like city hall was built as a meeting place for the guildsmen governing the city at the time. Although its massive bulk and towering campanile dominate Piazza della Signoria, its interior courtyard is a good deal less severe. Its main attraction, however, is the opulently vast, second-floor Sala dei Cinquecento (Room of the Five Hundred), named for the 500-member Great Council that met here. ✉ *Piazza della Signoria, Piazza della Signoria* ☎ *055/2768224* 🌐 *cultura.comune.fi.it/pagina/musei-civici-fiorentini/museo-di-palazzo-vecchio* 🎫 *From €12.50.*

Piazza della Repubblica

PLAZA/SQUARE | The square marks the site of an ancient forum, which was the core of the original Roman settlement and which was replaced in the Middle Ages by the Mercato Vecchio (Old Market). The current piazza, constructed between 1885 and 1895 as a neoclassical showpiece, is lined with cafés that

Florence through the Ages

Guelph vs. Ghibelline. Although Florence can lay claim to a modest importance in the ancient world, it didn't come into its own until the Middle Ages. In the early 1200s, the city, like most of the rest of Italy, was rent by civic unrest. Two factions, the Guelphs and the Ghibellines, competed for power. The Guelphs supported the papacy, and the Ghibellines supported the Holy Roman Empire. Bloody battles—most notably one at Montaperti in 1260—tore Florence and other Italian cities apart. By the end of the 13th century, the Guelphs ruled securely, and the Ghibellines had been vanquished. This didn't end civic strife, however: the Guelphs split into the Whites and the Blacks for reasons still debated by historians. Dante, author of *The Divine Comedy*, was banished from Florence in 1301 because he was a White.

The Guilded Age. Local merchants had organized themselves into guilds by some time beginning in the 12th century. In 1250, they proclaimed themselves the *primo popolo* (literally, "first people"), making a landmark attempt at elective, republican rule. Though the episode lasted only 10 years, it constituted a breakthrough in Western history. Such a daring stance by the merchant class was a by-product of Florence's emergence as an economic powerhouse. Florentines were papal bankers; they instituted the system of international letters of credit, and the gold florin became the international standard of currency. With this economic strength came a building boom. Sculptors such as Ghiberti and Donatello decorated the new churches; painters such as Giotto and Masaccio frescoed their walls.

Mighty Medici. Though ostensibly a republic, Florence was blessed (or cursed) with one very powerful family, the Medici, who came to prominence in 1434 and were initially the de facto rulers and then the absolute rulers of Florence for several hundred years. It was under patriarch Cosimo il Vecchio (1389–1464) that the Medici's position in Florence was securely established. Florence's golden age occurred during the reign of his grandson Lorenzo de' Medici (1449–92). Lorenzo was not only an astute politician but also a highly educated man and a great patron of the arts. Called "Il Magnifico" (the Magnificent), he gathered around him poets, artists, philosophers, architects, and musicians.

Lorenzo's son Piero (1471–1503) proved inept at handling the city's affairs. He was run out of town in 1494, and Florence briefly enjoyed its status as a republic while dominated by the Dominican friar Girolamo Savonarola (1452–98). After a decade of internal unrest, the republic fell and the Medici returned to power, but Florence never regained its former prestige. By the 1530s most of the major artistic talent had left the city—Michelangelo, for one, had settled in Rome. The now-ineffectual Medici, eventually attaining the title of grand dukes, remained nominally in power until the line died out in 1737, after which time Florence passed from the Austrians to the French and back again until the unification of Italy (1865–70), when it briefly became the capital under King Vittorio Emanuele II.

are the perfect spots from which to people-watch. ✉ *Piazza della Repubblica, Piazza della Repubblica.*

★ Piazza della Signoria

PLAZA/SQUARE | This is by far the most striking square in Florence. It was here, in 1497 and 1498, that the famous "bonfire of the vanities" took place, when the fanatical Dominican friar Savonarola induced his followers to hurl their worldly goods into the flames. The statues in the square and in the 14th-century Loggia dei Lanzi on the south side vary in quality. Cellini's famous bronze *Perseus* holding the severed head of Medusa is certainly the most important. ✉ *Piazza della Signoria, Piazza della Signoria.*

★ Ponte Vecchio (*Old Bridge*)

BRIDGE | This charmingly simple bridge was built in 1345 to replace an earlier bridge swept away by flood. Its shops first housed butchers, then grocers, blacksmiths, and other merchants. But in 1593, the Medici grand duke Ferdinand I, whose private corridor linking the Medici palace (Palazzo Pitti) with the Medici offices (the Uffizi) crossed the bridge atop the shops, decided that all this plebeian commerce under his feet was unseemly. So he threw out the butchers and blacksmiths and installed 41 goldsmiths and eight jewelers. The bridge has been devoted solely to these two trades ever since. ✉ *Ponte Vecchio, Duomo.*

Restaurants

Coquinarius

$$ | **ITALIAN** | This rustically elegant space, which has served many purposes over the past 600 years, offers some of the tastiest food in town at great prices. It's the perfect place to come if you aren't sure what you're hungry for, as it offers a bit of everything, including several fish dishes, among them carpaccio and grilled offerings, and a selection of pasta dishes that make choosing just one very hard, though the ravioli with pecorino and pears is particularly good. **Known for:** many vegetarian options; reasonably priced wine list; inconsistent service. [$] *Average main: €23* ✉ *Via delle Oche 11/r, Duomo* ☎ *055/2302153* 🌐 *www.coquinarius.it* 🕘 *No lunch Sun.*

Gucci Osteria

$$$$ | **FUSION** | Chef, artist, and visionary Massimo Bottura has joined forces with the creative folks at Gucci to develop a marvelous tasting menu that is both classic and innovative. Though he trained with Ducasse and Adrià, his major influence was his grandmother's cooking. **Known for:** Southern-Italian inspired dishes; an ever-changing menu; outdoor seating in one of Florence's most beautiful squares. [$] *Average main: €120* ✉ *Piazza della Signoria 10, Piazza della Signoria* ☎ *055/0621744* 🌐 *www.gucciosteria.com/it/florence.*

★ Rivoire

$$ | **ITALIAN** | One of the best spots in Florence for people-watching offers stellar service, light snacks, and terrific aperitivi. It's been around since the 1860s, and has been famous for its hot and cold chocolate (with or without cream) for more than a century. **Known for:** delicious (but expensive) hot chocolate; friendly bartenders; the view on the piazza. [$] *Average main: €23* ✉ *Piazza della Signoria 5/r, Piazza della Signoria* ☎ *055/214412* 🌐 *www.rivoire.it/firenze.*

Coffee and Quick Bites

★ 'ino

$ | **ITALIAN** | Grab a bite and/or a glass of wine after a visit to the nearby Uffizi. Only the very best ingredients go into owner Alessandro Frassica's delectable (if a bit pricey) panini. **Known for:** delicious bread; interesting panini combinations; top-notch ingredients. [$] *Average main: €11* ✉ *Via dei Georgofili 3/r–7/r, Piazza della Signoria* ☎ *055/214154* 🌐 *www.inofirenze.com.*

Continued on page 509

THE DUOMO

FLORENCE'S BIGGEST MASTERPIECE

For all its monumental art and architecture, Florence has one undisputed centerpiece: the Cathedral of Santa Maria del Fiore, better known as the Duomo. Its cupola dominates the skyline, presiding over the city's rooftops like a red hen over her brood. Little wonder that when Florentines feel homesick, they say they have "*nostalgia del cupolone.*"

The Duomo's construction began in 1296, following the design of Arnolfo di Cambio, Florence's greatest architect of the time. By modern standards, construction was slow and haphazard—it continued through the 14th and into the 15th century, with some dozen architects having a hand in the project.

In 1366, Neri di Fioravante created a model for the hugely ambitious cupola: it was to be the largest dome in the world, surpassing Rome's Pantheon. But when the time finally came to build the dome in 1418, no one was sure how—or even if—it could be done. Florence was faced with a 143 foot hole in the roof of its cathedral, and one of the greatest challenges in the history of architecture.

Fortunately, local genius Filippo Brunelleschi was just the man for the job. Brunelleschi won the 1418 competition to design the dome, and for the next 18 years he oversaw its construction. The enormity of his achievement can hardly be overstated. Working on such a large scale (the dome weighs 37,000 tons and uses 4 million bricks) required him to invent hoists and cranes that were engineering marvels. A "dome within a dome" design and a novel herringbone bricklaying pattern were just two of the innovations used to establish structural integrity. Perhaps most remarkably, he executed the construction without a supporting wooden framework, which had previously been thought indispensable.

Brunelleschi designed the lantern atop the dome, but he died soon after its first stone was laid in 1446; it wouldn't be completed until 1461. Another 400 years passed before the Duomo received its facade, a 19th-century neo-Gothic creation.

DUOMO TIMELINE

1296 Work begins, following design by Arnolfo di Cambio.

1302 Arnolfo dies; work continues, with sporadic interruptions.

1331 Management of construction taken over by the Wool Merchants guild.

1334 Giotto appointed project overseer, designs campanile.

1337 Giotto dies; Andrea Pisano takes leadership role.

1348 The Black Plague; all work ceases.

1366 Vaulting on nave completed; Neri di Fioravante makes model for dome.

1417 Drum for dome completed.

1418 Competition is held to design the dome.

1420 Brunelleschi begins work on the dome.

1436 Dome completed.

1446 Construction of lantern begins; Brunelleschi dies.

1461 Antonio Manetti, a student of Brunelleschi, completes lantern.

1469 Gilt copper ball and cross added by Verrocchio.

1587 Original facade is torn down by Medici court.

1871 Emilio de Fabris wins competition to design new facade.

1887 Facade completed.

WHAT TO LOOK FOR INSIDE THE DUOMO

The interior of the Duomo is a fine example of Florentine Gothic with a beautiful marble floor, but the space feels strangely barren—a result of its great size and the fact that some of the best art has been moved to the nearby **Museo dell'Opera del Duomo**.

Notable among the works that remain are two towering equestrian frescoes of famous mercenaries: Niccolò da Tolentino (1456) by Andrea del Castagno, and Sir John Hawkwood (1436) by Paolo Uccello. There's also fine terra-cotta work by Luca della Robbia. Ghiberti, Brunelleschi's great rival, is responsible for much of the stained glass, as well as a reliquary urn with gorgeous reliefs. A vast fresco of *the Last Judgment*, painted by Vasari and Zuccari, covers the dome's interior. Brunelleschi had wanted mosaics to go there; it's a pity he didn't get his wish.

In the crypt beneath the cathedral, you can explore excavations of a Roman wall and mosaic fragments from the late 6th century; entry is near the first pier on the right. On the way down you pass Brunelleschi's modest tomb.

1. Entrance; stained glass by Ghiberti
2. Fresco of Niccolò da Tolentino by Andrea del Castagno
3. Fresco of John Hawkwood by Paolo Uccello
4. *Dante and the Divine Comedy* by Domenico di Michelino
5. *Lunette: Ascension* by Luca della Robbia
6. Above altar: two angels by Luca della Robbia. Below the altar: reliquary of St. Zenobius by Ghiberti
7. *Lunette: Resurrection* by Luca della Robbia
8. Entrance to dome
9. Bust of Brunelleschi by Buggiano
10. Stairs to crypt
11. Campanile

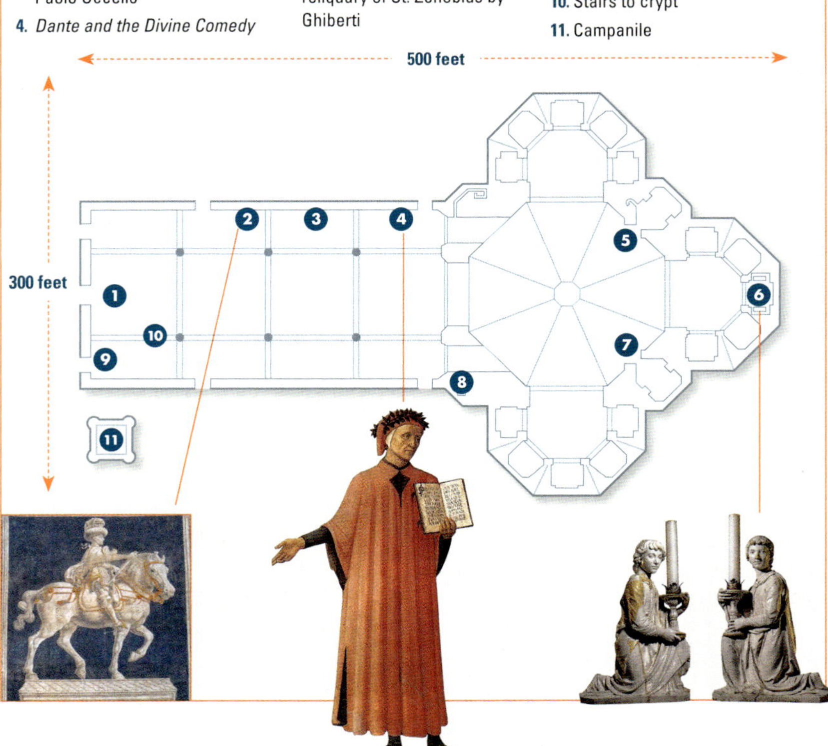

MAKING THE CLIMB

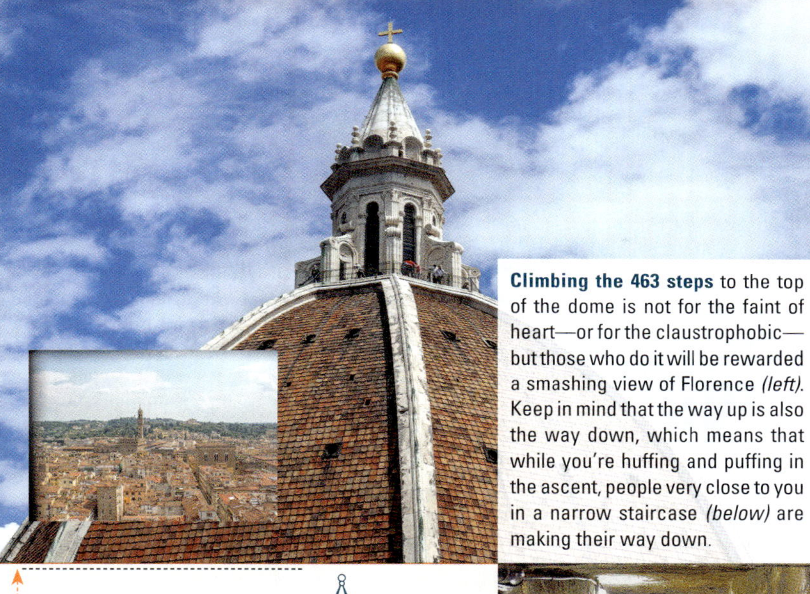

Climbing the 463 steps to the top of the dome is not for the faint of heart—or for the claustrophobic—but those who do it will be rewarded a smashing view of Florence *(left)*. Keep in mind that the way up is also the way down, which means that while you're huffing and puffing in the ascent, people very close to you in a narrow staircase *(below)* are making their way down.

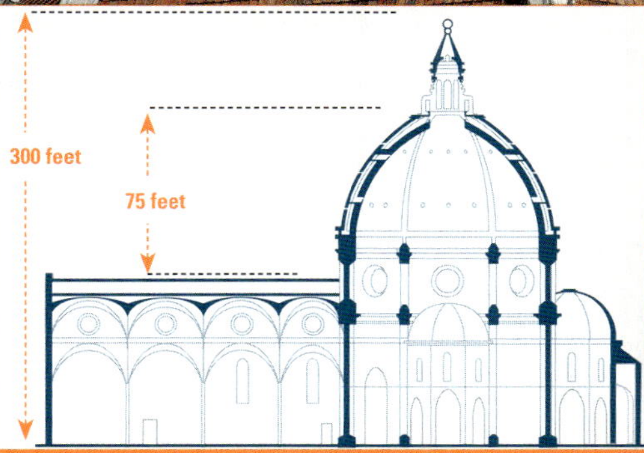

DUOMO BASICS

- Admission to the church is free, but there's a fee to visit the cupola, and timed-entry reservations are required.
- For an alternative to the dome, consider climbing the less trafficked campanile, which gives you a view from on high of the dome itself.
- Dress code essentials: covered shoulders, no short shorts, and hats off upon entering.

THE CRYPT

The crypt is worth a visit: computer modeling allows visitors to see its ancient Roman fabric and subsequent rebuilding. A transparent plastic model shows exactly what the earlier church looked like.

BRUNELLESCHI vs. GHIBERTI
The Rivalry of Two Renaissance Geniuses

In Renaissance Florence, painters, sculptors, and architects competed for major commissions, with the winner earning the right to undertake a project that might occupy him (and keep him paid) for a decade or more. Stakes were high, and the resulting rivalries fierce—none more so than that between Filippo Brunelleschi and Lorenzo Ghiberti.

The two first clashed in 1401, for the commission to create the bronze doors of the Baptistery. When Ghiberti won, Brunelleschi took it hard, fleeing to Rome, where he would remain for 15 years. Their rematch came in 1418, over the design of the Duomo's cupola, with Brunelleschi triumphant. Thereafter, neither man missed a chance to belittle the other's work.

FILIPPO BRUNELLESCHI (1377–1446)

MASTERPIECE: The dome of Santa Maria del Fiore.

BEST FRIENDS: Donatello, whom he stayed with in Rome after losing the Baptistery doors competition; the Medici family, who rescued him from bankruptcy.

SIGNATURE TRAITS: Paranoid, secretive, bad tempered, practical joker, inept businessman.

SAVVIEST POLITICAL MOVE: Feigned sickness and left for Rome after his dome plans were publicly criticized by Ghiberti, who was second-in-command. The project proved too much for Ghiberti to manage on his own, and Brunelleschi returned triumphant.

MOST EMBARRASSING MOMENT: In 1434, he was imprisoned for two weeks for failure to pay a small guild fee. The humiliation might have been orchestrated by Ghiberti.

OTHER CAREER: Shipbuilder. He built a huge vessel, *Il Badalone*, to transport marble for the dome up the Arno. It sank on its first voyage.

INSPIRED: The dome of St. Peter's in Rome.

LORENZO GHIBERTI (1378–1455)

MASTERPIECE: *The Gates of Paradise*, the ten-paneled east doors of the Baptistery.

BEST FRIEND: Giovanni da Prato, an underling who wrote diatribes attacking the dome's design and Brunelleschi's character.

SIGNATURE TRAITS: Instigator, egoist, know-it-all, shrewd businessman.

SAVVIEST POLITICAL MOVE: During the Baptistery doors competition, he had an open studio and welcomed opinions on his work, while Brunelleschi labored behind closed doors.

OTHER CAREER: Collector of classical artifacts, historian.

INSPIRED: *The Gates of Hell* by Auguste Rodin.

The Gates of Paradise detail

Hotels

Hermitage

$$ | **HOTEL** | Some rooms here have views of the Palazzo Vecchio, and others of the Arno; the rooftop terrace, where you can have breakfast or an aperitivo, is decked with flowers. **Pros:** views; friendly staff; enviable position a stone's throw from the Ponte Vecchio. **Cons:** short flight of stairs to reach elevator; might be time for a refurbishing; street noise sometimes a problem. *$ Rooms from: €285 ✉ Vicolo Marzio 1, Piazza della Signoria ☎ 055/287216 🌐 www.hermitagehotel.com 28 rooms 🍽 Free Breakfast.*

Hotel degli Orafi

$$$$ | **HOTEL** | A key scene in *A Room with a View* was shot in this pensione, which is today a luxury hotel adorned with chintz and marble. **Pros:** stellar Arno views; rooftop bar; quiet location during the evenings. **Cons:** some street noise in river-facing rooms; on the path of many tour groups during the day; somewhat pricey. *$ Rooms from: €605 ✉ Lungarno Archibusieri 4, Piazza della Signoria ☎ 055/5357722 🌐 www.hoteldegliorafi.it 50 rooms 🍽 Free Breakfast.*

Hotel Helvetia and Bristol

$$$$ | **HOTEL** | From the cozy yet sophisticated lobby, with its stone columns, to the guest rooms decorated with prints, you might feel as if you're a guest in a manor house. **Pros:** central location; excellent restaurant; old-world charm. **Cons:** rooms facing the street get some noise; breakfast is not always included in the price of a room; books up quickly. *$ Rooms from: €800 ✉ Via dei Pescioni 2, Piazza della Repubblica ☎ 055/26651 🌐 collezione.starhotels.com 89 rooms 🍽 No Meals.*

Hotel Renaissance

$$ | **HOTEL** | Nestled in an old building just a stone's throw from the main civic square (Piazza Signoria), this charming little boutique hotel offers peace and elegance. **Pros:** the staff; the sumptuous breakfast; the location. **Cons:** steps up to the elevator; some street noise in some rooms; books up quickly. *$ Rooms from: €190 ✉ Via della Condotta 4, Piazza della Signoria ☎ 055/213996 🌐 www.hotelrenaissancefirenze.com 9 rooms 🍽 No Meals.*

★ In Piazza della Signoria

$$ | **B&B/INN** | In this home that is part of a 15th-century palazzo, a cozy feeling permeates the charming rooms, all of which are uniquely decorated and lovingly furnished; some have damask curtains, others fanciful frescoes in the bathroom. **Pros:** marvelous staff; tasty breakfast with a view of Piazza della Signoria; some rooms easily accommodate three. **Cons:** short flight of stairs to reach elevator; some of the rooms have steps up into showers and bathtubs; books up quickly during high season. *$ Rooms from: €313 ✉ Via dei Magazzini 2, Piazza della Signoria ☎ 055/2399546 🌐 www.boutiquehotelinpiazza.com 13 rooms 🍽 Free Breakfast.*

Palazzo Vecchietti

$$$$ | **HOTEL** | If you're looking for a swank setting, and the possibility of staying in for a meal (each room has a tiny kitchenette), look no further than this hotel which, while thoroughly modern, dates to the 15th century. **Pros:** great service; central location; public room has a Renaissance fireplace and high ceilings. **Cons:** no restaurant; some street noise a possibility; it's expensive. *$ Rooms from: €835 ✉ Via degli Strozzi 4, Duomo ☎ 055/2302802 🌐 www.palazzovecchietti.com 12 rooms 🍽 Free Breakfast.*

Nightlife

Hard Rock Cafe

LIVE MUSIC | Hard Rock packs in young Florentines and travelers eager to sample the music hall chain's take on classic American grub. *✉ Via De' Brunelleschi 1, Piazza della Repubblica ☎ 055/277841 🌐 www.hardrock.com.*

Yab

DANCE CLUB | Yab never seems to go out of style, though it increasingly becomes the haunt of Florentine high school and university students intent on dancing and doing vodka shots. ✉ *Via Sassetti 5/r, Piazza della Repubblica* ☎ *055/215160* 🌐 *www.yab.it.*

Performing Arts

Orchestra da Camera Fiorentina

MUSIC | This orchestra performs various classical music concerts (many of them free) throughout the year at churches, villas, and museums. Past performances have filled Orsanmichele, the Bargello, and Santo Spirito Church with the orchestra's music. ✉ *Via Monferrato 2, Piazza della Signoria* ☎ *055/783374* 🌐 *www.orchestradacamerafiorentina.it.*

Shopping

★ **Bernardo**

CLOTHING | Come here for men's trousers, cashmere sweaters, and shirts with details like mother-of-pearl buttons. ✉ *Via Porta Rossa 87/r, Piazza della Repubblica* ☎ *055/283333* 🌐 *www.bernardofirenze.it.*

Diesel

CLOTHING | Trendy Diesel started in Vicenza; its gear is on the "must-have" list of many Italian teens. ✉ *Via degli Speziali 16/r, Piazza della Signoria* ☎ *055/2399963* 🌐 *shop.diesel.com.*

Fratelli Piccini

JEWELRY & WATCHES | Still in operation after four generations, this Florentine institution sells antique jewelry and makes pieces to order; you can also get old jewelry reset here. ✉ *Ponte Vecchio 21/23r, Duomo* ☎ *055/294768* 🌐 *www.fratellipiccini.com.*

Gherardi

JEWELRY & WATCHES | Florence's king of coral, Gherardi has the city's largest selection of finely crafted pieces, as well as cultured pearls, jade, and turquoise. ✉ *Ponte Vecchio 36/r, Piazza della Signoria* ☎ *055/211809* 🌐 *www.gherardigioielli.it.*

Mandragora Art Store

MUSEUM SHOP | This is one of the first attempts in Florence to cash in on the museum-store craze. Look for reproductions of valued works of art and jewelry. ✉ *Piazza del Duomo 50/r, Duomo* ☎ *055/292559* 🌐 *www.mandragora.it.*

Mercato dei Fiori e Piante (*Flower Market*)

MARKET | Every Thursday morning from September through June the covered loggia in Piazza della Repubblica hosts this lively market—a riot of plants, flowers, and difficult-to-find herbs. ✉ *Piazza della Repubblica, Piazza della Repubblica.*

Mercato del Porcellino

MARKET | FAMILY | If you're looking for cheery, inexpensive trinkets to take home, roam through the stalls under the loggia of the Mercato del Porcellino. ✉ *Via Por Santa Maria at Via Porta Rossa, Piazza della Repubblica* ☎ *339/3271143 mobile* 🌐 *www.mercatodelporcellino.it.*

Missoni Boutique

CLOTHING | Shop for knitwear at the Florence outpost of the Italian brand known for its bold pieces. ✉ *Via Porta Rossa 77–79/r, Piazza della Repubblica* ☎ *055/215774* 🌐 *www.missoni.com.*

Oro Due

JEWELRY & WATCHES | Gold jewelry and other beauteous objects are priced according to the level of craftsmanship and the value of gold bullion that day. ✉ *Via Lambertesca 12/r, Piazza della Signoria* ☎ *055/292143.*

★ **Paolo Penko**

JEWELRY & WATCHES | Renaissance goldsmiths provide the inspiration for this dazzling jewelry with a contemporary feel. There is another branch in the San Lorenzo district. ✉ *Via dell'Oche, 20r, Duomo* ☎ *055/2052577* 🌐 *www.paolopenko.com.*

Patrizia Pepe

CLOTHING | The Florentine designer has clothes for those with a tiny streak of rebelliousness. Sizes run small. ✉ *Piazza San Giovanni 12/r, Duomo* ☎ *055/2645056* 🌐 *www.patriziapepe.com.*

★ **Pegna**

FOOD | This shop has been selling both Italian and non-Italian food since 1860. If you're tired of mozzarella and feel the need for some cheddar, this is the place to find it. ✉ *Via dello Studio 8, Duomo* ☎ *055/282701* 🌐 *www.pegna.sangiustosrl.com.*

Quercioli & Lucherini

LINGERIE | This shop has been vending high-quality clothing—the kind that goes next to bare skin—since 1895. Remember that luxury comes at a price. ✉ *Via Porta Rossa 45/r, Piazza della Repubblica* ☎ *055/292035.*

San Lorenzo

A sculptor, painter, architect, and poet, Florentine native son Michelangelo was a consummate genius, and some of his finest creations remain in his hometown. The Biblioteca Medicea Laurenziana is perhaps his most fanciful work of architecture. A key to understanding Michelangelo's genius can be found in the magnificent Cappelle Medicee, where both his sculptural and architectural prowess can be clearly seen. Planned frescoes were never completed, sadly, for they would have shown in one space the artistic triple threat that he certainly was. The towering yet graceful *David,* perhaps his most famous work, resides in the Galleria dell'Accademia.

Sights

Basilica di San Lorenzo

CHURCH | Filippo Brunelleschi designed this basilica, as well as that of Santo Spirito in the Oltrarno, in the 15th century. He never lived to see either finished. The two interiors are similar in design and effect. San Lorenzo, however, has a grid of dark, inlaid marble lines on the floor, which considerably heightens the dramatic effect. Brunelleschi's Sagrestia Vecchia (Old Sacristy) has stucco decorations by Donatello; it's at the end of the left transept. ✉ *Piazza San Lorenzo, San Lorenzo* ☎ *055/214042* 🌐 *www.sanlorenzofirenze.it* 🎫 *€9* ⏲ *Closed Sun.*

Biblioteca Medicea Laurenziana

(Laurentian Library)

LIBRARY | Michelangelo the architect was every bit as original as Michelangelo the sculptor. He was interested in experimentation, invention, and the expression of a personal vision that was at times highly idiosyncratic. It was never more idiosyncratic than in the Laurentian Library, begun in 1524 and finished in 1568 by Bartolomeo Ammannati. Its famous *vestibolo,* a strangely shaped anteroom, has had scholars scratching their heads for centuries. In a space more than two stories high, why did Michelangelo limit his use of columns and pilasters to the upper two-thirds of the wall? Why didn't he rest them on strong pedestals instead of on huge, decorative curlicue scrolls, which rob them of all visual support? Why did he recess them into the wall, which makes them look weaker still? The architectural elements give the room a soft, rubbery look that is one of the strangest effects ever achieved by 16th-century architecture. ✉ *Piazza San Lorenzo 9, entrance to left of San Lorenzo, San Lorenzo* ☎ *055/2937911* 🌐 *www.bmlonline.it* ⏲ *Check ahead on admission price for special exhibitions, opening days and times as this site has seen temporary closures.*

Florence's Trial by Fire

One of the most striking figures of Renaissance Florence was Girolamo Savonarola, a Dominican friar who, for a moment, captured the spiritual conscience of the city. In 1491 he became prior of the convent of San Marco, where he adopted a life of austerity and delivered sermons condemning Florence's excesses and the immorality of his fellow clergy. Following the death of Lorenzo de' Medici in 1492, Savonarola was instrumental in the re-formation of the republic of Florence, ruled by a representative council with Christ enthroned as monarch. In one of his most memorable acts he urged Florentines to toss worldly possessions—from sumptuous dresses to Botticelli paintings—onto a "bonfire of the vanities" in Piazza della Signoria. Savonarola's antagonism toward church hierarchy led to his undoing: he was excommunicated in 1497, and the following year was hanged and burned on charges of heresy. Today, at the Museo di San Marco, you can visit Savonarola's cell.

★ **Cappelle Medicee** (*Medici Chapels*)
CHURCH | This magnificent complex includes the Cappella dei Principi, the Medici chapel and mausoleum begun in 1605 that kept marble workers busy for several hundred years, and the Sagrestia Nuova (New Sacristy), designed by Michelangelo and so called to distinguish it from Brunelleschi's Sagrestia Vecchia (Old Sacristy). Michelangelo received the commission for the New Sacristy in 1520 from Cardinal Giulio de' Medici, who later became Pope Clement VII. The cardinal wanted a new burial chapel for his cousins Giuliano, Duke of Nemours (1478–1534), and Lorenzo, Duke of Urbino (1492–1519). He also wanted to honor his father, also named Giuliano, and his uncle, Lorenzo il Magnifico. The result was a tour de force of architecture and sculpture.

The complex is also home to the Stanza Segreta di Michelangelo (Michelangelo's Secret Room), a small room—covered in exquisite charcoal sketches—where the artist was thought to have hidden for a few months in 1530, after having angered Pope Clement VII. For preservation reasons, access to this room is very limited, and the requisite reservations (🌐 *www.b-ticket.com/b-Ticket/uffizi*) tend to sell out very quickly several months in advance, so plan well ahead if you want to visit the site. ✉ *Piazza di Madonna degli Aldobrandini 6, San Lorenzo* ☎ *055/294883 reservations* 🌐 *www.bargellomusei.beniculturali.it* 🎫 *€9* 🕑 *Closed Tues.*

★ **Galleria dell'Accademia**
(*Accademia Gallery*)
ART MUSEUM | **FAMILY** | The collection of Florentine paintings, dating from the 13th to the 18th century, is largely unremarkable, but the sculptures by Michelangelo are worth the price of admission. The unfinished *Slaves*, fighting their way out of their marble prisons, were meant for the tomb of Michelangelo's overly demanding patron Pope Julius II. But the focal point is the original *David*, commissioned in 1501 by the Opera del Duomo (Cathedral Works Committee), which gave the 26-year-old sculptor a leftover block of marble that had been ruined 40 years earlier by two other sculptors. ✉ *Via Ricasoli 58/60, San Marco* ☎ *055/294883 reservations, 055/0987100 gallery* 🌐 *www.galleriaaccademiafirenze.it* 🎫 *€16* 🕑 *Closed Mon.* ✍ *€4 advanced booking fee.*

Mercato Centrale

MARKET | **FAMILY** | Some of the food at this huge, two-story market hall is remarkably exotic. The ground floor contains meat and cheese stalls, as well as some very good bars that have panini. The upstairs food hall is eerily reminiscent of food halls everywhere, but the quality of the food served more than makes up for this. The downstairs market is closed on Sunday; the upstairs food hall is always open. ✉ *Piazza del Mercato Centrale, San Lorenzo* ☎ *055/2399798* 🌐 *www.mercatocentrale.it/firenze.*

Museo di Casa Martelli

HISTORIC HOME | The wealthy Martelli family, long associated with the all-powerful Medici, lived, from the 16th century, in this palace on a quiet street near the Basilica of San Lorenzo. The last Martelli died in 1986, and, in October 2009, the *casa-museo* (house-museum) opened to the public. It's the only nonreconstructed example of such a house in all of Florence, and for that reason alone it's worth a visit. The family collected art, and while most of the stuff is B-list, a few gems by Beccafumi, Salvatore Rosa, and Piero di Cosimo adorn the walls. ✉ *Via Zanetti 8, San Lorenzo* ☎ *055/0649420* 🌐 *www.bargellomusei.beniculturali.it* 🎫 *Free* 🕒 *Closed Sun., Mon., Tues. morning, Wed.–Fri., and Sat. afternoon.*

Museo di San Marco

ART MUSEUM | A former Dominican convent adjacent to the church of San Marco houses this museum, which contains many stunning works by Fra Angelico (circa 1400–55), the Dominican friar famous for his piety as well as for his painting. When the friars' cells were restructured between 1439 and 1444, he decorated many of them with frescoes meant to spur religious contemplation. His unostentatious and direct paintings exalt the simple beauties of the contemplative life. Don't miss the famous *Annunciation,* on the upper floor, and the works in the gallery off the cloister as you enter. Here you can see his beautiful *Last Judgment*; as usual, the tortures of the damned are far more inventive and interesting than the pleasures of the redeemed. ✉ *Piazza San Marco 3, San Lorenzo* ☎ *055/0882000* 🌐 *museitoscana.cultura.gov.it* 🎫 *€8* 🕒 *Closed Sun. and Mon.*

Palazzo Medici-Riccardi

CASTLE/PALACE | The main attraction of this palace, begun in 1444 by Michelozzo for Cosimo de' Medici, is the interior chapel, the Cappella dei Magi, on the piano nobile (main floor). Painted on its walls is Benozzo Gozzoli's famous *Procession of the Magi,* finished in 1460 and celebrating both the birth of Christ and the greatness of the Medici family. The building also hosts rotating exhibits. ✉ *Via Cavour 3, San Lorenzo* ☎ *055/2760552* 🌐 *www.palazzomediciriccardi.it* 🎫 *Museum only €10* 🕒 *Closed Wed.*

Santissima Annunziata

CHURCH | Dating from the mid-13th century, this church was restructured in 1447 by Michelozzo, who gave it an uncommon (and lovely) entrance cloister with frescoes by Andrea del Sarto (1486–1530), Pontormo (1494–1556), and Rosso Fiorentino (1494–1540). Another fresco of note is the very fine *Holy Trinity with St. Jerome* in the second chapel on the left. Done by Andrea del Castagno (circa 1421–57), it shows a wiry and emaciated St. Jerome with Paula and Eustochium, two of his closest followers. ✉ *Piazza di Santissima Annunziata, San Lorenzo* ☎ *055/266181* 🎫 *Free.*

Spedale degli Innocenti

ART MUSEUM | **FAMILY** | The edifice built by Brunelleschi in 1419 to serve as an orphanage takes the historical prize as the very first Renaissance building. Brunelleschi designed its portico with his usual rigor, constructing it from the two shapes he considered mathematically (and therefore philosophically and aesthetically) perfect: the square and the circle. Below the level of the arches, the portico encloses a row of perfect cubes;

A
B
C
D
E
F
1
2
3
4
5
6
7
8
9
0
300 ft
0
100 m
Fortezza da Basso
Viale Spartaco Lavagnini
Viale Filippo Strozzi
Via G. Dolfi
V. V. Salvagnoli
Via E. Poggi
Via delle Ruote
Via F. Bartolommei
Via San Zanobi
Via C. Ridolfi
Via di Barbano
Via del Pratello
Via della Fortezza
Via Faenza
Palazzo dei Congressi
Via Guelfa
Via G. Montanelli
Via di Sante Caterina d' Alessandria
Via Ventisette Aprile
Via Santa Reparata
Via San Zanobi
Via Bernardo Cennini
Via Faenza
Via Guelfa
Via Santa Reparata
Via San Gallo
Via Fiume
Via Nazionale
Via Chiara
Via Panicale
Via Taddea
V. Sant'Orsola
Via Guelfa
Via Valfonda
Stazione Centrale
Via Nazionale
Via G.B. Zannoni
Via dell' Ariento
Piazza del Mercato
Via Rosina
Via Sant'Antonino
SAN LORENZO
Borgo la Noce
Via della Stufa
Via de Ginori
Via Cavour
Piazza della Stazione
Via S.Caterina
Via Sant'Antonino
Via dell' Amorino
Via Faenza
Piazza San Lorenzo
Santa Maria Novella
Piazza dell'Unità Italiana
Piazza Madonna Aldobrandini
San Lorenzo
Via del Pucci
Via d. Bitti
Via del Panzani
Via del Giglio
V. dell' Alloro
Via F. Zannetti
Borgo San Lorenzo
Via Martelli
Via Ricasoli
Piazza Santa Maria Novella
Via degli Avelli
Via dei Banchi
Via dei Cerretani
Piazza del Duomo
Duomo
Via della Scala
Via del Moro
Via d. Trebbio
Via del Pecori

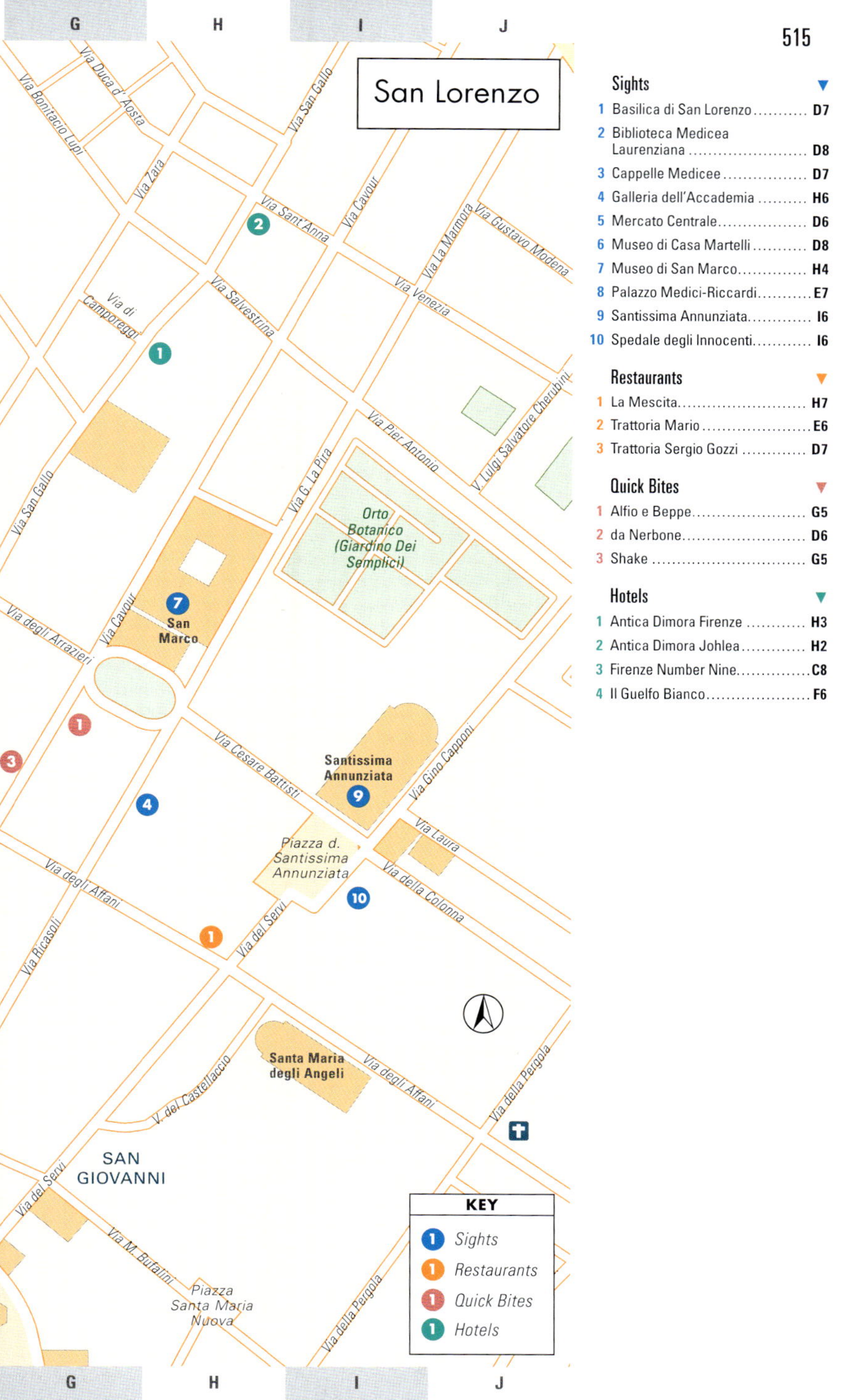

Sights

1 Basilica di San Lorenzo D7
2 Biblioteca Medicea Laurenziana D8
3 Cappelle Medicee D7
4 Galleria dell'Accademia H6
5 Mercato Centrale D6
6 Museo di Casa Martelli D8
7 Museo di San Marco H4
8 Palazzo Medici-Riccardi E7
9 Santissima Annunziata I6
10 Spedale degli Innocenti I6

Restaurants

1 La Mescita H7
2 Trattoria Mario E6
3 Trattoria Sergio Gozzi D7

Quick Bites

1 Alfio e Beppe G5
2 da Nerbone D6
3 Shake G5

Hotels

1 Antica Dimora Firenze H3
2 Antica Dimora Johlea H2
3 Firenze Number Nine C8
4 Il Guelfo Bianco F6

above the level of the arches, the portico encloses a row of intersecting hemispheres. The entire geometric scheme is articulated with Corinthian columns, capitals, and arches borrowed directly from antiquity.

At the time he designed the portico, Brunelleschi was also designing the interior of San Lorenzo, using the same basic ideas. But because the portico was finished before San Lorenzo, the Spedale degli Innocenti can claim the honor of ushering in Renaissance architecture. The 10 ceramic medallions depicting swaddled infants that decorate the portico are by Andrea della Robbia (1435–1525/28), done in about 1487.

Within the building is the Museo degli Innocenti. Although most of the objects are minor works by major artists, they're still worth a look. Of note is Domenico Ghirlandaio's (1449–94) *Adorazione dei Magi* (*Adoration of the Magi*), executed in 1488. The museum also hosts temporary exhibits primarily focused on contemporary art. ✉ *Piazza di Santissima Annunziata 13, San Lorenzo* ☎ *055/2037122* 🌐 *www.museodeglinnocenti.it* 🎟 *From €9.*

Restaurants

La Mescita

$ | TUSCAN | Come early (or late) to grab a seat at this tiny spot frequented by Florentine university students and businesspeople, who come to enjoy the day's primi (the lasagna is terrific), perhaps followed by the *polpettone* (meat loaf) and tomato sauce. Though seats are cramped, and the wine is no great shakes, the service is friendly, and the food hits the spot. **Known for:** its longevity (it's been around since the 1920s); delicious pastas at rock-bottom prices; local atmosphere. [$] *Average main: €12* ✉ *Via degli Alfani 70/r, San Lorenzo* ☎ *347/7951604 mobile* ▬ *No credit cards* ⏲ *No dinner.*

★ Trattoria Mario

$ | TUSCAN | Locals flock to this narrow, family-run trattoria to feast on Tuscan favorites served at simple tables under a wooden ceiling dating from 1536. Genuine Florentine hospitality prevails—you'll be seated wherever there's room, which often means with strangers—and, yes, there's a bit of extra oil in most dishes, which imparts calories as well as taste, but aren't you on vacation? **Known for:** grilled meats; roasted potatoes; festive atmosphere. [$] *Average main: €15* ✉ *Via Rosina 2/r, corner of Piazza del Mercato Centrale, San Lorenzo* ☎ *055/218550* 🌐 *www.trattoriamario.com* ⏲ *Closed Sun. and Aug. and Sun. No dinner Mon.–Thurs. and Sat.*

★ Trattoria Sergio Gozzi

$ | TUSCAN | This restaurant just across from the Basilica of San Lorenzo and run by the Gozzi family since 1915 serves food that's as delicious as it is affordable. The short menu changes daily, though the *lombatina alla griglia* (grilled veal T-bone steak) is almost always available, and meat eaters should not miss it. **Known for:** local favorite; ever-changing menu; terrific pastas. [$] *Average main: €14* ✉ *Piazza San Lorenzo 8/r, San Lorenzo* ☎ *055/281941* 🌐 *www.facebook.com/TrattoriaGozzi* ⏲ *Closed Sun. No dinner.*

Coffee and Quick Bites

Alfio e Beppe

$ | ITALIAN | Watch chickens roast over high flames while you decide which of the delightful side dishes you'd like to enjoy as well. Although this place is strictly takeout (there are no tables), it's open on Sunday when many places are not. **Known for:** roasted chicken to go; delicious roasted potatoes; good ribs. [$] *Average main: €9* ✉ *Via Cavour 118/r, San Marco* ☎ *055/214108* ⏲ *Closed Sat.*

★ da Nerbone

$ | **TUSCAN** | This *tavola calda* (cafeteria) in the middle of the covered Mercato Centrale has been serving Florentines since 1872. Tasty primi and secondi are always available, as are *bollitos* (boiled beef sandwiches), but the cognoscenti come for the *panino con il lampredotto* (tripe sandwich)—best when it's prepared *bagnato* (with the bread quickly dipped in the tripe cooking liquid) and served slathered with green and/or spicier red sauce. **Known for:** tripe sandwich; frequented by locals (and everyone else); favorite dishes sell out fast. *Average main: €10 Piazza Mercato Centrale, San Lorenzo 055/6480251 Closed Sun. No dinner.*

Shake

$ | **ITALIAN** | Handily located between Piazza San Marco and Piazza San Lorenzo, the first outpost of Shake (there are now five throughout the city) serves up creative juices, tasty baked goods, wonderful salads, and great bowls. It's committed to sustainability and to keeping its carbon footprint small. **Known for:** remarkable way with juices (the De-Tox is especially good); nice, cheerful staff; courtyard seating in a garden. *Average main: €10 Via Cavour 67/69r, San Lorenzo 055/0515418 www.shakecafe.it.*

Hotels

Antica Dimora Firenze

$$ | **B&B/INN** | Each simply furnished room in this *residenza* (guesthouse) is painted a different pastel color—peach, rose, powder-blue—and double-glazed windows ensure a peaceful night's sleep. **Pros:** ample DVD library; honor bar with Antinori wines; complimentary coffee, tea, and fresh fruit available all day in the sitting room. **Cons:** books up quickly; some might consider it too small; might be too removed for some. *Rooms from: €235 Via San Gallo 72, San Marco 055/4627296 www.antichedimorefiorentine.it 6 rooms Free Breakfast.*

★ Antica Dimora Johlea

$$ | **B&B/INN** | In addition to guest rooms with four-poster beds and sweeping drapes, this 19th-century palazzo has a charming, flower-filled terrace where you can sip a glass of wine while taking in a view of Brunelleschi's cupola. **Pros:** great staff; cheerful rooms; honor bar. **Cons:** staff goes home at 7:30; staircase to roof terrace is narrow; steps to breakfast room. *Rooms from: €336 Via San Gallo 80, San Marco 055/4633292 www.antichedimorefiorentine.it 6 rooms Free Breakfast.*

Firenze Number Nine

$$$$ | **HOTEL** | At this elegant hotel, swank reception rooms have comfortable couches and contemporary artwork, and guest rooms feature parquet floors, high ceilings, and furnishings that combine Scandinavian sleekness with the Italian love for fine fabric (think: damask draperies). **Pros:** historic center location; walk-in gym and spa; sumptuous breakfast. **Cons:** some street noise; might be too trendy for some; books up quickly. *Rooms from: €675 Via del Conti 9, San Lorenzo 055/293777 firenzenumbernine.com 45 rooms Free Breakfast.*

Il Guelfo Bianco

$$ | **HOTEL** | The 15th-century building has all modern conveniences, but Renaissance charm still shines in the high-ceiling rooms. **Pros:** great staff; beautiful floors made of either parquet or marble; sumptuous breakfast. **Cons:** rooms facing the street can be noisy; might be too removed for some; not all rooms are well lit. *Rooms from: €219 Via Cavour 29, San Marco 055/288330 www.ilguelfobianco.it 40 rooms Free Breakfast.*

Meet the Medici

The Medici were the dominant family of Renaissance Florence, wielding political power and financing some of the world's greatest art. You'll see their names at every turn around the city. These are some of the more notable family members.

Cosimo il Vecchio (1389–1464): incredibly wealthy banker to the popes and the first in the family line to act as de facto ruler of Florence. He was a great patron of the arts and architecture; he was the moving force behind the family palace and the Dominican complex of San Marco.

Lorenzo il Magnifico (1449–92): grandson of Cosimo il Vecchio who presided over a Florence largely at peace with its neighbors. A collector of cameos, a writer of sonnets, and a lover of ancient texts, he was the preeminent Renaissance man and, like his grandfather, the de facto ruler of Florence.

Leo X (1475–1521): also known as Giovanni de' Medici, he became the first Medici pope, helping extend the family power base to include Rome and the Papal States. His reign was characterized by a host of problems, the biggest one being a former friar named Martin Luther.

Catherine de' Medici (1519–89): was married by her great uncle Pope Clement VII to Henry of Valois, who later became Henry II of France. Wife of one king and mother of three, she was the first Medici to marry into European royalty. Lorenzo il Magnifico, her great-grandfather, would have been thrilled.

Cosimo I (1537–74): the first grand duke of Tuscany, not to be confused with his ancestor, Cosimo il Vecchio.

Shopping

★ Baroni Alimentari

FOOD | The cheese selection at Baroni may be the most comprehensive in Florence. It also sells high-quality truffle products, vinegars, and other delicacies. ✉ *Mercato Central, enter at Via Signa, San Lorenzo* ☎ *055/289576* 🌐 *www.baronialimentari.com.*

Mercato Centrale

MARKET | FAMILY | This huge indoor food market offers a staggering selection of all things edible. Downstairs is full of vendors hawking their wares—meat, fish, fruit, vegetables—upstairs (daily 8 am–midnight) is full of food stalls serving up an array of Italian and international foods. ✉ *Piazza del Mercato Centrale, San Lorenzo* ☎ *055/2399798* 🌐 *www.mercatocentrale.it/firenze.*

Mercato di San Lorenzo

MARKET | FAMILY | The clothing and leather-goods stalls at Mercato di San Lorenzo in the streets next to the San Lorenzo church have bargains for shoppers on a budget. ✉ *Via dell'Ariento, San Lorenzo.*

Santa Maria Novella

Piazza Santa Maria Novella is a gorgeous, pedestrian-only square, with grass (laced with roses) and plenty of places to sit and rest your feet. The streets in and around the piazza have their share of architectural treasures, including some of Florence's most tasteful palaces. Between Santa Maria Novella and the Arno is Via Tornabuoni, Florence's swankiest shopping street.

Sights

Museo Novecento

ART MUSEUM | It began life as a 13th-century Franciscan hostel offering shelter to tired pilgrims. It later became a convalescent home, and in the late 18th century it was a school for poor girls. Now the former Ospedale di San Paolo houses a museum devoted to Italian art of the 20th century. Admittedly, most of these artists are not exactly household names, but the museum is so beautifully well done that it's worth a visit. The second floor contains works by artists from the second half of the century; start on the third floor and go directly to the collection of Alberto della Ragione, a naval engineer who was determined to be on the cutting edge of art collecting. ✉ *Piazza Santa Maria Novella 10, Santa Maria Novella* ☎ *055/2768224* 🌐 *www.museonovecento.it* 🎫 *€9.50* 🕘 *Closed Thurs.*

★ Museo Salvatore Ferragamo

ART MUSEUM | A shrine to footwear, the shoes in this dramatically displayed collection were designed by Salvatore Ferragamo (1898–1960) beginning in the early 20th century. Born in southern Italy, Ferragamo jump-started his career in Hollywood by creating shoes for the likes of Mary Pickford and Rudolph Valentino. He then returned to Florence and set up shop in the 13th-century Palazzo Spini Ferroni. The collection includes about 16,000 shoes, and those on display are frequently rotated. Special exhibitions are also mounted here and are well worth visiting—past shows have been devoted to Audrey Hepburn, Greta Garbo, and Marilyn Monroe. ✉ *Piazza Santa Trinita 5/r, Santa Maria Novella* ☎ *055/3562846* 🌐 *museo.ferragamo.com* 🎫 *€10.*

Museo Stibbert

HISTORY MUSEUM | Frederick Stibbert (1838–1906), born in Florence to an Italian mother and an English father, liked to collect things. Over a lifetime of doing so, he amassed some 50,000 objects. This museum, which was also his home, displays many of them. He had a fascination with medieval armor, as well as costumes, particularly Uzbek costumes, which are exhibited in a room called the Moresque Hall. These are mingled with an extensive collection of swords and guns. ✉ *Via Federico Stibbert 26, Santa Maria Novella* ☎ *055/475520* 🌐 *www.museostibbert.it* 🎫 *€10* 🕘 *Closed Thurs.*

Palazzo Strozzi

CASTLE/PALACE | The Strozzi family built this imposing palazzo in an attempt to outshine the nearby Palazzo Medici. The exterior is simple, severe, and massive: it's a testament to the wealth of a patrician, 15th-century Florentine family. The interior courtyard is another matter altogether. It is here that the classical vocabulary—columns, capitals, pilasters, arches, and cornices—is given uninhibited and powerful expression. Inside, find rotating exhibits with a focus on contemporary art. ✉ *Piazza degli Strozzi, Piazza della Repubblica* ☎ *055/2645155* 🌐 *www.palazzostrozzi.org* 🎫 *Courtyard free; exhibits €15.*

Santa Maria Novella

CHURCH | The facade of this church looks distinctly clumsy by later Renaissance standards, and with good reason: it is an architectural hybrid. The lower half was completed mostly in the 14th century and about 100 years later (around 1456), architect Leon Battista Alberti was called in to complete the job, adding architectural motifs in an entirely different style.

Interior highlights include the 14th-century, stained-glass-rose window depicting the *Coronation of the Virgin* (above the central entrance); the Cappella Filippo Strozzi (to the right of the altar) containing late-15th-century frescoes and stained glass by Filippino Lippi; Masaccio's *Trinity* (on the left-hand wall, almost halfway down the nave) painted around 1426–27; the *cappella maggiore* (the area around the high altar) displaying frescoes by Ghirlandaio; and the Cappella

A
B
C
D
E
F
1
2
3
4
5
6
7
8
9
0
300 ft
0
100 m
Stazione Centrale
Piazza della Stazione
Via Luigi Alamanni
Via Valfonda
Via Fiume
Via Faenza
Via Nazionale
Via della Scala
Via degli Orti Oricellari
Via S.Caterina
Via Sant'Antonino
Piazza dell' Unità Italiana
Via Palazzuolo
Via degli Alberto
Via del Canacci
Via Benedetta
Via del Panzani
Via del Giglio
SANTA MARIA NOVELLA
Piazza Santa Maria Novella
Via degli Avelli
Via dei Banchi
Borgo Ognissanti
V. Maso Finiguerra
Via d. Trebbio
Piazza Paolino
Via Melegnano
Via Montebello
Via del Porcellaria
Via S.Paolino
Via del Moro
Via delle Belle Donne
Via della Spada
Via del Sole
Lungarno Amerigo Vespucci
Via de' Fossi
Via del Federighi
Via della Vigna Nuova
Piazza Goldoni
Via Purgatorio
Via de' Tornabuoni
Via Parioncino
Via del Parione
Piazza Santa Trinita
Lungarno Sederini
Ponte alla Carrala
Lungarno Corsini
Fiume Arno
V. de' Tornabuoni
KEY
Sights
Restaurants
Hotels
Borgo San Frediano
Lungarno Guiciardini
Via del Geppi
V. Maggio Pte. S.Trinita
Via Santo Spirito
Piazza del Carmine
Borgo delta Stelia
Via de' Serragli
SANTO SPIRITO
V. de Coverelli

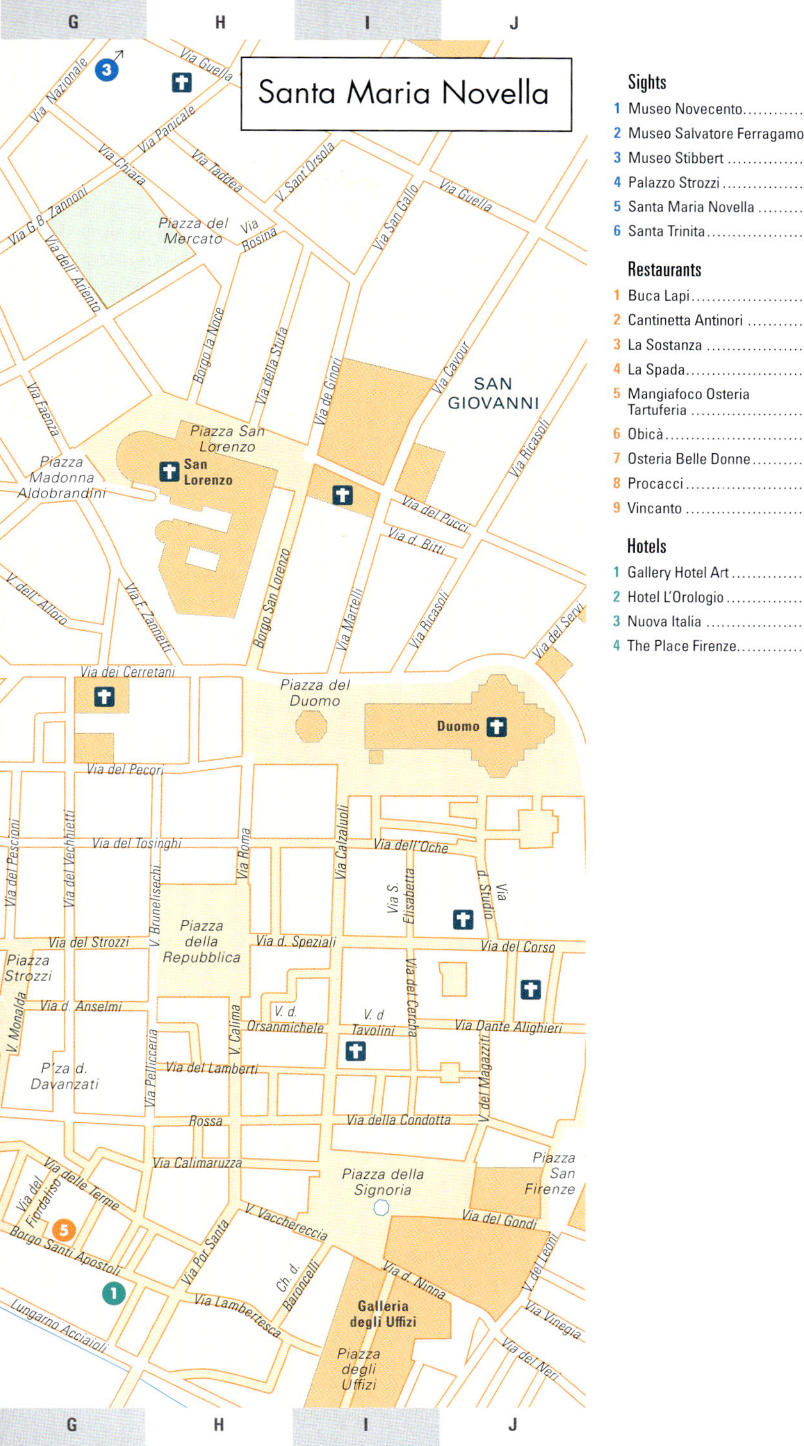

Sights

1 Museo Novecento D5
2 Museo Salvatore Ferragamo F8
3 Museo Stibbert G1
4 Palazzo Strozzi F7
5 Santa Maria Novella E4
6 Santa Trinita F8

Restaurants

1 Buca Lapi F5
2 Cantinetta Antinori F6
3 La Sostanza C5
4 La Spada E6
5 Mangiafoco Osteria Tartuferia G8
6 Obicà F6
7 Osteria Belle Donne E5
8 Procacci F6
9 Vincanto E4

Hotels

1 Gallery Hotel Art G9
2 Hotel L'Orologio E5
3 Nuova Italia F2
4 The Place Firenze E5

Gondi (to the left of the altar) with Filippo Brunelleschi's famous wooden crucifix, carved around 1410 and said to have so stunned the great Donatello when he first saw it that he dropped a basket of eggs. ✉ *Piazza Santa Maria Novella 18, Santa Maria Novella* ☎ *055/219257* 🌐 *www.smn.it/en* 🎫 *€7.50* 🕑 *Closed Sun. morning.*

Santa Trinita

CHURCH | Started in the 11th century by Vallombrosian monks and originally Romanesque in style, this church underwent a Gothic remodeling during the 14th century. (Remains of the Romanesque construction are visible on the interior front wall.) The major works are the fresco cycle and altarpiece in the Cappella Sassetti, the second to the high altar's right, painted by Ghirlandaio between 1480 and 1485. His work here possesses graceful decorative appeal and proudly depicts his native city, as most of the cityscapes show 15th-century Florence in all its glory. The wall frescoes illustrate scenes from the life of St. Francis, and the altarpiece, depicting the *Adoration of the Shepherds,* veritably glows. ✉ *Piazza Santa Trinita, Santa Maria Novella* ☎ *055/216912* 🕑 *Closed noon–4 pm.*

Restaurants

Buca Lapi

$$$ | **ITALIAN** | The Antinori family started selling wine from their palace's basement in the 15th century, and, 600 years later, this *buca* (hole) is a lively, subterranean spot filled with Florentine aristocrats chowing down on what might be the best—and the most expensive—*bistecca alla fiorentina* (flavorful, lightly seasoned beef) in town. The classic Tuscan menu has the usual suspects: *crostini di cavolo nero* (black cabbage on toasted garlic bread), along with *ribollita* (vegetable, bean, and bread soup) and *pappa al pomodoro* (tomato and bread soup). **Known for:** gargantuan bistecca; adherence to Tuscan classics; pet-friendly. 💲 *Average main: €40* ✉ *Via del Trebbio 1r, Santa Maria Novella* ☎ *055/213768* 🌐 *www.bucalapi.com/en* 🕑 *Closed Sun. No lunch.*

Cantinetta Antinori

$$$ | **TUSCAN** | After a morning of shopping on Via Tornabuoni, stop for lunch in this 15th-century palazzo, a place to see and be seen as well as to dine. The panache of the clientele is matched by that of the food, which is served with olive oil and vegetables from the family farm. **Known for:** chic clientele; most ingredients come from the family farm; outdoor seating in a 15th-century courtyard. 💲 *Average main: €31* ✉ *Piazza Antinori 3, Santa Maria Novella* ☎ *055/292234* 🌐 *www.cantinetta-antinori.com* 🕑 *Closed Sun.*

★ La Sostanza

$$ | **TUSCAN** | Since opening its doors in 1869, this trattoria has been serving top-notch, unpretentious food to Florentines who like their bistecca very large and, of course, very rare, as that's the only way to eat it. The *tartino di carciofi* (artichoke tart) and the *pollo al burro* (chicken with butter) are signature dishes. **Known for:** Tuscan classics; delicious desserts (especially the semifreddo); no-frills, simple decor and communal tables. 💲 *Average main: €24* ✉ *Via del Porcellana 25/r, Lungarno North* ☎ *055/212691* 🌐 *www.facebook.com/trattoriasostanzailtroia* 🕑 *Closed Sun.*

La Spada

$ | **ITALIAN** | **FAMILY** | Near Santa Maria Novella is La Spada. Walk in and inhale the fragrant aromas of meats cooking in the wood-burning oven. **Known for:** grilled meats and aromatic pastas; adherence to Tuscan cuisine; eat in or order takeout. 💲 *Average main: €15* ✉ *Via della Spada 62/r, Santa Maria Novella* ☎ *055/218757* 🌐 *www.ristorantelaspada.it.*

★ Mangiafoco Osteria Tartuferia

$$ | **TUSCAN** | On a romantic medieval side street in the heart of the centro storico, this small restaurant has two menus—one with Tuscan classics that reflect both the whims of the chef and what's in season, and the other that's focused on truffles, either white or black, again based on the season. On the first menu, look for creative salads and pasta, meat, and *taglieri* (mixed meat and cheese plates) that are often served with jams made from Chianti, vin santo, or balsamic vinegar. **Known for:** phenomenal wines by the glass or the bottle; house-made breads and desserts; truffle-focused menu. *Average main: €29 Borgo Santi Apostoli 26/r, Santa Maria Novella 055/2658170 www.mangiafoco.com No lunch weekdays.*

Obicà

$ | ITALIAN | With restaurants worldwide, Obicà, where mozarella takes center stage, has a strong following. This sleek eatery on Florence's swankiest street gets the cheese and its culinary cousin burrata (a fresh cheese filled with cream) from southern Italy and then makes it the centerpiece for various salads and pastas. You can pair your cheese with a number of accompaniments, including *caponata* (a Sicilian eggplant mélange) and mortadella from nearby Prato. **Known for:** mozzarella-laden menu; satisfying pizza and desserts; outdoor seating in nice weather. *Average main: €18 Via Tornabuoni 16, Santa Maria Novella 055/2773526 www.obica.com/restaurants/florence.*

Osteria Belle Donne

$$ | TUSCAN | Down the street from the church of Santa Maria Novella, this gaily decorated spot, festooned with plants and portraits of Marilyn Monroe and Audrey Hepburn, has an ever-changing menu and stellar service. The list of Tuscan standards is shaken up with alternatives such as stracciatella with shrimp and cherry tomatoes and truffles, when in season. **Known for:** seasonal ingredients; many dishes not typical of Tuscany; lively atmosphere. *Average main: €27 Via delle Belle Donne 16/r, Santa Maria Novella 055/2382609 www.belledonneosteria.it.*

★ Procacci

$$ | ITALIAN | At this classy Florentine institution dating from 1885, try one of the minitruffle panini and swish it down with a glass of prosecco. **Known for:** pane tartufato; excellent wines by the glass; serene (but tiny) space. *Average main: €21 Via Tornabuoni 64/r, Santa Maria Novella 055/211656 www.procacci1885.it.*

Vincanto

$$ | ITALIAN | It opens at 11 am and closes at midnight and also delivers: this is a rarity in Florentine dining. They do a little bit of everything here, including pastas, salads, pizzas, and even an American-style breakfast. **Known for:** a wide-ranging menu; kitchen stays open late; outside terrace with views of a beautiful square. *Average main: €24 Piazza Santa Maria Novella 23/r, Santa Maria Novella 055/2741555 www.ristorantevincanto.com.*

Hotels

Gallery Hotel Art

$$$ | HOTEL | High design resides at this art showcase near the Ponte Vecchio, where sleek, uncluttered rooms are dressed mostly in neutrals but have luxe touches such as leather headboards. **Pros:** trendy atmosphere; artistic touches; the in-house Fusion Bar serves delightful cocktails. **Cons:** some street noise; books up quickly; might be too trendy for some. *Rooms from: €450 Vicolo dell'Oro 5, Santa Maria Novella 055/27263 www.lungarnocollection.com/gallery-hotel-art 74 rooms No Meals.*

Hotel L'Orologio

$$$ | HOTEL | The owner of this understatedly elegant hotel has a real passion for watches, which is why he chose to name his hotel after them (and why you will see them throughout the property)—and

the location can't be beat, as it abuts the increasingly beautiful Piazza Santa Maria Novella. **Pros:** location; great staff; stunning breakfast room. **Cons:** some folks think it's too close to the train station; gets the occasional tour group; holds conferences from time to time. *$ Rooms from: €525 ✉ Piazza Santa Maria Novella 24, Santa Maria Novella ☎ 055/277380 🌐 www.hotelorologioflorence.com 🛏 55 rooms 🍽 Free Breakfast.*

Nuova Italia

$ | HOTEL | FAMILY | The genial Viti family oversees this property with clean and simple rooms near the train station and well within walking distance of the sights. **Pros:** reasonable rates; close to everything; great for those on a budget. **Cons:** no elevator; the neighborhood is highly trafficked; some street noise. *$ Rooms from: €162 ✉ Via Faenza 26, Santa Maria Novella ☎ 055/287508 🌐 www.hotel-nuovaitalia.com ⏲ Closed Dec. 20–Dec. 27 🛏 20 rooms 🍽 Free Breakfast.*

★ The Place Firenze

$$$$ | HOTEL | Hard to spot from the street, this sumptuous place provides all the comforts of a luxe home away from home—expect soothing earth tones in the guest rooms, free minibars, crisp linens, and room service offering organic dishes. **Pros:** private, intimate feel; stellar staff; small dogs allowed. **Cons:** breakfast seating a bit cramped; books up quickly; might be too trendy for some. *$ Rooms from: €960 ✉ Piazza Santa Maria Novella 7, Santa Maria Novella ☎ 055/2645181 🌐 www.theplacefirenze.com 🛏 20 rooms 🍽 Free Breakfast.*

Performing Arts

Maggio Musicale Fiorentino

MUSIC | The landmark Parco della Musica (Music Park) complex, designed by Paolo Desideri and associates, is the home of the Maggio Musicale Fiorentino. You can purchase tickets for its symphony performances and operas directly at the box office, by phone or online. *✉ Piazza Vittorio Gui 1, Santa Maria Novella ☎ 055/2779309 🌐 www.maggiofiorentino.it.*

Teatro Cartiere Carrara

CONCERTS | This large exhibition space, formerly Tuscany Hall, hosts a variety of events throughout the year, including concerts by visiting rock stars, performances by lesser-known bands from across Europe, and a large art market. *✉ Lungarno Aldo Moro 3, Lungarno North ☎ 055/6504112 🌐 www.teatrocartierecarrara.it.*

Shopping

★ Alberto Cozzi

STATIONERY | You'll find an extensive line of Florentine papers and paper products in this shop, where artisans also rebind and restore books. *✉ Via del Parione 35/r, Santa Maria Novella ☎ 055/294968 🌐 www.legatoriacozzifirenze.it.*

★ Angela Caputi

JEWELRY & WATCHES | Angela Caputi wows Florentine cognoscenti with her highly creative, often outsize, acrylic jewelry. A small but equally creative collection of women's clothing made of fine fabrics is also on offer. *✉ Borgo Santi Apostoli 44/46, Santa Maria Novella ☎ 055/292993 🌐 www.angelacaputi.com.*

Antica Officina del Farmacista Dr. Vranjes

FRAGRANCES | Dr. Vranjes elevates aromatherapy to an art form with scents for the body and home. *✉ Via della Vigna Nuova 30/r, Santa Maria Novella ☎ 055/0945851 🌐 www.drvranjes.it.*

Bottega Giotti

LEATHER GOODS | You'll find multiple lines of leather bags, wallets, and other accessories here. *✉ Piazza Ognissanti 3–4/r, Lungarno North ☎ 055/294265 🌐 www.bottegagiotti.com.*

Brandimarte

JEWELRY & WATCHES | Most people want to buy gold (for which Florence is justly famous) when they visit. That said, Brandimarte, which has specialized in exquisitely crafted silver jewelry, decorative objects, and housewares since 1955, is well worth a visit. ✉ *Via del Moro 92/r, Santa Maria Novella* ☎ *349/4220269 mobile* 🌐 *www.brandimarte.com.*

Cellerini

LEATHER GOODS | In a city where it seems just about everybody carries an expensive leather bag, Cellerini is an institution. ✉ *Via del Sole 9/r, Santa Maria Novella* ☎ *055/282533* 🌐 *www.cellerini.it.*

Emilio Pucci

CLOTHING | The aristocratic Marchese di Barsento, Emilio Pucci, became an international name in the late 1950s when the stretch ski clothes he designed for himself caught on with the *dolce vita* ("sweet life") crowd—his pseudopsychedelic prints and "palazzo pajamas" became all the rage. ✉ *Via Tornabuoni 20–22/r, Santa Maria Novella* ☎ *055/2658082* 🌐 *www.pucci.com.*

Ferragamo

SHOES | Set in a 13th-century palazzo, this classy institution displays designer clothing and accessories, though elegant footwear still underlies the Ferragamo success. ✉ *Via Tornabuoni 14/r, Santa Maria Novella* ☎ *055/292123* 🌐 *www.ferragamo.com.*

★ Loretta Caponi

CLOTHING | Synonymous with Florentine embroidery, this shop sells luxury lace, linens, and lingerie that have earned the eponymous signora worldwide renown. There's also beautiful (and expensive) clothing for children. ✉ *Via delle Belle Donne 28/r, Santa Maria Novella* ☎ *055/213668* 🌐 *www.lorettacaponi.it/en.*

★ Officina Profumo Farmaceutica di Santa Maria Novella

FRAGRANCES | The essence of a Florentine holiday is captured in perfumes, candles, and sachets at this cathedral-like emporium of herbal cosmetics and soaps that are made following centuries-old recipes created by friars. See a wire cutter used to make soap in the 19th century, a library of elixirs, and temporary exhibits that will make you feel like you're in a museum rather than the original shop of a brand that's now global. ✉ *Via della Scala 16, Santa Maria Novella* ☎ *055/216276* 🌐 *eu.smnovella.com.*

Pineider

STATIONERY | Although it has shops throughout the world, Pineider started out in Florence in 1774 and still does its printing here. Stationery and business cards are the mainstay, but the stores also sell colorful pens and fine-leather bags and desk accessories. ✉ *Lungarno degli Acciaiuoli 72–76/r, Santa Maria Novella* ☎ *055/284655* 🌐 *www.pineider.com.*

Principe

DEPARTMENT STORE | This Florentine institution sells casual clothes for men and women at far-from-casual prices. It also has a great housewares department. ✉ *Via del Sole 2, Santa Maria Novella* ☎ *055/292764* 🌐 *www.principedifirenze.com.*

Valli

FABRICS | Gifted seamstresses (and seamsters) should look no further than this place, which sells sumptuous silks, beaded fabrics, lace, wool, and tweeds by the meter. ✉ *Via della Vigna Nuova 81/r, Santa Maria Novella* ☎ *055/282485* 🌐 *www.vallitessuti.com.*

Santa Croce

The Santa Croce quarter, on the southeast fringe of the historic center, was built up in the Middle Ages outside the second set of medieval city walls. The centerpiece of the neighborhood was (and is) the basilica of Santa Croce, which could hold great numbers of worshippers; the vast piazza could accommodate any overflow and also served as a

Santa Croce
A
B
C
D
E
F
1
2
3
4
5
6
7
8
9
SAN GIOVANNI
SANTA CROCE
Duomo
Piazza del Duomo
Piazza d. Santissima Annunziata
Piazza Santa Maria Nuova
Piazza della Signoria
Piazza San Firenze
Galleria degli Uffizi
Piazza degli Uffizi
Piazza Santa Croce
Piazza d. Giudici
Piazza Mentana
Via Cesare Battisti
V. Gino Capponi
Via Laura
Via della Colonna
Via degli Affani
Via del Servi
Via Cavour
Via Ricasoli
Via de Ginori
Via del Pucci
Via d. Bitti
Via Martelli
V. del Castellaccio
Via della Pergola
Via Nuova dei Caccini
Via M. Bufalini
V. F. Portinari
V. dell' Orinolo
Via Sant' Egidio
Via dell' Orinolo
Borgo Pinti
Via Fiesolana
Bonizzi
Via dell'Oche
Via dei Calzaiuoli
Via S. Elisabetta
Via d. Studio
V.del Proconsolo
Via del Corso
Borgo degli Albizi
Via dei Tavolini
Via del Cercha
Via Dante Alighieri
V. del Magazziti
Via d. Giraldi
V. del Pandolfini
Via d. Senglole
Via Matteo Palmieri
Via d. Badesse
V. dell'
Via dell' Agnolo
Via Ghibellina
Via d. Rosa
Via della Condotta
Via dell Vecchia
Via del Burelli
Via dell' Anguillara
Via Torta
Via Giuseppe Verdi
V. G. d. Verrazzano
Via del Fico
Via del Gondi
Via d. Ninna
V. del Leoni
V. d. Corno
Via Vinegia
Borgo del Greci
Via dei Pepi
V. delle Pinzochere
Via san Cristofano
Via del Neri
Via d. Castellani
V. d. Castello d' Altafronte
Via Osteria del Guanto
Via del Magalotti
Via de' Rustici
V. del Brache
Via del Benci
Borgo Santa Croce
Via Antonio Magliabechi
Via del Saponai
V. d. Mosca
V. del Vagellai
1
2
3
4
5

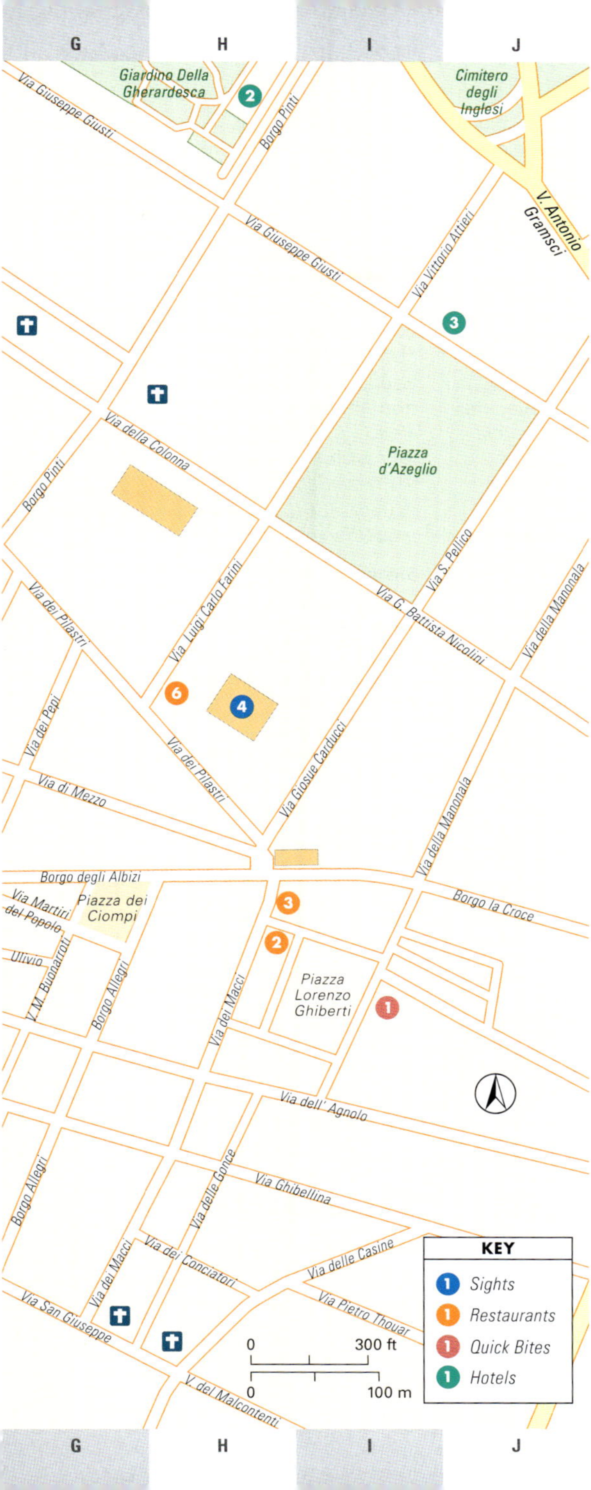

Sights

1 Casa Buonarroti F7
2 Piazza Santa Croce.................. E8
3 Santa Croce F8
4 Sinagoga............................ H5

Restaurants

1 Caffè Italiano D7
2 Cibrèo Ristorante H6
3 Cibrèo Trattoria H6
4 Enoteca Pinchiorri.................. F7
5 La Giostra.......................... E5
6 Ruth's H5

Quick Bites

1 da Rocco............................ I7
2 Perché No!.......................... A6

Hotels

1 Borgo Pinti......................... F4
2 The Four Seasons H1
3 Hotel Regency J2

Giardino Della Gherardesca
Cimitero degli Inglesi
Via Giuseppe Giusti
Borgo Pinti
V. Antonio Gramsci
Via Vittorio Alfieri
Via della Colonna
Piazza d'Azeglio
Via S. Pellico
Via G. Battista Nicolini
Via della Mannonala
Via Luigi Carlo Farini
Via dei Pilastri
Via dei Pepi
Via di Mezzo
Via Giosue Carducci
Via della Mannonala
Borgo degli Albizi
Piazza dei Ciompi
Via Martiri del Popolo
Borgo la Croce
Ulivio
V. M. Buonarroti
Borgo Allegri
Via dei Macci
Piazza Lorenzo Ghiberti
Via dell' Agnolo
Borgo Allegri
Via delle Gonce
Via Ghibellina
Via delle Casine
Via dei Macci
Via dei Conciatori
Via Pietro Thouar
Via San Giuseppe
V. del Malcontenti

0 300 ft
0 100 m

KEY

1 Sights
1 Restaurants
1 Quick Bites
1 Hotels

fairground and, allegedly since the middle of the 16th century, as a playing field for no-holds-barred soccer games. A center of leatherworking since the Middle Ages, the neighborhood is still packed with leatherworkers and leather shops.

Sights

Casa Buonarroti

ART MUSEUM | If you really enjoy walking in the footsteps of the great genius, you may want to complete the picture by visiting the Buonarroti family home. Michelangelo lived here from 1516 to 1525, and later gave it to his nephew, whose son, Michelangelo il Giovane (Michelangelo the Younger), turned it into a gallery dedicated to his great-uncle. The artist's descendants filled it with art treasures, some by Michelangelo himself. Two early marble works—the *Madonna of the Stairs* and *Battle of the Centaurs*—demonstrate his genius. ✉ *Via Ghibellina 70, Santa Croce* ☎ *055/241752* 🌐 *www.casabuonarroti.it* 🎫 *€8* ⏲ *Closed Tues.*

★ Piazza Santa Croce

PLAZA/SQUARE | **FAMILY** | Originally outside the city's 12th-century walls, this piazza grew with the Franciscans, who used it for public preaching. During the Renaissance, it hosted *giostre* (jousts), including one sponsored by Lorenzo de' Medici. Lined with many palazzi dating from the 15th and 16th centuries, the square remains one of Florence's loveliest and is a great place to people-watch. ✉ *Piazza Santa Croce, Santa Croce.*

★ Santa Croce

CHURCH | This Gothic church, whose facade dates from the 19th century, contains the skeletons of many Renaissance celebrities, including Michelangelo (1475–1564), Galileo Galilei (1564–1642), Niccolò Machiavelli (1469–1527), and Lorenzo Ghiberti (1378–1455). In addition, the collection of art here is by far the most important of any church in Florence. The most famous works are the Giotto frescoes in the two chapels immediately to the right of the high altar. They illustrate scenes from the lives of St. John the Evangelist and St. John the Baptist (in the right-hand chapel), as well as those from the life of St. Francis (in the left-hand chapel). Among the church's other highlights are Donatello's *Annunciation*; 14th-century frescoes by Taddeo Gaddi (circa 1300–66) illustrating scenes from the life of the Virgin Mary; and Donatello's *Crucifix*, criticized by Brunelleschi for making Christ look like a peasant. ✉ *Piazza Santa Croce 16, Santa Croce* ☎ *055/2466105* 🌐 *www.santacroceopera.it* 🎫 *Church and museum €8.*

Sinagoga

SYNAGOGUE | Jews were well settled in Florence by the end of the 14th century. By 1574, however, they were required to live within the large "ghetto" at the north side of today's Piazza della Repubblica, by decree of Cosimo I. Construction of the modern Moorish-style synagogue began in 1874 as a bequest of David Levi, who wished to endow a synagogue "worthy of the city." Falcini, Micheli, and Treves designed the building on a domed Greek cross plan with galleries in the transept and a roofline bearing three distinctive copper cupolas visible from all over Florence. The exterior has alternating bands of tan travertine and pink granite, reflecting an Islamic style repeated in Giovanni Panti's ornate interior. ✉ *Via Farini 6, Santa Croce* ☎ *055/245252* 🌐 *www.firenzebraica.it/sinagoga* 🎫 *Synagogue and museum €9 (reservations €1)* ⏲ *Closed weekends and Jewish holidays.*

Restaurants

Caffè Italiano

$$ | **PIZZA** | **FAMILY** | This small pizzeria is favored by locals. Make a reservation or come early to grab one of the few tables in front or round the back, and don't mind the fact that service here is intentionally rushed: turning tables is paramount.

Known for: pizza offerings; limited seating; local favorite. $ *Average main: €20* ✉ *Via Isole delle Stinche 11/r, Santa Croce* ☎ *055/289080* 🌐 *www.caffeitaliano.it.*

★ Cibrèo Ristorante

$$$ | **TUSCAN** | This upscale trattoria serves sumptuous options like the creamy crostini *di fegatini* (a savory chicken-liver spread) and melt-in-your-mouth desserts. Many Florentines hail this as the city's best restaurant, and justifiably so—late chef–owner Fabio Picchi (who left behind his Florence culinary legacy in 2022) knew Tuscan food better than anyone, and it shows. **Known for:** authentic Tuscan food, at the original Cibrèo outpost; seasonal menu; multilingual staff. $ *Average main: €40* ✉ *Via A. del Verrocchio 8/r, Santa Croce* ☎ *055/2341100* 🌐 *www.cibreo.com* ⏲ *No lunch Mon.–Thurs.*

Cibrèo Trattoria

$ | **TUSCAN** | This intimate trattoria, known to locals as Cibreino, shares its name and its kitchen with the famed Florentine restaurant but has a shorter, less-expensive menu. Save room for dessert, as the pastry chef has a deft hand with chocolate tarts. **Known for:** excellent meal at a moderate price; clever riffs on classic dishes; desserts to save room for. $ *Average main: €18* ✉ *Via dei Macci 122/r, Santa Croce* ☎ *055/2341100* 🌐 *www.cibreo.com.*

Enoteca Pinchiorri

$$$$ | **ITALIAN** | A sumptuous Renaissance palace with high, frescoed ceilings and bouquets in silver vases provides the backdrop for this restaurant, one of the most expensive in Italy. Some consider it one of the best, and others consider it inauthentic, as the cuisine extends far beyond Italian. **Known for:** creative food; wine cellar; exorbitantly high prices. $ *Average main: €120* ✉ *Via Ghibellina 87, Santa Croce* ☎ *055/26311* 🌐 *www.enotecapinchiorri.it* ⏲ *Closed Sun., Mon., and Aug. No lunch* 🧥 *Jacket.*

★ La Giostra

$$$ | **ITALIAN** | Passing by this restaurant at night, you may think there's a club beyond its doors, given the crowd gathering outside. Frequented by celebrities, its name means "carousel," and it was created by the late Prince Dimitri Kunz d'Asburgo Lorena and is now expertly run by Soldano, one of his twin sons. **Known for:** sublime desserts; lively atmosphere; vegetarian and vegan options. $ *Average main: €33* ✉ *Borgo Pinti 12/r, Santa Croce* ☎ *055/241341* 🌐 *www.ristorantelagiostra.com* ⏲ *No lunch weekends.*

Ruth's

$$ | **KOSHER** | The only kosher–vegetarian restaurant in Tuscany is Ruth's, adjacent to Florence's synagogue. On the menu are inexpensive vegetarian and Mediterranean dishes, and there's also a large selection of kosher wines. **Known for:** harissa; nice wine list; friendly staff. $ *Average main: €20* ✉ *Via Farini 2/a, Santa Croce* ☎ *055/2480888* 🌐 *www.kosheruth.com* ⏲ *Closed for dinner Fri. and lunch Sat. (unless a special reservation and payment is made in advance).*

Coffee and Quick Bites

da Rocco

$ | **TUSCAN** | **FAMILY** | At one of Florence's biggest markets, you can grab lunch to go, or you can cram into one of the booths and pour from the straw-cloaked flask (wine here is *da consumo,* which means they charge you for how much you drink). Food is abundant and Tuscan, service is fast, and locals pack in. **Known for:** tasty food at rock-bottom prices; ever-changing menu; takeout. $ *Average main: €9* ✉ *Mercato Sant'Ambrogio, Piazza Ghiberti, Santa Croce* ☎ *339/8384555 mobile* 🌐 *www.daroccotrattoria.com* ⏲ *Closed Sun. No dinner.*

★ Perché No!

$ | **ICE CREAM** | **FAMILY** | What many consider the best gelateria in the centro storico embodies the "practice makes perfect" adage. It's been making ice cream since 1939. **Known for:** gelati made daily; one of the oldest gelaterias in the city; unusual flavors and vegan options. *$ Average main: €3 ✉ Via dei Tavolini 19r, Duomo ☎ 055/2398969 🌐 www.facebook.com/GelateriaPercheNo.*

Hotels

Borgo Pinti

$ | B&B/INN | FAMILY | Nuns of the Oblates of the Assumption run this convent holiday house, where some of the simple but spotlessly clean rooms have views of the Duomo's cupola, and others look out onto a garden where you are welcome to relax. **Pros:** great location and (mostly) quiet rooms; Mass held daily; a soothing, somewhat untended garden. **Cons:** some have observed that there's hall noise; rooms facing the street can be noisy; check out is by 9 am. *$ Rooms from: €100 ✉ Borgo Pinti 15, Santa Croce ☎ 055/2346291 🌐 www.oblate.it 40 rooms Free Breakfast.*

The Four Seasons

$$$$ | HOTEL | This 15th-century palazzo is perhaps the city's most luxurious hotel, where many guest rooms have original 17th-century frescoes, and an 11-acre garden is dotted with centuries-old trees. **Pros:** pool; state-of-the-art spa; Michelin-starred Il Palagio restaurant. **Cons:** ultra-pricey; splashing children in the pool can be a nuisance for some; small rooms. *$ Rooms from: €2,275 ✉ Borgo Pinti 99, Santa Croce ☎ 055/26261 🌐 www.fourseasons.com/florence 117 rooms No Meals.*

Hotel Regency

$$$ | HOTEL | Though it's just 15 minutes from the Accademia and Michelangelo's *David,* this hotel—in a 19th-century mansion adorned with rich fabrics and period-appropriate furnishings—is a true retreat from the city's noise and crowds. **Pros:** faces one of the few green spaces in central Florence; quiet residential setting; lovely, on-site Relais le Jardin restaurant. **Cons:** somewhat removed from the city center; rooms facing the park can be noisy; books up quickly. *$ Rooms from: €536 ✉ Piazza d'Azeglio 3, Santa Croce ☎ 055/245247 🌐 www.regency-hotel.com ⏲ Closed Jan.–Mar. 31 rooms Free Breakfast.*

Nightlife

Caffè Sant'Ambrogio

BARS | Come here when it's summer for outdoor seating with a view of an 11th-century church (Sant'Ambrogio) directly across the street; the crowd gathers until past 2 am. Come here at any time of the year for perfectly mixed drinks and a lively atmosphere filled with (mostly) locals. *✉ Piazza Sant'Ambrogio 7–8/r, Santa Croce ☎ 055/2477277 🌐 www.caffesantambrogio.it.*

Jazz Club

LIVE MUSIC | Enjoy live music in this small basement club. *✉ Via Nuova de' Caccini 3, at Borgo Pinti, Santa Croce 🌐 www.facebook.com/jazzclubfirenze.it.*

Rex

BARS | A trendy, artsy clientele frequents this bar at aperitivo time. By 10 pm, the place is packed with mostly young folks sipping cocktails. *✉ Via Fiesolana 23–25/r, Santa Croce ☎ 055/2480331 🌐 www.rexfirenze.com.*

Shopping

★ Mercato di Sant'Ambrogio

MARKET | FAMILY | It's possible to strike gold at this lively market, where clothing stalls abut those with fruits and vegetables. *✉ Piazza Ghiberti, off Via dei Macci, Santa Croce ☎ 055/2480778 🌐 www.mercatosantambrogio.it.*

Continued on page 537

WHO'S WHO IN RENAISSANCE ART

Michelangelo. Leonardo da Vinci. Raphael. This heady triumvirate of the Italian Renaissance is synonymous with artistic genius. Yet they are only three of the remarkable cast of characters whose work defines the Renaissance, that extraordinary flourishing of art and culture in Italy, especially in Florence, as the Middle Ages drew to a close. The artists were visionaries, who redefined painting, sculpture, architecture, and even what it means to be an artist.

THE PIONEER. In the mid-14th century, a few artists began to move away from the flat, two-dimensional painting of the Middle Ages. Giotto, who painted seemingly three-dimensional figures who show emotion, had a major impact on the artists of the next century.

THE GROUNDBREAKERS. Brunelleschi and Botticelli took center stage in the 15th century. Ghiberti, Masaccio, Donatello, Uccello, Fra Angelico, and Filippo Lippi were other major players. Part of the Renaissance (or "re-birth") was a renewed interest in classical sources—the texts, monuments, and sculpture of Ancient Greece and Rome. Perspective (the illusion of three-dimensional space) in painting was another development during this era, known as the Early Renaissance. Suddenly the art appearing on the walls looked real, or more realistic than it used to.

Roman ruins were not the only thing to inspire these artists. There was an incredible exchange of ideas going on. In Santa Maria del Carmine, Filippo Lippi was inspired by the work of Masaccio, who in turn was a friend of Brunelleschi. Young artists also learned from the masters via the apprentice system. Ghiberti's workshop (*bottega* in Italian) included, at one time or another, Donatello, Masaccio, and Uccello. Botticelli was apprenticed to Filippo Lippi.

THE BIG THREE. The mathematical rationality and precision of 15th-century art gave way to what is known as the High Renaissance. Leonardo, Michelangelo, and Raphael were much more concerned with portraying the body in all its glory and with achieving harmony and grandeur in their work. Oil paint, used infrequently up until this time, became more widely employed. As a result, Leonardo's colors are deeper, more sensual, more alive. For one brief period, all three were in Florence at the same time. Michelangelo and Leonardo surely knew one another, as they were simultaneously working on frescoes (never completed) inside Palazzo Vecchio.

When Michelangelo went to Rome in 1508, it started an artistic exodus from which Florence never fully recovered.

A RENAISSANCE TIMELINE

IN THE WORLD

Black Death in Europe kills one third of the population, 1347-50.

Joan of Arc burned at the stake, 1431.

IN FLORENCE

Dante, a native of Florence, writes *The Divine Comedy*, 1302-21.

Founding of the Medici bank, 1397.

Medici family made official papal bankers.

1434, Cosimo il Vecchio becomes de facto ruler of Florence. The Medici family will dominate the city until 1494.

1300

1400

IN ART

EARLY RENAISSANCE

GIOTTO (ca. 1267-1337)

Giotto fresoes in Santa Croce, 1320-25.

1334, 67-year-old Giotto is appointed chief architect of Santa Maria del Fiore, Florence's Duomo *(below)*. He begins to work on the Campanile, which will be completed in 1359, after his death.

Masaccio and Masolino fresco Santa Maria del Carmine, 1424-28.

BRUNELLESCHI (1377-1446)

LORENZO GHIBERTI (ca. 1381-1455)

DONATELLO (ca. 1386-1466)

PAOLO UCCELLO (1397-1475)

FRA ANGELICO (ca. 1400-1455)

MASACCIO (1401-1428)

FILIPPO LIPPI (ca. 1406-1469)

Ghiberti wins the competition for the Baptistery doors *(above)* in Florence, 1401.

Donatello sculpts his bronze *David*, ca. 1440.

Fra Angelico frescoes friars' cells in San Marco, ca. 1438-45.

Uccello's *Sir John Hawkwood*, ca. 1436.

Brunelleschi wins the competition for the Duomo's cupola, 1418.

Gutenberg Bible is printed, 1455.

Columbus discovers America, 1492.

Martin Luther posts his 95 theses on the door at Wittenberg, kicking off the Protestant Reformation, 1517.

Constantinople falls to the Turks, 1453.

Machiavelli's *Prince* appears, 1513.

Copernicus proves that the earth is not the center of the universe, 1530-43.

Lorenzo "il Magnifico" *(right)*, the Medici patron of the arts, rules in Florence, 1449-92.

Two Medici popes Leo X (1513-21) and Clement VII (1523-34) in Rome.

Catherine de'Medici becomes Queen of France, 1547.

1450 | 1500 | 1550

HIGH RENAISSANCE | MANNERISM

Fra Filippo Lippi's *Madonna and Child*, ca. 1452.

Botticelli paints the *Birth of Venus*, ca. 1482.

1508, Raphael begins work on the chambers in the Vatican, Rome.

1504, Michelangelo's *David* is put on display in Piazza della Signoria, where it remains until 1873.

Michelangelo begins to fresco the Sistine Chapel ceiling, 1508.

Giorgio Vasari publishes his first edition of *Lives of the Artists*, 1550.

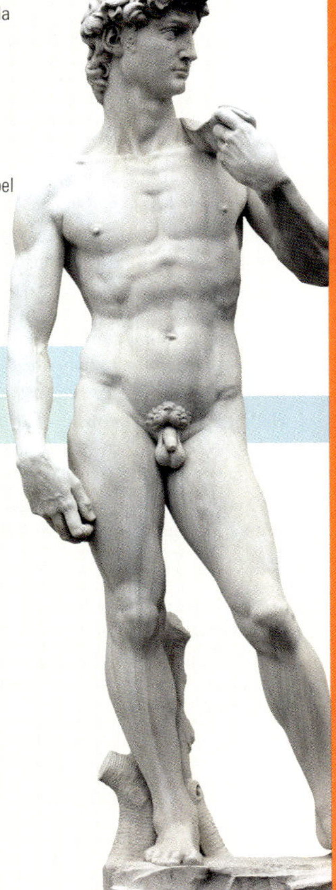

BOTTICELLI (ca. 1444-1510)

LEONARDO DA VINCI (1452-1519)

RAPHAEL (1483-1520)

MICHELANGELO (1475-1564)

Leonardo paints *The Last Supper (below)* in Milan, 1495-98.

Giotto's *Nativity*

Donatello's *St. John the Baptist*

Ghiberti's *Gates of Paradise*

GIOTTO (CA. 1267-1337)

Painter/architect from a small town north of Florence.

He unequivocally set Italian painting on the course that led to the triumphs of the Renaissance masters. Unlike the rather flat, two-dimensional forms found in then prevailing Byzantine art, Giotto's figures have a fresh, life-like quality. The people in his paintings have bulk, and they show emotion, which you can see on their faces and in their gestures. This was something new in the late Middle Ages. Without Giotto, there wouldn't have been a Raphael.

In Florence: Santa Croce; Uffizi; Campanile; Santa Maria Novella

Elsewhere in Italy: Scrovegni Chapel, Padua; Vatican Museums, Rome

FILIPPO BRUNELLESCHI (1377-1446)

Architect/engineer from Florence.

If Brunelleschi had beaten Ghiberti in the Baptistery doors competition in Florence, the city's Duomo most likely would not have the striking appearance and authority that it has today. After his loss, he sulked off to Rome, where he studied the ancient Roman structures first-hand. Brunelleschi figured out how to vault the Duomo's dome, a structure unprecedented in its colossal size and great height. His Ospedale degli Innocenti employs classical elements in the creation of a stunning, new architectural statement; it is the first truly Renaissance structure.

In Florence: Duomo; Ospedale degli Innocenti; San Lorenzo; Santo Spirito; Baptistery Doors Competition Entry, Bargello; Santa Croce

LORENZO GHIBERTI (CA. 1381-1455)

Sculptor from Florence.

Ghiberti won a competition—besting his chief rival, Brunelleschi—to cast the gilded bronze North Doors of the Baptistery in Florence. These doors, and the East Doors that he subsequently executed, took up the next 50 years of his life. He created intricately worked figures that are more true-to-life than any since antiquity, and he was one of the first Renaissance sculptors to work in bronze. Ghiberti taught the next generation of artists; Donatello, Uccello, and Masaccio all passed through his studio.

In Florence: Door Copies, Baptistery; Original Doors, Museo dell'Opera del Duomo; Baptistry Door Competition Entry, Bargello; Orsanmichele

DONATELLO (CA. 1386-1466)

Sculptor from Florence.

Donatello was an innovator who, like his good friend Brunelleschi, spent most of his long life in Florence. Consumed with the science of optics, he used light and shadow to create the effects of nearness and distance. He made an essentially flat slab look like a three- dimensional scene. His bronze sculpture of *David* is probably the first free-standing male nude since antiquity. Not only technically brilliant, his work is also emotionally resonant; few sculptors are as expressive.

In Florence: David, Bargello; St. Mark, Orsanmichele; Palazzo Vecchio; Museo dell'Opera del Duomo; San Lorenzo; Santa Croce

Elsewhere in Italy: Padua; Prato; Venice

Fra Angelico's *Déposition de Croix*

Masaccio's *Trinity*

Filippo Lippi's *Madonna and Child with Two Angels*

PAOLO UCCELLO (1397-1475)

Painter from Florence.

Renaissance chronicler Vasari once observed that had Uccello not been so obsessed with the mathematical problems posed by perspective, he would have been a very good painter. The struggle to master single-point perspective and to render motion in two dimensions is nowhere more apparent than in his battle scenes. His first major commission in Florence was the gargantuan fresco of the English mercenary Sir John Hawkwood (the Italians called him Giovanni Acuto) in Florence's Duomo.

In Florence: **Sir John Hawkwood, Duomo; Battle of San Romano, Uffizi; Santa Maria Novella**

Elsewhere in Italy: **Urbino, Prato**

FRA ANGELICO (CA. 1400-1455)

Painter from a small town north of Florence.

A Dominican friar, who eventually made his way to the convent of San Marco, Fra Angelico and his assistants painted frescoes for aid in prayer and meditation. He was known for his piety; Vasari wrote that Fra Angelico could never paint a crucifix without a tear running down his face. Perhaps no other painter so successfully translated the mysteries of faith and the sacred into painting. And yet his figures emote, his command of perspective is superb, and his use of color startles even today.

In Florence: **Museo di San Marco; Uffizi**

Elsewhere in Italy: **Vatican Museums, Rome; Fiesole; Cortona; Perugia; Orvieto**

MASACCIO (1401-1428)

Painter from San Giovanni Valdarno, southeast of Florence.

Masaccio and Masolino, a frequent collaborator, worked most famously together at Santa Maria del Carmine. Their frescoes of the life of St. Peter use light to mold figures in the painting by imitating the way light falls on figures in real life. Masaccio also pioneered the use of single-point perspective, masterfully rendered in his His friend Brunelleschi probably introduced him to the technique, yet another step forward in rendering things the way the eye sees them. Masaccio died young and under mysterious circumstances.

In Florence: **Santa Maria del Carmine; Trinity, Santa Maria Novella**

FILIPPO LIPPI (CA. 1406-1469)

Painter from Prato.

At a young age, Filippo Lippi entered the friary of Santa Maria del Carmine, where he was highly influenced by Masaccio and Masolino's frescoes. His religious vows appear to have made less of an impact; his affair with a young nun produced a son, Filippino (Little Philip, who later apprenticed with Botticelli), and a daughter. His religious paintings often have a playful, humorous note; some of his angels are downright impish and look directly out at the viewer. Lippi links the earlier painters of the 15th century with those who follow; Botticelli apprenticed with him.

In Florence: **Uffizi; Palazzo Medici Riccardi; San Lorenzo; Palazzo Pitti**

Elsewhere in Italy: **Prato**

Botticelli's *Primavera*

Leonardo's *Portrait of a Young Woman*

Raphael's *Madonna on the Meadow*

BOTTICELLI (CA. 1444-1510)

Painter from Florence.

Botticelli's work is characterized by stunning, elongated blondes, cherubic angels (something he undoubtedly learned from his time with Filippo Lippi), and tender Christs. Though he did many religious paintings, he also painted monumental, nonreligious panels—his *Birth of Venus* and *Primavera* being the two most famous of these. A brief sojourn took him to Rome, where he and a number of other artists frescoed the Sistine Chapel walls.

In Florence:
Birth of Venus, Primavera, Uffizi; Palazzo Pitti
Elsewhere in Italy:
Vatican Museums, Rome

LEONARDO DA VINCI (1452-1519)

Painter/sculptor/engineer from Anchiano, a small town outside Vinci.

Leonardo never lingered long in any place; his restless nature and his international reputation led to commissions throughout Italy, and took him to Milan, Vigevano, Pavia, Rome, and, ultimately, France. Though he is most famous for his mysterious *Mona Lisa* (at the Louvre in Paris), he painted other penetrating, psychological portraits in addition to his scientific experiments: his design for a flying machine (never built) predates Kitty Hawk by nearly 500 years. The greatest collection of Leonardo's work in Italy can be seen on one wall in the Uffizi.

In Florence: **Adoration of the Magi, Uffizi**
Elsewhere in Italy: **Last Supper, Santa Maria delle Grazie, Milan**

RAPHAEL (1483-1520)

Painter/architect from Urbino.

Raphael spent only four highly productive years of his short life in Florence, where he turned out made-to-order panel paintings of the *Madonna and Child* for a hungry public; he also executed a number of portraits of Florentine aristocrats. Perhaps no other artist had such a fine command of line and color, and could render it, seemingly effortlessly, in paint. His painting acquired new authority after he came up against Michelangelo toiling away on the Sistine ceiling. Raphael worked nearly next door in the Vatican, where his figures take on an epic, Michelangelesque scale.

In Florence: **Uffizi; Palazzo Pitti**
Elsewhere in Italy: **Vatican Museums, Rome**

MICHELANGELO (1475-1564)

Painter/sculptor/architect from Caprese.

Although Florentine and proud of it (he famously signed his St. Peter's *Pietà* to avoid confusion about where he was from), he spent most of his 89 years outside his native city. He painted and sculpted the male body on an epic scale and glorified it while doing so. Though he complained throughout the proceedings that he was really a sculptor, Michelangelo's Sistine Chapel ceiling is arguably the greatest fresco cycle ever painted (and the massive figures owe no small debt to Giotto).

In Florence: **David, Galleria dell'Accademia; Uffizi; Casa Buonarroti; Bargello**
Elsewhere in Italy: **St. Peter's Basilica, Vatican Museums, and Piazza del Campidoglio in Rome**

Oreria

JEWELRY & WATCHES | The two women who run Oreria create divine designs using silver and semiprecious stones. ✉ *Borgo Pinti 87/a, Santa Croce* ☎ *055/244708* 🌐 *www.oreria.net.*

★ Scuola del Cuoio

LEATHER GOODS | Leatherworkers ply their trade at Scuola del Cuoio (Leather School), a consortium in the former dormitory of the convent of Santa Croce. High-quality, fairly priced jackets, belts, and purses are sold here. ✉ *Piazza Santa Croce 16, Santa Croce* ☎ *055/244533* 🌐 *www.scuola-del-cuoio.com.*

The Oltrarno

A walk through the Oltrarno (literally "the other side of the Arno") takes in two very different aspects of Florence: the splendor of the Medici, manifest in the riches of the mammoth Palazzo Pitti and the gracious Giardino di Boboli; and the charm of the Oltrarno, a gentrified former working-class neighborhood with artisans' and antiques shops.

Sights

Giardino Bardini

GARDEN | FAMILY | Garden lovers, those who crave a view, and those who enjoy a nice hike should visit this lovely villa, whose history spans centuries. It had a walled garden as early as the 14th century; its "Grand Stairs"—a zigzag ascent well worth scaling—have been around since the 16th. In spring, the garden is filled with irises, roses, and heirloom flowers and its magnificent wisteria pergola is in bloom. It also has a Japanese garden and statuary. ✉ *Costa San Giorgio 2, San Niccolò* ☎ *055/294883* 🌐 *www.villabardini.it* 🎫 *€10 includes Giardino di Boboli* ⏲ *Closed the 1st and last Mon. of month.*

★ Giardino di Boboli (*Boboli Gardens*)

GARDEN | FAMILY | The main entrance to these gardens is from the right side of the courtyard of Palazzo Pitti. The landscaping began to take shape in 1549, when the Pitti family sold the palazzo to Eleanor of Toledo, wife of the Medici grand duke Cosimo I. Stone paths lead to vine-covered pergolas and grand staircases, and a walk here also affords excellent views. ✉ *Piazza de' Pitti, Palazzo Pitti* ☎ *055/294883* 🌐 *www.uffizi.it/giardino-boboli* 🎫 *€10 includes Giardino Bardini* ⏲ *Closed 1st and last Mon. of month.*

Museo Bardini

ART MUSEUM | The 19th-century collector and antiquarian Stefano Bardini turned his palace into his own private museum. Upon his death, the collection was turned over to the state and includes an interesting assortment of Etruscan pieces, sculpture, paintings, and furniture that dates mostly from the Renaissance and Baroque eras. ✉ *Via dei Renai 37, Oltrarno* ☎ *055/2768224* 🌐 *cultura.comune.fi.it/musei* 🎫 *€7* ⏲ *Closed Tues.–Thurs.*

★ Palazzo Pitti

ART MUSEUM | This is one of Florence's largest architectural set pieces. The original palazzo, built for the Pitti family around 1460, consisted of the main entrance and the sections extending as far as three windows on either side. In 1549, the property was sold to the Medici, who commissioned Bartolomeo Ammannati to make substantial additions.

Today, the palace houses several museums. The Museo degli Argenti contains Medici treasures; the Galleria del Costume showcases 300 years of fashion; the Galleria d'Arte Moderna has mostly Tuscan 19th- and 20th-century paintings; and the Galleria Palatina, where paintings from the 15th to the 17th century are displayed in rooms that remain much as the Lorena, the rulers who took over from the Medici in 1737, left them. ✉ *Piazza Pitti, Palazzo*

Sights

1 Giardino Bardini **G4**
2 Giardino di Boboli....... **C5**
3 Museo Bardini **G3**
4 Palazzo Pitti **D3**
5 Piazzale Michelangelo **J5**
6 San Miniato al Monte.................... **J7**
7 Santa Felicita............ **E2**
8 Santa Maria del Carmine.................. **B2**
9 Santo Spirito **C2**

Restaurants

1 Alla Vecchia Bettola **A2**
2 Fuori Porta................ **I4**
3 Il Santo Bevitore **C1**
4 La Casalinga............. **C3**
5 Osteria Antica Mescita San Niccolò **I4**
6 Zeb **I4**

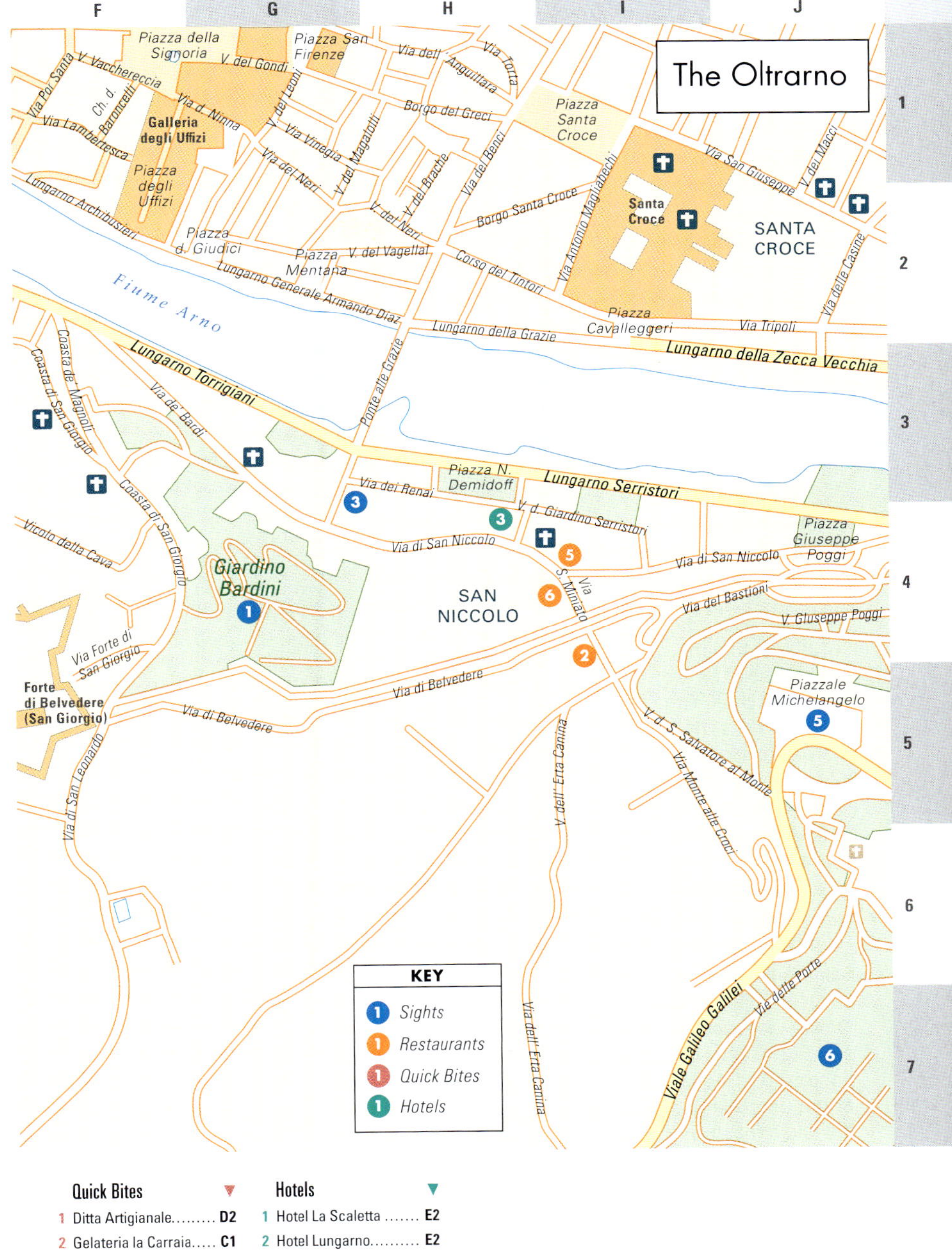

Quick Bites ▼

1 Ditta Artigianale......... **D2**

2 Gelateria la Carraia..... **C1**

Hotels ▼

1 Hotel La Scaletta **E2**

2 Hotel Lungarno.......... **E2**

3 Hotel Silla................ **H4**

Pitti ☎ *055/294883* 🌐 *www.uffizi.it/palazzo-pitti* 🎫 *From €16* ⏲ *Closed Mon.*

★ Piazzale Michelangelo

PLAZA/SQUARE | FAMILY | From this lookout you have a marvelous view of Florence and the hills around it, rivaling the vista from the Forte di Belvedere. A copy of Michelangelo's *David* overlooks outdoor cafés packed with tourists during the day and evening. In May, the Giardino dell'Iris (Iris Garden) off the piazza is abloom with more than 2,500 varieties of the flower. The Giardino delle Rose (Rose Garden) on the terraces below the piazza is also in full bloom in May and June. ✉ *Piazzale Michelangelo, San Niccolò.*

San Miniato al Monte

CHURCH | This abbey, like the Baptistery a fine example of Romanesque architecture, is one of the oldest churches in Florence, dating from the 11th century. A 12th-century mosaic topped by a gilt bronze eagle, emblem of San Miniato's sponsors, the Calimala (cloth merchants' guild), crowns the green-and-white marble facade. Inside are a 13th-century inlaid-marble floor and apse mosaic. Artist Spinello Aretino (1350–1410) covered the walls of the Sagrestia with frescoes of scenes from the life of St. Benedict. ✉ *Via delle Porte Sante 34, San Niccolò* ☎ *055/2342731* 🌐 *www.sanminiatoalmonte.it* ⏲ *Closed daily 1–3 pm.*

Santa Felicita

CHURCH | This late-Baroque church (its facade was remodeled between 1736 and 1739) contains the Mannerist Jacopo Pontormo's *Deposition,* the centerpiece of the Cappella Capponi (executed 1525–28) and a masterpiece of 16th-century Florentine art. The granite column in the piazza was erected in 1381 and marks a Christian cemetery. While following the Vasari Corridor, you can see the Medici family's private entrance to the church. ✉ *Piazza Santa Felicita 3, Palazzo Pitti* ☎ *055/213018* ⏲ *Closed Sun.*

Favorite Places

Liz Shemaria: If you time it right you can catch the vespers echoing off the Romanesque walls of San Miniato al Monte—a peaceful respite above the terra-cotta skyline and its crowds.

Santa Maria del Carmine

CHURCH | The Cappella Brancacci, at the end of the right transept of this church, contains a masterpiece of Renaissance painting: a fresco cycle that changed the course of Western art. It is the work of Masaccio (1401–28) and Masolino (1383–circa 1447), who began it around 1424, and Filippino Lippi (1457–1504), who finished it some 50 years later.

It was, however, Masaccio's work that opened a new frontier for painting, as he was among the first artists to employ single-point perspective. His style predominates in the *Tribute Money,* on the upper-left wall; *St. Peter Baptizing,* on the upper altar wall; the *Distribution of Goods,* on the lower altar wall; and the *Expulsion of Adam and Eve,* on the chapel's upper-left entrance pier. The figures of Adam and Eve possess a startling presence thanks to the dramatic way in which their bodies seem to reflect light. In their faces, you also see terrible shame and suffering depicted with a humanity rarely achieved in art. ✉ *Piazza del Carmine, Santo Spirito* ☎ *055/2768224 reservations* 🌐 *bigliettimusei.comune.fi.it* 🎫 *€11* ⏲ *Closed Tues. and Sun. morning* ✍ *Reservations to visit the Cappella Brancacci are required.*

Santo Spirito

CHURCH | It was here that Filippo Brunelleschi solved two major problems of interior Renaissance church design: how to build a cross-shape interior using architectural elements borrowed from antiquity (a religious taboo at the time) and how to incorporate the order and regularity that Renaissance scientists (among them Brunelleschi himself) were at the time discovering in the natural world.

His resolution of the first problem was brilliantly simple: while ancient Greek temples were walled buildings surrounded by classical colonnades, Brunelleschi's churches were classical arcades surrounded by walled buildings. His solution to the second problem was mathematically precise: he made it so that the church's components were proportionally related. That is, the transepts and nave have the same width; the side aisles are half as wide as the nave; the chapels off the side aisles are half as deep as the side aisles; the chancel and transepts are one-eighth the depth of the nave; and so on, with dizzying exactitude. ✉ *Piazza Santo Spirito 30, Oltrarno* ☎ *055/210030* 🌐 *www.basilicasantospirito.it* 🎫 *Church free; tour €2* ⏲ *Closed Wed.*

Restaurants

Alla Vecchia Bettola

$$ | **TUSCAN** | The name doesn't exactly mean "old dive," but it comes pretty close. The recipes here come from "wise grandmothers" and celebrate Tuscan food in its glorious simplicity—prosciutto is sliced to order, grilled meats are tender, service is friendly, and the wine list is well-priced and good. **Known for:** grilled meats; firmly Tuscan menu; just outside the centro storico but worth the taxi ride. $ *Average main: €20* ✉ *Viale Vasco Pratolini 3/5/7, Oltrarno* ☎ *055/224158* ⏲ *Closed Sun. and Mon.*

★ Fuori Porta

$ | **WINE BAR** | This wine bar on the way up the hill to Piazzale Michelangelo serves cured meats and cheeses, pastas, salads, and daily specials. Crostini and *crostoni*—grilled bread topped with a mélange of cheeses and meats—are the house specialty, and its grilled vegetables are divine. **Known for:** lengthy wine list; crostini and crostoni; changing daily specials. $ *Average main: €14* ✉ *Via Monte alle Croci 10, San Niccolò* ☎ *055/2342483* 🌐 *www.fuoriporta.it.*

★ Il Santo Bevitore

$$ | **TUSCAN** | Florentines and other lovers of good food flock to "The Holy Drinker" for Tuscan-inspired dishes—perhaps the exceptional verdure sott'olio or the *terrina di fegatini* (a creamy chicken-liver spread) to start, followed by one of the divine pastas. Unpretentious white walls, dark wood furniture, and paper placemats provide the simple decor. **Known for:** Tuscan dishes with flair; Norcini (cured meats) menu; friendly waitstaff. $ *Average main: €24* ✉ *Via Santo Spirito 64/r–66/r, Santo Spirito* ☎ *055/211264* 🌐 *www.ilsantobevitore.com.*

★ La Casalinga

$ | **TUSCAN** | *Casalinga* means "housewife," and this place, which has been around since 1963, has the nostalgic charm of a mid-century kitchen with Tuscan comfort food to match. If you eat ribollita anywhere in Florence, eat it here—it couldn't be more authentic. **Known for:** ribollita; black pepper beef stew; often packed. $ *Average main: €15* ✉ *Via Michelozzi 9/r, Santo Spirito* ☎ *055/218624* 🌐 *www.trattorialacasalinga.it* ⏲ *Closed Sun. and 2 wks in Dec. and Jan.*

Osteria Antica Mescita San Niccolò

$ | **TUSCAN** | Always crowded this osteria is next to San Niccolò church, and, if you sit in the lower part, you'll be in what was once a chapel dating from the 11th century. The subtle but dramatic background nicely complements the food, which is simple Tuscan. **Known for:** soup options; grilled meats; outdoor seating in a small, lovely square. $ *Average main: €14* ✉ *Via San Niccolò 60/r, San Niccolò* ☎ *055/2342836* 🌐 *www.anticamescitasanniccolo.com.*

Zeb

$ | **TUSCAN** | "Zeb" stands for *zuppa e bollito* (soup and boiled things), but you can't go wrong with anything at this small *alimentari* (delicatessen) with high-quality ingredients at a reasonable price. It's homestyle Tuscan cuisine at its very best, served in intimate surroundings (there's room for only about 20 diners). **Known for:** fantastic soup; terrific pasta; lovely wine list. *Average main: €18 Via San Miniato 2, Oltrarno 055/2342864 www.zebgastronomia.com Closed Wed. No dinner Sun. or Mon. and Tues. Nov.–Mar.*

Coffee and Quick Bites

Ditta Artigianale

$ | **CAFÉ** | Founded in 2013 as a micro coffee roaster on Via de' Neri, Ditta Artigianale now has six spots throughout Florence. Follow a side street off the Palazzo Pitti to take a coffee break with a classic espresso, drip coffee, or the inventive Coffemisu (espresso, cookies, cocoa, and mascarpone cream) in a space that's more like an airy mid-century modern living room, than a coffee shop. **Known for:** fair trade coffee; extensive brunch menu; lively atmosphere, popular with expats and study abroad crowd. *Average main: €10 Via dello Sprone 5/r, Oltrarno 055/0457163 www.dittaartigianale.it.*

Gelateria la Carraia

$ | **ICE CREAM** | **FAMILY** | At the foot of Ponte Carraia, two bridges down from the Ponte Vecchio, find standard gelato flavors or creative options such as *delizia carraia* (white chocolate with pistachio sauce). **Known for:** supercreamy gelato; generous cones; every flavor is worth a taste. *Average main: €3 Piazza Nazario Sauro 2, Santo Spirito 055/280695 www.gelaterialacarraia.it/en.*

Hotels

Hotel La Scaletta

$$ | **HOTEL** | In addition to a tremendous view of the Boboli Gardens, this mazelike pensione near the Ponte Vecchio and Palazzo Pitti has simply furnished but mostly large rooms and a sunny breakfast room. **Pros:** in-house restaurant with stunning views; wonderful, multilingual staff; in a lively neighborhood. **Cons:** small elevator, many steps and confusing corridors; books up quickly; standard rooms are showing wear and tear. *Rooms from: €277 Via Guicciardini 13, Palazzo Pitti 055/283028 www.hotellascaletta.it 36 rooms No Meals.*

Hotel Lungarno

$$$$ | **HOTEL** | Private terraces with views of the Arno and the Palazzo Vecchio are among the draws in many of this hotel's accommodations. **Pros:** upscale without being stuffy; lovely Arno views; Borgo San Jacopo, the hotel restaurant. **Cons:** rooms without Arno views feel less special; street noise happens; walls can be thin. *Rooms from: €800 Borgo San Jacopo 14, Oltrarno 055/27261 www.lungarnocollection.com 63 rooms No Meals.*

Hotel Silla

$$ | **HOTEL** | Rooms in this 15th-century palazzo, entered via a courtyard with potted plants and sculpture-filled niches, are simply furnished; some have Arno views, others have stuccoed ceilings. **Pros:** in the middle of everything except the crowds; cordial, friendly staff; great breakfast. **Cons:** street noise; small rooms; some rooms could use an update. *Rooms from: €240 Via de' Renai 5, San Niccolò 055/2342888 www.hotelsilla.it 36 rooms Free Breakfast.*

Shopping

★ Giulio Giannini e Figlio

STATIONERY | One of Florence's oldest paper-goods stores is *the* place to buy marbleized stock, which comes in many formats, from flat sheets to paper-covered boxes or even pencils. *Via dei Velluti 1/r, Oltrarno 055/212621 www.giuliogiannini.com.*

★ **Il Torchio**
STATIONERY | Photograph albums, frames, diaries, and other objects dressed in handmade paper are high quality and they also accept custom orders. ✉ *Via dei Bardi 17, San Niccolò* ☎ *055/2342862* 🌐 *www.legatoriailtorchio.com.*

★ **Madova**
HATS & GLOVES | Complete your winter wardrobe with a pair of high-quality leather gloves, available in a rainbow of colors and a choice of linings (silk, cashmere, and unlined), from Madova. It's been in business for more than 100 years. ✉ *Via Guicciardini 1/r, Palazzo Pitti* ☎ *055/2396526* 🌐 *www.madova.it.*

Pitti Mosaici
HOUSEWARES | Stones are worked into exquisite tables, pictures, and jewelry at Pitti Mosaici, which continues the *pietre dure* (mosaic) tradition that was all the rage of 16th-century Florence. ✉ *Piazza dei Pitti 23/r, Palazzo Pitti* ☎ *055/282127* 🌐 *www.pittimosaici.com.*

Side Trip from Florence

Fiesole

10 km (6 miles) north of Florence.

A half-day excursion to Fiesole, in the hills above Florence, gives you a pleasant respite from museums and a wonderful view of the city. From here the view of the Duomo offers a new appreciation for what the Renaissance accomplished. Fiesole began life as an ancient Etruscan and later Roman village that held some power until it succumbed to barbarian invasions. Eventually it gave up its independence in exchange for Florence's protection. The medieval cathedral, ancient Roman amphitheater, and lovely old villas behind garden walls are clustered on a series of hilltops. A walk around Fiesole can take from one to two or three hours, depending on how far you stroll from the main piazza.

GETTING HERE AND AROUND

The trip from Florence by car takes 20–30 minutes. Drive to Piazza Liberta and cross the Ponte Rosso heading in the direction of the SS65/SR65. Turn right on to Via Salviati and continue on to Via Roccettini. Make a left turn to Via Vecchia Fiesolana, which will take you directly to the center of town. There are several possible routes for the two-hour walk from central Florence to Fiesole. One route begins in a residential area of Florence called Salviatino (Via Barbacane, near Piazza Edison, on the No. 7 bus route), and after a short time, offers peeks over garden walls of beautiful villas, as well as the view over your shoulder at the panorama of Florence in the valley. Buses also run to Fiesole from the center of Florence; check Autolinee Toscane for timetables (🌐 *www.at-bus.it*).

VISITOR INFORMATION

CONTACT Fiesole Tourism Office. ✉ *Via Portigiani 3, Fiesole* ☎ *055/5961311* 🌐 *www.fiesoleforyou.it.*

Sights

Anfiteatro Romano (*Roman Amphitheater*)
RUINS | The beautifully preserved, 2,000-seat Anfiteatro Romano, near the Duomo, dates from the 1st century BC and is still used for summer concerts. To the right of the amphitheater are the remains of the Terme Romani (Roman Baths), where you can see the gymnasium, hot and cold baths, and rectangular chamber where the water was heated. Admission here also gets you access to the attached archaeological museum and the small Bandini Museum, which showcases sacred art including several Luca della Robbia ceramics. ✉ *Via Portigiani 1, Fiesole* ☎ *055/5961293* 🌐 *www.museidifiesole.it* 🎫 *€12, includes access to archaeological park and museum and Bandini Museum* ⏲ *Check website for seasonal closure days.*

Badia Fiesolana

CHURCH | From the church of San Domenico it's a five-minute walk northwest to Fiesole's original cathedral. Dating from the 11th century, it was first the home of the Camaldolese monks. Thanks to Cosimo il Vecchio de' Medici, the complex was substantially restructured. The facade, never completed owing to Cosimo's death, contains elements of its original Romanesque decoration. ✉ *Via della Badia dei Roccettini 9, Fiesole* ☎ *055/4685398* 🌐 *www.fiesoleforyou.it/en/badia-fiesolana* ⏲ *Closed weekends.*

Duomo *(Fiesole Cathedral)*

CHURCH | A stark medieval interior yields many masterpieces at Fiesole Cathedral (Cathedral of Saint Romulus of Fiesole). In the raised presbytery, the Cappella Salutati was frescoed by 15th-century artist Cosimo Rosselli, but it was his contemporary, sculptor Mino da Fiesole (1430–84), who put the town on the artistic map. The Madonna on the altarpiece and the tomb of Bishop Salutati are fine examples of the artist's work. ✉ *Piazza della cattedrale, 1, Fiesole* ☎ *055/59400* 🌐 *www.fiesoleforyou.it/en/cathedral-of-san-romolo.*

San Domenico

CHURCH | If you really want to stretch your legs, walk 4 km (2½ miles) toward the center of Florence along Via Vecchia Fiesolana, a narrow lane in use since Etruscan times, to the church of San Domenico. Sheltered in the church is the *Madonna and Child with Saints* by Fra Angelico, who was a Dominican friar here before he moved to Florence. ✉ *Piazza San Domenico, off Via Giuseppe Mantellini, Fiesole* ☎ *055/59230* 🌐 *www.fiesoleforyou.it/en/church-and-convent-of-san-domenico.*

San Francesco

CHURCH | This lovely hilltop church has a good view of Florence and the plain below from its terrace and benches. Off the little cloister is a small, eclectic museum containing, among other things, two Egyptian mummies. Halfway up the hill you'll see sloping steps to the right; they lead to a fragrant wooded park with trails that loop out and back to the church. ✉ *Via San Francesco 13, Fiesole* ☎ *055/59175* 🌐 *www.fiesoleforyou.it/en/church-convent-of-san-francesco* 🎫 *Free.*

Restaurants

La Reggia degli Etruschi

$$ | ITALIAN | Atop a steep hill, en route to the church of San Francesco, this lovely little eatery is certainly worth the trek. Indulge in inventive reworkings of Tuscan classics, like the *mezzaluna di pera a pecorino* (little half-moon pasta stuffed with pear and pecorino) served with Roquefort and poppy seeds. **Known for:** out-of-the-way location; good wine list and friendly service; small terrace with outdoor seating. 💲 *Average main: €28* ✉ *Via San Francesco 18, Fiesole* ☎ *333/3556126 mobile* 🌐 *www.lareggiadeglietruschi.com.*

Hotels

Villa San Michele

$$$$ | HOTEL | In the hills of Fiesole, a cypress-lined driveway provides an elegant preamble to this incredibly gorgeous (and very expensive) hotel, which is housed in a 16th-century building that was originally a Franciscan convent designed by Santi di Tito. **Pros:** exceptional convent conversion; stunning views; shuttle bus makes frequent forays to and from Florence. **Cons:** money must be no object; some rooms are small; you must either depend on the shuttle bus or have a car. 💲 *Rooms from: €1,726* ✉ *Via Doccia 4, Fiesole* ☎ *055/5678200* 🌐 *www.belmond.com/hotels* ⏲ *Closed Nov.–May* 🛏 *45 rooms* 🍽 *Free Breakfast.*

Chapter 12

TUSCANY

Updated by
Liz Shemaria

WELCOME TO TUSCANY

TOP REASONS TO GO

★ **Piazza del Campo, Siena:** Sip a cappuccino or enjoy some gelato as you take in the spectacle in and of this shell-shape piazza.

★ **Piero della Francesca's True Cross frescoes, Arezzo:** If your Holy Grail is great Renaissance art, seek out these 12 enigmatic scenes in Arezzo's Basilica di San Francesco.

★ **San Gimignano:** Grab a spot at sunset on the steps of the Collegiata as flocks of swallows swoop in and out of the famous medieval towers.

★ **Wine tasting in Chianti:** Sample the fruits of the region's gorgeous vineyards, either at the wineries themselves or in the wine bars found in the towns.

★ **Leaning Tower of Pisa:** It may be touristy, but it's still a whole lot of fun to climb to the top and admire the view.

1 **Lucca.** See 16th-century ramparts.

2 **Pisa.** Its bell tower is known the world over.

3 **Chianti.** A picturesque wine region.

4 **Volterra.** Breathtaking hilltop views.

5 **San Gimignano.** Lovely hill town.

6 **Colle di Val d'Elsa.** Laid-back hill town.

7 **Siena.** An enchanting medieval city.

8 **Arezzo.** Visit for the sublime frescoes.

9 **Cortona.** Sits above the flat Valdichiana.

10 **Montepulciano.** Its higher altitude means cooler summers.

11 **Pienza.** An ideal city planned by Pope Pius II.

12 **Montalcino.** Famed for its robust red wine.

13 **Abbazia di Sant'Antimo.** A Romanesque abbey.

TYRRHENIAN SEA

Portoferraio

ELBA

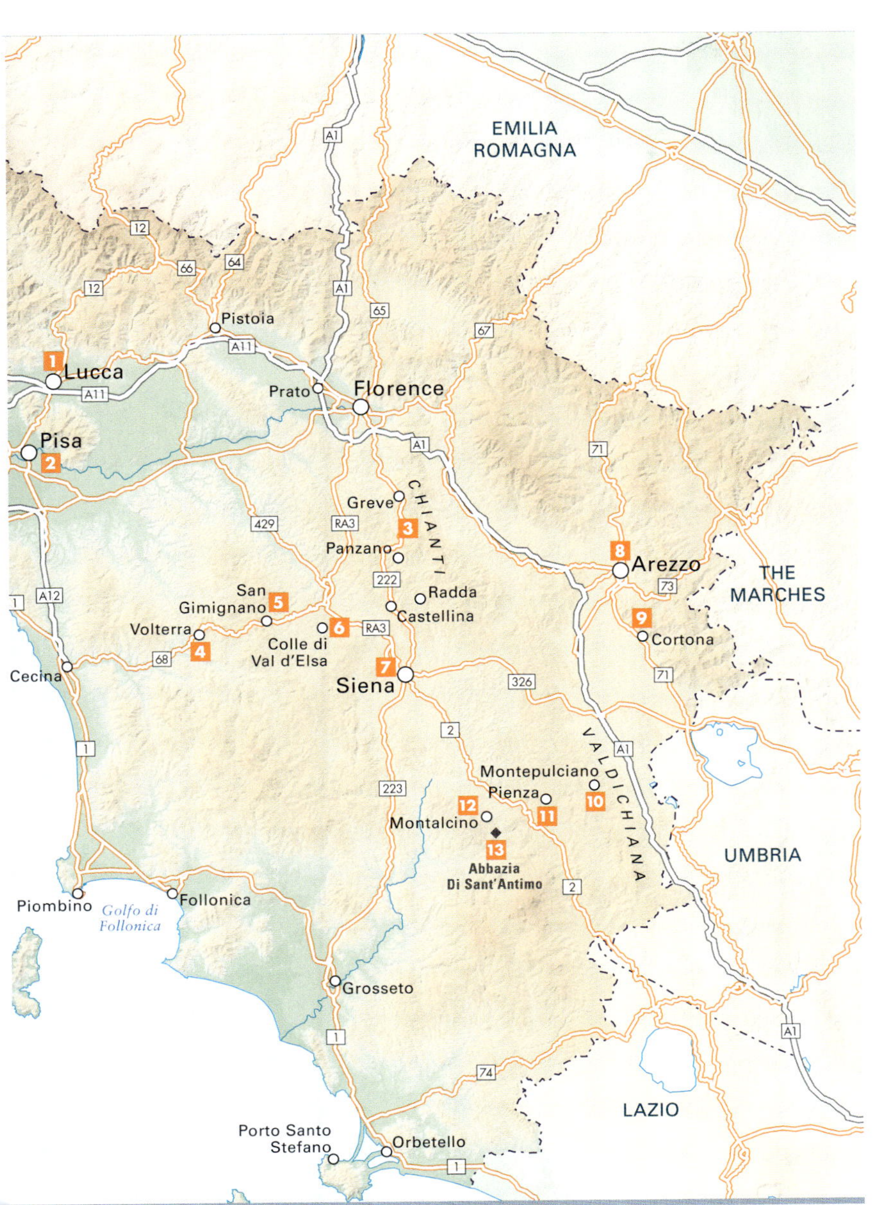
EMILIA
ROMAGNA
THE
MARCHES
UMBRIA
LAZIO
CHIANTI
VALDICHIANA
1 Lucca
2 Pisa
Pistoia
Prato
Florence
Greve
3
Panzano
Radda
Castellina
San Gimignano 5
Volterra 4
Colle di Val d'Elsa 6
7 Siena
8 Arezzo
9 Cortona
Cecina
Montepulciano 10
Pienza 11
12 Montalcino
13 Abbazia Di Sant'Antimo
Piombino
Golfo di Follonica
Follonica
Grosseto
Porto Santo Stefano
Orbetello
A1
A11
A12
RA3
12
64
65
66
67
68
71
73
74
222
223
326
429
1
2

EATING AND DRINKING WELL IN TUSCANY

Affettati misti (Italian cured meat platter)

The influence of the ancient Etruscans—who favored the use of fresh herbs—is still felt in Tuscan cuisine three millennia later. Simple and earthy, Tuscan food celebrates the seasons with fresh vegetable dishes, wonderful bread-based soups, and meats perfumed with sage, rosemary, and thyme.

Throughout Tuscany there are excellent upscale restaurants that serve elaborate dishes, but to get a real taste of the flavors of the region, head for the family-run trattorias found in every town. The service and setting are often basic, but the food can be memorable.

Few places serve lighter fare at midday, so expect substantial meals at lunch and dinner, especially in out-of-the-way towns. Dining hours are fairly standard: lunch between 12:30 and 2, dinner between 7:30 and 10.

HOLD THE SALT

Tuscan bread is famous for what it's missing: salt. That's because it's intended to pick up seasoning from the food it accompanies, not be eaten alone. That doesn't mean Tuscans don't like to start a meal with bread, but usually it's prepared in some way. It can be grilled and drizzled with olive oil (*fettunta*), covered with chicken liver spread (*crostino con fegatini*), or toasted, rubbed with garlic, and topped with tomatoes (*bruschetta*).

AFFETTATI MISTI

The name, roughly translated, means "mixed cold cuts," and it's something Tuscans do exceptionally well. A platter of cured meats, served as an antipasto, is sure to include *prosciutto crudo* (cured pork, cut paper-thin) and *salame* (dry sausage, prepared in dozens of ways—some spicy, some sweet). The most distinctly Tuscan affettati are made from *cinta senese* (a once nearly extinct pig found only in the heart of the region) and *cinghiale* (wild boar, which roam all over Italy). You can eat these delicious slices unadorned or layered on a piece of bread.

PASTA

Restaurants throughout Tuscany serve dishes similar to those in Florence, but they also have their own local specialties. Many recipes are from the *nonna* (grandmother) of the restaurant's owner, handed down over time but never written down.

Look in particular for pasta creations made with *pici* (a long, thick, hand-rolled spaghetti). Pappardelle (a long, ribbonlike pasta noodle) is frequently paired with sauces made with game, such as *lepre* (hare) or cinghiale. In the northwest, a specialty of Lucca is *tordelli di carne al ragù* (meat-stuffed pasta with a meat sauce).

Wines from Tuscany

Ribbonlike pasta with mushrooms

MEAT

Bistecca alla fiorentina (a thick T-bone steak, grilled rare) is the classic meat dish of Tuscany, but there are other specialties as well. Many menus will include *tagliata di manzo* (thinly sliced, roasted beef, drizzled with olive oil), *arista di maiale* (roast pork with sage and rosemary), and *salsiccia e fagioli* (pork sausage and beans). In the southern part of the region, don't be surprised to find *piccione* (pigeon), which can be roasted, stuffed, or baked.

WINE

Grape cultivation here also dates from Etruscan times, and vineyards are abundant, particularly in Chianti. The resulting medium-body red wine is a staple on most tables; however, you can select from a multitude of other varieties, including such reds as Brunello di Montalcino and Vino Nobile di Montepulciano and such whites as vermentino and vernaccia.

Super Tuscans (a fanciful name given to a group of wines by American journalists) now command attention as some of the best produced in Italy; they have great depth and complexity. The dessert wine vin santo is made throughout the region and is often sipped with biscotti (twice-baked almond cookies), perfect for dunking.

Midway down the Italian peninsula, Tuscany (Toscana in Italian) is distinguished by rolling hills, snowcapped mountains, cypress trees, and miles of coastline on the Tyrrhenian Sea—which all adds up to gorgeous views at practically every turn. The beauty of the landscape proves a perfect foil for the region's abundance of superlative art and architecture.

It also produces some of Italy's finest wines and olive oils. The combination of unforgettable art, sumptuous landscapes, and eminently drinkable wines that pair beautifully with its simple food makes a trip to Tuscany something beyond special.

Many of Tuscany's cities and towns have retained the same fundamental character over the past 500 years. Civic rivalries that led to bloody battles centuries ago have given way to soccer rivalries. Renaissance pomp lives on in the celebration of local feast days and centuries-old traditions such as the Palio in Siena and the Giostra del Saracino (Joust of the Saracen) in Arezzo. Often, present-day Tuscans look as though they might have served as models for paintings produced hundreds of years ago. In many ways, the Renaissance lives on in Tuscany.

MAJOR REGIONS

Hill towns southwest of Florence. The search for the best tiny hill town always leads to San Gimignano, known as the "medieval Manhattan" for its 13th-century stone towers.

Southern Tuscany. Among the highlights of Tuscany's southern reaches are the wine-producing centers of Montalcino and Montepulciano.

Northwest Tuscany. Head here to climb the Leaning Tower of Pisa and stroll medieval walls in Lucca, the birthplace of composer Giacomo Puccini.

Planning

Getting Here and Around

BUS

Buses are a reliable but time-consuming means of getting around the region because they tend to stop in every town. Trains are a better option in virtually every respect when you're headed to Pisa, Lucca, Arezzo, and other cities with good rail service. But for most smaller towns, buses are the only option. Be aware that making arrangements for bus travel, particularly for a non–Italian speaker, can be a test of patience.

CAR

Driving is the only way (other than hiking or biking) to reach many of Tuscany's small towns and vineyards. The cities west of Florence are easily accessed by the A11, which leads to Lucca and then to the sea. The A1 takes you south from Florence to Arezzo and Chiusi (where you turn off for Montepulciano). Florence and Siena are connected by a *superstrada* and also the scenic Via Cassia (SR2) and even more panoramic Strada Chiantigiana (SR222), both of which thread through Chianti, skirting rolling hills and vineyards. The hill towns north and west of Siena lie along superstradas and winding local roads—all are well marked, but you should still arm yourself with a good map.

TRAIN

Trenitalia trains (🌐 *www.trenitalia.com*) on Italy's main north–south rail line stop in Florence as well as Prato, Arezzo, and Chiusi. Another major line connects Florence with Pisa, and the coastal line between Rome and Genoa passes through Pisa as well. There's regular, frequent hourly service from Florence to Lucca, and several trips a day between Florence and Siena. Siena's train station is 2 km (1 mile) north of the *centro storico* (historic center), but cabs and city buses are readily available, as is a very handy funicular.

For other parts of Tuscany—Chianti, Montalcino, and Montepulciano, for example—you're better off traveling by bus or by car. Train stations, when they exist, are far from the historic centers (usually in the valleys below hill towns), and service is infrequent.

Hotels

A visit to the Tuscan countryside is a trip into absolute beauty. There are plenty of good hotels in the larger towns, but the classic experience is to stay in a villa rental or one of the rural accommodations—often converted private homes, sometimes working farms or vineyards (known as *agriturismi*).

Although it's tempting to think you can stumble upon a little out-of-the-way hotel at the end of the day, you're better off not testing your luck. Make reservations before you go. If you don't have a reservation, you may be able to get help finding a room from the local tourist office.

⇨ *Hotel and restaurant reviews have been shortened. For full information, visit Fodors.com. Prices in the hotel reviews are the lowest cost of a standard double room in high season. Prices in the dining reviews are the average cost of a main course at dinner, or, if dinner is not served, at lunch.*

What It Costs in Euros

$	$$	$$$	$$$$
RESTAURANTS			
under €20	€20–€30	€31–€40	over €40
HOTELS			
under €175	€175–€400	€401–€600	over €600

Making the Most of Your Time

Tuscany isn't the place for a jam-packed itinerary. One of the greatest pleasures here is indulging in rustic hedonism, marked by long lunches and showstopping sunsets. Whether by car, by bike, or on foot, you'll want to get out into the glorious landscape, but it's smart to keep your plans modest. Set a church or a hill town or an out-of-the-way restaurant as your destination, knowing that half the pleasure is in getting there—admiring as you go the stately palaces, the tidy geometry of row upon row of grapevines, and the fields vibrant with red poppies, sunflowers, and yellow broom.

You'll need to devise a strategy for seeing the sights. Take Siena: this beautiful, art-filled town simply can't be missed; it's compact enough that you can see the major sights on a day trip, and that's exactly what most people do. Spend the night, though, and you'll get to see the town breathe a sigh and relax on the day-trippers' departure. In Pisa, the famous tower and the rest of the Camposanto are not only worth seeing but a must-see, a highlight of any trip to Italy. But nearby Lucca must not be overlooked either. In fact, this walled town has greater charms than Pisa does, making it a better choice for an overnight, so you should come up with a plan that takes in both places.

Restaurants

A meal in Tuscany traditionally consists of five courses, and every menu you encounter will be organized along this plan of antipasto, primo, secondo, contorno, and dolce. The crucial rule of restaurant dining is that you should order at least two courses. Otherwise, you'll likely end up with a lonely piece of meat and no sides.

Visitor Information

Many towns in Tuscany have tourist information offices, which can be useful resources for trip-planning advice (and sometimes maps). Such offices are typically open from 8:30 to 1 and 3:30 to 6 or 7; those in smaller towns are usually closed Saturday afternoon and Sunday, and often shut down entirely from early November through Easter.

The tourist information office in Greve is an excellent source for general information about the Chianti wine region and its hilltop towns. In Siena, the centrally located tourist office in Piazza del Campo has information about Siena and its province. Both offices can help you book hotel rooms. Offices in smaller towns can also be a good place to check if you need last-minute accommodations.

Lucca

90 km (56 miles) west of Florence.

Ramparts built in the 16th and 17th centuries enclose a charming fortress town filled with churches (99 of them), terra-cotta–roofed buildings, and narrow cobblestone streets, along which locals maneuver bikes to do their daily shopping. Here Caesar, Pompey, and Crassus agreed to rule Rome as a triumvirate in 56 BC; Lucca was later the first Tuscan town to accept Christianity. The town still has a mind of its own, and when most of Tuscany was voting communist as a matter of course, Lucca's citizens rarely followed suit. The famous composer Giacomo Puccini (1858–1924) was born here; he is celebrated during the summer Opera Theater and Music Festival of Lucca. The ramparts circling the centro storico are the perfect place to stroll, bicycle, or just admire the view.

GETTING HERE AND AROUND

You can reach Lucca easily by train from Florence; the centro storico is a short walk from the station. If you're driving, take the A11/E76.

VISITOR INFORMATION

CONTACT Lucca Tourism Office. ✉ *Porta San Donato vecchia, Piazzale Verdi, Lucca* ☎ *0583/583150* 🌐 *www.turismo.lucca.it.*

Sights

Traffic (including motorbikes) is restricted in the walled historic center of Lucca. Walking is the best, most enjoyable way to get around. Or you can rent a bicycle; getting around on bike is easy, as the center is quite flat.

Duomo

CHURCH | The blind arches on the cathedral's facade are a fine example of the rigorously ordered Pisan Romanesque style, in this case happily enlivened by an extremely varied collection of small, carved columns. Take a closer look at the decoration of the facade and that of the portico below; they make this one of the most entertaining church exteriors in Tuscany.

The Gothic interior contains a moving Byzantine crucifix—called the Volto Santo, or Holy Face—brought here, according to legend, in the 8th century (though it probably dates from between the 11th and early 13th century). The masterpiece of the Sienese sculptor Jacopo della Quercia (circa 1371–1438) is the marble *Tomb of Ilaria del Carretto* (1407–08). ✉ *Piazza San Martino 8, Lucca* ☎ *0583/490530* 🌐 *www.museocattedralelucca.it* 🎫 *€3.*

Museo Nazionale di Villa Guinigi

ART MUSEUM | Although this museum presents a noteworthy overview of Lucca's artistic traditions up through the 17th century, you might find few other visitors exploring its extensive collections of local Etruscan, Roman, Romanesque, and Renaissance art. It's all housed in the 15th-century former villa of the Guinigi family, on the eastern end of the historic center. ✉ *Via della Quarquonia 4, Lucca* ☎ *0583/496033* 🌐 *www.luccamuseinazionali.it* 🎫 *€4* ⏲ *Closed Mon. and 2nd, 4th, and 5th Sun. of month.*

★ Passeggiata delle Mura

CITY PARK | **FAMILY** | On nice days, the citizens of Lucca cycle, jog, stroll, or kick a soccer ball in this green, beautiful, and very large circular park. It's neither inside nor outside the city but rather right atop and around the ring of ramparts that defines Lucca. Sunlight streams through two rows of tall plane trees to dapple the *passeggiata delle mura* (walk on the walls), which is 4 km (2½ miles) long. Ten bulwarks are topped with lawns, many with picnic tables and some with play equipment for children. Be aware at all times of where the edge is—there are no railings, and the drop to the ground outside the city is a precipitous 40 feet. ✉ *Lucca* ☎ *0583/583150* 🌐 *www.turismo.lucca.it.*

Piazza dell'Anfiteatro

PLAZA/SQUARE | **FAMILY** | Here's where the ancient Roman amphitheater once stood. Some of the medieval buildings built over the amphitheater retain its original oval shape and brick arches. ✉ *Piazza dell'Anfiteatro, Lucca.*

San Frediano

CHURCH | A 14th-century mosaic decorates the facade of this church just steps from the anfiteatro. Inside are works by Jacopo della Quercia and Matteo Civitali (1436–1501), as well as the lace-clad mummy of St. Zita (circa 1218–78), the patron saint of household servants. ✉ *Piazza San Frediano, Lucca* ☎ *349/8440290* 🌐 *www.sanfredianolucca.com* 🎫 *€3 (€7 with campanile).*

San Michele in Foro

CHURCH | The facade here is even more fanciful than that of the Duomo. Its upper levels have nothing but air behind them (after the front of the church was built, there were no funds to raise the nave), and the winged archangel Michael, who stands at the very top, seems precariously poised for flight. The facade, heavily restored in the 19th century, displays busts of such Italian patriots as Garibaldi and Cavour. Check out the superb Filippino Lippi (1457/58–1504) panel painting of Saints Jerome, Sebastian, Rocco, and Helen in the right transept. ✉ *Piazza San Michele, Lucca* ☎ *0583/53576* 🌐 *www.turismo.lucca.it/chiesa-san-michele.*

Torre Guinigi

NOTABLE BUILDING | **FAMILY** | The tower of the medieval Palazzo Guinigi contains one of the city's most curious sights: a grove of holm oaks. It is said that they were planted by the Guinigi family at the

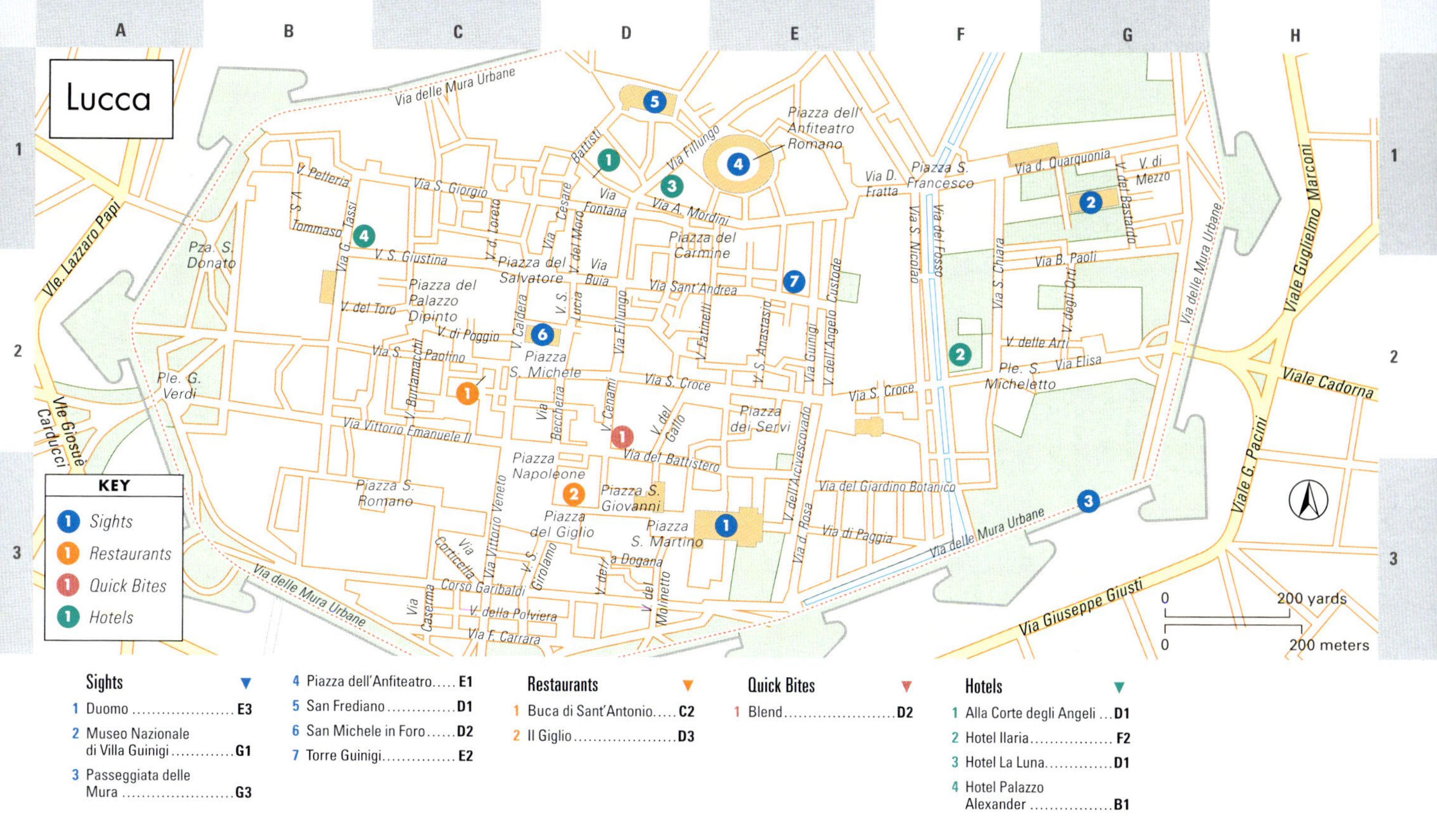

Lucca
A
B
C
D
E
F
G
H
1
2
3
KEY
Sights
Restaurants
Quick Bites
Hotels
Via delle Mura Urbane
Vle. Lazzaro Papi
Vle Giosuè Carducci
Pza. S. Donato
Ple. G. Verdi
V. Pelleria
V. S. Tommaso
Via G. Tassi
V. S. Giustina
V. del Toro
Via S. Giorgio
V. d. Loreto
Via Cesare Battisti
V. del Moro
Via Fontana
Piazza del Salvatore
Via Buia
Piazza del Palazzo Dipinto
V. di Poggio
V. Caldera
V. S. Lucia
Via S. Paolino
V. Burlamacchi
Piazza S. Michele
Via Vittorio Emanuele II
Via Beccheria
V. Cenami
Via Fillungo
Via S. Croce
V. del Gallo
Via del Battistero
Piazza Napoleone
Piazza S. Giovanni
Piazza S. Romano
Piazza del Giglio
Via Vittorio Veneto
Via Corticella
Corso Garibaldi
V. S. Girolamo
V. del
a Dogana
V. del Molinetto
Via Caserma
V. della Polviera
Via F. Carrara
Piazza S. Martino
Via A. Mordini
Piazza del Carmine
Via Sant'Andrea
V. Fatinelli
V. S. Anastasio
Via Guinigi
V. dell'Angelo Custode
Piazza dei Servi
V. dell'Arcivescovado
Via d. Rosa
Via del Giardino Botanico
Via di Paggia
Piazza dell' Anfiteatro Romano
Via D. Fratta
Piazza S. Francesco
Via S. Nicolao
Via del Fosso
Via S. Chiara
Via d. Quarquonia
V. del Bastardo
V. di Mezzo
Via B. Paoli
V. degli Orti
V. delle Arti
Via Elisa
Ple. S. Micheletto
Viale Guglielmo Marconi
Viale Cadorna
Viale G. Pacini
Via Giuseppe Giusti
0
200 yards
0
200 meters
Sights
1 Duomo E3
2 Museo Nazionale di Villa Guinigi G1
3 Passeggiata delle Mura G3
4 Piazza dell'Anfiteatro E1
5 San Frediano D1
6 San Michele in Foro D2
7 Torre Guinigi E2
Restaurants
1 Buca di Sant'Antonio C2
2 Il Giglio D3
Quick Bites
1 Blend D2
Hotels
1 Alla Corte degli Angeli D1
2 Hotel Ilaria F2
3 Hotel La Luna D1
4 Hotel Palazzo Alexander B1

top of the tower as a symbol of renewal, and their roots have pushed their way into the room below. From the top you have a magnificent view of the city and the surrounding countryside. (Only the tower is open to the public, not the palazzo.) ✉ *Via Sant'Andrea 45, Lucca* ☎ *0583/48090* 🌐 *cultura.comune.lucca.it* 🎫 *€8.*

Restaurants

★ Buca di Sant'Antonio

$$ | **TUSCAN** | The staying power of Buca di Sant'Antonio—it's been around since 1782—is the result of superlative Tuscan food brought to the table by waitstaff who don't miss a beat. The menu includes the simple but blissful *tortelli lucchesi al sugo* (meat-stuffed pasta with a tomato-and-meat sauce), as well as more daring dishes such as roast *capretto* (kid goat) with herbs. **Known for:** superlative pastas; excellent sommelier; classy, family-run ambience. $ *Average main: €26* ✉ *Via della Cervia 3, Lucca* ☎ *0583/55881* 🌐 *www.bucadisantantonio.com* ⏲ *Closed Mon., 1 wk in Jan., and 1 wk in July. No dinner Sun.*

★ Il Giglio

$$$ | **TUSCAN** | Divine, cutting-edge food and Tuscan classics are served in this one-room space, where in winter you may find a roaring fireplace, and in warmer months there's outdoor seating on a pretty little piazza. If mushrooms or tartufo are in season, try homemade pasta topped with them. **Known for:** creative menu with seasonal ingredients; fine service; the wine list, especially its selection of local wines. $ *Average main: €31* ✉ *Piazza del Giglio 2, Lucca* ☎ *0583/494058* 🌐 *www.ristorantegiglio.com* ⏲ *Closed Tues. and Wed. and 15 days in Nov.*

Favorite Places

Liz Shemaria: Tuscany's many towers are medieval symbols of power, but Lucca's Torre Guinigi is unlike the others. Its grove of holm oaks makes it worth climbing 230 stairs to the top.

Coffee and Quick Bites

Blend

$ | **ITALIAN** | If you're looking for a lovely spot to recharge, stop by this place (just around the corner from the Duomo), and have a fantastic sandwich, or a glass of wine, or a tasty salad, a coffee, or dessert. It's open from late morning to late in the evening. **Known for:** open late; near the Duomo; good salads. $ *Average main: €15* ✉ *Piazza S. Giusto 8, Duomo* ☎ *0583/050442.*

Hotels

Alla Corte degli Angeli

$$ | **B&B/INN** | This charming hotel with a friendly staff is right off the main shopping drag, Via Fillungo. **Pros:** many rooms are connecting, making them good for families; great location; fantastic on-site restaurant. **Cons:** some rooms have tubs but no showers; not all rooms are created equal; books up quickly. $ *Rooms from: €246* ✉ *Via degli Angeli 23, Lucca* ☎ *0583/469204* 🌐 *www.allacortedegliangeli.it* 🛏 *21 rooms* 🍴 *Free Breakfast.*

Hotel Ilaria

$$ | **HOTEL** | The former stables of the Villa Bottini have been transformed into a modern hotel with stylish rooms done in a warm wood veneer with blue-and-white fittings. **Pros:** modern; free bicycles; multilingual, pleasant staff. **Cons:** though in the city center, it's a little removed from

main attractions; some find it overpriced; books up quickly. $ *Rooms from: €194* ✉ *Via del Fosso 26, Lucca* ☎ *0583/47615* 🌐 *www.hotelilaria.com* 🛏 *44 rooms* 🍴 *Free Breakfast.*

Hotel La Luna

$$ | B&B/INN | On a quiet, airy courtyard close to the Piazza del Mercato, this hotel, run by the Barbieri family for more than four decades, occupies two renovated wings of an old building. **Pros:** professional staff; the annex has wheelchair-accessible rooms; central location. **Cons:** some rooms feel dated; street noise can be a bit of a problem; may be too central for some. $ *Rooms from: €200* ✉ *Corte Compagni 12, at Via Fillungo, Lucca* ☎ *0583/493634* 🌐 *www.hotellaluna.it* 🛏 *29 rooms* 🍴 *Free Breakfast.*

Hotel Palazzo Alexander

$$ | HOTEL | This hotel, in a building dating from the 12th century, has public rooms with timbered ceilings, warm yellow walls, and brocaded chairs and guest rooms with high ceilings and still more of that glorious damask. **Pros:** intimate feel; gracious staff; a short walk from San Michele in Foro. **Cons:** some complain of too-thin walls; books up quickly; might be too quiet for some. $ *Rooms from: €213* ✉ *Via S. Giustina 48, Lucca* ☎ *0583/583571* 🌐 *www.hotelpalazzoalexander.it* 🛏 *13 rooms* 🍴 *Free Breakfast.*

Shopping

Lucca's justly famed olive oils are available throughout the city (and exported around the world).

★ Antica Bottega di Prospero

FOOD | Stop by this shop for top-quality local food products, including farro, dried porcini mushrooms, olive oil, and wine. ✉ *Via San Lucia 13, Lucca* ☎ *0583/494875* 🌐 *www.bottegadiprospero1790.com.*

★ Caniparoli

CHOCOLATE | FAMILY | If you love sweets then you'll be pleased with the selection of artisanal chocolates, marzipan delights, and gorgeous cakes. Creations become even more fanciful during Christmas and Easter. ✉ *Via San Paolino 44, Lucca* ☎ *0583/53456* 🌐 *www.caniparolicioccolateria.it.*

★ Enoteca Vanni

WINE/SPIRITS | A huge selection of wines, as well as an ancient cellar, make this place worth a stop. For the cost of the wine only, tastings can be organized through the shopkeepers and are held in the cellar or outside in a lovely little piazza. All of this can be paired with *affettati misti* (sliced cured meats) and cheeses of the highest caliber. ✉ *Piazza San Salvatore 7, Lucca* ☎ *0583/491902* 🌐 *www.enotecavanni.com.*

★ Pasticceria Taddeucci

FOOD | FAMILY | A particularly delicious version of *buccellato*—the sweet, anise-flavored bread with raisins that is a Luccan specialty—is baked at Pasticceria Taddeucci. ✉ *Piazza San Michele 34, Lucca* ☎ *0583/494933* 🌐 *www.buccellatotaddeucci.it.*

Activities

A good way to spend the afternoon is to go biking around the large path atop the city's ramparts. There are two good spots right next to each other where you can rent bikes. The prices are about the same (about €15 per day and €5 per hour for city bikes) and they are centrally located, just beside the town wall.

Poli Antonio Biciclette

BIKING | FAMILY | This is one of the best options for bicycle rentals on the east side of town. ✉ *Piazza Santa Maria 42, Lucca East* ☎ *0583/493787* 🌐 *www.biciclettepoli.com.*

Pisa

19 km (11 miles) southwest of Lucca.

If you can get beyond the kitsch of the vendors hawking cheap souvenirs around the Leaning Tower, you'll find that Pisa has much to offer. Its treasures aren't as abundant as those of Florence, to which it is inevitably compared, but the cathedral-baptistery-tower complex of Piazza del Duomo, known collectively as the Campo dei Miracoli (Field of Miracles), is among the most dramatic settings in Italy.

Pisa may have been inhabited as early as the Bronze Age. It was certainly populated by the Etruscans and, in turn, became part of the Roman Empire. In the early Middle Ages this city on the Arno River flourished as an economic powerhouse—along with Amalfi, Genoa, and Venice, it was one of the four maritime republics. The city's economic and political power ebbed in the early 15th century as it fell under Florence's domination, though it enjoyed a brief resurgence under Cosimo I de' Medici in the mid-16th century. Pisa sustained heavy damage during World War II, but the Duomo and the Leaning Tower were spared, along with some other grand Romanesque structures.

GETTING HERE AND AROUND

Pisa is an easy hour's train ride from Florence. By car it's a straight shot on the Firenze–Pisa–Livorno ("Fi-Pi-Li") autostrada. The Pisa–Lucca train runs frequently and takes about 30 minutes.

VISITOR INFORMATION

CONTACT **Pisa Tourism Office.** ✉ *Piazza XX Settembre, Pisa* ☎ *050/550100* 🌐 *www.turismo.pisa.it.*

Pisa, like many Italian cities, is best explored on foot, and most of what you'll want to see is within walking distance. The views along the Arno River are particularly grand and shouldn't be missed—there's a feeling of spaciousness that isn't found along the Arno in Florence.

As you set out, note that there are various combination-ticket options for sights on the Piazza del Duomo.

Battistero

NOTABLE BUILDING | This lovely Gothic baptistery, which faces the Duomo's facade, is best known for the pulpit carved by Nicola Pisano (circa 1220–84; father of Giovanni Pisano) in 1260. Every half hour, an employee will dramatically close the doors, then intone, thereby demonstrating how remarkable the acoustics are in the place. ✉ *Piazza del Duomo, Pisa* ☎ *050/835011* 🌐 *www.opapisa.it* 🎫 *From €8; discounts available if bought in combination with tickets for other monuments* ⏲ *Check the website for seasonal hrs.*

Camposanto

CEMETERY | According to legend, the cemetery—a walled structure on the western side of the Piazza dei Miracoli—is filled with earth that returning Crusaders brought back from the Holy Land. Contained within are numerous frescoes, notably *The Drunkenness of Noah,* by Renaissance artist Benozzo Gozzoli (1422–97), and the disturbing *Triumph of Death* (14th century; artist uncertain), whose subject matter shows what was on people's minds in a century that saw the ravages of the Black Death. ✉ *Piazza del Duomo, Pisa* ☎ *050/835011* 🌐 *www.opapisa.it* 🎫 *From €8.*

Duomo

CHURCH | Pisa's cathedral brilliantly utilizes the horizontal marble-stripe motif (borrowed from Moorish architecture) that became common on Tuscan cathedrals. It is famous for the Romanesque panels on the transept door facing the tower that depict scenes from the life of Christ. The beautifully carved 14th-century pulpit is by Giovanni Pisano. ✉ *Piazza*

This cemetery—a walled structure on the western side of the Piazza dei Miracoli—is known for its frescoes.

del Duomo, Pisa ☎ *050/835011* 🌐 *www.opapisa.it* 🎫 *From €8.*

★ Leaning Tower (Torre Pendente)

NOTABLE BUILDING | FAMILY | Legend holds that Galileo conducted an experiment on the nature of gravity by dropping metal balls from the top of the 187-foot-high Leaning Tower of Pisa (whether it's true is a matter of debate). Work on this tower, built as a campanile for the Duomo, started in 1173. The lopsided settling began when construction reached the third story. The architects attempted to compensate by making the remaining floors slightly taller on the leaning side, but the extra weight made the problem worse. By the late 20th century, many feared the tower would simply topple over. The structure has since been firmly anchored to the earth and restored to its original tilt of 300 years ago.

Reservations, which are essential, can be made online or by calling the Museo dell'Opera del Duomo. It's also possible to arrive at the ticket office and book for the same day. Note, though, that children under eight aren't allowed to climb. ✉ *Piazza del Duomo, Pisa* ☎ *050/835011* 🌐 *www.opapisa.it* 🎫 *From €20.*

Museo Nazionale di San Matteo

ART MUSEUM | On the north bank of the Arno, this museum contains some beautiful examples of local Romanesque and Gothic art. Despite the fact that it has stunning works by Donatello and Benozzo Gozzoli (among others), here you'll find very few other visitors. ✉ *Piazza Matteo in Soarta 1, Pisa* ☎ *050/541865* 🌐 *museitoscana.cultura.gov.it* 🎫 *€5* ⏲ *Closed Mon.*

Piazza dei Cavalieri

PLAZA/SQUARE | The piazza, with its fine Renaissance Palazzo dei Cavalieri, Palazzo dell'Orologio, and Chiesa di Santo Stefano dei Cavalieri, was laid out by Giorgio Vasari in about 1560. The square was the seat of the Ordine dei Cavalieri di Santo Stefano (Order of the Knights of St. Stephen), a military and religious institution meant to defend the coast from possible invasion by the Turks.

Also in this square is the prestigious Scuola Normale Superiore, founded by Napoléon in 1810 on the French model. Here graduate students pursue doctorates in literature, philosophy, mathematics, and science. In front of the school is a large statue of Ferdinando I de' Medici dating from 1596. On the extreme left is the tower where the hapless Ugolino della Gherardesca (died 1289) was imprisoned with his two sons and two grandsons—legend holds that he ate them. Dante immortalized him in Canto XXXIII of his *Inferno.* Duck into the Church of Santo Stefano (if you're lucky enough to find it open) and check out Bronzino's splendid *Nativity of Christ* (1564–65). ✉ *Piazza dei Cavalieri, Pisa* 🌐 *www.turismo.pisa.it.*

Santa Maria della Spina

CHURCH | Originally an oratory dating from the 13th century, this delicate, tiny church is a fine example of Tuscan Gothic architecture. It has been restored several times, including in 1996–98, after having been damaged by a flood. The results of a recent face-lift are grand. ✉ *Lungarno Gambacorti, Pisa* ☎ *055/3215446* 🌐 *www.turismo.pisa.it* 🎫 *Free.*

Restaurants

Al Madina

$ | **MIDDLE EASTERN** | Pisa is an incredibly multicultural city, as evidenced by restaurants like this one, which serves the best Middle Eastern food in town. The tables are a little close together, but the atmosphere is lively, and you'll find all the classics—from falafel to hummus—as well as a delicious dessert of ricotta mousse with homemade quince jam. **Known for:** fresh, plentiful salads and sides; shish kebab; dips and pita bread. $ *Average main: €12* ✉ *Via San Martino 41/45, Pisa* ☎ *050/20409* 🌐 *www.ristorantealmadina.it* 🕓 *Closed Mon.*

Osteria dei Cavalieri

$$ | **ITALIAN** | This charming, white-walled restaurant, a few steps from Piazza dei Cavalieri, serves up exquisitely grilled fish dishes, pleases vegetarians, and prepares tagliata for meat lovers. Three set menus, from the sea, garden, and earth, are available, or you can order à la carte. **Known for:** location in the centro storico; classic Tuscan dishes; catch-of-the-day fish-tasting menu. $ *Average main: €21* ✉ *Via San Frediano 16, Pisa* ☎ *050/580858* 🌐 *www.osteriacavalieri.pisa.it* 🕓 *Closed Sun., 2 wks in Aug., and Dec. 29–Jan. 7. No lunch Wed.*

★ **V. Beny**

$$$ | **TUSCAN** | Apricot walls hung with etchings of Pisa make this small, single-room restaurant warmly romantic. Husband and wife Damiano and Sandra Lazzerini have been running the place for two decades, and it shows in their obvious enthusiasm while talking about the menu (fish is a focus) and daily specials, which often astound. **Known for:** superb fish dishes; gracious service; terrific wine list. $ *Average main: €33* ✉ *Piazza Chiara Gambacorti 22, Pisa* ☎ *050/25067* 🌐 *www.beny.eatbu.com* 🕓 *Closed Sun. and 2 wks in mid-Aug. No lunch Sat.*

★ **Vineria di Piazza**

$$ | **ITALIAN** | It's set in a lively, historic market square and frequented by locals. The menu adheres to Tuscan tradition, often including high-quality bistecca alla Fiorentina, but also indulges in some flights of fantasy, with inventive desserts. **Known for:** inventive pasta dishes; baccalà (salt cod) served in inventive ways; charming, energetic staff. $ *Average main: €20* ✉ *Piazza delle Vettovaglie 13, Pisa* ☎ *050/5207846* 🌐 *www.facebook.com/vineriadipiazzavettovaglie* 🕓 *No dinner Sun.–Tues.*

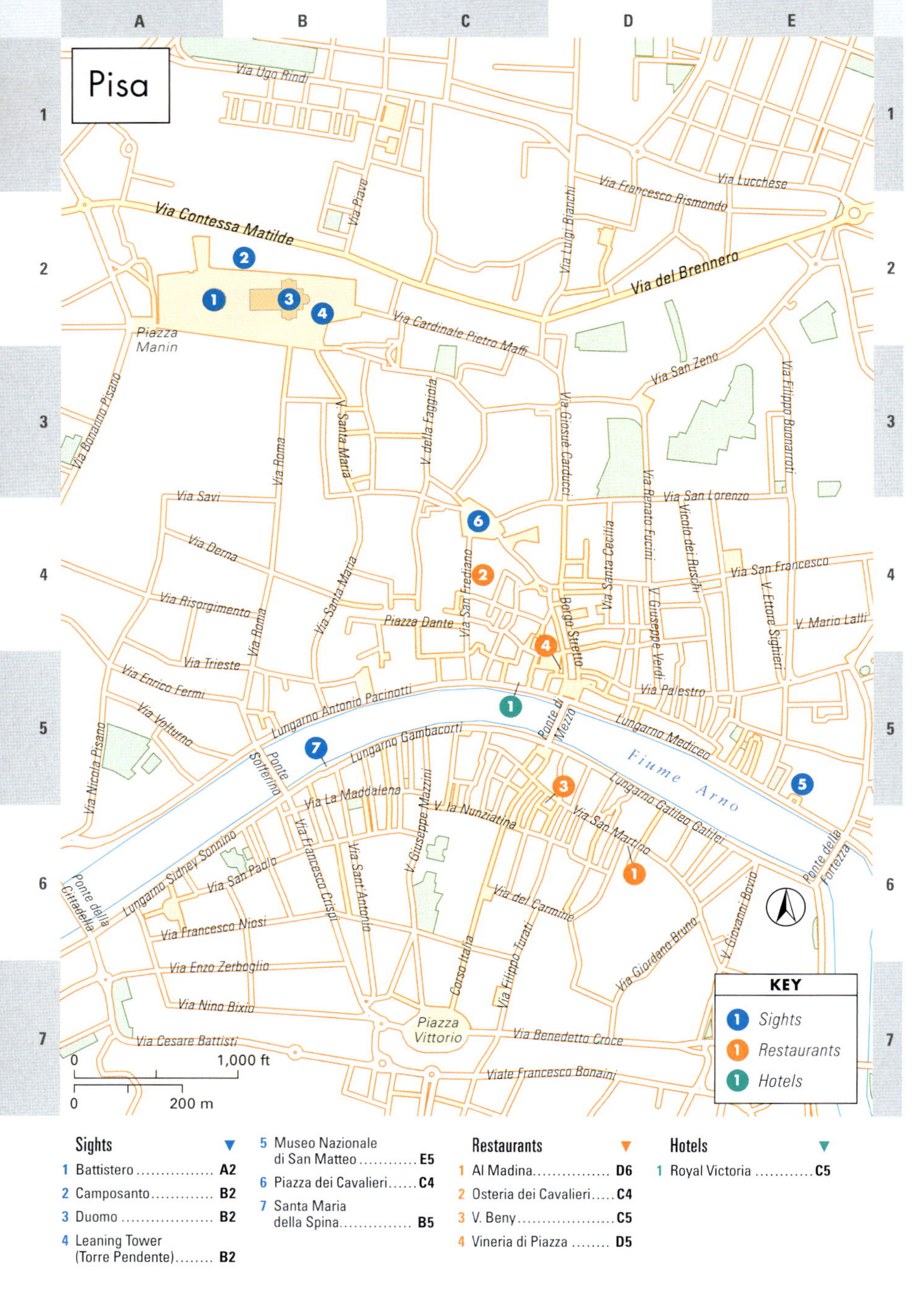

Sights

1 Battistero **A2**

2 Camposanto **B2**

3 Duomo **B2**

4 Leaning Tower (Torre Pendente)........ **B2**

5 Museo Nazionale di San Matteo **E5**

6 Piazza dei Cavalieri...... **C4**

7 Santa Maria della Spina............... **B5**

Restaurants

1 Al Madina............... **D6**

2 Osteria dei Cavalieri..... **C4**

3 V. Beny.................... **C5**

4 Vineria di Piazza **D5**

Hotels

1 Royal Victoria **C5**

Hotels

Royal Victoria

$ | **HOTEL** | In a pleasant palazzo facing the Arno, a 10-minute walk from the Campo dei Miracoli, this hotel has room styles that range from the 1800s, complete with frescoes, to the 1920s; the most charming are in the old tower. **Pros:** friendly staff; lovely views of the Arno from many rooms; old-world charm. **Cons:** rooms can be noisy; some rooms could use a dusting and refresh; spotty Wi-Fi. *Rooms from: €120* *Lungarno Pacinotti 12, Pisa* *050/940111* *www.royalvictoria.it* *38 rooms* *Free Breakfast.*

Performing Arts

Fondazione Teatro di Pisa

THEATER | Pisa has a lively performing-arts scene, most of which happens at the 19th-century Teatro Verdi. Music and dance performances are presented from September through May. Visit the website for schedules and information. *Via Palestro 40, Lungarni, Pisa* *050/941111* *www.teatrodipisa.pi.it.*

Chianti

This is the heartland: both sides of the Strada Chiantigiana (SR222) are embraced by glorious panoramic views of vineyards, olive groves, and castle towers. Traveling south from Florence, you first reach the aptly named one-street town of Strada in Chianti. Farther south, the number of vineyards on either side of the road dramatically increases—as do the signs inviting you in for a free tasting. Beyond Strada lies Greve in Chianti, completely surrounded by wineries and filled with wineshops. There's art to be had as well: Passignano, west of Greve, has an abbey that shelters a 15th-century *Last Supper* by Domenico and Davide Ghirlandaio. Farther still, along the Strada Chiantigiana, are Panzano and Castellina in Chianti, both hill towns. It's from near Panzano and Castellina that branch roads head to the other main towns of eastern Chianti: Radda in Chianti, Gaiole in Chianti, and Castelnuovo Berardenga.

The Strada Chiantigiana gets crowded during the high season, but no one is in a hurry. The slow pace gives you time to soak up the beautiful scenery.

Greve in Chianti

40 km (25 miles) north of Siena, 28 km (17½ miles) south of Florence.

If there is a capital of Chianti, it is Greve, a friendly market town with no shortage of cafés, enoteche, and crafts shops lining its streets.

GETTING HERE AND AROUND

Driving from Florence or Siena, Greve is easily reached via the Strada Chiantigiana (SR222). Autolinee Toscane buses travel frequently between Florence and Greve. The bus system also connects Siena and Greve, but a direct trip is virtually impossible. There is no train service to Greve.

VISITOR INFORMATION

CONTACT Greve in Chianti Tourism Office. *Piazza Matteotti 10, Greve in Chianti* *055/8546299* *www.visitchianti.net.*

Sights

Montefioralle

TOWN | A tiny hilltop hamlet, about 2 km (1 mile) west of Greve in Chianti, Montefioralle is the ancestral home of Amerigo Vespucci (1454–1512), the mapmaker, navigator, and explorer who named America. (His cousin-in-law, Simonetta, may have been the inspiration for Sandro Botticelli's *Birth of Venus*, painted sometime in the 1480s.) *Greve in Chianti.*

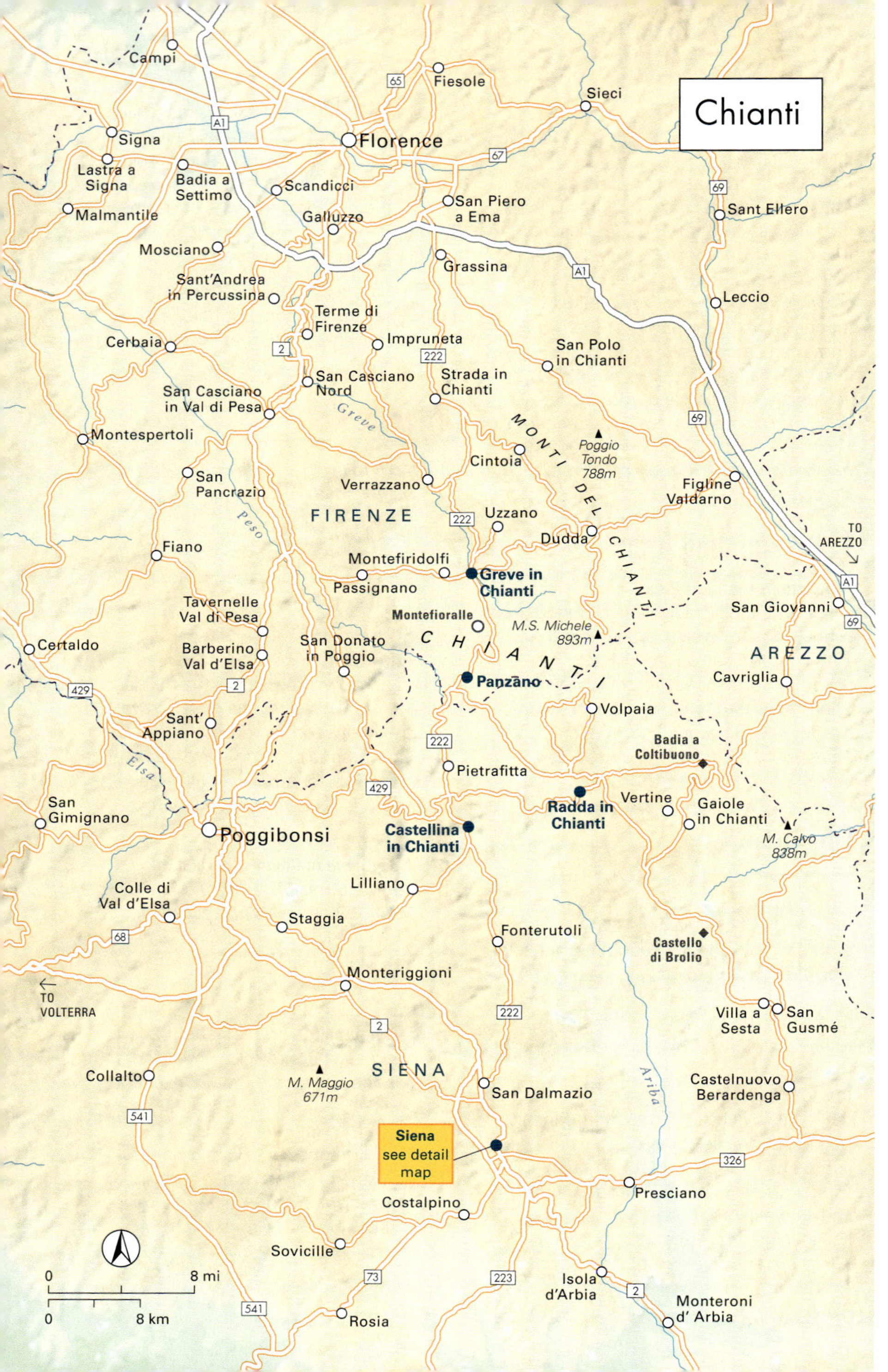

Chianti
Campi
Fiesole
Sieci
Signa
Florence
Lastra a Signa
Badia a Settimo
Scandicci
Malmantile
Galluzzo
San Piero a Ema
Sant Ellero
Mosciano
Grassina
Sant'Andrea in Percussina
Leccio
Terme di Firenze
Impruneta
Cerbaia
San Polo in Chianti
San Casciano Nord
Strada in Chianti
San Casciano in Val di Pesa
Greve
MONTI DEL CHIANTI
Montespertoli
Poggio Tondo 788m
Cintoia
San Pancrazio
Verrazzano
Figline Valdarno
FIRENZE
Uzzano
Peso
Dudda
TO AREZZO
Fiano
Montefiridolfi
Greve in Chianti
Passignano
San Giovanni
Tavernelle Val di Pesa
Montefioralle
M.S. Michele 893m
CHIANTI
AREZZO
Certaldo
San Donato in Poggio
Barberino Val d'Elsa
Panzano
Cavriglia
Volpaia
Sant' Appiano
Badia a Coltibuono
Elsa
Pietrafitta
Vertine
Radda in Chianti
Gaiole in Chianti
San Gimignano
Poggibonsi
Castellina in Chianti
M. Calvo 838m
Colle di Val d'Elsa
Lilliano
Staggia
Fonterutoli
Castello di Brolio
Monteriggioni
TO VOLTERRA
Villa a Sesta
San Gusmé
Collalto
SIENA
M. Maggio 671m
San Dalmazio
Castelnuovo Berardenga
Arbia
Siena see detail map
Presciano
Costalpino
Sovicille
Isola d'Arbia
Monteroni d' Arbia
Rosia
0
8 mi
0
8 km
A1
65
67
69
2
222
429
68
541
73
223
326

Piazza Matteotti

PLAZA/SQUARE | FAMILY | Greve's gently sloping and asymmetrical central piazza is surrounded by an attractive arcade with shops of all kinds. In the center stands a statue of the discoverer of New York harbor, Giovanni da Verrazzano (circa 1480–1527). Check out the lively market held here on Saturday morning. ✉ *Piazza Matteotti, Greve in Chianti.*

Restaurants

Enoteca Fuoripiazza

$ | TUSCAN | Detour off Greve's flower-strewn main square for food that relies heavily on local ingredients (like cheese and salami produced nearby). The lengthy wine list provides a bewildering array of choices to pair with affettati misti or one of the primi (first courses)—the *pici* (a thick, hand-rolled spaghetti) are deftly prepared here. **Known for:** alfresco dining; local cheese and salami; attentively prepared food. *$ Average main: €18 ✉ Via I Maggio 2, Greve in Chianti ☎ 055/8546313 🌐 www.enotecaristorantefuoripiazza.it ⏲ Closed Mon. No dinner Sun.*

★ **Falorni**

$ | ITALIAN | This institution—it's been around since 1806—began life as a butcher shop and, indeed, it still is, but it also has a little restaurant that serves great *taglieri* (plates of mixed cured pork products, usually, though cheese does prominently figure as well). Soups, lasagne, various tartares, and sandwiches are also on hand; the quality of the products is exceptional. **Known for:** cured meats using centuries' old recipes; great wines by the glass; outdoor seating. *$ Average main: €13 ✉ Piazza G. Matteotti 66, Greve in Chianti ☎ 055/853029 🌐 www.falorni.it.*

★ **Ristoro di Lamole**

$$ | TUSCAN | Up a winding road lined with olive trees and vineyards, this place is worth the effort it takes to find. The view from the outdoor terrace is divine, as is the simple, exquisitely prepared Tuscan cuisine—start with the bruschetta drizzled with olive oil or the sublime *verdure sott'olio* (marinated vegetables) before moving on to any of the fine secondi. **Known for:** coniglio (rabbit) is a specialty; sweeping view from the terrace; your hosts Paolo and Filippo. *$ Average main: €20 ✉ Via di Lamole 6, Località Lamole, Greve in Chianti ☎ 055/8547050 🌐 www.ristorodilamole.it ⏲ Closed Dec.–Feb.*

Hotels

Albergo del Chianti

$$ | B&B/INN | FAMILY | Simple but pleasantly decorated bedrooms with plain modern cabinets and wardrobes and wrought-iron beds have views of the town square or out over the tile rooftops toward the surrounding hills. **Pros:** central location; best value in Greve; swimming pool. **Cons:** rooms facing the piazza can be noisy; hotel could use an overall update; remote: a car is a necessity. *$ Rooms from: €215 ✉ Piazza Matteotti 86, Greve in Chianti ☎ 055/853763 🌐 www.albergodelchianti.it ⏲ Closed Jan.–early Mar. 🛏 16 rooms 🍽 No Meals.*

Castello Vicchiomaggio

$$ | B&B/INN | FAMILY | Stay in a fortified castle, which was built more than a millennium ago, was rebuilt during the Renaissance, and is now a charming inn and a prestigious wine estate where you can taste local vintages. **Pros:** spacious rooms; spectacular views; very helpful staff. **Cons:** some rooms lack air-conditioning; might be too remote for some; you need a car to get around. *$ Rooms from: €231 ✉ Via Vicchiomaggio 4, Località Vicchiomaggio, Greve in Chianti ☎ 055/854079 🌐 www.vicchiomaggio.it ⏲ Closed Dec.–mid-Mar. 🛏 15 rooms 🍽 Free Breakfast.*

★ Villa Bordoni

$$ | **B&B/INN** | Scotts David and Catherine Gardner transformed a ramshackle, 16th-century villa into a retreat where no two rooms are alike—all have stenciled walls; some have four-poster beds, others small mezzanines. **Pros:** splendidly isolated in the hills above Greve; beautiful decor; wonderful hosts. **Cons:** on a long and bumpy dirt road; need a car to get around; books up quickly. *Rooms from: €234 Via San Cresci 31/32, Greve in Chianti 055/8546230 www.villabordoni.com Closed Dec.–mid-Mar. 12 rooms Free Breakfast.*

★ Villa Il Poggiale

$$ | **B&B/INN** | **FAMILY** | Renaissance gardens, beautiful rooms with high ceilings and elegant furnishings, a panoramic pool, and expert staff are just a few of the things that make a stay at this 16th-century villa memorable. **Pros:** beautiful gardens and panoramic setting; elegant historical building; exceptionally professional staff. **Cons:** private transportation necessary; some rooms face a country road and may be noisy during the day; it may be too isolated for some. *Rooms from: €220 Via Empolese 69, San Casciano Val di Pesa 20 km (12 miles) northwest of Greve 055/828311 www.villailpoggiale.it Closed Jan. 26 rooms Free Breakfast.*

Panzano

7 km (4½ miles) south of Greve, 36 km (22 miles) south of Florence.

The magnificent views of the valleys of the Pesa and Greve rivers easily make Panzano one of the prettiest stops in Chianti. The triangular Piazza Bucciarelli is the heart of the new town. A short stroll along Via Giovanni da Verrazzano brings you up to the old town, Panzano Alto, which is still partly surrounded by medieval walls. The town's 13th-century castle is now almost completely absorbed by later buildings (its central tower is now a private home).

GETTING HERE AND AROUND

From Florence or Siena, Panzano is easily reached by car along the Strada Chiantigiana (SR222). Autolinee Toscane buses travel frequently between Florence and Panzano and less often from Siena. There is no train service to Panzano.

Sights

Pieve di San Leolino

CHURCH | Ancient even by Chianti standards, this hilltop church probably dates from the 10th century, but it was completely rebuilt in the Romanesque style sometime in the 13th century. It has a 14th-century cloister worth seeing. The 16th-century terra-cotta tabernacles are attributed to Giovanni della Robbia, and there's also a remarkable triptych (attributed to the Master of Panzano) that was executed sometime in the mid-14th century. Open days and hours are unpredictable; check with the tourist office in Greve in Chianti for the latest information. *Località San Leolino, Panzano 3 km (2 miles) south of Panzano 055/852003 www.sanleolino.org Free.*

Restaurants

★ Officina della Bistecca

$$$$ | **ITALIAN** | **FAMILY** | Local butcher and restaurateur, Dario Cecchini, has extended his empire of meat to include this space above his butcher's shop. In addition to two tasting menus—one heavily meat-laden, the other with none—you'll find a stellar version of *giardiniera sott'olio* (pickled and preserved vegetables), and exceptional bread (the product of much experimentation). **Known for:** convivial atmosphere; performing waitstaff; enormously popular, especially in summer. *Average main: €50 Via XX Luglio 11, Panzano 055/852020 www.dariocecchini.com/officina.*

★ Solociccia

$$$ | TUSCAN | FAMILY | As at his other eateries, Dario Cecchini, Panzano's local merchant of meat, offers two set menus for lunch—one where beef products dominate every course and the other vegetarian. The *musetto al limone e brodo vero* (an interesting salame served with stunning beef broth) might kick off the proceedings, and on the table you'll find *pinzimonio*, a dish of raw sliced vegetables (carrot, fennel, onions) to be dipped into terrific olive oil and sprinkled with Dario's special house-made herbed salt. **Known for:** choice of two set menus; great service; party atmosphere. *$ Average main: €40 ✉ Via XX Luglio 11, Panzano ☎ 055/852020 🌐 www.dariocecchini.com/solociccia ⏲ No dinner.*

Hotels

★ Villa Le Barone

$$ | B&B/INN | Once the home of the Viviani della Robbia family, this 16th-century villa in a grove of ancient cypress trees retains many aspects of a private country dwelling, including homey guest quarters. **Pros:** beautiful location; wonderful restaurant; great base for exploring the region. **Cons:** some rooms are a bit small; 15-minute walk to nearest town; a car is a must. *$ Rooms from: €272 ✉ Via San Leolino 19, Panzano ☎ 055/852621 🌐 www.villalebarone.com ⏲ Closed Nov.–early Apr. 28 rooms Free Breakfast.*

Radda in Chianti

26 km (15 miles) southeast of Panzano, 55 km (34 miles) south of Florence.

Radda in Chianti sits on a ridge stretching between the Val di Pesa and Val d'Arbia. It is easily reached by following the SR429 from Castellina. It's another one of those tiny villages with steep streets for strolling; follow the signs that point you toward the *camminamento medioevale,* a covered 14th-century walkway that circles part of the city inside the walls.

GETTING HERE AND AROUND

Radda can be reached by car from either Siena or Florence along the SR222 (Strada Chiantigiana), and from the A1 autostrada. A few buses each day travel from Siena to Radda on Autolinee Toscane. There is no direct bus from Florence or train service convenient to Radda.

VISITOR INFORMATION

CONTACT Radda in Chianti Tourism Office. *✉ Piazza del Castello 6, Radda in Chianti ☎ 0577/738494 🌐 www.visitchianti.net.*

Sights

★ Badia a Coltibuono (*Abbey of the Good Harvest*)

WINERY | This Romanesque abbey has been owned by internationally acclaimed cookbook author Lorenza de' Medici's family for more than a century and a half (the family isn't related to the Florentine Medici). Wine has been produced here since the abbey was founded by Vallombrosan monks in the 11th century. Today, the family continues the tradition, making wines, cold-pressed olive oil, and various flavored vinegars. Don't miss the jasmine-draped courtyard and the inner cloister with its antique well. *✉ Località Badia a Coltibuono, Gaiole in Chianti ✥ 4 km (2½ miles) north of Gaiole ☎ 0577/74481 tours 🌐 www.coltibuono.com Tour and tasting from €27 Reservations essential.*

★ Castello di Brolio

CASTLE/PALACE | If you have time for only one castle in Tuscany, this should be it. At the end of the 12th century, when Florence conquered southern Chianti, Brolio became Florence's southernmost outpost, and it was often said, "When Brolio growls, all Siena trembles." It was built about AD 1000 and owned by the monks of the Badia Fiorentina. The "new" owners, the Ricasoli family, have been in possession since 1141.

Bettino Ricasoli (1809–80), the so-called Iron Baron, was one of the founders of modern Italy and is said to have invented the original formula for Chianti wine; you can also visit the on-site Barone Ricasoli winery for a guided cellar tour and wine tasting.

Brolio, one of Chianti's best-known labels, is still justifiably famous. The grounds are worth visiting, and some of the guided tours do provide a glimpse of the castle's interior. The entrance fee includes a wine tasting in the enoteca. A small museum, where the Ricasoli Collection is housed in a 12th-century tower, displays objects that relate the long history of the family and the origins of Chianti wine. There are various options for an overnight here. ✉ *Località Madonna a Brolio, Gaiole in Chianti* ✣ *2 km (1 mile) southeast of Gaiole* ☎ *0577/730280* 🌐 *www.ricasoli.com* 🎫 *Gardens €7; tour and tasting from €45* 🕓 *Gardens closed mid-Dec.–late Mar.* ✍ *Reservations essential for wine tours.*

Palazzo del Podestà

GOVERNMENT BUILDING | Radda's town hall (aka Palazzo Comunale), in the middle of town, was built in the second half of the 14th century and has always served the same function. The 51 coats of arms (the largest is the Medici's) embedded in the facade represent the past governors of the town, but unless you have official business, the building is closed to the public. ✉ *Piazza Ferrucci 1, Radda in Chianti* 🎫 *Free.*

Restaurants

Osteria Le Panzanelle

$ | **TUSCAN** | Silvia Bonechi's experience in the kitchen—with the help of a few precious recipes handed down from her grandmother—is one of the reasons for the success of this small restaurant in the tiny hamlet of Lucarelli; the other is the front-room hospitality of Nada Michelassi. These two *panzanelle* (women from Panzano) serve a short menu of tasty and authentic dishes at what the locals refer to as *il prezzo giusto* (the right price). **Known for:** fine home cooking; good wine list; unpretentious atmosphere. 💲 *Average main: €16* ✉ *Località Lucarelli 29, Radda in Chianti* ✣ *8 km (5 miles) northwest of Radda on road to Panzano* ☎ *0577/733511* 🌐 *www.lepanzanelle.it* 🕓 *Closed Mon. and Jan. and Feb. No dinner Sun.*

Hotels

La Bottega di Giovannino

$ | **B&B/INN** | This is a fantastic place for the budget-conscious traveler, as rooms are immaculate and most have a stunning view of the surrounding hills. **Pros:** great location in the center of town; close to restaurants and shops; super value. **Cons:** some rooms are small; books up quickly; basic decor. 💲 *Rooms from: €85* ✉ *Via Roma 6–8, Radda in Chianti* ☎ *057/735601* 🌐 *www.labottegadigiovannino.it* 🕓 *Closed mid-Dec.–Mar.* 🛏 *9 rooms* 🍴 *No Meals.*

Palazzo San Niccolò

$ | **HOTEL** | The wood-beam ceilings, terra-cotta floors, and some of the original frescoes of a 19th-century town palace remain, but the marble bathrooms have all been updated, some with whirlpool tubs. **Pros:** central location; friendly staff; pool (though a car is necessary to get there at a nearby hotel). **Cons:** some rooms face a main street; room sizes vary; street noise in some rooms. 💲 *Rooms from: €144* ✉ *Via Roma 16, Radda in Chianti* ☎ *0577/735666* 🌐 *www.hotelsanniccolo.com* 🕓 *Closed Nov.–Mar.* 🛏 *18 rooms* 🍴 *No Meals.*

★ Relais Fattoria Vignale

$$ | **B&B/INN** | A refined and comfortable country house offers numerous sitting rooms with terra-cotta floors and attractive stonework, as well as wood-beamed guest rooms filled with simple wooden furnishings and handwoven rugs.

Pros: intimate public spaces; excellent restaurant; nice grounds and pool. **Cons:** single rooms are small; annex across a busy road; a car is necessary. *$ Rooms from: €195 ✉ Via Pianigiani 9, Radda in Chianti ☎ 0577/738300 🌐 www.vignale.it ⏲ Closed Nov.–late Mar. 41 rooms 🍽 Free Breakfast.*

Castellina in Chianti

13 km (8 miles) south of Panzano, 59 km (35 miles) south of Florence, 22 km (14 miles) north of Siena.

Castellina in Chianti—or simply Castellina—is on a ridge above three valleys: the Val di Pesa, Val d'Arbia, and Val d'Elsa. No matter what direction you turn, the panorama is bucolic. The strong 15th-century medieval walls and fortified town gate give a hint of the history of this village, which was an outpost during the continuing wars between Florence and Siena. In the main square, the Piazza del Comune, there's a 15th-century palace and a 15th-century fort constructed around a 13th-century tower. It now serves as the town hall.

GETTING HERE AND AROUND

As with all the towns along the Strada Chiantigiana (SR222), Castellina is an easy drive from either Siena or Florence. From Siena, Castellina is also well served by Autolinee Toscane. There's no direct bus from Florence. The closest train station is at Castellina Scalo, some 15 km (9 miles) away.

VISITOR INFORMATION

CONTACT Castellina in Chianti Tourism Office. *✉ Via Ferruccio 40, Castellina in Chianti ☎ 0577/741392 🌐 www.visitchianti.net.*

Restaurants

Albergaccio di Castellina

$$$ | TUSCAN | The fact that the dining room can seat only about 35 guests makes a meal here an intimate experience, and the ever-changing menu mixes traditional and creative dishes. In late September and October, mushrooms and chestnuts are featured in gnocchi and ravioli; grilled meats and seafood are on offer throughout the year. **Known for:** creative menu; superb wine list; marvelous waitstaff. *$ Average main: €33 ✉ Via Fiorentina 63, Castellina in Chianti ☎ 0577/741042 🌐 www.ristorantealbergaccio.com ⏲ Closed Sun.*

Ristorante Le Tre Porte

$$ | TUSCAN | Grilled meat dishes are the specialty at this popular restaurant, with a bistecca alla fiorentina (served very rare, as always) taking pride of place; paired with grilled fresh porcini mushrooms when in season (spring and fall), it's a heady dish. The panoramic terrace is a good choice for dining in summer; inside, the upper floor offers an unmistakably Tuscan setting, while the downstairs is more modern and intimate. **Known for:** views from the terrace; their way with mushrooms; fine wine list with lots of local bottles. *$ Average main: €25 ✉ Via Trento e Trieste 8, Castellina in Chianti ☎ 0577/741163 🌐 www.treporte.com.*

Sotto Le Volte

$$ | TUSCAN | As the name suggests, you'll find this small restaurant under the arches of Castellina's medieval walkway, and the eatery's vaulted ceilings make for a particularly romantic setting. The menu is short and eminently Tuscan, with typical soups and pasta dishes; the *costine d'agnello alle erbe* (herbed lamb chops) are especially tasty. **Known for:** unique setting; flair for Tuscan classics; attentive waitstaff. *$ Average main: €20 ✉ Via delle Volte 14–16, Castellina in Chianti ☎ 0577/741299 🌐 www.*

sottolevolteristorante.it ⏲ *Closed Tues. and Wed. and Jan.–Mar.*

Hotels

★ **Palazzo Squarcialupi**

$$ | B&B/INN | In this lovely 15th-century palace, spacious rooms have high ceilings, tile floors, and 18th-century furnishings, and many have views of the valley below. **Pros:** great location in town center; elegant public spaces; nice spa, pool, and grounds. **Cons:** on a street with no car access; across from a busy restaurant; rooms facing the street can experience some noise. [$] *Rooms from: €199* ✉ *Via Ferruccio 22, Castellina in Chianti* ☎ *0577/741186* 🌐 *www.squarcialupirelaxinchianti.com* ⏲ *Closed Nov.–Mar.* *17 rooms* *Free Breakfast.*

Volterra

30 km (18 miles) southwest of San Gimignano.

As you approach the town through bleak, rugged terrain, you can see that not all Tuscan hill towns rise above rolling green fields. Volterra stands mightily over Le Balze, a stunning series of gullied hills and valleys formed by erosion that has slowly eaten away at the foundation of the town—now considerably smaller than it was during its Etruscan glory days some 2,000 years ago.

GETTING HERE AND AROUND

By car, the best route from San Gimignano follows the SP1 south to Castel San Gimignano and then the SS68 west to Volterra. Coming from the west, take the SS1, a coastal road to Cecina, then follow the SS68 east to Volterra. Either way, there's a long, winding climb at the end of your trip. Traveling to Volterra by bus or train is complicated; avoid it if possible, especially if you have lots of luggage. From Florence or Siena the journey by public transit is best made by bus and involves a change in Colle di Val d'Elsa. From Rome or Pisa, it is best to take the train to Cecina and transfer to the Volterra-Saline station. The latter is 10 km (6 miles) from town.

VISITOR INFORMATION

CONTACT Volterra Tourism Office. ✉ *Piazza dei Priori 20, Volterra* ☎ *0588/87257* 🌐 *www.volterratur.it.*

Sights

Duomo

CHURCH | Behind the textbook 13th-century Pisan–Romanesque facade is proof that Volterra counted for something during the Renaissance, when many important Tuscan artists came to decorate the church. Three-dimensional stucco portraits of local saints are on the gold, red, and blue ceiling (1580) designed by Francesco Capriani, including St. Linus, the successor to St. Peter as pope and claimed by the Volterrans to have been born here.

The highlight of the Duomo is the brightly painted, 13th-century, wooden, life-size *Deposition* in the chapel of the same name. The unusual Cappella dell'Addolorata (Chapel of the Grieved) has two terra-cotta Nativity scenes; the depiction of the arrival of the Magi has a background fresco by Benozzo Gozzoli. ✉ *Piazza San Giovanni, Volterra* ☎ *0588/286300* 🌐 *www.animadivolterra.it/il-duomo* 🎟 *€8, includes baptistry* ⏲ *Closed Jan. 7–Mar. and Mon.–Thurs. Nov. 4–Dec. 24.*

★ **Museo Etrusco Guarnacci**

HISTORY MUSEUM | An extraordinary collection of Etruscan relics is made all the more interesting by clear explanations in English. The bulk of the collection is comprised of roughly 700 carved funerary urns. The oldest, dating from the 7th century BC, were made from tufa (volcanic rock). A handful are made of terra-cotta, but most—dating from the 3rd to 1st century BC—are done in alabaster. The urns are grouped by subject, and, taken together, they form a fascinating testimony about Etruscan life and death. ✉ *Via Don Minzoni 15, Volterra* ☎ *0588/86347* 🌐 *www.comune.volterra.pi.it/turismo* 🎫 *€10.*

Pinacoteca

ART MUSEUM | One of Volterra's best-looking Renaissance buildings contains an impressive collection of Tuscan paintings arranged chronologically on two floors. Head straight for Room 12, with Luca Signorelli's (circa 1445–1523) *Madonna and Child with Saints* and Rosso Fiorentino's later *Deposition*. Though painted just 30 years apart, they illustrate the shift in style from the early 16th-century Renaissance ideals to full-blown Mannerism: the balance of Signorelli's composition becomes purposefully skewed in Fiorentino's painting, where the colors go from vivid but realistic to emotively bright. Other important paintings in the small museum include Ghirlandaio's *Apotheosis of Christ with Saints* and a polyptych of the *Madonna and Saints* by Taddeo di Bartolo, which once hung in the Palazzo dei Priori. ✉ *Via dei Sarti 1, Volterra* ☎ *0588/87580* 🌐 *www.comune.volterra.pi.it/turismo* 🎫 *€10.*

Porta all'Arco Etrusco

RUINS | Even if a good portion of the arch was rebuilt by the Romans, three dark, weather-beaten, 4th-century-BC heads (thought to represent Etruscan gods) still face outward to greet those who enter here. A plaque on the outer wall recalls the efforts of the locals who saved the arch from destruction by filling it with stones during the German withdrawal at the end of World War II. ✉ *Via Porta all'Arco, Volterra* ☎ *0588/86099* 🌐 *www.volterratur.it* 🎫 *Free.*

Teatro Romano

RUINS | Just outside the walls, past Porta Fiorentina, are the ruins of the 1st-century-BC Roman theater, one of the best-preserved in Italy, with adjacent remains of the Roman *terme* (baths). You can enjoy an excellent bird's-eye view of the theater from Via Lungo le Mura. ✉ *Viale Francesco Ferrucci, Volterra* ☎ *0588/87257* 🌐 *www.volterratur.it* 🎫 *€10.*

Restaurants

Il Sacco Fiorentino

$ | TUSCAN | This lovely trattoria has been around for a long time, and with good reason—the Tuscan classics rely heavily on the local cheese (pecorino) and local meats (especially wild boar, among others), and the wine list is long and very well-priced. The white walls, tile floors, and red tablecloths create an understated tone that is unremarkable, but once the food starts arriving, it's easy to forgive the lack of decoration. **Known for:** convenient location near Duomo and Piazza dei Priori; gentle prices; excellent wine list. 💲 *Average main: €17* ✉ *Via Giusto Turazza 13, Volterra* ☎ *0588/88537* 🕓 *Closed Wed.*

Trattoria Da Badò

$ | TUSCAN | Family-run Da Badò—with Lucia in the kitchen and her sons, Giacomo and Michele, waiting tables—is the best place in town to eat traditional food elbow-to-elbow with locals; Lucia likes to concentrate on just a few dishes, so it won't take long to decide between the standards, all prepared with a sure hand. Consider the *zuppa alla volterrana* (a soup made with vegetables and bread), *pappardelle alla lepre* (wide fettuccine with rabbit sauce), or a stew of either rabbit or wild boar—for dessert, a slice of homemade almond tart is a must. **Known for:** excellent traditional dishes; small menu; local favorite. 💲 *Average main: €16* ✉ *Borgo San Lazzaro 9, Volterra* ☎ *0588/80402* 🕓 *Closed Wed.*

Hotels

Albergo Etruria

$ | HOTEL | The rooms are modest, and there's no elevator, but the central location, the ample buffet breakfast, and the reasonable rates make this a good choice. **Pros:** great central location; friendly staff; tranquil garden with rooftop views. **Cons:** some rooms can be noisy during the day; books up quickly as it's good value; no elevator. $ *Rooms from: €103 ✉ Via Matteotti 32, Volterra ☎ 0588/87377 ⊕ www.albergoetruria.it ⏲ Closed early Dec.–early Feb. 15 rooms Free Breakfast.*

Hotel San Lino

$ | **HOTEL** | Within the town's medieval walls, this convent-turned-hotel has wood-beam ceilings, graceful archways, and terra-cotta floors, with nice contemporary furnishings and ironwork in the rooms. **Pros:** steps from center of town; friendly and helpful staff; convenient parking. **Cons:** rooms facing the street can be noisy; books up quickly; though in the center, somewhat removed from things. $ *Rooms from: €115 ✉ Via San Lino 26, Volterra ☎ 0588/85250 ⊕ www.hotelsanlino.net ⏲ Closed early Nov.–late Mar. 43 rooms Free Breakfast.*

San Gimignano

14 km (9 miles) northwest of Colle di Val d'Elsa, 38 km (24 miles) northwest of Siena, 54 km (34 miles) southwest of Florence.

When you're on a hilltop surrounded by soaring medieval towers silhouetted against the sky, it's difficult not to fall under the spell of San Gimignano. Its tall walls and narrow streets are typical of Tuscan hill towns, but it's the medieval "skyscrapers" that set the town apart from its neighbors. Today 14 towers remain, but at the height of the Guelph–Ghibelline conflict there was a forest of more than 70, and it was possible to cross the town by rooftop rather than by road.

Today San Gimignano isn't much more than a gentrified walled city, touristy but still very much worth exploring because, despite the profusion of cheesy souvenir shops lining the main drag, there's some serious Renaissance art to be seen here.

GETTING HERE AND AROUND

You can reach San Gimignano by car from the Florence–Siena superstrada. Exit at Poggibonsi Nord and follow signs for San Gimignano. Although it involves changing buses in Poggibonsi, getting to San Gimignano by bus from Florence is a relatively straightforward affair. There's also direct bus service from Siena to San Gimignano several times daily. All the buses are operated by Autolinee Toscane. You cannot reach San Gimignano by train.

VISITOR INFORMATION

CONTACT San Gimignano Tourism Office. *✉ Piazza Duomo 1, San Gimignano ☎ 0577/940008 ⊕ www.sangimignano.com.*

Sights

★ Collegiata

CHURCH | The town's main church is not officially a duomo (cathedral), because San Gimignano has no bishop. But behind the simple facade of the Romanesque Collegiata lies a treasure trove of fine frescoes, covering nearly every wall. Bartolo di Fredi's 14th-century fresco cycle of Old Testament scenes extends along one wall. Their distinctly medieval feel, with misshapen bodies, buckets of spurting blood, and lack of perspective, contrasts with the much more reserved scenes from the Life of Christ (attributed to 14th-century artist Lippo Memmi) painted on the opposite wall just 14 years later. *✉ Piazza Pecori 1–2, entrance on left side of church, San Gimignano ☎ 0577/286300 ⊕ www.duomosangimignano.it €5.*

Museo Civico

CASTLE/PALACE | The impressive civic museum occupies what was the "new" Palazzo del Popolo; the Torre Grossa is adjacent. Dante visited San Gimignano for only one day as a Guelph ambassador from Florence to ask the locals to join the

Florentines in supporting the pope—just long enough to get the main council chamber named after him.

Upstairs, paintings by famous Renaissance artists Pinturicchio (*Madonna Enthroned*) and Benozzo Gozzoli (*Madonna and Child*), and two large *tondi* (circular paintings) by Filippino Lippi (circa 1457–1504) attest to the importance and wealth of San Gimignano. ✉ *Piazza Duomo 2, San Gimignano* ☎ *0577/286300* 🌐 *www.sangimignanomusei.it* 🎫 *€9 cumulative ticket, €13 San Gimignano Pass (museums and duomo).*

Sant'Agostino

CHURCH | Make a beeline for Benozzo Gozzoli's superlative 15th-century fresco cycle depicting scenes from the life of St. Augustine. The saint's work was essential to the early development of church doctrine. Benozzo's 17 scenes on the choir wall depict Augustine as a man who traveled and taught extensively in the 4th and 5th centuries. The 15th-century altarpiece by Piero del Pollaiolo (1443–96) depicts *The Coronation of the Virgin* and the various protectors of the city. ✉ *Piazza Sant'Agostino 10, San Gimignano* ☎ *0577/904313* 🌐 *www.conventosantagostino.it* 🎫 *Free.*

Restaurants

★ Cum Quibus

$$ | ITALIAN | This is, without a doubt, one of the region's most creative restaurants—an intimate place with a menu that's Tuscan but not (its signature egg yolk starter is done with élan). Not a step is missed, and although it's possible to order à la carte, the tasting menu is also a good way to go. **Known for:** courtyard dining in nice weather; incorporation of non-Tuscan ingredients into Tuscan food; amazing wine list with prices to suit all budgets. $ *Average main: €26* ✉ *Via San Martino 17, San Gimignano* ☎ *0577/943199* 🌐 *en.mktn.it/cumquibus* ⏲ *Closed Wed. and Thurs. and Jan. and Feb.*

Enoteca Gustavo

$ | WINE BAR | There's no shortage of places to try Vernaccia di San Gimignano, the justifiably famous white wine with which San Gimignano is often singularly associated. At this wine bar, you can buy a glass of Vernaccia di San Gimignano and sit down with a cheese plate or one of the fine crostini. **Known for:** quality products; fine list of wines by the glass; friendly staff. $ *Average main: €15* ✉ *Via San Matteo 7, San Gimignano* ☎ *0577/940057* 🌐 *www.facebook.com/enotecagustavo.*

Osteria del Carcere

$$ | ITALIAN | Although it calls itself an *osteria* (tavern), this place much more resembles a wine bar, with a bill of fare that includes several different types of pâtés and a short list of seasonal soups and salads. The sampler of goat cheeses, which can be paired with local wines, should not be missed. **Known for:** excellent chef–proprietor; inventive dishes; housed in a former jail. $ *Average main: €20* ✉ *Via del Castello 13, San Gimignano* ☎ *0577/941905* ⏲ *Closed Wed. and early Jan.–Mar. No lunch Thurs.*

Hotels

★ Hotel La Collegiata

$$ | HOTEL | After serving as a Franciscan convent and then the residence of the noble Strozzi family, the Collegiata has been converted into a fine hotel, with no expense spared in the process. **Pros:** gorgeous views from terrace; elegant rooms in main building; wonderful staff. **Cons:** long walk into town; service can be impersonal; some rooms are dimly lit. $ *Rooms from: €241* ✉ *Località Strada 27, San Gimignano* ✣ *1 km (½ mile) north of San Gimignano town center* ☎ *0577/943201* 🌐 *www.lacollegiatahotel.com* ⏲ *Closed Nov.–Mar.* 🛏 *20 rooms* 🍽 *Free Breakfast.*

Hotel Pescille

$$ | **HOTEL** | A rambling farmhouse has been transformed into a handsome hotel with understated contemporary furniture in the bedrooms and country-classic motifs in the bar. **Pros:** splendid views; quiet atmosphere; 10-minute walk to town. **Cons:** furnishings a bit austere; there's an elevator for luggage but not for guests; a vehicle is a must. *Rooms from: €250 Località Pescille, San Gimignano 4 km (2½ miles) south of San Gimignano 0577/940186 www.pescille.it Closed mid-Oct.–mid-Apr. 38 rooms Free Breakfast.*

Torraccia di Chiusi

$$ | **B&B/INN** | **FAMILY** | A perfect retreat for families, this tranquil hilltop *agriturismo* (farm stay) offers simple, comfortably decorated accommodations on extensive grounds 5 km (3 miles) from the hubbub of San Gimignano. **Pros:** great walking possibilities; family-run hospitality; delightful countryside view. **Cons:** 30 minutes from the nearest town on a winding gravel road; need a car to get here; might be too remote for some. *Rooms from: €200 Località Montauto 16, San Gimignano 0577/941972 www.torracciadichiusi.it 11 rooms Free Breakfast.*

Colle di Val d'Elsa

12 km (7 miles) west of Monteriggioni, 25 km (16 miles) northwest of Siena, 51 km (32 miles) south of Florence.

Most people pass through on their way to and from popular tourist destinations Volterra and San Gimignano—a shame, since Colle di Val d'Elsa has a lot to offer. It's another town on the Via Francigena that benefited from trade along the pilgrimage route to Rome. Colle got an extra boost in the late 16th century when it was given a bishopric, probably related to an increase in trade when nearby San Gimignano was cut off from the well-traveled road. The town is arranged on two levels, and from the 12th century onward the flat lower portion was given over to a flourishing papermaking industry; today the area is mostly modern, and efforts have shifted toward the production of fine glass and crystal.

GETTING HERE AND AROUND

You can reach Colle di Val d'Elsa by car on either the SR2 from Siena or the Florence–Siena superstrada. Bus service to and from Siena and Florence is frequent.

VISITOR INFORMATION

CONTACT Colle di Val d'Elsa Tourism Office. *Via del Castello 33, Colle di Val d'Elsa 0577/922791 www.visitcolledivaldelsa.com.*

Sights

Make your way from the newer lower town (Colle Bassa) to the prettier, upper part of town (Colle Alta). The best views of the valley are to be had from Viale della Rimembranza, the road that loops around the western end of town, past the church of San Francesco. The early-16th-century Porta Nuova was inserted into the preexisting medieval walls, just as several handsome Renaissance palazzi were placed into the medieval neighborhood to create what is now called the Borgo.

Chiesa di Santa Caterina

CHURCH | Visit this 15th-century church to view the excellent stained-glass window in the apse, executed by Sebastiano Mainardi (circa 1460–1513), as well as a haunting *Pietà* created by local artist Zacchia Zacchi (1473–1544). *Via Campana 35, Colle di Val d'Elsa 0577/922791 www.visitcolledivaldelsa.com Free.*

Duomo

CHURCH | Several reconstructions have left little to admire of the once-Romanesque Duomo. Inside is the Cappella del Santo Chiodo (Chapel of the Holy Nail), built in the 15th century to hold a nail allegedly from the cross upon which Christ was

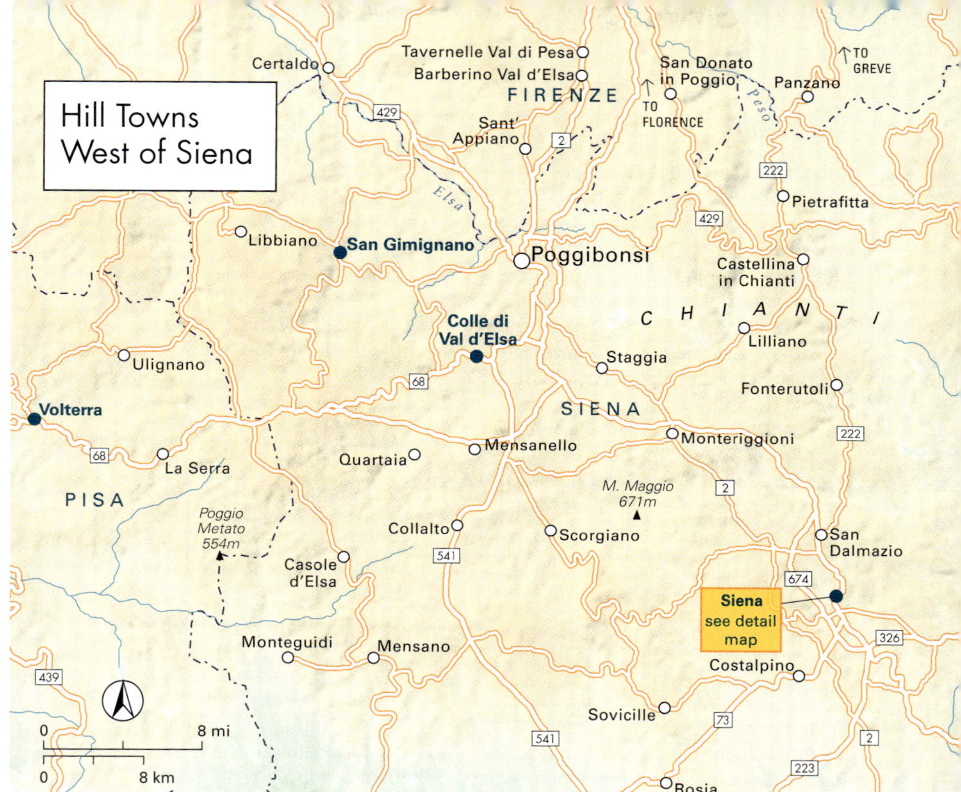

crucified. (Perhaps it inspired the locals to go into the nail-making business, which became another of the town's flourishing industries.) ✉ *Piazza del Duomo, Colle di Val d'Elsa* ☎ *0577/920389* 🌐 *www.visitcolledivaldelsa.com* 🎫 *Free.*

Museo San Pietro

ART MUSEUM | The museum of sacred art displays religious relics as well as triptychs from the Sienese and Florentine schools dating from the 14th and 15th centuries. It also contains the town's tribute to Arnolfo di Cambio, with photos of the buildings he designed for other towns. Down Via del Castello, at No. 63, is the house-tower where Arnolfo was born in 1245. (It's not open to the public.) ✉ *Via Gracco del Secco 102, Colle di Val d'Elsa* ☎ *0577/286300* 🌐 *www.museisenesi.org* 🎫 *€8* 🕒 *See the website for seasonal hrs.*

Restaurants

★ Ristorante Arnolfo

$$$$ | **MODERN ITALIAN** | Food lovers should not miss Arnolfo, one of Tuscany's most highly regarded restaurants, where chef Gaetano Trovato sets high standards of creativity in dishes that daringly ride the line between innovation and tradition, almost always with spectacular results. The menu changes frequently, but you are always sure to find fish and lots of fresh vegetables in the summer. **Known for:** tasting menus; imaginative dishes; superb wine list. $ *Average main: €200* ✉ *Viale della Rimembranza 24, Colle di Val d'Elsa* ☎ *0577/920549* 🌐 *www.arnolfo.com* 🕒 *Closed Tues. and Wed., and mid-Feb.–early Mar., 10 days in early Apr., and mid-Nov.–early Dec.*

Hotels

Palazzo San Lorenzo Hotel & Spa

$$ | **HOTEL** | A 17th-century palace in the historic center of Colle has rooms that exude warmth and comfort, with light-color wooden floors, soothingly tinted fabrics, and large windows. **Pros:** central location; lovely spa area; extremely well maintained. **Cons:** caters to business groups; some of the public spaces feel rather sterile; a car is a necessity. *Rooms from: €180* *Via Gracco del Secco 113, Colle di Val d'Elsa* *0577/923675* *www.palazzosanlorenzo.it* *48 rooms* *Free Breakfast.*

Siena

76 km (47 miles) south of Florence, 27 km (16 miles) southeast of Colle di Val d'Elsa.

With its narrow streets and steep alleys, a Gothic Duomo, a bounty of early Renaissance art, and the glorious Palazzo Pubblico overlooking its magnificent Campo, Siena is often described as Italy's best-preserved medieval city. It is also remarkably modern: many shops sell clothes by up-and-coming designers. Make a point of catching the *passeggiata* (evening stroll), when locals throng the Via di Città, Banchi di Sopra, and Banchi di Sotto, the city's three main streets.

Victory over Florence in 1260 at Montaperti marked the beginning of Siena's golden age. Even though Florentines avenged the loss 29 years later, Siena continued to prosper. During the following decades Siena erected its greatest buildings (including the Duomo); established a model city government presided over by the Council of Nine; and became a great art, textile, and trade center. All of these achievements came together in the decoration of the Sala della Pace in Palazzo Pubblico. It makes you wonder what greatness the city might have gone on to achieve had its fortunes been different, but in 1348 the Black Death decimated the population, brought an end to the Council of Nine, and left Siena economically vulnerable. Siena succumbed to Florentine rule in the mid-16th century, when a yearlong siege virtually eliminated the native population. Ironically, it was precisely this decline that, along with Sienese pride, prevented further development, to which we owe the city's marvelous medieval condition today.

But although much looks as it did in the early 14th century, Siena is no museum. Walk through the streets and you can see that the medieval contrade—17 neighborhoods into which the city has been historically divided—are a vibrant part of modern life. You may see symbols of the *contrada* emblazoned on banners and engraved on building walls: Tartuca (turtle), Oca (goose), Istrice (porcupine), Torre (tower)—among others. The Sienese still strongly identify themselves with the contrada where they were born and raised; loyalty and rivalry run deep. At no time is this more visible than during the centuries-old Palio, a twice-yearly horse race held in the Piazza del Campo, but you need not visit then to come to know the rich culture of Siena, evident at every step.

GETTING HERE AND AROUND

From Florence, the quickest way to Siena is via the Florence–Siena superstrada. Otherwise, take the Via Cassia (SR2) for a scenic route. Coming from Rome, leave the A1 at Valdichiana, and follow the Siena–Bettole superstrada. Autolinee Toscane provides frequent bus service between Florence and Siena. Because buses are direct and speedy, they are preferable to the train, which sometimes involves a change in Empoli.

If you come by car, you're better off leaving it in one of the parking lots around the perimeter of town. Driving is difficult or impossible in most parts of the city center. Practically unchanged since medieval times, Siena is laid out in a "Y" over the slopes of several hills, dividing the city into *terzi* (thirds).

TIMING

It's a joy to walk in Siena—hills notwithstanding—as it's a rare opportunity to stroll through a medieval city rather than just a town. (There is quite a lot to explore, in contrast to tiny hill towns that can be crossed in minutes.) The walk can be done in as little as a day, with minimal stops at the sights. But stay longer and take time to tour the churches and museums, and to enjoy the streetscapes themselves. Many of the sites have reduced hours Sunday afternoon and Monday.

VISITOR INFORMATION

CONTACT Siena Tourism Office. ✉ *Il Campo 1, Siena* ☏ *0577/292222* 🌐 *www.visitsienaofficial.it.*

Battistero

RELIGIOUS BUILDING | The Duomo's 14th-century Gothic Baptistery was built to prop up the apse of the cathedral. There are frescoes throughout, but the highlight is a large bronze 15th-century baptismal font designed by Jacopo della Quercia. It's adorned with bas-reliefs by various artists, including two by Renaissance masters: the *Baptism of Christ* by Lorenzo Ghiberti (1378–1455) and the *Feast of Herod* by Donatello. ✉ *Piazza San Giovanni, Città* ☏ *0577/286300* 🌐 *www.operaduomo.siena.it* 🎫 *From €14 combined ticket includes the Duomo, Cripta, and Museo dell'Opera.*

★ Cripta

CEMETERY | Routine excavation work revealed this crypt, which had been hidden for centuries under the grand *pavimento* (floor) of the Duomo and was opened to the public in 2003. In the late 13th century, an unknown master executed the crypt's breathtaking frescoes, which have sustained remarkably little damage and have retained their original colors. The *Deposition/Lamentation* proves that the Sienese school could paint emotion just as well as the Florentine school—and that it did so some 20 years before Giotto. ✉ *Scale di San Giovanni, Città* ✥ *Down steps to right side of cathedral* ☏ *0577/286300* 🌐 *www.operaduomo.siena.it* 🎫 *€16 combined ticket includes the Duomo, Battistero, roof terrace, and Museo dell'Opera.*

★ Duomo

CHURCH | Siena's cathedral, completed in two brief phases at the end of the 13th and 14th centuries, is beyond question one of the finest Gothic churches in Italy. The multicolored marble and painted decoration are typical of the Italian approach to Gothic architecture, and the amazingly detailed facade has few rivals. Highlights of the Duomo's striking interior include dark-green-and-white striping; a coffered and gilded dome; a stained-glass window that's the oldest (circa 1288) example of such work in Italy; a carousel pulpit carved around 1265; and magnificent Renaissance frescoes in the Biblioteca Piccolomini.

The Duomo is most famous, though, for its inlaid-marble floors, which took almost 200 years to complete. More than 40 artists contributed to the magnificent work, made up of 56 separate compositions depicting biblical scenes, allegories, religious symbols, and civic emblems. The floors are covered for most of the year but are unveiled from the end of June until the end of July and from mid-August until mid-October. ✉ *Piazza del Duomo, Città* ☏ *0577/286300* 🌐 *www.operaduomo.siena.it* 🎫 *€16 combined ticket includes Cripta, Battistero, roof terrace, and Museo dell'Opera.*

★ Museo dell'Opera

ART MUSEUM | Part of the unfinished nave of what was to have been a new cathedral, the museum contains the Duomo's treasury and some of the original decoration from its facade and

Sights

1 Battistero C4
2 Cripta C4
3 Duomo C4
4 Museo dell'Opera C4
5 Palazzo Pubblico C4
6 Piazza del Campo C4
7 Pinacoteca Nazionale C5
8 San Domenico B3
9 Santa Maria della Scala B4

Restaurants

1 Antica Trattoria Papei ... C4
2 Osteria Il Grattacielo C3

Hotels

1 Grand Hotel Continental C3
2 Hotel Santa Caterina E6
3 Palazzo Ravizza B5

interior. The first room on the ground floor displays weather-beaten 13th-century sculptures by Giovanni Pisano that were brought inside for protection and replaced by copies, as was a tondo of the *Madonna and Child* (now attributed to Donatello) that once hung on the door to the south transept. The masterpiece is unquestionably Duccio's *Maestà,* one side with 26 panels depicting episodes from the Passion, the other side with a *Madonna and Child Enthroned.* The second floor is divided between the treasury, with a crucifix by Giovanni Pisano, and *La Sala della Madonna degli Occhi Grossi* (the Room of the Madonna with the Big Eyes), named after the 13th-century painting. There is a fine view from the tower inside the museum. ✉ *Piazza del Duomo 8, Città* ☎ *0577/286300* 🌐 *www.operaduomo.siena.it* 🎫 *€16 combined ticket includes Cripta, Battistero, roof terrace, and Museo dell'Opera.*

Palazzo Pubblico

GOVERNMENT BUILDING | The Gothic Palazzo Pubblico, the focal point of the Piazza del Campo, has served as Siena's town hall since the 1300s. It now also contains the Museo Civico, with walls covered in early Renaissance frescoes. The nine governors of Siena once met in the Sala della Pace, famous for Ambrogio Lorenzetti's frescoes called *Allegories of Good and Bad Government*, painted in the late 1330s to demonstrate the dangers of tyranny. The good government side depicts utopia, showing first the virtuous ruling council surrounded by angels and then scenes of a perfectly running city and countryside. Conversely, the bad government fresco tells a tale straight out of Dante. The evil ruler and his advisers have horns and fondle strange animals, and the town scene depicts the seven mortal sins in action.

The Torre del Mangia, the palazzo's famous bell tower, is named after one of its first bell ringers, Giovanni di Duccio (called Mangiaguadagni, or earnings eater). The climb up to the top is long and steep, but the view makes it worth every step. ✉ *Piazza del Campo 1, Città* ☎ *0577/292368* 🌐 *museocivico.comune.siena.it* 🎫 *Museum €6, museum and tower €15.*

★ Piazza del Campo

PLAZA/SQUARE | The fan-shape Piazza del Campo, known simply as Il Campo (The Field), is one of the finest squares in Italy. Constructed toward the end of the 12th century on a market area unclaimed by any contrada, it's still the heart of town. Its brickwork is patterned in nine different sections—representing each member of the medieval Council of Nine.

At the top of the Campo is a copy of the early 15th-century Fonte Gaia by Siena's greatest sculptor, Jacopo della Quercia. The 13 sculpted reliefs of biblical events and virtues that line the fountain are 19th-century copies; the originals are in the museum complex of Santa Maria della Scala. On Palio horse-race days (July 2 and August 16), the Campo and all its surrounding buildings are packed with cheering, frenzied locals and tourists craning their necks to take it all in. ✉ *Piazza del Campo, Città.*

Pinacoteca Nazionale

ART MUSEUM | The superb collection of five centuries of local painting in Siena's national picture gallery can easily convince you that the Renaissance was by no means just a Florentine thing. Accordingly, the most interesting section of the collection, chronologically arranged, has several important firsts. Room 1 contains a painting of the *Stories of the True Cross* (1215) by the so-called Master of Tressa, the earliest identified work by a painter of the Sienese school, and is followed in Room 2 by late-13th-century artist Guido da Siena's *Stories from the Life of Christ,* one of the first paintings ever made on canvas (earlier painters used wood panels).

Rooms 3 and 4 are dedicated to Duccio, a student of Cimabue (circa 1240–1302) and considered to be the last of the proto-Renaissance painters. Ambrogio Lorenzetti's landscapes in Room 8 are among the first truly secular paintings in Western art. Among later works in the rooms on the floor above, keep an eye out for the preparatory sketches used by Domenico Beccafumi (1486–1551) for the 35 etched marble panels he made for the floor of the Duomo. ✉ *Via San Pietro 29, Città* ☎ *0577/281161* 🌐 *www.pinacotecanazionalesiena.it* 🎫 *€6* ⏲ *Closed Sun. and Mon. after 1:30.*

San Domenico

CHURCH | Although the Duomo is celebrated as a triumph of 13th-century Gothic architecture, this church, built at about the same time, turned out to be an oversize, hulking brick box that never merited a finishing coat in marble, let alone a graceful facade. Named for the founder of the Dominican order, the church is now more closely associated with St. Catherine of Siena. Just to the right of the entrance is the chapel in which she received the stigmata. On the wall is the only known contemporary portrait of the saint, made in the late 14th century by Andrea Vanni (circa 1332–1414). Farther down is the famous Cappella delle Santa Testa, the church's official shrine.

On either side of the chapel are well-known frescoes by Sodoma (aka Giovanni Antonio Bazzi, 1477–1549) of *St. Catherine in Ecstasy.* Don't miss the view of the Duomo and town center from the apse-side terrace. ✉ *Piazza San Domenico, Camollìa* ☎ *0577/286848* 🌐 *www.basilicacateriniana.it* 🎫 *Free.*

★ Santa Maria della Scala

ART MUSEUM | For more than 1,000 years, this complex across from the Duomo was home to Siena's hospital, but it now serves as a museum. Restored 15th-century frescoes in the Sala del Pellegrinaio tell the history of the hospital, which was created to give refuge to passing pilgrims and others in need and to distribute charity to the poor. Incorporated into the complex is the church of the Santissima Annunziata, with a celebrated *Risen Christ* by Vecchietta (also known as Lorenzo di Pietro, circa 1412–80). Down in the dark, Cappella di Santa Caterina della Notte is where St. Catherine went to pray at night. Displays in the subterranean archaeological museum are clearly marked and serve as a good introduction to the history of regional excavations. Don't miss della Quercia's stunning original sculpted reliefs from the Fonte Gaia. ✉ *Piazza del Duomo 2, Città* ☎ *0577/292615* 🌐 *www.santamariadellascala.com* 🎫 *€9* ⏲ *Closed Tues. Nov.–mid-Mar.*

Restaurants

Antica Trattoria Papei

$ | TUSCAN | This place, which has been in the Papei family for three generations, attracts both locals and visitors with basic but fine Sienese specialties and reasonable prices. Tucked away behind the Palazzo Pubblico in a square that serves as a parking lot for most of the day, the restaurant's location isn't great, but the food is; thanks to portable heaters, there is outdoor seating all year-round. **Known for:** great place to sample local specialties; lively atmosphere; outdoor seating. [$] *Average main: €15* ✉ *Piazza del Mercato 6, Città* ☎ *0577/280894* 🌐 *www.anticatrattoriapapei.com.*

Osteria Il Grattacielo

$ | TUSCAN | If you're wiped out from too much sightseeing, consider a meal at this hole-in-the-wall restaurant where locals congregate for a simple lunch. There's a collection of verdure sott'olio, a wide selection of affettati misti, and pasta—all of which can be washed down with the cheap, yet eminently drinkable, house wines. **Known for:** simple, good-value food; earthy ambience; outdoor seating in summer. [$] *Average main: €12* ✉ *Via Pontani 8, Camollìa* ☎ *331/7422835*

🌐 www.sites.google.com/view/ilgrattacielo1840 ⏲ No dinner Sun.

Hotels

★ Grand Hotel Continental

$$$ | **HOTEL** | Pope Alexander VII of the famed Sienese Chigi family gave this palace to his niece as a wedding present in 1600, and, through the centuries, it has been a private home as well as a grand hotel—one that exudes elegance from its stately pillared entrance to its crisp-linen sheets. **Pros:** luxurious accommodations; great location on the main drag; first-rate concierge. **Cons:** sometimes stuffy atmosphere; lots of noise if your room is street-side; breakfast costs extra. *$ Rooms from: €420 ✉ Banchi di Sopra 85, Camollìa ☎ 0577/56011 🌐 collezione.starhotels.com 51 rooms No Meals.*

Hotel Santa Caterina

$$ | **B&B/INN** | The atmosphere here is welcoming, hospitable, and enthusiastic, and the staff goes out of their way to ensure a fine stay; rooms in the back look out onto the lush grounds or the countryside in the distance. **Pros:** friendly staff; a short walk to center of town; breakfast in the garden. **Cons:** on a busy intersection; outside city walls; 15-minute (easy) walk into the historic center. *$ Rooms from: €200 ✉ Via Piccolomini 7, San Martino ☎ 0577/221105 🌐 www.hotelsantacaterinasiena.com 22 rooms Free Breakfast.*

Palazzo Ravizza

$ | **HOTEL** | Exuding the charm of a bygone era, this palazzo has guest rooms featuring high ceilings and antique furnishings, as well as bathrooms decorated with hand-painted tiles. **Pros:** 10-minute walk to the center of town; pleasant garden with a view beyond the city walls; professional staff. **Cons:** not all rooms have views; some rooms are a little cramped; somewhat removed from the center of things. *$ Rooms from: €150 ✉ Pian dei Mantellini 34, Città ☎ 0577/280462 🌐 www.palazzoravizza.it 41 rooms Free Breakfast.*

Arezzo

63 km (39 miles) northeast of Siena, 81 km (50 miles) southeast of Florence.

Arezzo is best known for the magnificent Piero della Francesca frescoes in the church of San Francesco. It's also the birthplace of the poet Petrarch (1304–74), the Renaissance artist and art historian Giorgio Vasari, and Guido d'Arezzo (aka Guido Monaco), the inventor of contemporary musical notation. Arezzo dates from pre-Etruscan times, when around 1000 BC the first settlers erected a cluster of huts. Arezzo thrived as an Etruscan capital from the 7th to the 4th century BC, and was one of the most important cities in the Etruscans' anti-Roman 12-city federation, resisting Rome's rule to the last.

The city eventually fell and in turn flourished under the Romans. In 1248 Guglielmino degli Ubertini, a member of the powerful Ghibelline family, was elected bishop of Arezzo. This sent the city headlong into the enduring conflict between the Ghibellines (pro-emperor) and the Guelphs (pro-pope). In 1289 Florentine Guelphs defeated Arezzo in a famous battle at Campaldino. Among the Florentine soldiers was Dante Alighieri (1265–1321), who often referred to Arezzo in his *Divine Comedy*. Guelph–Ghibelline wars continued to plague Arezzo until the end of the 14th century, when Arezzo lost its independence to Florence.

GETTING HERE AND AROUND

Arezzo is easily reached by car from the A1, the main highway running between Florence and Rome. Direct trains connect Arezzo with Rome (2½ hours) and Florence (1 hour). Direct bus service is available from Florence but not from Rome.

VISITOR INFORMATION

CONTACT Arezzo Tourism Office. ✉ *Via Giorgio Vasari, 13, Arezzo* ☎ *0575/377468* 🌐 *www.discoverarezzo.com.*

Sights

★ Basilica di San Francesco

CHURCH | The famous Piero della Francesca frescoes depicting *The Legend of the True Cross* (1452–66) were executed on the three walls of the Capella Bacci, the apse of this 14th-century church. What Sir Kenneth Clark called "the most perfect morning light in all Renaissance painting" may be seen in the lowest section of the right wall, where the troops of Emperor Maxentius flee before the sign of the cross. Reservations are required and can be made online. ✉ *Piazza San Francesco 2, Arezzo* ☎ *0575/1696256* 🌐 *www.museiarezzo.it* 🎫 *€9* 🕒 *Closed Wed. and Sun. morning.*

Duomo

CHURCH | Arezzo's medieval cathedral at the top of the hill contains a fresco of a tender *Maria Maddalena* by Piero della Francesca (1420–92); look for it in the north aisle next to the large marble tomb near the organ. Construction of the Duomo began in 1278 but twice came to a halt, and the church wasn't completed until 1510. The ceiling decorations and the stained-glass windows date from the 16th century. The facade, designed by Arezzo's Dante Viviani, was added later (1901–14). ✉ *Piazza del Duomo 1, Arezzo* ☎ *0575/377468* 🌐 *www.discoverarezzo.com.*

Museo Archeologico

HISTORY MUSEUM | FAMILY | The Archaeological Museum in the Convento di San Bernardo, just outside the Anfiteatro Romano, exhibits a fine collection of Etruscan bronzes. The ticket allows admission to the Anfiteatro Romano. ✉ *Via Margaritone 10, Arezzo* ☎ *0575/1696266* 🌐 *www.museiarezzo.it* 🎫 *€9* 🕒 *Closed Sun. after 2 pm.*

Piazza Grande

PLAZA/SQUARE | FAMILY | With its irregular shape and sloping brick pavement, framed by buildings of assorted centuries, Arezzo's central piazza echoes Siena's Piazza del Campo. Though not quite so magnificent, it's lively enough during the outdoor antiques fair the first weekend of the month and when the Giostra del Saracino (Saracen Joust), featuring medieval costumes and competition, is held here on the third Saturday of June and on the first Sunday of September. ✉ *Piazza Grande, Arezzo* ☎ *0575/377468* 🌐 *www.discoverarezzo.com.*

Santa Maria della Pieve (*Church of Saint Mary of the Parish*)

CHURCH | The curving, tiered apse on Piazza Grande belongs to a church that was originally an early Christian structure—itself constructed over the remains of a Roman temple. The church was rebuilt in Romanesque style in the 12th century. The splendid facade dates from the early 13th century but includes granite Roman columns. A magnificent polyptych, depicting the Madonna and Child with four saints, by Pietro Lorenzetti (circa 1290–1348), embellishes the high altar. ✉ *Corso Italia 7, Arezzo* ☎ *0575/377468* 🌐 *www.discoverarezzo.com.*

Restaurants

Il Grottino

$ | ITALIAN | FAMILY | It's small, but the very cheery staff is only too happy to provide you with wonderful plates of typical Tuscan food. The kitchen stays open a little bit later than most, which makes this a perfect stop after seeing some of the amazing art that Arezzo has to offer. **Known for:** delicious soups; surprisingly well-composed mixed salads; inventive desserts. $ *Average main: €16* ✉ *Via della Madonna del Prato 1, Arezzo* ☎ *0575/302537* 🌐 *www.facebook.com/ilgrottinoarezzo.*

Hotels

★ Castello di Gargonza

$$ | HOTEL | FAMILY | Enchantment reigns at this tiny 13th-century countryside hamlet, part of the fiefdom of the aristocratic Florentine Guicciardini family and reinvented by the modern Count Roberto Guicciardini. **Pros:** romantic, one-of-a-kind accommodation in a medieval castle; peaceful, isolated setting; on-site restaurant. **Cons:** standard rooms are extremely basic; a little out of the way for exploring the region; private transportation is a necessity. *Rooms from: €250 ✉ SR73, Località Gargonza, Monte San Savino ✣ 32 km (19 miles) southwest of Arezzo ☎ 0575/847021 ⊕ www.gargonza.it ⏲ Closed 2nd wk of Jan.–Mar. 47 rooms Free Breakfast.*

★ Il Borro

$$$$ | HOTEL | The location has been described as "heaven on earth," and a stay at this elegant Ferragamo estate—situated near a medieval village and with accommodations that include a 10-bedroom villa (rented out as a single unit) that was once a luxurious hunting lodge—is sure to bring similar descriptions to mind. **Pros:** exceptional service; great location for exploring eastern Tuscany; unique setting and atmosphere. **Cons:** off the beaten track, making private transport a must; not all suites have country views; very expensive. *Rooms from: €880 ✉ Località Il Borro 1 ✣ Outside village of San Giustino Valdarno, 20 km (12 miles) northwest of Arezzo ☎ 055/977053 ⊕ www.ilborro.it ⏲ Closed Dec.–Mar. 61 rooms Free Breakfast.*

Shopping

Ever since Etruscan goldsmiths set up their shops here more than 2,000 years ago, Arezzo has been famous for its jewelry. Today the town lays claim to being one of the world's capitals of jewelry design and manufacture, and you can find an impressive display of big-time baubles in the town center's shops.

Arezzo is also famous, at least in Italy, for its antiques dealers. The first weekend of every month, between 8:30 and 5:30, a popular and colorful flea market selling antiques and not-so-antique items takes place in the town's main square, Piazza Grande, and in the streets and parks nearby.

Cortona

29 km (18 miles) south of Arezzo, 79 km (44 miles) east of Siena, 117 km (73 miles) southeast of Florence.

Brought into the limelight by Frances Mayes's book *Under the Tuscan Sun* and a subsequent movie, Cortona is no longer the destination of just a few specialist art historians and those seeking reprieve from busier tourist venues. The main street, Via Nazionale, is now lined with souvenir shops and fills with crowds during summer. Although the main sights of Cortona make braving the bustling center worthwhile, much of the town's charm lies in its maze of quiet backstreets. It's here that you will see laundry hanging from windows, find children playing, and catch the smell of simmering pasta sauce. Wander off the beaten track and you won't be disappointed.

GETTING HERE AND AROUND

Cortona is easily reached by car from the A1 autostrada: take the Valdichiana exit toward Perugia, then follow signs for Cortona. Regular bus service, provided by Autolinee Toscane, is available between Arezzo and Cortona (one hour). Train service to Cortona is made inconvenient by the location of the train station, in the valley 3 km (2 miles) steeply below the town itself. From there, you have to rely on bus or taxi service to get up to Cortona.

VISITOR INFORMATION

CONTACT Cortona Tourism Office. *Piazza Signorelli 9, Cortona* *0575/637274* *www.comunedicortona.it.*

Sights

Museo Diocesano

ART MUSEUM | Housed in part of the original cathedral structure, this nine-room museum has an impressive number of large, splendid paintings by native son Luca Signorelli (1445–1523), as well as a delightful *Annunciation* by Fra Angelico (1387/1400–55). The church was built between 1498 and 1505 and restructured by Giorgio Vasari in 1543. Frescoes depicting sacrifices from the Old Testament by Doceno (1508–56), based on designs by Vasari, line the walls. *Piazza Duomo 1, Cortona* *0575/286300* *www.cortonatuseibellezza.it* *€6* *Closed Mon.–Thurs. Nov.–Mar.*

Santa Maria al Calcinaio

CHURCH | Legend has it that an image of the Madonna appeared on a wall of a medieval *calcinaio* (lime pit used for curing leather), the site on which the church was then built between 1485 and 1513. The linear gray-and-white interior recalls Florence's Duomo. Sienese architect Francesco di Giorgio (1439–1502) most likely designed the sanctuary: the church is a terrific example of Renaissance architectural principles. *Località Il Calcinaio 227, Cortona* *3 km (2 miles) southeast of Cortona's center* *3291605624 mobile* *www.calcinaio.it.*

Restaurants

Osteria del Teatro

$$ | TUSCAN | Photographs from theatrical productions spanning many years line the walls of this tavern off Cortona's large Piazza del Teatro. The food is simply delicious—try the *filetto al lardo di colonnata e prugne* (beef cooked with bacon and prunes); service is warm and friendly. **Known for:** food that's in season; lively atmosphere; pretty dining room. *Average main: €20* *Via Maffei 2, Cortona* *0575/630556* *osteria-del-teatro.com* *Closed Wed. and 2 wks in Nov.*

Hotels

★ Il Falconiere

$$$ | B&B/INN | Options at this sumptuous lodging include rooms and suites in an 18th-century villa, or, for more seclusion, private suites and villas at the far end of the property. **Pros:** attractive setting in the valley beneath Cortona; excellent service; elegant, but relaxed. **Cons:** a car is a must; some find rooms in main villa a little noisy; might be too isolated for some. *Rooms from: €520* *Località San Martino 370, Cortona* *3 km (2 miles) north of Cortona* *0575/612679* *www.ilfalconiere.it* *Closed Nov.–Jan.* *33 rooms* *Free Breakfast.*

Montepulciano

610 km (6 miles) northeast of Chianciano Terme, 65 km (40 miles) southeast of Siena, 114 km (70 miles) southeast of Florence.

Perched on a hilltop, Montepulciano is made up of a pyramid of redbrick buildings set within a circle of cypress trees. At an altitude of almost 2,000 feet, it is cool in summer and chilled in winter by biting winds sweeping down its spiraling streets. The town has an unusually harmonious look, the result of the work of three architects: Antonio da Sangallo "il Vecchio" (circa 1455–1534), Vignola (1507–73), and Michelozzo (1396–1472). The group endowed it with fine palaces and churches in an attempt to impose Renaissance architectural ideals on an ancient Tuscan hill town.

GETTING HERE AND AROUND

From Rome or Florence, take the Chiusi–Chianciano exit from the A1 (Autostrada del Sole). From Siena, take the SR2 south

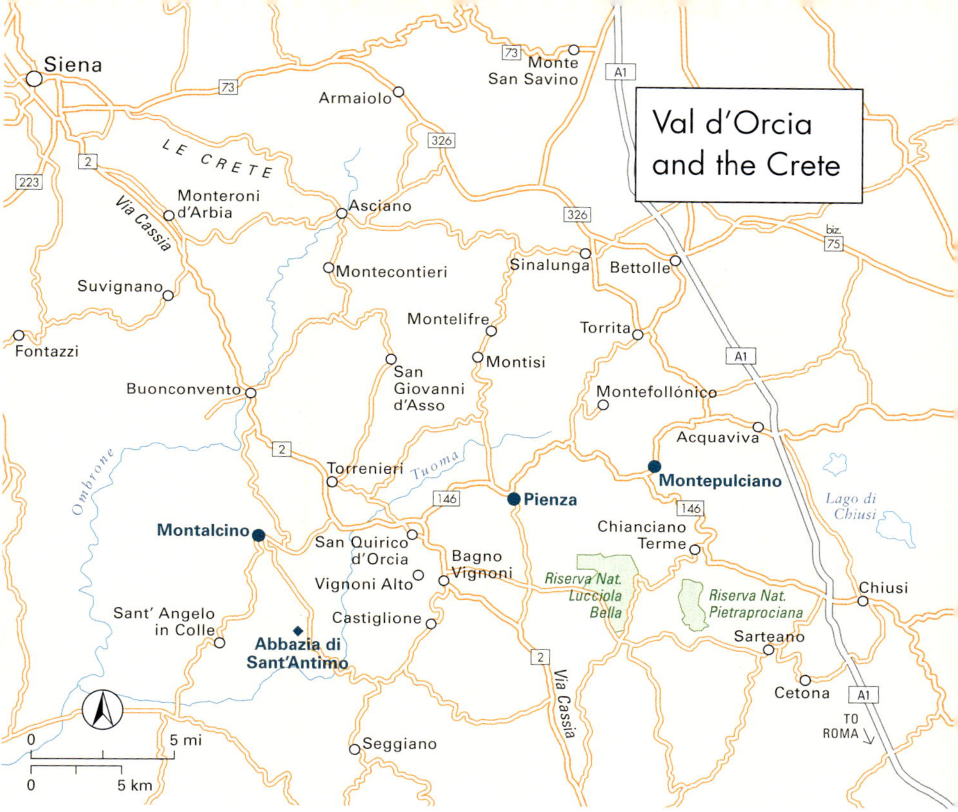

Val d'Orcia and the Crete

to San Quirico and then the SP146 to Montepulciano. Autolinee Toscane offers bus service from Siena to Montepulciano several times a day. Montepulciano's train station is in Montepulciano Stazione, 10 km (6 miles) away.

VISITOR INFORMATION

CONTACT Montepulciano Tourism Office. ✉ *Piazza Don Minzoni 1, Montepulciano* ☎ *0578/757341* 🌐 *www.prolocomontepulciano.it.*

Sights

Duomo

CHURCH | The unfinished facade of Montepulciano's cathedral doesn't measure up to the beauty of its neighboring palaces. On the inside, however, its Renaissance roots shine through. The high altar has a splendid triptych painted in 1401 by Taddeo di Bartolo (circa 1362–1422), and you can see fragments of the tomb of Bartolomeo Aragazzi, secretary to Pope Martin V, that was sculpted by Michelozzo between 1427 and 1436. ✉ *Piazza Grande, Montepulciano* ☎ *0578/71951.*

Piazza Grande

PLAZA/SQUARE | Filled with handsome buildings, this large square on the heights of the old historic town is Montepulciano's pièce de résistance. ✉ *Piazza Grande, Montepulciano.*

★ San Biagio

CHURCH | Designed by Antonio da Sangallo il Vecchio, and considered his masterpiece, this church sits on the hillside below the town walls and is a model of High Renaissance architectural perfection. Inside is a painting of the Madonna that, according to legend, was the only thing remaining in an abandoned church that two young girls entered on April 23, 1518. The girls saw the eyes of the Madonna moving, and that same afternoon so did a farmer and a cow, who knelt down in front of the painting. In 1963, the image was proclaimed the *Madonna del Buon Viaggio* (Madonna of the Good Journey), the protector of tourists in Italy. ✉ *Via di San Biagio, Montepulciano* ☎ *0578/286300* 🌐 *www.tempiosanbiagio.it* 🎫 *€4.50.*

Restaurants

Le Logge del Vignola

$$ | ITALIAN | In this small and cozy dining room, owner and sommelier Massimo Stella, his daughter Virginia, and chef Carlo Gutierrez bring fine dining flair to traditional Tuscan dishes like handmade pici pasta with black garlic and potato gnocchi. The wine list, which has many options by the glass, focuses on regional favorites. **Known for:** attentive service; well-curated wine list; elegant desserts. $ *Average main: €24* ✉ *Via delle Erbe 6, Montepulciano* ☎ *0578/717290* 🌐 *www.leloggedelvignola.com* ⏲ *Closed Tues. No lunch Wed.*

★ Osteria del Conte

$ | ITALIAN | As high in Montepulciano as you can get, just behind the Duomo, this small and intimate restaurant is expertly run by the mother-and-son team of Lorena and Paolo Brachi. Passionate about the food they prepare, both have a flair for the region's traditional dishes—the *pici all'aglione* (pasta with garlic sauce) and the *filetto ai funghi porcini* (steak with porcini mushrooms) are mouthwateringly good. **Known for:** fine home cooking; good local wines; attentive service. $ *Average main: €16* ✉ *Via di San Donato 19, Montepulciano* ☎ *0578/756062* 🌐 *www.osteriadelconte.it* ⏲ *Closed Mon. No dinner Sun.*

Hotels

La Terrazza

$ | B&B/INN | FAMILY | On a quiet street in the upper part of town, these unpretentious lodgings are given sparkle by the welcoming and friendly service of the owners, Roberto and Vittoria Giardinelli. **Pros:** family-friendly atmosphere; quiet central location; great value for money. **Cons:** no air-conditioning; no night porter; books up quickly. $ *Rooms from: €110* ✉ *Via del Piè al Sasso 16, Montepulciano* ☎ *0578/757440* 🌐 *www.laterrazzadi-montepulciano.it* *14 rooms* 🍽 *Free Breakfast.*

Pienza

12 km (7 miles) west of Montepulciano, 52 km (31 miles) southeast of Siena, 120 km (72 miles) southeast of Florence.

Pienza owes its appearance to Pope Pius II (1405–64), who had grand plans to transform his hometown of Corsignano—its former name—into a compact model Renaissance town. The man entrusted with the transformation was Bernardo Rossellino (1409–64), a protégé of the great Renaissance architectural theorist Leon Battista Alberti (1404–72). His mandate was to create a cathedral, a papal palace, and a town hall that adhered to the vainglorious pope's principles. Gothic and Renaissance styles were fused, and the buildings were decorated with Sienese paintings. The net result was a project that expressed Renaissance ideals of art, architecture, and civilized good living in a single scheme: it stands as an exquisite example of the architectural canons that Alberti formulated in the early Renaissance and that were utilized by later architects, including Michelangelo, in designing many of Italy's finest buildings and piazzas. Today the cool nobility of Pienza's center seems almost surreal in this otherwise unpretentious village, renowned for its smooth sheep's-milk pecorino cheese.

GETTING HERE AND AROUND

From Siena, drive south along the SR2 to San Quirico d'Orcia and then take the SP146. The trip should take just over an hour. Autolinee Toscane buses travel from Siena to Pienza with a change in Buonconvento. There is no train service to Pienza.

VISITOR INFORMATION

CONTACT Pienza Tourism Office. ✉ *Corso il Rossellino, Pienza* ☎ *0578/749905* 🌐 *comune.pienza.si.it/vivere-pienza/ufficio-turistico.*

Sights

Duomo

CHURCH | This 15th-century cathedral was built by the architect Bernardo Rossellino (1409–64) under the influence of Leon Battista Alberti. The travertine facade is divided into three parts, with Renaissance arches under the pope's coat of arms encircled by a wreath of fruit. Inside, the cathedral is simple but richly decorated with Sienese paintings. The building's perfection didn't last long—the first cracks appeared immediately after it was completed, and its foundations have shifted slightly ever since as rain erodes the hillside behind. You can see this effect if you look closely at the base of the first pier as you enter the church and compare it with the last. ✉ *Piazza Pio II, Pienza* ☎ *0578/286300* 🌐 *www.pienzacittadiluce.it/duomo.*

Museo Diocesano

ART MUSEUM | This museum, which sits to the left of Pienza's Duomo, is small but has a few interesting papal treasures and rich Flemish tapestries. The most precious piece is a rare mantle that belonged to Pope Pius II: it's woven in gold and embellished with pearls and embroidered religious scenes. ✉ *Corso Il Rossellino 30, Pienza* ☎ *0578/749905* 🌐 *www.pienzacittadiluce.it* 🎟 *€8 or €13 with Palazzo Piccolomini, Duomo and its crypt* ⏲ *Closed Tues.*

Palazzo Piccolomini

CASTLE/PALACE | In 1459, Pius II commissioned Bernardo Rossellino to design the perfect palazzo for his papal court. The architect took Florence's Palazzo Rucellai by Alberti as a model and designed this 100-room palace. Three sides of the building fit perfectly into the urban plan around it, while the fourth, looking over the valley, has a lovely loggia uniting it with the gardens in back. Guided tours departing every 30 minutes take you to the papal apartments, including a beautiful library, the Sala delle Armi (with an impressive weapons collection), and the music room, with its extravagant wooden ceiling forming four letter Ps, for Pope, Pius, Piccolomini, and Pienza. The last tour departs 30 minutes before closing. ✉ *Piazza Pio II, Pienza* ☎ *0577/286300* 🌐 *www.palazzopiccolominipienza.it* 🎟 *€8 or €13 including Museo Diocesano, Duomo, and its crypt* ⏲ *Closed Tues., early Jan.–mid-Feb., and mid-Nov.–late Nov.*

Restaurants

★ Osteria Sette di Vino

$ | TUSCAN | Tasty dishes based on the region's cheeses are the specialty at this simple osteria on a quiet, pleasant, central square. Try versions of pici or the starter of radicchio baked quickly to brown the edges. **Known for:** pecorino tasting menu; bean soup; awesome vegetable options. 💲 *Average main: €10* ✉ *Piazza di Spagna 1, Pienza* ☎ *0578/749092* ⏲ *Closed Wed., July 1–15, and Nov.*

Climb to the top of La Fortezza for the views and then slake your thirst in the on-site enoteca.

Montalcino

19 km (12 miles) northeast of Bagno Vignoni, 41 km (25½ miles) south of Siena, 109 km (68 miles) south of Florence.

Tiny Montalcino, with its commanding view from high on a hill, can claim an Etruscan past. It saw a fair number of travelers, as it was directly on the road from Siena to Rome. During the early Middle Ages it enjoyed a brief period of autonomy before falling under the orbit of Siena in 1201. Now Montalcino's greatest claim to fame is that it produces Brunello di Montalcino, one of Italy's most esteemed reds. Driving to the town, you pass through the brunello vineyards. You can sample the excellent but expensive red in wine cellars in town or visit a nearby winery, such as Fattoria dei Barbi, for a guided tour and tasting; you must email or call ahead for reservations.

GETTING HERE AND AROUND

By car, follow the SR2 south from Siena, then follow the SP45 to Montalcino. Autolinee Toscane buses travel between Siena and Montalcino daily with a change in Buonconvento. There is no train service available.

VISITOR INFORMATION

CONTACT Montalcino Tourism Office. ✉ *Via Ricasoli 31, Montalcino* ☎ *0577/846014* 🌐 *www.visitvaldorcia.it.*

Sights

★ La Fortezza

CASTLE/PALACE | FAMILY | Providing refuge for the last remnants of the Sienese army during the Florentine conquest of 1555, the battlements of this 14th-century fortress are still in excellent condition. Climb the narrow, spiral steps for the 360-degree view of most of southern Tuscany. An on-site enoteca serves delicious snacks that pair beautifully with the local wines. ✉ *Piazzale Fortezza, Montalcino* ☎ *0577/849221 enoteca* 🌐 *www.enotecalafortezza.com* 🎫 *Fortress free, walls €4, tastings from €25* 🕓 *Closed Mon. Nov.–Mar.*

Museo Civico e Diocesano d'Arte Sacra

ART MUSEUM | This fine museum is in a building that belonged to Augustinian friars in the 13th-century. The ticket booth is in the glorious refurbished cloister, and the sacred art collection, gathered from churches throughout the region, is displayed on two floors in former monastic quarters. Although the art here might be called B-list, a fine altarpiece by Bartolo di Fredi (circa 1330–1410), the *Coronation of the Virgin,* makes dazzling use of gold. In addition, there's a striking 12th-century crucifix that originally adorned the high altar of the church of Sant'Antimo. Also on hand are many wood sculptures, a typical medium in these parts during the Renaissance. ✉ *Via Ricasoli 31, Montalcino* ☎ *0577/286300* 🌐 *www.museisenesi.org* 🎫 *€10* 🕓 *Check the website for updated seasonal hrs.*

Restaurants

Il Grappolo Blu

$$ | ITALIAN | Any one of this restaurant's *piatti tipici* (typical plates) is worth trying, though the local specialty, pici all'aglione (thick, long noodles served with sautéed cherry tomatoes and many cloves of garlic), is done particularly well. The chef also has a deft touch with vegetables; if there's fennel on the menu, make sure to order it. **Known for:** great quality and price; kind, caring staff; convivial atmosphere. 💲 *Average main: €21* ✉ *Scale di Via Moglio 1, Montalcino* ☎ *0577/847150* 🌐 *www.grappoloblu.it* 🕓 *Closed Tues.*

Taverna dei Barbi

$ | TUSCAN | This rustic taverna with a large stone fireplace is amid vineyards that produce excellent Brunello—as well as its younger cousin, Rosso di Montalcino—a few minutes south of Montalcino, in the direction of Sant'Antimo. Many of the ingredients used in soup, gnocchi, bruschetta, and other traditional specialties are grown on the estate farm. **Known for:** heavenly aromas coming from grilled meat on a spit; fantastic wines; superb staff. 💲 *Average main: €15* ✉ *Podere Podernuovo 170, Montalcino* ☎ *0577/847143* 🌐 *www.fattoriadeibarbi.it* 🕓 *Closed weekends and Jan.–Mar.*

Hotels

★ **Rosewood Castiglion del Bosco**

$$$$ | RESORT | This estate, one of the largest still in private hands in Tuscany, was purchased at the beginning of this century and meticulously converted into a second-to-none resort that incorporates a medieval *borgo* (village) and surrounding farmhouses and has luxurious suites, as well as opulent three- to five-bedroom villas, each with its own pool. **Pros:** exclusive and tranquil location; breathtaking scenery; acclaimed golf course. **Cons:** well off the beaten track, nearest town is 12 km (7½ miles) away; private transportation required; truly exorbitant prices. 💲 *Rooms from: €1,906* ✉ *Località Castiglion del Bosco, Montalcino* ☎ *0577/1913001* 🌐 *www.castigliondelbosco.com* 🕓 *Closed Jan. to mid-March* 🛏 *53 units* 🍴 *No Meals.*

Abbazia di Sant'Antimo

10 km (6 miles) south of Montalcino, 51 km (32 miles) south of Siena, 19 km (74 miles) south of Florence.

It's well worth your while to go out of your way to visit this 12th-century Romanesque abbey, as it's a gem of pale stone in the silvery green of an olive grove.

GETTING HERE AND AROUND

The Abbazia di Sant'Antimo, nestled below the town of Castelnuovo dell'Abate, is a 15-minute drive from Montalcino. Autolinee Toscane bus service is extremely limited, and the abbey cannot be reached by train.

Sights

★ Abbazia di Sant'Antimo

CHURCH | The exterior and interior sculpture of this Romanesque abbey, dating from the 12th century, is outstanding, particularly the nave capitals, a combination of French, Lombard, and even Spanish influences. The sacristy (seldom open) forms part of the primitive Carolingian church (founded in AD 781), its entrance flanked by 9th-century pilasters. The small vaulted crypt dates from the same period. ✉ *Localita' S. Antimo 222, Castelnuovo dell'Abate* ☎ *0577/286300* 🌐 *www.antimo.it* 🕑 *Closed for mass on Sun. and religious holidays until 11 am.*

Chapter 13

UMBRIA AND THE MARCHES

Updated by
Liz Humphreys

WELCOME TO UMBRIA AND THE MARCHES

TOP REASONS TO GO

★ **Palazzo Ducale, Urbino:** A visit here reveals more about the ideals of the Renaissance than a shelf of history books could.

★ **Assisi, shrine to St. Francis:** Recharge your soul in this rose-color hill town with a visit to the gentle saint's majestic basilica, adorned with great frescoes.

★ **Spoleto, Umbria's musical mecca:** Crowds descend and prices ascend here during summer's Festival dei Due Mondi, but Spoleto's hushed charm enchants year-round.

★ **Tantalizing truffles:** Are Umbria's celebrated "black diamonds" coveted for their pungent flavor, their rarity, or their power in the realm of romance?

★ **Orvieto's Duomo:** Arresting visions of heaven and hell on the facade and brilliant frescoes within make this Gothic cathedral a dazzler.

1 **Perugia.** Umbria's largest town, filled with university students.

2 **Assisi.** The fascinating city of St. Francis.

3 **Gubbio.** A medieval mountainous town in north Umbria.

4 **Deruta.** A 14th-century town famous for its ceramics.

5 **Spello.** A pretty hilltop town known for its art.

6 **Montefalco.** A wine town nicknamed "balcony over Umbria."

7 **Spoleto.** Come to see the Piazza del Duomo.

8 **The Valnerina.** Valley of the River Nera.

9 **Todi.** Considered Umbria's prettiest hill town.

10 **Orvieto.** Carved out of volcanic rock and known for its cathedral.

11 **Urbino.** See the Palazzo Ducale here.

12 **Loreto.** Home to the House of the Virgin Mary.

13 **Ascoli Piceno.** A major producer of fruit and olives in the region.

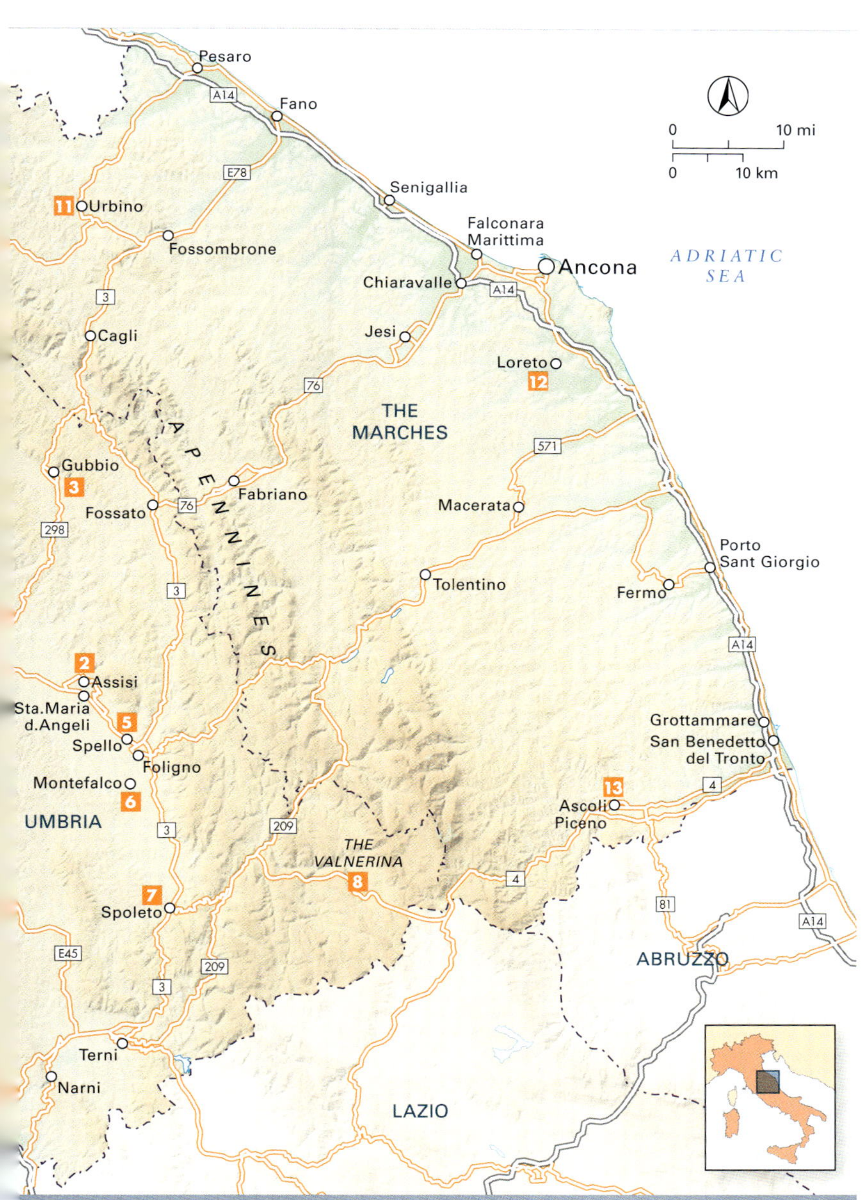
Pesaro
Fano
Senigallia
Falconara Marittima
Ancona
Chiaravalle
Jesi
Loreto
12
ADRIATIC SEA
0 10 mi
0 10 km
11 Urbino
Fossombrone
Cagli
APENNINES
THE MARCHES
Gubbio
3
Fossato
Fabriano
Macerata
Porto Sant Giorgio
Tolentino
Fermo
2
Assisi
Sta.Maria d.Angeli
5
Spello
Foligno
Montefalco
6
UMBRIA
Grottammare
San Benedetto del Tronto
13
Ascoli Piceno
THE VALNERINA
8
7
Spoleto
ABRUZZO
Terni
Narni
LAZIO
A14
E78
3
76
571
298
209
4
81
E45

EATING AND DRINKING WELL IN UMBRIA AND THE MARCHES

Porchetta (roasted pork)

Central Italy is mountainous, and its food is hearty and straightforward, with a stick-to-the-ribs quality that sees hardworking farmers and artisans through a long day's work and helps them make the steep climb home at night.

In restaurants here, as in much of Italy, you're rewarded for seeking out the local cuisines, and you'll often find better and cheaper food if you're willing to stray a few hundred yards from the main sights. Spoleto is noted for its good food and service, probably a result of high expectations from the international arts crowd. For gourmet food, however, it's hard to beat Montefalco and Bevagna, which have both excellent restaurants and first-rate wine merchants.

A rule of thumb for eating well throughout Umbria is to order what's in season; stroll through local markets to see what's for sale. Also, a number of restaurants in the region offer *degustazione* (tasting) menus that give you a chance to try different local specialties without breaking the bank.

TASTY TRUFFLES

More truffles are found in Umbria than anywhere else in Italy. Spoleto and Norcia are prime territory for the *tartufo nero* (reddish-black interior and fine white veins), prized for its extravagant flavor and intense aroma.

The mild summer truffle, *scorzone estivo* (black outside and beige inside), is in season from May through December. The *scorzone autunnale* (burnt brown color and visible veins inside) is found from October through December.

OLIVE OIL

Nearly everywhere you look in Umbria, olive trees grace the hillsides. The soil of the Apennines allows the olives to ripen slowly, guaranteeing low acidity, a cardinal virtue of fine oil. Look for restaurants that proudly display their own oil, often a sign that they care about their food.

Umbria's finest oil is found in Trevi, where the local product is intensely green and fruity. You can sample it in the town's wine bars, which often offer olive-oil tastings.

Green and black olives

PORK PRODUCTS

Much of traditional Umbrian cuisine revolves around pork. It can be cooked in wood-fired stoves, sometimes basted with a rich sauce made from innards and red wine. The roasted pork known as *porchetta* is grilled on a spit and flavored with fennel and herbs, leaving a crisp outer sheen.

In Norcia, the art of pork processing has been handed down through generations, so much so that charcuterie producers throughout Italy are often known as *norcini.* Don't miss *prosciutto di Norcia,* which is aged for two years.

LENTILS AND SOUPS

Throughout Umbria, look for *imbrecciata,* a soup of beans and grains, delicately flavored with local herbs. The town of Castelluccio di Norcia is particularly known for its lentils and its farro (a grain used by the Romans, similar to wheat), as well as for the variety of beans used in its soups. Other ingredients that find their way into thick Umbrian soups are wild beets, sorrel, mushrooms, spelt, chickpeas, and the elusive, fragrant saffron, grown in nearby Cascia.

Salad with spelt

WINE

Sagrantino grapes are the star in Umbria's most notable red wines. For centuries they've been used in Sagrantino *passito,* a semisweet wine made by leaving the grapes to dry for a period after picking to intensify their sugar content. In recent decades, Montefalco Sagrantino *secco* (dry) has occupied the front stage. Both passito and secco have a deep, ruby-red color, with a full body and rich flavor.

The abundance of *enotecas* (wineshops and wine bars) has made it easier to arrange tastings. Many establishments also let you sample different olive oils on toasted bread, known as bruschetta. Some wine information centers, such as La Strada del Sagrantino in the town of Montefalco, will help set up appointments for tastings.

Birthplace of saints and home to some of the country's greatest artistic treasures, central Italy is a collection of misty green valleys and picture-perfect hill towns laden with centuries of history.

Umbria and the Marches are the Italian countryside as you've imagined it: verdant farmland, steep hillsides topped with medieval fortresses, and winding country roads. Orvieto's cathedral and Assisi's basilica are two of the most important sights in Italy, while Perugia, Todi, Gubbio, and Spoleto are rich in art and architecture.

East of Umbria, the Marches (Le Marche to Italians) stretch between the Apennines and the Adriatic Sea. It's a region of great turreted castles on high peaks defending passes and roads—a testament to the centuries of battle that have taken place here. Rising majestically in Urbino is a splendid palace, while the town of Ascoli Piceno can lay claim to one of the most beautiful squares in Italy.

MAJOR REGIONS

Northern Umbria. Umbria's largest town, Perugia, is home to some of Perugino's great frescoes. Assisi, the city of St. Francis, is a major pilgrimage site that retains its medieval hill-town character. The quiet towns lying around Perugia include Deruta, which produces exceptional ceramics; Gubbio, a charming medieval town on the Monte Ingino slopes; Spello, a beautiful art-filled town with a mix of ancient frescoes, Roman ruins, and contemporary art; and Montefalco, known for its Sagrantino wine production, best sampled in its pretty square.

Southern Umbria. A massive castle towers over Spoleto, which is home to the Piazza del Duomo and Filippo Lippi frescoes in its cathedral. Of central Italy's many hill towns, none has a more impressive setting than Orvieto, perched on a plateau 1,000 feet above the surrounding valley. Nearby Todi also has a lovely central square, Piazza del Popolo, offering magnificent countryside views. Farther east, the Valnerina, on the Nera River, impresses with its forests and waterfalls, as well as Norcia's culinary treats of black truffles and pork.

The Marches. East of Umbria, the steep, twisting roads of this region lead to well-preserved medieval towns before settling down to the sandy beaches of the Adriatic. The main attraction is Urbino, the best surviving example of the ideal Renaissance city. Hilltop Loreto houses a major religious site, Santuario della Santa Casa (House of the Virgin Mary), while medieval Ascoli Piceno, near the Abruzzo border, has one of the most elegant piazzas in the country.

Planning

Festivals

If you want to attend an event, make arrangements in advance. During festival time, hotel rooms and restaurant tables are at a premium. A similar caveat applies for Assisi during religious festivals at Christmas, Easter, the feast of St. Francis (October 4), and Calendimaggio (May 1), when pilgrims arrive en masse.

★ **Eurochocolate Festival**

FESTIVALS | FAMILY | If you've got a sweet tooth and are visiting in fall, book early and head to Perugia for Europe's largest chocolate festival, held for 10 days in mid- to late November. ✉ *Piazza Moncada, Perugia* ☎ *075/5003848* 🌐 *www.eurochocolate.com.*

★ **Festival dei Due Mondi**

FESTIVALS | The annual event, held in late June and early July, is one of the most important cultural happenings in Europe, attracting big names in all branches of the arts, particularly music, opera, and theater. ✉ *Via Vaita Sant'Andrea, 10, Spoleto* ☎ *0743/69080* 🌐 *www.festivaldispoleto.com.*

★ **Umbria Jazz Festival**

FESTIVALS | One of the world's biggest jazz festivals attracts big names and big crowds to Perugia for 10 days in July, and to Orvieto for five days in December or January. ✉ *Piazza Danti, 28, Perugia* ☎ *075/5732432* 🌐 *www.umbriajazz.it.*

Getting Here and Around

BUS

Perugia's bus station is in Piazza Partigiani, which you can reach by taking the escalators from the town center.

Local bus services between all the major and minor towns of Umbria are good. Some of the routes in rural areas are designed to serve as many places as possible and are, therefore, quite roundabout and slow. Schedules change often, so consult with local tourist offices before setting out.

CAR

The steep hills and deep valleys that make Umbria and the Marches so idyllic also make for challenging driving. Fortunately, the area has an excellent, modern road network, but be prepared for tortuous roads if your explorations take you off the beaten track.

On the western edge of the region is the Umbrian section of the Autostrada del Sole (A1), Italy's principal north–south highway. It links Florence and Rome with Orvieto and passes near Todi and Terni. The SS3 intersects with the A1 and leads on to Assisi and Urbino. The Adriatica superhighway (A14) runs north–south along the coast, linking the Marches to Bologna and Venice.

Central Umbria is served by a major highway, the RA6, which passes along the shore of Lake Trasimeno and ends in Perugia. Assisi is served by the modern highway S75; the S75 connects to the S3 and S3bis, which cover the heart of the region. Major inland routes connect coastal A14 to large towns in the Marches, but inland secondary roads in mountain areas can be winding and narrow.

TRAIN

Several direct daily trains, run by the Italian state railway, Trenitalia, link Florence and Rome with Perugia and Assisi, and local service to the same area is available from Terontola (on the Rome–Florence line) and from Foligno (on the Rome–Ancona line).

Intercity trains between Rome and Florence make stops in Orvieto. The main Rome–Ancona line passes through Narni, Terni, Spoleto, and Foligno.

Hotels

Virtually every older town, no matter how small, has some kind of hotel. A trend, particularly around Gubbio, Orvieto, and Todi, is to convert old villas, farms, and monasteries into first-class hotels. The natural splendor of the countryside more than compensates for the distance from town—provided you have a car. Hotels in town tend to be simpler than their country cousins, with a few notable exceptions in Spoleto, Gubbio, and Perugia.

Making the Most of Your Time

Umbria is a nicely compact collection of character-rich hill towns; you can settle in one, then explore the others, as well as the countryside and forest in between, on day trips.

Perugia, Umbria's largest and liveliest city, is a logical choice for your base, particularly if you're arriving from the north. If you want something a little quieter, virtually any other town in the region will suit your purposes; even Assisi, which overflows with bus tours during the day, is delightfully quiet in the evening and early morning. Spoleto and Orvieto are the most developed towns to the south, but they're still of modest proportions. Charming Montefalco is a required stop for wine lovers.

If you have the time to venture farther afield, consider trips to Gubbio, northeast of Perugia, and Urbino, in the Marches. Both are worth the time it takes to reach them, and both make for pleasant overnight stays. In southern Umbria, Valnerina and the Piano Grande are out-of-the-way spots with the region's best hiking.

Restaurants

As befits a landlocked territory, the cuisine of Umbria is firmly based on local produce. Consequently, most restaurants in the region offer menus that are strictly seasonal, though locals have ensured that the food most associated with Umbria—*tartufi,* or truffles—is available year-round thanks to their mastery of freezing, drying, and preserving techniques.

Truffles are added to a variety of dishes, especially local pastas *stringozzi* (also written *strengozzi* or *strangozzi*) and *ombrichelli.* Lamb, pork, and boar are the most common meats consumed in Umbria, and lentils grown around Castelluccio are highly prized.

Seafood from the Adriatic predominates in the coastal Marches region, often made into *brodetto,* a savory fish soup. Inland, Ascoli Piceno is renowned for its stuffed green olives.

⇨ *Hotel and restaurant reviews have been shortened. For full information, visit Fodors.com. Prices in the hotel reviews are the lowest cost of a standard double room in high season. Prices in the dining reviews are the average cost of a main course at dinner, or, if dinner is not served, at lunch.*

What It Costs in Euros

$	$$	$$$	$$$$
RESTAURANTS			
under €20	€20–€30	€31–€40	over €40
HOTELS			
under €175	€175–€400	€401–€600	over €600

Visitor Information

CONTACT Umbria Regional Tourism Office. ✉ *Via Mario Angeloni 61, Perugia* ☎ *075/5681260* 🌐 *www.umbriatourism.it.*

Perugia

157 km (98 miles) southeast of Florence, 65 km (40 miles) east of Montepulciano.

Perugia is a majestic, handsome, wealthy city, and with its trendy boutiques, refined cafés, and grandiose architecture, it doesn't try to hide its affluence. A student population of around 30,000 means that the city, with a permanent population of about 165,000, is abuzz with activity throughout the year. Umbria Jazz, one of the region's most important music festivals, attracts music lovers from around the world every July, and Eurochocolate, the international chocolate festival, is an

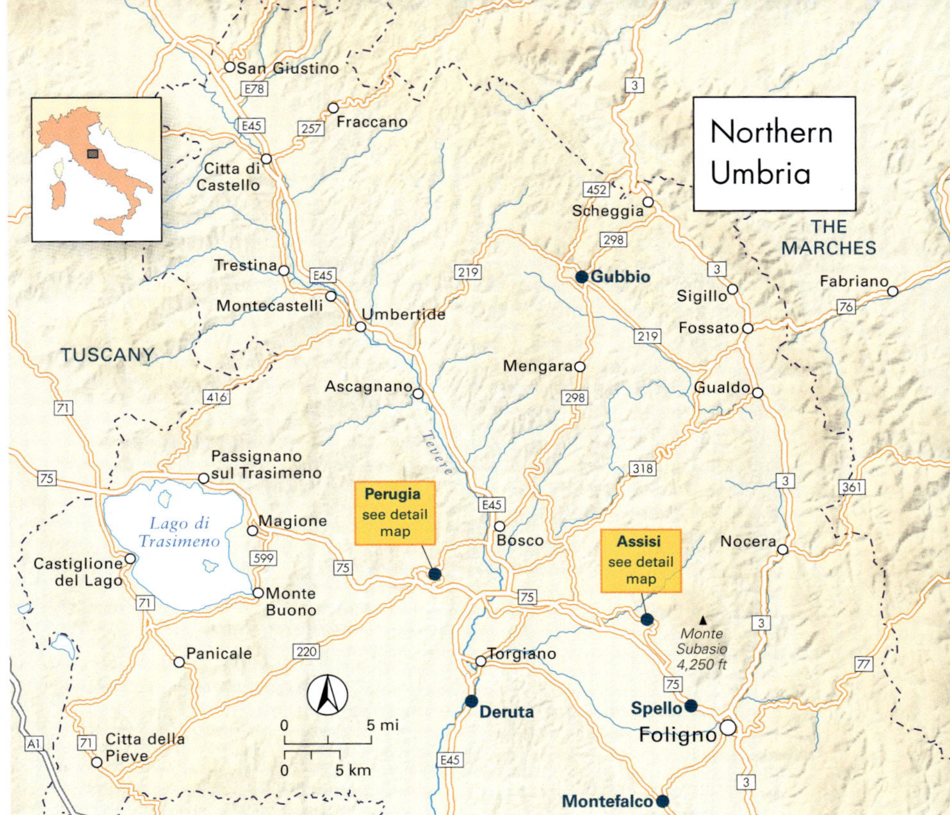

irresistible draw each October for anyone with a sweet tooth.

GETTING HERE AND AROUND

The best approach to the city is by train. The area around the station doesn't attest to the rest of Perugia's elegance, but buses running from the station to Piazza d'Italia, the heart of the old town, are frequent. If you're in a hurry, take the *minimetro,* a one-line subway, to Stazione della Cupa.

If you're driving to Perugia and your hotel doesn't have parking facilities, leave your car in one of the lots close to the center. Electronic displays indicate the location of lots and the number of available spaces. If you park in the Piazza Partigiani, take the escalators that pass through the fascinating subterranean excavations of the city's Roman foundations and lead to the town center.

Sights

Collegio del Cambio (*Bankers' Guild Hall*)
HISTORIC SIGHT | These elaborate rooms, on the ground floor of the Palazzo dei Priori, served as the meeting hall and chapel of the guild of bankers and money changers. Most of the frescoes were completed by the most important Perugian painter of the Renaissance, Pietro Vannucci, better known as Perugino. He included a remarkably honest self-portrait on one of the pilasters. The iconography includes common religious themes, such as the Nativity and the Transfiguration seen on the end walls. Booking a time for your visit in advance online or by phone is recommended. ✉ *Corso Vannucci 25, Perugia* ☎ *075/9372110* 🌐 *www.collegiodelcambio.it* 🎫 *€6* 🕑 *Closed Sun. and Mon. afternoon.*

Umbria Through the Ages

The earliest inhabitants of Umbria, the Umbri, were thought by the Romans to be the most ancient inhabitants of Italy. Little is known about them: with the coming of Etruscan culture, the tribe fled into the mountains in the eastern portion of the region. The Etruscans, who founded some of the great cities of Umbria, were in turn supplanted by the Romans. Unlike Tuscany and other regions of central Italy, Umbria had few powerful medieval families to exert control over the cities in the Middle Ages—its proximity to Rome ensured that it would always be more or less under papal domination.

In the center of the country, Umbria has, for much of its history, been a battlefield where armies from north and south clashed. Hannibal destroyed a Roman army on the shores of Lake Trasimeno, and the bloody course of the interminable Guelph–Ghibelline conflict of the Middle Ages was played out here. Dante considered Umbria the most violent place in Italy. Trophies of war still decorate the Palazzo dei Priori in Perugia, and the little town of Gubbio continues a warlike rivalry begun in the Middle Ages—every year it challenges the Tuscan town of Sansepolcro to a cross-bow tournament. Today the bowmen shoot at targets, but neither side has forgotten that 500 years ago they were shooting at each other.

In spite of—or perhaps because of—this bloodshed, Umbria has produced more than its share of Christian saints. The most famous is St. Francis, the decidedly pacifist saint whose life shaped the Church of his time. His great shrine at Assisi is visited by hundreds of thousands of pilgrims each year. St. Clare, his devoted follower, was Umbria-born, as were St. Benedict, St. Rita of Cascia, and the patron saint of lovers, St. Valentine.

Corso Vannucci

STREET | A string of elegantly connected palazzi expresses the artistic nature of this city center, the heart of which is concentrated along Corso Vannucci. Stately and broad, this pedestrian-only street runs from Piazza Italia to Piazza IV Novembre. Along the way, the entrances to many of Perugia's side streets might tempt you to wander off and explore. But don't stray too far as evening falls, when Corso Vannucci fills with Perugians out for their evening *passeggiata,* a pleasant predinner stroll that may include a pause for an aperitif at one of the many bars that line the street. ✉ *Perugia.*

Duomo (*Cathedral of San Lorenzo*)

CHURCH | Severe yet mystical, the Cathedral of San Lorenzo is most famous for being the home of the wedding ring of the Virgin Mary, stolen by the Perugians in 1488 from the nearby town of Chiusi. The ring, kept high up in a red-curtained vault in the chapel immediately to the left of the entrance, is stored under lock and key—15 locks, to be precise—most of the year. It's shown to the public on July 29 (the day it was brought to Perugia) and September 12. The cathedral itself dates from the Middle Ages, and has many additions from the 15th and 16th centuries. The museum displays historical artworks and treasures, plus don't miss walking the underground foundation layers, some of which date to the 7th century BC; book a timeslot online when you buy a ticket. ✉ *Piazza IV Novembre, Perugia* ☎ *075/5723832 cathedral, 075/5724853 museum and*

Underground Perugia 🌐 *isolasanlorenzo.it* 🎫 *Cathedral audio guide €4, museum €8, Underground Perugia tour €10, Cloister Pass (museum and Underground Perugia) €15, Isola Pass (museum, Underground Perugia, and cathedral audio guide) €18* 🕒 *Closed during religious services.*

★ Galleria Nazionale dell'Umbria

ART MUSEUM | The region's most comprehensive art gallery is housed on the fourth floor of the Palazzo dei Priori. The collection includes work by native artists—most notably Pintoricchio (1454–1513) and Perugino (circa 1450–1523). In addition to paintings, the gallery has frescoes, sculptures, and some superb examples of crucifixes from the 13th and 14th centuries. ✉ *Corso Vannucci 19, Piazza IV Novembre, Perugia* ☎ *075/5721009* 🌐 *gallerianazionaledellumbria.it* 🎫 *€10* 🕒 *Closed Mon. Nov.–June.*

Museo Archeologico Nazionale

HISTORY MUSEUM | An excellent collection of Etruscan artifacts from throughout the region sheds light on Perugia as a flourishing city long before it fell under Roman domination in 310 BC. Little else remains of Perugia's mysterious ancestors, although the Arco di Augusto, in Piazza Fortebraccio, the northern entrance to the city, is of Etruscan origin. ✉ *Piazza G. Bruno 10, Perugia* ☎ *075/5727141* 🌐 *www.musei.umbria.beniculturali.it* 🎫 *€5* 🕒 *Closed Mon. and 3rd Sun. of the month.*

Palazzo dei Priori (*Palace of the Priors*)

GOVERNMENT BUILDING | A series of elegant, connected buildings serves as Perugia's city hall and houses three museums. The buildings string along Corso Vannucci and wrap around the Piazza IV Novembre, where the original entrance is located. The steps here lead to the *Sala dei Notari* (Notaries' Hall). Other entrances lead to the Galleria Nazionale dell'Umbria, the Collegio del Cambio, and the Collegio della Mercanzia.

The Sala dei Notari, which dates from the 13th century and was the original meeting place of the town merchants, had become the seat of the notaries by the second half of the 15th century. Wooden beams and an array of interesting frescoes attributed to Maestro di Farneto embellish the room. ✉ *Piazza IV Novembre 25, Perugia* 🎫 *Free.*

Rocca Paolina

HISTORIC SIGHT | A labyrinth of little streets, alleys, and arches, this underground city was originally part of a fortress built at the behest of Pope Paul III between 1540 and 1543 to confirm papal dominion over the city. Parts of it were destroyed after the end of papal rule, but much still remains. Begin your visit by taking the escalators that descend through the subterranean ruins from Piazza Italia down to Via Masi. In summer, this is the coolest place in the city. ✉ *Piazza Italia, Perugia* 🎫 *Free.*

Restaurants

Antica Trattoria San Lorenzo Simone Ciccotti

$$$ | UMBRIAN | Both the food and the service are outstanding at this popular small, brick-vaulted eatery next to the Duomo. Particular attention is paid to adapting traditional Umbrian cuisine to the modern palate, and there's also a nice variety of seafood dishes on the menu, both à la carte and in good-value tasting menus—the *pacchero* (pasta with smoked eggplant, cod, and scampi) is a real treat. **Known for:** impeccable service; modernized versions of local recipes; fish and truffle tasting menus. $ *Average main: €35* ✉ *Piazza Danti 19/a, Perugia* ☎ *075/5721956* 🌐 *anticatrattoriasanlorenzo.com* 🕒 *Closed Tues. No lunch Wed., Thurs., and Sat.*

★ Civico 25

$ | UMBRIAN | You won't see many tourists inside this lively bistro-style eatery tucked into an alleyway of Perugia. But

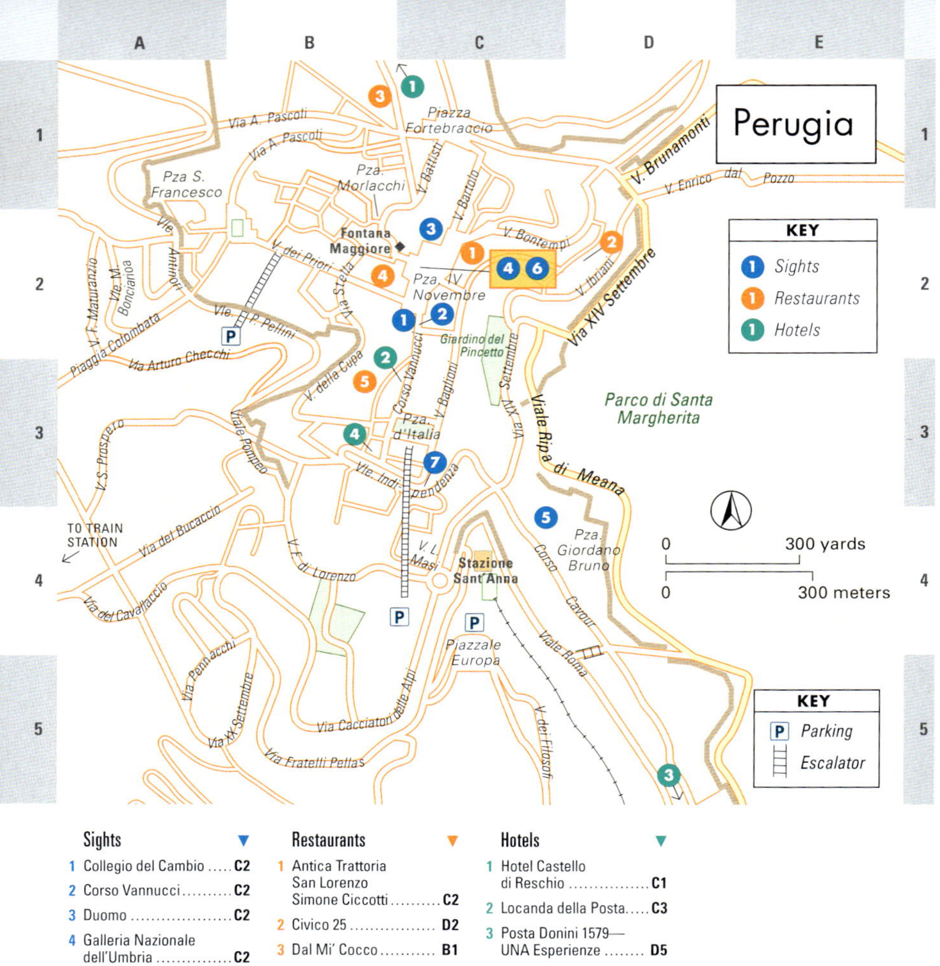

Sights

1 Collegio del Cambio **C2**
2 Corso Vannucci **C2**
3 Duomo **C2**
4 Galleria Nazionale dell'Umbria **C2**
5 Museo Archeologico Nazionale................. **C4**
6 Palazzo dei Priori **C2**
7 Rocca Paolina............ **C3**

Restaurants

1 Antica Trattoria San Lorenzo Simone Ciccotti.......... **C2**
2 Civico 25 .... **D2**
3 Dal Mi' Cocco **B1**
4 Osteria a Priori.......... **B2**
5 Ristorante La Taverna............... **B3**

Hotels

1 Hotel Castello di Reschio **C1**
2 Locanda della Posta..... **C3**
3 Posta Donini 1579— UNA Esperienze **D5**
4 Sina Brufani **B3**

you will find tasty Umbrian cuisine, such as Chianina beef tartare and strangozzi pasta, spruced up with an innovative flair and served with a fine choice of wines, including many made by natural producers. **Known for:** local dishes with a gourmet twist; extensive wine selection; friendly service. $ *Average main: €18* ✉ *Via della Viola 25, Perugia* ☏ *075/5716376* 🌐 *civico25.com* ⏲ *Closed Sun. No lunch.*

Dal Mi' Cocco

$ | **UMBRIAN** | Favored by Perugia's university students, this casual spot with vaulted ceilings is fun, crowded, and inexpensive. Fixed-price meals change with the season and include starters, pasta, a main meat course, and dessert; each day of the week brings some new creation *dal cocco* (from the "coconut," or head) of the chef. **Known for:** authentically casual feel; honest prices; abundant portions. $ *Average main: €18* ✉ *Corso Garibaldi 12, Perugia* ☏ *075/5732511* 🌐 *www.facebook.com/ristorantedalmicocco* ⏲ *Closed Mon. and late July–mid-Aug.*

★ Osteria a Priori

$ | **MODERN ITALIAN** | This charming wine-and-olive-oil shop with a restaurant (featuring vaulted ceilings and exposed brick) tucked into the back offers up small plates using ingredients with a "zero-kilometer" philosophy: everything comes from local and artisanal Umbrian producers. Regional cheeses, homemade pastas, and slow-cooked meats steal the show, and, as might be expected, the selection of wine is top-notch. **Known for:** all Umbrian products; knowledgeable servers; local, nontouristy atmosphere. $ *Average main: €15* ✉ *Via dei Priori 39, Perugia* ☏ *075/5727098* 🌐 *osteriaapriori.it* ⏲ *Closed Sun.*

Ristorante La Taverna

$$ | **UMBRIAN** | Medieval steps lead to a rustic two-story space where wine bottles and artful clutter decorate the walls. The regional menu features lots of delicious homemade pastas and grilled meats prepared by chef Claudio and served up in substantial portions, plus generous shavings of truffle in season. **Known for:** Umbrian specialties; swift and efficient service; welcoming ambience. $ *Average main: €25* ✉ *Via delle Streghe 8, off Corso Vannucci, Perugia* ☏ *075/5732536* 🌐 *www.ristorantelataverna.com.*

Hotels

★ Hotel Castello di Reschio

$$$$ | **RESORT** | Dating from 1050, this imposing castle-turned-hotel includes two restaurants, tennis courts, an equestrian center, a spa inspired by Roman baths, and exquisite guest rooms featuring beamed ceilings and bespoke furniture designed by the hotel's owners. **Pros:** truly a destination in itself; situated amid gorgeous landscapes; excellent food options. **Cons:** service is standoffish at times; incredibly expensive; room decor feels a bit cluttered. $ *Rooms from: €1,812* ✉ *34 km (21 miles) SE of Perugia, Tabaccaia di Reschio, Lisciano Niccone* ☏ *075/844362* 🌐 *www.reschio.com* ⏲ *Closed Jan.–mid-Mar.* *36 rooms* *Free Breakfast.*

★ Locanda della Posta

$$ | **HOTEL** | This friendly, centrally located, converted 18th-century palazzo off the bustling pedestrian-only Corso Vannucci features spacious rooms soothingly decorated in muted colors; some include original frescoes and beamed ceilings. **Pros:** some fine views; central location; exudes good taste and refinement. **Cons:** some street noise; no real lobby; no gym or spa. $ *Rooms from: €178* ✉ *Corso Vannucci 97, Perugia* ☏ *075/5728925* 🌐 *www.locandadellapostahotel.it* *17 rooms* *Free Breakfast.*

★ Posta Donini 1579 – UNA Esperienze

$ | **HOTEL** | **FAMILY** | Beguilingly comfortable guest rooms set on lovely grounds—where gardeners go quietly about their business—along with a small but charming spa and a well-regarded restaurant make this historical hotel south of Perugia worth a stay. **Pros:** plush atmosphere; a quiet and private getaway; great restaurant. **Cons:** outside Perugia; uninteresting village; parking area can get full. *Rooms from: €129 ✉ Via Deruta 43, San Martino in Campo ✥ 15 km (9 miles) south of Perugia ☎ 075/609132 🌐 www.postadonini.it 48 rooms Free Breakfast.*

Sina Brufani
$$ | HOTEL | Though a tad old-fashioned, this elegant, centrally located hotel dating from 1884 with a magnificent spa is the most upscale accommodation in town. **Pros:** wonderful location; unique spa area; excellent views from many rooms. **Cons:** could use a refresh; in-house restaurant not up to par; service can be hit-or-miss. *Rooms from: €181 ✉ Piazza Italia 12, Perugia ☎ 075/5732541 🌐 www.sinahotels.com 94 rooms Free Breakfast.*

Nightlife

With its large student population, the city has plenty to offer in the way of bars and clubs. The best ones are around the city center, off Corso Vannucci.

Bottega del Vino
WINE BAR | This cozy wine bar offers a large selection of *vino* from around Italy as well as light meals; you can't go wrong with the *antipasti* (appetizers), cheese platter, or bruschetta. A live jazz band plays on Wednesday night. *✉ Via del Sole 1, Perugia ☎ 075/5716181 🌐 www.facebook.com/labottegadelvinopg.*

★ Living Café
BARS | Get the best views in town from the large terrace of this café–bar, attached to Ristorante del Sole. It's the most scenic spot in town for aperitivo; happy hour starts daily at 7 pm. *✉ Via della Rupe 1, Perugia ☎ 075/5735031 🌐 www.ristorantesole.com.*

Marla
COCKTAIL BARS | This eclectic cocktail bar–art gallery showcases DJs and live music, including funk bands on Wednesday evenings. *✉ Via Bartolo 9/11, Perugia ☎ 0320/9728186 🌐 www.instagram.com/marlaperugia.*

Shopping

Stroll down any of Perugia's main streets, including Corso Vannucci, Via dei Priori, Via Oberdan, and Via Sant'Ercolano, and you'll see many well-known designer boutiques and specialty shops.

The most typical thing to buy is chocolate, which you can find almost anywhere. The best-known confections made by Perugina (now owned by Nestlé) are the chocolate-and-hazelnut-filled nibbles called Baci (literally, "kisses"). They're wrapped in silver foil that includes a sliver of paper, like the fortune in a fortune cookie, with multilingual romantic sentiments or sayings.

★ Chocostore by Eurochocolate
CHOCOLATE | FAMILY | The official store of the Eurochocolate festival sells bars, truffles, dipped fruits, and more chocolate goodies year-round. There's also a second store at Corso Vannucci 2, as well as a location devoted to Perugina products at Piazza IV Novembre 26/28. *✉ Piazza IV Novembre 7, Perugia ☎ 075/5732885 🌐 chocostore.eurochocolate.com.*

Perugina
CHOCOLATE | FAMILY | At Baci Perugina's original home, you'll find these iconic chocolates in all shapes and sizes, along with chocolate bars and candies. *✉ Corso Vannucci 101, Perugia ☎ 075/5736677 🌐 www.sweetcityperugia.it.*

Assisi

28 km (17 miles) southeast of Perugia.

The small town of Assisi is one of the Christian world's most important pilgrimage sites and home of the Basilica di San Francesco—built to honor St. Francis (1182–1226) and erected swiftly after his death. The peace and serenity of the town are a welcome respite from the hustle and bustle of Italy's major cities.

GETTING HERE AND AROUND

Assisi lies on the Terontola–Foligno rail line, with almost hourly connections to Perugia and direct trains to Rome and Florence several times a day. The Stazione Centrale is 4 km (2½ miles) from town, with a bus service about every half hour.

Assisi is easily reached from the A1/E35 autostrada (Rome–Florence) and the SS75 highway. The walled town is closed to traffic, so cars must be left in the parking lots at Porta San Pietro, near Porta Nuova, or beneath Piazza Matteotti. Pay your parking fee at the *cassa* (ticket booth) before you return to your car to get a ticket to insert in the machine that will allow you to exit. It's a short but sometimes steep walk into the center of town; frequent minibuses (buy tickets from a newsstand or tobacco shop near where you park your car) make the rounds for weary pilgrims.

Sights

Assisi is pristinely medieval in architecture and appearance, owing in large part to relative neglect from the 16th century until 1926, when the celebration of the 700th anniversary of St. Francis's death brought more than 2 million visitors. Since then, pilgrims have flocked here in droves, and today several million arrive each year to pay homage. The hill on which Assisi sits rises dramatically from the flat plain, and the town is dominated by a medieval castle at the very top.

★ Basilica di San Francesco

CHURCH | The basilica isn't one church but two: the Gothic church on the upper level, and the Romanesque church on the lower level. Work on this two-tiered monolith was begun in 1228. Both churches are magnificently decorated artistic treasure houses, covered floor to ceiling with some of Europe's finest frescoes: the Lower Basilica is dim and full of candlelight shadows, while the Upper Basilica is bright and airy.

In the Upper Church, the magnificent frescoes from 13th-century Italian painter Giotto, painted when he was only in his twenties, show that he was a pivotal artist in the development of Western painting. The Lower Church features frescoes by celebrated Sienese painters Simone Martini and Pietro Lorenzetti, as well as by Giotto (or his assistants). ✉ *Piazza di San Francesco, Assisi* ☎ *075/8190084* 🌐 *www.sanfrancescoassisi.org* 🎫 *Free.*

Basilica di Santa Chiara

CHURCH | The lovely, wide piazza in front of this church is reason enough to visit. The red-and-white-striped facade frames the piazza's panoramic view over the Umbrian plains. Santa Chiara is dedicated to St. Clare, one of the earliest and most fervent of St. Francis's followers and the founder of the order of the Poor Ladies—or Poor Clares—which was based on the Franciscan monastic order. The church contains Clare's body, and in the Cappella del Crocifisso (on the right) is the cross that spoke to St. Francis. A heavily veiled nun of the Poor Clares order is usually stationed before the cross in adoration of the image. ✉ *Piazza Santa Chiara, Assisi* ☎ *075/812216* 🌐 *www.assisisantachiara.it* 🎫 *Free.*

Cattedrale di San Rufino

CHURCH | St. Francis and St. Clare were among those baptized in Assisi's Cattedrale, which was the principal church in

Assisi
KEY
Sights
Restaurants
Hotels
Steps
Rocca Maggiore
Anfiteatro Romano
San Pietro
Pza. San Francesco
Pza. Unità d'Italia
Pza. San Pietro
Pza. d. Comune
Pza. San Rufino
Pza. Matteotti
Via Merry del Val
Via Santa Croce
Via del Colle
V. della Rocca
Via Metastasio
Via S. Francesco
Via S. Maria delle Rose
Via S. Paolo
Via Giotto
Via Portica
Via del Seminario
Via Fontebella
Via del Fosso Cupo
V. degli Ancajani
Via Borgo S. Pietro
Via Brizi
V. B. da Quintavalle
Via A. Cristofani
Via Rocchi
Via S. Antonio
Via S. Agnese
V. di San Rufino
V. Dono Doni
Via S. Gabriele
Corso Mazzini
Via Bovi
V. Santuario d. Carceri
Viale Umberto I
Via Galeazzo Alessi
Via Borgo Aretino
Viale Vittorio Emanuele II
Viale Vittorio Emanuele
Viale G. Marconi
S147
S444
TO SANTA MARIA DEGLI ANGELI AND TRAIN STATION
TO SAN DAMIANO
0
200 yards
0
200 meters
A
B
C
D
E
F
G
H
1
2
3
Sights
1 Basilica di San Francesco A1
2 Basilica di Santa Chiara F2
3 Cattedrale di San Rufino F2
4 Eremo delle Carceri H2
5 Santa Maria Sopra Minerva E2
Restaurants
1 Buca di San Francesco D2
2 Osteria Piazzetta dell'Erba E2
3 Ristorante Bar San Francesco B1
4 Trattoria Pallotta Assisi E2
Hotels
1 Borgo Castello Panicaglia G1
2 Hotel Umbra E2
3 Nun Assisi Relais & Spa Museum G1

town until the 12th century. The baptismal font has since been redecorated, but it's possible to see the crypt of St. Rufino, the bishop who brought Christianity to Assisi and was martyred on August 11, 238 AD (or 236 AD by some accounts), as well as climb to the bell tower. Admission to the crypt includes the small Museo della Cattedrale, with its detached frescoes and artifacts. ✉ *Piazza San Rufino, Assisi* ☎ *075/812712* 🌐 *www.assisimuseodiocesano.it* 🎫 *Church free, crypt and museum €4, bell tower and museum €5, bell tower €2* ⏲ *Museum closed Wed.*

Eremo delle Carceri

RELIGIOUS BUILDING | About 4 km (2½ miles) east of Assisi is a monastery set in a dense wood against Monte Subasio: the Hermitage of Prisons. This was the place where St. Francis and his followers went to "imprison" themselves in prayer. The only site in Assisi that remains essentially unchanged since St. Francis's time, the church and monastery are the kinds of tranquil places that St. Francis would have appreciated. The walk out from town is very pleasant, and many trails lead from here across the wooded hillside of Monte Subasio. ✉ *Via Eremo delle Carceri 38, Assisi* ✢ *4 km (2½ miles) east of Assisi* ☎ *075/812301* 🌐 *www.santuarioeremodellecarceri.org* 🎫 *Donations accepted.*

Santa Maria Sopra Minerva

CHURCH | Dating from the time of the Emperor Augustus (27 BC–AD 14), this structure was originally dedicated to the Roman goddess of wisdom, and in later times it was used as a monastery and prison before being converted into a church in the 16th century. The expectations raised by the perfect classical facade are not met by the interior, which was subjected to a thorough Baroque transformation in the 17th century. ✉ *Piazza del Comune 14, Assisi* ☎ *075/812361* 🎫 *Free.*

Restaurants

Buca di San Francesco

$ | UMBRIAN | In summer, dine in a cool green garden; in winter, under the low brick arches of the cozy cellars. The unique settings and the first-rate (though straightforward) fare make this central restaurant one of Assisi's busiest; try the namesake homemade spaghetti *alla buca*, served with a roasted mushroom sauce. **Known for:** cozy atmosphere; historical surroundings; warm and welcoming service. $ *Average main: €16* ✉ *Via Eugenio Brizi 1, Assisi* ☎ *075/812204* ⏲ *Closed Mon. and 10 days in late July.*

★ Osteria Piazzetta dell'Erba

$$ | UMBRIAN | Hip service and sophisticated presentations attract locals, who enjoy Italian cuisine with unusual twists (think porcini mushroom risotto with blue cheese and blueberries), a nice selection of salads—unusual for an Umbrian restaurant—plus sushi options and intriguing desserts. The enthusiastic young team keep things running smoothly and the energy high. **Known for:** friendly staff; inventive dishes; intimate ambience. $ *Average main: €22* ✉ *Via San Gabriele dell'Addolorata 15/b, Assisi* ☎ *075/815352* 🌐 *www.osteriapiazzetta-dellerba.it* ⏲ *Closed Mon. and a few wks in Jan. or Feb.*

Ristorante Bar San Francesco

$$ | UMBRIAN | An excellent view of the Basilica di San Francesco from the covered terrace is just one reason to patronize this traditional restaurant, where Umbrian dishes are made with aromatic locally grown herbs. Menus change seasonally and include a fine selection of pastas and mains; appetizers and desserts are also especially good. **Known for:** prime Assisi location; tasty seasonal dishes; pleasant staff. $ *Average main: €23* ✉ *Via di San Francesco 52, Assisi* ☎ *075/812329* 🌐 *www.ristorante-sanfrancesco.com.*

Trattoria Pallotta Assisi

$$ | UMBRIAN | At this homey, family-run trattoria with a crackling fireplace and stone walls, the women do the cooking and the men serve the food; try the *strangozzi alla pallotta* (thick spaghetti with a pesto of olives and mushrooms). Connected to the restaurant is an inn whose eight rooms have firm beds and some views across the rooftops of town. **Known for:** traditional local dishes; delicious meat plates, including pigeon and rabbit; fast and courteous service. *Average main: €22 Vicolo della Volta Pinta 3, Assisi 075/8155273 www.trattoriapallotta.it Closed Tues.*

Hotels

Advance reservations are essential at Assisi's hotels between Easter and October and over Christmas. Latecomers are often forced to stay in the modern town of Santa Maria degli Angeli, 8 km (5 miles) away. As a last-minute option, you can always inquire at restaurants to see if they're renting out rooms.

Until the early 1980s, pilgrim hostels outnumbered ordinary hotels in Assisi, and they present an intriguing and economical alternative to conventional lodgings. They're usually called *conventi* or *ostelli* ("convents" or "hostels") because they're run by convents, churches, or other Catholic organizations. Rooms are spartan but peaceful.

★ Borgo Castello Panicaglia

$$ | HOTEL | FAMILY | This small, rustic-chic hotel between Assisi and Gubbio, dating from 1266 but thoroughly modernized inside, is a relaxing base for exploring the pretty Umbrian countryside. **Pros:** modern amenities in a historical building; extremely family-friendly atmosphere; tasty and inventive meals. **Cons:** no spa; location is quite rural; need a car to get around the area. *Rooms from: €295 Località Panicaglia, Nocera 24 km (15 miles) northeast of Assisi 0742/81663 www.borgocastello-panicaglia.com 17 rooms Free Breakfast.*

Hotel Umbra

$ | HOTEL | Rooms on the upper floors of this charming 16th-century town house near Piazza del Comune look out over the Assisi rooftops to the valley below, as does the sunny, vine-covered terrace. **Pros:** very central; pleasant small garden; excellent valley views from some rooms. **Cons:** difficult parking; some small rooms; uninspiring breakfast. *Rooms from: €125 Via degli Archi 6, Assisi 075/812240 www.hotelumbra.it Closed Nov.–late Mar. 24 rooms Free Breakfast.*

★ Nun Assisi Relais & Spa Museum

$$$$ | HOTEL | Within walking distance of Assisi's restaurants and shops, this monastery built in 1275 has been converted into a thoroughly contemporary, high-end place to stay with a fabulous spa carved out of 2,000-year-old Roman baths. **Pros:** fantastic blend of the historical and modern; excellent restaurant; wonderful place to relax. **Cons:** on the expensive side; on-site parking costs extra; split-level rooms with stairs difficult for those with mobility issues. *Rooms from: €664 Via Eremo delle Carceri 1A, Assisi 075/8155150 www.nunassisi.com 18 rooms Free Breakfast.*

Gubbio

39 km (24 miles) northeast of Perugia, 92 km (57 miles) east of Arezzo.

There's something otherworldly about this jewel of a medieval town, tucked away on the slopes of Monte Ingino. Even in the height of summer, the so-called Città del Silenzio (City of Silence) stays comparatively cool, and its dramatically steep streets remain

Continued on page 610

ASSISI'S BASILICA DI SAN FRANCESCO

The legacy of St. Francis, founder of the Franciscan monastic order, pervades Assisi. Each year the town hosts several million pilgrims, but the steady flow of visitors does nothing to diminish the singular beauty of one of Italy's most important religious centers. The pilgrims' ultimate destination is the massive Basilica di San Francesco, which sits halfway up Assisi's hill, supported by graceful arches.

The basilica is not one church but two. The Romanesque Lower Church came first; construction began in 1228, just two years after St. Francis's death, and was completed within a few years. The low ceilings and candlelit interior make an appropriately solemn setting for St. Francis's tomb, found in the crypt below the main altar. The Gothic Upper Church, built only half a century later, sits on top of the lower one, and is strikingly different, with soaring arches and tall stained-glass windows (the first in Italy). Inside, both churches are covered floor to ceiling with some of Europe's finest frescoes: the Lower Church is dim and full of candlelit shadows, and the Upper Church is bright and airy.

VISITING THE BASILICA

THE LOWER CHURCH

The most evocative way to experience the basilica is to begin with the dark Lower Church. As you enter, give your eyes a moment to adjust. Keep in mind that the artists at work here were conscious of the shadowy environment—they knew this was how their frescoes would be seen.

In the first chapel to the left, a superb fresco cycle by Simone Martini depicts scenes from the life of St. Martin. As you approach the main altar, the vaulting above you is decorated with the *Three Virtues of St. Francis* (poverty, chastity, and obedience) and *St. Francis's Triumph*, frescoes attributed to Giotto's followers. In the transept to your left, Pietro Lorenzetti's *Madonna and Child with St. Francis and St. John* sparkles when the sun hits it. Notice Mary's thumb; legend has it Jesus is asking which saint to bless, and Mary is pointing to Francis. Across the way in the right transept, Cimabue's *Madonna Enthroned Among Angels and St. Francis* is a famous portrait of the saint. Surrounding the portrait are painted scenes from the childhood of Christ, done by the assistants of Giotto. Nearby is a painting of the crucifixion attributed to Giotto himself.

You reach the crypt via stairs midway along the nave—on the crypt's altar, a stone coffin holds the saint's body. Steps up from the transepts lead to the cloister, where there's a gift shop, and the treasury, which contains holy objects.

THE UPPER CHURCH

The St. Francis fresco cycle is the highlight of the Upper Church. *(See facing page.)* Also worth special note is the 16th-century choir, with its remarkably delicate inlaid wood. When a 1997 earthquake rocked the basilica, the St. Francis cycle sustained little damage, but portions of the ceiling above the entrance and altar collapsed, reducing their frescoes (attributed to Cimabue and Giotto) to rubble. The painstaking restoration of the Upper Church took two years. ⚠ The dress code is strictly enforced—no bare shoulders or bare knees.

FRANCIS, ITALY'S PATRON SAINT

St. Francis was born in Assisi in 1181, the son of a noblewoman and a well-to-do merchant. His troubled youth included a year in prison. He planned a military career, but after a long illness Francis heard the voice of God, renounced his father's wealth, and began a life of austerity. His mystical embrace of poverty, asceticism, and the beauty of man and nature struck a responsive chord in the medieval mind; he quickly attracted a vast number of followers. Francis was the first saint to receive the stigmata (wounds in his hands, feet, and side corresponding to those of Christ on the cross). He died on October 4, 1226, in the Porziuncola, the secluded chapel in the woods where he had first preached the virtue of poverty to his disciples. St. Francis was declared patron saint of Italy in 1939, and today the Franciscans make up the largest of the Catholic orders.

THE UPPER CHURCH'S ST. FRANCIS FRESCO CYCLE

The 28 frescoes in the Upper Church depicting the life of St. Francis are the most admired works in the entire basilica. They're also the subject of one of art history's biggest controversies. For centuries they were thought to be by Giotto (1267-1337), the great early Renaissance innovator, but inconsistencies in style, both within this series and in comparison to later Giotto works, have thrown their origin into question. Some scholars now say Giotto was the brains behind the cycle, but that assistants helped with the execution; others claim he couldn't have been involved at all.

Two things are certain. First, the style is revolutionary—which argues for Giotto's involvement. The tangible weight of the figures, the emotion they show, and the use of perspective all look familiar to modern eyes, but in the art of the time there was nothing like it. Second, these images have played a major part in shaping how the world sees St. Francis. In that respect, who painted them hardly matters.

Starting in the transept, the frescoes circle the church, showing events in the saint's life (and afterlife). Some of the best are grouped near the church's entrance—look for the nativity at Greccio, the miracle of the spring, the death of the knight at Celano, and, most famously, the sermon to the birds.

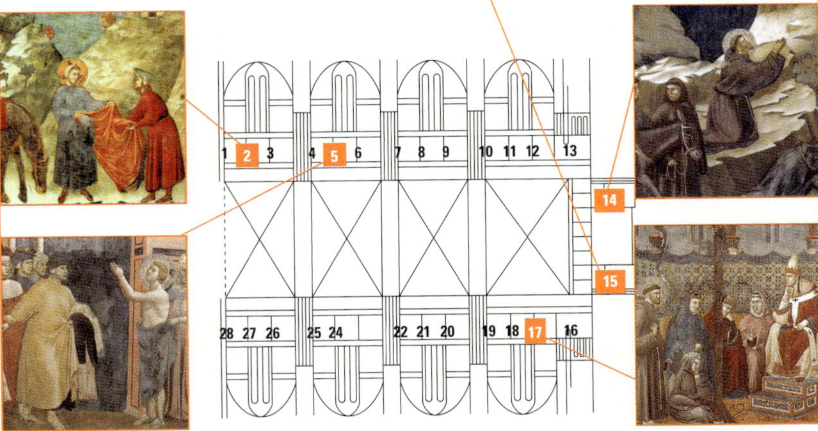

The St. Francis fresco cycle

1. Homage of a simple man
2. Giving cloak to a poor man
3. Dream of the palace
4. Hearing the voice of God
5. Rejection of worldly goods
6. Dream of Innocent III
7. Confirmation of the rules
8. Vision of flaming chariot
9. Vision of celestial thrones
10. Chasing devils from Arezzo
11. Before the sultan
12. *Ecstasy of St. Francis*
13. Nativity at Greccio
14. Miracle of the spring
15. Sermon to the birds
16. Death of knight at Celano
17. Preaching to Honorius III
18. Apparition at Arles
19. Receiving the stigmata
20. *Death of St. Francis*
21. Apparition before Bishop Guido and Fra Agostino
22. Verification of the stigmata
23. *Mourning of St. Clare*
24. Canonization
25. Apparition before Gregory IX
26. Healing of a devotee
27. Confession of a woman
28. Repentant heretic freed

relatively serene. At Christmas, kitsch is king. From December 7 to January 10, colored lights are strung down the mountainside in a shape resembling an evergreen, creating the world's largest Christmas tree.

Parking in the central Piazza dei Quaranta Martiri—named for 40 hostages murdered by the Nazis in 1944—is easy and secure. It's wise to leave your car there and explore the narrow streets on foot.

GETTING HERE AND AROUND

If you're driving from Perugia, take the SS318, which rises steeply up toward the Gubbio hills. The trip will take you 40 to 50 minutes. The closest train station is Fossato di Vico, about 20 km (12 miles) from Gubbio. Daily buses connect the train station with the city, a 30-minute trip. There are also many buses a day that leave from Perugia's Piazza Partigiani, the main Perugia bus terminal.

VISITOR INFORMATION

CONTACT Gubbio Tourism Office. ✉ *Via Repubblica 15, Gubbio* ☎ *075/9220693* 🌐 *www.ilikegubbio.com.*

Sights

Basilica di Sant'Ubaldo

CHURCH | Gubbio's famous *ceri*—three 16-foot-tall pillars crowned with statues of Saints Ubaldo, George, and Anthony—are housed in this basilica atop Monte Ingino. The pillars are transported to the Palazzo dei Consoli on the first Sunday of May, in preparation for the Festa dei Ceri, one of central Italy's most spectacular festivals. ✉ *Via Monte Ingino 5, Gubbio* ☎ *075/9273872* 🌐 *www.santubaldogubbio.it* 🎫 *Free.*

Duomo di Gubbio

CHURCH | Set on a narrow street on the highest tier of the town, the Duomo dates from the 13th century, with some Baroque additions—in particular, a lavishly decorated bishop's chapel. ✉ *Via Ducale, Gubbio* ☎ *075/922138* 🌐 *diocesigubbio.it* 🎫 *Free.*

Funivia Colle Eletto

TRANSPORTATION | FAMILY | For a bracing ride to the top of Monte Ingino (where you can see the Basilica di Sant'Ubaldo), hop on the funicular that climbs the hillside just outside the city walls at the eastern end of town. It's more like an oversize metal birdcage than a cable car, and it's definitely not for those who suffer from vertigo. Operating hours vary considerably from month to month; check the funicular's website. ✉ *Via San Girolamo, Gubbio* ☎ *075/9273881* 🌐 *www.funiviagubbio.it* 🎫 *€7 round-trip* ⏲ *Closed Wed. Nov.–Mar.*

Palazzo dei Consoli

HISTORY MUSEUM | Gubbio's striking Piazza Grande is dominated by this medieval palazzo, attributed to a local architect known as Gattapone, who is still much admired by today's residents (though some scholars have suggested that the palazzo was in fact the work of another architect, Angelo da Orvieto). In the Middle Ages, the Parliament of Gubbio assembled in the palace, which has become a symbol of the town and now houses a museum with a collection famous chiefly for the Tavole Eugubine—seven bronze tablets that are written in the ancient Umbrian language, employing Etruscan and Latin characters, and that provide the best key to understanding this obscure tongue.

Also in the museum is a fascinating miscellany of rare coins and earthenware pots. A lofty loggia provides exhilarating views over Gubbio's roofscape and beyond. For a few days at the beginning of May, the palace also displays the famous ceri, the ceremonial wooden pillars at the center of Gubbio's annual festivities. ✉ *Piazza Grande, Gubbio* ☎ *075/9274298* 🌐 *www.palazzodeiconsoli.it* 🎫 *€9.*

Palazzo Ducale

CASTLE/PALACE | This scaled-down copy of the Palazzo Ducale in Urbino (Gubbio was once the possession of that city's ruling family, the Montefeltro) contains a small museum and a courtyard. Some of the public rooms offer magnificent views. ✉ *Via Federico da Montefeltro 2, Gubbio* ☎ *075/9275872* 🌐 *www.facebook.com/palazzoducalegubbio* 🎟 *€5* ⏲ *Closed Mon. Nov.–Mar.*

Restaurants

Ristorante Grotta dell'Angelo
$$ | UMBRIAN | In summer, the handful of outdoor tables are in high demand at this rustic trattoria, which is situated in a hotel of the same name at the lower part of the old town near the main square. The menu features simple local specialties, including *capocollo* (a type of salami), *stringozzi* (Umbrian wheat pasta), and lasagna *tartufata* (with truffles). **Known for:** reasonable prices; good antipasti and grilled meats; homey atmosphere. $ *Average main: €15* ✉ *Via Gioia 47, Gubbio* ☎ *075/9271747* 🌐 *www.grottadellangelo.it* ⏲ *Closed Tues. and early Jan.–early Feb.*

★ **Taverna del Lupo**
$$ | UMBRIAN | One of the city's most famous taverns has a menu that includes such indulgences as lasagna made in the Gubbian fashion, with ham and truffles, and the *suprema di faraono* (guinea fowl in a delicately spiced sauce); save room for the excellent desserts. The restaurant also has two fine wine cellars and an extensive wine list. **Known for:** wide menu choice; alluring presentation; good wine list. $ *Average main: €25* ✉ *Via Ansidei 21, Gubbio* ☎ *075/9274368* 🌐 *www.tavernadellupo.it.*

Hotels

★ **Castello di Petroia**
$ | HOTEL | This atmospheric, 12th-century castle 15 km (9 miles) from Gubbio has spacious, antiques-filled, individually decorated rooms—some with decorated or beamed ceilings and stained glass, many with whirlpool tubs—as well as excellent in-house breakfasts and dinners. **Pros:** charming atmosphere; lovely breakfast buffet with handmade cakes and jams; seasonal outdoor swimming pool. **Cons:** decor is on the simple side; beds could be comfier; temperature can be difficult to regulate in guest rooms. $ *Rooms from: €160* ✉ *Località Petroia, Gubbio* ☎ *075/920287* 🌐 *www.petroia.it* ⏲ *Closed early Jan.–late Mar.* 🛏 *16 rooms* 🍽 *Free Breakfast.*

Hotel Bosone Palace
$ | HOTEL | A former palace is now home to an elegant, if faded, hotel, where elaborate frescoes grace the ceilings of the two enormous suites and delightful breakfast room. **Pros:** friendly welcome; excellent location; low rates. **Cons:** needs a refresh; rooms and bathrooms on the small side; can hear church bells ringing during the night. $ *Rooms from: €78* ✉ *Via XX Settembre 22, Gubbio* ☎ *075/9220688* 🌐 *www.hotelbosone.com* 🛏 *30 rooms* 🍽 *No Meals.*

★ **Vocabolo Moscatelli**
$$$ | HOTEL | Set inside a 12th-century monastery, this romantic boutique hotel is surrounded by greenery and filled with art. **Pros:** gorgeous outdoor pool; breakfast offered all day; supremely comfortable beds. **Cons:** no spa; only kids aged 14 and up allowed; a fair distance from restaurants and sights. $ *Rooms from: €495* ✉ *Via del Refari 2, Umbertide* ✥ *44 km (27 miles) west of Gubbio* ☎ *075/5455815* 🌐 *www.vocabolomoscatelli.com* ⏲ *Closed Dec. and mid-Jan.–mid-Apr.* 🛏 *12 rooms* 🍽 *Free Breakfast.*

Deruta

19 km (11 miles) southeast of Perugia, 60 km (37 miles) southwest of Gubbio.

This 14th-century hill town is most famous for its ceramics. A drive through the countryside to visit the workshops is a good way to spend a morning, but be sure to stop in the medieval town itself.

GETTING HERE AND AROUND

From Perugia, follow the directions for Rome and the E45 highway; Deruta has its own exits. There are also buses from Perugia that take about 30 minutes to reach Deruta.

VISITOR INFORMATION

CONTACT Deruta Tourism Office. ✉ *Via Biordo Michelotti 27, Deruta* ☏ *075/9728612* 🌐 *visitderuta.com.*

Sights

Museo Regionale della Ceramica (*Regional Ceramics Museum*)
HISTORY MUSEUM | It's only fitting that Deruta is home to an impressive ceramics museum, which is housed in the 14th-century former convent of San Francesco. The most notable pieces are Renaissance vessels made using the *lustro* technique, which originated in Arab and Middle Eastern cultures some 500 years before coming into use in Italy in the late 1400s and which incorporates crushed precious materials such as gold or silver to create a rich, lustrous finish. ✉ *Largo San Francesco, Piazza del Consoli 12, Deruta* ☏ *075/9711000* 🌐 *www.museoceramicadideruta.it* 🎫 *€7, includes Pinacoteca Comunale* ⏲ *Closed Tues. and Wed. Nov.–Mar. and Tues. Apr., May, and Oct.*

Pinacoteca Comunale
ART MUSEUM | The 14th-century Palazzo dei Consoli houses Deruta's Municipal Picture Gallery. The rich collection displayed over two floors includes frescoes and paintings by the Renaissance artists Perugino and L'Alunno, among other works from local churches. Upstairs, the Pascoli Collection features 17th- and 18th-century canvases, donated by a descendant of the prominent art collector and writer Lione Pascoli. Artists represented include Giovanni Battista Gaulli, Sebastiano Conca, and Francesco Trevisani. Note that outside of the summer months, the museum is only open on Sunday. ✉ *Piazza dei Consoli 12, Deruta* ☏ *075/9711000* 🎫 *€7, includes Museo Regionale Della Ceramica* ⏲ *Closed Tues. Apr., May, and Oct., and Mon.–Sat. Nov.–Mar.*

Shopping

Deruta is home to dozens of ceramics shops that offer a range of items, including extra pieces commissioned by well-known British and North American tableware manufacturers. A drive along Via Tiberina Nord takes you past one shop after another. If you ask, most owners will take you to see where they actually throw, bake, and paint their wares.

Spello

30 km (19 miles) southeast of Perugia, 12 km (7 miles) southeast of Assisi, 33 km (21 miles) north of Spoleto.

With well-appointed hotels, this hilltop town at the edge of Monte Subasio, just a short drive or train ride from Perugia or Assisi, makes an excellent base for exploring the region. Spello's art scene includes first-rate frescoes by Pinturicchio and Perugino, and contemporary artists can be observed at work in studios around town. If antiquity is your passion, the town also has some intriguing Roman ruins. And the warm, rosy-beige tones of the local *pietra rossa* stone on the buildings brighten even cloudy days.

GETTING HERE AND AROUND

Spello is an easy half-hour drive from Perugia. From the E45 highway, take the exit toward Assisi and Foligno. Merge onto the SS75 and take the Spello exit. There are also regular trains on the Perugia–Assisi line. Spello is 1 km (½ mile) from the train station, and it's a short, steep walk up to Porta Consolare.

From Porta Consolare, continue up the steep main street, which begins as Via Consolare and changes names several times as it crosses the little town. It also follows the original Roman road, so, as it curves around, you'll see winding medieval alleyways to the right and more uniform, Roman-era blocks to the left.

Sights

Santa Maria Maggiore

CHURCH | The two great Umbrian artists Pinturicchio and Perugino hold sway in this 16th-century basilica. Pinturicchio's vivid frescoes in the Cappella Baglioni (1501) are striking for their rich colors, finely dressed figures, and complex symbolism. Among his finest works are the *Nativity, Christ Among the Doctors,* and the *Annunciation* (look for Pinturicchio's self-portrait in the Virgin's room). Two pillars on either side of the apse are decorated with frescoes by Perugino (circa 1450–1523). ✉ *Piazza Matteotti 18, Spello* ☎ *0742/301792* 🌐 *smariamaggiore.com* 🎫 *€3 for Cappella Baglioni* ⏲ *Closed Mon.*

Hotels

La Bastiglia

$ | HOTEL | Polished wooden planks and handwoven rugs have replaced the rustic flooring of a former grain mill, and comfortable sitting rooms and cozy bedrooms are filled with a mix of antique and modern pieces. **Pros:** friendly staff; leisure and wellness facilities; fine views from top-floor rooms, some with terraces. **Cons:** some shared balconies; no elevator and plenty of steps, so pack light; can use an overall refresh. $ *Rooms from: €140* ✉ *Via Salnitraria 15, Spello* ☎ *0742/651277* 🌐 *labastiglia.com* ⏲ *Closed 3 wks in Jan.* 🛏 *34 rooms* 🍽 *Free Breakfast.*

Montefalco

18 km (11 miles) south of Spello, 34 km (21 miles) south of Assisi, 48 km (30 miles) southeast of Perugia.

Nicknamed the "balcony over Umbria" for its high vantage point over the valley that runs from Perugia to Spoleto, Montefalco began as an important Roman settlement along the Via Flaminia. The town owes its current name ("Falcon's Mount") to Emperor Frederick II (1194–1250). Obviously a greater fan of falconry than Roman architecture, he destroyed the ancient town, which was known as Coccorone, in 1249, and built in its place what would later become Montefalco. Aside from a few fragments incorporated in a private house just off Borgo Garibaldi, no traces remain of the old Roman center.

However, Montefalco has more than its fair share of interesting art and architecture and is well worth the drive up the hill. It's also a good place to stop for a meal, as is nearby Bevagna. You need go no farther than the main squares to find a restaurant or bar with a hot meal, and most establishments—both simple and sophisticated—offer a splendid combination of history and small-town hospitality.

GETTING HERE AND AROUND

If you're driving from Perugia, take the E45 toward Rome. Take the Foligno exit, then merge onto the SP445 and follow it into Montefalco. The drive takes around 50 minutes. The nearest train station is in Foligno, about 7 km (4½ miles) away. From there you can take a taxi or a bus into Montefalco.

VISITOR INFORMATION

CONTACT La Strada del Sagrantino. ✉ *Piazza del Comune 17, Montefalco* ☎ *0742/378490* 🌐 *www.stradadelsagrantino.it.*

The Sagrantino Story

Sagrantino grapes have been used to produce red wine for centuries. The wine began as Sagrantino *passito*, a semisweet version in which the grapes are left to dry for a period after picking to intensify the sugar content. One theory traces the origin of Sagrantino back to ancient Rome in the works of Pliny the Elder, the author of the *Natural History*, who referred to the Itriola grape that some researchers think may be Sagrantino. Others believe that, in medieval times, Franciscan friars returned from Asia Minor with the grape. ("Sagrantino" perhaps derives from *sacramenti*, the religious ceremony in which the wine was used.)

The passito is still produced today and is preferred by some. But the big change in Sagrantino wine production came in the past decades, when Montefalco Sagrantino *secco* (dry) came onto the market. Both passito and secco have a deep ruby-red color that tends toward garnet highlights, with a full body and rich flavor.

For the dry wines, producers not to be missed are Paolo Bea, Terre di Capitani, Antonelli, Perticaia, and Arnaldo Caprai. Try those labels for the passito as well, in addition to Ruggeri and Scacciadiavoli. Paolo Bea's biodynamic wines are robust and long-lasting. Terre di Capitani is complex and has vegetable and mineral tones that join tastes of wild berries, cherries, and chocolate—this winemaker pampers his grapes and it shows. Antonelli is elegant, refined, and rich. Perticaia has a full, rounded taste. Caprai is bold and rich in taste. The Ruggeri passito is one of the best, so don't be put off by its homespun label.

At La Strada del Sagrantino in Montefalco's main square, you can pick up a map of the wine route, set up appointments, and book accommodations. Some wineries are small and not equipped to receive visitors. Visit the local *enoteche* (wineshops) and ask the sommeliers to guide you to the smaller producers.

Restaurants

★ Enoteca L'Alchimista

$$ | UMBRIAN | "The Alchemist" is an apt name, as the chef's transformations are magical, and everything can be paired with wines from the restaurant's extensive selection. Though pasta, veggie, and meat dishes change seasonally, the homemade gnocchi in Sagrantino wine sauce, always on offer, wins raves from guests, plus all the delicious desserts are made on the premises. **Known for:** extensive wine list; congenial setting and atmosphere; refined but relaxed dining. *Average main: €22* *Piazza del Comune 14, Montefalco* *0742/378558* *www.ristorantealchimista.it* *Closed Tues.*

Hotels

★ Palazzo Bontadosi Hotel & Spa

$ | HOTEL | This charming boutique hotel, set in an 18th-century palace overlooking the main square, has spacious, individually decorated rooms, where original frescoes and beamed ceilings contrast with modern furnishings and some bathrooms have deep soaking tubs. **Pros:** sophisticated, design-focused vibe; spa in medieval cellars has a private Turkish bath and soaking pool; friendly service. **Cons:** rooms facing the square can be noisy; no gym; small breakfast selection. *Rooms from: €152* *Piazza del Comune 19, Montefalco* *0742/379357* *hotelbontadosi.it* *12 rooms* *Free Breakfast.*

Villa Pambuffetti

$ | **HOTEL** | If you want to be pampered in the refined atmosphere of a private villa, this is the spot, with the warmth of a fireplace in the winter, a pool to cool you down in summer, and cozy reading nooks and guest rooms year-round. **Pros:** peaceful gardens; cooking courses offered; excellent dining room. **Cons:** outside the town center; grounds could be better kept; dated feel. *$ Rooms from: €158 ✉ Viale della Vittoria 20, Montefalco ☎ 0742/379417 🌐 www.villapambuffetti.it 🛏 15 rooms 🍽 Free Breakfast.*

Spoleto

24 km (15 miles) southeast of Montefalco, 46 km (29 miles) south of Assisi, 63 km (39 miles) southeast of Perugia, 80 km (50 miles) east of Orvieto.

For most of the year, Spoleto is one more in a pleasant succession of sleepy hill towns, resting regally atop a mountain. But for more than two weeks every summer the town shifts into high gear for a turn in the international spotlight during the Festival dei Due Mondi (Festival of Two Worlds), an extravaganza of theater, opera, music, painting, and sculpture.

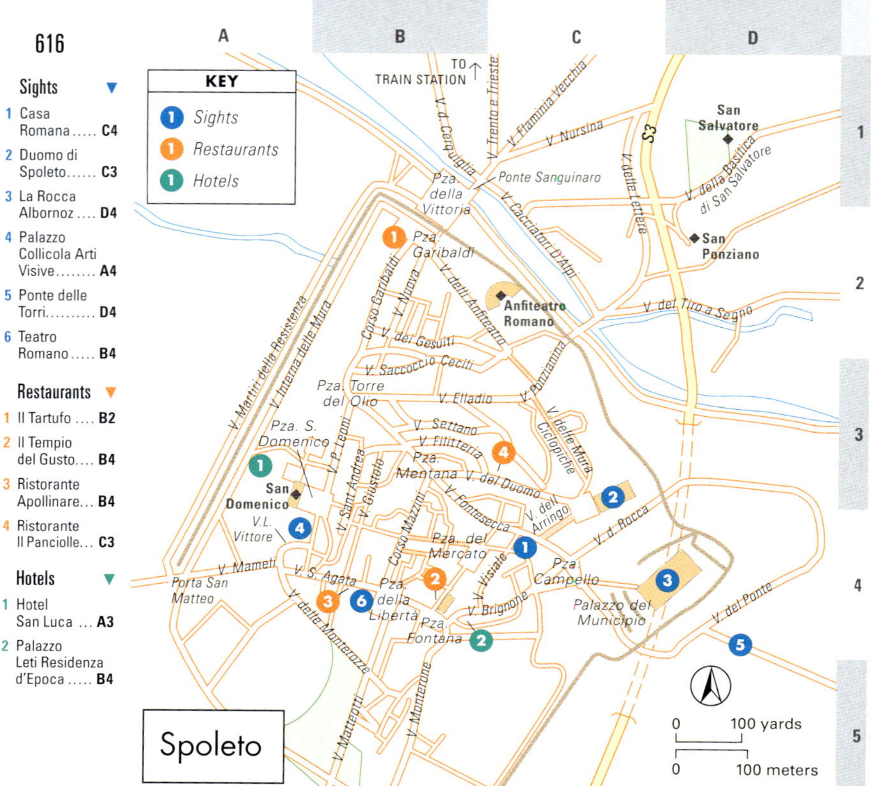

As the world's top artists vie for honors, throngs of art aficionados vie for hotel rooms. If you plan to spend the night in Spoleto during the festival, make sure you have confirmed reservations, or you may find yourself scrambling at sunset.

GETTING HERE AND AROUND

Spoleto is an hour's drive from Perugia. From the E45 highway, take the exit toward Assisi and Foligno, then merge onto the SS75 until you reach the Foligno Est exit. Merge onto the SS3, which leads to Spoleto. Parking options inside the city walls include Piazza Campello (just below the Rocca) on the southeast end, Via del Trivio to the north, and Piazza San Domenico on the west end. You can also park at Piazza della Vittoria farther north, just outside the walls, or at one of several well-marked lots near the train station.

There are regular trains on the Perugia–Foligno line. If you arrive by train, you can walk 1 km (½ mile) from the station to the entrance to the lower town, but it's a 15-minute uphill walk to the center, so you may want to take a local bus or a taxi. Regular bus connections are every 15–30 minutes.

Consider purchasing the Spoleto Card (€12), which provides entry to several museums—the Casa Romano, La Rocca Albornoz, and the Teatro Romano among them—as well as access to guided tours. It's sold online (🌐 *www.spoletocard.it*), at the included sights, and at some hotels.

VISITOR INFORMATION

CONTACT **Spoleto Tourism Office.** ✉ *Largo Ferrer 6, off Corso Mazzini, Spoleto* ☎ *0743/218620* 🌐 *www.comune.spoleto.pg.it.*

Sights

The walled city is set on a slanting hillside, with the most interesting sections clustered toward the upper portion. Like most other towns with narrow, winding streets, Spoleto is best explored on foot. Bear in mind that much of the city is on a steep slope, so there are lots of stairs and steep inclines. The well-worn stones can be slippery even when dry; wear rubber-sole shoes for good traction.

Casa Romana (*Roman House*)
RUINS | FAMILY | Spoleto became a Roman colony in the 3rd century BC, but the best excavated remains date from the 1st century AD. Well preserved among them is the Casa Romana. According to an inscription, it belonged to Vespasia Polla, the mother of Emperor Vespasian (one of the builders of the Colosseum and perhaps better known by the Romans for taxing them to install public toilets, later called "Vespasians"). The rooms, arranged around a large central atrium built over an *impluvium* (rain cistern), are decorated with black-and-white geometric mosaics. ✉ *Palazzo del Municipio, Via di Visiale 9, Spoleto* ☎ *0743/40255* 🎫 *€3; included with Spoleto Card* ⏲ *Closed Tues. and Wed.*

★ **Duomo di Spoleto** (*Spoleto Cathedral*)
CHURCH | One of the finest cathedrals in the region is lit by eight rose windows that are especially dazzling in the late afternoon sun. Above the church's entrance is Bernini's bust of Pope Urban VIII (1568–1644), who had the church redecorated in 17th-century Baroque; fortunately he didn't touch the 15th-century frescoes painted in the apse by Fra Filippo Lippi (circa 1406–69) between 1466 and 1469. These immaculately restored masterpieces—the *Annunciation, Nativity,* and *Dormition*—tell the story of the life of the Virgin. The *Coronation of the Virgin,* adorning the half dome, is the literal and figurative high point. Portraits of Lippi and his assistants are on the right side of the central panel. ✉ *Piazza del Duomo 2, Spoleto* ☎ *0577/286300* 🌐 *www.duomospoleto.it* 🎫 *Cathedral is free, €5 for cathedral audio guide, €10 for full audio guide including the upper part of the cathedral, bell tower, Sala della Grande Bellezza, Diocesan Museum, and Church of Sant'Eufemia.*

La Rocca Albornoz
CASTLE/PALACE | FAMILY | Built in the mid-14th century for Cardinal Egidio Albornoz, this massive fortress served as a seat for the local pontifical governors, a tangible sign of the restoration of the Church's power in the area when the pope was ruling from Avignon. Several popes spent time here, and, in 1499, one of them, Alexander VI, sent his capable teenage daughter, Lucrezia Borgia (1480–1519), to serve as governor for three months. The Gubbio-born architect Gattapone (14th century) used the ruins of a Roman acropolis as a foundation and incorporated materials from many Roman-era sites, including the Teatro Romano.

La Rocca's plan is long and rectangular, with six towers and two grand courtyards, an upper loggia, and grand interior reception rooms. In the largest tower, Torre Maestà, you can visit an apartment with some interesting frescoes. ✉ *Piazza Campello, Spoleto* ☎ *0743/224952* 🎫 *€7.50, including the Museo Nazionale del Ducato; free with Spoleto Card.*

★ **Palazzo Collicola Arti Visive**
ART MUSEUM | Spoleto's compact but delightful modern art museum, housed in an 18th-century palace, features a fine collection of works from Italian contemporary artists, including renowned Spoleto sculptor Leoncillo and Umbria-based American sculptor Barbara Pepper. International artists such as Alexander Calder and Richard Serra are also represented, and an entire room is devoted to a large-scale wall drawing by Sol Lewitt. The Appartamento Nobile is a reproduction of an 18th-century nobleman's house, and the Pictures Gallery has paintings from

the 16th to 19th centuries. ✉ *Piazza Collicola 1, Spoleto* ☎ *0743/46434* 🌐 *www.palazzocollicola.it* 🎟 *€9; included with Spoleto Card* ⏲ *Closed Tues. and Wed.*

★ **Ponte delle Torri** (*Bridge of the Towers*)
BRIDGE | Standing massive and graceful through the deep gorge that separates Spoleto from Monteluco, this 14th-century bridge is one of Umbria's most photographed monuments, and justifiably so. Built over the foundations of a Roman-era aqueduct, it soars 262 feet above the forested gorge—higher than the dome of St. Peter's in Rome. A must-see sight, the bridge offers spectacular views of Monteluco, and is particularly impressive on a starry night. ✉ *Via del Ponte, Spoleto* 🎟 *Free.*

Teatro Romano
RUINS | **FAMILY** | The Romans who colonized the city in 241 BC constructed this small theater in the 1st century AD; for centuries afterward it was used as a quarry for building materials. The most intact portion is the hallway that passes under the *cavea* (stands). The rest was heavily restored in the early 1950s and serves as a venue for Spoleto's Festival dei Due Mondi. The theater was the site of a gruesome episode in Spoleto's history: during the medieval struggle between Guelph (papal) and Ghibelline (imperial) forces, Spoleto took the side of the Holy Roman Emperor. Afterward, 400 Guelph supporters were massacred in the theater, their bodies burned in an enormous pyre. In the end, the Guelphs were triumphant, and Spoleto was incorporated into the states of the Church in 1354. ✉ *Piazza della Libertà, Spoleto* ☎ *0743/223277* 🎟 *€4, free with Spoleto Card* ⏲ *Closed Mon.–Wed.*

Restaurants

Il Tartufo
$$ | **UMBRIAN** | As the name indicates, dishes prepared with truffles are the specialty here—don't miss the risotto al tartufo. Incorporating the ruins of a Roman villa, the surroundings are rustic on the ground floor and more modern upstairs; in summer, tables appear outdoors, and the traditional fare is spiced up to appeal to the cosmopolitan crowd attending (or performing in) the Festival dei Due Mondi. **Known for:** recipes incorporating truffles; charming staff; abundant portions, well presented. [$] *Average main: €22* ✉ *Piazza Garibaldi 24, Spoleto* ☎ *0743/40236* 🌐 *www.ristoranteiltartufo.it* ⏲ *Closed Mon. and early Jan.–early Feb. No dinner Sun.*

Il Tempio del Gusto
$ | **UMBRIAN** | In charming shabby-chic environs, this welcoming eatery near the Arco di Druso (ancient Roman arch) serves up Italian with a subtle twist. Along with an extensive selection of thoughtfully chosen Umbrian wines, you'll find lots of veggie options, mounds of truffles in season, and, to finish things off, a superlative version of Spoleto sponge cake. **Known for:** flavorful Umbrian cuisine; friendly atmosphere; quaint setting. [$] *Average main: €19* ✉ *Via Arco di Druso 11, Spoleto* ☎ *0743/47121* 🌐 *www.iltempiodelgusto.com* ⏲ *Closed Thurs.*

★ **Ristorante Apollinare**
$$ | **UMBRIAN** | Low wooden ceilings and flickering candlelight make this monastery from the 10th and 11th centuries Spoleto's most romantic spot; in warm weather, you can dine under a canopy on the piazza. The kitchen serves sophisticated, innovative variations on local dishes, including long, slender strengozzi pasta with such toppings as cherry tomatoes, mint, and a touch of red pepper or (in season) porcini mushrooms or truffles. **Known for:** modern versions of traditional Umbrian dishes; intimate and elegant setting; impeccable service. [$] *Average main: €24* ✉ *Via Sant'Agata 14, Spoleto* ☎ *0743/223256* 🌐 *www.ristoranteapollinare.it* ⏲ *Closed Tues.*

Ristorante Il Panciolle

$ | **UMBRIAN** | A small garden filled with lemon trees in the heart of Spoleto's medieval quarter provides one of the most appealing settings you could wish for. Dishes, which change throughout the year, might include pastas served with asparagus or mushrooms, as well as grilled meats; more expensive dishes prepared with fresh truffles are also available in season. **Known for:** authentic local cuisine; affable staff; panoramic terrace. *$ Average main: €14 ✉ Via del Duomo 3/5, Spoleto ☎ 0743/45677 🌐 www.ilpanciolle.it.*

Hotels

★ Hotel San Luca

$ | **HOTEL** | Hand-painted friezes decorate the walls of the spacious guest rooms, and elegant comfort is the grace note throughout—you can sip afternoon tea in oversize armchairs by the fireplace or take a walk in the sweet-smelling rose garden. **Pros:** very helpful staff; spacious rooms; close to escalators for exploring city. **Cons:** outside the town center; restaurant only open for groups; can feel soulless in winter. *$ Rooms from: €104 ✉ Via Interna delle Mura 21, Spoleto ☎ 0743/223399 🌐 www.hotelsanluca.com 35 rooms 🍴 Free Breakfast.*

★ Palazzo Leti Residenza d'Epoca

$ | **HOTEL** | Fabulously landscaped gardens, complete with fountains and sculptures, along with panoramic views provide a grand entrance to this late 13th-century residence turned charming hotel high up in Spoleto's old town. **Pros:** feels like a private hideaway; unbeatable views; friendly owners happy to help. **Cons:** reaching on-site parking can be tricky; often booked far in advance; few amenities (no restaurant, gym, or spa). *$ Rooms from: €125 ✉ Via degli Eremiti 10, Spoleto ☎ 0743/224930 🌐 www.palazzoleti.com 12 rooms 🍴 Free Breakfast.*

The Valnerina

The Valnerina is 27 km (17 miles) southeast of Spoleto.

The Valnerina (the valley of the River Nera, to the southeast of Spoleto) is the most beautiful of central Italy's many well-kept secrets. The twisting roads that serve the rugged landscape are poor, but the drive is well worth the effort for its forgotten medieval villages and dramatic mountain scenery.

GETTING HERE AND AROUND

You can head into the area from Terni on the S209, or on the SP395 bis north of Spoleto, which links the Via Flaminia (SS3) with the middle reaches of the Nera Valley through a tunnel.

Sights

Cascata delle Marmore

WATERFALL | **FAMILY** | The road east of Terni (SS3 Valnerina) leads 10 km (6 miles) to the Cascata delle Marmore (Waterfalls of Marmore), which, at 541 feet, are the highest in Europe. A canal was dug by the Romans in the 3rd century BC to prevent flooding in the nearby agricultural plains. Nowadays, the waters are often diverted to provide hydroelectric power for Terni, reducing the roaring falls to an unimpressive trickle, so check with the information office at the falls (there's a timetable on its website) or with Terni's tourist office before heading here. On summer evenings, when the falls are in full spate, the cascading water is floodlit to striking effect. The falls are usually at their most energetic at midday and at around 4 pm. This is a good place for hiking, except in December and January, when most trails may be closed. *✉ SP79, Terni ↔ 10 km (6 miles) east of Terni ☎ 0744/67561 🌐 www.cascatadellemarmore.info €12.*

Hiking the Umbrian Hills

Magnificent scenery makes the heart of Italy excellent walking, hiking, and mountaineering country. In Umbria, the area around Spoleto is particularly good; several pleasant, easy, and well-signed trails begin at the far end of the Ponte alle Torri bridge over Monteluco. From Cannara, an easy half-hour walk leads to the fields of Pian d'Arca, the site of St. Francis's sermon to the birds.

For slightly more arduous walks, follow the saint's path uphill from Assisi to the Eremo delle Carceri, and then continue along the trails that crisscross Monte Subasio. At 4,250 feet, the treeless summit affords views of Assisi, Perugia, far-off Gubbio, and the distant mountain ranges of Abruzzo. For even more challenging hiking, the northern reaches of the Valnerina are exceptional; the mountains around Norcia should not be missed.

Throughout Umbria and the Marches, most recognized trails are marked with the distinctive red-and-white blazes of the Club Alpino Italiano. Tourist offices are a good source for walking and climbing itineraries to suit all ages and levels of ability, and bookstores *tabacchi* (tobacconists) and *edicole* (newsstands) often have maps and guides that detail the best area routes. Wear comfortable walking shoes or hiking boots, depending on your route, and bring plenty of water.

Norcia

TOWN | The birthplace of St. Benedict, Norcia is best known for its Umbrian pork and truffles, which you can sample at shops throughout town. Norcia exports truffles to France and hosts a truffle festival, Nero Norcia, every February. Though the town itself is still under reconstruction following a devastating 2016 earthquake, the surrounding mountains provide spectacular hiking. ✉ *42 km (25 miles) east of Spoleto, 67 km (42 miles) northeast of Terni, Norcia.*

★ Piano Grande

VIEWPOINT | A spectacular mountain plain 25 km (15 miles) to the northeast of the valley, Piano Grande is a hang glider's paradise and a wonderful place for a picnic or to fly a kite. It's also nationally famous for the quality of the lentils grown here, which are a traditional part of every Italian New Year's feast. ✉ *Piano Grande, Teramo* 🎟 *Free.*

Hotels

★ Palazzo Seneca

$ | **HOTEL** | The Bianconi family oversees this elegant hotel, which is housed in a 16th-century palace—just around the corner from Norcia's main square—and features stone floors, vaulted ceilings, and a Michelin-star restaurant. **Pros:** fabulous restaurant (book well in advance); lots of style and charm; central location. **Cons:** breakfast not up to par; no gym; no parking at the hotel. [$] *Rooms from: €170* ✉ *Via Cesare Battisti 12, Norcia* ☎ *0743/817434* 🌐 *www.palazzoseneca.com* 🕓 *Closed Dec.–Mar.* *24 rooms* 🍴 *Free Breakfast.*

Todi

34 km (22 miles) south of Perugia, 34 km (22 miles) northeast of Orvieto, 46 km (29 miles) northwest of Spoleto.

As you stand on Piazza del Popolo, looking out onto the Tiber Valley below, it's easy to see why Todi is often described as Umbria's prettiest hill town. Legend has it that the town was founded by the Umbri, who followed an eagle who had stolen a tablecloth. They liked this lofty perch so much that they settled here for good. The eagle is now perched on the insignia of the medieval palaces in the main piazza.

GETTING HERE AND AROUND

Todi is best reached by car, as the town's two train stations are way down the hill and connected to the center by infrequent bus service. From Perugia, follow the E45 toward Rome. Take the Todi/Orvieto exit, then follow the SS79 bis into Todi. The drive takes around 40 minutes.

VISITOR INFORMATION

CONTACT **Todi Tourism Office.** ✉ *Piazza del Popolo 29–30, Todi* ☎ *075/8956227.*

Sights

Duomo di Todi *(Todi Cathedral)*

CHURCH | One end of the Piazza del Popolo is dominated by this 12th-century Romanesque-Gothic masterpiece, built over the site of a Roman temple. The simple facade is enlivened by a finely carved rose window. Look up at that window as you step inside and you'll notice its peculiarity: each "petal" of the rose has a cherub's face in the stained glass. Also take a close look at the capitals of the double columns with pilasters: perched between the acanthus leaves are charming medieval sculptures of saints—Peter with his keys, George and the dragon, and so on. You can see the rich brown tones of the wooden choir near the altar, but unless you have binoculars or request special permission in advance, you can't get close enough to see all the exquisite detail in this Renaissance masterpiece of woodworking (1521–30). The severe, solid mass of the Duomo is mirrored by the Palazzo dei Priori (1595–97) across the way. ✉ *Piazza del Popolo 1, Todi* ☎ *335/5420520* 🌐 *www.chiesaditodi.it* 🎫 *Free.*

Piazza del Popolo

PLAZA/SQUARE | Built above the Roman Forum, Piazza del Popolo is Todi's high point, a model of spatial harmony with stunning views of the surrounding countryside. In the best medieval tradition, the square was conceived to house both the temporal and the spiritual centers of power. ✉ *Piazza del Popolo, Todi* 🎫 *Free.*

Restaurants

★ **Pane & Vino**

$$ | **ITALIAN** | This charmingly rustic restaurant in Todi's historic center specializes in "dishes of the past" made from local ingredients. Choose from a fine selection of meat and cheese antipasti, housemade pastas and soups, and hearty meat dishes—accompanied by truffles in season—along with tempting daily specials, served with well-priced wines from a comprehensive list. **Known for:** focus on organic products from small producers; fabulous selection of wines from across Italy; friendly, knowledgeable service. $ *Average main: €20* ✉ *Via Augusto Ciuffelli 33, Todi* ☎ *075/8945448* 🌐 *panevinotodi.com* ⊙ *Closed Wed.*

Ristorante Umbria

$$ | **UMBRIAN** | Todi's most popular restaurant for more than four decades is reliable for its sturdy country food and the wonderful view from its terrace; because it has only 16 tables outside, make sure you reserve ahead. In winter, try lentil soup, risotto with saffron and porcini mushrooms, or wild boar with polenta; steaks, accompanied by a rich darkbrown wine sauce, are good any time of year. **Known for:** traditional Umbrian dishes; terrific vista from terrace; friendly atmosphere. *Average main: €26 Via San Bonaventura 13, Todi 075/8942737 www.ristoranteumbria.it Closed Tues. and 3–4 wks in Jan. and Feb.*

Hotels

★ Relais Todini
$$ | **HOTEL** | Inside a 14th-century manor house 9 km (6 miles) southeast of Todi, this elegant hotel sits adjacent to working vineyards (don't forget to sample the Todini wines) and features such welcome amenities as a spa, outdoor pool, and gym. **Pros:** quiet location; lots of relaxing public spaces, including a spa; walking paths around the grounds. **Cons:** spa feels a bit small; priced on the high side; reception not staffed 24/7. *Rooms from: €270 Frazione Collevalenza, Todi 075/887521 www.relaistodini.com Closed weekdays Nov.–Mar. 12 rooms Free Breakfast.*

Residenza D'Epoca San Lorenzo Tre
$ | **HOTEL** | Magnificent valley views are paired with 19th-century charm at this property filled with paintings, antique furnishings, and period knickknacks. **Pros:** old-world atmosphere; excellent central location; spectacular views. **Cons:** few modern amenities; long flight of steps to enter; small basic bathrooms. *Rooms from: €115 Via San Lorenzo 3, Todi 075/8944555 www.sanlorenzo3.it Closed Nov.–early Apr. 6 rooms Free Breakfast.*

Orvieto

30 km (19 miles) southwest of Todi, 78 km (48 miles) southwest of Perugia, 81 km (51 miles) west of Spoleto.

Carved from an enormous plateau of volcanic rock high above a green valley, Orvieto has natural defenses that made the high walls seen in many Umbrian towns unnecessary. The Etruscans were the first to settle here, digging a honeycombed network of more than 1,200 wells and storage caves out of the soft stone.

The Romans attacked, sacked, and destroyed the city in 283 BC. Since then, it has grown up out of the rock into an enchanting maze of alleys and squares. Orvieto was solidly Guelph in the Middle Ages, and, for several hundred years, popes sought refuge in the city, at times needing protection from their enemies, at times seeking respite from the summer heat in Rome.

When painting his frescoes inside the Duomo, Luca Signorelli asked that part of his contract be paid in Orvietan wine, and he was neither the first nor the last to appreciate the region's popular white. In past times, the caves carved underneath the town were used to ferment the Trebbiano grapes used in making Orvieto Classico. Although local wine production has moved out to more traditional vineyards, you can still while away the afternoon with tastings at any number of shops in town.

GETTING HERE AND AROUND

Orvieto is well connected by train to Rome, Florence, and Perugia. It's also adjacent to the A1 autostrada that runs between Florence and Rome. Parking areas in the upper town tend to be crowded. A better idea is to follow the signs for the Campo Della Fiera parking lot, then take the escalators or elevator that carry people up the hill.

VISITOR INFORMATION

CONTACT Orvieto Tourism Office. *Piazza del Duomo 24, Orvieto 0763/341772 liveorvieto.com.*

Sights

★ Duomo di Orvieto (*Orvieto Cathedral*)
CHURCH | Orvieto's stunning cathedral was built to commemorate the Miracle at Bolsena. In 1263, a young priest who questioned the miracle of

transubstantiation (in which the Communion bread and wine become the flesh and blood of Christ) was saying Mass at nearby Lago di Bolsena. A wafer he had just blessed suddenly started to drip blood, staining the linen covering the altar. Thirty years later, construction began on a duomo in Orvieto to celebrate the miracle and house the stained altar cloth.

The cathedral's interior is rather vast and empty; the major works are in the transepts. To the left is the Cappella del Corporale, where the square linen cloth (*corporale*) is kept in a golden reliquary that's modeled on the cathedral and inlaid with enamel scenes of the miracle. In the right transept is the Cappella di San Brizio, which holds one of Italy's greatest fresco cycles, notable for its influence on Michelangelo's *Last Judgment*, as well as for the extraordinary beauty of the figuration. In these works, a few by Fra Angelico and most by Luca Signorelli, the damned fall to hell, demons breathe fire and blood, and Christians are martyred. The Museo dell'Opera dell Duomo next to the cathedral is worth a short visit to see its small collection of historical paintings and sculptures, along with the Museo Emilio Greco, which houses 32 bronze sculptures from its namesake sculptor, who created the cathedral's bronze doors. ✉ *Piazza del Duomo, Orvieto* ☎ *0763/342477* 🌐 *www.duomodiorvieto.it* 🎫 *€8, includes Cappella di San Brizio, Museo dell'Opera dell Duomo, Duomo Underground, and Museo Emilio Greco; included with Carta Unica.*

Museo Etrusco Claudio Faina

HISTORY MUSEUM | This superb private collection, beautifully arranged and presented, goes far beyond the usual smattering of local remains displayed at many museums. The collection is particularly rich in Greek- and Etruscan-era pottery, from large Attic amphorae (6th–4th century BC) to Attic black- and red-figure pieces to Etruscan *bucchero* (dark-reddish clay) vases. Other interesting items include a 6th-century sarcophagus and a substantial display of Roman-era coins. ✉ *Piazza del Duomo 29, Orvieto* ☎ *0763/341511* 🌐 *museofaina.it* 🎫 *€6; included with Carta Unica* 🕒 *Closed Tues.*

Favorite Places

Liz Humphreys: Orvieto's beautiful Duomo always makes my heart sing. Between the gold mosaics and rose window outside and the Cappella di San Brizio frescoes inside – pure magic.

Orvieto Underground

RUINS | **FAMILY** | More than just about any other town, Orvieto has grown from its own foundations. The Etruscans, the Romans, and those who followed dug into the tufa (the same soft volcanic rock from which catacombs were made) to create more than 1,000 separate cisterns, caves, passages, storage areas, and production areas for wine and olive oil. Much of the tufa removed was used as building blocks for the city that exists today, and some was partly ground into *pozzolana*, which was made into mortar. You can see the labyrinth of dugout chambers beneath the city on the Orvieto Underground tour, which runs daily at 11, 12:15, 4, and 5:15 (reservations recommended), departing from Piazza del Duomo 23. ✉ *Piazza del Duomo 23, Orvieto* ☎ *0763/344891* 🌐 *www.orvietounderground.it* 🎫 *Tours €8; included with Carta Unica* ✍ *Reservations recommended 1 day prior in summer.*

Pozzo della Cava

RUINS | If you're short on time but want a quick look at the cisterns and caves beneath the city, head for the Pozzo della Cava, an Etruscan well for spring water. On a walk through nine excavated caves you can see the fascinating ruins of medieval houses and unearthed archaeological artifacts. ✉ *Via della Cava 28, Orvieto* ☎ *0763/342373* 🌐 *www.pozzodellacava.it* 🎫 *€4; included with Carta Unica* 🕐 *Closed mid- –late Jan.*

Restaurants

Le Grotte del Funaro

$ | UMBRIAN | Dine inside tufa caves under central Orvieto, where the two windows afford splendid views of the hilly countryside. The traditional Umbrian food is reliably good, with simple grilled meats and vegetables and pizzas—oddly, though, the food is outclassed by an extensive wine list, with top local and Italian labels and quite a few rare vintages. **Known for:** unusual setting; crusty pizzas; good choice of wines. $ *Average main: €17* ✉ *Via Ripa Serancia 41, Orvieto* ☎ *0763/343276* 🌐 *www.grottedelfunaro.com* 🕐 *Closed Mon. and 10 days in July.*

Ristorante Maurizio

$ | UMBRIAN | Off a busy pedestrian street near the Duomo, this welcoming, family-owned restaurant has an ultra contemporary look but is actually housed in a 14th-century medieval building with arched ceilings. The Martinelli family's own products, including balsamic vinegar, olive oil, and pasta, are used in their robustly flavored dishes, and you can also sample their well-regarded Montefalco wines. **Known for:** complimentary balsamic vinegar tasting to start; traditional Umbrian dishes; local wines. $ *Average main: €17* ✉ *Via del Duomo 78, Orvieto* ☎ *0763/343212* 🌐 *www.ristorante-maurizio.com.*

Trattoria La Grotta

$ | UMBRIAN | The vaulted, plant-filled dining area—where white walls are adorned with paintings, antique vases, and other knickknacks—makes a congenial setting for this small, rustic-style trattoria, which is lauded for its homemade pasta, perhaps with an artichoke, duck, or wild-boar sauce. Roast lamb, veal, and pork are all also good, and the desserts are supplied by Orvieto's most eminent *pasticceria* (pastry shop). **Known for:** tasty homemade pastas; fresh, local ingredients; warm and welcoming service. $ *Average main: €15* ✉ *Via Luca Signorelli 5, Orvieto* ☎ *0763/341348* 🌐 *www.trattorialagrottaorvieto.com* 🕐 *Closed Tues.*

Hotels

Eremito

$$ | GUESTHOUSE | For a more spiritual slant to your vacation, spend a night or two at this "modern monastery," where you'll sleep in a cell, eat vegetarian food by candlelight, practice yoga, and relax in a whirlpool tub. **Pros:** truly getting away from it all; chance to meet other travelers; lovely scenery. **Cons:** very simple accommodations (and no Wi-Fi); on the pricey side; need a car to get there. $ *Rooms from: €370* ✉ *Località Tarina 2, Parrano* ✥ *28 km (17 miles) north of Orvieto* ☎ *0763/891010* 🌐 *www.eremito.com* 🛏 *14 rooms* 🍽 *All-Inclusive.*

Hotel Palazzo Piccolomini

$ | HOTEL | This 16th-century family palazzo has been beautifully restored, with inviting public spaces and handsome guest quarters where contemporary surroundings are accented by old beams, vaulted ceilings, and other distinctive touches. **Pros:** private parking; efficient staff; good location. **Cons:** underwhelming breakfasts; four-star category not completely justified; some rooms and bathrooms are small. $ *Rooms from: €150* ✉ *Piazza Ranieri 36, Orvieto* ☎ *0763/341743* 🌐 *www.palazzopiccolomini.it* 🕐 *Closed Jan. and Feb.* 🛏 *32 rooms* 🍽 *No Meals.*

★ Locanda Palazzone

$$ | HOTEL | Spending the night in this 13th-century building just 5 km (3 miles) northwest of Orvieto is like staying in a sophisticated country home, albeit one with vineyard views, a private chef, and two-level rooms with modern furnishings. **Pros:** tranquil surroundings;

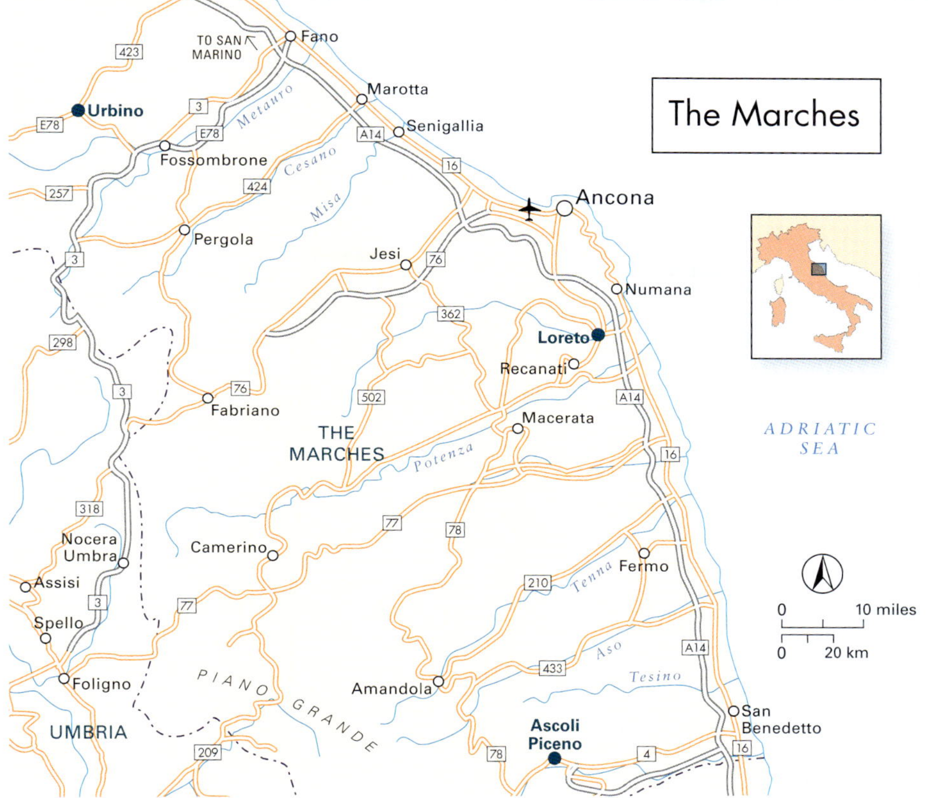

extremely friendly owners and staff; tasty meals served nightly. **Cons:** can hear noise from other guest rooms; Wi-Fi can be iffy; split-level rooms can be difficult for those with mobility issues or young children. *Rooms from: €263* *Località Rocca Ripesena 68, Orvieto* *0763/393614* *www.locandapalazzone.it* *Closed mid-Dec.–mid-Mar.* *7 rooms* *Free Breakfast.*

Urbino

230 km (143 miles) east of Florence, 116 km (72 miles) northeast of Perugia, 75 km (47 miles) north of Gubbio.

Majestic Urbino, atop a steep hill with a skyline of towers and domes, is something of a surprise to come upon. Though quite remote, it was once a center of learning and culture almost without rival in western Europe. The town looks much as it did in the glory days of the 15th century: a cluster of warm brick and pale stone buildings, all topped with russet-color tile roofs. The focal point is the immense and beautiful Palazzo Ducale.

The city is also home to the small but prestigious Università di Urbino—one of the oldest in the world—so its streets are usually filled with students, and it has the usual college town array of bookshops, bars, and coffeehouses. In summer, the Italian student population is replaced by foreigners who come to study Italian language and arts at several prestigious, private, fine-arts academies.

Urbino's fame rests on the reputation of three of its native sons: Duke Federico da Montefeltro (1422–82), the enlightened warrior–patron who built the Palazzo

Ducale; Raffaello Sanzio (1483–1520), or Raphael, one of the most influential painters in history and an embodiment of the spirit of the Renaissance; and the architect Donato Bramante (1444–1514), who translated the philosophy of the Renaissance into buildings of grace and beauty. Unfortunately there's little work by either Bramante or Raphael in the city, but the duke's influence can still be felt strongly.

GETTING HERE AND AROUND

Take the SS3 bis from Perugia, and follow the directions for Gubbio and Cesena. Exit at Umbertide and take the SS219, then the SS452, and at Calmazzo, the SS73 bis to Urbino.

VISITOR INFORMATION

CONTACT Urbino Tourism Office. ✉ *Via Puccinotti 35, Urbino* ☎ *0722/2613* 🌐 *www.vieniaurbino.it.*

Sights

Casa Natale di Raffaello (*House of Raphael*)
HISTORIC HOME | This is the house in which the painter was born and where he took his first steps in painting, under the direction of his artist father. There's some debate about the fresco of the Madonna here; some say it's by Raphael, whereas others attribute it to the father—with Raphael's mother and the young painter himself standing in as models for the Madonna and Child. ✉ *Via Raffaello 57, Urbino* ☎ *0722/320105* 🌐 *www.casaraffaello.com* 🎫 *€4.*

★ **Palazzo Ducale di Urbino** (*Ducal Palace*)
ART MUSEUM | The Palazzo Ducale holds a place of honor in the city. If the Renaissance was, ideally, a celebration of the nobility of man and his works, of the light and purity of the soul, then there's no place in Italy, the birthplace of the Renaissance, where these tenets are better illustrated. From the moment you enter the peaceful courtyard, you know you're in a place of grace and beauty, and the harmony of the building indeed reflects the high ideals of the time.

The palace houses the Galleria Nazionale delle Marche (National Museum of the Marches), with a superb collection of paintings, sculpture, and other objets d'art. Some pieces originally belonged to the Montefeltro family; others were brought here from churches and palaces throughout the region. Masterworks include Paolo Uccello's *Profanation of the Host,* Titian's *Resurrection* and *Last Supper,* and Piero della Francesca's *Madonna of Senigallia.* But the gallery's highlight is Piero's enigmatic work long known as *The Flagellation of Christ.* Much has been written about this painting, and although few experts agree on its meaning, most agree that this is one of the painter's masterpieces. ✉ *Piazza Rinascimento 13, Urbino* ☎ *0722/350077 ticket office* 🌐 *gndm.it* 🎫 *€12* ⏲ *Closed Mon.*

Restaurants

La Fornarina
$$ | **ITALIAN** | Locals often crowd this small, two-room trattoria near the Piazza della Repubblica. The specialty is meaty country fare, such as *coniglio* (rabbit) and *vitello alle noci* (veal cooked with walnuts) or *ai porcini* (with mushrooms); there's also a good selection of pasta dishes. **Known for:** excellent starters; welcoming atmosphere; hospitable staff. *$ Average main: €20* ✉ *Via Mazzini 14, Urbino* ☎ *0722/320007.*

Hotels

Hotel Bonconte
$ | **HOTEL** | Just inside the city walls and close to the Palazzo Ducale, this hotel has pleasant, if worn, rooms decorated with a smattering of antiques; those in front also have views of the valley below Urbino. **Pros:** pleasant views; central but away from the bustle; good breakfast. **Cons:** an uphill walk to town center; some rooms are cramped; rooms and public

spaces getting a bit shabby. *Rooms from: €105* *Via delle Mura 28, Urbino* *0722/2463* *www.viphotels.it* *23 rooms* *No Meals.*

★ **Palazzo Giusti Suites and Spa**

$ | **HOTEL** | This hotel in a renovated, 14th-century, historic center palace is an appealing mix of antiquity and modernity, including an expansive spa with a sauna and Turkish bath; a swimming pool that features a glass bottom so you can see the Roman ruins beneath it; and magnificent guest rooms with frescoed walls, vaulted ceilings, and charming decorative fireplaces. **Pros:** ultrarelaxing spa area; convenient location; beautiful historical setting. **Cons:** no restaurant; can be confusing to reach the hotel due to pedestrian streets; no gym. *Rooms from: €130* *Via Vittorio Veneto 37, Urbino* *0722/078023* *www.palazzogiustiurbino.com* *5 rooms* *Free Breakfast.*

Loreto

150 km (93 miles) northeast of Perugia, 121 km (75 miles) southeast of Urbino.

There's a strong Renaissance feel to this hilltop town, which is home to one of the most important religious sites in Europe, the Santuario della Santa Casa (House of the Virgin Mary). Bramante and Sansovino gave the church its Renaissance look, although many other artists helped create its special atmosphere.

Today, the town revolves around the religious calendar. If you can be here on December 10, you will witness the Feast of the Translation of the Holy House, when huge bonfires are lighted to celebrate the miraculous arrival, in 1295, of the house in Nazareth where the Virgin Mary was living at the time of the Annunciation.

GETTING HERE AND AROUND

If you're driving from Perugia, take the SS318 and then the SS76 highway to Fabriano and then on to Chiaravalle, where it merges with the A14 autostrada. The drive takes around two hours. Trains also go to Loreto, but the station is about 1½ km (1 mile) outside the town center. Regular buses leave from the station to the center.

VISITOR INFORMATION

CONTACT Loreto Tourism Office. *Via Solari 3, Loreto* *071/970276* *letsmarche.it.*

Sights

★ **Basilica della Santa Casa**

CHURCH | Loreto is famous for one of the best-loved shrines in the world: the Santuario della Santa Casa (House of the Virgin Mary), within the Basilica della Santa Casa. Legend has it that angels moved the house from Nazareth, where the Virgin Mary was living at the time of the Annunciation, to this hilltop in 1295. The reason for this sudden and divinely inspired move was that Nazareth had fallen into the hands of Muslim invaders, who the angelic hosts viewed as unsuitable keepers of this important shrine.

The house itself consists of three rough stone walls contained within an elaborate marble tabernacle. Built around this centerpiece is the giant Basilica of the Holy House, which dominates the town. Millions of pilgrims come to the site every year (particularly at Easter and on the December 10 Feast of the Translation of the Holy House), and the little town of Loreto can become uncomfortably crowded.

Many great Italian architects—including Bramante, Antonio da Sangallo the Younger (1483–1546), Giuliano da Sangallo (circa 1445–1516), and Sansovino (1467–1529)—contributed to the design of the basilica. It was begun in the Gothic style in 1468 and continued in Renaissance style through the late Renaissance. ✉ *Piazza della Madonna 1, Loreto* ☎ *071/9747213* 🌐 *www.santuarioloreto.va* 🎫 *Free.*

Ascoli Piceno

156 km (97 miles) southeast of Perugia, 88 km (55 miles) south of Loreto.

Ascoli Piceno sits in a valley ringed by steep hills and cut by the Tronto River. In Roman times, it was one of central Italy's best-known market towns. Today, with around 45,000 residents, it's a major fruit and olive producer, making it one of the most important towns in the region.

Despite growth during the Middle Ages and at other times, the streets in the town center continue to reflect the grid pattern of the ancient Roman city. You'll even find the word *rua,* from the Latin *ruga,* used for "street" instead of the Italian *via.* Now largely closed to traffic, the city center is great to explore on foot.

GETTING HERE AND AROUND

From Perugia, take the SS75 to Foligno, then merge onto the SS3 to Norcia. From here, take the SS4 to Ascoli Piceno. There are also trains, but the journey would be quite long, taking you from Perugia to Ancona, 105 km (65 miles) to the north, before changing for Ascoli Piceno.

VISITOR INFORMATION

CONTACT Ascoli Piceno Tourism Office. ✉ *Piazza Aringo 7, Ascoli Piceno* ☎ *0736/298334.*

Sights

Piazza del Popolo

PLAZA/SQUARE | The heart of the town is the majestic Piazza del Popolo, dominated by the Gothic church of San Francesco and the Palazzo del Popolo, a 13th-century town hall that contains a graceful Renaissance courtyard. The square functions as the living room of the entire city and at dusk each evening is packed with people strolling and exchanging news and gossip—the sweetly antiquated ritual called a passeggiata—performed all over the country. ✉ *Piazza del Popolo, Ascoli Piceno* 🎫 *Free.*

Hotels

★ Hotel Palazzo dei Mercanti

$ | HOTEL | This tastefully renovated convent right nearby Ascoli Piceno's historic center includes everything you need for a pleasant stay—a well-regarded restaurant, a relaxing spa, and modern guest rooms that have comfy beds and bathrooms with showers. **Pros:** elegant guest rooms; delicious breakfast buffet; prime central location. **Cons:** rooms can seem too dark; some rooms on the small side; restaurant can be noisy. $ *Rooms from: €131* ✉ *Corso Trento e Trieste 35, Ascoli Piceno* ☎ *0736/256044* 🌐 *www.palazzodeimercanti.it* *25 rooms* *Free Breakfast.*

Hotel Pennile

$ | HOTEL | This pleasant and affordable family-run hotel in a quiet residential area outside the old city center is pleasantly set amid a grove of olive trees. **Pros:** peaceful environment; a good budget option; easy parking. **Cons:** distance from town center; no restaurant; can hear some noise from other rooms. $ *Rooms from: €90* ✉ *Via G. Spalvieri 13/a, Ascoli Piceno* ☎ *0736/41645* 🌐 *www.hotelpennile.it* *33 rooms* *Free Breakfast.*

Chapter 14

NAPLES AND CAMPANIA

Updated by
Nick Bruno

WELCOME TO NAPLES AND CAMPANIA

TOP REASONS TO GO

★ **Naples, Italy's most operatic city:** Walk through the energy, chaos, and beauty that is Spaccanapoli, the city's historic artery, and you'll create an unforgettable memory.

★ **Pompeii:** The excavated ruins of Pompeii offer a unique, occasionally spooky glimpse into everyday life—and sudden death—in Roman times.

★ **"The Living Room of the World":** Pose oh-so-casually with the beautiful people on La Piazzetta, the central crossroads of the island of Capri—a stage-set square that always seems ready for a gala performance.

★ **Ravello:** High above the famously blue Bay of Salerno, this Amalfi Coast charmer is a contender for the title of "most beautiful village in the world."

★ **Positano, a world made of stairs:** Built like a vertical amphitheater, Positano's only job is to look enchanting on the Amalfi Coast—and it does that very well.

1 Naples. Italy's third-largest city is lush, chaotic, friendly, amusing, confounding, and very beautiful.

2 Herculaneum. The famous archaeological site was once a wealthy seaside resort.

3 Pompeii. The most famous dig of all—the one that arguably kick-started archaeological studies—is Pompeii.

4 Vesuvius. Dominating the skyline southeast of Naples is the destructive Vesuvius caldera.

5 Oplontis (Torre Annunziata). Fascinating lesser-known ruins.

6 Ischia. More than twice the size of Capri, lesser-known Ischia has volcanic-sand beaches, thermal hot-spring spas, and fewer day-trippers.

7 Procida. Sun, cliffs, and sea combine to create the distinctive atmosphere so memorably immortalized in the film *Il Postino.*

8 Capri. The rocky island mixes natural beauty and dolce vita glamour.

9 Sorrento. Perched over the Bay of Naples with an incomparable view of Mt. Vesuvius, this Belle Époque resort town is sheer delight.

10 Positano. The ultimate pastel-brushed, tumbling-to-the-seaside village moves between sophisticated-luxe, beachcomber casual, and selfie-reverential posing.

11 Conca dei Marini. Put on the map by 1960s jet-setters, this tiny but exceedingly picturesque harbor hideaway rubs shoulders with the luminous Emerald Grotto.

12 Amalfi. This buzzy resort is threaded with beguiling, rambling passages, testimony to its Norman and Arab-Sicilian past. The glory of the city's days as a medieval maritime republic is most evident in its fantastic cathedral.

13 Ravello. Just beyond the Valley of the Dragon lies Ravello, perched "closer to the sky than the sea" atop Monte Cereto and set over the breath-taking Bay of Salerno. Ravello is one of Italy's most beautiful towns.

14 Paestum. With its Greek temples and Roman ruins in flowery meadows, this vision of a lost city makes a rousing finale to any Grand Tour.

MOLISE
PUGLIA
LAZIO
A1
87
372
Telese
Teano
7
Benevento
Grottaminarda
A1
Caserta
7
A16
Nola
Avellino
Naples
4 Vesuvius
Pozzuoli
A30
1
2
Herculaneum
5
3
Pompeii
Oplontis
(Torre Annunziata)
A3
7
PROCIDA
6
ISCHIA
Golfo di Nápoli
Castellammare
SORRENTINE PENINSULA
13
Ravello
Salerno
Sorrento
9
12
10
Amalfi
Positano
Battipaglia
Eboli
8
CAPRI
11
Conca dei Marini
Golfo di Salerno
18
Paestum
14
Agropoli
TYRRHENIAN SEA
Castellabate
0
20 mi
0
20 km

EATING AND DRINKING WELL IN NAPLES AND CAMPANIA

Cappuccinos at a coffee bar

Think of Neapolitan food and you conjure up images of pasta, pizza, and tomatoes. The stereotype barely scratches the surface of what's available in Naples—to say nothing of the rest of Campania, where the cuisine reflects an enormously diverse landscape.

The region is known for its enclaves of gastronomy, notable among them the tip of the Sorrentine Peninsula. You may well come across *cucina povera,* a cuisine inspired by Campania's *contadino* (peasant) roots, with all the ingredients sourced from a nearby garden. Expect to see roadside stalls selling stellar local produce, including *annurca* apples (near Benevento), giant lemons (Amalfi Coast), roasted chestnuts (especially near Avellino), and watermelons (the plains around Salerno). Try to get to one of the local *sagre,* village feasts celebrating a *prodotto tipico* (local specialty), which could be anything from snails to wild boar to cherries to (commonly) wine.

A TIPPING TIP

Neapolitans are easily recognized in bars elsewhere in Italy by the tip they leave on the counter when ordering. This habit does not necessarily ensure better service in bars in Naples, notorious for their fairly offhand staff, but you do blend in better with the locals.

In restaurants, a service charge is often included (alternatively, 5%–10% is reasonable). In pizzerias, tips are given less often unless you've splurged on side dishes or sweets, or have had particularly good service.

PIZZA

Naples is the undisputed homeland of pizza, and you'll usually encounter it here in two classic forms: *margherita* and *marinara*. Given the large portions, some choose to ask for a *mignon* (kids' portion), or even to share, divided between two plates. Take-away outlets in most town centers sell pizza by the slice, along with the usual range of fried *arancini* (rice balls) and *crocchè di patate* (potato fritters).

COFFEE

Given the same basic ingredients—coffee grounds, water, a machine—what makes *caffè* taste so much better in Naples than elsewhere remains a mystery. If you find the end product too strong, ask to have it with a dash of milk (caffè *macchiato*) or a little diluted (caffè *lungo*). Many bars serve with sugar already added; for without, request *senza zucchero* or *amaro*.

BUFFALO

Long feted for the melt-in-your-mouth mozzarella cheese made from its milk, the water buffalo is also the source of other culinary delights. Throughout the region, look for buffalo ricotta and mascarpone, as well as buffalo *provola* and *scamorza*, which may be lightly smoked (resulting in a golden crust). Caserta has *nero di bufala* (with activated carbon that aids digestion), while around Salerno you'll find smoked *caciocavallo* cheese as well as *carne di bufala* (buffalo meat).

Buffalo mozzarella

Margherita pizza

THE ORAL TRADITION

Locals in Campania like to bypass the restaurant menu and ask what the staff recommend. Take this approach and you'll often wind up with a daily special or the house specialty. Although you're unlikely to get multilingual staff outside the larger hotels and main tourist areas, the person you talk to will spare no effort to get the message across.

WINE

Wine in Campania has an ancient pedigree. Some say fancifully that Campania's undisputed king of reds, the *aglianico*, got its name from the word "Hellenic"; and *fiano*, the primary white grape, closely resembles the Roman variety *apianus*. Horace, the Latin poet, extolled the virtues of drinking wine from Campania. A century later, Pliny the Elder was harsher in his judgment.

In recent decades, though, Campania has gained respect for its boutique reds. Due to the rugged landscape, small farms, and limited mechanization, prices can be relatively high, but the quality is high as well.

A region of evocative names—Capri, Sorrento, Pompeii, Positano, Amalfi—Campania conjures up visions of cliff-shaded, sapphire-hue coves, sun-dappled waters, and mighty ruins. More travelers visit this corner than any other in southern Italy, and it's no wonder.

Home to Vesuvius, the area's unique geology is responsible for Campania's photogenic landscape. A spectacular coastline stretches out along a deep blue sea, punctuated by rocky islands.

Through the ages, the area's temperate climate, warm sea, fertile soil, and natural beauty have attracted Greek colonists, then Roman emperors—who called the region "Campania Felix," or "the happy land"—and later Saracen raiders and Spanish invaders. The result has been a rich and varied history, reflected in everything from architecture to mythology. The highlights span millennia: the near-intact Roman towns of Pompeii and Herculaneum, the Greek temples in Paestum, the Norman and Baroque churches in Naples, the white-dome fisherman's houses of Positano, the dolce vita resorts of Capri. Campania piles them all onto one mammoth must-see-and-taste *panuozzo napoletano* sandwich.

The region's complex identity is most intensely felt in its major metropolis, Naples. Few who visit remain ambivalent. You needn't participate in the mad whirl of the city, however. The best pastime in Campania is simply finding a spot with a stunning view and indulging in *il dolce far niente* ("the sweetness of doing nothing").

MAJOR REGIONS

Herculaneum and Pompeii. Volcanic ash and mud preserved the Roman towns of Herculaneum and Pompeii almost exactly as they were on the day Vesuvius erupted in AD 79, leaving them not just archaeological ruins but museums of daily life in the ancient world. The two cities and the volcano that buried them can be visited from either Naples or Sorrento, thanks to the Circumvesuviana, the suburban railroad that provides fast, frequent, and economical service.

Capri, Ischia, and Procida. Capri may get star billing among the islands that line the Bay of Naples, but Ischia and Procida also have their own lower-key appeal. Once entirely dependent on its thermal springs, Ischia is now the archaeological front-runner in the bay, thanks to the noted museum in Lacco Ameno. Procida has opened up to tourism and in 2022 was celebrated for sparking rejuvenation through culture as *Capitale Italiana della Cultura*, helping expand access to its chief natural asset, the unspoiled isle of Vivara.

The Sorrentine Peninsula. As the hub for a whole banquet of must-see sites—Pompeii and Naples to the north, Capri to the west, and the Amalfi Coast to the south—the beautiful, Belle Époque resort town of Sorrento is unequaled.

The rest of the peninsula, with plains and limestone outcroppings, watchtowers and Roman ruins, groves and beaches, monasteries and villages, winding paths leading to isolated coves, and panoramic views of the bays of both Naples and Salerno, remains relatively undiscovered.

The Amalfi Coast. One of the most gorgeous places on Earth is the corner of the Campania region called the Amalfi Coast. The justly famed jewels along the water are Positano, Amalfi, and Ravello. Considering the natural splendor of this region, it's no surprise that it has some of the most beautiful beaches in the world. White, sunbaked villages rise above cliffs hollowed out with grottoes and crystal lagoons lapped by emerald green water. Larger beaches, like those in Positano and Amalfi, are easily accessible, but the magic often lies in finding hidden coves and scenic spots, such as the picture-perfect Marina di Praia.

Planning

Getting Here and Around

BOAT

Several companies offer a variety of fast craft and passenger and car ferries connecting the islands of Capri, Ischia, and Procida with Naples and Pozzuoli year-round. Hydrofoils and other fast craft leave from Naples's Molo Beverello, adjacent to Piazza Municipio, with some departures in high season also from Mergellina, about 1½ km (1 mile) west of Piazza Municipio. Slower car ferries leave from the berths at Calata Porta di Massa, a 10-minute walk, or three-minute shuttle bus ride, east of Molo Beverello.

Information on departures is published every day in the local paper, *Il Mattino*. Alternatively, ask at the tourist office or at the port, check websites (🌐 *www.caremar.it*, 🌐 *www.navlib.it*, 🌐 *www.snav.it*) or contact these companies directly. Always double-check schedules in stormy weather.

BUS

Within Campania there's an extensive network of local SITA buses (🌐 *www.sitasudtrasporti.it*), although finding information about it can be trying.

CAR

You can get along fine without a car in Campania, and there are plenty of reasons not to have one. Much of Naples is pedestrianized, meaning motorized arteries are often bottlenecked; you can't bring a car to Capri (except in winter, when everything's closed); and parking in the towns of the Amalfi Coast is hard to come by and expensive.

Italy's main north–south route, the A1 (aka the Autostrada del Sole), connects Rome with Naples and Campania. In good traffic the drive to Naples from Rome takes a little more than two hours. The A3 autostrada, a somewhat perilous continuation of the A1, runs south from Naples through Campania and into Calabria. Herculaneum (Ercolano) and Pompeii (Pompei) both have marked exits off the A3. For Vesuvius, take the Portici Ercolano exit. For the Sorrento Peninsula and the Amalfi Coast, exit at Castellammare di Stabia. To get to Paestum, take the A3 to the Battipaglia exit, and follow the road to Capaccio Scalo–Paestum. Roads on the Sorrento Peninsula and Amalfi Coast are narrow and twisting, but they have outstanding views.

If you come to Naples by car, find a garage such as Petraglia (🌐 *garagepetraglia.it*), agree on the rate, and leave it there for the duration of your stay. (If you park on the street, you run the risk of theft.)

TAXI

You may be able to hail a taxi if you see one driving, but your best bet is to call Taxi Napoli (🌐 *www.taxinapoli.it*) ask someone at your hotel to book one. Taxi ranks can be found outside the central Piazza Garibaldi train station and the port (Molo Beverello), as well as throughout the city. Watch out for overcharging at three locations: the airport, the railway station, and the hydrofoil marina. The official fixed rate (be sure to ask for *tariffa predeterminata*!) from the airport to the central station is €21/port area €24, which covers three people and baggage. City Airport Taxis (🌐 *www.city-airport-taxis.com*) offers a private service.

TRAIN

There are up to five trains every hour between Rome and Naples. Both the Alta Velocità Frecciarossa and Italo trains (the fastest types of train service) make the trip in a little more than an hour, with the Intercity taking two. All trains to Naples stop at the refurbished but forever scuzzy Stazione Centrale (🌐 *www.trenitalia.com*,🌐 *www.italotreno.it*).

The frequent (though run-down) suburban Circumvesuviana (🌐 *www.eavsrl.it*) runs from Naples's Porta Nolana and stops at Stazione Centrale before continuing to Herculaneum, Pompeii, and Sorrento. Travel time between Naples and Sorrento on the Circumvesuviana line is about 75 minutes.

For ticketing purposes, the region is divided into travel zones by distance from Naples. If you're traveling from Naples to anywhere else in Campania, be sure to ask for a *biglietto integrato*. It's slightly more expensive than the direct ticket (€0.50 more), but there will be no need to buy a separate ticket for your subway, tram, or bus ride to the train station as the biglietto integrato covers the whole journey. An integrato ticket to Herculaneum costs €3.10, to Pompeii €4.10, and to Sorrento €5.80. Tap and Go Ticketless now allows you to use your bank card for your journeys.

Hotels

Most parts of Campania have accommodations in all price categories, but they tend to fill up in high season, so reserve well in advance. In summer, on the coast and the islands, hotels that serve meals often require you to take half board.

⇨ *Hotel and restaurant reviews have been shortened. For full information, visit Fodors.com. Prices in the hotel reviews are the lowest cost of a standard double room in high season. Prices in the dining reviews are the average cost of a main course at dinner, or, if dinner is not served, at lunch.*

What It Costs in Euros

	$	$$	$$$	$$$$
RESTAURANTS				
	under €20	€20–€30	€31–€40	over €40
HOTELS				
	under €175	€175–€400	€401–€600	over €600

Making the Most of Your Time

In Campania there are three primary travel experiences: Naples, with its restless exuberance; the resorts (Capri, Sorrento, the Amalfi Coast), dedicated to leisure and indulgence; and the archaeological sites (Pompeii, Herculaneum, Paestum), where the ancient world is frozen in time. Each is wonderful in its own way. If you have a week, you can get a good taste of all three. With less time, you're better off choosing between them rather than stretching yourself thin.

Pompeii, being a day trip, is the simplest to plan for. To get a feel for Naples, you should give it a couple of days at a minimum. The train station makes a harsh first impression (an overhaul has softened the blow), but the city grows on you as you take in the sights and interact with the locals.

That said, many people bypass Naples and head right for the resorts. These places are all about relaxing—you'll miss the point if you're in a rush. Although Sorrento isn't as spectacular as Positano or Capri, it makes a good base because of its central location.

DISCOUNTS AND DEALS

Government-run sites are free on the first Sunday of each month—good for those on a budget, but less so for avoiding crowds. The **Campania ArteCard** with app entitles users to free or discounted admission to about four dozen museums and monuments in Naples and beyond. These are the main passes: Naples, three days (€27), has three sights included and up to 50% off the rest, plus transportation; Campania region, three days (€41), including Pompeii and other Bay of Naples sights and Ravello and Paestum with two sights included and others up to 50% off, plus transportation; Campania region, seven days (€43), with five sights included and many others up to 50% off, but no transportation. For longer stays the new 365 Gold Pass allows two entries to principle attractions and up to 50% off entry to others over an entire year (€50). Other benefits (which vary depending on the pass) include discounts on audio guides, theater tickets, city tours, and other activities. Visitors ages 18–25 receive generous discounts (10 free admissions) with the three-day Napoli Young card (€16) and 365 Gold Pass Young (€36) for entry to the Arte-Card circuit sights over a year.

Confusingly, there's an e-commerce-driven **Naples Pass** (app only). It includes some free sights, tours, and added discounts. Transport passes and other attractions, including the Vesuvius Express trip can be added. The cheapest three-day option Naples Pass is €37 while the seven-day Region Area Pass is €99. For more information, visit ⊕ *www.campaniartecard.it* and ⊕ *www.naples-pass.eu*, or the tourist office in the Piazza Garibaldi station, which distributes a helpful booklet about the various passes.

Restaurants

As the birthplace of pizza, Naples prides itself on its vast selection of pizzerias, among the most famous of which are Da Michele (where Julia Roberts filmed her pizza scene in *Eat Pray Love*) or Sorbillo. Many Neapolitans make lunch their big meal of the day and then have a pizza for supper.

Dining on the Amalfi Coast, Capri, Ischia, and Procida revolves largely around seafood. Dishes are prepared using the short, rolled handmade *scialatielli* or large *paccheri* pasta and adorned with local *vongole* (clams) or *cozze* (mussels) and other shellfish. Octopus, squid, and the fresh fish of the season are always on the menu for the second course. Cetara has been famous for its *alici* (anchovies) since Roman times, and even produces alici bread. Eateries range from beach-side trattorias to beacons of fine dining with stupendous views.

Tours

City Sightseeing

BUS TOURS | **FAMILY** | Close to the port, beside the main entrance to Castel Nuovo, is the terminal for double-decker buses belonging to City Sightseeing. For €26 you can take two different excursions, giving you reasonable coverage of the downtown sights and outlying attractions like the Museo di Capodimonte; tickets are valid for 24 hours, and you can join the tour at any stop. City Sightseeing also offers a shuttle service to Pompeii. ✉ *Piazza Municipio, Naples* ☎ *081/5517279, 335/7803812 mobile/WhatsApp* ⊕ *www.city-sightseeing.it/naples.*

Lino Tour

GUIDED TOURS | Lino Tour offers tailor-made tours of the attractions in and around Naples. ✉ *Naples* ☎ *081/8772244* 🌐 *www.linotourcarservice.com.*

Naples

Located under the shadow of Vesuvius, Naples is the most vibrant city in Italy—a steaming, bubbling, reverberating minestrone in which each block is a small village and everything seems to be a backdrop for an opera not yet composed.

It's said that northern Italians vacation here to remind themselves of the time when Italy was *molto italiana—really* Italian. In this respect, Naples (Napoli in Italian) doesn't disappoint: Neapolitan rainbows of laundry wave in the wind over alleyways, mothers caress children, men break out into impromptu arias at sidewalk cafés, and street scenes offer an intricate theater of human exchanges.

Everywhere contrasting elements of faded gilt and romance, grandeur and squalor form a pageant of pure *Napoletanità*, a distillation of *Italianità*—Italy at its most Italian.

As the historic capital of the region known as Campania, Naples has been perpetually and tumultuously in a state of flux. Neapolitans are instinctively the most hospitable of people, and they've often paid a price for being so, having unwittingly extended a warm welcome to wave after wave of invaders. Lombards, Goths, Normans, Swabians, Spanish viceroys and kings, and Napoleonic generals arrived in turn; most of them proved to be greedy and self-serving. Still, if these foreign rulers bled the populace dry with taxes, they left the impoverished city with a rich architectural inheritance.

GETTING HERE AND AROUND

Public transportation in Naples is decent, and includes two subway lines, three funiculars, and a multitude of buses. Tickets cost €1.30 per journey, but a Ticket Integrato Campania costs €1.80 and is valid for 90 minutes on all transport for as far as Pozzuoli to the west and Portici to the east; €5.40 buys a *biglietto giornaliero* (all-day ticket).

Now with a couple of art-decorated stations (Toledo and Università) voted among Europe's most attractive, Naples's Metropolitana provides fairly frequent service and can be the fastest way to get across the traffic-clogged city. Linea 1, Metropolitana Collinare, links the hill area of the Vomero and beyond with the National Archaeological Museum and Piazza Municipio near the port, as well as Stazione Centrale. The older Linea 2 stretches from the train station to Pozzuoli. Trains on both lines run 5:45 am–11 pm. To check journey costs and download the app visit 🌐 *www.unicocampania.it.*

Bus service is viable, especially with the introduction of larger buses on the regular R1, R2, R3, and R4 routes. Electronic signs display wait times at many stops. Three tram routes now thread through the streets with new tram rolling stock introduced in 2020, but the service is unreliable and regularly suspended.

VISITOR INFORMATION

Many tourist offices in Naples have closed in recent years (government cuts) and those open have sporadic hours. Handily placed in the Centro Storico is the old Infopoint office run by Campania Turismo in Piazza del Gesù. Pick up a free map and info about possible savings through the Campania ArteCard.

CONTACTS **Info Turismo Regionale Piazza del Gesù.** ✉ *Piazza del Gesù Nuovo 7, Centro Storico* ☎ *081/5512701* 🌐 *www.visitnaples.eu/en.*

Campania Through the Ages

Ancient history. Lying on Mediterranean trade routes plied by several pre-Hellenic civilizations, Campania was settled by the ancient Greeks from approximately 800 BC onward. Here myth and legend blend with historical fact. The town of Herculaneum is said—rather improbably—to have been established by Hercules himself; and Naples in ancient times was called Parthenope, the name attributed to one of the sirens who preyed on hapless sailors in antiquity.

Thanks to archaeological research, some of the layers of myth have been stripped away to reveal a pattern of occupation and settlement well before Rome became established. Greek civilization flourished for hundreds of years all along this coastline, but there was nothing in the way of centralized government until centuries later when the Roman Republic, uniting all Italy for the first time, absorbed the Greek colonies with little opposition. Generally, the peace of Campania was undisturbed during these centuries of Roman rule.

Foreign influences. Naples and Campania, like Italy in general, decayed along with the Roman Empire and was thereafter squabbled over by Europe's foreign dynasties. Naples regained some importance under the rule of the Angevins in the latter part of the 13th century and continued its progress in the 1440s under Aragonese rule. The nobles who served under the Spanish viceroys in the 16th and 17th centuries enjoyed their pleasures, even as Spain milked the area for taxes.

After a short Austrian occupation, Naples became the capital of the Kingdom of the Two Sicilies, which the Bourbon kings established in 1738. Their rule was generally benevolent as far as Campania was concerned, and their support of papal authority in Rome was important in the development of the country as a whole. Their rule was important artistically, too, contributing to the architecture of the region, and attracting great musicians, artists, and writers who were drawn by the easy life at court. Finally, Giuseppe Garibaldi launched his famous expedition, and in 1860 Naples was united with the rest of Italy.

Modern times. Things were relatively tranquil through the years that followed—with visitors thronging to Capri, Sorrento, Amalfi, and, of course, Naples—until World War II. Allied bombings did considerable damage in and around Naples. At the fall of the fascist government, the sorely tried Neapolitans rose up against Nazi occupation troops and in four days of street fighting drove them out of the city. A monument was raised to the *scugnizzo* (the typical Neapolitan street urchin), celebrating the youngsters who participated in the battle. With the end of the war, artists, tourists, writers, and other lovers of beauty returned to the Campania region.

As time passed, some parts of Campania gained increased attention from visitors, while others lost their cachet. Years of misgovernment have left their mark, yet the region's cultural and natural heritage is finally being revalued as local authorities and inhabitants recognize the importance of the area's largest industry—tourism.

Centro Storico

To experience the true essence of Naples, you need to explore the Centro Storico, an unforgettable neighborhood that is the heart of old Naples. This is the Naples of peeling building facades and hanging laundry, with small alleyways fragrant with fresh flowers laid at the many shrines to the Blessed Virgin. Here the cheapest pizzerias in town feed the locals like kings, and the raucous street carnival of Neapolitan daily life is punctuated with oases of spiritual calm. All the contradictions of Naples—splendor and squalor, palace and slum, triumph and tragedy—meet here and sing a full-throated chorale.

Sights

Duomo di Napoli

CHURCH | Although this cathedral was established in the 1200s, the current building was erected a century later and has since undergone radical changes—especially during the baroque period. Inside, the 350-year-old wooden ceiling is supported by 110 ancient columns salvaged from pagan buildings. The 4th-century church of Santa Restituta, incorporated into the cathedral, was redecorated in the late 1600s in the baroque style, though the mosaics in the Battistero (Baptistery) are claimed to be the oldest in the Western world.

In the Cappella del Tesoro di San Gennaro, multicolor marbles and frescoes honor St. Januarius, the miracle-working patron saint of Naples. Three times a year his dried blood is believed to liquefy during rites in his honor. The most spectacular painting is Ribera's *San Gennaro in the Furnace* (1647), depicting the saint emerging unscathed from the furnace. The Museo del Tesoro di San Gennaro houses a rich collection of treasures associated with the saint. ✉ *Via Duomo 149, Centro Storico* ☎ *081/449097 Duomo, 081/294980 Tesoro di San Gennaro* 🌐 *tesorosangennaro.it* 🎫 *Tesoro di San Gennaro with audio guide €13, guided visits €25* Ⓜ *Duomo, Cavour.*

Gesù Nuovo

CHURCH | A stunning architectural contrast to the plain Romanesque frontage of other nearby churches, the strikingly austere, recently restored (2023) stone facade of this elaborate Baroque church dates to the late 16th century. Originally a palace, the building was seized by Pedro of Toledo in 1547 and sold to the Jesuits with the condition that the facade remain intact. Behind the entrance is Francesco Solimena's action-packed *Heliodorus' Eviction from the Temple*. You can find the work of familiar Baroque sculptors (Naccherino, Finelli) and painters inside. The gracious *Visitation* above the altar in the second chapel on the right is by Massimo Stanzione, who also contributed the fine frescoes in the main nave: they're in the presbytery (behind and around the main altar). ✉ *Piazza Gesù Nuovo, Centro Storico* ☎ *081/5578111* Ⓜ *Dante.*

★ LAPIS Museum

RUINS | **FAMILY** | The beautifully restored 17th-century Basilica di Pietrasanta, a Cosimo Fanzago Baroque masterpiece built on the site of the Roman Temple of Diana, hosts regular multimedia exhibitions, but the star attraction here is the underground visit to a section of Naples's oldest aqueduct. Four tours a day descend 40 meters (131 feet) below the busy Via dei Tribunali to large lavishly illuminated cisterns hewed from excavated tuff two millennia ago, still filled with running water (thanks to a collaboration with the city's waterworks). ✉ *Piazzetta Pietrasanta 17/18, Centro Storico* ☎ *081/19230565* 🌐 *www.lapismuseum.com* 🎫 *€10* ✍ *Reservations essential on weekends* Ⓜ *Dante.*

The Madonna and Pistol

PUBLIC ART | This piece is by controversial street artist Banksy. Located on a wall in front of the grand facade of the chiesa dei Girolamini, the church where the 17th-century philosopher Giambattista Vico is buried, the stencilled *La Madonna con la Pistola* sits behind a protective glass screen and attracts a regular trickle of devotees. ✉ *Piazza Girolamini, Centro Storico* Ⓜ *Cavour.*

Madre (*Museum of Contemporary Art Donnaregina*)

ART GALLERY | With 86,111 square feet of exhibition space, a host of young and helpful attendants, and occasional late-night events, the Madre is one of the most visited museums in Naples. Most of the artworks on the first floor were installed in situ by their creators, but the second-floor gallery exhibits works by international and Italian contemporary artists. The museum also hosts temporary shows by major international artists. ✉ *Via Settembrini 79, San Lorenzo, Centro Storico* ☎ *081/19528498* 🌐 *www.madrenapoli.it/en* 🎫 *€8* 🕒 *Closed Tues.* Ⓜ *Cavour.*

Monumento Nazionale dei Girolamini

RELIGIOUS BUILDING | *I Girolamini* is another name for the Oratorians, followers of St. Philip Neri, to whom the splendid church I Girolamini is dedicated. The church is part of a larger complex managed as the Monumento Nazionale dei Girolamini. The Florentine architect Giovanni Antonio Dosio designed I Girolamini, which was erected between 1592 and 1619; the dome and facade were rebuilt (circa 1780) in the most elegant neoclassical style after a design by Ferdinando Fuga. Inside the entrance wall is Luca Giordano's grandiose fresco (1684) of Christ chasing the money changers from the temple. The intricate carved-wood ceiling, damaged by Allied bombs in 1943, has now been restored to its original magnificence. ✉ *Via Duomo 142, Centro Storico* ☎ *081/294444* 🌐 *www.bibliotecadeigirolamini.beniculturali.it* 🎫 *€5* 🕒 *Closed Mon.* Ⓜ *Cavour.*

★ **Museo Archeologico Nazionale** (*National Museum of Archaeology*)

HISTORY MUSEUM | Also known as MANN, this legendary museum, located on the northern edge of the Centro Storico district, has experienced something of a rebirth in recent years. Its unrivaled collections include world-renowned archaeological finds that put most other museums to shame, from some of the best mosaics and paintings from Pompeii and Herculaneum to the legendary Farnese collection of ancient sculpture. The core masterpiece collection is almost always open to visitors, while seasonal exhibitions feature intriguing cultural events, collaborations, and contemporary artists. Some of the newer rooms, covering archaeological discoveries in the Greco-Roman settlements and necropolises in and around Naples, have helpful informational panels in English. ✉ *Piazza Museo 19, Centro Storico* 🌐 *mann-napoli.it* 🎫 *€20* 🕒 *Closed Tues.* Ⓜ *Museo.*

★ **Museo Cappella Sansevero** (*Sansevero Chapel Museum*)

NOTABLE BUILDING | The dazzling funerary chapel of the Sangro di Sansevero princes combines noble swagger, overwhelming color, and a touch of the macabre—which expresses Naples perfectly. The chapel was begun in 1590 by Prince Giovan Francesco di Sangro to fulfill a vow to the Virgin if he were cured of a dire illness. The seventh Sangro di Sansevero prince, Raimondo, had the building modified in the mid-18th century and is generally credited for its current baroque styling, the noteworthy elements of which include the splendid marble-inlay floor and statuary, including Giuseppe Sanmartino's spine-chillingly lifelike *Cristo Velato* (Veiled Christ). ✉ *Via Francesco de Sanctis 19, off Vicolo Domenico Maggiore, Centro Storico* ☎ *081/5524936* 🌐 *www.museosansevero.it* 🎫 *€12* 🕒 *Closed Tues.* Ⓜ *Dante.*

Sights

1 Duomo di Napoli D2
2 Gesù Nuovo A5
3 LAPIS Museum B4
4 The Madonna and Pistol D3
5 Madre.................... D1
6 Monumento Nazionale dei Girolamini D3
7 Museo Archeologico Nazionale................ A2
8 Museo Cappella Sansevero............... B4
9 Napoli Sotterranea C3
10 Ospedale delle Bambole D4
11 Pio Monte della Misericordia.............. E3
12 San Lorenzo Maggiore C3
13 Santa Chiara A5

Restaurants

1 Di Matteo D3
2 Gino Sorbillo............ B4
3 L'Etto...................... A3
4 Palazzo Petrucci Pizzeria................... B5

Quick Bites

1 Scaturchio............... B5

Hotels

1 Costantinopoli 104 ...... A3
2 Hotel Palazzo Decumani................ D4

Napoli Sotterranea (*Underground Naples*)
HISTORIC SIGHT | FAMILY | Fascinating 90-minute tours of a portion of Naples's fabled underground city provide an initiation into the complex history of the city center. Efforts to dramatize the experience—amphoras lowered on ropes to draw water from cisterns, candles given to navigate narrow passages, objects shifted to reveal secret passages—combine with enthusiastic English-speaking guides to make this particularly exciting for older children. Be prepared on the underground tour to go up and down many steps and crouch in very narrow corridors. ✉ *Piazza San Gaetano 68, along Via dei Tribunali, Centro Storico* ☎ *081/296944* 🌐 *www.napolisotterranea.org* 🎫 *€15* Ⓜ *Dante, Cavour.*

★ **Ospedale delle Bambole**
SPECIALTY MUSEUM | FAMILY | In the courtyard of the 16th-century Palazzo Marigliano is this world-famous hospital for dolls, which has a small museum dedicated to its poignant mission. Doll limbs, eyes and well-cuddled, antique characters of all shapes and descriptions spill from packed shelves. In business since 1895, it's a wonderful place to take kids (and their injured toys) and for anyone who retains a childhood sense of wonder with a penchant for the uncanny. ✉ *Via San Biagio dei Librai 39, Centro Storico* ☎ *081/18639797* 🌐 *ospedaledellebambole.com* 🎫 *€3* 🕒 *Closed Tues.–Thurs.* Ⓜ *Duomo.*

★ **Pio Monte della Misericordia**
RELIGIOUS BUILDING | One of the Centro Storico's defining sites, this octagonal church was built around the corner from the Duomo for a charitable institution seven noblemen founded in 1601. The institution's aim was to carry out acts of Christian charity like feeding the hungry, clothing the poor, nursing the sick, sheltering pilgrims, visiting prisoners, and burying the indigent dead—acts immortalized in the history of art by Caravaggio's famous altarpiece depicting the *Sette Opere della Misericordia* (*Seven Acts of Mercy*). Pride of place is given to the great Caravaggio above the altar. ✉ *Via Tribunali 253, Centro Storico* ☎ *081/446973* 🌐 *piomontedellamisericordia.it* 🎫 *€10* 🕒 *Closed Sun. afternoon* Ⓜ *Cavour, Duomo.*

★ **San Lorenzo Maggiore**
RELIGIOUS BUILDING | The church of San Lorenzo features a very unmedieval facade of 18th-century splendor. Due to the effects and threats of earthquakes, the church was reinforced and reshaped along Baroque lines in the 17th and 18th centuries. Begun by Robert d'Anjou in 1270 on the site of a previous 6th-century church, the church has a single, barnlike nave that reflects the Franciscans' desire for simple spaces. Also found here is the church's most important monument: the tomb of Catherine of Austria (circa 1323), by Tino da Camaino. ✉ *Via dei Tribunali 316, Centro Storico* ☎ *081/2110860* 🌐 *www.laneapolissotterrata.it* 🎫 *Excavations and museum €9* Ⓜ *Cavour, Dante.*

★ **Santa Chiara**
RELIGIOUS BUILDING | Offering a stark contrast to the opulence of the nearby Gesù Nuovo, Santa Chiara is the leading Angevin Gothic monument in Naples. The fashionable house of worship for the 14th-century nobility, the church of St. Clare was intended to be a great dynastic monument by Robert d'Anjou. Built in a Provençal Gothic style between 1310 and 1328 (probably by Gagliardo Primario) and dedicated in 1340, the church had its aspect radically altered in the baroque period. A six-day fire started by Allied bombs on August 4, 1943, put an end to all that, as well as to what might have been left of the important cycle of frescoes by Giotto and his Neapolitan workshop. Around the left side of the church is the Chiostro delle Clarisse, the most famous cloister in Naples. ✉ *Piazza Gesù Nuovo, Centro Storico* ☎ *081/5516673* 🌐 *www.monasterodisantachiara.it*

Museum and cloister €7 Cloister closed Sun. afternoon M Dante, Università.

Restaurants

Di Matteo

$ | **PIZZA** | **FAMILY** | Every pizzeria along Via dei Tribunali is worth the long wait—and trust us, all the good ones will be jam-packed—but just one can claim to have served a U.S. president: Bill Clinton enjoyed a Margherita here when the G8 was held in Naples in 1994. Today the superlative *pizzaioli* (pizza makers) turn out a wide array of pizzas, all to the utmost perfection. **Known for:** functional decor and pizzaioli working at front; funny pics of Clinton and the "Pizzaiolo del Presidente" Ernesto Cacialli in 1994; top value, including filling pizza fritta (fried). *$ Average main: €9 Via Tribunali 94, Centro Storico 081/455262 www.pizzeriadimatteo.com Closed Sun. M Cavour, Dante.*

Gino Sorbillo

$ | **PIZZA** | **FAMILY** | There are a few restaurants called Sorbillo along Via dei Tribunali, but this one is world-renowned. Order the same thing the locals do, namely a basic Neapolitan pizza (try the unique pizza al pesto or the stunningly simple marinara, with just San Marzano tomatoes, wild garlic, and oregano) that's cooked to perfection by the third generation of pie makers who run the place. **Known for:** the crowd waiting outside; leave your name at the door and listen to be called; head honcho Gino is a celebrity and pizza ambassador. *$ Average main: €12 Via Tribunali 32, Centro Storico 081/446643 www.sorbillo.it Closed Sun. M Dante.*

L'Etto

$ | **SOUTHERN ITALIAN** | This innovative eatery offers a menu of fixed-price bowls such as the *squisita* (exquisite) with rice, octopus, hummus, and fennel or the *vivace* (lively) with seared tuna fillet, chopped hazelnuts, and three types of rice. The open kitchen looks over a large, high, communal table with stools, and outdoor seating overlooks the bustling Piazza Bellini. **Known for:** healthy Mediterranean (including vegan and vegetarian) dishes; communal interior eating area; outdoor plaza seating. *$ Average main: €15 Via Santa Maria di Costantinopoli 102, Centro Storico 081/3145078 www.ettoexperience.it M Dante, Museo.*

Palazzo Petrucci Pizzeria

$ | **PIZZA** | **FAMILY** | Here you can dine under vaulted ceilings in the former stables of a 17th-century mansion, eat outdoors overlooking the grand Piazza San Domenico Maggiore, or feast from a table on the roof terrace, facing the *giuglia* (obelisk) di San Domenico. Options include *pizze* or *pizze fritte*—with classic or unusual toppings—as well as robust salads and antipasti. **Known for:** grandest palazzo venue for a pizza feast; atmospheric views and sounds over the piazza; craft beer, pizze fritte, and vegan options. *$ Average main: €12 Piazza San Domenico Maggiore 5–7, Centro Storico 081/5512460 palazzopetrucci.it Closed 2 wks in Aug. M Dante.*

Coffee and Quick Bites

★ Scaturchio

$ | **CAFÉ** | Established in 1905, this Neapolitan institution on Spaccanapoli is a buzzy place to sample some of the finest pastries in town—plus it also makes classic savory dishes, ice cream, and mighty decent coffee. **Known for:** sumptuous babà, sfogliatelle, and pastiera; Ministeriale liquor-filled chocolates; zucchine a scapece, arancini, and other savory bites. *$ Average main: €6 Piazza San Domenico Maggiore 19, Centro Storico 081/5516944 www.scaturchio.it M Dante.*

Hotels

Costantinopoli 104

$$ | **HOTEL** | An oasis of what Italians call *stile liberty* (Art Nouveau style), with impressive stained-glass fittings and striking artwork, this serene, elegant hotel is well placed for touring the Centro Storico and visiting the Museo Archeologico Nazionale. **Pros:** pool (a rarity in Neapolitan hotels) and garden; pleasant service; tranquil oasis in the heart of the city. **Cons:** rooms are getting dated; can be difficult to find; some rooms suffer from nightlife disturbance from Piazza Bellini. *Rooms from: €324 Via Costantinopoli 104, Centro Storico 081/5571035 www.costantinopoli104.it 19 rooms Free Breakfast Museo.*

★ Hotel Palazzo Decumani

$$ | **HOTEL** | This contemporary upscale hotel near the Centro Storico's major sights occupies an early-20th-century palazzo, but you won't find heavy, ornate furnishings—the emphasis is on light and space, both in short supply in old Naples. **Pros:** guests-only lounge-bar; large rooms and bathrooms; service on par with fancier hotels. **Cons:** pricey parking in nearby garage; unkempt neighborhood; disappointing breakfast. *Rooms from: €200 Piazzetta Giustino Fortunato 8, Centro Storico 081/4201379 www.palazzodecumani.com 28 rooms Free Breakfast Duomo.*

Nightlife

Lento Hi-Fi Bar

COCKTAIL BARS | Deep in the Centro Storico between the buzzy Piazza Bellini and edgy Piazza Mercato, you'll find this sophisticated spot opened in 2025 for fab cocktails and light *stuzzichini* bites. The area's first listening bar-cum-modern speakeasy is backdropped by stylish, design-lit interiors and a top sound system with resident and visiting DJs behind the altar-like console tweaking the nobs of the bespoke rotary mixer into the early hours. *Giovanni Paladino 23, Centro Storico 392/2192837 mobile www.lentohifi.it.*

Shopping

Ferrigno

CRAFTS | Shops selling Nativity scenes cluster along the Via San Gregorio Armeno off Spaccanapoli, and they're all worth a glance. The most famous is Ferrigno. Although Maestro Giuseppe Ferrigno died in 2008, the family business continues, still faithfully using 18th-century techniques. *Via San Gregorio Armeno 8, Centro Storico 081/5523148 www.arteferrigno.it Cavour, Duomo.*

Toledo

Naples's setting on what is possibly the most captivating bay in the world has long been a boon for its inhabitants—the expansive harbor has always brought great mercantile wealth to the city—and, intermittently, a curse. Throughout history, a who's who of Greek, Roman, Norman, Spanish, and French despots has quarreled over this gateway to Campania. Each set of conquerors recognized that the area around the city harbor—today occupied by the Molo Beverello hydrofoil terminal and the 1928 Stazione Marittima—functioned as a veritable welcome mat to the metropolis and consequently should be a fitting showcase of regal authority. This had become imperative because of explosive population growth, which, by the mid-16th century, had made Naples the second-largest city in Europe, after Paris. With the mass migration of the rural population to the city, Naples had grown into a capricious, unplanned, disorderly, and untrammeled capital. Thus, the central aim of the ruling dynasties became the creation of a *Napoli nobilissima*—a "most noble" Naples.

Sights
1 Castel Nuovo C5
2 Galleria Umberto I ... B5
3 Gallerie d'Italia – Palazzo Banco di Napoli B4
4 Palazzo Reale B6
5 Piazza del Plebiscito ... B6
6 Sant'Anna dei Lombardi.... B1
7 Teatro San Carlo and Memus Museum B5
8 Via Toledo... B2
Restaurants
1 A' Cucina Ra Casa Mia.... A5
2 A Pignata ... A2
3 Trattoria San Ferdinando . A5
Hotels
1 Palazzo Turchini C3
2 Renaissance Naples Hotel Mediterraneo........ B3
A
B
C
D
1
2
3
4
5
6
7
8
9
Santa Chiara
Largo Bianchi Nuovi
Centro Storico
Universita'
Piazza Bovio
Corso Umberto I
Via Mezzocannone
V. Sedile di Porto
Via Donnalbina
Via G. Sanfelice
Piazza G. Matteotti
Via A. Diaz
Via Cesare Battisti
Via Monteoliveto
V. Carrozzieri alla Posta
Calata Trinità Maggiore
Piazza Carità
Via Toledo
Toledo
Via Pasquale Scura
Via San Liborio
Via Pignasecca
Str. Formale
Vc. 1° Portapiccola
Via Girardi
V. G. Simonelli
V. Concezione a Montecalvario
Vico San Matteo
Vico Nuovo
Vico Lungo del Gelso
Vico San Sepolcro
Via de Deo
Vico Giardinetto
Vico Lungo
Lungo Teatro
Vico Speranzella
Vico della Tofa
Via P. E. Imbriani
Vc. d'Afflitto
Via Santa Brigida
Via San Mattia
Vc. Berio
Vico Sergente Maggiore
Vico Carlo de Cesare
Via Nardones
Piazza Trieste e Trento
Via San Carlo
Via Chiaia
Via Serra
Via Ponte di Tappia
V. S. Giacomo
V. Cervantes de Saavedra
Via Medina
Rua Catalana
Via F. Gioia
Via A. Depretis
Via Alcide de Gasperi
Via Cristoforo Colombo
Calata S. Marco
Municipio
Toledo
Piazza Municipio
Via Vittorio Emanuele II
Palazzo Reale
Piazza del Plebiscito
Via A. F. Acton
Bacino Vittorio Emanuele III
Via de Cesare
Galleria della Vittoria
Via Pallonetto Santa Lucia
Via Cesario Console
Pizzo-Falcone
Via Santa Lucia
Via Cuma
Via R. de Cesare
Via M. Turchi
Via Generale Orsini
Via Palepoli
Via Nazario Sauro
Golfo di Napoli
Santa Lucia
Via Chiatamone
Via Lucilio
Via Partenope
0
1/8 mi
0
1/8 km
KEY
Line 1 Metropolitana Collinare
Line 6
Sights
Restaurants
Hotels
Toledo

Sights

★ Castel Nuovo

CASTLE/PALACE | Known to locals as Maschio Angioino, in reference to its Angevin builders, this imposing castle is now used more for marital than for military purposes—a portion of it serves as a government registry office. A white four-tiered triumphal entrance arch, ordered by Alfonso of Aragon after he entered the city in 1443 to seize power from the increasingly beleaguered Angevin Giovanna II, upstages the building's looming Angevin stonework. Across the courtyard within the castle is the Sala Grande, also known as the Sala dei Baroni, which has a stunning vaulted ceiling 92 feet high. **TIP→ Guided tours (in English and Italian), which provide greater access to the castle's rooms, are available once inside the castle.** ✉ *Piazza Municipio, Toledo* ☎ *081/7957722* 🌐 *www.comune.napoli.it/maschioangioino* 🎟 *€6, tours €10* 🕒 *Closed Sun.* Ⓜ *Municipio.*

Galleria Umberto I

NOTABLE BUILDING | The galleria was erected during the "cleanup" of Naples following the devastating cholera epidemic of 1884. With facades on Via Toledo—the most animated street in Naples at the time—the Liberty-style arcade with curvy glass and wrought-iron dome and vaulted wings, built between 1887 and 1890 according to a design by Emanuele Rocco, had a prestigious and important location. ✉ *Entrances on Via San Carlo, Via Toledo, Via Santa Brigida, and Via Verdi, Toledo* Ⓜ *Toledo.*

Gallerie d'Italia – Palazzo Banco di Napoli

ART GALLERY | Once the headquarters of the Banco di Napoli, this vast 20th-century building houses a small museum that's worth seeking out for its outstanding collection of 17th- and 18th-century paintings. Relocated from the nearby 17th-century Palazzo Zevallos Stigliano in 2022, the star attraction is Caravaggio's last work, *The Martyrdom of Saint Ursula.* The saint here is, for dramatic effect, deprived of her usual retinue of a thousand followers. On the left, with a face of pure spite, is the king of the Huns, who has just shot Ursula with an arrow after his proposal of marriage has been rejected. A changing program "L'Ospite Illustre" introduces pieces by an "Ilustrious guest," such as Raphael and Velázquez from renowned collections. ✉ *Via Toledo 177, Toledo* ☎ *800/167619* 🌐 *gallerieditalia.com* 🎟 *€7* 🕒 *Closed Mon.* Ⓜ *Toledo.*

★ Palazzo Reale

CASTLE/PALACE | **FAMILY** | Created to express Bourbon power and values, the Palazzo Reale (circa 1600) was originally commissioned by the Spanish viceroys as a residence for King Philip III, should he chance to visit Naples. He died in 1621 before ever doing so. The palace was subsequently renovated by successive rulers—including dim-witted Ferdinand IV who liked to fire his hunting rifles at the birds in his tapestries—and is filled with lavish, 18th century–style salons.

To the right after climbing the monumental Scalone d'Onore (Staircase) is the Court Theater, built for Charles III and his private opera company. Highlights beyond include the Throne Room, with its ponderous titular object dating to sometime after 1850; the Ambassadors' Room, with choice Gobelin tapestries and a ceiling painted by Belisario Corenzio (1610–20) that honors Spanish military victories; Room IX, which was bedroom to Charles's queen, Maria Cristina; the Great Captain's Room, with ceiling frescoes by Battistello Caracciolo (1610–16) and a jolly wall-mounted series by Federico Zuccari depicting 12 proverbs; Room XIII, a writing room with some furnishings by Adam Weisweiler, cabinetmaker to Marie Antoinette; and the huge Room XXII featuring Sèvres porcelain.

The heavily gilt Palatine Chapel has a multicolor marble intarsia altar, as well as a Nativity scene with some pieces sculpted by Giuseppe Sammartino. Another wing holds the Biblioteca Nazionale Vittorio Emanuele III. Starting out from Farnese bits and pieces, it was enriched with the papyri from Herculaneum found in 1752. There's also a terrace that looks onto Castel Nuovo. In the Bourbon stables, the Galleria del Tempo (open afternoons and evenings only) offers a multimedia trip through the history of Naples. The Museo Caruso (open mornings only) in the monumental Sala Dorica is dedicated to the great Neapolitan tenor Enrico Caruso. ✉ *Piazza Plebiscito, Toledo* ☎ *081/400547 ticket office, 848/800288* 🌐 *palazzorealedinapoli.org* 🎫 *Palazzo, museums and galleria €15; gardens €2; guided visits to the attics and belvedere €7* ⏲ *Closed Wed.* Ⓜ *Toledo, Municipio.*

Piazza del Plebiscito

PLAZA/SQUARE | In 1994, after a period of having been used as a parking lot, this square was restored to create one of Napoli Nobilissima's most majestic spaces, with a Doric semicircle of columns resembling St. Peter's Square in Rome. The piazza was erected in the early 1800s under the Napoleonic regime, and after the regime fell, Ferdinand, the new King of the Two Sicilies, ordered the addition of the Church of San Francesco di Paola. On the left as you approach the church is a statue of Ferdinand and on the right one of his father, Charles III, both of them clad in Roman togas. Around dusk, floodlights come on, creating a magical effect. A delightful sea breeze airs the square, and most days one corner becomes an improvised soccer stadium where local youths emulate their heroes. ✉ *Piazza del Plebiscito, Toledo* Ⓜ *Toledo, Municipio.*

★ Sant'Anna dei Lombardi

CHURCH | This church, simple and rather anonymous from the outside, houses some of the most important ensembles of Renaissance sculpture in southern Italy. Begun with the adjacent convent of the Olivetani and its four cloisters in 1411, it was given a Baroque makeover in the mid-17th century by Gennaro Sacco.

To the left of the Ligorio Altar is the Mastrogiudice Chapel, whose altar contains *Scenes from the Life of Jesus* (1489) by Benedetto da Maiano, a great name in Tuscan sculpture. On the other side of the entrance is the Piccolomini Chapel, with a *Crucifixion* by Giulio Mazzoni (circa 1550), a refined marble altar (circa 1475), and a funerary monument to Maria d'Aragona by another prominent Florentine sculptor, Antonello Rossellino (circa 1475). ✉ *Piazza Monteoliveto 15, Toledo* ☎ *081/4420039* 🌐 *www.santannadeilombardi.com* 🎫 *Side chapels, oratory, and sacristy €6; Abbots' Crypt €2* ⏲ *Side chapels, oratory, and sacristy closed Sun. morning* Ⓜ *Dante.*

Teatro San Carlo and Memus Museum

PERFORMANCE VENUE | Of Italy's opera houses, La Scala in Milan is the most famous, but San Carlo is perhaps the most beautiful, and Naples is, after all, the most operatic of cities. The neoclassical structure, designed by Antonio Niccolini, was built in a mere nine months after an 1816 fire destroyed the original. Many operas, including Donizetti's *Lucia di Lammermoor* and Rossini's *La Donna del Lago,* were composed for the house. Its nearly 200 boxes are arranged on six levels, and its 12,000-square-foot stage permits large-scale productions.

If you're not attending an opera, you can still experience the splendid theater on a 30-minute guided tour and a visit to Memus (Museo Memoria e Musica). The theatrically lit museum and archive have props, costumes, stage sets, multimedia displays, and documents galore. ✉ *Via San Carlo 98/F, Toledo* ☎ *081/7972331 ticket office, 081/7972412 tours, 081/7972449 Memus* 🌐 *www.teatrosancarlo.it* 🎫 *Tours €9; museum €3* ⏲ *Museum closed Wed.* Ⓜ *Municipio.*

Via Toledo

HISTORIC DISTRICT | Sooner or later you'll wind up at one of the busiest commercial arteries, also known as Via Roma, which is thankfully closed to through traffic—at least along the stretch leading from the Palazzo Reale. Don't avoid dipping into this parade of shops and coffee bars where plump pastries are temptingly arranged. ✉ *Via Toledo, Toledo* Ⓜ *Toledo.*

Restaurants

A' Cucina Ra Casa Mia

$ | SOUTHERN ITALIAN | Just off bustling Via Toledo on the basalti flagstones of a narrow Quartieri Spagnoli street, this small trattoria does superb-value, classic Neapolitan dishes. Take a seat at one of the small tables with checkered tablecloths and ask the amiable staff about the day's freshest seafood, meat, and vegetable dishes while taking in the atmospheric surroundings. **Known for:** homey place popular with locals; fresh seafood pasta dishes; veggie and gluten-free options. $ *Average main: €16* ✉ *Via Carlo De Cesare 14, Toledo* ☎ *081/4976297* 🌐 *www.acucinaracasamia.it* ⏲ *Closed Tues.*

A Pignata

$ | SOUTHERN ITALIAN | A hidden gem in the Quartieri Spagnoli, A Pignata is a favorite with locals for its typical Neapolitan cooking. Each antipasto of land and sea is a meal in itself, but save space for the grilled calamari or *involtini di cotica di maiale*, rolled pork rind stuffed with garlic, parsley, pine nuts, and sultanas. **Known for:** sumptuous local dishes; relaxed atmosphere; a favorite with locals. $ *Average main: €15* ✉ *Vico Lungo del Gelso 110/112, Toledo* ☎ *081/413526* 🌐 *www.trattoriapignata.it* ⏲ *Closed Mon.* Ⓜ *Toledo.*

Trattoria San Ferdinando

$ | SOUTHERN ITALIAN | This family-run trattoria exudes a calm, relaxed atmosphere, offering traditional Neapolitan dishes without fuss or ostentation. Try the excellent fish or the pasta dishes, which are cooked with a light, modern touch, especially those with *verdure* (fresh leafy vegetables) or with *patate con la provola* (potatoes and smoked mozzarella). **Known for:** excellent, fresh seafood specialties; popular with locals in the evening, so reserve ahead; near Teatro San Carlo. $ *Average main: €17* ✉ *Via Nardones 117, Toledo* ☎ *081/421964* 🌐 *www.trattoriasanferdinando.com* ⏲ *Closed Sun. and last 3 wks of Aug. No dinner Sat. and Mon.* Ⓜ *Toledo, Municipio.*

Hotels

Palazzo Turchini

$$ | HOTEL | Just a few minutes' walk from the Castel Nuovo, Palazzo Turchini is one of the city center's more attractive smaller hotels. **Pros:** close to port and Metro stop; more intimate than neighboring business hotels; rooftop terrace. **Cons:** close to a busy traffic hub; rooms a tad businesslike; rooms on the small and stuffy side. $ *Rooms from: €180* ✉ *Via Medina 21, Toledo* ☎ *081/5510606* 🌐 *www.palazzoturchini.it* *27 rooms* 🍽 *Free Breakfast* Ⓜ *Municipio.*

Renaissance Naples Hotel Mediterraneo

$$ | HOTEL | Within walking distance of both the Teatro San Carlo and the Centro Storico, this efficient, Marriott-affiliated business hotel has a lobby and guest rooms that are bright and airy. **Pros:** convenient to the port; pleasant rooftop breakfast terrace; good for those who want a modern hotel. **Cons:** in a busy part of town; looking tired in places; not for those who want historic atmosphere. $ *Rooms from: €371* ✉ *Via Nuova Ponte di Tappia 25, Toledo* ☎ *081/7970001* 🌐 *www.marriott.com* *189 rooms* 🍽 *Free Breakfast* Ⓜ *Toledo, Municipio.*

Shopping

Ascione

JEWELRY & WATCHES | A family firm established in 1855 and known for its traditionally made coral jewelry and artwork, Ascione has a showroom/gallery on the second floor of a shabby wing of the Galleria Umberto. Don't miss the 30-minute guided tour (€5, book ahead), which explains the company's rich history and takes in displays that include Egypt's King Farouk's elaborate wedding gift to his bride, Farida, as well as what many consider to be the most beautiful cameo in existence. ✉ *Piazzetta Matilde Serao 19, Piazza Municipio* ☎ *081/421111* 🌐 *www.ascione.it* Ⓜ *Municipio.*

Chiaia, Santa Lucia, and Nearby

The Lungomare is the city's grandest stretch of waterfront. In the 19th century, Naples's waterfront harbored the picturesque quarter that was called Santa Lucia, a district dear to artists and musicians and known for its fishermen's cottages. The fishermen were swept away when an enormous landfill project extended the land out to what is now Via Nazario Sauro and Via Partenope, the address for some of Naples's finest hotels. Huge stretches of the waterfront are blessedly traffic-free, only enhancing their distinctly Neapolitan charm. The area also boasts the chic Chiaia neighborhood surrounding Piazza dei Martiri and the gilded 19th-century Villa Pignatelli.

Sights

Castel dell'Ovo (*Castle of the Egg*)

CASTLE/PALACE | **FAMILY** | This 12th-century castle, the oldest in Naples, was built atop the ruins of an ancient Roman villa on a thin promontory that dangles over the Porto Santa Lucia. Legend has it that the poet Virgil hid inside the villa an egg that had protective powers as long as it remained intact. The belief was taken so seriously that to quell the people's panic after Naples suffered an earthquake, an invasion, and a plague in quick succession, its monarch felt compelled to produce an intact egg, solemnly declaring it to be the original.

Today, the castle shares its views with some of the city's top hotels, and its gigantic rooms, rock tunnels, and belvederes over the bay are among the city's most striking sights. **■ TIP→ Note that Castel dell'Ovo is closed for renovation work. Although it's scheduled to reopen in 2025, check on its status before visiting.** ✉ *Santa Lucia waterfront, Via Eldorado 3, off Via Partenope, Santa Lucia* ☎ *081/7956180* 🌐 *www.comune.napoli.it/casteldellovo* 🎫 *Free* Ⓜ *Municipio.*

★ **Lungomare** (*Seafront*)

PROMENADE | The first thing Mayor Luigi de Magistris did after his 2011 election was to banish traffic from the city's seafront. Strolling, skating, or biking along Via Caracciolo and Via Partenope with Capri, Vesuvius, and the Castel dell'Ovo in your sights is a favorite Neapolitan pastime. ✉ *Via Caracciolo, Chiaia* Ⓜ *Mergellina, Municipio.*

Restaurants

★ **Amici Miei**

$$ | **SOUTHERN ITALIAN** | Favored by meat eaters who can't abide another bite of bream, this cozy, dimly lit dining den is known for dishes such as tender carpaccio with fresh artichoke hearts. There are also excellent house-made pasta selections, including orecchiette with chickpeas or *pappardelle al sugo di agnello* (pasta with lamb sauce), but the highlights are the extravagant grilled meat plates. **Known for:** a choice of quality meat dishes; held in high esteem locally; warm, friendly service befitting the name. 💲 *Average main: €23* ✉ *Via Monte di Dio 78, Chiaia* ☎ *081/7646063* 🌐 *www.*

ristoranteamicimiei.com ⏲ *Closed Mon. and late July–early Sept. No dinner Sun.* Ⓜ *Chiaia.*

Da Dora

$$ | **SEAFOOD** | Despite its location on an unpromising-looking *vicolo* (alley) off the Riviera di Chiaia, this small restaurant has achieved cult status for its seafood platters. It's remarkable what owner–chef Renato can produce in his tiny kitchen—start with linguine *alla Dora,* laden with local seafood and fresh tomatoes, and perhaps follow up with grilled *pezzogna* (blue-spotted bream). **Known for:** freshest seafood, both raw and cooked; simple, attractive nautical-theme decor; good quality but slow service when busy. Ⓢ *Average main: €26* ✉ *Via Ferdinando Palasciano 30, Chiaia* ☎ *081/680519* ⏲ *Closed Mon.* Ⓜ *San Pasquale.*

'O Tabaccaro

$ | **SEAFOOD** | If you're trying to keep to a budget but want to enjoy a seafood feast alongside the yachts of the Borgo Marinaro harbor, head to this former tobacco store, now a family-run trattoria. While your eyes feast on all the pretty boats, the Lungomare hotels, the Castel dell'Ovo, and Vesuvius, you can savor classic Neapolitan seafood spaghetti or an *impepata di cozze* (mussels with pepper and garlic, available May–Aug.). **Known for:** relatively inexpensive fare; harborside dining; family service. Ⓢ *Average main: €15* ✉ *Via Luculliana 28, Santa Lucia* ☎ *081/7646352* 🌐 *www.facebook.com/brunaruoppolo.1990* Ⓜ *Municipio.*

★ **Pescheria Mattiucci**

$$ | **SOUTHERN ITALIAN** | This fourth-generation fish shop run by brothers is also a trendy, if rough-and-ready, spot to enjoy a super-fresh but pricey seafood meal—including superb Neapolitan sushi—and cold wine while sitting on a buoy stool. **Known for:** pescheria counter displaying today's catch; intimate and small place, so get here early or call ahead; fish lunches. Ⓢ *Average main: €26* ✉ *Vico Belledonne a Chiaia 27, Chiaia* ☎ *081/2512215* 🌐 *www.pescheriamattiucci.com* ⏲ *Closed Sun. and Mon.* Ⓜ *San Pasquale.*

★ **Umberto**

$ | **SOUTHERN ITALIAN** | Run by the Di Porzio family since 1916, Umberto is one of the city's classic restaurants, combining the poshness of its neighborhood, Chiaia, and the friendliness found in other parts of Naples. Try the *paccheri d'o treddeta* ("three-finger" pasta with octopus, tomato, olives, and capers), which bears the nickname of the original Umberto, who happened to be short a few digits. **Known for:** authentic Pizza DOC (smaller, with chunky cornicione rim); charming hosts; classic Neapolitan meat sauce alla Genovese. Ⓢ *Average main: €19* ✉ *Via Alabardieri 30–31, Chiaia* ☎ *081/418555* 🌐 *www.umberto.it* ⏲ *No lunch Mon.* Ⓜ *Chiaia.*

Coffee and Quick Bites

Gran Caffè Cimmino

$ | **CAFÉ** | Connoisseurs often say the most refined pastries in town can be found at Gran Caffè Cimmino. Many of the city's lawyers congregate here, to celebrate or commiserate with crisp, light cannoli; airy lemon eclairs; choux paste in the form of a mushroom laced with chocolate whipped cream; and delightful wild-strawberry tartlets. **Known for:** Neapolitan breakfast favorite; babà (rum-soaked sponge cake) to die for; terrace for watching Chiaia's finest. Ⓢ *Average main: €4* ✉ *Via G. Filangieri 12/13, Chiaia* ☎ *081/418303* 🌐 *www.facebook.com/cimminofilangieri* Ⓜ *Chiaia.*

Moccia Panefìcio

$ | **NEAPOLITAN** | Established in 1936, this *quartiere* Chiaia favorite is the locals' choice for classic Neapolitan pastries like babà (rum-soaked sponge cake), *torta caprese* (chocolate-and-nut cake), *pastiera* (tart), and *sfogliatelle* (shell-shape pastry), freshly baked bread and panini for picnics and buffet/pastry trays

Chiaia, Santa Lucia, and Nearby
Sights
1 Castel dell'Ovo D8
2 Lungomare . B7
Restaurants
1 Amici Miei .. C6
2 Da Dora A5
3 'O Tabaccaro .. D8
4 Pescheria Mattiucci ... B5
5 Umberto..... B6
Quick Bites
1 Gran Caffè Cimmino..... B5
2 Moccia Paneficio.... A5
Hotels
1 Chiaja Hotel de Charme .. D5
2 Grand Hotel Parker's A4
3 Grand Hotel Saint Lucia .. D7
4 Grand Hotel Vesuvio...... D7
5 Il Transatlantico Napoli D8
6 Palazzo Alabardieri .. C6
7 Weekend a Napoli..... A1
TO CIMITERO DELLE FONTANELLE
Vomero
Castel Sant'Elmo
Certosa e Museo di San Martino
Largo San Martino
Funicolare di Montesanto
Funicolare di Chiaia
Funicolare Centrale
Quartieri Spagnoli
Piazza Fuga
Piazza Carità
Via Toledo
Corso Vittorio Emanuele
Amadeo
Chiaia
Via dei Mille
Largo del Vasto a Chiaia
Piazza dei Martiri
Piazza Santa Maria degli Angeli
Piazza Plebiscito
Galleria della Vittoria
San Pasquale
Riviera di Chiaia
Aquarium
Villa Comunale
Piazza della Vittoria
Via Arcoleo
Via Francesco Caracciolo
Pizzofalcone
Santa Lucia
Via Chiatamone
Via Partenope
LUNGOMARE
Golfo di Napoli
Borgo Marinaro
KEY
Line 2 Metropolitana FS
Line 6
Sights
Restaurants
Quick Bites
Hotels
0
1/4 mi
0
1/4 km
A
B
C
D
1
2
3
4
5
6
7
8
9

for parties. **Known for:** zeppola di San Giuseppe (cream-filled pastry); pizzette and other savory snacks; taralli (crackers) and other crunchy goodies. *Average main: €5 Via Pasquale di Chiaia 21, Chiaia 081/402131 www.mocciapanificio.com Piazza Amedeo.*

Hotels

Chiaja Hotel de Charme

$ | **HOTEL** | This 18th-century palazzo has a great location, and its apartments, all on the first floor, have plenty of atmosphere. **Pros:** good location near Piazza del Plebiscito and the Palazzo Reale; on a bustling pedestrian-only street; some antiques in guest rooms. **Cons:** no views in a town with some great ones; even with air-conditioning some rooms get hot in summer; entrance up a flight of stairs. *Rooms from: €140 Via Chiaia 216, Chiaia 081/415555 www.hotelchiaia.it 33 rooms Free Breakfast Chiaia.*

★ Grand Hotel Parker's

$$$ | **HOTEL** | A little up the hill from Chiaia, with fine views of the bay and distant Capri, this landmark hotel first opened in 1870 and continues to offer a supreme dose of elegance. **Pros:** excellent restaurant; fabulous views; historical hotel. **Cons:** a very long walk or taxi ride from city center and seafront; not much going on in immediate neighborhood; terrace sometimes closed when hosting weddings. *Rooms from: €557 Corso Vittorio Emanuele 135, Chiaia 081/7612474 www.grandhotelparkers.it 67 rooms Free Breakfast Piazza Amedeo.*

Grand Hotel Santa Lucia

$$ | **HOTEL** | Neapolitan Lungomare enchantment can be yours if you stay at this luxurious, quietly understated hotel, which overlooks the port immortalized in the song "Santa Lucia." Hundreds of boats bob in the water, seafood restaurants line the harbor, and the medieval Castel dell'Ovo presides over it all. **Pros:** great views from most rooms; proximity to the port is convenient for trips to the islands; fab pastries and baked goods. **Cons:** rooms can be small and dated; extra charges at breakfast; not near a metro stop. *Rooms from: €330 Via Partenope 46, Santa Lucia 081/7640666 www.santalucia.it 85 rooms Free Breakfast Municipio.*

★ Grand Hotel Vesuvio

$$$ | **HOTEL** | You'd never guess from the blandly modern exterior that this is the oldest of the city's great seafront hotels—the place where Enrico Caruso died, where Oscar Wilde dallied with lover Lord Alfred Douglas, and where Bill Clinton charmed the waitresses—but, fortunately, the spacious, soothing interior compensates for what's lacking on the outside. **Pros:** luxurious atmosphere; historical setting and traditionally furnished rooms; directly opposite Borgo Marinaro. **Cons:** pool closes Sundays/public holidays; some rooms are small; public spaces and some rooms need updating. *Rooms from: €495 Via Partenope 45, Santa Lucia 081/7640044 www.vesuvio.it 160 rooms Free Breakfast Municipio.*

★ Il Transatlantico Napoli

$$ | **B&B/INN** | Enjoying perhaps the most enchanting setting in all of Naples, this modestly priced hotel tops many a traveler's dream list of places to stay. **Pros:** fabulous views; great location at a reasonable price; boat hire available. **Cons:** basic, somewhat dated rooms; no elevator; sometimes loud music in the Borgo. *Rooms from: €205 Via Lucculliana 15, Santa Lucia 081/7648842 www.transatlanticonapoli.com 8 rooms No Meals Municipio.*

★ Palazzo Alabardieri

$$ | **HOTEL** | Just off the chic Piazza dei Martiri, this intimate hotel pairs modern facilities with a traditional feel. **Pros:** impressive public salons; central location

close to fancy shops and restaurants; polite, pleasant, and professional staff. **Cons:** no sea view; cell reception, Wi-Fi, and air-conditioning are patchy; small rooms. *Rooms from: €220 Via Alabardieri 38, Chiaia 081/415278 www.palazzoalabardieri.it 33 rooms Free Breakfast Chiaia.*

★ Weekend a Napoli

$$ | B&B/INN | Patrizia and Paolo run this homey upscale B&B in a handsome stile-liberty (Italian Art Nouveau) palazzo on the well-to-do Vomero hill. **Pros:** residential Vomero atmosphere with family pics and presepi; quality bedding and tasteful decor with interesting artworks; passionate, knowledgeable hosts who run tours. **Cons:** basic rooms lack light and are noisy; some rooms have precarious steps to mezzanine beds; away from the downtown sights. *Rooms from: €178 Via Enrico Alvino 157, Vomero 081/5781010 weekendanapoli.com Closed Jan. 6 rooms Free Breakfast Quattro Giornate.*

Nightlife

★ Enoteca Belledonne

WINE BAR | Between 8 and 9 some evenings, it seems as though the whole upscale Chiaia neighborhood has descended into this tiny space for an aperitivo. The small tables and low stools can be awkward, but the cozy atmosphere, friendly staff, and the pleasure of being surrounded by glass-front cabinets full of wine bottles with beautiful labels more than makes up for it. Excellent local wines are available by the glass at great prices. *Vico Belledonne a Chiaia 18, Chiaia 081/403162 www.enoteca-belledonne.eu San Pasquale.*

Shopping

Marinella

ACCESSORIES | Count the British royal family among the customers of this shop, which has been selling traditional made-to-measure ties for more than 100 years. It also sells scarves and other small accessories for both men and women. *Via Riviera di Chiaia 287, Chiaia 081/2451182 www.emarinella.eu Chiaia, San Pasquale.*

Tramontano

LEATHER GOODS | Since 1865, this place has been crafting fine leather luggage, bags, belts, and wallets. *Via Chiaia 143, Chiaia 081/414837 www.tramontano.it Chiaia.*

Piazza Garibaldi

The first place many see in Naples thanks to the city's main train station, there is not a lot to hold your attention here. Recently completely rebuilt, it now features a swanky new underground shopping mall based around the train station, but is still a gathering point for street sellers and hawkers and is best avoided at night. The surrounding area is scruffy with some notable churches as well as the famed Porta Capuana, one of the historic gates to the city walls.

Restaurants

Da Michele

$ | PIZZA | FAMILY | You may recognize Da Michele from the movie *Eat, Pray, Love,* but for more than 140 years before Julia Roberts arrived, this place was a culinary reference point. Despite offering only four types of pizza—marinara (tomato, garlic, and oregano), Margherita (tomato, mozzarella, and basil), *cosacca* (tomato, pecorino, and basil), and *marita* (half marinara, half Margherita)—plus a small selection of drinks, it still manages to draw long lines. **Known for:** pizza purists' favorite; stripped-down choice of pizzas; long lines outside the humble, historic flagship location. *Average main: €6 Via Sersale 1/3, off Corso Umberto, between Piazza Garibaldi and Piazza Nicola*

Amore, Piazza Garibaldi ☏ *081/5539204* 🌐 *www.damichele.net* ⏲ *Closed 2 wks in Aug.* Ⓜ *Garibaldi, Duomo.*

Mimì alla Ferrovia

$ | **NEAPOLITAN** | Patrons of this local institution have included the filmmaker Federico Fellini and that truly Neapolitan comic genius and self-styled aristocrat Totò. It's in a fairly seedy area, but it's worth taking a taxi (especially at night) to get here and sample updated versions of such classics as grilled octopus or *tubettoni* (short, tubular pasta shapes) with sausage-meat, mushrooms, and provola cheese. **Known for:** crammed with photos of Italian VIPs; classic Neapolitan dishes with modern touches; a merry crowd of diners. $ *Average main: €19* ✉ *Via A. D'Aragona 19/21, Piazza Garibaldi* ☏ *081/5538525* 🌐 *www.mimiallaferrovia.it* ⏲ *Closed Sun. and last wk in Aug.* Ⓜ *Garibaldi.*

Capodimonte and Vomero

The Parco di Capodimonte is the crowning point of the vast mountainous plain that slopes down through the city to the waterfront. With views over the entire city and bay, the park was first founded in the 18th century as a hunting preserve by Charles of Bourbon. Before long he commissioned a spectacular Palazzo Reale for the park. Today this palace is the Museo di Capodimonte, which contains among its treasures the city's greatest collection of Old Master paintings.

To the west is the largely residential Vomero. From the balcony belvedere of the Museo di San Martino, a rich spread of southern Italian amplitude fills the eye: hillsides dripping with luxuriant greenery interspersed with streets short and narrow, countless church spires, and far below, the reason it all works, the intensely blue Bay of Naples. To tie together the lower parts with Vomero, everyone uses the *funicolare*—the funicular system that runs up and down the hill.

Sights

Castel Sant'Elmo

CASTLE/PALACE | Perched on the Vomero, this massive castle is almost the size of a small town. Built by the Angevins in the 14th century to dominate the port and the old city, it was remodeled by the Spanish in 1537. The parapets, configured in the form of a six-pointed star, provide fabulous views. Once a major military outpost, the castle these days hosts occasional cultural events. Within the castle, the Museo del Novecento traces Naples's 20th-century artistic output. For sunset and golden-hour views, plus half-price entry come after 4 pm. ✉ *Largo San Martino, Vomero* ☏ *081/5587708* 🌐 *www.beniculturali.it* 🎫 *€5* Ⓜ *Vanvitelli.*

★ **Certosa e Museo di San Martino**

RELIGIOUS BUILDING | Atop a rocky promontory with a fabulous view of the entire city, this monastery seems more like a palace. Indeed, the *certosa,* or charter house, started in 1325, was so sumptuous that by the 18th century Ferdinand IV threatened to halt the religious order's government subsidy. Highlights include the Cappella del Tesoro, with Luca Giordano's ceiling fresco of Judith holding aloft Holofernes's head and Jusepe de Ribera's masterful *Pietà;* the Quarto del Priore (Prior's Quarters), an extravaganza of salons filled with frescoes and paintings; and the Sezione Presepiale, the world's greatest collection of Christmas cribs. ✉ *Piazzale San Martino 8, Vomero* ☏ *081/2294503* 🌐 *www.beniculturali.it* 🎫 *€6* ⏲ *Closed Wed.* Ⓜ *Vanvitelli.*

★ **Museo di Capodimonte**

ART MUSEUM | The grandiose, 18th-century, neoclassical, Bourbon royal palace houses fine and decorative art in 124 rooms. The main galleries on the first floor are devoted to the Farnese collection, as well as work from the 13th to the 18th century, including many pieces by Dutch masters, as well as an El Greco and 12 Titian paintings. On the second floor look for stunning paintings by Simone Martini (circa 1284–1344) and Caravaggio (1573–1610). ✉ *Via Miano 2, Capodimonte* ☎ *081/7499111* 🌐 *capodimonte.cultura.gov.it* 🎫 *€15* 🕒 *Closed Wed.* Ⓜ *Museo then Bus C63, 168, 178, 204, or 3M.*

Fonoteca

BARS | By day, this is the city's best independent record store. By night, it's *the* place to hear eclectic tunes and mingle in Vomero. It serves decent bar snacks, pasta dishes, cakes, and drinks. ✉ *Via Morghen 31, Vomero* ☎ *081/5560338* 🌐 *www.fonoteca.net* Ⓜ *Vanvitelli.*

Herculaneum

10 km (6 miles) southeast of Naples.

A visit to the archaeological site of Herculaneum neatly counterbalances the hustle of its larger neighbor, Pompeii. Although close to the heart of busy Ercolano—indeed, in places right under the town—the ancient site seems worlds apart.

GETTING HERE AND AROUND

To get to Herculaneum by car, take the A3 Naples–Salerno autostrada and exit at Ercolano. Follow signs for the "Scavi" (excavations). The Circumvesuviana railway connects Herculaneum to Naples, Portici, Torre del Greco, Torre Annunziata, Pompeii, and Sorrento.

★ Herculaneum Ruins

ARCHAEOLOGICAL SITE | Lying more than 50 feet below the present-day town of Ercolano, the ruins of Herculaneum are set among the acres of greenhouses that make this area an important European flower-growing center. In AD 79, the gigantic eruption of Vesuvius, which also destroyed Pompeii, buried the town under a tide of volcanic mud. Excavation first began in 1738 under King Charles of Bourbon. Today less than half of Herculaneum has been excavated. Nevertheless, what has been found is generally better preserved than Pompeii. In some cases, you can even see the original wooden beams, doors, and staircases. At the entrance, pick up a free map showing the gridlike layout of the dig. Splurge on an audio guide app via 🌐 *www.ercolano.tours* (€10): the standard audio guide (€8 for one, €13 for two) may be available for those without a smartphone. You can also join a group with a local guide (around €15 per person). Most of the houses are open, and a representative cross section of domestic, commercial, and civic buildings can be seen. ✉ *Corso Resina 6, Ercolano* ☎ *081/0106490* 🌐 *ercolano.beniculturali.it* 🎫 *€16; €5 supplement for Teatro Antico.*

Museo Archeologico Virtuale (MAV)

HISTORY MUSEUM | **FAMILY** | With dazzling "virtual" versions of Herculaneum's streets and squares and a multidimensional simulation of Vesuvius erupting, Herculaneum's 1st-century-meets-the-21st-century museum is a must for kids and adults alike. After stopping at the ticket office, you descend, as in an excavation, to a floor below. You'll experience Herculaneum's Villa dei Papiri before and (even more dramatically) during the eruption, courtesy of special effects: enter "the burning cloud" of AD 79; then emerge, virtually speaking, inside Pompeii's House of the Faun, which can be seen both as it is and as it was for two centuries BC. The next re-creation is again Villa dei Papiri. Then comes a stellar pre- and postflooding view of Baia's Nymphaeum, the now-displaced statues arrayed as they were in the days of Emperor Claudius, who commissioned them.

Bay of Naples
Naples see detail maps
Sorrento & Amalfi Coast see detail map
Capri see detail map
Marina di Lago di Pátria
Marina di Varcature
Cumae
Qualiano
Marano di Nápoli
Casavatore
Miano
Casória
Capodimonte
Solfatara
Pozzuoli
Agnano Terme
Mergellina
Marechiaro
Baia
Bacoli
Miseno
Capo Misene
Golfo di Pozzuoli
Isola di Nisida
Golfo di Napoli
Procida Porto
Procida
Vivara
ISOLA DI PROCIDA
Punta Solchiaro
Punta Cornacchia
Lacco Ameno
Ischia Porto
Forio
Monte Epomeo
Spiaggia di Citard
Ischia
Ischia Ponte
Giardini Poseidon Terme
Barano d'Ischia
Sant' Angelo
Punta Sant'Angelo
ISOLA D'ISCHIA
TYRRHENIAN SEA
Nola
Pomigliano
Volla
Somma
S Anastasia
Cércola
Ottaviano
Vesuvius
Parco del Vesùvio
S Giuseppe
Terzigno
Pogglomarino
Boscotrecase
Boscoreale
Pompeii
Portici
Herculaneum
Torre del Greco
Oplontis (Torre Annunziata)
Circumvesuviana Rail Line
Palma
Parco Regionale del Partenio
Monteforte
Sarno
Pagani
Nocera
S António
Castellammare di Stábia
Gragnana
Vico Equense
Marina di Equa
Piano di Sorrento
Meta
Alimuri
Sorrento
Marina di Puolo
Massa Lubrense
SORRENTINE PENINSULA
Positano
Sant'Agata sui Due Golfi
Metrano
Termini
Punta Campanella
Praiano
Amalfi
Ravello
Maiori
Cetara
THE AMALFI COAST
Bocca Piccola
Grotta Azzurra
Punta dell'Arcera
Anacapri
Marina Grande
Capri
Marina Piccola
ISOLA DI CAPRI
A1
A16
A30
A3
18
145
0
10 mi
0
10 km

Planning for Your Day in Pompeii

Getting There

The archaeological site of Pompeii has its own stop (Pompei–Villa dei Misteri) on the Circumvesuviana line to Sorrento, close to the main entrance at the Porta Marina, which is the best place from which to start a tour. If, like many visitors every year, you get the wrong train from Naples (stopping at the other "Pompei" station), all is not lost. There's another entrance to the excavations at the far end of the site, just a seven-minute walk to the Amphitheater.

Admission

Single tickets for the vast main sight plus suburban villas cost €22 and are valid for one full day. The site is open April–October, daily 9–7 (last admission at 5:30); and November–March, daily 9–5 (last admission at 3:30). For more information call ☎ *081/8575347* or visit 🌐 *www.pompeiisites.org.*

What to Bring

The only restaurant inside the site is both overpriced and busy, so bring along water and snacks. There are some shady, underused picnic tables outside the Porta di Nola, to the northeast of the site. Luggage is not allowed in the site.

Timing

Visiting Pompeii does have its frustrating aspects: many buildings are blocked off by locked gates, and enormous group tours tend to clog up more popular attractions. But the site is so big that it's easy to lose yourself. To really see the site, you'll need four or five hours, a bit less if you hire a guide.

To get the most out of Pompeii, rent an audio guide and opt for one of the three itineraries (two hours, four hours, or six hours). If hiring a guide, make sure the guide is registered for an English tour and standing inside the gate; agree beforehand on the length of the tour and the price, and prepare yourself for sound bites of English mixed with dollops of hearsay. For a higher-quality (and more expensive) full-day tour, try Context Travel (🌐 *www.contexttravel.com*).

Visitors here are invited to take a front-row seat for "Day and Night in the Forum of Pompeii," with soldiers, litter-bearing slaves, and toga-clad figures moving spectrally to complete the spell; or to make a vicarious visit to the Lupanari brothels, their various pleasures illustrated in graphic virtual frescoes along the walls. A wooden model of Herculaneum's theater, its virtual re-creation, reminds us that it was here that a local farmer, while digging a well, first came across what proved to be not merely a single building but a whole town. Equally fascinating are the virtual baths. There's also a 3D film of Vesuvius erupting, replete with a fatalistic narrative and cataclysmic special effects: the words of Pliny the Younger provide a timeless commentary while the floor vibrates under your feet. ✉ *Via IV Novembre 44, Ercolano* ☎ *081/7776843* 🌐 *www.museomav.it* 🎫 *€11.*

Continued on page 666

ANCIENT POMPEII
TOMB OF A CIVILIZATION

The site of Pompeii, petrified memorial to Vesuvius's eruption in AD 79, is the largest, most accessible, and probably most famous of excavations anywhere.

A busy commercial center with a population of 10,000–20,000, ancient Pompeii covered about 170 acres on the seaward end of the fertile Sarno Plain. Today Pompeii is choked with both the dust of 25 centuries and more than 3 million visitors every year; only by escaping the hordes and lingering along its silent streets can you truly fall under the site's spell.

On a quiet backstreet, all you need is a little imagination to picture life in this ancient town. Come in the late afternoon when the site is nearly deserted and you will understand the true pleasure of visiting Pompei.

Top: Plaster cast of human remains, Pompeii.
Bottom: Standing columns, House of the Faun

A FUNNY THING HAPPENS ON THE WAY TO THE FORUM

as you walk through Pompeii. Covered with dust and decay as it is, the city seems to come alive. Perhaps it's the familiar signs of life observed along the ancient streets: bakeries with large ovens just like those for making pizzas, *thermopolia* (snack bars) tracks of cart wheels cut into the road surface, graffiti etched onto the plastered surfaces of street walls. But a glance up at Vesuvius, still brooding over the scene like an enormous headstone, reminds you that these folks—whether imagined in your head or actually wearing a mantle of

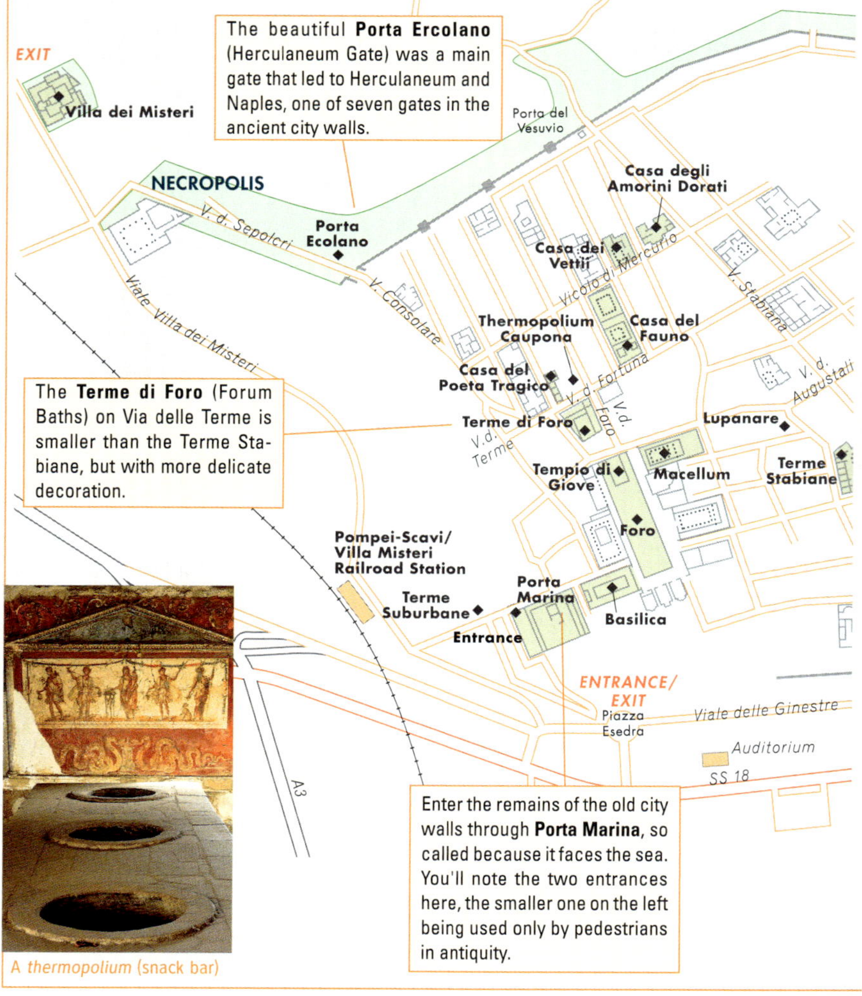

The beautiful **Porta Ercolano** (Herculaneum Gate) was a main gate that led to Herculaneum and Naples, one of seven gates in the ancient city walls.

The **Terme di Foro** (Forum Baths) on Via delle Terme is smaller than the Terme Stabiane, but with more delicate decoration.

Enter the remains of the old city walls through **Porta Marina**, so called because it faces the sea. You'll note the two entrances here, the smaller one on the left being used only by pedestrians in antiquity.

A *thermopolium* (snack bar)

Pompeii's cemetery, or Necropolis

lava dust—have not taken a breath for centuries. The town was laid out in a grid pattern, with two main intersecting streets. The wealthiest took a whole block for themselves; or built a house and rented out the front rooms, facing the street, as shops. There were good numbers of *tabernae* (taverns) and thermopolia on almost every corner, and frequent shows at the amphitheater.

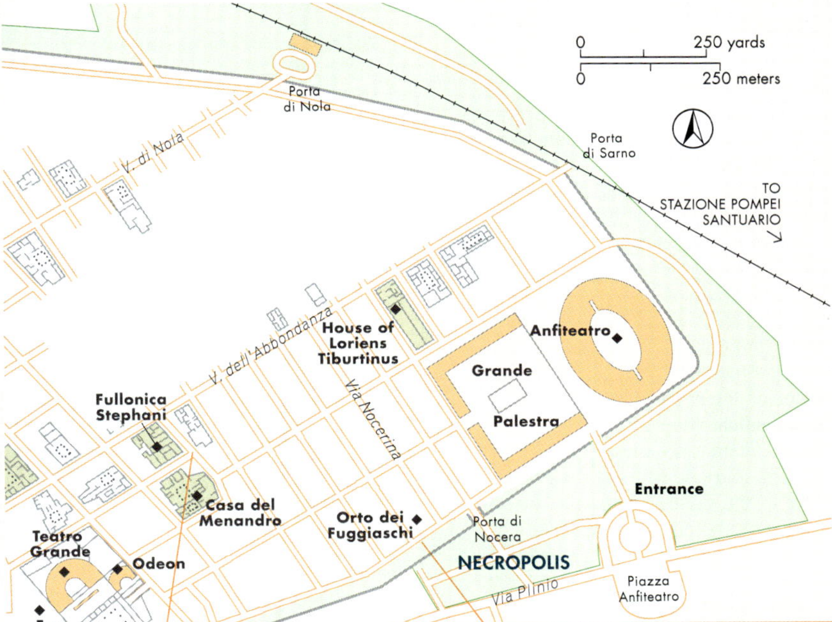

0 250 yards
0 250 meters
Porta di Nola
V. di Nola
Porta di Sarno
TO STAZIONE POMPEI SANTUARIO
House of Loriens Tiburtinus
V. dell' Abbondanza
Anfiteatro
Grande Palestra
Via Nocerina
Fullonica Stephani
Casa del Menandro
Orto dei Fuggiaschi
Entrance
Porta di Nocera
Teatro Grande
Odeon
NECROPOLIS
Via Plinio
Piazza Anfiteatro
Foro Triangolare
Porta di Stabia
Via Plinio

The **Orto dei Fuggiaschi** (Garden of the Fugitives) contains poignant plaster casts of those overwhelmed by the eruption in AD 79 and left *in situ*. Many of the victims were claimed a day after the initial eruption not by the rain of lapilli and ash but by the first surge— a dense cloud of vapor, ash, and other solids that swept down the slopes of the volcano like a boiling avalanche at 40–50 miles per hour.

Togas, the required Roman attire, were washed and wool was dyed at a *fullonica* (fullery). Urine was used to bleach and clean garments in large stone vats and basins, that you can see all over Pompeii.

PUBLIC LIFE IN ANCIENT POMPEII

Forum

THE CITY CENTER

As you enter the ruins at Porta Marina, make your way uphill to the **Foro** (Forum), which served as Pompeii's commercial, cultural, political, and religious center. You can still see some of the two stories of colonnades that used to line the square. Like the ancient Greek *agora* in Athens, the Forum was a busy shopping area, complete with public officials to apply proper standards of weights and measures. Fronted by an elegant three-column portico on the eastern side of the forum is the **Macellum**, the covered meat and fish market dating to the 2nd century BC; here vendors sold goods from their reserved spots in the central market. It was also in the Forum that elections were held, politicians let rhetoric fly, speeches and official announcements were made, and worshippers crowded around the **Tempio di Giove** (Temple of Jupiter), at the northern end of the forum.

Basilica

On the southwestern corner is the **Basilica**, the city's law court and the economic center. These rectangular aisled halls were the model for early Christian churches, which had a nave (central aisle) and two side aisles separated by rows of columns. Standing in the Basilica, you can recognize the continuity between Roman and Christian architecture.

THE GAMES

The **Anfiteatro** (Amphitheater) was the ultimate in entertainment for Pompeians and offered a gamut of experiences, but essentially this was for gladiators rather than wild animals. By Roman standards, Pompeii's amphitheater was quite small (seating 20,000). Built in about 70 BC,

Amphitheater

making it the oldest extant permanent amphitheater in the Roman world, it was oval and divided into three seating areas. There were two main entrances—at the north and south ends—and a narrow passage on the west called the Porta Libitinensis, through which the dead were probably dragged out. A wall painting found in a house near the theater (now in the Naples Museum) depicts the riot in the amphitheater in AD 59 when several citizens from the nearby town of Nocera were killed. After Nocerian appeals to Nero, shows were suspended for three years.

BATHS AND BROTHELS

In its day, Pompeii was celebrated as the Côte d'Azur of the ancient Roman empire. Evidence of a Sybaritic bent is everywhere—in the town's grandest villas, in its baths and rich decorations, and murals revealing a worship of hedonism. Satyrs, bacchantes, hermaphrodites, and acrobatic couples are pictured.

The first buildings to the left past the ticket turnstiles are the **Terme Suburbane** (Suburban Baths), built—by all accounts without permission—right up against the city walls. The baths have eyebrow-raising frescoes in the *apodyterium* (changing room) that strongly suggest that more than just bathing and massaging went on here. On the walls of **Lupanari** (brothels) are scenes of erotic games in which clients could engage. The **Terme Stabiane** (Stabian Baths) had underground furnaces, the heat from which circulated beneath the floor, rose through flues in the walls, and escaped through chimneys. The sequence of the rooms is standard: changing room (apoditerium), tepid (tepidarium), hot (calidarium), and cold (frigidarium). A vigorous massage with oil was followed by rest and conversation.

Fresco of Pyramus and Thisbe in the House of Loreius Tiburtinus

Thanks to those deep layers of pyroclastic deposits from Vesuvius that protected the site from natural wear and tear over the centuries, graffiti found in Pompeii provide unique insights into the sort of things that the locals found important 2,000 years ago. A good many were personal and lend a human dimension to the disaster that not even the sights can equal.

At the baths: **"What is the use of having a Venus if she's made of marble?"**

At the entrance to the front lavatory at a private house: **"May I always and everywhere be as potent with women as I was here."**

On the Viale ai Teatri: **"A copper pot went missing from my shop. Anyone who returns it to me will be given 65 bronze coins."**

In the Basilica: **"A small problem gets larger if you ignore it."**

PRIVATE LIFE IN ANCIENT POMPEII

The facades of houses in Pompeii were relatively plain and seldom hinted at the care and attention lavished on the private rooms within. When visitors arrived they passed the shops and entered an atrium, from which the occupants received air, sunlight, and rainwater, the latter caught by the *impluvium*, a rectangular-shaped receptacle under the sloped roof. In the back was a receiving room, the *tablinum*, and behind was another open area, the peristyle. Life revolved around this uncovered inner courtyard, with rows of columns and perhaps a garden with a fountain. The atrium was surrounded by *cubicula* (bedrooms) and the *triclinium* (dining area). Interior floors and walls were covered with colorful marble tiles, mosaics, and frescoes.

Mosaic, Casa del Poeta Tragico

Several homes were captured in various states by the eruption of Vesuvius, each representing a different slice of Pompeiian life. The **Casa del Fauno** (House of the Faun) displayed wonderful mosaics, now at the Museo Archeologico Nazionale in Naples. The **Casa del Poeta Tragico** (House of the Tragic Poet) is a typical middle-class house. On the floor is a mosaic of a chained dog and the inscription *cave canem* ("Beware of the dog"). The **Casa degli Amorini Dorati** (House of the Gilded Cupids) is an elegant, well-preserved home with original decorations. Many paintings and mosaics were executed at **Casa del Menandro** (House of Menander), a patrician's villa named for a fresco of the Greek playwright. Two blocks beyond the Stabian Baths you'll notice on the left the current digs at the **Casa dei Casti Amanti** (House of the Chaste Lovers). A team of plasterers and painters were at work here when Vesuvius erupted, redecorating one of the rooms and patching up the cracks in the bread oven near the entrance—possibly caused by tremors a matter of days before.

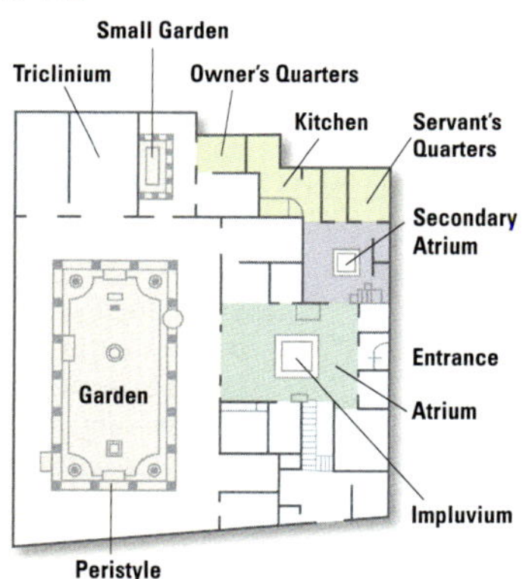

CASA DEI VETTII

The House of the Vettii (reopened in January 2023 after two decades of restoration) is the best example of a house owned by wealthy *mercatores* (merchants). It contains vivid murals—a magnificent *pinacoteca* (picture gallery) within the very heart of Pompeii. The scenes here—except for those in the two wings off the atrium—were all painted after the earthquake of AD 62. Once inside, look at the delicate frieze around the wall of the triclinium (on the right of the peristyle garden as you enter from the atrium), depicting cupids engaged in various activities, such as selling oils and perfumes, working as goldsmiths and metalworkers, acting as wine merchants, or performing in chariot races. Another of the main attractions in the Casa dei Vettii is the small cubicle beyond the kitchen area (to the right of the atrium) with its faded erotic frescoes now protected by Perspex screens.

UNLOCKING THE VILLA DEI MISTERI

Villa dei Misteri

There is no more astounding, magnificently memorable evidence of Pompeii's devotion to the pleasures of the flesh than the frescoes on view at the **Villa dei Misteri** (Villa of the Mysteries), a palatial abode 400 yards outside the city gates, northwest of Porta Ercolano. Unearthed in 1909, this villa had many beautiful rooms painted with frescoes; the finest are in the *triclinium*. Painted in the most glowing Pompeiian reds and ochers, the panels may relate the saga of a young bride (Ariadne) and her initiation into the mysteries of the cult of Dionysus, who was a god imported to Italy from Greece and then given the Latin name of Bacchus. The god of wine and debauchery also represented the triumph of the irrational—of all those mysterious forces that no official state religion could fully suppress.

Pompeii's best frescoes, painted in glowing reds and oranges, retain an amazing vibrancy.

The Villa of the Mysteries frescoes were painted circa 50 BC, most art historians believe, and represent the peak of the Second Style of Pompeiian wall painting. The triclinium frescoes are thought to have been painted by a local artist, although the theme may well have been copied from an earlier cycle of paintings from the Hellenistic period. In all there are 10 scenes, depicting children and matrons, musicians and satyrs, phalluses and gods. There are no inscriptions (such as are found on Greek vases), and after 2,000 years historians remain puzzled by many aspects of the triclinium cycle. Scholars endlessly debate the meaning of these frescoes, but anyone can tell they are among the most beautiful paintings left to us by antiquity. In several ways, the eruption of Vesuvius was a blessing in disguise, for without it, these masterworks of art would have perished long ago.

Pompeii

22 km (14 miles) southeast of Naples, 17 km (10½ miles) southeast of Herculaneum.

Mention Pompeii and most travelers think of ancient Roman villas, prancing bronze fauns, plaster casts of writhing Vesuvius victims, and the fabled days of the emperors.

GETTING HERE AND AROUND

To get to Pompeii by car, take the A3 Napoli–Salerno highway to the Pompei exit and follow signs for the nearby "Scavi." There are numerous guarded parking lots near the Porta Marina, Piazza Essedra, and Anfiteatro entrances, where you can leave your vehicle for a fee.

Pompeii has two central Circumvesuviana railway stations served by two separate train lines. The Naples–Sorrento train stops at "Pompei Scavi–Villa dei Misteri," 100 yards from the Porta Marina ticket office of the archaeological site, while the Naples–Poggiomarino train stops at Pompei Santuario, more convenient for the Santuario della Madonna del Rosario and the hotels and restaurants in the modern town center. A third Ferrovie della Statale (FS) train station south of the town center is only convenient if arriving from Salerno or Rome.

Sights

★ Pompeii

ARCHAEOLOGICAL SITE | Petrified memorial to Vesuvius's eruption in AD 79, Pompeii is the largest, most accessible, and most famous excavation anywhere. Ancient Pompeii had a population of 10,000–20,000 and covered about 170 acres on the seaward end of the Sarno Plain. Today it attracts more than 2 million visitors every year, but if you come in the quieter late afternoon, you can truly fall under the site's spell. Highlights include the Foro (Forum), which served as Pompeii's cultural, political, commercial, and religious hub; homes that were captured in various states by the eruption of Vesuvius, including the Casa del Poeta Tragico (House of the Tragic Poet), a typical middle-class residence with a floor mosaic of a chained dog, and the Casa dei Vettii (House of the Vettii), the best example of a wealthy merchant's home; the Villa dei Misteri (Villa of the Mysteries), a palatial abode with many fresco-adorned rooms; and the Anfiteatro (Amphitheater), built around 70 BC. Consider renting an audio guide and opt for one of the three itineraries (two hours, four hours, or six hours) available at Porta Marina. If hiring a guide, agree beforehand on the length of the tour and the price. Advance tickets can be purchased online at 🌐 *www.ticketone.it/en/artist/scavi-pompei* (there's a link on the official Pompeii website). ✉ *Pompei* ☎ *081/8575347* 🌐 *www.pompeiisites.org* 🎫 *€18 (Pompeii Express ticket) for the main ancient site; €22 (Pompeii+ ticket) includes the Ville Suburbane: Villa dei Misteri etc; €26 ("3 Days" ticket) also includes Oplontis, Villa Arianna, Villa San Marco, Museo Libero D'Orsi plus shuttle bus.*

Vesuvius

8 km (5 miles) northeast of Herculaneum, 16 km (10 miles) east of Naples.

Vesuvius may have lost its plume of smoke for now, but it has lost none of its fascination—especially for those who live in the towns around the cone.

GETTING HERE AND AROUND

To arrive by car, take the A3 Napoli–Salerno autostrada to the Torre del Greco exit and follow Via E. De Nicola from the tollbooth and then signs for the Parco Nazionale del Vesuvio.

Vesuvio Express (🌐 *www.vesuvioexpress.it*) operates a shuttle-bus service with timed entrance ticket included (€30) departing from Ercolano Circumvesuviana station (eight round-trips per day); and one per day from Napoli Centrale (€40). The vehicles thread their way rapidly up back roads, reaching the top in 20/40 minutes.

Sights

Vesuvius

VOLCANO | Although Vesuvius's destructive powers are on hold, the threat of an eruption remains ever present. Seen from the other side of the Bay of Naples, Vesuvius appears to have two peaks: on the northern side is the steep face of Monte Somma, possibly part of the original crater wall in AD 79; to the south is the present-day cone of Vesuvius, which has actually formed within the ancient crater. The AD 79 cone would have been considerably higher, perhaps peaking at around 9,000 feet. The upper slopes bear the visible scars left by 19th- and 20th-century eruptions, the most striking being the lava flow from 1944 lying to the left (north side) of the approach road from Ercolano on the way up.

As you tour the cities that felt the volcano's wrath, you may be overwhelmed by the urge to explore Vesuvius itself, and it's well worth the trip. The view when the air is clear is magnificent, with the curve of the coast and the tiny white houses among the orange and lemon blossoms. When the summit becomes lost in mist, though, you'll be lucky to see your hand in front of your face. If you notice the summit clearing—it tends to be clearer in the afternoon—head for it. If possible, see Vesuvius after you've toured the ruins of buried Herculaneum to appreciate the magnitude of the volcano's power. Admission to the crater includes a compulsory guide, usually a young geologist who speaks a smattering of English. At the bottom you'll be offered a stout walking stick (a small tip is appreciated when you return it). The climb can be tiring if you're not used to steep hikes. Because of the volcanic stone, you should wear athletic or sturdy shoes, not sandals. Entry requires a timed ticket and must be purchased in advance at 🌐 *vesuviopark.vivaticket.it* unless you buy entry as a package from Vesuvio Express. ☎ *081/7775720, 081/8653911* 🌐 *www.parconazionaledelvesuvio.it* 🎫 *€12.*

Oplontis (Torre Annunziata)

20 km (12 miles) southeast of Naples, 5 km (3 miles) west of Pompeii.

Surrounded by the fairly drab 1960s urban landscape of Torre Annunziata, Oplontis justifies its reputation as one of the more mysterious archaeological sites to be unearthed in the 20th century. The villa complex has been imaginatively ascribed—from a mere inscription on an amphora—to Nero's second wife, Poppaea Sabina. Her family was well known among the landed gentry of neighboring Pompeii, although, after a kick in the stomach from her emperor husband, she died some 15 years before the villa was overwhelmed by the eruption of 79.

GETTING HERE AND AROUND

By car, take the A3 Napoli–Salerno autostrada to the Torre Annunziata exit. Follow Via Veneto west, then turn left onto Via Sepolcri for the excavations. By train, take the Circumvesuviana railway to Torre Annunziata, the town's modern name (€3.30 from Naples).

Sights

Oplontis

ARCHAEOLOGICAL SITE | For those overwhelmed by the throngs at Pompeii, a visit to the site of Oplontis offers a chance for contemplation and intellectual stimulation. What has been excavated so far of the Villa of the Empress Poppaea covers more than 75,000 square feet, and because the site is bound by a road to the west and a canal to the south, its full extent may never be known.

Complete with porticoes, a large peristyle, a pool, baths, and extensive gardens, the villa is thought by some to have been a school for young philosophers and orators. You have to visit to appreciate the full range of Roman wall paintings; one highlight is found in Room 5, a sitting room that overlooked the sea. ✉ *Via Sepolcri 1, Torre Annunziata* ☎ *081/8575347* 🌐 *www.pompeiisites.org* 🎫 *€8* ⏲ *Closed Tues.*

Ischia

45 minutes by hydrofoil, 90 minutes by car ferry from Naples, 60 minutes by ferry from Pozzuoli.

Although Capri leaves you breathless with its charm and beauty, Ischia (pronounced "EES-kee-ah") takes time to cast its spell. In fact, an overnight stay is not long enough; you have to look harder here for the signs of antiquity, the traffic can be reminiscent of Naples, and the island displays all the hallmarks of rapid, uncontrolled urbanization. Ischia does have many jewels, though. There are the wine-growing villages beneath the lush volcanic slopes of Monte Epomeo, and unlike Capri, the island enjoys a life of its own that survives when the tourists head home.

GETTING HERE AND AROUND

Ischia is well connected with the mainland in all seasons. The last boats leave for Naples and Pozzuoli at about 8 pm (though in the very high season there is a midnight sailing), and you should allow plenty of time for getting to the port and buying a ticket. Ischia has three ports—Ischia Porto, Casamicciola, and Forio (hydrofoils only)—so you should choose your ferry or hydrofoil according to your destination. Non-Italians can bring cars to the island relatively freely. Up-to-date schedules are published at 🌐 *www.traghetti-ischia.info.*

Ischia's bus network reaches all the major sites and beaches on one of its 18 lines. The principal lines are CD and CS, circling the island in clockwise and counterclockwise directions—in the summer months runs continue until after midnight. The main bus terminus is in Ischia Porto at the start of Via Cosca, where buses run by the company EAV radiate out around the island. Be warned: it's often chaotic with buses filling quickly with scrambling school kids. There are convenient *fermate* (stops) at the two main beaches—Citara and Maronti—with timetables displayed at the terminus. Tickets cost €1.70 per ride, €2.10 for 100 minutes. A one-day pass is €5.10, a seven-day pass €14.50. Note that conditions can get hot and crowded.

VISITOR INFORMATION

CONTACT Pro Loco Ischia: Isola Verde. ✉ *Via Iasolino 3, Ischia* ☎ *081/984163* 🌐 *www.prolococomuneischia.it.*

Sights

Forio

TOWN | FAMILY | The far-western and southern coasts of Ischia are more rugged and attractive than other areas. Forio, at the extreme west, has a waterfront church, Chiesa del Soccorso, and is a good spot for lunch or dinner. **■ TIP→ Head to the whitewashed Soccorso church to watch a gorgeous sunset—perhaps the best spot on the island to do so.** ✉ *Forio.*

Giardini Poseidon Terme

HOT SPRING | FAMILY | The largest spa on the island has the added boon of a natural sauna hollowed out of the rocks. Here you can sit like a Roman senator on stone chairs recessed in the rock and let the hot water cascade over you. With countless thermally regulated pools, promenades, and steam pools, plus lots of kitschy toga-clad statues of the

Caesars, Poseidon exerts a special pull on tourists, many of them grandparents shepherding grandchildren. On certain days, the place is overrun with people, so be prepared for crowds and wailing babies. ✉ *Baia di Citara, Via Giovanni Mazzella, Forio* ☎ *081/9087111* 🌐 *www.giardiniposeidonterme.com* 🎫 *€45, €50 in Aug.* ⏲ *Closed Nov.–late Apr.*

★ Ischia Ponte

NEIGHBORHOOD | **FAMILY** | Most of the hotels are along the beach in the part of town called Ischia Ponte, which gets its name from the *ponte* (bridge) built by Alfonso of Aragon in 1438 to link the picturesque castle on a small islet offshore with the town and port. For a while the castle was the home of Vittoria Colonna, poetess, granddaughter of Renaissance Duke Federico da Montefeltro (1422–82), and platonic soulmate of Michelangelo, with whom she carried on a lengthy correspondence. The Castello Aragonese itself is a fascinating place to explore, a citadel with atmospheric corners and various exhibition spaces including the stylish Lo Studio art space/craft shop. There are wonderful views amid battlements, gardens, former places of worship and a Napoleonic prison. Plus there's the panoramic Il Terrazzo café and the lofty Il Monastero hotel-café-restaurant. It's all run by the Mattera family who bought the abandoned fortress from the State in 1912: "25,000 lire for 25 centuries of abandoned history" they say. Expect lots of steps but there's a lift if you prefer to avoid the climb. The surrounding area has countless cafés, shops, and restaurants, and a 1-km (½-mile) fine-sand beach. ✉ *Ischia Ponte* ☎ *081/992834* 🌐 *www.castelloaragoneseischia.com* 🎫 *€12* ⏲ *Closed Jan. and Feb.*

Ischia Porto

TOWN | **FAMILY** | This is the island's largest town and the usual point of debarkation. It's no workaday port, however, but rather a lively resort with plenty of hotels, restaurants, the island's best shopping area, and low, flat-roof houses on terraced hillsides overlooking the water. Its narrow streets and villas and gardens are framed by pines. ✉ *Ischia Porto.*

Monte Epomeo

VOLCANO | The inland town of Fontana is the base for excursions to the top of this long-dormant volcano that dominates the island landscape. You can reach its 2,589-foot peak in less than 1½ hours of relatively easy walking. ✉ *Ischia.*

★ Sant'Angelo

TOWN | **FAMILY** | On the southern coast, this is a charming village with a narrow path leading to its promontory; the road doesn't reach all the way into town, so it's free of traffic. It's a five-minute boat ride from the beach of Maronti, at the foot of cliffs. ✉ *Sant'Angelo.*

Restaurants

À Paranza - Sea Restaurant

$$ | **NEAPOLITAN** | Book a table by the water's edge with views over Ischia Ponte at this elegant white/azure dining spot, whose ambience and cuisine shines at lunch and twinkles come evening. Young thirtysomething owner Stefano and professional staff guide you through the *mare* and *terra* menu that mixes classic Neapolitan dishes with novel creations like stuffed squid stuffed with *friarielli* (broccoli rabe), all served on artsy ceramic plates. **Known for:** fried-seafood medley; wonderful harbor setting; Ischia rabbit and catch of the day. 💲 *Average main: €23* ✉ *Via Luigi Mazzella 11, Ischia Ponte* ☎ *081/843 0183* 🌐 *www.instagram.com/aparanza-searestaurant* ⏲ *Closed Nov.–Mar.*

Da Cocò

$$ | **SOUTHERN ITALIAN** | This inviting restaurant with a terrace is on the causeway that links the Aragonese castle to the rest of Ischia. It's renowned for its fresh seafood, which is highly prized by the Ischitani: shoreline classics dominate, starting with the antipasto da Cocò platter including chunky octopus pieces and marinated anchovies followed by spaghetti with *calameretti* (squidlets), tomatoes, and chilli peppers. **Known for:** magical setting near the castello; deliciously light lemon and almond cake; good spot to just sit with an aperitivo and nibbles. *Average main: €22* *Via Aragonese 1, Ischia Ponte* *081/981823* *www.facebook.com/ristorantecoco* *Closed Jan. and Feb.*

★ Umberto a Mare

$$$ | **SOUTHERN ITALIAN** | This iconic eatery has occupied the space below the Santuario del Soccorso since 1936, when the original Umberto began to grill the local catch on the seafront. The setting is divine, with a terrace overlooking the Bay of Citara and the green tuff *scogli degli innamorati* (lovers' rocks). **Known for:** breathtaking sunset sea views; changing displays of artworks; decades-long reputation for exquisite seafood. *Average main: €32* *Via Soccorso 8, Forio* *081/997171* *www.umbertoamare.it* *Closed Nov.–Mar.*

Coffee and Quick Bites

Ice da Luciano

$ | **ICE CREAM** | A stop here for some gelato or granita is a must upon arriving in Ischia Ponte. **Known for:** the best ice cream on the island; inexpensive prices; large selection. *Average main: €3* *Via Luigi Mazzella 140, Ischia Ponte* *081/0123228* *www.facebook.com/icedaluciano.*

Hotels

★ Albergo Il Monastero

$$ | **HOTEL** | The Castello Aragonese, on its own island, is the unrivaled location for this unique hotel with a peaceful ambience and simple but comfortable rooms overlooking the Mediterranean. **Pros:** stunning views and peaceful garden; fab breakfast and restaurant with terrace views; artsy L'Altana Suite with private terraces. **Cons:** a long way from the entrance to your room; perhaps too far from the town's action; some may not like the understated decor. *Rooms from: €220* *Castello Aragonese 3, Ischia Ponte* *081/992435* *www.ilmonasteroischia.com* *Closed Nov.–late Apr.* *20 rooms* *Free Breakfast.*

★ Botania Relais & Spa

$$$ | **HOTEL** | Nestled in the verdant hills between Lacco and Forio, Botania is a serene, chic retreat with white washed lodges in beautiful grounds dotted with pools, olive-arbored corners, and top-notch facilities. **Pros:** wonderful, lush grounds near La Mortella; gorgeous modern spa, gym, and various pools; produce from their on-site market garden. **Cons:** a bit isolated from the beach action; live music and evening events can be loud; on the pricey side. *Rooms from: €561* *Via Provinciale Lacco 284, Ischia* *081/997978* *www.botaniarelais.com* *50 rooms* *Free Breakfast.*

Mezzatorre Hotel & Thermal Spa

$$$$ | **HOTEL** | Far from the madding, sunburned crowds—in a sleekly renovated former fortress on Punta Cornacchia above the Bay of San Montano—this luxurious getaway (part of the chic Pellicano Hotels Group) tempts its privileged guests to stay put and *relax*, with a glamorous heated pool overlooking a storybook cove, fine restaurants, spa treatments, and hundreds of pretty pine and pomegranate trees. **Pros:** tranquil retreat with wonderful views; fab restaurants and spa; private bay, exclusive atmosphere. **Cons:** very isolated; pricey and maybe too posey for some; far from the action. *Rooms from: €1,050* *Via Mezzatorre 23, Forio* *081/986111* *www.mezzatorre.com* *Closed Nov.–Apr.* *48 rooms* *Free Breakfast.*

Procida

35 minutes by hydrofoil, 1 hour by car ferry from Naples.

Lying barely 3 km (2 miles) from the mainland and 10 km (6 miles) from the nearest port (Pozzuoli), Procida is an island of enormous contrasts. It's the most densely populated island in Europe—just more than 10,000 people crammed into less than 2 square miles—and yet there are oases like Marina Corricella and Vivara, which seem to have been bypassed by modern civilization. The inhabitants of the island—the Procidani—have an almost symbiotic relationship with the Mediterranean: many join the merchant navy, others either fish or ferry vacationers around local waters. And yet land traffic here can be more intense than on any other island in the Bay of Naples.

GETTING HERE AND AROUND

Procida's ferry timetable caters to the many daily commuters who live on the island and work in Naples or Pozzuoli. The most frequent—and cheapest—connections are from the Port of Pozzuoli. After stopping at Procida's main port, Marina Grande (the locals call it "Sent-Co" from Sancio Cattolico), many ferries and hydrofoils continue on to Ischia, for which Procida is considered a halfway house.

Restaurants

La Conchiglia "Da Tonino"

$$ | SOUTHERN ITALIAN | A meal at this restaurant, on the beach about a half-mile east of Corricella, encapsulates Procida's seaside simplicity. Lapping waves and views of the marina and Capri form the backdrop for the fresh seafood and vegetable creations. **Known for:** beach-side views and breezes through open windows; freshest ingredients; boat trips and bathing nearby. *$ Average main: €21 ✉ Via Pizzaco 10, Procida ☎ 081/8967602 🌐 www.laconchigliaristorante.com ⏲ Closed mid-Nov.–Mar.*

Coffee and Quick Bites

Bar Dal Cavaliere

$ | CAFÉ | This busy café-bar has outside seating on the *basalti* flagstones with views of the port, so you can watch the boats coming in and out while munching on island-specialty *lingue di bue* and classic sfogliatelle pastries, panini, or *semifreddi* (frozen desserts similar to ice cream). **Known for:** pastries sold by weight—great for groups; near the ferry port; stuzzichini snacks with beers and aperitivi. *$ Average main: €5 ✉ Via Roma 42, Marina Grande, Procida ☎ 081/8101074.*

Capri

50 minutes by hydrofoil, 50–85 minutes by car ferry from Naples.

Gorgeous grottoes, soaring conical peaks, caverns great and small, plus villas of the emperors and thousands of legends brush Capri with an air of whispered mystery. Emperor Augustus was the first to tout the island's pleasures by nicknaming it Apragopolis (City of Sweet Idleness), and Capri has drawn escapists of all kinds ever since. Ancient Greek and Roman goddesses were moved aside by the likes of Jacqueline Onassis, Elizabeth Taylor, and Brigitte Bardot, who made the island into a paparazzo's playground in the 1960s. Today, new generations of glitterati continue to answer the island's call.

Life on Capri gravitates around the two centers of Capri Town (on the saddle between Monte Tiberio and Monte Solaro) and Anacapri, higher up (902 feet). The main road connecting Capri Town with the upper town of Anacapri is well plied by buses. On arriving at the main harbor, the Marina Grande, everyone heads for the famous funicular, which ascends (and descends) several times an hour. Once you're lofted up to Anacapri by bus, you can reach the island heights by taking the spectacular chairlift that ascends to the top of Monte Solaro (1,932 feet) from Anacapri's town center. Within Capri Town and Anacapri foot power is the preferred mode of transportation, as much for convenience as for the sheer delight of walking along the fragrant flower-fringed lanes.

GETTING HERE AND AROUND

Capri is well connected with the mainland in all seasons, though there are more sailings April–October. Hydrofoils, Sea Cats, and similar vessels leave from Molo Beverello (below Piazza Municipio) in Naples, while far less frequent car ferries leave from Calata Porta di Massa, 1,000 yards to the east. There's also service to and from Sorrento's Marina Piccola and Salerno Masuccio. Much of Capri is pedestrianized, and a car is a great hindrance, not a help.

Several ferry and hydrofoil companies ply the waters of the Bay of Naples, making frequent trips to Capri. Schedules change from season to season; the tourist office's website (🌐 *www.capritourism.com*) gives updated departure times. However, you can't return to Naples after the last sailing (11 pm in high season, often 8 pm or even earlier in low season). There's little to be gained—sometimes nothing—from buying a round-trip ticket, which will just tie you down to the return schedule of one line. However, book in advance in spring and summer for a Sunday return to the mainland.

VISITOR INFORMATION

CONTACT Infopoint Isola di Capri. ✉ *Piazza Umberto I, Capri* ☎ *081/8370686* 🌐 *www.facebook.com/capritourism.*

Sights

★ Anacapri

TOWN | A tortuous road leads up to Anacapri, the island's "second city," about 3 km (2 miles) from Capri Town. Crowds are thick down Via Capodimonte leading to Villa San Michele and around Piazza Vittoria, the square where you catch the chairlift to the top of Monte Solaro. Via Finestrale leads to the noted Le Boffe quarter, centered on the Piazza Diaz. Elsewhere, Anacapri is quietly appealing. It's a good starting point for walks, such as the 80-minute round-trip journey to the Migliara Belvedere, on the island's southern coast. ✉ *Anacapri.*

Capri Town

TOWN | On arrival at the port, pick up the excellent map of the island at the tourist office. You may have to wait for the funicular railway (€2.40 one-way) to Capri Town, some 450 feet above the harbor. So this might be the time to splurge on an open-top taxi—it could save you an hour in line and a sweaty ride packed into a tiny, swaying bus. From the upper station, walk out into Piazza Umberto I, better known as the Piazzetta, the island's social hub. ✉ *Capri.*

★ Certosa di San Giacomo

HISTORIC SIGHT | An eerie atmosphere hangs around neglected corners of this once grand, palatial complex between the Castiglione and Tuoro hills, founded between 1371 and 1374. After the monastery was sacked by the pirates Dragut and Barbarossa in the 16th century, it was restored and rebuilt—thanks in part to heavy taxes exacted from the populace. The Quarto del Priore hosts occasional art exhibitions, but the showstopper here is the Museo Diefenbach, with restored canvases by German painter K.W. Diefenbach, who visited Capri in 1899 and stayed until his death in 1913. ✉ *Via Certosa, Capri Town* ☎ *081/8376218* 🌐 *www.beniculturali.it/luogo/certosa-di-san-giacomo* 🎫 *€10* ⏲ *Closed Mon.*

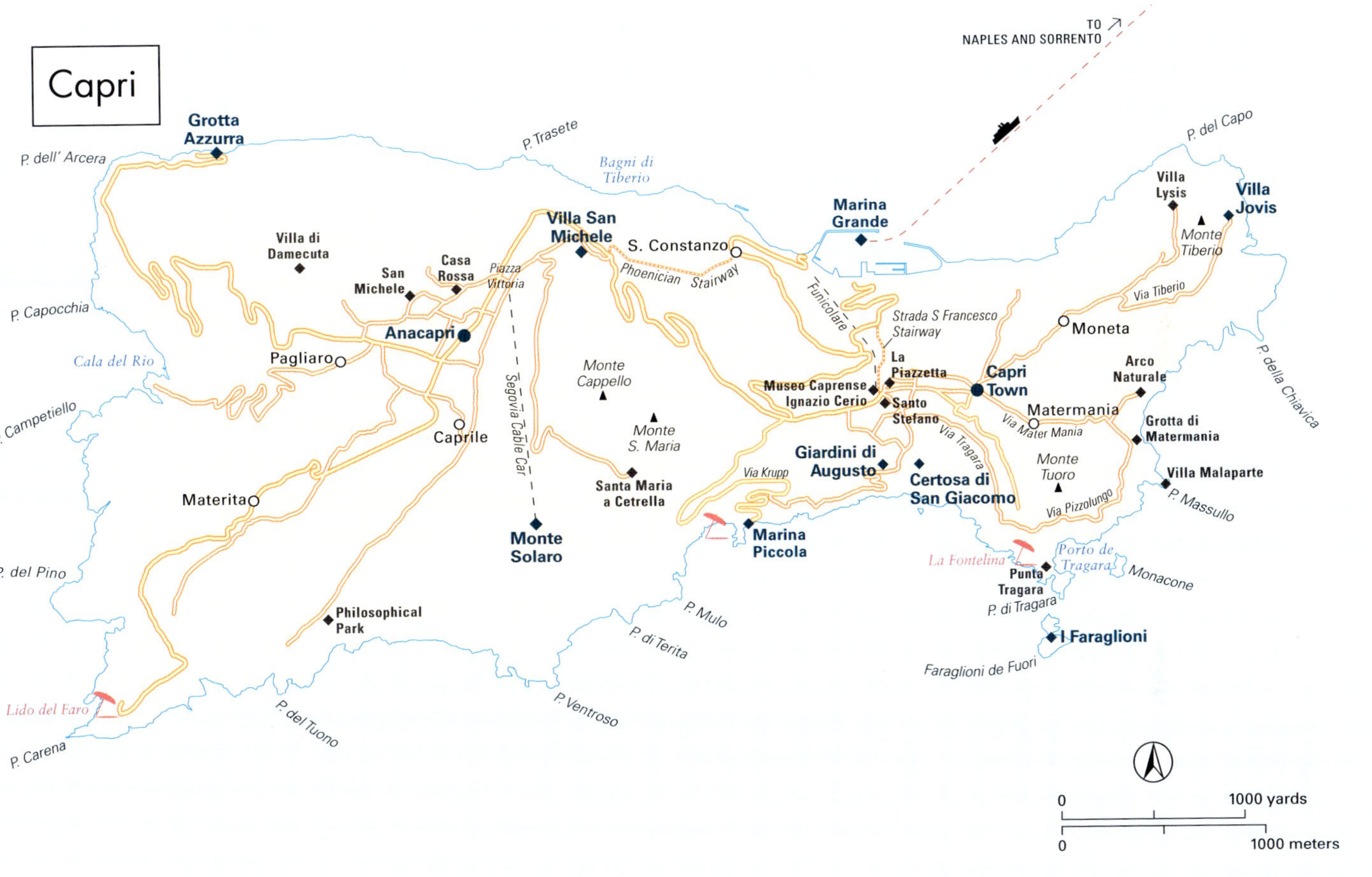
Capri
TO NAPLES AND SORRENTO
Grotta Azzurra
P. dell' Arcera
P. Trasete
Bagni di Tiberio
P. del Capo
Villa Lysis
Villa Jovis
Monte Tiberio
Marina Grande
Villa San Michele
S. Constanzo
Phoenician Stairway
Funicolare
Villa di Damecuta
San Michele
Casa Rossa
Piazza Vittoria
P. Capocchia
Anacapri
Strada S Francesco Stairway
Via Tiberio
Moneta
Cala del Rio
Pagliaro
Monte Cappello
La Piazzetta
Capri Town
Museo Caprense Ignazio Cerio
Santo Stefano
Arco Naturale
P. della Chiavica
Segovia Cable Car
Matermania
Via Mater Mania
Grotta di Matermania
P. Campetiello
Caprile
Monte S. Maria
Via Tragara
Giardini di Augusto
Monte Tuoro
Via Krupp
Certosa di San Giacomo
Villa Malaparte
Materita
Santa Maria a Cetrella
P. Massullo
Via Pizzolungo
Monte Solaro
Marina Piccola
La Fontelina
Porto de Tragara
Punta Tragara
Monacone
P. del Pino
P. di Tragara
Philosophical Park
P. Mulo
P. di Terita
I Faraglioni
Faraglioni de Fuori
Lido del Faro
P. Ventroso
P. del Tuono
P. Carena
0
1000 yards
0
1000 meters

★ Giardini di Augusto

(*Gardens of Augustus*)

GARDEN | From the terraces of this beautiful public garden, you can see the village of Marina Piccola below—restaurants, cabanas, and swimming platforms huddle among the shoals—and admire the steep, winding Via Krupp, actually a staircase cut into the rock. Friedrich Krupp, the German arms manufacturer, loved Capri and became one of the island's most generous benefactors. ✉ *Via Matteotti, beyond monastery of San Giacomo, Capri Town* ☎ *353/4523908 mobile* 🌐 *www.capriculturaeturismo.it* 🎫 *€2.50.*

Grotta Azzurra

CAVE | Only when the Grotta Azzurra was "discovered" in 1826, by the Polish poet August Kopisch and Swiss artist Ernest Fries, did Capri become a tourist destination. The watery cave's blue beauty became a symbol of the return to nature. In reality, the grotto had long been a local landmark. During the Roman era it had been the elegant, mosaic-decorated nymphaeum of the adjoining villa of Gradola. The water's extraordinary sapphire color is caused by a hidden opening in the rock that refracts the light. Locals say the afternoon light is best from April to June, and the morning in July and August. The Blue Grotto can be reached from Marina Grande or from the small embarkation point below Anacapri on the northwest side of the island, accessible by bus from Anacapri. You board one boat to get to the grotto, then transfer to a smaller boat that takes you inside. ✉ *Anacapri* 🎫 *From €24 from Marina Grande via various companies, then €18 by rowboat with Coop. Battellieri* ⏲ *Closed if the sea is even minimally rough.*

★ I Faraglioni

NATURE SIGHT | Few landscapes set more artists dreaming than that of the famous Faraglioni—three enigmatic, pale-ocher limestone colossi that loom out of the sea just off the Punta Tragara on the southern coast of Capri. Soaring almost 350 feet above the water, the Faraglioni have become a beloved symbol of Capri. The first rock is called Faraglione di Terra, since it's attached to the land; at its base is the famous restaurant and bathing lido Da Luigi. The second is called Faraglione di Mezzo, or Stella, and little boats can often be seen going through its picturesque tunnel. The rock farthest out to sea is Faraglione di Scopolo and is inhabited by a wall lizard species with a striking blue belly. ✉ *End of Via Tragara, Capri.*

Favorite Places

Nick Bruno: On Capri, do yourself a favor and just get lost... I escape the crowds and head towards Villa Jovis and Parco Astarita for its natural wonders, serene views, and resident goats.

★ Marina Piccola

BEACH | FAMILY | Marina Piccola is a delightfully picturesque inlet that provides the Capresi and other sun worshippers with their best access to beaches and safe swimming. The entire cove is lined with *stabilimenti*—elegant bathing lidos where the striped cabanas are often air-conditioned. The most famous of these lidos (there's a fee to use the facilities) is La Canzone del Mare. Its seaside restaurant offers a dreamy view of the Faraglioni and a luncheon here, although pricey, can serve as an indelible Capri moment. Jutting out into the bay at the center of the marina is the Scoglio delle Sirene, or Sirens' Rock—a small natural promontory—which the ancients believed to be the haunt of the Sirens, the mythical temptresses whose song seduced Odysseus in Homer's *Odyssey.* ✉ *Via Marina Piccola, Capri.*

★ Monte Solaro

VIEWPOINT | An impressive limestone formation and the highest point on Capri (1,932 feet), Monte Solaro affords gasp-inducing views toward the bays of both Naples and Salerno. A serene 13-minute chairlift ride will take you right to the top (refreshments available at the bar), where you can launch out on a number of scenic trails on the western side of the island. Picnickers should note that even in summer it can get windy at this height, and there are few trees to provide shade or refuge. ✉ *Piazza Vittoria, Anacapri* ☎ *081/8371438* 🌐 *www.capriseggiovia.it* 🎫 *€11 one-way, €14 return* ⏲ *Chairlift closed in adverse weather.*

★ Villa Jovis

RUINS | In Roman times, Capri was the site of 12 spacious villas, but Villa Jovis is both the best preserved and the largest. Named in honor of the ancient Roman god Jupiter, or Jove, the villa of the emperor Tiberius is riveted to the towering Rocca di Capri like an eagle's nest overlooking the strait separating Capri from Punta Campanella. The Salto di Tiberio (Tiberius's Leap) is where ancients believed Tiberius had enemies (among them his discarded lovers and even unfortunate cooks) hurled over the precipice into the sea some 1,000 feet below. ✉ *Via A. Maiuri, Capri* ☎ *081/8374549* 🌐 *www.capri.com* 🎫 *€6, with audio guide* ⏲ *Closed Mon., Jan. and Feb., and weekdays in Mar.*

★ Villa San Michele

HISTORIC HOME | From Anacapri's Piazza Vittoria, picturesque Via Capodimonte leads to Villa San Michele, the charming former home of Swedish doctor and philanthropist Axel Munthe (1857–1949). At the ancient entranceway to Anacapri at the top of the Scala Fenicia, the villa is set around Roman-style courtyards and marble walkways. Rooms display the doctor's varied collections, which range from bric-a-brac to antiquities. A spectacular pergola path overlooking the entire Bay of Naples leads from the villa to the famous Sphinx Parapet, where an ancient Egyptian sphinx looks out toward Sorrento. ✉ *Viale Axel Munthe 34, Anacapri* ☎ *081/8371401* 🌐 *www.villasanmichele.eu* 🎫 *€12.*

Restaurants

Al Grottino

$$ | **SOUTHERN ITALIAN** | In a 14th-century building close to the Piazzetta, this small, friendly, family-run restaurant has arched ceilings, autographed photos of famous patrons, and lots of atmosphere. Specialties include scialatielli *ai fiori di zucchine e gamberetti* (with zucchini flowers and shrimp) and *cocotte* (house-made pasta with mussels, clams, and shrimp), but the owner delights in taking his guests through the menu of regional dishes. **Known for:** good value for Capri; Caprese specialties with the freshest ingredients; gluten-free options. $ *Average main: €23* ✉ *Via Longano 27, Capri* ☎ *081/8370584* 🌐 *www.ristorantealgrottino.net* ⏲ *Closed Nov.–late Mar.*

Aurora

$$$$ | **SOUTHERN ITALIAN** | Often frequented by celebrities, whose photographs adorn the walls inside and out, the island's oldest restaurant offers courtesy and *simpatia* (irrespective of your star status), a sleekly minimalist interior, and tables outside along a chic thoroughfare. The cognoscenti start by sharing a pizza *all'Acqua*—thin-crust, with mozzarella and a sprinkling of *peperoncino* (chili)—but the *gnocchetti al pesto con fagiolini croccanti e pinoli* (dumplings with pesto, beans, and pine nuts) and house-made sweets are good, too. **Known for:** historic and pricey jet-set hangout; Papà Gennaro's unusually light pizza all'Acqua; incredible wine cellar and choice. $ *Average main: €42* ✉ *Via Fuorlovado 18/22, Capri Town* ☎ *081/8370181* 🌐 *www.auroracapri.com* ⏲ *Closed Nov.–Easter.*

★ Da Gelsomina

$$ | **SOUTHERN ITALIAN** | Amid its own terraced vineyards with inspiring views to the island of Ischia and beyond, this is much more than just a well-reputed restaurant. The owner's mother was a friend of Axel Munthe, and he encouraged her to open a food kiosk, which evolved into Da Gelsomina; today the specialties include *pollo a mattone* (chicken grilled under bricks) and locally caught rabbit. **Known for:** opened in the 1960s with family links to Axel Munthe; chicken grilled under bricks; fresh produce and wine from their verdant gardens. *Average main: €26 Via Migliara 72, Anacapri 081/8371499 www.dagelsomina.com Closed Nov.–Mar.*

Il Geranio

$$$ | **SOUTHERN ITALIAN** | Take the steps up to the right just before the Giardini di Augusto to find this romantic spot, where outdoor seating is staggered on the layered terraces, commanding a fine view of the Fariglioni. The menu combines the best of local and international cooking, specializing in both meat and seafood dishes. **Known for:** wonderful long-serving staff including Lello; panoramic terrace and stylish dining room with bar; desserts including a lighter Caprese cake al limone. *Average main: €35 Via Matteotti 8, Capri Town 081/8370616 www.geraniocapri.com Closed mid-Oct.–mid-Apr.*

★ Il Solitario

$$ | **NEAPOLITAN** | **FAMILY** | Tucked away from Via G. Orlandi, there's always a warm, relaxed family welcome and deliciously simple Caprese food here. **Known for:** sumptuous ravioli; cheery dining room and leafy pergola; grilled fish and meat. *Average main: €21 Via Giuseppe Orlandi 96, Anacapri 081/8371382 www.instagram.com/ilsolitarioanacapri No dinner Sun.*

La Canzone del Mare

$$$ | **SOUTHERN ITALIAN** | Although it's not primarily a restaurant, a luncheon dominated by fresh seafood and vegetables in the covered pavilion of this legendary bathing lido of the Marina Piccola is Capri at its most picture-perfect. With two seawater pools, a rocky beach, and I Faraglioni in the distance, it was the erstwhile haunt of Gracie Fields, Emilio Pucci, Noël Coward, and any number of 1950s and '60s glitterati. **Known for:** open terrace overlooking Marina Piccola; sunset wine and peaches served with stuzzichini (appetizers); famous dolce vita–era haunt—popular and pricey. *Average main: €38 Via Marina Piccola 93, Marina Piccola 081/8370104 www.lacanzonedelmare.com No dinner. Closed Oct.–late Apr.*

★ La Capannina

$$$ | **SOUTHERN ITALIAN** | Near the busy piazzetta and long one of Capri's most celebrity-haunted restaurants, La Capannina has a discreet flower-decked veranda that's ideal for dining by candlelight. Specialties change daily depending on the season, but the menu always includes ravioli capresi, linguine *con lo scorfano* (with scorpion fish), and an exquisite "Pezzogna" (sea bream cooked whole and topped with a layer of potatoes). **Known for:** walls strewn with photos of celebrity clientele; wine bar next door; family-run since 1931. *Average main: €37 Via Le Botteghe 12b, Capri Town 081/8370732 www.capanninacapri.com Closed Nov.–mid-Mar.*

La Fontelina

$$$ | **SOUTHERN ITALIAN** | Given its position right on the water's edge, seafood classics like mixed grilled seafood and mussel soup are almost de rigueur here, but also expect fabulous fresh vegetable creations like linguine with zucchini. La Fontelina also functions as a lido, with steps and ladders into fathoms-deep blue water, and this location—accessible on foot from Punta

Tragara or by boat from Marina Piccola (10 minutes; €40 up to four passengers)—makes it a good place to spend a delightfully comatose day. **Known for:** lunch stop for beach-club bathers; shuttle boat from Marina Piccola; daily seafood specials. *Average main: €32* *Via Faraglioni 2, Località Faraglioni, Capri* *081/8370845* *www.fontelina-capri.com* *Closed mid-Oct.–Easter. No dinner.*

Le Grottelle

$$ | **SOUTHERN ITALIAN** | This extremely informal trattoria enjoys a distinctive setting up against limestone rocks not far from the Arco Naturale, with the kitchen in a cave at the back. Whether you stumble over it (and are lucky enough to get a table) or intentionally head for it after an island hike, Le Grottelle will prove memorable, thanks to the ambience, the views of Li Galli islands, and a menu that includes ravioli and local rabbit but is best known for seafood dishes such as homemade *mezzi paccheri* pasta with swordfish and eggplant. **Known for:** breathtaking cliff-clinging location; seafood and rabbit dishes; cool grotto interiors and rustic terrace. *Average main: €29* *Via Arco Naturale 13, Capri* *081/8375719* *Closed Tues., and Nov.—Mar.*

Villa Margherita

$$$ | **NEAPOLITAN** | With twinkly lit tables on a large terrace, plus a stylish bar for apertivi and *dopo-cena* carousing this place is a good bet for sophisticated versions of Caprese and Neapolitan classics. Warm host Pietro and the capable crew will guide you through the changing menu—standouts may include the *candele alla Genovese*, slow-cooked beef and onion pasta with novel additions, and roasted turbot with shallot cream. **Known for:** seafood and vegetarian pasta dishes; seafood secondi and prime meat cuts like wagyu and tomahawk; lovely terrace and chic bar with music and late DJ sets. *Average main: €34* *Via Campo di Teste 4, Capri* *081/8377532* *www.ristorantevillamargheritacapri.com.*

Coffee and Quick Bites

★ Buonocore

$ | **ITALIAN** | **FAMILY** | Follow your nose to this legendary, sweet-smelling Caprese fave for breakfast, beach picnics, and on-the-hoof snacks. Buonocore lures you down its steps on a Capri Town lane with all manner of pizze, panini, gelati, and paste, including their specialty almond and lemon Caprilú biscotti. **Known for:** tempting smells of freshly made cones and pastries; small pizze to take away; very popular so may have to fare la coda. *Average main: €9* *Via Vittorio Emanuele 35, Capri Town* *081/8377826* *www.facebook.com/capri.gelateriabuonocore.*

Hotels

★ Capri Palace Jumeirah

$$$$ | **RESORT** | This Anacapri icon with unique design, spa, exquisite food, and luxurious retreat atmosphere throughout has amassed a noted art collection and even launched a fashion and home line and hosted A-list cultural events. **Pros:** noted art collection; stunning (and sometimes surprising) design; award-winning spa and dining. **Cons:** all that glam comes at a price; some may find the quiet Anacapri location removed from the action (and water); service can be slow. *Rooms from: €1,083* *Via Capodimonte 14, Anacapri* *081/9780111* *www.capripalace.com* *Closed mid-Oct.–mid-Apr.* *67 rooms* *Free Breakfast.*

★ Capri Tiberio Palace

$$$$ | **HOTEL** | Offering guests comfort, style, luxury, and sigh-inducing views since the 19th century, this hotel is a short walk from the piazzetta—near the action, but not quite in the thick of it. **Pros:** friendly staff; pure luxury; fabulous design. **Cons:** no port-to-door guest shuttle; the pool is too close to the restaurant; tiny gym. *Rooms from: €1,211* *Via Croce 11–15, Capri Town* *081/9787111* *www.*

capritiberiopalace.com ⏲ *Closed Nov.–mid-Apr.* 🛏 *54 rooms* 🍽 *Free Breakfast.*

Il Gatto Bianco

$$ | **HOTEL** | The spot where Jacqueline Kennedy famously sought refuge from the paparazzi is still a wonderful place to experience a quintessentially Caprese atmosphere, particularly in the public spaces, featuring a blue-on-white bar/breakfast area, 1950s majolica-lined stairs, and antique-y accents. **Pros:** central location; price semi-decent for Capri; historical yet faded jet-set resort. **Cons:** perhaps too close to the action; no sea view; dated decor, tech, and tiny showers in many rooms. [$] *Rooms from: €350* ✉ *Via Vittorio Emanuele 32, Capri Town* ☎ *081/8370203* 🌐 *www.gattobianco-capri.com* ⏲ *Closed Nov.–mid-Mar.* 🛏 *40 rooms* 🍽 *Free Breakfast.*

★ La Minerva

$$$$ | **HOTEL** | A onetime private home, this chic yet friendly small hotel has become a Capri favorite of those seeking intimate luxury, where most of the bright, airy rooms have panoramic terraces—shaded in bougainvillea and with views of the gardens and the sea in the background. **Pros:** fab views and tranquil ambience; family-run and genuinely warm service; cool, understated design with vibrant artworks. **Cons:** a 10-minute climb with steps to the Piazzetta; some rooms not the most spacious; pricey and gets booked up early as small. [$] *Rooms from: €1,290* ✉ *Via Occhio Marino 8, Capri Town* ☎ *081/8377067* 🌐 *www.laminervacapri.com* ⏲ *Closed Nov.–Mar.* 🛏 *18 rooms* 🍽 *Free Breakfast.*

La Tosca

$$ | **HOTEL** | Up a tiny side street above the Certosa, this simple, quiet hotel offers unassuming vibes, terrace views, and reasonable rates. **Pros:** simple, unadorned whitewashed charm; pleasant, helpful owner; quiet spot near Capri Town. **Cons:** not all rooms have good views; books up early; sparsely decorated rooms might seem to lack panache. [$] *Rooms from: €239* ✉ *Via Birago 5, Capri Town* ☎ *081/8370989* 🌐 *www.latoscahotel.com* ⏲ *Closed Nov.–Feb.* 🛏 *11 rooms* 🍽 *Free Breakfast.*

Punta Tragara

$$$$ | **HOTEL** | Designed by Le Corbusier, this former private villa became a satellite headquarters for America's central command during World War II and hosted Churchill and Eisenhower; today, it's one of Capri's most beautiful hotels, with a breathtaking location on Punta Tragara; public areas adorned with baronial fireplaces, gilded antiques, and travertine marble; and guest rooms that are simultaneously sumptuous and cozy-casual. **Pros:** decadent and luxurious; wonderful views of the famed Faraglioni rocks; two gorgeous pools. **Cons:** a 15-minute walk from the center; some find the style dated (others find it a plus); small gym. [$] *Rooms from: €1,380* ✉ *Via Tragara 57, Capri* ☎ *081/8370844* 🌐 *www.hoteltragara.com* ⏲ *Closed mid-Oct.–mid-Apr.* 🛏 *43 rooms* 🍽 *Free Breakfast.*

Quisisana

$$$$ | **HOTEL** | Some say Capri has three villages: Capri Town, Anacapri, and this landmark hotel, which looms large in island mythology, attracts utterly devoted guests, and has an enormous lobby and theater-cum-convention center that are 1930s jewels designed by noted modernist Gio Ponti. **Pros:** luxe atmosphere on a large scale; stumbling distance from La Piazzetta; top spa facilities. **Cons:** patchy service; convention-size and far from cozy; not quite as ritzy as in bygone days. [$] *Rooms from: €1,050* ✉ *Via Camerelle 2, Capri Town* ☎ *081/8370788* 🌐 *www.quisisana.com* ⏲ *Closed late Oct.–Apr.* 🛏 *140 rooms* 🍽 *Free Breakfast.*

Villa Sarah

$$ | **HOTEL** | This yellow, two-story, Mediterranean-style hostelry built in 1974—complete with Capri's signature round windows and a setting amid lovely gardens in a tranquil residential district—has lots of Caprese family spirit and simple

but homey, brightly accented rooms that will make you feel like a guest in a private villa. **Pros:** one of the few remaining family-run not profit-obsessed places; lush garden full of fruits and lovely pool; unfussy decor with original '70s features. **Cons:** a long and steep climb from the Piazzetta; many rooms tiny and some may find too dated; not for the fashionistas. *Rooms from: €250 Via Tiberio 3/a, Capri Town 081/8377817 www.villasarah.it Closed Nov.–Mar. 20 rooms Free Breakfast.*

Sorrento

50 km (31 miles) south of Naples.

Winding along a cliff above a small beach and two harbors, the town is split in two by a narrow ravine formed by a former mountain stream. To the east, dozens of hotels line busy Via Correale along the cliff—many have "grand" included in their names, and some indeed are. To the west, however, is the historic sector, which still enchants. It's a relatively flat area, with winding, stone-paved lanes bordered by balconied buildings, some joined by medieval stone arches. The bustling, coach- and car-traffic-fringed central piazza is named after the poet Torquato Tasso, born here in 1544. Away from the vehicles this part of town is a delightful place to walk through. Craftspeople are often at work in their stalls and shops and are happy to let you watch; in fact, that's the point. Music spots and bars cluster in the side streets near Piazza Tasso.

GETTING HERE AND AROUND

From downtown Naples, take a Circumvesuviana train from Stazione Centrale (Piazza Garibaldi) or a hydrofoil from Molo Beverello. If you're coming directly from the airport in Naples, pick up a direct bus to Sorrento. By car, take the A3 Naples–Salerno autostrada, exiting at Castellammare, and then following signs for Penisola Sorrentina, then for Sorrento.

VISITOR INFORMATION

CONTACT Ufficio Campania Turismo. *Via L. De Maio 35, Sorrento 081/8074033 www.facebook.com/aziendaautonomadisoggiornodisorrentoesantagnello.*

Sights

★ Chiesa e Chiostro di San Francesco

CHURCH | Near the Villa Comunale gardens and sharing its view over the Bay of Naples, the church and convent is celebrated for its 12th-century cloister. Filled with greenery and flowers, the Moorish-style cloister has interlaced pointed arches of tufa rock, alternating with octagonal columns, supporting smaller arches. The combination makes a suitably evocative setting for summer concerts and theatrical presentations. The interior's 17th-century decoration includes an altarpiece by a student of Francesco Solimena, depicting St. Francis receiving the stigmata. Above the cloisters **Galleria Raffaele Celentano** exhibits the candid black-and-white photographs of Italian life by a contemporary local photographer. There's an adjoining panoramic terrace ripe for sunset views and a joyous installation featuring an arbor rope swing, a cut-up Fiat 500 and washing line of photos and clothes. *Piazza S. Francesco, Sorrento 081/8781269 www.raffaelecelentano.com Cloisters free; gallery €5.*

Marina Grande

MARINA/PIER | Close to the historic quarter (but not that close—many locals prefer to use the town bus to shuttle up and down the steep hill), the port, or *borgo,* of the Marina Grande is Sorrento's fishing harbor. In recent years it has become unashamedly touristy, with outdoor restaurants and cafés encroaching on what little remains of the original harbor. The marina still remains a magical location for an evening out on the waterfront. Don't

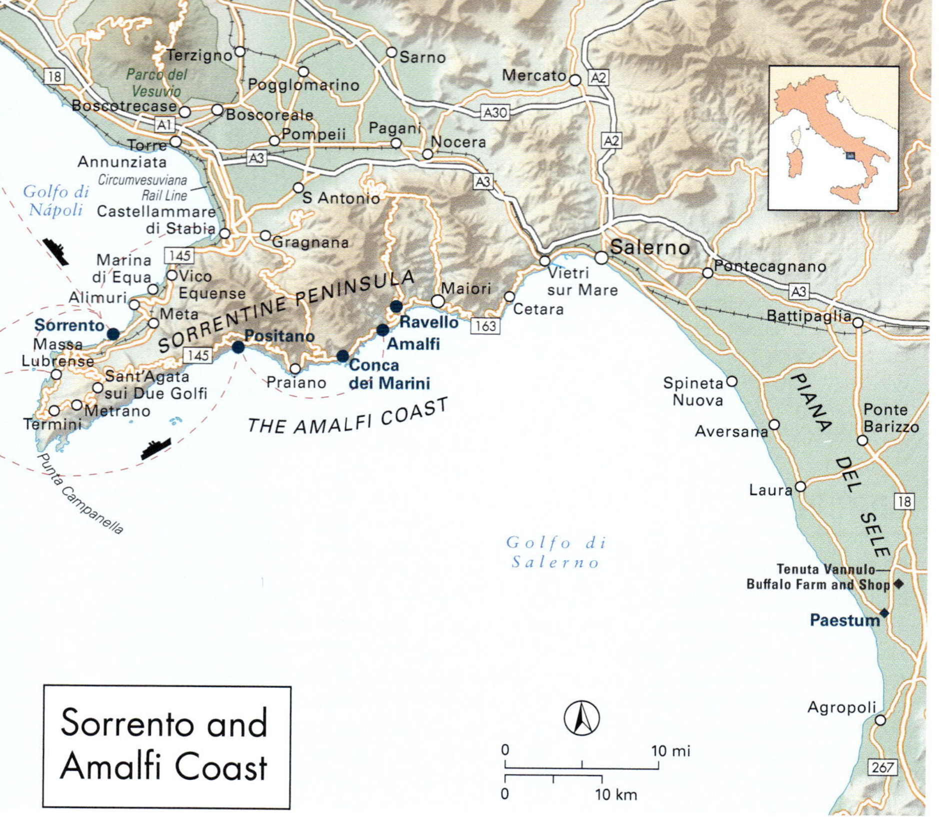

confuse this harbor with Marina Piccola, at the base of the cliff, below Piazza Tasso and the Hotel Excelsior Vittoria; that's the area where ferries and hydrofoils dock. ✉ *Via del Mare, Sorrento.*

Museo Correale di Terranova

ART MUSEUM | In an 18th-century villa with a lovely garden, on land given to the patrician Correale family by Queen Joan of Anjou in 1428, this museum is a highlight of Sorrento. It has an eclectic private collection amassed by the count of Terranova and his brother—one of the finest devoted to Neapolitan paintings, decorative arts, and porcelains. Magnificent 18th- and 19th-century inlaid tables by Giuseppe Gargiulo, Capodimonte porcelains, and Rococo portrait miniatures are reminders of the age when pleasure and delight were everything in wealthy circles. Also on view are regional Greek and Roman archaeological finds, Old Master paintings, and 17th-century majolicas—even the poet Tasso's death mask. ✉ *Via Correale 50, Sorrento* ☎ *081/8781846* 🌐 *www.museocorreale.it* 🎫 *€15; included in the €31 Sorrento Musei ticket* ⏲ *Closed Mon.*

Sedile Dominova

NOTABLE BUILDING | Enchanting showpiece of the Largo Dominova—the little square that is the heart of Sorrento's historic quarter—the Sedile Dominova is a picturesque open loggia with expansive arches, balustrades, and a green-and-yellow-tile cupola, originally constructed in the 16th century. The open-air structure is frescoed with 18th-century trompe-l'oeil columns and the family coats of arms, which once belonged to the *sedile* (seat), the town council where nobles met to discuss civic problems as early as the

Angevin period. Today, Sorrentines still like to congregate around the umbrella-topped tables near the tiny square. ✉ *Largo Dominova, at Via S. Cesareo and Via P.R. Giuliani, Sorrento* 🎫 *Free.*

★ Villa Comunale

VIEWPOINT | The largest public park in Sorrento sits on a cliff top overlooking the entire Bay of Naples. It offers benches, flowers, palms, and people/sunset-watching, plus a seamless vista that stretches from Capri to Vesuvius. From here steps lead down to Sorrento's main harbor, the Marina Piccola. ✉ *Adjoining church of San Francesco, Sorrento.*

Restaurants

Da Emilia

$$ | **SOUTHERN ITALIAN** | Near the steps of the Marina Grande, this reliable choice for seafood (established in 1947) might not be Sorrento's most visually prepossessing place, but its homespun, family feel—complete with wooden tables and checked tablecloths—is a refreshing change from the town's (occasionally pretentious) elegance. **Known for:** tasty and fresh seafood combos like mussels with Sorrentine lemons; harbor terrace above the rocks; competed in Italian TV show 4 Ristoranti. $ *Average main: €22* ✉ *Via Marina Grande 62, Sorrento* ☎ *081/8072720* 🌐 *www.daemilia.it* 🕓 *Closed Nov.–Feb.*

★ Don Alfonso 1890

$$$$ | **SOUTHERN ITALIAN** | A gastronomic giant and pioneer in upscale farm-to-table cuisine (it even grows its own produce on a small farm nearby), Don Alfonso is considered one of Italy's best restaurants. It's a family affair, with mamma (Livia) handling the dining room, papà (former chef Alfonso Iaccarrino) tending to the organic plot, one son working as the current chef (preparing classic dishes alongside edgier creations), and the other serving as maître d'. **Known for:** stellar tasting menus; slow-food pioneer; Punta Campanella local garden produce. $ *Average main: €42* ✉ *Corso Sant'Agata 13, Sant'Agata sui Due Golfi* ✣ *SITA Bus to via Nastro Verde or taxi from Sorrento* ☎ *081/8780026* 🌐 *www.donalfonso.com* 🕓 *Closed Nov.–Apr. No lunch weekdays. No dinner Mon. and Tues.*

★ Ristorante Bagni Delfino

$$ | **SOUTHERN ITALIAN** | At this informal, waterside restaurant and snack bar, you won't see many locals—they're unlikely to be impressed by the four-language menus—but the seafood platters are fresh and flavorful, and you can eat alfresco in the sunshine or inside a glass-enclosed dining area with a nautical motif. You can even go for a swim. **Known for:** bountiful portions; sunny terrace beside a sunbathing/swimming jetty; great views of the Marina Grande and beyond. $ *Average main: €30* ✉ *Via Marina Grande 216, Sorrento* ☎ *081/8782038* 🌐 *www.ristoranteildelfinosorrento.com* 🕓 *Closed Nov.–Mar.*

★ Ristorante Museo Caruso

$$$ | **SOUTHERN ITALIAN** | Seafood classics, including *tartara di pescato del giorno* (raw catch-of-the-day antipasto) and linguine with *riccio* (sea urchin), are tweaked creatively here. The staff is warm and helpful, the singer on the sound system is the long-departed "fourth tenor" himself, and the operatic memorabilia (including posters and old photos of Caruso) and subtle lighting add to the atmosphere. **Known for:** Caruso memorabilia aplenty; Torna a Surriento and the Neapolitan songbook; tasting menus from €80 and a few à la carte choices. $ *Average main: €35* ✉ *Via S. Antonino 12, Sorrento* ☎ *081/8073156* 🌐 *www.ristorantemuseocaruso.com.*

Ristorante 'o Parrucchiano La Favorita

$$ | **SOUTHERN ITALIAN** | Opened in 1868 by an ex-priest (*'o parrucchiano* means "the priest" in the local dialect), this restaurant serves classic Sorrentine cuisine in a 19th-century setting that's enchanting, although it can feel overly touristy: a sprawling, multilevel greenhouse packed with tables and chairs amid fruit trees and enough tropical foliage to fill a Victorian conservatory. **Known for:** fecund greenhouse and terrace foliage and fruit; signature cannelloni created in 1870; gorgeous setting but may disappoint food/service-wise. *Average main: €22 Corso Italia 71, Sorrento 081/8781321 www.parrucchiano.com Closed Jan.*

Coffee and Quick Bites

★ A'Marenna

$ | ITALIAN | FAMILY | Run with enthusiasm and love by two young Sorrentine women, this small rustic-styled bakery and bistro makes generously filled panini using fresh ingredients on ciabatta and *panuozzo* pizza-dough bread. It's also a fab spot to linger with some local wine and a cheese platter. **Known for:** friendly service; local wines; vegan and veggie options. *Average main: €8 Via Tasso 23, Sorrento 081/18495183 www.facebook.com/amarennasorrento.*

Hotels

Bellevue Syrene

$$$$ | HOTEL | This luxurious retreat, magnificently set on a bluff high over the Bay of Naples, is one of Italy's most legendary hotels, complete with Art Deco touches throughout; lounges and salons decorated with avant-garde artwork and trompe-l'oeil frescoes; and guest rooms that range from sleekly modern to sumptuously fanciful. **Pros:** impeccable design elements; elegant common areas; incredible views. **Cons:** wallet-melting rates; pricey parking; small pool. *Rooms from: €2,300 Piazza della Vittoria 5, Sorrento 081/8781024 www.bellevue.it Closed Jan.–Mar. 49 rooms Free Breakfast.*

★ Excelsior Vittoria

$$$$ | HOTEL | Overlooking the Bay of Naples, this luxurious Belle Époque dream has been in the same family since 1834, which means that public spaces are virtual museums—with elegant Victorian love seats and *stile liberty* (Art Nouveau) ornamentation—and guest rooms are spacious, with soigné furnishings and balconies and terraces that overlook gardens or the bay. **Pros:** beyond the protected gates, you're in the heart of town; gardens buffer city noise; grand spaces and handsome furnishings. **Cons:** not all rooms have sea views; some rooms are comparatively small; dated gym. *Rooms from: €909 Piazza Tasso 34, Sorrento 081/8777111 www.exvitt.it Closed Jan.–Mar. 83 rooms Free Breakfast.*

La Favorita

$$$$ | HOTEL | The lobby might be a glamorous white-on-white extravaganza of Caprese columns, tufted sofas, shimmering crystal chandeliers, silver ecclesiastical objects, and gilded Baroque mirrors, but the charming staff ensure the vibe is elegantly casual, the guest rooms are well equipped and spacious, and the rooftop pool area has magnificent bay and Vesuvius vistas. **Pros:** central location; beautiful terrace; idyllic garden. **Cons:** no views to speak of from guest rooms; lack of decent air-conditioning and room thermostat control; rooms near the bar noisy after midnight. *Rooms from: €689 Via T. Tasso 61, Sorrento 081/8782031 www.hotellafavorita.com Closed Jan.–Mar. 85 rooms Free Breakfast.*

Positano

14 km (9 miles) east of Sorrento, 57 km (34 miles) south of Naples.

When John Steinbeck visited Positano in 1953, he wrote that it was difficult to consider tourism an industry because "there are not enough [tourists]." Alas, there are more than enough now, and the town's vertical landscape with pastel-hue houses, drapes of bright pink bougainvillea, and sapphire-blue sea make it easy to understand why.

The most photographed fishing village in the world, this fabled locale is home to some 4,000 Positanesi, who are joined daily by hordes arriving from Capri, Sorrento, and Amalfi. The town clings to the Monti Lattari with arcaded, cubist buildings, set in tiers up the mountainside, in shades of rose, peach, purple, and ivory.

GETTING HERE AND AROUND

SITA buses leave from the Circumvesuviana train station in Sorrento. Buses also run from Naples and, in summer, Rome. There are hydrofoils from Naples, Salerno and Sorrento in the summer months.

A word of advice: wear comfortable walking shoes and be sure your back and legs are strong enough to negotiate those picturesque but daunting and ladderlike *scalinatelle*. In the center of town, where no buses can go, you're on your own from Piazza dei Mulini. To begin your explorations, make a left turn onto the boutique-flanked Via dei Mulini and head down to the Palazzo Murat, Santa Maria Assunta, and the beach—one of the most charming walks of the coast.

VISITOR INFORMATION

CONTACT Ufficio del Turismo Luca Vespoli. ✉ *Via Regina Giovanna 13, Positano* ☎ *331/2085821 mobile* 🌐 *www.facebook.com/prolocopositano.*

Sights

★ MAR – Museo Archeologico Romano

ARCHAEOLOGICAL SITE | Painstaking excavations begun in 2003 below the oratory of Santa Maria Assunta are now open to the public and showcase tantalizing traces of Positano's vast Roman settlement buried by the AD 79 eruption. Through volcanic debris some 30 feet below the *piazzetta* is a cool subterranean world with different captivating chambers and crypts. The new entrance leads to the most recently discovered Roman villa excavations, which sit below the Cripta Superiore with its spine-tingling funereal seating, reserved for Positano's most upstanding 18th-century citizens. Among the Roman artifacts are vibrant frescoes, ornate stucco reliefs, and intricate bronzes. Another entrance nearby leads to the Cripta Inferiore, with two naves, marble columns, and later additions. ✉ *Piazza Flavio Gioia 7, Positano* ☎ *331/2085821 WhatsApp* 🌐 *marpositano.it* 🎫 *€15.*

Palazzo Murat

NOTABLE BUILDING | Past a bevy of resort boutiques, head to Via dei Mulini to view the prettiest garden in Positano: the 18th-century courtyard of the Palazzo Murat, named for Joachim Murat, who sensibly chose the palazzo as his summer residence. This was where Murat, designated by his brother-in-law Napoleon as king of Naples in 1808, came to forget the demands of power and lead a simpler life. He built this grand abode (now a hotel) near the church of Santa Maria Assunta, just steps from the main beach. ✉ *Via dei Mulini 23, Positano* ☎ *089/875177* 🌐 *www.palazzomurat.it.*

Santa Maria Assunta

CHURCH | The Chiesa Madre, or parish church of Santa Maria Assunta, lies just south of the Palazzo Murat, its green-and-yellow majolica dome topped by a perky cupola. Built on the site of the former Benedictine abbey of St. Vito, the 13th-century Romanesque structure was almost completely rebuilt in 1700. At the altar is a Byzantine 13th-century painting on wood of Madonna with Child, known popularly as the Black Virgin. A replica is carried to the beach every August 15 to celebrate the Feast of the Assumption. Embedded over the doorway of the church's bell tower is a medieval bas-relief of fish, a fox, and a pistrice (the mythical half-dragon, half-dog sea monster). This is one of the few relics of the medieval abbey of Saint Vito. ✉ *Piazza Flavio Gioia, Positano* ☎ *089/875480* 🌐 *www.chiesapositano.it.*

Marina Grande Beach in Positano is a nice, long stretch of sand that attracts a cosmopolitan crowd.

Spiaggia Grande

BEACH | FAMILY | The walkway from the Piazza Flavio Gioia leads down to Spiaggia Grande, Positano's main beach, bordered by an esplanade and some of the town's busiest restaurants. Surrounded by the spectacular amphitheater of houses and villas that leapfrog up the hillsides of Monte Comune and Monte Sant'Angelo, this remains one of the most picturesque beaches in the world. **Amenities:** food and drink; lifeguards; showers; toilets; water sports. **Best for:** swimming. ✉ *Spiaggia Grande, Positano.*

★ Via Positanesi d'America

PROMENADE | FAMILY | Just before the ferry ticket booths to the right of Spiaggia Grande, a tiny road that is the loveliest seaside walkway on the entire coast rises up and borders the cliffs leading to Fornillo Beach. The road is named for the town's large number of 19th-century emigrants to the United States—Positano virtually survived during World War II thanks to the money and packages their descendants sent back home. Halfway up the path lies the Torre Trasìta (Trasìta Tower), the most distinctive of Positano's three coastline defense towers. Now a residence occasionally available for summer rental, the tower was used to spot pirate raids. As you continue along the Via Positanesi d'America, you'll pass a tiny inlet and an emerald cove before Fornillo Beach comes into view. ✉ *Via Positanesi d'America, Positano.*

Restaurants

★ Da Vincenzo

$$ | SOUTHERN ITALIAN | Established in 1958, this buzzy family-run place pairs generations of tradition and genuine love of hospitality with ever-evolving innovation, reflected in the exceptional takes on classic Neapolitan dishes and the stylish, up-to-date yet rustic decor. Expect warm banter with busy staff, who greet passersby while introducing a menu with both sea and robust land mainstays such as grilled octopus, linguine with anchovies, lamb chops with braised artichokes, and eggplant Parmesan. **Known**

for: charming hosts, from the owner to the young waitstaff; entertaining outside terrace on street; sumptuous dolci, including cheesecake. *Average main: €28 Via Pasitea 172/178, Positano 089/875128 www.davincenzo.it Closed Nov.–Mar. No lunch Tues.*

Il Ritrovo

$$$ | **SOUTHERN ITALIAN** | **FAMILY** | In the tiny town square of Montepertuso, 1,500 feet up the mountainside from Positano (call for the free shuttle service to and from), the Ritrovo has been noted for its cucina for more than 20 years. The menu showcases food from both the sea and the hills: try the scialatielli *ai frutti di mare* accompanied by well-grilled vegetables; the house specialty *zuppa saracena,* a paella-like affair brimming with assorted seafood; and the lemon tiramisu, perhaps paired with one of 80 different kinds of a homemade liqueur, including carob and chamomile options. **Known for:** airy, tranquil mountainside location; local spigola (sea bass) grilled or poached; amiable padrone Salvatò, who also runs a cooking school. *Average main: €32 Via Montepertuso 77, Montepertuso 089/812005 www.ilritrovo.com Closed mid-Jan.–mid-Feb.*

★ Next2

$$$ | **SOUTHERN ITALIAN** | Wrought-iron gates open from scenic Via Pasitea into Next2's *bianco e nero*–chic courtyard, replete with a cocktail bar and a cozy salon filled with wine bottles and prime window seats for sunset views. Calmly charming Carmela and her friendly crew including a young, talented chefs in the semi-open kitchen deliver elegant, subtly flavored creations including: grilled octopus antipasto with green beans and potato foam, a flavor-packed Datterino tomato spaghettoni and—*spigola al vapore (*steamed seabass wrapped in an eye-catching zucchini jacket served with baby vegetables). **Known for:** exquisite-looking small-portioned dishes; delectable desserts like lemon meringue tartlet with lemon sorbet; cocktails with novel, fresh infusions. *Average main: €36 Via Pasitea 242, Positano 089/8123516 next2.it No lunch.*

★ Saraceno D'Oro

$$ | **SOUTHERN ITALIAN** | Although open for lunch, this reliable restaurant and its wonderful staff—tellingly popular with the *Positanesi*—truly comes into its own in the evening. Living up to its name, the ambience is distinctly Moorish without being kitschy; wood-fired pizza and hearty costiera seafood dishes dominate the menu. **Known for:** friendly staff; one of the best scialatielli di scoglio (classic seafood pastas) around; delizia di limone dessert. *Average main: €25 Via Pasitea 254, Positano 089/812050 www.saracenodoro.it Closed Nov.–Dec. 26 and Jan. and Feb.*

Coffee and Quick Bites

Bar Paradise

$ | **SANDWICHES** | **FAMILY** | With an outdoor terrace overlooking the Spiaggia Grande, this is an ideal stop for a coffee, a sandwich, or an ice cream. By night, the latest music pumps from the stereo and the clamor of sporting events blares from the large-screen TVs, as movers, groovers, and soccer fans from around the globe sip cocktails after a hard day on the beach. **Known for:** fab gelato artigianale; selection of beers and cocktails; pastries, pizza, and panini. *Average main: €7 Via del Saracino 32, Positano 089/811915 www.bucapositano.it/en/bar-paradise Closed Mon.*

Hotels

Hotel Pupetto

$$ | **HOTEL** | Hidden away from the Positano crowds, a short passeggiata away from the hydrofoil port, lovely host Gabriella and her long-serving team run a laid-back but well-run hotel blessed by Spiaggia Fornillo beachside bliss, with 34 tiled suites and practical bathrooms with

balconies and facilities galore including restaurant, bar and bathing services. **Pros:** wonderful staff and intimate beach; fab breakfast on the restaurant beachside terrace; quieter location with interesting walks nearby. **Cons:** those craving chic may not dig the simplicity; shortcut walk to Via Pasitea may be too hilly for some; restaurant and bar now Positano pricey. *$ Rooms from: €370 ✉ Via Fornillo 37, Positano ☎ 089/875087 🌐 www.hotel-pupetto.it ⏲ Nov.–Easter 🛏 34 rooms 🍽 Free Breakfast.*

★ La Fenice

$$ | HOTEL | This tiny, unpretentious hotel on the outskirts of Positano beckons with bougainvillea-laden views, castaway cottages, terraces growing produce, and a turquoise seawater pool—all perched over a private beach where a boat can whisk you away to Capri. **Pros:** small private beach with kayaks; famiglia Mandara's home-grown small-holding produce; secluded pool with bar service. **Cons:** a 10-minute walk to town; roadside rooms are small and noisy; lots of steps. *$ Rooms from: €260 ✉ Via G. Marconi 4, Positano ☎ 089/875513 🌐 www.lafenicepositano.com ⏲ Sometimes closed Dec.–Feb. 🛏 14 rooms 🍽 Free Breakfast.*

★ Le Sirenuse

$$$$ | HOTEL | As legendary as its namesake sirens, this 18th-century palazzo has long set the standard for luxury in Italian hotels: it opened in 1951 with just 12 rooms (John Steinbeck stayed here while writing "Positano" for *Harper's Bazaar* in 1953) and now sprawls over eight floors, where extravagantly stylish guest rooms are accented with antiques and fine linens. **Pros:** unrivaled views, including from poolside terrace; many rooms have whirlpool tubs; gorgeous artworks around every corner. **Cons:** a bit of a climb from the town center; lower-priced rooms are small; can be noisy. *$ Rooms from: €2,100 ✉ Via Cristoforo Colombo 30, Positano ☎ 089/875066 🌐 www.sirenuse.it ⏲ Closed Nov.–Mar. 🛏 58 rooms 🍽 Free Breakfast.*

Palazzo Murat

$$$$ | HOTEL | A central-yet-secreted location, an infinity pool below the cupola of Santa Maria Assunta, and a magical bougainvillea-draped patio garden are among the things that make the Murat much coveted by hotel bucket-listers. **Pros:** once a regal residence with a sense of history; stunning garden and surroundings; shops and passeggiata on the doorstep. **Cons:** only five rooms have seaside views; staff can be snooty; not all balconies secluded. *$ Rooms from: €750 ✉ Via dei Mulini 23, Positano ☎ 089/875177 🌐 www.palazzomurat.it ⏲ Closed Nov.–Mar. 🛏 31 rooms 🍽 Free Breakfast.*

Nightlife

L'Alternativa

GATHERING PLACE | The Tiffany-blue hut by the ferry ticket office at the far end of Spiaggia Grande is a refreshingly no-frills spot for a granita or snack by day or late-night cocktail or bottle of Peroni beer. Expect a friendly and unpretentious crowd, where local fishermen mix with young visitors who congregate in and around the harbor seats into the evening enjoying the reasonable (shock!)-for-Positano prices. *✉ Molo Spiaggia Grande, Positano.*

La Zagara

COCKTAIL BARS | Come evening, things heat up at this bar/restaurant/ *pasticceria* (pastry shop) where a local pianist tickles the ivories and summer sees DJ jams on the leafy terrace. *✉ Via dei Mulini 8, Positano ☎ 089/875964 🌐 www.lazagara.com.*

Conca dei Marini

13 km (8 miles) east of Positano, 29 km (18 miles) east of Sorrento.

A longtime favorite of the off-duty rich and famous, Conca dei Marini (the name means "seafarers' basin") hides many of its charms, as any sublime hideaway should. On a curve in the road sits the village's most noteworthy attraction, the Emerald Grotto.

Sights

Grotta dello Smeraldo (*Emerald Grotto*)
BODY OF WATER | **FAMILY** | The tacky road sign, squadron of tour buses, Dean Martin–style boatmen, and free-form serenading (Andrea is the king of the grotto crooners) scream tourist trap, but there is, nevertheless, a compelling, eerie *bellezza* in the rock formations and luminous waters here. The karstic cave was originally part of the shore, but the lowest end sank into the sea. Intense greenish light filters into the water from an arch below sea level and is reflected off the cavern walls. You visit the Grotta dello Smeraldo, which is filled with huge stalactites and stalagmites, on a large rowboat. Don't let the boatman's constant spiel detract from the experience—just tune out and enjoy the sparkles, shapes, and brilliant colors. The light at the grotto is best from noon to 3 pm. You can take an elevator from the coast road down to the grotto, or in the summer you can drive to Amalfi and arrive by boat (from €30 including admission fee). Companies in Positano, Amalfi, and elsewhere along the coast provide passage to the grotto, but consider one of the longer boat trips that also explore Punta Campanella, Li Galli, and the more secluded spots along the coast. *Via Smeraldo, west of Capo di Conca, Conca dei Marini 089/831535 €10 Closed in adverse weather conditions.*

Hotels

★ **Monastero Santa Rosa Hotel & Spa**
$$$$ | **HOTEL** | One of Italy's most exclusive retreats—in a 17th-century monastery on dramatic coastal cliffs—this boutique hotel has just 20 rooms, all with vaulted ceilings, Italian antiques, modern amenities, sumptuous bathrooms, and dazzling views framed by Mediterranean gardens. **Pros:** excellent service; meticulously restored property with spa; gorgeous gardens and infinity pool. **Cons:** out of reach for many budgets; some rooms could be more spacious; a bit remote. *Rooms from: €1,155 Via Roma 2, Conca dei Marini 089/8321199 www.monasterosantarosa.com Closed Nov.–mid-Apr. 20 rooms Free Breakfast.*

Amalfi

18 km (11 miles) east of Positano, 35 km (22 miles) east of Sorrento.

At first glance, it's hard to imagine that this resort destination was one of the world's great naval powers and a sturdy rival of Genoa and Pisa for control of the Mediterranean in the 11th and 12th centuries. Once the seat of the Amalfi Maritime Republic, the town is set in a verdant valley of the Lattari Mountains, with cream-color and pastel-hue buildings tightly packing a gorge on the Bay of Salerno. The harbor, which once launched the greatest fleet in Italy, now bobs with ferries and blue-and-white fishing boats. The main street, lined with shops and pasticcerie, has replaced a raging mountain torrent, and terraced hills flaunt the green and gold of lemon groves. Bearing testimony to its great trade with Tunis, Tripoli, and Algiers, Amalfi remains honeycombed with Arab-Sicilian cloisters and covered passages. In a way Amalfi has become great again, showing off its medieval glory days with sea pageants, convents-turned-hotels, ancient paper mills, covered streets, and its glimmering cathedral.

GETTING HERE AND AROUND

From April to October the optimal way to get to Amalfi is by ferry from Salerno or Naples (sometimes via Sorrento). Sita Sud buses run from Naples and Sorrento throughout the year. By car, take the Statale 163 (Amalfitana) from outside Sorrento or Salerno, or take the Angri exit on the A3 autostrada and cross the mountainous Valico di Chiunsi.

VISITOR INFORMATION

CONTACT Amalfi Tourist Board. (*Amalfi Tourist Office*) ✉ *Arsenale della Repubblica e Molo Pennello, Piazza Flavio Gioia e Largo Cesareo Console, Amalfi* ☎ *089/8736222* 🌐 *www.visitamalfi.info.*

Sights

Arsenale di Amalfi

HISTORIC SIGHT | Get a feel of the architecture and naval might of the *repubblica marinara* (maritime republic) of Amalfi at this fascinating museum within the impressive Arsenale shipyard, which was first documented in 1059. As well as a cultural and performance space, the Arsenal contains the Museo della Bussola e del Ducato Marinaro, which largely focuses on the golden age of the Amalfi Republic between 839 and 1139, displaying artifacts such as money, manuscripts, navigational and other nautical instruments, costumes, art, and religious objects. ✉ *Largo Cesario Console 3, Amalfi* ☎ *089/8731293* 🌐 *arsenalediamalfi.it* 🎫 *€3.*

★ Duomo di Sant'Andrea

CHURCH | Complicated, grand, delicate, and dominating, the 9th-century Amalfi cathedral has been remodeled over the years with Romanesque, Byzantine, Gothic, and Baroque elements but retains a predominantly Arab-Norman style. Built around 1266 as a burial ground for Amalfi's elite, the cloister, the first stop on a tour of the cathedral, is one of southern Italy's architectural treasures. Its flower-and-palm-filled quadrangle has a series of exceptionally delicate intertwining arches on slender double columns. The chapel at the back of the cloister leads into the 9th-century basilica, now a museum housing sarcophagi, sculpture, Neapolitan goldsmiths' artwork, and other treasures from the cathedral complex. Steps from the basilica lead down into the Cripta di Sant'Andrea (Crypt of St. Andrew). The cathedral above was built in the 13th century to house the saint's bones, which came from Constantinople. Following the one-way traffic up to the cathedral, you can admire the elaborate polychrome marbles and painted, coffered ceilings from its 18th-century restoration. ✉ *Piazza Duomo, Amalfi* ☎ *089/871324* 🌐 *museodiocesanoamalfi.it* 🎫 *€4* 🕑 *Generally closed early Jan. and Feb. except for daily services.*

★ Museo della Carta (*Paper Museum*)

HISTORY MUSEUM | FAMILY | Uphill from town, the Valle dei Mulini (Valley of the Mills) was for centuries Amalfi's center for paper-making, an ancient trade learned from the Arabs, who learned it from the Chinese. Beginning in the 12th century, former flour mills were converted to produce paper made from cotton and linen. The paper industry was a success, and by 1811 more than a dozen mills here, with more along the coast, were humming. Natural waterpower ensured that the handmade paper was cost-effective. Yet, by the late 1800s the industry had moved to Naples and other more geographically accessible areas. Flooding in 1954 closed most of the mills for good, and many have been converted into private housing. The Museo della Carta (Museum of Paper) opened in 1971 in a 15th-century mill. Paper samples, tools of the trade, old machinery, and the audiovisual presentation are all enlightening. You can also participate in a paper-making laboratory. ✉ *Via delle Cartiere 23, Amalfi* ☎ *089/8304561* 🌐 *www.museodellacarta.it* 🎫 *€4.50, €7 with guided tour and paper-making experience* 🕑 *Closed weekdays Jan. and Feb., and Mon. Nov. and Dec.*

Restaurants

★ Da Ciccio: Cielo Mare Terra

$$ | **SOUTHERN ITALIAN** | Featuring, as its name suggests, stunning views of sky, sea, and land and run by the fourth generation of the *famiglia* Cavaliere (sommelier Giuseppe, front-of-house manager Antonio, and chef Marco), this restaurant just outside of town serves exquisite dishes made with fresh local produce—often from its own *orto* garden and the sea below. Many diners opt for the aromatic theater *al tavolo* of the signature *spaghetti al cartoccio dal 1965* (spaghetti with clams, olives, capers, tomatoes, and oregano), which the ever-smiling Antonio removes from baking paper, mixes, and serves. **Known for:** warm family-run place with home-grown produce; aperitivo on the panoramic terrace; free shuttle service from Amalfi and around. *Average main: €26 Via Giovanni Augustariccio 21, Amalfi 089/831265, 0345/3538935 for shuttle service www.ristorantedaciccio.com Closed Tues. No lunch weekdays.*

Coffee and Quick Bites

Andrea Pansa

$ | **CAFÉ** | Amalfi's historic pasticceria is famed for its candied fruits and assortment of tempting Neapolitan pastries. If you have no time to linger and indulge at their piazza tables, order at the bar for a cheaper stand-up coffee and *sflogliatella* (shell-shaped pastry) fix. **Known for:** historic facade and interiors on Piazza Duomo; delizia di limone cake; excellent but pricey. *Average main: €7 Piazza Duomo 40, Amalfi 089/871065 www.pasticceriapansa.it.*

Hotels

Albergo Sant'Andrea

$$ | **HOTEL** | Just across from the magnificent steps leading to Amalfi's cathedral, this tiny, family-run *pensione* has a cute "Room with a View" lobby that's as big as a Victorian closet and guest rooms (most overlooking the Duomo) that range from cozy to a family-friendly triple, plus a mini-apartment. **Pros:** great location on the main square; divine Duomo views; old-school family-run pensione (with half-board available). **Cons:** steep flight of steps to entrance; simple, dated decor; on the piazza, so expect noise. *Rooms from: €300 Salita Costanza D'Avalos 1, Amalfi 089/871145 www.albergo-santandrea.it Closed Feb. and Mar. 8 rooms Free Breakfast.*

★ Anantara Hotel Convento di Amalfi

$$$$ | **RESORT** | This fabled medieval monastery was lauded by such guests as Longfellow and Wagner, and after a luxurious overhaul by the esteemed Anantara hotel group, it still retains its historic charm and features, including a celebrated Arab-Sicilian cloister and Baroque church. **Pros:** a slice of paradise; impeccable service; sublime terrace and garden walkways. **Cons:** food pricey and inconsistent; 15-minute walk to town; noise from occasional wedding and events. *Rooms from: €1,626 Via Annunziatella 46, Amalfi 089/8736711 www.anantara.com/en/convento-di-amalfi Closed Jan.–mid-Mar. 52 rooms Free Breakfast.*

Shopping

Leading off from Piazza Duomo is the main street of Amalfi, Via Lorenzo d'Amalfi, which is lined with some of the loveliest shops on the coast. While it can be crowded during the day, be sure to take a stroll along here in the evening.

Ravello

5 km (3 miles) northeast of Amalfi, 40 km (25 miles) northeast of Sorrento.

Positano may focus on pleasure, and Amalfi on history, but cool, serene Ravello revels in refinement. Thrust over the

Ravello's History

The town itself was founded in the 9th century, under Amalfi's rule. Residents prosperous from cotton tussled with the superpower republic and elected their own doge in the 11th century; Amalfitani dubbed them *ribelli* (rebels). In the 12th century, with the aid of the Norman King Roger, Ravello even succeeded in resisting Pisa's army for a couple of years, though the powerful Pisans returned to wreak destruction along the coast. Even so, Ravello's skilled seafaring trade with merchants and Moors from Sicily and points east led to a burgeoning wealth, which peaked in the 13th century, when there were 13 churches, four cloisters, and dozens of sumptuous villas. Neapolitan princes built palaces and life was privileged.

Ravello's bright light eventually diminished, first through Pisa's maritime rise in the 14th century, then through rivalry between its warring families in the 15th century. When plague cast its shadow in the 17th century, the population plummeted from upward of 30,000 to perhaps a couple of thousand souls, where it remains today. When Ravello was incorporated into the diocese of Amalfi in 1804, a kind of stillness settled in. Despite the decline of its power and populace, Ravello's cultural heritage and special loveliness continued to blossom. Gardens flowered and music flowed in the ruined villas, and artists, sophisticates, and their lovers filled the crumbling palazzi. Grieg, Wagner, D.H. Lawrence, Chanel, Garbo and her companion, conductor Leopold Stokowski, and then, slowly, tourists followed in their footsteps.

S163 and the Bay of Salerno on a mountain buttress, below forests of chestnut and ash, above terraced lemon groves and vineyards, it early on beckoned the affluent with its island-in-the-sky views and secluded defensive positioning. Gardens out of the *Arabian Nights,* pastel palazzi, tucked-away piazzas with medieval fountains, architecture ranging from Romano-Byzantine to Norman-Saracen, and those sweeping blue-water, blue-sky vistas have inspired a panoply of large personalities. Today, many visitors flock here to discover this paradisiacal place, some to enjoy the town's celebrated two-month-long summer music festival (the Ravello Festival 🌐 *www.ravellofestival.com*), others just to stroll through the hillside streets to gape at the bluer-than-blue panoramas of sea and sky.

GETTING HERE AND AROUND

Buses from Amalfi make the 20-minute trip along white-knuckle roads. From Naples, take the A3 Naples–Salerno autostrada; then exit at Angri and follow signs for Ravello. The journey takes about 75 minutes. Save yourself the trouble of driving by hiring a car and driver.

VISITOR INFORMATION

CONTACT Infopoint. ✉ *Piazza Fontana Moresca 10, Ravello* ☎ *089/857096.*

Sights

Auditorium Oscar Niemeyer

ARTS CENTER | Crowning Via della Repubblica and the hillside, which overlooks the spectacular Bay of Salerno, Auditorium Niemeyer is a startling piece of modernist architecture. Designed with a dramatically curved, all-white roof by the Brazilian architect Oscar Niemeyer (designer of Brasília), it was conceived as an alternative indoor venue for concerts, including those of the famed summer Ravello Festival and is now also used as a cinema. The subject of much controversy since its first conception back in 2000, it raised the wrath of some locals who denounced such an ambitious modernist building in medieval Ravello. They need not have worried. The result, inaugurated in 2010, is a design masterpiece—a huge, overhanging canopied roof suspended over a 400-seat concert area, with a giant eye-shape window allowing spectators to contemplate the extraordinary bay vista during performances. ✉ *Via della Repubblica 12, Ravello* ☎ *089/857096.*

★ Duomo

CHURCH | Ravello's first bishop, Orso Papiciò, founded this cathedral, dedicated to San Pantaleone, in 1086. Rebuilt in the 12th and 17th centuries, it retains traces of medieval frescoes in the transept, an original mullioned window, a marble portal, and a three-story 13th-century bell tower playfully interwoven with mullioned windows and arches. The 12th-century bronze door has 54 embossed panels depicting Christ's life, and saints, prophets, plants, and animals, all narrating biblical lore. Ancient columns divide the nave's three aisles, and treasures include sarcophagi from Roman times and paintings by the southern Renaissance artist Andrea da Salerno. Most impressive are the two medieval pulpits: the earlier one is inset with a mosaic scene of Jonah and the whale, while the more famous one opposite boasts exquisite mosaic work and six twisting columns sitting on lion pedestals. In the crypt is the **Museo del Duomo**, which displays 13th-century treasures from the reign of Frederick II of Sicily. ✉ *Piazza del Duomo, Ravello* ☎ *089/858029* 🌐 *www.duomoravello.it* 🎫 *€4.*

Giardini del Vescovo (*Monsignore*)

GARDEN | A onetime bishop's residence that dates from at least the 12th century, the Villa Episcopio (formerly Villa di Sangro) today hosts concerts and exhibitions and has an open-air theater in its splendid gardens—the same gardens where André Gide found inspiration for his novel *The Immoralist,* where Italy's King Vittorio Emanuele III abdicated in favor of his son in 1944, and where Jackie Kennedy enjoyed breaks from her obligations as First Lady during a much publicized 1962 visit. Wheelchair access is via a new ramp on via San Giovanni del Toro. ✉ *Via Richard Wagner/Via dei Episcopio, Ravello* 🎫 *Free.*

Mamma Agata

COOKING CLASSES | Learn about Costiera Amalfitana cooking traditions with Mamma Agata, known for a popular cookbook, delicious meatballs and eggplant parmigiana, and for hosting Astaire, Bogart, Burton and Taylor, and Jackie Kennedy; while cheerful daughter Chiara has swapped spoons with Michael Jordan, Pierce Brosnan, and Woody Harrelsen among others. The family will walk you through the preparation of its many generation-spanning recipes. A morning session is followed by lunch and an introduction to the family's organic lemons, zucchini, tomatoes, and abundant produce grown in their wonderful garden and sent around the world. Classes now include a pizza-making course, and must be arranged in advance (they are not offered on Wednesday). ✉ *Piazza San Cosma 9, Ravello* ☎ *089/857845* 🌐 *www.mammaagata.com* 🎫 *Cooking class and lunch from €250* ⏱ *Closed Wed., weekends, Dec.–Mar., Easter and Aug. 10–25.*

Museo del Corallo (*Coral Museum*)

ART MUSEUM | To the left of the Duomo, the entrance to this private museum is through the tempting shop CAMO, and both are the creation of master-craftsman-in-residence Giorgio Filocamo. The museum celebrates the venerable tradition of Italian workmanship in coral, harvested in bygone centuries from the gulfs of Salerno and Naples and crafted into jewelry, cameos, and figurines. The fascinating collection, not confined solely to coral work, includes a painting of Sisto IV from the 14th century. Look also in particular for a carved Christ from the 17th century, for which the J. Paul Getty Museum offered $525,000 in 1987 (the offer was refused), and a tobacco box covered in cameos, one of only two in the world. There is also a statue of the Madonna dating to 1532. Giorgio has crafted coral for Pope John Paul II, the Clintons, and Princess Caroline, as well as numerous Hollywood stars. ✉ *Piazza Duomo 9, Ravello* ☎ *089/857461* 🌐 *www.museodelcorallo.com* 🎫 *Free* ⏲ *Closed Fri.–Sun.*

★ Villa Cimbrone

GARDEN | To the south of Ravello's main square, a somewhat hilly 15-minute walk along Via San Francesco brings you to Ravello's showstopper, the Villa Cimbrone, whose dazzling gardens perch 1,500 feet above the sea. This medieval-style fantasy was created in 1905 by England's Lord Grimthorpe and made world-famous in the 1930s when Greta Garbo found sanctuary from the press here. The Gothic *castello-palazzo* sits amid idyllic gardens that are divided by the grand Avenue of Immensity pathway, leading in turn to the literal high point of any trip to the Amalfi Coast—the Belvedere of Infinity. This grand stone parapet, adorned with stone busts, overlooks the entire Bay of Salerno and frames a panorama that the late writer Gore Vidal, a longtime Ravello resident, described as the most beautiful in the world. The villa itself is now a five-star hotel. ✉ *Via Santa Chiara 26, Ravello* ☎ *089/857459* 🌐 *www.villacimbrone.it* 🎫 *€10.*

★ Villa Rufolo

GARDEN | Directly off Ravello's main piazza is the Villa Rufolo, home to some of the most spectacular gardens in Italy, framing a stunning vista of the Bay of Salerno, often called the "bluest view in the world." If one believes the master storyteller Boccaccio, the villa was built in the 13th century by Landolfo Rufolo, whose immense fortune stemmed from trade with the Moors and the Saracens. Norman and Arab architecture mingle in a welter of color-filled gardens so lush the composer Richard Wagner used them as inspiration for Klingsor's Garden, the home of the Flower Maidens, in his opera *Parsifal.* Beyond the Arab-Sicilian cloister and the Norman tower lie the two terrace gardens. The lower one, the "Wagner Terrace," is often the site of Ravello Festival concerts. Highlights of the house are its Moorish cloister—an Arabic-Sicilian delight with interlacing lancet arcs and polychromatic palmette decoration—and the 14th-century Torre Maggiore, or Klingsor's Tower. ✉ *Piazza del Duomo, Ravello* ☎ *089/857621* 🌐 *villarufolo.com* 🎫 *€8, extra charge for concerts.*

Restaurants

Vittoria

$$ | **PIZZA** | **FAMILY** | Just south of the Duomo, this airy, unfussy place with coved stone ceilings is a good bet for an informal bite. The *pizza al forno di legna* with fresh toppings is the star attraction: locals praise it, and even Gore Vidal allegedly approved. **Known for:** extensive menu; very popular with locals and tourists; Campanian classics like seafood-heaped spaghettoni allo scoglio. 💲 *Average main: €25* ✉ *Via dei Rufolo 3, Ravello* ☎ *089/857947* 🌐 *www.ristorantepizzeriavittoria.it.*

Hotels

Belmond Hotel Caruso

$$$$ | **HOTEL** | In a grand palazzo on the highest point of Ravello, with some buildings dating from the 16th century and with a Bay of Salerno panorama that's incomparable and timeless, this member of the exclusive Belmond hotel brand has been a slice of hospitality paradise since the 19th century; today it shimmers with modern luxuries amid its frescoes, Norman arches, and beautifully terraced garden. **Pros:** infinity pool; spacious suites with terraces; complimentary boat and shuttle services. **Cons:** way out of most visitors' price range; service can be inconsistent; food may disappoint. *Rooms from: €2,155 Piazza San Giovanni del Toro 2, Ravello 089/858801 www.hotelcaruso.com Closed Nov.–mid-Apr. 50 rooms Free Breakfast.*

Hotel Parsifal

$$ | **HOTEL** | In 1288, this diminutive property overlooking the coastline housed an order of Augustinian friars; today the intact cloister hosts travelers intent on enjoying themselves under the coved ceilings of the former *eremitani scalzi* (shaved hermit) cells. **Pros:** staying in a former Ravello convent; charming manager and his family dote on Americans; open year-round. **Cons:** some may not like the '70s vibe; tiny rooms; can be chilly in colder months. *Rooms from: €200 Viale Gioacchino d'Anna 5, Ravello 089/857144 www.hotelparsifal.com 17 rooms Free Breakfast.*

Hotel Rufolo

$$ | **HOTEL** | The quarters might be snug and simply furnished, but many have balconies with gorgeous sea and sky vistas framed by the palm trees of the Villa Rufolo, just below the hotel. **Pros:** parking included in room rates; beautiful views over Villa Rufolo; great pool and spa services. **Cons:** car park clutters the entrance; dated decor; paying for the location. *Rooms from: €313 Via San Francesco 1, Ravello 089/857133 www.hotelrufolo.it Closed Jan.–Mar. 34 rooms Free Breakfast.*

Hotel Villa Cimbrone

$$$$ | **HOTEL** | Suspended over the azure sea and set amid legendary rose-filled gardens, this Gothic-style castle was once home to Lord Grimthorpe and a hideaway for Greta Garbo; since the 1990s, it's been an exclusive if pricey visitors haven, with guest rooms ranging from palatial to cozy. **Pros:** gorgeous pool and views; surrounded by beautiful gardens; top-rated restaurant. **Cons:** a longish hike from town center (porters can help with luggage); daily arrival of respectful day-trippers; some rooms outdated and overpriced. *Rooms from: €900 Via Santa Chiara 26, Ravello 089/857459 www.villacimbrone.com Closed Nov.–mid-Apr. 19 rooms Free Breakfast.*

Villa Amore

$$ | **HOTEL** | A 10-minute walk from the Piazza Duomo, this secluded hotel with a garden is family-run and shares the same exhilarating view of the Bay of Salerno as Ravello's most expensive hotels. **Pros:** wonderful views; inexpensive alternative to its illustrious neighbors; good-value restaurant. **Cons:** away from the main drag; some rooms are very cramped and without views; long flight of steps to reach entrance. *Rooms from: €260 Via dei Fusco 5, Ravello 089/857135 www.villaamore.it Closed Nov.–Mar. 12 rooms Free Breakfast.*

Paestum

99 km (62 miles) southeast of Naples.

For history buffs, a visit to Campania is not complete without seeing the ancient ruins of Paestum. A visit to the ruins to stroll past the incredibly well-preserved temples and see the top-notch collection at the Museo Nazionale is a great day trip from the Amalfi Coast or Naples.

GETTING HERE AND AROUND

By car, take the A3 autostrada south from Salerno, take the Battipaglia exit to SS18. Exit at Capaccio Scala. You can also take a Busitalia or an FS train from Salerno. The archaeological site is a 10-minute walk from the station.

VISITOR INFORMATION

CONTACT Infopoint Paestum. *(Paestum Tourist Office)* ✉ *Via Magna Grecia 887, Paestum* ☎ *0828/811016.*

Sights

★ Paestum Archaeological Park

ARCHAEOLOGICAL SITE | One of Italy's most majestic sights lies on the edge of a flat coastal plain: the remarkably preserved Greek temples of Paestum. This is the site of the ancient city of Poseidonia, founded by Greek colonists probably in the 6th century BC. When the Romans took it over in 273 BC, they Latinized the name to Paestum and changed the layout of the settlement, adding an amphitheater and a forum. Much of the archaeological material found on the site is displayed in the Museo Nazionale within the park, and several rooms are devoted to the unique tomb paintings—rare examples of Greek and pre-Roman pictorial art—discovered in the area.

At the northern end of the site opposite the ticket barrier is the Tempio di Cerere (Temple of Ceres). Built in about 500 BC, it is thought to have been originally dedicated to the goddess Athena. Follow the road south past the Foro Romano (Roman Forum) to the Tempio di Nettuno (Temple of Poseidon), a showstopping Doric edifice with 36 fluted columns and an entablature (the area above the capitals) that rivals those of the finest temples in Greece. Beyond is the so-called Basilica, which dates from the early 6th century BC. The name is an 18th-century misnomer, though, since it was, in fact, a temple devoted to Hera, the wife of Zeus. Try to see the temples in the early morning or late afternoon when the stone takes on a golden hue. ✉ *Via Magna Grecia, Paestum* ☎ *0828/811023 ticket office* 🌐 *www.museopaestum.beniculturali.it* 🎫 *Site and museum: Mar.–Nov. €15, Dec.–Feb. €10.*

★ Tenuta Vannulo—Buffalo Farm and Shop

FARM/RANCH | **FAMILY** | Foodies, families, and the curious flock to this novel farm attraction that celebrates humane animal husbandry, organic mozzarella di bufala, and other wonderful products. A tour of the ranch run by the Palmieri family—headed by the serene octogenerian Antonio—brings you nose to glistening snout with probably the most pampered buffalo in the world. Some 600 of them wallow in pools, get a mechanical massage, and flap their ears to classical music. The shop/restaurant is the place to taste and take away cheese, ice cream, yogurt, chocolate, and leather products. ✉ *Contrada Vannulo, Via Galileo Galilei 101, Capaccio, Paestum* ☎ *0828/727894* 🌐 *www.tenutavannulo.com* 🎫 *€5 guided group tours; book in advance.*

Hotels

Tenuta Seliano

$ | **B&B/INN** | At this working farm about 3 km (2 miles) from Paestum's Greek temples, befriend the resident dogs so they will accompany you on country walks or bike rides, and opt for half board to enjoy home-produced mozzarella and rich buffalo stew. **Pros:** a great taste of a working farm; a banquet every evening; cooking classes. **Cons:** confusing to find; not for non–dog fans; rustic, dated decor. $ *Rooms from: €122* ✉ *Via Seliano, Paestum* ✥ *About 1 km (½ mile) down dirt track west off main road from Capaccio Scalo to Paestum* ☎ *0828/723634* 🌐 *www.agriturismoseliano.it* ⏲ *Closed Nov.–Mar.* *14 rooms* 🍽 *Free Breakfast.*

Chapter 15

PUGLIA, BASILICATA, AND CALABRIA

Updated by
Nick Bruno

WELCOME TO PUGLIA, BASILICATA, AND CALABRIA

TOP REASONS TO GO

★ **A wander through Sassi:** The Basilicata town of Matera is endowed with one of the most unusual landscapes in Europe—a complex network of ancient cave dwellings partially hewn from rock, some of which now house chic bars and restaurants.

★ **A trip to peasant-food heaven:** Dine on Puglia's famous puree of fava beans with chicory and olive oil in a humble country restaurant.

★ **Lecce and its Baroque splendors:** The beautiful, friendly city of Lecce might be known for its peculiar brand of fanciful Baroque architecture, but it's not yet famous enough to have lost its Pugliese charm.

★ **The trulli of the Valle d'Itria:** Strange conical houses—many of them still in use—dot the rolling countryside of Puglia, centering on Alberobello, a town still composed almost entirely of these *trulli*. They must be seen to be believed.

1 **Bari.** An atmospheric *centro storico* is a highlight of this busy Adriatic port.

2 **Trani.** Don't miss this harbor town's stunning cathedral.

3 **Polignano a Mare.** Steep cliffs draw thrill-seekers and those looking to relax overlooking gorgeous inlets.

4 **Castel del Monte.** This town's octagonal, eponymous fortress is mysterious.

5 **Mattinata.** The Gulf of Manfredonia beaches here will dazzle you.

6 **Vieste.** The spectacular Gargano Promontory is the site of this resort town.

7 **Alberobello.** It's hard not to be enchanted by Alberobello's fairy-tale stone trulli.

8 **Ostuni.** The so-called Città Bianca (White City) is perched above azure waters.

9 **Ceglie Messapica.** The heart of this town is beguilingly medieval.

10 **Martina Franca.** Lose yourself in a maze of alleys and piazzas.

11 **Taranto.** An engaging archaeological museum is the main draw of this port town with a naval base.

12 **Lecce.** Here, it's all about Baroque beauty and lively locals.

13 **Otranto.** Look out over the sea from Otranto's medieval fortress.

14 **Gallipoli.** This fishing town is famed for its island *borgo antico.*

15 **Matera.** The so-called City of Sassi is filled with the intriguing cave dwellings.

16 **Maratea.** The mountains here seem to fall into the sea.

17 **Diamante.** This Calabrese resort is lively.

18 **Castrovillari.** For hiking, this gateway to mountainous Pollino National Park is a great hub.

19 **Cosenza.** Come to explore attractive medieval sights.

20 **Camigliatello.** The mountainous Sila National Park surrounds this town.

21 **Crotone.** The Treasure of Hera is among Crotone's draws.

22 **Tropea.** Gorgeous beaches will beckon you to Tropea.

23 **Reggio Calabria.** This busy port city plays footsie with Sicily.

ADRIATIC SEA
0 30 mi
0 30 km
Peschici
6 Vieste
GARGANO PROMONTORY
5 Mattinata
Manfredonia
San Severo
Foggia
Barletta
2 Trani
Canosa
1 Bari
4 Castel del Monte
3 Polignano a Mare
Monopoli
Fasano
Ostuni 8
PUGLIA
Altamura
Alberobello 7
CAMPANIA
Martina Franca 10
9 Ceglie Messapica
Brindisi
Potenza
15 Matera
Salerno
Taranto 11
SALENTO
Lecce 12
13 Otranto
BASILICATA
Manduria
Aliano
Bernalda
LUCANO
Gallipoli 14
Gagliano
Golfo di Taranto
16 Maratea
Castrovillari 18
17 Diamante
Cosenza 19
Camigliatello 20
Paola
TYRRHENIAN SEA
CALABRIA
Crotone 21
Catanzaro
IONIAN SEA
Vibo Valentia
AEOLIAN ISLANDS
Tropea 22
Salina
Lipari
Vulcano
Rosarno
Palmi
Siderno
Locri
Messina
Reggio Calabria 23
SICILY
Cape Spartivento

EATING AND DRINKING WELL IN PUGLIA, BASILICATA, AND CALABRIA

Meat and cheese products flavored with chili peppers

The Mediterranean diet was born in the south of Italy. The cuisine here is based on seasonal local produce, so don't expect to find, say, grapes in May or watermelon in November, although the mild climate and fertile soil, linked to modern farming methods, mean that most vegetable products have a long growing season.

Traditional cuisine reflects its peasant origins, with hearty homemade pasta, thick bean soups, and grilled meat and fish. The emphasis, though, is on vegetables, with zucchini, eggplant, beans, sweet peppers, and at least a dozen varieties of tomatoes transformed into imaginative dishes. Naturally, the local olive oil is never lacking on the table. Dribbled over soup or a thick chunk of bread, it can transform the plainest dish into a gourmet treat. One defining principle of Italian cooking is to use excellent ingredients in simple preparations. That philosophy reaches its purest expression here.

FABULOUS FAVA

Puré di fave e cicorielle, a puree of fava beans topped with sautéed chicory, is unique to Puglia and Basilicata. The simple recipe has been prepared here for centuries and continues to be a staple of the local diet. The dried favas are soaked overnight, cooked with potatoes, seasoned with salt and olive oil, and served warm with wild green chicory, often with a sprinkling of ground *peperoncino* (chili pepper). Mix it together before eating, and wash it down with a glass of *primitivo* or *aglianico*.

MEAT

In addition to its excellent beef, Basilicata is known for its *salsicce lucane* (sausages), seasoned with salt, cayenne pepper, and fennel seeds. Enormous grills are a feature of many of the region's restaurants, infusing the dining area with the aroma of freshly cooked meat. Adventurous eaters in Puglia should look for *turcinieddhri* (a blend of lamb's innards) and *pezzetti di cavallo* (braised horse meat).

PASTA

Puglia is the home of orecchiette with *cime di rapa* (broccoli rabe) and olive oil, a melodious dish that's wondrous in its simplicity. Try cavatelli and *strascinati* (rectangles of pasta with one rough side and one smooth side). For a crunchy, spicy kick, *spaghetti all'assassina,* invented in 1960s Bari, pairs pan-charred pasta with tomato, garlic, and chili sauce.

PEPPERS

Calabria is known for its use of little hot peppers that can range from a mild sprinkling in tomato sauce to the tongue-scorching *'nduja* (spicy pork salami) paste. Local cured meats like *soppressata* (dried spicy salami) and *salsiccia piccante* (hot sausage), often sold by street vendors on a roll with peppers and onions.

Orecchiette pasta

Baked fish with potatoes

SEAFOOD

Fish can be grilled (*alla griglia*), baked (*al forno*), roasted (*arrosto*), or steamed (*in umido*). Among the highlights are delicate *orata* (sea bream), branzino (sea bass), *gamberi rossi* (sweet red shrimp), and calamari. Puglia is the home of *cozze pelose* (hairy-shelled mussels), and Calabria's version of sushi is freshly caught *ricci di mare* (sea urchins), considered a delicacy—and an aphrodisiac!

WINES

Puglia produces around 16% of Italy's wine, more than the output of Australia. In the past, most of it was *vino sfuso* (jug wine), but over the past 25 years, producers have been concentrating on quality—with impressive results. The ancient *primitivo* grape (an ancestor of California's zinfandel) yields strong, heady wines like Primitivo di Manduria. The *negroamaro* grape is transformed into palatable *rosati* (rosés), as well as the robust Salice Salentino. Pair a dessert with the sweet red Aleatico di Puglia or Moscato di Trani.

In Basilicata, producers use the aglianico grape to outstanding effect in the prestigious Aglianico del Vulture. In Calabria, they've worked wonders with another thick-skinned ancient Greek variety, *gaglioppo*.

Venture off the traffic-filled highways and explore the countryside of Italy's boot, made up of three separate regions—Puglia, Basilicata, and Calabria—each one with its own character. This is Italy's deep south, where whitewashed buildings stand silently over three turquoise seas, castles guard medieval alleyways, and grandmothers dry their handmade orecchiette in the afternoon heat.

At every turn, these three regions boast dramatic scenery. Geographical divides have preserved an astonishing cultural and linguistic diversity that's unequaled elsewhere on the Italian mainland. Southern Italians are extremely proud of their hometowns and will gladly direct you to some forgotten local chapel in an olive grove, an unmarked monument, or an obscure work of art.

One of southern Italy's most popular vacation destinations is the Gargano Promontory, where safe sandy shores and secluded coves are nestled between whitewashed coastal towns and craggy limestone cliffs. You'll also find many beautiful stretches of sandy beaches along the coast of the Salento Peninsula and the Mediterranean shoreline of Calabria and Basilicata.

MAJOR REGIONS

Bari and the Adriatic Coast. The busy port of Bari offers architectural nuggets in its labyrinthine old quarter. In nearby Trani a distinctive Apulian-Romanesque church stands by the sea, while Polignano a Mare has cliff-top medieval charm above sparkling waters. For a unique excursion, head to Castel del Monte, home to an enigmatic 13th-century octagonal castle.

The Gargano Promontory. Amid the Foresta Umbra's landscape of craggy limestone, pine trees, and scrubby Mediterranean *macchia* (underbrush) are the beguiling coastal resorts of Vieste and Mattinata.

The Trulli District. The inland area southeast of Bari has a mostly flat, rock-strewn terrain that's been given over to olive cultivation. The area is also interspersed with idiosyncratic limestone habitations called *trulli*. The center of the Trulli District is Alberobello in the enchanting Valle d'Itria. Amid this fairy-tale-like landscape are the dazzling whitewashed hilltop market towns of Martina Franca, Ceglie Messapica, and Ostuni.

The Salento Penninsula. South of the Trulli District the monotony of endless olive trees is redeemed by an alluring coastline of dramatic sandstone cliffs and intimate fishing towns such as Otranto and Gallipoli. Taranto has a captivating archaeological museum amid its rusty, industrial surroundings, while Lecce is an oasis of grace and sophistication, with swirling Baroque architecture and a lively cultural scene.

Basilicata. Occupying the instep and part of the heel of Italy's boot, this and the neighboring Calabria region formed part of Magna Graecia, southern Italy's Greek colonies. Today, Basilicata attracts travelers in search of bucolic settings, great food, and archaeological treasures. The village of Aliano was made famous by writer Carlo Levi (1902–75). Matera, a recently rejuvenated city with Baroque splendor, is built on the side of a ravine honeycombed with Sassi that have been transformed into swanky homes, restaurants, and hotels. On a spectacularly mountainous section of the Tyrrhenian coast is the gorgeous resort Maratea.

Calabria. Italy's southernmost mainland region has fantastic beaches in lively resort communities such as Tropea and Diamante. Castrovillari, Cosenza, and Camigliatello are great rustic bases for exploring the Sila Mountains and Pollino National Park. Crotone was a major ancient cultural center, and, toward Sicily, the busy port of Reggio Calabria is home to two arresting ancient Greek statues, the *Bronzi di Riace.*

Planning

Discounts

If you're planning to visit many museums and attractions consider each region's cumulative tickets. The Puglia Musei Card (€20 🌐 *museipuglia.cultura.gov.it/ticket*) offers superb value entrance to over a dozen regional attractions including Castel del Monte and Castelli Svevo di Bari e Trani. The Valle d'Itria Card (€14 🌐 *hello.valleditria.it*) includes sights in Martina Franca, Locorotondo, and Ceglie Messapica. LeccEcclesiae Baroque Tour Ticket (€11/€21 with bell-tower 🌐 *chiese-lecce.it/en) includes entrance to various museums and churches.*

Getting Around

BUS

There is direct, if not always frequent, service between most destinations within Calabria, Puglia, and Basilicata. In many cases, bus service is the backup when problems with train service arise. Matera is linked with Bari by frequent Ferrovie Appulo Lucane trains and buses and with Taranto by SITA bus. In Calabria the Romano bus company runs a regular service between various towns. Ferrovie della Calabria operates many of the local routes.

CAR

Although roads are generally good in the south, and major cities are linked by fast autostradas, driving here is a major test of navigation skills. Driving into the center of many cities and towns can be particularly complicated, owing to mazes of one-way streets, pedestrianized zones, and limited parking facilities. The good news is that you can bypass many communities via ring roads. Also, if you're staying at an in-town hotel, check with the staff about parking: the more upscale properties often have garage facilities or valet services for guests.

If you're squeamish about getting lost, don't drive at night in the countryside—roads can be confusing without the visual aid of landmarks, and GPS is far from infallible. Also, Bari, Brindisi, and Reggio Calabria are notorious for car thefts and break-ins. In these cities, don't leave valuables in the car, and find a guarded parking space if possible.

The E45/A3 autostrada from Naples and its toll-free continuation the A2

(Salerno–Reggio Calabria) links Naples to the south, with major exits at Sicignano (for the interior of Basilicata and Matera), Cosenza (the Sila Massif and Crotone), and Pizzo (for Tropea). Parts of the A2 in northern Calabria cross uplands more than 3,000 feet high, and snow chains may be required during winter months. In the summer and during holiday weekends this is the main north–south route for Italy's sun seekers, so factor in plenty of time for delays and avoid peak travel times.

Take the SS18 for coastal destinations on the Tyrrhenian side and the E90 for the Ionian, alongside various state roads that crisscross toward the Adriatic. Given speed detectors and driver-tracking technology, it's best to stick to speed limits and be careful not to enter ZTL (*zona a traffico limitato*) restricted traffic areas (cameras are set up in towns such as Matera and Altamura): you'll be spared an unwelcome ticket when you get home.

TRAIN

Trenitalia runs to Calabria, either following the Ionian Coast as far as Reggio Calabria or swerving inland to Cosenza and the Tyrrhenian Coast. Italo runs high-speed services along the coasts to Bari and Reggio Calabria.

Making the Most of Your Time

If your priority is relaxing on the beach, plan on a few days at a seaside resort in one of the Gargano Promontory's fishing villages, such as Peschici, Rodi Garganico, and Vieste, and perhaps a further stay at one of the Calabrian coastal resorts, such as Diamante or Tropea, or Maratea in Basilicata.

Otherwise, choose a base like Polignano a Mare or Trani, especially if you land or dock in Bari. Take day trips out to the Valle d'Itria, or to the remarkable octagonal Castel del Monte. Then head east along the Adriatic route (SS16), stopping to see the idyllic hilltop Ostuni before continuing on to Lecce, where you'll want to spend at least two to three nights exploring the city's Baroque wonders and taking a day trip down to Otranto and Gallipoli.

Next, take regional roads and the Via Appia (SS7) to reach Matera, whose Sassi cave dwellings are a southern Italian highlight; allow at least two nights here. Then it's back out to the SS106 to Calabria, along the coast dotted with ancient Greek settlements, as far as Tropea. At this point, cut inland on the SS107 across the Sila Massif, stopping at the hill resort of Camigliatello or carrying on to the more vibrant lowland Cosenza. Reggio Calabria is worthwhile just to see the celebrated Riace bronzes.

Restaurants

Italy's southern region is home to numerous restaurants that feature home cooking or Slow Food–inspired menus, which boils down to everything is made with the freshest ingredients. Meals are meant to be enjoyed at leisure, however, and service is not swift. Whether you decide to dine in a well-known restaurant or at a humble country trattoria, plan to give some thought to your menu choices (it's expected) and ask questions (also expected).

Hotels

Hotels in the region range from grand upscale establishments to small and stylish bijou inns to family-run rural *agriturismi* (country hostelries, often part of farms) that compensate for a lack of amenities with their famous southern hospitality. *Fattorie* and *masserie* (small farms and grander farm estates) offering accommodations are listed at local tourist offices.

In beach areas such as the Gargano Promontory and Salento, campgrounds and bungalow lodgings are ubiquitous and popular with families and budget travelers. Note that many seaside hotels open up just for the summer season, when they often require several-day stays with full or half board. And do remember that in a region like this—blazingly hot in summer and chilly in winter—air-conditioning and central heating can be important.

⇨ *Hotel and restaurant reviews have been shortened. For full information, visit Fodors.com. Prices in the hotel reviews are the lowest cost of a standard double room in high season. Prices in the dining reviews are the average cost of a main course at dinner, or, if dinner is not served, at lunch.*

What It Costs in Euros

$	$$	$$$	$$$$
RESTAURANTS			
under €20	€20–€30	€31–€40	over €40
HOTELS			
under €175	€175–€400	€401–€600	over €600

Bari

260 km (162 miles) southeast of Naples, 450 km (281 miles) southeast of Rome.

The biggest city in the region, Bari is a major port and a transit point for travelers catching ferries across the Adriatic to Greece, Croatia, and Albania. This cosmopolitan city has an atmospheric historic center and wonderful seafront. In recent years, it has become a major center of pilgrimage for Russian Orthodox visitors, due to its connection with St. Nicholas, the patron saint of Russia, as well as of Bari. The old quarter of the city, around the basilica and the harbor castle, is a lively maze of whitewashed alleyways buzzing with bars, cafés, restaurants, and crafts shops. Most of the modern town is set out in a logical 19th-century grid, following the designs of Joachim Murat (1767–1815), Napoléon's brother-in-law and King of the Two Sicilies. The heart is **Piazza della Libertà,** where old and young gather in the evenings. Explore Bari's *lungomare* seafront, taking in the old town walls and labyrinthine lanes, cathedral, Liberty-style Teatro Margherita, and Porto Vecchio, where you can sample "Il Crudo Barese," raw seafood.

GETTING HERE AND AROUND

By car, take the Bari-Nord exit from the A14 autostrada. Bari's train station is a hub for Puglia-bound trains. ITA Airways and Ryanair fly to Bari Airport from Rome and Milan. Bari, Brindisi, and Milan are also connected by easyJet.

VISITOR INFORMATION

CONTACT Infopoint Turistico Bari. ✉ *Piazza del Ferrarese 29, Bari* ☎ *080/5242244* 🌐 *www.viaggiareinpuglia.it.*

Sights

★ Bari Vecchia and Via Sparano

HISTORIC DISTRICT | **FAMILY** | By day, you can lose yourself in the maze of white alleyways in Bari Vecchia, the Old Town stretching along the harbor, now humming with restaurants, cafés, and crafts shops. Residents tend to leave their doors wide open, so you can catch a glimpse into the daily routine of southern Italy: matrons hand-rolling orecchiette, their grandchildren home from school for the midday meal, and workers busy patching up centuries-old arches and doorways. Back in the new town, join the evening passeggiata on pedestrian-only Via Sparano, then, when night falls, saunter out among the outdoor bars and restaurants in Piazza Mercantile, past Piazza Ferrarese at the end of Corso Vittorio Emanuele. ✉ *Via Sparano, Bari.*

Puglia, Past and Present

Puglia has long been inhabited and invaded. On sea voyages to their colonies and trading posts in the west, the ancient Greeks invariably headed for Puglia first—it was the shortest crossing—before filtering southward into Sicily and westward to the Tyrrhenian Coast. In turn, the Romans—often bound in the opposite direction—were quick to recognize the strategic importance of the peninsula. Later centuries would see a procession of other empires raiding or colonizing Puglia: Byzantines, Saracens, Normans, Swabians, Turks, and Spaniards all swept through, each group leaving their mark. Romanesque churches and the powerful castles built by 13th-century Holy Roman Emperor Frederick II (who also served as king of Sicily and Jerusalem) are among the most impressive buildings in the region. Frederick II, dubbed "Stupor Mundi" (Wonder of the World) for his wide-ranging interests in literature, science, mathematics, and nature, was one of the foremost personalities of the Middle Ages.

The region experienced a huge economic revival after decades of neglect following World War II. Since then, EU funding, state incentive programs, and irrigation subsidies have helped Puglia to become Italy's top regional producer of wine, with the remainder of land devoted to olives, citrus, and vegetables. The main ports of Bari, Brindisi, and Taranto are thriving economic centers, though there remain serious problems of unemployment and poverty. However, the much-publicized arrival of thousands of asylum seekers from Eastern Europe and beyond has not significantly destabilized these cities (as had been feared), and economic and political refugees have dispersed throughout Italy. Today, despite years of regionwide *recessione*, an air of prosperity still wafts through the smarter streets of Lecce, Trani, and smaller towns like Otranto and Peschici.

★ Basilica di San Nicola

CHURCH | The 11th-century Basilica di San Nicola, overlooking the sea in the *città vecchia* (old city), houses the bones of St. Nicholas, the inspiration for Santa Claus. His relics were stolen from Myra, in present-day Turkey, by a band of sailors from Bari and are now buried in the crypt. Because St. Nicholas is also the patron saint of Russia, the church draws both Roman Catholic and Russian Orthodox pilgrims; souvenir shops in the area display miniatures of the Western saint and his Eastern counterpart side by side. ✉ *Largo Abate Elia 13, Piazza San Nicola, Bari* ☎ *080/5737111* 🌐 *www.basilicasannicola.it.*

Castello Svevo

CASTLE/PALACE | Looming over the cathedral is the symbol of Bari: huge Castello Svevo, which houses a number of archaeological and art collections within its evocative courtyards, towers, and rooms. The current building dates from the time of Holy Roman Emperor Frederick II (1194–1250), who rebuilt an existing Norman-Byzantine castle to his own exacting specifications. Designed more for power than beauty, it looks out beyond the cathedral to the small Porto Vecchio (Old Port). Inside are displays that include plaster-cast reproductions of the city's sculptural riches, Byzantine archaeological finds, immersive multimedia projections, photo collections, and historic ceramics and other precious objects. ✉ *Piazza Federico II di Svevia, Bari* ☎ *080/8869304* 🌐 *www.musei.puglia.beniculturali.it* 🎫 *€10* ⏲ *Closed Mon.*

★ **Cattedrale di San Sabino**

CHURCH | Bari's 12th-century Romanesque cathedral is the seat of the local bishop and was the scene of many significant political marriages between important families in the Middle Ages. The cathedral is dedicated to San Sabino, a 6th-century bishop who apparently lived to be 105. The main draw is the subterranean **Museo del Succorpo della Cattedrale** with ancient basilica, a Byzantine church and Roman remains, including mosaic-tiled flooring swirling with fish, octopi, and plants. ✉ *Piazza dell'Odegitria, Bari* ☎ *080/5210605* 🌐 *www.arcidiocesibaribitonto.it/luoghi-di-culto/cattedrale* 🎫 *€9.*

Restaurants

Ristorante al Pescatore

$$ | **SEAFOOD** | In the lively heart of the old town, opposite the castle, stands one of Bari's best seafood restaurants with tables packed together. The interior is rather sparse, with whitewashed walls and a vaulted ceiling, and the dining room can be crowded and noisy, but during the summer you can sit on the quieter outdoor veranda. **Known for:** seafood antipasto (crudo misto); ricci di mare—a taste of the Puglian sea; fish by weight so be careful what you order. 💲 *Average main: €27* ✉ *Piazza Federico II di Svevia 6/8, Bari* ☎ *080/5237039* 🌐 *www.alpescatorebari.com* ⏲ *Closed Tues.*

Ristorante Opera

$ | **SOUTHERN ITALIAN** | Don't be put off by its nondescript modernist street location, as Opera delivers a well-crafted menu of superb-value seafood dishes, from sushi-style *crudi* to beautifully grilled seabass. The always innovative food is served on arty tableware in the smart yet welcoming contemporary space or on the street-side terrace outside. **Known for:** loved by locals and families; freshest seafood with a twist; innovative vegetarian options. 💲 *Average main: €19* ✉ *Via Nicolo' Piccinni 151, Bari* ☎ *340/1774153 mobile* 🌐 *ristoranteoperabari.eatbu.com* ⏲ *Closed Mon. No dinner Sun.*

Coffee and Quick Bites

★ **Caffè Vergnano 1882 Amendola**

$ | **SOUTHERN ITALIAN** | Grand stone rooms and a pretty terrazza sprouting olive trees make this a flexible and fab venue to breakfast, brunch, and lunch—and to socialize with evening drinks. As well as a constant stream of excellent coffee, they do a selection of pastries, great-value daily specials (pasta for just €7), and various snacks. **Known for:** historic stone building and courtyard seating; daily pasta, grilled meat, and veggie dishes; evening buffet and DJ sets. 💲 *Average main: €8* ✉ *Via Amendola 128/b, Bari* ☎ *080/5586586* 🌐 *www.facebook.com/caffevergnanobari.*

Hotels

★ **Dilman Luxury Stay**

$$ | **B&B/INN** | Contemporary minimalism, a soothing color palate, and cool design, including travertine-lined spa-like bathrooms and mood lighting, make this central boutique B&B a reliably serene and clean choice. **Pros:** well-maintained rooms; warm and knowledgeable staff; Jacuzzi and saunas in the chicest suites. **Cons:** decor and breakfast choice may be too sparse for some; costly parking at nearby garage; reception not always manned. 💲 *Rooms from: €290* ✉ *Via Calefati 14, Bari* ☎ *080/5940165* 🌐 *www.dilman.it* 🛏 *16 rooms* 🍽 *Free Breakfast.*

Palazzo Zippitelli

$ | **APARTMENT** | The second floor of this handsome 1930s palazzo in the modern Madonnella district near the lungomare houses spacious contemporary apartments with vibrant color-blocks, well-equipped kitchens, living spaces,

Puglia

30 miles
50 km
0
0
ADRIATIC SEA
Isole Tremiti
I Cameroni
Isole S. Domino
Peschici
Vieste
Rodi Garganico
Lago di Varano
Foresta Umbra
TO TERMOLI
GARGANO PROMONTORY
Mattinata
Monte Sant'Angelo
Manfredonia
San Giovanni Rotondo
L' Annunziata
Golfo di Manfredonia
San Severo
Zapponeta
PUGLIA
Lucera
Foggia
Barletta
Trani
Molfetta
Bari
Polignano a Mare
Cerignola
Andria
Corato
Castel del Monte
Grotte di Castellana
Fasano
TRULLI DISTRICT
Ostuni
Brindisi
CAMPANIA
Alberobello
Locorotondo
PUGLIA
Santeramo in Colle
Gioia del Colle
Martina Franca
Ceglie Messapica
Via Appia
Mesagne
Melfi
Spinazzola
Altamura
Gravina in Puglia
Massafra
Francavilla Fontana
Campi
Lecce
S. Angelo dei Lombardi
Matera
Taranto
Grottaglie
Manduria
Mare Piccolo
Mare Grande
SALENTO
Otranto
Via Appia
Potenza
Castellaneta Marina
Nardo
Maglie
Santa Cesarea Terme
BASILICATA
Lido di Metaponto
Gallipoli
Castro
TO NAPLES
Eboli
Auletta
Scanzano
Leuca
Salerno
Battipaglia
LUCANO
Golfo di Taranto
Golfo di Salerno

comfortable bedrooms, and small balconies. **Pros:** great-value, spacious apartments; live and shop like a Madonnella local; good location near the lungomare and local shops. **Cons:** bit of a walk to Bari Vecchia; part of building maybe undergoing renovation; some traffic noise. *Rooms from: €140 Largo Francesco Carabellese 5, Bari 337/3842565 mobile www.palazzozippitelli.com 8 apartments No Meals.*

Trani

43 km (27 miles) northwest of Bari.

Trani has a harbor filled with fishing boats and a quaint old town with cobblestone streets, gleaming medieval churches, and palazzi built from local limestone. The town is also justly famous for its sweet dessert wine, Moscato di Trani. It's smaller than the other ports along this coast.

GETTING HERE AND AROUND

By car, take the Trani exit from the A14 autostrada. Frequent trains run from Bari.

VISITOR INFORMATION

CONTACT Info Point Trani. *Palazzo Palmieri, Piazza Trieste 8, Trani 393/3757734 mobile and WhatsApp messaging www.prolocotrani.it.*

Sights

Castello Svevo

CASTLE/PALACE | One of Frederick II's most imposing fortresses, the quadrangular Trani Castle guarded the Adriatic sea route throughout the Middle Ages. It was the scene of several royal weddings of the Swabian and Anjou houses, as well as the place of imprisonment for life of Siffridina, Countess of Caserta, who had supported the losing Swabian dynasty against Charles I of Anjou. In the early 20th century it became a state prison and remained so until 1974. The ground floor contains a museum telling the story of the castle alongside archaeological finds, sculpture, and a wealth of ceramics. *Piazza Re Manfredi 14, Trani 0883/506603 €8.*

★ Cattedrale

CHURCH | The stunning pinkish-white 11th-century cathedral, considered one of the finest in Puglia, is built on a spit of land jutting into the sea. Dedicated to St. Nicholas the Pilgrim, it was a favorite place of prayer for crusaders embarking for war in the Holy Land. Its lofty bell tower can be visited, and guided tours arranged by request at the nearby Museo Diocesiano and via the website calendar slots; the views are worth the climb. *Piazza Duomo, Trani 0883/500293 www.cattedraletrani.it Free, bell tower €5.*

Polo Museale Trani

SPECIALTY MUSEUM | Four floors of the handsome 18th-century Palazzo Lodispoto, near the Duomo, contain two very different collections: the Museo Diocesano showcases Trani's wealth of religious artifacts, while the Museo della Macchina per Scrivere follows the evolution of the typewriter. Among the highlights in the former are fragments from the 6th-century basilica, medieval and Baroque architectural elements, and funereal treasures commissioned by Charles I of Anjou on the death of his son Philip. The latter collection has 400 examples of typewriters from around the world, including some iconic Olivetti models as well as those used to type Braille, Arabic, and Japanese. Nearby at Via La Giudea, the **Sinagoga Museo Sant'Anna** has exihbits detailing the history of Trani's Jewish community. *Palazzo Lodispoto, Piazza Duomo 8/9, Trani 0883/582470 www.fondazioneseca.it Main museum site €8, Sinagogo Museo €4, combined €9 Closed Mon.*

Hotels

★ Palazzo Filisio

$ | **HOTEL** | Superbly positioned in front of the Duomo on a quiet seaside piazza, this small, handsome, beautifully maintained hotel has guest rooms with contemporary wooden furniture, white and azure fabrics, and marbled bathrooms. **Pros:** right next to the cathedral; superb breakfast and restaurant; most rooms have sea views. **Cons:** no parking outside hotel; often occupied by wedding parties; books up in high season. *$ Rooms from: €140 ✉ Via M. Reginaldo Giuseppe Maria Addazi 2, Trani ☎ 0883/500931 🌐 www.palazzofilisio.it ⏲ Restaurant closed Mon. 🛏 14 rooms 🍽 Free Breakfast.*

Polignano a Mare

35 km (22 miles) southeast of Bari, 14 km (9 miles) north of Castellana.

This well-preserved, whitewashed old town, perched on limestone cliffs overlooking the Adriatic, makes an atmospheric base for exploring the surrounding area. Film crews and adrenaline junkies come to experience the town's spectacular cliff-diving championships, which usually take place in June. In recent years a social media buzz has led to an influx of day-trip crowds in the summer months.

GETTING HERE AND AROUND

From Bari, take the Polignano exit from the SS16. Frequent trains run from Bari.

VISITOR INFORMATION

CONTACT Prololo Turismo F.F. Favale. *✉ Via Dante Alighieri, Polignano a Mare ☎ 080/4252336 🌐 www.prolocopolignanoamare.com.*

Restaurants

★ Antica Trattoria Comes Dal 1926

$ | **SOUTHERN ITALIAN** | **FAMILY** | Run by genial Giuseppe, this family-run trattoria serves classic seafood dishes in a relaxed, modern dining room. Freshly netted catches are heaped on hearty plates, like *insalata di mare* (seafood salad), seafood cavatelli pasta, and grilled *gamberoni* (prawns). **Known for:** superb Pugliese seafood antipasti; big helpings, big value; cold cuts, cheeses, and Angus steaks. *$ Average main: €19 ✉ Via Pompeo Sarnelli 14, Polignano a Mare ☎ 080/4248888 ⏲ Closed Wed. No lunch Sun.*

Hotels

Borgobianco Resort & Spa

$$ | **RESORT** | **FAMILY** | Housed in a handsome masseria farmhouse building, this countryside resort provides a tranquil base for relaxing by the pool, eating alfresco in courtyards and terraces, and spa pampering. **Pros:** cool, whitewashed luxury in tranquil location; shuttle bus to town; gorgeous pool, spa, and outdoor spaces. **Cons:** town not in easy walking distance; service can be patchy; decor could be a tad soulless for some. *$ Rooms from: €358 ✉ Contrada Casello Cavuzzi, Polignano a Mare ☎ 080/2049060 🌐 borgobianco.it 🛏 48 rooms 🍽 Free Breakfast.*

Castel del Monte

56 km (35 miles) southwest of Bari.

The isolated Norman Castel del Monte dominates the surrounding countryside from the top of a 1,778-foot-high hill. The nearest town is Andria, 17 km (10½ miles) away, largely modern and congested—avoid traffic by taking the ring road around it.

The imposing Castel del Monte is a 13th-century structure built by Emperor Frederick II on land he inherited from his mother, Constance of Sicily.

GETTING HERE AND AROUND

Take the Andria-Barletta exit from the A14 autostrada, then follow the SS170dir to Castel del Monte. From April through October (and weekends November–March) there's a daily minibus service from Piazza Bersaglieri d'Italia in Andria.

VISITOR INFORMATION

CONTACT Castel del Monte Tourism Office. ✉ *Via Vespucci 114, Andria* ☎ *0883/592283* 🌐 *www.proloco.andria.ba.it.*

Sights

Castel del Monte

CASTLE/PALACE | Crowning an isolated hill 1,778 feet above sea level in the heart of the Alta Murgia National Park, this enigmatic octagonal fortress, built by Frederick II in the first half of the 13th century, has puzzled historians and researchers for centuries. Rooms are arranged in a seemingly illogical sequence through eight towers around a central courtyard. Recent interpretations suggest it was an elaborate cultural center conceived by Frederick to study various scientific disciplines of the Western and the Arabic worlds. Umberto Eco used it as his inspiration for riddles in *The Name of the Rose*. To avoid disappointment: it's an impressive if largely empty building, and can be tricky to get to and pricey to visit when adding parking, guided tours, and so on. ✉ *On signposted minor road, 17 km (10½ miles) south of Andria, Andria* ☎ *327/9805551 mobile* 🌐 *aditusculture.com* 🎟 *€10; audioguide €6; guided tour (Italian only) €7; €6 parking and €2 return shuttle bus from lot.*

Mattinata

138 km (86 miles) northwest of Bari.

The town of Mattinata is a good center for hikes in the Foresta Umbra and for visiting the Santuario di San Michele. It also has attractive stretches of sandy beach.

GETTING HERE AND AROUND

From Foggia (the chief city in Puglia's northernmost province), take the winding SS89. Regular buses leave from Foggia's and San Severo's train stations.

VISITOR INFORMATION

CONTACT Info Point Mattinata. ✉ *Corso Matino 64, Mattinata* ☎ *0884/552425 municipal office* 🌐 *instagram.com/infopointmattinata.*

Sights

Foresta Umbra

NATURE PRESERVE | In the middle of the Gargano Promontory is the majestic Foresta Umbra (Shady Forest), a dense growth of beech, maple, pine, and oak generally found in more northerly climates, thriving here because of the altitude, which reaches 3,200 feet above sea level. Between the trees in this national park are occasional dramatic vistas opening out over the Golfo di Manfredonia. There are nature trails and picnic areas easily reached from Vieste, Peschici, and Mattinata. A seasonal lakeside visitor center (bike hire and guide hikes available) and **Museo Naturalistico della Foresta Umbra,** offers information, a small natural history exhibition and family-friendly deer-feeding area. ✉ *Visitor center, Laghetto Umbra, SP52bis, Monte Sant'Angelo* ☎ *0884/568911 national park, 376/163 3650 visitor center (mobile)* 🌐 *www.doveandiamosulgargano.it/en/visit-umbra-forest; museoforestaumbra.it* 🕒 *Visitor center closed Oct.–Easter.*

Santuario di San Michele

RELIGIOUS BUILDING | Pilgrims have flocked to the mountain community of Monte Sant'Angelo for nearly 1,500 years—among them St. Francis of Assisi and crusaders setting off for the Holy Land from the then-flourishing port of Manfredonia. Monte Sant'Angelo is centered on the Santuario di San Michele, built over the grotto where the archangel Michael is believed to have appeared before shepherds in the year 490. Walk down a long series of steps to get to the grotto itself; on its walls you can see the hand tracings left by pilgrims. The Sanctuary was declared a UNESCO World Heritage site in 2011. To learn more about the history and myth surrounding the site visit the adjoining Musei TECUM. ✉ *Via Reale Basilica 127, Monte Sant'Angelo* ☎ *0884/561150* 🌐 *www.santuariosanmichele.it* 🎟 *Musei TECUM €5.*

Restaurants

Trattoria dalla Nonna

$$ | SEAFOOD | Waves lap at the shore just inches from your table at this elegant but unpretentious trattoria, which often has a cozy fireplace ablaze in winter. You must follow a narrow twisting lane to get here, but it's worth the effort for specialties like the raw seafood antipasto, which features shellfish you might not find anywhere else. **Known for:** unique cozze pelose mussels; fabulous sea views; also run a B&B. $ *Average main: €26* ✉ *Contrada Funni al Lido, Località Funni, Mattinata* ✥ *Off the main road (watch for signs)* ☎ *0884/559205* 🌐 *www.facebook.com/trattoria.dallanonna* 🕒 *Closed Tues., Nov., and Jan.*

Hotels

Baia delle Zagare

$$ | HOTEL | Overlooking one of the Gargano Peninsula's loveliest bays, this secluded cluster of whitewashed buildings houses simply furnished modern rooms, some of which have balconies. **Pros:** incredible views and location; fab pool and gardens; access to wonderful beach. **Cons:** impossible to get to without a car; rooms may be a tad sparse for some; lots of steps. $ *Rooms from: €293* ✉ *Litoranea Mattinata–Vieste, 17 km (10 miles) northeast of Mattinata, Mattinata* ☎ *0884/550155* 🌐 *www.hotelbaiadellezagare.it* 🕒 *Closed Nov.–mid-May* 🛏 *143 rooms* 🍽 *Free Breakfast.*

Vieste

93 km (58 miles) northeast of Foggia, 179 km (111 miles) northwest of Bari.

This large whitewashed town jutting off the tip of the spur of Italy's boot is an attractive place to wander around. Although curvy mountain roads render it slightly less accessible from autostradas and main rail stations than, say, Mattinata, it is, nevertheless, a good base for exploring Gargano. The resort attracts legions of tourists in summer, some bound for the Isole Tremiti, a tiny archipelago connected to Vieste by regular ferries.

GETTING HERE AND AROUND

If you're driving from Foggia, take the winding SS89. Regular buses leave from Foggia's train station.

VISITOR INFORMATION

CONTACT IAT Vieste Tourism Office. ✉ *Piazza John Fitzgerald Kennedy, Vieste* ☎ *0884/708806* 🌐 *www.viaggiareinpuglia.it.*

Sights

Castello Svevo

CASTLE/PALACE | Originally built by Frederick II, this impressive structure was enlarged by the Spanish to defend against attacks from the Turks, and it has remained a military base ever since. It is only open to the public for guided visits and temporary exhibitions and events; call ahead for the latest information. ✉ *Via Duomo, Vieste* ☎ *0884/708806* 🌐 *www.viaggiareinpuglia.it.*

Museo Civico Archeologico Michele Petrone

HISTORY MUSEUM | Opened in 2019 and housed in the Beata Vergine degli Angeli convent, next to the church of SS. Sacramento, there's a small municipal museum with Greco-Roman artifacts excavated in the area here, plus temporary art shows (Warhol and Banksy in recent years). Multimedia displays bring to life handsome amphorae, Roman bathhouse bronze statuary, and finds from the necropolis at nearby Villa di Santa Maria di Merino. ✉ *Lungomare A. Vespucci, Vieste* ☎ *0884/712223* 🌐 *www.facebook.com/poloculturalevieste* *€10 including art show* ⏲ *Closed weekends.*

Restaurants

★ Al Dragone

$$ | SOUTHERN ITALIAN | Dine on exquisite Gargano fare at this atmospheric eatery set in a natural grotto just next to the cathedral in the heart of the old center. The menu is dominated by locally caught fish, and although dishes draw on traditional recipes, you can expect the occasional innovation. **Known for:** small plates of beautifully crafted seafood; gorgeous setting; impressive wine cellar and cigar selection. $ *Average main: €26* ✉ *Via Duomo 8, Vieste* ☎ *0884/701212* 🌐 *www.instagram.com/ristorante_al_dragone_vieste* ⏲ *Closed Tues. and mid-Oct.–Mar.*

Hotels

Navicri

$ | B&B/INN | FAMILY | Run by the friendly *famiglia* De Mauro, this modern B&B ticks all the boxes for those seeking great value in a tranquil, scenic setting near the beach. **Pros:** fab rooftop pool and Jacuzzi; great breakfast spread, including homemade jams; immaculate rooms. **Cons:** having to walk to town and beach might not appeal to some; one triple doesn't have a balcony; minimum night stays in high season. $ *Rooms from: €110* ✉ *Via Saragat, Vieste* ☎ *0884/705022* 🌐 *www.bbnavicri.it* *6 rooms* *Free Breakfast.*

Alberobello

59 km (37 miles) southeast of Bari, 45 km (28 miles) north of Taranto.

With more than 1,000 trulli along its steep, narrow streets, Alberobello has been designated a UNESCO World Heritage site. It is one of the more popular and well-established destinations in Puglia and has some excellent restaurants (and some less-than-excellent trinket shops).

GETTING HERE AND AROUND

By car, take the Monopoli exit from the SS16, follow the SP237 to Putignano, then SS172 to Alberobello. The FSE Trulli Link bus or Bari-Martina Franca bus are quickest (both 70 mins). A longer (130 mins) alternative route involves a train to Putignano, where you then take a bus.

VISITOR INFORMATION

CONTACT Alberobello Tourism Office. ✉ *Via Monte Nero 1, Alberobello* ☎ *379/2987173 mobile* 🌐 *www.prolocoalberobello.it.*

Sights

Alberobello–Martina Franca Road

SCENIC DRIVE | The trulli in Alberobello itself are impressive, but the most scenic concentration of these unique conical structures is along a 15-km (9-mile) stretch of the SS172 (Alberobello–Martina Franca) through the tranquil Valle d'Itria. Stop to visit some of the area's vineyards and oil mills—many of which have a welcoming open-door policy—surrounded by vast groves of ancient gnarled olive trees. ✉ *Alberobello.*

Trullo Sovrano

MUSEUM VILLAGE | FAMILY | Although this 18th-century house, Alberobello's largest trullo, originally belonged to a wealthy family, it has been furnished in a traditional style, providing insight into what everyday life was like in these unique beehive constructions. Check out the classic film *Casanova '70*, starring Marcello Mastroianni and Moira Orfei, which was partly filmed in and around the trullo. ✉ *Piazza Sacramento 10, Alberobello* ✣ *Follow Corso Vittorio Emanuele up past the obelisk and basilica* ☎ *080/4326030* 🌐 *www.trullosovrano.eu* 🎫 *€2.50.*

Restaurants

Il Poeta Contadino

$$ | SOUTHERN ITALIAN | There are actually two eateries here, but superior is the well-regarded Poeta Contadino, which specializes in regional cooking with a creative twist and offers a refined dining experience amid candlelight that casts shadows on ancient stone walls. If you're on a budget, though, the more affordable Osteria del Poeta also serves bite-size traditional dishes. **Known for:** exquisite seafood and meat dishes; stunning vaulted ceiling; extensive wine list. $ *Average main: €28* ✉ *Via Indipendenza 21–27, Alberobello* ☎ *080/4321917* 🌐 *www.ilpoetacontadino.it* ⏲ *Closed Mon.*

★ L'Aratro

$$ | SOUTHERN ITALIAN | Welcoming and rustic, this eatery set inside adjoining trulli is run by the ever nattily dressed and playful host Domenico alongside son Luca and a wonderful family team who deliver fabulous Slow Food-certified Pugliese dishes. Local ingredients figure prominently in the traditional, seasonal dishes: share the multi-dish feast-in-itself antipasto dell'Aratro, then the orrecchiete with anchovies and *cime di rapa* (broccoli rabe), and the hearty *tiella di agnello* (lamb casserole with, tomatoes, potatoes and wild onions). **Known for:** diligent use of local produce; gregarious host Domenico; gorgeous trulli venue. $ *Average main: €25* ✉ *Via Monte San Michele 25–29, Alberobello* ☎ *080/4322789* 🌐 *www.ristorantearatro.it.*

★ **Le Alcove**

$$ | **HOTEL** | This cluster of trulli has been transformed into luxury suites with original architectural features with exposed stone everywhere, modern comforts, and tasteful flourishes, and breakfast is taken in an intimate inner courtyard and two pleasant rooms. **Pros:** centrally located near the Trullo Sovrano; quaint, unusual accommodations; excellent breakfast choice. **Cons:** some rooms and bathrooms are rather small; three rooms aren't in the main building; some rooms have a narrow, awkward metal staircase to upper areas. *Rooms from: €265* *Piazza Ferdinando IV 7, Alberobello* *080/4323754* *www.lealcove.it* *9 rooms* *Free Breakfast.*

Activities

Fiat 500 tours and Giardini Pistola

DRIVING TOURS | Setting off from the gorgeous Giardini Pistola, these fun driving escapades around Valle d'Itria in a dinky vintage Fiat 500 include a three-hour photo quest tour, a Culinary Quest visiting local producers to assemble an aperitivo feast, and an Alberbello tour. Included is a visit to the farm shop and four-hectare gardens designed by Urquhart & Hunt, a series of terraces and meandering paths to wander around, including a maze and a cutting garden. Southern Visions run various other tours and offer accommodation including the chic trulli villa near Alberobello, Casa Badra. *Strada Provinciale 1, Canale di Pirro, Fasano, Alberobello* *349/0510376 500 Tours (mobile), 327/1092505 Giardino (mobile)* *500journeys.com; giardinipistola.com* *Tours from €129; gardens €10* *Closed Mon.*

Ostuni

50 km (30 miles) west of Brindisi, 85 km (53 miles) southeast of Bari.

This sun-bleached medieval town lies on three hills not far from the coast. From a distance, Ostuni is a jumble of blazing white houses and churches spilling over a hilltop and overlooking the sea. Don't be surprised if you hear a lot of English and German spoken in the cobbled streets. The Città Bianca (White City) as it is called, and its maze of hilly lanes and terraces with stunning views, has cast its spell on day-tripping hordes and many British and German nationals, who have bought second homes here. That doesn't mean that the town has lost its local flavor; fairs, religious festivals, and colorful traditional events are held as always with the same enthusiasm and fervor.

GETTING HERE AND AROUND

By car, take the Ostuni exit from the SS16. Trenitalia runs frequent trains from Bari. The station, however, is 5 km (3 miles) from the town—there is almost hourly local bus service.

VISITOR INFORMATION

CONTACT Info-Point Ostuni. *Piazza della Libertà 69, Ostuni* *0831/1982471* *www.facebook.com/infopointostuni.*

Ostuni Old Town

HISTORIC DISTRICT | Known as the Città Bianca for its dazzling white buildings and cobbled streets, Ostuni commands stupendous views out over the coast and the surrounding plain. Its unpolluted sea and clean beaches have earned it international Blue Flag recognition since 1994. The surrounding countryside contains a number of interesting 17th- and 18th-century masserie, many of which have been converted into agriturismi. *Old Town, Ostuni* *www.viaggiareinpuglia.it.*

Piazza Libertà

PLAZA/SQUARE | The city's main square divides the new town to the west and the old town to the east. The triangular piazza contains the town symbol: the towering Guglia di Sant'Oronzo (Spire of St. Oronzo), named after the patron of Ostuni, in whose honor an elaborate festival is held every year in late August. ✉ *Piazza Libertà, Ostuni* 🌐 *www.viaggiareinpuglia.it.*

Beaches

★ Torre Guaceto

BEACH | The transparent water and chalky sand of this marine reserve extend 19 km (12 miles) along the coast and 6 km (4 miles) inland, where the wetlands are a haven for wildlife. Those seeking a spectacular walk in an unspoiled expanse head to the Spiaggia delle Conchiglie, which consists of tiny white shells. Note: it's protected and off-limits to bathers. A shuttle bus operates from the main car park. **Amenities:** food and drink; lifeguards; parking (fee); toilets. **Best for:** snorkeling; sunrise; sunset; swimming; walking. ✉ *Riserva Naturale di Torre Gauceto, Ostuni* ☎ *0831/989976 for info and guided visits* 🌐 *www.riservaditorreguaceto.it.*

Restaurants

Osteria Piazzetta Cattedrale

$$ | **SOUTHERN ITALIAN** | Gentle front-of-house Roberto welcomes and chef wife Marilea creates exquisite, delicately flavored dishes amid a whitewashed room filled with antique mirrors, oddities, and assorted bottles. You could start with smoked eggplant and ricotta flan or dive into adventurous territory with the risotto of foie gras and sea-urchin ice cream, but it's best to concentrate on the mains that feature lamb, amberjack, and baccalà cod. **Known for:** intimate, relaxed dining; tarollomisu (tiramisù with taralli); tasting menus. $ *Average main: €25* ✉ *Largo Arcid Teodoro Trinchera 7, Matera* ☎ *0831/335026* 🌐 *www.piazzettacattedrale.it.*

Hotels

Paragon 700

$$$ | **HOTEL** | Housed within the handsome Palazzo Rosso, the former residence of Ostuni's first mayor has been transformed from near dereliction to a stunning boutique hotel. **Pros:** gorgeous rooms some with large tubs, showers, and a Turkish bath; excellent breakfast in the restaurant or shaded terrace; some rooms have balconies. **Cons:** some may find the old steps tricky; feel of lifestyle store (lots of things for sale) may be grating for some; no in-room kettles or coffee facilities. $ *Rooms from: €550* ✉ *Largo Michele Ayroldi Carissimo 14, Ostuni* ☎ *0831/369219* 🌐 *paragon700.com* *15 rooms and suites* *Free Breakfast.*

Primo Ostuni

$ | **HOTEL** | Located beside the bus and parking space, and a short walk to Piazza Libertà, Primo is a sleek modern hotel, with great staff, whitewashed spaces and comfortable rooms with some interesting lighting and design throughout. **Pros:** spotlessly clean and new; near the parking and bus stop; some rooms have sea views and a small balcony. **Cons:** view and ambience spoiled by the buses parked outside; self-service coffee machine and no à la carte breakfast; some may find it a tad soulless. $ *Rooms from: €161* ✉ *Via Tenente Specchia, Ostuni* ☎ *0131/217538* 🌐 *primoostunihotel.it* *50 rooms* *Free Breakfast.*

Ceglie Messapica

11 km (7 miles) southwest of Ostuni, 18 km (11 miles) southeast of Martina Franca.

With its 14th-century Piazza Vecchia, tattered Baroque balconies, and lordly medieval castles, the little whitewashed town of Ceglie Messapica is the epitome of everyone's notion of the sleepy southern Italian town. Situated at the center of the triangle formed by Taranto, Brindisi, and Fasano, this town was once the military capital of the region and often defended itself against invasions from the Taranto city-state, which wanted to clear a route to the Adriatic. Nowadays, Ceglie Messapica is a gourmet destination with a surprising number of excellent restaurants.

GETTING HERE AND AROUND

By car, take the Ostuni exit from the SS16, and follow the SP22 to Ceglie Messapica. Ferrovie del Sud-Est runs frequent but complicated (slow with changes) bus and train connections from Bari.

VISITOR INFORMATION

CONTACT Info-Point Ceglie Messapica. ✉ *Via G. Elia 16, Ceglie Messapica* ☎ *0831/371003.*

Restaurants

★ Al Fornello Da Ricci

$$$$ | **SOUTHERN ITALIAN** | The cuisine served in the elegant dining room of this restaurant, complete with a verdant garden and run by couple Antonella and Vinod—both creative chefs—marries exotic influences with tradition. It's a great place to splurge on a tasting menu; note, though, that hours can be erratic, especially during winter months, so call ahead. **Known for:** imaginative dishes and cocktails; magical outside space; friendly service. [$] *Average main: €90* ✉ *Via delle Grotte 11, Ceglie Messapica* ☎ *0831/377104* 🌐 *www.antonellariccivinodsookar.it* ⏲ *Closed Mon. and Tues.*

★ Cibus

$ | **SOUTHERN ITALIAN** | Amid the stone vaults and vine-leafy, light-dappled courtyard of this highly acclaimed old-town osteria turned Slow Food destination, the freshest Pugliese meat and produce are transformed into exquisite tapas-like dishes. Be sure to ask the amiable owner to show you his wine cellar and equally impressive cheese larder, where he personally controls the maturing process. **Known for:** gorgeous setting; friendly service and Slow Food ethos; noteworthy wine and cheese. [$] *Average main: €19* ✉ *Via Chianche di Scarano, Ceglie Messapica* ☎ *0831/388980* 🌐 *www.ristorantecibus.it* ⏲ *Closed Mon. and Tues. No dinner Sun.*

Martina Franca

29 km (18 miles) southwest of Ostuni, 36 km (22 miles) north of Taranto.

Martina Franca is a beguiling town with a dazzling mixture of medieval and Baroque architecture in the light-color local limestone. Developed as a military stronghold in the 14th century, all that remains of the defensive walls are the four gates that divide the old part from the modern suburbs. Lose yourself in the maze of twisting white alleyways, where erstwhile palaces jostle with a dozen churches and narrow stairways leading up to humbler abodes. No longer a little-known backwater, the centro storico can be crowded with sightseers on the weekends. The positive side is that this has led to the emergence of top-quality restaurants, and you'll be spoiled for choice. Each July into early August, the town hosts the Valle d'Itria music festival, which showcases classical music and opera.

GETTING HERE AND AROUND

By car, take the Fasano exit from the SS16, then follow the SS172. The Ferrovie Sud-Est runs frequent but slow trains and buses from Bari and Taranto.

VISITOR INFORMATION

CONTACT Martina Franca Tourism Office. ✉ *Via Dottor Adolfo Ancona 5, Martina Franca* ☎ *366/1266045 mobile* 🌐 *www.facebook.com/prolocomartina.*

Favorite Places

Nick Bruno: I like wandering the labyrinthine lanes of hilltop Martina Franca, with its whitewashed Escher-like angled dwellings, staircases, and palazzi, eventually emerging by the Basilica di San Martino in Piazza Plebiscito.

Sights

Basilica di San Martino

CHURCH | A splendid example of southern Italian Baroque architecture, the basilica contains rows of lavishly decorated altars in polychrome marbles, as well as treasures like the silver statues of the two patron saints, San Martino and Santa Comasia. Eyes are drawn to the the gorgeous main altar (1773) by Neapolitan master Sanmartino (of San Severo, Naples fame). Among the other artistic, allegorical highlights is the vibrant sculpture of the Madonna Pastorella as a shepherd girl in a gown of cloth-of-gold, defending Christ's flock from demons. MuBa, a fab free museum nearby at via Stabile 4, exhibits religious artefacts from the basilica and archival art. ✉ *Via Vittorio Emanuele 30, Martina Franca* ☎ *080/4302664* *€3 donation museum; €2 for guided tour* *Museum closed Mon.*

Restaurants

I Templari

$ | SOUTHERN ITALIAN | Away from the central hubbub, engaging couple Giampiero and Maria Pia's charming restaurant serves hearty, traditional Martina Franca classics and grilled seafood amid a beguilling rustic-walled room and panoramic terrace. Build up an appetite before ordering a bountiful primo and secondo, such as the homemade orecchiette pasta with five-hour-cooked Podolica-beef ragù followed by sausages and *bombette* (pork filled with cheese). **Known for:** carpaccio, prime cuts, sausages, and capocollo (pork shoulder); twinkly lights and Valle d'Itria views; smart rooms upstairs with views. *Average main: €19* ✉ *Vico 1 Bellini 7, Martina Franca* ☎ *080/9673070* 🌐 *ristorantetemplari.net.*

Hotels

★ Casa degli Uccellini

$ | B&B/INN | Beautifully restored trulli complex set within wild-flower meadows, wheat fields, and woods, wonderfully warm host Marilù's agriturismo offers instant relaxation, simple yet cozy, rustic domed-ceiling rooms and a flowery courtyard and kitchen for all to use at any time. **Pros:** Marilù's hospitality; fab courtyard breakfast of homemade cakes and use of kitchen; idyllic fields with two resident dogs and a cat. **Cons:** minimum two-night stay but not really a con; own transport preferable; rural location not for everyone. *Rooms from: €120* ✉ *Str. Lamia Nuova, Martina Franca* ☎ *335/5838637 mobile* 🌐 *www.lacasadegliuccellini.it* *3 rooms* *Free Breakfast.*

Dimora Felice

$ | APARTMENT | Two beautifully furnished, architect-renovated apartments within historic palazzi in the Centro Storico, with whitewashed coved ceilings, intriguing Pugliese crafts and fabrics, plus large comfortable beds. **Pros:** Graziana and Francesco the most helpful hosts; original features mixed with thoughtful decor and excellent facilities; near all the sights and the underground carpark. **Cons:** apartment one has steep steps so not suitable for all; living like a local without hotel reception not for all; may become popular so book early. *Rooms from: €160 ✉ Vico II Via Salvator Rosa 11, Martina Franca ☎ 389/6272099 mobile 🌐 www.dimorafelice.it 2 apartments No Meals.*

Taranto

100 km (62 miles) southeast of Bari, 40 km (25 miles) south of Martina Franca.

Taranto (stress the first syllable) was an important port even in Greek times, and it's still Italy's largest naval base. It lies toward the back of the instep of the boot on the broad Mare Grande bay, which is connected to a small internal Mare Piccolo basin by two narrow channels. The old town is a collection of palazzi (in varying states of decay) along narrow cobblestone streets on an island between the two bodies of water, linked by causeways to the modern city, which stretches inward along the mainland.

GETTING HERE AND AROUND

By car, the A14 autostrada takes you almost directly to Taranto. Trenitalia runs frequent trains from Bari and Brindisi.

VISITOR INFORMATION

CONTACT Infopoint Taranto. *✉ Galleria Comunale di Taranto, Piazza Castello, Taranto ☎ 334/2844098 mobile.*

Sights

Castel Sant'Angelo

CASTLE/PALACE | The monumental Castel Sant'Angelo, more commonly referred to as the Castello Aragonese, guards the drawbridge leading from the island center of Taranto to the newer city on the mainland. The castle is occupied by the Italian navy, but it's open to the public, and navy personnel conduct regular, free guided tours. The castle, built in its present form by King Ferdinand of Aragon, King of Naples, in the 15th century, contains ruins of older Greek, Byzantine, and Norman constructions as well as the Renaissance Chapel of San Leonardo. *✉ Piazza Castello 4, Taranto ☎ 099/7753438 call to book a free guided tour 🌐 www.castelloaragonesetaranto.com Free.*

Cattedrale di Di San Cataldo

CHURCH | Originally dedicated to Santa Maria Maddalena before San Cataldo (St. Cathal of Munster) got the Papal nod, Puglia's oldest Duomo has 5th-century origins and been rebuilt several times—its present shape layered on top of an 11th-century Byzantine layout. Striking features include the ornate Baroque facade (1713) by the Leccese Mauro Manieri, geometric motifs in the nave and transept, 16 ancient marble columns with ornate capitals, and a recently rebuilt campanile and 1657 cupola. *✉ Piazza Duomo, Taranto ☎ 099/4608268 🌐 www.cattedraletaranto.com.*

★ MArTA – Museo Archeologico Nazionale Taranto

SPECIALTY MUSEUM | Taranto's outstanding National Archaeological Museum (MArTA) occupies the historic premises of the ex-monastery of San Pasquale. The museum dates from 1887, and its collection of Greek and Roman antiquities is considered to be one of the most important in Italy. Admire the rich cache of tomb goods, including magnificent gold jewelry, objects in ivory and bone, and rare colored glass. A display of Jewish, Christian, and Muslim funeral epitaphs, dating from the 4th century, demonstrate the peaceful coexistence of the three religions in this multicultural Mediterranean hub from the Byzantine era to the Middle Ages. *✉ Via Cavour 10,*

Taranto ☎ 099/4532112 🌐 aditusculture.com 🎫 €10 🕑 Closed Mon.

San Domenico Maggiore

CHURCH | Taranto's most important monument is the ancient church and monastery of San Domenico in the heart of the centro storico. Situated on the narrow strip of land that divides Taranto's two bays, Mare Piccolo and Mare Grande, the present, rather neglected church rises over the ancient Greek acropolis of Taranto where the city is considered to have originated. The statue of Our Lady of Sorrows, much venerated by the local people, stands in the last chapel on the left. Pop into the beautiful 13th-century cloister for a moment's respite from sightseeing. ✉ *Via Duomo 33, Taranto* ☎ *099/4707733* 🎫 *Free* 🕑 *Erratic hrs; cloister closed Sun.*

Restaurants

Al Gatto Rosso

$$ | SOUTHERN ITALIAN | Set in a handsome Stile Liberty palazzo, with outdoor seating and a smart, minimalist dining room, the well-regarded "Red Cat" has been serving elegant seafood since 1952. The third-generation owner and head chef Agostino Bartoli is renowned for his innovative dishes using the freshest fish and seasonal vegetables. **Known for:** raw seafood antipasti; delicious gelato and semifreddo desserts; near MArTA. $ *Average main: €26* ✉ *Via Cavour 2, Taranto* ☎ *340/5337800 mobile* 🌐 *www.ristorantegattorosso.com* 🕑 *Closed Mon.*

Hotels

Hotel L'Arcangelo

$ | HOTEL | Set in a handsome 17th-century palazzo on slightly scruffy but charming Piazza Fontana, this self-styled "boutique hotel" has limestone walls, coved ceilings and warm off-white hues throughout, with many guest rooms having sea or church views and terraces. **Pros:** central piazza location near San Nicola church; gorgeous roof terrace; fish restaurants nearby. **Cons:** area undergoing renovation works; noise from piazza; some corners dated. $ *Rooms from: €110* ✉ *Piazza Fontana, angolo via Garibaldi 3, Taranto* ☎ *099/4715940* 🌐 *www.hotelarcangelotaranto.it* *11 rooms* *Free Breakfast.*

Lecce

40 km (25 miles) southeast of Brindisi, 87 km (54 miles) east of Taranto.

Lecce is the crown jewel of the Mezzogiorno. The city is called "the Florence of the south," but that term doesn't do justice to Lecce's uniqueness in the Italian landscape. Although its pretty boutiques, lively bars, laid-back student cafés, and evening passeggiata draw comparisons to the cultural capitals of the north, Lecce's impossibly intricate Baroque architecture and its hyperanimated crowds are distinctively southern. Summer is a great time to visit, when courtyards and piazzas host dramatic productions or performances. Baroque music concerts are often held in Lecce's beautiful churches and cultural spaces.

GETTING HERE AND AROUND

By car from Bari, take the main coast road via Brindisi and continue along the SS613 to Lecce. Frequent trains run along the coast from Bari and beyond. The closest airport is in Brindisi.

VISITOR INFORMATION

CONTACT Infopoint Castello. ✉ *Castello Carlo V, Via XXV Luglio, Lecce* ☎ *0832/246517* 🌐 *www.facebook.com/castellocarlov.*

Sights

★ Duomo

CHURCH | Dominating a vast square concealed by a maze of alleyways, Lecce's magnificent cathedral of Santa Maria Assunta never fails to take visitors by surprise. The goal when building the 17th-century structure was to stun the faithful with a vision of opulence and power. Constructed in rosy local stone, the church is flanked by the ornate Bishops' Palace (1694), the seminary, whose first-floor Museum of Sacred Art (MuDAS) displays papier-mâché sculptures alongside brooding Caravaggio-esque paintings. Adding to this melodious architectural scene is the under-restoration 236-foot-high *campanile* (bell tower), which dominates the centro storico skyline. ✉ *Piazza Duomo, off Corso Vittorio Emanuele II, Lecce* ☎ *0832/308557* 🌐 *www.cattedraledilecce.it* 🎫 *Duomo free; LeccEcclesiae ticket museum and religious sites €11; ticket "completo," including campanile €21.*

Fondazione Biscozzi Rimbaud

ART GALLERY | Contemporary and modern art enthusiasts should seek out this 2018-established collection lovingly amassed since the late '60s by a wealthy Pugliese couple. Among the 200-plus works, striking geometric and abstract paintings and sculpture from 1950–80 predominate. The permanent exhibits are a wonderful introduction to masters of *modernismo italiano* and less well-known Pugliese artists from Burri to Zorio. ✉ *Piazzetta Baglivi 4, Lecce* ☎ *0832/1994743* 🌐 *www.fondazionebiscozzirimbaud.it* 🎫 *€8* 🕒 *Closed Mon.*

★ Museo Faggiano

HISTORY MUSEUM | **FAMILY** | Wannabe restauranteur Luciano Faggiano excavated fascinating discoveries when he bought this building and investigated the blocked toilet back in the year 2000. After initially finding a false floor that led to a Messapian tomb, more digging with the help of family and friends unearthed incredible artifacts including Roman devotional bottles, ancient vases, a ring with Christian symbols, and dusty frescoes. With encouragement and help from the Lecce government and university, an atmospheric homespun museum was born that allows visitors to explore the layers of history beneath the site's seemingly mundane masonry and toilet cisterns. The sprawling roof terrace affords wonderful views over the city. ✉ *Via Ascanio Grandi 56, Lecce* ☎ *0832/300528* 🌐 *www.museofaggiano.it* 🎫 *€5.*

Piazza Sant'Oronzo

PLAZA/SQUARE | This is the buzzing hub of Lecce's social life in the heart of the maze of pedestrianized alleyways lined with cafés, little restaurants, and crafts shops. Named after Oronzo, the city's patron saint, who crowns a Roman column that once marked the end of the Via Appia Antica, the piazza is also occupied by Roman amphitheater (I–II century AD) and the 16th-century Renaissance-Gothic style Palazzo del Seggio or "Il Sedile." ✉ *Piazza Sant'Oronzo, Lecce.*

Santa Croce

CHURCH | Although Lecce was founded before the time of the ancient Greeks, it's often associated with the term *Barocco leccese,* the result of a citywide impulse in the 17th century to redo the town in an exuberant fashion. But this was Baroque with a difference: generally, such architecture is heavy and monumental, but here it took on a lighter, more fanciful air, and the church of Santa Croce is a fine example, along with the adjoining Palazzo della Prefettura. The facade is a riot of sculptures of saints, angels, leaves, vines, and columns—all in glowing local honey-color stone, creating an overall lighthearted effect. ✉ *Via Umberto I 3, Lecce* ☎ *0832/241957* 🌐 *www.chieselecce.it/en/santa-croce* 🎫 *Church €7; LeccEcclesiae ticket €11.*

Restaurants

Alle Due Corti

$ | **SOUTHERN ITALIAN** | **FAMILY** | Renowned local culinary experts run this cove-ceilinged trattoria, where traditional Salentine cuisine is treated with both respect and originality. The white-walled interior is stark, but there's plenty of character in the simple, tasty fare and the gregarious chatter of local families. **Known for:** cookery courses; small plates of hearty Pugliese food; Anthony Bourdain dined here for his Parts Unknown series. *Average main: €18 Corte dei Giugni 1, corner of Via Prato 42, Lecce 0832/242223 www.alleduecorti.com Closed Sun.*

★ La Cucina di Mamma Elvira

$$ | **SOUTHERN ITALIAN** | Down a side street with relaxed seating inside and outside a handsome palazzo, this spot delivers hearty and tasty traditional Leccese food with the occasional international twist. Meaty mainstays include the chunky orrecchiettoni pasta with Scottona (heifer) ragù and various beef, lamb, and offal dishes. **Known for:** sister spots Scantè next door and Enoteca nearby; seafood including baccalà and polpo; Verdure di Stagione seasonal veg side. *Average main: €24 Via Ludovico Maremonti 33, Lecce 331/5795127 mobile mammaelvira.com Closed Tues.*

Coffee and Quick Bites

Caffè Alvino

$ | **SOUTHERN ITALIAN** | This historic caffè-gelateria is in the heart of Lecce, with handsome interiors and seating out on Piazza Sant'Oronzo. From early morning to late at night this is a buzzy place where Leccesi come to meet and refuel on classic Salentino pastries like *pasticciotti* (ricotta- or egg-filled pastry) and zeppole. **Known for:** arguably the best pastries in town; great coffee and gelato; centrally located. *Average main: €7 Piazza Sant'Oronzo 30, Lecce 0832/246748 www.facebook.com/alvino.catamo.*

Hotels

★ 8piuhotel

$ | **HOTEL** | **FAMILY** | Its design is more "international style" than "rustic Pugliese," but this hotel offers superb value, combining contemporary creature comforts with fancy tech. **Pros:** fitness center and guest cycles; abundant breakfast; on-site restaurant, Negroamaro. **Cons:** lack of local character might not appeal to some; a bit out of town; tech overload. *Rooms from: €97 Viale del Risorgimento, Lecce 0832/306686 www.8piuhotel.com 83 rooms Free Breakfast.*

★ Fiermontina Museum

$$$ | **HOTEL** | If you ever fancied a luxury stay in a small museum, Fiermontina is a magical world set within a courtyard, with four stunning suites dedicated to the arts and a museum you can wander around at night with a lantern, all the captivating legacy of painter Antonia Fiermonte and her love and friendship with two sculptors. **Pros:** wonderful personalized service and attention to detail; fabulous à la carte breakfast; sister hotels including the not-to-missed Palazzo Bozzi Corso. **Cons:** quality comes with a price; if you don't like art maybe not you; some may not like the proximity of the surrounding buildings. *Rooms from: €550 Vicolo dei Raynò 4, Lecce 0832/1516129 www.fiermontemuseum.com 4 suites Free Breakfast.*

★ Palazzo Zimara

$$ | **HOTEL** | An imposing Leccese stone palazzo dating back to 1557 reborn in 2024 with spacious suites mixing moodily lit architectural features with contemporary style, sleek bathrooms, large comfy beds, a rooftop pool, and refined restaurant dining at La Bocca. **Pros:** a balance of modern style, comforts and history; some rooms have balconies and standalone tubs; fabulous, friendly staff. **Cons:** minimalist design may not be for

everyone; may get booked up early; glass and metal lift gets hot. *Rooms from: €254 ✉ Via Giuseppe Libertini 44, Lecce ☎ 083/2405261 🌐 palazzozimara.it 18 suites Free Breakfast.*

Otranto

36 km (22 miles) southeast of Lecce, 188 km (117 miles) southeast of Bari.

In one of the first great Gothic novels, Horace Walpole's *The Castle of Otranto*, published in 1764, the English writer immortalized this city and its mysterious medieval fortress, and indeed Otranto (stress the first syllable) has had more than its share of dark thrills. As the easternmost point in Italy—and, therefore, closest to the Balkan Peninsula—it's often borne the brunt of foreign invasions, including the massacre of 800 citizens by the Moors in 1480 because they refused to give up their faith. From here, you can see across the sea to Albania on a clear day. If you are a fan of the Neolithic, you will be interested in the Grotta dei Cervi, a few miles down the coast. The walls of the cave are covered with hundreds of prehistoric images, painted with red ocher and black bat guano.

GETTING HERE AND AROUND

By car from Lecce, take the southbound SS16 and exit at Maglie. To follow the coast, take the SS53 from Lecce, then follow the SS611 south. There's regular train (via Maglie) and bus services from Lecce both run by Ferrovie del Sud-Est (FSE).

VISITOR INFORMATION

CONTACT Pro Loco Otranto Tourism Office. *✉ Via Lopez 2, Otranto ☎ 0836/806585 🌐 www.prolocotranto.it.*

Sights

Castello Aragonese

CASTLE/PALACE | The massive Aragonese Castle is considered a masterpiece of 16th-century military architecture. Rebuilt by the Spanish viceroy Don Pedro di Toledo in 1535 after it was badly damaged in the siege of Otranto (1480), when invading Ottoman armies destroyed the city, its impressive walls and bastions dominate the port and seashore. Escape the heat with a walk around its cool interiors and more fascinating cellars (underground tours available for extra €4) that snake around its recently landscaped moats. Various art and photographic exhibitions are held here in the summer, although it lacks engaging interpretation materials. *✉ Piazza Castello, Otranto ☎ 0836/212745 🌐 www.comune.otranto.le.it €12 during exhibitions.*

★ Cattedrale

CHURCH | By far the best sight in Otranto is the cathedral, Santa Maria Annunziata, consecrated in 1088. Its highlight is a 12th-century Pantaleone mosaic: covering the entire length of the nave, the sanctuary, and the apse, it depicts scenes from the Old Testament and traditional medieval chivalric tales and animals set alongside a Tree of Life. The walls behind the main altar are lined with glass cases containing the skulls and tibias of the 800 martyrs of Otranto, slain by the Ottomans after the seige of 1480 for not renouncing their faith. *✉ Piazza Basilica, Otranto ☎ 0836/802720 🌐 www.comune.otranto.le.it.*

Hotels

Corte di Nettuno

$$ | **HOTEL** | Handily moored near the marina and the castello, this hotel has a nautical theme with wrought-iron gates in the shape of waves, a statue of the sea god Neptune at the entrance, the owner's maritime antiques throughout, and guest rooms accented by shades of blue. **Pros:** good location near the marina and sights; quirky decor full of artsy surprises; decent food. **Cons:** some people may find the sea theme overly eccentric; clinical feel in some dated and gloomy rooms; bottled water is not free. *$ Rooms from: €204 ✉ Via Madonna del Passo, Otranto ☎ 0832/351321 ⊕ www.cdshotels.it ⏲ Closed Nov.–Mar. 28 rooms 🍽 Free Breakfast.*

Masseria Montelauro

$$ | B&B/INN | FAMILY | Beautifully restored, with high-style interiors, this 19th-century former masseria is an oasis of comfort just a short drive from lovely Otranto. **Pros:** interesting building; lovely grounds and pool; friendly, helpful service. **Cons:** a car is absolutely necessary; food is pricey; some rooms rather stuffy. *$ Rooms from: €250 ✉ SP358, Località Montelauro, Otranto ☎ 0836/806203 ⊕ www.masseriamontelauro.it ⏲ Closed Nov.–Apr. 29 rooms 🍽 Free Breakfast.*

Gallipoli

37 km (23 miles) south of Lecce, 190 km (118 miles) southeast of Bari.

The fishing port of Gallipoli, on the eastern tip of the Golfo di Taranto, is divided between a new town, on the mainland, and the beautiful fortified *borgo antico* (old town) across a 17th-century bridge, crowded onto its own small island in the gulf. The Greeks called it Kallipolis ("the fair city"), the Romans Anxa. Like the infamous Turkish town of the same name on the Dardanelles, the Italian Gallipoli occupies a strategic location and thus was repeatedly attacked through the centuries—by the Normans in 1071, the Venetians in 1484, and the British in 1809. Today life in Gallipoli revolves around fishing. Boats in primary colors breeze in and out of the bay during the day, and Gallipoli's fish market, below the bridge, throbs with activity all morning.

GETTING HERE AND AROUND

From Lecce, take the SS101. From Taranto, follow the coastal SS174. Frequent trains and buses run by FSE from Lecce.

VISITOR INFORMATION

CONTACT Pro Loco Gallipoli Tourism Office. *✉ Via Kennedy, Gallipoli ☎ 0833/264283 ⊕ www.facebook.com/prolocogallipoliufficiale.*

Sights

Castello Aragonese

CASTLE/PALACE | The massive bulk of Gallipoli's castle guards the entrance to the island of the borgo antico, which is linked to the new town by a bridge. Rising out of the sea, the present fortress, dating from the 17th to 18th century, is built on the foundations of an earlier Byzantine citadel. It has four towers, plus a separate fifth known as the Rivellino, where open-air shows are held in summer. A visit allows grandstand sea views, but there's little to see inside between exhibitions. *✉ Rampa Castello, Gallipoli ☎ 0833/262775 €5.*

Duomo

CHURCH | In the center of the borgo antico, Gallipoli's Duomo is a notable Baroque cathedral from the late 17th century, dedicated to Sant'Agata, patron saint of the city. Built in local limestone, the ornate facade is matched by an equally elaborate interior with columns and altars in fine polychrome marble and paintings by leading local Gallipoli and Neapolitan maestros of the time. Particularly interesting are the stone carvings that depict episodes from the city's history. *✉ Via Duomo 1, Gallipoli ☎ 0833/261987 ⊕ www.cattedralegallipoli.it.*

La Purità

CHURCH | A fine example of Gallipoli Baroque, the 17th-century Church of Santa Maria della Purità stands at the end of the borgo antico overlooking famed Purità Beach. It contains an eye-popping wealth of art and decoration, including the painting at the high altar by Luca Giordano (1634-1705), intricately carved wooden choir stalls, and a 19th-century majolica pavement. ✉ *Riviera Nazario Sauro, Gallipoli* ☎ *0833/261699*.

Beaches

★ Beaches of Gallipoli

BEACH | FAMILY | Ample swimming and clean, fine-grained sand make Gallipoli's beaches a good choice for families. For a stunning Borgo Antico backdrop there's La Purità. The 5-km (3-mile) mainland strand from the Punta Pizzo nature reserve to the more developed Lido San Giovanni is divided among a series of bathing establishments, providing sun beds, umbrellas, showers, changing facilities, and snack bars. Parco Gondar hosts a fun fair and music events. Water-sports equipment can be bought or rented at the waterfront shops in town. **Amenities:** food and drink; lifeguards; parking (fee); showers; toilets; water sports. **Best for:** partiers; snorkeling; sunset; swimming; walking; windsurfing. ✉ *Gallipoli* 🌐 *www.prolocogallipoli.it*.

Restaurants

La Vinaigrette

$$ | SEAFOOD | Within shell-like earshot of the sea, this professionally run trattoria with sleek white interiors and a panoramic terrace serves some of the finest seafood in the Salento. Expect classic Pugliese salty preparations like *crudi, grigliate,* and *fritture* (raw, grilled, and fried) beautifully cooked and elegantly presented. **Known for:** pick from the freshest catch on display; well-considered wine list; sea views and sushi-like crudi like tuna carpaccio. [$] *Average main: €22* ✉ *Riviera Armando Diaz 75, Gallipoli* ☎ *0833/264501* 🌐 *www.lavinaigrette.it*.

Hotels

★ Relais Corte Palmieri

$ | HOTEL | Set in an aristocratic 18th-century house in the center of the borgo antico and near Purità Beach, the Relais Corte Palmieri has been tastefully renovated to meet modern standards while preserving its frescoes, mosaics, antique doors, and other historical features. **Pros:** individually decorated rooms; roof garden with spectacular views; on-site spa. **Cons:** difficult to reach; parking is mighty tricky in narrow alleys; noisy rooms street-side and near breakfast room. [$] *Rooms from: €153* ✉ *Corte Palmieri 3, Gallipoli* ☎ *0833/265318* 🌐 *www.relaiscortepalmieri.it* ⏲ *Closed late Oct.–late Mar. or early Apr.* *20 rooms* *Free Breakfast*.

Matera

62 km (39 miles) south of Bari.

This town of unique Sassi (cave dwellings) is one of southern Italy's most intriguing places. The so-called New Town is full of elegant Baroque churches, palazzi, and broad piazzas, which are filled to bursting during the evening passeggiata. It's perched on the verge of a steep gully crowded with ancient rock churches, some of which you can tour, and other Sassi converted into modern-day homes as well as hotels and restaurants. This is a particularly good time to visit: Matera's designation as the European Capital of Culture for 2019 and Capitale Mediterranea della Cultura 2026 has reenergized the community with investment, cultural initiatives, and plenty of buzz.

GETTING HERE AND AROUND

From Bari, take the SS96 to Altamura, then the SS99 to Matera. One or two trains per hour (Ferrovie Appulo Lucane) leave Bari Centrale for Matera (two hours), although a few bus operators, including Marino Bus, provide a faster (one hour) connection.

Basilicata and Calabria
ADRIATIC SEA
Bari
Andria
Polignano a Mare
PUGLIA
Fasano
Spinazzola
Gravina in Puglia
Altamura
Gioia del Colle
Ostuni
Massafra
CAMPANIA
Matera
Francavilla Fontana
Potenza
Grassano
Via Appia
Taranto
TO NAPLES
Eboli
Battipaglia
Auletta
Ferrandina
Pisticci
Metaponto
Lido di Metaponto
BASILICATA
Sala Consilina
Aliano
Colobraro
Agropoli
CILENTO
LUCANO
Francaville in Sinni
Parco Nazionale del Pollino
Lagonegro
Acquafredda
San Severino Lucano
Terranova di Pollino
Golfo di Taranto
Maratea
Amendolara
Marina di Camerota
Marina di Maratea
Rotonda
Cerchiara di Calabria
Praia a Mare
Morano Calabro
Castrovillari
Sibari
Scalea
Cirella
Diamante
Rossano
Parco Nazionale della Sila—La Fossiata
Point Alice
Parco Nazionale della Calabria
Lago di Cecita
Cetraro
Camigliatello
TYRRHENIAN SEA
Paola
Cosenza
San Giovanni in Flore
Rende
SILA GRANDE
Lorica
Museo e Parco Archeologico Nazionale di Capo Colonna
Crotone
SILA MASSIF
Amantea
Capo Rizzuto
Capo Colonna
CALABRIA
Falerna
0
30 miles
0
50 km
Lamezia Terme
Catanzaro
Capo Rizzuto
Pizzo
Soverato
Briatico
Stromboli
Tropea
Capo Vaticano
Panarea
Nicotera
Stilo
Marina di Monasterace
AEOLIAN ISLANDS
Rosarno
Salina
IONIAN SEA
Filicudi
Lipari
Palmi
Lipari
ASPROMONTE
Gerace
Bagnara Calabra
Locri
Vulcano
Villa San Giovanni
Scilla
Milazzo
Bovalino
Messina
Gambárie
Reggio Calabria
Gallico
Parco Nazionale della Calabria
Barcellona
SICILY
Melito di Porto Salvo
A14
16
100
A14
172
172
7
93
7
165
7
407
A3
407
97
106
166
598
598
A3
653
18
106
A3
105
18
106
107
18
280
A3
522
18
106
A3
111
183
106
A20
A18
185

VISITOR INFORMATION

CONTACT Proloco Matera Città dei Sassi (Tourism Office). ✉ *ia Dante 3/1, Matera* ☎ *328/9333548 mobile* 🌐 *www.materawelcome.it.*

Sights

★ Duomo

CHURCH | Matera's splendidly restored cathedral, dedicated to the Madonna della Bruna and Sant'Eustachio, was built in the late 13th century and occupies a prominent position between the two Sassi. Lavishly decorated, it has a typical Puglian Romanesque flavor; inside, there's a recovered fresco, probably painted in the 14th century, showing scenes from the Last Judgment. On the Duomo's facade the figures of Sts. Peter and Paul stand on either side of a sculpture of Matera's patron, the Madonna della Bruna. ✉ *Piazza Duomo, Matera* ☎ *0835/332012* 🎫 *Museo €3.50.*

Museo Nazione di Matera (MNM) – Domenico Ridola Archaeological Museum

HISTORY MUSEUM | Named after local 19th-century medical doctor Domenico Ridola, who investigated archaeological sites in the surrounding area, this seat of the MNM highlights his excavations of the remains of Paleolithic and Neolithic settlements, as well as a richly endowed 4th-century-BC tomb. Ridola's finds are on view in the museum, which is housed in the former monastery of Santa Chiara. The collection includes an extensive selection of prehistoric and classical artifacts, notably Bronze Age implements and beautifully decorated red-figure pottery from Magna Graecia. ✉ *Via Ridola 24* ☎ *0835/310058* 🌐 *www.museonazionaledimatera.it* 🎫 *€10; cumulative 2-day museum ticket €15* ⏲ *Closed Mon.*

Museo Nazione di Matera (MNM) – Museo Nazionale d'Arte Medievale e Moderna della Basilicata

ART MUSEUM | Housed within the handsome 17th-century Palazzo Lanfranchi, this part of the MNM is divided into three contrasting thematic sections: Sacred Art, Collectibles, and Contemporary Art. You may want to skim through the many restored artifacts from Basilicata's churches and the 300-plus works of the Neapolitan school: the main attraction are the 70-plus paintings of Carlo Levi and his must-stop-to-absorb humanist masterpiece *Lucania '61*. MNM also manages the **Former Hospital of San Rocco** (founded in 1348 and rebuilt in 1610), at Via San Biagio 31. It's worth visiting if you buy the cumulative ticket (€3 otherwise) for its fascinating history, architecture, and changing exhibitions. ✉ *Piazza G. Pascoli 1, Matera* ☎ *0835/310058* 🌐 *www.museonazionaledimatera.it* 🎫 *€10; cumulative 2-day museum ticket €15* ⏲ *Closed Tues., Ex Ospedale San Rocco closed Wed.*

MUSMA (Museo della Scultura Contemporanea)

ART GALLERY | Amid otherworldly cave interiors, medieval courtyards, frescoed corners, and the grand spaces of 17th-century Palazzo Pomarici, this museum charts the evolution of Italian sculpture from the early 1800s to the present. Innovative curation, atmospheric lighting, and eerie acoustics make for a one-of-a-kind gallery experience. ✉ *Palazzo Pomarici, Via San Giacomo, Matera* ☎ *366/9357768 mobile* 🌐 *www.musma.it* 🎫 *€10.*

San Giovanni Battista

CHURCH | Considered a jewel of medieval architecture, the 13th-century Romanesque church of San Giovanni Battista was restored to its pre-Baroque simplicity in 1926. The elaborately carved portal is a riot of entwining stone vines, flowers, leaves, human figures, and allegorical creatures. Inside, the three naves are flanked by columns crowned with capitals, each one decorated with symbolic animal forms and other images—no two are alike. ✉ *Via San Biagio, Matera* ☎ *0835/334182.*

★ **Sassi di Matera**
HISTORIC DISTRICT | Matera's Sassi are piled chaotically atop one another down the sides of a steep ravine. Some date from Paleolithic times, when they were truly just caves. Over time, they were transformed into enclosed houses. In the 1960s, most inhabitants moved into ugly apartment blocks. The 1993 designation as a UNESCO World Heritage site, however, resulted in a cleanup and gentrification, with hotels, bars, and restaurants taking over many structures. From the upper town, the Strada Panoramica walk offers stellar views of the two areas known as Sasso Caveoso and Sasso Barisano. ✉ *Sasso Caveoso, Matera* 🌐 *www.materawelcome.it.*

★ **Storica Casa Grotta di Vico Solitario**
MUSEUM VILLAGE | Head to this house-museum in the Sasso Caveoso district for moving insights into what peasant life was like in a limestone cave dwelling. The cramped quarters are filled with traditional utensils and furniture, the belongings of its last inhabitants, who left in 1956 as part of a forced relocation of some 15,000 Sassi residents to apartment blocks. With its rainwater cistern, hand loom, storage niches, and tiny kitchen area and other living spaces (for both the family and their animals), the cave also demonstrates the ingenuity that made living here possible. ✉ *Vicinato di vico Solitario 11, Matera* ☎ *0835/310118* 🌐 *www.casagrotta.it* 🎫 *€5.*

Restaurants

Il Terrazzino
$ | SOUTHERN ITALIAN | The dining area is carved out of a cliff, and the terrace overlooks the famous Sassi ravine. From both you can enjoy such rustic specialties as *foglie d'ulivo* (stuffed olive leaves), *zuppa di grano e ceci* (cheese and chickpea soup), and *pignata* (lamb stew with seasonal vegetables). **Known for:** stupendous views; classic Basilicata meat dishes and fresh pasta; interesting interiors (including a spectacular three-level wine cellar). $ *Average main: €18* ✉ *Vico S. Giuseppe 7, Matera* ☎ *0835/332503* 🌐 *www.ilterrazzino.it* ⏲ *Closed Tues.*

★ **Vitantonio Lombardo**
$$$$ | MODERN ITALIAN | An open kitchen and contemporary table lamps heighten the culinary theater of Matera's fanciest restaurant, set in a cool, minimalist Rione Sassi grotto. The chef's innovative 5-, 7-, or 10-course tasting menus feature vibrant seasonal creations served on artsy ceramics and in wooden bowls. **Known for:** glass-screened wine cellar; imaginative, changing tasting menu; exquisite bread and olive oil. $ *Average main: €140* ✉ *Via Madonna delle Virtù 13/14, Matera* ☎ *0835/335475* 🌐 *www.vlristorante.it* ⏲ *Closed Tues. No lunch Wed.–Fri.*

Coffee and Quick Bites

I Vizi degli Angeli – Laboratorio di Gelateria Artigianale
$ | SOUTHERN ITALIAN | FAMILY | As befitting the "artisan gelato laboratory" moniker, this whitewashed parlor with vibrant colors has an array of vegan-friendly and alchemical ice-cream combos. Among the more unusual "angels' vices" flavors served in *coppe* (tubs) and freshly made *coni* (cones) are hibiscus, pineapple and ginger, lavender and licorice. **Known for:** refreshing granita di melone; fruity smoothies; icy frappè and caffè shakerato. $ *Average main: €4* ✉ *Via Domenico Ridola 36, Matera* ☎ *0835/310637* 🌐 *www.ivizidegliangeli.it.*

Hotels

Il Palazzotto
$$ | HOTEL | Interestingly renovated residence hewn out of the tufa rock, with a relaxed lounge/reception backdropped by a large Guerricchio canvas and atmospheric, sculptured breakfast room and cozy niche; a choice of high-dome ceiling, multishape rooms and suites—a mix modern and rustic furniture offset

by sleek lighting. **Pros:** larger rooms in the sassi caves are more spacious and unique; decent if unspectacular buffet breakfast; Radino wine tasting and bistro. **Cons:** some glazed doors face wandering tourists and terrace bar chat; free water not provided in rooms; basic showers and fiddly lighting switches. *$ Rooms from: €232 ✉ Rione Sasso Barisano, Accesso da Via Fiorentini, Via Sette Dolori, 39, Matera ☎ 0835/334519 ⊕ ilpalazzottomatera.com 12 rooms Free Breakfast.*

★ Locanda di San Martino
$ | HOTEL | Situated at the bottom of the Sassi ravine on Via Fiorentini (limited car access), the Locanda is a more upscale cave-dwelling hotel, with all modern comforts, including an elevator to whisk you up the cliff to your room. **Pros:** convenient location if you come by car; comfortable rooms; on-site ancient Roman–style spa. **Cons:** rooms reached via outdoor walkway; limited parking nearby; spa may be a tad intimate for some. *$ Rooms from: €150 ✉ Via Fiorentini 71, Matera ☎ 0835/256600 ⊕ www.locandadisanmartino.it 40 rooms Free Breakfast.*

★ Moyseion
$$ | HOTEL | An immersive, experiential stay in Magna Graecia amid twinkly lit ancient caves and scattered stone dwellings, with attention to every detail from the breakfast menu, crafted reproduction furniture, vases and fabrics, plus an enchanting spa that stages the daily Water Sanctuary ritual performance. **Pros:** a truly unique experience including dancing and harp-playing storyteller; wonderful, talented staff who perform and assist; rituals: Xenia, the welcome; symposium with food. **Cons:** the unusual atmosphere and provided Greek costume maybe not for all; reception not 24 hours; lacks some hotel services. *$ Rooms from: €229 ✉ Radelle del Sole 3, Matera ☎ 0835/1971880 ⊕ moyseion.com 16 rooms Free Breakfast.*

Maratea

217 km (135 miles) south of Naples.

The high, twisty road into the Maratea region affords breathtaking glimpses of the turquoise sea and a gigantic statue of Cristo Redentore (reminiscent of the one in Rio de Janeiro) atop a hill. Steep crags separate the area into villages that include Maratea Porto, Marina di Maratea, Fiumicello, and Cersuta. The main inland town of Maratea proper is a tumble of cobblestone streets, where the ruins of a much older settlement (Maratea Antica) can be seen. Between the rocky headlands, there's no shortage of secluded beaches, which can get crowded in August. A summer minibus service connects all the different points once or twice an hour.

GETTING HERE AND AROUND

By car, take the Lagonegro exit from the A3 autostrada and continue along the SS585. Intercity, regional, and seasonal high-speed Frecciarossa trains from Reggio Calabria and Naples stop at Maratea. In the summer months there's a bus linking the train station to the upper town 4 km (2½ miles) away.

VISITOR INFORMATION

CONTACT Pro Loco di Maratea La Perla. *✉ Via Santavenere 144, Maratea ☎ 0973/876026 ⊕ marateaproloco.it.*

Beaches

Cala Jannita
BEACH | FAMILY | Maratea's dramatic rock topography is best experienced from this fab little bay and its Spiaggia Nera (Black Beach) with sparkling limpid waters and striking dark, volcanic pebbles. Bring sandals or shoes as it's a tricky approach. **Amenities:** food and drink; lifeguards; parking (fee); showers; toilets. **Best for:** swimming. **TIP→ For a kayak adventure around Maratea's beaches and sea caves visit www.flymaratea.it, which also offers**

guided treks for all abilities. ✉ *Maratea* ☎ *375/7723896 mobile.*

Restaurants

Da Cesare

$$ | SOUTHERN ITALIAN | With an open kitchen and a veranda—so you can keep an eye on both the chef and the azure waters of the Golfo di Policastro—there's always something to see at this family-run seafood restaurant. Even better: it serves some of the freshest catches in town, with specialties like linguine *con nero di seppia* (with cuttlefish ink sauce), grilled squid, and *grigliata mista* (mixed grilled fish and seafood). **Known for:** seafood dishes aplenty; open veranda with views; prominent position on coastal road. $ *Average main: €23* ✉ *Via Nazionale Cersuta 52, Maratea* ✣ *On the SS18 (main coast road) in village of Cersuta, about 5 km (3 miles) north of Maratea, 3 km (2 miles) south of Acquafredda* ☎ *0973/871840* ⏲ *Closed Thurs. Nov.–Mar.*

Hotels

Villa Cheta

$$ | HOTEL | FAMILY | This Stile Liberty villa in the seaside village of Acquafredda has original features and period pieces, a tranquil garden, a pool where you can idle the days away, and a flowery terrace for sunset dining. **Pros:** surrounded by Mediterranean greenery; beautiful coast and mountain views; lovely Art Nouveau building. **Cons:** hotel is quite remote, so shops and the town require a car; popular in high season; steps to entrance and Porticello beach. $ *Rooms from: €190* ✉ *Via Timpone 46, Località Acquafredda, Maratea* ☎ *0973/878134* 🌐 *www.villacheta.it* ⏲ *Closed Oct.–Apr.* 🛏 *22 rooms* 🍴 *Free Breakfast.*

Diamante

51 km (32 miles) south of Maratea, 225 km (140 miles) south of Naples.

A lively and attractive little resort on Calabria's north Tyrrhenian Coast, Diamante styles itself as "the town of murals and *peperoncini* (hot chili peppers)." Its walls are peppered with quirky murals by mainly local artists, and the pedestrianized seafront promenade is lined with shops, ice-cream parlors, and bars. Flanking the broad palm-lined prom are sparkling beaches and interesting archaeological remains in the nearby Cirella district. September's annual Peperoncino Festival brings spicy cultural and gastronomic events.

GETTING HERE AND AROUND

Driving from Maratea, take the SS18; from Cosenza, take the SS107 to Paola, then the SS18. Regional trains leave from Naples a few times a day, with regular service from Paola and Cosenza.

VISITOR INFORMATION

CONTACT Proloco Diamante & Cirella. ✉ *Via Gullo 1, Diamante* ☎ *0985/81130.*

Restaurants

A' Cucchiarella

$ | SEAFOOD | FAMILY | One of Diamante's most popular restaurants, in the old town center just off the seafront promenade, has atmospheric stone interiors. In the summer, sidewalk tables are the perfect relaxed place to watch the evening passeggiata while savoring inventive fish dishes. **Known for:** exceptional seafood with arty presentation; good vegetarian options; handsome stone-walled dining rooms and a terrace. $ *Average main: €19* ✉ *Via Cavour 6, Diamante* ☎ *0985/877287* ⏲ *Closed Mon.–Thurs. Oct.–Mar.*

Hotels

Grand Hotel San Michele

$ | HOTEL | Set in a Belle Époque–style villa surrounded by gardens, atop a cliff near the village of Cetraro, the San Michele offers Mediterranean charm and old-style elegance. **Pros:** beautiful setting; 9-hole golf course; pool and private beaches. **Cons:** some garden levels accessed by steps; breakfast lacks variety; isolated, if you lack your own transport. *Rooms from: €170 Località Bosco 8/9, Cetraro 20 km (12 miles) south of Diamante on the SS18 0982/91012 www.san-michele.it Closed Nov.–Easter 65 rooms Free Breakfast.*

Castrovillari

68 km (43 miles) northeast of Diamante, 75 km (48 miles) northwest of Cosenza.

Stress the first "i" when you pronounce the name of this provincial Calabrian city, nestled in the deep valley beneath 7,375-foot Mt. Pollino. The town is notable as a venue for summer's Calabria-wide Peperoncino Jazz Festival (*www.facebook.com/peperoncinojazzfestival*). Its synagogue, which you can visit, dates from the early Middle Ages; its San Giuliano church from the 16th century.

GETTING HERE AND AROUND

By car, take the A3 autostrada and exit at Frascineto-Castrovillari. Inter SAJ runs around four buses per day (except Sunday) from Cosenza.

Sights

Parco Nazionale del Pollino

NATIONAL PARK | FAMILY | Italy's largest national park straddles Calabria and Basilicata, rises to over 7,000 feet at Serra Dolcedorme, and offers many opportunities for outdoors enthusiasts. Its ancient wooded valleys are home to Europe's oldest tree, a 1,230-year-old Heldreich's pine. There are five summits all over 6,562 feet, the highest point being Serra Dolcedorme at 7,438 feet above sea level, the highest point of the Southern Apennines. It's the only peak from where it's possible to see three seas: the Ionian, the Tyrrhenian, and the Adriatic. Hiking trails dot the landscape with excursions for most abilities—and there are popular picnicking viewpoints, often near *rifugi* (rustic hostels that tend to offer food). *Via Cairoli 80, Castrovillari 334/1005054 Club Alpino Italiano–Sezione di Castrovillari, 0973/669311 Ente Parco Nazionale del Pollino parconazionalepollino.it; www.caicastrovillari.it.*

Restaurants

★ **La Locanda di Alia**

$$ | MODERN ITALIAN | International food magazines have lauded this restaurant, where the wine cellar is well stocked and renowned chef-owner Gaetano Alia incorporates local produce and imaginative twists into the Calabrese dishes on the changing menu. La Locanda also has guest rooms in its adjoining Alia Jazz Hotel, which is surrounded by a lush garden and has a swimming pool. **Known for:** award-winning but unpretentious cuisine; candele pasta with spicy Calabrese 'nduja sauce; gorgeous setting with a leafy terrace. *Average main: €26 Via Ietticelli 55, Castrovillari Off the main street in Castrovillari (look for signs) 0981/46370 www.facebook.com/locandadialia No dinner Sun.*

Cosenza

75 km (48 miles) southeast of Diamante, 185 km (115 miles) northeast of Reggio Calabria.

A construction boom in the 1950s and '60s encased Cosenza's medieval city—which winds up the hillsides between the Busento and Crati rivers. Respite from the sprawling, traffic-clogged modern town can be found on pedestrianized Corso Mazzini, where you can dine, shop and *passeggiare* amid the sculptures of the MAB open-air museum. Highlights include Dalì's *St. George and the Dragon* and haunting works by De Chirico. South of the Busento, the steep, stair-filled centro storico truly hails from another age: wrought-iron balconies overlook narrow alleyways lined with old-fashioned storefronts and bars. The palazzi that line the route to the 12th-century Duomo, a UNESCO World Heritage monument, once housed nobility but today serve as studio spaces for many artists and artisans. The medieval castle, open to the public, crowns Pancrazio Hill, where the views of the town and the surrounding countryside are magnificent.

Cosenza is also the gateway to the cool and silent forests of the Sila mountains, hilltop villages and nearby university town Rende (only 13 km [8 miles] away), and the Pollino National Park area (less than 80 km [50 miles]).

GETTING HERE AND AROUND

By car, take the Cosenza exit from the A3 autostrada. By train, change at Paola or Napoli on the main Rome–Reggio Calabria line. Regional trains run from Naples. Ferrovie della Calabria and Inter SAJ runs buses from Castrovillari, Spezzano della Sila and Camigliatello.

VISITOR INFORMATION

CONTACT Cosenza Tourist Office. ✉ *Piazza XI Settembre, Cosenza* ☎ *0984/813015, 328/1754422 mobile.*

Sights

Castello Svevo

CASTLE/PALACE | Castello Normanno Svevo crowns Pancrazio Hill above the old city, and the uphill walk rewards with wonderful views across to the Sila Mountains. Its origins are lost to memory: the locals' fort was built upon by the Byzantines and the Saracens. Before being enlarged by the Normans, it was the residence of the Arab caliph Saati Cayti. What is known is that the castle takes its name from the great Swabian emperor Frederick II (1194–1250), who added two octagonal towers. Angevin, Aragonese, and Bourbon dynasties made additions. Although extensively restored and open to the public, with audio guide/tablet tours and occasional cultural events amid its sparse spaces, the castle shows the ravages of successive earthquakes and a lightning strike that ignited gunpowder once stored within. ✉ *Via del Castello, Colle Pancrazio, Cosenza* ☎ *0984/1811234* *€5* *Closed Mon.*

Duomo

CHURCH | Cosenza's original Duomo, probably built in the middle of the 11th century, was destroyed by an earthquake in 1184. A new cathedral was consecrated in the presence of Emperor Frederick II in 1222. After many Baroque additions, later alterations have restored some of the Provençal Gothic style. Inside, on the left of the main altar, you'll see the lovely monument to Isabella of Aragon, who died after falling from her horse en route to France in 1271. ✉ *Piazza del Duomo 1, Cosenza* ☎ *0984/77864* *Closed daily 12:30 pm–4 pm.*

Museo Diocesano di Cosenza

HISTORY MUSEUM | Situated between the archbishop's palace and the Duomo, the museum contains paintings, silverware, vestments, and other precious objects collected by the archbishops of Cosenza over centuries. Look for the filigreed silver cup known as "the Pope," the 15th-century "Torquemada" chalice, and paintings by Luca Giordano, Andrea Vaccaro, and Giuseppe Pascaletti. The heart of the museum contains La Stauroteca, emblem of Cosenza and the city's greatest treasure: a unique reliquary cross dating back to the 13th century. ✉ *Piazza Aulo Giano Parrasio 16, Cosenza* ☎ *0984/687750* *www.museodiocesanocosenza.it* *Free* *Closed after 1:30 and Sun. (except by appointment).*

Take a break from sightseeing and enjoy the great outdoors in La Fossiata nature preserve.

Restaurants

★ **Hippocampus**
$$ | SEAFOOD | Renowned for its simply crafted dishes made with the freshest seasonal catch, Cosenza's best seafood restaurant has (appropriately enough) a minimalist, blue-and-white, nautical-theme interior. Guided by a waiter, you might start with a selection of antipasti to share, followed by a classic pasta *allo scoglio* (spaghetti with mixed seafood) and a main *fritto misto di mare* (medley of fried seafood). **Known for:** exceptional, superfresh seafood; a chef happy to create vegetarian dishes; unfussy, welcoming vibe. *Average main: €27 Via Piave 33, Cosenza 0984/22103 Closed Mon. No dinner Sun. No lunch Tues.–Fri.*

Hotels

Royal Hotel
$ | HOTEL | Like most hotels in Cosenza, the Royal caters mainly to a business clientele, yet it's nevertheless a good choice for a stopover: what it lacks in local flavor, it makes up for with excellent central location, functional yet dated rooms, and reasonable room rates. **Pros:** close to pedestrian-only shopping area; garage parking available; good customer service. **Cons:** 20-minute walk from centro storico; beige '70s time-capsule decor in parts; can be busy during events. *Rooms from: €90 Via delle Medaglie d'Oro 1, Cosenza 0984/412165 www.hotelroyalcosenza.it 34 rooms Free Breakfast.*

Camigliatello

30 km (19 miles) east of Cosenza.

Lined with chalets, Camigliatello is one of the Sila Massif's major resort towns. Most of the Sila isn't mountainous at all; rather, it's an extensive, sparsely populated plateau with areas of thick forest. There was, at one point, considerable deforestation, but in 1968 the area received a special designation as the Parco Nazionale della Sila, and strict rules have limited the felling of timber, which has allowed the forests to regenerate. There are well-marked trails through pine and beech woods and ample opportunities for horseback riding. Autumn sees droves of locals hunting mushrooms and gathering chestnuts; winter brings crowds to nearby ski slopes.

GETTING HERE AND AROUND

By car, take the Cosenza Nord exit from the A3 autostrada, then follow the SS107, or if you are following the SS106 along the Ionian Coast, branch off at Sibari and follow the signs.

VISITOR INFORMATION

CONTACT Proloco Camigliatello Tourism Office. *Via Roma 147, Camigliatello* *0984/452850* *www.prolococamigliatello.it.*

Sights

Il Treno della Sila

TRAIN/TRAIN STATION | FAMILY | In spring and summer, and on special dates, this narrow-gauge steam railway takes visitors through stunning countryside from Moccone and Camigliatello Silano to San Nicola-Silvana Mansio. The journey takes 40–50 minutes; in 2024 major works were carried out, including Sculca station, enabling it to stage cultural events, historical reenactments and culinary tastings. Check the website for the latest schedules, events, etc. *Via Forgitelle 11, Camigliatello* *366/6237773 mobile* *www.trenodellasila.it* *From €30.*

★ **Parco Nazionale della Sila—La Fossiata**

NATIONAL PARK | Calabria's granite plateau of Sila National Park is a wonderful place for lovers of the wild outdoors. Rising to nearly 7,000 feet at its highest peak, Botte Donato, the park was inaugurated in 2002, with forests, valleys, and rivers home to 175 species of vertebrates, including the park's now protected symbol, *il lupo,* the wolf. The forestry commission office in nearby Cupone can provide tourist information, maps, and assistance, such as arranging guides. *Via Nazionale, Lorica di San Giovanni in Fiore, Camigliatello* *0984/537109 Forestry Commission Office* *www.parcosila.it* *Office closed weekends.*

Hotels

Tasso

$ | HOTEL | FAMILY | On the edge of Camigliatello, less than 1 km (½ mile) from the ski slopes, this hotel is in a peaceful, picturesque location. **Pros:** beautiful surroundings; lively evening and family entertainment; conveniently located near the ski area. **Cons:** nondescript architecture and out-of-date decor; scant breakfast choice lacking Calabrese products; dated bathrooms. *Rooms from: €85* *Via Torquato Tasso, Spezzano della Sila, Camigliatello* *0984/578113* *www.hoteltasso.it* *82 rooms* *Free Breakfast.*

Crotone

105 km (65 miles) east of Cosenza, 150 km (94 miles) northeast of Locri.

One of the most important Magna Graecia colonies in Italy, Crotone was a major cultural center in the 5th century BC, when it was the home of thinkers like philosopher and mathematician Pythagoras. Sadly, modern development has eclipsed much of its former beauty, but it preserves something of an old-town feel, with its imposing 16th-century castle and an archaeological museum of some importance. Its coastal waters, stretching to Capo Rizzuto, make up Italy's largest protected marine area; and the island castle Le Castella, 15 km (9 miles) from Crotone, is a vision out of a fairy tale.

GETTING HERE AND AROUND

By car, take the Cosenza Nord exit from the A3 autostrada, then follow the SS107. There are regular Trenitalia train/bus connections (three hours) from

Cosenza via Sibari, and quicker (two hours) direct buses run by Autolinee Romano and FlixBus.

VISITOR INFORMATION

CONTACT Proloco Crotone Tourism Office. ✉ *Via Molo Sanità 2, Crotone* ☎ *329/8154963 mobile* 🌐 *prolococrotone.it.*

Sights

Museo Archeologico Nazionale

HISTORY MUSEUM | Constructed to house the treasures found at the Sanctuary of Hera Lacinia, as well as many antiquities recovered from the surrounding seabed, the museum is situated in the heart of the old city of Crotone, close to the seafront castle. The most precious part of the collection is the so-called Treasure of Hera, with the goddess's finely wrought gold diadem and belt pendant. You can also see the rare 5th-century-BC bronze *askos* (container for oil) in the form of a mermaid, illegally exported to the United States and subsequently recovered by the Italian government from the Getty Museum in California. ✉ *Via Risorgimento 121, Crotone* ☎ *0962/23082* 🌐 *inktr.ee/museo-archeologicocrotone* 🎫 *€4* ⏲ *Closed Mon.*

★ Museo e Parco Archeologico Nazionale di Capo Colonna

RUINS | Il Santuario di Hera Lacinia (Sanctuary of Hera Lacinia) was once one of the most important shrines of Magna Graecia. Only one column remains standing, but the site (known as Capo Colonna because of that single pillar) occupies a stunning position on a promontory 11 km (7 miles) south of the town of Crotone. The ruins are part of a vast park, which also contains a well-appointed museum documenting finds from prehistory to the Roman era. The sanctuary itself, which dates from the 7th century BC, is fenced off for safety reasons, but a walkway allows viewing. ✉ *Via Michele Di Donato, Capo Colonna, Crotone* ☎ *0962/934814* 🌐 *musei.calabria.beniculturali.it* 🎫 *Free* ⏲ *Closed Mon.*

Beaches

★ Capo Rizzuto—Spiagge Rosse

BEACH | FAMILY | If practicalities and time allow, make the short trip toward Capo Rizzuto just down the coast for some of the most fabulous bathing and snorkeling in the region. Among its bays and protected marine reserve waters is Spiagge Rosse, whose orange-red sand beach and crystalline waters make it the most alluring on this stretch of coast. **Amenities:** food and drink; lifeguards; parking (no fee); showers; toilets. **Best for:** snorkeling; swimming. ✉ *Contrada Fratte, Capo Rizzuto, Crotone* ☎ *0962/1916760* 🌐 *www.villaggiospiaggerosse.it.*

Hotels

Hotel Helios

$ | HOTEL | On the coastal road between Crotone and Capo Colonna, a little out of town and just 8 km (5 miles) from the Sanctuary of Hera Lacinia, the '70s-style Helios has crystal clear shores nearby and a pool, terrace, restaurant, and snack bar—all on-site. **Pros:** elevated sea views; efficient, courteous staff; on bus route into town and open year-round. **Cons:** uninspiring architecture and grounds; lacks room soundproofing; rooms need a refresh. $ *Rooms from: €135* ✉ *Viale Magna Grecia at Via Makalla 2, Crotone* ☎ *0962/901291* 🌐 *www.helioshotels.it* 🛏 *42 rooms* 🍴 *Free Breakfast.*

Tropea

120 km (75 miles) southwest of Cosenza, 107 km (66 miles) north of Reggio Calabria.

Ringed by cliffs and wonderful sandy beaches, the Tropea promontory is still just beginning to be discovered by foreign tourists. The main town of Tropea, its old palazzi built in simple golden stone, easily wins the contest for prettiest town on Calabria's Tyrrhenian

Coast. On a clear day the seaward views from the waterfront promenade take in Stromboli's cone and at least four of the other Aeolian Islands; you can visit them by motorboat, departing daily in summer. Accommodations are good, and beach addicts won't be disappointed by the choice of magnificent sandy bays within easy reach. The beach beside Santa Maria dell'Isola is said to be one of the Mediterranean's most beautiful, but there are other fine beaches south at Capo Vaticano and north at Briatico.

GETTING HERE AND AROUND

By car, exit the A3 autostrada at Pizzo and follow the southbound SP6/SS522. Frequent trains depart daily from Lamezia Terme, a useful transport hub.

VISITOR INFORMATION

CONTACT Proloco Tropea Tourism Office. ✉ *Piazza Ercole 19–23, Tropea* ☎ *0963/61475* 🌐 *www.facebook.com/prolocotropeavv.*

Sights

Cattedrale

CHURCH | In Tropea's beguiling warren of lanes, seek out the old Norman cathedral, whose main altar contains the locally revered icon of the Madonna di Romania, protectress of the city. Also of interest are the imposing 14th-century "Black Crucifix," in one of the side chapels, and the adjoining Museo Diocesano, which contains an archaeological section and a collection of sacred art, including a life-size statue of Santa Domenica in solid silver, dating from 1738. **TIP→ November through March, the cathedral is open for church services only, but if you're quiet and respectful, you can probably sneak a peek.** ✉ *Largo Duomo, Tropea* ☎ *0963/61034* 🎟 *Cathedral free, Museo Diocesano €5* ⏲ *Closed Nov.–Mar., except for services.*

★ Santa Maria dell'Isola

VIEWPOINT | The sanctuary of Santa Maria dell'Isola is the symbol of Tropea, and it is easy to see why. Perched high on a rocky promontory and accessible only by a winding flight of stone steps cut into the cliffside, it dominates the sea view from Piazza Ercole, the main town square. Believed to date from the 4th century AD, it has been rebuilt many times and took its present form in the 18th century, after it was damaged by an earthquake. The inside of the church is unadorned, but visitors can climb up to the roof to admire the splendid view or wander through the pleasant garden set on the rocks behind the building. The beach below the rock is considered to be among the most beautiful in Italy. ✉ *Largo Marina dell'Isola, Tropea* ☎ *377/306 5825 mobile* 🌐 *www.facebook.com/santuariosantamariadellisola* 🎟 *Church free, garden €3.*

Beaches

★ Marasusa

BEACH | FAMILY | The most famous of Calabria's beaches is backed by sheer cliffs topped by Tropea's stacked buildings—seemingly growing out of the rock. Beyond this popular vacation destination stretch sits the gleaming island promontory sanctuary of Santa Maria dell'Isola. For bathers, snorkelers, and frolickers the light-hued sand is quite fine underfoot and the greenish-blue waters are wonderful. Adding to the drama is the smoking cone of island volcano Stromboli on the western horizon. **Amenities:** lifeguards; parking (no fee); showers; toilets. **Best for:** snorkeling; surfing; swimming; windsurfing. ✉ *Via Lungomare, Tropea.*

Restaurants

Osteria Antico Androne

$$ | **SOUTHERN ITALIAN** | With intimate tables around the interior courtyard and mezzanine of the 18th-century Palazzo Teotino, this osteria is a truly atmospheric place to dine. The menu is a mix of traditional local dishes and classic southern Italian pasta combinations—with subtle Tropeana twists here and there. **Known for:** grilled and fried seafood; Calabrese fileja pasta with Tropea onions; meat and vegetarian options. *Average main: €20* *Via Boiano 6, Tropea* *349/2887969 mobile* *Closed Mon.*

Hotels

★ **Hotel Rocca della Sena**

$$ | **HOTEL** | Overlooking Tropea's golden sands and azure waters, this intimate, self-styled boutique hotel—with modern, quirky, equatorial-theme rooms—is a reliable option. **Pros:** tranquil location on Tropea's periphery; fab sea views; a terrace with a large whirlpool bath. **Cons:** standard rooms on the cramped and gloomy side; lack of bar menu options; some may find the LED mood lighting and furnishings tacky. *Rooms from: €325* *Via Paolo Orsi, Tropea* *0963/62374* *www.hotelroccadellasena.it* *Closed Nov.–early Apr.* *15 rooms* *Free Breakfast.*

Villa Paola

$$$ | **HOTEL** | Converted from an elegant 16th-century Franciscan convent and immersed in gorgeous, flowery grounds and cloisters on the outskirts of Tropea, this pastel-hued retreat-style hotel has stylish, minimalist interiors and wonderful tranquil terraces replete with infinity pool and breathtaking views. **Pros:** large beds and quality linen bedding; warm Calabrese staff; elevated views over Tropea and the sea. **Cons:** lacks the full five-star facilities and attentiveness; a 15-minute walk from the beach; occasional weddings may break the exclusive retreat feel. *Rooms from: €558* *Contrada Paola 6, Tropea* *0963/62370* *www.villapaolatropea.it* *11 rooms* *Free Breakfast.*

Reggio Calabria

115 km (71 miles) south of Tropea, 499 km (311 miles) south of Naples.

This raw city is one of Italy's busiest ports, where you can find not only container ships and cranes but also the wonderful Lungomare Falcomatà, a promenade made for lazy passeggiatas. Hydrofoils for Sicily depart from here; vehicle-carrying ferries depart from Villa San Giovanni, 13 km (8 miles) north.

Reggio Calabria is also a great base for visiting *borghi* (historic villages) like the beautiful town of Stilo, which is known for being the birthplace and home of the philosopher Tommaso Campanella (1568–1639), whose magnum opus was the socialistic *La Città del Sole* (*The City of the Sun*, 1602). Stilo is 138 km (86 miles) northeast of Reggio Calabria along the Ionian coastal road, SS106. Regular trains run from Lamezia Terme.

GETTING HERE AND AROUND

The A3 autostrada runs directly to Reggio Calabria. A dozen direct trains depart from Naples and Rome daily. There are daily flights from all over Italy and seasonal services from around Europe.

VISITOR INFORMATION

CONTACT I.A.T. Reggio Calabria Tourism Office. *329 Corso Garibaldi, Reggio Calabria* *0965/89212* *turismo.reggiocal.it.*

Sights

Lungomare Falcomatà

PROMENADE | FAMILY | Reggio's panoramic palm tree–lined promenade, with views across the Straits of Messina toward Sicily and Etna (on nice days), is named after the former mayor who helped the city's 1990s "Reggio Spring" rebirth. Join the joggers, teens, and families along the 1.6-km (1-mile) route taking in the sea air, handsome Stile Liberty architecture, and Arena dello Stretto, an open-air Greek-style theater, which hosts summer events, performances, and concerts. ✉ *Lungomare Falcomatà, Reggio Calabria.*

★ Museo Archeologico Nazionale di Reggio Calabria (MArC)

HISTORY MUSEUM | Reggio Calabria is home to one of southern Italy's most important archaeological museums. Its prize exhibit, of course, is the two ancient Greek statues known as the Bronzi di Riace, which were discovered by an amateur deep-sea diver off Calabria's Ionian Coast in 1972. After a lengthy but necessary conservation effort, these 5th-century-BC statues of two Greek warriors, thought to be the work of either Pheidias or Polykleitos, now take pride of place in their special temperature-controlled room, complete with earthquake-resistant bases. ✉ *Piazza de Nava 26, Reggio Calabria* ☎ *0965/613988* 🌐 *www.museoarcheologicoreggiocalabria.it* 🎫 *€10* 🕒 *Closed Mon.*

Hotels

Excelsior Grand Hotel

$ | HOTEL | Inviting modern decor, all the amenities one expects from a top international hotel, and a prime location near the town's seafront make this a popular choice with business travelers as well as tourists. **Pros:** centrally located near Museo Nazionale della Magna Grecia; rooftop restaurant with views and truly unique dishes; near the beach. **Cons:** standard, dated business hotel decor; street noise in some rooms; some rooms are tiny. [$] *Rooms from: €170* ✉ *Via Vittorio Veneto 64, Reggio Calabria* ☎ *0965/812211* 🌐 *www.grandhotelexcelsiorrc.it* 🛏 *84 rooms* 🍽 *Free Breakfast.*

★ Hotel Medinblu

$ | HOTEL | The sleek, contemporary guest rooms at this hotel in an imaginatively renovated 1915 palazzo are warmed up a bit by fabrics with bold prints; fabulous public areas include a spacious, chic roof terrace and cocktail bar that serve aperitivi. **Pros:** central location; warm, professional customer service; rooftop breakfast and seasonal evening concerts. **Cons:** hotel's garage a short walk away; traffic noise in some rooms; some may find decor lacks character. [$] *Rooms from: €142* ✉ *Via Demetrio Tripepi 98, Reggio Calabria* ☎ *0965/312982* 🌐 *www.hotelmedinblu.com* 🛏 *20 rooms* 🍽 *Free Breakfast.*

Chapter 16

SICILY

Updated by
Nick Bruno

WELCOME TO SICILY

TOP REASONS TO GO

★ **Taormina, Sicily's most beautiful resort:** The view of the sea and Mount Etna from its jagged cactus-covered cliffs is as close to perfection as a panorama can get.

★ **A walk on Siracusa's Ortigia Island:** Classical ruins rub elbows with Baroque palaces and fish markets in Sicily's most striking port city, where the Duomo is literally built atop an ancient Greek temple.

★ **Palermo's palaces, churches, and crypts:** Virtually every great European empire ruled Sicily's strategically positioned capital at some point, and it shows most of all in the diverse architecture, from Roman to Byzantine to Arab-Norman.

★ **Valley of the Temples, Agrigento:** This stunning set of ruins is proudly perched above the sea in a grove full of almond trees; not even in Athens will you find Greek temples this finely preserved.

1 **Palermo.**

2 **Monreale.**

3 **Segesta.**

4 **Erice.**

5 **Trapani.**

6 **Marsala.**

7 **Selinunte.**

8 **Agrigento.**

9 **Enna.**

10 **Piazza Armerina.**

11 **Caltagirone.**

12 **Ragusa.**

13 **Modica.**

14 **Scicli.**

15 **Noto.**

16 **Siracusa.**

17 **Catania.**

18 **Acireale.**

19 **Mount Etna.**

20 **Taormina.**

21 **Castelmola.**

22 **Messina.**

23 **Milazzo.**

24 **Cefalù.**

25 **Lipari.**

26 **Salina.**

27 **Panarea.**

28 **Stromboli.**

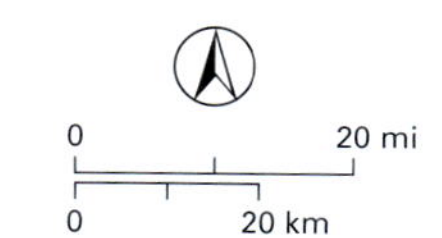

MEDITERR

TYRRHENIAN SEA
28
Stromboli
Panarea
27
26
Salina
Filicudi
Alicudi
Lipari
25
AEOLIAN ISLANDS
Vulcano
Villa San Giovanni
Milazzo
23
A20
22
Messina
Capo d'Orlando
A20
Barcellona Pozzo di Gotto
Reggio Calabria
1
Palermo
Bagheria
24
Cefalù
A19
A20
Termini Imerese
TYRRHENIAN COAST
116
A18
21
Castelmola
Randazzo
120
Taormina
20
19
Mount Etna 3,323m
284
A19
A18
Adrano
18
Acireale
Paterno
189
Enna
A19
17
Catania
IONIAN SEA
9
Caltanissetta
640
Piazza Armerina
10
417
Lentini
115
Canicattì
11
194
Augusta
8
Agrigento
Caltagirone
123
626
16
Siracusa
115
Ortygia
124
Licata
Gela
115
12
Ragusa
15
Vittoria
13
Modica
Noto
RANEAN SEA
14
Scicli
Pachino

EATING AND DRINKING WELL IN SICILY

Street vegetable market

Sicilian cuisine is one of the oldest in existence, with records of cooking competitions dating to 600 BC. Food in Sicily today reflects the island's unique cultural mix, imaginatively combining fish, fruits, vegetables, and nuts with Italian pastas and Arab and North African elements—couscous is a staple in Palermo.

It's hard to eat badly here. From the lowliest of trattorias to the most highfalutin *ristorante*, you'll find classic dishes that have long been staples of the family dinner table—basically pasta and seafood. In more formal restaurants, you'll find greater attention to detail and a more sophisticated atmosphere, while less pretentious trattorias tend to be family-run affairs, occasionally without so much as a menu to guide you. There's also a new wave of creative restaurants that have come up with interesting versions of old standbys, using local and often organic ingredients and changing menus with the season. No matter where you choose to eat in the most gregarious of regions in the most convivial of countries, you can expect a lively dining experience.

SICILIAN MARKETS

Sicily's natural fecundity is evident wherever you look, from the prickly pears sprouting on roadsides, to the slopes of vineyards and citrus groves covering the interior, to the ranks of fishing boats moored in every harbor. You can come face-to-face with this bounty in the clamorous street markets of Palermo and Catania where you'll encounter teetering piles of olives and oranges, enticing displays of cheeses and meats, and vegetables of every description.

WINES

The earthy *nero d'avola* grape bolsters many of Sicily's traditionally sunny, expansive reds, and it's often softened with fruity, bright *frappato* to make Sicily's only DOCG wine, Cerasuolo di Vittoria. Red wines from around Mount Etna that use the grapes *nerello mascalese* and *nerello cappuccio* have also gained renown. Sicily produces crisp white varieties, too, such as *carricante, catarratto bianco, inzolia*, and *grillo*. When it comes to sweet accompaniments, the small island of Pantelleria produces the smooth *passito* dessert wine, made from *zibibbo* grapes, while the Aeolian Islands are known for Malvasia delle Lipari.

DELICIOUS FISH

Pasta *con le sarde,* with fresh sardines, olive oil, raisins, pine nuts, and wild fennel gets a different treatment at every restaurant. Grilled *tonno* (tuna) and *orata* (dorado) are coastal staples, while delicate *ricci* (sea urchins) are a specialty. King, however, is *pesce spada* (swordfish), best enjoyed *marinato* (marinated), *affumicato* (smoked), or as the traditional *involtini di pesce spada* (roulades).

LOCAL SPECIALTIES

In Catania, you'll be offered *caserecci alla Norma* (a short pasta with a sauce of tomato, eggplant, salted ricotta, and basil). The *mandorla* (bitter almond), the pride of Agrigento and Noto, plays into everything from risotto *alle mandorle* (with almonds, butter, Grana cheese, and parsley) to almond granita—a must in summer. Pistachios produced around Bronte, on the lower slopes of Etna, go into pasta sauces as well as ice cream and granita, while salted capers from the Aeolian Islands and Pantelleria add zest to salads and fish sauces.

Arancini (deep-fried rice balls)

Sardines

SNACKS

Two favorite Sicilian snacks are *arancini* ("little oranges," or deep-fried rice croquettes with a cheese or meat filling) and *panelle* (seasoned chickpea flour boiled to a paste, cooled, sliced, and fried). Also look for special foods associated with festivals, such as the ominously named *ossa dei morti* ("bones of the dead," or hard almond cookies). But the most eye-catching of all are the *frutta martorana*: sweet fruit-shaped marzipan confections sold in *pasticcerie* (pastry shops). The Baroque town of Modica is famous for its chocolate, produced using an Aztec recipe brought to Sicily by Spanish conquistadores.

The island of Sicily has an abundance of history, its legacy tangible in magnificent Greek temples, prehistoric cave-towns, extravagant Roman mosaics, flamboyant Baroque palaces, and Arab-Norman cathedrals bejeweled with Byzantine mosaics. Add the spectacular sights of Mount Etna and Stromboli—two of Europe's most active volcanoes—and Sicily's unique cuisine—mingling Arab, Roman and Greek, Spanish and French—and you understand why visitors continue to be drawn here.

Sicily has beckoned seafaring wanderers since the trials of Odysseus were first sung in Homer's *Odyssey*—an epic that is sometimes called the world's first travel guide. Strategically poised between Europe and Africa, this mystical land of three corners and a fiery volcano once hosted two of the most enlightened capitals of the West: Siracusa and Palermo. And it has been a melting pot of every great civilization on the Mediterranean—Greek and Roman, then Arab and Norman, and finally French, Spanish, and Italian. Invaders through the ages weren't just attracted by its strategic location, however; they recognized a paradise in Sicily's deep blue skies and temperate climate, in its lush vegetation and rich marine life—all of which prevail to this day.

In modern times, the traditional graciousness and nobility of the Sicilian people have survived alongside the destructive influences of the Mafia under Sicily's semiautonomous government. The island has more recently emerged as something of an international travel hot spot, drawing increasing numbers of visitors. Brits and Germans flock in ever-growing numbers to Agrigento and Siracusa, and in high season Chinese and American tour groups seem to outnumber the locals in Taormina and the Baroque hill towns. And yet, in Sicily's windswept heartland, vineyards, olive groves, and lovingly kept dirt roads leading to family farmhouses still tie Sicilians to the land and to tradition, forming a happy connectedness that can't be defined by economic measures.

Planning

Getting Here and Around

AIR

The cost of flights within Italy (even one-way) may compare favorably with train and ferry travel, and there are frequent internal flights from Milan, Rome, and other regional airports to Sicily's two major airports, Palermo's Falcone Borsellino Airport (PMO 🌐 *www.aeroportodipalermo.it*) and Catania's Fontanarossa Airport (CTA 🌐 *www.aeroporto.catania.it/en*), as well as to Trapani-Birgi's Vincenzo Florio Airport (TPS 🌐 *www.airgest.it*) and Comiso Airport (CIY 🌐 *www.aeroportodicomiso.eu*), located between Ragusa and Caltagirone.

BUS

Air-conditioned buses connect major and minor cities in Sicily and are often faster and more convenient than local trains—still single track on many stretches—but also slightly more expensive. Various companies serve different routes. See the individual destination sections for specific recommendations.

Major companies include AST (🌐 *www.astsicilia.it*); Autoservizi Russo (🌐 *www.russoautoservizi.it*); Autoservizi Salemi (🌐 *www.autoservizisalemi.it*); Prestia e Comandè (🌐 *www.prestiaecomande.it*); SAIS (🌐 *www.saisautolinee.it*); Segesta Autolinee (🌐 *www.segesta.it*); and Tarantola e Cuffaro (🌐 *www.tarantolacuffaro.it*).

SAIS, for example, runs frequently between Palermo and Catania, Messina, and other cities, in each case arriving in and departing from the vicinity of the train stations.

CAR

Driving is the ideal way to explore Sicily. Modern highways circle and bisect the island, making all main cities easily reachable. Along the north coast, the A20 autostrada (also known as E90) connects Messina, Cefalù, and Palermo while along the eastern coast, Messina, Taormina, Catania, and Siracusa are linked by the A18/E45, which is being extended (slowly) as far as Gela. At the time of writing the Modica-Gela stretch was yet to be completed. Running through the interior, from Catania to west of Cefalù, is the A19, a beautiful and rarely busy route; threading west from Palermo, the A29/E933 runs to Trapani, with a leg stretching down to Mazara del Vallo. In general, the south side of the island is less well served, though stretches of the SS115 west of Agrigento are relatively fast and traffic-free. The A18 between Messina and Catania and the A20 autostradas are subject to tolls. You'll likely hear stories about the dangers of driving in Sicily. In the big cities—especially Palermo, Catania, and Messina—streets can be a honking mess, with lane markings and stop signs taken as mere suggestions; you can avoid the chaos by driving through at off-peak times or on weekends. However, once outside the urban areas and resort towns, most of the highways and regional state roads are a driving enthusiast's dream—they're winding, sparsely populated, and reasonably well maintained, with striking new views around many bends. The worst roads are in the remote center, around Vallelunga Pratameno, which are subject to landslides. Obviously, don't leave valuables in your car, and make sure baggage is stowed out of sight, if possible.

TRAIN

All trains in Sicily are operated by Italy's national rail company Trenitalia (🌐 *www.trenitalia.com*). There are direct express trains from Rome to Palermo, Catania, and Siracusa. The Rome–Palermo and Rome–Siracusa trips take at least 11 hours. After Naples, the run is mostly along the coast, so try to book a window seat on the right if you're not on an overnight train. At Villa San Giovanni, in Calabria, the train is separated and loaded onto a ferryboat to cross the strait to Messina—a favorite for kids.

There are no high-speed lines within Sicily, but main lines connect Messina, Taormina, Siracusa, Catania, and Palermo. The Messina–Palermo run, along the northern coast, and Messina–Taormina, along the eastern coast, are especially scenic. Secondary lines are generally very slow and may be unreliable. For schedules, check the Trenitalia website.

Hotels

Luxurious grand hotels tend to be confined to the major cities and resorts of Palermo, Catania, Taormina, and Siracusa. More recently there has been a Renaissance of extremely chic, charming, exquisitely designed, and often very expensive boutique and rural hotels in the southeast towns of Modica, Ragusa, and Noto and surrounding countryside, on Mount Etna, and in the Aeolian Islands. B&Bs exist everywhere, with the greatest choice in Palermo, Catania, and Taormina, including both period and more modern designer places. Beach resorts tend to have a range of options, while rural lodgings range from sophisticated wine estates to agriturismi (farm-stays), some quite basic, others extremely comfortable, and usually offering half-board plans that can make for some of Sicily's most memorable meals. There are also excellent-quality villas available to rent—a perfect option for large groups and families.

⇨ *Hotel and restaurant reviews have been shortened. For full information, visit Fodors.com. Prices in the hotel reviews are the lowest cost of a standard double room in high season. Prices in the dining reviews are the average cost of a main course at dinner, or, if dinner is not served, at lunch.*

What It Costs in Euros

$	$$	$$$	$$$$
RESTAURANTS			
under €20	€21–€30	€31–€40	over €40
HOTELS			
under €175	€176–€400	€401–€600	over €600

Restaurants

As befits a major city, Palermo has a huge selection of interesting and varied restaurants, while Catania is best known for its high-quality seafood. In the tourist-heavy coastal towns, dining can be hit or miss, while inland there has been a mini-explosion of new-wave gourmet restaurants in the Baroque towns of Ragusa, Modica, and Noto, as well as some intriguing options popping up on Mount Etna.

In the west of the island, expect to find a Sicilian variant of North African couscous on the menus, often made with seafood and well worth sampling. In the countryside, *agriturismi* (farm bed-and-breakfasts), country hotels, and wineries are your best bets for a good meal.

When to Go

Sicily's high season (mid-June through mid-September) is hot, often humid, expensive, and busy. During the peak season from late July to late August, beaches are crowded, and hotels and restaurants are often booked up, so advance reservations are necessary—often several weeks or even months for hotels and a day or two for restaurants.

April–May and mid-September–October are the ideal months for more temperate weather, more elbow room on the beaches, and more capacity and availability at hotels and restaurants. Keep in mind that the Mediterranean takes a long time to warm up, and a long time to cool down, so if beaches and swimming are a priority, autumn is better than spring. The Easter period (lasting a few days around Good Friday) can be very busy, and some resort destinations may close in late October.

The winter months of November through March see many places outside the cities closed, if only for a few weeks, while tourist facilities at most of Sicily's beach resorts and on all the offshore islands shut down for the entire period. Flights, accommodation rates, and car rentals are at their lowest at this time of year, but bear in mind that November and December can see a lot of rain while January and February are the coldest months.

Palermo

Once the intellectual capital of southern Europe, Palermo has always been at the crossroads of Mediterranean civilization. Favorably located on a crescent bay at the foot of Monte Pellegrino, it has attracted almost every culture touching the Mediterranean world. To Palermo's credit, it's absorbed these diverse cultures into a unique personality that's at once Arab and Christian, Byzantine and Roman, Norman and Italian. The city's heritage encompasses all of Sicily's varied ages, but its distinctive aspect is its Arab-Norman identity, an improbable marriage that, mixed in with Byzantine and Jewish elements, resulted in resplendent works of art. These are most notable in its churches, from small jewels such as San Giovanni degli Eremiti to larger-scale works such as the cathedral. No less noteworthy than the architecture is Palermo's chaotic vitality, on display at some of Italy's most vibrant outdoor markets, public squares, street bazaars, and food vendors, and, above all, in its grand, discordant symphony of motorists, motorcyclists, and pedestrians that triumphantly climaxes in the new town center each evening with one of Italy's busiest passeggiatas.

Sicily's capital is a multilayered, vigorous metropolis with a strong historical profile; approach it with an open mind. You're likely to encounter some frustrating instances of inefficiency and, depending on the season, stifling heat. If you have a car, park it in a garage as soon as you can, and don't take it out until you're ready to depart.

Palermo's old center is easily explored on foot, but you may choose to spend a morning taking a bus tour to help you get oriented. The Quattro Canti, or Four Corners, is the hub that separates the four sections of the old city: La Kalsa (the old Arab section) to the southeast, Albergheria to the southwest, Capo to the northwest, and Vucciria to the northeast. Each of these is a tumult of activity during the day, though at night the narrow alleys empty out and are best avoided in favor of the more animated avenues of the new city north of Teatro Massimo. Most of the important sights to visit by day are scattered along three major axes: Via (or Corso) Vittorio Emanuele, Via Maqueda, and Via Roma.

GETTING HERE AND AROUND

Palermo is home to one of Sicily's two major international airports, Aeroporto Falcone Borsellino at Punta Raisi, 30 km (18 miles) west of town, and as such is a main gateway for those arriving in Sicily by plane. Along with international flights, there are regular connections from and to other Italian cities such as Milan, Rome, and Naples, as well as to Sicily's far-flung isles of Pantelleria and Lampedusa. There's a tourist information desk in the arrivals hall.

Trains run from the station below Palermo's airport to the city center every half hour or so, with tickets dispensed from machines. Don't forget to validate your ticket before travel by punching it at one of the station's machines. Prestia e Comandè buses run every 30 minutes to the bus station behind the main train station, with stops en route including Piazza Ruggero Settimo in the modern city center. Buy tickets from the driver. A taxi from Palermo's airport to the center should cost €40–€50, while shared taxis cost €8 per person, with drop-offs at a range of points within the city (though you may have to wait for the minimum of five passengers before setting off). Journey time by taxi or bus between Palermo airport and city center is 30 minutes to one hour, depending on traffic; by train, it's around one hour, with stops within walking distance of Palazzo Reale and Via della Libertà before reaching the main station (Palermo Centrale).

You'll find you can walk to most spots within central Palermo, though it's worth taking advantage of city bus services, run by AMAT (🌐 *www.amat.pa.it*), for longer stretches—for example, between the main train station and Piazza Ruggero Settimo (Bus 101); between the main train station and Piazza dell'Indipendenza, for the Palazzo Reale (Bus 109); and out to Monreale (Bus 389 from Piazza dell'Indipendenza) and Mondello (Bus 806 from Piazza Francesco Crispi off Via della Libertà, which is reachable on Bus 101). Monreale can also be reached on the less frequent but faster AST bus service that runs from Corso Tukory, near the central station.

Bus tickets can be purchased from kiosks and shops showing the AMAT sticker and cost €1.40 for any journeys made within 90 minutes (timed from when you punch your ticket in the machine onboard the bus) with a €0.40 supplement if you purchase on board; €3.50 for tickets lasting an entire day; €6 for tickets lasting two days; €8 for three days; and €16.50 for a week.

VISITOR INFORMATION

You'll find helpful visitor information offices (🌐 *turismo.comune.palermo.it* or 🌐 *turismo.cittametropolitana.pa.it*) at the airport and in the heart of the old city, near Piazza Bellini.

Sights

Catacombe dei Cappuccini

CEMETERY | The spookiest sight in all of Sicily, this 16th-century catacomb houses more than 8,000 corpses of men, women, and young children—some in tombs but many mummified, preserved, and hanging in rows on the walls, divided by social caste, age, or gender. Most wear signs indicating their names and the years they lived, and many are Capuchin friars, who were founders and proprietors of this bizarre establishment from 1599 to 1911. The site is still managed by the nearby Capuchin church, but was closed to new corpses when an adjacent cemetery was opened, making the catacombs redundant. Though memorable, this is not a spot for the faint of heart; children might be frightened or disturbed. ✉ *Piazza Cappuccini 1, off Via Cappuccini, Near Palazzo Reale* ☎ *091/6527389* 🌐 *www.catacombepalermo.it* 🎫 *€5.*

Cattedrale di Palermo

CHURCH | This church is a lesson in Palermitano eclecticism—originally Norman (1182), then Catalan Gothic (14th to 15th century), then fitted out with a Baroque and neoclassical interior (18th century). Its turrets, towers, dome, and arches come together in the kind of meeting of diverse elements that King Roger II (1095–1154), whose tomb is inside along with that of Frederick II, fostered during his reign. The exterior is more intriguing than the interior, and it's worth walking round to the gracefully decorated back of the apse to view the interlacing Arab arches inlaid with limestone and black volcanic tufa. The climb to the cathedral's roof is also recommended for some fabulous city views. ✉ *Via Vittorio Emanuele,*

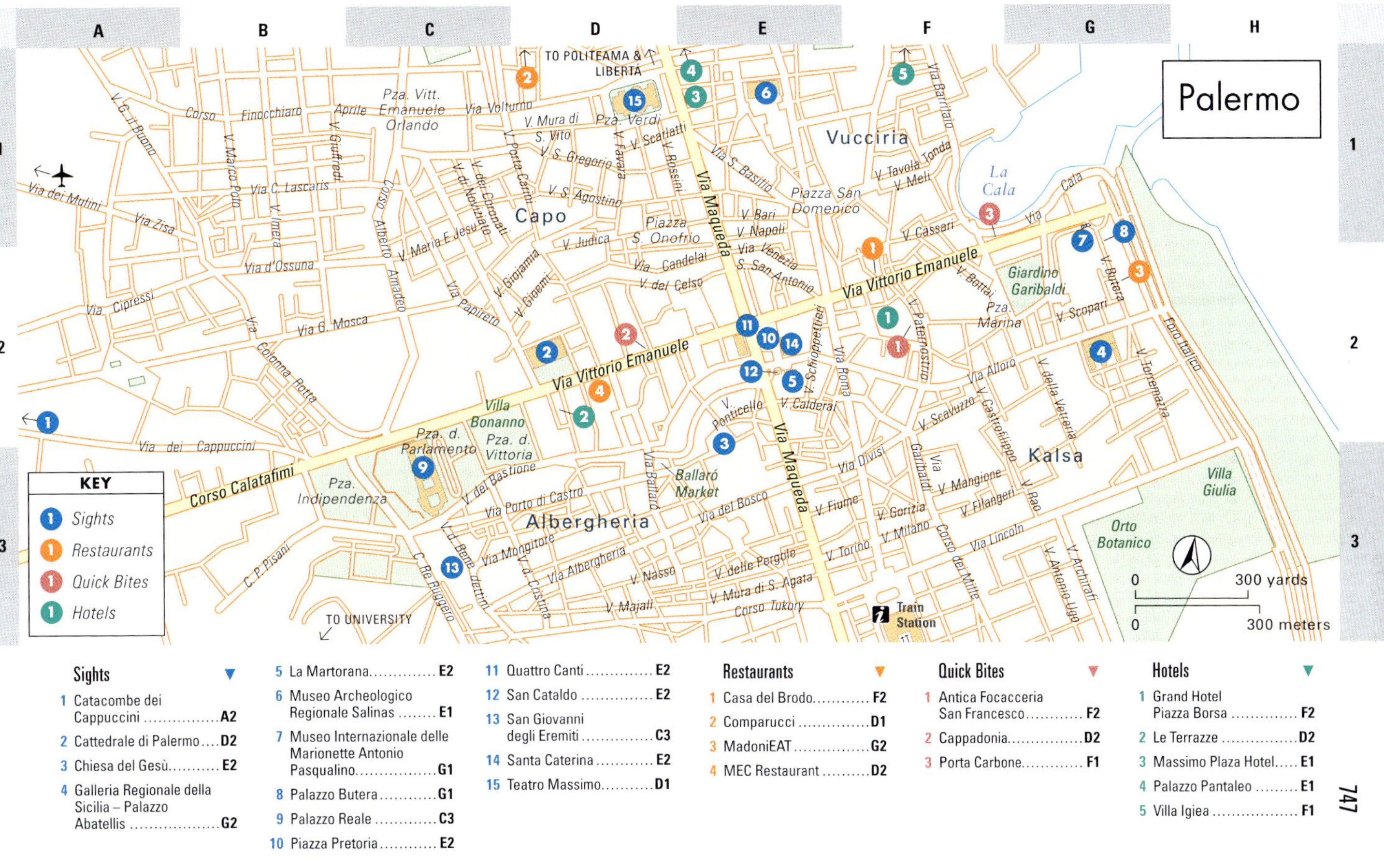
Palermo
A
B
C
D
E
F
G
H
1
2
3
KEY
Sights
Restaurants
Quick Bites
Hotels
TO POLITEAMA & LIBERTÀ
TO UNIVERSITY
Vucciria
Capo
Albergheria
Kalsa
La Cala
Via Maqueda
Via Vittorio Emanuele
Corso Calatafimi
Foro Italico
Via dei Mulini
Via Zisa
V. G. il Buono
Corso Finocchiaro Aprile
Pza. Vitt. Emanuele Orlando
Via Volturno
V. Mura di S. Vito
Pza. Verdi
V. Scarlatti
V. Favara
V. S. Gregorio
V. S. Agostino
V. Porta Carini
V. dei Coronati
V. di Noviziato
V. Maria E Jesu
Corso Alberto Amadeo
V. Giuffredi
V. Marco Polo
Via C. Lascaris
V. Imera
Via d'Ossuna
Via Cipressi
Via G. Mosca
Via Colonna Rotta
Via dei Cappuccini
Via Papireto
V. Giojamia
V. Gioeni
V. Judica
Piazza S. Onofrio
Via Candelai
V. del Celso
V. Rossini
Via S. Basilio
Piazza San Domenico
V. Bari
V. Napoli
Via Venezia
S. San Antonio
V. Schioppettieri
Via Roma
V. Calderai
V. Ponticello
Via Ballarò
Ballarò Market
Via del Bosco
Via Porto di Castro
V. del Bastione
Pza. d. Parlamento
Villa Bonanno
Pza. d. Vittoria
Pza. Indipendenza
V. d. Bene dettini
C. Re Ruggero
C. P. Pisani
Via Mongitore
V. d. Cristina
Via Albergheria
V. Nasso
V. Majali
V. delle Pergole
V. Mura di S. Agata
Corso Tukory
V. Fiume
V. Torino
Via Divisi
Via Garibaldi
V. Gorizia
V. Milano
Corso dei Mille
Via Lincoln
V. Mangione
V. Filangeri
V. Rao
V. Castrofilippo
V. Scavuzzo
Via Alloro
V. della Vetreria
V. Paternostro
V. Bottai
Pza. Marina
V. Scopari
Giardino Garibaldi
V. Butera
V. Torremazza
Via Cala
V. Cassari
V. Tavola Tonda
V. Meli
Via Barrilaio
V. Archirafi
V. Antonio Ugo
Orto Botanico
Villa Giulia
Train Station
0
300 yards
0
300 meters
Sights
1 Catacombe dei Cappuccini A2
2 Cattedrale di Palermo D2
3 Chiesa del Gesù E2
4 Galleria Regionale della Sicilia – Palazzo Abatellis G2
5 La Martorana E2
6 Museo Archeologico Regionale Salinas E1
7 Museo Internazionale delle Marionette Antonio Pasqualino G1
8 Palazzo Butera G1
9 Palazzo Reale C3
10 Piazza Pretoria E2
11 Quattro Canti E2
12 San Cataldo E2
13 San Giovanni degli Eremiti C3
14 Santa Caterina E2
15 Teatro Massimo D1
Restaurants
1 Casa del Brodo F2
2 Comparucci D1
3 MadoniEAT G2
4 MEC Restaurant D2
Quick Bites
1 Antica Focacceria San Francesco F2
2 Cappadonia D2
3 Porta Carbone F1
Hotels
1 Grand Hotel Piazza Borsa F2
2 Le Terrazze D2
3 Massimo Plaza Hotel E1
4 Palazzo Pantaleo E1
5 Villa Igiea F1

Capo ☎ 329/3977513 🌐 www.cattedrale.palermo.it 🎫 Church free; €6 treasury, crypt, apses and royal tombs; €15 treasury, crypt, apses, royal tombs, and roof.

Chiesa del Gesù

CHURCH | It is more than worth the short detour from the lively Ballarò Market to step into the serene Baroque perfection of the "Church of Jesus." The ornate church was built by the Jesuits not long after their arrival in Palermo in the late 16th century, and was constructed at the site of their religious seat in the city, so the church is also sometimes known as Casa Professa (motherhouse). The interior is almost completely covered with intricate marble bas-reliefs and elaborate black, tangerine, and cream stonework. The splendid church was severely damaged in World War II, but careful restoration has returned it to its shiny, swirling glory. ✉ *Piazza Casa Professa 21, Albergheria ☎ 377/3397612 mobile (WhatsApp text messages only) 🌐 www.casaprofessa.it 🎫 €2, €6 includes museum ⏲ Closed Sun.*

Galleria Regionale della Sicilia – Palazzo Abatellis

ART MUSEUM | Housed in this late-15th-century Catalan Gothic palace with Renaissance elements is the Galleria Regionale, holding Palermo's foremost collection of medieval and Renaissance art. Among its treasures are the *Annunciation* (1474), a painting by Sicily's prominent Renaissance master Antonello da Messina (1430–79), and an arresting fresco spanning two floors (and visible from both the ground floor and a first-floor gallery) by an unknown 15th-century painter, titled *The Triumph of Death*, a macabre depiction of the plague years. ✉ *Via Alloro 4, Kalsa ☎ 331/6581788 mobile 🌐 www.facebook.com/abatellis 🎫 €9; free 1st Sun. of month ⏲ Closed Mon.*

★ La Martorana

(Santa Maria dell'Ammiraglio)

CHURCH | One piazza over from the dancing nymphs of Fontana Pretoria, this church, with its elegant Norman campanile, was erected in 1143 but had its interior altered considerably during the Baroque period. High along the western wall, however, is some of the oldest and best-preserved mosaic artwork of the Norman period. Near the entrance is a fascinating mosaic that shows the Norman King Roger II being crowned by Christ. In it Roger is dressed in a bejeweled Byzantine stole, reflecting the Norman court's penchant for all things Byzantine. Archangels along the ceiling wear the same stole wrapped around their shoulders and arms. The much plainer San Cataldo is next door. ✉ *Piazza Bellini 3, Quattro Canti ☎ 345/8288231 mobile 🌐 turismo.comune.palermo.it 🎫 €2 ⏲ Closed Sun.*

Museo Archeologico Regionale Salinas *(Salinas Regional Museum of Archaeology)*

HISTORY MUSEUM | This archaeology museum is the oldest public museum in Sicily, with a small but excellent collection, including a marvelously reconstructed Doric frieze from the Greek temple at Selinunte, which reveals the high level of artistic culture attained by the Greeks in Sicily some 2,500 years ago. There are also lion's head water spouts from 480 BC, as well as other excavated pieces from around Sicily, including Taormina and Agrigento, which make up part of an informative exhibition on the broader history of the island. After admiring the artifacts, wander through the two plant-filled courtyards, and be sure to check the website for special culture nights, when the museum is open late to host musical performances. ✉ *Piazza Olivella 24, Via Roma, Olivella ☎ 091/6116807 🌐 turismo.comune.palermo.it 🎫 €7, free 1st Sun. of month ⏲ Closed Mon.*

Museo Internazionale delle Marionette Antonio Pasqualino

SPECIALTY MUSEUM | FAMILY | This collection of more than 4,000 masterpieces showcasing the traditional Opera dei Pupi (puppet show), both Sicilian and otherwise, will delight visitors of all ages with their glittering armor and fierce expressions. The free audio guide to the colorful displays is only available in Italian, but the well-designed exhibits include video clips of the puppets in action, which requires no translation. There are also regular live performances in the museum's theater (Monday 11 am and Tuesday–Saturday 5 pm), which center on the chivalric legends of troubadours of bygone times. The museum can be hard to find: look for the small alley just off Piazzetta Antonio Pasqualino 5. ✉ *Piazzetta Antonio Pasqualino 5, near Via Butera, Kalsa* ☎ *091/328060* 🌐 *www.museodellemarionette.it/en* 🎫 *€5.*

★ **Palazzo Butera**

ART MUSEUM | Dating from the 18th century but closed for most of the last four decades, the Palazzo Butera has been transformed by its gallerista owners, Massimo and Francesca Valsecchi, into one of Sicily's (and Italy's) most imaginative museum collections. Its labyrinthine rooms now display a heady mixture of old and new art. The collection's strength lies in its bold juxtapositions, with works by an international roster of experimental modern artists of the likes of Gilbert and George, and David Tremlett, exhibited alongside classical landscapes and graceful Sicilian furniture from the 19th century. Painted ceilings remain from the palace's Baroque beginnings, some of them artfully peeled back to reveal the wooden construction behind them. Diverse temporary exhibitions displayed on the ground floor add to the mix. There's a lot to take in, but if you need a break from all the hectic creativity, head for the terrace, accessed from the second floor, which provides benches and a walk around one of the two courtyards as well as views over the harbor. You can get even better views from the viewing platform reached from the roof, while further up, steps lead to a lofty view of the harbor, Monte Pellegrino, and, inland, the whole of the Conca d'Oro plain in which the city sits. ✉ *Via Butera 18, Kalsa* ☎ *091/7521754* 🌐 *www.palazzobutera.it* 🎫 *€12.50* 🕒 *Closed Mon.*

★ **Palazzo Reale** (*Royal Palace*)

CASTLE/PALACE | This historic palace, also called Palazzo dei Normanni (Norman Palace), was the seat of Sicily's semiautonomous rulers for centuries; the building is a fascinating mesh of 10th-century Norman and 17th-century Spanish structures. Because it now houses the Sicilian Parliament, parts of the palace are closed to the public from Tuesday to Thursday when the regional assembly is in session. The must-see Cappella Palatina (Palatine Chapel) remains open. Built by Roger II in 1132, it's a dazzling example of the harmony of artistic elements produced under the Normans and the interweaving of cultures in the court. Here the skill of French and Sicilian masons was brought to bear on the decorative purity of Arab ornamentation and the splendor of 11th-century Greek Byzantine mosaics. The interior is covered with glittering mosaics and capped by a splendid 10th-century Arab honeycomb stalactite wooden ceiling. Biblical stories blend happily with scenes of Arab life—look for one showing a picnic in a harem—and Norman court pageantry.

Upstairs are the royal apartments, including the Sala di Re Ruggero (King Roger's Hall), decorated with ornate medieval mosaics of hunting scenes—an earlier (1120) secular counterpoint to the religious themes seen elsewhere. During the time of its construction, French, Latin, and Arabic were spoken here, and Arab astronomers and poets exchanged ideas with Latin and Greek scholars in one of the most interesting marriages of culture in the Western world. From Friday to Monday, the Sala is included with entry to the palace or chapel; it sometimes hosts special art exhibits. ✉ *Piazza del Parlamento, Near Palazzo Reale* ☎ *091/7055611* 🌐 *www.federicosecondo.org* 🎫 *€15.50–19 Fri.–Mon.; €11–15 Tues.–Thurs.* ⏲ *Royal Apartments closed Tues.–Thurs.*

Piazza Pretoria

FOUNTAIN | The square's centerpiece, a lavishly decorated fountain with 500 separate pieces of sculpture and an abundance of nude figures, so shocked some Palermitans when it was unveiled in 1575 that it got the nickname "Fountain of Shame." It's even more of a sight when illuminated at night. Sadly, there is no water in the fountain at present while it awaits a major repair. ✉ *Piazza Pretoria, Quattro Canti.*

Quattro Canti

STREET | The Four Corners is the decorated intersection of two main thoroughfares: Via Vittorio Emanuele and Via Maqueda. Four rather exhaust-blackened Baroque palaces from Spanish rule meet at concave corners, each with its own fountain and representations of a Spanish ruler, patron saint, and one of the four seasons. These days it's one of Palermo's major tourist hot spots and a favorite venue for street performers. ✉ *Corso Vittorio Emanuele and Via Maqueda, Quattro Canti.*

San Cataldo

CHURCH | Three striking Saracenic pink domes mark this church, built in 1154 during the Norman occupation of Palermo. The church now belongs to the Knights of the Holy Sepulchre and has a spare but intense stone interior. ✉ *Piazza Bellini 3, Kalsa* ☎ *091/2713837* 🌐 *turismo.comune.palermo.it* 🎫 *€2.50.*

San Giovanni degli Eremiti

CHURCH | Distinguished by its five reddish-orange domes and stripped-clean stone interior, this 12th-century church was built by the Normans on the site of an earlier mosque—one of 200 that once stood in Palermo. The emirs ruled Palermo for nearly two centuries and brought to it their passion for lush gardens and fountains. One is reminded of this while sitting in San Giovanni's delightful cloister of twin half columns, surrounded by palm trees, jasmine, oleander, and citrus trees. ✉ *Via dei Benedettini 14–20, Near Palazzo Reale* ☎ *091/6515019* 🌐 *turismo.comune.palermo.it* 🎫 *€7, free 1st Sun. of month.*

Santa Caterina

CHURCH | The walls of this splendid Baroque church (1596) in Piazza Bellini are covered with extremely impressive decorative 17th-century inlays of precious marble. There are marvelous views from the terrace, and a bakery selling delicacies made using the nuns' recipes. ✉ *Piazza Bellini, Quattro Canti* ☎ *091/2713837* 🌐 *www.monasterosantacaterina.com* 🎫 *€3; €10 combined ticket, includes church, monastery, and rooftop.*

Teatro Massimo

PERFORMANCE VENUE | Construction of this formidable neoclassical theater, the largest in Italy, was started in 1875 by Giovanni Battista Basile and completed by his son Ernesto in 1897. A reconstruction project started in 1974 ran into severe delays, and the facility remained closed until just before its centenary, in 1997. Its interior is as glorious as ever, but the exterior remains more famous thanks to *The Godfather Part III,* which ended with a famous shooting scene on the theater's steps. Visits, by 40-minute guided tour only, are available in five languages, including English, while a tour of the current production's *palcoscenico* (stage set) is also available daily at changing times (call to check). ✉ *Piazza Verdi 9, at top of Via Maqueda, Olivella* ☎ *091/6053267 tours, 091/6053580 ticket office* 🌐 *www.teatromassimo.it* 🎫 *€12 tour; €5 stage visit.*

Restaurants

Casa del Brodo

$ | SICILIAN | On the edge of the Vucciria, this is one of Palermo's oldest restaurants, dating back to 1890, and still dear to the hearts of locals for its wintertime namesake dish, tortellini *in brodo* (in beef broth), the specialty of the house. There's an extensive antipasto buffet, and you can't go wrong with the *fritella di fave, piselli,* and *carciofi e ricotta* (fried fava beans, peas, artichokes, and ricotta). **Known for:** large selection of antipasti; tortellini in brodo; good choice of traditional offal dishes. $ *Average main: €16* ✉ *Corso Vittorio Emanuele 175, Vucciria* ☎ *091/321655* 🌐 *www.casadelbrodo.it* ⏲ *Closed Tues. Oct.–May. Closed Sun. June–Sept., and 2 wks in Jan.*

Comparucci

$ | PIZZA | FAMILY | One of Palermo's best modern pizzerias serves delicious Neapolitan-style pies from a big oven in the open kitchen—the genius is in the crust, which is seared in a matter of seconds. The toppings, too, are delicious, and the place attracts big crowds on weekends and in summer (when it often stays open until midnight—later than almost any other restaurant in the neighborhood). **Known for:** pizza, pizza, and more pizza; outdoor seating in summer; late-night dining. $ *Average main: €10* ✉ *Via Messina 36/e, Libertà* ☎ *091/6090467* 🌐 *www.pizzeriacomparucci.com* ⏲ *No lunch.*

MadoniEAT

$ | SICILIAN | Only the finest agricultural produce of the nearby Madonie mountains goes into the simple but satisfying dishes served in this informal eatery attached to the Palazzo Butera art gallery. The frequently changing menu—dependent on the season and what's available from their suppliers—offers vegetarian, vegan, and gluten-free dishes alongside meat choices, and might include busiate pasta with a sauce of cardoncelli mushrooms and breadcrumbs, and beef nuggets cooked in nero d'avola wine with carrots and mashed potatoes. **Known for:** seasonal, fresh, and locally produced ingredients; vegetarian, vegan, and gluten-free choices; convenient for lunch after a visit to Palazzo Butera. $ *Average main: €15* ✉ *Palazzo Butera, Via Butera 20, Kalsa* ☎ *091/7521749* 🌐 *www.madonieat.com* ⏲ *Closed Mon. and 2 wks in Jan. No dinner Sun.*

★ MEC Restaurant

$$$$ | SICILIAN | Here's a novelty for Palermo in the form of a superb modern restaurant located within a museum dedicated to Steve Jobs and Apple products, a surprisingly successful combination; you not only have the ability to revisit ancient IT devices and learn about the history of the tech company, but the food is pretty excellent. Each of the dishes is a revelation, from the house-made tonnarello pasta with mullet and smoked provola cheese sauce to the pigeon with red-wine scented quince and, among the desserts, semifreddo meringue with ricotta cheese, mango chutney, and passion fruit ice cream. **Known for:** restaurant and museum in one gorgeous, historic building; innovative modern dishes; attentive service. $ *Average main: €41* ✉ *Via Vittorio Emanuele 452, Quattro Canti* ☎ *091/9891901* 🌐 *www.mecrestaurant.it* ⏲ *Closed Sun. No lunch.*

Coffee and Quick Bites

Antica Focacceria San Francesco

$ | SICILIAN | Marble-top tables, cast-iron ovens, and walls adorned with turn-of-the-20th-century black-and-white photographs characterize this neighborhood bakery, celebrated for the Sicilian snacks and inexpensive meals it has been doling out since 1834. The big pot on the counter holds the delicious regional specialty pani cà meusa (boiled calf's spleen with caciocavallo cheese and salt), but the squeamish can opt for chickpea fritters or enormous arancini. **Known for:** Sicilian street food; historic atmosphere;

meat and pasta specialties. *Average main: €6 Via A. Paternostro 58, Kalsa 091/320264 www.anticafocacceria.it Closed Jan.*

★ Cappadonia

$ | **ICE CREAM** | **FAMILY** | To enhance a postprandial passeggiata along one of Palermo's main strolling thoroughfares, make a stop at this modern gelateria to pick up one of its exceptional gourmet ice creams. The flavors change with the seasons, but you should find the tangerine sorbet that bursts with sweet citrus tang and the classic *cannolo siciliano* available year-round. **Known for:** delicious ice cream; seasonal flavors; central promenading location. *Average main: €4 Via Vittorio Emanuele 401, Capo 392/5689784 mobile cappadonia.it Closed Jan. and Feb.*

Porta Carbone

$ | **SANDWICHES** | A civic institution facing Palermo's old fishing port, this venerable (but modernized) snack stop has been serving pani cà meusa (calf's spleen sandwich) for more than 70 years. This local specialty comes sprinkled with a bit of salt and a squeeze of lemon and served with or without cheese to a buzzing crowd of Palermo's elders and youngsters alike. **Known for:** calf's spleen sandwich that might be the best in town; a bit of Sicilian history; buzzing atmosphere. *Average main: €3 Via Cala 62, Kalsa 091/323433 www.facebook.com/panicameusaportacarbone Closed Sun.*

Hotels

Grand Hotel Piazza Borsa

$ | **HOTEL** | Cleverly converted from three historic buildings—a bank, a palazzo, and a monastery—this hotel with modern, unadorned rooms is ideally located just off the central axis of Via Vittorio Emanuele. **Pros:** quiet but central location; beguiling architecture and courtyard; wellness center with fitness equipment, rare for Sicily hotels. **Cons:** most rooms have showers in the bathtubs; staff sometimes inattentive; limited parking. *Rooms from: €129 Via dei Cartari 18, Kalsa 091/320075 piazzaborsa.it 127 rooms No Meals.*

★ Le Terrazze

$ | **B&B/INN** | Although just steps from the bustling Cattedrale area, this small, beautifully restored B&B is enveloped in complete calm. **Pros:** convenient location for the sights; alfresco breakfasts on the glorious rooftop; period-style rooms. **Cons:** parking can be difficult; books up quickly; Wi-Fi sometimes patchy. *Rooms from: €150 Via Pietro Novelli 14, Albergheria 320/4328567 www.leterrazzebb.it No credit cards 2 rooms Free Breakfast.*

Massimo Plaza Hotel

$ | **HOTEL** | Small and select, this hotel enjoys one of Palermo's best locations—opposite the Teatro Massimo, on the border of the old and new towns—and has guest rooms that are spacious, comfortably furnished, and well insulated from the noise on pedestrianized Via Maqueda. **Pros:** central location; very attentive staff; tasty breakfast made to order. **Cons:** 21 steps (no elevator) up to the rooms; in pedestrian zone, so vehicles have to keep their distance; cheaper rooms have no views. *Rooms from: €160 Via Maqueda 437, Olivella 091/325657 www.massimoplazahotel.com 11 rooms Free Breakfast.*

★ Palazzo Pantaleo

$ | **B&B/INN** | Accessed from a quiet courtyard situated between Palermo's two great theaters, with large, airy rooms and a charming host, this top-floor apartment is part of a beautifully renovated palazzo dating from the mid-19th century. **Pros:** convenient modern town location; pleasant and welcoming host; free private parking. **Cons:** no lounge; a little hard to find; often booked up. *Rooms from: €140 Via Ruggero Settimo 74, Libertà 335/7006091 mobile www.*

palazzopantaleo.it *7 rooms* *Free Breakfast.*

★ Villa Igiea

$$$$ | HOTEL | Following a magnificent renovation by the Rocco Forte group, this Art Nouveau fantasy created by architect Ernesto Basile for the Florio family at the turn of the 20th century has been restored to its original glamour and glory. **Pros:** secluded setting; historic building with lots of atmosphere; free shuttle to city center in the summer. **Cons:** price range out of reach for most; no amenities in the nearby area; a bit far from Palermo attractions. *Rooms from: €1350* *Salita Belmonte 43, Acquasanta* *091/6312111* *www.roccofortehotels.com* *100 rooms* *Free Breakfast.*

Nightlife

BARS AND CAFÉS

★ Maison Bocum

COCKTAIL BARS | This multilevel cocktail bar between the Vucciria market and the marina is serious about mixology and has created a dedicated oasis in the city's trendiest area. Linger over complex cocktails while lounging on vintage chairs under sparkling chandeliers, all while rubbing elbows with Palermo's cool crowd as records spin on the audiophile turntable in the corner. Tapas and expertly prepared meat and seafood dishes are also available. *Via dei Cassari 6, Vucciria* *091/332009* *www.bocum.it.*

Performing Arts

CONCERTS AND OPERA

★ Teatro Massimo

CONCERTS | As the biggest theater in Italy, Teatro Massimo is truly larger than life. Concerts and operas are presented throughout the year, though in summer concerts are usually held outdoors. An opera at the Massimo is an unforgettable Sicilian experience. *Piazza Verdi, at top of Via Maqueda, Olivella* *091/6053580 tickets, 091/8486000 call center, 091/6053267 tours* *www.teatromassimo.it* *Performances from €20, tours €12.*

Shopping

Ballarò Market

MARKET | Wind your way through the Albergheria district and this historic market, where the Saracens did their shopping in the 11th century—joined by the Normans in the 12th. The market's name is said to come from nearby Monreale, named Bahlara when Arab traders resided there, and it remains faithful to their original commerce of fruit, vegetables, and grain. These days the stalls are dotted with bars and outdoor restaurants where you can sample the produce, but the market has lost none of its authenticity—just keep a close eye on your belongings in the crowd. And go early: the action dies out by 4 pm most days. Take a wander around the district to view the wonderful "Postcards of Ballarò" project murals (documented in a 2018 Netflix film), including Fulvio di Piazza's *Turbo Ballarò*, a vibrant whirlpool of fish alluding to the market. *Vla Ballarò, Albergheria* *South and west of Chiesa del Gesù.*

Pasticceria Alba

$ | BAKERY | One of the most famous pastry shops in Sicily, this modern and capacious place is one of Palermo's best spots to find sweet favorites like cannoli and *cassata siciliana*. It's also a meeting place for all ages, where you can relax with a drink or an excellent gelato. **Known for:** delicious pastries and ice creams; trendy spot for meeting up; hot snacks served till late. *Average main: €8* *Piazza Don Bosco 7/c, Libertà* *Off Via della Libertà near La Favorita Park* *091/309016.*

Vucciria Market

MARKET | A ghost of its former self, Vucciria—whose name translates to "voices" or "hubbub"—was once the most vibrant market in Palermo, memorably captured in Renato Guttuso's canvas of the same name (now exhibited in Palazzo Steri). It is now reduced to barely more than a single street and piazza. It takes on more of a street food/block party atmosphere at night, when no-name bars open to sell cheap cocktails to the crowds gathering around the smoking grills that are wheeled outside after dark. ✉ *Vucciria Market, Vucciria.*

Monreale

10 km (6 miles) southwest of Palermo.

Only a short drive or bus ride from Palermo, the sleepy town of Monreale is well worth the effort of a visit just to see the spectacular gold mosaics inside its Duomo. Try to arrive early in the morning or later in the afternoon to avoid the tour bus hordes.

GETTING HERE AND AROUND

You can reach Monreale on frequent AMAT buses that depart from Palermo's Piazza Indipendenza or on the less frequent but faster AST buses from Corso Tukory, outside the central station. From Palermo, drivers can follow Corso Calatafimi west, though the going can be slow. Park in the car park a little way outside Monreale's center.

Sights

Cloister of Santa Maria La Nuova

RELIGIOUS BUILDING | The lovely Benedictine cloister of the abbey adjacent to the Duomo was built at the same time as the church but enlarged in the 14th century. The enclosure is surrounded by 216 intricately carved double columns, every other one decorated in a unique glass mosaic pattern. Afterward, don't forget to walk behind the cloister to the belvedere, with stunning panoramic views over the Conca d'Oro (Golden Conch) plain toward Palermo. If you wish to visit, reserve a tour online at least a week in advance. ✉ *Piazza del Duomo, Monreale* 🌐 *www.coopculture.it* 🎫 *€8; €13 including entire monumental complex (Duomo, Diocesan Museum).*

★ Duomo di Monreale

CHURCH | Monreale's splendid cathedral is lavishly executed with mosaics depicting events from the Old and New Testaments. It's a glorious fusion of Eastern and Western influences, widely regarded as the finest example of Norman architecture in Sicily. After the Norman conquest of Sicily, the new princes showcased their ambitions through monumental building projects. William II (1154–89) built the church complex with a cloister and palace between 1174 and 1185, employing Byzantine craftsmen.

The major attraction is the 68,220 square feet of glittering gold mosaics decorating the cathedral interior. Christ Pantocrator dominates the apse area; the nave contains narratives of the Creation; and scenes from the life of Christ adorn the walls of the aisles and the transept. The painted wooden ceiling dates from 1816–37 while the roof commands a great view (a reward for climbing 172 stairs). The wood and metal organ, the only one in Europe with six keyboards and 10,000 pipes, was restored after lightning damage in 2015, and played by Mick Jagger on a private visit in 2021.

Bonnano Pisano's bronze doors, completed in 1186, depict 42 biblical scenes and are considered among the most important medieval artifacts still in existence. Barisano da Trani's 42 panels on the north door, dating from 1179, present saints and evangelists. To visit, book a spot on 🌐 *www.coopculture.it* at least a week in advance. ✉ *Piazza del Duomo, Monreale* ☎ *327/3510886* 🌐 *www.duomomonreale.com* 🎫 *€6; €13 including entire monumental complex (Cloister, Diocesan Museum).*

Restaurants

Osteria Peper's

$ | **SICILIAN** | Just a few steps down the cobbled hill from the cathedral, this small and colorful osteria offers simple but enthusiastically prepared meals from a menu that reads like a list of your Sicilian nonna's favorite dishes. Sure, it's somewhat touristy, but for once that doesn't equate with either brisk service or formulaic fare. **Known for:** down-home Sicilian cooking; relaxed and friendly atmosphere; lively decor. *Average main: €14 Via Cappuccini 6/10, Monreale 091/7525157 No lunch Mon.*

Segesta

85 km (53 miles) southwest of Palermo.

Segesta is the site of one of Sicily's most impressive temples, constructed on the side of a barren windswept hill overlooking a valley of giant fennel. Virtually intact today, the temple is considered by some to be finer in its proportions and setting than any other Doric temple left standing.

GETTING HERE AND AROUND

Every day except Sunday, at least four buses travel from Trapani to Segesta (50 minutes) and three from Palermo (90 minutes), both services operated by Tarantola e Cuffaro (*www.tarantolacuffaro.it*). If you are in the area already, the site is easily reached via the A29 autostrada.

Sights

★ **Parco Archeologico di Segesta** (*Doric Temple*)

ARCHAEOLOGICAL SITE | Segesta's imposing temple was actually started in the 5th century BC by the Elymians, who may have been refugees from Troy—or at least non-Greeks, since it seems they often sided with Carthage. In any case, the style of the temple is in many ways Greek, but it was never finished; the walls and roof never materialized, and the columns were never fluted.

Wear comfortable shoes; even if you drive, you'll need to park your car in the lot at the bottom of the hill and walk about five minutes up to the temple. If you're up for a longer hike, a little more than 1 km (½ mile) away near the top of the hill are the remains of a fine theater with impressive views, especially at sunset, of the plains and the Bay of Castellammare (there's also a shuttle bus to the theater for €2.50 round-trip that leaves every 15–30 minutes). Concerts and plays are staged here in summer. *Contrada Barbaro, SR22, Segesta 0924/952356 www.parcodisegesta.com €12.*

Erice

38 km (24 miles) south of San Vito Lo Capo, 15 km (9 miles) northeast of Trapani.

Perched 2,450 feet above sea level, Erice is an enchanting medieval mountaintop aerie of palaces, fountains, and cobblestone streets. Shaped like an equilateral triangle, the town was the ancient landmark Eryx, dedicated to Aphrodite (Venus). When the Normans arrived, they built a castle on Monte San Giuliano, where today there's a lovely public park with benches and belvederes offering striking views of Trapani, the Egadi Islands offshore, and, on a very clear day, Cape Bon and the Tunisian coast. Because of Erice's elevation, clouds conceal much of the view for most of winter. Sturdy shoes (for the cobblestones) and something warm to wear are recommended.

GETTING HERE AND AROUND

Make your approach via Trapani, which is on the A29 autostrada and well connected by bus and train with Marsala and Palermo. In late March to early January, a

Western Sicily
TO LIVORNO & GENOA
TO NAPLES & ROME
Di Ustica
TO SARDINIA
TYRRHENIAN SEA
TO SARDINIA
TO TUNIS
Capo San Vito
San Vito Lo Capo
Golfo di Castellammare
Mondello
Golfo di Palermo
Palermo see detail map
Monreale
Golfo di Termini Imerese
Termini Imerese
Castellammare di Golfo
Levanzo
Trapani
Erice
Marèttimo
Favignana
Segesta
Càccamo
Mt. S. Calogero
Marsala Salt Pans
Marsala
Gibellina
Salaparuta
Corleone
Prizzi
Castelvetrano
Mazara del Vallo
Selinunte
Sciacca
Ribera
Raffadali
Agrigento
Valle dei Templi
TO PANTELLERIA
MEDITERRANEAN SEA
Pantelleria
0
20 mi
0
20 km
TO LINOSA
TO LAMPEDUSA
A29
A19
113
187
115
188
118
121
285
624
386
189
640

funivia (suspended cable car) runs from the outskirts of Trapani to Erice (🌐 *www.funiviaerice.it* 🕓 *Mon. 2–8, Tues.–Thurs. 8:30–8, extended hours weekends and daily from late June to mid-September*); however, it is often closed in windy weather, so always check first. The trip by car or bus from Trapani takes around 40 minutes. By car, take the route via Valderice, not the "direct route," to avoid an extremely winding and steep country road. Buses depart from the terminal on Trapani's Piazza Malta.

Restaurants

Monte San Giuliano

$ | **SICILIAN** | At this traditional restaurant located on a side street near the main piazza, you can sit on a tree-lined patio overlooking the sea or in the white-walled dining room and munch on free *panelle* (chickpea fritters) while waiting for your main dish, which will be served tableside, spooned from the cooking pots to your plate by the friendly staff. The fresh pastas and couscous are exemplary, and there are also a few seafood mains (tuna and baccalà often) and a glut of meat (lamb, beefsteak, and veal). **Known for:** great pasta and couscous; charming setting; extensive and interesting wine list. [$] *Average main: €18* ✉ *Vicolo San Rocco 7, Erice* ☎ *0923/869595* 🌐 *www.montesangiuliano.it* 🕓 *Closed Mon., 6 wks in Jan.–Feb., and 4 wks in Nov.–Dec.*

Coffee and Quick Bites

★ La Tonda Fritta

$ | **SICILIAN** | Arancine—fried rice balls—are ubiquitous all over Sicily, but rarely do you find them prepared while you wait or offered in such a range as in this little snack shop near Porta Trapani. The menu lists more than 30 varieties, which include swordfish, smoked salmon, and curry fillings, as well as vegetarian and vegan options. **Known for:** more than 30 types of arancine; great snacks on the go; fast service. [$] *Average main: €4* ✉ *Via Vittorio Emanuele 100, Erice* ☎ *328/1378708 mobile* 🌐 *www.facebook.com/latondafritta* 🕓 *Closed Nov.–Feb.*

Pasticceria Grammatico

$ | **BAKERY** | Fans of Sicilian sweets and pastries make a beeline for this place run by Maria Grammatico, who gained international fame with *Bitter Almonds,* her life story of growing up in a convent orphanage, cowritten with Mary Taylor Simeti. Her almond-paste creations are works of art, molded into striking shapes, including dolls and animals. **Known for:** nice views; uniquely shaped desserts; delicious pastries, sweets, and biscuits. [$] *Average main: €5* ✉ *Via Vittorio Emanuele 14, Erice* ☎ *0923/869390* 🌐 *www.mariagrammatico.it* 🕓 *Closed Wed.*

Hotels

Moderno

$ | **HOTEL** | This delightful hotel has a creaky old feel to it, but that's part of the charm—the lobby area, scattered with books, magazines, and tchotchkes, calls to mind an elderly relative's living room; but the rooms themselves are simple, light, and comfortable. **Pros:** central location; great rooftop terrace; well-regarded restaurant. **Cons:** very modest rooms; street-facing rooms can be noisy; old-fashioned feel not for everyone. [$] *Rooms from: €100* ✉ *Via Vittorio Emanuele 67, Erice* ☎ *0923/869300* 🌐 *www.hotelmodernoerice.it* *35 rooms* *Free Breakfast.*

Shopping

Ceramica Ericina

CERAMICS | Among Italians, Erice is known for the quality and delicate floral designs of its majolica ceramics, well represented in this ceramics store off Piazza San Domenico, one of the best in town. ✉ *Via Guarnotti 20, Erice* ☎ *334/2303855 mobile* 🌐 *www.facebook.com/CeramicaEricina.*

Trapani

11 km (7 miles) southwest of Erice, 30 km (19 miles) northwest of Segesta, 75 km (47 miles) southwest of Palermo.

The provincial capital of Trapani (both province and city share the same name) was originally founded by the ancient Elymians, who claimed descent from the Trojans, as a port for Eryx (Erice). Its Greek name, Drepanon, meaning "sickle," refers to the long, curving limb of land trailing into the sea on which the city is built. Much of its later wealth was founded on the salt pans lying to the south that are still active today.

Although the outskirts of town are uninspiring, Trapani's old town has a busy, buzzy feel to it, especially in the evenings when families crowd the main, pedestrianized Corso Vittorio Emanuele and bars and restaurants spill onto the street. Via Garibaldi, linking the old and new districts, is also a busy shopping and promenading thoroughfare. North of the hydrofoil port, the old Jewish quarter is a warren of somewhat down-at-heel alleys centered on the 16th-century Palazzo della Giudecca on Via della Giudecca.

Linked to Palermo and Castellammare del Golfo by autostrada A29, the town has its own airport and is also an important nexus for trips to Erice, Mozia, San Vito Lo Capo, and the Egadi Islands.

GETTING HERE AND AROUND

Trapani–Birgi Airport (🌐 *www.airgest.it*) is 15 km (9 miles) south of town, and is linked to Palermo by the A29 autostrada and by infrequent slow trains. Most visitors without cars will prefer the much faster bus services, which all terminate at Piazza Malta, though fast buses from the airport, Palermo, Palermo's airport, and Agrigento also make a stop at the ferry and hydrofoil port.

With much of the old town closed to traffic and available parking spots hard to find, drivers should take advantage of the large and inexpensive car park on Piazza Vittorio Emanuele, at the bottom of Via Garibaldi. The old town is easy to negotiate on foot, though visitors to the Museo Pepoli and Santuario Annunziata should either drive or make use of the frequent city bus services.

While you can book online, tickets to the Egadi islands can be picked up from the ticket offices at the port or from Egatour (✉ *Via ammiraglio Staiti 13, Trapani* 🌐 *www.egatourviaggi.it*), which also offers island tours, tickets for Pantelleria, and bus tickets.

Sights

Museo Regionale Pepoli

ART MUSEUM | Trapani's foremost museum collection is located in a former Carmelite monastery that was attached to the important religious site of Santuario dell'Annunziata. The art sections take in some excellent examples of medieval and Renaissance art, including statuary by Antonello Gagini and a painting by Titian. Among the archaeological exhibits is a selection of low-key finds from Mozia and Selinunte. There's also a guillotine from 1800, and a good collection of memorabilia from Garibaldi's Sicilian campaign against the Bourbons in 1860.

The usual entrance to the museum is in the Villa Pepoli public garden; when this is closed enter from Via Madonna, behind the garden. ✉ *Via Conte Agostino Pepoli 180, Trapani* ☎ *0923/553269* 🌐 *www2.regione.sicilia.it/beniculturali/museopepoli/museopepoli.html* 🎟 *€7, free 1st Sun. of month* ⏲ *Closed Mon.*

Restaurants

Ai Lumi

$ | **SICILIAN** | This popular restaurant on the pedestrianized Corso Vittorio Emanuele occupies some former stables, though the modern art on the walls and its candlelit tables evoke far more romantic associations. Dishes are predominantly local and traditional, including such starters as a delicious fish couscous and busiate pasta with Trapani-style pesto (which is made with ground almonds instead of pine nuts and tomatoes) and eggplant, while among the mains you'll be tempted by *ghiotta di pesce misto* (mixed seafood in a rich sauce of tomatoes, olives, and capers), and grilled swordfish. **Known for:** congenial ambience; traditional local dishes; friendly staff. *$ Average main: €18 ✉ Corso Vittorio Emanuele 75, Trapani ☎ 0923/872418 ⊕ www.ailumi.it.*

Coffee and Quick Bites

★ Meno Tredici

$ | ICE CREAM | FAMILY | There's a regular trickle of locals to this gelateria conveniently located opposite the hydrofoil port. Most opt for the local favorite: ice cream in a brioche with a couple of wafer biscuits poking out. **Known for:** tangy ice creams; thirst-quenching granitas; tasty desserts. *$ Average main: €3 ✉ Via Staiti 61, Trapani ☎ 0923/1781797 ⊕ www.gelateriamenotredici.it.*

Hotels

Room of Andrea

$ | HOTEL | A 19th-century palazzo opposite a public garden in central Trapani has been converted to a comfortable hotel that provides pampering accommodation in swish surroundings. **Pros:** small rooftop pool; characterful surroundings and decor; good location. **Cons:** some rooms cramped; most rooms lack much of a view; no hotel parking. *$ Rooms from: €151 ✉ Viale Regina Margherita 31, Trapani ☎ 0923/365728 ⊕ www.roomofandrea.it ⇆ 46 rooms 🍴 Free Breakfast.*

Marsala

30 km (19 miles) south of Trapani.

Marsala is readily associated with its world-famous, richly colored eponymous fortified wine, and your main reason for stopping may be to visit some of the many wineries in the area and sample the product. But this quiet seaside town, together with the nearby island of Mozia, was also once the main Carthaginian base in Sicily: it was from here that Carthage fought for supremacy over the island against Greece and Rome, leaving behind intriguing archaeological sites. In 1773, a British merchant named John Woodhouse happened upon the town and discovered that the wine here, once fortified, was as good as the port long imported by the British from Portugal. Two other wine merchants, Whitaker and Ingham, rushed in, and by 1800 Marsala was exporting wine all over the British Empire. Later in the 19th century, Marsala played a significant role in the Risorgimento, the movement for Italian liberty. It was here that the swashbuckling national hero Giuseppe Garibaldi landed in 1860 with his thousand Redshirts to begin the campaign to oust the Bourbons from southern Italy.

Between Marsala and Trapani, the Stagnone Islands sit amid the shallow lagoon that forms part of a nature reserve, fringed by the eye-catching salt pans that dominate the local landscape. The best known of the islands is tiny Mozia, once an important Phoenician settlement, later fortified by the Carthaginians under whom it became one of the three main Punic strongholds in Sicily. Motya, as it was known, was completely destroyed by Dionysius of Syracuse in 397–396 BC, and its population transferred to the more defensible site of Lilybaeum (modern Marsala), after which most of the Carthaginian city vanished beneath fields and orchards. There was some Roman settlement here, but it was not until the

17th century that the island was identified as the site of ancient Motya, and not until it was acquired in the late 19th century by the Anglo-Sicilian polymath Joseph (or Giuseppe) Whitaker, scion of one of the most prominent Marsala wine dynasties, that excavations began. The Fondazione Whitaker still owns the island and manages Mozia's excellent archaeological museum that displays some of the most significant finds dug up here (though many now reside in Palermo's archaeological museum).

GETTING HERE AND AROUND

There are good bus services from Palermo and Trapani to Marsala, and frequent trains also run from Trapani. Drivers can take the coastal SS115.

VISITOR INFORMATION

Marsala Tourism Office (✉ *Via XI Maggio 100* 🌐 *www.turismocomunemarsala.com*)

Sights

★ Donnafugata Winery

WINERY | Founded and still run by the Rallo family, whose involvement in wine production dates from 1851, the Donnafugata Winery is open for tastings and tours of its *cantina* (wine cellar); reservations are required and can be made online or by phone. It's an interesting look at the wine-making process in Sicily, and it ends with a sampling of several whites and reds, an optional food pairing, and a chance to buy a bottle. Don't miss the delicious, full-bodied red Mille e Una Notte, and the famous Ben Ryè Passito di Pantelleria, a sweet dessert wine made from dried grapes. ✉ *Via Sebastiano Lipari 18, Marsala* ☎ *0923/724245* 🌐 *www.donnafugata.it* 🎫 *Tastings from €30* ⏲ *Closed Sun.*

★ Marsala Salt Pans

OTHER ATTRACTION | Driving along the flat and winding coast road north of Marsala, you'll soon come across the extraordinary series of salt pans glistening in the shallows of Sicily's largest lagoon, the Stagnone di Marsala. The shallow depth of the lagoon, ranging from 2 to 6 feet, has made it perfect for the production of salt, and it has been put to this purpose since Phoenician times. The sheer flatness of the scene is varied only by the conical heaps of salt and a scattering of the disused windmills once used to supply power. The scene is still and quiet most of the time, but you'll sometimes see pockets of activity, with full wheelbarrows of salt being hauled to the conveyor belts that create the mounds. The stacks of earthenware tiles you'll see everywhere are used to weigh down the salt to prevent it being from blown away by gusts of wind. It's an extremely photogenic tableau, with the light changing through the day, the occasional presence of spindly pink flamingos in the lagoon, and Mozia and the Egadi archipelago looming through the haze. The narrow coastal road is one-way for much of its length, and the cycle track running alongside it enables the area to be comfortably toured on two wheels.

There's a small museum dedicated to the salt extraction industry in a restored windmill at the Ettore e Infersa embarcation point, where souvenir samples of salt can be purchased. You'll also find the Mamma Caura bar-restaurant here (🌐 *www.seisaline.it* ⏲ *Closed Tues. Oct.–May*), with outdoor tables and a rooftop terrace. ✉ *Marsala.*

Museo Archeologico Baglio Anselmi

HISTORY MUSEUM | A sense of Marsala's past as a Carthaginian stronghold is captured by the well-preserved Punic warship displayed in this museum, along with some of the amphorae and other artifacts recovered from the wreck. The vessel, which was probably sunk during the great sea battle that ended the First Punic War in 241 BC, was dredged up from the mud near the Egadi Islands in the 1970s. There's also a good display of maritime and archaeological finds, as well as some Roman ruins with mosaics just beyond the museum's doors. A combined ticket allows you to take in the rather sparse archaeological area behind the museum, too. ✉ *Lungomare Boeo 30, Marsala* ☎ *0923/952535* 🌐 *www.turismocomunemarsala.com/museo-archeologico-lilibeo* 🎫 *€7, €8 with archaeological site* 🕓 *Closed Mon.*

Selinunte

35 km (22 miles) southeast of Mazara del Vallo, 114 km (71 miles) southwest of Palermo.

Numerous ruined Greek temples perch on a high, undulating plateau overlooking the Mediterranean at Selinunte (or Selinus). The town is named after a local variety of wild celery (*Apium graveolens*, or *petroselinum*) that in spring grows in profusion among the ruined columns and overturned capitals. Although the nearest village of Marinella di Selinunte is a rather unremarkable seaside resort, there are some very nice places to stay just inland as well as some good beaches, including Porto Palo and the wild dunes of the Foce del Belice nature reserve. Although many travelers treat Selinunte as a quick stop between the temples of Segesta and Agrigento, the area makes a charming holiday base, especially if you're looking for a slower pace with fewer visitors.

GETTING HERE AND AROUND

Selinunte is a half-hour drive from Mazara del Vallo, and an 90-minute drive from Agrigento, which means it can be easily visited via car as a day trip from any of the towns south along the coast. Getting here by public transport is trickier. There are five buses daily to Selinunte from the town of Castelvetrano, 11 km (7 miles) north, which is itself accessible from Palermo by bus and train.

Sights

★ Greek Temple Ruins

ARCHAEOLOGICAL SITE | Selinunte was one of the most important colonies of ancient Greece, recently discovered to have been home to the largest industrial quarter found in any ancient European city. Founded in the 7th century BC, the city became the rich and prosperous rival of Segesta, making its money on trade and manufacturing ceramics. When in 409 BC Segesta turned to the Carthaginians for help in vanquishing their rival, the Carthaginians sent an army to destroy Selinunte. The temples were demolished, the city was razed, and 16,000 of Selinunte's inhabitants were slaughtered. Archaeologists recently discovered pots with the remains of food inside, proof that some were in the middle of eating when the attackers arrived. The remains of Selinunte are in many ways unchanged from the day of its sacking—burn marks still scar the Greek columns, and much of the site still lies in rubble at its exact position of collapse. The original complex held seven temples scattered over two sites separated by a harbor. Of the seven, only one—reconstructed in 1958—is whole. **TIP→ This is a large archaeological site, so you might make use of the private navetta (shuttle) to save a bit of walking. Alternatively, if you have a car, you can visit the first temples close to the ticket office on foot and then drive westward to the farther site. Be prepared to show your ticket at various stages.** ✉ *SS115, Marinella Selinunte* ✣ *13 km (8 miles) southeast of Castelvetrano* ☎ *0924/923970* 🌐 *parchiarcheologici.regione.sicilia.it* 🎫 *€10.*

Restaurants

Da Vittorio

$ | **SEAFOOD** | Located right on the beach at Porto Palo, Da Vittorio is something of a local legend, highly regarded and much loved by everyone from wine and olive oil makers to celebrating families. The focus is on fresh fish and seafood, with pasta for the first course, and grilled fish for a second, all enhanced with traditional Sicilian flavors such as capers, almonds, and wild fennel. **Known for:** creative seafood on the beach; neighborhood institution since the 1960s; open all year long. $ *Average main: €17* ✉ *Via Friuli Venezia Giulia 9, Porto Palo* ☎ *0925/78381* 🌐 *www.ristorantevittorio.it* ⏲ *Closed mid-Dec.–mid-Jan.*

Agrigento

8 km (5 miles) northeast of Porto Empedocle, 128 km (80 miles) south of Palermo.

Agrigento owes its fame almost exclusively to its stunning ancient Greek temples—though it was also the birthplace of playwright Luigi Pirandello (1867–1936) and the setting for the Montelusa scenes of Andrea Camilleri's Inspector Montalbano books. For fans of the books, the old town is an evocative place for a wander, culminating in a visit to nuns for an almond pastry and the fascinating Museo di Santo Spirito.

Beyond its historical and archaeological allure, Agrigento will capture the hearts of gourmands with its delectable produce grown in the surrounding farms. Beyond the citrus, prickly pear, and wheatgrass, you will also encounter rows of vineyards on the outskirts of the city producing a range of varietals including the classic Sicilian grapes, Grillo and Nero D'Avola.

Located slightly inland on the Mediterranean coast, it is also an excellent base for those who want to stay in a city environment for more dining and entertainment options in the evening but still have easy access to beaches, historical sights, and vineyards.

GETTING HERE AND AROUND

you're driving, take the A19 autostrada to Caltanissetta, then follow the SS640 to Agrigento. Motorists can also access the town easily via the coastal SS115 and, from Palermo, by the SS189. Buses and trains run from Enna, Palermo, and Catania, with centrally located bus and train stations. Trenitalia optimized their nonstop routes from Palermo, with over a dozen direct trains daily, which take around 2 hours each way.

VISITOR INFORMATION

Agrigento Tourist Information (✉ *Via Empedocle 73, Agrigento* 🌐 *www.visitsicily.info/en/localita/agrigento*)

Sights

Monastero di Santo Spirito

CONVENT | First built in 1299, these cloisters and their courtyard, up the hill above the Valle dei Templi near the modern city, are open to the public. However, most visitors only stop by the adjacent abbey for a treat and tour of the church, so be sure to ring the doorbell and try the chewy almond cookies. On special occasions, there may be *kus-kus dolce*—a sweet dessert dish made from pistachios, almonds, and chocolate—made from a recipe that the Cistercian nuns learned from Tunisian servants back in the 13th century. For the full abbey experience, visitors can choose to stay at the monastery guesthouse, which offers seven single rooms and four double rooms. ✉ *Cortile Santo Spirito 9, Agrigento* ✣ *Off Via Porcello* ☎ *0922/1552737* 🌐 *monasterosspirito.wixsite.com/agrigento.*

★ Valle dei Templi

ARCHAEOLOGICAL SITE | The temples of Agrigento, a UNESCO World Heritage site, are considered some of the world's finest and best-preserved Greek temples. Whether you first come upon the Valley in the early morning light, bathed by golden floodlights after sunset, or in January and February when it's awash in the fragrant blossoms of thousands of almond trees, it's easy to see why the poet Pindar celebrated Akragas (Agrigento's Greek name) as "the most beautiful city built by mortals." The temples were originally erected as a showpiece to flaunt the Greek victory over Carthage. They have since withstood a later sack by the Carthaginians, mishandling by the Romans, and neglect by Christians and Muslims.

Although getting to, from, and around the dusty ruins of the Valle dei Templi is pretty easy, this important archaeological zone still deserves at least several hours, and it's pretty easy to spend a whole day at the park. The temples are spread out, but the Valley is all completely walkable and usually toured on foot. However, since there's only one hotel (Villa Athena) that's close enough to walk to the ruins, you'll most likely have to drive to reach the site. The best place to park is at the entrance to the temple area. The site opens at 8:30 am and is divided into western and eastern sections, linked by a bridge. The best way to see them both is to park at the Temple of Juno entrance and walk downhill through the eastern zone, across the footbridge into the western zone, and then return uphill, so that you see everything again from a different angle and in a different light. The best time to go is either first thing in the morning or couple of hours before sunset. However, if you are in Agrigento in high summer you might want to consider a night visit; the gates open shortly before sunset, with the temples floodlit as night falls.

You'll want to see the eight pillars of the Tempio di Ercole (Temple of Hercules) that make up Agrigento's oldest temple complex, dating from the 6th century BC. The Tempio di Giunone (Temple of Juno) at the top of the hill is perhaps the most beautiful of all the temples, partly in ruins and commanding an exquisite view of the Valley (especially at sunset). The low wall of mighty stone blocks in front of it was an altar used to sacrifice animals as an offering to the goddess. Next down the hill is the almost perfectly complete Tempio della Concordia (Temple of Concord), perhaps the best-preserved Greek temple currently in existence, thanks to its conversion into a Christian church in the 6th century, though it was restored to its current form in the 18th century. Below it is the Valley's oldest surviving temple, the Temple of Hercules, with nine of its original 38 columns standing, the rest tumbled around like a child's upended bag of building bricks.

Continuing over the pedestrian bridge, you reach the Tempio di Giove (Temple of Jupiter). It was meant to be the largest temple in the complex; it was never completed, but it would have occupied approximately the size of a soccer field. It was an unusual temple, with half columns backing into a continuous wall and 25-foot-high telamon, or male figures, inserted in the gaps in between. Some telamon have been roughly reassembled horizontally on the ground near the temple. Beyond is the so-called Temple of Castor and Pollux, which is picturesque but actually a folly created in the 19th century from various columns and architectural fragments.

We recommend a guided tour for those wanting to learn more about this fascinating yet complex history. You can book guided tours directly via the website, and there are licensed tour guides at the entrance of the temple offering tours. The ticketing office also rents audio guides in multiple languages for those looking to explore independently. Plan to stay at the park for at least half a day; there are plenty of bathrooms and small cafés throughout the park that offer snacks like arancini and even full-sized pasta dishes. **■ TIP→ Save time by booking your tickets in advance online.** ✉ *Zona Archeologica, Via dei Templi, Agrigento* ☎ *0922/1839996* 🌐 *www.parcovalledeitempli.it* 🎫 *€17,*

€22.50 with Museo Regionale Archeologico Pietro Griffo (free 1st Sun. of month).

Restaurants

★ Il Re di Girgenti

$$ | **SICILIAN** | You might not expect to find an ultramodern place to dine within a few minutes' drive of Agrigento's ancient temples. Yet, this restaurant offers pleasing versions of Sicilian classics in a trendy, country-chic atmosphere (think moody lighting and funky geometric tile floors mixed with walls lined with old-fashioned crockery and cookware) and is popular with young locals. **Known for:** Sicilian dishes with a twist; contemporary setting with lovely views; delightful wine selections. *Average main: €24 ✉ Via Panoramica dei Templi 51, Agrigento ☏ 0922/401388 🌐 www.ilredigirgenti.it ⏲ Closed Tues.*

Trattoria dei Templi

$$ | **SICILIAN** | Along a road on the way up to Agrigento proper from the temple area, this vaulted family-run restaurant serves up tasty traditional food, namely daily house-made pasta specials and plenty of fresh fish dishes, all prepared with Sicilian flair. Your best bet is to ask the advice of brothers Giuseppe and Simone, the owners and chief orchestrators in the restaurant, who can also help select a Sicilian wine to pair with your meal. **Known for:** exceptional antipasti, like carpaccio of cernia (grouper); fresh fish; good choice of local wines. *Average main: €20 ✉ Via Panoramica dei Templi 15, Agrigento ☏ 0922/403110 🌐 www.instagram.com/trattoria_dei_templi__rist ⏲ Closed Sun.*

Hotels

Foresteria Baglio della Luna

$$ | **HOTEL** | In the valley below the temples, fiery sunsets and moonlight cast a glow over the ancient 12th-century watchtower at the center of this farmhouse-hotel complex, which is composed of stone buildings surrounding a peaceful geranium- and ivy-filled courtyard and the garden beyond. **Pros:** quiet setting; pretty gardens; top-notch restaurant. **Cons:** hotel a little dark inside; no pool; location a bit remote. *Rooms from: €244 ✉ Via Serafino Amabile Guastella 1, Contrada Maddalusa, Agrigento ☏ 0922/511061 🌐 www.bagliodellaluna.com ⏲ Closed Dec.–Feb. 23 rooms Free Breakfast.*

★ Villa Athena

$$$ | **HOTEL** | The 18th-century Villa Athena, updated into a sleek, luxurious place to stay, complete with gorgeous manicured gardens and swimming pool, holds a privileged position directly overlooking the Temple of Concordia, a 10-minute walk away—an amazing sight both during the day and when it's lit up at night. **Pros:** unbeatable views, and the only hotel within walking distance of the Valle dei Templi; good restaurant and spa; plenty of free parking. **Cons:** lobby on the small side; expensive compared to other area options; lack of information on other local attractions. *Rooms from: €400 ✉ Via Passeggiata Archeologica 33, Agrigento ☏ 0922/596288 🌐 www.hotelvillaathena.it 27 rooms Free Breakfast.*

Enna

33 km (21 miles) northwest of Piazza Armerina.

Deep in Sicily's interior, the fortress city of Enna (altitude 2,844 feet) commands exceptional views of the surrounding rolling plains, and, in the distance, Mount Etna. Thanks to its central location, it's the highest provincial capital in Italy and is nicknamed the "Navel of Sicily." Virtually unknown to tourists and relatively untouched by industrialization, this lively town charms and prospers in a distinctly old-fashioned Sicilian way. Its surrounding towns and areas are also worth exploring and will take you further off the beaten track. Nature lovers will love the many nature trails throughout the region. Contrary to the arid southern coast, you will see many rolling green hills and a cooler microclimate.

Due to its historic lack of tourists, the most appealing lodgings are outside town. Those who are short on time will discover that Enna makes a good stop-over for sightseeing with lunch, as it is right along the autostrada about halfway between Palermo and Catania.

GETTING HERE AND AROUND

Just off the A19 autostrada, Enna is easily accessible by car. With the train station 5 km (3 miles) below the upper town, the most practical public transportation is by the efficient bus service from Palermo or Catania. There's also a train from Palermo to Enna, but it takes almost two hours to get there, which is longer than the 90-minute bus ride.

Sights

Piazza Vittorio Emanuele

PLAZA/SQUARE | In town, head straight for Via Roma, which leads to Piazza Vittorio Emanuele—the center of Enna's shopping scene and evening passeggiata. The attached Piazza Crispi, dominated by what used to be the grand old Hotel Belvedere, affords breathtaking panoramas of the hillside and smoking Etna looming in the distance. The bronze fountain in the middle of the piazza is a reproduction of Gian Lorenzo Bernini's famous 17th-century sculpture *The Rape of Persephone,* a depiction of Hades abducting Persephone. ✉ *Piazza Vittorio Emanuele, Enna.*

Torre di Federico II

VIEWPOINT | This mysterious octagonal tower stands above the lower part of town and has been celebrated for millennia as marking the exact geometric center of the island—thus the tower's (and the city's) nickname, Umbilicus Siciliae (Navel of Sicily). Climb the 97 steps of the spiral staircase for views over the city and beyond. ✉ *Via Torre di Frederico II, Enna* ☎ *329/8965116 mobile* 🌐 *www.pro-loco-enna-proserpina.it/torre-di-federico* 🎟 *€4, combined ticket with Castello di Lombardia.*

Restaurants

Centrale di Pirrera

$$ | SICILIAN | Housed in an old palazzo, this casual place has served meals since 1889 and famously keeps a medieval specialty, *controfiletto all'Ennese* (a veal fillet with onions, artichokes, guanciale, and white wine), on the menu, in addition to a range of slightly more modern seasonal dishes. Choose from a decent selection of Sicilian wines to accompany your meal while you take in the large mirrored wall and local pottery. **Known for:** antipasti buffet; classic Sicilian dishes and local wines; atmospheric outdoor terrace in summer. $ *Average main: €21* ✉ *Piazza VI Dicembre 9, Enna* ☎ *0935/500963* 🌐 *www.ristorantecentrale.net* ⏲ *Closed Mon.*

Piazza Armerina

30 km (18 miles) northwest of Caltagirone.

Crowned by a mighty cathedral, the medieval hill town of Piazza Armerina is a magnificent sight from afar. Up close, the historic center's crumbling yellow-stone architecture with Sicily's trademark bulbous balconies creates quite an effect despite a feeling of dilapidation and abandonment (most locals have moved to the modern suburbs). It is a place to visit rather than stay, with the most appealing lodging options in the surrounding countryside.

Piazza Armerina is most famous for the ancient Roman mosaics down the road at Villa Romana del Casale, but lovers of ancient history may be even more entranced by the huge and rarely visited Greek town of Morgantina and the incredible finds from the site, which once graced the galleries of the Getty museum in Malibu, California.

GETTING HERE AND AROUND

Piazza Armerina is linked to Catania, Enna, and Palermo by regular buses, with less frequent buses also connecting to Caltagirone. There's no train station.

TOURS

Serena Raffiotta

PRIVATE GUIDES | A freelance archaeologist and researcher, Serena is the perfect guide to Morgantina and Aidone as well as the Villa Romana del Casale. She has also helped identify objects illegally excavated from Sicily's archaeological sights, including a blue-painted curl of terra-cotta that was on display at the Getty Museum in Malibu. She identified it as belonging to the head of a god from Morgantina; it was repatriated to Italy in 2016 and is now displayed in the village of Aidone. ✉ *Piazza Armerina* ☎ *329/1561022 mobile* 🌐 *www.facebook.com/morgantinavilladelcasale* 🎟 *Half-day tour €150; full-day tour €250.*

VISITOR INFORMATION

Piazza Armerina Tourism Office (✉ *Gen.le Muscarà 47/A, Piazza Armerina* 🌐 *www.visitsicily.info/en/informazioni-turistiche*)

Sights

★ **Villa Romana del Casale** (*Imperial Roman Villa*)

ARCHAEOLOGICAL SITE | The exceptionally well-preserved Imperial Roman Villa is thought to have been a hunting lodge of the emperor Maximian (3rd–4th century AD) and offers some of the best mosaics of the Roman world, artfully covering more than 12,000 square feet. The excavations were not begun until 1950, and most of the wall decorations and vaulting have been lost, but the shelter over the site hints at the layout of the original building. The mosaics were probably made by North African artisans; they're similar to those in the Tunis Bardo Museum, in Tunisia. The entrance was through a triumphal arch that led into an atrium surrounded by a portico of columns, which line the way to the *thermae*, or bathhouse. It's colorfully decorated with mosaic nymphs, a Neptune, and enslaved people massaging bathers. The peristyle leads to the main villa, where in the Salone del Circo you look down on mosaics illustrating scenes from the Circus Maximus in Rome. A theme running through many of the mosaics—especially the long hall flanking one entire side of the peristyle courtyard—is the capturing and shipping of wild animals, which may have been a major source of the owner's wealth. Yet the most famous mosaic is the floor depicting 10 girls wearing the ancient equivalent of bikinis, going through what looks like a fairly rigorous set of training exercises. ✉ *SP15 Contrada Casale, 4 km (2½ miles) southwest of Piazza Armerina, Piazza Armerina* ☎ *0935/680036 ticket office, 0935/687667 office* 🌐 *www.villaromanadelcasale.it* 🎟 *€14 (free 1st Sun. of month).*

Restaurants

★ **Al Fogher**

$$ | **MODERN ITALIAN** | This culinary beacon in Sicily's interior features ambitious—and successful—dishes with the creative flair of chef Angelo Treno, whose unforgettable pastas topped with truffles or caviar, for example, offer a decidedly different expression of traditional regional ingredients. The unassuming and elegant dining room is inside an old railway house and is the perfect place to enjoy a bottle from the 500-label wine list; in cold weather, you can cozy up to a fireplace, but the terrace is the place to be in summer. **Known for:** sophisticated preparations; local ingredients; well-thought-out wine list. 💲 *Average main: €21* ✉ *Contrada Bellia, Piazza Armerina* ✣ *Near SS117* *bis, Aidone exit, about 1 km (½ mile) north of Piazza Cascino ☎ 0935/684123 🌐 www.facebook.com/ristorantealfogher ⏲ Closed Mon. No dinner Sun.*

Caltagirone

72 km (41 miles) northeast of Licata.

Caltagirone's functional modern periphery, built over three hills, gives way to an imposing, if slightly run-down, Baroque town center. Beyond the visit, driving into the town is also impressive, as you can see it sitting high from the highway. The city is one of the main centers of Sicily's ceramics industry, evidenced by churches and palazzi featuring majolica decorations on their balustrades, domes, windowsills, and facades. The best-known sight is the monumental Scala Santa Maria del Monte. After Caltanissetta, it is the second-most populous *comune* in central Sicily, giving visitors a glimpse of the local central Sicilian urban lifestyle.

GETTING HERE AND AROUND

Driving is the best way to get to Caltagirone. Regular buses from Catania stop in the lower town, which is a pleasant stroll from the center. Connections by bus with other towns in Sicily are infrequent. There are two Trenitalia trains—one in the midafternoon and another in the evening coming from Catania.

VISITOR INFORMATION

Caltagirone Tourist Office (✉ *Via Volta Libertini 3, Caltagirone* ☎ *0933/53809* 🌐 *www.cittadicaltagirone.it*).

Museo della Ceramica

SPECIALTY MUSEUM | Caltagirone was declared a UNESCO World Heritage site for its ceramics as well as for its numerous Baroque churches. Although the museum offers little information in English about the beautiful items displayed in its many glass cases, you can still see one of Sicily's most extensive ceramics collections, ranging from Neolithic finds to red-figure pottery from 5th-century-BC Athens and 18th-century terra-cotta Nativity figures. ✉ *Giardini Pubblici, Via Roma, Caltagirone* ☎ *0933/58418* 🌐 *parchiarcheologici.regione.sicilia.it/catania-valle-aci/biglietti/museo-della-ceramica-caltagirone* 🎫 *€4.*

★ Scala Santa Maria del Monte

OTHER ATTRACTION | While you can see examples of Caltagirone's long ceramic tradition throughout the city, the most impressive display can be found in the 142 individually decorated tiled steps of this monumental staircase leading up to the neglected Santa Maria del Monte church. On July 25 (the feast of San Giacomo, the city's patron saint) and again on August 15th (the feast of the Assumption), the stairs form a tapestry design with illuminated candles. Months of work go into preparing the 4,000 *coppi,* or cylinders of colored paper, that hold oil lamps—then, at 9:30 pm on the nights of July 24, July 25, August 14, and August 15, a squad of hundreds of youngsters (tourists are welcome to participate) spring into action to light the lamps, so that the staircase flares up all at once. ✉ *Piazza Municipio, Caltagirone.*

Ragusa

21 km (13 miles) northwest of Modica.

Ragusa, with its undulating topography, is divided into two parts: a modern city (Ragusa Superiore) with some handsome architecture amid a modern mess, and a lower, unspoiled historic core (Ragusa Ibla) that is blessed with beguiling Baroque buildings and fabulous vantage points throughout the narrow, twisty, and steep streets. With its tiny squares and narrow lanes, the area was completely rebuilt after the devastating earthquake of 1693.

The city is known for some great local red wines and wonderful cheese—a creamy, doughy, flavorful version of caciocavallo. It also has some fabulous restaurants.

GETTING HERE AND AROUND

Trains and buses leave from Siracusa four or five times daily (once on Sunday), and there is also regular service from Modica, Scicli, and Noto.

VISITOR INFORMATION

Hi! Hybla Infopoint (✉ *Corso XXV Aprile 42* 🌐 *www.ragusawelcome.com/en*)

Sights

★ Cinabro Carrettieri

CRAFT MUSEUM | Sicilian carts—brightly painted and led by either a horse or donkey—were an important part of Sicilian history in the 19th and early 20th centuries (at least until the advent of the truck), and they have become a symbol of the island, often sold in miniature form as tourist souvenirs. For fascinating insight into the crafts and their role in Sicilian history, this workshop-museum, which is run by Biagio and Damiano, is a cultural highlight. They'll take you through the fascinating history of the cart, its place in Sicilian society, and the many skills involved in decorating them, including those eye-popping painted designs that advertised the wares transported and status of the driver. A visit can also be part of a 75-minute tour that takes in two other nearby sights: the Circolo di Conversazione (1850), an exclusive club with frescoed ceiling, scene of debate, intrigue, and card playing that is reserved for Ragusa's nobility to this day; plus the lavish Palazzo Arezzo di Trifiletti. Talk to Biagio about a visit to the Antico Mercato (✉ *Via del Mercato 124–144*), where botteghe (craft workshops)—including those devoted to sculpture, blacksmithing, and a puppet theater—are run by young artisans to help keep these traditions alive, often accompanied by tables of bountiful food and wine by Putia del Vino wine bar, under the market's beautifully restored arcades. ✉ *Via Orfanotrofio 22, Ragusa* ☎ *340/8444804* 🌐 *www.facebook.com/cinabrocarrettieri* 🎫 *€7; €15 tour including Circolo and palazzo.*

Duomo di San Giorgio

CHURCH | Designed by Rosario Gagliardi in 1738 (and completed in 1791), Ragusa's main cathedral, a fine example of the Sicilian Baroque, was further modified in the 19th century with the addition of a Neoclassical cupola. The flamboyant convex facade with bell tower rises 203 feet, looking like a wedding cake from the sloping piazza below to provide sightlines for the 141-foot dome. Although visitors enter via side entrances, the ornate portal frames wooden doors that are decorated with six episodes in the martyrdom of San Giorgio, all carved by Fiorello (1793). The three-nave interior is more subdued in comparison and contains numerous paintings and statuary by mostly 18th-century Sicilian artists, as well as an impressive 3,383-pipe Organum Maximum made in Bergamo in 1881; that alone is well worth hearing and a reason to visit. But you may wish to linger to take in the artworks and sunlight-bathed atmosphere from 20 vibrant, stained-glass windows, each detailing more saintly scenes and allegories. ✉ *Salita Duomo 15, Ragusa* ☎ *0932/220085* 🌐 *www.duomosangiorgioragusa.it* 🎫 *Free.*

Giardino Ibleo

GARDEN | On the edge of the old town, this tranquil public garden is lined with palm trees and dotted with fountains and churches along stone paths with numerous benches for contemplation and picnicking. The ambling walkways skirt the cliffside and offer dramatic views of the valley below. Among the three churches here, the Chiesa dei Cappuccini is notable for the beautiful wooden altar featuring a triptych by Pietro Novelli (1635) depicting the Assumption, flanked by Saints Agata and Catherina. ✉ *Via Giardino, Ragusa* ☎ *0932/652374.*

Restaurants

Duomo Ciccio Sultano

$$$$ | **SICILIAN** | In an understated palazzo on a cobblestone street near the Duomo, star chef Ciccio Sultano prepares imaginative and beautifully plated splurge-worthy dinners and a three-course prix-fixe lunch menu that include unforgettable variations on classic Sicilian cuisine. Although dishes can be ordered à la carte, tasting menus convey a fuller sense of the chef's signature style, which uses the finest ingredients from around the island in subtly extravagant combinations. **Known for:** being one of Sicily's most renowned restaurants; imaginative wine pairings; intriguing range of set menus. *$ Average main: €45* ✉ *Via Capitano Bocchieri 31, Ragusa* ☎ *0932/651265* 🌐 *www.cicciosultano.it* ⏲ *Closed Sun. and Mon. (except Aug.), and early Jan.–mid-Mar.*

Locanda Gulfi

$ | **SICILIAN** | On gorgeous grounds of the Gulfi winery, this is a tranquil spot for a sophisticated lunch or dinner, with sweeping views of the Chiaramonte hills and vineyards (about a half-hour drive north of Ragusa). Expect Sicilian dishes with a twist in the modern dining room, which features hand-blown chandeliers and black-and-red color scheme. **Known for:** seasonal, local Sicilian dishes; renowned organic Gulfi wine; vineyard terrace views and an inn to stay the night. *$ Average main: €19* ✉ *Contrada Patria, Chiaramonte Gulfi* ✥ *19 km (12 miles) north of Ragusa* ☎ *0932/928081 reservations, 0932/921654 winery* 🌐 *www.gulfi.it* ⏲ *Closed Mon. No dinner Sun.*

Hotels

Eremo della Giubiliana

$ | **B&B/INN** | In the countryside about 20 minutes by car south of Ragusa, this charming family-run monastery-turned-hotel features friendly service and a relaxed but luxurious vibe, with unique rooms in former monks' chambers that vary in size and lay-out but are all quiet and well-appointed. **Pros:** peaceful atmosphere; rooms filled with character; top-notch service. **Cons:** grounds, while lovely, could use better upkeep; restaurant food could be better; no other nearby eateries due to remote location. *$ Rooms from: €180* ✉ *Contrada Giubiliana, Marina di Ragusa* ☎ *0932/669119* 🌐 *www.eremodellagiubiliana.it* *24 rooms* *Free Breakfast.*

★ Giardino sul Duomo

$ | **HOTEL** | **FAMILY** | With a selection of smartly appointed rooms scattered among traditional stone buildings and a modern breakfast room and reception area, this ideally located *albergo diffuso* with chic citrus-grove gardens provides a perfect Val di Noto base. **Pros:** reliable, friendly, hands-on owner Michele; incredible views of Ragusa Ibla, the Duomo, and hills from the garden and pool; range of lodging options. **Cons:** gets booked up in advance; not all rooms have stunning views; not everyone may be able to negotiate Ibla's hilly lanes. *$ Rooms from: €149* ✉ *Via Dottor Solarino 26/A, Ragusa* ☎ *366/5794027* 🌐 *www.giardinosulduomo.it* *14 rooms* *Free Breakfast.*

Modica

37 km (23 miles) west of Noto.

Modica and Ragusa are the two chief cities in Sicily's smallest province (also called Ragusa), and the centers of a region dominated by the limestone hills of the Monti Iblei. The dry, rocky, and gentle countryside filled with canyons and grassy knolls is a unique landscape for Sicily. In Modica, the main artery—Corso Umberto I—is lined with shops and restaurants and is in the valley at the bottom of the town (called Modica Bassa), while the old town of Modica Alta is built atop a ridge. That's part of this UNESCO-listed area's charm; it's a joy to wander its steep 14th-century lanes traversed by endless staircases and lined with Baroque architecture. Modica is also famed for its chocolate—cooked at a low temperature and possessed of a distinctive granular texture—is sold in many stores on Corso Umberto I.

GETTING HERE AND AROUND

Trains leave from Siracusa around four times from Monday to Saturday (twice on Sunday); the same line also serves Noto, Sampieri, and Scicli. It's a 20-minute journey from Ragusa. If there's a strike or limited service (especially on a Sunday) you can take buses from all these towns as well as Catania.

VISITOR INFORMATION

Ufficio Turistico Modica (✉ *Corso Umberto I 14* 🌐 *comunemodica.rg.it/site/ufficio-turistico/*)

Sights

Duomo di San Pietro Apostolo

CHURCH | Statues of the apostles line the staircase of Modica's honey-colored stone cathedral, which was originally constructed in the 14th century, then rebuilt in an impressive Baroque style following its destruction in the 1693 earthquake. Look down to marvel at the ornate intarsia stone tiling and above at the vaulted ceiling frescoes (1760-80) depicting Biblical scenes by local artist Gian Battista Ragazzi and his son Stefano. Flanked by an impressive wooden choir the main altar has a vibrant marble statue *Madonna del Soccorso* (also called *Madonna della Mazza*), which dates from 1507. This curious image of

Favorite Places

Nick Bruno: A monumental staircase leads up to the 200-foot-high facade of Modica's Duomo di San Giorgio, but the towering campanile offers a panorama of Baroque beauty with a dash of drama.

Mary, who is wielding a club to smash a Satanic figure while cradling the baby Jesus, has its origins in the legend of 14th-century Nicola La Bruna from Palermo, whose vision of Mary is said to have cured a grave illnes. On a political note, there was a long and bitter dispute with lofty rival San Giorgio (Modica's other cathedral) regarding which church was rightfully Modica's "Chiesa Madre" (Mother Church); thankfully, they now share that status more amicably. If you're a glutton for churches, consult 🌐 *www.laviadellecollegiate.it* for information and itineraries that cover Modica's plethora of places of worship. ✉ *Corso Umberto I, 120, Modica* ☎ *0932/941074* 🌐 *www.laviadellecollegiate.it/collegiata-di-san-pietro-apostolo* 🎟 *€2.50; €6 for "Camino Mariano di Modica" church pass.*

★ Duomo di San Giorgio

CHURCH | This Baroque beauty and so-called Mother Church of Modica Alta is reached by climbing 250 steps that crisscross in a monumental staircase leading up to the main doors. Dating back to medieval times—and after a series of calamities, including the 1693 earthquake—its present form took shape during the 17th and 18th centuries, largely under Spanish rule. The imposing 200-foot-high facade and tower were remodeled by Rosario Gagliardi (1698–1762); the church was finally crowned by an iron cross in 1842. You'll want to linger amid the white-stuccoed, eggshell blue and gold-leafed interior, taking in the artistic flamboyance of its five naves and numerous chapels, which are surrounded and supported by 22 Corinthian columns. One chapel houses the equestrian statue of San Giorgio that is paraded through Modica every April. A towering polyptych attributed to Bernardino Nigro (1538–1590) consists of nine Biblical scenes capped by a lunette of God and two golden adoring angels. Don't miss the meridian sundial with the signs of the zodiac near the the main altar; it was designed by the mathematician Armando Perini in 1895. Mass is held year-round on Sunday at 11 am, daily at 7 pm from April through October, as well as 7:30 pm in July and August; from November through March, the daily evening mass is at 6 pm. **TIP→ For the best views in town, climb the campanile. (For a cacophonous experience, you can also time your ascension to 30 minutes before mass when the mighty bells chime. Cover your ears, though.)** ✉ *Corso San Giorgio, Modica* ☎ *0932/941279* 🌐 *www.scoprimodica.it/cosa-vedere/le-chiese/san-giorgio* 🎟 *Free; campanile €2.*

Museo della Pipa

CRAFT MUSEUM | Charming Salvatore Amorelli, known affectionarly as Totò, has been crafting pipes since 1982, and his evocative, tobacco-perfumed workshop-museum, which is hidden away within a historic courtyard lined with beautifully gnarled pieces of wood, is a joy to visit. As you enter his workshop, smiling Salvatore will take you through the fascinating history of the pipe, the different types of wood and techniques he uses, with displays of pipes laid out on tables. Totò's pipes are sculptural works of art, enjoyed by people from around world, including Bill Clinton, who has a sax-shaped number. Visitors may drop by any day but Sunday, but it's better to call ahead to make an appointment (long lunches are sacred here, of course). ✉ *Corso Garibaldi 58, Modica* ☎ *327/9352071* 🎟 *Free* ⏲ *Closed Sun.*

Restaurants

★ Accursio Ristorante

$$$$ | **SICILIAN** | There are just a few tables at this intimate, Michelin-starred restaurant with subdued lighting, where chef Accursio Craparo delivers exquisite plates with influences and produce from throughout Sicily. The tasting menu is special but very expensive, so for a more affordable, relaxed setting head a few doors down to sister spot Radici (meaning Roots), which offers heartier, simpler options like fried pasta with meaty ragù. **Known for:** excellent 150-bottle wine selection; beautifully presented seasonal dishes; sophisticated atmosphere. $ *Average main: €135* ✉ *Via Grimaldi 41, Modica* ☎ *0932/941689* 🌐 *www.accursioristorante.it* ⏲ *Closed Mon. No dinner Sun. No lunch Tues.*

Coffee and Quick Bites

Pasticceria Di Lorenzo

$ | **BAKERY** | **FAMILY** | Wood lined and unadorned, this family-run pastry shop is one of the best places to try Modica's signature crescent-shape cookies, the *'mpanatigghi*. These soft cookies are filled with a mixture of chocolate, almonds, and veal, a combination that works surprisingly well. **Known for:** chocolate squares that resemble the city's cobblestones; specialty cookies; family run. $ *Average main: €5* ✉ *Corso Umberto I 225, Modica* ☎ *0932/945324* 🌐 *www.pasticceriadilorenzo.it* ⏲ *Closed Wed.*

Shopping

★ Antica Dolceria Bonajuto

CHOCOLATE | Bonajuto is the oldest chocolate producer in town, dating from 1880. This busy shop on Modica Bassa's main street lets you sample many varieties of their delightful product before you buy, and also makes renowned cannoli and candied orange peel. ✉ *Corso Umberto I 159, Modica* ☎ *0932/941225* 🌐 *www.bonajuto.it.*

Scicli

44 km (27 miles) west of Noto.

Overshadowed by its larger neighbors, Modica and Ragusa, Scicli is a Baroque beauty in its own right and one of the eight villages designated by UNESCO in the Val di Noto. In recent years, it has entered Italian popular culture as the filming location of the hugely popular *Montalbano* series, but its decorated stone palaces, art-filled churches, serene surrounding hills, and proximity to beautiful beaches like Sampieri, will delight visitors whether or not they know the Sicilian detective show.

GETTING HERE AND AROUND

Trains and buses from Siracusa, Modica, Ragusa, and Noto stop in Scicli on a regular basis.

Sights

Chiesa di San Bartolomeo

CHURCH | The fabulously voluptuous facade makes a stunning contrast with the limestone cliffs soaring above the edge of the town's historic center. A dizzying fusion of the Baroque and rococo lies behind the lace grate doors of this single-nave church; your eyes eventually lead to the central altarpiece painting, *Martyrdom of Saint Bartholomew* (1779) by Francesco Pasucci. Most enchanting is the Neapolitan wooden nativity scene conceived in the 16th century and remodeled by Pietro Padula (1773–76). ✉ *Via S. Bartolomeo, Scicli* ☎ *0932/931251* 🎫 *Free.*

Chiesa Madre di Sant'Ignazio

CHURCH | Founded in the 17th century by the Jesuits, Scicli's "mother church" was rebuilt following the 1693 earthquake. Housing the remains of the town's patron saint, Guglielmo the Hermit, a side chapel also hosts the life-size papier-mâché statue of the Madonna *su cavallo* (on a horse), also known as the *Madonna delle Milizie.* She is paraded through the streets on the last Saturday in May to celebrate her feast day. ✉ *Piazza Italia, Scicli* ☎ *0932/931278* 🎫 *Free.*

Noto

38 km (23 miles) southwest of Siracusa.

If Siracusa's Baroque beauties whet your appetite for that over-the-top style, head to Noto, a UNESCO World Heritage site. Lying about 40 minutes away on the A18, the compact and easy-to-navigate city is doable as a day trip—though staying overnight lets you see the lovely buildings glow in the setting sun after the tourist hordes have departed. Noto's remarkable architectural integrity is due to the fact that the original town—known as Noto Antica and located 14 km (8 miles) away from the current town—was decimated by an earthquake in 1693. When it came to rebuilding, the present site was selected. It lies on a steep slope, with the palaces of the aristocrats concentrated in the lower town, with simpler housing for more ordinary folk set on a grid plan in the upper town. The two sections are a short, steep walk from one another. A prime example of design from the island's Baroque heyday, it presents a pleasing ensemble of honey-color buildings. Simply walking Corso Vittorio Emanuele, the pedestrianized main street, qualifies as an aesthetic experience. You may also recognize the town from Michelangelo Antonioni's movie *L'Avventura* (or from the more recent *White Lotus*). Tours of Noto's municipal sights were mired in a legal dispute in 2024, but this should be resolved in 2025.

GETTING HERE AND AROUND

Trains leave from Siracusa at least five times daily (no service Sunday); there are also four trains a day from Ragusa (none on Sunday), though the station is a bit outside of town. Buses depart numerous times a day from Siracusa, Catania, and Ragusa.

VISITOR INFORMATION

Noto Tourism Office (✉ *Corso Vittorio Emanuele 135* 🌐 *www.travelnoto.com*)

Sights

★ Cattedrale di San Nicolò

CHURCH | Noto's domed cathedral is an undisputed highlight of the extraordinary Baroque architecture for which the town is world-famous. Climb the monumental staircase to get a glimpse of the interior—restored over a 10-year period after the dome collapsed in 1996—which is simple and unloved by some (its newness and painting style may appear strange at first) compared to the magnificent exterior, but still worth a look. Indeed, it's become so popular that an entrance fee has been introduced, mainly to help the informative volunteers to cope with the foot flow. ✉ *Corso Vittorio Emanuele, Noto* ☎ *0931/835286* 🌐 *www.diocesinoto.it* 🎫 *€2.*

Palazzo Nicolaci di Villadorata

CASTLE/PALACE | On a steep hill above the main corso, the palace's magnificent balconies, which are supported by mythical monsters, have made it one of the most iconic—and photographed—sights in Sicily. For a rare insight into the lifestyle of social climbers in the 18th century, you can take a tour of the interior to see some of the 90 rooms belonging to the noble Nicolaci family, the highlight being the splendid frescoed ballroom, the Salone delle Feste, which hosts regular classical music recitals. A legal dispute in 2024 halted tours, but this should be resolved at some point. Between tours and concerts, you can wander into the courtyard for a gander during the day. ✉ *Via Corrado Nicolaci, Noto* ☎ *338/7427022.*

Restaurants

★ Anche gli Angeli

$$ | **ITALIAN** | Under the atmospheric arches of Chiesa di San Carlo's 1700s-era crypt, renowned chef Salvatore Vicari's food ethos is all about deceptively simple yet sophisticated combinations of the finest Sicilian ingredients. Let the wonderful waitstaff guide you through the changing seasonal menu of high-end takes on local pasta, meat, and seafood dishes. **Known for:** elegant design under historic vaulted ceiling; sommelier tips on finest wines and cocktails; haute 'n' hearty plates like barbecue pork-belly chunks with foraged greens. 💲 *Average main: €23* ✉ *Via Arnaldo da Brescia 2, Noto* ☎ *0931/576023* 🌐 *www.anchegliangeli.it.*

Ristorante Crocifisso

$$$$ | **SICILIAN** | One of the Baroque town's fanciest restaurants reframes traditional Sicilian dishes in a contemporary style in an understated modern dining room. With a wonderful wine list that includes many Sicilian natural wines, a meal here is pricey but one to remember. **Known for:** new takes on classic Sicilian dishes; small but well-crafted plates; fantastic wine selection with a focus on Sicilian and natural wines. 💲 *Average main: €100* ✉ *Via Principe Umberto 48, Noto* ☎ *0931/968608* 🌐 *www.ristorante-crocifisso.it* 🕒 *Closed mid-Jan.–late Feb. and Wed. No lunch.*

Ristorante Manna

$$ | **SICILIAN** | Having relocated to a handsome,1700s-era former vineyard in seaside Lido di Noto, much-loved Manna still serves its famous dishes—from fresh pastas to creative seafood and exceptional daily specials—that bring out the tasty natural goodness of local premium ingredients. Choose from the beguiling cobbled courtyard or rustic-cum-chic dining area mixing stone structures with cool artworks, a stylish complement to the refined modern takes on *la cucina Siciliana*. **Known for:** modern, creative Sicilian cuisine; seaside location so you need a car; cool, contemporary-meets-rustic setting. 💲 *Average main: €26* ✉ *Lungomario Ionio, 1, Noto* ☎ *0931/836051* 🌐 *www.mannanoto.it* 🕒 *Closed Nov., Jan.–Mar., and Tues. No lunch weekdays.*

 Coffee and Quick Bites

Caffè Sicilia
$ | **BAKERY** | When you need a break from the architectural eye candy, indulge in an edible sweet (and a restorative coffee or granita) at this wondrous cake shop. Their cannoli, biscotti, and gelato are particularly highly rated and considered some of the best in the country. **Known for:** perfect almond granita; delicious cannoli; house-made ice cream. *Average main: €6 Corso Vittorio Emanuele 125, Noto 0931/835013 www.caffesicilia.it Closed Nov. and mid-Jan.–late Mar.*

 Hotels

Gagliardi Boutique Hotel
$$ | **HOTEL** | In a converted 18th-century palace on a quiet street behind Palazzo Ducezio, this smart hotel's main draw is its wonderful panoramic roof terrace bar, while offering less striking but nevertheless spacious, understated rooms. **Pros:** extremely central location; excellent breakfast, including almond granita; sunset apertivi on the roof. **Cons:** only one room has a bathtub; some rooms could do with a refresh; short on amenities (no restaurant, spa, or pool). *Rooms from: €250 Via Silvio Spaventa 41, Noto 0931/839730 www.gagliardihotel.com 11 rooms Free Breakfast.*

Siracusa

28 km (17 miles) northeast of Noto.

Siracusa, known to English speakers as Syracuse, is a wonder to behold. One of the great ancient capitals of Western civilization, the city was founded in 734 BC by Greek colonists from Corinth and soon grew to rival—and even surpass—Athens in splendor and power. It became the largest, wealthiest city-state in the west and a bulwark of Greek civilization. Although Siracusa lived under tyranny, rulers such as Dionysius filled their courts with Greeks of the highest cultural stature—among them the playwrights Aeschylus and Euripides and the philosopher Plato. The Athenians, who didn't welcome Siracusa's rise, set out to conquer Sicily, but the natives outsmarted them in what was one of the greatest military campaigns in ancient history (413 BC). The city continued to prosper until it was conquered two centuries later by the Romans.

Present-day Siracusa still has some of the finest examples of Baroque art and architecture; dramatic Greek and Roman ruins; and a Duomo that's the stuff of legend—a microcosm of the city's entire history in one building. The modern city also has a wonderful, lively Baroque old town worthy of extensive exploration, as well as pleasant piazzas, outdoor cafés and bars, and a wide assortment of excellent seafood. There are essentially two areas to explore in Siracusa: the Parco Archeologico (Archaeological Zone) on the mainland, and the island of Ortigia, the ancient city first inhabited by the Greeks, which juts out into the Ionian Sea and is connected to the mainland by two small bridges.

Ortigia has become increasingly popular with tourists, and although it's filled with lots of modern boutiques (and tourist shops), it still retains its charm despite the crowds. Wandering off the main streets you'll find ornate Baroque palazzi and atmospheric leafy courtyards. Walking along the splendid *lungomare,* there are plenty of terraces to linger and watch the waves, sometimes foaming and dramatically crashing, sometimes serene and azure blue. On warm days intimate rocky beaches and a wooden bathing platform below the winding promenade, become joyous places to swim and sunbathe.

GETTING HERE AND AROUND

On the main train line from Messina and Catania, Siracusa is also linked to Noto, Ragusa, Modica, and Scicli via the

At the Parco Archeologico della Neapolis, walk inside the Ear of Dionysius (the Greek god of wine, fertility, and religious ecstasy), which was used as a prison in ancient Greek times.

improved Ferrovia Siracusa–Gela–Canicattì line. Catania and the nearby Val di Noto are also served by frequent buses.

Although Ortigia is a compact area and a pleasure to amble around without making you unduly tired, mainland Siracusa is a grid of wide modern avenues with heavy car traffic. At the northern end of Corso Gelone, above Viale Paolo Orsi, the orderly grid gives way to the ancient quarter of Neapolis, where the sprawling Parco Archeologico is accessible from Viale Teracati (an extension of Corso Gelone). East of Viale Teracati, about a 10-minute walk from the Parco Archeologico, the old district of Tiche holds the archaeological museum and the church and catacombs of San Giovanni, both off Viale Teocrito (drive or take a taxi or city bus from Ortigia). Coming from the train station, it's a 15-minute trudge to Ortigia along Via Francesco Crispi and Corso Umberto. If you're not up for that, take a taxi. Siracusa's bus system is terribly unreliable and best avoided.

VISITOR INFORMATION

Siracusa Tourism Office (✉ *Via Roma 31* 🌐 *www.siracusaturismo.net*)

Archaeological Zone

Sights

Catacomba di San Giovanni

RUINS | Not far from the Archaeological Park, off Viale Teocrito, the catacombs below the church of San Giovanni are one of the earliest known Christian sites in the city. Inside the crypt of San Marciano is an altar where it is believed that St. Paul preached on his way through Sicily to Rome. The frescoes in this small chapel are mostly bright and fresh, though some dating from the 4th century AD show their age. To visit the catacombs, you must take a 45-minute guided tour (included with the admission price), which leaves about every half hour and is conducted in Italian and English. ✉ *Piazza San Giovanni, Tyche* ☎ *0931/64694* 🌐 *www.kairos-web.com* 🎫 *€10* 🕐 *Closed Mon. and Jan.*

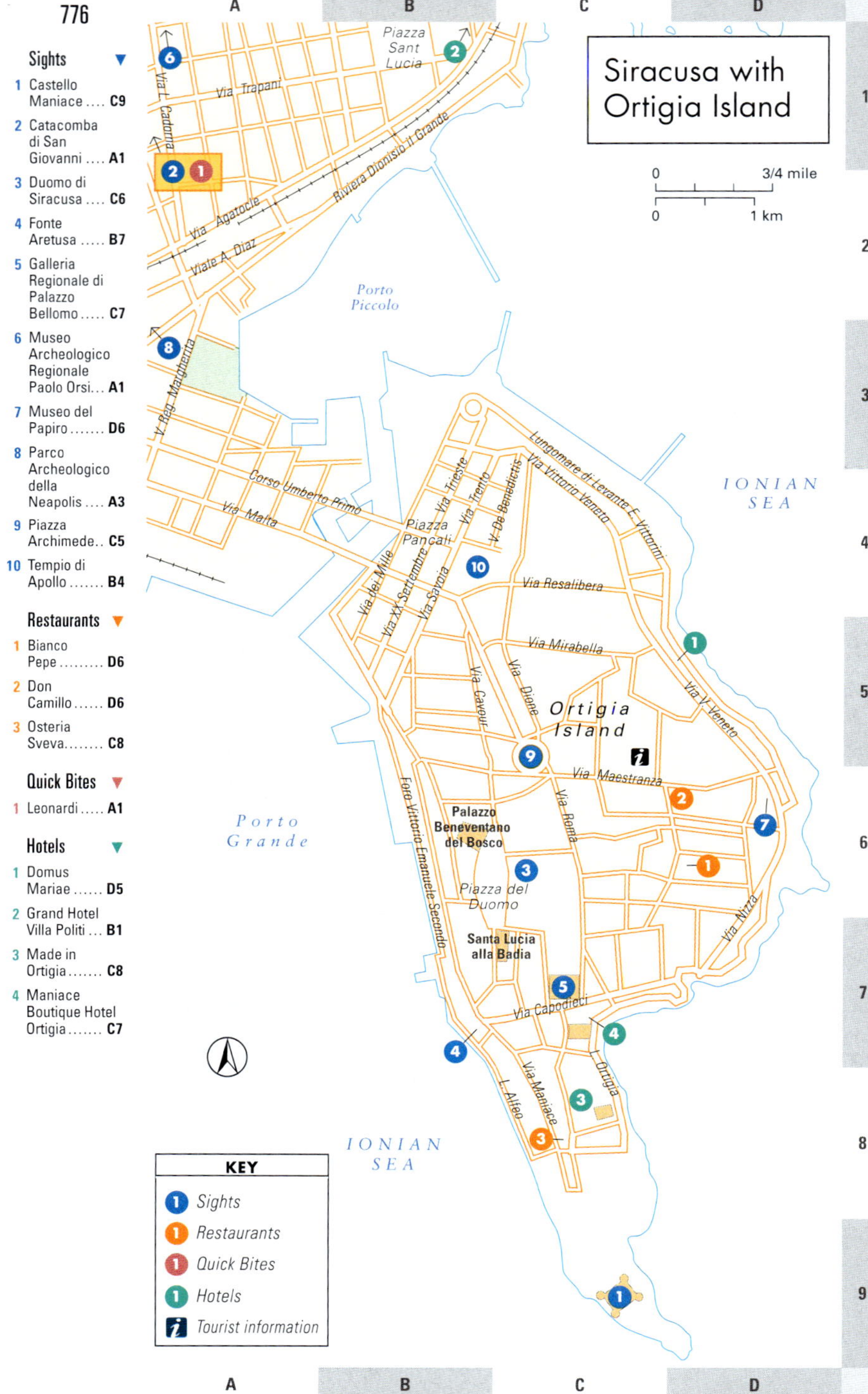

Siracusa with Ortigia Island
Sights
1 Castello Maniace C9
2 Catacomba di San Giovanni A1
3 Duomo di Siracusa C6
4 Fonte Aretusa B7
5 Galleria Regionale di Palazzo Bellomo C7
6 Museo Archeologico Regionale Paolo Orsi... A1
7 Museo del Papiro D6
8 Parco Archeologico della Neapolis A3
9 Piazza Archimede.. C5
10 Tempio di Apollo B4
Restaurants
1 Bianco Pepe D6
2 Don Camillo D6
3 Osteria Sveva........ C8
Quick Bites
1 Leonardi A1
Hotels
1 Domus Mariae D5
2 Grand Hotel Villa Politi ... B1
3 Made in Ortigia C8
4 Maniace Boutique Hotel Ortigia C7
KEY
Sights
Restaurants
Quick Bites
Hotels
Tourist information
0 3/4 mile
0 1 km
A B C D
1 2 3 4 5 6 7 8 9
Piazza Sant Lucia
Via Trapani
Via L. Cadorna
Riviera Dionisio il Grande
Via Agatocle
Viale A. Diaz
Porto Piccolo
V. Reg. Margherita
Corso Umberto Primo
Via Malta
Lungomare di Levante E. Vittorini
Via Vittorio Veneto
Via Trieste
Via Trento
V. De Benedictis
Piazza Pancali
Via dei Mille
Via XX Settembre
Via Savoia
Via Resalibera
Via Mirabella
Via Cavour
Via Dione
Ortigia Island
Via V. Veneto
Via Maestranza
Via Roma
IONIAN SEA
Porto Grande
Foro Vittorio Emanuele Secondo
Palazzo Beneventano del Bosco
Piazza del Duomo
Via Nizza
Santa Lucia alla Badia
Via Capodieci
L. Ortigia
Via Maniace
L. Alfeo
IONIAN SEA

Museo Archeologico Regionale Paolo Orsi
HISTORY MUSEUM | The impressive collection of Siracusa's splendid if scruffy archaeological museum is organized by region and time period around a central atrium and ranges from Neolithic pottery to fine Greek statues and vases. Compare the Landolina Venus—a headless goddess of love who rises out of the sea in measured modesty (a 1st-century-AD Roman copy of the Greek original)—with the much earlier (300 BC) elegant Greek statue of Hercules in Section C. Of a completely different style is a marvelous fanged Gorgon, its tongue sticking out, that once adorned the cornice of the Temple of Athena to ward off evildoers. It's a massive collection so be prepared to be fatigued at some point while walking around the disheveled space-station-esque modernist (1961) complex. ✉ *Viale Teocrito 66, Tyche* ☎ *0931/489514* 🌐 *www.aditusculture.com* 🎟 *€10; combined ticket with Parco Archeologico della Neapolis €22* ⏲ *Closed Mon.*

★ **Parco Archeologico della Neapolis**
RUINS | Siracusa is most famous for its dramatic set of Greek and Roman ruins, which are considered to be some of the best archaeological sites in all of Italy and should be combined with a stop at the Museo Archeologico. If the park is closed, go up Viale G. Rizzo from Viale Teracati to the belvedere overlooking the ruins, which are floodlit at night.

Before the park's ticket booth is the gigantic Ara di Ierone (Altar of Hieron), which was once used by the Greeks for spectacular sacrifices involving hundreds of animals. The first attraction in the park is the Latomia del Paradiso (Quarry of Paradise), a lush tropical garden full of palm and citrus trees. This series of quarries served as prisons for the defeated Athenians, who were enslaved; the quarries once rang with the sound of their chisels and hammers. At one end is the famous Orecchio di Dionisio (Ear of Dionysius), with an ear-shape entrance and unusual acoustics inside, as you'll hear if you clap your hands. The legend is that Dionysius used to listen in at the top of the quarry to hear what the enslaved people were plotting below.

The Teatro Greco is the chief monument in the Archaeological Park. Indeed it's one of Sicily's greatest classical sites and the most complete Greek theater surviving from antiquity. Climb to the top of the seating area (which could accommodate 15,000) for a fine view: all the seats converge upon a single point—the stage—which has the natural scenery and the sky as its backdrop. Hewn out of the hillside rock in the 5th century BC, the theater saw the premieres of the plays of Aeschylus, and Greek tragedies are still performed here every year in May and June. Above and behind the theater runs the Via dei Sepulcri, in which streams of running water flow through a series of Greek sepulchres.

The well-preserved and striking Anfiteatro Romano (Roman Amphitheater) reveals much about the differences between the Greek and Roman personalities. Where drama in the Greek theater was a kind of religious ritual, the Roman amphitheater emphasized the spectacle of combative sports and the circus. This arena is one of the largest of its kind and was built around the 2nd century AD. The corridor where gladiators and beasts entered the ring is still intact, and the seats (some of which still bear the occupants' names) were hauled in and constructed on the site from huge slabs of limestone. ✉ *Viale Teocrito, entrance on Via Agnello, Archaeological Zone* ☎ *0931/489511* 🌐 *www.aditusculture.com* 🎟 *€16.50, combined ticket with Museo Archeologico €22.*

Coffee and Quick Bites

Leonardi
$ | **BAKERY** | For some great Sicilian cakes and ice cream on your way to the Archaeological Park, visit this bar-cum- *pasticceria*. It's popular with locals, especially on Sunday for a late breakfast and takeaway golden trays of exquisite pastries for lunch, so you may have to line up for your cakes. **Known for:** great coffee and cakes; a favorite of locals; handy location near the Archaeological Park. *Average main: €4* *Viale Teocrito 123, Tyche* *0931/61411* *pasticcerialeonardi.com.*

Hotels

Grand Hotel Villa Politi
$ | **HOTEL** | Winston Churchill, European royalty, and other VIPs have frequented the grand 18th-century Villa Politi, and although it's now a little faded, it retains a sense of elegance with rococo furnishings alongside basic modern luxuries like comfy beds. **Pros:** handy for the Neapolis archaeological site; free parking in the hotel lot; expansive outdoor pool and nearby private beach. **Cons:** a fair distance from the sights of Ortigia; not many restaurants in the neighborhood; not as sparkling and fresh as in the past. *Rooms from: €145* *Via M. Politi 2, Archaeological Zone* *0931/412121* *www.villapoliti.com* *100 rooms* *Free Breakfast.*

Performing Arts

Teatro Greco (*Greek Theater*)
THEATER | From early May to mid-July, Siracusa's ancient Teatro Greco stages performances of classical tragedy and comedy. Tickets begin from €30. The ticket office is at *Corso Matteotti 29*, in Ortigia. *Via del Teatro Greco, Archaeological Zone* *0931/487248 ticket office* *www.indafondazione.org.*

Ortigia

Sights

Castello Maniace
CASTLE/PALACE | The southern tip of Ortigia island is occupied by this castle built by Frederick II (1194–1250), from which there are fine sea views (until recently, it was an army barracks). The grounds (with bar) are open to the public and have become a popular spot for picnics and lunch breaks. Highlights of the castle are the vaulted main hall and the cannon emplacements in the basement—at their most evocative on stormy days when you can hear the waves crashing against the walls. Contemporary art shows, usually featuring sculpture, are staged in the cathedral-like interiors and even in the surrounding waters. *Via del Castello Maniace 51, Ortigia* *0931/4508211* *www.aditusculture.com* *€5; €9 with exhibition.*

★ **Duomo di Siracusa**
CHURCH | Siracusa's Duomo is an archive of more than 2,000 years of island history, and has creatively incorporated ruins through the many time periods it has survived, starting with the bottommost, where excavations have unearthed remnants of Sicily's distant past, when the Siculi inhabitants worshipped their deities here. During the 5th century BC (the same time Agrigento's Temple of Concord was built), the Greeks erected a temple to Athena over it, and in the 7th century, Siracusa's first Christian cathedral was built on top of the Greek structure. The massive columns of the original Greek temple were incorporated into the present structure and are clearly visible, embedded in the exterior wall along Via Minerva. The Greek columns were also used to dramatic advantage inside, where on one side they form chapels connected by elegant wrought-iron gates. The Baroque facade, added in the 18th century, displays a harmonious

rhythm of concaves and convexes. In front, the sun-kissed stone piazza is encircled by pink and white oleanders and elegant buildings ornamented with filigree grillwork, and is typically filled with frolicking children and street musicians. Check with the tourist office for guided tours of its underground tunnels, which are located to the right when you stand facing the cathedral. ✉ *Piazza del Duomo, Ortigia* ☎ *0931/65328* 🌐 *arcidiocesi.siracusa.it/chiesa-cattedrale* 🎟 *€2.*

Fonte Aretusa

FOUNTAIN | A freshwater spring, the Fountain of Arethusa sits next to the sea, studded with Egyptian papyrus that's reportedly natural. This anomaly is explained by a Greek legend that tells how the nymph Arethusa was changed into a fountain by the goddess Artemis (Diana) when she tried to escape the advances of the river god Alpheus. She fled from Greece, into the sea, with Alpheus in close pursuit, and emerged in Sicily at this spring. It's said if you throw a cup into the Alpheus River in Greece, it will emerge here at this fountain, which is home to a few tired ducks and some faded carp—but no cups. If you want to stand right by the fountain, you need to gain admission through the aquarium; otherwise look down on it from Largo Aretusa. ✉ *Largo Aretusa, Ortigia* ✣ *Off promenade along harbor* ☎ *0931/65861* 🌐 *www.fontearetusasiracusa.it* 🎟 *€5* ⏲ *Closed Tues.*

Galleria Regionale di Palazzo Bellomo

ART MUSEUM | Palazzo Bellomo looks unlike any other palace in Ortigia, a formidable 13th-century building, whose austere minimalist facade (with scarcely a window) could almost seem contemporary but dates from a time when Sicily was part of the Holy Roman Empire. Conflicts between Emperor Frederick II and the Pope were rife—the Pope was encouraging the mercantile cities Venice and Genoa to make war on Sicily, promising Siracusa as prize. That defense was paramount is not surprising. The Gothic upper floor was added, along with the courtyard—a perfect Shakespearean film set—in the 15th century. Highlight of the collection is an Annunciation by Antonello da Messina, painted for a church in Palazzolo Acreide, with the Hyblaean mountains visible through the windows behind the angel and the Madonna. Early Christian sculpture and a fine collection of altarpieces and icons are fascinating evidence of the enduring Byzantine and Gothic influence in Sicily. While the rest of Italy was swept by the Renaissance, Siracusa's artists were still painting heavily stylized Byzantine or Gothic works. ✉ *Via Capodieci 14, Ortigia* ☎ *0931/69511* 🌐 *aditusculture.com* 🎟 *€9* ⏲ *Closed Mon.*

Museo del Papiro

SPECIALTY MUSEUM | Housed in the 16th-century former convent of Sant'Agostino, the small but intriguing Papyrus Museum uses informative exhibits and videos to demonstrate how papyri are prepared from reeds and then painted—an ancient tradition in the city. Siracusa, it seems, has the only climate outside the Nile Valley in which the papyrus plant—from which the word "paper" comes—thrives. ✉ *Via Nizza 14, Ortigia* ☎ *0931/22100* 🌐 *www.museodelpapiro.it* 🎟 *€5* ⏲ *Often closed for conferences and sporadic hours, so call ahead.*

Piazza Archimede

PLAZA/SQUARE | The center of this piazza has a Baroque fountain, the Fontana di Diana, festooned with fainting sea nymphs and dancing jets of water. Look for the Chiaramonte-style **Palazzo Montalto,** an arched-window gem just off the piazza on Via Montalto. ✉ *Piazza Archimede, Ortigia.*

Tempio di Apollo

RUINS | Scattered through the piazza just across the bridge to Ortigia are the ruins of a temple dedicated to Apollo, which dates back to the 6th century BC. A model of this is in the Museo Archeologico.

In fact, little of this noble Doric temple remains except for some crumbled walls and shattered columns; the window in the south wall belongs to a Norman church that was built much later on the same spot. *Largo XXV Luglio, Ortigia* *Free.*

Restaurants

Bianco Pepe

$$ | **PIZZA** | With tables on one of Ortigia's most picturesque piazzas—right below the rose-window of the roofless church of San Giovannino—the pizza chef here creates magnificent light crisp, blistered pizzas made of a tasty dough slow-risen for 48 hours. There's a dazzling and inspired choice, but the best pizzas are those with gourmet toppings—San Daniele prosciutto, buffalo mozzarella, burrata, chopped cherry tomatoes, homemade pesto, and even raw prawns, smoked tuna, and thyme-infused octopus—added as soon as the pizza base leaves the oven. **Known for:** pizza with burrata, cherry tomatoes, and homemade pesto; romantic but casual outdoor dining on a beautiful piazza; inventive, original, and delicious gourmet pizza. *Average main: €15* *Piazza del Precursore 7–9, Ortigia* *0931/1852406* *www.facebook.com/biancopepe.pepe* *No lunch.*

★ Don Camillo

$$ | **SICILIAN** | A gracious series of delicately arched stone rooms at Giovanni Guarneri's famed eatery, which opened in 1985, are lined with wine bottles and sepia-toned images of old Ortigia. It's all about the freshest seafood and inspired creativity here: from the historic Radici tasting menu sample for instance, a 1986-classic spaghetti *delle serene* (with sea urchin and shrimp in butter), or partake in a special from 1999, seared tuna with red and green bell pepper dipping sauces. **Known for:** top-quality fish, meat, and vegetarian ingredients; impeccable, engaging service; exquisite tasting menus. *Average main: €25* *Via Maestranza 96, Ortigia* *0931/67133* *www.ristorantedoncamillosiracusa.it* *Closed Sun., 2 wks in Jan., and 2 wks in July.*

Osteria Sveva

$ | **SICILIAN** | At this slow-food tavern, conveniently located right behind the Castello Maniace, you can sit back and enjoy both surf and turf dishes in the vaulted interior or—even better—on the outdoor terrace. One major plus is that you can order half portions of several pasta dishes or opt for a *secondo,* like the unusual *pesce in crosta di patate* (grilled fish in a potato crust)—all served on hand-painted ceramic ware. **Known for:** homestyle Sicilian dishes; chirpy owner Emmanuele; charming setting on a square. *Average main: €18* *Piazza Federico di Svevia 1, Ortigia* *0931/24663* *www.instagram.com/osteriasveva* *Closed Wed., Jan., and Nov.*

Hotels

★ Domus Mariae

$ | **HOTEL** | On Ortigia's eastern shore, this hotel, in an unusual twist, is owned by Ursuline nuns, who help to make the mood placid and peaceful, but the accommodations are simple rather than monastic. **Pros:** decent breakfast; gorgeous sea views and rooftop terrace; enthusiastic staff. **Cons:** stairs to climb; not much street parking near the hotel; not all rooms spacious or with sea views. *Rooms from: €170* *Via Vittorio Veneto 76, Ortigia* *0931/60087* *www.domusmariaebenessere.com* *12 rooms* *Free Breakfast.*

Made in Ortigia

$ | **APARTMENT** | Down a narrow lane near the castello, you'll find these four good-value, simply furnished apartments of various sizes with kitchenettes. **Pros:** living like a local; near restaurants, the sea, and the castello; good value, especially in low season. **Cons:** studio may feel cramped; spiral staircases in two apartments tricky for some; Studio 2 bathroom smells musty and needs a refurb. *Rooms from: €110 Via Salomone, 35/46, Ortigia 320/1982946 www.casavacanzaortigia.com 4 apartments No Meals.*

★ **Maniace Boutique Hotel Ortigia**
$$ | HOTEL | Opened in 2024, the UNA group's stunning contemporary renovation of this lungomare limestone palazzo offers stylish public spaces and individual guest rooms, some with vibrant *cassata*-inspired pop art, others with antiquity-inspired mosaics. **Pros:** sea views across the from Cala Rossa beach; top-quality breakfast choice in chic bar area; superb reception, bar, and breakfast staff. **Cons:** design ethos may not be for everyone; prices bound to rise once established; poor mobile-phone reception in the lobby. *Rooms from: €225 Lungomare d'Ortigia 13, Ortigia 371/5233520 maniaceboutiquehotel.com 21 rooms Free Breakfast.*

Shopping

★ **Ortigia Street Market**
MARKET | This historic food market is still the daily shopping center for residents of Ortigia and mainland Siracusa. Seafood stalls display the catch of the day, ranging from local clams that you'll find in most restaurants to sea urchins that normally only appear on the more expensive menus. Even in the colder months, the vegetable and fruit stalls are still vibrant and inviting. One thing to look out for is the local Pachino tomato. It has protected status and can be found fresh, dried, or reduced to a gloriously intense thick paste called *strattu*, dried in the sun, which adds fantastic deep flavors to soups and pasta sauces. Intertwined within the stalls are several local bars where you can rest and take in the hustle and bustle of local Italian food culture. The market is open every day except for Sunday, from 7 am to 1:45 pm. *Vicolo Bagnara, Ortigia.*

Catania

210 km (130 miles) southeast of Palermo, 60 km (37 miles) north of Siracusa.

The chief wonder of Catania, Sicily's second city, is that it's there at all. Nearly every century has seen its share of tragedy for the Catanesi: a Greek tyrant that cast the population out, another who sold the majority of the citizens into slavery, Carthaginians who drove the successive occupants away once again. Each time, the city was rebuilt, only to meet more destruction. The plague hit hard in the Middle Ages, severely decimating the population. Mount Etna erupted in 1669, with a mile-wide stream of lava covering part of the city, and just 25 years after that, a disastrous earthquake forced Catania to begin again.

Today Catania is in the midst of yet another resurrection—this time from crime, filth, and urban decay. Although the city remains loud and full of traffic, signs of gentrification are everywhere. The elimination of vehicles from the Piazza del Duomo and the main artery of Via Etnea, and the cleaning of many of the historic buildings have added to its newfound charm. Home to what is arguably Sicily's best university, Catania is full of youthful exuberance, which comes through in its designer bistros, the chic osterias that serve wine, and the trendy boutiques that have cropped up all over town. Even more impressive is the vibrant cultural life.

GETTING HERE AND AROUND

Catania is well connected by bus and train with Messina, Taormina, Siracusa, Enna, and Palermo. The airport of Fontanarossa serves as a transportation hub for the eastern side of the island. From here you can get buses to most major destinations without going into the city center. The Alibus runs a loop from the airport through the city center (*€4; approximately every 25 mins*).

Within the city, use the AMTS bus service (*€1, €2.50 all day* *www.amts.ct.it*), which also connects to outlying areas such as Aci Castello. The website can be difficult to use, but the AMT Catania app offers useful route suggestions, online ticket purchasing, and timetables—and it's available in English. Catania also has an underground Metro line (*€1, €2 all day* *www.circumetnea.it*), but with only 10 stations centered on the downtown area, it's often easier to just walk.

From the Borgo station in Catania you can circle Mount Etna on the single-track Circumetnea railway line, which runs to Riposto, with a change at Randazzo. The one-way trip takes about 3½ hours, with departures every 90 minutes or so. After you've made the trip, you can get back on the conventional rail service between Riposto and Catania.

VISITOR INFORMATION

Catania Tourism Office (*www.comjune.catania.it/la-citta/turismo*)

Sights

Fontana dell'Amenano

FOUNTAIN | The underground Amenano River flows beneath much of Catania. You can glimpse it at the Fontana dell'Amenano, a Carrara marble fountain on the Piazza del Duomo that was built in 1867. It's a popular meeting point and tourist attraction. However, one of the best places to experience the river is at the bar-restaurant A Putia dell'Ostello (*Piazza Currò 6* *095/7233010* *www.agorahostel.com*). Here you can sit at a lantern-lit underground table as the water swirls through. If you're not planning to stay for a drink, someone from the bar will sell you a €1 ticket to walk into the cavelike seating area. Aside from the underground river, the bar area aboveground is a lively, fun spot to hang out on a Monday evening when many other places are closed. *Piazza del Duomo, Catania.*

Cattedrale di Sant'Agata (Duomo)

CHURCH | Giovanni Vaccarini designed the contrasting black lava and white limestone facade of city's cathedral, which dominates the Piazza del Duomo and which houses the tomb of composer Vincenzo Bellini. Also of note are the three apses of lava that survive from the original Norman structure and a fresco from 1675 in the sacristy that portrays Catania's submission to Etna's eruption. Guided tours of the cathedral, which is dedicated to Catania's protector, are available in English if reserved in advance. The cathedral's treasures are on view in the Museo Diocesano Catania (*www.museodiocesanocatania.com*), and underneath the cathedral are the ruins of Greco-Roman baths. *Piazza del Duomo, bottom end of Via Etnea, Catania* *095/320044, 339/4859942 mobile, for tours* *www.cattedralecatania.it* *Museum €7, sacristy €3, baths €5; combined ticket €10.*

Centro Storico

HISTORIC DISTRICT | Black lava stone from Etna, combined with largely Baroque architecture, give Catania's historic center a very distinctive feel. After Catania's destruction by lava and earthquake at the end of the 17th century, the city was rebuilt and its informal mascot "U Liotru" (an elephant carved out of lava balancing an Egyptian obelisk) was placed outside the cathedral as a kind of talisman. This square also marks the entrance to Catania's famous *pescheria* (fish market) and is one of the few points in the city where you can see the Amenano River aboveground. Another point of interest is Via Garibaldi, which runs from Piazza del Duomo up toward the impressively huge Porta Garibaldi, a black-and-white triumphal arch built in 1768 to commemorate the marriage of Ferdinando I. Also of note in the center are Castello Ursino, which is now a museum, the Greco-Roman theater off Via Vittorio Emanuele II, the Roman amphitheater in Piazza Stesicoro, and the

Monastero dei Benedettini, now a part of the university. ✉ *Catania.*

Via Etnea

STREET | With the ever-looming volcano perfectly framed at the end of the road, this main street is lined with cafés and stores selling high-street jewelry, clothing, and shoes. At sunset, it plays host to one of Sicily's most enthusiastic passeggiatas, in which Catanesi of all ages take part. Starting in 2022, the central stretch became a pedestrianized zone, limiting all vehicle traffic. ✉ *Via Etnea, Catania.*

Restaurants

Oasi Frutti di Mare da Nitto

$$ | **SEAFOOD** | Located in the Ognina port, the little Nitto empire has exploded: what began as a mobile market in the 1960s (from the back of a Piaggio Ape) is now a standing fresh fish market and series of restaurants. Locals line up outside the little market to get their daily catch, while next door the fast-casual restaurant serves some of the best-prepared seafood in the area, including squid ink pastas, skewers of grilled fish, and raw seafood platters. **Known for:** vivacious atmosphere; tuna agrodolce, a sweet-and-sour tuna side dish studded with pine nuts and raisins; fresh-off-the-boat seafood. [$] *Average main: €20* ✉ *Piazza Mancini Battaglia 6, Catania* ☎ *095/491165* 🌐 *www.nittopescheria.it.*

Pamochã

$ | **ITALIAN** | An acronym for "Pane, Mortadella, and Champagne," Pamocha indeed specializes in bubbles, masterful salumi plates, all the bruschetta, and raw seafood towers of oysters, sweet red shrimp, tuna, and caviar. Typically the portions at this glam-meets-rustic café are small, making it perfect for aperitivo or a late-night snack (it's open until 2 am). **Known for:** French-grower Champagne; Instagram-worthy meat case; outside seating on a busy pedestrian street. [$] *Average main: €16* ✉ *Via Gemmellaro 46, Catania* ☎ *338/8158024* 🌐 *www.pamocha.it* ⏲ *Closed Tues. No lunch.*

Coffee and Quick Bites

Caffè del Duomo

$ | **CAFÉ** | Dive right into the hustle and bustle of Catania at Caffè del Duomo, which has handmade cookies and cakes and a great local atmosphere. The piazza-front location is the main draw, but the fantastic cannoli are another reason to stop for coffee and watch the world go by. **Known for:** great spot for people-watching; handmade treats; typical Sicilian breakfast. [$] *Average main: €5* ✉ *Piazza Duomo 11–13, Catania* ☎ *095/7150556* 🌐 *www.caffedelduomo-catania.com.*

★ **Scirocco Sicilian Fish Lab**

$ | **SEAFOOD** | In the heart of the fish market, you'll find the best fritto misto (fried seafood mix) in the area. Walk up to the little counter on the stone balcony overlooking the action and place your order for a paper cone of fried seafood made with the lightest and crispiest batter. **Known for:** unique seafood sandwiches called tramezzini; superfresh seafood; fast service. [$] *Average main: €7* ✉ *Piazza Alonzo di Benedetto 7, Catania* ☎ *095/8361194* 🌐 *www.sciroccolab.com.*

Hotels

★ **Palazzo Marletta**

$$ | **HOTEL** | Baroque architecture punctuates the city, and one of the best ways to see it up close is with a stay at Palazzo Marletta, a private palace turned plush hotel. **Pros:** arrangement with a local car valet service for parking; copious breakfast; prime location just off the Duomo. **Cons:** not all rooms have a view of the Duomo; modern rooms lack some of the charm of historic ones; can be difficult to navigate the historic district if arriving by car. [$] *Rooms from: €288* ✉ *Via Erasmo Merletta 7, Catania* ☎ *095/6680166*

www.palazzomarletta.it *7 rooms* *Free Breakfast.*

Palace Catania|Una Esperienze

$$ | **HOTEL** | For great views of Etna, this centrally located hotel overlooking Catania's main shopping street has a rooftop terrace where you can enjoy breakfast or take in the scenery during happy hour over a cocktail and antipasti buffet. **Pros:** amazing rooftop views; extremely central location; eager-to-please staff. **Cons:** bit of a generic feel; some noisy rooms; fee for parking. *Rooms from: €206* *Via Etnea 218, Catania* *095/2505111* *www.gruppouna.it* *94 rooms* *Free Breakfast.*

Acireale

6 km (4 miles) north of Aci Trezza, 16 km (10 miles) north of Catania.

Acireale sits amid a cluster of rocky pinnacles and lush lemon groves. The craggy coast is known as the Riviera dei Ciclopi, after the legend narrated in the *Odyssey* in which the blinded cyclops, Polyphemus, hurled boulders at the retreating Ulysses, thus creating spires of rock, or faraglioni (pillars of rock rising dramatically out of the sea). Tourism has barely taken off here, so it's a good destination if you feel like putting some distance between yourself and the busloads of tourists in Taormina, or if you are seeking an easy day trip from Catania. And though the beaches are rocky, there's good swimming here, too.

GETTING HERE AND AROUND

Buses arrive frequently from Taormina and Catania. Acireale is on the main coastal train route, though the station is a long walk south of the center. Local buses pass by every 20 minutes or so.

VISITOR INFORMATION

Acireale Tourism Office (*www.visitsicily.info/en/acireale*)

Sights

Belvedere di Santa Caterina

VIEWPOINT | Lord Byron (1788–1824) visited the Belvedere di Santa Caterina to look out over the Ionian Sea during his Italian wanderings. Today, the viewpoint is south of the old town, near the Terme di Acireale, off SS114, and is a tranquil spot for photos or quiet reflection on one of the several benches positioned toward the water. *Off SS114, Acireale.*

Duomo di Acireale (*Cattedrale Maria Santissima Annunziata*)

CHURCH | With its cupola and twin turrets, Acireale's cathedral is an extravagant Baroque construction dating from the 17th century. Look out for the 19th-century, horizontal sundial on the floor of the transept which incorporates the signs of the zodiac, and in the chapel to the right of the altar, the 17th-century silver statue of Santa Venera (patron saint of Acireale) by Mario D'Angelo. Climb up to the belvedere for stunning views. *Piazza del Duomo, Acireale* *095/601102* *www.diocesiacireale.it* *Tower access €2.50.*

Santa Maria La Scala

TOWN | A steep, half-hour walk (or a very twisty drive) from Acireale's center, this picturesque harbor, with lava stone steps leading to the water, is filled with fishermen unloading brightly colored boats. Inexpensive lunches are served in the many restaurants along the harbor; your fresh fish dish is priced by weight. *Santa Maria La Scala, Acireale* *www.visitsicily.info/en/santa-maria-la-scala.*

Restaurants

★ **La Grotta**

$$ | **SEAFOOD** | With its dining room set in a cave above the harbor of Santa Maria La Scala, this rustic trattoria specializes in seafood. Try the *insalata di mare* (a selection of delicately boiled fish served with lemon and olive oil), pasta with clams or cuttlefish ink, or fish grilled over

charcoal. **Known for:** the catch of the day; superfresh seafood; unique cave setting. $ *Average main: €27* ✉ *Via Scalo Grande 46, Acireale* ☎ *095/7648153* 🌐 *www.facebook.com/77saro* ⏲ *Closed Tues. and late Oct.–Nov.*

Coffee and Quick Bites

Gran Caffè Eldorado

$ | ICE CREAM | Delicious ice creams and granita *di mandorla* (almond granita) make Eldorado a must-visit when in Acireale. Just steps from the cathedral, it makes for a nice *pausa caffè* during a day of sightseeing. **Known for:** great ice creams; wonderful desserts; friendly staff. $ *Average main: €3* ✉ *Corso Umberto 3, Acireale* ☎ *347/9717926 mobile.*

Mount Etna

30 km (19 miles) northwest of Acireale, 35 km (22 miles) north of Catania, 64 km (40 miles) southwest of Taormina.

The first time you see Mount Etna, whether it's trailing clouds of smoke or emitting fiery streaks of lava, is certain to be unforgettable. The best-known symbol of Sicily and one of the world's major active volcanoes, Etna is the largest and highest volcano in Europe—the cone of the crater rises 11,014 feet above sea level. Etna is so important to locals that she's often affectionately called Mamma Etna. Although you'll get wonderful vantage points of Etna from Taormina, Castelmola, and Catania in particular, it also makes a rewarding day or overnight trip to see the mountain up close, with a hike or climb; you can find routes suitable for every fitness level. It's also become a popular destination for wine lovers thanks to the many boutique wineries on its slopes; most accept visitors with an appointment.

The villages that surround Mount Etna make good bases for visiting nearby cities like Catania, Acireale, and Taormina. **Zafferana Etnea** is famous for orange-blossom honey and pizza *siciliana*; **Nicolosi,** at nearly 3,000 feet, is known as "La Porta dell'Etna" (the Door to Etna); the medieval village of **Milo** is known as the City of Wine; **Trecastagni** (the Three Chestnut Trees) has beautiful Renaissance churches; **Randazzo,** the largest of the surrounding towns, sells objects made of lava, wood, and wrought iron at its market; and **Bronte** is Italy's center of pistachio cultivation.

GETTING HERE AND AROUND

From Catania you can circle the lower slopes of Mount Etna by the Circumetnea railway, but it's easier and quicker to access these foothills either by car or bus. Getting to the more interesting, higher levels requires taking one of the stout four-wheel-drive minibuses that leave from Piano Provenzana on the north side and from Rifugio Sapienza on the south side. A cable car, called the Funivia dell'Etna, from Rifugio Sapienza (✉ *Piazzale Funivia* 🌐 *www.funiviaetna.com*) takes you part of the way.

TOURS

★ Etna Experience

ADVENTURE TOURS | Your answer to all things outdoors in the area, the company offers wide range of excursions around Etna, including full-day hikes to volcanic caves and the Alcantara gorges, half-day sunset hikes, wine-tasting jaunts, and the signature Mount Etna Summit tour, which includes high-level trekking up to 10,800 feet to get you as close to the crater as humanly possible. ✉ *Piazza Federico di Svevia 32, Catania* ☎ *349/3053021* 🌐 *www.etnaexperience.com* 🎫 *From €44.*

Eastern Sicily, the Tyrrhenian Coast, and the Aeolian Islands
TO NAPLES
TO NAPLES
Stromboli
TO TROPEA
AEOLIAN ISLANDS
Panarea
Alicudi
Filicudi
Salina
Lipari
TYRRHENIAN SEA
Vulcano
0
20 mi
0
20 km
Pescina di Venere
Capo di Milazzo
Milazzo
Golfo di Milazzo
Villa San Giovanni
Capo D'orlando
St Agata di Militello
Messina
Patti
Cefalù
Caldura
TYRRHENIAN COAST
Reggio Calabria
Pizzo Carbonara
Randazzo
Castelmola
Taormina
Linguaglossa
Giardini-Naxos
Bronte
Mount Etna
Riposto
Nicosia
Milo
Giarre
Barone di Villagrande
Adrano
Zafferara Etnea
Trecastagni
Santa Maria La Scala
Biancavilla
Nicolosi
Acireale
Enna
Paterno
Aci Castello
Caltanisetta
Aci Trezza
Catania
Villa Romana del Casale
Piazza Armerina
Golfo di Catania
Casale
Mazzarino
Palagonia
Agnone
Lentini
Caltagirone
Augusta
Vizzini
IONIAN SEA
Euryalus
Gela
Palazzolo Acreide
Siracusa with Ortigia Island
see detail map
Golfo di Gela
Vittoria
Comiso
Ragusa
Noto
Avola
Modica
Golfo di Noto
KEY
Ferry lines
Ski Area
Scicli
Pachino
TO MALTA
MEDITERRANEAN SEA
Capo Passero

Etna Wine School

FOOD AND DRINK TOURS | For a comprehensive overview of the wine world on Mount Etna, look to Benjamin North Spencer, an American-born wine expert, Etna resident, and author of *The New Wines of Mount Etna*. He and his team offer half-day and full-day courses suitable for professionals and casual enthusiasts alike. You'll visit a vineyard, taste wines based on Carricante and Nerello Mascalese grapes, eat local delicacies, and learn about Etna wine-making traditions at the source. Transportation is not included in these tours but is an additional cost. ☎ *347/3348782* 🌐 *www.etnawineschool.com* 🎫 *½-day tours from €140.*

Gruppo Guide Alpine Etna Sud

ADVENTURE TOURS | Led by highly qualified alpine guides, excursions leave from the Rifugio Sapienza, near the cable car station. The price includes the ascent by cable car followed by a trip by Jeep to 9,514 feet, from where you continue on foot to the Summit Craters, at 10,958 feet, then down back along slopes of volcanic ash to the cable car station for the descent. Sunset trips, easier excursions for families with children, and two- and five-day treks can also be organized. Their website is in English, and English-speaking guides are available. ✉ *Piazza Vittorio Emanuele 43, Nicolosi* ☎ *095/7914755* 🌐 *www.etnaguide.eu* 🎫 *From €120.*

VISITOR INFORMATION

Nicolosi Tourism Office (🌐 *www.nicolosietna.it*)

Sights

★ Barone di Villagrande

WINERY | At the oldest winery on Etna, the expansive terrace shaded by oak trees looks out over vineyards and down to the sea. The staff offers friendly and informative tours (with excellent English) followed by a tasting of five wines with food pairings or a more formal lunch. Reservations are required. There are also four charming guest rooms overlooking the vineyards for overnight stays (minimum two nights). ✉ *Via del Bosco 25, Milo* ☎ *095/7082175* 🌐 *www.villagrande.it* 🎫 *Tours and tastings from €45.*

★ Mount Etna

VOLCANO | Affectionally called Idda (or "she" in Sicilian dialect), Etna is basically always active, and occasionally there are airspace closures due to the spewing ash. But for the locals who live in her shadow, Etna is not some ever-present doomsday reminder. She's a living part of the dynamic landscape, loved and revered.

In 387 BC, Plato sailed in just to catch a glimpse of it; in the 9th century AD, the first granita of all time was shaved off its snowy slopes; in 1669, it erupted continuously for four months and lava flows reached Catania; and in the 21st century, the volcano still grabs headlines on an annual basis. Significantly notable eruptions have occurred in the modern era, such as in 1971 (when lava buried the Etna Observatory), in 1981 (when the village of Randazzo narrowly missed destruction), in 2001 (when there was a large flank eruption), in 2002 (when a column of ash spewed that could be seen from space), and in 2008 (when the eruption lasted 417 days and triggered some 200 earthquakes). In February and March 2021, she erupted 11 times in a matter of three weeks, scattering windblown ash throughout the towns below, including Catania. July and August of 2024 saw major eruptions, disrupting flights at Catania airport. Traveling to the proximity of the crater depends on Mount Etna's temperament, but you can walk up and down the enormous lava dunes and wander over its moonlike surface of dead craters. The rings of vegetation change markedly as you rise, with vineyards and pine trees gradually giving way to birch forests and growths of broom and lichen. ✉ *Parco dell'Etna* ☎ *095/821111* 🌐 *www.parcoetna.it.*

Restaurants

★ Cave Ox

$ | ITALIAN | This casual osteria is frequented by local winemakers who come for pizza dinners and rustic daily lunch specials, but most visitors are smitten with the small but amazing cellar focused on Etna natural wines. Everything's fresh, simple, and delicious—and made to pair with one of the delightful wines suggested by owner and wine enthusiast Sandro. **Known for:** superlative selection of natural wines from Etna; filling lunches and pizza dinners; local winemaker crowd. *$ Average main: €13 ✉ Via Nazionale Solicchiata 159, Castiglione di Sicilia ☎ 0942/986171 🌐 www.caveox.it ⏲ Closed Tues.*

★ Shalai Restaurant

$$$$ | MODERN ITALIAN | You might not expect to find a thoroughly contemporary restaurant on the slopes of Mount Etna, but Shalai, in the boutique hotel of the same name, is truly a modern oasis, where young chef Giovanni Santoro prepares updated and beautifully presented versions of Sicilian classics. For the full Michelin-starred experience, choose from the six-course meat or fish tasting menus; to finish, the deconstructed cannoli are a true delight. **Known for:** innovative modern Sicilian dishes; delicious tasting menus; excellent wine list. *$ Average main: €70 ✉ Shalai, Via Marconi 25, Linguaglossa ☎ 095/643128 🌐 www.shalai.it ⏲ No lunch weekdays.*

Hotels

★ Monaci delle Terre Nere

$$$$ | HOTEL | This cozy boutique hotel in the foothills of Mount Etna features spacious rustic-chic rooms on a working organic farm with vineyards, along with an elegant Slow Food–inspired restaurant. **Pros:** eco-conscious atmosphere and policies; delicious food and wine; pool with countryside views. **Cons:** accommodations may be a little quirky for some; no televisions in bedrooms; bathrooms can be quite minimalist. *$ Rooms from: €603 ✉ Via Monaci, Zafferana Etnea ☎ 095/7083638, 38/2257939 mobile 🌐 www.monacidelleterrenere.it ⏲ Closed Jan.–mid-Mar. 27 rooms Free Breakfast.*

Taormina

35 km (22 miles) north of Riposto, 54 km (34 miles) northeast of Catania.

The view of the sea and Mount Etna from Taormina's jagged, cactus-covered cliffs is as close to perfection as a panorama can get—especially on clear days, when the snowcapped volcano's white puffs of smoke rise against the blue sky. Even when overrun with tourists, its natural beauty is hard to dispute. Writers have extolled Taormina's charms almost since it was founded in the 6th century BC by Greeks from nearby Naxos; Goethe and D. H. Lawrence were among its well-known enthusiasts. The town's boutique-lined main streets lose their charm pretty quickly, but the many hiking paths that wind through the beautiful hills surrounding Taormina promise a timeless alternative. A trip up to stunning Castelmola (whether on foot or by car) should also be on your itinerary. It should be noted that in general, Taormina becomes a ghost town in January and February, and almost every hotel and restaurant is closed.

GETTING HERE AND AROUND

Buses from Messina or Catania arrive near the center of Taormina, while trains from these towns pull in at the picturesque station, at the bottom of the hill. Local buses bring you the rest of the way. A cable car takes passengers up the hill from a parking lot about 2 km (1 mile) north of the train station.

VISITOR INFORMATION

Taormina Tourist Office (🌐 *www.comune.taormina.me.it*)

Sights

Casa Cuseni

HISTORIC HOME | Luminaries such as Picasso, Bertrand Russell, Ernest Hemingway, and Tennessee Williams all fell for the charms of this house, which from 1947 was set up as a hotel for writers and artists. It was run for over 50 years by Daphne Phelps, the niece of the painter Robert Kitson, who with the artist Frank Brangwyn designed and built the villa in the early 1900s. A guided tour reveals its stories and the works of art donated by artists. The dining room holds distinctive frescoes and furniture by Frank Brangwyn, and the library has the desk where Roald Dahl wrote *Charlie and the Chocolate Factory*. There are five antiques-filled rooms where guests can stay. ✉ *Via Leonardo da Vanci, Taormina* ☏ *0942/558111* 🌐 *www.casacuseni.it* 🎟 *Tours daily, reserve at least a week ahead; €20* 🕒 *Closed Nov.–Mar.*

Castello Saraceno

VIEWPOINT | An unrelenting 20-minute walk up the Via Crucis footpath takes you to the church of the Madonna della Rocca, hollowed out of the limestone rock. Above it towers the 1,000-year-old stone walls of Castello Saraceno, which is built on the site of earlier Greek and Roman fortifications. Although the gate to the castle has been locked for decades, it's worth the climb just for the panoramic views. ✉ *Monte Tauro, Taormina.*

Palazzo Corvaja

NOTABLE BUILDING | Many of Taormina's 14th- and 15th-century palaces have been carefully preserved. Especially beautiful is the crenellated Palazzo Corvaja, with characteristic black-lava and white-limestone inlays and the seat of the first Sicilian parliament in 1411. The interior is presently closed. ✉ *Largo Santa Caterina, Taormina.*

★ Teatro Greco

RUINS | The Greeks put a premium on finding impressive locations to stage their dramas, such as Taormina's hillside Teatro Greco. Beyond the columns, you can see the town's rooftops spilling down the hillside, the arc of the coastline, and Mount Etna in the distance. The theater was built during the 3rd century BC and rebuilt by the Romans during the 2nd century AD. Its acoustics are exceptional: even today a stage whisper can be heard in the last rows. In summer, many music and dance performances are held in the Teatro Greco after sunset, when the marvelous vistas of the sparkling Ionian Sea are shrouded in darkness, but the glow of Sicily's most famous volcano can sometimes be seen in the distance. ✉ *Via Teatro Greco, Taormina* ☏ *0942/23220* 🌐 *www.aditusculture.com* 🎟 *€12.*

★ Villa Comunale

GARDEN | Stroll down Via Bagnoli Croce from the main Corso Umberto to the Villa Comunale to enjoy the stunning views from the seaside city's best terrace walkways. Also known as the Parco Duca di Cesarò, the lovely public gardens were designed by Florence Trevelyan Cacciola, a Scottish lady "invited" to leave England following a romantic liaison with the future Edward VII (1841–1910). Arriving in Taormina in 1889, she married a local professor and devoted herself to the gardens, filling them with native Mediterranean and exotic plants, ornamental pavilions, and fountains. ✉ *Via Bagnoli Croce, Taormina.*

Beaches

Mazzarò

BEACH | Below the main city of Taormina is Mazzarò (reached via a cable car called the funivia), where summertime beachgoers jostle for space on a pebble beach against the scenic backdrop of the aptly named Isola Bella. The first section of beach is reserved for expensive resorts but the far end, next to Isola Bella, has a large free area. The tiny "beautiful island" of Isola Bella was once the private residence of Florence Trevelyan and now houses a small exhibition. This and the surrounding grottoes and nature reserve can be visited by walking or paddling across a narrow strip of sand. **Amenities:** none. **Best for:** walking. *Taormina Mare, Taormina* *www.parconaxostaormina.com* *€5 for Isola Bella.*

Restaurants

L'Arco dei Cappuccini

$$ | **SEAFOOD** | Just off Via Costantino Patricio, by the far side of the Cappuccini arch, lies this diminutive restaurant. Outdoor seating and an upstairs kitchen help make room for a few extra tables—a necessity, as locals are well aware that neither the price nor the quality is equaled elsewhere in town. **Known for:** fine dining; authentic local cooking; a great wine list. *Average main: €25* *Via Cappuccini 7, off Via Costantino Patricio, Taormina* *0942/480750* *www.arcodeicappuccini.com* *Closed late Nov.*

★ Trattoria Il Barcaiolo

$$ | **SEAFOOD** | Just behind the public beach in Mazzarò Bay, this intimate little terrace restaurant is shrouded by an enormous old grapevine and looks out onto postcard-perfect views of paradise. Since 1981, the family-owned trattoria has been serving pristine seafood to discerning locals and in-the-know tourists. **Known for:** extensive wine list; swordfish carpaccio with citrus and capers; cassata and cannoli for dessert. *Average main: €30* *Via Castelluccio 43, Taormina* *379/2089564* *www.barcaiolo.altervista.org* *Closed Tues. and late Nov.–March. No lunch.*

Coffee and Quick Bites

Pasticceria Etna

$ | **BAKERY** | Fans of marzipan will delight at the range of almond sweets on offer here in the shape of the ubiquitous *fico d'India* (prickly pear) and other fruit. A block of almond paste makes a good souvenir—you can bring it home to make an almond latte or granita. **Known for:** almond sweets; fresh cannoli; house-made granita. *Average main: €3* *Corso Umberto I 112, Taormina* *0942/24735* *www.pasticceriaetna.com.*

Hotels

★ Belmond Grand Hotel Timeo

$$$$ | **HOTEL** | On a princely perch overlooking the town, the Greek theater, and the bay, this truly grand hotel, Taormina's oldest, wears a graceful patina that suggests la dolce vita, with a splash of Baroque and a dash of Mediterranean design in the lobby, which has tile- and brickwork walls and vaulted ceilings. **Pros:** feeling of indulgence; amazing location with fantastic views; exemplary service. **Cons:** very expensive; lower category rooms only have partial views; spa is on the small side. *Rooms from: €1380* *Via Teatro Greco 59, Taormina* *0942/6270200* *www.belmond.com/grand-hotel-timeo-taormina* *Closed Jan.–mid-Mar.* *70 rooms* *Free Breakfast.*

★ Belmond Villa Sant'Andrea

$$$$ | **HOTEL** | **FAMILY** | In a prime location on its own private beach at Taormina Mare, this elegant hotel in a late-1800s villa offers phenomenal views of the water, attentive service, and luxurious and comfortable guest rooms. **Pros:** glorious private beach; flawless service; free shuttle service to Taormina town. **Cons:** limited on-site parking; spa is small; pricey food and drinks. *Rooms from: €1200* *Via Nazionale 137, Taormina* *0942/6271200* *www.belmond.com/villa-sant-andrea-taormina-mare* *Closed*

Nov.–late Mar. 70 rooms Free Breakfast.*

Hotel Villa Paradiso

$$ | HOTEL | On the edge of the town's historic center, overlooking lovely public gardens and facing the sea, this under-the-radar family-run hotel was renovated in 2023, but still maintains its antique furnishings, paintings, and Persian rugs, as well as its delightful service, good rooftop restaurant, and Etna views from many guest rooms. **Pros:** fab, bountiful table-service breakfast; shuttle bus to beach; great rooftop views. **Cons:** not all rooms have views; valet parking costs extra; shuttle bus is extra. *Rooms from: €350 Via Roma 2, Taormina 0942/23921 www.hotelvillaparadisotaormina.com Closed Nov. and Dec. 37 rooms Free Breakfast.*

San Domenico Palace, A Four Seasons Hotel

$$$$ | HOTEL | The sweeping views of the castle, the sea, and Mount Etna from this converted 14th-century Dominican monastery will linger in your mind, along with the equally memorable levels of luxury and wonderful food in the hotel's highly lauded restaurant, Principe Cerami. **Pros:** strong sense of history and grandeur; gorgeous infinity pool with amazing views; gorgeous grounds. **Cons:** very expensive parking and bar; events can be noisy; beach access through partner affiliates. *Rooms from: €2000 Piazza San Domenico 5, Taormina 0942/613111 www.fourseasons.com/taormina Closed mid-Nov.–Feb. 111 rooms Free Breakfast.*

Castelmola

5 km (3 miles) west of Taormina.

Although many believe that Taormina has the most spectacular views, tiny Castelmola—floating 1,800 feet above sea level—takes the word "scenic" to a whole new level. Along the cobblestone streets within the ancient walls, 360-degree panoramas of mountain, sea, and sky are so ubiquitous that you almost get used to them (but not quite). Collect yourself with a sip of the sweet almond wine (best served cold) made in local bars, or with lunch at one of the humble pizzerias or panino shops.

A 10-minute drive on a winding but well-paved road leads from Taormina to Castelmola; you must park in one of the public lots below the village and walk up to the center, only a few minutes away. On a nice day, hikers are in for a treat if they make the trip from Taormina on foot instead. It's a serious uphill climb, but the 1½-km (¾-mile) path offers breathtaking views, which compensate for the somewhat poor maintenance of the path itself. You'll begin at Porta Catania in Taormina, with a walk along Via Apollo Arcageta past the Chiesa di San Francesco di Paola on the left. The Strada Comunale della Chiusa then leads past Piazza Andromaco, revealing good views of the jagged promontory of Cocolonazzo di Mola to the north. Allow around an hour for the ascent, a half hour for the descent. There's another, slightly longer (2-km [1-mile]) path that heads up from Porta Messina past the Roman aqueduct, Convento dei Cappuccini, and the northeastern side of Monte Tauro. You could take one up and the other down. In any case, avoid the midday sun, wear comfortable shoes, and carry plenty of water with you.

GETTING HERE AND AROUND

Regular buses bound for Castelmola leave from Taormina's bus station on Via Pirandello.

Sights

★ Castello di Mola

RUINS | In all of Sicily there may be no spot more scenic than atop this crumbling hilltop fortification reached by a set of steep staircases rising out of the town center. From here you can gaze upon two coastlines, smoking Mount Etna, and the town spilling down the mountainside. Mention of its foundations go back to the 4th-century Hellenistic Siceliote inhabitants; it was remodeled by 9th-century Byzantines and then the Normans, but all that stands today are remains of the 16th-century castle walls. Come during daylight hours to take full advantage of the vista. ✉ *Castello Normanno, Castelmola* 🌐 *www.comune.castelmola.me.it.*

Restaurants

Il Vicolo

$ | **SICILIAN** | Located on a side street, this trattoria is one of the simpler dining choices in town, and also one of the better ones—what it lacks in views it makes up for with a pleasant rustic ambience plus a great selection of handmade pasta and, in the evening, *forno a legna* (from a wood-fired oven). In winter, pizzas are served weekends only. **Known for:** cozy, homey environs; pasta and pizza; signature totano (flying squid) ragù. [$] *Average main: €15* ✉ *Via Papa Pio IX 26, Castelmola* ☎ *0942/28481* 🌐 *www.facebook.com/ilvicolo.difalcone* 🕒 *Closed Tues. Sept.–June and 2 wks late Jan.–early Feb.*

Hotels

Villa Sonia

$ | **HOTEL** | Many of the guest rooms at this well-situated hotel have private terraces with gorgeous Instagrammable views of Etna without the crowds (or high prices) of nearby Taormina. **Pros:** bus stop to Taormina outside door; on-site sauna and pool; friendly service. **Cons:** some rooms are quite small; not much to do in the evening; lots of steps to get here. [$] *Rooms from: €150* ✉ *Via Porta Mola 9, Castelmola* ☎ *0942/28082* 🌐 *www.hotelvillasonia.com* 🕒 *Closed mid-Nov.–Mar.* *44 rooms* *Free Breakfast.*

Messina

42 km (26 miles) north of Savoca, 94 km (59 miles) northeast of Catania, 237 km (149 miles) east of Palermo.

Messina's ancient history recounts a series of disasters, but the city once vied with Palermo in a bid to become the island's capital, developing a fine university, a bustling commercial center, and a thriving cultural environment. At 5:20 am on December 28, 1908, Messina was reduced from a flourishing metropolis of 120,000 to a heap of rubble, shaken to pieces by an earthquake that turned into a tidal wave; 80,000 people died as a result, and the city was almost completely leveled. As you approach by ferry, you won't notice any outward indication of the disaster, just the modern countenance of a 3,000-year-old city. The somewhat flat look is a precaution of seismic planning: tall buildings are not permitted.

GETTING HERE AND AROUND

Frequent hydrofoils and ferries carry passengers, cars, and trains across the Strait of Messina from Villa San Giovanni, from just below the train station. There are also regular hydrofoil departures for foot passengers from Reggio Calabria. Cruise ships also stop in Messina's port. There is at least one hydrofoil departure daily for the Aeolian Islands.

From within Sicily, Messina is easily reachable by car, as it sits just off the E45 autostrada from Catania and the E90 autostrada from Palermo. There are regular train and bus services from both cities as well.

VISITOR INFORMATION

Messina Tourist Office (✉ *Via Consolato del Mare 19* 🌐 *turismoecultura.cittametropolitana.me.it*)

Sights

★ Duomo

CHURCH | The reconstruction of Messina's Norman and Romanesque cathedral, originally built by the Norman king Roger II and consecrated in 1197, has retained much of the original plan—including a handsome crown of Norman battlements, an enormous apse containing glittering mosaics, and a splendid wood-beamed ceiling. The adjoining bell tower contains one of the largest and most complex mechanical clocks in the world: constructed in 1933, it has a host of gilded automatons (a roaring lion and crowing rooster among them) that spring into action every day at the stroke of noon, lasting for 12 minutes. Don't miss the chance to climb the bell tower itself. As you head up the internal stairs, you'll see the system of levers and counterweights that operates the movements of the gilded bronze statues that parade through the open facade high over the Duomo's square. At the top, an open-air terrace offers 360-degree views of Messina and the strait. ✉ *Piazza del Duomo 29, Messina* ☎ *090/774895* 🌐 *www.messinarte.it* 🎟 *Clock tower €5.*

Restaurants

★ A Cucchiara

$$ | **MODERN ITALIAN** | Light and elegance permeate this stone-walled restaurant, where the open kitchen provides theater and owner Peppe Giamboi takes the stage as a gustatory storyteller, roaming from table to table. The menu is constantly changing, but you'll find excellent work with vegetables (a rarity in Sicily) and really lovely preparations of local cod. **Known for:** elegant food in a relaxed, welcoming atmosphere; locally, sustainably sourced seafood; robust wine program. 💲 *Average main: €23* ✉ *Strada San Giacomo 19, Messina* ☎ *090/711023* 🕑 *Closed Sun. No lunch Sat.*

Milazzo

41 km (25 miles) east of Patti, 39 km (24 miles) west of Messina.

Milazzo is a bustling ferry-port city filled with a mixture of history and natural beauty, not to mention a vibrant array of fresh seafood markets and restaurants to enjoy. It's also the main port of entry to the Aeolian Islands.

GETTING HERE AND AROUND

Milazzo is easily reached by car via the Messina–Palermo Autostrada. There are also regular trains from both Messina and Palermo.

VISITOR INFORMATION

For information, go to Servizio Turistico Regionale di Milazzo (✉ *20 Piazza Caio Duilio).*

Sights

Capo di Milazzo

SCENIC DRIVE | This rustic piece of coastline juts out from the naturally formed port of Milazzo, showing off classic Mediterranean scrub, a kind of coastal vegetation common to Sicily. The road leading to the cape is perfect for a scenic drive, and there are rustic beaches you can stop to enjoy along the way. Follow the signs from the city center to reach the cape or follow the main local road toward Palermo. ✉ *SP72 98057, Milazzo.*

Castello di Milazzo

CASTLE/PALACE | **FAMILY** | It is common to see castles along Sicily's coastline as the Normans used them to defend the island from invaders throughout the Middle Ages. Castello di Milazzo lies high above the town and is a beautiful example of an authentic medieval castle. It's well worth the hike up for the views out to the sea. ✉ *Salita Castello, Milazzo* ☎ *090/9221291* 🌐 *www.comune.milazzo.me.it* 🎟 *€7 includes Museum of the Sea and other exhibitions.*

Museum of the Sea

SPECIALTY MUSEUM | FAMILY | The Castello di Milazzo is home to this museum founded by Sicilian marine biologist Carmelo Isgro who recovered the remains of a sperm whale that died after it was caught in an illegal fishing net off the Aeolian Islands. Isgro reconstructed the whale's skeleton, and it became the central figure of the museum along with other exhibits that highlight the relationship between man and the sea and how it can be improved. While the museum is free, you still have to book your ticket online at least 24 hours in advance. ✉ *Castello di Milazzo, Bastione di Santa Maria, Complesso Monumentale, Milazzo* ☎ *380/7641409* 🌐 *www.mumamilazzo.com* 🎫 *€7 includes Castello di Milazzo and other exhibitions* ⏲ *Closed Mon.*

Pescina di Venere

POOL | This secluded natural sea pool is located at the end of Milazzo's long, wild cape. A meandering rustic path will take you on a 20-minute walk down to the unique natural rock formations that create pools of variable depths. You're able to swim in them, but there are no changing rooms, toilets, or places to buy food or drinks so be sure to bring everything you need. ✉ *SP72, Milazzo* 🎫 *Free.*

Restaurants

M'arricriu Tratto-Bistrot

$$ | SICILIAN | The fresh and beautifully presented interpretations of classic Sicilian seafood dishes make this a fabulous spot to dine. Call in advance to reserve a table on the sunny but shaded modern terrace with splendid sea views or a seat in the cozy dining room that mixes modern with the traditional. **Known for:** raw seafood antipasti; inventive pasta dishes; classic Pepata di Cozze alla Messinese mussels. $ *Average main: €25* ✉ *Via Marina Garibaldi 249, Milazzo* ☎ *090/3695695* 🌐 *marricriutrattobistrot.it* ⏲ *Closed Mon.*

Hotels

Hotel La Bussola

$ | HOTEL | For a convenient, short stay near the port, this sleek, modern hotel offers comfortable rooms, a lounge bar, a bistro restaurant, and a lovely roof garden. **Pros:** excellent for Aeolian Island ferries; helpful staff; relaxing roof terrace. **Cons:** maybe too businesslike for some; not near the beach; limited breakfast choices. $ *Rooms from: €90* ✉ *Via Nino Bixio 11/13, Milazzo* ☎ *090/9221244* 🌐 *www.hotelabussola.it* *26 rooms* 🍽 *Free Breakfast.*

Shopping

Parco Commerciale Corolla

MALL | FAMILY | As the largest shopping mall in Messina province, Parco Corolla offers a nice selection of Italian fashion stores, including children's clothing, accessories, perfume, and jewelry. In addition, a shopping district surrounds the mall with many other diverse stores, including a food hall and a cinema. ✉ *Parco Commerciale Corolla Via Firenza, Milazzo* ☎ *090/931824* 🌐 *www.parcocorolla.it.*

Cefalù

69 km (42 miles) east of Palermo.

The jewel of the Tyrrhenian Coast is no doubt Cefalù, a classically appealing old Sicilian town built on a spur jutting out into the sea.

The city's medieval origins have left behind many interesting historical sites to explore. The Palazzo Maria in Piazza Duomo and the Osteria Magno in Corso Ruggero are palaces that date back to the 13th century. They were both owned by the Ventimiglia family, an influential aristocratic family that dominated and owned most of the agricultural wealth of this part of the island in the Middle Ages.

Among its many evocative historic locations is the medieval washhouse. Carved out of rustic lava stone and used until the early 20th century, the ancient bathhouse is home to a series of basins fed by the waters of the Cefalino River, which flow out from 22 iron lion-shape spouts. Here, you can get a sense of how life was in Sicily in the Middle Ages.

Cefalù's historical heritage continues with remnants of the Baroque period from the 18th century, which gave birth to the elaborate decorations and style that are quite unique to Sicily. There are the ornate facades of the church of the Monte della Pietà, which dates from 1716, and the stunning Church of Purgatory (1668). The town's historical center is dotted with endless portholes, squares, facades, and architectural details. The visual, photogenic highlight is around the old quayside, with its pier, cobbled walkways, and various panoramic niches.

West of the old town is the longer sandy beach and promenade, whose backdrop is a string of far less attractive modern resorts and their busy restaurants, bars, car parks, boxy hotel buildings, and traffic-ridden sprawl, which climbs the hill.

GETTING HERE AND AROUND

Trains and buses run between Palermo and Messina, and stop at the station about a 10-minute walk from town. Drivers can take the A20 autostrada, though the traffic going in and out of Cefalù can be heavy in summer and the 50-minute train ride from Palermo may be the better option.

VISITOR INFORMATION

Cefalù Tourism Office (✉ *Corso Ruggero 139* 🌐 *www.visitcefalu.com*)

Sights

★ Duomo

CHURCH | Cefalù is dominated by a massive headland—*la rocca*—and a 12th-century Romanesque Duomo, which is one of the finest Norman cathedrals in Italy. Roger II began the church in 1131 as an offering of thanks for having been saved here from a shipwreck. Its mosaics rival those of Monreale. (Whereas Monreale's Byzantine Christ figure is an austere and powerful image, emphasizing Christ's divinity, the Cefalù Christ is softer, more compassionate, and more human.)
At the Duomo you must be respectfully attired—no shorts or beachwear permitted. Three themed tours explore the Duomo complex, taking in the museum, cloisters, roof, and towers (from €10). ✉ *Piazza del Duomo, Cefalù* ☎ *0921/926366* 🌐 *duomocefalu.it/en* 🎫 *"Green" Museum and Cloister 30-min tour €10; "Red" 55-min panoramic tour including the towers €12* 🕒 *Cloister closed weekends.*

Restaurants

Al Porticciolo

$$ | **SICILIAN** | Nicola Mendolia's seaside restaurant is comfortable, casual, and faithfully focused on food—primarily pizza, but with an extensive selection of seafood, pasta, and meat, too. Dark, heavy wooden tables create a comfortable environment filled with a mix of jovial locals and businesspeople, though the most memorable option is to dine on the spacious terrace. **Known for:** extensive selection of pizzas; local seafood; lovely terrace overlooking the water. $ *Average main: €22* ✉ *Via Carlo Ortolani di Bordonaro 66, Cefalù* ☎ *0921/921981* 🌐 *www.alporticcioloristorante.com* 🕒 *Closed Dec.–Mar.*

Hotels

Bohémien Boutique Guesthouse

$ | **B&B/INN** | The fanciest, contemporary-design-led B&B in town offers top-of-the-line showers, striking lighting, and sumptuous beds in a converted family apartment building from the 19th century. **Pros:** free hot drinks and water in the cozy guest lounge; lovely owner Mari; decadent freestanding bath in two rooms. **Cons:** self check-in and lack of 24/7 reception; underwhelming breakfast at nearby Golden Bar; no elevator. *Rooms from: €155 Via Umberto I 15C, Cefalù 331/7583397 www.bohemienbeb.it 5 rooms Free Breakfast.*

Lipari

2 hours 10 minutes from Milazzo by ferry, 1 hour by hydrofoil; 1 hour 45 minutes from Reggio Calabria and 2 hours 30 minutes from Messina by hydrofoil.

The largest and most developed of the Aeolians, Lipari welcomes you with distinctive pastel-color houses. Fields of spiky agaves dot the northernmost tip of the island, Acquacalda, indented with disused pumice and obsidian quarries. In the west is San Calogero, where you can explore hot springs and mud baths. From the red lava base of the island rises a plateau crowned with a 16th-century castle and a 17th-century cathedral.

GETTING HERE AND AROUND

Ferries and hydrofoils from Milazzo via Vulcano stop here, and there are also connections with the other Aeolian Islands. There's also a more limited hydrofoil service from Messina via Reggio di Calabria, a daily hydrofoil from Palermo in summer, and ferries year-round from Naples. On the island, if you plan to explore extensively, you should rent a car or a scooter. Lipari is the largest of the Aeolians and navigating it can be difficult without your own mode of transport.

Sights

★ Museo Archeologico Regionale Eoliano Luigi Bernabò Brea

HISTORY MUSEUM | This vast, multibuilding museum is terrific, with an intelligently arranged collection of prehistoric finds—some dating as far back as 5000 BC—from various sites in the archipelago, as well as Greek and Roman artifacts, including an outstanding collection of Greek theatrical masks, and even interesting information on volcanoes. Basic descriptions about the exhibits are provided in both English and Italian: panels in each room and captions in the showcases. That said, there is so much to see, and the museum is worth at least a few hours of your time. *Via Castello 2, Lipari 090/9880174 €7 Closed Sun. afternoon.*

★ Vulcano

ISLAND | True to its name, the island of Vulcano has a profusion of fumaroles sending up jets of hot vapor, and although the volcano itself is dormant, emissions have recently reached dangerous levels, occasionally resulting in parts of the island being evacuated. When it is safe, visitors can come to soak in the strong-smelling sulfur springs or to sunbathe and walk on some of the archipelago's best beaches, though the volcanic black sand can be off-putting at first glance. Volcanic conditions permitting, you can climb the volcano and walk right around the crater. Advenzu offer a number of guided trekking tours around Vulcano, as well as kayaking, sailing, tandem paragliding, snorkeling, and other activities. *389/1447708 mobile www.advenzu.com from €55 for an Advenzu 2½-hr guided trek of the Gran Cratere della Fossa.*

Restaurants

★ Osteria San Bartolo

$ | ITALIAN | Chef Danilo Conti started with a passion for wine and subsequently grew deeper respect for the soil of his home territory. The dishes at his osteria just steps from the port in Lipari are clean and balanced—the opposite of fussy—but primarily celebrate the fishing and agricultural traditions of the island, highlighting their seasonal, locally grown citrus and herbs. **Known for:** natural wine (chef owns a wine shop a few doors down); swordfish parmigiana, tuna caponata; showcasing the best of both sea and land. *Average main: €16 Via Francesco Crispi 109, Lipari 090/8961317 www.sanbartolovineriaedispensa.com Closed Wed.*

Hotels

Hotel Villa Enrica

$$ | HOTEL | This hotel's hillside position gives it one of the best views on the island, looking south over Marina Lunga and the castle, and it seems like nearly every part of the hotel (from rooms to common areas) takes advantage of that vista. **Pros:** complimentary access to pool and amenities of sister property Hotel Mea; shuttle service to beach; cliffside infinity pool with snack bar for light lunches. **Cons:** no heated pool; service can be slow; often hosts events, so can get crowded with nonguests. *Rooms from: €245 Strada Serra Pirrera 11, Lipari 090/9880826 www.hotelvillaenricalipari.com Closed late Oct.–Easter 20 rooms Free Breakfast.*

Les Sables Noirs

$$ | HOTEL | Named for the black sands of the beach it sits on, this luxury hotel is superbly sited on the beautiful Porto di Ponente, and its cool modern furnishings and inviting pool and spa induce a sybaritic mood. **Pros:** stunning beachfront location; delicious breakfasts; quick five-minute walk to town. **Cons:** no on-site restaurant; four-night minimum stay in August; the spa is not included in the price. *Rooms from: €280 Porto di Ponente, Vulcano 335/090950 www.lessablesnoirs.it Closed Oct. 5–mid-May 53 rooms Free Breakfast 4-night minimum stay in Aug.*

Tenuta di Castellaro Winery & Resort

$$ | RESORT | Driven by their passion for wine and the island of Lipari, the visionary Lentsch family decided to embark on a project of great scale beginning in 2006 (spanning 2,000 square meters) ending with the beautiful and unique result that you see today: three micro-residences designed with the most modern amenities and plant technologies in keeping with full respect of nature. **Pros:** full immersion of nature and serenity with the most incredible views of all of the islands; sustainable property; secluded private outdoor patios and baths overlook the vineyards. **Cons:** in the countryside hamlet of Quattropani (7 km [4.5 miles] from Lipari port); if you want to explore the city center you will need a car or a taxi; no formal restaurant on-site. *Rooms from: €250 Via Caolino s/n, Lipari 345/4342755 www.tenutadicastellaro.it Closed Oct.–Apr. 3 units Free Breakfast.*

Salina

50 minutes from Lipari by ferry, 25 minutes by hydrofoil.

The second largest of the Aeolians, Salina is also the most fertile, which accounts for its excellent Malvasia wine. Salina is the archipelago's lushest and highest island, too: Mount Fossa delle Felci rises to more than 3,000 feet and offers a challenging two-hour hike to the summit, and the vineyards and fishing villages along its slopes add to the allure. Pollara, in the west of the island, has capitalized on its fame as one of the locations in the 1990s cult movie *Il Postino* (*The Postman*) and is an ideal location for sunset watching and an evening passeggiata on well-maintained paths along the volcanic terrain.

GETTING HERE AND AROUND

Ferries and hydrofoils arrive from Milazzo connecting Salina to all islands of the archipelago. There's also a more limited hydrofoil service from Messina via Reggio di Calabria, a daily hydrofoil from Palermo in summer, and ferries year-round from Naples. Note that there are two ports on Salina: Santa Marina Salina and Rinella. Not all ferries and hydrofoils arrive at both ports, so double-check your tickets and timetables. Once on the island, you can get around by taxi, rental car, or a scooter. The island's bus service, C.I.T.I.S., runs reliably and (usually) on time between the island's towns. Tickets cost €1.90 to €2.90, depending on distance.

TOURS

Sogno Eoliano

BOAT TOURS | An island perhaps best experienced by water, there is no one better to show you around Salina than native sailor Samuele and his partner in business (and in life) Federica. Sogno Eoliano specializes in private boat excursions completely tailored to you. From their own favorite secret spots to whatever you wish to see of the island (logistically possible and within reason), Federica and Samuele, also the most gracious hosts and gentlest of souls, are ready with open arms to create a special experience for you on the open sea. *Salina 331/9928032 mobile www.sognoeoliano.it From €200 (up to 5 people).*

Restaurants

Capofaro Restaurant

$$ | SICILIAN | Thanks to a recent revamp in the kitchen, this hotel restaurant is a great new dining destination. Their philosophy of "*cucina* terroir" (territory cooking) and "short kilometer" focuses first and foremost on using the vegetables grown on the estate's own garden, the island's local seafood, other Mediterranean products (most of all capers), and applying the traditional techniques to bread making using ancient grains. **Known for:** beautiful setting; fabulous wines straight from their vineyards; innovative dishes that are beautifully plated, including their homemade breads, anything crudo, homemade desserts. *Average main: €30 Capofaro Locanda & Malvasia, Via Faro 3, Malfa, Salina 090/9844330 www.capofaro.it Closed mid-Oct.–mid-May.*

★ Da Alfredo

$ | SICILIAN | Starting in 1968, the mini-empire of owner Alfredo Olivieri was built one granita and one pane cunzato at a time, and no summer on Salina is complete without a stop at his little shop off the Marina Garibaldi piazza in Lingua. You'll find all the classic granita flavors (almond, coffee, lemon, pistachio), but it's the seasonal fruits that shine here: mulberry, fig, wild blackberries, watermelon, and cantaloupe. **Known for:** charismatic owner; seasonally focused granita; joyous atmosphere. *Average main: €15 Via Marina Garibaldi, Santa Marina, Salina 090/9843980 www.facebook.com/daalfredosalina Closed Nov.–Easter.*

Hotels

La Locando di Postino

$ | HOTEL | In a converted 150-year-old farmhouse that once housed local priests, this really special boutique hotel in Pollara is a family affair, run by husband and wife Mauro and Amelia (and their children Mariachiara and Francesco). **Pros:** eco-certified hotel; private patio and hammock with every room; restaurant on-site. **Cons:** not so centrally located within Salina and far from all of the ports; a car or scooter is necessary if you want to explore other parts of the island; restaurant is open to the public. *Rooms from: €180* *Via Picone 10, Pollara, Salina* *090/9843958* *www.lalocandadelpostino.it* *Closed Nov.–Apr.* *10 rooms* *Free Breakfast.*

★ Principe di Salina
$$ | **HOTEL** | Awash in white with vibrant pops of color, this family-run boutique property that hugs the Malfa hillside defines barefoot chic. **Pros:** excellent wine and cocktail list; house-made sourdough breads and pastries; Ortigia bath products. **Cons:** no kids under 12; restaurant closed for external guests; not directly on the sea. *Rooms from: €250* *SP 182 3, Malfa, Salina* *090/9844415* *www.principedisalina.it* *Closed late Oct.–late Apr.* *16 rooms* *Free Breakfast.*

Panarea

2 hours 15 minutes from Lipari by ferry, 55 minutes by hydrofoil; 25 minutes from Salina by hydrofoil.

Panarea is the smallest of the islands but has some of the most dramatic scenery, including wild caves carved out of rock and dazzling flora. The exceptionally clear water and the richness of life on the seafloor make Panarea especially suitable for underwater exploration. The outlying rocks and islets make a gorgeous sight, and you can enjoy the panorama on an easy excursion to the small Bronze Age village at Capo Milazzese.

GETTING HERE AND AROUND

Ferries and hydrofoils arrive here from Milazzo, Lipari, Salina, and Stromboli. There is a less frequent hydrofoil service from Messina via Reggio di Calabria, and in summer a daily connection with Palermo. There are also weekly ferries to and from Naples. For a splurge, you can book a helicopter flight with Air Panarea (*www.airpanarea.com*) from the airports of Palermo, Catania, Naples, Lamezia Terme, and Reggio Calabria. The Milazzo flight is 17 minutes and €1,520 for up to six people (other journeys and prices upon request). Once on the island, you'll need to rely on walking, Vespas, or electric golf carts to get around—cars are banned.

Restaurants

Ristorante Broccia
$$ | **SICILIAN** | The stylish restaurant ("broccia" means fork in the ancient Sicilian dialect) offers local and regional cuisine in a refined setting. Chef Daniela Cappelli (sister of hotel owner Maria) uses elements of the surrounding Aeolian Islands in dishes that are both traditional and inventive. **Known for:** sophisticated setting; creative cuisine; gracious host. *Average main: €24* *Quartara Boutique Hotel, Via San Pietro 15, Panarea* *331/8695713* *www.quartarahotel.com* *Closed late Oct.–mid-Apr.*

Hotels

Hotel Raya
$$$ | **HOTEL** | Although some visitors say it's resting on past laurels and is in need of renovations, Raya is perfectly in keeping with the elite style of Panarea—discreet and expensive, with a pool and terrace that enjoy views over the sea toward Stromboli. **Pros:** great views of Stromboli; hippie-chic ambience; lovely pool area. **Cons:** snooty staff; uphill trudge to rooms; no young children allowed. *Rooms from: €500* *Via San Pietro, San Pietro, Panarea* *090/983013* *www.hotelraya.it* *Closed mid-Oct.–mid-Apr.* *34 rooms* *Free Breakfast.*

Stromboli

Approx. 4 hours from Lipari by ferry, 65–90 minutes by hydrofoil; 80 minutes from Salina by hydrofoil; approx. 10 hours from Naples by ferry, 4 hours 30 minutes by hydrofoil.

This northernmost of the Aeolians consists entirely of the cone of an active volcano. The view from the sea—especially at night, as an endless stream of glowing red-hot lava flows into the water—is unforgettable. Stromboli is in a constant state of activity, with minor explosions happening every 20 minutes or so. In periods of high activity and visibility, eruptions can be seen from the other islands. The volcano is closely monitored, and the main danger would be from an underwater landslide that could trigger a tsunami. Access to the volcano is permitted only with an official guide. The main town has a small selection of reasonably priced hotels and restaurants, a choice of lively clubs and cafés, and plenty of trekking outfits. In addition to the island tour, excursions might include boat trips around the sea stack of Strombolicchio, which is all that remains of the original volcano that gave rise to Stromboli. At night, boats offer trips to see the Sciara del Fuoco, the lava channel that rises out of the blue waters.

GETTING HERE AND AROUND

Ferries and hydrofoils arrive here from Milazzo via Vulcano, Lipari, Salina, and Panarea. There's also a more limited hydrofoil service from Messina via Reggio di Calabria, one hydrofoil daily from Palermo in summer, and ferries year-round from Naples. Once on the island, you'll need to navigate by foot, or you can book one of the golf cart taxis located near the port.

TOURS

Pippo Navigazione

BOAT TOURS | The best way to see Stromboli's eruptions is with a boat tour such as those run by Pippo Navigazione. Boat trips include three-hour day cruises and night tours that explore the area where the lava reaches the sea. Group trips can have up to 30 people. You can also book private excursions. ✉ *Porto Scari, Stromboli* ☎ *348/0559296 mobile* 🌐 *www.facebook.com/pippoNavigazionestromboli* 🎫 *From €30.*

Restaurants

Da Zurro

$$ | **SEAFOOD** | The energy of eclectic but endearing chef Francesco (aka Zurro) exudes from his open kitchen into each delectable dish served. Da Zurro is the last of its kind on Stromboli, a simple yet robust restaurant focused on fresh fish and the old island recipes, while also keeping alive the old-school art of Italian hospitality. **Known for:** charismatic owner; fun and warm atmosphere; Strombo-li-Siciliano recipes, including ravioli stuzzi (fish-stuffed squid ink pasta). 💲 *Average main: €23* ✉ *Via Crivelli 5, Stromboli* ☎ *338/1342495* 🕑 *No lunch Nov.–Mar.*

Chapter 17

SARDINIA

Updated by
Robert Andrews

WELCOME TO SARDINIA

TOP REASONS TO GO

★ **Relax on idyllic beaches:** Covering more than 1,900 km (1,200 miles) of coastline, Sardinia's beaches beckon with their turquoise waters, white sand, and rippled dunes.

★ **Discover natural beauty:** A network of trails explores Sardinia's resplendent mountains, deep gorges, lush forests, and cascading waterfalls.

★ **Explore charming towns and villages:** From coastal towns to rural villages, the island is dotted with a variety of settlements that take pride in their history and tradition. Each has its own culture, cuisine, and unique way of life.

★ **Dive or snorkel the outer reefs:** Crystalline waters, warm weather, and outer reefs make Sardinia a paradise for underwater adventurers. Sunken ships and marine reserves provide the ideal place to discover marine life.

★ **Savor Sardinian delicacies:** From pasta and prosciutto to lamb and cheese, the island's cuisine is sure to satisfy any appetite.

1 Cagliari. Sardinia's capital is a hive of cultural attractions, dining hot spots, and glamorous shops.

2 Pula. Just south of Cagliari, Pula is home to resorts, beaches, and a major archaeological site.

3 Sant'Antioco. A significant archaeological site and museum merit a visit on this west-coast island, once a major Carthaginian base.

4 San Pietro. This offshore isle makes a perfect bolt-hole, with its lively port and undeveloped beaches.

5 Costa Verde. A high, cliffy coastline and alluring beaches are the main attractions on Sardinia's "Green Coast."

6 Barumini. The island's ancient and enigmatic nuraghic culture are showcased at Su Nuraxi, just outside Barumini.

7 Oristano. Little visited by tourists, this provincial center makes an appealing base for the nearby Sinis Peninsula.

8 Tharros. Explore Carthaginian and Roman ruins at this site near the town of Oristano.

9 Nuoro. The largest inland town is a must-see for anyone interested in Sardinia's traditional culture.

10 Fonni. Near the island's highest peaks, Fonni makes an ideal hiking base.

11 Alghero. Alghero's historic center is a warren of traffic-free lanes lined with lively bars, shops, and restaurants.

12 Sassari. Sardinia's second city has an atmospheric old quarter.

13 Castelsardo. This former north coast stronghold is renowned for its basketware.

14 Santa Teresa Gallura. On the island's northern tip, this resort is surrounded by excellent beaches.

15 La Maddalena. Garibaldi's former home is a highlight of any tour of this archipelago.

16 Porto Cervo. Day-trippers are drawn to this jet-setter enclave on the famed Costa Smeralda.

17 Olbia. Sardinia's northern gateway is a short drive from some of Italy's most exclusive hotels and beaches.

FRANCE
La Maddalena
Santa Teresa
Gallura
Palau
Porto Cervo
COSTA SMERALDA
Bassacutena
Arzachena
Golfo Aranci
Golfo di Olbia
Olbia
Punta Caprara
Isola Asinara
Stintino
Golfo dell'Asinara
Castelsardo
Tempio Pausania
Sedini
Telti
Monti
Padru
Porto Torres
Sorso
Chiaramonti
Oschiri
Sassari
Siniscola
Ozieri
Budduso
Alghero
Villanova Monteleone
Sas Linnas Siccas
Bitti
Bultei
Orosei
Padria
Nuoro
Dorgali
Cala Gonone
Monte Ortobene
Golfo di Orosei
Orotelli
Bosa
Macomer
Tresnuraghes
TYRRHENIAN SEA
Abbasanta
Fonni
Tortolì
Cabras
Oristano
Tharros
Asuni
Laconi
Bari Sardo
Golfo di Oristano
Nurallao
MEDITERRANEAN SEA
Marrubiu
Uras
Barumini
Su Nuraxi
Porto Palma
COSTA VERDE
Furtei
Guspini
Piscinas
Samassi
Muravera
Buggerru
Villasor
Monastir
Dolianova
Decimomannu
Iglesias
Cagliari
Portoscuso
Carloforte
Isola San Pietro
Carbonia
Golfo di Cagliari
Villasimius
Sant'Antioco
Giba
Sarroch
Pula
Isola Sant'antioco
Golfo di Palmas
Chia
Capo Teulada
Capo Spartivento
0
10 mi
0
10 km

EATING AND DRINKING WELL IN SARDINIA

Traditional Sardinian ravioli

Wining and dining in Sardinia is not just a richly delicious experience, it's also a way to have a close-up encounter with the history, geography, and cultural traditions of the island. Sardinian food has its own culinary identity, a complex and eclectic mix that makes for mouthwatering and often revelatory dishes.

Sardinia's proximity to North Africa and its long Spanish occupation mean that elements of both cultures can be found in the island's kitchens, including couscous and paella. There are also strong regional variations within Sardinia itself, as well as a traditional division between the land-based fare of the interior and the fresh seafood on the coasts. Wherever you go here, you'll find a strong emphasis on seasonal ingredients and ancient cooking techniques.

BREADS, CHEESES, AND SWEET SPECIALTIES

Sardinia has a strong tradition of bread making and is famous for crispy paper-thin *pane carasau* flatbread (*carta di musica* in Italian).

Ever wondered about all those sheep roaming the rugged slopes of the interior? They're there to produce the raw materials for Italy's original and best pecorino. It's ubiquitous in Sardinia, and comes in various strengths and consistencies.

Sardinian desserts include *sospiri* (morsels of almond dough stuffed with citrus-infused almond paste), *torrone di mandorle* (almond nougat), and *seadas* (cheese-filled pastries topped with honey, also called *sebadas*). The *candelaus,* a fruit-and-almond dessert, and sweet ricotta-stuffed *pardula* cakes are popular in Cagliari. Unmissable is *amaro di corbezzolo,* made by bees that suck nectar from a plant known as *arbutus,* the tree strawberry.

MEAT

The most popular meat dishes are veal, roast *agnello* (lamb), and *porcheddu* (spit-roasted suckling pig). *Cavallo,* or *carne equino* (horse meat), is also commonly found on restaurant menus, particularly in Sassari, where it's generally served in the form of a *bistecca* (thin steak). Donkey (*asino*) and wild boar (*cinghiale*) are other Sardinian specialties. Sometimes cinghiale is roasted on a spit or prepared using the ancient Sardinian technique of *incarralzadu*, for which it's placed in a large hole lined with fragrant myrtle leaves. Another option is *zuppa cuata*, a hearty soup that's made from beef broth, bread, and aged pecorino cheese.

SEAFOOD

Whole fish are best eaten roasted or grilled, though you may also find them sautéed in pasta or incorporated into *copaxa de peix*, a fish soup from Alghero. The most famous Alghero dish is lobster, known as *langouste* or *aragosta*. Lobster doesn't appear on restaurant menus in winter—fortunately, the very time when *riccio di mare* (sea urchin), another local specialty, is best enjoyed. Winter is also the best season for *bottarga*, the dried, cured roe of gray mullet or tuna.

Almond nougat

Roast lamb

STARTERS

Opt for antipasti *di mare* or *di terra* to kick off your meal. Traditional pastas include *malloreddus* (small shells), *culurgiones* (ravioli), and *maccarones de busa* (thick pasta twists). Homemade pastas might be topped with a wild-boar sauce; *fregola*, a semolina pasta, is often served with *arselle* (clams).

WINE

Among the whites, the dry *torbato* of the Alghero Coast and the slightly sparkling *vermentino* from Gallura are standouts. The Oristano region produces the dry, sherrylike *vernaccia* (unrelated to the Tuscan variety), Bosa produces amber-tone *malvasia*, and inland Barbagia is one of the best sources of *cannonau*, a red wine with an ancient pedigree. The traditional liqueur *mirto,* which makes a fine after-dinner drink, is made from native wild myrtle berries.

The second-largest island in the Mediterranean, Sardinia remains unique and enigmatic with its rugged coastline and white-sand beaches, dramatic granite cliffs, and mountainous inland tracts. Glamorous resorts lie within a short distance of quiet, medieval villages, and ruined castles and ancient churches testify to an eventful history.

But although conquerors from all directions—Phoenicians, Carthaginians, Romans, Catalans, Pisans, Genoans, Piedmontese—have left their traces, no outside culture has had a dominant impact. Pockets of foreign influence persist along the coasts, but inland, a proud Sardinian culture flourishes.

As a travel destination, Sardinia's identity is split: the island has some of Europe's most expensive resorts, but it's also home to pristine terrain untouched by commercial development. Fine sand and clean waters draw summer sun worshippers to beaches that rank among the Mediterranean's best. Most famous are those along the Costa Smeralda (Emerald Coast), where the ultrarich have anchored their yachts since the 1960s.

Away from the glamorous shores and upscale locales found in the northeast, much of Sardinia's coast is rugged and unreachable, a jagged series of wildly beautiful inlets accessible only by sea. Inland, Sardinia remains shepherd's country, silent and stark.

MAJOR REGIONS

Cagliari and the Southern Coast. Sardinia's capital and largest city, Cagliari (pronounced *cahl*-yah-ree) contains the island's principal art and archaeology museums as well as an intact old citadel with lofty views of the sea, lagoons, and mountains. To the southwest is Pula, an inland resort within easy reach of good beaches and the excavations at Nora.

Su Nuraxi to the Costa Smeralda. Inland and north of Cagliari, explore the apogee of the island's prehistoric Nuraghic civilization at Su Nuraxi, just outside the village of Barumini. Northwest of here, Oristano makes an ideal stopover for exploring the ruins at Tharros. In the mountainous interior, Nuoro has a first-rate ethnographic museum highlighting Sardinia's traditional shepherd's culture. The rugged granite landscape of Sardinia's northeast is probably best known for the Costa Smeralda, a short strip of elite hotels and beaches.

Did You Know?

The gorgeous Costa Smeralda was a luxury hideaway in the 1960s for celebrities. These days, the area is more accessible, with an airport in Olbia and some budget dining and lodging options.

Planning

Getting Here and Around

AIR

Flying is by far the fastest and easiest way to get to the island. Sardinia's major airport, Aeroporto di Elmas, is in Cagliari, with smaller ones at Alghero (Aeroporto Fertilia) and Olbia (Aeroporto Costa Smeralda).

BUS

Cagliari is linked with the other towns of Sardinia by a network of buses. All major cities and most local destinations are served by ARST (🌐 *www.arst.sardegna.it*). City buses in Cagliari, Oristano, Olbia, Alghero, and Sassari operate on the same system as those on the mainland: either buy your ticket first, at a tobacco shop, ticket booth, or machine, and punch it in the machine on the bus, or buy onboard incurring a supplementary charge.

CAR

Sardinia is about 270 km (167 miles) long from north to south, which takes three to four hours to drive on main roads; it's roughly 120 km (75 miles) across, but there are no fast east–west routes. Most of the ferries that connect the island with the mainland transport cars.

Roads are generally in good condition, with clear signposting. Superstrada double-lane routes are well developed and toll-free. Expect winding inland mountain and coastal roads with hairpin turns. Most gas stations are closed in the afternoon, at night, and on Sunday, though at those times you can still use cards to automatically gas up. Try to avoid driving at night, when mountain roads are particularly hazardous and roadside facilities are infrequent, especially in the east. Be alert for sheep on rural routes. Fog and snow may be issues in winter.

FERRIES

Large modern ferries operated by Grimaldi Lines (🌐 *www.grimaldi-lines.com*), Tirrenia Lines (🌐 *www.en.tirrenia.it*), Moby Lines (🌐 *www.mobylines.com*), Corsica Ferries (🌐 *www.corsica-ferries.it*), and Grandi Navi Veloci (🌐 *www.gnv.it*), connect mainland Italy (Genoa, Livorno, Piombino, Civitavecchia, and Naples) and Sicily (Palermo) with Sardinian ports at Porto Torres, Olbia, Arbatax, and Cagliari. Crossing time is 8–12 hours; the longer crossings are usually overnight. Moby Lines operates much smaller ferries year round between Santa Teresa di Gallura and Bonifacio, Corsica, taking less than an hour. These ferries are a popular mode of transport, however, and should be booked ahead in July and August.

TRAIN

Trenitalia (🌐 *www.trenitalia.com*), or Ferrovie dello Stato (FS), is the national railway of Italy. You can plan itineraries, purchase tickets, and look for special deals online. The Stazione Centrale in Cagliari is next to the bus station on Piazza Matteotti. There are fairly good connections between Olbia, Cagliari, Sassari, and Oristano. Service on the few other local lines is infrequent and slow. The fastest train between Olbia and Cagliari takes a little over 3½ hours. Local trains run by ARST connect Sassari with Alghero (around 40 minutes).

If you can stand a little agitation and are a fan of slow travel, consider taking a trip on the rickety old narrow-gauge railroad operated by Trenino Verde della Sardegna through the island's interior. The service, which started as a public transport utility in 1893, now only operates limited routes once or twice weekly throughout the year in the form of tourist excursions that take in some of Sardinia's most panoramic landscapes. The main Trenino Verde (🌐 *www.treninoverde.com*) routes currently run from the village of Mandas (linked to Cagliari by local trains) to Laconi via Serri, Isili, and Nurallao; from

Arbatax, a small port on the island's east coast, to the mountain village of Lanusei; and from the inland town of Tempio Pausania, in the northeast of the island, to the village of Luras. Check on the latest routes and itineraries. Journeys take between 40 minutes and 2¾ hours, and may include guided tours of some of the places en route plus lunch stops.

Hotels

In Sardinia, there are numerous luxury resorts with stunning beachfront vistas, bed-and-breakfast inns in medieval villages, private villas tucked away on lush hills, modern hotels in the trendy capital, and farmhouses on tranquil mountainsides. During summer months, the most popular destination on the island is the Costa Smeralda in the east. High demand during July and August raises nightly rates to an astronomical range, above €2,000 for the most deluxe accommodations. Find more reasonable hotel rates in other parts of the island, which are equally breathtaking and less crowded. Plan dates well in advance, as many hotels close at the end of September until the following April or May.

⇨ *Hotel and restaurant reviews have been shortened. For full information, visit Fodors.com. Prices in the hotel reviews are the lowest cost of a standard double room in high season. Prices in the dining reviews are the average cost of a main course at dinner, or, if dinner is not served, at lunch.*

What It Costs in Euros

$	$$	$$$	$$$$
RESTAURANTS			
under €20	€20–€30	€31–€40	over €40
HOTELS			
under €175	€175–€400	€401–€600	over €600

Restaurants

The full range of eateries can be found in every Sardinian town, from pizzerias to gourmet restaurants, and you'll be especially spoiled for choice in the island's capital, Cagliari, and the resort of Alghero, where good-value fixed-price menus are common. Seafood is ubiquitous, though the most authentic Sard cuisine is based on land products, such as lamb, boar, and suckling pig, not to mention mushrooms, artichokes, and other seasonal produce. Note that, as in other parts of Italy, fish dishes are often priced according to weight (usually by the *etto,* or 100 grams). Many places close in winter; in summer, book ahead to be sure of a table.

Tours

Visos Viaggi
PRIVATE GUIDES | This travel agent and tour operator specializes in individual tours and villa and hotel accommodations. ✉ *Via Puccini 41, Cagliari* ☎ *070/658772* 🌐 *www.visosviaggi.com.*

When to Go

The best time to visit Sardinia is Easter through September. European vacationers flock to the island for sunshine in July and August. Expect to pay the highest rates during these two peak summer months, when roads, tourist sites, and beaches are most crowded. Nature is at its most exuberant during the spring, while from September to October, when accommodations start to shut down for the year, you'll find end-of-season deals and fewer tourists. During the winter months, the smaller resorts can resemble ghost towns—with closed restaurants, hotels, and shops.

Cagliari

268 km (166 miles) south of Olbia.

Known in the local dialect as Casteddu, the island's capital has a warren of pedestrianized streets at its heart and a range of impressive Italianate architecture, from modern to medieval. The city comprises around 170,000 people and has a busy commercial port and waterfront with broad avenues and arched arcades, while the old hilltop citadel (called, simply, Castello) makes a good starting point to a visit, not least for the Museo Archeologico located here. The imposing Bastione di Saint Remy gateway to the Castello district is a must-see.

GETTING HERE AND AROUND

The easiest way to arrive in Cagliari is by plane or boat. From the airport, it's easy to get into the city center by train. You can also rent a car at the airport; booking before arrival is highly recommended. If you arrive by boat, travel from Palermo (Sicily), Civitavecchia (Rome), or Naples. The port is near the city center.

Piazza Matteotti is the terminal for long-distance buses and Cagliari's city buses, which are operated by Consorzio Trasporti e Mobilità (CTM). Buy city bus tickets (€1.30 for a ticket valid for 90 minutes, or €3.30 for an all-day ticket) at the kiosk or machine here before boarding. From nearby Via Roma or Piazza Yenne, you can pick up the circular Bus 7, useful for reaching the old quarter in the upper town. If you don't mind the steep walk, you could get there on foot (about 10 minutes from Piazza Yenne), but you can't drive there—only residents' cars are allowed. Most of Cagliari's restaurants and bars are located in the Marina area, near the port, which is only accessible on foot.

VISITOR INFORMATION

CONTACTS Cagliari Tourism Office. ✉ *Palazzo Civico, Piazza Matteotti, Cagliari* ☎ *070/6777397, 338/6498498 mobile* 🌐 *cagliariturismo.comune.cagliari.it.* **Infopoint Aeroporto Elmas.** ✉ *Arrivals hall, Cagliari airport, Via dei Trasvolatori, Elmas* ☎ *070/21121281* 🌐 *www.sardegnaturismo.it.*

Sights

Anfiteatro Romano

RUINS | This substantial amphitheater arena dating from the 2nd century AD attests to the importance of Karalis (modern-day Cagliari) to the Romans. Used for gladiatorial and animal contests, its squeezed, elliptical shape is due to the constrictions of the surrounding calcareous rock, but it could still hold up to 10,000 spectators—about half of Cagliari's population at the time. At time of writing, the site can be viewed from a raised walkway, but plans are afoot to allow visitors to enter the seating area and underground passages. **TIP→ If you don't want to enter the site, good views can be had from the adjacent Viale Sant'Ignazio.** ✉ *Viale Sant'Ignazio da Laconi, Cagliari* ☎ *070/6777900* 🌐 *www.monumenti-cagliari.it* *€3.*

Castello

VIEWPOINT | Perched over the vast expanse of Cagliari and its port, this hillside quarter has narrow streets that hold ancient monuments and piazzas amid apartments with wash hung out to dry on elaborate wrought-iron balconies. The most impressive entrance is through the commanding late-19th-century archway of the Bastione di St. Remy on Piazza Costituzione. Entering this way means climbing numerous steps; if this is a problem, walk up Viale Regina Elena or to the top of Piazza Yenne (behind Santa Chiara church) to find an elevator, or take the 7 bus. You'll be greeted by an impressive panorama of the cityscape and across the Gulf of Cagliari. From Piazza Palazzo, holding Cagliari's cathedral, it's a level walk to Piazza Indipendenza and the Museo Archeologico. ✉ *Cagliari.*

Duomo

CHURCH | The Cattedrale di Santa Maria, also known as the Duomo, was begun in the 12th century, but major renovation in the 17th century and reconstruction during the mid-1930s have left little of the original medieval church. The tiers of columns on the facade resemble those of medieval Romanesque Pisan churches, but only sections of the central portal, the bell tower, and the two side entrances are from the 13th century. Look for one of the most memorable features inside—the oversize marble pulpit sculpted in the 1300s and divided in half to fit into the church nave; it now lies on either side of the main entrance. ✉ *Piazza Palazzo, Cagliari* 🌐 *www.duomodicagliari.it* ⏲ *Closed Sun. 1–4 pm.*

★ Museo Archeologico

HISTORY MUSEUM | Built within the walls of the Pisan castle erected in the early 1300s, Cagliari's archaeological museum is the world's foremost authority on Sardinia's ancient Nuraghic civilization, named after the curious stone towers, or *nuraghi*, that are unique to the island. Archaeologists date most of these enigmatic structures to about 1300–1200 BC, the same time the ancient Israelites were establishing themselves in Canaan. Relics from this period are dispersed throughout the museum, notably the *bronzetti* (bronze statuettes) from Nuraghic towers and tombs, and, on the top floor, the much-celebrated Giganti di Mont'e Prama, giant Nuraghic stone statues representing warriors and boxers, unearthed in the 1970s and only recently restored and displayed to the public. Among the museum's other highlights are, on the first floor, quirky images excavated from a sanctuary dedicated to Bes, the ancient Egyptian deity whose cult reached far across the Mediterranean in the 3rd to 1st centuries BC, and the "Nora Stele", an inscribed stone said to be the earliest written document in Sardinia (and one of the earliest in Europe), which has the first mention of the name Sardinia, dating from between 850 and 725 BC.

The same entry ticket also allows you to visit the Pinacoteca, or art collection (accessed from the top floor), which includes some outstanding examples of religious art from the 15th and 16th centuries—well worth a look. ✉ *Piazza Arsenale, Cagliari* ☎ *070/655911* 🌐 *museinazionalicagliari.cultura.gov.it* 🎫 *€10* 🕑 *Closed Tues. Nov.–Feb.*

Orto Botanico

GARDEN | FAMILY | Located just below Cagliari's amphitheater, the city's Botanical Garden offers a welcome refuge from the summer's heat, and a shady spot for a pause from sightseeing. The 12-acre site is managed by Cagliari university and includes plants from all over the Mediterranean as well as Africa and further afield, plus herbariums, ponds, and a scattering of Roman remains, notably cisterns, tanks, and a well. As the only green space in the city center, it's ideal for kids to let off steam, and perfect for a picnic. Guided tours are also available (book ahead). ✉ *Viale Sant'Ignazio da Laconi 11, Cagliari* ☎ *070/6753512* 🌐 *sites.unica.it/hbk* 🎫 *€4* 🕑 *Closed Mon.*

Torre dell'Elefante

HISTORIC SIGHT | Part of Cagliari's imposing Pisan defenses, this medieval fortified tower was built in 1307 by Giovanni Capula as one of the main entrances to the Castello quarter. It is named after the small carving of an elephant visible on one wall. The side facing the old citadel was left entirely open, allowing you to view the series of wooden stairs and landings inside without climbing a step. If you are tempted to climb to the top, you'll be rewarded by a fabulous panorama of the city and its surrounding lagoons. Visits are only possible on guided tours, scheduled at 15 minutes past the hour; under-12s are not permitted for safety reasons. The structure is the twin of Torre San Pancrazio, located near the archaeological museum and currently closed for renovation work. ✉ *Piazza San Giuseppe 5, Cagliari* ☎ *070/6777900* 🌐 *www.monumenticagliari.it* 🎫 *€3.*

Beaches

★ Poetto Beach

BEACH | FAMILY | Only 5 km (3 miles) southeast of the city center, Poetto Beach is one of the most enticing spots to relax in summer for both locals and tourists. Its clean, shallow, turquoise waters stretch for some 8 km (5 miles), and the beach is lined with cafés, restaurants, snack bars, and parks. Beach chairs and umbrellas are available for rent for around €15. Away from the sea, you can explore the nearby Molentargius lagoon, and admire the pink flamingos that nest in the marshy reeds there. **TIP→ Poetto is easy to reach on the frequent public transport services: take Bus PF, PQ, or, in summer, Poetto Express or 5ZE, all from Piazza Matteotti.** **Amenities:** food and drink; lifeguards; parking (fee in summer); showers; toilets; water sports. **Best for:** swimming; walking; windsurfing. ✉ *Cagliari* ✢ *By car, take Viale Diaz from Cagliari to Viale Poetto.*

Restaurants

Sa Ide e S'Ollia

$ | SOUTHERN ITALIAN | Take a tour of contemporary Sardinian gastronomy in this trendsetting place that has become a hit with the *cagliaritani*. You can choose between eating à la carte or the small dishes offered on the tasting menus (€30, €35, and €40, including desserts), which might include such bold pairings as tagliatelle with pesto, hazelnut, cherry, and fresh orange, beef strips with berries and myrtle liqueur, and sea bream fillet with cherry, thyme, and orange oil. **Known for:** innovative food pairings; enthusiastic service; good-value set menus. *Average main: €17 Corso Vittorio Emanuele II 370, Cagliari 327/9649391 mobile www.facebook.com/saideesollia June–Oct. no lunch Sun., no dinner Tues.; Nov.–May no dinner Sun.*

Su Cumbidu

$ | ITALIAN | A meal at this restaurant in Cagliari's lively Marina quarter, near the port, makes for a quick and affordable introduction to Sardinia's rural cuisine. Dishes can be ordered as part of a fixed-price meal or separately, and portions are large, so go easy on antipasti to leave room for main courses of lamb, sausage, and the famous Sardinian *maialetto* (roast suckling pig, aka *porcheddu*). **Known for:** traditional meat-based dishes; casual, friendly atmosphere; range of set-price menus. *Average main: €15 Via Napoli 13, Cagliari 070/670712 www.facebook.com/sucumbiduterra.*

Trattoria Lillicu

$ | SEAFOOD | Seafood is the name of the game in this no-frills eatery at one end of the Marina's main restaurant alley. Below a gallery of paintings and old black-and-white photographs, two rows of marble-top tables line the walls, invariably filled with local families cheerfully tucking into such dishes as seafood risotto, grilled eels, and *pesce al pomodoro fresco* (a mix of sea-bream, red mullet, sea-bass, and sole in a fresh tomato sauce). **Known for:** simple but delicious seafood; brisk and boisterous atmosphere; authentic feel. *Average main: €18 Via Sardegna 78, Cagliari 070/652970 www.facebook.com/tratt.lillicu Closed Mon. No dinner Sun.*

Coffee and Quick Bites

Antico Caffè

$$ | ITALIAN | The gilded Antico Caffè once served as an intellectual haunt for famous writers like D.H. Lawrence and Grazia Deledda, who won the Nobel Prize in Literature in 1926. **Known for:** traditional ambience; swift lunches; late closing. *Average main: €20 Piazza Costituzione 10/11, Cagliari 070/658206 www.anticocaffe1855.it.*

Caffè Svizzero

$ | ITALIAN | Entering this antique, arched bar a stone's throw from the port is like stepping back to 1901, when the Caffè Svizzero first opened its doors. Order a steaming cappuccino, a glass of the local vermentino wine, or a freshly squeezed fruit juice, and nibble on a panino, a pizzetta, or a pastry. **Known for:** historic interior; great pastries; courteous staff. *Average main: €5 Largo Carlo Felice 6–8, Cagliari 070/664578 Closed Tues.*

Il Gusto dei Cannas

$ | SOUTHERN ITALIAN | Conveniently located a few steps from Cagliari's cathedral and archaeological museum in the Castello quarter, this tiny, welcoming spot offers a range of delicious lunchtime snacks to eat in at a counter or take out in a small or large box. Choices may include chicken salad, tripe and peas, caponata, and parmigiana, as well as freshly prepared filled panini. **Known for:** a range of freshly prepared snacks; take-out boxes; service with a smile. *Average main: €5 Via Lamarmora 60, Cagliari 351/9795417 No dinner Oct.–May.*

Hotels

Hotel AeR BJ Vittoria

$ | B&B/INN | The airy white rooms, period-style furnishings, and ceramic flooring make this third-floor pension directly opposite the port cozy and characterful.

Pros: clean rooms; central location near port; old-style family atmosphere. **Cons:** breakfast is not served in the hotel; no parking; shabby entrance. *$ Rooms from: €130 ✉ Via Roma 75, Cagliari ☎ 349/4473556 mobile, 070/667970 🌐 www.hotelbjvittoria.it 🛏 14 rooms 🍴 Free Breakfast.*

Hotel Regina Margherita

$ | **HOTEL** | Close to the port and the main downtown sights, this large, modern hotel attracts both vacationers and businesspeople with a quiet, friendly ambience and spacious, sober rooms. **Pros:** central location; higher rooms have harbor views; free parking. **Cons:** lacks local character; few leisure facilities; breakfast sometimes disappoints. *$ Rooms from: €159 ✉ Viale Regina Margherita 44, Cagliari ☎ 070/670342 🌐 www.hotelreginamargherita.com 🛏 100 rooms 🍴 Free Breakfast.*

Il Gallo Bianco

$ | **B&B/INN** | A broad sun terrace and white, plant-filled decor make this sleek boutique hotel a good choice, as do the spacious and surprisingly quiet—given the busy location—guest rooms, all of which have modern bathrooms and some of which have private balconies. **Pros:** sun terrace; central location near the train and bus stations; friendly staff. **Cons:** no parking; neighborhood is traffic-heavy and run-down; no staff present at night. *$ Rooms from: €139 ✉ Via Roma 237, Cagliari ☎ 334/9533149 mobile 🌐 www.gallobiancocagliari.it 🛏 16 rooms 🍴 Free Breakfast.*

★ THotel

$ | **HOTEL** | In the vicinity of Parco di Monte Claro, about a 15-minute taxi or bus ride from Cagliari's center, this trendy hotel offers contemporary styling and upscale guest rooms in a 15-floor circular tower with sweeping city views. **Pros:** great views from most rooms; free parking; outstanding service. **Cons:** 2 km (1¼ miles) from port; spa facilities can get busy; constant bustle in public areas. *$ Rooms from: €130 ✉ Via Dei Giudicati 66, Cagliari ☎ 070/47400 🌐 thotel.it 🛏 207 rooms 🍴 Free Breakfast.*

Nightlife

Al Merlo Parlante

PUB | This backstreet *birroteca* ("beer bar") has been dispensing distinguished brews for the last 40 years, and is a favorite haunt of students and beer aficionados of all ages. Local Sardinian craft beers and lagers and ales from around the world feature on its extensive and changing menu, many of them hand-pulled. The list of panini is almost equally long and equally impressive, and nachos are also served. *✉ Via Portoscalas 69, Cagliari ☎ 351/6638849 mobile 🌐 www.facebook.com/al.merlo.parlante.*

Caffè Libarium Nostrum

WINE BAR | A dim bohemian haunt full of wooden beams and brick-lined nooks and crannies, Libarium Nostrum is one of Cagliari's coolest café-bars. It's an occasional venue for live music and DJs, but the real draw is the outdoor terrace high atop medieval ramparts, the perfect spot for enjoying cocktails and sunset views. Food is available, from panini and other snacks to meat and fish dishes, and it stays open late. *✉ Via Santa Croce 33/35, Cagliari ☎ 346/5220212 moblie.*

Performing Arts

The Teatro Lirico stages concerts with local and well-known European artists throughout the year. See 🌐 *www.teatroliricodicagliari.it* or contact the tourist office for information.

Shopping

Cagliari's best shopping street—full of boutiques and specialty shops for clothes, shoes, bags, and jewelry—is **Via Manno,** just up from the port off Piazza Yenne. Via Manno climbs to Piazza Costituzione, from where **Via Garibaldi** trails back downhill, with an equally good range of slightly cheaper stores. Both streets are pedestrian-only.

Galinanoa

CRAFTS | This smart store in the Marina neighborhood holds a cornucopia of original and eye-catching artifacts inspired by traditional Sardinian arts and crafts, but with an original modern slant. Particularly appealing are the vividly colored ceramics, woven and wooden goods, elegant handbags, and highly stylized sculptures of sheep and bulls. Ask about shipping items home. ✉ *Via Baylle 71, Cagliari* ☎ *070/7563543* 🌐 *www.facebook.com/galinanoa.*

Sapori di Sardegna

FOOD & DRINK | Drop into this shop opposite the port for Sardinian food products, including local wines, artisanal biscuits, pecorino cheeses, carasau flatbread, honey, and olives. There's a great range of items, and the English-speaking staff are always willing to help you out. ✉ *Vico dei Mille 1, Cagliari* ☎ *070/6848747* 🌐 *saporidisardegna.com.*

Activities

WINDSURFING

Windsurfing Club Cagliari

WINDSURFING | FAMILY | Sardinia has some of Europe's best windsurfing spots. This outfit located in Cagliari's beach resort of Poetto provides advice, lessons, and courses for everyone from beginners to experts. ✉ *Viale Marina Piccola, Cagliari* ☎ *070/372694* 🌐 *www.windsurfingclub.it.*

Pula

29 km (18 miles) southwest of Cagliari, 314 km (195 miles) southwest of Olbia.

Resort villages sprawl along the coast southwest of the capital, which has its share of fine scenery and good beaches. On the marshy shoreline between Cagliari's Aeroporto di Elmas and Pula, huge flocks of flamingos are a common sight. Beaches and lodging catering to summer crowds are concentrated 4 km (2½ miles) south of Pula, a little more than 1½ km (1 mile) south of Nora, in a conglomeration that makes up Santa Margherita di Pula. At Chia, 19 km (12 miles) southwest of Pula, is one of Sardinia's most magnificent coastal stretches, with white-sand beaches, powdery dunes, placid coves, and turquoise waters.

GETTING HERE AND AROUND

From Cagliari, drive approximately 40 km (25 miles) on the SS195. Follow directions for Pula/Chia. From Olbia, take SS729 and SS131 toward Cagliari; then, follow SP2 and SS195bis toward Pula/Chia. The journey is approximately 300 km (190 miles).

Sights

★ **Nora**

ARCHAEOLOGICAL SITE | The narrow promontory outside Pula was the site of a Phoenician, Carthaginian, and then, later, Roman settlement that was first inhabited some 2,800 years ago. Nora was a prime location as a stronghold and an important trading town; Phoenician settlers scouted for good harbors, cliffs to shelter their craft from the wind, and an elevation from which they could defend themselves. An old Roman paved road passes the temple ruins, which include baths, a Roman theater, and an amphitheater now used for summer music festivals. ✉ *3 km (2 miles) south of Pula, Pula* ☎ *329/6715230 mobile* 🌐 *www.fondazionepulacultura.it* 🎫 *€10.*

Sant'Efisio

CHURCH | Behind its inappropriate modern frontage, the simple interior of this 11th-century church at the base of the Nora promontory retains its ancient and atmospheric character. Viewed from the rear, too, the exterior reveals its original lines. The church plays a key role in one of Sardinia's most colorful annual events—the Festa di Sant'Efisio, when a four-day procession accompanies a statue of the martyred St. Efisius all the way from Cagliari to here and back again, culminating in a huge parade of costumed Sardinians and decorated *traccas* (ox-drawn carriages) along Cagliari's main avenue. Try to catch this if you're in the area from May 1 to May 4 (the last day being the most spectacular). ✉ *Nora Beach, Pula* ✣ *3 km (2 miles) south of Pula* ☎ *389/1675008 mobile* 🌐 *www.facebook.com/confraternitadisantefisio.pula* ⏲ *Closed weekdays and Sat. morning.*

 Beaches

★ Chia Beach

BEACH | FAMILY | Although there is a perfectly serviceable sandy beach right outside the archaeological site of Nora, infinitely more enticing is the series of long expanses of sand 18 km (11 miles) farther south toward the cape of Capo Spartivento, Sardinia's southernmost tip. **Amenities:** food and drink; lifeguards; parking (fee in summer); toilets. **Best for:** swimming. ✉ *Santa Margherita di Pula* ✣ *By car, head south down the SS195 past Santa Margherita di Pula.*

 Restaurants

★ Su Furriadroxu

$ | SOUTHERN ITALIAN | Amid the lime and lemon trees in this courtyard trattoria in the center of Pula, you'll find down-home Sard cooking at its most authentic, with the accent firmly on meat dishes. The menu (in the local Campidanese dialect, with Italian and English translations) lists a selection of meaty fare, with pride of place going to the most famous of island dishes, *porceddu* (roast suckling pig), which you'll find displayed sizzling on a spit to satisfy the most purist of local gourmands. **Known for:** authentic Campidanese cooking; traditional outdoor setting; carnivorous feast. Ⓢ *Average main: €19* ✉ *Via XXIV Maggio 11, Pula* ☎ *070/5923819* 🌐 *www.instagram.com/sufurriadroxu* ⏲ *Closed Nov.; Wed. June–Sept.; and Tues. and Wed. Oct.–May. No lunch.*

★ Conrad Chia Laguna Sardinia

$$$ | RESORT | FAMILY | Now relaunched under Hilton's Conrad banner, the Chia Laguna hotel still has its captivating position overlooking Monte Cogoni beach and the sleek expanse of Chia lagoon, and its five-star facilities are geared to maximizing guests' enjoyment of these natural advantages. **Pros:** first-class facilities; choice of fine restaurants; proximity to some of Sardinia's best beaches. **Cons:** extravagant room rates, restaurant prices, and extras; pool closes early; remote location. Ⓢ *Rooms from: €493* ✉ *Viale dei Fenicotteri 52, Chia* ☎ *070/92391* 🌐 *www.chialagunaresort.com* ⏲ *Closed Nov.–mid-Apr.* 🛏 *107 rooms* 🍴 *Free Breakfast.*

Costa dei Fiori

$$ | HOTEL | FAMILY | Worry and stress seem to melt away upon arriving at this beach hideaway, where modern guest rooms with stone floors, big windows, and rural Sardinian touches are surrounded by peaceful gardens planted with pines and palms. **Pros:** great leisure facilities; lovely grounds; good low-season rates. **Cons:** you need a car; unexciting restaurant food; the beach may disappoint. Ⓢ *Rooms from: €311* ✉ *SS195 Km 33, Santa Margherita di Pula* ☎ *070/9245333* 🌐 *www.costadeifiori.it* ⏲ *Closed late Oct.–late Apr.* 🛏 *82 rooms* 🍴 *Free Breakfast.*

★ Faro Capo-Spartivento

$$$$ | HOTEL | Atop a cliff at the end of a rocky track on Sardinia's southernmost tip, a working lighthouse dating from 1856 contains this unusual hotel—a self-described "door suspended between the sky and the sea"—where it's easy to switch off and tune out amid luxurious surroundings. **Pros:** select and secluded; excellent restaurant; unique character and setting. **Cons:** remote and isolated location; rooms in annex lack much character; access road is in terrible condition. *Rooms from: €944* ✉ *Viale Spartivento* *5 km (3 miles) southwest of Chia* ☎ *393/8276800 mobile* *www.farocapospartivento.com* *Closed Nov.–Mar.* *10 rooms* *Free Breakfast.*

Sant'Antioco

75 km (47 miles) west of Pula, 100 km (62 miles) west of Cagliari.

Off Sardinia's southwest coast is the sleepy island of Sant'Antioco, whose good beaches have made it a popular holiday spot. Outside the peak summer months, though, the most hectic activity seems to be the silent repairing of nets by local fishermen who have already pulled in their daily catch. The island has been connected to the mainland since Carthaginian times by a causeway that's still standing (the modern causeway that you cross runs parallel), and Sant'Antioco town (the island and its main town share the same name) has a fascinating collection of archaeological remains from this period.

GETTING HERE AND AROUND

Sant'Antioco is about 90 minutes from Cagliari by bus or car. Drive on the SS130 as far as Iglesias, then the SS126 in the direction of Carbonia and Sant'Antioco.

Sights

Calasetta

TOWN | On the island of Sant'Antioco, off the southwestern coast of Sardinia, the fishing village and port of Calasetta draws visitors year-round for its beautiful beaches and fresh-seafood dishes. The pristine beaches of Spiaggia Grande and Le Saline, alternating with rocky areas, dunes, and local vegetation, form a rugged paradise. Founded by Ligurian settlers who worked as coral and tuna fishermen, Calasetta is connected daily by ferry boats with the smaller island of San Pietro, which also keeps intact its Ligurian cultural history and dialect. ✉ *10 km (6 miles) northwest of Sant'Antioco town, Sant'Antioco.*

Carbonia

TOWN | If you like to seek out the esoteric, explore the rugged inland hills and town of Carbonia, less than 30 minutes' drive from Sant'Antioco and about an hour by car or train from Cagliari. Built in 1938 by Mussolini to serve as an administrative center of a once-booming coal-mining area, its time-frozen architecture—ordered rows of workers' houses around a core of monumental public buildings on the broad Piazza Roma—has been called an urban UFO set down in the Sardinian landscape. ✉ *Piazza Roma 1, Carbonia* ☎ *0781/6941 tourist office* *www.carboniaturismo.it.*

Iglesias

TOWN | Perched at about 600 feet in the southwest hills of the island, this authentic Sardinian town 35 km (22 miles) north of Sant'Antioco has two notable medieval churches: the Cattedrale di Santa Chiara and Madonna delle Grazie. The town is famous for its theatrical, Spanish-inflected Easter festivities. A short drive away, on the Costa Verde, you can enjoy unspoiled, uncrowded beaches, including the beautiful Masua cove at Porto Cauli beach. ✉ *Piazza Municipio, Iglesias* ☎ *0781/274507 tourist office* *www.iglesiasturismo.it.*

Monte Sirai

ARCHAEOLOGICAL SITE | Just outside Carbonia and strategically positioned atop a plateau that provides views inland and far out to sea, the remains of one of Sardinia's most important Carthaginian military strongholds were discovered by chance in 1962. The walls of Mt. Sirai were erected around 375 BC, and they continued to function as impregnable fortress barriers until the Roman conquest in 238 BC. For the full picture, try to combine your visit with a look at Carbonia's archaeological museum on Via Campania. *✉ Off SS126, Km 17, Località Sirai ✣ 1 km (½ mile) north of Carbonia, direction Sant'Antioco ☎ 345/7559751 archaeological site (mobile), 345/8886058 museum (mobile) ⊕ www.carboniamusei.it 🎫 Site €6, museum €6, or €10 for both ⏲ Closed Mon., also Tues. Oct.–Mar.*

Zona Archeologica

RUINS | The chief point of interest in Sant'Antioco island's eponymous main town is the Archaeological Zone at the top of the old section, which has terrific views of the Sardinian mainland. Here you can see a *tophet*—a Punic sanctuary, necropolis, and burial site—which is scattered with urns that contained the cremated remains of stillborn children. Below the site is Sant'Antioco's excellent archaeological museum that showcases artifacts from the tophet as well as from the Neolithic, Byzantine, and Roman eras. You can also visit a nearby ethnographic collection and a Piedmontese fort. Various combined tickets are available. *✉ Via Sabatino Moscati, Sant'Antioco ☎ 0781/82105, 389/7962114 mobile ⊕ www.mabsantantioco.it 🎫 Archaeological zone €4, museum €6, combined tickets for both €7, ethnographic collection €3, Piedmontese fort €2.50.*

San Pietro

5 km (3 miles) northwest of Sant'Antioco.

A ferry at the small northern port of Calasetta connects Sant'Antioco with Carloforte, the main town on the smaller island of San Pietro. This classic little Italian port and its surrounding coastline are a favorite of wealthy Cagliaritans, many of whom have built weekend cottages here. The best views are from Capo Sandalo, on San Pietro's rugged western coast, but head to the island's southern tip for the beaches. Accommodation is especially scarce during the annual music festival (*⊕ www.carlofortefestival.com*) that takes place over 10 days in early August. During daylight hours the ferry departs approximately hourly in summer and every 90 minutes in winter—the trip takes 30 minutes.

GETTING HERE AND AROUND

Car ferries operated by Delcomar (*⊕ www.delcomar.it*) connect San Pietro with Calasetta on Sant'Antioco, or Portoscuso near Iglesias on the Sardinian mainland. Round-trip tickets are from €10 per person, from €20 for a car.

Hotels

Hotel Hieracon

$ | HOTEL | This hotel on Carloforte's harborfront combines its elegant, historic flavor with modern whitewashed accommodation. **Pros:** helpful English-speaking staff; characterful historic ambience; good location. **Cons:** cheaper rooms are cramped; few sea-facing rooms; not up to its four-star grading. *[$] Rooms from: €108 ✉ Corso Cavour 62, Carloforte ☎ 0781/854028, 393/7953214 mobile ⊕ www.hotelhieracon.com ⏲ Closed mid-Oct.–mid-Apr. 🛏 23 rooms 🍽 Free Breakfast.*

Costa Verde

80 km (50 miles) northwest of Cagliari.

If you've come to Sardinia in search of untrammeled wilderness and sweeping sands as far as the eye can see, this semideserted coast will fit the bill. Hidden away in the forgotten southwest corner of the island, the Costa Verde, or Green Coast, is a succession of cliffs and beaches, many of them accessible only by bumpy, unpaved tracks. The effort is worth it. The dune-backed sands shelter rare grasses and birdlife, and the area offers magnificent swimming along stretches of beach that seem endless.

GETTING HERE AND AROUND

The best way to access the Green Coast is by car, though roads can be dangerously steep and winding. Take precautions and drive during daytime, also because roads and exits are poorly lit. Roads designated "SS" are developed freeways with fast-flowing traffic.

You can approach one of the most evocative stretches of the coast, Piscinas, either from the town of Guspini, on the straggling S126, or from a turnoff a couple of miles farther south, which leads through the abandoned mining town of Ingurtosu. It's a strange, ghostly cluster of chimneys and workers' dwellings, forlorn amid the encroaching scrubland. Drive down the dirt track another 10 km (6 miles) or so, through woods of juniper, to reach the sea.

Beaches

Piscinas

BEACH | FAMILY | Sea and nature are the big draws of Sardinia's Costa Verde, where you'll find such wild and unpopulated beaches as Piscinas, at the southern end of the coast and reached via a rough mountain road that passes deserted mines and herds of goats. **Amenities:** none; parking (fee in summer). **Best for:** solitude; sunset; swimming; walking. ✉ *Via Bau, Arbus.*

Torre dei Corsari

BEACH | FAMILY | At the northern end of the Costa Verde, Torre dei Corsari is a long and wide stretch of quartz sand, easily accessible and with plenty of facilities including bars, restaurants, and sun beds to rent. **Amenities**: food and drink; parking (fee in summer); toilets. **Best for:** sunset; swimming. ✉ *Viale della Torre, Arbus.*

Hotels

Hotel Le Dune

$$$ | HOTEL | A remote Green Coast oasis on lovely Piscinas Beach—between Capo Pecora and Capo Frasca—this designer hotel occupies a former warehouse, built in the late 1800s to house minerals excavated from surrounding hills. **Pros:** beachfront property; breathtaking setting; gym, pool, and spa available. **Cons:** remote location; five-star prices for sometimes mediocre facilities and services; restaurant menu a bit samey. *Rooms from: €522 ✉ Via Bau 1, Piscinas di Ingurtosu, Arbus ☎ 070/7058030 www.ledunepiscinas.com Closed mid-Oct.–mid-Apr. 28 rooms Free Breakfast.*

Barumini

65 km (40 miles) north of Cagliari.

Take a detour along good roads into Sardinia's interior to visit the extraordinary stone village-fortress of Su Nuraxi, just outside the quiet village of Barumini.

GETTING HERE AND AROUND

The best way to reach Su Nuraxi is by car. From the capital, follow SS131 to SS197. Direct buses to the site are few and far between.

Sights

★ Su Nuraxi

RUINS | FAMILY | The most extensive of the island's 7,000 discovered nuraghi, Su Nuraxi is on the UNESCO World Heritage list. Concentric rings of thick stone walls conceal dark chambers and narrow passages in a central beehive-shape tower. In the ruins of the surrounding village there are benches, ovens, wells, and other Bronze Age remnants. Tours start every 30 minutes and last about an hour. The same ticket includes entry to a museum and exhibition center in Barumini. **TIP→ If you're driving from**

Su Nuraxi to the Costa Smeralda
CORSICA
FRANCE
Bonifacio
Isola Santa Maria
Isola Maddalena
Isola Caprera
Compendio Garibaldino
Santa Teresa Gallura
Capo Testa
La Maddalena
Palau
Porto Cervo
COSTA SMERALDA
Arzachena
Bassacutena
Sant'Antonio di Gallura
Capo Figari
Golfo Aranci
Golfo di Olbia
Olbia
I. Tavolara
I. Molara
Punta Caprara
Isola Asinara
0
10 mi
0
10 km
Stintino
Golfo dell'Asinara
Castelsardo
Tempio Pausania
Telti
Porto Torres
Sedini
Monti
Padru
Sorso
Chiaramonti
Oschiri
Sassari
Ozieri
Budduso
Siniscola
S'Ena 'e sa Chitta
Grotta di Nettuno
Capo Caccia
Alghero
Villanova Monteleone
Bitti
Bultei
Sas Linnas Siccas
Orosei
Padria
Monte Ortobene
Nuoro
Dorgali
Cala Gonone
Golfo di Orosei
Bosa
Macomer
Orotelli
Tresnuraghes
Abbasanta
Fonni
TYRRHENIAN SEA
Tortolì
Cabras Beach
Cabras
San Giovanni di Sinis
Oristano
Capo San Marco
Tharros
Golfo di Oristano
Asuni
Laconi
Bari Sardo
Sadali
Nurallao
Capo di Frasca
Marrubiu
Tertenia
Sant'Antonio de Santadi
Uras
Su Nuraxi
Barumini
Porto Palma
Mandas
Cantoniera San Giorgio
MEDITERRANEAN SEA
Furtei
Guspini
San Nicolo Gerrei
Samassi
Muravera
Fluminimaggiore
Monastir
Buggerru
Villasor
Dolianova
Decimomannu
90
133
427
125
200
127
392
199
291
597
389
105
292
49
129
131
128
388
198
442
126
197

SS131, don't be misled to other, lesser nuraghi—follow the signs all the way to Barumini. ✉ *Viale Su Nuraxi, Barumini* ✣ *SP5 Barumini–Tuili, 1 km (½ mile) west of Barumini* ☎ *070/9368128* 🌐 *www.fondazionebarumini.it* 🎫 *€15.*

Oristano

60 km (37 miles) northwest of Barumini, 93 km (58 miles) northwest of Cagliari.

The elegant and compact old quarter of this provincial center off the tourist track exudes a distinct serenity. At its pedestrianized center is Piazza Eleonora, which retains an old-world charm thanks to a neoclassical town hall, a marble monument to Giudichessa Eleonora, the warrior queen who opposed the Spanish incursions at the end of the 14th century, and the 18th-century Mameli palace with its beautiful wrought-iron balconies. The piazza is one of the focal points of Oristano's relaxed evening passeggiata, and at other times teems with vivacious children.

GETTING HERE AND AROUND

Oristano is easily accessible and well connected to other major areas of Sardinia by car, train, or bus. Trains and buses between Cagliari, Sassari, Olbia, and Nuoro stop here several times per day. The central bus station is in the city center, the train station on the outskirts, a short bus or taxi ride away. By car, turn off the SS131 highway for Oristano. The part-pedestrianized old center is easily negotiable on foot.

VISITOR INFORMATION

CONTACT Oristano Tourist Office. ✉ *Piazza Eleonora 18, Oristano* ☎ *0783/308693* 🌐 *www.oristanoinfo.it.*

Sights

Cabras

BEACH | FAMILY | Extensive marshlands and shallow lagoons teeming with eels, crayfish, and wildlife surround this calm and compact 11th-century town. Make a stop at the archaeological museum here for its awe-inspiring nuraghic statues, then venture north and west into the Sinis Peninsula to access the pristine beaches of Is Arutas, Maimoni, and Mari Ermi, characterized by fine white quartzified sand grains. The flat terrain and quiet roads of the peninsula make it ideal for exploring by bike. ✉ *SP3 off SP1, 10 km (6 miles) northwest of Oristano, Cabras.*

Restaurants

Bar Pasticceria Eleonora

$ | SOUTHERN ITALIAN | Steps from Oristano's tourist office, you can take a refreshing break with a coffee and a pastry or panino at this relaxed café on the corner of Piazza Eleonora. The outdoor tables are ideal for people-watching, and ice creams are also available. **Known for:** fresh pastries and snacks; traditional local flavor; central people-watching spot. 💲 *Average main: €6* ✉ *Piazza Eleonora d'Arborea 1, Oristano* ☎ *0783/71454* ⏲ *Closed Sun.*

Cocco e Dessi

$ | SOUTHERN ITALIAN | The building dates from 1925 but the interior shows a diversity of styles, with the main dining area (one of five) inside a glass gazebo. Dishes featuring fresh catches of the day, meat dishes, and herb-infused sauces are complemented by pizzas and such pastas as *lados di Dorgali*—a handmade pasta served with wild boar sauce and cheese. Just save room for a dessert of *tumbarelle di Stintino*, a delicious concoction of ricotta, walnuts, and orange zest. **Known for:** quirky decor; convivial atmosphere; great local dishes. 💲 *Average* *main: €19* ✉ *Via Tirso 31, Oristano* ☎ *0783/252648* 🌐 *www.coccoedessi.it.*

Ristorante Craf da Banana

$ | **SOUTHERN ITALIAN** | The brick walls, dim lighting, and vaulted ceilings here make you feel as if you've stepped into a wine cellar. Aged photographs of Oristano's Sa Sartiglia jousting festival and specialty dishes from Oristano and Montiferru do a good job capturing local flavor. **Known for:** traditional Sardinian dishes; historical setting; cozy, romantic atmosphere. [$] *Average main: €19* ✉ *Via de Castro 34, Oristano* ☎ *0783/70669* 🌐 *www.ristorantecrafdabanana.com* ⏲ *No lunch Sun. June–Sept. No dinner Sun. Oct.–May.*

Trattoria Gino

$ | **SOUTHERN ITALIAN** | Light-color walls adorned with old photos and shelves of local wine provide the setting for the two rows of tables in Trattoria Gino, a presence in Oristano for nearly a century. The menu emphasizes simple, traditional dishes, such as *culurgiones* (ravioli) with creamed zucchini and scampi, *gnocchetti alla campidanese* (with a sausage-meat sauce), and spaghetti *ai ricci* (with sea urchins). **Known for:** simple, traditional dishes; reasonable prices; plain but elegant surroundings. [$] *Average main: €17* ✉ *Via Tirso 13, Oristano* ☎ *0783/71428* ⏲ *Closed Sun. and 3 wks Sept. and Oct.*

Hotels

Mariano IV Palace Hotel

$ | **HOTEL** | This central downtown hotel has a reassuringly old-fashioned style, with its grand, columned exterior and elegant neoclassical lobby hung with chandeliers. **Pros:** convenient location; good restaurant; low online rates. **Cons:** dated feel; caters mostly to business travelers; no parking for cars. [$] *Rooms from: €90* ✉ *Piazza Mariano 50, Oristano* ☎ *0783/360101* 🌐 *www.hotelmarianoiv.com* 🛏 *67 rooms* 🍴 *Free Breakfast.*

Residenza d'Epoca Regina d'Arborea

$ | **B&B/INN** | One floor of a 19th-century palazzo, next to the town hall on Oristano's traffic-free main square, has been tastefully converted into a small but stylish guest house, with rich furnishings, chandeliers, antique murals, and domed ceilings. **Pros:** rich period character; very central location; helpful hosts. **Cons:** quirky style not to everyone's taste; no car access possible; not suitable for children. [$] *Rooms from: €144* ✉ *Piazza Eleonora d'Arborea 4, Oristano* ☎ *0783/302101* 🌐 *www.reginadarborea.it* ⏲ *Closed 10 days in Dec.* 🛏 *6 rooms* 🍴 *Free Breakfast.*

Tharros

16 km (10 miles) west of Oristano, 52 km (32 miles) northwest of Barumini.

Spread across a thin tongue of land that dangles off the Sinis Peninsula, the archaeological site of Tharros ranks as one of Sardinia's most important Phoenician, Carthaginian, and Roman settlements. It's not hard to understand why this evocative site was selected by the ancients, given its sweeping views across the Gulf of Oristano, its defensibility, and the shelter it provides vessels. Founded around 800 BC, the city was finally abandoned in the 11th century AD, in favor of Oristano.

GETTING HERE AND AROUND

Whether you're heading to Tharros from the north or south, follow the SS131 to Oristano. Drive through Oristano toward Cabras, branching off on SP6 for San Giovanni di Sinis and Tharros. There's frequent bus service from Oristano.

Sights

Museo Civico di Cabras

HISTORY MUSEUM | This lagoon-side archaeological museum displays many of the better-preserved urns and other artifacts recovered from nearby excavation sites, including Tharros. It is also the main home of the Giganti di Mont'e Prama—unique nuraghic stone statues recovered from the Sinis Peninsula in the 1970s but only recently viewable in their restored state. The visit takes about an hour. Buy a combination ticket to see the Museo Civico and the ruins at Tharros. ✉ *Via Tharros 121, off SP6, 10 km (6 miles) northwest of Oristano, Cabras* ☎ *0783/290636* 🌐 *www.museocabras.it* 🎫 *€9; €13 combined ticket, includes Tharros* ⏲ *Closed Mon. Nov.–Mar.*

San Giovanni di Sinis
CHURCH | Just before the entrance of Tharros, you'll see the small, squat, and pink-domed church of San Giovanni di Sinis, dating from the 11th century. The simplicity of its bare and perfectly preserved interior, with three low-vaulted naves lit by tiny window apertures, offers a fascinating insight into the religious practises of the time. ✉ *SP6, San Giovanni di Sinis, Cabras* ☎ *0783/370019* 🌐 *monteprama.it* 🎫 *Free.*

Tharros
RUINS | FAMILY | The spectacular site of the Carthaginian and Roman city of Tharros was, like Nora to the south, chosen because it commanded the best views of the gulf and could provide an easy escape route if inland tribes threatened. The Phoenician-Punic city planning here includes sophisticated water channeling and masonry foundations. Two reconstructed Corinthian columns stand as testament to the site's Roman history, and there are baths visible and mosaic fragments from the Roman city. ✉ *Off SP6, 16 km (10 miles) west of Oristano, 113 km (70 miles) northwest of Cagliari, San Giovanni di Sinis* ☎ *0783/370019* 🌐 *monteprama.it/tharros* 🎫 *€9; €13 combined ticket, includes Museo Civico di Cabras; €11 combined ticket, Tharros and tower* ⏲ *Closed Mon. Nov.–Mar.*

En Route

On the way to the archaeological ruins in Tharros you pass the ghost town of **San Salvatore,** revived briefly in the 1960s as a locale for spaghetti Westerns and since abandoned, except for a few days every summer, when it is the focus of a religious pilgrimage. The small dwellings here are used to accommodate the pilgrims. The saloon from the movie set still stands (and offers drinks and snacks). Among the dunes past San Salvatore are large huts formerly used by fishermen and now much in demand as vacation homes.

Nuoro

107 km (67 miles) northeast of Tharros, 181 km (113 miles) north of Cagliari.

The strongly traditional but somewhat nondescript provincial capital of Nuoro stands on the edge of the Gennargentu massif, home to the island's highest peaks (6,000 feet). Apart from a brace of engaging museums, a lively restaurant scene and a well-attended evening *passeggiata* along the part-pedestrianized main street of the old town, not much happens here; you can do some shopping amid strolling locals, or try the local Barbagia sausage, which is great.
■ TIP→ Entry to Nuoro's museums is free on the first Sunday of the month.

GETTING HERE AND AROUND

From Cagliari, the drive to Nuoro takes about two hours. Take the SS131 toward Sassari/Oristano/Nuoro, then continue on SS131 DCN toward Nuoro/Olbia. After 55 km (34 miles), turn off, following signs for Nuoro Centro. The town is also reachable by train on a service (run by ARST) from

Macomer, which is on the main north-south train network.

Sights

Monte Ortobene

MOUNTAIN | About 7 km (4 miles) north-east of Nuoro is Monte Ortobene, a granite peak at 2,900 feet offering lofty views over the gulch below. Here you can also see up close the imposing bronze statue of the Rendentore, or Christ the Redeemer, overlooking the valley. Pilgrimages and Masses take place in summer here. Picnic tables make this a favorite spot for an alfresco lunch throughout the year. The mountain is easily reachable from Nuoro by bus or car via SP45. ✉ *Nuoro* 🌐 *www.comune.nuoro.it.*

Museo Deleddiano

HISTORIC HOME | Nuoro is the literary capital of Sardinia and was the home of the island's most celebrated writer, the Nobel Prize–winner Grazia Deledda (1871–1936), who was born and grew up in this dwelling in the old center. The restored building is now a museum dedicated to the novelist, elegantly furnished in the style of the late 19th century and permitting a fascinating insight into how people lived in that period. The kitchen and garden are especially interesting, and letters and photographs relating to Deledda are displayed on the top floor. ✉ *Via Grazia Deledda 42, Nuoro* ☎ *0784/242900* 🌐 *www.isresardegna.it* 🎫 *€5, or €8 with the Ethnographic Museum* 🕒 *Closed Mon. Nov.–mid-Mar.*

★ Museo Etnografico Sardo

HISTORY MUSEUM | Also known as the Museo del Costume, this ethnographic collection is a must for anyone interested in the cultural context of Sardinia's customs and traditions. Among the 8,000 items in the museum's collection, you can view domestic and agricultural implements, splendid jewelry, traditional musical instruments, and dozens of local costumes. Audio guides are available, and guided tours can be booked. The nearby park on Sant'Onofrio Hill affords magnificent views over Nuoro and the surrounding country. ✉ *Via A. Mereu 56, Nuoro* ☎ *0784/257035* 🌐 *www.isresardegna.it* 🎫 *€5, or €8 with the Museo Deleddiano* 🕒 *Closed Mon. Nov.–mid-Mar.*

Favorite Places

Rob Andrews: Nuoro's Museo Etnografico Sardo is the place to get in touch with Sardinia's rural roots, a fantastic showcase for the richness of the island's village culture in all its forms.

Restaurants

★ Il Portico

$ | **ITALIAN** | Brotherly love (and ownership) and quality seafood are among the things that make this old-town restaurant so exceptional. Modern artwork, stone pillars, and arched ceilings help to provide a fitting setting for the predominantly traditional cuisine livened up with modern elements. **Known for:** innovative takes on traditional cuisine; locals' choice; welcoming atmosphere. 💲 *Average main: €18* ✉ *Via Mons. Bua 13, Nuoro* ☎ *0784/232909* 🌐 *www.ilporticonuoro.it* 🕒 *Closed Mon., 2 wks in July and Aug., and 2 wks in Jan. and Feb. No dinner Sun.*

Il Rifugio

$$ | **SOUTHERN ITALIAN** | **FAMILY** | At this family-run local spot, the rustic dining area—with terra-cotta floors, brick pillars, and a wood-burning stove—is packed nearly every night. The service, presentation, and wine list are as exceptional as the food: only the freshest local meats and cheeses are served, and all the dishes are made from scratch, including the

pizza (available evenings only), the pasta, and the semifreddo ice cream drizzled with honey. **Known for:** lively and convivial air; authentic and expertly prepared local dishes; good wine cellar. *$ Average main: €20 ✉ Via A. Mereu 28/36, Nuoro ☎ 0784/232355 🌐 www.trattoriarifugio.com ⏲ Closed Wed. No dinner Tues.*

Hotels

★ Casa Solotti

$ | **B&B/INN** | You don't have to venture far out of Nuoro to appreciate its magnificent mountainous setting, and mountain views don't get much grander than from this excellent lodging immersed in the oak forests of Monte Ortobene. **Pros:** beautiful mountain views; warm and friendly hospitality; terrific breakfasts. **Cons:** remote rural location; not ideal for anyone with impaired mobility; few facilities. *$ Rooms from: €70 ✉ Località Monte Ortobene, Nuoro ☎ 0784/33954, 328/6028975 mobile 🌐 www.casasolotti.it ⏲ Closed mid-Nov.–late Dec. and late Jan.–late Mar. 6 rooms Free Breakfast.*

Su Gologone Experience Hotel

$$$ | **HOTEL** | Just southeast of Nuoro, in the foothills of the Supramonte range, Su Gologone combines luxury with rural flavor in guest rooms that feel like country retreats (exposed beams, wooden chests, traditional Sardinian fabrics) and a rustic restaurant that pairs local cannonau reds with such Sardinian specialties as *maccarones de busa* (thick homemade pasta twists), *culurgiones* (ravioli), suckling pig, and, for dessert, *sebadas* (fried-dough pockets stuffed with cheese and lemon peel). **Pros:** locally influenced restaurant; great opportunities for hiking in the Supramonte Valley; museumlike decor. **Cons:** used by groups and wedding parties; many stairs to negotiate; remote location. *$ Rooms from: €440 ✉ Località Su Gologone ☎ 0784/287512 🌐 www.sugologone.it ⏲ Closed early Nov.–mid-Apr. 68 rooms Free Breakfast.*

Shopping

Latteria Zia Marianna 1936

FOOD | Named after the nonna of the current generation that runs this specialty food shop dating from 1936, this place on the main axis of Nuoro's old town offers an enticing array of jams, wines, pastas, cheeses, hams, and bread—in short all the great food and drink that this part of the island is famous for. You can sample the various wares, too, in the adjacent bar/bistro. *✉ Corso Garibaldi 174–176, Nuoro ☎ 0784/1823005 🌐 www.facebook.com/latteriaziamarianna1936.*

Fonni

30 km (19 miles) south of Nuoro, 137 km (85 miles) south of Olbia.

In the heart of the Barbagia region, Fonni is the highest town on the island. This mountainous district, including Monte Spada and the Bruncu Spina refuge on the Gennargentu massif, is Sardinia's most primitive. Life in some villages seems not to have changed much since the Middle Ages.

GETTING HERE AND AROUND

To reach Fonni, the highest town in Sardinia, drive or take a bus from Nuoro. There is no train service.

From Nuoro, take SS389var to Mamoiada, then SS389, or, for a more scenic route, branch off on SS128 to go via the town of Gavoi. From Cagliari, follow SS131, exiting at Ghilarza toward the village of Ottana. Continue on SS128 to Gavoi, then follow signs for Fonni. From Sassari, follow SS131 south, turning east onto SS129 at Macomer. Continue on SS128, following signs for Fonni.

Shopping

Special candies made from honey and nougat are sold in hilltop Tonara, 15 km (9 miles) southwest of Fonni.

In the mountain village of Aritzo, about 45 km (28 miles) south of Fonni, high up in the Barbagia, look for handcrafted wooden utensils and furniture.

Torronificio Marotto
CANDY | Tonara, a short and scenic drive southwest of Fonni, is the capital of *torrone* (nougat) production in Sardinia. You'll find some of the sweetest and nuttiest examples in this traditional store in the heart of the village, all handmade and available in a range of flavors. ✉ *Via Roma 6, Tonara* ☎ *0784/63824* 🌐 *www.torronificiomarotto.com.*

Alghero

137 km (85 miles) southwest of Olbia.

A tourist-friendly town of about 43,000 inhabitants, with a distinctly Spanish flavor, Alghero is also known as "Barcelonetta" (Little Barcelona) for its strong Catalan ties. Rich wrought-iron scrollwork decorates balconies and screened windows, street names appear in the Catalan-tinged local dialect as well as Italian, and Spanish motifs can be seen in stone portals and bell towers.

Besides its historic architectural gems, the fortified town is well worth a visit to simply stroll along its narrow cobblestone lanes, admire the sea views from its mighty city walls, and browse its pretty boutiques. To dip into the local culture, pick up from the tourist office or one of the participating attractions an "Alghero Ticket," allowing free entry into all the principal sights (€25, or €50 for a family ticket). It's available between April and October.

GETTING HERE AND AROUND

Alghero Airport is 15 km (9 miles) from the city center, which you can reach by car, taxi, or public transport. Regional buses and local trains connect the town with Sassari, and there are buses from Via Catalogna in the public gardens to local beaches, sights outside town, and nearby villages. In summer, the Beach Bus also connects the beaches and sights to Alghero's center. The closest passenger port is Porto Torres, approximately 40 km (25 miles) north, with links to Genoa, Civitavecchia (Rome), Corsica, and France.

VISITOR INFORMATION

CONTACT Alghero Tourism Office. ✉ *Via Cagliari 2, in the public gardens, Alghero* ☎ *079/979054* 🌐 *www.algheroturismo.eu.*

Sights

Capo Caccia
NATURE SIGHT | Head 25 km (16 miles) west of Alghero for the spectacular heights of the imposing limestone headland of Capo Caccia. The rugged promontory, blanketed by thick maquis, forms part of the Porto Conte nature reserve and is home to deep caves such as the Grotta di Nettuno. Close by are the beaches of Porto Ferro, Cala Viola, and, on the beautiful Porto Conte inlet, Cala Dragunara. ✉ *West of Alghero, Alghero* ☎ *079/945005* 🌐 *www.algheroparks.it* 🎫 *Free.*

★ **Grotta di Nettuno** (*Neptune's Cave*)
CAVE | **FAMILY** | At the base of a sheer cliff, the pounding sea has carved an entrance to a vast fantastic cavern filled with stunning water pools, stalactites, and stalagmites. The dramatic cave and coves, discovered by fishermen in the 18th century, are popular tourist attractions for their sheer natural beauty. You must visit with a guide; tours start on the hour. It's possible to reach the caves by boat or by land. Between April and November, boat trips depart regularly from the port of Alghero for €17 round-trip (admission to the grotto is extra). To reach the grotto by land, you can descend the 654 dizzying steps of Escala del Cabirol ("Goat Steps"), which are cut into the steep cliff here. **TIP→ By public bus or, in**

summer, the Beach Bus from Alghero's Via Catalogna, the trip to the top of the stairway takes about 50 minutes. Allow 15 minutes for the descent by foot. Visitors arriving by land must book beforehand by telephone or online at *www.algheroexperience.it.* *Off SP55, 13 km (8 miles) west of Alghero, Alghero 345/7418361 grotto (mobile) www.grottadinettuno.it €14 Closed in rough seas.*

Museo del Corallo

SPECIALTY MUSEUM | The coast around Alghero is one of the Mediterranean's most abundant sources of red coral, the subject of this entertaining and informative museum housed in a Liberty-era villa near Piazza Sulis. Old photographs and films show the process of harvesting the substance, and there are impressive displays of coral jewelry and ornaments. *Via Venti Settembre 8, Alghero 079/4134690 www.museialghero.it €5 Closed mornings Mon. and Wed., afternoons Tues. and Thurs.*

San Francesco

RELIGIOUS BUILDING | Alghero's cathedral on Via Manno hosts most of the town's official religious functions, but this 15th–16th-century church built in the Catalan-Gothic style is closest to the hearts of the *algheresi* and where you might come across the local dialect, used in some of the masses here. The simple interior holds a particularly emaciated-looking wooden Christ, while the crypt and cloister have an atmospheric charm, but the highlight of a visit is to climb the hexagonal bell tower—not too arduous—for some great views of the Old Town (open mornings: April and May, Tuesday, Friday, and Saturday; June–October, daily; November–March, Tuesday and Friday). Evening concerts are held in the cloister in the summer months. *Via Carlo Alberto 46, Alghero 351/6428081 mobile www.complessosanfrancescoalghero.com €6, €3 church and cloister only, €4 tower only Closed Mon. morning, Thurs. afternoon, and Sun.*

Beaches

Le Bombarde and Lazzaretto Beaches

BEACH | FAMILY | A couple of kilometers north of Alghero's old town, backed by pine woods, Maria Pia beach offers a convenient though unspectacular spot for an afternoon of bathing and sunbathing, but if you don't mind going farther afield, head for the altogether superior beaches of Le Bombarde and Lazzaretto, on adjacent inlets 10 km (6 miles) west of town. Sheltered from the wind and equipped with bars and facilities for renting pedalos and canoes, the beaches are similar in style—both curves of soft sand studded with a few rocks, and both packed in August. **TIP→ The beaches are easy to reach on public buses or the private tourist bus service, Beach Bus (May–September), both leaving from Via Catalogna in the public gardens.** **Amenities:** food and drink; lifeguards; parking (fee in summer); showers; toilets; water sports. **Best for:** snorkeling; swimming; windsurfing. *Alghero By car, take Via Garibaldi and then SS127bis north and west along the coast toward Fertilia.*

Restaurants

★ Al Vecchio Mulino

$ | SOUTHERN ITALIAN | Slightly off the tourist track but well known to locals, this grotto-like former mill has two long rooms with low, vaulted ceilings and a brisk but cheerful atmosphere. There's a good balance between meat and seafood dishes, the menu taking in everything from *malloreddus alla sarda* (local pasta with sausage-meat sauce) and *fritto misto di mare* (fried squid, prawns, and fresh fish) to crusty pizzas. **Known for:** abundant portions reasonably priced; locals' choice; vivacious and cozy ambience. *Average main: €19 Via Don Deroma 3, Alghero 079/977254 www.facebook.com/alvecchiomulinoalghero Closed Tues., 2 wks in late Jan., and Nov.–mid-Dec. No lunch.*

Il Pavone

$$ | **ITALIAN** | Fresh flowers on white linen tablecloths add color to the bright glass-enclosed dining area of this delightful eatery on busy Piazza Sulis; gold-framed paintings and oversize wine bottles capped in wax add Italian charm—as does the seasonally changing menu of pasta and seafood dishes such as potato-stuffed *culurgiones* (a ravioli-like pasta) topped with pecorino cheese, dried tomatoes, and wild rocket, and fillet of suckling pig in a Vermentino sauce. Many opt for the three- or four-course prix-fixe menus (€50 and €60), which include a traditional dessert. **Known for:** delicious mains and desserts; impressive wine list; attentive and knowledgeable service. $ *Average main: €25* *Piazza Sulis 3, Alghero* *079/979584* *www.ilpavone-ristorante.com* *Closed Mon., Tues., and late Nov.–late Dec. No dinner Sun. late Nov.–Easter.*

La Lepanto

$$ | **SEAFOOD** | A covered veranda by the seafront marks out Alghero's top seafood restaurant, an expansive and sunny room complete with crustacean-filled aquarium. Summer sees crowds of both locals and tourists, many of whom come for the specialty *aragosta* (lobster) cooked different ways, including with fettuccine or *alla Lepanto* (with tomato, onions, and orange). **Known for:** superior seafood in all its forms; bright interior with covered veranda seating; central location. $ *Average main: €23* *Via Carlo Alberto 135, Alghero* *079/979116* *www.lalepanto.com* *Closed Feb. and Tues.*

Mabrouk

$$$$ | **SEAFOOD** | There's always a lively crowd at this backstreet trattoria, where diners pack into three rooms to enjoy the same multicourse set menu of seafood. If this seems limiting, think again—you'll be presented with a range of fresh, delicious, seasonally appropriate dishes (perhaps prawns, squid, swordfish, or sea bass) in abundant portions. **Known for:** prix-fixe menus with unlimited drinks; fresh seafood; cheerful atmosphere. $ *Average main: €55* *Via Santa Barbara 4, Alghero* *079/970000* *www.facebook.com/mabroukalghero* *Closed Mon. and mid-Oct.–Mar. No dinner Sun.; no lunch Tues.–Sat.*

Coffee and Quick Bites

Bar Pasticceria Ciro

$ | **ITALIAN** | For a delicious cannolo, fruit tart, or *bignè* (cream puff), local cognoscenti make a beeline for this classic bar and pastry shop near Piazza Sulis, where the sweet delights displayed are made with the lightest pastry and the freshest fillings. Good coffees, ice creams, and sandwiches are also available, and there are tables inside and out back. **Known for:** light pastries; old-fashioned style; cordial service. $ *Average main: €5* *Via Sassari 35/b, Alghero* *079/979960* *www.instagram.com/pasticceria.ciro* *Closed Mon.*

Cafè Latino

$ | **ITALIAN** | In prime position with tables arrayed on Alghero's broad city walls and views down to the yachting marina and across to Capo Caccia, this makes a wonderful place to pause by day or night with a spritz or fruit juice. The menu has a number of food items, too. **Known for:** superb views over the port; good selection of snacks and cocktails; friendly service. $ *Average main: €10* *Bastioni Magellano 10, Alghero* *079/6766044* *www.cafelatino.it* *Closed Jan.–mid-Feb. and Tues. mid-Feb.–June and Sept.–Dec.*

Hotels

Hotel San Francesco

$ | **HOTEL** | The only hotel located in Alghero's central Catalan quarter occupies an ex-convent once attached to the church of San Francesco. **Pros:** historic ambience; central location; breakfast in the cloister. **Cons:** no frills or extras; not a good choice for kids; no parking nearby. *Rooms from: €108 Via Machin 2, Alghero 079/980330 www.sanfrancescohotel.com Closed Nov.–Mar. 20 rooms Free Breakfast.*

★ Villa Las Tronas Hotel & Spa

$$$ | HOTEL | A stunning mansion dating from the 1880s has been transformed into this elegant secluded hotel that blends gold tapestries, crystal chandeliers, marble floors, canopy-draped beds, vaulted ceilings, and other Belle Époque treasures with modern amenities such as a luxury spa with a gym and an illuminated pool. **Pros:** promontory setting with regal sea views; incredible service; luxury spa. **Cons:** usually a two-night minimum stay in July and August; no meat dishes served at dinner; very expensive. *Rooms from: €475 Lungomare Valencia 1, Alghero 079/981818 www.hotelvillalastronas.it 24 rooms Free Breakfast.*

Nightlife

Poco Loco

LIVE MUSIC | For live music, bowling, or just a slice of pizza, this long-standing establishment has been a fixture for generations of Alghero's youth. The music is mainly jazz, blues, and rock, while a range of beers and cocktails are served as well as pizza cooked in a wood oven and dispensed by the meter. *Via Gramsci 8, Alghero 079/983604 www.pocolocoalghero.com.*

Shopping

De Filippis

JEWELRY & WATCHES | On the so-called Riviera del Corallo, Alghero has long been famed for its coral products, fashioned into elegant jewelry. This shop, with three outlets within a few yards of each other in the old town, has an impressive range of coral bracelets, brooches, and necklaces. *Via Carlo Alberto 22, Alghero 079/979394 www.defilippis.it.*

Sassari

34 km (21 miles) northeast of Alghero, 212 km (132 miles) north of Cagliari.

With a population of about 125,000, Sassari, the island's second-largest city, is an important university town and administrative center, notable for its history of intellectualism and bohemian student culture. Look for downtown vendors of *fainè,* a pizzalike chickpea-flour pancake glistening with olive oil, which is a Genoan and Sassarese specialty. The mazelike old town is blissfully isolated from the chaotic traffic swirling through the newer neighborhoods—Sassari is the hub of several highways and secondary roads leading to various coastal resorts, among them Stintino and Castelsardo.

GETTING HERE AND AROUND

Sassari can be reached by plane, ferry, train, bus, or car. The nearest airport is Alghero-Fertilia, about 30 km (19 miles) from Sassari. Inexpensive buses can get you to the center of Sassari. The closest port is Porto Torres, about 20 km (12½ miles) away, connected by ferry to Spain, France, Corsica, Genoa, and Civitavecchia (Rome). Frequent bus and train services operate between Sassari and Cagliari, Olbia, and Alghero.

VISITOR INFORMATION

CONTACT Sassari. *Via Sebastiano Satta 13, Sassari 079/2008072.*

Sights

Duomo

CHURCH | The highly ornate stone Duomo is Sassari's must-see sight. The cathedral, dedicated to St. Nicolas (of Santa Claus inspiration), took more than half a millennium to build: the foundations were laid in the 12th century, and the Spanish colonial–style facade was completed in the 18th. Of particular interest in the plainer interior are the ribbed Gothic vaults, the 14th-century painting of the

Madonna del Bosco on the high altar, and the early-19th-century tomb of Placido Benedetto di Savoia, the uncle of united Italy's first king. Look out, too, for the *candelieri* displayed in the lateral chapels here—10-foot-tall wooden candlesticks which, festooned with ribbons and flowers, are carried through the streets of Sassari every August 14th by members of the local guilds in one of the city's major festivals. ✉ *Piazza Duomo 3, Sassari* ☎ *079/232574* 🎫 *Free.*

Restaurants

L'Assassino

$ | **SOUTHERN ITALIAN** | Get a true taste of regional cuisine at this family-run trattoria near the tourist office in the Old Town. The menu is not for the squeamish or for vegetarians: horse, donkey, and—one of the standouts—roasted suckling pig feature prominently, as do typical Sassarese dishes such as *trippa alla parmigiana* (tripe with Parmesan), *lumaconi in rosso* (snails in a rich tomato sauce), and *cordula con piselli* (sheep's intestines with peas). **Known for:** authentic Sassarese dishes; superb roasted suckling pig; pleasant courtyard seating in summer. $ *Average main: €18* ✉ *Via Pettenadu 19, Sassari* ☎ *079/233463* 🌐 *www.trattoriatipica.sassari.it* ⏱ *Closed late Dec.–late Jan.*

Castelsardo

32 km (20 miles) northeast of Sassari.

The seaside citadel of Castelsardo is surmounted by an impressive fortress, which now contains a museum highlighting the basketware for which the town is famous. Wandering the upper town's maze of steep alleys is a delight, as is browsing the numerous shops in the lower town. Good souvenirs include not only woven baskets but also rugs and wrought-iron items. On the road into Castelsardo from the east, note the **Roccia dell'Elefante** (Elephant Rock), which was hollowed out by primitive man to be used as a burial chamber. The local name for this type of structure is *domus de janas* (literally, "fairy house").

GETTING HERE AND AROUND

Castelsardo is a 40-minute drive from Sassari on SS200. Frequent ARST buses also connect the two towns. Cars cannot enter Castelsardo's historic center, though you can drive part of the way up from Piazza La Pianedda. Parking is extremely limited, however, and if you're fit enough to tackle the steep streets you're best off leaving your car in the lower town and walking up.

VISITOR INFORMATION

CONTACT Castelsardo Tourism Office. ✉ *Piazza Maestro di Castelsardo, Castelsardo* ☎ *079/6762792* 🌐 *www.comune.castelsardo.ss.it.*

Sights

★ **Museo dell'Intreccio Mediterraneo**

CASTLE/PALACE | Castelsardo is best known in Sardinia for its intricate and colorful basketwork, numerous examples of which can be seen in the stores lining the main road and on the walls of the old center. The Museo dell'Intreccio Mediterraneo, located in the formidable 13th-century castle that dominates the town, puts it all into context, displaying a diverse range of woven baskets, culinary equipment, fishing equipment, and even an example of *fassonis*, the reed-constructed fishing boats once used around Oristano. The well-preserved castle was the Sardinian base of the powerful Doria family in the Middle Ages and has replicas of armor, catapults, and other medieval weaponry on the walls; try to time your visit to be here at sunset for the unforgettable views. The castle stays open till midnight and beyond in July and August. Your entry ticket includes admission to a museum dedicated to Castelsardo and its Genoan origins, housed nearby in an old Franciscan convent and mainly consisting of panels and videos—from here, too, there are awesome panoramic views of the coast. ✉ *Via Marconi, Castelsardo* ☎ *079/6014769* 🌐 *www.mimcastelsardo.it* 🎫 *€5.*

Restaurants

Ristorante Spaghetteria Aragona

$ | **SEAFOOD** | Tucked out of sight in a sequestered corner of Castelsardo's old center, this simple trattoria enjoys magnificent sea views from its outdoor terrace. The stunning panorama makes a wonderful setting for the simple and abundant seafood dishes offered on the menu, including shellfish risotto, prawn tagliolini, a mixed fish grill, and whatever else is fresh and seasonal. **Known for:** terrace for alfresco dining; spectacular panoramic views; abundant portions. [$] *Average main: €18* ✉ *Via Manganella 3, Castelsardo* ☎ *340/6303312 mobile* 🌐 *www.ristorantearagona.com* ⏲ *Closed Dec.–Mar. and Wed. Apr.–June and Oct. and Nov.*

Santa Teresa Gallura

70 km (43 miles) northeast of Castelsardo, 65 km (41 miles) northwest of Olbia.

At the northern tip of Sardinia, Santa Teresa Gallura has the fun and carefree vibe of a resort that has retained the relaxed air of the fishing village from which it developed. Nearby beaches rival those farther down the coast yet somehow aren't as crowded with tourists.

GETTING HERE AND AROUND

Ferry crossings from Bonifacio in Corsica operated by Moby Lines (🌐 *www.mobylines.com*) and Ichnusa Lines (🌐 *ichnusalines.com*) run seven times per day. The trip lasts about 50 minutes.

By car, you can drive from Olbia following the SS125 in the direction of Arzachena-Palau. At the fork in Palau, turn left to Santa Teresa Gallura. Continue for 25 km (16 miles). From Cagliari, follow SS131 to Sassari. Before the city center, exit at Sassari Latte Dolce, heading in the direction of Platamona/Castelsardo, which leads to the scenic coastal road Porto Torres–Santa Teresa.

From Alghero, follow SS291 until Sassari and continue to the coast on SS200 and SP90 to Santa Teresa. From Castelsardo, take SP134 then turn left on SP90 for Santa Teresa.

There are frequent bus connections with Olbia, but there is no train station in Santa Teresa Gallura. The nearest main-line train station is in Olbia.

FERRY CONTACT Ichnusa Lines. ✉ *Santa Teresa Gallura* ☎ *800/959369 call center, 1676530 Santa Teresa ticket office* 🌐 *ichnusalines.com.* **Moby Lines.** ✉ *Santa Teresa Gallura* ☎ *0789/751449* 🌐 *www.mobylines.com.*

VISITOR INFORMATION

CONTACT Santa Teresa Gallura Tourist Office. ✉ *Piazza Vittorio Emanuele 24, Santa Teresa Gallura* ☎ *0789/740986* 🌐 *www.santateresagalluraturismo.com.*

Hotels

★ **Hotel Canne al Vento**

$ | **B&B/INN** | Family-run Canne al Vento has been a quiet, cheerful haven in town since the late 1950s. **Pros:** abundant and memorable breakfasts; personal, friendly service; convenient parking. **Cons:** on a main road; some rooms are on the small side; no elevator for upper-floor rooms. [$] *Rooms from: €120* ✉ *Via Nazionale 23, Santa Teresa Gallura* ☎ *0789/754219, 366/4215601 mobile* 🌐 *hotelcannealvento.com* ⏲ *Closed Jan.* 🛏 *22 rooms* 🍽 *Free Breakfast.*

Hotel Corallaro

$$ | **HOTEL** | **FAMILY** | A brief walk from the town center, this hotel occupies a panoramic spot right by the splendid Rena Bianca beach and has functional

rooms—most of them spacious, a few of them with balconies and sea views. **Pros:** welcoming management and staff; steps away from the beach; airy rooms with plenty of storage space. **Cons:** some rooms overlook car park; steep uphill walk to town center; attracts groups. [$] *Rooms from: €280* ✉ *Spiaggia Rena Bianca, Santa Teresa Gallura* ☎ *0789/755475* 🌐 *www.hotelcorallaro.it* ⏲ *Closed early Oct.–mid-May* *83 rooms* 🍽 *Free Breakfast.*

La Maddalena

45 km (20 miles) northwest of Olbia, 68 km (42 miles) northeast of Castelsardo.

From the port of Palau you can visit the archipelago of La Maddalena, seven granite islands embellished with aromatic scrub and wind-bent pines. The most significant of the handful of sites to see here is Giuseppe Garibaldi's home and tomb. Explore the lively port (also called La Maddalena), then head to one of several picture-postcard coves, the perfect spot for a picnic and a swim in the crystal clear waters.

GETTING HERE AND AROUND

The only way to get to this small island is by boat or ferry. From Olbia, take a bus or drive to Palau, then catch the ferry to La Maddalena. During the day, car ferries make the 3-km (2-mile) trip two to four times an hour. The town center is right in front of the dock. Local buses are available for accessing the beaches, although the island is best explored by scooter or bike.

VISITOR INFORMATION

CONTACT La Maddalena Tourist Office. ✉ *Via XX Settembre 20, La Maddalena* ☎ *0789/736321* 🌐 *www.facebook.com/lamaddalenaturismo.*

Sights

★ Compendio Garibaldino

HISTORIC HOME | FAMILY | Pilgrims from around the world converge on the Compendio Garibaldino, a complex on the island of Caprera that contains not only the restored home of Giuseppe Garibaldi (1807–82) but also his tomb. The national hero and military leader who laid the groundwork for the unification of Italy in 1861 lived a simple life as a farmer on Caprera, the island that he eventually owned. Exhibits include a collection of weaponry, numerous items of furniture belonging to the family, Garibaldi's famous red shirt, and the poncho he wore during his South American campaigns. The grounds contain the hero's tomb alongside those of his family, all surrounded by the olive grove that he planted. There are explanatory panels in Italian and English, and visitors can also download an app providing more comprehensive information. A combined ticket takes in the Memoriale Giuseppe Garibaldi, 4 km (2½ miles) away—a multimedia museum, housed within a stern fortress dating from 1895, that chronicles the swashbuckling career of the Italian hero.

To visit the Compendio and Memoriale, take the ferry from Palau to Isola Maddalena, from where a causeway bridge crosses to Caprera. Note that visits to the Compendio Garibaldino must always be booked ahead for a specific time slot. A tour of the house and grounds should take less than an hour. **TIP→ Caprera island is now a nature reserve, its woods and Mediterranean scrub crisscrossed by a network of waymarked trails that offer great opportunities for scenic walks and picnics.** ✉ *7 km (4½ miles) east of Isola Maddalena, Caprera, La Maddalena* ☎ *0789/727162 for information, 335/7505401 for booking visits (mobile)* 🌐 *www.garibaldicaprera.beniculturali.it* 🎫 *€8; €12 combined ticket includes Memoriale Giuseppe Garibaldi* ⏲ *Closed Sun.* ✍ *Book tickets by telephone or online.*

Porto Cervo

35 km (22 miles) southeast of La Maddalena, 30 km (19 miles) north of Olbia.

Sardinia's northeastern coast is fringed with beaches, cliffs, inlets, and small bays. This has become an upscale vacationland, with glossy resorts such as Baia Sardinia and Porto Rotondo just outside the confines of the famed Costa Smeralda. Some of Italy's most expensive hotels are here, and magnificent yachts anchor in the waters of Porto Cervo. Golf courses, yacht clubs, and numerous alfresco restaurants and bars cater to those who want to see and be seen.

GETTING HERE AND AROUND

Porto Cervo is accessible by boat, car, taxi, and bus. Buses run regularly from Olbia and Palau.

Whichever airport or port of entry into Sardinia you choose, head to Olbia. By car, follow SS125 north toward Arzachena and Costa Smeralda. After 10 km (6 miles), turn right onto SP73 toward Porto Rotondo/Porto Cervo. Continue on SP94 and turn onto SP59 to Porto Cervo. The trip takes about 30 minutes.

Beaches

The beaches around the Costa Smeralda are some of the most exclusive in Europe, and they don't disappoint—with fine golden sand sheltered by red cliffs and fronting azure waters. Many can only be reached by boat, and there are regular launches from Porto Cervo. Rentals of sun beds and towels are as expensive as you'd expect.

Spiaggia del Principe

BEACH | FAMILY | Among the less developed of the Costa Smeralda's five-star beaches, the Spiaggia del Principe is tucked well away from the crowds, mainly because it is not so readily accessible as some of the others. The rewards, however, are all the greater. Edged by jagged, gold-tinted rocks, the beach has fine white sand and water ranging from emerald to a Caribbean shade of turquoise. Access from the car park is tricky—a 10-minute walk along a rough path (stout sneakers needed)—but a tuk-tuk service is sometimes on hand for a small charge. **Amenities:** food and drink; parking (fee in summer); toilets. **Best for:** swimming; walking. ✉ *Porto Cervo* ✣ *3 km (2 miles) east of Cala di Volpe on Via Romazzino and Via delle Mimose.*

Restaurants

I Frati Rossi

$$$ | SOUTHERN ITALIAN | In the hills above Porto Cervo, this soothing hideaway—where a sheltered terrace looks out onto a verdant garden—is a great place to take a break from the coast's glossy trappings. Recommended antipasti include *sa cannacca* (dried sausage with pecorino cheese) and octopus salad with potatoes; *ravioli di cernia e carciofi* (homemade ravioli with grouper fish, artichokes, and truffle) is a great pasta choice; and the grilled fish is an excellent main. **Known for:** secluded dining; tasty seafood dishes; terrace seating with garden views. [$] *Average main: €35* ✉ *Via Paolino Azara, Pantogia, off SP59, Pantogia* ☎ *0789/94395* 🌐 *www.fratirossi.it* ⏲ *Closed Nov.–early Jan. No lunch Mon.*

Hotels

★ Cala di Volpe

$$$$ | RESORT | Long a magnet for the beautiful people, this hyperglamorous Marriott Luxury Collection hotel was designed by Jacques Couëlle to evoke a traditional Mediterranean village, complete with its own bay and covered bridge; the exterior is complemented by a rustic-elegant interior with beamed ceilings, terra-cotta floors, Sardinian arts and crafts, and porticoes overlooking the Cala di Volpe Bay. There's an Olympic-size saltwater pool, boat service to a private

beach, and access to the Pevero Golf Club. **Pros:** stunning architecture and grounds; luxurious ambience; exceptional staff. **Cons:** some rooms disappoint; astronomical rates for room, additional amenities, drinks, and meals; car necessary. *Rooms from: €1,146 ✉ Cala di Volpe, Porto Cervo ☎ 0789/976111, 800/4484066 toll-free 🌐 www.caladivolpe.com ⊙ Closed mid-Oct.–mid-Apr. 121 rooms Free Breakfast.*

★ Petra Segreta Resort and Spa

$$$ | **HOTEL** | Sea and mountain views, top-quality cuisine, and chic and spacious guest rooms are the main draws at this romantic boutique hotel outside the picturesque village of San Pantaleo. **Pros:** tranquil mountainside setting with spectacular views; blend of traditional surroundings and modern amenities; two good restaurants. **Cons:** two-night minimum stay applies in July and August; remote and isolated; not suitable for families. *Rooms from: €582 ✉ Via Buddeu, San Pantaleo, Olbia ☎ 0789/1876441 🌐 www.petrasegretaresort.com ⊙ Closed Nov.–early Apr. 27 rooms Free Breakfast.*

Activities

Pevero Golf Course

GOLF | Designed by Robert Trent Jones Sr. and opened in 1972, Pevero is a world-class course with some of Europe's most beautiful fairways. Stretching nearly 6½ km (4 miles) between the Gulf of Pevero and Cala di Volpe (Bay of Foxes), it provides challenging playing conditions that incorporate 70 bunkers, several rock formations, and vegetation. The dress code is formal on the course and in the upscale clubhouse. Note that the course and clubhouse are closed on Monday and Tuesday between November and February. *✉ Località Cala di Volpe 20, Porto Cervo ☎ 0789/976400 🌐 www.peverogolfclub.com From €80, depending on season and course; from €45 for club car 18 holes, 6,348 yards, par 72.*

Yacht Club Costa Smeralda

SAILING | The Aga Khan IV founded this yacht club with some local associates in 1967 in order to promote nautical activities. The club provides use of its pool, restaurant, bar, and guest rooms to those with memberships at associated yacht clubs. Watch for regattas from June to September, and check out the YCCS Sailing School, which organizes courses on dinghies and cabin cruisers. *✉ Via della Marina, Porto Cervo ☎ 0789/902200 🌐 www.yccs.it.*

Olbia

30 km (19 miles) south of Porto Cervo.

Amid the resorts of Sardinia's northeastern coast, Olbia, a town of about 62,000, is a lively little seaport and port of call for mainland ferries at the head of a long, wide bay.

GETTING HERE AND AROUND

The main airport, Olbia–Costa Smeralda, is only 1½ km (1 mile) from the town center. Inexpensive city buses and taxis are available outside the terminal. Trains operate between Olbia and Cagliari and take about four hours.

The Olbia–Isola Bianca harbor provides daily connections with the Italian mainland, less than 300 km (186 miles) away. Regular ferries arrive from Genoa, Civitavecchia (Rome), and Livorno. Most ferries take 8–12 hours.

VISITOR INFORMATION

CONTACT Olbia. *✉ Municipio, Piazza Terranova Pausania 1, at Corso Umberto I, Olbia ☎ 0789/52206, 334/9809802 mobile 🌐 www.helloolbia.com.*

Sights

Basilica San Simplicio

CHURCH | Olbia's little basilica, a short walk from the main Corso Umberto I, is the city's unmissable sight. The simple granite structure dates from the 11th century, part of the great Pisan church-building program, using pillars and columns recycled from Roman buildings. The basilica has a bare, somewhat somber interior; its three naves are separated by a series of Romanesque arches, and fragments of frescoes are visible behind the altar. **TIP→ Recent renovations of the monument have unearthed the remains of a Greek and Roman necropolis, which is now open to the public (the entrance is in the car park beneath the piazza).** *Piazza San Simplicio, Olbia* *0789/396241* *www.museumtempioampurias.it/polo-museale-civitatense.*

Restaurants

Il Gambero

$$ | SOUTHERN ITALIAN | This backstreet trattoria has a strong rustic flavor, its two rooms adorned with brass cooking pots, colorful embroideries, old photographs, and agricultural knickknacks. The menu, too, has a local focus and might include roast pecorino with honey, and *bottarga* (mullet roe) with fennel and orange. **Known for:** simple, rustic decor; fresh, local meat and seafood dishes; informal but discreet service. *Average main: €22* *Via Lamarmora 6, Olbia* *0789/23874* *www.facebook.com/ilgamberotrattoria* *Closed Mon. and Nov.*

Hotels

La Locanda del Conte Mameli

$$ | HOTEL | Housed in a remodeled palazzo built at the end of the 19th century for the count after which it is named, this small and select hotel occupies a quiet location on a traffic-free backstreet just a few steps from Corso Umberto. **Pros:** small hotel with personal service; antique furnishings; central but quiet location. **Cons:** tricky to access by car; some rooms are slightly cramped and gloomy; no parking. *Rooms from: €209* *Via delle Terme 8, Olbia* *366/9098653 mobile* *www.lalocandadelcontemameli.com* *11 rooms* *Free Breakfast.*

Index

N

O

P

Photo Credits

Front Cover: Leonid Andronov/GettyImages [Descr.:Galleria Vittorio Emanuele II in Milan, Italy.] **Back cover, from left to right:** Fabiomax/iStockphoto. Shaiith/iStockphoto. Aleh Varanishcha/iStockphoto. **Spine:** ChiccoDodiFC/iStockphoto. **Interior, from left to right:** Liubomir Paut/iStockphoto (1). Resulmuslu/iStockphoto (2-3). Gaspar Janos/Shutterstock (5). Aleh Varanishcha/iStockphoto (8). Anton Aleksenko/iStockphoto (9). **About Our Writers:** All photos are courtesy of the writers except for the following. Nick Bruno courtesy of Graeme Ogston. Laura Itzkowitz courtesy of Melissa Itzkowitz. Elizabeth Shemaria courtesy of Ian Tuttle. **Chapter 1: Experience Italy:** Bluejayphoto/iStockphoto (10-11). Mapics/Dreamstime (12-13). Fivepointsix/Shutterstock (13). Pcruciatti/Shutterstock (13). ItalyDrones/Shutterstock (14). Figurniysergey.com/iStockphoto (14). HuangZheng/Shutterstock (14). Chen Min Chun/Shutterstock (14). Janoka82/iStockphoto (15). Jaroslaw Pawlak/Shutterstock (15). Mi.Ti./Shutterstock (16). Inguaribile Vlaggiatore/Shutterstock (16). Alessandro Cristiano/Shutterstock (16). Parilov/Shutterstock (16). Cheryl Ramalho/iStockphoto (17). Alexirina27000/Dreamstime (18). Siempreverde22/Dreamstime (18). Gaspar Janos/Shutterstock (18). Andrei Molchan/Shutterstock (18). Wirestock/iStockphoto (19). Stefanodeang/Shutterstock (19). Marianceccarelli/iStockphoto (20). Cge2010/Shutterstock (20). Emicristea/iStockphoto (20). Den-belitsky/iStockphoto (20). Omas_Photo/Shutterstock (21). StevanZZ/Shutterstock (28). StevanZZ/Shutterstock (28). Nicola Pulham/Shutterstock (28). Kavalenkava/Shutterstock (28). Jenifoto/iStockphoto (28). GagliardiPhotography/Shutterstock (29). Vololibero/Shutterstock (29). Tour Liguria/Volver (29). Lucamato/iStockphoto (29). Baarssen2/Dreamstime (29). Taste Bologna (30). Montese Cooking Experiences (30). Monni & Pirisi/Tasting Sardinia (30). Joaquin Corbalan P/Shutterstock (31). Dr. Ronald Pitcock/Cook with us in Rome (31). AndrewSoundarajan/iStockphoto (32). AndreaAstes/iStockphoto (32). Robert Zehetmayer/Dreamstime (32). LizCoughlan/Shutterstock (32). Jlabouyrie/Dreamstime (33). **Chapter 3: Rome:** Max Zolotukhin/iStockphoto (63). Alexandros Michailidis/Shutterstock (66). Barmalini/iStockphoto (67). Natalia_maroz/Shutterstock (67). Gush Photography/Shutterstock (88-89). TTaylor/Wikimedia Commons (88). RPBaiao/Shutterstock (90). Imaengine/Dreamstime (92-93). Imaengine/Dreamstime (94-95). **Chapter 4: Venice:** Ratnakorn Piyasirisorost/GettyImages (145). FotoGablitz/iStockphoto (148). Jess_h/Shutterstock (149). Iz89/Shutterstock (149). Mapics/Dreamstime (198). **Chapter 5: The Veneto and Friuli–Venezia Giulia:** Gistel Cezary Wojtkowski/iStockphoto (205). C Teubner/Shutterstock (208). From_my_point_of_view/iStockphoto (209). ChiccoDodiFC/iStockphoto (209). **Chapter 6: The Dolomites:** Boerescu/Shutterstock (255). Tati Liberta/Shutterstock (258). Davide Bianco Photo/Shutterstock (259). CuboImages srl/Alamy (259). Elena Brunelli/Shutterstock (282). Paolo Graziosi/iStockphoto (288). **Chapter 7: Milan, Lombardy, and the Lakes:** Boris Stroujko/Shutterstock (299). OlgaBombologna/Shutterstock (302). Nagy Julia/Shutterstock (303). Valerio Pardi (303). Photophonico/iStockphoto (336). Michelangeloop/iStockphoto (339). **Chapter 8: Piedmont and the Valle d'Aosta:** Freesurf69/Dreamstime (365). S74/Shutterstock (368). Alessandro Cristiano/Shutterstock (369). B Work et Art/Shutterstock (369). MikeDotta/Shutterstock (389). **Chapter 9: The Italian Riviera:** Proslgn/Dreamstime (397). Zagorulko Inka/Shutterstock (400). Alessio Orru/Shutterstock (401). Maxsala/Dreamstime (401). Gaspar Janos/Shutterstock (407). Whatafoto/Shutterstock (408). F11photo/Shutterstock (408). Elephotos/Shutterstock (408). Nightcap/Shutterstock (408). Sanga Park/iStockphoto (409). Aliaksandr Antanovich/Shutterstock (409). Viviane Teles (409). Philippe Paternolli/iStockphoto (441). **Chapter 10: Emilia–Romagna:** AleMasche72/iStockphoto (443). Fabiomax/iStockphoto (446). Dietmarrauscher/Dreamstime (447). Alemasche72/Dreamstime (447). ESstock/Shutterstock (459). Piccerella/iStockphoto (460). Alessia Pierdomenico/Shutterstock (460). Consorzio del Prosciutto di Parma (460). Udo Schröter/Flickr (460). Grischa Georgiew/iStockphoto (460). Consorzio del Formaggio (461). Consorzio del Formaggio (461). M Laky/Shutterstock (461). Roberto A Sanchez/iStockphoto (461). Consorzio del Formaggio (461). AGF Srl/Alamy (462). Verysmallplanet/Shutterstock (462). ESstock/Shutterstock (463). Foodlove/Shutterstock (463). Giorgio Morara/Shutterstock (463). Archivio Fotografico Di Bologna Turismo (463). Claudio Baldini/Shutterstock (463). **Chapter 11: Florence:** Emi Cristea/iStockphoto (487). Thekovtun/Shutterstock (490). George M. Groutas/Flickr (491). Lesya Dolyuk/Shutterstock (491). George Diamonds/Shutterstock (504-505). Sailko/WikimediaCommons (506). Sailko/WikimediaCommons (506). Sailko/WikimediaCommons (506). Skovalsky/Shutterstock (507). Alberto Valenzuela/Shutterstock (507). Rough Guides/Alamy (507). Mary Evans Picture Library/Alamy (508). Library of Congress Prints and Photographs Division (508). Kritskaya/Shutterstock (508). Fae/WikimediaCommons (531). Gustav Schauer/WikimediaCommons (531). Marzolino/Shutterstock (531). Romas_Photo/Shutterstock (532). Steve Allen/Shutterstock (532). Allen Lugmayer/Shutterstock (533). Giannit/Dreamstime (533). MisterStock/Shutterstock (533). Yuri Turkov/Shutterstock (533). Web Gallery of Art/Wikimedia Commons (534). Virtusincertus/Flickr (534). Cysun/Shutterstock (534). Jean louis mazieres/Flickr (535). Bill Perry/Shutterstock (535). Deb Nystrom/Flickr (535). Sailko/WikimediaCommons (536). Oursana/WikimediaCommons (536). Dguendel/WikimediaCommons (536). **Chapter 12: Tuscany:** Christopher Salerno/Shutterstock (545). Kuvona/Dreamstime (548). Kwasny221/iStockphoto (549). Frantic00/Shutterstock (549). Kiev.Victor/Shutterstock (558). Simona Bottone/Shutterstock (586). **Chapter 13: Umbria and the Marches:** Sergey Dzyuba/Shutterstock (589). Vividaphoto/Dreamstime (592). 5 second Studio/Shutterstock (593). Bonchan/Shutterstock (593). StevanZZ/Shutterstock (607). Santiago Urquijo/Getty Images (608). Threerivers11/Dreamstime (608). Frans Vandewalle/Flickr (609). Petrusbarbygere/Wikimedia Commons (609). Eloquence/WikimediaCommons (609). Petrusbarbygere/WikimediaCommons (609). Petrusbarbygere/Wikimedia Commons (609). **Chapter 14: Naples and Campania:** E55evu/Dreamstime (629). Look Die Bildagentur der Fotografen GmbH/Alamy (632). Sprmaxsr/Dreamstime (633). CuboImages srl/Alamy (633). Wjarek/Shutterstock (659). Pablo Debat/Shutterstock (659). Kated/Shutterstock (660). Erica Ruth Neubauer/Alamy (661). Balounm/Shutterstock (661). Leonid Andronov/Shutterstock (662). Dennis Degnan/GettyImages (662). Maurizio De Mattei/Shutterstock (662). Leonid Andronov/Shutterstock (663). Smartshots International/GettyImages (664). Alfiya Safuanova/Shutterstock (665). Arcady/Shutterstock (684). **Chapter 15: Puglia, Basilicata, and Calabria:** Josefskacel/Dreamstime (695). Jcartwright01/Dreamstime (698). Fanfo/Dreamstime (699). Claudia Longo/Shutterstock (699). Fabio Dell/Shutterstock (709). Marco Fine/Shutterstock (731). **Chapter 16: Sicily:** Peeter Viisimaa/iStockPhoto (737). Pramen/Shutterstock (740). Gyro/iStockphoto (741). ChiccoDodiFC FotoOk.it/iStockphoto (741). Vvoe/Shutterstock (775). **Chapter 17: Sardinia:** Eva Bocek/Shutterstock (801). Marmo81/Shutterstock (804). Marmo81/Shutterstock (805). Oxana Denezhkina/Shutterstock (805). Travelwild/Shutterstock (807). **Every effort has been made to trace the copyright holders, and we apologize in advance for any accidental errors. We would be happy to apply the corrections in the following edition of this publication.*

Notes

Fodor's ESSENTIAL ITALY 2026

Publisher: Stephen Horowitz, *General Manager*

Editorial: Douglas Stallings, *Editorial Director;* Jill Fergus, Alexis Kelly, Amanda Sadlowski, *Senior Editors;* Brian Eschrich, *Editor;* Angelique Kennedy-Chavannes, Yoojin Shin, *Associate Editors*

Design: Tina Malaney, *Director of Design and Production*; Jessica Gonzalez, *Senior Designer,* Jaimee Shaye, *Graphic Design Associate*

Production: Jennifer DePrima, *Editorial Production Manager,* Elyse Rozelle, *Senior Production Editor;* Carol Seigler, *Production Editor*

Maps: Rebecca Baer, *Map Director,* David Lindroth, Mark Stroud (Moon Street Cartography), *Cartographers*

Photography: Viviane Teles, *Director of Photography;* Namrata Aggarwal, Neha Gupta, Payal Gupta, Ashok Kumar, *Photo Editors;* Zamantta Larios Salazar, Shanelle Jacobs, *Photo Production Interns*

Business and Operations: Chuck Hoover, *Chief Marketing Officer;* Robert Ames, *Group General Manager*

Public Relations and Marketing: Joe Ewaskiw, *Senior Director of Communications and Public Relations*

Fodors.com: Jeremy Tarr, *Editorial Director;* Rachael Levitt, *Managing Editor*

Writers: Robert Andrews, Nick Bruno, Liz Humphreys, Laura Itzkowitz, Natalie Kennedy, Elizabeth Shemaria

Editor: Jill Fergus

Production Editor: Carol Seigler

8th Edition

ISBN 978-1-64097-857-7

ISSN 2476-0692

All details in this book are based on information supplied to us at press time. Always confirm information when it matters, especially if you're making a detour to visit a specific place. Fodor's expressly disclaims any liability, loss, or risk, personal or otherwise, that is incurred as a consequence of the use of any of the contents of this book.

SPECIAL SALES

This book is available at special discounts for bulk purchases for sales promotions or premiums. For more information, e-mail SpecialMarkets@fodors.com.

PRINTED IN CANADA

10 9 8 7 6 5 4 3 2 1